Argentina
Uruguay & Paraguay

Wayne Bernhardson

LONELY PLANET PUBLICATIONS
Melbourne • Oakland • London • Paris

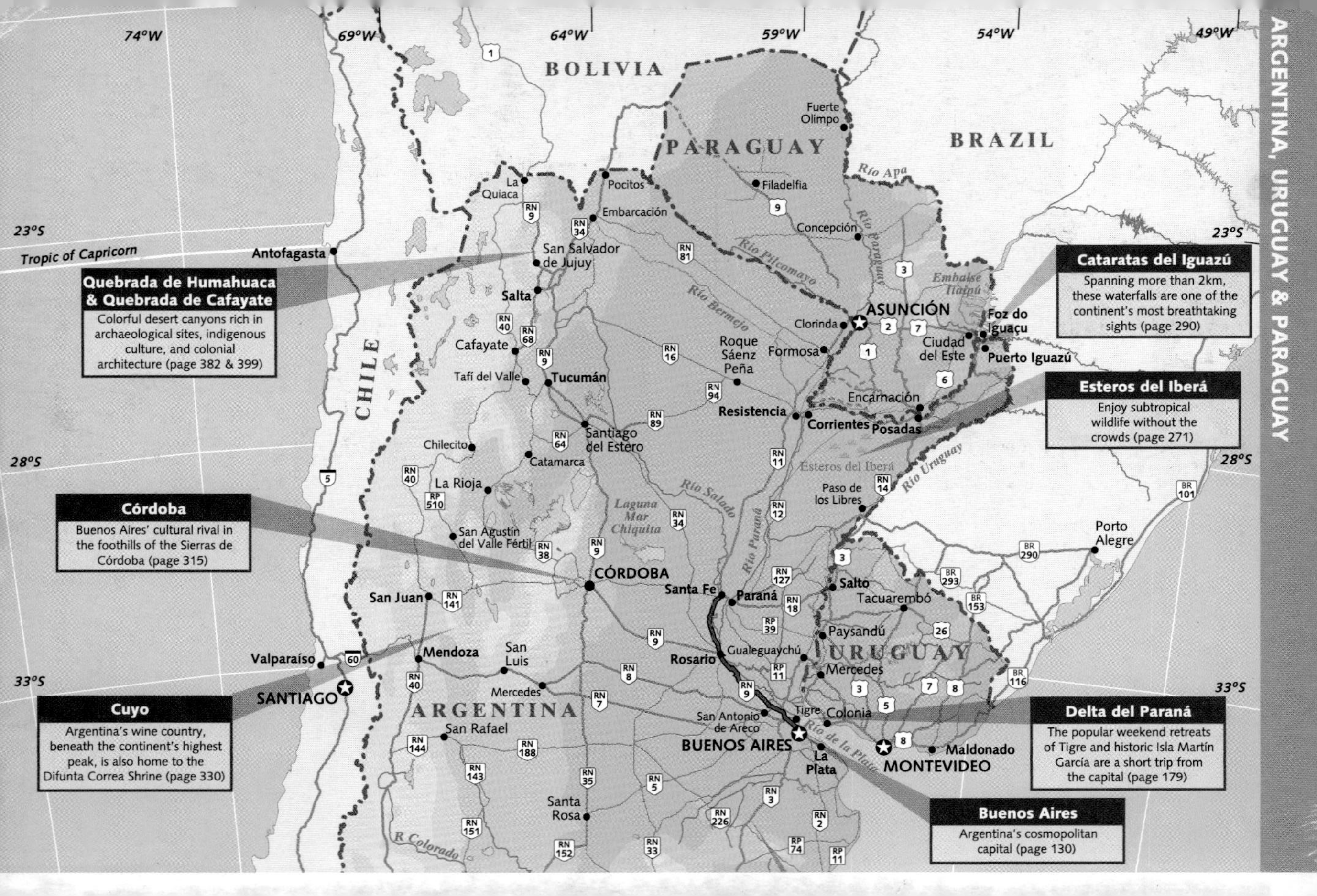
Quebrada de Humahuaca & Quebrada de Cafayate
Colorful desert canyons rich in archaeological sites, indigenous culture, and colonial architecture (page 382 & 399)
Córdoba
Buenos Aires' cultural rival in the foothills of the Sierras de Córdoba (page 315)
Cuyo
Argentina's wine country, beneath the continent's highest peak, is also home to the Difunta Correa Shrine (page 330)
Cataratas del Iguazú
Spanning more than 2km, these waterfalls are one of the continent's most breathtaking sights (page 290)
Esteros del Iberá
Enjoy subtropical wildlife without the crowds (page 271)
Delta del Paraná
The popular weekend retreats of Tigre and historic Isla Martín García are a short trip from the capital (page 179)
Buenos Aires
Argentina's cosmopolitan capital (page 130)
BOLIVIA
PARAGUAY
BRAZIL
CHILE
ARGENTINA
URUGUAY
74°W
69°W
64°W
59°W
54°W
49°W
23°S
28°S
33°S
Tropic of Capricorn
Antofagasta
Valparaíso
SANTIAGO
La Quiaca
Pocitos
Embarcación
San Salvador de Jujuy
Salta
Cafayate
Tafí del Valle
Tucumán
Santiago del Estero
Chilecito
Catamarca
La Rioja
San Agustín del Valle Fértil
CÓRDOBA
San Juan
Mendoza
San Luis
Mercedes
San Rafael
Santa Rosa
Santa Fe
Paraná
Rosario
Gualeguaychú
San Antonio de Areco
Tigre
BUENOS AIRES
La Plata
Colonia
MONTEVIDEO
Maldonado
Mercedes
Paysandú
Salto
Tacuarembó
Paso de los Libres
Esteros del Iberá
Resistencia
Corrientes
Posadas
Encarnación
Roque Sáenz Peña
Formosa
Clorinda
ASUNCIÓN
Ciudad del Este
Foz do Iguaçu
Puerto Iguazú
Embalse Itaipú
Concepción
Filadelfia
Fuerte Olimpo
Porto Alegre
Río Apa
Río Paraguay
Río Pilcomayo
Río Bermejo
Río Salado
Río Paraná
Río Uruguay
Río de la Plata
R. Colorado
Laguna Mar Chiquita

FACTS ABOUT URUGUAY 646

History 646
Geography & Climate 649
Flora & Fauna 650
Government & Politics 650
Economy 651
Population & People 651
Education 652
Arts 652
Religion 652
Language 652

FACTS FOR THE VISITOR 653

Highlights 653
Planning 653
Tourist Offices 653
Visas & Documents 654
Embassies & Consulates 654
Customs 655
Money 655
Post & Communications 656
Books 657
Films 657
Newspapers 657
Radio & TV 657
Health 657
Senior Travelers 657
Useful Organizations 658
Business Hours & Public Holidays 658
Food 658
Drinks 659
Entertainment 659
Spectator Sports 659
Shopping 659

GETTING THERE & AWAY 660

GETTING AROUND 662

MONTEVIDEO 663

History 663
Orientation 664
Information 665
Walking Tour 666
Museo Histórico Nacional 667
Museo del Gaucho y de la Moneda 668
Museo Torres García 668
Museo Pedagógico José Pedro Varela 668
Museo Naval 668
Other Museums 668
Palacio Legislativo 669
Teatro Solís 669
Mercado del Puerto 669
Organized Tours 669
Special Events 669
Places to Stay 672
Places to Eat 673
Entertainment 674
Spectator Sports 674
Shopping 675
Getting There & Away 675
Getting Around 677

URUGUAYAN LITTORAL 679

Colonia 679
Colonia Suiza 686
Colonia Valdense 686
Carmelo 686
Around Carmelo 688
Fray Bentos 688
Mercedes 690
Paysandú 692
Termas De Guaviyú 694
Salto 694
Around Salto 696
Tacuarembó 696
Valle Edén 697
Rivera 698

URUGUAYAN RIVIERA 699

Atlántida 699
Piriápolis 699
Pan de Azúcar 702
Minas 702
Around Minas 703
Maldonado 703
Around Maldonado 706
Punta del Este 706
Around Punta del Este 712
Rocha 712
La Paloma 712
Cabo Polonio 714
Aguas Dulces 714
Parque Nacional Santa Teresa 715
Chuy 715
Treinta y Tres 716
Melo 716

FACTS ABOUT PARAGUAY 718

History 718
Geography & Climate 722
Flora & Fauna 723
National Parks & Reserves 723
Government & Politics 725
Economy 727
Population & People 727
Education 728
Arts 728
Society & Conduct 729
Language 729
Religion 730

Tucumán 407
Around Tucumán 415
Tafí del Valle 415
Quilmes 418
Santiago del Estero Province 418
Santiago del Estero 418
Termas de Río Hondo 423
La Rioja & Catamarca Provinces 425
La Rioja 427
Around La Rioja 432
Villa Sanagasta 433
Anillaco 433
Chilecito 433
Nonogasta 436
Cuesta de Miranda 436
Parque Nacional Talampaya 436
Catamarca 437
Around Catamarca 442
Andalgalá 443
Belén 443
Around Belén 444
Hualfín 444
Santa María 444

PATAGONIA 446

Río Negro & Neuquén Provinces 449
Carmen de Patagones . . . 451
Viedma 453
Coastal Río Negro 456
Bariloche 458
Parque Nacional Nahuel Huapi 469
El Bolsón 473
Around El Bolsón 477
Neuquén 478
Zapala 482
Around Zapala 484
Aluminé 484
Junín de los Andes 484
San Martín de los Andes . . 487
Around San Martín de los Andes 491
Parque Nacional Lanín . . . 492
Villa La Angostura 494
Villa Traful 496
Chubut Province 497
Puerto Madryn 498
Around Puerto Madryn . . . 504
Reserva Faunística Península Valdés 504
Trelew 509
Gaiman 514
Around Gaiman 516
Dolavon 516
Rawson 516
Reserva Provincial Punta Tombo 517
Camarones 518
Around Camarones 518
Comodoro Rivadavia 518
Around Comodoro Rivadavia 523
Río Mayo 524
Gobernador Costa 524
Esquel 525
Around Esquel 531
Trevelin 531
Around Trevelin 533
Parque Nacional Los Alerces 533
El Maitén 536
Santa Cruz Province 537
Río Gallegos 538
Around Río Gallegos 542
Río Turbio 543
Estancia Tapi Aike 544
El Calafate 544
Around El Calafate 548
Parque Nacional Los Glaciares 548
Fitzroy Range 551
Caleta Olivia 554
Puerto Deseado 556
Around Puerto Deseado . . 559
Monumento Natural Bosques Petrificados 559
Puerto San Julián 560
Gobernador Gregores 561
Comandante Luis Piedrabuena 561
Around Comandante Luis Piedrabuena 562
Perito Moreno 562
Around Perito Moreno . . . 564
Bajo Caracoles 564
Cueva de las Manos 564
Parque Nacional Perito Moreno 565
Los Antiguos 566

TIERRA DEL FUEGO & CHILEAN PATAGONIA 569

Tierra del Fuego 573
Río Grande 573
Around Río Grande 575
Ushuaia 576
Around Ushuaia 582
Parque Nacional Tierra del Fuego 583
Chilean Patagonia 586
Punta Arenas 587
Around Punta Arenas 598
Puerto Natales 600
Around Puerto Natales . . . 605
Parque Nacional Torres del Paine 606
Porvenir 611
Cerro Sombrero 613
Lago Blanco 613
Puerto Williams 613

FALKLAND ISLANDS (ISLAS MALVINAS) 616

Facts about the Falklands . . . 616
Facts for the Visitor 624
Getting There & Away 629
Getting Around 630
Stanley 630
Around Stanley 635
The Camp 637
East Falkland 637
West Falkland 640

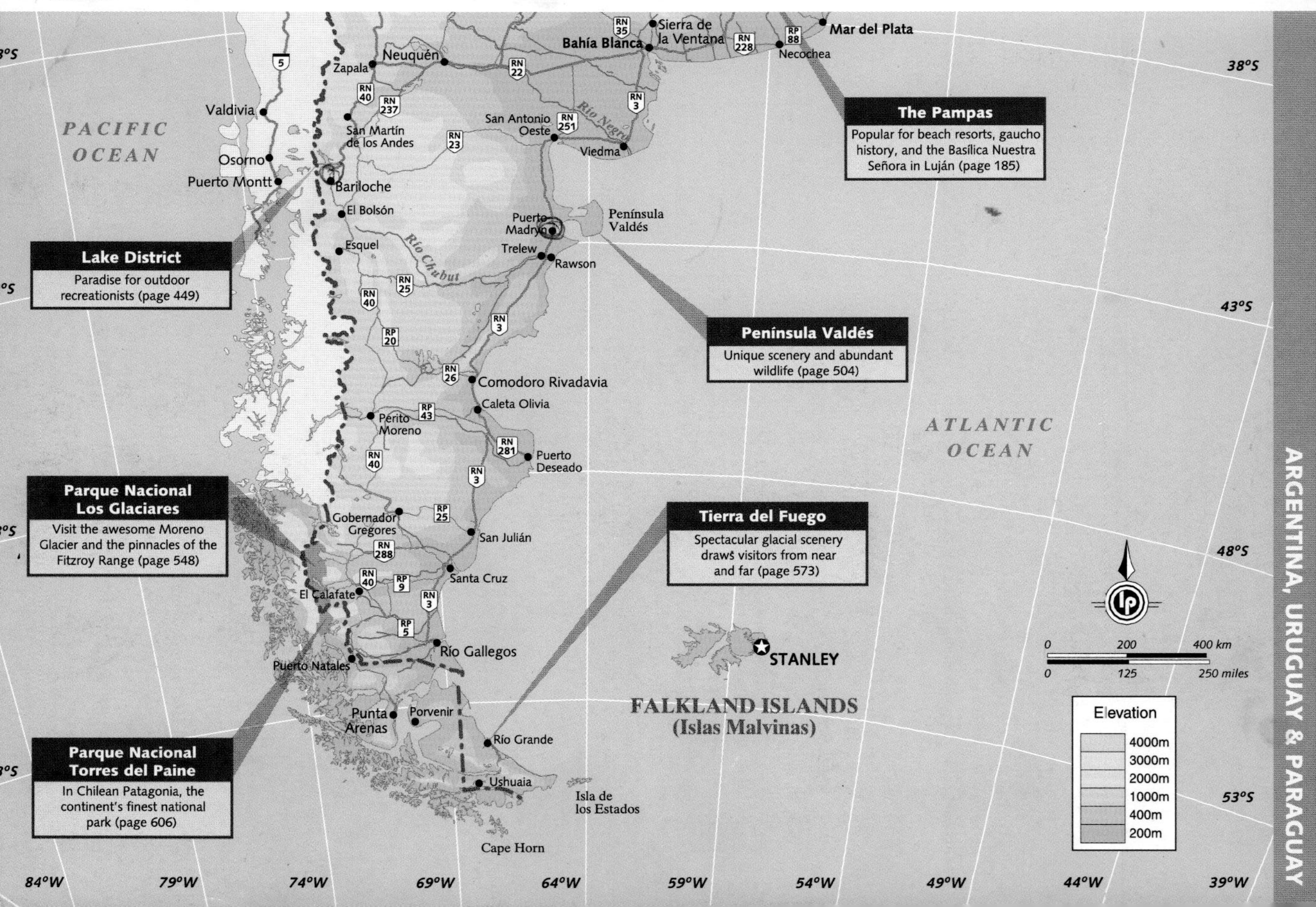

The Pampas
Popular for beach resorts, gaucho history, and the Basílica Nuestra Señora in Luján (page 185)
Península Valdés
Unique scenery and abundant wildlife (page 504)
Tierra del Fuego
Spectacular glacial scenery draws visitors from near and far (page 573)
Lake District
Paradise for outdoor recreationists (page 449)
Parque Nacional Los Glaciares
Visit the awesome Moreno Glacier and the pinnacles of the Fitzroy Range (page 548)
Parque Nacional Torres del Paine
In Chilean Patagonia, the continent's finest national park (page 606)
PACIFIC OCEAN
ATLANTIC OCEAN
FALKLAND ISLANDS (Islas Malvinas)
STANLEY
Mar del Plata
Necochea
Sierra de la Ventana
Bahía Blanca
Neuquén
Zapala
Valdivia
Osorno
Puerto Montt
Bariloche
San Martín de los Andes
El Bolsón
Esquel
San Antonio Oeste
Viedma
Río Negro
Península Valdés
Puerto Madryn
Trelew
Rawson
Río Chubut
Comodoro Rivadavia
Caleta Olivia
Perito Moreno
Puerto Deseado
Gobernador Gregores
San Julián
Santa Cruz
El Calafate
Puerto Natales
Río Gallegos
Punta Arenas
Porvenir
Río Grande
Ushuaia
Isla de los Estados
Cape Horn
RN 35
RN 228
RP 88
RN 22
RN 3
RN 40
RN 237
RN 23
RN 251
RN 25
RP 20
RN 26
RP 43
RN 281
RP 25
RN 288
RP 9
RP 5
5
38°S
43°S
48°S
53°S
84°W
79°W
74°W
69°W
64°W
59°W
54°W
49°W
44°W
39°W
0
200
400 km
125
250 miles
Elevation
4000m
3000m
2000m
1000m
400m
200m

Argentina, Uruguay & Paraguay
3rd Edition – August 1999
First published – August 1992

Published by
Lonely Planet Publications Pty Ltd A.C.N. 005 607 983
192 Burwood Rd, Hawthorn, Victoria 3122, Australia

Lonely Planet Offices
Australia PO Box 617, Hawthorn, Victoria 3122
USA 150 Linden St, Oakland, CA 94607
UK 10a Spring Place, London NW5 3BH
France 1 rue du Dahomey, 75011 Paris

Photographs
Sandra Bao, Wayne Bernhardson, Frank S Balthis, Andrea Booner/Tony Stone Images, D Donne Bryant, David R Frazier, Robert Frerck/Odyssey Productions, Robert Fried, Sarah J Hawkins, Ken Laffal, Library of Congress, Robert Rattner, Secretaría de Turismo Argentina, Sylvia Stevens
Some of the images in this guide are available for licensing from Lonely Planet Images.
email: lpi@lonelyplanet.com.au

Front cover photograph
Perito Moreno Glacier, Patagonia, Argentina (Hans Strand/Tony Stone Images)

ISBN 0 86442 641 0

Printed by Colorcraft Ltd, Hong Kong

Contents

INTRODUCTION 13

FACTS ABOUT ARGENTINA 16

History 16
Geography & Climate 29
Ecology & Environment . . . 32
Flora & Fauna 32
National & Provincial Parks . . 34
Government & Politics 37
Economy 41
Population & People 43
Education 45
Arts 45
Society & Conduct 52
Religion 52
Language 53

FACTS FOR THE VISITOR 54

Highlights 54
Suggested Itineraries 55
Planning 55
Tourist Offices 56
Visas & Documents 62
Customs 63
Money 63
Post & Communications . . . 67
Internet Resources 70
Books 70
Film 73
Newspapers & Magazines . . 74
Radio & TV 75
Photography & Video 76
Time 76
Electricity 76
Weights & Measures 76
Laundry 76
Toilets 76
Health 76
Women Travelers 87
Gay & Lesbian Travelers . . . 88
Disabled Travelers 88
Senior Travelers 88
Travel with Children 88
Useful Organizations 89
Dangers & Annoyances . . . 90
Business Hours 91
Public Holidays & Special Events 91
Activities 92
Language Courses 93
Work 93
Accommodations 94
Food 96
Drinks 99
Entertainment 100
Spectator Sports 102
Shopping 103

GETTING THERE & AWAY 104

Air 104
Land 114
River & Sea 117
Organized Tours 117
Warning 119

GETTING AROUND 120

Air 120
Bus 122
Train 123
Car & Motorcycle 124
Bicycle 127
Hitchhiking 128
Boat 128
Local Transport 128
Organized Tours 129

BUENOS AIRES 130

History 130
Orientation 131
Information 133
Things to See & Do 138
Language Courses 151
Organized Tours 151
Special Events 154
Places to Stay 155
Places to Eat 158
Entertainment 163
Spectator Sports 168
Shopping 169
Getting There & Away . . . 170
Getting Around 175
Around Buenos Aires 179
Tigre & The Delta del Paraná 179
Isla Martín García 180

THE PAMPAS 185

Northern Buenos Aires Province 188
La Plata 188
Around La Plata 194
Luján 195
San Antonio de Areco . . . 197
Around San Antonio de Areco 203
Atlantic Coast Beaches . . 203
Mar del Plata 203
Around Mar del Plata . . . 212
Villa Gesell 212
Pinamar 215
San Clemente del Tuyú . . . 217
Necochea 217
Southern Buenos Aires Province 220
Bahía Blanca 220

Sierra de la Ventana 224
Around Sierra de la Ventana 226
Tandil 227
Around Tandil 229
Santa Fe Province 229
Santa Fe 229
Around Santa Fe 236
Rosario 236
La Pampa Province 242
Santa Rosa 242
Around Santa Rosa 246
Parque Nacional Lihué Calel 246

ARGENTINE MESOPOTAMIA 249

Entre Ríos Province 251
Paraná 251
La Paz 256
Gualeguaychú 257
Concepción 259
Palacio San José 260
Colón 260
Parque Nacional El Palmar 261
Concordia 262
Corrientes Province 265
Corrientes 266
Paso de la Patria 270
Mercedes 270
Esteros del Iberá 271
Paso de los Libres 272
Yapeyú 274
Santo Tomé 274
Misiones Province 274
Posadas 279
Around Posadas 283
San Ignacio & San Ignacio Miní 284
Montecarlo 286
Puerto Iguazú 286
Parque Nacional Iguazú . . 290
Parque Nacional do Iguaçu (Brazil) 294
Foz do Iguaçu (Brazil) 295

THE GRAN CHACO 299

Resistencia 300
Parque Nacional Chaco . . . 305
Roque Sáenz Peña 306
Formosa 308
Clorinda 311
Parque Nacional Río Pilcomayo 311

CÓRDOBA 313

Córdoba 315
La Calera 323
Villa Carlos Paz 323
Cosquín 324
La Falda 324
Candonga 325
Jesús María 325
Santa Catalina 326
Alta Gracia 326
Villa General Belgrano . . . 327
Candelaria 327
Mina Clavero 327
Around Mina Clavero 329
Villa de las Rosas 329
Yacanto 329

CUYO 330

Mendoza Province 330
Mendoza 332
Around Mendoza 344
Uspallata 346
Parque Provincial Aconcagua 347
San Rafael 350
Around San Rafael 352
General Alvear 353
Malargüe 353
Around Malargüe 354
Las Leñas 355
San Juan Province 356
San Juan 356
Around San Juan 361
Difunta Correa Shrine 363
San José de Jáchal 363
Around San José de Jáchal 365
San Agustín de Valle Fértil 365
Parque Provincial Ischigualasto 367
San Luis Province 368
San Luis 368
Parque Nacional Sierra de las Quijadas 371
Merlo 371

THE ANDEAN NORTHWEST 373

Jujuy Province 375
San Salvador de Jujuy 376
Around Jujuy 382
Quebrada de Humahuaca 382
Tilcara 383
Humahuaca 385
Around Humahuaca 386
La Quiaca 386
Around La Quiaca 388
Monumento Natural Laguna de dos Pozuelos 389
Parque Nacional Calilegua 389
Salta Province 390
Salta 391
National Parks of Salta Province 398
Quebrada de Cafayate . . . 399
Cafayate 400
Valles Calchaquíes 402
El Tren a las Nubes & the Chilean Crossing . . . 405
Tucumán Province 406

FACTS FOR THE VISITOR 731

Highlights ... 731
Planning ... 731
Tourist Offices ... 731
Visas & Documents ... 732
Embassies & Consulates ... 732
Customs ... 733
Money ... 733
Post & Communications ... 734
Books ... 734
Newspapers & Radio ... 734
Film & Photography ... 735
Time ... 735
Health ... 735
Women Travelers ... 735
Useful Organizations ... 735
Dangers & Annoyances ... 736
Business Hours & Public Holidays ... 736
Food ... 736
Drinks ... 737
Entertainment ... 737
Spectator Sports ... 737
Shopping ... 737

GETTING THERE & AWAY 738

GETTING AROUND 740

ASUNCIÓN 742

History ... 742
Orientation ... 743
Information ... 744
Walking Tour ... 746
Panteón de los Héroes ... 747
Museo Etnográfico Andrés Barbero ... 747
Mercado Petirossi & Mercado Cuatro ... 747
Jardín Botánico ... 747
Museo del Barro ... 747
Museo Boggiani ... 750
Art Galleries ... 750
Organized Tours ... 750
Places to Stay ... 750
Places to Eat ... 751
Entertainment ... 753
Shopping ... 753
Getting There & Away ... 754
Getting Around ... 756

EASTERN PARAGUAY 757

Circuito Central ... 757
Areguá ... 757
Itauguá ... 757
San Bernardino ... 759
Caacupé ... 759
Around Caacupé ... 759
Piribebuy ... 760
Around Piribebuy ... 760
Yaguarón ... 760
Itá ... 760
Southeastern Paraguay ... 761
Villa Florida ... 762
Encarnación ... 762
Around Encarnación ... 765
San Ignacio Guazú ... 766
Santa María ... 766
Northeastern Paraguay ... 767
Ciudad del Este ... 767
Around Ciudad del Este ... 770
Coronel Oviedo ... 771
Villarrica ... 771
Pedro Juan Caballero ... 771
Parque Nacional Cerro Corá ... 772
Concepción ... 772

THE PARAGUAYAN CHACO 773

Villa Hayes ... 773
Pozo Colorado ... 775
Filadelfia ... 775
Around Filadelfia ... 777
Loma Plata ... 777
Neu-Halbstadt ... 777
Parque Nacional Defensores del Chaco ... 779
Mariscal Estigarribia ... 780
Estancia La Patria ... 780

LANGUAGE 781

GLOSSARY 787

CLIMATE CHARTS 794

INTERNET RESOURCES 795

ACKNOWLEDGEMENTS 797

INDEX 804

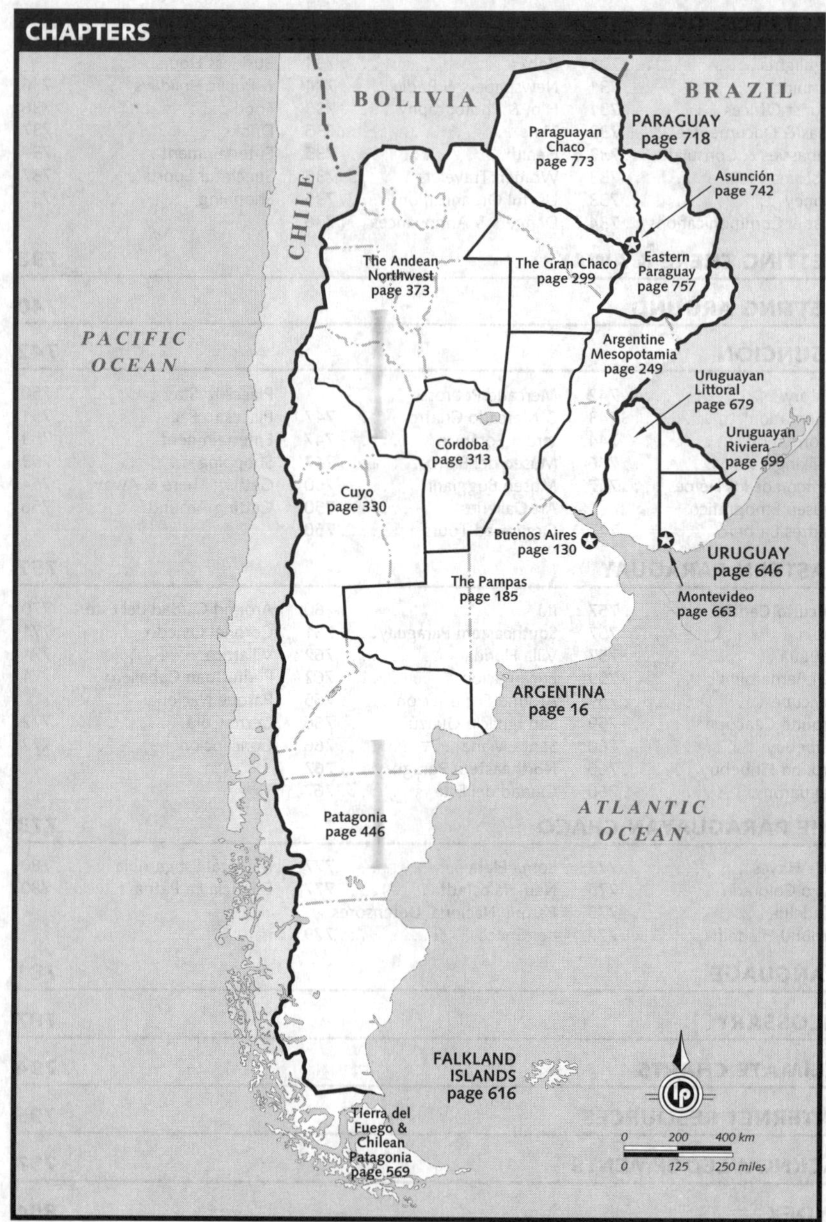
CHAPTERS
BOLIVIA
BRAZIL
CHILE
PARAGUAY
page 718
Paraguayan
Chaco
page 773
Asunción
page 742
The Andean
Northwest
page 373
The Gran Chaco
page 299
Eastern
Paraguay
page 757
PACIFIC
OCEAN
Argentine
Mesopotamia
page 249
Uruguayan
Littoral
page 679
Córdoba
page 313
Uruguayan
Riviera
page 699
Cuyo
page 330
Buenos Aires
page 130
URUGUAY
page 646
The Pampas
page 185
Montevideo
page 663
ARGENTINA
page 16
ATLANTIC
OCEAN
Patagonia
page 446
FALKLAND
ISLANDS
page 616
Tierra del
Fuego &
Chilean
Patagonia
page 569
0 200 400 km
0 125 250 miles

The Author

PHOTO BY MARÍA LAURA MASSOLO

Wayne Bernhardson

Wayne Bernhardson was born in Fargo, North Dakota, grew up in Tacoma, Washington, and earned a PhD in geography at the University of California, Berkeley. He has traveled extensively in Mexico and Central and South America, and lived for extended periods in Chile, Argentina, and the Falkland (Malvinas) Islands. His other LP credits include Buenos Aires, Chile & Easter Island, South America on a shoestring, Baja California, Mexico, and the 1st edition of the Rocky Mountains. Wayne resides in Oakland, California, where his Alaskan malamute Gardel smiles as charismatically as his legendary porteño namesake.

FROM THE AUTHOR

Special mention to Fito and Mary Massolo of Olavarría, Buenos Aires province, my Argentine family for so many years, and to all their sons and daughters, nieces and nephews, and others.

Many others in Buenos Aires and elsewhere were exceptionally helpful and hospitable in the process of pulling this all together. The list could go on forever, but special mention goes to the following Buenos Aires residents: Mónica Kapusta of the Subsecretaría de Turismo; Pablo Fisch; Federico Kirbus, Joaquín Allolio; Diego Allolio, Dori Lieberman; Jochen Hoettcke; Michael Soltys and Andrew Graham-Yooll of the Buenos Aires Herald; Diego Curubeto of Ámbito Financiero; Ernesto Seman of Clarín; Mario Banchik of Librerías Turísticas; Monique Larraín of the Guía Argentina de Tráfico Aéreo; Carlos Felipe Arnedo of the Casa de Formosa; and Armando Schlecker of the Guía Latinoamericana de Transportes. A huge and special thanks to Georges and Marion Helft of San Telmo for their willingness to permit photography of their extraordinary collection of modern Argentine art.

In the provinces, thanks to Vicky Holzkan of Resistencia; Mariana Juri, Rosemary Fayad, Alberto Albino, Daniel Cadile, Ariadna López, María Leonor Bajouth, and Cecilia Díaz of Mendoza; María Graciela Viollaz of Malargüe, Mendoza; Julio César Lovece and Natalie Prosser de Goodall of Ushuaia, Tierra del Fuego; Adrian Falcone and Tammy Olsen of Parque Nacional Perito Moreno, Santa Cruz; Judith López and Rubén Montivero of La Rioja; Mariano Besio, now of El Calafate, and the rest of the staff at the Casa de Santa Cruz in Buenos Aires; Martín Jáuregui of Rawson, Chubut; Nathalia Bilotti, Cecilia Torrejón and Gustavo Wofcy Diez of Puerto Madryn, Chubut; Daniel Rojas Lanús of the Museo Egidio Feruglio, Trelew, Chubut; Estela Maris Williams of the Municipalidad de Trelew, Chubut; Ana Ruiz of Enprotur, San Juan; Rubén Vásquez of El Chaltén, Santa Cruz; Lilián Díaz and Mario Feldman of El Calafate; Sonia Nasif of Esquel; Raúl Morales, José María Lucero, and Ricardo Clark of Salta; Analía Loren Taverna of Puerto Deseado, Santa Cruz; and David Rivarola of San Luis and his colleague Luis Chiappe of the American Museum of Natural History in New York.

In Chilean Patagonia, thanks to Julio Arenas Coloma of Sernatur, Punta Arenas; Hernán Jofré of Amerindia, Puerto Natales; Edmundo Martínez G of Andescape, Puerto Natales; and Miguel Ángel Muñoz of Sernatur, Puerto Natales. Special mention to Yerko Ivelic of Cascada Expediciones, Santiago de Chile, for harboring my truck while I returned to California to write up this material; and to customs agent Juan Alarcón Rojas of Santiago for guidance through the Chilean bureaucracy.

Chris McAsey, coauthor of LP's Brazil guide, provided supplementary information on Foz do Iguaçu (Brazil) and Chuy/Chui (Uruguay/Argentina). In Montevideo, as always, I appreciate the help from Manuel Pérez Bravo of the Asociación de Hoteles y Restaurantes del Uruguay. Jorge C Margariños Micoud of Montevideo and Alejandra Canela of Colonia were also helpful. Paula Braun, of Paula's Tours in Asunción, Paraguay, was particularly patient in updating material on the Chaco. Thanks also to Antonio van Humbeeck of the Fundación Moisés Bertoni in Asunción.

In the Falkland Islands, thanks to Stanley residents John Fowler and Deborah Gilding of the Falkland Islands Tourist Board, Governor Richard Ralph, Ian and Maria Strange, Kay McCallum, Sue Binnie, Jane Cameron, Tony Smith, Montana Short, John and Margaret Leonard, Shirley Peck, Dave Eynon, and Ray and Nancy Poole. In the camp, thanks to Dave and Pat Grey of Sea Lion Island, Richard and Toni Stevens of Port Sussex, Tony McMullen of Goose Green, William and Lynda Anderson of San Carlos, James McGhie of Pebble Island, John Ferguson of Weddell Island, all the Pole-Evanses on Saunders Island, Robin Lee and Ron Reeves of Port Howard, Richard and Griz Cockwell of Fox Bay East for lunch and transport back to Port Howard, and Jerome and Sally Poncet of Beaver Island.

In Oakland, thanks to James T Smith for paying my bills and to María Laura Massolo for permission to adapt material from her contribution to LP's Travel with Children. Thanks also to Miguel Helft of San Francisco, to Ted Oberlander of UC Berkeley for an interpretation of La Olla, and to Scott Stine of California State University, Hayward, for sharing the results of his research on the Moreno Glacier.

In Los Angeles, Buddy Lander of LanChile was most helpful in arranging flight details, along with Alberto Cortés of LanChile in Miami.

Thanks again to Tony and Maureen Wheeler for keeping me employed these several years, to former LP publishing director Caroline Liou, and to Eric Kettunen and other Oakland office editors, cartographers, and staff.

This Book

FROM THE PUBLISHER

This book was edited and proofed in Lonely Planet's Oakland office by Ben Greensfelder and Maureen Klier, who was project editor. Many thanks to Carolyn Hubbard for her guidance, support, and supply of mate, with a tip of the fedora to relief pitcher Tom Downs. Tracey Croom and Colin Bishop drew the maps, with help from Patrick Bock, Mary Hagemann, Monica Lepe, and Margaret Livingston. Amy Dennis and Alex Guilbert oversaw the cartography. Design was spearheaded by Henia Miedzinski. Hayden Foell drew the illustrations, with help from Hugh D'Andrade and Mark Butler. Layout was done by Richard Wilson and Shelley Firth, guided by Margaret Livingston. The cover was designed by Rini Keagy with assistance from Hugh. The book was indexed by Ken DellaPenta.

Sandra Bao provided invaluable assistance in implementing the changes to all Argentine phone numbers. Thanks also to Tara Duggan and Wade Fox for proofreading, Kevin Anglin and Joslyn Leve for editorial assistance, Josh Schefers for hunting down photographs, Robert Reid for Buenos Aires updates, and Kate Hoffman, 'La Comandante' of the second edition of this book.

THANKS
Many thanks to the travellers who used the last edition and wrote to us with helpful hints, advice and interesting anecdotes. Your names appear in the back of this book.

Foreword

ABOUT LONELY PLANET GUIDEBOOKS

The story begins with a classic travel adventure: Tony and Maureen Wheeler's 1972 journey across Europe and Asia to Australia. Useful information about the overland trail did not exist at that time, so Tony and Maureen published the first Lonely Planet guidebook to meet a growing need.

From a kitchen table, then from a tiny office in Melbourne (Australia), Lonely Planet has become the largest independent travel publisher in the world, an international company with offices in Melbourne, Oakland (USA), London (UK) and Paris (France).

Today Lonely Planet guidebooks cover the globe. There is an ever-growing list of books, and there's information in a variety of forms and media. Some things haven't changed. The main aim is still to help make it possible for adventurous travelers to get out there – to explore and better understand the world.

At Lonely Planet we believe travelers can make a positive contribution to the countries they visit – if they respect their host communities and spend their money wisely. Since 1986 a percentage of the income from each book has been donated to aid projects and human-rights campaigns.

Updates Lonely Planet thoroughly updates each guidebook as often as possible. This usually means there are around two years between editions, although for more unusual or more stable destinations the gap can be longer. Check the imprint page (following the color map at the beginning of the book) for publication dates.

Between editions, up-to-date information is available in two free newsletters – the paper *Planet Talk* and email *Comet* (to subscribe, contact any Lonely Planet office) – and on our website at www.lonelyplanet.com. The *Upgrades* section of the website covers a number of important and volatile destinations and is regularly updated by Lonely Planet authors. *Scoop* covers news and current affairs relevant to travelers. And, lastly, the *Thorn Tree* bulletin board and *Postcards* section of the site carry unverified, but fascinating, reports from travelers.

Correspondence The process of creating new editions begins with the letters, postcards and emails received from travelers. This correspondence often includes suggestions, criticisms and comments about the current editions. Interesting excerpts are immediately passed on via newsletters and the website, and everything goes to our authors to be verified when they're researching on the road. We're keen to get more feedback from organizations or individuals who represent communities visited by travelers.

Lonely Planet gathers information for everyone who's curious about the planet – and especially for those who explore it firsthand. Through guidebooks, phrasebooks, activity guides, maps, literature, newsletters, image library, TV series and website, we act as an information exchange for a worldwide community of travelers.

Research Authors aim to gather sufficient practical information to enable travelers to make informed choices and to make the mechanics of a journey run smoothly. They also research historical and cultural background to help enrich the travel experience and allow travelers to understand and respond appropriately to cultural and environmental issues.

Authors don't stay in every hotel because that would mean spending a couple of months in each medium-size city and, no, they don't eat at every restaurant because that would mean stretching belts beyond capacity. They do visit hotels and restaurants to check standards and prices, but feedback based on readers' direct experiences can be very helpful.

Many of our authors work undercover; others aren't so secretive. None of them accept freebies in exchange for positive write-ups. And none of our guidebooks contain any advertising.

Production Authors submit their raw manuscripts and maps to offices in Australia, the USA, the UK or France. Editors and cartographers – all experienced travelers themselves – then begin the process of assembling the pieces. When the book finally hits the shops, some things are already out of date, we start getting feedback from readers and the process begins again....

WARNING & REQUEST

Things change – prices go up, schedules change, good places go bad and bad places go bankrupt – nothing stays the same. So, if you find things better or worse, recently opened or long since closed, please tell us and help make the next edition even more accurate and useful. We genuinely value all the feedback we receive. Julie Young coordinates a well-traveled team that reads and acknowledges every letter, postcard and email and ensures that every morsel of information finds its way to the appropriate authors, editors and cartographers for verification.

Everyone who writes to us will find their name in the next edition of the appropriate guidebook. They will also receive the latest issue of *Planet Talk*, our quarterly printed newsletter, or *Comet*, our monthly email newsletter. Subscriptions to both newsletters are free. The very best contributions will be rewarded with a free guidebook.

Excerpts from your correspondence may appear in new editions of Lonely Planet guidebooks, the Lonely Planet website, *Planet Talk* or *Comet*, so please let us know if you *don't* want your letter published or your name acknowledged.

Send all correspondence to the Lonely Planet office closest to you:

Australia: PO Box 617, Hawthorn, Victoria 3122
USA: 150 Linden St, Oakland, CA 94607
UK: 10A Spring Place, London NW5 3BH
France: 1 rue du Dahomey, 75011 Paris

Or email us at: talk2us@lonelyplanet.com.au

For news, views and updates, see our website: www.lonelyplanet.com

HOW TO USE A LONELY PLANET GUIDEBOOK

The best way to use a Lonely Planet guidebook is any way you choose. At Lonely Planet, we believe the most memorable travel experiences are often those that are unexpected, and the finest discoveries are those you make yourself. Guidebooks are not intended to be used as if they provided a detailed set of infallible instructions!

Contents All Lonely Planet guidebooks follow the same format. The Facts about the Country chapters or sections give background information ranging from history to weather. Facts for the Visitor gives practical information on issues like visas and health. Getting There & Away gives a brief starting point for researching travel to and from the destination. Getting Around gives an overview of the transport options available when you arrive.

The peculiar demands of each destination determine how subsequent chapters are broken up, but some things remain constant. We always start with background, then proceed to sights, places to stay, places to eat, entertainment, getting there and away, and getting around information – in that order.

Heading Hierarchy Lonely Planet headings are used in a strict hierarchical structure that can be visualized as a set of Russian dolls. Each heading (and its following text) is encompassed by any preceding heading that is higher on the hierarchical ladder.

Entry Points We do not assume guidebooks will be read from beginning to end, but that people will dip into them. The traditional entry points are the list of contents and the index. In addition, however, some books have a complete list of maps and an index map illustrating map coverage.

There may also be a color map that shows highlights. These highlights are dealt with in greater detail later in the book, along with planning questions and suggested itineraries. Each chapter covering a geographical region usually begins with a locator map and another list of highlights. Once you find something of interest in a list of highlights, turn to the index.

Maps Maps play a crucial role in Lonely Planet guidebooks and include a huge amount of information. A legend is printed on the back page. We seek to have complete consistency between maps and text, and to have every important place in the text captured on a map. Map key numbers usually start in the top left corner.

Although inclusion in a guidebook usually implies a recommendation, we cannot list every good place. Exclusion does not necessarily imply criticism. In fact, there are a number of reasons why we might exclude a place – sometimes it is simply inappropriate to encourage an influx of travelers.

Introduction

Argentina, Uruguay, and Paraguay comprise the bulk of the region commonly known as South America's 'Southern Cone,' which stretches from the tropics to, by some accounts, the South Pole. Within this region are a remarkable variety of both natural and cultural attractions. The magnificent desolation of Patagonia and the high Andes contrasts dramatically with the urban frenzy of Buenos Aires, one of the world's largest and most cosmopolitan cities.

For many travelers, the region's natural wonders will be the primary attraction. In the early 20th century, Argentina was one of the first South American countries to designate national parks. Its southern Andean cordillera offers a string of alpine parks where awesome glaciers spill icebergs into blue-green lakes of incomparable beauty. The central cordillera features the highest peaks in the Western Hemisphere, while the northern deserts are, in their own way, no less impressive; these thinly populated areas also contain unusual wildlife. In vivid contrast are the massive concentrations of sub-Antarctic wildlife on the southern Patagonian coastline. Argentina also shares the awesome Iguazú Falls with Brazil and Paraguay.

Because of the cultural domination of overseas immigrants, ecological historian Alfred Crosby has called Buenos Aires and its immediate hinterlands a 'neo-Europe,' in which trans-Atlantic arrivals and their cultural baggage – domestic plants and animals, and weeds – transformed the natural environment and ensured the eventual demise of the relatively few indigenous people who inhabited the area in the 16th century. According to Crosby, the most aggressive weeds were the Europeans themselves, whose overwhelming numbers created a society that never truly accepted its New World uniqueness nor its ultimately derivative nature. It did, however, maintain important economic and cultural links with Europe, feeding its parent with grains and beef, contributing to world literature through Borges and others, and exporting the tango to European salons. For such reasons, Argentina is one Latin American country in which Europeans, North Americans, and Anglophones can feel at ease and travel relatively inconspicuously.

Uruguay, whose economy and culture closely resemble those of the Argentine Pampas, is a political buffer between giant Brazil and Argentina, while isolated Paraguay is South America's 'empty quarter,' a hot, sparsely populated, subtropical lowland best known, until recently, for the unusually durable military dictatorship of General Alfredo Stroessner. Historically, Uruguay is the most stable and democratic of the three countries, but the recent regional democratic revival has made all three countries

more inviting destinations. There is still uncertainty whether democratic institutions will endure, but many signs are positive, and, at present, one can travel through all three countries without fear of arbitrary arrest and detention.

This was not the case through the 1970s and early 1980s, when Argentina's military dictatorship fought its infamous Dirty War against 'subversives' before losing both power and prestige during the military confrontation with Britain in the South Atlantic war of 1982, commonly referred to as the Falklands War. Uruguay suffered a similar, if slightly less brutal, experience at the hands of its military, while Paraguay endured institutionalized authoritarian rule for decades until 1989 when General Stroessner was ousted and replaced with a reform-minded (if not entirely untainted) colleague. Though now headed by a civilian president, it is still the most politically volatile of the three countries in this book.

Present-day Argentina also includes northwestern areas with significant indigenous populations once more closely integrated with the pre-Columbian civilizations of Peru and Bolivia. Throughout the colonial era, when Buenos Aires was a nearly forgotten backwater, cities such as Tucumán and Salta provided mules and essential provisions for the vital mining economy of the central Andes.

Only late in the 19th century, following a brutal war of extermination against mounted Indians and with the assistance of a new wave of European immigration, did the Argentine state incorporate enormous, thinly populated Patagonia into its effective orbit. These persistent regional distinctions challenge the nebulous but frequently expressed ideal of *argentinidad*, a uniform Argentine nationality.

Even today, despite economic disorder, Argentina's relative prosperity attracts immigrants from adjacent lands like Chile and Bolivia. It also presents the visitor with a greater geographical and cultural diversity than one might expect. With Uruguay and Paraguay, it offers a multitude of complementary natural and cultural attractions for an extended stay.

The Falkland Islands (Islas Malvinas) are a special case. Politically, they are one of the world's last colonial relics, yet there is no doubt that the people, by and large, are content with their political status.

Though the Falkland Islands are steeped in history, visitors will be most impressed by the wild landscape and especially by the tame, abundant, and accessible wildlife. Except for the nearly constant wind, the climate is surprisingly benign. Yet short of Antarctica itself, there is no better place to see the birds and mammals characteristic of the world's most southerly regions.

ARGENTINA

WAYNE BERNHARDSON

Facts about Argentina

HISTORY

Despite its relative brevity, at least in a global sense, Argentine history is a complex and contentious topic. Many Argentine historians, and historians who write about Argentina, have explicit or implicit political perspectives that color both their choice of facts and their interpretation.

Pre-Columbian Argentina

Conventional histories portray Argentina as a homogeneous society founded on European immigration, but the country's pre-Columbian and colonial past (not to mention the present) are more complex than this misleading stereotype. When Europeans first arrived in the 16th century, South America's diverse economic and social systems ranged from densely settled civilizations in the central Andes to semisedentary agriculturalists of the tropical and temperate forests to nomadic hunters and gatherers of the Amazon and the Patagonian steppes.

On the eastern slopes of the central Andes – the periphery of the civilizations of Peru and Bolivia – Diaguita Indians irrigated maize fields that supported permanent villages between present-day Salta and San Juan in northwestern Argentina. Other groups, like the Comechingones near Córdoba, practiced a similar livelihood. To the east, in the forested Río Paraná delta across the Chaco scrubland, smaller Guaraní populations of shifting cultivators relied on maize, along with tuber crops like manioc (cassava) and sweet potatoes. Over most of the region, though, highly mobile peoples hunted the guanaco (a wild relative of the Andean llama) and the rhea (a flightless bird resembling the ostrich) with bow and arrow or *boleadoras* (heavily weighted thongs). In the far south, coastal groups like the Yahgans gathered shellfish and bird eggs.

Invasion of the New World

Ironically, even after a papal treaty ratified the Spanish-Portuguese division of the Americas in 1494, the structure of Indian societies more strongly influenced the economic and political structure of colonial society than did the edicts of peninsular authorities. The first Spaniards sought gold and silver above all, and ruthlessly appropriated precious metals through outright robbery when possible or by other more brutal means, such as forced labor. El Dorado, the legendary city of gold, eluded them, but they soon realized that the true wealth of the Indies consisted of the surprisingly large Indian populations they encountered in Mexico, Peru, and elsewhere.

The Spaniards exploited the indigenous populations of the New World through legal mechanisms like the *encomienda*, best translated as 'entrustment,' by which the Crown granted individual Spaniards rights to Indian labor and tribute in a particular village or area. Institutions like the Catholic Church also held encomiendas. In theory, Spanish legislation required the holder of the encomienda to reciprocate at least with instruction in the Spanish language and the Catholic religion, but in practice imperial administration was inadequate to ensure compliance and avoid the worst abuses. Spanish overseers worked Indians mercilessly in the mines and extracted the maximum in agricultural produce.

In the most densely populated parts of the Americas, some *encomenderos* became extraordinarily wealthy, but the system failed when Indian populations died off rapidly. This was less because of overwork and physical punishment than because the Indians, isolated for at least 10,000 years from Old World diseases, could not withstand the onslaught of smallpox, influenza, typhus, and other microbial killers brought in by colonists. In some parts of the New World, introduced diseases reduced the native population by more than 95%.

In most of Argentina and the other modern River Plate countries (Uruguay and Paraguay), the encomienda was less significant than in the Andes. Ironically, the most highly organized Indian peoples were the easiest to subdue and control, since they were accustomed to similar forms of exploitation. In hierarchical states like the Inca empire, the Spaniards rather easily assumed the apex of the pyramid.

The semisedentary and nomadic peoples of the riverine lowlands and the southern Pampas, though, put up determined resistance. In 1536, Querandí Indians routed Pedro de Mendoza's garrison at Buenos Aires within five years of its establishment, and even into the late 19th century, parts of the Pampas were not safe for settlers. Abandoned Spanish livestock multiplied rapidly on the lush pastures of the Pampas, where horses greatly aided the Indians' mobility and ability to strike. Not until the so-called Conquista del Desierto, a de facto war of extermination against the Pampas Indians in the late 19th century, could the European usurpers relax their guard.

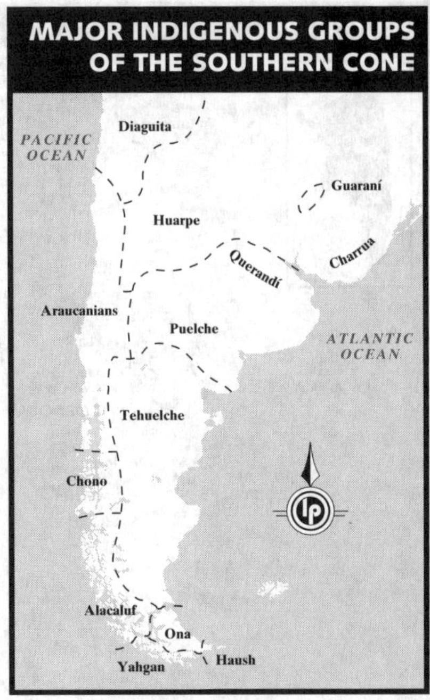

Colonial Times

Indian resistance discouraged early settlement of the lower River Plate, and potential settlers preferred Asunción, founded in 1537 on the upper Paraná. The region's most significant early economic links were not directly with Spain, but with silver-rich Alto Perú (now Bolivia), where the bonanza mine at Potosí financed Spanish expansion, and with Lima, capital of the Viceroyalty of Peru. Although Spanish forces reestablished Buenos Aires by 1580, it remained a backwater in comparison to Andean settlements like Tucumán (founded 1571), Córdoba (1573), Salta (1582), La Rioja (1591), and Jujuy (1593). Spaniards from Chile settled the cities of Mendoza (1561), San Juan (1562), and San Luis (1596) in what became known as the Cuyo region. The Tucumán region provided mules, cloth, and foodstuffs for Alto Perú; Cuyo produced wine and grain, while Buenos Aires languished.

The colonial-era decline of northwestern Argentina's Indian population and the relatively small indigenous numbers elsewhere produced a maldistribution of land that mirrored similar shifts in other Latin American countries but took on particularly Argentine characteristics. The appearance of *latifundios* (large landholdings) came about after the virtual disappearance of the Indian population made the encomienda obsolete. Spanish immigrants and *criollos* (American-born Spaniards) responded by acquiring large tracts of the best land for agriculture and livestock; this new institution, the *hacienda*, bore some resemblance to its feudal Spanish namesake, though it differed greatly in detail. As Indian populations gradually recovered or merged with the Spanish to form a mixed-race *mestizo* population, they found that the best lands had been monopolized and that their only economic alternatives were cultivation of *minifundios* (small plots) on inferior lands or dependent labor on the large estates.

Although the hacienda was never as important in Argentina as it was in Peru or Mexico, the livestock *estancia* came to play a critical role in the development of Argentine

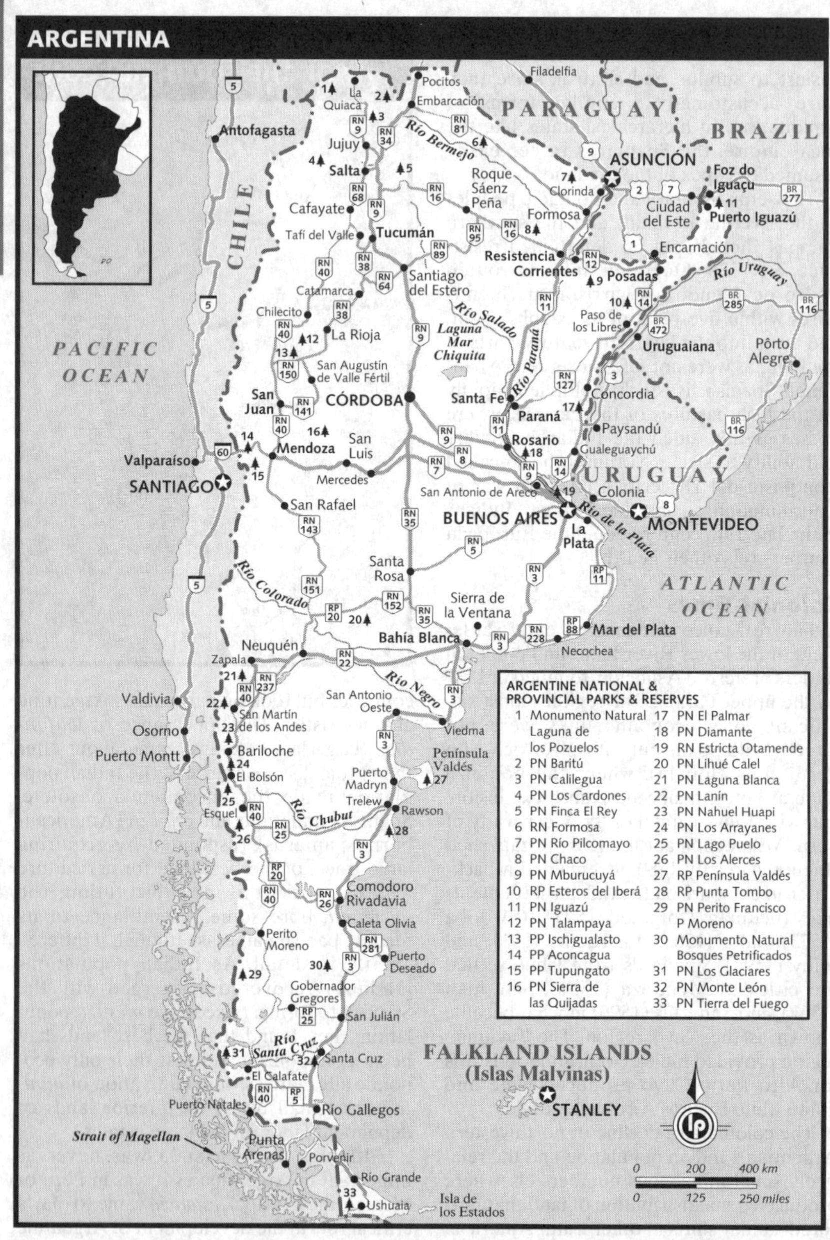
ARGENTINA
PARAGUAY
BRAZIL
CHILE
URUGUAY
PACIFIC OCEAN
ATLANTIC OCEAN
FALKLAND ISLANDS (Islas Malvinas)
STANLEY
ASUNCIÓN
SANTIAGO
BUENOS AIRES
MONTEVIDEO
CÓRDOBA
Antofagasta
Filadelfia
Pocitos
Embarcación
La Quiaca
Jujuy
Salta
Cafayate
Tafí del Valle
Tucumán
Santiago del Estero
Catamarca
Chilecito
La Rioja
San Augustín de Valle Fértil
San Juan
Mendoza
San Luis
Mercedes
Valparaíso
San Rafael
Roque Sáenz Peña
Clorinda
Formosa
Resistencia
Corrientes
Posadas
Foz do Iguaçu
Puerto Iguazú
Ciudad del Este
Encarnación
Paso de los Libres
Uruguaiana
Pôrto Alegre
Concordia
Paysandú
Gualeguaychú
Santa Fe
Paraná
Rosario
San Antonio de Areco
Colonia
La Plata
Santa Rosa
Sierra de la Ventana
Bahía Blanca
Mar del Plata
Necochea
Neuquén
Zapala
Valdivia
Osorno
Puerto Montt
San Martín de los Andes
Bariloche
El Bolsón
Esquel
San Antonio Oeste
Viedma
Península Valdés
Puerto Madryn
Trelew
Rawson
Comodoro Rivadavia
Caleta Olivia
Perito Moreno
Puerto Deseado
Gobernador Gregores
San Julián
Santa Cruz
El Calafate
Puerto Natales
Río Gallegos
Strait of Magellan
Punta Arenas
Porvenir
Río Grande
Ushuaia
Isla de los Estados
Río Bermejo
Río Salado
Río Paraná
Río Uruguay
Río de la Plata
Río Colorado
Río Negro
Río Chubut
Río Santa Cruz
Laguna Mar Chiquita
0 200 400 km
0 125 250 miles
ARGENTINE NATIONAL & PROVINCIAL PARKS & RESERVES
1 Monumento Natural Laguna de los Pozuelos
2 PN Baritú
3 PN Calilegua
4 PN Los Cardones
5 PN Finca El Rey
6 RN Formosa
7 PN Río Pilcomayo
8 PN Chaco
9 PN Mburucuyá
10 RP Esteros del Iberá
11 PN Iguazú
12 PN Talampaya
13 PP Ischigualasto
14 PP Aconcagua
15 PP Tupungato
16 PN Sierra de las Quijadas
17 PN El Palmar
18 PN Diamante
19 RN Estricta Otamende
20 PN Lihué Calel
21 PN Laguna Blanca
22 PN Lanín
23 PN Nahuel Huapi
24 PN Los Arrayanes
25 PN Lago Puelo
26 PN Los Alerces
27 RP Península Valdés
28 RP Punta Tombo
29 PN Perito Francisco P Moreno
30 Monumento Natural Bosques Petrificados
31 PN Los Glaciares
32 PN Monte León
33 PN Tierra del Fuego

PROVINCES OF ARGENTINA
PARAGUAY
CHILE
Jujuy
Salta
Formosa
San Salvador de Jujuy
ASUNCIÓN
Salta
Santiago del Estero
Formosa
Tucumán
Tucumán
Chaco
Misiones
PACIFIC OCEAN
Catamarca
Resistencia
Corrientes
Posadas
Santiago del Estero
Catamarca
Corrientes
La Rioja
La Rioja
Santa Fe
BRAZIL
San Juan
Córdoba
Santa Fe
Paraná
San Juan
Córdoba
Entre Ríos
San Luis
Mendoza
URUGUAY
San Luis
SANTIAGO
Mendoza
MONTEVIDEO
BUENOS AIRES
La Plata
Santa Rosa
Buenos Aires
La Pampa
Neuquén
Neuquén
Río Negro
Viedma
Rawson
ATLANTIC OCEAN
Chubut
Santa Cruz
FALKLAND ISLANDS
(Islas Malvinas)
STANLEY
Río Gallegos
Tierra del Fuego
Ushuaia
0 200 400 km
0 125 250 miles

society. When the Spaniards returned to the River Plate estuary in the late 16th century, they found that the cattle and horses abandoned decades earlier had proliferated almost beyond belief as the primary agents in what historian Alfred Crosby has called 'ecological imperialism.' With commerce severely restricted under Spanish regulation, the inhabitants of colonial Buenos Aires looked to livestock for their livelihood. Without these livestock, the legendary gaucho of the Pampas could never have existed, but their growing commercial importance also brought his extinction.

Growth & Independence

Though isolated and legally prohibited from direct European commerce for nearly two centuries, the people of Buenos Aires pursued a flourishing contraband trade with Portuguese Brazil and nonpeninsular European powers. Governed for too long at the tail end of an indirect supply line via the Caribbean, Panama, and Peru, frustrated criollos wished to carry on direct trade with Spain. In naming Buenos Aires capital of the new Viceroyalty of the River Plate in 1776, the Spanish crown explicitly acknowledged that the region had outgrown the mother country's political and economic domination.

Toward the end of the 18th century, criollos became increasingly dissatisfied and impatient with peninsular authority in all parts of the continent. The expulsion of British troops who briefly occupied Buenos Aires in 1806 and 1807 gave the people of the River Plate new confidence in their ability to stand alone, which they asserted in the revolution of May 25, 1810.

Independence movements throughout South America united to expel Spain from the continent by the 1820s. Under the leadership of General José de San Martín and others, the United Provinces of the River Plate, the direct forerunner of Argentina, declared formal independence at Tucumán in 1816. Ironically, British financial and logistical support had made it possible for Argentina to break the Spanish yoke. In the process, Bolivia and Paraguay became independent countries rather than remaining part of the former Viceroyalty.

Despite achieving independence, the provinces were united in name only. Lacking any effective central authority, the regional disparities obscured by Spanish rule became more obvious. This resulted in the rise of the *caudillos* (local strongmen), who resented and resisted Buenos Aires as strongly as Buenos Aires had resisted Spain. Argentine educator and president Domingo F Sarmiento, himself a product of the provinces, indicted the excesses of demagogic caudillos in his classic *Life in the Argentine Republic in the Days of the Tyrants* (1845). At the same time the caudillos commanded great personal loyalty and respect. In 1833 Charles Darwin observed in his notes that Juan Manuel de Rosas 'by conforming to the dress and habits of the Gauchos ... obtained an unbounded popularity in the country' and that he 'never saw anything like the enthusiasm for Rosas ... '

In theory, the great controversy in Argentine politics was between the Federalists of the interior, who advocated provincial autonomy, and the Unitarists of Buenos Aires, who upheld central authority. The Federalists, associated with conservative provincial landowners but supported by much of the rural working class (including a substantial Afro-Argentine population that has almost completely disappeared), resented Buenos Aires as much as Madrid. The Unitarists, led by intellectuals like Bernardino Rivadavia, were more cosmopolitan and looked to Europe for capital, immigrants, and ideas. For nearly two decades, bloody and vindictive conflicts between the two factions left the country nearly exhausted. A common salutation on documents of the period was 'Death to the Unitarist savages!'

The Reign of Rosas

In practice, differences between Federalists and Unitarists sometimes owed as much to convenience as conviction. Juan Manuel de Rosas came to prominence as a caudillo in Buenos Aires province and undoubtedly represented the interests of rural elites

The Paths of the Liberators

José de San Martín

The two major figures of South American independence, Simón Bolívar and José de San Martín, converged on the center from the periphery. Bolívar, born wealthy in Caracas, advanced from the north, while San Martín, of more humble origins on the former Jesuit mission of Yapeyú on the Río Uruguay, led the charge from the south.

In retrospect, it is no surprise that the leaders should come from the backwaters of the Spanish empire, since Spanish control was strongest in Peru, where it had been established on the foundation of the indigenous Inca state. In the far-flung viceroyalties of Nueva Granada (present-day Venezuela) and the Río de la Plata, Bolívar and San Martín developed a criollo sense of identity that their privileged educations in Spain did nothing to eradicate.

Still, the two differed greatly in temperament. Bolívar, by all accounts, was a passionate man who, when his young Spanish wife died, sublimated his energy first in grandiose plans for Spanish American independence, which took many years to win. Despite early setbacks, his intensity and populist ability to inspire the masses – even when they failed to understand or did not agree with his ideas – proved a greater strength than his limited military skills. By sheer persistence and force of will, he turned former adversaries into supporters, and his movement gained strength.

San Martín, by contrast, was more methodical and conservative. Though he immediately prepared to return to Buenos Aires from Europe upon hearing of the events of the Revolution of May 1810, his actions were those of a professional soldier who had spent 20 years in the ranks. Rather than leap into battle, he first trained and organized his forces; especially in the logistically and strategically demanding liberation of Chile, for example, which involved crossing the high Andes and surprising royalist forces at Chacabuco, his troops' discipline served them well.

After liberating Chile, San Martín, who disdained political ambition for himself, sailed north to drive the royalists out of Lima (though they remained strong elsewhere) and then north to a now famous meeting with Bolívar at Guayaquil, Ecuador. The apolitical Argentine found himself in conflict with Bolívar, whose political ambitions were boundless, if largely praiseworthy. San Martín saw the essential expediency of installing a powerful leader, even a monarch, to avoid the disintegration of Peru, while Bolívar insisted on a constitutional republic. In a complicated exchange that aroused ill feeling among partisans of both leaders, the Venezuelan won the day and San Martín returned to the south.

Simón Bolívar

In the long run, though, both were disappointed. The proliferation of caudillos appalled both great soldier-statesmen and set an often deplorable pattern for most of the 19th century. San Martín returned to an Argentina racked by internal dissension and left for self-imposed exile in France almost as soon as he arrived, never to return. Bolívar's dream of the strong republic of Gran Colombia was shattered by difficulties which led to the secession of Ecuador and the separation of Colombia and Venezuela. Just before being exiled, he died of pulmonary tuberculosis in the Colombian town of Santa Marta.

whose power depended on their estancias and *saladeros* (tanneries and salting works). But he also helped centralize political power in Buenos Aires and set other ominous precedents in Argentine political life, creating the *mazorca*, his ruthless political police force, and institutionalizing torture. In the words of Sarmiento:

> The central consolidated despotic government of the landed proprietor, Don Juan Manuel Rosas ... applied the knife of the Gaucho to the culture of Buenos Ayres, and destroyed the work of centuries – of civilization, law and liberty.

Even allowing for Sarmiento's partisan rhetoric, Rosas' opportunism and continual military adventures required a large standing army, consuming an increasing percentage of public expenditures, and the dictator required all overseas trade to be funneled through the port of Buenos Aires rather than shipped directly to the provinces.

Despite Federalist efforts, Buenos Aires continued to dominate the new country. After the Unitarists and even some of Rosas' former allies forced him from power in 1852, succeeding decades and economic developments confirmed the city's primacy. Rosas himself spent the last 25 years of his life in exile in Southampton, England.

The Roots of Modern Argentina

Rosas' expulsion ushered in a new era in Argentine development. Sheep estancias, producing enormous quantities of wool in response to the nearly inexhaustible demand of English mills, supplanted the relatively stagnant cattle estancias. According to Argentine historian Hilda Sábato, the province of Buenos Aires was in the vanguard of this process, integrating Argentina into the global economy and, simultaneously, consolidating the country as a political entity. Steadily, European immigrants assumed important roles in crafts and commerce. In nearby areas of Buenos Aires province, small farms known as *chacras* supplied the city's food, but sheep displaced the semiwild cattle of the surrounding estancias. In the periphery of the province, though, cattle estancias operated much as before.

Politically, the Constitution of 1853, still in force today despite its frequent suspension, signified the triumph of Unitarism, even allowing the president to dissolve provincial administrations despite lip service to federal principles. The economic expression of Unitarism was Liberalism, an openness to foreign capital, which even now raises the hackles of many Argentine nationalists – both leftists and rightists. As used in Argentina, the term Liberalism means something very different from what it does in Western Europe and North America.

According to historian David Rock, Liberalism had three main aspects: foreign investment, foreign trade, and immigration. In the late 19th century, all three inundated the Humid Pampas, Mesopotamia, and Córdoba, if barely lapping at the edges of some interior provinces. Basque and Irish refugees became the first shepherds, as both sheep numbers and wool exports increased nearly tenfold between 1850 and 1880. Some herders were independent family farmers on relatively small units, but the majority were sharecroppers, and the land itself remained in the hands of large landowners.

After 1880, Argentina became a major producer of cereal crops for export, and it still is today. The Humid Pampas were the focus of this development, whose origins lay in mid-century colonization projects focused on attracting European settlers. *Estancieros* rarely objected to occupation of lands that were nominally theirs, because new settlers provided a buffer between themselves and the still troublesome Indians. Swiss, German, French, and Italian farmers proved successful in provinces like Santa Fe and Entre Ríos.

Such developments did not eliminate latifundios. The government sold public lands at giveaway prices to pay its debts, encouraging speculators and reducing independent opportunities for immigrants, whose only agricultural alternatives were sharecropping or seasonal labor. Many remained in Buenos Aires, steadily increasing the city's share of the country's population.

British capital, amounting to one-third of Britain's total Latin American investment by 1890, dominated the Argentine economy. Most went to infrastructural improvements such as railroads, which rapidly made the cart roads of the Pampas obsolete. By the turn of the century, Argentina had a highly developed rail network, fanning out from Buenos Aires in all directions, but the economy remained vulnerable to international fluctuations like the 1879 depression that followed the Franco-Prussian War.

These conditions stimulated a debate over foreign investment that anticipated 20th-century controversies over 'dependence' and economic autonomy through industrial diversification and protectionism. In fact, the only industries that benefited from protection were agricultural commodities like wheat, wine, and sugar. These in turn benefited large landholders and encouraged further land speculation and concentration. Speculation led to a boom in land prices and paper money loans that depreciated in value, causing near collapse of the financial system toward the end of the 19th century.

By reducing opportunities for family farming, land speculation and commodity exports also encouraged urban growth. The port city of Buenos Aires, which rapidly modernized in the 1880s, nearly doubled its population through immigration during that decade alone. Urban services such as transportation, power and water improved steadily. Because of the capital's increasing importance, it became an administratively distinct federal zone (the Capital Federal), effectively seceding from its namesake province. Outside the Pampas, uneven development exaggerated regional inequality.

From the mid-1890s until WWI, Argentina's economy recovered enough to take advantage of the opportunities presented by beef, mutton, and wheat exports. Because of inequities in land distribution, though, this prosperity was less broad-based than it might have been. Industry could not absorb all the immigrants, and with the onset of the Great Depression, the military took power under conditions of indecisive and ineffectual civilian government, as well as considerable social unrest. An obscure but oddly visionary colonel, Juan Domingo Perón, was the first leader to try to come to grips with the economic crisis.

Juan Perón & His Legacy

Born in Lobos, Buenos Aires province, in 1895, Juan Perón emerged in the 1940s to become Argentina's most revered, and most despised, political figure. During his youth and rather mediocre military career, he became familiar with virtually the entire country from its subtropical north to its sub-Antarctic south. As Perón grew to maturity, Argentina was one of the world's most prosperous countries, but its prosperity was narrowly based on commodity exports such as meat, grain, and wool.

The *oligarquía terrateniente* (landed elite) benefited most from the export economy and resisted attempts to promote diversification through domestic industrialization. Correctly or not, many Argentines came to perceive the country's agricultural sector as beholden to foreign 'liberal,' especially British, interests.

This interpretation carried some credibility. British capital built most of the railways that radiated from Buenos Aires like spokes from the hub of a wheel, bringing agricultural commodities to the capital for shipment to Europe. In return, inexpensive

Juan Perón

Teniente General Juan Domingo Perón

Lieutenant General Juan Perón (diehard supporters refuse to separate his name and rank) was an Argentine enigma, embodying the contradictions of the country itself. Rising to power through the elitist institution of the military, he still enjoyed broad popularity among the public at large. Leader of a Roman Catholic country, he incited his followers to attack the Church. Attracting people of intense and passionate convictions, he could appeal ambiguously to followers from across the political spectrum. Irreconcilable factions within Perón's Justicialist party warred with each other, sometimes with words and often with bullets and bombs, while each ardently professed its allegiance to the man and his ideals.

During the era of Argentina's greatest power and prestige, Perón insightfully assessed the country's shortcomings as well as its strengths. When the Perón family relocated to Patagonia for an unsuccessful attempt at sheep farming, he saw firsthand the most unsavory aspects of large, paternalistic sheep estancias, controlled almost exclusively by British interests. Recognizing that the sheepherders and other workers of the Pampas were not far removed from his own humble origins, he treated them on a basis of equality. As a young military officer, he witnessed the miserable physical and educational state of rural conscripts, casualties of an inequitable social order. Sent to restore order in several labor disputes, he proved an attentive listener to working-class concerns, mediating labor settlements on the railways and sugar *ingenios* (factories) of the subtropical north.

Perón first came to national prominence after a military coup deposed President Ramón Castillo in 1943. Sensing an opportunity to assist the country's forgotten working class, Perón settled for a relatively minor post as head of the National Department of Labor. In this post, his success at organizing relief efforts after a major earthquake in the Andean city and province of San Juan earned praise throughout the country. In the process he also met Eva Duarte, the actress who would become his second wife and make her own major contribution to Argentine history. Both occupy an enduring place in the country's political mythology.

During sojourns as Argentine military attaché in Fascist Italy and Nazi Germany, Perón had grasped the importance of spectacle in public life, and he had the personal charisma to put it into practice. With the equally charismatic 'Evita' at his side, he transformed the country's political culture and economy, and addressed massive rallies from the balcony of the Casa Rosada. Giving voice to the disenfranchised masses, the Peróns enlisted them in their cause and alienated traditionally powerful sectors of Argentine society. He created a powerful institution, the General Confederation of Labor (CGT), which overwhelmed rival labor organizations.

There was no disguising the Perons' demagoguery and ambition. Evita once wrote that 'there are two things of which I am proud: my love for the people and my hatred for the oligarchy.' Despite huge congressional majorities, Perón's authoritarian tendencies led him to govern by decree rather than by consultation and consensus. His excessively personalistic approach created a political party, known formally as 'Justicialist' but popularly and universally as 'Peronist,' which has never completely transcended a stagnant reliance on its founder's charisma. He did not hesitate to use or condone intimidation and torture for political ends, although such activities never reached the level they did during the state terrorism of the late 1970s. Argentine literary great Jorge Luis Borges was among those who suffered Perón's caprice.

Yet during the decade they lived together, the Peróns also broadened the range and popular appeal of Argentine politics in many positive ways. Besides legitimizing the trade-union movement and extending political rights and economic benefits to working-class people, they managed to secure voting rights for women by 1947. Unfortunately, they could not or would not overcome the atmosphere of tension and confrontation that colored Argentine politics for more than three decades after Evita's death in 1952.

British products flooded domestic markets and retarded local industry.

Perón associated a new economic order with domestic industrialization and economic independence. In this sense, he appealed to both conservative nationalists, who distrusted the cosmopolitan landowning elite, and to intellectuals and working-class radicals, who resented the role of foreign capital. Almost until his death, Perón avoided alienating either sector even as they conducted a virtual civil war with each other.

After being dislodged from an influential labor post and briefly incarcerated by jealous fellow officers, Perón ran for and won the presidency in 1946 and again in 1952. Until his ouster in 1955, his reforms and programs benefited working-class interests in matters of wages, pensions, job security, and working conditions. University education ceased to be the privilege of the elite, but instead became available to any capable individual. Many Argentines gained employment in the expanding state bureaucracy.

Coming to power at a time of global crisis, just after WWII, Perón may have had no alternative but to foster state involvement since Europe, the traditional source of capital, was in utter ruin. In any event, his policies had broad support from both traditional working-class supporters and a military concerned about dependence on foreign sources for raw materials and munitions.

Economic shortcomings, including rising inflation, undermined the latter stages of Perón's presidency. He also failed to disavow a virulent and often violent anticlerical campaign that divided the country toward the end of his first presidency. In late 1955, he himself fell victim to the so-called Revolución Libertadora, a coup that sent him into exile and initiated nearly three decades of catastrophic military rule, with only brief interludes of civilian government.

Perón's Exile & Return

After Perón left the country, Argentina's military government banned his Justicialist party, which split into several factions. Even to speak Perón's name in public was suspect; Anglo-Argentines might refer to him as

Eva Perón

'Johnny Sunday,' a gloss on Perón's Christian names 'Juan Domingo.' Perón himself wandered to Paraguay, Panama (where he met his third wife, dancer María Estela Martínez, known better by her stage name, Isabelita), Venezuela, the Dominican Republic, and eventually to Spain, where he remained from 1961 to 1973.

During exile, Perón and his associates constantly plotted their return to Argentina. He acquired a bizarre retinue of advisors, including his personal secretary, José López Rega, a spiritualist and extreme right-wing nationalist who was Perón's Svengali or Rasputin. At Perón's Puerta de Hierro mansion in Madrid, where Evita Perón's embalmed body lay in state after being rescued from an anonymous grave in Italy in 1971, López Rega reportedly conducted rituals over the casket to imbue Isabelita with Evita's charismatic qualities.

In the late 1960s, increasing economic problems and political instability, including strikes, political kidnappings, and guerrilla warfare, marked Argentine political life. In the midst of these events, Perón's opportunity to return finally arrived in 1973, when the beleaguered military relaxed their objections to the Justicialist party and loyal Peronist Hector Cámpora was elected president. Cámpora himself was merely a stalking-horse for Perón and soon resigned, paving the way for new elections handily won by Perón.

After an 18-year exile, Perón once again symbolized Argentine unity, but there was no substance to his rule. His anticipated arrival at Buenos Aires' Ezeiza airport, attended by hundreds of thousands of people on a dark winter's night, resulted in violent clashes between supporters across the broad spectrum of Argentine politics. Chronically ill, Perón died in mid-1974, leaving a fragmented country. His ill-qualified wife Isabelita, elected as his literal running mate but under the spell of López Rega, inherited the presidency.

In this chaotic political climate, armed conflict was the rule rather than the exception. The urban Montoneros, a left-wing, anti-imperialist Peronist faction, went underground, kidnapping and executing enemies, bombing foreign enterprises, and robbing banks to finance armed struggle. The Ejército Revolucionario Popular (People's Revolutionary Army, known by its acronym ERP) waged guerrilla warfare in the mountainous forests of Tucumán. López Rega's Alianza Anticomunista Argentina (AAA, or Argentine Anti-Communist Alliance) took the law into its own hands, assassinating labor leaders, academics, and others it considered subversive.

La Guerra Sucia (1976-83)

In March 1976, unable to maintain civil order or control inflation that sometimes exceeded 50% per month, Isabelita Perón's government fell in a bloodless and widely anticipated military coup. Placed under house arrest, she eventually went into exile in Spain, where her main interest appeared to be challenging Imelda Marcos and Nancy Reagan for the world's most extravagant wardrobe.

If the coup itself was bloodless, its aftermath was not. During the so-called Proceso de Reorganización Nacional, General Jorge Rafael Videla's military regime instituted a reign of terror unparalleled since the days of Rosas. Military officers occupied nearly every position of political importance in the entire country.

In theory and rhetoric, the Proceso was a comprehensive effort at reforming the bloated state sector and stabilizing the economy by eliminating corruption, thus creating the basis for economic growth and an enduring democracy; in practice, it was one more chapter in a history of large-scale government corruption in the name of development, accompanied by an orgy of state-sponsored or tolerated violence and anarchy.

The army's superior firepower quickly eliminated the naive, inept, and outmanned ERP in Tucumán. The more sophisticated and intricately organized Montoneros posed a greater challenge but were eventually eliminated in the infamous Guerra Sucia (Dirty War), which claimed thousands of innocent victims. Operating with state complicity, paramilitary death squads like the AAA were responsible for countless other casualties.

The 'Disappeared'

In eliminating ERP and the Montoneros, the dictatorship made little effort to distinguish among those who actively fought against it and aided the guerrillas, those who openly or privately sympathized with the guerrillas without assisting them, and those who expressed reservations about the military's indiscriminate brutality. Only a few highly visible and courageous individuals and organizations publicly criticized the regime at great personal risk.

During these years, to 'disappear' meant to be abducted, detained, tortured, and probably killed with no hope or pretense of legal process. The armed forces and police ran numerous illegal detention centers, the most notorious of which was the Escuela de Mecánica de la Armada (ESMA, or Naval Mechanics School) in an exclusive northern suburb of Buenos Aires. For anyone crossing the street, even at midday, the presence of a black Ford Falcon, without numbered plates and occupied by four men in sunglasses, induced outright terror.

The dictatorship almost never acknowledged illegal detention of individuals, although it sometimes reported their deaths in battles or skirmishes with 'security forces.' Inexplicably, a few escaped or were released, but their stories gained more notoriety outside Argentina than within. A few courageous individuals, like Nobel Peace Prizewinner Adolfo Pérez Esquivel, and groups, such as the famous 'Madres de la Plaza de Mayo,' kept their stories in public view. The Madres still parade in front of Buenos Aires' Casa Rosada presidential palace every Thursday.

No one knows exactly how many people died during the Dirty War. In 1986 *Nunca Más*, the official report commissioned by civilian president Raúl Alfonsín and presented by the prestigious novelist Ernesto Sábato, listed 9000 cases, but some estimates are three times greater. Ironically, the Dirty War ended only when the Argentine military attempted a real military objective.

Falklands War

In mid-1982, a cartoon in the Buenos Aires magazine *Humor* depicted 'La Libertad Argentina' (a female symbol equivalent to the US Statue of Liberty or England's Britannia) in a public playground with her four children and their toys: an army general with a tank, an admiral with a destroyer, an air force brigadier with a jet fighter, and a smartly dressed civilian with a bridge. When another woman remarks how expensive it is to raise children, La Libertad responds, 'You're telling me!'

Despite public homage to economic growth and stabilization, Argentina's economy continued to decline during military rule. On the one hand, the government enacted strict economic measures, including a fixed exchange rate to eliminate speculation on the dollar, but it failed to reduce annual inflation below three digits. It did, however, aggravate unemployment and undermine local industry through cheap imports. Lip service to austerity brought in billions of dollars in loans, which were invested in grandiose public works projects like the toll road between downtown Buenos Aires and the airport at Ezeiza, while public officials pocketed much of the money and sent it overseas to Swiss bank accounts. Meanwhile, the military acquired the latest in European technology, including the deadly Exocet missile.

Under the weight of its import splurge and debt burden, the economy collapsed in chaos. Almost overnight, devaluation reduced the peso to a fraction of its former value, and inflation again reached astronomical levels. The Proceso was coming undone.

In an orderly transition in early 1981, General Roberto Viola replaced General Videla as de facto president, but before the end of the year General Leopoldo Galtieri replaced the ineffectual Viola. Under Galtieri, rapid economic deterioration and popular discontent, manifested in the first mass demonstrations at Casa Rosada since before the 1976 coup, led to desperate measures. To stay in power, Galtieri launched an April 1982 invasion to dislodge the British from the Falkland Islands, which had been claimed by Argentina as the Malvinas for nearly a century and a half.

Overnight, the nearly unopposed occupation of the Malvinas unleashed a wave of nationalist euphoria that subsided almost as fast as it crested. Acting on faulty advice from civilian foreign minister Nicanor Costa Méndez, Galtieri underestimated the determined response of British Prime Minister Margaret Thatcher. Thatcher herself was having political difficulties, and Britain was willing and able to absorb heavy naval losses to attain a remote goal. After only 74 days, Argentina's ill-trained, poorly motivated, and ineffective forces surrendered ignominiously, and the military meekly prepared to return government to civilian hands. In 1983, Argentines elected Raúl Alfonsín, of the Unión Cívica Radical (UCR, or Radical Civic Union), to the presidency.

For more details on the war, see the Falkland Islands chapter.

Aftermath

In his successful presidential campaign, Alfonsín pledged to try military officers responsible for human-rights violations during the Dirty War. Evidence uncovered by the commission that produced *Nunca Más* contributed to the conviction of junta members including Videla, Viola, and Admiral Emilio Massera for kidnapping, torture, and homicide. Videla and Massera received life sentences, though in virtual luxury accommodations in a military prison.

When the government attempted to extend trials to junior officers, many of whom protested that they had been merely 'following orders,' those officers responded with uprisings in several different parts of the country. These might have toppled the government, but had they been more forcefully resisted, they might have effectively subjugated the military to civilian control. The timid administration succumbed to military demands and produced a *Ley de la Obediencia Debida* (Law of Due Obedience), allowing lower-ranking officers to use the defense that they were following orders, as well as a *Punto Final* (Stopping Point), beyond which no criminal or civil prosecutions could take place. These measures eliminated prosecutions of notorious individuals such as navy captain Alfredo Astiz (the 'Angel of Death'), who was implicated in the disappearance of a Swedish-Argentine teenager and the highly publicized deaths of two French nuns thrown into the Río de la Plata from an airplane.

The Law of Due Obedience and the Stopping Point did not eliminate the Dirty War's divisive impact on Argentine politics; after 1987, the military reasserted its role in politics despite internal factionalism. In December 1990, prior to a visit by US president George Bush, a dissident junior officer movement known as the *carapintadas* (so-called after their custom of painting their faces with camouflage markings) occupied army headquarters across from the Casa Rosada and elsewhere in Buenos Aires in the hope of encouraging the military establishment to join them in overthrowing President Carlos Menem, himself a prisoner during the Dirty War.

Ironically and astonishingly, Menem himself contributed to the controversy in an unexpected and unwarranted manner. Just after Christmas of that year, he pardoned Videla, Massera, and their cohorts even though the Argentine public overwhelmingly opposed such measures. He also pardoned former Montonero guerrilla Mario Firmenich who, some speculated, still had access to substantial funds that might benefit Menem's Peronist party. (US journalist Martin Anderson has argued that Firmenich was a double agent who collaborated with the military government's intelligence services while participating in armed resistance, but the evidence for this is scanty.)

In 1991, Menem aroused further controversy when he ordered Argentine warships to the Persian Gulf in support of the allied effort to liberate Kuwait (the ships gave logistical support, but did not participate in combat). Both right- and left-wing nationalists resented the president's apparent obsequiousness toward the USA, but the definition of an overtly military mission for Argentine forces was something of a novelty; since then they have undertaken other international missions, such as serving as peacekeepers in the former Yugoslavia. Kept busy with such tasks, the military has been remarkably quiet over the past few years, and no one anticipates overt military domination of Argentina, but it would be premature to dismiss completely the specter of military intervention in civilian matters.

During the 1995 presidential campaign, Dirty War issues resurfaced spectacularly when journalist Horacio Verbitsky wrote *The Flight* (New York, New Press, 1996), a book based on interviews with former navy captain Adolfo Scilingo. Troubled but unrepentant, Scilingo acknowledged that he himself participated in regular weekly flights in which the navy threw political prisoners, alive but drugged, into the Atlantic. While such reports had long circulated, this was the first time any participant had openly admitted responsibility, and it ignited a clamor of protest for a more complete accounting of the disappeared – even though Alfonsín's due-obedience law and Menem's pardons had eliminated any possibility of further prosecutions. Another revelation was that military chaplains had counseled and comforted the perpetrators of the killings.

Taken by surprise, Menem attacked Scilingo's credibility and encouraged the country not to reopen old wounds, though some suggested that the president was trying to cover a bleeding gash with a Band-Aid. Inconsistencies among the administration's spokespersons as to the possibility of lists of the disappeared undercut the president's statements, and, despite initial denials, more material soon became available. A complete accounting still seems a long-range goal, since the military destroyed many records before surrendering power in 1983 and probably hid others overseas. Nevertheless, many Argentines believe that, because so many of the participants are still alive, a more complete record is likely to come about – even though some groups, like the Madres de la Plaza de Mayo, have vowed to seek a list of the murderers, not the disappeared.

Recent Developments

Scilingo's 'confession' set off a chain of events that has yet to end. Despite Menem's continued pleas to put the matter aside, Army Chief of Staff General Martín Balza went on nationwide television to apologize to the country for the army's conduct during the Dirty War, Air Force Chief of Staff General Juan Paulik did likewise for his branch, and Roman Catholic Bishop Jorge Novak regretfully admitted the Church's collaboration. Navy officials, however, remained conspicuously silent and even spoke of promoting the disreputable Astiz, precipitating a minor diplomatic confrontation with France.

In both France and Spain, cases remain pending against former Argentine military officers, who, because of Interpol warrants against them, cannot leave the country without risking arrest. French objections forced Astiz's retirement from the navy, but the former officer's inability to shut up (in a magazine interview, he declared himself 'the best-trained person in the country to kill a politician or journalist') cost him both his retired military status and pension. More recently, a Buenos Aires judge has ordered the incarceration of Videla during investigations as to his responsibility for the kidnapping of children born to political prisoners and given to military families for adoption – a crime not covered by the Punto Final and presidential pardons.

At the same time, public outcry led to congressional repeal of the Punto Final and Obediencia Debida laws in 1998. This was not, however, retroactive, and most of the criminals of 1976-83 still walk the streets. Victims and human-rights activists in Buenos Aires have responded with the tactic of *escrache*, plastering the city with posters publicizing the faces and addresses of Dirty War criminals and demonstrating outside their residences.

Tucumán governor Antonio Domingo Bussi, a former general who led the army against the ERP insurrection and won the governorship by a small plurality in 1995, encountered a different problem when it was discovered he had hidden a large Swiss bank account alleged to come from Dirty War spoils. Though weakened politically and facing criminal charges, Bussi's Fuerza Republicana party held enough seats in the provincial legislature to prevent his impeachment in the short term.

GEOGRAPHY & CLIMATE

With a total land area of about 2.8 million sq km, excluding the South Atlantic islands and the Antarctic quadrant it claims as national territory, Argentina is the world's eighth-largest country, only slightly smaller than India. On the South American continent, only neighboring Brazil is larger. The distance from La Quiaca on the Bolivian border to Ushuaia in Tierra del Fuego is nearly 3500km, about the same as from Havana to Hudson's Bay or from the Sahara to Scotland.

Argentine geographers acknowledge four major physiographic provinces: the Andes, the lowland North, the Pampas, and Patagonia. Each of these, however, has considerable variety in its own right, since altitude as well as latitude plays a major role in Argentine geography. Most of the country is a mid-latitude lowland, but the Andean chain runs the length of the country's western border, diminishing in altitude toward the south. The Andes separate Argentina from Chile, while rivers form its borders with Uruguay, Brazil, and Paraguay. The relatively short

Bolivian frontier has both mountainous and riverine areas.

The Andes

The Andean chain runs the length of Argentina, from the Bolivian border in the north to the South Atlantic, where the chain disappears. Its greatest elevations presented a formidable western barrier to colonizers entering from Peru after the Spanish invasion of the New World. In this northwestern region, a string of oasis settlements from Jujuy and Salta southward to Mendoza developed, with communications links to Lima rather than to Buenos Aires. This area's colonial architecture, primarily but not exclusively ecclesiastical, is the most significant in Argentina. The mestizo population most closely resembles that of Peru and Bolivia, where indigenous traits are dominant.

Rainfall can be erratic, although rain-fed agriculture is feasible from Tucumán northward. In most areas, perennial streams descending from the Andes provide irrigation water. In the extreme north lies the southern extension of the Bolivian *altiplano*, a thinly populated high plain between 3000 and 4000 meters altitude, punctuated by even higher volcanic peaks. The inhabitants reside in scattered mining settlements, and there are a few llama herders; the zone is too arid for the more valuable but delicate alpaca. Although days can be surprisingly hot (sunburn is a serious hazard in the high altitude tropics), frosts occur almost nightly. In the summer rainy season, travelers should be prepared for potential flash floods and even snow at higher elevations.

South of Tucumán, rainfall is inadequate for crops, but irrigation has brought prosperity to the wine-producing Cuyo region, consisting of the provinces of Mendoza, San Juan, and San Luis. La Rioja and Catamarca are much less well-to-do. Much of this area resembles the Great Basin of the western US, with north-south mountain ranges separated by salt flats or shallow lakes.

On the region's far western edge is the massive Andean crest, featuring 6960m Aconcagua, South America's highest peak. Hot in summer, the area is pleasant the rest of the year despite cool winter nights. On occasion the *zonda*, a dry wind descending from the Andes, causes dramatic temperature increases and, consequently, serious physical discomfort.

The Chaco & Mesopotamia

East of the Andes and their foothills, northern Argentina consists of mostly subtropical lowlands, though parts lie north of the Tropic of Capricorn. The arid western area, known as the Argentine Chaco, is part of the much larger Gran Chaco region which extends into Bolivia, Paraguay, and Brazil. Here, in the provinces of Santiago del Estero, Chaco, Formosa, and northern Santa Fe and Córdoba, summers are brutally hot.

Between the Paraná and Uruguay rivers, the climate is mild, and rainfall is heavy in the provinces of Entre Ríos and Corrientes, which comprise most of the area known as Mesopotamia. The hot and humid province of Misiones, a politically important salient surrounded on three sides by Brazil and Paraguay, contains part of the awesome Iguazú Falls, which descend from southern Brazil's Paraná Plateau.

Rainfall decreases from east to west; for example, Corrientes' annual average rainfall of about 1200mm contrasts with Santiago del Estero's 500mm, which is insufficient for rain-fed agriculture because evaporation is so high. Shallow summer flooding is common throughout Mesopotamia and the eastern Chaco, while only the immediate river floodplains become inundated in the west. The Chaco has a well-defined winter dry season, which is even more pronounced the farther west one travels, while Mesopotamia's rainfall is more evenly distributed throughout the year.

The Pampas

Bordering the Atlantic Ocean and the Río de la Plata and stretching nearly to Córdoba and the central Andean foothills, the Pampas are modern Argentina's political and economic heartland. Industry and agriculture are both concentrated here; outside the federal capital of Buenos Aires and its industrial suburbs, most settlements are cookie-cutter farm towns resembling, in some ways, their counterparts in the US Midwest.

The Pampas are more properly subdivided into the Humid Pampas, along the littoral, and the Arid Pampas of the western interior and the south. More than a third of the country's population lives in and around Buenos Aires, whose humid climate resembles New York City's in the spring, summer, and autumn. Annual rainfall exceeds 900mm, but several hundred kilometers westward it is less than half that. Buenos Aires' winters are humid but mild.

The Pampas are an almost completely level plain of wind-borne loess (fine-grained silt or clay ranging in color from beige to gray) and river-deposited sediments. The absence of relief makes the area vulnerable to flooding from the relatively few small rivers that cross it. Only the granitic Sierra de Tandil (484m) and the Sierra de la Ventana (1273m), in southwestern Buenos Aires province, and the Sierra de La Pampa disrupt the otherwise monotonous terrain. The seacoast of Buenos Aires province features attractive, sandy beaches at resorts like Mar del Plata and Necochea, which *porteños* (inhabitants of the capital) overrun in January and February.

Patagonia & the Lake District

Patagonia is the region south of the Río Colorado, consisting of the provinces of Neuquén, Río Negro, Chubut, and Santa Cruz. It is separated from Chilean Patagonia by the Andes, although their crest is much lower than in the north; at 3554m, Cerro Tronador, the highest peak in Parque Nacional Nahuel Huapi near San Carlos de Bariloche dwarfs all surrounding summits by at least 1000m.

The cordillera is still high enough, though, that Pacific storms drop most of their rain and snow on the Chilean side. In the extreme southern reaches of Patagonia, this rain-shadow effect does not prevent the accumulation of sufficient snow and ice to form the largest Southern Hemisphere glaciers outside Antarctica. Hiking, trekking, skiing, and mountaineering are common recreational activities, depending on the season. Outdoors enthusiasts should be prepared for changeable, often inclement weather.

East of the Andean foothills, the cool, arid Patagonian steppes support huge flocks of sheep, almost all of whose wool is exported to Europe. In organization and operation, Patagonian sheep estancias resemble their counterparts in New Zealand and Australia, although environmental conditions are very different. The Atlantic maritime influence generally keeps temperatures relatively mild, even in winter when more uniform atmospheric pressure moderates the strong gales that blow most of the year.

Except for urban clusters like Comodoro Rivadavia (center of the petroleum industry) and Río Gallegos (wool and meat packing), Patagonia is thinly populated. Tidal ranges along the Atlantic coast are too great for major port facilities. In the valley of the Río Negro and at the outlet of the Río Chubut, there is farming and fruit orchards.

Tierra del Fuego

The world's southernmost permanently inhabited territory, the 'Land of Fire' consists of one large island (Isla Grande), unequally divided between Chile and Argentina, and many smaller ones, some of which have been objects of longtime contention between the two Southern Cone powers. When Europeans first passed through the Strait of Magellan, which separates Isla Grande from the Patagonian mainland, the fires stemmed from the activities of the now almost extinct Yahgan Indians; nowadays, they result from the flaring of natural gas in the region's oil fields.

The northern half of Isla Grande, resembling the Patagonian steppes, is devoted to sheep grazing for wool and mutton, while its southern half is mountainous and partly covered by forests and glaciers. Despite its reputation for inclemency, it would be more accurate to call the weather changeable. As in Patagonia, winter conditions are rarely extreme, although trekking and outdoor camping are not advisable except for experienced mountaineers. For most visitors, the brief daylight hours in winter may be a greater deterrent than the weather. Skiing is possible in Ushuaia, along with outstanding views of the famous Beagle Channel.

ECOLOGY & ENVIRONMENT

Argentina's diverse environments have spawned environmental challenges ranging from industrial pollution to deforestation to overgrazing. The single most palpable example of industrial problems is the visible contamination of waterways like the Riachuelo in the Buenos Aires barrio of La Boca, but the concentration of industrial chemicals and heavy metals in the sediments beneath the surface is even more serious than floating oil slicks. Supposedly the Riachuelo is the Menem administration's number one environmental priority, but nobody takes seriously Environment Secretary María Julia Alsogaray's pledge to swim in the river when the cleanup finally ends.

Thanks to diesel-spewing buses, countless private vehicles, and fleets of taxis, the capital's dense traffic has the usual impact on air quality. The frequent rains, however, clear the air with some regularity. One real plague is the seemingly infinite numbers of feral cats, fed by bag ladies who dump the kittens into virtually any green space – schools, for instance, must post signs asking people not to abandon cats on their property. The impact on songbirds is palpable.

Like other world megacities, Buenos Aires long ago outgrew local energy resources. Despite Argentina's self-sufficiency in petroleum and abundant (if sometimes remote) hydroelectric capacity, Argentine governments have promoted nuclear power since 1950. The 344-megawatt Atucha I reactor, near Buenos Aires, has supplied energy to the capital since 1974, but it operated only at half-capacity through the 1980s because cheaper hydroelectricity made nuclear power less competitive. There is another functioning reactor at Río Tercero, in Córdoba province.

A joint Argentine-Paraguayan hydroelectric project in Itaipú has proved an economic and ecological boondoggle, but it limps along nevertheless, thanks to government subsidies. Government officials have proposed dredging the Río Paraná into Paraguay and southern Brazil to provide deep-water access for ocean-going vessels – a project that might desiccate the famous wetlands of the Pantanal – but Brazil's apparent retreat from the project has reduced this danger for the moment.

Among the contemporary major issues has been the proposed placement of a nuclear waste dump in the Patagonian province of Chubut, a development that has induced many towns to declare themselves 'non-nuclear municipalities.'

FLORA & FAUNA

Because Argentina is so large and varied in its environments, it supports a wide range of flora and fauna. The country's subtropical rainforests, palm savannas, high-altitude deserts, high-latitude steppes, humid temperate grasslands, alpine and sub-Antarctic forests, and coastal areas all support distinctive biota that will be unfamiliar to most visitors, or at least to those from the Northern

Endangered Species

The Convention on International Trade in Endangered Species of Wild Fauna and Flora (CITES) is a diplomatic agreement regulating trade in biotic resources, including plants and animals, that are either in immediate danger of extinction, or else threatened or declining so rapidly that they may soon be in danger of extinction. Regulations are complex, but in general such species are either protected from commercial or noncommercial exploitation or subject to severe restrictions. In many instances, all commerce of a given species is prohibited; in most others, the export of plants and animals in a given country is prohibited without express authorization from that country's government.

Under CITES, most species are assigned either to Appendix I (endangered, under immediate threat of extinction without remedial action) or Appendix II (threatened, perhaps regionally endangered); some recovering species have been reassigned from Appendix I to Appendix II. Appendix III listings cover species that require close monitoring to determine their degree of vulnerability to extinction.

Travelers should take special care not to hunt, purchase, or collect the following species of plants and animals found in Argentina, Uruguay, Paraguay, and the Falkland Islands, nor should they purchase products made from these plants and animals. Note that US customs no longer permits the importation of birds even with CITES permits from the appropriate country, and that the US Marine Mammal Protection Act prohibits the importation of any marine mammal products whatsoever.

Appendix I

Flora

Alerce (Chilean falsh larch) *(Fitzroya cupressoides)*

Mammals

Andean cat *(Felis jacobita)*
Beaked whales *(Berardius* or *Mesoplodon* spp)
Blue whale *(Balaenoptera musculus)*
Bottlenosed whales *(Hyperodon* spp)
Brazilian tapir *(Tapirus terrestris)*
Chacoan giant peccary *(Catagonus wagneri)*
Fin whale *(Balaenoptera physalus)*
Giant armadillo *(Priodontes maximus)*
Humpback whale *(Megaptera novaeangliae)*
Jaguarundi *(Felis yagouarundi)*
Long-tailed otter *(Lutra platensis)*
Maned wolf *(Chrysocyon brachyrus)*
Marine otter *(Lutra felina)*
Marsh deer *(Blastocerus dicotemus)*
Minke whale *(Balaenoptera acutorostrata)*
Pampas deer *(Ozotocerus bezoarticus)*
Pink fairy armadillo *(Clamyphorus truncatus)*
Pudú *(Pudu pudu)*
Pygmy right whale *(Caperea marginata)*
Sei whale *(Balaenoptera borealis)*
South Andean huemul *(Hippocamelus bisulcus)*
Southern right whale *(Eubalaena australis)*
Southern river otter *(Lutra provocax)*
Sperm whale *(Physeter catodon)*
Vicuña *(Vicugna vicugna)*

Birds

Andean condor *(Vultur gryphus)*
Black-fronted piping-guan *(Pipile jacutinga)*
Darwin's rhea *(Pterocnemia pennata)*
Eskimo curlew *(Numenius borealis)*
Glaucous macaw *(Anodorhynchous glaucus)*
Harpy eagle *(Harpia harpyja)*
Red-spectacled parrot *(Amazona pretrei pretrei)*
Solitary tinamou *(Tinamus solitarius)*

Reptiles

Argentine boa constrictor *(Boa constrictor occidentalis)*
Broad-snouted caiman *(Caiman latirostris)*
Yacaré (caimán) *(Caiman crocodilus yacare)*

Appendix II

Mammals

Argentine gray fox *(Dusicyon griseus)*
Guanaco *(Lamo guanicoe)*
La Plata river dolphin
Pontoporia (Stenodelphis blainvillei)
Pampas fox *(Dusicyon gymnocercus)*
Southern elephant seal *(Mirounga leonina)*
Southern fur seal *(Arctocephalus australis)*

Birds

Caracaras *(Falconidae* all species in family except those on Appendix I)
Chilean flamingo *(Phoenicopterus ruber chilensis)*
Greater rhea *(Rhea americana albescens)*

Hemisphere. To protect these environments, Argentina has created an extensive system of national parks, briefly described below. More detailed descriptions of both the parks and their characteristic species can be found in separate entries in geographical chapters and boxed text.

In the high northern Andes, vegetation consists of sparse bunch grasses *(ichu)* and low, widely spaced shrubs, known collectively as *tola*. The most conspicuous animal is the domestic llama, but its wild cousins the guanaco and vicuña are also present, while migratory birds (including flamingos) inhabit the high saline lakes. In a few favored sites at lower elevations, most notably in Salta and Tucumán provinces, the summertime rains create geographical islands of dense subtropical forest, but wild animals other than the occasional bird are much more difficult to spot.

In the Chaco, open savannas alternate with nearly impenetrable thorn forests, while Mesopotamian rainfall is sufficient to support swampy lowland forests as well as upland savanna. One of the best areas on the continent to enjoy wildlife is the swampy Esteros del Iberá, in Corrientes province, where animals such as swamp deer, capybara, and caiman, along with many large migratory birds, are tame and common. Misiones' native vegetation is mostly dense subtropical forest, though its upper elevations are studded with Araucaria pines.

The once lush native grasses of the Argentine Pampas have suffered under grazing pressure from introduced European livestock and the proliferation of grain farms, so that very little native vegetation remains, except along watercourses like the Río Paraná. In less densely settled areas, including the arid Pampas of La Pampa province, guanacos, foxes, and even pumas are not unusual sights. Many surface water bodies, both permanent and seasonal, provide migratory bird habitats.

Most of Patagonia lies in the rain shadow of the Chilean Andes, so the vast steppes of southeastern Argentina resemble the sparse grasslands of the arid Andean highlands. But closer to the border there are pockets of dense *Nothofagus* (southern beech) and coniferous woodlands that owe their existence to the winter storms which sneak through and over the cordillera. Northern Tierra del Fuego is a grassy extension of the Patagonian steppe, but the heavy rainfall of the mountainous southern half supports verdant southern beech forests. As in the farther north, the guanaco is the most conspicuous mammal, but the flightless rhea, resembling the Old World ostrich, runs in flocks across the plains.

More particularly notable in Patagonia and Tierra del Fuego is the wealth of coastal wildlife, ranging from penguins, cormorants, and gulls to sea lions, fur seals, elephant seals, and whales. Several coastal reserves, from Río Negro province south to Tierra del Fuego, are home to enormous concentrations of wildlife that are one of the region's greatest visitor attractions.

NATIONAL & PROVINCIAL PARKS

Argentina's national parks lure visitors from around the world. One of Latin America's first national park systems dates from the turn of the century, when explorer and surveyor Francisco P Moreno donated 7500 hectares (29 sq miles) near Bariloche to the state in return for guarantees that the parcel would be preserved for the enjoyment of all Argentines. This area is now part of Parque Nacional Nahuel Huapi in the Andean lake district.

Since then, the country has established many other parks and reserves, mostly but not exclusively in the Andean region. There are also important provincial parks and reserves, such as Península Valdés, that do not fall within the national park system but deserve attention. In general, the national parks are more visitor-oriented than the provincial parks, but there are exceptions; Parque Nacional Perito Moreno has few visitor services, for example, while at Reserva Provincial Península Valdés they are extensive.

Note that Argentine park personnel, including rangers, are generally very cautious and patronizing with respect to activities beyond the most conventional, and will often exaggerate the difficulty of hikes and climbs.

Before seeing the national parks, visitors to Buenos Aires should stop at the capital's national parks office (see Information in the Buenos Aires chapter) for maps and brochures, which are often in short supply in the parks themselves; there may be a charge for some of these. The following parks are listed generally north to south, west to east.

Monumento Natural Laguna de los Pozuelos

A large, high-altitude lake in Jujuy province supports abundant bird life, including three species of flamingos, on its 16,000 hectares.

Parque Nacional Baritú

On the Bolivian border in Salta province and accessible by road only through Bolivia, this park contains 72,000 hectares of nearly virgin subtropical montane forest.

Parque Nacional Calilegua

In Argentina's Jujuy province, this scenic unit of 76,000 hectares protects a variety of ecosystems, from *yungas* (transitional, subtropical lowland forest) to humid, subtropical montane forest to sub-Alpine grassland.

Parque Nacional Los Cardones

Finally granted national park status after many years in limbo, this scenic montane desert park (70,000 hectares) in the highlands west of Salta protects the striking cardón cactus, which in the past has been used for timber and other purposes. Visitor services are still few, but increasing.

Parque Nacional Finca El Rey

In the eastern part of Salta province, this lush, mountainous park protects 44,000 hectares of subtropical and coniferous Andean forest.

Parque Nacional Río Pilcomayo

On the Paraguayan border in the province of Formosa, this reasonably accessible park protects 60,000 hectares of subtropical marshlands and palm savannas harboring birds, mammals, and reptiles, such as the caiman or *yacaré*.

Reserva Natural Formosa

In western Formosa province, on the north bank of the Río Bermejo, this 10,000-hectare gallery-forest reserve is a winter-only destination – summer temperatures are brutally, dangerously hot. It also features mammals like puma, peccary and anteater, as well as diverse bird life.

Parque Nacional Chaco

In Chaco province, this very accessible but little-visited park offers 15,000 hectares of dense, subtropical thorn forests, marshes, and palm savannas, as well as colorful birds.

Parque Nacional Mburucuyá

On the north side of the famous Esteros del Iberá, this newly declared 15,060-hectare marshland reserve is southeast of the city of Corrientes.

Parque Nacional Iguazú

In the northeastern province of Misiones, on the border with Brazil and Paraguay, this very popular park contains the awesome Iguazú Falls, featured in the popular film *The Mission*. It also preserves nearly 55,500 hectares of subtropical rain forest, with abundant birds, mammals, and reptiles.

Reserva Provincial Esteros del Iberá

In Corrientes province on the south side of the Esteros, this tranquil wetland reserve may be a better wildlife site than Brazil's famous Pantanal.

Parque Nacional El Palmar

Readily accessible from Buenos Aires, this 8500-hectare park on the Río Uruguay in Entre Ríos province protects the last extensive stands of *yatay* palm savanna, elsewhere destroyed or threatened by grazing. It is also an excellent place to see birds.

Parque Nacional Talampaya

In western La Rioja province, among desert landscapes reminiscent of the southwestern

US, this 270,000-hectare unit recently gained national park status, thanks partly to the intervention of provincial native President Carlos Menem. However, its rich scenery, plus extraordinary geological, paleontological, and archaeological resources, make it more than deserving.

Parque Provincial Ischigualasto

In northern San Juan province, also popularly known as Valle de la Luna (Valley of the Moon), this park is a scenic paleontological preserve between sedimentary ranges of the Cerros Colorados and Cerro Los Rastros.

Parque Nacional Diamante

In the province of Entre Ríos, south of the city of Paraná, this 2458-hectare unit protects the islands and gallery forests (forests that grow along streams in regions that otherwise cannot support them) of the northern delta region.

Reserva Natural Estricta Otamendi

In the province of Buenos Aires, between Tigre and Zárate, this riverside reserve on the south bank of the Paraná is the closest unit to the federal capital.

Parque Nacional Sierra de las Quijadas

In the northwestern corner of San Luis province, the polychrome desert canyons of this scenic 150,000-hectare unit have been the site of major dinosaur discoveries.

Parque Provincial Aconcagua

The province of Mendoza has set aside 71,000 hectares surrounding the Western Hemisphere's highest peak, 6960m Aconcagua, a major destination for mountaineers from around the world.

Parque Provincial Tupungato

Tupungato, the 6650m summit of Mendoza's second major provincial park is, according to most mountaineers, a more interesting and challenging objective than nearby Aconcagua.

Parque Nacional Lihué Calel

Relieving the desert monotony, this picturesque 9900-hectare park in La Pampa province has salmon-colored peaks and isolated valleys that support a surprising range of fauna and flora, including pumas, guanacos, foxes, rheas, vizcachas, and flowering cacti. There are also numerous Indian petroglyphs and some historical buildings.

Parque Nacional Laguna Blanca

Surrounded by ancient volcanoes and lava flows near the city of Zapala in Neuquén province, this lake supports nesting colonies of black-necked swans, plus Andean flamingos and other distinctive birds. The lake and surrounding parklands cover more than 11,000 hectares.

Parque Nacional Lanín

The snow-covered, symmetrical cone of Volcán Lanín is the centerpiece of this large (378,000 hectares) northern Patagonian park, near the mountain resort of San Martín de los Andes. Equally worthwhile, if less imposing, are the extensive forests of 'monkey puzzle trees' *(Araucaria* spp) and southern beech *(Nothofagus* spp). Fishing is a popular pastime.

Parque Nacional Nahuel Huapi

Lago Nahuel Huapi, an enormous trough carved by Pleistocene glaciers, filled by meltwater, and surrounded by impressive peaks, is the focus of this scenic, 758,000-hectare park. The city of San Carlos de Bariloche is the main base for visiting the park, the most highly developed in the Argentine system.

Parque Nacional Los Arrayanes

Surrounded on all sides by the much larger Parque Nacional Nahuel Huapi, this park, on a small peninsula near the resort of Villa La Angostura, protects pure stands of the unique *arrayán* tree, a member of the myrtle family.

Parque Nacional Lago Puelo

High Andean peaks surround Lago Puelo, an aquamarine, low-altitude lake in northwestern Chubut province, which drains into the Pacific near the town of El Bolsón (Río Negro province). Covering 23,700 hectares along the Chilean border, the park offers an interesting if infrequently used border crossing.

Parque Nacional Los Alerces

Along the Andean crest in Chubut province, west of the city of Esquel, this very attractive park protects 263,000 hectares of the unique Valdivian forest ecosystem, which includes impressive specimens of the *alerce* tree, resembling the California redwoods.

Reserva Provincial Península Valdés

While not part of the national park system, the Chubut provincial reserve of Península Valdés is an important destination for wildlife enthusiasts. Marine mammals, including whales, sea lions, and elephant seals, are the main attraction, but there are also Magellanic penguins and other unusual seabirds.

Along the Patagonian coast there are a number of smaller reserves with breeding colonies of seabirds and marine mammals.

Reserva Provincial Punta Tombo

Also not part of the national park system, this provincial reserve south of Trelew in Chubut has an enormous nesting colony of burrowing Magellanic penguins and other seabirds.

Parque Nacional Perito Francisco P Moreno

Named for the founder of the Argentine park system, the 115,000 hectares of this unit in northwestern Santa Cruz province protect a series of awesome glacial lakes, surrounding alpine peaks and Andean-Patagonian forest. Wildlife includes herds of guanaco. For real solitude, this park and Monumento Natural Bosques Petrificados are the best bets in the Argentine system.

Monumento Natural Bosques Petrificados

On the Patagonian steppe in northern Santa Cruz province, this isolated 10,000-hectare park features immense specimens of petrified *Proaraucaria* trees from an era prior to the creation of the Andes, when the region contained a dense, humid forest.

Parque Nacional Monte León

In the province of Santa Cruz, a short distance south of the town of Piedrabuena, this newly designated unit is Argentina's first coastal national park outside Tierra del Fuego.

Parque Nacional Los Glaciares

One of Argentina's must-see attractions is the famous Moreno Glacier – one of few in the world that is currently advancing – but the awesome pinnacles of the Fitzroy Range invite an even longer stay. Southern beech forests cover substantial zones of the 600,000-hectare park.

Parque Nacional Tierra del Fuego

Argentina's first shoreline national park, this unit on the Beagle Channel west of Ushuaia stretches inland to envelop alpine glaciers and peaks within its 63,000 hectares. There are marine mammals, seabirds, shorebirds, and extensive southern beech forests.

GOVERNMENT & POLITICS

After the end of military dictatorship in 1983, Argentina returned to the Constitution of 1853, which established a federal system similar to that of the USA. There are separate executive and bicameral legislative branches, an ostensibly independent judiciary, and a theoretical balance of power among the three.

In 1994 a constitutional convention amended the document to permit the president's reelection while reducing the term to four years (from the previous six-year single term). It also eliminated the legal requirement that the president be a Roman Catholic, added an additional senator for each province and the city of Buenos Aires, and lengthened the legislative year.

The president and the Congreso Nacional (comprising a 254-member Cámara de Diputados and a 72-member Senado) are popularly elected, as are provincial governors and legislatures. In practice, the president is far more powerful than his US counterpart and frequently governs by decree without consulting the Congreso; the president can also, and frequently does, intervene in provincial matters. When the constitutional convention established reelection of the president, it also created the office of Jefe de Gabinete, a sort of executive prime minister responsible to the Congreso.

Administratively, the country consists of a federal district (the city of Buenos Aires proper), plus 23 provinces, the territories of the South Atlantic islands (including the Falklands/Malvinas and South Georgia, under British administration), and the Argentine Antarctic (where territorial claims are on hold by international agreement).

Political Parties

Although personality is often more important than party, the spectrum of Argentine political parties is broad. At least 18 different parties are represented in the Congreso, but the most numerous are the Peronists (Justicialists) of the late Juan Perón and current President Carlos Menem, and the Unión Cívica Radical (misleadingly called the 'Radicals,' despite the fact that they usually represent middle-class interests) of former President Raúl Alfonsín. Though Argentines of all classes normally participate in political discussion, which does not always constitute dialogue, some observers have expressed concern about the apathy among younger voters, who have traditionally formed the activist sector of their parties.

Until the 1940s, when Perón revolutionized Argentine politics by overtly appealing to labor unions and other underrepresented sectors of society, the Radicals vied against parties tied to traditional conservative landowning interests for electoral supremacy. Within the Peronist party, there remain deeply divided factions, which, in the mid-1970s, even conducted open warfare against each other. Former *Buenos Aires Herald* editor James Neilson has described the party as a 'promiscuous mixture of fascists, trotskyites, militarists, nationalists, Christian Democrats, socialists, feudalists, liberals, conservatives, and infinitely flexible opportunists.'

Currently these divisions are less violent, but there is still friction between the official neoliberal adherents of President Menem, who has attempted to reduce the state's role in economic matters and limit the influence of militant labor, and leftist and nationalist elements that see Menem's policies as capitulation to foreign institutions such as the World Bank and International Monetary Fund. Ultranationalist factions within the Justicialist party are not much happier despite their loathing of the left.

Menem has forged an open association with the conservative Unión del Centro Democrático (UCeDé, or Democratic Center Union) and its leader, Alvaro Alsogaray, whose counsel is a source of great irritation to leftists and nationalists. Other parties, much less numerous and influential, include the Partido Intransigente (PI, or Intransigent Party), the Democracia Cristiana (Christian Democrats), and the Movimiento para Integración y Desarollo (MID, or Movement for Integration and Development). The Movimiento Para la Dignidad e Independencia (MODIN, or Movement for Dignity and Independence) is a right-wing extremist party formed by former carapintada leader Aldo Rico, a retired colonel who attempted to overthrow the elected government of former Radical President Raúl Alfonsín, but Rico (mayor of the Buenos Aires suburb of San Miguel) recently joined the Peronist party.

Local parties and leaders dominate some provinces. In Neuquén, for instance, the Sapag family's Partido Popular Neuquino has been responsible for some of the country's most progressive social policies. In the province of Catamarca, the Saadi family is known for the most egregious corruption – even by Argentine standards – but their links to principals in a highly publicized murder case have dimmed their fortunes.

Current Politics

Rising Peronist political figures include ex-Governor Ramon 'Palito' Ortega of Tucumán, a former crooner who once attempted to get the federal government to subsidize a financial disaster he suffered in bringing Frank Sinatra to Buenos Aires but now occupies an important federal post; ex-Santa Fe Governor Carlos Reutemann, who first came to public prominence as a Formula One racing driver; and Buenos Aires provincial Governor Eduardo Duhalde, Menem's former vice-president. Duhalde, however, has become persona non grata among pro-Menem forces for his harsh criticism of the presidential economic policies and official corruption.

Former economy minister Domingo Cavallo, author of the government's controversial but, to this point, effective 'convertibility' policy, formed his own Partido Acción para la República (Action for the Republic) after a falling out with Menem and is presently a congressional deputy.

Many Argentines think the Radical party lost its identity by acquiescing to the so-called 'Pacto de Olivos,' which permitted Menem to run for re-election despite a constitutional prohibition, but a somewhat tenuous Alianza (alliance) with the center-left coalition known as Frente del País Solidario (Frepaso, the national arm of Frente Grande, which has done well in Buenos Aires municipal elections) has helped revive its fortunes. The leading opposition candidates for the presidency in 1999 are Radical mayor Fernando De la Rúa of Buenos Aires and Frepaso's Deputy Carlos 'Chacho' Alvarez. The two parties have an agreement to divide the presidential and vice-presidential nominations between them, but who gets the top spot is an issue that could still undercut the Alianza. The MID and the Unidad Socialista (Socialist Unity) are part of Frepaso, which has yet to prove itself at the national level.

In the 1997 congressional elections, generally viewed as a repudiation of Peronist corruption, the Partido Justicialista lost its majority in the Cámara de Diputados and now has only 119 seats. The Radicals have 68 seats, Frepaso 38 (these two together form the opposition Alianza), while the remaining 32 seats come from 19 different parties (in a triumph of Argentine individualism, nine of these parties have one member each!). In the Senate, the Peronists have 37 seats, the Radicals 19, and the remaining 14 belong to 11 lesser regional parties, sometimes allied with the major parties.

In addition to the Menem-Cavallo economic policies, major issues have been Menem's authoritarian tendencies and corruption in his administration (one influential banker referred to the country as a 'kleptocracy'). Even before winning a second term, he spoke of running again in 1999 (which would have required a further constitutional amendment), he has not refrained from ruling by decree, rather than consulting with Congress over legislation, and he has even interfered in the federal courts. The president's supporters even attempted to circumvent constitutional term limits to permit their man to run again – in effect, trying to declare the Constitution unconstitutional.

Certain issues have aroused suspicion of the administration, including a drug-money laundering case involving the president's in-laws and sluggish and unsuccessful police investigations of the bombings of the Israeli embassy and Asociación Mutua Israelita Argentina (AMIA) cultural center (see Population & People later in this chapter). There have also been revelations that Argentina's ambassador to Saudi Arabia had apparently accepted large bribes to grant citizenship to Middle Eastern terrorists, and the administration has links to mysterious businessman Alfredo Yabrán, who committed suicide in 1998 while under investigation in the murder of a prominent photojournalist.

Nevertheless, the divided opposition has been ineffective in pursuing such matters, and many Argentines seem uninterested. Perhaps the most effective criticism has come from the vox populi, where Menem is referred to as *El Mufa* – a slang term implying a 'jinx.' (Professional athletes have suffered misfortunes such as broken bones soon after meeting the president, who regularly scrimmages with the national soccer team. One racing boat driver, shortly after shaking hands with him, lost the hand in an accident). According to popular belief, it is bad luck to use the president's name, so many now obliquely refer to him as 'Méndez.'

The Military

Since 1930, when it overthrew Radical President Hipólito Yrigoyen, the military has played a crucial, if not always public, role in Argentine politics. Generals have often worn the presidential sash – most recently between 1976 and 1983. It is sometimes difficult to determine whether the frequent coups occur when the military feel themselves 'obliged' to intervene because of civilian incompetence, corruption, and disorder, or whether military activities themselves create conditions that undermine the civil order.

The military coup that overthrew constitutional President María Estela Martínez de Perón ('Isabelita') in 1976 was bloodless, expected, and, even welcome among moderate sectors. After Juan Perón's death, people yearned for relief from economic chaos and the erosion of public order, in which violent strikes, bombings, and kidnappings were everyday occurrences.

In the aftermath of the coup, though, military rule was savage. The services operated dozens of clandestine detention centers, most notably the infamous Escuela de Mecánica de la Armada (ESMA, or Naval Mechanics' School) in Buenos Aires, where the government's opponents and presumed opponents were tortured and frequently murdered under the ideology of the 'national security doctrine' (see History earlier in this chapter).

The military themselves are traditionally a privileged sector in Argentine society. More frequently used to control the civilian population than to fight foreign enemies, they failed miserably in confronting Britain during the Falklands/Malvinas War of 1982 but soon recovered their technological capacity in spite of heavy losses. The air force, which suffered the heaviest material losses despite a creditable performance under difficult conditions, quickly replaced lost hardware even in the midst of a grave economic crisis that foolish military action had aggravated.

President Menem has made some headway in redefining the military's mission by involving them, despite nationalist objections, in international operations, such as the 1991 Gulf War and peacekeeping operations in the Balkans and elsewhere. At the same time, despite his own incarceration at the hands of the military during the Dirty War, he inexplicably pardoned the highest-ranking criminals and even gratuitously praised them for saving the country from 'chaos' at the end of 1994. In response, human-rights groups, such as the Madres de La Plaza de Mayo, have continued to publicize the whereabouts and activities of individuals like the notorious Astiz, and, in an extraordinary episode, Army Chief of Staff Eduardo Bauza apologized on nationwide television for his branch's role in the repression. The navy, however, has remained unrepentant.

The abolition of compulsory military service, once universal for all males above the age of 18, is a sign of the military's diminished influence; it has also reduced the army's size. Even with higher salaries and better working conditions, though, the services have been unable to achieve recruitment quotas, and even officers have suffered salary cuts due to budget crises.

Many Argentines continue to view the military with a mixture of distaste and anxiety over its ambiguous role in society. The cover photograph of a magazine article on the 'power of secretaries' in business once depicted several young women in military dress uniform rather than the presidential sash, a symbol of civilian authority.

Geopolitics

Besides the national security doctrine, one of the mainstays of military ideology and influence is the idea of geopolitics, a 19th-century European doctrine interpreted in a peculiarly Argentine way. According to this worldview, first elaborated by German geographer Friedrich Ratzel and later exaggerated in National Socialist (Nazi) ideology in the 1930s, the state resembles a biological organism that must grow (expand) or die. This means effective occupation of the territories that the state claims as its own, through which the state comes into conflict with other states. Such thinking was a major factor in General Galtieri's decision to invade the Falkland Islands in 1982.

Other South American countries, particularly Brazil and Chile, share this perspective. Chile's former dictator, General Augusto Pinochet, has even written a textbook titled *Geopolítica*, while his Argentine and Brazilian counterparts discuss topics like the 'Fifth Column' of Chilean immigrants (largely illiterate sheep shearers from the economically depressed island of Chiloé) in Patagonia or the justification of territorial claims in the Antarctic, in accordance with each country's longitudinal 'frontage' on the icebound continent. In one instance, an Argentine military government transported a pregnant woman to Antarctica to give birth there and strengthen its case for 'effective settlement.'

The tenets of geopolitics are most popular among, but not restricted to, the military, who publish obsessively complex articles in journals like *Estrategia* (Strategy). Although some of these analyses are much more sophisticated than others, it would be a mistake to dismiss any of them too easily. Once during an interview with the author, an Argentine naval officer observed that, 'For us, the Malvinas are a pact sealed in blood.' So long as such attitudes persist, the militarization of Argentine society remains a serious issue.

ECONOMY

Relating the tale of a relative who found an unusable 'treasure' of 10 billion old pesos in the mountains of Córdoba, one of the characters in Osvaldo Soriano's novel *Una Sombra Ya Pronto Serás* (Shadows) remarks that 'a country where finding a fortune is a waste of time isn't a serious country.'

Indeed, Argentina's inability to achieve its potential, despite abundant natural resources and its literate and sophisticated population, has mystified foreign observers for decades. The country resembled Australia and Canada in the early 20th century, but has regressed instead of keeping pace with those countries. Burdened with a monstrous foreign debt unlikely to ever be repaid, Argentina has a shrinking middle class, while the working class and poor have little hope of advancement. Despite the recent stability of the Menem administration, it remains difficult to find any Argentine truly optimistic about the country's future.

Since colonial times, the Argentine economy has relied on agricultural exports – hides, wool, beef, and grains – gleaned from the fertile Pampas. Self-sufficient in petroleum and other energy resources, the country has been unable to capitalize on these advantages despite a superficial prosperity. With a per capita GDP of US$8900 (a figure exaggerated by an overvalued peso), Argentina is one of Latin America's wealthiest countries, but its economy is in a state of perpetual chaos. To repay international debts of US$100 billion (thousand million) would require all export earnings for nearly four years; by contrast, Mexico's foreign debt equals only 18 months of its exports.

Encouraged by international institutions, Argentina's borrowing binge of the 1970s and 1980s funded gigantic, capital-intensive projects offering no obvious economic advantages to the country but myriad opportunities for graft and corruption. These undertakings, like the Yacyretá Dam on the upper Río Paraná, fostered economic speculation that contributed to the country's chronic inflation, which consistently exceeded 100% per annum and was often much higher.

One of Argentina's problems has been inequities in the rural sector, where problems resemble those of other Latin American countries. The richest agricultural lands of the Pampas remained under the control of relatively few individuals – unlike Canada or the US, where family farmers benefited from a more broadly based prosperity. With other rural people relegated to marginal lands or a role as dependent labor on large estates, Argentina reproduced the classic Latin American pattern of latifundio versus minifundio. Institutions like the powerful Sociedad Rural maintained the power of the landholding elite.

Perón's rise to power demonstrated that the rural social structure was inadequate for broader prosperity, that Argentina needed to develop its industrial base, and that workers needed to share in industrial development. At the time, there was probably no alternative to state involvement, but it long outlived its usefulness.

In the early years of the Menem administration, Economy Minister Domingo Cavallo drastically slashed the state sector, once the economy's largest, by selling off corrupt or inefficient state enterprises like Entel (the state telephone company), Aerolíneas Argentinas, and Yacimientos Petrolíferos Fiscales (YPF, the state oil monopoly). Some agencies had so many superfluous employees that their only usual presence was on the payroll; the day after the announcement of the impending privatization of Entel, so many people came to work that there were insufficient desks for all of them.

Argentines refer to individuals who hold multiple government jobs as *ñoquis*, after the traditional potato pasta served in Argentine households on the 29th of each month – the implication is that they appear on the job just before their monthly paychecks are due. Such practices have contributed to ruinous inflation rates, often exceeding 50% per month. While the prevalence of ñoquis has declined in the federal bureaucracy (between 1990 and 1995, federal employment fell from one million to 370,000), reform has barely touched provincial governments.

To its credit, the Menem administration has broken the inflationary spiral by reducing the public sector and its deficit, selling off inefficient state enterprises, and restricting the activities of militant labor unions. Cavallo managed to tame inflation by means of a 'convertibility' law that pegged the peso at one to one with the dollar – in effect establishing a gold standard as the government would print no more pesos than its hard currency reserves would support. Economy Minister Roque Fernández, who replaced Cavallo in mid-1996, has continued his predecessor's macroeconomic policies, and inflation for 1997 was only 1% – an astonishingly low figure by Argentine standards.

Selling off state assets like Aerolíneas Argentinas, YPF, and Entel was a one-time bonanza that reduced or eliminated budget deficits in the short term and increased productivity, but a more efficient tax system will have to achieve such gains in the future. The legacy of state domination has fostered a large informal sector that operates parallel to the official economy in providing goods and services. One study claimed that only 40% of Argentina's workers functioned in the 'official' economy – the remainder labored independently, were often paid in cash, and avoided taxes entirely.

The reduction of the state sector has also brought costs that often do not fit into conventional accounting systems. In April 1995, for instance, the privatized YPF dumped waste oil into the Río de la Plata, near Buenos Aires' popular Reserva Ecológica, on the rationale that 'we had to get rid of the waste somehow and this looked like the only solution.' A state-controlled YPF might not have done things any differently, but this intentional discharge also came at a time when the company had contracted to clean up the area's waters.

Whether the 'rationalization' of the Argentine economy envisaged by Menem and Cavallo will be successful is uncertain, but similar measures over the last 22 years have failed many times. The administration's pleas for austerity and promises that things will get better ring false when the president himself accepts a US$50,000 sports car as a gift from potential foreign investors, and a prominent labor leader declares that 'nobody in Argentina ever got rich by working.' Corruption remains such a serious problem that Transparency International ranked Argentina a poor 64th out of 85 countries in its 1998 survey of international government practices, eliciting a hostile rebuke from President Menem.

One of the side effects of privatization has been increasing unemployment, which the government sees as an essential structural adjustment but which ordinary people worry may be a more enduring problem. In late 1997, official unemployment figures stood at 13.7%, with a probable undercount in rural areas. In part, provincial governments have taken up the slack by hiring more people for their own state-run enterprises, but their reliance on federal government revenue-sharing causes serious difficulties. Even then, the legal monthly minimum wage is only US$200 in a country where living expenses are comparable to Europe or North America.

The crash of the Mexican peso in January 1995 put considerable pressure on the Argentine economy, as has the Asian meltdown of 1998, but to this point the convertibility policy has resisted devaluation pressures that could unleash a new round of serious inflation. Argentine policy makers have cast a nervous eye on Brazil, the dominant partner in the Mercosur customs union, whose shaky markets could also cast the much smaller Argentine economy into recession. Despite 6% growth in 1997, the government has backed off expensive public-works measures such as an ambitious highway improvement program.

Mercosur

The customs union of Brazil, Argentina, Uruguay, and Paraguay, known as 'Mercosur,' is the first attempt by developing countries to establish a free-trade area, and the union should in theory facilitate commerce among the four countries and reduce prices for imported goods. Nobody should get too excited too soon, however. At present the policy only requires the four countries to impose a common external tariff on most imported goods, but internal customs barriers remain in place to protect local and national industries.

There is no common labor market, such as in the European Union, so Brazilian, Paraguayan, and Uruguayan workers are officially unwelcome in Argentina, and vice versa. At present, undocumented foreign laborers are being persecuted in much the same manner as Mexican and Central American workers residing in the USA.

Tourism

Tourism makes a substantial contribution to the Argentine economy; in 1996, nearly 4.3 million foreigners visited the country, while the 1993 income from *turismo receptivo* exceeded US$3600 million (this figure does not include domestic tourism, also an important economic factor). Excluding citizens of the neighboring countries of Brazil, Chile, Uruguay, and Paraguay, the greatest number of foreign visitors to Argentina are European (539,000), followed by Americans (317,000). Tourism employs nearly half a million Argentines and accounts for about 20% of the country's export earnings.

POPULATION & PEOPLE

Argentina's population of 36.1 million is unevenly distributed. More than a third reside in Gran Buenos Aires (Greater Buenos Aires), which includes the Capital Federal and its suburbs in the Buenos Aires province. Nearly 90% live in urban areas (defined as places with population greater than 2000); the other major population centers are Rosario (Santa Fe province), Córdoba, Tucumán, Mendoza, and Bahía Blanca (Buenos Aires province). South of Patagonia's Río Colorado the population is small and dispersed. The population growth rate is barely 1%, with a doubling time of 62 years.

From the early 19th century, the Unitarist faction in Argentine politics had followed the dictum of Juan Bautista Alberdi, a native of Tucumán, who argued that 'to govern is to populate.' Unitarists saw Europe as a model for independent Argentina's aspirations and did everything possible to promote European immigration. Alberdi's ideas retain great appeal, surviving especially among geopoliticians who fantasize filling the country's vast empty spaces, Patagonia, and even Antarctica, with more Argentines.

Unlike the central Andean countries, which had large, urbanized Indian populations when Europeans appeared on the scene, the Pampas core of present-day Argentina was sparsely populated by hunting and gathering peoples. Except in the northwest, where early colonization proceeded from Peru and Bolivia, European immigrants displaced relatively small numbers of indigenous peoples. From the mid-19th century on, the trickle of Europeans became a flood, as Italians, Basques, Welsh, English, Ukrainians, and immigrants of other nationalities inundated Buenos Aires as they did New York City. Italian surnames are even more common than Spanish ones, though Italo-Argentines do not constitute a cohesive, distinctive group in the way that Italian-Americans do in many cities in the US.

Some groups have retained a distinctive cultural identity, such as Anglo-Argentines throughout the country and the Welsh-Argentines in Chubut province (despite the near eclipse of Welsh as a living language). In some areas there are agricultural settlements with a definable ethnic heritage, for instance, the Germans of Eldorado in Misiones province, the Bulgarians and Yugoslavs of Roque Sáenz Peña in the Chaco, and the Ukrainians of La Pampa.

Buenos Aires' Jewish community of about 400,000, the world's eighth largest, has drawn unfortunate attention due to the bombing of the Israeli embassy in 1992 and the particularly lethal terrorist destruction of the Asociación Mutua Israelita Argentina (AMIA) in July 1994, when a bomb killed at least 86 people as it leveled the Jewish cultural center. Progress in identifying the culprits has been agonizingly slow, even though in late 1995 some 15 people (10 of them noncommissioned army officers) were arrested and charged with planning or facilitating the attack; there are as yet no convictions, however. The bombing has had a chilling effect on the capital's Jewish community; most synagogues and other Jewish centers have been heavily fortified, and security guards check everyone upon entry.

Middle Eastern immigrants, though not numerous, have attained great political influence. The most obvious case is President Carlos Menem, of Syrian ancestry, who rose to prominence in the province of La Rioja. Although he is a vocal and perhaps opportunistic Catholic (Catholicism was a formal requirement for the presidency when he was first elected), his marriage to his now-estranged wife, Zulema Yoma, was arranged; both Zulema and their daughter, Zulemita, are active Muslims who planned a pilgrimage to Mecca after the death of Carlos Jr in a helicopter accident.

The Saadis in Catamarca and the Sapags in Neuquén are other influential political families of Middle Eastern origins, while Colonel Mohammed Alí Seineldín (a fanatical Catholic despite his name) is an imprisoned leader of the army's fascist carapintada movement. Argentines refer indiscriminately to anyone of Middle Eastern ancestry (except Jews or Israelis) as a *turco* (Turk), sometimes though not always with racist connotations.

The Buenos Aires suburb of Escobar has a conspicuous Japanese community, but non-European immigrants have generally not been welcome; despite the upheavals in Asia over the past decade-plus, only a relative handful of immigrants from that region have entered Argentina. Nevertheless, an abundance of Chinese restaurants have opened in the past decade, the common Korean surname Kim fills nearly a page in the Buenos Aires telephone directory, and Asian faces are a more common sight than in the past.

Many Chileans live in Argentine Patagonia, but their usual status as dependent laborers on sheep estancias marginalizes their position in Argentine society. Bolivian highlanders often serve as seasonal laborers *(peones golondrinas,* or swallows) in the sugar harvests of northwestern Argentina; some have moved to Buenos Aires, where they mainly work in construction. Numerous Paraguayans and Uruguayans also reside permanently in Argentina. As the Menem administration's increasingly rigid economic policies have swelled unemployment, some Argentines have begun to scapegoat undocumented foreign workers, even though those workers (like Mexicans in the USA) fill economic niches that few Argentines choose to fill themselves.

Estimates of the country's indigenous population range from 60,000 to 150,000, but the Instituto Nacional de Estadística places the figure around 100,000. The largest groups are the Quechua of the northwest and the Mapuche of northern Patagonia, but there are important populations of Matacos, Tobas, and others in the Chaco and in northeastern cities such as Resistencia and Santa Fe. The Alfonsín administration was surprisingly sympathetic to Indian issues, but the Menem government appears indifferent.

EDUCATION

Argentina's 94% literacy rate is one of Latin America's highest. From the ages of five to 12, education is free and compulsory, though attendance is low in some rural areas. The comprehensive secondary-education system follows the French model, with no elective courses. Elite public secondary schools like the Colegio Nacional Buenos Aires, where the teachers are also university instructors, are unequaled by other public or private institutions, although some bilingual schools are very prestigious. Many government officials have graduate degrees from universities in Europe and the US – former Economy Minister Domingo Cavallo, for instance, is a Harvard PhD.

Universities are traditionally free and open, but once students have chosen a specialization, their course of study is extremely rigid. Ready access to higher education has glutted Buenos Aires with large numbers of professionals, like doctors and lawyers, who are not easily absorbed into the city's economy, but are reluctant to relocate to the provinces. Private universities exist, but public universities like Buenos Aires, Córdoba, and La Plata are more prominent.

In addition to university education, there is a tertiary system for the preparation of teachers, who do not need a university degree. Individuals who are not academically oriented can choose vocational training.

Argentina has had two Nobel Prize winners, Bernardo Houssay (Medicine, 1946), and Luis Federico Leloir (Chemistry, 1972). Traditionally, however, many Argentine scientists have worked overseas because of the turbulent political situation, especially in the universities, and for economic reasons.

Once associated with the working class and brothels, the tango attained broad popularity in the early 20th century.

ARTS

Many Argentine intellectuals have been educated in European capitals, particularly Paris. In the 19th and early 20th centuries, Buenos Aires self-consciously emulated French trends in art, music, and architecture, but many Argentines have made their mark outside the country's borders.

Music & Dance

Music and dance are difficult to separate in Argentina. The palatial Teatro Colón, home of the Buenos Aires opera, is one of the finest facilities of its kind in the world. Classical music and ballet, as well as modern dance, appear there and at similar venues like the Teatro Avenida.

Tango & Folk Probably the best-known manifestation of Argentine popular culture is the tango, both as music and dance, with important figures such as the legendary Carlos Gardel, the late Julio Sosa and Astor

Folk singer Mercedes Sosa

Piazzolla, and contemporaries like Susana Rinaldi, Eladia Blásquez, and Osvaldo Pugliese. Tango is constantly on the radio (Buenos Aires has a 24-hour all-tango FM station), tops the bill at the capital's finest nightclubs, and is even heard in the streets. North American tango enthusiasts can ask for a free, sample copy of the monthly newsletter *El Firulete* by contacting ☎ 408-720-9506, fax 732-2690, tangoman@hooked.net, 1111 W El Camino Real, Suite 109, Sunnyvale, CA 94087.

The late Atahualpa Yupanqui was a giant of Argentine folk music, which takes much of its inspiration from the northwestern Andean region and the countries to the north, especially Bolivia and Peru. Los Chalchaleros are a northern folk institution who recently celebrated their 50th anniversary.

Other contemporary performers include Mercedes Sosa of Tucumán (probably the best-known Argentine folk artist outside the South American continent), Suna Rocha (also an actress) of Córdoba, Antonio Tarragó Ross, Leon Gieco (modern enough to adopt and adapt a rap style at times), and the Conjunto Pro Música de Rosario.

Jazz There are many jazz venues in Buenos Aires, mostly in the downtown area and San Telmo. Internationally, Argentina's best-known jazz musician is probably Rosario-born saxophonist Gato Barbieri, though he rarely performs in the capital.

Known best for his Hollywood soundtracks, porteño composer and pianist Lalo Schifrin moved to the United States in the 1950s in order to play with jazz legends like Dizzy Gillespie and Eric Dolphy.

Rock & Pop Rock musicians such as Charly García (formerly a member of the pioneering group Sui Generis) and Fito Páez (dismissed by some as excessively commercial) are national icons. García's version of the Argentine national anthem does what Jimi Hendrix did for 'The Star-Spangled Banner.' After a judge dismissed a lawsuit alleging that García lacked 'respect for national symbols,' the *Buenos Aires Herald* editorialized that García's defense was a victory over 'extremist nationalist sectors' which had too long 'imposed their warped and often authoritarian views on the rest of society'.

Les Luthiers, an irreverent group who build many of their unusual instruments from scratch, satirize those sectors in the middle class and the military. Many performers are more conventional and derivative, but before you report an Elvis sighting in Buenos Aires, make sure it isn't Sandro, a living Argentine clone of the King. The advent of Sandro impersonators in the raucous *boliches* (nightclubs) of La Boca may be sending a message to the man known to his devotees as 'El Maestro'.

Popular Argentine groups playing 'rock nacional' include the now defunct Soda Stereo, Los Divididos (descendants of an earlier group known as Sumo), the wildly unconventional Babasónicos, Patricio Rey y Sus Redonditos de Ricota, and Los Ratones Paranóicos, who opened for the Rolling Stones on their spectacularly successful five-night stand in Buenos Aires in February 1995 (Stones associate Andrew Loog Oldham has produced one of the Ratones' albums). Also on the bill with the Stones were Las Pelotas and the Buenos Aires blues artist Pappo.

Los Fabulosos Cadillacs (winners of a Grammy as best alternative Latin rock group and a favorite crossover act among

Anglophone audiences) have popularized ska and reggae, along with groups like Los Auténticos Decadentes, Los Pericos, Los Cafres, and Espías Secretos. Almafuerte, descended from the earlier Hermética, is Buenos Aires' leading (but surprisingly literate) heavy metal band. Actitud María Marta is a young but politically conscious rap group whose songs deal with topics like the children of the disappeared.

Porteño blues band Memphis La Blusera, [illegible]ve act, has worked with North [illegible]gend Taj Mahal (the current [illegible]y of blues in Buenos Aires perhaps adds a new dimension to the old question 'Can blue men sing the whites?'). Las Blacanblus is a female vocal ensemble doing humorous, near a cappella versions of blues standards.

Singer Patricia Sosa's closest counterparts in the English-speaking world would be Janis Joplin or, today, perhaps Melissa Ethridge. The appropriately named Dos Minutos emulates the Ramones, who themselves played Buenos Aires several times.

Literature

Argentine writers of international stature include Jorge Luis Borges, Julio Cortázar, Ernesto Sábato, Manuel Puig, Osvaldo Soriano, and Adolfo Bioy Casares, much of whose work is readily available in English translation. Argentine women writers are best known for poetry and essays, but little of their work has appeared in translation. One exception is Victoria Ocampo, whose essays were included in Doris Meyer's biography *Against the Wind and Tide* (University of Texas, 1990). Dates below refer to the initial Spanish edition, followed by the English translation.

Borges, best known for his short stories but also for his works of poetry, wrote with references that sometimes make him inaccessible to readers without a solid grounding in the classics, though his material often deals with everyday porteño and provincial life. James Woodall has recently analyzed (mostly in the Freudian sense of the word) Argentina's most famous literary figure in *Borges: A Life* (Basic Books, 1997), originally published in Britain under the title *The Man in the Mirror of the Book* (Hodder & Stoughton, 1996).

Originally published in 1961 and a cult favorite among Argentine youth, Sábato's *On Heroes and Tombs* (Ballantine, 1991) is a psychological novel that explores people and places in Buenos Aires. Try also his novella *The Tunnel* (1950; Ballantine 1988), the engrossing story of a porteño painter so obsessed with his art that it distorts his relationship to everything and everyone else.

Cortázar, though a Parisian resident most of his life, nonetheless featured clearly Argentine characters in novels like the experimentally structured *Hopscotch* (1963; Random House, 1966) and *62: A Model Kit* (1968). The landmark 1960s film *Blow-Up* was based on one of his short stories. Manuel Puig's novels, including *Kiss of the Spider Woman* (New York, Vintage, 1991), *The Buenos Aires Affair* (Dutton, 1968), *Betrayed by Rita Hayworth* (1968), and *Publis Angelical* (Vintage, 1986), focus on

Writer Jorge Luis Borges

the ambiguous role of popular culture in Argentina.

Bioy Casares' hallucinatory novella *The Invention of Morel* (University of Texas, 1985) also deals with the inability or unwillingness to distinguish between fantasy and reality; it was a partial inspiration for the highly praised film *Man Facing Southeast*. His *Diary of the War of the Pig* (McGraw Hill, 1972), set in Buenos Aires, is also available in translation.

The late Osvaldo Soriano, perhaps Argentina's most popular contemporary novelist, wrote *A Funny Dirty Little War* and *Winter Quarters*, both published by Readers International. In Soriano's *Shadows* (Knopf, 1993), the protagonist is lost in an Argentina where the names are the same, but all the familiar landmarks and points of reference have lost their meaning. The original title, *Una Sombra Ya Pronto Serás*, comes from the lyrics of a popular tango.

The most notorious Argentine fiction of recent years is Federico Andahazi's sexually explicit but unquestionably literary *The Anatomist* (Doubleday, 1998), which caused an uproar when the wealthy sponsor of an national literary prize tried to overturn the award her committee gave the author.

Architecture

Argentina lacks the great pre-Columbian monuments of Peru and Bolivia, though a few significant archaeological sites dot the Andean Northwest. This region has notable if not abundant Spanish colonial architecture in cities such as Salta and Tucumán, and in villages in isolated areas like the Quebrada de Humahuaca. Other areas for colonial architecture, or at least atmosphere, include San Antonio de Areco and Carmen de Patagones in Buenos Aires province. The city of Buenos Aires itself has scattered colonial examples, but is essentially a turn-of-the-century city whose architectural influences are predominantly French. Recent architecture tends to the pharaonic and impersonal, with a substantial number of modernistic buildings in the downtown area.

Architects in the Andean lake district of northern Patagonia have adapted Middle European styles into some of the region's most appealing urban landscapes, but recent tacky construction in cities like San Carlos de Bariloche has overwhelmed its appeal. Southern Patagonia, while not famous for its architecture, has an intriguing and unique 'Magellanic' style of wooden houses with metal cladding, also present in southern Chile.

Painting & Sculpture

Like much of Argentine culture, the visual arts express a tension between the European derivative and criollo originality – the European influence has been so powerful that porteño art critic Jorge Glusberg has argued the 'colonial period' in Argentine art lasted into the mid-20th century, to be severed only by the outbreak of WWII. Buenos Aires is the focus of the country's arts community, but there are also unexpected outliers, such as the city of Resistencia, capital of Chaco province. Still, many of the most innovative artists go abroad, usually to Europe or North America, to make a living.

Early Argentine painting can pride itself on figures like self-taught Cándido López, a 19th-century military officer who lost his right hand in the war against Paraguay but rehabilitated himself well enough to paint more than 50 extraordinary oils on the conflict. The many Argentine artists who studied in France or Italy produced work with demonstrably European themes, but some local manifestations of their work are memorable, such as the restored ceiling murals of Antonio Berni, Lino Spilimbergo, and others in Buenos Aires' Galerías Pacífico shopping center. The late Benito Quinquela Martín, who put the working-class barrio of La Boca on the artistic map, painted brightly colored oils of life in the factories and on the waterfront.

Contemporary painting has eschewed the romantic without abandoning its regard for the countryside. Tucumán-born Víctor Hugo Quiroga's paintings, for instance, deal with provincial rather than porteño themes, but they successfully reflect the impact of modern global developments on criollo life.

Porteño painter Guillermo Kuitca makes an imaginative use of cartographic images by integrating them with events like the genocide against European Jews in works like *Kristallnacht II*. Graciela Sacco is a multimedia artist who incorporates audio and video narratives into her arrangements of ready-made objects like plastic spoons and bar codes.

Given its French origins, official public art tends toward hero worship and the pompously monumental, expressed through equestrian statues of military figures such as José de San Martín, Justo José Urquiza, and Julio Argentino Roca. A welcome exception is the work of the late Rogelio Yrurtia, some of whose works deal sympathetically with the struggles and achievements of working people – see his *Canto al Trabajo* on the Plazoleta Olazábal on Av Paseo Colón at Av Independencia in San Telmo.

An even stronger counterpoint to nationalist idolatry are modern works by individuals including sculptor Alberto Heredia,

The Legend of Che Guevara

Many people still do not realize that one of Cuba's greatest revolutionary heroes, in some ways eclipsing even Fidel Castro, was an Argentine. Ernesto Guevara, known by the common Argentine interjection *che*, was officially born in the city of Rosario in 1928, grew up in Buenos Aires and the Córdoba mountain resort of Alta Gracia, and studied medicine in the capital. He traveled extensively throughout his own country, as well as South and Central America, before finding his calling in Mexico, where he met Fidel Castro and other exiles who remarkably overthrew Cuban dictator Fulgencio Batista in 1959.

Unable to resign himself to the bureaucratic task of building Cuban socialism, Guevara became an icon by trying, unsuccessfully, to spread revolution in the Congo, in Argentina and Bolivia, where Che himself died in 1967 after a particularly inept campaign further undercut by political factionalism in Bolivia. Che himself didn't make it any easier to repeat his early successes in Cuba, giving away many of his secrets through his extensive writings, but his high profile, eloquent writings and speeches, and early death made him a global figure.

The 30th anniversary of Che's death, in 1997, produced a spate of biographies of varying quality, most of them simultaneously sympathetic to the guerrilla leader but critical of his shortcomings. Journalist John Lee Anderson's *Che Guevara: A Revolutionary Life* (Grove Press) is a workmanlike chronology, which has the best material on Che's Argentine childhood and youth, and his long term goal of spreading the revolution to Argentina. Mexican academic Jorge Castañeda's *Compañero: The Life and Death of Che Guevara* (Knopf) is more analytical but still accessible. Castañeda's countryman, journalist-novelist Paco Ignacio Taibo, has written *Guevara, also Known as Che* (St Martin's Press), which uses a hybrid style of biography and fiction, frequently using Che's own words.

The year also produced some unlikely tributes – two decades earlier, no one could have guessed that the Argentine government, then under the thumb of a vicious right-wing military dictatorship, would one day issue a postage stamp honoring Che's Argentine roots. Though Che detested Perón and Peronism, Peronist president Carlos Menem defended the stamp by declaring that' . . . Guevara is an Argentine and a world figure, and this is one way to advance towards peace and understanding in Argentina.'

whose work ridicules the solemnity of official public art and even national icons like José de San Martín. Heredia's powerful and controversial statue *El Caballero de la Máscara* depicts a 19th-century caudillo as a headless horseman; during the military dictatorship of 1976-83, the sculpture could not be exhibited under its original title *El Montonero*, which implied associations with guerrilla forces that had nothing to do with the artist's theme. Heredia has also dealt with environmental issues in works like the ghostly *Chernobyl*.

Another overtly political sculptor is Juan Carlos Distéfano, whose disconcerting *El Rey y La Reina* (The King and the Queen), an image of two figures shot to death in the front seat of an automobile, actually appeared in a prominent Buenos Aires gallery during the dictatorship. For comic relief, the surrealistic junk sculptures of Yoël Novoa are accessible to audiences of almost any age or political persuasion.

Visitors should not overlook manifestations of (often anonymous) folk art in the streets – even political graffiti can be remarkably elaborate and eloquent. Of particular interest is *filete*, the ornamental line painting that once graced the capital's horsecarts, trucks, and buses.

Buenos Aires has a multitude of art galleries, most of which are very conventional but some of which deal with audacious modern art.

Contemporary Argentine art has gained recognition in international markets, where Berni's 1954 painting *Juanito Laguna bañándose entre latas* (Juanito Laguna washing amongst the trash), a protest against social and economic inequality, sold in New York for US$150,000 in 1997. Another Berni work, *Emigrantes*, sold for US$500,000 in 1996.

For a brief survey of modern Argentine art in English, look for Glusberg's *Art in Argentina* (Milan, Giancarlo Politi Editore, 1986). Readers who understand Spanish can try Rafael Squirru's *Arte Argentino Hoy* (Buenos Aires, Ediciones de Arte Gaglianone, 1983), a selection of work from 48 contemporary painters and sculptors illustrated in color.

Film

Despite the limited resources available to directors, Argentine cinema has achieved international stature, especially since the end of the military dictatorship of 1976-83. Many Argentine films, both before and after the Dirty War, are available on video.

María Luisa Bemberg, perhaps Argentina's best-known contemporary director, died in 1995. Her historically based films often illuminate the Argentine experience, particularly the relationship between women and the church. *Camila* (nominated for a best foreign film Oscar in 1984) recounts the tale of Catholic socialite Camila O'Gorman, who fell in love and ran away from Buenos Aires with a young Jesuit priest in 1847, before the repressive government of Rosas found and executed them both.

Bemberg's English-language film *Miss Mary* (1986), starring Julie Christie, focuses on the experience of an English governess of upper-class Argentine children, while *I, the Worst of All* (1990) tells the life of the 17th-century Mexican nun Sor Juana Inés de la Cruz. Bemberg's last directorial effort, *I Don't Want to Talk About It* (1992), was an offbeat love story starring Marcelo Mastroianni. Filmed in the Uruguayan city of Colonia, across the river from Buenos Aires, it metaphorically explores issues of power and control in a provincial town.

Director Luis Puenzo's *The Official Story* (1985) deals with the delicate, controversial theme of adoption of the children of missing or murdered parents by those responsible for their disappearance or death during the Dirty War; it stars Norma Leandro, a popular stage actress who has also worked in English-language films in the US. Some critics, however, have rebuked Puenzo for an apparent subtext implying that Argentines were innocently ignorant of the period's flagrant atrocities, and the issue has resurfaced with the arrest of former dictator Jorge Rafael Videla on kidnapping charges. William Hurt, the late Raúl Julia, and Robert Duvall all appeared in Puenzo's English-language film version of Albert Camus' novel *The Plague* (1992), which the director set in Buenos Aires.

Eliseo Subiela's *Man Facing Southeast* (1986) takes part of its inspiration from Adolfo Bioy Casares' ingenious novella *The Invention of Morel*. Uruguayan poet Mario Benedetti has a cameo in Subiela's *The Dark Side of the Heart* (1992), a compellingly melancholy love story, set in Buenos Aires and Montevideo, with a surprise ending.

Héctor Babenco directed the English-language *Kiss of the Spider Woman* (1985), also starring Hurt and Julia. Set in Brazil but based on Manuel Puig's novel, it's an intricate portrayal of the way in which the police and military abuse political prisoners and exploit informers. Babenco also directed the engrossing *Pixote* (1981), a brutally frank drama about Brazilian street children.

Director Fernando 'Pino' Solanas politicized the tango in *The Exile of Gardel* (1985), dealing with the disrupted lives of a group of displaced Argentines during the Dirty War (the film's Parisian setting was ironically apropos for Francophile Argentina). The late tango legend Astor Piazzola composed the soundtrack and appears in the film. Solanas, a leftist candidate for president in 1995, has also directed the films *El Viaje* and *Sur*.

Marcelo Piñeyro's *Wild Horses* (1995) is, despite the director's denials, a road movie that starts with a bizarre Robin Hood-style bank robbery in Buenos Aires and ends with a chase in the province of Chubut. It stars veteran actor Héctor Alterio.

Héctor Olivera's *La Patagonia Rebelde* (1974), which often plays university campuses and repertory houses in the USA, is a historical account of the anarchist rebellion in Santa Cruz province at the turn of the century. Olivera also adapted Osvaldo Soriano's satirical novels to the big screen in *A Funny Dirty Little War* (1983) and *Una Sombra Ya Pronto Serás* (1994). Despite its title, the former has nothing to do with the horrors of the Proceso, except perhaps metaphorically. But his *The Night of the Pencils* (1986) deals directly with the Dirty War – through the notorious case of half a dozen La Plata high-school students abducted, tortured, and killed by the military.

Manuel Antín's *Don Segundo Sombra* (1969), based on Ricardo Güiraldes' gauchesco novel, is a coming-of-age-on-the-Pampas film, set in the village of San Antonio de Areco. Antín's 1980 film *Long Ago and Far Away* mines similar material from William Henry Hudson's writings about his youth in Buenos Aires province.

Filmed around the scenic city of Tandil, in Buenos Aires province, Luis César D'Angiolillo's *Killing Grandpa* (1991) is a family drama with touches of humor and magical realism, starring veteran stage and screen actor Federico Luppi. Luppi appears in Adolfo Aristarain's *A Place in the World*, which was disqualified from the Best Foreign Language Film competition at the 1992 Academy Awards since it was submitted by Uruguay, but produced mainly in Argentina; the film has drawn comparisons to the classic Hollywood Western *Shane*. Luppi also plays the lead in Mexican director's Guillermo del Toro's *Cronos* (1992), an offbeat science-fiction gangster film, and in US director John Sayles' Spanish-language *Men with Guns* (1997), an allegorical exploration of political violence in Latin America.

Although not himself a filmmaker, porteño composer Lalo Schifrin wrote much music for Hollywood, including themes and soundtracks for *Mission Impossible*, *Bullitt*, *Cool Hand Luke*, and *Dirty Harry*, among many others.

For information and recommendations on movies about Argentina, see the Film section in the Facts for the Visitor chapter.

Theater

Buenos Aires has a vigorous theater community, equivalent in its own way to New York, London, or Paris, but even in the provinces, live theater is an important medium of expression. Legendary Argentine performers include Luis Sandrini and Lola Membrives, and famous European writers like Federico García Lorca and Jean Cocteau have explored the Buenos Aires theater scene. Probably Argentina's most famous contemporary playwright is Juan Carlos Gené, until recently director of the Teatro General San Martín.

The theater season is liveliest from June through August, but there are always performances on the docket. Av Corrientes is the capital's Broadway or West End, but throughout the city are large and small theater venues and companies, some very improvisational and unconventional. Many of the capital's most popular (and vulgar) shows move to the provincial beach resort of Mar del Plata for the summer.

Unlike stage actors in some countries, those in Argentina seem to move seamlessly among stage, film, and television. Perhaps performers like Norma Leandro, Federico Luppi, and China Zorrilla feel less self-conscious about moving among the various media, since the Argentine public is smaller and work opportunities fewer than in London, New York, or Los Angeles. Some 150 Argentine plays have passed from the theater to film since the silent era.

SOCIETY & CONDUCT

English-speaking visitors may find Argentina more accessible than other Latin American countries because of its superficial resemblance to their own societies. In contrast to countries like Peru and Bolivia, with their large indigenous populations, foreign travelers are relatively inconspicuous and can more easily integrate themselves into everyday life. Argentines are gregarious and, once you make contact with them, much more likely to invite you to participate in their regular activities than would, say, Quechua llama herders in Bolivia.

One of these activities, which you should never refuse, is the opportunity to *tomar un mate* (drink mate). Drinking mate (pronounced 'mah-tay'), or Paraguayan tea, is an important ritual throughout the River Plate countries and to a lesser degree in Chile, but especially so in Argentina. In the south, it is drunk bitter, but in the north people take it with sugar and *yuyos*, or herbs (see 'Mate & Its Ritual' in the Facts for the Visitor chapter).

RELIGION

Roman Catholicism is the official state religion but, as in many other Latin American countries, evangelical Protestantism is making inroads among traditionally Catholic believers. Even within the Catholic religion, popular beliefs diverge from official doctrine – one of the best examples is the cult of the Difunta Correa, based in San Juan province, to which hundreds of thousands of professed Argentine Catholics make annual pilgrimages and offerings, despite an aggressive campaign by the Church hierarchy against her veneration.

Spiritualism and veneration of the dead have remarkable importance for a country that prides itself on European sophistication. Novelist Tomás Eloy Martínez has observed that Argentines honor their national heroes, such as San Martín, not on the anniversary of their birth but of their death, a habit that indirectly parallels the celebrations of saints' days. Visitors to Recoleta and Chacarita cemeteries in Buenos Aires – essential sights for comprehending Argentine culture – will see steady processions of pilgrims communing with icons, including Juan and Evita Perón, psychic Madre María, and tango singer Carlos Gardel, by laying hands on their tombs and leaving arcane offerings.

Official Catholicism has provided Argentina some of its finest monuments, from the modest but picturesque churches of the Andean Northwest to the Jesuit missions of Mesopotamia, the colonial cathedral in Córdoba, and the neo-Gothic basilica of Luján in Buenos Aires province. Insufficient attention to the role of religion will limit anyone's understanding of Argentine society.

Like other Argentine institutions, the Church has many factions. During the late 1970s and early 1980s, the official Church generally supported the de facto military government despite persecution, kidnapping, torture, and murder of religious workers. These workers, adherents of the 'Liberation Theology' movement, often worked among the poor and dispossessed in both rural areas and the *villas miserias* (shantytowns) of Buenos Aires and other large cities. Such activism has resumed in today's more permissive political climate, but the Church hierarchy remains obstinate: the late Archbishop

Antonio Quarracino of Buenos Aires, for example, defended President Menem's pardon of the convicted murderers and torturers of the Proceso, and it appears that official chaplains acquiesced in Dirty War atrocities by counseling the perpetrators.

LANGUAGE

Spanish is the official language, but some immigrant communities retain their language as a badge of identity. Italians are the single largest immigrant group, and the Italian language is widely understood, while the Anglo-Argentine community retains a precise, clipped English – short-wave listeners who stumble onto Radio Argentina Al Exterior may momentarily assume they've found the BBC. While many Argentines study English as a second language, outside Buenos Aires it is often only in tourist offices, major hotels, and travel agencies catering to foreigners that you will encounter individuals with a good working knowledge of the language. In Chubut province, despite the persistence of many Welsh cultural traditions, the Welsh language itself has nearly disappeared, though there are some indications of a revival.

No one should ignore the country's 17 native languages, though some are spoken by very few individuals. In the Andean Noroeste, Quechua speakers are numerous, although most are bilingual in Spanish. In the southern Andes, there are at least 40,000 Mapuche-speaking Indians. In northeastern Argentina, there are about 15,000 Guaraní speakers, an equal number of Tobas, and about 10,000 Matacos.

Facts for the Visitor

HIGHLIGHTS

For most visitors from overseas, Argentina's principal attractions are both cultural and natural. But as in all countries, some of the least-frequented sights deserve more attention, while a few of the best-known destinations hardly warrant a stop.

The following list, starting in the north and working south, includes some of the country's best-known tourist attractions and some lesser but still deserving ones in its most remote corners.

Quebrada de Humahuaca & Quebrada de Cafayate The scenic desert canyons of the Andean Northwest, with their large Indian populations, archaeological sites, and colonial churches, are an outlier of the central Andean countries.

Cataratas del Iguazú Despite the increasing commercialization of the surrounding area, the thunderous falls at Iguazú remain one of the continent's most breathtaking sights.

Esteros del Iberá For approachable, abundant subtropical wildlife, some travelers find this marshland in Corrientes province even more impressive than Brazil's Pantanal, but it's much less visited.

Córdoba Argentina's second-largest city is Buenos Aires' cultural rival, with monumental colonial and ecclesiastical architecture, not to mention the nearby Sierras.

Buenos Aires A self-consciously European sophistication, combined with the romantic image of the tango, is only the stereotypical trademark of a city that has much more to offer.

Delta del Paraná Less than an hour from Buenos Aires, the myriad channels of the Río de la Plata are a welcome escape from the noise, heat, and congestion of the capital.

The Pampas The gaucho, a cultural icon and modern anachronism, remains Argentina's enduring image in towns like San Antonio de Areco and surrounding estancias, many of which encourage paying guests. Religious pilgrimage centers such as Luján, with its monumental cathedral, are worth a visit.

Cuyo Argentina's wine country also features recreational attractions like Mendoza's Parque Provincial Aconcagua and San Juan's offbeat Difunta Correa shrine.

Lake District Soaring volcanoes, shimmering lakes, sprawling forests, and trout-rich rivers make the eastern slopes of the Andes a recreational paradise. Its traditional focus is San Carlos de Bariloche, on Lago Nahuel Huapi, but many other places are more suitable for extended visits.

Península Valdés The unique, abundant wildlife and desert scenery of the Patagonian coast draw visitors to this popular wildlife reserve near Puerto Madryn, in Chubut province. Punta Tombo is a comparable attraction, but even the barren Patagonian steppe exercises a powerful hold on the imagination.

Parque Nacional Los Glaciares In Santa Cruz province, the breathtaking Moreno Glacier is even more awesome when the lake behind it causes it to burst at irregular intervals. The pinnacles of the Fitzroy range, in the park's northern sector, pull in climbers and mountaineers from around the world.

Parque Nacional Torres del Paine In Chilean Patagonia, South America's finest national park is a miniature Alaska.

Tierra del Fuego The town of Ushuaia is itself overrated, but the wild coastal and alpine scenery around it justify a trip to the terminus of Ruta Nacional (RN) 3.

SUGGESTED ITINERARIES

Since Argentina is a very large country, itineraries will depend on time and mode of transport. Visiting the country's most popular attractions – the city of Buenos Aires, the Cataratas del Iguazú, and the Moreno Glacier in Parque Nacional Los Glaciares – would require a minimum of about 10 days by airplane, but this would be very rushed, and at least two weeks is desirable. Add other key destinations like Península Valdés, the city of Ushuaia, the lake district around Bariloche, and Chile's Parque Nacional Torres del Paine (a popular stop for visitors to Los Glaciares) and at least a month is on the docket.

Traveling overland on a budget, the same destinations would justify two months or more, with the possible addition of Cuyo and the Andean Northwest. If the money holds out, dedicated overland travelers could easily spend six months in the country with little backtracking or repetition.

PLANNING

When to Go

For residents of the Northern Hemisphere, Argentina offers the inviting possibility of enjoying two summers in the same year, but the country's great variety can make a visit in any season worthwhile. Buenos Aires' urban attractions transcend the seasons, but popular Patagonian destinations, like the Moreno Glacier in Santa Cruz province, are best in summer. The Iguazú Falls, in subtropical Misiones province, are best in the southern winter or spring, when heat and humidity are less oppressive; at this time, skiers could also visit Andean resorts such as Bariloche or Las Leñas.

Maps

The Automóvil Club Argentino (ACA), at Av del Libertador 1850 in Buenos Aires, publishes regularly updated maps of the country and each province. You may also find them at specialty bookstores, like Edward Stanford's in London, or in the map rooms of major university libraries. At about US$10 each, an entire set of provincial maps costs upward of US$200, but they are indispensable for motorists and an excellent investment for any other traveler in Argentina – members of foreign automobile clubs can purchase them at discount prices. In most major cities, ACA has a service center that sells these maps, although not every center stocks all of them.

Tourist offices in Buenos Aires and the provinces stock maps of considerable use to visitors – the province of Neuquén does an exemplary job. These vary in quality but are usually free. Members of the American Automobile Association (AAA) and its affiliates can obtain that organization's South American road map, which is adequate for initial planning but not for on-the-road use. Published by International Travel Maps (ITMB), the vivid three-sheet *South America*, by the late Australian cartographer Kevin Healy, is really reference material, packed with information, but not suitable for taking along on a trip.

More suitable for field use, ITMB's more detailed *Argentina* map, at a scale of 1:4,000,000, also includes most of Chile and Uruguay, large parts of Paraguay, and smaller areas of Brazil and Bolivia.

For topographic maps, the best source is Buenos Aires' Instituto Geográfico Militar, open 8 am to 1 pm weekdays, at Cabildo 381 in Palermo (Subte: Ministro Carranza, but also reached by bus No 152). These maps are difficult to obtain outside the capital.

What to Bring

Argentina is a mostly temperate, mid-latitude country, and seasonally appropriate clothing for North America or Europe will be equally suitable here. In the subtropical north, especially in summer, carry lightweight cottons, but at higher elevations in the Andean Northwest and the high latitudes of Patagonia, warm clothing is important even in summer.

Argentines have no prejudice against backpackers, and many young Argentines take to Patagonia and other remote parts of the country on a shoestring themselves. Cheaper Argentine outdoor equipment, though, is generally inferior to that made in North America or Europe, so bring camping

TOURIST TRAPS

Argentina has its share of gaudy and costly tourist traps, or places that are simply distasteful or overrated. Like the previous list, this one starts in the north and works south.

Villa Carlos Paz On a large artificial reservoir outside the city of Córdoba, Villa Carlos Paz is an even more ghastly version of Mar del Plata in summer, without the appeal of surf or sea lions.

Mar del Plata Your best chance of becoming a traffic fatality is to attempt to drive down Ruta Provincial (RP) 2 from Buenos Aires to this summer madhouse, where porteños flock to socialize with the same people they see the rest of the year, elbowing them for space on the beach. The rest of the year, it's a relatively normal and even attractive place.

Bariloche The setting is incomparable, but the lake district's largest city has encroached on Parque Nacional Nahuel Huapi, and its high-rise timeshares have overwhelmed the architectural integrity of its landmark Centro Cívico.

El Calafate At the gateway to the Moreno glacier, Calafate's merchants are notorious for disregard of their captive clientele – where else in the world would a restaurant owner blame a customer for a fly in the beer glass? It's only fair to say, though, that new blood is improving the level of services, and the government's convertibility policy has eliminated the once-rampant currency speculation.

supplies from home. Higher quality products will be very expensive.

TOURIST OFFICES

Almost every city or town has a tourist office, usually on or near the main plaza or at the bus terminal. Each Argentine province also has its own representation in Buenos Aires; most, though not all, of these are well organized, often offering a computerized database of tourist information, and are well worth a visit before heading for the provinces. A few municipalities, mostly the Atlantic coastal resorts of Buenos Aires province, have separate offices in Buenos Aires.

The best-organized provincial offices are those of Buenos Aires, Chubut, Entre Ríos, Jujuy, Misiones, Río Negro, Santa Cruz, and Tierra del Fuego.

Local Tourist Offices

The offices listed below are provincial tourist offices located in Buenos Aires unless indicated otherwise.

Buenos Aires
(☎ 4371-7045)
Av Callao 235

Catamarca
(☎ 4374-6891)
Córdoba 2080

Chaco
(☎ 4476-0961)
Av Callao 322

Chubut
(☎ 4382-8126)
Sarmiento 1172

Córdoba
(☎ 4373-4277)
Av Callao 332

Corrientes
(☎ 4394-7432)
4th floor, San Martín 333

Entre Ríos
(☎ 4328-9327)
Suipacha 844

Formosa
(☎ 4381-7048)
Hipólito Yrigoyen 1429

Jujuy
(☎ 4393-6096)
Av Santa Fe 967

La Pampa
(☎ 4326-0511)
Suipacha 346

La Rioja
(☎ 4815-1929)
Av Callao 745

Mar del Plata (municipal)
(☎ 4384-5658)
Av Corrientes 1660

Mendoza
(☎ 4371-7301)
Av Callao 445

Misiones
(☎ 4393-1812)
Av Santa Fe 989

Neuquén
(☎ 4326-6812)
Perón 687

Pinamar (municipal)
(☎ 4315-2680)
5th floor, Florida 930

Río Negro
(☎ 4371-7066)
Tucumán 1916

Salta
(☎ 4326-1314)
Diagonal Norte (Roque Sáenz Peña) 933

San Clemente del Tuyú (municipal)
(☎ 4381-0764)
Bartolomé Mitre 1135

San Juan
(☎ 4382-9241)
Sarmiento 1251

San Luis
(☎ 4822-3641)
Azcuénaga 1087

Santa Cruz
(☎ 4325-3098/3102, estancias@interlink.com.ar)
Suipacha 1120

Santa Fe
(☎ 4375-4570)
Montevideo 373

Santiago del Estero
(☎ 4326-9418)
Florida 274

Tierra del Fuego (Instituto Fueguino de Turismo)
(☎ 4322-8855)
Av Santa Fe 919

Tucumán
(☎ 4322-0010)
Suipacha 140

Villa Carlos Paz
(☎ 4322-0053)
Lavalle 623, Oficinas 38/39

Villa Gesell (municipal)
(☎/fax 4374-5199)
Bartolomé Mitre 1702

Tourist Offices Abroad

The larger Argentine consulates, such as those in New York City and Los Angeles, usually have a tourism representative in their delegation. Local representatives of Aerolíneas Argentinas often have similar information at their disposal. The US delegate for Argentina's Secretaría de Turismo is Eduardo Piva (☎ 305-442-1366, fax 441-7029), 2655 Le Jeune Rd-PH1, Suite F, Coral Gables, FL 33134.

Australia
(☎ 02-6282-4555)
MLC Tower, 1st floor, Woden, ACT 2606

Canada
(☎ 613-236-2351)
90 Sparks St, Suite 620, Ottawa, Ontario K1P 514
(☎ 514-842-6582)
2000 Peel St, Suite 710,
Montreal, Quebec H3A 2W5

UK
(☎ 020-7318-1340)
27 Three Kings Yard, London W1Y 1FL

USA
(☎ 202-238-6460)
1718 Connecticut Ave NW,
Washington, DC 20009
(☎ 212-603-0403)
12 W 56th St, New York, NY 10019
(☎ 213-954-9155)
5550 Wilshire Blvd, Suite 210,
Los Angeles, CA 90036
(☎ 305-373-1889)
800 Brickell Ave, Penthouse 1, Miami, FL 33131
(☎ 312-819-2610)
205 N Michigan Ave, Suite 4209,
Chicago, IL 60601
(☎ 713-871-8935)
1990 Post Oak Blvd, Suite 770,
Houston, TX 77056

Embassies & Consulates

Argentine Embassies & Consulates

Argentina has diplomatic representation throughout Latin America, North America, Western Europe, and many other regions, including Australia. The following are most likely to be useful to prospective visitors. For more detailed information on overseas delegations, see the Tourist Offices Abroad section in this chapter.

Australia
Embassy:
(☎ 02-6282-4555)
MLC Tower, 1st floor, Woden, ACT 2606
Consulate:
(☎ 02-9251-3402)
Gold Fields House
1 Alfred St, Sydney, NSW 2000

Bolivia
Embassy:
(☎ 02-353233, 417737)
Sánchez Lima and Aspiazú, La Paz 64

Brazil
Consulates:
(☎ 045-574-2969)
Travessa Eduardo Bianchi 26, Foz do Iguaçu
(☎ 021-533-1569)
Entrepiso, Praia de Botafogo 228
Rio de Janeiro
(☎ 011-285-2274)
9th floor, Av Paulista 1106, São Paulo

Canada
Embassy:
(☎ 613-236-2351)
90 Sparks St, Suite 620
Ottawa, Ontario K1P 514
Consulates:
(☎ 416-955-0232)
1 First Canadian Place, Suite 5840
Toronto, Ontario M5X 1K2
(☎ 514-842-6582)
2000 Peel St, Suite 710
Montreal, Québec H3A 2W5

Chile
Consulates:
(☎ 02-222-6853)
Vicuña Mackenna 41, Santiago
(☎ 65-253966)
2nd floor, Cauquenes 94, Puerto Montt
(☎ 61-261912)
21 de Mayo 1878, Punta Arenas

Paraguay
Embassy:
(☎ 021-442151)
Banco Nación, 1st floor, Palma 319, Asunción
Consulates:
(☎ 071-203446)
Mallorquín 788, Encarnación

UK
Embassy:
(0171-318-1300, 020-7318-1300 after April 2000)
65 Brook St, London W1Y 1YE
Consulate:
(☎ 0171-318-1340, 020-7318-1340 after April 2000)
27 Three Kings Yard, London W1Y 1FL

USA
Embassy:
(☎ 202-238-6460)
1600 New Hampshire Ave
Washington, DC 20009
Consulates:
(☎ 202-238-6460)
1718 Connecticut Ave NW
Washington, DC 20009
(☎ 212-603-0403)
12 W 56th St, New York, NY 10019
(☎ 323-954-9155)
5550 Wilshire Blvd, Suite 210
Los Angeles, CA 90036

Embassies & Consulates

(☎ 305-373-1889)
800 Brickell Ave, Penthouse 1,
Miami, FL 33131

(☎ 312-819-2610)
205 N Michigan Ave, Suite 4209
Chicago, IL 60601

(☎ 713-871-8935)
1990 Post Oak Blvd, Suite 770
Houston, TX 77056

(☎ 504-523-2823)
2 Canal St, Suite 915,
New Orleans, LA 70130

(☎ 404-880-0805)
229 Peach Tree St, Suite 1401
Atlanta, GA 30303

Uruguay
Embassy:
(☎ 903-0084)
Wilson Ferreira Aldunate 1281, Montevideo
Consulates:
(☎ 542-2266)
Franklin D Roosevelt 442, Carmelo
(☎ 0522-2093)
Av General Flores 230, Colonia
(☎ 535-2638)
Sarandí 3193, Fray Bentos
(☎ 0722-2253)
Leandro Gómez 1034, Paysandú
(☎ 042-41106)
Edificio Santos Dumont, Punta del Este
(☎ 073-2931)
General Artigas 1134, Salto

Embassies & Consulates in Argentina

As a tourist, it's important to realize what your own embassy – the embassy of the country of which you are a citizen – can and can't do.

Generally speaking, it won't be much help in emergencies if the trouble you're in is remotely your own fault. Remember that you are bound by the laws of the country you are in. Your embassy will not be sympathetic if you end up in jail after committing a crime locally, even if such actions are legal in your own country.

In genuine emergencies you might get some assistance, but only if other channels have been exhausted. For example, if you need to get home urgently, a free ticket is exceedingly unlikely – the embassy would expect you to have insurance. If you have all your money and documents stolen, it might assist in getting a new passport, but a loan for onward travel is out of the question.

Australia
Embassy:
(☎ 011-4777-6580)
Villanueva 1400, Palermo, Buenos Aires

Belgium
Embassy:
(☎ 011-4331-0066)
8th floor, Defensa 113
Montserrat, Buenos Aires

Bolivia
Embassy:
(☎ 011-4381-0539)
Av Belgrano 1670, 1st floor
Montserrat, Buenos Aires

Consulates:
(☎ 0261-429-2458)
Eusebio Blanco and 25 de Mayo, Mendoza
(☎ 0387-421-1040)
Mariano Boedo 34, Salta
(☎ 0388-423-3156)
Güemes 779, 2nd floor,
San Salvador de Jujuy
(☎ 0381-421-0956, 422-2217)
Balcarce 173, Tucumán

Brazil
Embassy:
(☎ 011-4394-5264)
Carlos Pellegrini 1363, 5th floor
Retiro, Buenos Aires

Embassies & Consulates

Consulates:
(☎ 03772-425441)
Mitre 842, Paso de los Libres
(☎ 03752-424830)
Av Corrientes 1416, Posadas
(☎ 03757-420601)
Esquiú and El Mensú, Puerto Iguazú

Canada
Embassy:
(☎ 011-4805-3032)
Tagle 2828, Palermo, Buenos Aires

Chile
Embassy:
(☎ 011-4394-6582)
9th floor, San Martín 439, Buenos Aires
Consulates:
(☎ 0291-452-5808)
Güemes 102, Bahía Blanca
(☎ 02944-422842)
Juan Manuel de Rosas 180, Bariloche
(☎ 0297-462414)
Rivadavia 671, Comodoro Rivadavia
(☎ 02945-51189)
Molinari 754, Esquel (honorary)
(☎ 0261-425-5024)
Olascoaga 1071, Mendoza
(☎ 0299-422727)
La Rioja 241, Neuquén
(☎ 02966-422364)
Mariano Moreno 148, Río Gallegos
(☎ 0387-431-1857)
Santiago del Estero 965, Salta
(☎ 0381-430-0714)
Laprida 130, Tucumán

Denmark
Embassy:
(☎ 011-4312-6901)
9th floor, Leandro N Alem 1074, Buenos Aires

France
Embassy:
(☎ 011-4312-2409)
3rd floor, Santa Fe 846, Buenos Aires
Consulates:
(☎ 0261-423-1542)
Houssay 790, Mendoza
(☎ 03752-426182)
Ayacucho 211, Posadas
(☎ 0387-431-4726)
Santa Fe 156, Salta
(0381-243-921)
Laprida 19, Tucumán

Germany
Embassy:
(☎ 011-4778-2500)
Villanueva 1055, Palermo, Buenos Aires
Consulates:
(☎ 02944-425695)
Ruiz Moreno 65, Bariloche (honorary)
(☎ 0261-429-6539)
Montevideo 127, 1st floor, No 6, Mendoza
(☎ 0387-421-6525)
Córdoba 202, Salta
(☎ 0381-424-2658)
9 de Julio 1042, Tucumán

Ireland
Embassy:
(☎ 011-4325-8588)
Suipacha 1380, Buenos Aires

Israel
Embassy:
(☎ 011-4342-6932)
10th floor, Av de Mayo 701, Buenos Aires
Consulate:
(☎ 0261-438-0642)
Olascoaga 838, Mendoza

Italy
Embassy:
(☎ 011-4816-6132)
M T de Alvear 1149, Buenos Aires
Consulates:
(☎ 02944-422603)
Vicealmirante O'Connor 467
Bariloche (honorary)

Embassies & Consulates

(☎ 0261-423-1640)
Necochea 712, Mendoza
(☎ 0299-424457)
Perito Moreno 549, 1st floor, Neuquén
(☎ 0387-431-4455)
Alvarado 1632, Salta
(☎ 0388-422-3199)
Av Fascio 660, San Salvador de Jujuy
(☎ 0381-431-0426)
San Martín 623, 1st floor, Tucumán

Japan
Embassy:
(☎ 011-4318-8220)
Bouchard 547, 15th floor, Buenos Aires

Mexico
Embassy:
(☎ 011-4821-7170)
Larrea 1230, Buenos Aires

Netherlands
Embassy:
(☎ 011-4334-4000)
Ave de Mayo 701, 19th floor, Buenos Aires

Norway
Embassy:
(☎ 011-4312-2204)
3rd floor, Esmeralda 909, Buenos Aires

Paraguay
Embassy:
(☎ 011-4812-0075)
Viamonte 1851, Buenos Aires
Consulates:
(☎ 0378-342-6576)
Gobernador Ruiz 2746, Corrientes
(☎ 03752-423850)
San Lorenzo, between Santa Fe and Sarmiento, Posadas

Perú
Embassy:
(☎ 011-4811-4619)
Av Córdoba 1345
Buenos Aires

Spain
Embassy:
(☎ 011-4811-0078)
Guido 1760, Buenos Aires
Consulates:
(☎ 02944-468011)
Rolando 268, Bariloche (honorary)
(☎ 0261-425-3947)
Agustín Álvarez 455, Mendoza
(☎ 422466)
Alberdi 72, Neuquén
(☎ 0381-435-3042)
Mate de Luna 4107, Tucumán

Sweden
Embassy:
(☎ 011-4342-1422)
Tacuarí 147, Buenos Aires

Switzerland
Embassy:
(☎ 011-4311-6491)
10th floor, Santa Fe 846, Buenos Aires
Consulate:
(☎ 0381-431-1180)
24 de Setiembre 524, Tucumán

UK
Embassy:
(☎ 011-4803-7070)
Dr Luis Agote 2412, Buenos Aires

USA
Embassy:
(☎ 011-4777-4533)
Colombia 4300, Buenos Aires

Uruguay
Embassy:
(☎ 011-4807-3040)
Las Heras 1907, Buenos Aires
Consulates:
(☎ 0345-421-0380)
Pellegrini 709, Concordia
(☎ 03446 426168)
Rivadavia 510, Gualeguaychú

VISAS & DOCUMENTS

Passports

Passports are obligatory for all visitors except for citizens of bordering countries. Argentina presently enjoys civilian government, and the police and military presence are relatively subdued, but the police can still demand identification at any moment. It is advisable to carry your passport at all times, especially if there is political unrest. In general, Argentines are very document oriented, and a passport is essential for cashing traveler's checks, checking into a hotel, and many other routine activities.

Visas

Argentina has eliminated visas for many but not all foreign tourists. In theory, upon arrival all non-visa visitors must obtain a free tourist card, good for 90 days and renewable for 90 more. In practice, immigration officials issue these only at major border crossings, such as airports and on the ferries and hydrofoils between Buenos Aires and Uruguay.

Although you should not toss your card, losing it is no major catastrophe. At most exit points, officials will provide immediate replacement; that is, the bureaucracy may require you to fill one in even though you're leaving the country.

Nationals of the USA and most Western European countries, including Britons, do not need visas. Australians no longer need visas, but New Zealanders, who do need them, must submit their passports with a payment of NZ$44 and may need to show a return or onward ticket; ordinarily, the visa will be ready the following day. Verify whether the visa is valid for 90 days from date of issue, or 90 days from first entry.

Children under the age of 14 traveling without both parents theoretically need a parent's consent form, but the author's 10-year-old daughter has traveled many times to and from the country with only one parent without ever being asked for such a form.

Argentina has a wide network of embassies and consulates, both in neighboring countries and overseas. Some are very accommodating, while others (most notably those in Colonia, Uruguay, and La Paz, Bolivia) may treat your visit as a major nuisance. Renewing a nearly expired visa at a consulate other than the one that issued it can be almost impossible; it is easier to get a new passport and then request a new Argentine visa.

Individuals born in Argentina, even of foreign parents, are considered Argentines and may encounter difficulties entering the country with non-Argentine documents – in one instance, officials harassed a retired US army colonel who was born in Buenos Aires for lacking proof of completing obligatory military service in Argentina. Argentine passports renewed overseas expire upon reentry into Argentina, and renewing them with the Policía Federal can be a tiresome process on a short trip.

Very short visits to neighboring countries usually do not require visas. Most importantly, you need not waste time obtaining a Brazilian visa to cross from the Argentine town of Puerto Iguazú to Foz do Iguaçu and/or Ciudad del Este, Paraguay, if you return the same day, although you must normally show your passport. The same is true at the Bolivian border town of Villazón, near La Quiaca, and the Paraguayan crossing at Encarnación, near Posadas.

Visa Extensions As mentioned, Argentine tourist cards are valid for 90 days. For a 90-day extension, visit the Dirección Nacional de Migraciones (☎ 4312-8661), at Av Antártida Argentina 1355 in Retiro (Buenos Aires) or in provincial capitals, or at provincial delegations of the Policía Federal. There may be a nominal charge. In areas where the police are unaccustomed to dealing with immigration, the process can be tedious and time-consuming.

Travelers wishing to stay longer than six months will find it simpler to cross the border into a neighboring country for a few days and then return for an additional six months. Although it is possible to obtain residence, leaving the country then becomes problematic and you cannot take advantage of tourist regulations with respect to Argentine customs and duties.

Travel Insurance

In addition to health and accident insurance, a policy that protects baggage and valuables, like cameras and camcorders, is a good idea. Keep your insurance records separate from other possessions in case you have to make a claim.

Driver's License & Permits

Motorists need an International Driving Permit to complement their national or state licenses, but should not be surprised if police at the numerous roadside checkpoints do not recognize it or, even worse, claim it is invalid and try to exact a bribe. Politely refer them to the Spanish translation on the card.

Drivers of Argentine vehicles must carry their title document *(tarjeta verde* or 'green card'; for foreign vehicles, customs permission is the acceptable substitute). Liability insurance is obligatory, and police often ask to see proof of insurance at checkpoints.

Hostel Cards

In Buenos Aires, the Red Argentina de Albergues Juveniles (RAAJ; ☎ 4511-8712, fax 4312-0089; raaj@hostels.org.ar), at Florida 835, 3rd floor, is part of Argentina's energetic, nonprofit student-travel agency Asatej. It sells the Hostelling International card for US$20. RAAJ is rapidly displacing the moribund Asociación Argentina de Albergues de la Juventud (☎ 4476-1001), Talcahuano 214, 2nd floor, which also sells the card.

Student & Youth Cards

The International Student Identity Card (ISIC), available from RAAJ and Asatej (see Useful Organizations later in this chapter), may help travelers obtain discounts on public transportation, museum admissions, and the like, but virtually any official-looking university identification may be an acceptable substitute.

Seniors' Cards

Travelers over the age of 60 may also obtain *tercera edad* (senior citizen) discounts on museum and other admissions. Usually a passport with date of birth will be sufficient evidence of age.

Photocopies

In the event of loss or theft, it's a good idea to keep photocopies of important documents, such as a passport, plane tickets, traveler's checks, and credit cards. Store copies separately from the originals.

CUSTOMS

Argentine customs officials generally defer to foreign visitors, but if you cross the border frequently and carry electronic equipment, like cameras or a laptop computer, it is helpful to have a typed list of your equipment, including serial numbers, to be stamped by authorities. At Buenos Aires' Aeropuerto Internacional Ezeiza, you will likely be asked whether you are carrying such goods, which are costlier in Argentina than overseas. Entering Argentina from Paraguay or Chilean Patagonia, where cheap electronics are also available, you may experience very thorough baggage checks.

Depending on where you have been, customs authorities focus on different things. Travelers arriving from the central Andean countries may be searched for drugs, while those from central Chile or Brazil should know that fruit and vegetables are likely to be confiscated. Even after passing customs, which may be some distance from the actual border, you are subject to inspection by police at checkpoints that are usually at provincial borders or important highway junctions. *Never* carry firearms.

MONEY

In the not-so-distant past, Argentine money presented real problems for visitors unaccustomed to hyperinflation and without sufficient zeros on their pocket calculators – when Argentine economists spoke hopefully of single-digit inflation, they meant *per month*. Since the institution of Domingo Cavallo's convertibility policy in early 1991, however, inflation has fallen to record lows, and the peso has remained fixed against the dollar. Still, given Argentina's legacy of financial instability, travelers should keep a close watch on the exchange markets and current economic events; it's still not wise to keep large amounts of cash in local currency.

All prices in this book are given in US dollars (US$) unless otherwise indicated.

Currency

The past decade of economic stability has all but closed the former revolving door of Argentine currencies. The present unit is the peso ($), which replaced the inflation-ravaged *austral* on January 1, 1992. The austral had replaced the *peso argentino* in 1985, which had replaced the *peso ley* in 1978, which had replaced the ordinary *peso* some years earlier. One new peso equals 10,000 australs, at par with the US dollar.

Paper money comes in denominations of 2, 5, 10, 20, 50, and 100 pesos. One new peso equals 100 *centavos*; coins come in denominations of 1, 5, 10, 25, and 50 centavos, and one peso. Few merchants want anything to do with one centavo coins and even five centavo coins get scant attention.

At present, dollars are de facto legal tender almost everywhere, but it's wise to carry some pesos; institutions like the post office and some bus companies, as well as a few nationalistic merchants, refuse to accept US currency.

Tattered, nearly shredded Argentine banknotes seem to stay in circulation for decades, but few banks or businesses accept torn, worn, or defaced dollars. Counterfeiting, of both local and US bills, has become a problem in recent years, and some merchants may be skeptical of large denominations.

Traditionally, the provinces of Jujuy, Salta, and Tucumán sometimes issue their own paper money, known as *bonos* (bonds), for local use; these are only valid in the province of issue and have expiration dates beyond which they become worthless, so dispose of them locally and on time. If traveling through the northern provinces, do not accept bonos unless you are staying for some days in the province.

Exchanging Money

US dollars are by far the preferred foreign currency, although Chilean and Uruguayan pesos can be readily exchanged at the borders. Even when the dollar is relatively weak, only Buenos Aires will have a ready market for European currencies.

Cash & Traveler's Checks Cash dollars can be exchanged at banks, *casas de cambio* (exchange houses), hotels, and some travel agencies, and often in shops or on the street. Cash dollars earn a much better rate of exchange and avoid commissions of up to 10% or more levied on traveler's checks, which are increasingly difficult to cash anywhere and specifically *not* recommended. Cash (if you are confident in your ability to carry it safely) or an ATM card is a much better alternative

ATMs *Cajeros automáticos* (ATMs) are increasingly abundant in Argentina and can also be used for cash advances on major credit cards like MasterCard and Visa. System crashes, especially when rainfall is heavy, can make it impossible to retrieve money from ATMs, however. Many but not all ATMs dispense dollars as well as Argentine pesos.

Credit Cards The most widely accepted credit cards are Visa and MasterCard. A MasterCard, which is affiliated with the local Argencard, is more widely accepted than Visa, and travelers with UK Access should insist on their affiliation to MasterCard. American Express, Diner's Club, and others are also valid in many places. Because lost or stolen credit cards are vulnerable to abuse, credit-card holders should consider a protection plan to insure themselves against serious financial loss.

Credit-card users should be aware of two complications. First, some businesses add a *recargo* (surcharge) of 10% or more to credit card purchases because of high bank charges and the often lengthy period between the purchase and their own receipt of payment. The flip side of this practice is that some merchants give a discount of 10% or more for cash purchases.

Second, the amount you pay depends upon the exchange rate at the time your pur-

The *Menem* Trucho

For more than two decades of economic chaos and inflation, Argentines coped with changing currencies, from the peso ley to the peso argentino to the austral to the current peso. At times, walletfuls of million-peso notes barely bought a cup of coffee, while balancing bank accounts consistently challenged the capacities of handheld calculators. Merchants and consumers would barely learn to deal with strings of zeros before they were slashed in the latest monetary reform.

No one, though, was quite prepared for the crisp new notes that appeared at the end of 1991 bearing a portrait of President Carlos Menem, the numeral '1' and the text 'Un Valor Que Estabilizó El País' – 'A Courage That Stabilized the Country.' On the reverse side appeared an etching of the Casa Rosada, the presidential palace, and the imprint of the 'Partido Justicialista Nacional,' Menem's own Peronist party.

After the initial success of former Economy Minister Domingo Cavallo's convertibility plan, the administration was justifiably proud of Argentina's almost unprecedented single-digit inflation. So proud was Menem's personal friend Armando Gostanian, a wealthy clothing tycoon and director of the Casa de Moneda (National Mint), that he ordered the production of thousands of these superficially credible banknotes on embossed official paper in honor of the president.

To the administration's opponents, however, these 'Menem truchos' (bogus Menems) became yet another symbol of corruption, arrogance, and impunity. Although Gostanian's partisan indiscretion apparently didn't cost the state any money, it fell into a gray area under a counterfeiting law that prohibits the production of anything resembling official currency.

Seven years later, the 'Menem trucho' has become a minor collector's item, while Gostanian remains head of the mint and continues to test the limits of political propriety. Anticipating the 10th anniversary of Menem's accession to power and promoting the President's hoped-for second re-election in 1999 (despite an unambiguous constitutional prohibition), the director arranged the printing of similar bills on unofficial paper – Menem Trucho 2.0? – with the numeral '10' followed by 'Años de Estabilidad' (Years of Stability). Printed on cheaper paper, with the punning disclaimer 'Muestra de Capacidad' ('Sample of Ability),' it praises Menem's political skills while explicitly denying any official cachet – unlike the original Menem Trucho.

chase is posted to your overseas account, which can be weeks later. If the local currency is depreciating, your purchase price may be a fraction of the dollar cost you calculated at the time. Conversely, if the local is appreciating, you may get an unpleasant surprise.

International Transfers Travelers who have suffered lost or stolen cash and credit cards have found the American Express MoneyGram a quick and efficient (if costly) means of transferring funds from their home country to Argentina. AmEx has a major office in Buenos Aires, as well as representatives throughout the country, which are indicated in the text.

Exchange Rates

Despite the current stability, for most of the past half-century exchange rates have been volatile. For example, in mid-December of

1990 the dollar sunk below 5000 australs until a minor economic crisis and intensified domestic demand by Argentines planning overseas holidays drove the rate up dramatically. By September 1991, the rate for the previous currency was just below 10,000 australs per US dollar.

At present, there is no black market, and you can change money freely, but in times of crisis visitors should be aware of changes in the so-called 'parallel rate.' For the most up-to-date information, see *Ámbito Financiero*, Argentina's equivalent of *The Wall Street Journal* or *Financial Times*, or the English-language daily *Buenos Aires Herald*.

Australia	A$1	=	Arg$0.63
Bolivia	Bol$1	=	Arg$0.17
Brazil	BraR$1	=	Arg$0.58
Canada	C$1	=	Arg$0.67
Chile	Ch$1000	=	Arg$2.06
Euro	€1	=	Arg$1.07
France	1FF	=	Arg$0.17
Germany	DM1	=	Arg$0.55
Italy	L1000	=	Arg$0.55
Japan	¥100	=	Arg$0.82
Netherlands	*f*1	=	Arg$.049
New Zealand	NZ$1	=	Arg$0.53
Paraguay	₲1000	=	Arg$0.34
Spain	100pta	=	Arg$0.65
Switzerland	SF1	=	Arg$0.67
United Kingdom	UK£1	=	Arg$1.60
United States	US$1	=	Arg$1
Uruguay	Ur$10	=	Arg$0.90

Costs

At times of instability, which have been often enough in the past half-century, panicky Argentines buy US dollars, the local exchange rate collapses, and the country can become absurdly cheap for the visitor with hard currency. Presently, though, the economy is relatively stable, and the country is nearly as expensive as Europe or North America. Inflation has remained relatively high in some sectors, so that prices for hotels, restaurants, and similar travelers' services have increased more rapidly than others in the economy at large. Some Argentines prefer to take their holidays in less-expensive countries like the USA and have acquired the ironic nickname 'démedos' because, on their visits to Miami, they find consumer items so cheap that they tell the clerk to 'give me two.'

This does not mean that budget travel is impossible. Certain key costs, such as modest lodging, food, and some transportation, will be lower than in Europe or North America, though higher than in surrounding countries. After overcoming the initial shock, travelers arriving from inexpensive countries like Bolivia should be able to spend a rewarding time in Argentina by adapting to local conditions. By seeking out cheaper hospedajes and residenciales, carrying a tent to take advantage of campgrounds, and dining selectively, judicious travelers can control costs. In particular, those accustomed to eating every meal in a restaurant in neighboring countries will not be able to do so in Argentina; consider sandwich fixings from the market and splurge on an occasional treat elsewhere.

Still, everyone but compulsive shoestring travelers should probably allow a minimum of US$35 to US$40 per day for food and lodging, and pat themselves on the back if they can get by on less. It's possible to spend much more, and prices in this book are subject to wild fluctuations.

Tipping & Bargaining

In restaurants, it is customary to tip about 10% of the bill, but in times of economic distress Argentines themselves frequently overlook the custom. In general, waiters are ill-paid, so if you can afford to eat out, you can afford to tip. Even a small *propina* will be appreciated.

Bargaining is not the way of life in Argentina as it is in Bolivia or Peru, but it is customary in the Andean Northwest and in artisan markets throughout the country. Even in Buenos Aires, downtown shops selling leather and other tourist items will listen to offers. Late in the evening, some hotels may give a break on room prices; if you plan to stay several days, they almost certainly will. Many better hotels will give discounts up to 30% for payment in cash.

Taxes & Refunds

Under limited circumstances, foreign visitors may obtain refunds of the *impuesto de valor agregado* (IVA, or value-added tax) on purchases of Argentine products upon their departure from the country. A 'Tax Free' (in English) window decal identifies participating merchants in this program, but always verify their status before making your purchase.

To obtain a refund of this 21% tax, present your passport and tourist card to the merchant for purchases of US$200 or more; the merchant must enter the amount of the refund on the reverse of the invoice and paste an equivalent quantity of stamps on the form, the triplicate of which you will also receive. On leaving the country, you must have your purchase separate from the rest of your baggage for inspection; a customs official will check it and seal the invoice.

With this invoice, branches of Banco de la Nación at Buenos Aires' Aeropuerto Internacional Ezeiza, Aeroparque Jorge Newbery (for flights to some neighboring countries), and the capital's river ports at Dársena Norte and Dársena Sur will refund your money in pesos, then change it into US dollars. These branch banks are open 24 hours a day.

POST & COMMUNICATIONS

The post office and telephone services have been among Argentina's most intractable problems – both are traditionally corrupt and inefficient. Telephone service has improved rapidly in the past few years, but not as rapidly as costs have risen.

Still more dependable than the post office are Argentine domestic couriers, such as Andreani and OCA, and international couriers, like DHL and Federal Express. The latter two have offices only in the largest cities, like Buenos Aires, while the former two usually serve as their connections to the interior of the country.

Postal Rates

Argentina's postal rates are among the world's highest. Domestic letters weighing 150 grams or less cost US$0.75, and postcards cost US$0.50. International letters weighing 20 grams or less cost US$0.75 to bordering countries, US$1 elsewhere in the Americas, and US$1.25 outside the Americas.

Certified and international express mail services are more expensive but a better value because of their dependability. Certified letters start at US$2.75 for up to 20 grams, and international express service begins at US$5.50 for up to 100 grams.

Airmail packages are expensive, while surface mail is much cheaper but even less dependable.

Sending Mail

Encotesa or Correo Argentino is the recently privatized postal and telegraph service. It is frequently paralyzed by strikes and 'work-to-rule' stoppages, resulting in enormous accumulations of mail that never reach a final destination. Send essential overseas mail *certificado* (registered) or *puerta a puerta* (express, literally 'door to door') to ensure its arrival. Mail containing money or anything else of value is likely to be opened, the valuable contents expropriated, and anything else tossed in the trash.

The Number You Dialed Has Been Changed...

In January 1999, the Argentine phone system made major changes. All ordinary telephone numbers (excepting toll-free) throughout the country now have an initial 4 so that, for example, the seven-digit numbers in all of Gran Buenos Aires became eight-digit numbers beginning with 4 (the number 123-4567 would become 4123-4567). Simultaneously, an initial 1 was added to the Gran Buenos Aires area code, making the new area code ☎ 11.

Outside Gran Buenos Aires, the area codes were also changed, along with the addition of an initial 4. In Telecom services areas, generally north of Buenos Aires, an initial 3 was added, so that Córdoba's ☎ 51 area code became ☎ 351. In Telefónica service areas, generally south of Buenos Aires, an initial 2 was added to the area code, so that La Plata's ☎ 21 area code is now 221.

Toll-free numbers now repeat their initial digit three times. For instance MCI Worldphones' 51002 became 555-1002.

Note that while the new system formally took effect in January 1999, there will be a transition period in which both systems will operate simultaneously. We've done our best to change the numbers in this book in accordance with the new system.

When addressing a letter to Argentina, note that the house number usually follows rather than precedes the street name, while the postal code precedes rather than follows the name of the town or city. Thus a typical postal address would be as follows:

Carlos Saúl Méndez
Avenida Corrientes 1724
1013 Buenos Aires
ARGENTINA

Receiving Mail

You can receive mail via poste restante or lista de correos, both equivalent to general delivery, at any Argentine post office. Instruct your correspondents to address letters clearly and to indicate a date until which the post office should hold them; otherwise, they will be returned or destroyed.

Post offices have imposed heavy charges, up to US$1.50 per letter, on poste restante services, so if you can arrange to have mail delivered to a private address, such as a friend's residence or a hotel, you will avoid this surprisingly costly and irritatingly bureaucratic nuisance.

It is also worth remembering that Argentines often refer to Buenos Aires proper as the 'Capital Federal,' which works as a destination on mail.

Telephone

Argentina's country code is ☎ 54; the Spanish term for area code is *característica.*

Argentine telephone rates remain very high, despite the prospect of cheaper calls with the end of the Telecom/Telefónica duopoly at the end of 1999. Some rates, however, have fallen enough that making overseas calls collect or by credit card is not necessarily cheaper than calling from long-distance offices. Domestic collect calls are impossible within Argentina.

Telecom and Telefónica have assumed control of most of Entel's long-distance offices, although some provinces and smaller towns operate their own telephone cooperatives, and there are now many privately run *locutorios* (long-distance offices). If possible, make overseas calls outside costly peak business hours; there is usually a 20% discount between 10 pm and 8 am weekdays and all day on weekends. Even these rates are no bargain, though.

Some locutorios do not care to handle collect or credit-card calls, which must be placed at Telecom or Telefónica offices or from a private telephone. If you're calling from a private phone, use Discado Directo Internacional (International Direct Dialing), which provides direct access to home-country operators for long-distance collect and credit-card calls. The system is hopelessly overloaded on and near major holidays like Christmas.

Most public telephones operate on tokens known as *fichas* or *cospeles*, which are basically of equal value but differ for local and long-distance service. For local calls, one cospel gives you about three minutes. Both fichas and cospeles are available from street-corner kiosks and phone company offices, but kiosks normally tack on 10% or more for their own profit. Phone cards are now widely available and more convenient than a pocketful of tokens. Phone debit cards *(tarjetas)* are available in values of 25, 50, 100, and 150 fichas.

Most public phones are inexplicably located on noisy corners that make hearing very difficult. In most of Patagonia, though, enclosed phone booths shut out the noise. Note that some hotel telephones will register a call as completed within 20 or 30 seconds, whether or not anyone has answered, so hang up quickly if there's no response.

When calling or answering the telephone, the proper salutation is *hola* (hello). Exchange pleasantries before getting to the point of your conversation. When calling a central number or business switchboard, you may be asked for an *interno* (extension number).

Emergency & Information Convenient three-digit numbers are available for Asistencia Pública (Emergency; ☎ 107), Policía (Police; ☎ 101), Bomberos (Fire Department; ☎ 100), and Información (Directory Assistance; ☎ 110).

International Direct Dialing From those parts of Argentina that have Discado Directo Internacional (DDI, or International Direct Dialing), it is now possible to get direct access to home-country operators for collect and credit-card calls from both private and public telephones; this is usually much cheaper than going through the Argentine carriers. Note that private locutorios will only rarely permit their facilities to be used for such calls, since they make no profit on them.

The following toll-free numbers provide direct connections to home-country operators; for other countries dial Telintar at ☎ 000 (a number blocked at many locutorios that do permit access to 800 numbers). The first number for each country corresponds to the 800 number used from public telephones; the second to the number used from private telephones.

Australia
☎ 0800-56100
☎ 0061-8066-6111

Canada
☎ 0800-55500
☎ 001-800-222-1111

France
☎ 0800-53300
☎ 0033-800-999111

Germany
☎ 0800-54900
☎ 00449-800-99111

Italy
☎ 0800-53900
☎ 0039-800-555111

UK (British Telecom)
☎ 0800-54401
☎ 0044-800-555111

UK (Mercury)
☎ 0800-24400
☎ 0044-800-333111

USA (AT&T)
☎ 0800-21001, 0800-54288
☎ 001-800-200-1111

USA (MCI)
☎ 0800-51002
☎ 001-800-333-1111

USA (Sprint)
☎ 0800-51003
☎ 001-800-777-1111

Fax & Email

Most locutorios offer fax services. In addition to fax services, Encotesa also provides telegraph and telex services.

Online access is rapidly increasing in Argentina, with a proliferation of Internet cafés and ISPs, but their cost is far higher than in the US or Europe. Recent reductions in phone charges for Internet connections, however, may result in reduced costs for end users. Still, the best bet for sending or retrieving electronic communications is to rely on a friend with access.

INTERNET RESOURCES

The World Wide Web can be a very useful resource for travelers aware of its shortcomings, particularly unverified (and unverifiable) information. It's most helpful for reading foreign newspapers, hunting down bargain airfares, and checking weather conditions; less so for booking hotels, as responses are often very slow.

The Lonely Planet website (www.lonelyplanet.com) provides summaries on travel to most places on earth, postcards from other travelers, and the Thorn Tree bulletin board, where you can ask questions before you go or offer advice when you get back. You can also find travel news and updates to many of our most popular guidebooks, and the subWWWay section links you to the most useful travel resources elsewhere on the Web. For a list of helpful links, see the Website Appendix.

BOOKS

Buenos Aires is a major publishing center and has many excellent bookstores on or near Av Corrientes, which is a delightful area to browse. For details, see the Buenos Aires chapter. For information on Argentine literature see Arts in the Facts about Argentina chapter.

Most books are published in different editions by different publishers in different countries. As a result, a book might be a hardcover rarity in one country while it's readily available in paperback in another. Fortunately, bookstores and libraries can search by title or author, so your local bookstore or library is the best place to find out about the availability of the following recommended titles.

Guidebooks

Other guidebooks can supplement and complement this one, especially if you are visiting additional South American countries. One obvious endorsement is Lonely Planet's *Buenos Aires* city guide, which provides far more detail on the Argentine capital. *South America on a shoestring* is a collaborative effort by several authors.

LP also has guides for Ecuador & the Galápagos Islands, Peru, Colombia, Venezuela, Bolivia, Brazil, and Chile & Easter Island, as well as the *Latin American Spanish phrasebook*.

If you plan to do trekking, or even some short walks, a good companion is Clem Lindenmayer's *Trekking in the Patagonian Andes* (Lonely Planet), a detailed guide to walking in Chilean and Argentine Patagonia, which includes contour maps.

The APA Insight Guides series has volumes on Buenos Aires and Argentina that are excellent in cultural and historical analyses, with outstanding photographs, but lacking on the nuts-and-bolts of everyday travel. While not really suitable for field use, these are good for pre-trip reading, though many typographical errors mar the Argentina volume.

Readers competent in Spanish will find *La Guía Pirelli: Buenos Aires, Sus Alrededores y Costas del Uruguay* full of illuminating historical and cultural material on the capital and nearby areas. It suffers from inadequate maps, though, and seems to assume that every visitor has a new BMW and stays in five-star hotels – by Pirelli's standards, Hotel Plaza Francia, luxurious and pricey by most accounts, ranks as budget accommodation. Pirelli also publishes a guide to the entire country with the same strengths and shortcomings; both may be available in English, but the English-language editions are less up-to-date than the Spanish versions.

Travel

Argentina has inspired some excellent travel writing, most notably Bruce Chatwin's indispensable *In Patagonia* (1977), one of the most informed syntheses of life and landscape for any part of South America or the entire world. Avoid Paul Theroux's irritatingly patronizing *The Old Patagonian*

Express (1980), whose best-selling author unquestionably succeeds in his efforts to distance himself from the people and places he travels among.

American scientist George Gaylord Simpson's *Attending Marvels: A Patagonian Journal* (1934) starts, surprisingly but excitingly, with an account of the 1930 coup against President Hipólito Yrigoyen. AF Tschifferly's *Southern Cross to Pole Star* (1933, but frequently reprinted) recounts the Swiss author's ride from Buenos Aires to Washington, DC, with two Argentine criollo horses, though only a small portion of the book deals with Argentina proper.

The late British naturalist Gerald Durrell wrote several frivolous but entertaining accounts of his travels in Argentina, from Jujuy to Patagonia, in *The Drunken Forest* and *The Whispering Land*, available in inexpensive paperback editions. Make a special effort to locate Lucas Bridges' *The Uttermost Part of the Earth* (1947), which describes his life among the Indians of Tierra del Fuego. Bridges' father was one of the earliest missionary settlers from the Falkland Islands and compiled an important dictionary of the Yahgan language.

Don't overlook works of greater antiquity. Charles Darwin's *Voyage of the Beagle* (1838) is as vivid as yesterday; his account of the gauchos on the Pampas and in Patagonia evokes a way of life to which Argentines still pay symbolic homage, though it no longer really exists. Frequently reprinted, William Henry Hudson's *Idle Days in Patagonia* (1893) is a romantic account of the 19th-century naturalist's adventures in search of migratory birds. Also check out his *The Purple Land* (1885) and *Far Away and Long Ago* (1918).

One of the more improbable pieces of travel literature in recent years is Ernesto Guevara's *The Motorcycle Diaries: A Journey Around South America* (Verso, 1995), an early 1950s account of two Argentine medical students who rode a dilapidated motorcycle across northern Patagonia and into Chile before abandoning it to continue their trip by stowing away on a coastal freighter. Guevara, a Cuban resident who died in 1967 in Bolivia, is better known by his nickname, 'Che,' derived from the common Argentine interjection meaning, basically, 'hey!'

History

General For an account of early European exploration in Argentina and elsewhere in South America, see JH Parry's *The Discovery of South America* (1979). Although it does not focus specifically on Argentina, James Lockhart and Stuart Schwartz's *Early Latin America* (1983) makes the unconventional but persuasive argument that the structures of native societies were more important than Spanish domination in the cultural transitions of colonial times. Uruguayan writer Eduardo Galeano presents a bitter indictment of European conquest and its consequences in *The Open Veins of Latin America: Five Centuries of the Pillage of a Continent* (1973). Do not miss Alfred Crosby's exceptional account of the ecological transformation of the Pampas in comparison with other midlatitude lands settled by Europeans in his *Ecological Imperialism: The Biological Expansion of Europe, 900-1900* (1986).

For the South American wars of independence, including Argentina's, a standard work is John Lynch's *The Spanish-American Revolutions 1808-1826* (1973). One of the best-known contemporary accounts of post-independence Argentina, often used as a university text, is Domingo Faustino Sarmiento's *Life in the Argentine Republic in the Days of the Tyrants*, an eloquent but often condescending critique of the Federalist caudillos and their followers from the Unitarist perspective of the country's second constitutional president. Also worthwhile is Lynch's *Argentine Dictator: Juan Manuel de Rosas, 1829-1852* (1981). José Luis Romero analyzes the conflict between Unitarism and Federalism in *A History of Argentine Political Thought* (Stanford, 1968).

James Scobie's *Argentina: A City and a Nation* (Oxford, 1964), a standard account of the country's development, has gone through many editions.

The most up-to-date, comprehensive history of the country is David Rock's

Domingo Faustino Sarmiento

Argentina 1516-1987: From Spanish Colonization to the Falklands War and Alfonsín (University of California, 1987).

For an account of Britain's role in Argentina's 19th-century development, see HS Ferns' *Britain and Argentina in the Nineteenth Century* (Oxford, 1960). More recent is Alistair Henessy and John King's edited collection of essays, *The Land That England Lost: Argentina and Britain, A Special Relationship* (London, British Academic Press, 1992), which goes beyond the strictly political to deal with intriguing cultural topics like the English tango fad just prior to WWI.

Several historians have compared Argentina, Australia, and Canada as exporters of primary products such as beef and wheat, and their subsequent economic development. These include Tim Duncan and John Fogarty's *Australia and Argentina: On Parallel Paths* (Melbourne, 1984), DC Platt and current Argentine foreign minister Guido di Tella's edited *Argentina, Australia, and Canada: Studies in Comparative Development, 1970-1985* (Macmillan, 1985), and Carl Solberg's *The Prairies and the Pampas: Agrarian Policy in Canada and Argentina, 1880-1930* (Stanford, 1987).

For an interpretation of the gaucho's role in Argentine history, see Richard W Slatta's *Gauchos and the Vanishing Frontier* (Nebraska, 1983). More recently, Slatta has compared the gauchos with stockmen of other countries in the beautifully illustrated *Cowboys of the Americas* (Yale, 1990). Nicholas Shumway's *The Invention of Argentina* (University of California, 1991) offers a kind of intellectual history of the country.

The Peróns & Their Legacy A standard biography is Robert Alexander's *Juan Domingo Perón* (Boulder, Westview Press, 1979). Another important book is Frederick Turner and José Enrique Miguens' *Juan Perón and the Reshaping of Argentina* (Pittsburgh, 1983). Also look at Joseph Page's *Perón: A Biography* (Random House, 1983), and Robert Crassweller's *Perón and the Enigma of Argentina* (Norton, 1987). A fascinating, fictionalized version of Perón's life, culminating in his return to Buenos Aires in 1973, is Tomás Eloy Martínez's *The Perón Novel* (New York, Pantheon, 1988).

Eva Perón speaks for herself, to some degree, in her ghost-written biography *La Razón de Mi Vida (My Mission in Life)*. VS Naipaul suggests that political violence and torture have long permeated Argentine society in his grim but eloquent essay *The Return of Eva Perón* (Knopf, 1980). Also try JM Taylor's *Eva Perón: The Myths of a Woman* (University of Chicago, 1979) or Martínez's novel *Santa Evita* (Knopf, 1996).

The Military, Politics & Geopolitics One good general overview of the military in Latin America is John J Johnson's *The Military and Society in Latin America* (Stanford, 1964). Robert Potash has published two complementary books on military interference in Argentine politics: *The Army and Politics in Argentina, 1928-1945: Yrigoyen to Perón* (Stanford, 1969), and *The Army and Politics in Argentina, 1945-1962: Perón to Frondizi* (Stanford, 1980).

For analysis of the notion of geopolitics in Argentina, see Philip Kelly and Jack Child's edited volume, *Geopolitics of the Southern Cone & Antarctica* (London, Lynne Rienner, 1980). A more general account, dealing with Chile, Brazil, and Paraguay as well, is César Caviedes' *The Southern Cone: Realities of the Authoritarian State* (Rowman & Allenheld, 1984).

The Dirty War The classic first-person account of state terrorism in the late 1970s is Jacobo Timmerman's *Prisoner Without a Name, Cell Without a Number* (Knopf, 1981). *Nunca Más*, the official report of the National Commission on the Disappeared, systematically details military abuses during the 1976 to 1983 period. John Simpson and Jana Bennett's *The Disappeared: Voices from a Secret War* (Robson Books, 1985) is a good general account. A highly regarded first novel on the Dirty War is US writer Lawrence Thornton's *Imagining Argentina* (Bantam, 1988).

Contemporary Argentine Politics

For an analysis of the contradictions in Argentine society, read Gary Wynia's *Argentina in the Postwar Era: Politics and Economic Policy Making in a Divided Society*. A recent collection on the democratic transition is Monica Peralta-Ramos and Carlos Waisman's *From Military Rule to Liberal Democracy in Argentina*. David Erro's *Resolving the Argentine Paradox: Politics and Development, 1966-1992* provides a good analysis of contemporary Argentine politics and policies through the early Menem years, though it may be overly optimistic about current trends.

Geography & Natural History

There are several readable texts that integrate Latin American history with geography. Try Arthur Morris' *South America* (Hodder & Stoughton, 1979), Harold Blakemore and Clifford Smith's collection *Latin America* (Methuen, 1983), which includes a detailed chapter on the River Plate countries, and the *Cambridge Encyclopedia of Latin America* (1992), which is rather broader.

For Argentina's national parks, do not overlook William Leitch's beautifully written and comprehensive *South America's National Parks* (Seattle, 1990), which is superb on environment and natural history though weak on practical aspects of South American travel. Birders might acquire the 4th edition of T Narosky and D Yzurieta's *Guía para la Identificación de las Aves de Argentina y Uruguay* (Buenos Aires: Vásquez Massini, 1993), also available in English as *Birds of Argentina and Uruguay*.

Foreign Literature

Writers from other countries have dealt with Argentine themes. Banned by the military dictatorship of the Proceso, Peruvian novelist Mario Vargas Llosa's *Aunt Julia and the Scriptwriter* offers amusing but ironic and unflattering observations of what other Latin Americans think of Argentines. Graham Greene's satirical novel *The Honorary Consul* recounts the kidnapping of an insignificant British diplomat by a small but committed revolutionary group in the slums of Corrientes.

FILM

Argentina has left its mark on Hollywood and vice versa. Carlos Gardel flashed his smile in several Spanish-language films, including *El Día Que Me Quieras*, and Hollywood used Argentina as a location under forced circumstances – Juan Perón's economic policies prohibited studios from exporting profits made from their movies, so some studios used the proceeds to film in Argentina; the epic *Taras Bulba* (1962), for instance, was filmed partly around Salta.

Faye Dunaway appeared much later in the truly atrocious *Eva Perón* (filmed in 1981 as an NBC-TV miniseries and now available on video), for which Dunaway's salary probably comprised 90% of the budget. A recent atrocity, filmed partly in Buenos Aires, is director Alan Parker's musical *Evita*, confirming Mick Jagger's judgment of Madonna as 'a thimbleful of talent in an ocean of ambition.' Even more recently, Buenos Aires gets obliterated in the cartoonish sci-fi epic *Starship Troopers* (1997), whose ostensible hero is a porteño, and parts of the Brad Pitt epic *Seven Years in Tibet* (1997) were shot in Mendoza province, near the Chilean border.

An all-star cast of Richard Gere, Michael Caine, and Bob Hoskins couldn't redeem director John Mackenzie's *Beyond the Limit* (1983), an atrocious adaptation of Graham Greene's Corrientes-based novel *The Honorary Consul*, which was filmed in Veracruz, Mexico. Set during the Dirty War and more intelligent than most English-language films about Argentina, Martin Donovan's creepy *Apartment Zero* (1989) simultaneously depicts many amusing aspects of porteño life as it follows an Anglo-Argentine film buff (played by Colin Firth) who takes a morbid interest in his mysterious North American housemate.

Readers who know Spanish may enjoy *Ámbito Financiero* film critic Diego Curubeto's *Babilonia Gaucha*, an entertaining exploration of the relationship between Hollywood and Argentina.

See Arts in the Facts about Argentina chapter for information on the local film industry and its personalities.

NEWSPAPERS & MAGAZINES

Argentina is South America's most literate country, supporting a wide spectrum of newspapers and magazines despite unceasing economic crisis.

Buenos Aires has a thriving daily press of 11 nationwide dailies, several of them now online, with unambiguous political tendencies. Part of a multimedia consortium that also includes radio and TV stations, the centrist tabloid *Clarín* sells about 600,000 copies daily and more than a million on Sunday - the largest circulation of any newspaper in the Spanish-speaking world. It has an excellent Sunday cultural section, and is also the publisher of the new sports-oriented daily *¡Ole!* (circulation 60,000).

La Nación, founded in 1870 by future president Bartolomé Mitre, has moved from the right toward the center, but has come to resemble some of its less-thoughtful competitors in the process. Its circulation is about 200,000 daily, double that on Sunday. *La Prensa* is equally venerable, but is less influential.

The tabloid *Página 12* provides refreshing leftist perspectives and often breaks important stories that mainstream newspapers are slow to cover, but has lost much of the innovative fervor that characterized its early years, in the aftermath of the military dictatorship. Many articles are long and repetitive, but political columnist Horacio Verbitsky is widely acknowledged as the best in the country. Circulation is about 30,000 weekdays, 45,000 Sunday; it does not publish Monday.

The tabloid *Crónica*, with a weekday circulation of 400,000, is the yellow journalism counterpart to the US *National Enquirer* or Rupert Murdoch's *Sun*. Its circulation diminishes on weekends, since most of its public read it on the way to work.

Ámbito Financiero, the morning voice of the capital's financial community and a strong supporter of the Menem administration's economic policies, also has an excellent entertainment and cultural section. *El Cronista* is its afternoon rival. Both have circulations of around 30,000 and, along with the less influential *Buenos Aires Económico*, are published weekdays only.

The English-language daily *Buenos Aires Herald* (more influential than its circulation of about 8000 would suggest) covers Argentina and the world from an Anglo-Argentine perspective, emphasizing commerce and finance. Its perceptive weekend summaries of political and economic developments are a must for visitors with limited Spanish; the Sunday edition now includes Britain's *Guardian Weekly*. *Argentinisches Tageblatt* is a German-language weekly that is published Saturday.

Noticias is the local magazine equivalent to *Time* or *Newsweek*, while the recent startup *trespuntos* takes a more aggressive investigative stance. Monthlies like *La Maga* and *El Porteño* offer a forum for Argentine intellectuals and contribute greatly to the capital's cultural life. The monthly *Humor* caricatured the Argentine military during the Dirty War and even during the early nationalist hysteria of the Falklands conflict; in safer times, it has lost much of its edge but is still worth reading. Avoid its soft-porn spinoff *Humor Sexo*. In a country known for conservative Catholicism and male machismo, downtown kiosks in Buenos Aires sell (or at least display) a surprising amount of gay pornography.

In Buenos Aires, North American and European newspapers like *The New York Times*, *USA Today*, *The Guardian*, and *Le Monde*, are sold at kiosks on the corner of Florida and Av Córdoba, at premium prices (US$10 or more for the Sunday *Times*, for example). Magazines such as *Time*, *Newsweek*, and *The Economist* are also easy to obtain in larger cities.

Many Argentine newspapers and magazines are now available on the Internet, including the following:

Ámbito Financiero
www.ambitofinanciero.com
Buenos Aires' leading financial daily

Buenos Aires Herald
www.buenosairesherald.com
Abbreviated but still informative weekly version of the capital's venerable English-language daily

Clarín
www.clarin.com.ar
Very complete version of the world's' largest-circulation Spanish-language daily, but their graphics overkill often means very slow downloading

La Nación
www.lanacion.com.ar
One of Buenos Aires' oldest and most prestigious dailies

Página 12
www.pagina12.com
Left-of-center daily known for the capital's best investigative journalism

UkiNet
www.ukinet.com/
Human-rights-oriented website by a committed and talented independent journalist

Freedom of the Press?

Freedom of the press is far greater than under the military dictatorship of 1976-83, but abuses still occur – provincial journalists have been threatened with beatings and even death, and, in one case, Mendoza police may have illegally entered a hotel room and intimidated three visiting Chilean journalists. The present government has withheld official advertising from newspapers that have investigated official corruption too vigorously for its taste and even won a libel suit against the respected weekly magazine *Noticias*, despite everyone's admission that the facts of the case – the birth of a son to President Menem out of wedlock – were in fact true.

Threats have also come from the private sector, though. In early 1997, the discovery of the handcuffed, charred, and bullet-ridden body of photojournalist José Luis Cabezas in Mar del Plata was linked to a former Buenos Aires provincial policeman and to Gregorio Ríos, the security chief of Alberto Yabrán, a businessman intimate of the Menem administration whom the courts designated a 'potential instigator' of the crime. Yabrán later committed suicide under suspicious circumstances at one of his several estancias in Entre Ríos province.

RADIO & TV

In the post-Proceso years, the end of government monopoly in the electronic media has opened up the airwaves to a greater variety of programming than in the past. The most popular station, the nationwide Radio Rivadavia, is a combination of Top 40 and talk radio, but there are many other choices on the AM band, including Radio Mitre (AM 800 in Buenos Aires).

Dozens of FM stations specialize in styles ranging from classical to pop to tango – FM Tango 92.7 in Buenos Aires has tango all day, every day. Radio Nacional (FM 96.5 in Buenos Aires), which is widely diffused throughout the country, has good news coverage.

As in other countries, media conglomerates have great influence. *Clarín* is only the print flagship of a group that includes Radio Mitre, two TV stations and other outlets. Likewise, *El Cronista*'s holding company controls two major TV stations and a substantial amount of cable service throughout the country.

Legalization of privately owned television and the cable revolution, however, have brought a wider variety of programming to the small screen. To be sure, there are countless game shows, dance parties and soap-opera drivel *(novelas)*, but there is also serious public-affairs programming on major stations at prime viewing times like Sunday evening. Foreigners can tune to CNN for news and ESPN for sports. Spanish and Chilean stations are also available.

PHOTOGRAPHY & VIDEO

The latest in consumer electronics is available, but import duties make cameras and film very expensive – up to three times their cost in North America or Western Europe. Developing is equally expensive. Bring as much film as you can; you can always sell anything you don't need to other travelers. Locally manufactured film is reasonably good, but no cheaper than imported.

Color slide film can be purchased cheaply in Asunción, Paraguay, or in the free zones at Iquique and Punta Arenas, Chile. These are also good places to replace lost or stolen camera equipment, as prices are only slightly higher than in North America, even if the selection is not so great.

TIME

For most of the year, Argentina is three hours behind Greenwich Mean Time (GMT), but this varies among provinces. The city and province of Buenos Aires observe daylight saving time (summer time), but most provinces do not. Exact dates for the changeover vary from year to year.

ELECTRICITY

Electric current operates on 220V, 50 cycles. In downtown Buenos Aires, Calle Talcahuano has a large concentration of shops specializing in transformers and adapters for appliances.

WEIGHTS & MEASURES

The metric system is universal and obligatory for legal purposes, but country folk commonly use the Spanish *legua* (league, about 5km) to indicate distance. Hands are used to measure horses, while carpenters regularly use English measurements. Tire pressure is commonly measured in pounds per square inch.

See the inside back cover for a conversion chart.

LAUNDRY

In recent years, self-service laundries have become more common in both Buenos Aires and provincial cities, but they tend to be more expensive than their equivalent in the USA or Europe. Laverap has branches in most major cities. Most inexpensive hotels will have a place where you can wash your own clothes and hang them to dry. In some places maid service will be reasonable, but agree on charges in advance.

TOILETS

In terms of cleanliness and sanitation, Argentine toilets are probably better than in most of the rest of South America, but there is considerable regional variation – in subtropical rural areas like the Gran Chaco and parts of the Andean Northwest, standards can be lower. For the truly squeamish, the better restaurants and cafés are good alternatives. Always carry your own toilet paper.

HEALTH

Although emergency medical care in Argentina's public hospitals is good and usually free of charge, international travelers should take out comprehensive travel insurance before they leave home. If you're from a country with socialized medicine, you should find out what you'll need to do in order to be reimbursed for out-of-pocket money expenses.

In general, Argentina presents few serious health hazards. Before traveling, US residents can contact the international travel hotline (☎ 404-332-4559), a voicemail service at the Centers for Disease Control and Prevention (CDC) in Atlanta. Even more useful is CDC's automated fax information service (☎ 404-332-4565), which provides printouts of the most current information on health conditions in specific regions by immediate return fax. Just call the number, indicate which country you want information on (the number for Argentina, the Falklands, Paraguay, and Chile is 220180; Paraguay's is 220170), and provide a fax number. For the latest details while in Argentina, contact your country's consulate in Buenos Aires.

If you do become ill in Argentina, don't hesitate to seek medical help at hospitals or clinics. While some (like the British Hospital in Buenos Aires) will have more English-speaking staff than others, most doctors have a working knowledge of English.

Travel Health Guides

A number of books provide good information on travel health:

Staying Healthy in Asia, Africa & Latin America, Dirk Schroeder, Moon Publications, 1994. Probably the best all-around guide to carry; it's compact, detailed and well organized.

Travelers' Health, Dr Richard Dawood, Oxford University Press and Random House, 1994. Comprehensive, easy to read, authoritative and highly recommended, although it's rather large to lug around.

Where There is No Doctor, David Werner, Macmillan and Hesperian Foundation. A very detailed guide intended for someone, such as a Peace Corps worker, working in an underdeveloped country.

Backpacking in Chile and Argentina (Bradit Publications, 1994), by Andrew Dixon and Clare Hargreaves, has a good section on the hazards of hiking and camping in the Southern Cone countries.

Travel with Children, Maureen Wheeler, Lonely Planet Publications, 1995. Includes advice on travel health for younger children.

There are also a number of excellent travel health sites on the Internet. From the Lonely Planet website, there are links to the World Health Organization and the Centers for Disease Control & Prevention.

Predeparture Planning

Make sure you're healthy before you start traveling. If embarking on a long trip, make sure your teeth are in good shape, though Argentine dentists are excellent, especially those in Buenos Aires. If you wear glasses, take a spare pair and your prescription. You can get new eyeglasses made quickly and competently, depending on the prescription and frame you choose; replacing contacts may prove a bit more time-consuming. If you require a particular medication, take an adequate supply and bring a prescription in case you lose your supply.

Immunizations Argentina requires no vaccinations for entry from any country, but if you are visiting neighboring tropical countries you should consider prophylaxis against typhoid, malaria, and other diseases. The farther off the beaten track you go, the more necessary it is to take precautions.

It is important to understand the distinction between vaccines recommended for travel in certain areas and those required by law. Essentially the number of vaccines subject to international health regulations has been dramatically reduced over the last 10 years. Currently, yellow fever is the only vaccine subject to international health regulations. Vaccination as an entry requirement is usually only enforced when coming from an infected area.

On the other hand, a number of vaccines are recommended for travel in certain areas. These may not be required by law but are suggested for your personal protection. All vaccinations should be recorded on an International Health Certificate, which is available from your physician or government health department.

Plan ahead for getting your vaccinations: Some of them require an initial shot followed by a booster, while some vaccinations should not be given together. It is recommended you seek medical advice at least six weeks prior to travel. Note that smallpox has now been wiped out around the world, so immunization is no longer necessary.

Most travelers from Western countries will have been immunized against various diseases during childhood, but your doctor may still recommend booster shots against measles or polio, diseases still prevalent in many developing countries. The period of protection offered by vaccinations differs widely, and some are contraindicated if you are pregnant.

In some countries immunizations are available from airport or government health centers. Travel agents or airline offices will tell you where. Vaccinations include:

Tetanus & Diphtheria Boosters are necessary every 10 years, and protection is highly recommended.

Polio Polio is a serious, easily transmitted disease, still prevalent in many developing countries. Everyone should keep up to date with this vaccination. A booster every 10 years maintains immunity.

Hepatitis A The most common travel-acquired illness can be prevented by vaccination. Protection can be provided in two ways: with the antibody gamma globulin (see below) or with the Havrix vaccine, which provides long-term immunity (possibly more than 10 years) after an initial course of two injections and a booster at one year. It may be more expensive than gamma globulin but certainly has many advantages, including length of protection and ease of administration. It is important to know that as a vaccine it will take about three weeks to provide satisfactory protection – hence the need for careful planning prior to travel.

Gamma globulin is not a vaccination but a ready-made antibody that has proven very successful in reducing the chance of hepatitis infection. Because it may interfere with the development of immunity, it should not be given until at least 10 days after administration of the last vaccination you require; it should also be given as close as possible to departure because it is at its most effective in the first few weeks after administration, and the effectiveness tapers off gradually between three and six months.

Hepatitis B This disease is spread by blood or by sexual activity. Travelers who should consider a hepatitis B vaccination include those visiting countries where there are known to be many carriers, where blood transfusions may not be adequately screened or where sexual contact is a possibility. It involves three injections, the quickest course being over three weeks with a booster at 12 months.

Health Insurance It's a good idea to get travel insurance to cover theft, loss, and medical problems. There are a wide variety of policies, and your travel agent will have recommendations. International student travel policies handled by STA Travel, Council Travel, or other student travel organizations are usually good values. Some policies offer lower and higher medical expenses options, but the higher one is chiefly for countries that like the USA have extremely expensive medical costs. Check the small print.

- Some policies specifically exclude 'dangerous activities' like scuba diving, motorcycling, and even trekking. If these activities are on your agenda, avoid this sort of policy.
- You may prefer a policy that pays doctors or hospitals directly, rather than one that requires you to pay first and claim later. If you have to claim later, keep all documentation. Some policies ask you to call back (reverse charges) to a center in your home country for an immediate assessment of your problem.
- Check whether the policy covers ambulance fees or an emergency flight home. If you have to stretch out, you will need two seats, and somebody has to pay for it!

Medical Kit All standard medications are available in well-stocked pharmacies, and many common prescription drugs can be purchased legally over-the-counter in Argentina. A possible kit list includes:

- Aspirin or paracetamol (acetaminophen in the US) – for pain or fever.
- Antihistamine (such as Benadryl) – a decongestant for colds and allergies; eases the itch from insect bites or stings; and helps to prevent motion sickness. Antihistamines may cause sedation and interact with alcohol, so care should be taken when using them; take one you know and have used before, if possible.
- Antibiotics, which are useful for traveling off the beaten track, but they must be prescribed, and you should carry the prescription with you (see note below).
- Lomotil or Imodium – to treat diarrhea; prochlorperazine (eg, Stemetil) or metaclopramide (eg, Maxalon) is good for nausea and vomiting.
- Rehydration mixture, to treat severe diarrhea, which is particularly important if you're traveling with children.
- Antiseptic, such as povidone-iodine (eg, Betadine) – for cuts and scrapes.

- Calamine lotion, to ease irritation from bites or stings.
- Multivitamins – especially useful for long trips when dietary vitamin intake may be inadequate.
- Bandages and band-aids for minor injuries (minimize use in hot climates).
- Scissors, tweezers, and a thermometer (note that airlines prohibit mercury thermometers).
- Insect repellent, sunscreen lotion, lip balm, and water-purification tablets
- Cold and flu tablets and throat lozenges – Pseudoephedrine hydrochloride (Sudafed) may be useful if you're flying with a cold, to avoid ear damage.

Antibiotics are specific to the infections that they treat. Ideally, they should be administered only under medical supervision and never taken indiscriminately. Take only the recommended dose at the prescribed intervals and continue using it for the prescribed period, even if symptoms disappear earlier. Stop immediately if there are any serious reactions, and don't use the antibiotic at all if you are unsure if you have the correct one.

Basic Rules

Care in what you eat and drink is the most important health rule; stomach upsets are the most likely travel health problem (between 30% and 50% of travelers in a two-week stay experience this), but the majority of these upsets will be relatively minor. Don't become paranoid; after all, trying the local food is part of the experience of travel.

Food North Americans, Europeans, and Australians who are not vegetarians will find Argentine food relatively bland and easy on the stomach. Salad greens and other fresh vegetables are safe to eat in virtually every part of the country.

Remember that if your food is poor or limited in availability, if you're traveling hard and fast and therefore missing meals, or if you simply lose your appetite, you can soon start to lose weight and compromise your immune system.

Water Although Buenos Aires' aging water supply system has come under scrutiny for its chemical content, there is almost no danger of dysentery or similar ailments. In remote rural areas, where latrines may be close to wells, exercise caution. One geographical area of concern is the 'Impenetrable' of the central Chaco, north of Roque Sáenz Peña, which has been the only region in the country to experience cholera outbreaks.

Bottled drinking water, both carbonated and noncarbonated, is widely available in Argentina.

Water Purification If you prefer to purify water yourself, the simplest way is to boil it thoroughly – vigorous boiling for 10 minutes should be satisfactory even at high altitude (where water boils at a lower temperature, and germs are less likely to be killed).

Simple filtering will not remove all dangerous organisms, so if you cannot boil water it should be treated chemically. Chlorine tablets (Puritabs, Steritabs, or other brand names) will kill many pathogens, but not some parasites such as giardia and amoebic cysts. Iodine is very effective in purifying water and is available in tablet form (such as Potable Aqua), but follow the directions carefully – too much iodine can be harmful.

If you can't find tablets, tincture of iodine (2%) or iodine crystals can be used. Four drops of tincture of iodine per liter or quart of clear water is the recommended dosage; let the treated water stand for 20 to 30 minutes before drinking. Iodine crystals can also be used to purify water, but this is a more complicated process, as you must first prepare a saturated iodine solution (iodine loses its effectiveness if exposed to air or becomes damp, so keep it in a tightly sealed container). Flavored powder will help disguise the taste of treated water and is a good idea if you are traveling with children.

Everyday Health

Normal body temperature is 98.6°F or 37°C; more than 4°F (2°C) higher indicates a 'high' fever. The normal adult pulse rate is 60 to 80 per minute (children 80 to 100, babies 100 to 140). It is important to know how to take a temperature and a pulse rate.

Respiration (breathing) rate is also an indicator of illness. Count the number of breaths per minute: Between 12 and 20 is normal for adults and older children (up to 30 for younger children, 40 for babies). People with a high fever or serious respiratory illness (like pneumonia) breathe more quickly than normal. More than 40 shallow breaths a minute is usually an indication of pneumonia.

Medical Problems & Treatment

Potential medical problems can be broken down into several categories. First, there are the problems caused by extremes of temperature, altitude, or motion. Then there are diseases and illnesses caused through poor environmental sanitation, animal or human contact, and insect bites or stings. Simple cuts, bites, and scratches can also cause problems.

Self-diagnosis and treatment can be risky, so wherever possible, seek qualified help. Although we do give drug dosages in this section, they are for emergency use only. Medical advice should be sought where possible before administering any drugs. An embassy or consulate can usually recommend a good place to go for such advice.

Environmental Hazards

Altitude Sickness From the passes between Mendoza and Chile northward to the Bolivian border, altitude sickness *(apunamiento* or *soroche)*, also known as acute mountain sickness (AMS), represents a potential health hazard. In the thinner atmosphere above 3000m, or even lower in some cases, lack of oxygen causes many individuals to suffer headaches, nausea, shortness of breath, physical weakness, and other symptoms that can lead to very serious consequences, especially if combined with heat exhaustion, sunburn, or hypothermia.

There is no hard and fast rule as to how high is too high: AMS has been fatal at altitudes of 3000m, although it is much more common above 3450m. It is always wise to sleep at a lower altitude than the greatest height reached during the day. There are a number of other measures that can prevent or minimize AMS.

For mild cases, everyday painkillers such as aspirin or *chachacoma*, an herbal tea made from a common Andean shrub, will relieve symptoms until your body adapts. In the Andean Northwest, coca leaves are a common remedy, but authorities frown upon their usage, even by native peoples who sell them surreptitiously in the markets of Jujuy, Salta, and other towns. If you experience AMS symptoms, avoid smoking, drinking alcohol, eating heavily, or exercising strenuously. Most people recover within a few hours or days as their body produces more red blood cells to absorb oxygen, but if symptoms persist, it is imperative to descend to lower elevations. Following some simple guidelines will help:

- Ascend slowly – take frequent rest days, spending two to three nights for each climb of 1000m (3000 feet). If you reach a high altitude by trekking, acclimatization takes place gradually, and you are less likely to be affected than if you fly direct.
- It is always wise to sleep at a lower altitude than the greatest height reached during the day, if possible. Also, once above 3000m, care should be taken not to increase the sleeping altitude by more than 300m per day.
- Drink extra fluids. Mountain air is dry and cold, and you lose moisture as you breathe.
- Eat light, high-carbohydrate meals for more energy. Snacks such as chocolate or dried fruit are easily available in Argentina.
- Avoid alcohol, which may increase the risk of dehydration.
- Avoid sedatives, which decrease respiration.

Fungal Infections Fungal infections, which occur with greater frequency in hot weather, are most likely to occur on the scalp, between the toes (athlete's foot) or fingers, in the groin, and on the body (ringworm). You can get ringworm (which is a fungal infection, not a worm) from infected animals or other people. Athlete's foot can be picked up by walking on damp areas, such as shower floors.

To prevent fungal infections wear loose, comfortable clothes, avoid underwear made of artificial fibers, wash frequently, and dry carefully. If you do get an infection, wash the infected area daily with a disinfectant or medicated soap and water, and rinse and dry well. Apply an antifungal powder, try to expose the infected area to air or sunlight as much as possible, and wash all towels and underwear in hot water as well as changing them often.

Heat Exhaustion & Sunburn Although Argentina is mostly a temperate country, its northern provinces lie within the Tropic of Capricorn, where the sun's direct rays can be devastating – sunburn is a particularly serious matter at high altitudes. In the western Chaco and other desert regions, where summer temperatures can exceed 40°C, dehydration is equally a problem. In far southern Patagonia and Tierra del Fuego, where the protective ozone layer has dissipated because of aerosol fluorocarbons, sun protection is also a good idea despite the frequent overcast weather.

Use sunscreen and take extra care to cover areas not normally exposed to sun. Quality sunglasses and a Panama hat or baseball cap are excellent ideas. You should also use zinc cream or some other barrier cream for your nose and lips. Calamine lotion is good for mild sunburn. Protect your eyes with good-quality sunglasses, particularly if you will be near water, sand or snow.

Dehydration or salt deficiency can cause heat exhaustion. Take time to acclimatize to high temperatures and make sure that you get enough liquids. Salt tablets may also help, but adding extra salt to your food is better. Salt deficiency is characterized by fatigue, lethargy, headaches, giddiness, and muscle cramps. Vomiting or diarrhea can also deplete your liquid and salt levels. Anhydrotic heat exhaustion, caused by the inability to sweat, is quite rare. Unlike the other forms of heat exhaustion it is likely to strike people who have been in a hot climate for some time, rather than newcomers. Always carry a water bottle on long trips and take frequent drinks.

Heatstroke This serious, occasionally fatal, condition can occur if the body's heat-regulating mechanism breaks down and body temperature rises to dangerous levels. Long, continuous periods of exposure to high temperatures and insufficient fluids can leave you vulnerable to heatstroke. Avoid excessive alcohol intake or strenuous activity when you first arrive in a hot climate.

Symptoms include feeling unwell, not sweating very much (or at all) and a high body temperature (39°C to 41°C or 102°F to 106°F). Where sweating has ceased, the skin becomes flushed and red. Severe, throbbing headaches and lack of coordination also occur, and the sufferer may be confused or aggressive. Eventually the victim becomes delirious or convulses. Hospitalization is essential, but in the interim get victims out of the sun, remove their clothing, cover them with a wet sheet or towel and then fan continually. Give fluids if they are conscious.

Hypothermia At high altitudes in the mountains or high latitudes in Patagonia, cold and wet conditions can kill. Changeable weather at high altitudes can leave you vulnerable to exposure: After dark, temperatures in the mountains or desert (even when simply taking a long bus trip) can drop from balmy to below freezing, while high winds and a sudden soaking can lower your body temperature too rapidly. If possible, avoid traveling alone; partners are more likely to avoid hypothermia successfully. If you must travel alone, especially when hiking, be sure someone knows your route and when you expect to return. In some areas, you should always be prepared for cold, wet or windy conditions even if you're just out walking or hitchhiking.

Hypothermia occurs when the body loses heat faster than it can produce heat and the core temperature of the body falls. It is surprisingly easy to progress from very cold to dangerously cold due to a combination of wind, wet clothing, fatigue and hunger, even if the air temperature is above freezing. It is best to dress in layers; silk, wool and some of the new artificial fibers are all good insulating materials. A hat is important, as a lot of heat is lost through the head. A strong, waterproof outer layer (and a 'space' blanket for emergencies) are essential.

Always carry basic supplies, including food containing simple sugars to generate heat quickly, and fluid to drink.

Symptoms of hypothermia are exhaustion, numbness (particularly in the toes and fingers), shivering, slurred speech, irrational or violent behavior, lethargy, stumbling, dizzy spells, muscle cramps and violent bursts of energy. Irrationality may take the form of sufferers claiming they are warm and trying to take off their clothes.

To treat mild hypothermia, first get victims out of the wind and/or rain, remove their clothing if it's wet and replace it with dry, warm clothing. Give them hot liquids – not alcohol – and some high-calorie, easily digestible food. Do not rub victims; instead, allow them to slowly warm themselves. This should be enough to treat the early stages of hypothermia. Early recognition and treatment of mild hypothermia are the only ways to prevent severe hypothermia, which is a critical condition. In advanced stages it may be necessary to place victims in warm sleeping bags and get in with them.

Jet Lag Jet lag usually occurs when a person travels by air across more than three time zones (each time zone usually represents a one-hour time difference); however, some people experience it crossing only two zones. Many of the functions of the human body (such as temperature, pulse rate, and emptying of the bladder and bowels) are regulated by internal 24-hour cycles called circadian rhythms. When we travel long distances rapidly, our bodies take time to adjust to the 'new time' of our destination, and we may experience fatigue, disorientation, insomnia, anxiety, impaired concentration, and loss of appetite. These effects will usually be gone within three days of arrival, but there are ways of minimizing the impact of jet lag:

- Rest for a couple of days prior to departure; try to avoid late nights and last-minute dashes for traveler's checks, passports, and other important items.
- Try to select flight schedules that minimize sleep deprivation; arriving late in the day means you can go to sleep soon after you arrive. For very long flights, try to organize a stopover.
- Avoid excessive eating (which bloats the stomach) and alcohol (which causes dehydration) during the flight. Instead, drink plenty of noncarbonated, nonalcoholic drinks such as fruit juice or water.
- Avoid smoking, as this reduces the amount of oxygen in the airplane cabin even further and causes greater fatigue.
- Make yourself comfortable by wearing loose-fitting clothes and perhaps bringing an eye mask and ear plugs to help you sleep.

Motion Sickness Eating lightly before and during a trip will reduce the chance of motion sickness. If you are prone to motion sickness, try to sit in a place that minimizes disturbance, for example, near the wing on aircraft or near the center on a bus. Fresh air usually helps; reading and cigarette smoke do not. Commercial motion-sickness preparations, which can cause drowsiness, have to be taken before the trip commences – once you already feel sick, it's too late. Ginger, a natural preventative, is available in capsule form.

Infectious Diseases

Cholera The cholera outbreak that swept Peru and some other South American countries in the early 1990s has so far not spread among the general population of Argentina, Uruguay, and Paraguay, but it would be wise to take minimum precautions. Avoid raw seafood, and do not consume ice in drinks in areas where drinking water may be suspect. Little frequented by foreigners, the 'Impenetrable' of the mid-Chaco has been the site of Argentina's only cholera outbreaks.

The disease is characterized by a sudden onset of acute diarrhea with 'rice water' stools, vomiting, muscular cramps, and extreme weakness. Seek medical help fast and treat for dehydration, which can be extreme.

If there is an appreciable delay in getting to the hospital, then begin taking tetracycline (one 250mg capsule four times daily for adults). Note that tectracycline is not recommended for children under nine years, nor for pregnant women.

A cholera vaccine exists, but is not very effective, and is not required as a condition of entry to any country in the world.

Diarrhea A change of water, food, or climate can all cause the runs; diarrhea brought on by contaminated food or water is more serious. Despite all your precautions you may still have a mild bout of travelers' diarrhea, but a few rushed toilet trips with no other symptoms is not indicative of a serious problem. Moderate diarrhea, involving half a dozen loose movements in a day, is more of a nuisance.

Dehydration is the main danger with any diarrhea, particularly for children who can dehydrate quite quickly. Weak herbal tea with a little sugar, soda water, or soft drinks allowed to go flat and diluted 50% with water are all good fluid replacements. With severe diarrhea a rehydrating solution is necessary to replace minerals and salts.

Commercially available oral rehydration salts (ORS) are very useful; add the contents of one packet to a liter of boiled or bottled water. In an emergency you can make up a solution of eight teaspoons of sugar to a liter of boiled water and provide salted crackers at the same time. Stick to a bland diet as you recover.

Lomotil or Imodium can bring relief from the symptoms, although they do not actually cure the problem. Only use these drugs if absolutely necessary – eg, if you *must* travel. For children Imodium is preferable. Do not use these drugs if the person has a high fever or is severely dehydrated. Antibiotics may be useful in treating diarrhea that is watery, with blood and mucous, and/or accompanied by a fever.

The recommended drugs (adults only) would be either norfloxacin, 400mg twice daily for three days, or ciprofloxacin, 500mg twice daily for three days.

The drug bismuth subsalicylate has also been used successfully. The dosage for adults is two tablets or 30ml and for children it is one tablet or 10ml. This dose can be repeated every 30 minutes to one hour, with no more than eight doses in a 24-hour period.

The drug of choice for children would be co-trimoxazole (Bactrim, Septrin, Resprim) with dosage dependent on weight.

Dysentery This serious illness, caused by contaminated food or water, is characterized by severe diarrhea, often with blood or mucus in the stool. There are two kinds of dysentery: bacillary and amoebic. Bacillary dysentery is characterized by a high fever and rapid onset; headache, vomiting, and stomach pains are also symptoms. It generally does not last longer than a week, but it is highly contagious. Amoebic dysentery is often more gradual in the onset of symptoms, with cramping abdominal pain and vomiting less likely; fever may not be present. It is not a self-limiting disease: It will persist until treated and can recur and cause long-term health problems.

A stool test is necessary to diagnose which kind of dysentery you might have, so you should seek medical help urgently. In case of an emergency the drugs norfloxacin or ciprofloxacin can be used as presumptive treatment for bacillary dysentery, and metronidazole (Flagyl) can be used for amoebic dysentery.

For bacillary dysentery, norfloxacin 400mg twice daily for seven days or ciprofloxacin 500mg twice daily for seven days are the recommended dosages.

If you're unable to find either of these drugs, then a useful alternative is co-trimoxazole 160/800mg (Bactrim, Septrin, Resprim) twice daily for seven days. This is a sulpha drug and must not be used by people with a known sulpha allergy.

In the case of children the drug cotrimoxazole is a reasonable first-line treatment. For amoebic dysentery, the recommended adult dosage of metronidazole (Flagyl) is one 750mg to 800mg capsule three times daily for five days. Children ages 8 to 12 years should have half the adult dose; the dosage for younger children is one-third the adult dose.

An alternative to Flagyl is Fasigyn, taken as a 2-gram daily dose for three days. Alcohol must be avoided during treatment and for 48 hours afterward.

Giardiasis Commonly known as Giardia, and sometimes 'Beaver Fever,' this intestinal parasite is present in contaminated water. Giardia has even contaminated apparently pristine rushing streams in the backcountry.

Symptoms are stomach cramps, nausea, a bloated stomach, watery, foul-smelling diarrhea, and frequent gas. Giardia can appear several weeks after exposure to the parasite; symptoms may disappear for a few days and then return, a pattern which may continue. Tinidazole, known as Fasigyn, or metronidazole (Flagyl) are the recommended drugs for treatment. Either can be used in a single treatment dose. Antibiotics are useless.

Hepatitis Hepatitis is a general term for inflammation of the liver. There are many causes of this condition: drugs, alcohol, and infections are but a few. The discovery of new strains has led to a virtual alphabet soup, with hepatitis A, B, C, D, E, and a rumored G. These letters identify specific agents that cause viral hepatitis. Viral hepatitis is an infection of the liver, which can lead to jaundice (yellow skin), fever, lethargy, and digestive problems. It can have no symptoms at all, with the infected person not aware that he or she has the disease. Travelers shouldn't be too paranoid about this apparent proliferation of hepatitis strains; hep C, D, E, and G are fairly rare (so far), and following the same precautions as for A and B should be all that's necessary to avoid them.

Viral hepatitis can be divided into two groups on the basis of how it is spread. The first route of transmission is via contaminated food and water, and the second route is via blood and bodily fluids.

Hepatitis A is a very common disease in most countries, especially those with poor standards of sanitation. Most people in developing countries are infected as children; they often don't develop symptoms, but do develop lifelong immunity. The disease poses a real threat to the traveler, as people are unlikely to have been exposed to hepatitis A in developed countries.

The symptoms are fever, chills, headache, fatigue, feelings of weakness, and aches and pains, followed by loss of appetite, nausea, vomiting, abdominal pain, dark urine, light-colored feces, and jaundiced skin; the whites of the eyes may also turn yellow. You should seek medical advice, but in general there is not much you can do apart from resting, drinking lots of fluids, eating lightly, and avoiding fatty foods. People who have had hepatitis must forgo alcohol for six months after the illness, as hepatitis attacks the liver, and it needs that amount of time to recover.

The routes of transmission are via contaminated water, shellfish contaminated by sewerage, or foodstuffs sold by food handlers with poor standards of hygiene. Taking care with what you eat and drink can go a long way toward preventing this disease. If there is any risk of exposure, additional cover is highly recommended. This cover comes in two forms: gamma globulin and Havrix. See Immunizations earlier in this section.

Hepatitis B, which used to be called serum hepatitis, is spread through contact with infected blood, blood products, or bodily fluids; for example, through sexual contact, unsterilized needles, and blood transfusions. Other risk situations include having a shave or getting a tattoo in a local shop, or having your ears pierced. The symptoms of type B are much the same as type A except that they are more severe and may lead to irreparable liver damage or even liver cancer. Although there is no treatment for hepatitis B, a cheap and effective vaccine is available; see Immunizations earlier in this section.

Hepatitis C is similar to B but seems to lead to liver disease more rapidly. Often referred to as the 'Delta' virus, Hepatitis D only occurs in chronic carriers of hepatitis B. Hepatitis E is a very recently discovered virus, of which little is yet known. It appears to be rather common in developing countries, generally causing mild hepatitis, although it can be very serious in pregnant women. Care with water supplies is the only current prevention, as there are no specific vaccines for this type of hepatitis. At present it doesn't appear to be too great a risk for travelers.

Hydatidosis Spread by contact with dogs that have eaten the entrails of infected sheep, this highly contagious disease is prevalent in areas like Argentine and Chilean Patagonia, where sheep numbers are very high, and dogs may come into contact with them. Though not cause for panic, it is a potentially serious matter; do not eat homemade sausages in this region, and avoid contact with sheepdogs in particular.

Sexually Transmitted Diseases Sexual contact with an infected partner spreads these diseases. While abstinence is the only 100% effective preventative, using condoms also reduces your risk. Gonorrhea and syphilis are the most common of these diseases; sores, blisters, or rashes around the genitals, discharges, or pain when urinating are common symptoms. Symptoms may be less marked or not observed at all in women. Syphilis symptoms eventually disappear completely, but the disease continues and can cause severe problems in later years. The treatment of gonorrhea and syphilis is by antibiotics.

There are numerous other sexually transmitted diseases, and effective treatment is available for most. However, there is no cure for herpes, and there is also currently no cure for AIDS (see below).

'En Argentina no hay SIDA, porque hay 35 millones de forros.' (In Argentina, there's no AIDS, because there are 35 million scumbags (condoms). – slogan on a T-shirt in Santiago del Estero.

Despite this self-deprecating but misleading comment on Argentine society, HIV/AIDS exists, though not on the scale that it does in Brazil or parts of the USA – according to government statistics, about 3500 AIDS patients have died since 1982, there are roughly 12,000 cases with active symptoms and perhaps 80-100,000 infected with HIV. AIDS also certainly exists in Uruguay and Paraguay, but it is not (yet) the widespread disaster that it is in Brazil; Paraguay may be more under threat in the long term due to its close Brazilian connections.

Buenos Aires has two AIDS-related support organizations. Cooperación, Información y Ayuda al Enfermo de SIDA (Coinsida; ☎ 4304-6664) is an information and assistance center for victims of AIDS and HIV at Finocchietto 1263 in the barrio of Barracas. Línea SIDA (☎ 4922-1617) is at Zuviría 64 (Subte: Av La Plata) in the barrio of Parque Chacabuco, near Caballito.

HIV (the Human Immunodeficiency Virus) may develop into AIDS (Acquired Immune Deficiency Syndrome). HIV is a major problem in many countries. Any exposure to blood, blood products, or bodily fluids may put the individual at risk. Infection can come from practicing unprotected sex or sharing contaminated needles. Apart from abstinence, the most effective preventative is always to practice safe sex using condoms. It is impossible to detect the HIV-positive status of an otherwise healthy-looking person without a blood test.

HIV/AIDS can also be spread through infected blood transfusions; many countries cannot afford to screen blood for transfusions. It can also be spread by dirty needles – vaccinations, acupuncture, tattooing, and ear or nose piercing can potentially be as dangerous as intravenous drug use if the equipment is not clean. If you do need an injection, ask to see the syringe unwrapped in front of you, or better still, take a needle and syringe pack with you overseas – it is a cheap insurance package against the chance of HIV infection.

Fear of HIV infection should never preclude treatment for serious medical conditions. Although there may be a risk of infection, it is very small indeed. A good resource for help and information is the US Centers for Disease Control AIDS hotline (☎ 800-343-2347).

Insect-Borne Diseases

Chagas' Disease Darwin may have suffered from this parasitic disease, transmitted by a bug that lives in mud (adobe) huts and comes out to feed at night. The bite is often mistaken for that of a bedbug, but early symptoms of Chagas' disease include a hard, violet-colored swelling appearing in about a week at the site of the bite, followed by swelling of the lymph glands or by a fever.

The long-term complications can be quite serious and can eventually lead to death years later. Most cases of Chagas' disease have appeared in Brazil, but travelers should avoid sleeping in or near mud huts. If you have no other choice, sleep under a mosquito net, use insecticides and insect repellents, and check for hidden insects.

Hantavirus Northern Patagonia, particularly the area around Bariloche and El Bolsón, has been the site of recent outbreaks of a particularly lethal strain of hantavirus, spread through contact with rat urine or feces. The virus loses its potency on contact with sunlight or fresh air, so travelers should take caution to avoid places where rodents congregate, especially but not only abandoned buildings. While the odds of contracting hantavirus are statistically small, the consequences are potentially fatal.

Malaria There is a minor risk of malaria in rural areas of northern Argentina, bordering Bolivia in Salta and Jujuy provinces. Chloroquine is the recommended medication here.

Less Common Diseases

Rabies Dogs are noted carriers of rabies. Any bite, scratch, or even lick from a warm-blooded, furry animal should be cleaned immediately and thoroughly. Scrub with soap and running water, and then clean with an alcohol solution. If there is any possibility that the animal is infected, medical help should be sought immediately. Even if the animal is not rabid, all bites should be treated seriously as they can become infected or can result in tetanus. A rabies vaccination is now available and should be considered if you are in a high-risk category – eg, if you intend to explore caves (bat bites can be dangerous) or work with animals.

Shellfish Poisoning In Argentine and Chilean Patagonia, most notably in Tierra del Fuego, collection of shellfish is not advisable and, in many cases, not permitted because of toxic 'red tide' conditions.

Tetanus Tetanus is difficult to treat but is preventable with immunization. Tetanus occurs when a wound becomes infected by a germ that lives in the feces of animals or people, so thoroughly clean all cuts, punctures, or animal bites. Tetanus is also known as lockjaw, and the first symptom may be discomfort in swallowing, or stiffening of the jaw and neck; this is followed by painful convulsions of the jaw and the whole body.

Yellow Fever Yellow fever is a very low-risk matter in Argentina and Uruguay, which do not require vaccination certificates, and is only slightly higher in Paraguay. Nevertheless, a certificate is a good idea for anyone visiting neighboring tropical countries.

Cuts, Bites & Stings

Cuts & Scratches Skin punctures can easily become infected in hot climates and may be difficult to heal. Treat any cut with an antiseptic such as Betadine. When possible avoid bandages and band-aids, which can keep wounds wet.

Bites & Stings Bee and wasp stings are usually painful rather than dangerous. Calamine lotion will give relief, and ice packs will reduce the pain and swelling. Some spiders have dangerous bites, and scorpion stings are very painful, but neither is likely to be fatal. Bites are best avoided by not using bare hands to turn over rocks or large pieces of wood.

Snakebites do not cause instantaneous death, and antivenins are usually available. Seek medical help, if possible with the dead snake for identification, but don't attempt to catch the snake if there is even a remote possibility of being bitten again. In the case of a snakebite, avoid slashing and sucking the wound, avoid tight tourniquets (a lightly constricting band above the bite can help), avoid ice, keep the affected area below the level of the heart, and move it as little as possible. Do not ingest alcohol or any drugs. Stay calm and get to a medical facility as soon as possible.

In the case of spiders and scorpions, there are no special first-aid techniques. A black widow spider bite may be barely noticeable, but the venom can be dangerous, and if you're bitten you should seek medical attention immediately. Centipede, bee, wasp, and ant bites and stings may be relieved by application of ice.

If you are hiking a long way from the nearest phone or other help, and you are bitten or stung, you should hike out and get help, particularly in the case of snake and spider bites. Reactions are often delayed for up to 12 hours, and you can hike out before then. It is recommended that you always hike with a companion.

Ticks Ticks are parasitic arachnids that may be present in brush, forest, and grasslands, where hikers often get them on their legs or in their boots. The adults suck blood from hosts by burying their head into skin, but are often found unattached and can simply be brushed off. However, if one has attached itself to you, pulling it off and leaving the head in the skin increases the likelihood of infection or disease.

To avoid ticks, use insect repellent. To remove an attached tick, use a pair of tweezers, grab it by the head and gently pull it straight out – do not twist it. (If no tweezers are available, use your fingers, but protect them from contamination with a piece of tissue or paper.) Do not touch the tick with a hot object like a match or a cigarette – this can cause it to regurgitate noxious gut substances or saliva into the wound. And do not rub oil, alcohol, or petroleum jelly on it. If you get sick in the next couple of weeks or notice a rash where you were bitten, consult a doctor.

Bedbugs & Lice Bedbugs live in various places, but particularly in dirty mattresses and bedding. Spots of blood on linen or on the wall around the bed can be read as a suggestion to find another hotel. Bedbugs leave itchy bites in neat rows. Calamine lotion may help.

All lice cause itching and discomfort. They make themselves at home in your hair (head lice), your clothing (body lice), or in your pubic hair (crabs). You catch lice through direct contact with infected people or by sharing combs, clothing, and the like. Powder or shampoo treatment will kill the lice, and infected clothing should then be washed in hot water.

Women's Health

Gynecological Problems Poor diet, lowered resistance due to the use of antibiotics for stomach upsets, and even contraceptive pills can lead to vaginal infections when traveling in hot climates. Wearing skirts or loose-fitting trousers and cotton underwear helps prevent infections.

Yeast infections, characterized by a rash, itching, and discharge, can be treated with a vinegar or even lemon-juice douche or with yogurt. Nystatin, miconazole or clotrimazole pessaries or vaginal cream are the usual treatments. Trichomonas is a more serious infection; symptoms are a discharge and a burning sensation when urinating. Sexual partners must also be treated, and if a vinegar-water douche is not effective, seek medical attention. Flagyl is the prescribed drug.

Pregnancy Most miscarriages occur during the first three months of pregnancy, so this is the riskiest time to travel. The last three months should also be spent within reasonable distance of good medical care, as serious problems can develop at this time. Pregnant women should avoid unnecessary medication, but vaccinations and malarial prophylactics should still be taken where possible. Additional care should be taken to prevent illness, and particular attention should be paid to diet and nutrition. Abortion is illegal, though not unheard of, in Argentina.

WOMEN TRAVELERS

Attitudes toward Women

In Argentina, International Women's Day becomes yet another occasion to 'send her flowers,' but for women traveling alone, the country is probably safer than Europe, the USA, and most other Latin American countries – although you should not be complacent. Buenos Aires is more notorious than the provinces for annoyances like unwelcome physical contact, particularly on crowded buses or trains. If you're physically confident, a slap or a well-aimed elbow should discourage any further contact. If not, a scream is also very effective.

Other nuisances include crude language and *piropos*. Crude language, generally in the presence of other males, usually emphasizes feminine physical attributes. If you respond aggressively ('Are you talking to me?'), you will probably put your aggressor to shame. One clever New Yorker found that a bogus wedding ring worked wonders in deterring unwanted admirers.

There is no good definition of the piropo, but most Argentine males would consider it the masculine art of approaching a woman in public and commenting on her femininity or attractiveness. This is an idealized definition because piropos are most often vulgar, even though some are creative and even eloquent (one cited in the *Buenos Aires Herald* was, 'Oh God, the sky is parting and angels are falling'). While it can be irritating, such verbal aggression rarely becomes physical. On occasions when persistent suitors trail you for blocks, the best means of discouraging their pursuit is to completely ignore them.

Safety Precautions

Single women checking in at low-budget hotels, both in Buenos Aires and the provinces, may find themselves objects of suspicion, since prostitutes often frequent such places. In the provinces, women traveling alone are objects of curiosity, since Argentine women rarely do so. You should interpret questions as to whether you are running away from parents or a husband as expressions of concern.

If you hitchhike, always exercise judgment and avoid getting into a vehicle with more than one man: Argentine males rarely find it necessary to demonstrate their machismo except in the company of other males.

GAY & LESBIAN TRAVELERS

While Argentina is a strongly Catholic country, and homosexuality is taboo to many (former military dictator Juan Carlos Onganía once caused a furor by stating he would not have a homosexual friend), there are enclaves of tolerance in Buenos Aires (particularly Av Santa Fe and Recoleta), the Paraná Delta, and some other areas. Argentine males in general are more physically demonstrative than their counterparts in North America and Europe, so certain behaviors like kissing (at least on the cheek, in greeting) or a vigorous embrace may seem innocuous even to some who object to homosexuals. Lesbians walking hand-in-hand will attract relatively little attention, since Argentine women frequently do so, but this would be very conspicuous behavior for males. When in doubt, it's better to be discreet.

DISABLED TRAVELERS

Travelers with disabilities will find Argentina difficult at times; the wheelchair-bound in particular will find Buenos Aires' narrow sidewalks, which are frequently in disrepair, difficult to negotiate. Crossing streets is also a problem, since Argentine drivers are a challenge to even the most agile and physically fit adults. Nevertheless, Argentines with disabilities get around – one of the most famous works of contemporary Argentine fiction is Ernesto Sábato's *On Heroes and Tombs*, which includes an extraordinary 'Report on the Blind' based, in part, on the author's observations in Buenos Aires (Sábato, however, is not himself blind).

SENIOR TRAVELERS

Senior travelers should encounter no particular difficulties traveling in Argentina, where older citizens traditionally enjoy a great deal of respect; on crowded buses, for instance, most Argentines will readily offer their seat to an older person. Senior discounts on transportation and most other services are, however, virtually a thing of the past.

TRAVEL WITH CHILDREN

Argentina is extremely child-friendly in terms of safety, health, people's attitudes, and family-oriented activities, although there are regional differences. The country's numerous plazas and public parks, many with playgrounds, are popular gathering spots for families.

Once children are old enough to cross the street safely and find their way back home, parents don't hesitate to send unaccompanied preadolescents on errands and on visits to friends or neighbors. While most visiting parents are not likely to feel comfortable doing this, they can usually count on children's safety in public places.

For smaller children, a stroller is a good idea – even good walkers need rest, and it's much easier than carrying children in your arms and a good way of keeping track of them.

Argentines are very helpful on public transport. Often someone will give up a seat for a parent and child, but if that does not occur, an older person may offer to put the child on his or her lap. Sometimes this is so spontaneous that foreigners find someone pulling the child out of their arms. This is also a country where people frequently touch each other, so your children may be patted on the head or gently caressed.

Basic restaurants provide a wide selection of food suitable for children (vegetables, pasta, meat, chicken, fish), but adult portions are normally so large that small children rarely need a separate order. Waiters are accustomed to providing extra plates and cutlery for children, though some places may add a small additional charge. Argentina's high quality ice cream is a special treat.

Breast-feeding in public is uncommon, but mothers can always retreat into a café and cover themselves with a baby blanket during feedings.

Poorly maintained public bathrooms may be a concern for some parents. Always carry toilet paper, which is rarely stocked. While a woman may take a young boy into the ladies' room, it would be socially unacceptable for a man to take a girl of any age into the men's room.

USEFUL ORGANIZATIONS

Asatej (☎ 4311-6953, fax 4311-6840), Argentina's nonprofit student-travel agency and an affiliate of STA Travel, is on the 3rd floor, Florida 835, in Buenos Aires. The organization is eager to encourage budget travelers, and you need not be a student to take advantage of their services. Asatej is also affiliated with Hostelling International through the Red Argentina de Albergues Juveniles (RAAJ; see Hostel Card under Visas & Documents, earlier in this chapter, for details), and is helping to expand and promote the Argentine hostel system.

Travelers can also contact the Asociación Argentina de Albergues de la Juventud (AAAJ; ☎/fax 4476-1001), 2nd floor, Oficina 6, Talcahuano 214, 1013 Buenos Aires, for information on Argentine youth hostels. This office also serves as a travel agency, issues international student cards, and maintains a message board for travelers (mostly young Argentines) seeking companions for extended trips. AAAJ is, however, moribund in comparison with Asatej and RAAJ. The two hostel representatives overlap affiliations with some hostels, but also represent others exclusively.

The Administración de Parques Nacionales (APN; ☎ 4312-0783), Av Santa Fe 690 in Buenos Aires, provides information on national parks and stocks a small number of publications of interest to conservationists and wildlife enthusiasts. Inquiries out of the ordinary, however, usually draw blank stares. Visitors specifically interested in fly-fishing should contact the Asociación Argentina de Pesca de Mosca (☎ 4773-0821) at Lerma 452, 1414 Buenos Aires.

Another address of interest to conservationists is the pro-wildlife organization Fundación Vida Silvestre Argentina (☎ 4331-4864), Defensa 245, just south of Plaza de Mayo in Buenos Aires. Membership starts at US$35 per year and includes the Fundación's newsletter, *Otioso*; a US$60 membership includes the group's magazine, *Revista Vida Silvestre*. Hours are 9:30 am to 6 pm weekdays.

Birding enthusiasts might contact the Asociación Ornitológica del Plata (☎ 4312-8958), at 25 de Mayo 749, 2nd floor, in Buenos Aires. The Argentine affiliate of Greenpeace (☎ 4962-2291) is at Mansilla 3046 in Buenos Aires, a few blocks from the

Agüero station on Línea D of the Subte (underground).

DANGERS & ANNOYANCES

While violent crime is relatively rare, and personal security is a lesser concern than in most other Latin American countries, parts of the barrio of Buenos Aires – most notably La Boca – have seen armed robberies against visitors. More commonly, though, travelers cannot afford to be complacent with their possessions – pickpockets, purse-snatchers, and the like certainly exist.

Watch particularly for diversions like the 'inadvertent' collision that results in ice cream or some other substance being spilled on an unsuspecting visitor, who loses precious personal possessions while distracted by the apologetic perpetrator working in concert with a thief (one LP reader has eloquently called them 'mustard artists'). Some travelers have had similar problems with ambulatory street vendors at sidewalk cafés.

Most Argentine drivers jump the gun when the signal is about to change to green. Be especially wary of vehicles turning right; even though pedestrians at corners and crosswalks have legal right-of-way, almost nobody behind the wheel respects it. In 1997 in Buenos Aires, 423 pedestrians died in traffic accidents – a figure roughly equal to the number of citations issued for failure to cede right-of way – for a rate approximately 10 times that of pedestrian traffic deaths in Paris or Madrid.

Other troublesome and even potentially deadly hazards include potholes and loose tiles on city sidewalks, which can also be slippery when wet – pedestrians have died after falling and striking their heads.

US residents concerned with domestic travel conditions in Argentina or any other country can obtain recorded travel information from the United States Department of State Bureau of Consular Affairs by calling ☎ 202-647-5225.

Police & Military

The police and military may be of more concern than common criminals. Both military and police officials have been found responsible for extrajudicial killings of prisoners and conscripts, for which some officials have gone to prison, but foreign visitors are more likely to experience petty harassment. For motorists, so-called safety campaigns often result in citations for very minor equipment violations, which ostensibly carry very high fines – up to US$200 for an inadequate emergency brake.

In most cases, corrupt officers will settle for less expensive *coimas* (bribes), but this requires considerable caution and tact on your part. A discreet hint that you intend to phone your consulate may limit or eliminate such problems – often the police count on foreigners' ignorance of Argentine law – or a feigned inability with Spanish may mean it's too much trouble for them. For further information, see the Getting Around chapter.

The military retains considerable autonomy despite civilian government. Avoid approaching military installations, which often display the warning, 'No stopping or photographs – the sentry will shoot.' Though a military coup or similar emergency may seem unlikely, state-of-siege regulations suspend all civil rights; carry identification at all times, and make sure someone knows your whereabouts. Contact your embassy or consulate for advice.

Fireworks

A recent cause for concern is the widespread availability of fireworks, which are high-powered, poorly regulated, and very dangerous. Especially around holidays like Christmas and New Year's, thoughtless fireworks enthusiasts set off firecrackers in the streets and even toss them from high-rise apartments (when these go off between tall buildings, the echo-chamber effect mimics the bombing of Hanoi). It may be better to refrain from walking the streets of Buenos Aires at these times.

Terrorism

The state terrorism of the 1970s and 1980s has subsided, but deadly attempts on Jewish/Israeli centers in Buenos Aires, the worst occurring in March 1992 and July 1994, have

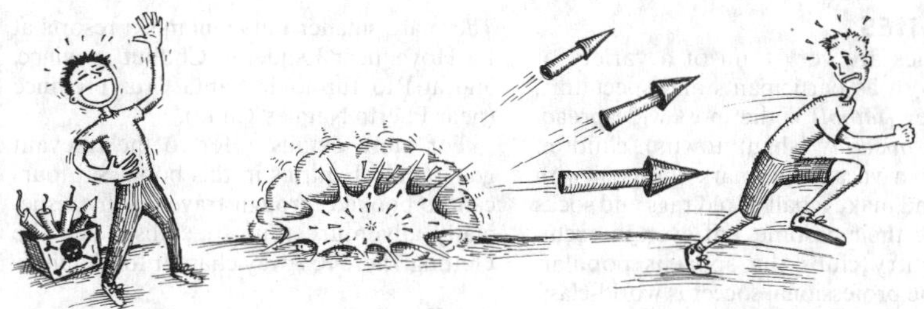

raised questions as to the government's commitment to public safety. In the months prior to the bombings, anti-Semitic incidents were increasingly common. As long as the government apparently remains disinterested in solving these crimes, terrorism will remain an issue.

Smoking

Many Argentines are heavy smokers – women as well as men – even though most will acknowledge the habit is unhealthy. If lung cancer is not the leading cause of death in the country, it's only because so many Argentines perish in traffic accidents first. In what might be the ultimate example of 'unclear on the concept,' the author once saw a porteño jogger with a lighted *pucho* in his mouth.

Long-distance and local buses, the Buenos Aires subway, and some other areas are legally smoke-free, even if enforcement is lax – moviegoers seem to think that the credits at the end of a film include orders to light up. Thanks to recent municipal legislation, many Buenos Aires restaurants and confiterías have set aside smoke-free areas.

Travelers bothered by secondhand smoke in an inappropriate setting, such as a taxi, will find it more productive to appeal to common courtesy by pleading that they have an *alergia* (allergy) rather than to act indignant.

BUSINESS HOURS

Traditionally, business hours in Argentina commence by 8 am and break at midday for three or even four hours, during which people return home for lunch and a brief siesta. After the siesta, shops reopen until 8 or 9 pm. This schedule is still common in the provinces, but government offices and many businesses in Buenos Aires have adopted a more conventional 8 am to 5 pm schedule in the interests of 'greater efficiency' and, especially in the case of government, reduced corruption.

PUBLIC HOLIDAYS & SPECIAL EVENTS

There are numerous national holidays on which government offices and businesses are closed. The following list of events does not include provincial holidays, which may vary considerably.

January 1
: Año Nuevo (New Year's Day)

March/April (dates vary)
: Viernes Santo/Pascua (Good Friday/Easter)

May 1
: Día del Trabajador (Labor Day)

May 25
: Revolución de Mayo (May Revolution of 1810)

June 10
: Día de las Malvinas (Malvinas Day, commemorating the establishment of the 'Comandancia Política y Militar de las Malvinas' in 1829)

June 20
: Día de la Bandera (Flag Day)

July 9
: Día de la Independencia (Independence Day, 1816)

August 17
: Día de San Martín (Anniversary of San Martín's death)

October 12
: Día de la Raza (Columbus Day)

December 25
: Navidad (Christmas Day)

ACTIVITIES

Argentines are very fond of a variety of sports, both as participants and spectators, but soccer *(fútbol)* is the most widespread. In *villas miserias* (shantytowns), children will clear a vacant lot, mark the goal with stones, and make a ball of old rags and socks to pursue their pastime, but even in exclusive country clubs the sport is popular. Argentine professional soccer is world-class, although many of the best athletes play in Europe because salaries there are higher. Argentina is almost always a World Cup contender and won the championship in 1978 (when it hosted the festivities in a politically charged environment) and 1986.

Other popular sports include tennis, auto racing, basketball, cycling, rugby, field hockey, and polo. Some of these, especially rugby and polo, are confined to elite sectors. Skiing, although expensive, is gaining popularity, as are other outdoor recreational activities, like canoeing, climbing, kayaking, trekking, windsurfing, and hang gliding. Paddle ball (a sort of hybrid between tennis and handball) has gained major popularity, with courts springing up around the country.

Skiing

Although surprisingly little-known to outsiders, Argentine skiing can be outstanding. Most locations offer superb powder, good cover, and plenty of sunny days, but prices are not cheap. Many fields are near large towns, so you don't even need to stay on the mountain but can stay cheaply nearby. Many resorts have large ski schools with instructors from all over the world, so even language is not a problem. At some of the older resorts equipment can be a little antiquated, but in general the quality of skiing more than compensates.

There are three main areas where skiers can indulge themselves: the southern Cuyo region, featuring Las Leñas and Los Molles near Malargüe; the lakes district, including the Cerro Catedral complex near Bariloche and Chapelco near San Martín de los Andes; and the world's most southerly commercial skiing near Ushuaia in Tierra del Fuego. There are smaller Patagonian ski resorts at La Hoya, near Esquel in Chubut province, and at Río Turbio, in Santa Cruz province (near Puerto Natales, Chile).

For more details, refer to the relevant geographical entries in this book. Ski tours can be booked through travel agents, especially adventure tour specialists; see the Getting There & Away chapter for details.

Cycling

Cycling has become one of the most popular participant activities in the country, and many Argentines make take long bike trips in summer. Both road and mountain bikes are common, but the latter are better for riding on bad roads in remote areas. For more information, see the Getting Around chapter.

Hiking

Argentina's vast open spaces offer plenty of wilderness walks for foreigners and Argentines alike. The most popular areas are the southern Andean national parks along the Chilean border, from Lanín south to Los Glaciares, and Tierra del Fuego, though the high Andean reaches around Aconcagua, west of Mendoza, are increasingly popular. The northern Andes around the Valle de Humahuaca are also good, but plenty of Argentines enjoy the gentler Sierra de la Ventana, in Buenos Aires province, and Sierras de Córdoba.

See the 2nd edition of LP's *Trekking in the Patagonian Andes* (1998) by Clem Lindenmayer for more information on southern Andean walks.

Mountaineering

Aconcagua, west of Mendoza, is a magnet for climbers, but there are plenty of other high peaks in the Andes – many of them more interesting than South America's highest point, which is a relatively straightforward walk up for experienced mountaineers in peak physical condition. The Fitzroy Range, in Parque Nacional Los Glaciares, Santa Cruz province, is another popular area, as are the mountains of Parque Nacional Nahuel Huapi, around Bariloche.

In southern Buenos Aires province, the Sierra de la Ventana is a good area for technical climbing, but provincial park rangers can be patronizing toward anyone interested in anything other than a simple hike.

Whitewater Rafting & Kayaking

This increasingly popular activity takes place on the rivers that descend from the Andean divide, from San Luis and Mendoza south into Chubut province. The main possibilities are the Río Mendoza and Río Diamante in the Cuyo region, the Río Hua Hum and Río Meliquina near San Martín de los Andes, and the Río Limay and Río Manso near Bariloche. Some of these, most notably the Limay, are gentle Class II floats, but most of the rest are Class III-plus whitewater.

Golf

Golf is an increasingly popular avocation with Argentina's leisured class; some clubs and courses are very elitist, but most are open to the public. For a complete list of courses in the country, contact the Asociación Argentina de Golf (☎ 4325-7498), Av Corrientes 538, 1043 Buenos Aires.

Polo

December's annual Campeonato Argentino Abierto de Polo (Argentine Open Polo Championship), held in the Buenos Aires barrio of Palermo, celebrated its centenary in 1993. Participation is not exactly for the masses, but most polo events are open to the public free of charge; for current information, contact the Asociación Argentina de Polo (☎ 4331-4646), Hipólito Yrigoyen 636 in Buenos Aires, which keeps a list of activities scheduled throughout the country.

La Picaza, at Guido 1923 in Recoleta (☎ 4804-8267) and at Av Callao 1423 in Barrio Norte (☎ 4801-1887), carries what is probably the best selection of polo equipment and souvenirs in Buenos Aires. Shoppers interested in polo gear can also visit La Polera (☎ 4806-0586), Uriburu 1710, or La Martina (☎ 4478-9366), Paraguay 661, which also organizes full-day polo lessons (with afternoon matches) on the outskirts of the capital.

Rugby

Rugby, like soccer, traces its origins to English influence, but is popular as an amateur participant sport rather than a professional activity – even the asthmatic Ernesto 'Che' Guevara was an enthusiastic rugby player during his youth in Córdoba. The national team, the Pumas, plays the best international competition.

LANGUAGE COURSES

Buenos Aires offers many opportunities for Spanish-language instruction. Consult the Sunday classified section of the *Buenos Aires Herald*, which offers several columns' worth of possibilities, including individual tutoring and even opportunities for teaching English. The *Herald* also publishes an occasional education supplement that details a variety of learning alternatives, primarily but not exclusively oriented toward Spanish-speakers wishing to learn English.

Before signing up for a course, read the description carefully, note all fees, and try to determine whether it suits your particular needs. Remember that small-group instruction or individual tutoring offer the best opportunities for improving language skills, but the latter is usually considerably more expensive.

WORK

It's not unusual for visiting travelers to work as English-language instructors in Buenos Aires, but wages are much lower than they would be in the US or UK, and it takes time to build up enough clientele to make it worthwhile. Check the classified section of the *Buenos Aires Herald*. Residence and work permits are fairly easy to obtain, but the effort may not be worth it.

Street artists, including musicians and mimes, are common in Buenos Aires, but there's so much competition that anyone without a distinctive skill will have a hard time earning his or her way.

Travelers can obtain work during the fruit harvests in areas like Río Negro Valley and El Bolsón in northern Patagonia, but wages are so low that you shouldn't expect to do much more than break even.

Ideally, in Argentina and the rest of Latin America, there should be work for someone who can mend the fractured English that so often appears in tourist brochures.

ACCOMMODATIONS

The spectrum of accommodations in Argentina ranges from campgrounds to five-star luxury hotels. Where you stay will depend on your budget, standards, and your location, as well as how thorough a search you care to make in an unfamiliar destination, but you should be able to find something reasonable by North American, European, or Australian criteria. You may also find yourself invited into Argentine homes and should not hesitate to accept under most conditions.

Note that, in many circumstances, tourist offices are reluctant to recommend budget accommodations or even to admit that they exist. This is partly because some of the cheapest accommodations can be pretty squalid, but mostly because the staff have the idea that foreigner visitors should stay in *hoteles de categoría*, the best available (and usually very expensive) lodging. Often, with gentle persistence, you can extract information on more economical alternatives.

Hotel checkout times vary but are often as early as 10 am and rarely later than noon. While most places are flexible within reason, some will add on an extra day; it's a good idea to verify each hotel's policy and to give advance notice if you need extra time.

Many establishments offer *media pensión* (half-board, meaning breakfast and lunch or dinner) or *pensión completa* (full board, all three meals) for an additional charge.

Camping & Refugios

If traveling on a budget, especially coming overland from the central Andean countries, do not dismiss the idea of camping in Argentina – by doing so, you may be able to keep expenses for accommodations at roughly what you would pay for hotels in Bolivia or Peru. Nearly every Argentine city and many smaller towns have municipal (or recently privatized) campgrounds, where you can pitch a tent for about US$5 per night – sometimes more, sometimes less, occasionally even free. Most Argentines arrive in their own automobiles, but backpackers are welcome.

These usually woodsy sites have excellent facilities – hot showers, toilets, laundry, a *fogón* (firepit) for cooking, a restaurant or *confitería* (café), a grocery, sometimes even a swimming pool – and are often very central. Personal possessions are generally secure, since attendants keep a watchful eye on the grounds, but don't leave cash or costly items like cameras lying around unnecessarily.

There are drawbacks, though. Argentines are renowned *trasnochadores* (night people). During summer vacation, it is not unusual for them to celebrate their *asado* (barbecue) until almost daylight, so in extreme cases you may find sleep difficult unless you can isolate yourself on the margins of the campground – often the least-appealing areas. On the other hand, you may be invited to join in one of these gregarious groups. Otherwise, avoid the most popular tourist areas in the prime vacation months of January and February.

For comfort, invest in a good, dome-style tent with rainfly before coming to South America, where camping equipment is costlier and often inferior. A three-season sleeping bag should be adequate for almost any weather conditions. A good petrol or kerosene-burning stove is also a good idea, since white gas *(bencina)* is expensive and available only at chemical supply shops or hardware stores. Firewood is a limited and often expensive resource, which, in any event, smudges pots and pans. Bring or buy mosquito repellent, since many campsites are near rivers or lakes.

There are, of course, opportunities for more rugged camping in the national parks and their backcountry. Parks have both organized sites resembling those in the cities and towns, and more isolated, rustic alternatives. Some parks have *refugios*, basic shelters for hikers in the high country. For details, see the entries under the respective national parks.

Hostels

There are several youth hostels in Buenos Aires (Capital Federal) and throughout the provinces. Most do not insist on a youth hostel card, but they usually charge a bit more for nonmembers. Since many hostels are generally open in summer only, especially in the provinces, it's a good idea to phone before heading over.

Argentina's two competing hostel organizations, both based in Buenos Aires, are the Red Argentina de Alojamiento para Jóvenes (RAAJ; ☎ 4511-8712, fax 4312-0089; raaj@hostels.org.ar), 3rd floor, Oficina 319B, and the Asociación Argentina de Albergues de la Juventud (AAAJ; ☎ 4476-1001), Talcahuano 214, 2nd floor. See Hostel Card under Visas & Documents, earlier in this chapter.

RAAJ and AAAJ hostels overlap jurisdictions, but the former has a smaller and generally better list than the AAAJ. A few hostel-style places belong to neither system, but some of these are nevertheless very good.

RAAJ affiliates are in the following provinces: Salta (capital); Jujuy (Tilcara); Misiones (Puerto Iguazú); Entre Ríos (Villa Paranacito); Mendoza (capital, Guaymallén, San Rafael); Córdoba (Villa Carlos Paz); Río Negro (Bariloche, El Bolsón); Chubut (Puerto Madryn, Esquel); Santa Cruz (El Calafate, El Chaltén); and Tierra del Fuego (Ushuaia).

AAAJ affiliates are in the following provinces: Buenos Aires (Tigre, Pinamar, Mar del Plata, San Bernardo); Córdoba (Villa General Belgrano, Villa Carlos Paz, Capilla del Monte, Cura Brochero); Mendoza (Guaymallén); Río Negro (Bariloche, El Bolsón); Chubut (Esquel, Puerto Madryn, Comodoro Rivadavia); Santa Cruz (El Calafate, El Chaltén, Puerto Deseado); Misiones (Puerto Iguazú); Jujuy (Humahuaca, Tilcara); Salta (capital); and Tucumán (capital).

Hospedajes, Pensiones & Residenciales

These offer cheap accommodations but the differences between them are sometimes ambiguous; all may even be called hotels. Rooms and furnishings are modest, usually including beds with clean sheets and blankets. Never hesitate to ask to see a room. While some have private bathrooms, more often you will share toilet and shower facilities with other guests.

An *hospedaje* is usually a large family home with a few extra bedrooms (the bath is shared). Often they are not permanent businesses but temporary expedients in times of economic distress. Similarly, a *pensión* offers short-term accommodations in a family home but may also have permanent lodgers. Meals may be available.

Residenciales, which are permanent businesses, figure more commonly in tourist office lists. In general, they occupy buildings designed for short-stay accommodations, although some (known euphemistically as *albergues transitorios)* cater to clientele who intend only *very* short stays – two hours maximum. Occasionally prostitutes frequent them, but so do young Argentine couples with no other indoor alternative for their passion. It's not always obvious whether a place is an albergue transitorio, though some are very candid about their business; except for a little noise, such activities should not deter you, even if you have children.

Hotels

Hotels proper vary from utilitarian one-star accommodations to five-star luxury, but do not assume a perfect correlation between these classifications and their standards – many one-star places are a better value than three- and four-star lodgings. In general, hotels provide a room with attached private bath, often a telephone, and sometimes *música funcional* (Muzak) or television. Normally they have a confitería or restaurant and may include breakfast in the price. In the top categories you will have room and laundry service, a swimming pool, and perhaps a gym, a bar, shopping galleries, plus other luxuries.

Rentals & Homestays

House and apartment rentals can save you money if you're staying in a place for an extended period. In resort locations, such as Mar del Plata, Bariloche, or Paso de la Patria, you can lodge several people for the price of one by seeking an apartment and cooking your own meals. Check tourist offices or newspapers for listings. In some cases, individuals with places to rent frequent the bus terminal or line the main thoroughfare into town.

During the tourist season, mostly in the interior, families rent rooms to visitors. Often these are excellent bargains, permitting access to cooking and laundry facilities and hot showers, as well as encouraging contact with Argentines. Tourist offices in most smaller towns, but even in cities as large as Salta and Mendoza, maintain lists of such accommodations.

Estancias

An increasingly popular way of passing an Argentine vacation is to stay at an estancia, both in the area around Buenos Aires and even in remotest Patagonia. Many estancias that have only recently begun to take guests are barely prepared for a regular tourist influx and may even boot their own children out of bed to accommodate them.

FOOD

There are different kinds of eating places in Argentina. If you're on a very low budget in the northern provinces, you may want to frequent the markets, where meals are often very cheap, but otherwise try the *rotiserías* (delis), which sell dairy products, roast chicken, pies, turnovers, and *fiambres* (processed meats). Such places often have restaurant-quality food for a fraction of the price.

Avoid fast-food clones such as *Pumper Nic*, which are neither as cheap nor even as good as their admittedly awful North American cousins. For fast food, try the bus or train terminal cafeterias or the common *comedor*, which usually has a limited menu, often including simple but filling fixed-price meals. Comedores also often serve *minutas* (short orders), such as steak, eggs, *milanesa* (breaded steak), salad, and french fries.

Confiterías serve mostly sandwiches, including *lomito* (steak), *panchos* (hot dogs), and hamburgers. *Restaurantes* are distinguished by much larger menus – including pasta dishes, *parrillada* (barbecue), and fish – professional waiters, and often more elaborate decor. There is, though, a great difference between the most humble and the most extravagant.

Restaurant meals are generally relaxed affairs. Breakfasts are negligible, but other meals can last for hours. Lunch starts around midday, but dinner starts later, much later, than in English-speaking countries. Almost nobody eats before 9 pm, and it's not unusual to dine after midnight even on weeknights.

An important part of the meal, whether at home or in the restaurant, is the *sobremesa*, dallying at the table to discuss family matters or other events of the day. No matter how long the lines outside, no Argentine restaurateur would even dream of nudging along a party that has lingered over coffee long after the food itself is history.

The Argentine Diet

Ever since Spanish livestock transformed the Pampas into enormous cattle ranches, the Argentine diet has relied on meat, but there is more ethnic and regional variety to Argentine cuisine than most people expect. The Andean Northwest is notable for spicy dishes, more closely resembling the food of the central Andean highlands than the bland fare of the Pampas. From Mendoza north, Middle Eastern food is commonplace.

Argentine seafood, while less varied than Chilean, deserves attention, even though Argentines are not big fish-eaters. In the Patagonian lake district, game dishes like trout, boar, and venison are regional specialties, while river fish in Mesopotamia and Misiones are outstanding. In the extreme south, where sheep graze the drier pastures, lamb often replaces beef in the typical asado.

Beef, though, is the focus of the diet; no meal is truly complete without it. Here, in fact, the Spanish word *carne* (meat) is synonymous with beef – lamb, venison, and poultry are all something else. Since the early 1980s, health food and vegetarian fare have won a niche in the diets of some Argentines, but outside Buenos Aires and a few other large cities vegetarian restaurants are less common. You will find Chinese food in the capital but not often elsewhere; the quality is not outstanding but some offer *tenedor libre* or *diente libre* (all you can eat) for those on a budget. High-cost and high-quality international cuisine is readily available if your budget is unlimited.

Snacks

One of the world's finest snacks is the *empanada*, a tasty turnover filled with vegetables, hard-boiled egg, olive, beef, chicken, ham, and cheese, or other fillings. These are cheap and available almost everywhere – buy them by the dozen in a *rotisería* before a long bus or train trip. Empanadas *al horno* (baked) are lighter than empanadas *fritas* (fried). Travelers coming from Chile will find Argentine empanadas very different.

Pizza, a common snack in markets and restaurants, is one of the cheapest things on the menu when purchased by the slice. In many *pizzerías*, it is cheaper to eat standing at the counter than to take a seat. Toppings are standardized – not customized as in North America – but there are more options when buying an entire pizza rather than slices. If an entire pizza is too large, it's worth asking if they'll prepare a half pizza). For slices, try *fugazza*, a delicious cheeseless variety with sweet onions that is very cheap, or *fugazzeta*, which adds cheese. Mozzarella is the most popular cheese. Many Argentines eat their pizza with *fainá*, a dense chickpea (garbanzo) dough baked and sliced to match.

For Argentines at home or on the road, a common afternoon snack is *mate con facturas*, mate with sweet pastries. If you go to visit an Argentine family in the afternoon, stop by the bakery to bring some along.

Breakfast

Argentines eat little or no breakfast. The most common breakfast items are coffee, tea, or *yerba mate* with *tostadas* (toast), *manteca* (butter), and *mermelada* (jam). In cafés, *medialunas* (small croissants), either sweet or *saladas* (plain), accompany your *café con leche* (coffee with milk). A mid-morning breakfast may consist of coffee plus a *tostado*, a thin-crust toasted sandwich with ham and cheese, and a glass of fresh-squeezed orange juice.

Main Dishes

Argentines compensate for skimpy breakfasts with enormous lunches, usually begun about noon or 1 pm, and dinners, never earlier than 9 pm and often much later. Beef, in a variety of cuts and styles of preparation, is the most common main course.

The most popular form is the *asado* or *parrillada*, a mixed grill of steak and other cuts, which is ideally prepared over charcoal or a wood fire and accompanied by *chimichurri*, a tasty marinade. A traditional parrillada also includes offal-like *chinchulines* (small intestines), *tripa gorda* (large intestine), *ubre* (udder), *riñones* (kidneys), and *morcilla* (blood sausage), but don't let that

Meatless Meals in Cattle Country

Argentine cuisine is known for red meat, but vegetarians no longer have much trouble making do except, perhaps, in the most out-of-the-way places. Since the 1980s, vegetarian restaurants have become commonplace in Buenos Aires and not unusual elsewhere, and nearly all of them have the additional appeal of being tobacco-free.

Even standard parrillas serve items acceptable to most vegetarians, such as green salads (often large enough for two people) and pasta dishes, like raviolis, *canelones* (cannelloni), and *ñoquis* (gnocchi) – but before ordering pasta be certain it doesn't come with a meat sauce. To be served a meatless dish in out of the way places, try pleading allergies and remember that *carne* (meat) is beef – chicken, pork, and the like are something else, though sometimes referred to as *carne blanca* (white meat). Vegans will find far fewer menu options.

Breaking Your Diet

Ice cream first appeared in Argentina in the mid-19th century when, in the absence of freezers, blocks of ice were shipped to Buenos Aires from Europe and the United States. In the province of Tucumán, ice was brought by fast riders from Cerro Aconquija – and they must have been very fast, given Tucumán's overpowering summer heat.

The Italian tradition has made Argentine *helado* (ice cream) the continent's best and comparable to the finest anywhere else in the world. Chains like *Massera*, located throughout the country, are not bad, but the best Argentine ice cream comes from smaller *heladerías*, which make their own in small batches on the premises or nearby – look for the words *elaboración propia* or *elaboración artesanal*. Such places often have dozens of flavors, from variations on conventional vanilla and chocolate to common and exotic fruits and unexpected mixtures. During winter, when Argentines rarely eat ice cream, the best heladerías often close.

Rarely will Argentine ice cream disappoint you, but only truly special shops are mentioned in the text. When restaurant desserts seem a bit expensive, a quarter kilo is a relatively economical alternative, especially when shared.

put you off unless you're a vegetarian. French fries or salad will usually accompany the parrillada.

Serious carnivores should not miss *bife de chorizo*, a thick, tender, juicy steak. *Bife de lomo* is short loin, *bife de costilla* or *chuleta* is T-bone steak, while *asado de tira* is a narrow strip of roast rib. *Vacío* is sirloin. *Matambre relleno* is stuffed and rolled flank steak, baked or eaten cold as an appetizer. Thinly sliced, it makes excellent sandwiches and is usually available at rotiserías.

Most Argentines prefer their beef *cocido* (well done), but on request restaurants will serve it *jugoso* (rare) or *a punto* (medium). *Bife a caballo* comes with two eggs and french fries.

Carbonada is a beef stew with rice, potatoes, sweet potatoes, maize, squash, chopped apples, and peaches. *Puchero* is a slow-cooking casserole with beef, chicken, bacon, sausage, blood sausage, maize, peppers, tomatoes, onions, cabbage, sweet potatoes, and squash; the cook may also add garbanzos or other beans. It is accompanied by rice cooked in the broth. *Milanesa*, a breaded steak, usually fried but sometimes baked, is one of the cheapest and most common short-order items on the menu. More elaborate versions are available: *milanesa napolitana* with tomato sauce and mozzarella, and *milanesa maryland*, made with chicken and accompanied by fried bananas and creamed corn.

Pollo (chicken) sometimes accompanies the standard parrillada, but also comes separately with french fries or salad. The most common fish is *merluza* (hake), usually fried in batter and served with mashed potatoes. Spanish restaurants are good for well-prepared seafood.

Most people will quickly recognize the influence of Italian immigrants in such pasta dishes as spaghetti, lasagna, cannelloni, and ravioli, but should not overlook the tasty *ñoquis* (gnocchi in Italian), an inexpensive staple when the budget runs low at the end of the month. Traditionally, ñoquis are a restaurant special on the 29th of each month, but in times of economic crisis people may joke that 'this month we'll have ñoquis on the 15th.'

Desserts

Fresh fruit is the most common *postre* in Argentine homes, where uncouth Americans and Australians will find that cultured Argentines peel oranges and all other fruit (except grapes) carefully with a knife. In restaurants, *ensalada de fruta* (fruit salad), *flan* (egg custard), or *queso y dulce* (cheese with preserved fruit, sometimes known as *postre vigilante)* are frequent choices. The 'dulce' can consist of *batata* (sweet potato) or *membrillo* (quince). Flan will be topped with *crema* (whipped cream) or *dulce de leche*, a sweet caramelized milk that is an Argentine specialty. *Almendrado*, vanilla ice cream rolled in almonds, is also common.

DRINKS

Everything from marriage proposals to business transactions to revolutions may start in cafés, where many Argentines spend hours on end over a single cup of coffee. Cafés also serve beer, wine, and hard liquor.

Bars are where people go to drink alcohol. In large cities, gentrified bars may be called pubs (pronounced as in English). In small towns, bars are a male domain, and the few women who frequent them are likely to be prostitutes.

The most famous and distinct Argentine drink is *mate*, a cultural bellwether. There are few drinking restrictions of any kind, although legally you must be 18 years old to drink alcohol in public.

Soft Drinks

Argentines drink prodigious amounts of soft drinks, from the ubiquitous Coca-Cola to 7UP to the local tonic water, Paso de los Toros, which is probably your best choice. Mineral water, both carbonated *(con gas)* and plain *(sin gas)*, is widely available, but tap water is potable almost everywhere. If there is no carbonated mineral water, ask for *soda*, which in small-town cafés and restaurants comes in large siphon bottles. Soda is usually the cheapest thirst quencher.

Juice

Jugos are not so varied as in tropical South America. For fresh-squeezed orange juice, ask for *jugo de naranja exprimido* – otherwise you may get tinned juice (oranges are very cheap in Argentina but, when turned into fresh juice, their value miraculously increases tenfold). *Pomelo* (grapefruit), *limón* (lemon), and *ananá* (pineapple) are also common. *Jugo de manzana* (apple juice) is a specialty of the Río Negro region of Patagonia, but it's available everywhere.

Licuados are milk-blended fruit drinks, but on request can be made with water. Common flavors are banana, *durazno* (peach), and *pera* (pear).

Coffee, Tea & Hot Chocolate

Caffeine junkies will be delighted to learn that even in the smallest town, their fix will be an espresso (accompanied by enough packets of sugar to fuel a Brazilian Volkswagen). *Café chico* is a thick, dark coffee served in a very small cup. *Cortado* is a small coffee with a touch of milk, usually served in a glass – for a larger portion ask for *cortado doble*. *Café con leche* (a latte) is similar but contains more milk, and is served for breakfast – don't make the mistake of ordering it after lunch or dinner in a restaurant, when you should request a cortado.

Tea, produced domestically in Corrientes and Misiones provinces, is also a common drink. Usually it comes with lemon slices, but if you drink it with milk, do not order *té con leche*, a tea bag immersed in warm milk. Rather, ask the waiter for *un poquito de leche* after being served.

Argentine hot chocolate can be delicious. For breakfast, try a *submarino*, a semisweet chocolate bar dissolved in a glass of steamed milk. Prices vary greatly. Even *chocolate*, made with powdered cocoa, can be surprisingly good, especially in Bariloche.

Alcoholic Drinks

Beer, wine, whiskey, and gin should satisfy most visitors' alcoholic thirst, but don't refrain from *ginebra bols* (which differs from gin) and *caña* (cane alcohol), both national specialties.

Quilmes, brewed in the Buenos Aires suburb but available everywhere, is an excellent beer. Bieckert is another popular brand. In bars or cafés, ask for the excellent *chopp* (draft or lager).

Argentine wines get less publicity abroad than Chilean ones, but *tintos* (reds) and *blancos* (whites) are both excellent and inexpensive (when prices on almost everything else skyrocket, wines miraculously remain reasonable, and a bottle of good wine may be cheaper than a liter of Coca-Cola). Especially at home, where jug wines are present at almost all meals, Argentines often mix their wine with soda water.

Wineries in the major growing areas, near Mendoza, San Juan, La Rioja, and Salta,

Mate & Its Ritual

No other trait captures the essence of *argentinidad* ('argentinity') as well as the preparation and consumption of mate (pronounced **mah**tay), perhaps the only cultural practice that transcends barriers of ethnicity, class, and occupation. More than a simple drink like tea or coffee, mate is an elaborate ritual, shared among family, friends, and coworkers. In many ways, sharing is the whole point.

Yerba mate is the dried, chopped leaf of *Ilex paraguayensis*, a relative of the common holly. Also known as 'Paraguayan tea,' it became commercially important during the colonial era on the plantations of the Jesuit missions in the upper Río Paraná. Europeans quickly took to the beverage, crediting it with many admirable qualities. The Austrian Jesuit Martin Dobrizhoffer wrote that mate 'provokes a gentle perspiration, improves the appetite, speedily counteracts the languor arising from the burning climate, and assuages both hunger and thirst.' Unlike many American foods and beverages, though, mate failed to make the trip back to Europe. After the Jesuits' expulsion in 1767, production declined, but it has increased dramatically since the early 20th century.

Argentina is the world's single largest producer and consumer of yerba mate. Argentines consume an average of 5kg per person per year, more than four times their average intake of coffee (although Uruguayans consume twice as much per capita as Argentines). It is also popular in parts of Chile, in southern Brazil, and in Paraguay.

Preparing mate is a ritual in itself. In the past, upper-class families even maintained a slave or servant whose sole responsibility was preparing and serving it. Nowadays, one person takes responsibility for filling the mate (gourd) almost to the top with yerba, heating but not boiling the water in a *pava* (kettle), and pouring it into the vessel. People sip the liquid from a *bombilla*, a silver straw with a bulbous filter at its lower end that prevents the leaves from entering the tube.

Gourds can range from simple calabashes to carved wooden vessels to the ornate silver museum pieces of the 19th century. Bombillas also differ considerably, ranging in materials

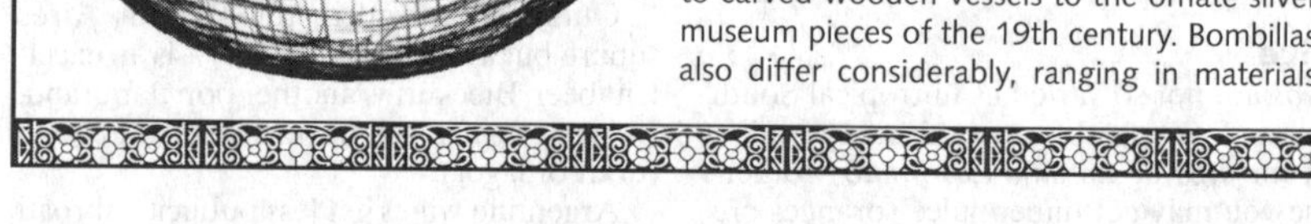

offer tours and tastings. Among the best-known brands are Orfila, Suter, San Felipe, Santa Ana, and Etchart. Try to avoid cheap boxed wines like Termidor.

ENTERTAINMENT

Argentines are fond of music and dancing. Dance clubs both in Buenos Aires and the provinces open late and close even later – nobody goes before midnight, and things don't really jump until 2 am. After sunrise, when the clubs close, partygoers head to a confitería or home for breakfast before collapsing in their beds. This is nearly as common on weekdays as on weekends. Recorded rather than live music is the norm.

Except in Buenos Aires, where there are good tango, rock, and jazz clubs, nightclubs tend to be disreputable places. Places listed in the *Buenos Aires Herald* as nightclubs are usually the more respectable ones; but in a Spanish context, the word 'nightclub' tends

Mate & Its Ritual

from inexpensive aluminum to silver and gold with intricate markings, and in design from long straight tubes to short curved ones.

There is an informal etiquette for drinking mate. The *cebador* (server) pours water slowly near the straw to produce a froth as he or she fills the gourd. The gourd then passes clockwise and this order, once established, continues. A good cebador will keep the mate going without changing the yerba for some time. Each participant drinks the gourd dry each time. A simple *gracias* will tell the server to pass you by.

There are marked regional differences in drinking mate. From the Pampas southward, Argentines take it *amargo* (without sugar), while to the north they drink it *dulce* (sweet) with sugar and *yuyos* (aromatic herbs). Purists, who argue that sugar ruins the gourd, will keep separate gourds rather than alternate the two usages. In summer, Paraguayans drink mate ice-cold as *tereré*.

Another style of mate is mate cocido, prepared as a weaker boiled infusion in a teacup (it is possible to purchase this in teabags). One of Argentina's best ice creameries, Heladería Jauja, with branches in Bariloche, Esquel, and El Bolsón, serves an improbable but remarkably tasty *mate cocido* flavor that even most Argentines find a little unusual.

An invitation to mate is a sign of acceptance and should not be refused, even though mate is an acquired taste and novices may find it bitter and very hot at first. On the second or third round, both the heat and bitterness will diminish. It is poor etiquette to hold the mate too long before passing it on. Drinking it is unlikely to affect either your health or finances despite Dobrizhoffer's warning:

> . . . by the immoderate and almost hourly use of this potation, the stomach is weakened, and continual flatulence, with other diseases, brought on. I have known many of the lower Spaniards who never spoke ten words without applying their lips to the gourd containing the ready-made tea. If many topers in Europe waste their substance by an immoderate use of wine and other intoxicating liquors, there are no fewer in America who drink away their fortunes in potations of the herb of Paraguay.

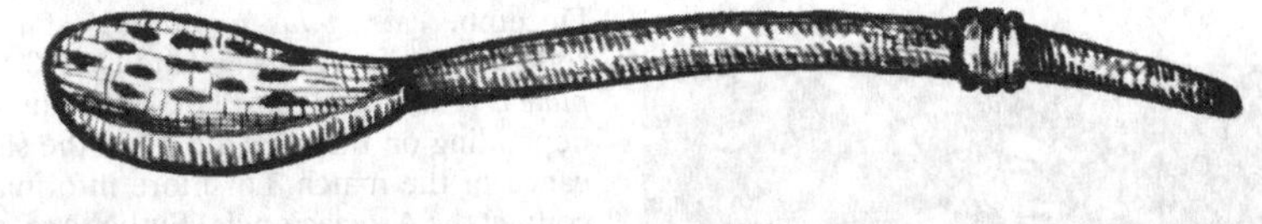

to imply a fairly seedy place with bar girls who are thinly disguised prostitutes.

Traditionally, Argentines jam the cinemas, although outside Buenos Aires the video revolution has meant the closure of many theaters that once counted on being the only show in town. Still, in the capital and larger cities, major theaters offer the latest films from Europe, the US, and the rest of Latin America. Repertory houses, cultural centers, and universities provide a chance to see classics or less-commercial films you may have missed.

In Buenos Aires, the main cinema districts are along Lavalle, Av Corrientes, and Av Santa Fe, and the inner suburb of Belgrano. Prices have risen in recent years and now match those in North America or Europe, but most cinemas offer substantial discounts midweek. On weekends, there are *transnoches* (late-night showings) around or after midnight.

Both in Buenos Aires and the provinces, live theater is well attended and high quality, from the classics and serious drama to burlesque. Av Corrientes is Buenos Aires' Broadway or West End, but even in places like Villa Regina, a small town in Río Negro province, there are several active theater groups and venues for performances.

There are two main types of theater: a well-supported official theater and a more underground type that improvises and operates on a shoestring budget, often performing in public places like parks and plazas, or even in rented houses. Despite their limited budgets, these productions can be surprisingly professional.

SPECTATOR SPORTS

Spectator sports are limited primarily to soccer, horse racing, polo, and boxing, though tennis, rugby, cricket, basketball, and Formula One automobile racing have their adherents (visiting pedestrians and drivers may conclude that most Argentine drivers consider themselves Formula One competitors). Among the best-known Argentine athletes and sports figures are soccer legend Diego Maradona, tennis stars Guillermo Vilas and Gabriela Sabatini, the late boxers Oscar Bonavena and Carlos Monzón, and ex-Formula One standout Carlos Reutemann, now a Peronist politician in the province of Santa Fe.

Diego Maradona

By any standard, Argentine soccer is world-class – the national team won the World Cup in 1978 (at home) and 1986, and made the quarter-finals at Paris in 1998. Buenos Aires has the highest density of first-division soccer teams in the world – eight of the country's 20 are based in the capital, with another five in the suburbs of Gran Buenos Aires.

Argentine fans are no less rabid than in Europe, and violence has become an unfortunate byproduct in a country whose *barras bravas* are the equivalent of British 'football hooligans.' Then again, it may just be the frustration of having paid extortionate prices to watch 90 minutes of apparently vigorous exercise that always seems to end in a scoreless tie.

Club officials themselves apparently contribute to the problem by giving their barras free tickets and transport, encouraging confrontations between fans of arch rivals (visitors should take special caution *not* to wear colors of the opposing teams; neutral single colors like black or tan would be best). In early 1998, a Buenos Aires judge briefly suspended all matches because of the clubs' failure to control fan disorder.

The season extends from March to December. *Entradas populares* (standing-room admission) costs around US$10, while *plateas* (fixed seats) cost US$20 and upward, depending on their location and the significance of the match. For more information, contact the Asociación del Fútbol Argentino (☎ 4371-4276), at Viamonte 1366, Buenos Aires.

For an account of soccer's development and history in the Southern Cone, see British sociologist Tony Mason's brief and rather misleadingly titled *Soccer in South America*, which deals almost exclusively with Argentina, Uruguay, and Brazil (London, Verso, 1994). Uruguayan writer Eduardo Galeano has recently published *Soccer in Sun & Shadow* (Verso, 1998), which contains many observations on Argentine soccer.

SHOPPING

As Argentine food is famous for beef, so Argentine clothing is famous for leather. In Buenos Aires, many downtown shops cater to the tourist trade in leather jackets, handbags, and shoes. Quality and prices can vary greatly, so shop around before buying. Shopkeepers are aggressive but sometimes open to bargaining.

Argentines are very fashion-conscious, with the latest styles displayed along Florida and Santa Fe in Buenos Aires and on main shopping streets in cities throughout the country. Bariloche is especially well known for woolen goods. The best prices are available just before seasonal changes, as shops try to liquidate their inventory. Jewelry is another quality Argentine product, made frequently with 18-karat gold.

Mate paraphernalia make good souvenirs. Gourds and bombillas range from simple and inexpensive aluminum, often sold in street kiosks, to elaborate and expensive gold and silver from jewelry stores or specialty shops. In the province of Salta, the distinctive *ponchos de Güemes* are a memorable choice.

In artisans' *ferias*, found throughout the country, the variety of handicrafts is extensive. There are good places in Buenos Aires (San Telmo's Plaza Dorrego, Recoleta's Plaza Francia, and Belgrano's Plaza General Belgrano), Mendoza, Bariloche, and El Bolsón. In the summer, the Atlantic Coast has many others.

Argentines are well read and interested in both national and world literature, and Buenos Aires has a superb selection of general- and special-interest bookstores. Since the end of the military dictatorship, the capital has re-established itself as a publishing center; April's Feria Internacional del Libro (book fair) is South America's largest, with over 600 exhibitors drawing more than a million visitors.

Foreign and foreign-language books tend to be very expensive, but there's a good selection (including this and other Lonely Planet guides) at Buenos Aires' better bookstores and, occasionally, those in the interior.

Getting There & Away

AIR

Argentina enjoys excellent air connections from North America, Europe, the UK, Australia, and New Zealand; from southern Africa across the Atlantic directly and via Brazil; and from all South American countries except the Guianas. Alternately, travelers can fly to a neighboring country, such as Chile or Brazil, and continue overland to Argentina. Be aware that international flights within South America tend to be costly unless purchased for intercontinental travel, though limited student and discount fares are available. One-way international tickets are usually very expensive.

Some travelers wishing to visit widely separated regions (ie, from Asia to South America) take advantage of Round-the-World (RTW) fares on the same trip. One possibility is the Qantas/Aerolíneas Argentinas ticket that lets you circle the globe with stops in New Zealand, Europe, and Southeast Asia. Similar fares are also available on other airlines.

Airports & Airlines

Buenos Aires' Aeropuerto Internacional Ministro Pistarini (more commonly known as Ezeiza) is the main international airport. Some regional flights use the more convenient Aeropuerto Jorge Newbery, commonly known as Aeroparque, which is due to be phased out over the next several years (though probably not during the life of this book). What will replace Aeroparque is as yet uncertain.

Airports in several provincial capitals and tourist destinations also enjoy international status, though far fewer flights use them. Among them are Jujuy, Salta, Tucumán, Mendoza, Puerto Iguazú, Córdoba, Rosario, Bariloche, Río Gallegos, and Ushuaia. In addition, border-hopping carriers sometimes serve Chile from Neuquén.

Major international airlines serving Argentina include: Aeroflot, AeroContinente, Air France, Alitalia, American Airlines, Aerolíneas Argentinas, Avianca, British Airways, Canadian Airlines, Cubana, Ecuatoriana, Iberia, Japan Airlines, KLM, LanChile, Lloyd Aéreo Boliviano (LAB), Lufthansa, Malaysia Airlines, Pluna, Qantas, South Africa Airways, Swissair, Transportes Aéreos Mercosur (TAM), TAP (Air Portugal), TransBrasil, United Airlines, Varig, and VASP.

Buying Tickets

From almost everywhere, South America is a relatively costly destination, but discount fares can reduce the bite considerably. In addition to a straightforward round-trip ticket, a ticket to Argentina can also be part of a Round-the-World ticket. There are often significant seasonal discounts, so try to avoid peak travel times, which include the month of December, the summer months, and religious and patriotic holidays. It's best to consult individual airlines about these holidays because dates can vary.

The plane ticket will probably be the single most expensive item in your budget, and buying it can be intimidating. It is always worth putting aside a few hours to research the current state of the market. Start shopping for a ticket early – some of the cheapest tickets must be purchased months in advance, and some popular flights sell out early. Also talk to other recent travelers – they just might be able to stop you from making some of the same old mistakes. Look at the ads in newspapers and magazines, consult reference books, and watch for special offers.

Airlines can supply information on routes and timetables, but they do not supply the cheapest tickets except during fare wars and the competitive low season. Travel agents are usually a better source of bargains. Whether you go directly through an airline or use an agent, always ask the representative to clarify the fare, the route, the duration of the journey, and any restrictions on the ticket.

One of the cheapest means of getting to South America is via a courier flight, in which a traveler trades all or part of her/his baggage allowance for a highly discounted fare and agrees to accompany business equipment or documents. The major drawbacks to this, in addition to having baggage limited to carry-on items, are the relatively short travel period and the very limited number of gateway airports in Europe and North America.

Most major airlines have ticket 'consolidators' offering substantial discounts on fares to Latin America, but things change so frequently that even weekly newspaper listings are soon out of date. Among the best sources of information on cheap tickets are the travel pages of major newspapers such as *The New York Times*, *Los Angeles Times*, and *San Francisco Examiner* for US departures, and Australia's *Sydney Morning Herald* and *The Age*. Similar listings are available in the travel sections of magazines such as *Time Out* and *TNT* in the UK. Ads in university newspapers and other local publications also offer cheap fares, but don't be surprised if they happen to be sold out when you contact the agents – they're usually low-season fares on obscure airlines with many conditions attached.

You may decide to pay more than the rock-bottom fare by opting for the safety of a better known travel agent. Established firms like STA Travel, which has offices worldwide, Council Travel in the USA, and Travel CUTS in Canada are valid alternatives and they offer good prices to most destinations (see individual country headings for a list of offices).

Cheap tickets are available in two distinct categories: official and consolidator. Official ones have a variety of names, including advance-purchase fares, budget fares, APEX (advance purchase excursion) and Super-APEX. Consolidator tickets are simply discounted tickets that the airlines release through selected travel agents (not through airline offices). The cheapest tickets are often nonrefundable and require an extra fee for changing your flight. Many insurance policies will cover this loss if you have to change your flight for emergency reasons. Return (roundtrip) tickets usually work out cheaper than two one-way fares – often *much* cheaper.

See 'Ticket Options' for information on the types of tickets you can purchase. Discounts on such fares are often available from travel agents, but usually not in Latin America, where discount ticketing is unusual. Standby can be a cheap way of getting from Europe to the US, but there are no such flights to Argentina or other parts of South America. Foreigners in Argentina may now pay for international air tickets in local currency, but since the new Argentine peso has stabilized at par with the dollar, there is presently no advantage to doing so.

Once you have your ticket, write down its number, together with the flight number and other details, and keep the information somewhere separate. If the ticket is lost or stolen, this will help you get a replacement.

Remember to buy travel insurance as early as possible.

Note: Use the fares quoted in this book as a guide only. They are approximate and based on rates advertised by travel agents and airlines at press time. Quoted airfares do not necessarily constitute a recommendation for the carrier.

Round-the-World Tickets Round-the-World (RTW) tickets have become very popular in the last several years. Airline RTW tickets are often real bargains and can work out to be no more expensive or even cheaper than an ordinary return ticket. Prices have risen in recent years, however, and now start around UK£1220, A$3100 or US$2700. However, partnerships among various airlines are changing rapidly and prices vary dramatically depending on departure dates and length of ticket, so this is one more issue that requires thorough research before committing.

The official airline RTW tickets are usually put together by a combination of two airlines, and permit you to fly anywhere you want on their route systems as long as you do not backtrack. Other restrictions are that you must usually book the first sector in advance, and cancellation penalties apply. There may be restrictions on the number of stops permitted, and tickets are usually valid from 90 days up to a year. An alternative type of RTW ticket is one put together by a travel agent using a combination of discounted tickets.

Although most airlines restrict the number of sectors that can be flown within the USA and Canada to four, and some airlines black out a few heavily traveled routes

Air Travel Glossary

Baggage Allowance This amount will be written on your ticket. Usually one 20kg item, which goes in the hold, and one carry-on item are the maximum, but many airlines allow more for international flights.

Bucket Shop An unbonded travel agency specializing in discounted airline tickets.

Bumped Just because you have a confirmed seat doesn't mean you're going to get on the plane (see Overbooking).

Cancellation Penalties If you have to cancel or change an APEX ticket, there are often heavy penalties involved; insurance can sometimes be taken out against these penalties. Some airlines impose penalties on regular tickets as well, particularly against 'no show' passengers.

Check-In Airlines ask you to check in a certain amount of time prior to flight departure (usually two hours for international flights). If you fail to check in by 30 minutes before the flight and it is overbooked, the airline can cancel your booking and give your seat to somebody else.

Confirmation Having a ticket written out with the flight and date you want doesn't mean you have a seat until the agent has checked with the airline that your status is 'OK' or confirmed. Meanwhile, you might only have 'on request' status.

Lost Tickets If you lose your ticket, an airline will usually treat it like a traveler's check and, after inquiries, issue you another one. Legally, however, an airline is entitled to treat it like cash and if you lose it, then it's gone forever. Take good care of your tickets.

No-Shows Passengers who fail to show up for their flight, sometimes due to unexpected delays or disasters, sometimes due to simply forgetting, sometimes because they made more than one booking and didn't bother to cancel the one they didn't want. Full-fare passengers who fail to turn up are sometimes entitled to travel on a later flight. The rest of us are penalized (see Cancellation Penalties).

On Request An unconfirmed booking for a flight (see Confirmation).

Onward Tickets Many countries enforce an entry requirement that you have a ticket out of the country. If you're not sure what you intend to do next, the easiest solution is to buy the cheapest onward ticket to a neighboring country or a ticket from a reliable airline that can later be refunded if you do not use it.

Open Jaws A return ticket with which you fly out to one place but return from another. If available, this can save you backtracking to your arrival point.

(like Honolulu to Tokyo), stopovers are otherwise generally unlimited. In most cases a 14-day advance purchase is required. After the ticket is purchased, dates can be changed without penalty and tickets can be rewritten to add or delete stops for US$50 each.

The majority of RTW tickets restrict you to just two airlines. For instance, Qantas flies in conjunction with American Airlines, Delta Air Lines, Northwest Airlines, Canadian Airlines, Air France, LanChile, and KLM. Qantas RTW tickets, with any of the

Air Travel Glossary

Overbooking Airlines hate to fly planes with empty seats, and since every flight has some passengers who fail to show up (see No-Shows), airlines often book more passengers than they have seats. Usually the excess passengers balance those who fail to show up, but occasionally somebody gets bumped. If this happens, guess who it is most likely to be? The passengers who check in late.

Reconfirmation At least 72 hours prior to the departure time of an onward or return flight, you must contact the airline and 'reconfirm' that you intend to be on the flight. If you don't do this, the airline can delete your name from the passenger list and you could lose your seat. You don't have to reconfirm the first flight on your itinerary or if your stopover is less than 72 hours. It doesn't hurt to reconfirm more than once.

Restrictions Discounted tickets often have various restrictions on them – advance purchase is the most usual one (see APEX). Others include restrictions on the minimum and maximum period you must be away, such as a minimum of 14 days or a maximum of one year (see Cancellation Penalties).

Transferred Tickets Airline tickets cannot be transferred from one person to another. Travelers sometimes try to sell the return half of their ticket, but officials can ask you to prove that you are the person named on the ticket. This is unlikely to happen on domestic flights, but on an international flight, tickets may be compared against passports.

Travel Agencies Travel agencies vary widely, and you should ensure that you use one that suits your needs. Some simply handle tours, while full-service agencies handle everything from tours and tickets to car rental and hotel bookings. A good one will do all these things and can save you a lot of money, but if all you want is a ticket at the lowest possible price, then you really need an agency specializing in discounted tickets. A discounted ticket agency, however, may not be useful for other things, such as booking hotels.

Travel Periods Some officially discounted fares, APEX fares in particular, vary with the time of year. There is often a low (off-peak) season and a high (peak) season. Sometimes there's an intermediate, or shoulder, season as well. At peak times, when everyone wants to fly, not only will the officially discounted fares be higher but so will unofficially discounted fares. Or there may simply be no discounted tickets available. Usually the fare depends on your outward flight – if you depart in the high season and return in the low season, you pay the high-season fare.

aforementioned partner airlines, cost US$3247 or A$3099.

For travelers starting in Australia or Argentina, one possibility is the combined ticket offered by Qantas and Aerolíneas Argentinas. Beginning from Sydney or Buenos Aires, you can stop in New Zealand, London, Paris, Bahrain, Singapore, and other cities, although you must arrange the itinerary in advance. It does not, unfortunately, permit North American stopovers, but similar fares are available in the USA and Canada. The price for the Aerolíneas-Qantas ticket is A$3299 in Sydney or US$3218 in Buenos Aires (the former figure represents about 35% less than the latter, so it is far cheaper in Australia).

Aerolíneas has additional RTW agreements with Air New Zealand, Cathay Pacific, KLM, Malaysia Airlines, Singapore Airlines, and Thai Airways International. British Airways, LanChile, and Qantas Airways offer a RTW ticket that allows you to combine routes, including across the Pacific via Easter Island, for US$3344 or A$2550.

Travelers with Special Needs

If you have special needs of any sort – a broken leg, dietary restrictions, need for a wheelchair, responsibility for a baby, fear of flying – you should let the airline know as soon as possible so they can make arrangements accordingly. You should remind them when you reconfirm your booking (at least 72 hours before departure) and again when you check in at the airport. It may also be worth calling several airlines before you make your booking to find out how they would handle your particular needs.

Airports and airlines can be surprisingly helpful, but they do need advance warning. Most international airports can provide escorts from the check-in desk to plane where needed, and there should be ramps, lifts, accessible toilets, and reachable phones. Aircraft toilets, on the other hand, are likely to present a problem; travelers should discuss this with the airline at an early stage and, if necessary, with their doctor.

Guide dogs for the blind will often have to travel in a specially pressurized baggage compartment with other animals, away from their owner, though smaller guide dogs may be admitted to the cabin. Guide dogs are not subject to quarantine as long as they have proof of being vaccinated against rabies.

Travelers with hearing difficulties can ask that airport and in-flight announcements be written down for them.

Children under two usually travel for 10% of the standard fare (for free on some airlines) as long as they don't occupy a seat, but they don't get a baggage allowance. 'Skycots' should be provided by the airline if requested in advance; these will take a child weighing up to about 10kg. Children between two and 12 can usually occupy a seat for half to two-thirds of full fare, and do get a baggage allowance. Strollers can often be taken on as carry-on luggage.

Departure Tax

International passengers leaving from Buenos Aires' Ezeiza pay a US$18 departure tax, also payable in local currency; with the application of the 21% IVA, it is due to rise to US$21.78. On flights of less than 300km to neighboring countries, such as Uruguay, the tax is only US$5, likely to increase by a 21% IVA.

Baggage & Other Restrictions

On most domestic and international flights you are limited to two checked bags, or three if you don't have a carry-on. There could be a charge if you bring more or if the size of the bags exceeds the airline's limits. It's best to check with the individual airline if you are worried about this. On some international flights the luggage allowance is based on weight, not size. Again, check with the airline.

If your luggage is delayed upon arrival (which is rare), some airlines will give a cash advance to purchase necessities. If sporting equipment is misplaced, the airline may pay for rentals. Should the luggage be lost, it is important to submit a claim. The airline doesn't have to pay the full amount of the claim; rather, they can estimate the value of your lost items. It may take them anywhere from six weeks to three months to process the claim and pay you.

Smoking Flights to and from Argentina, as well as those within the country, have non-smoking sections, but Argentine airports allow smoking throughout.

Illegal Items Items that are illegal to take on a plane, either in checked or carry-on baggage, include aerosols, polishes, waxes, and so on; tear gas and pepper spray; camp stoves with fuel; and divers' tanks that are full. Matches should not be checked.

The USA

From the USA, the principal gateways to South America are Miami, New York, and Los Angeles. Aerolíneas Argentinas is the national carrier, but other airlines serving Buenos Aires with direct flights include American Airlines, LanChile, Lloyd Aéreo Boliviano, and United Airlines. Other Latin American airlines have good connections via their home bases or Brazil, including Avianca, Ecuatoriana, Japan Airlines (with Varig), Korean Air (with Varig), Trans Brasil, Varig, and VASP.

Aerolíneas Argentinas and Austral offer a domestic air pass that is convenient for visiting widely separated parts of the country (for more details, see the Getting Around chapter), but note that such tickets must usually be bought outside the country, and sometimes can only be bought in conjunction with an international ticket.

Council Travel (CIEE; ☎ 800-226-8624, cts@ciee.org) has agencies in the following cities and in many other college towns:

Austin, TX
(☎ 512-472-4931)
2000 Guadalupe St

Berkeley, CA
(☎ 510-848-8604)
2486 Channing Way

Boston, MA
(☎ 617-266-1926)
273 Newbury St

Denver, CO
(☎ 303-571-0630)
900 Auraria Parkway, Tivoli Bldg

La Jolla, CA
(☎ 619-452-0630)
UCSD Price Center B-023

Los Angeles, CA
(☎ 213-208-3551)
10904 Lindbrook Drive

Miami, FL
(☎ 305-670-9261)
9100 S Dadeland Blvd, Suite 220

New York, NY
(☎ 212-822-2700)
205 E 42nd St, ground floor

Pacific Beach, CA
(☎ 619-270-6401)
953 Garnett Ave

San Francisco, CA
(☎ 415-421-3473)
530 Bush St

Seattle, WA
(☎ 206-632-2448)
1314 NE 43rd St, Suite 210

Washington, DC
(☎ 202-337-6464)
3300 M Street, NW, 2nd floor

Like Council Travel, the Student Travel Network (STA; ☎ 800-777-0112) has offices in the following cities plus many other college towns:

Berkeley, CA
(☎ 510-642-3000)
ASUC Travel Center, Univ of California

Boston, MA
(☎ 617-266-6014)
297 Newbury St

Chicago, IL
(☎ 312-786-9050)
429 S Dearborn St

Los Angeles, CA
(☎ 213-934-8722)
7202 Melrose Ave
(☎ 310-824-1574)
920 Westwood Blvd

Coral Gables, FL
(☎ 305-284-1044)
Univ of Miami, 1306 Stanford Drive

New York, NY
(☎ 212-627-3111)
10 Downing St

Philadelphia, PA
(☎ 215-382-2928)
3730 Walnut St

San Francisco, CA
(☎ 415-391-8407)
51 Grant Ave

Seattle, WA
(☎ 206-633-5000)
4341 University Way NE

Washington, DC
(☎ 202-887-0912)
2401 Pennsylvania Ave, Suite G

Courier Flights In the USA, New York and Miami are the only choices for courier flights to South America. For the widest selection of destinations, try Now Voyager (☎ 212-431-1616, fax 334-5253), 74 Varick St, Suite 307, New York, NY 10013; or Air Facility (☎ 718-712-1769), 153 Rockaway Blvd, Jamaica, NY 11434.

For up-to-date information on courier and other budget fares, send US$5 for the latest newsletter or US$25 for a year's subscription from Travel Unlimited, PO Box 1058, Allston, MA 02134. Another source of information is the International Association of Air Travel Couriers (☎ 407-582-8320, fax 582-1581, iaatc@courier.org), PO Box 1349, Lake Worth, FL 33460; its US$45 annual membership fee includes the monthly newsletter *Shoestring Traveler* (not related to Lonely Planet).

Canada

Canadian Airlines' Buenos Aires-Toronto route offers the only direct flights to Canada, daily except Thursday, but numerous airlines make connections in New York, Miami, and Los Angeles. The Brazilian airline VASP, which flies five times weekly to Toronto, is the only other carrier that flies to Canada, but this requires changing planes in Rio de Janeiro or São Paulo.

Travel CUTS, the Canadian national student-travel agency, is the Canadian counterpart of Council Travel and STA. Travel CUTS (☎ 416-966-2887 in Toronto, 604-659-2887 in Vancouver) has offices in all major cities. The Toronto *Globe and Mail* and *Vancouver Sun* carry travel agents' ads.

Mexico

Some LanChile flights from Buenos Aires to Los Angeles stop in Mexico City after Santiago. American, Avianca, Cubana, Lloyd Aéreo Boliviano, and Varig provide less-direct services.

Aerolíneas Argentinas flies twice weekly to and from Cancún. LAB and Varig also fly to Cancún, but less directly.

The UK & Europe

Direct services to Buenos Aires are available with Aeroflot, Aerolíneas Argentinas, Air France, Alitalia, British Airways, Iberia, KLM, Lufthansa, Pluna, Swissair, TAP (Air Portugal), and Trans Brasil. Varig has easy connections via Rio de Janeiro and São Paulo.

London's numerous bucket shops can provide the best deals; check out newspapers or magazines such as the Saturday *Independent*, *Time Out*, or *TNT* for suggestions. Currently the cheapest fares from London to Buenos Aires run about £357 one-way, £581 return in low season (March 1 to June 30), and £424 one-way, £702 return the rest of the year.

Since bucket shops come and go, it's worth inquiring about their affiliation with the Association of British Travel Agents (ABTA), which will guarantee a refund or alternative if the agent goes out of business. The following are reputable London bucket shops. Note that the second telephone number should be used after April 1999.

Campus Travel
(☎ 0171-730-3402, 020-7730-3402)
52 Grosvenor Gardens, London SW1W 0AG

Journey Latin America
(☎ 0181-747-3108, 020-8747-3108)
16 Devonshire Rd, Chiswick, London W4 2HD

Passage to South America
(☎ 0181-767-8989, 020-8767-8989)
Fovant Mews, 12 Noyna Rd, London SW17 7PH

South American Experience
(☎ 0171- 976-5511, 020-7976-5511)
47 Causton St, London SW1

STA Travel
(☎ 0171-581-4132, 020-7581-4132)
86 Old Brompton Rd, London SW7 3LQ
117 Euston Rd London NW12SX

Trailfinders
(☎ 0171-937-5400, 020-7937-5400, trailfinder.com/travelc.htm)
194 Kensington High St, London W8 7RG
(☎ 0171-938-3366, 020-7938-3366)
42-50 Earls Court Rd, London W8

In Berlin, check out the magazine *Zitty* for bargain-fare ads. In Berlin and other European capitals, the following agencies are good possibilities for bargain fares:

France
Council Travel
(☎ 01-44-41-89-80)
1 Place de l'Odeon, 75006 Paris

Germany
Council Travel
(☎ 089-39-50-22)
Adalbert Strasse 32, 80799 Munich 40

STA Travel
(☎ 030-283-3903)
Marienstraße 25, Berlin
(☎ 4969-43-01-91)
Berger Strasse 118, Frankfurt 1

Ireland
USIT Travel
(☎ 01-602-1600)
19 Aston Quay, Dublin

Italy
CTS
(☎ 06-462-0431)
Via Genova 16, Rome

Netherlands
NBBS
(☎ 020-642-0989)
Rokin 38, Amsterdam

Malibu Travel
(☎ 020-623-6814)
Damrak 30 Amsterdam

Spain
TIVE
(☎ 91-347-7778)
José Ortega y Gasset 71, Madrid

Switzerland
SSR
(☎ 01-297-1111)
Leonhardstrasse 10, Zürich

The only apparent Europe-South America courier flights are with British Airways (☎ 0181-564-7009; 020-8546-7009 after April 1999), which has roundtrips to Buenos Aires for £400, taxes included. More information is available by sending a stamped, self-addressed envelope to British Airways Travel Shop, World Cargo Centre, Export Cargo Terminal, S 126 Heathrow, Hounslow, Middlesex TW6 2JS.

Australia & New Zealand

The most direct service is Aerolíneas Argentinas' Tuesday, Thursday, and Saturday transpolar flight from Sydney via Auckland, which is an obvious connection for buyers of the Qantas-Aerolíneas RTW fare. Otherwise, LanChile's trans-Pacific flights from Tahiti to Santiago (including a possible stopover on Easter Island) have easy connections to Buenos Aires, but some travelers have found it cheaper to go via London or Los Angeles.

For travelers starting in Australia, the combined Qantas-Aerolíneas Argentinas ticket allows stopovers in Auckland, London, Paris, Bahrain, Singapore, and other cities, but you must arrange the itinerary in advance. The price for the Aerolíneas-Qantas ticket is A$3299 in Sydney or US$3218 in Buenos Aires (the former figure represents about 35% less than the latter, so it is far cheaper in Australia).

STA Travel (☎ 1-800-637-444) is a good place to inquire for bargain air fares; again, student status is not necessary to use their services.

Adelaide
(☎ 08-223-6620, 223-6244)
Level 4, Union House, Adelaide Univ

Brisbane
(☎ 07-3221-3722)
Shop 25 & 26, 111-117 Adelaide St

Canberra
(☎ 06-247-0800)
Arts Centre, ANU

Hobart
(☎ 02-243-496)
Ground Floor, Union Bldg, Univ of Tasmania

Melbourne
(☎ 03-9349-2411)
224 Faraday St, PO Box 75 Carlton S

Perth
(☎ 09-380-2302)
1st floor, New Guild Bldg, Univ of W Australia, Crawley

Sydney
(☎ 02-360-1822)
9 Oxford St, Paddington

STA also has offices at the following New Zealand locations:

Auckland
(☎ 0800-100-677, 309-0458)
10 High St
Christchurch
(☎ 03-379-909)
90 Cashel St
Wellington
(☎ 04-385-0561)
233 Cuba St

Asia & Africa

Carriers serving Buenos Aires directly from Asia, usually via North America, are Japan Airlines and Korean Air. Varig and VASP also have good connections via Rio de Janeiro or São Paulo.

Malaysia Airlines flies Wednesday and Sunday from Kuala Lumpur to Buenos Aires via Cape Town and Johannesburg. South Africa Airways flies Thursday from Johannesburg to Buenos Aires via São Paulo and Sunday via Cape Town.

Neighboring Countries

Air connections with Chile, Bolivia, Paraguay, Brazil, and Uruguay are primarily but not exclusively via capital cities.

Bolivia La Paz is the principal destination, but most flights from Buenos Aires stop in Santa Cruz de la Sierra (also known as Viru Viru after the local airport's name). The main carriers are Aerolíneas Argentinas and Lloyd Aéreo Boliviano. LAB also flies from Salta to Santa Cruz, Cochabamba, and La Paz, and from Tucumán and Jujuy to Santa Cruz, Cochabamba, and La Paz.

Ticket Options

There are several types of discount tickets to South America. The following are the main ones:

APEX Advance purchase excursion (APEX) tickets must be bought well before departure, but they can be a good deal if you know exactly where you will be going and how long you will be staying. Usually only available on a return basis, with a 14- or 21-day advance purchase requirement, these have minimum- and maximum-stay requirements (usually 14 and 180 days respectively), allow no stopovers, and stipulate cancellation charges.

Courier Flights This relatively new system, which businesses use to ensure the arrival of urgent freight without excessive customs hassles, can mean phenomenal bargains for travelers who can tolerate fairly strict requirements, such as short turnaround time – some tickets are valid for only a week or so, others for a month, but rarely any longer. In effect, the courier company ships business freight as your baggage, so that you can usually take only carry-on luggage, but you may pay as little as US$480 for a ticket from New York to Buenos Aires and back.

Discounted Tickets There are two types of discounted fares – officially discounted (see Promotional Fares) and unofficially discounted. The lowest prices often impose limitations such as flying with unpopular airlines, inconvenient schedules, or unpleasant routes and connections. A discounted ticket can save you other things than money – you may be able to pay APEX prices without the associated advance booking and other requirements. Discounted tickets only exist where there is fierce competition.

Economy Class Valid for 12 months, economy-class (Y) tickets have the greatest flexibility within their time period. However, if you try to extend beyond a year, you'll have to pay the difference of any price increase in the interim period.

Brazil From Ezeiza, Rio de Janeiro and São Paulo are the main destinations for many airlines, including Aerolíneas Argentinas (which also has some Buenos Aires flights that stop in Puerto Iguazú), Canadian Airlines, KLM, LAB, Swissair, TAM (via Asunción), TAP, Trans Brasil, Varig, and VASP. The latter three carriers have the greatest number of destinations other than the two Brazilian megalopolises. Varig also flies from Rosario and Córdoba to São Paulo and Belo Horizonte.

Pluna flies from Buenos Aires' Ezeiza to Rio de Janeiro and Salvador via Montevideo, and from Buenos Aires' Aeroparque to Florianópolis, Porto Alegre, São Paulo, and Rio, also via Montevideo. LAB flies from Ezeiza to Manaus via Santa Cruz.

Chile Many airlines fly between Buenos Aires and Santiago, a route on which heavily discounted tickets are available (with some restrictions). Only LanChile flies between Mendoza and the Chilean capital.

The privatized TAN, formerly the regional airline of Neuquén province but now owned by VASP, connects the provincial capital and San Martín de los Andes with Temuco and Concepción. Several small regional carriers fly between Punta Arenas, Chile, and destinations in Santa Cruz province and Argentine Tierra del Fuego.

Paraguay Asunción is Paraguay's only air connection with Buenos Aires; flights leave from both Aeroparque and Ezeiza. The only direct carriers are Aerolíneas Argentinas

Ticket Options

Excursion Fares Priced midway between APEX and full economy fare, these have no advance booking requirements but may require a minimum stay. Their advantage over advance purchase is that you can change bookings and/or stopovers without surcharge.

Full Fares Airlines traditionally offer first-class (coded F), business-class (coded J), and economy-class (coded Y) tickets. These days there are so many promotional and discounted fares available from the regular economy class that few passengers pay full economy fare.

MCO 'Miscellaneous charges orders' (MCOs) are open vouchers for a fixed US dollar amount, which can be exchanged for a ticket on any IATA (International Air Transport Association) airline. In countries that require an onward ticket as a condition for entry, such as Panama or Colombia, this will usually satisfy immigration authorities. In a pinch, you can turn it into cash at the local offices of the airline from which you purchased it.

Point-to-Point This discount ticket is available on some routes in return for waiving stopover rights, but some airlines have entirely eliminated stopovers.

Promotional Fares Officially discounted fares like APEX fares that are available from travel agents or direct from the airline.

RTW Some excellent bargains are possible on 'Round-the-World' tickets, sometimes for less than the cost of a return excursion fare. You must travel round the world in one direction and cannot backtrack; you are usually allowed five to seven stopovers.

Standby A discounted ticket with which you can fly only if there is a seat free at the last moment. Standby fares are usually only available on domestic routes.

and TAM, though Pluna has connections in Montevideo.

Uruguay There are numerous flights from Aeroparque to Montevideo, while a few long-distance international flights continue from Ezeiza to Montevideo. From Aeroparque, the only other Uruguayan destinations is Punta del Este, with LAPA, twice on Friday and Sunday, and more frequently with Aerolíneas Argentinas.

LAND

There are multitudinous crossings from the neighboring countries of Chile, Bolivia, Paraguay, Brazil, and Uruguay. Some are very easy, others very difficult and time-consuming (the latter are usually far more interesting).

Chile Border Crossings Except in far southern Patagonia, every land-crossing border with Chile involves crossing the Andes. Some passes close in winter. The only rail crossing, from Salta to Baquedano, is not a regular passenger service.

Chilean visas (probably best obtained in the traveler's home country or in Buenos Aires) are obligatory for citizens from: African countries, France, Guyana, Haiti, Kuwait, Mexico, New Zealand, Suriname, and Communist countries (the latter a shrinking category, presumably). The rest usually only need a Chilean tourist card, obtainable at the border.

Andean Routes The most frequented of the four crossings in this region is that between Mendoza and Santiago.

Salta to Calama Buses from Salta to Calama, with connections to Antofagasta and Iquique, now cross the Andes via a combination of national and provincial highways to Jujuy, Susques, and the Paso de Jama in the summer months only. The 4275m Huaytiquina Pass to the south, reached from Salta via RN 51 and RP 37, is still open to automobiles and trucks but carries almost no traffic, so forget about hitching. There may be passenger rail service to the Chilean border at Socompa, but only freight service beyond, though the Chilean train will sometimes take passengers. See the Andean Northwest chapter for details.

San Juan to La Serena Dynamited by the Argentine military during the Beagle Channel dispute of 1978-9, the 4779m Agua Negra Pass, at the western end of RN 150, is now open to automobiles and trucks, but regular bus service is still on hold.

Mendoza to Santiago Many bus companies serve the Libertadores border crossing, the most popular between the two countries, via RN 7 from the city of Mendoza. *Taxi colectivos*, which carry up to five passengers, are faster, more comfortable, and only slightly more expensive. Winter snow sometimes closes the route, but never for long. See the Mendoza entry of the Cuyo chapter for details.

Malargüe to Talca In summer only, weekly bus service crosses the narrow, precipitous road over the 2553m Paso Pehuenche and down the unforgettable canyon of Chile's Río Maule. For those with the time and patience, it's a real highlight.

Lake District Routes There are a number of scenic crossings between the Argentine and Chilean lake districts, some involving bus-boat shuttles. These are popular routes in summer, so make advance bookings whenever possible.

Neuquén & Zapala to Temuco The most northerly lake district route, RN 22, reaches the border at 1884m Paso Pino Hachado Pass, directly east of Zapala and Neuquén, and continues to Temuco, via Lonquimay and Curacautín, along the upper Río Biobío. Alternative RP 13, slightly to the south, uses the 1298m Paso Icaima. Both have occasional bus traffic in summer.

San Martín/Junín de los Andes to Temuco On the Argentine side, RP 60 skirts the northern slopes of Volcán Lanín to 1207m Paso Tromen (known to Chileans as

Mamuil Malal), which is closed in winter. On the Chilean side, the road passes Curra-rehue, Pucón, and Villarrica. There is summer bus service, often heavily booked, on this route.

San Martín de los Andes to Valdivia From San Martín, a daily ferry sails up Lago Lacar to Argentine customs at 659m Paso Hua Hum. Buses use the shoreline RP 48 to arrive at the same spot, which is served by local buses to the Chilean settlement of Pirehueico, where a ferry crosses the lake of the same name to Puerto Fuy. From Puerto Fuy there is bus service via Choshuenco and Panguipulli to Valdivia.

Bariloche to Osorno via Puyehue On the north shore of Lago Nahuel Huapi, 1308m Paso Cardenal Samoré on RN 231 is the quickest land crossing in the lake district; on the Chilean side, the highway traverses Parque Nacional Puyehue.

Bariloche to Puerto Montt via Lago Todos los Santos Extraordinarily popular in summer, the bus-boat combination is feasible as a single through ticket or in stages via several scenic villages.

From Bariloche, there are frequent bus services to Llao Llao's Puerto Pañuelo, where a ferry sails west on Lago Nahuel Huapi to Puerto Blest. After a short bus ride, passengers cross Lago Frías by launch, go through Argentine immigration at Puerto Frías, and continue by bus over the 1202m Paso de Pérez Rosales to Peulla for the ferry to Petrohué, at the west end of Lago Todos los Santos.

Southern Patagonian Routes Since the opening of Chile's Carretera Austral (Southern Highway) beyond Puerto Aysén, it has become more common to cross between Chile and Argentina south of Puerto Montt. There are also several crossing points in extreme southern Patagonia and Tierra del Fuego.

Lago Puelo to Puelo South of El Bolsón, a footpath/stock trail leads across the Chilean border to the Seno de Reloncaví (Reloncaví Sound), with connections to the city of Puerto Montt. This is approximately a three-day journey.

Esquel to Puerto Ramírez There are two possible crossings in this area. From Esquel there are colectivos on RN 259 to Futaleufú, across the Chilean border, with connections to Chaitén; on the Chilean side, the highway continues southwest to Puerto Ramírez and then turns northwest to Puerto Piedra and Chaitén. The alternative takes RP 17 and RP 44 to Corcovado (there is bus service along this route) to Argentine customs at Carrenleufú. Soon after the border is the town of Palena, where the road jogs northwest to meet the highway from Futaleufú.

Comodoro Rivadavia to Coihaique There are several weekly buses, often heavily booked, from Comodoro Rivadavia to Río Mayo via RP 26, RP 20, and RP 22. A more southerly route, with no public transport, goes over the Paso Huemules to Balmaceda and Coihaique via RP 55.

Los Antiguos to Chile Chico & Puerto Ibáñez A bus from Los Antiguos (where there are connections to the Patagonian coastal town of Caleta Olivia) goes to Chile Chico several times daily. From Chile Chico there's a ferry to Puerto Ibáñez on Lago General Carrera (which is called Lago Buenos Aires on the Argentine side). An alternative goes northwest from Perito Moreno via RP 45 and RP 72 to Puerto Ibáñez, avoiding the ferry crossing, but there's no public transport.

Calafate & Río Turbio to Puerto Natales & Parque Nacional Torres del Paine There are frequent buses between Puerto Natales and the Argentine coal town of Río Turbio, where many Chileans work; from Río Turbio there are connections to Río Gallegos. Twice weekly or more in summer, there are direct buses from Torres del Paine and Puerto Natales to Calafate, the gateway to Argentina's Parque Nacional Los Glaciares.

Río Gallegos to Punta Arenas There are many buses daily between Punta Arenas and Río Gallegos, a six-hour trip.

Tierra del Fuego to Punta Arenas From Río Grande there are two buses weekly via paved RN 3 to the Chilean border at San Sebastián. The buses continue to Porvenir, in Chilean Tierra del Fuego, where a three-hour ferry trip or a 15-minute flight takes you to Punta Arenas. There are also direct buses twice weekly from Ushuaia to Punta Arenas via the Primera Angostura ferry crossing.

An alternative crossing via RC-b, open November 1 to April 1 only, goes from Estancia José Menéndez, southwest of Río Grande, to the Argentine border at Radman, then fords the shallow Río Bellavista and continues 10km via a dirt road to the Chilean border station at Vicuña; from there, a good gravel road heads north to Camerón and Porvenir. Make sure your paperwork is in order, because very few foreigners cross the border here.

Bolivia Border Crossings The Bolivian border offers one major and two minor crossing points into Argentina. There are both rail and road connections at La Quiaca-Villazón in the province of Jujuy, while the Aguas Blancas and Yacuiba crossings are in the province of Salta.

La Quiaca to Villazón From Jujuy and Salta, there are many daily buses up the Quebrada de Humahuaca on RN 9 to La Quiaca, but there is no longer any passenger rail service on the Argentine side. At La Quiaca, you must walk or take a cab across the Bolivian border to catch a bus or train north to Tupiza, Uyuni, and Oruro.

Aguas Blancas to Bermejo From Orán, reached by bus from either Salta or Jujuy via RN 34 and RN 50, take a bus to Aguas Blancas and the Bolivian border town of Bermejo, where a bridge now crosses the river of the same name. From Bermejo, you can catch a bus to Tarija.

Pocitos to Yacuiba From Jujuy or Salta there are buses on RN 34 to Tartagal and on to the border at Pocitos-Yacuiba. From Yacuiba, there are trains to Santa Cruz de la Sierra.

Paraguay Border Crossings There are two direct border crossings between Argentina and Paraguay, and one requiring a brief detour through Brazil. Another may open across the massive Yacyretá hydroelectric project on the Río Paraná.

Clorinda to Asunción There are frequent bus services between Asunción and Clorinda (in Formosa province) via the Puente Internacional Ignacio de Loyola, which is infamous for ferocious customs checks (on the Argentine side) and corruption (on both sides).

Posadas to Encarnación Buses run frequently on the Puente Internacional Beato Roque González, the international bridge across the Río Paraná. However, it's still possible to take a launch between the river docks even though the rising waters behind Yacyretá Dam have submerged low-lying parts of both cities.

Puerto Iguazú to Ciudad del Este Frequent buses connect Puerto Iguazú in Misiones province to Ciudad del Este (formerly Puerto Presidente Stroessner) via the Brazilian city of Foz do Iguaçu.

Brazil Border Crossings The most common overland crossing is between Puerto Iguazú in Misiones province and Foz do Iguaçu, but you can also go from Paso de los Libres, in Corrientes province, to Uruguaiana, Brazil, and on to Porto Alegre. There is a new bridge across the Río Uruguay from Santo Tomé (north of Paso de los Libres) to the Brazilian village of São Borja, and a ferry in the province of Misiones, from San Javier to Puerto Xavier.

Direct bus service connects Buenos Aires with Rio de Janeiro and São Paulo.

Uruguay Border Crossings Travelers worried about seasickness on the ferry or hydrofoil will find direct buses from Buenos Aires to Montevideo, but these are slower and less convenient than the land-river combinations across the Río de la Plata, which are detailed below. All other land connections are across the Río Uruguay in Entre Ríos province.

Gualeguaychú to Fray Bentos Several buses daily cross the Puente Internacional Libertador General San Martín, with good connections to Montevideo from Mercedes, the first town beyond Fray Bentos.

Colón to Paysandú The Puente Internacional General José Gervasio Artigas links these two cities, south of Parque Nacional El Palmar.

Concordia to Salto The bridge across the Salto Grande hydroelectric complex, north of Concordia, unites these two cities north of Parque Nacional El Palmar. There are also scheduled launches across the river.

RIVER & SEA

From Buenos Aires, there are several ways to Uruguay that involve ferry and hydrofoil, and often require combinations with buses. The only other maritime service is the erratic boat from Ushuaia, Tierra del Fuego, to Puerto Williams, on Chile's Isla Navarino. For details, see the appropriate geographical entries.

Departure Tax

There is no tax for land departures, but users of the new hydrofoil port at Dársena Norte pay US$6 to travel to Colonia, Uruguay, or US$10 to Montevideo. These are now usually included in the fare, but ask to be sure.

Uruguay

Buenos Aires to Colonia From Buenos Aires there are two ferries (2½ hours) and several hydrofoils (45 minutes) daily to Colonia, with direct bus connections to Montevideo (three hours more).

Buenos Aires to Montevideo The most convenient river services to Montevideo are the comfortable, high-speed ferries that carry passengers to the Uruguayan capital in only 2½ hours from downtown Buenos Aires.

Tigre to Carmelo & Nueva Palmira Passenger launches cross the estuary of the Río de la Plata from the Buenos Aires suburb of Tigre. You can reach the docks from Retiro Station or via the No 60 bus ('Tigre') from Av Callao. From Carmelo there are good connections to Montevideo.

Chile

Puerto Almanza to Puerto Williams Traversing the Beagle Channel from Ushuaia to Puerto Williams on Isla Navarino (reached by plane or boat from Punta Arenas) has always been difficult, but a recent agreement between the two countries will permit ferries to cross the 7km of the Beagle Channel from the tiny cove of Puerto Almanza, east of Ushuaia.

ORGANIZED TOURS

Myriad companies offer tours to Argentina, but most focus on Buenos Aires, Iguazú, and the Moreno Glacier, sometimes including extensions to Ushuaia, Tierra del Fuego and/or Península Valdés. Other parts of the country get short shrift, so if you're interested in those areas, you may have to make arrangements in Buenos Aires. Increasingly, both Argentine and foreign companies have become involved in nature-oriented tourism (popularly, but not always accurately, known as *turismo ecológico* or *turismo aventura)*.

North America

Well-established North American companies operating in Argentina include Wilderness Travel (☎ 510-548-0420, 800-247-6700), 801 Allston Way, Berkeley, CA 94710; and Mountain Travel Sobek (☎ 510-527-8100, 800-227-2384), 6420 Fairmount Ave, El Cerrito, CA 94530. Both have lavishly illustrated catalogs of their numerous excursions to Patagonia and the Andean Lake District, which range from easy day hikes with accommodations at hotels and campgrounds, to strenuous treks and climbs with nights spent camping in the backcountry.

Wildland Adventures (☎ 206-365-0686, 800-345-4453, fax 363-6615, info@wildland.com), 3516 NE 155th St, Seattle, WA 98155, arranges 10-day itineraries through local guides and outfitters in Patagonia and the Andean Northwest for as few as two persons from around US$1800 per person (land cost). Another possibility is Lost World Adventures (☎ 404-373-5820, 800-999-0558, fax 377-1902, info@lostworldadventures.com), 220 Second Ave, Decatur, GA 30030. For visitors with limited time, such trips may be ideal, especially in areas like Patagonia where logistics can be difficult.

For bicyclists, Backroads (☎ 800-462-2848, 510-527-1555, fax 510-527-1444, www.backroads.com), 801 Cedar St, Berkeley, CA 94710, conducts 11-day mountain-biking (US$3298) and hiking (US$3398) trips in the Chilean-Argentine lake district, with stays in elegant hotels and cozy inns. Backroads also offers a 10-day Patagonia trip featuring hiking, rafting, and horseback riding.

For fishing enthusiasts, Orvis (☎ 800-778-4778), 10 River Rd, Manchester, VT 05254, arranges extended vacations in the Patagonian Lake District through Argentina Estancias (☎ 0972-27311, fax 27391), Casilla de Correo 25, 8730 San Martín de los Andes, Provincia de Neuquén.

Study tours sponsored by nonprofit organizations are another alternative. The Oceanic Society (☎ 800-326-7491, 415-441-1106, fax 474-3395), Fort Mason Center, Bldg E, San Francisco, CA 94123, does 10-day whale-watching tours to Península Valdés, also taking in the Punta Tombo penguin reserve, for US$3790 including airfare from Miami; a possible extension to Iguazú costs US$764. Smithsonian Study Tours (☎ 202-357-4700, fax 633-9250) does a 12-day trip to Buenos Aires, the Pampas, and Iguazú, cruising from Ushuaia to Cape Horn and back through the Beagle Channel to Puerto Natales, then overland to Torres del Paine and Punta Arenas, returning from Santiago. Prices range from US$8445 to US$10,545 per person.

For travelers at least 55 years of age, Elderhostel (☎ 617-426-8056), 76 Federal St, Boston, MA 02110, operates two-week tours to Buenos Aires and Salta, and to Argentine and Chilean Patagonia, for about US$4000 including airfare.

The UK

Journey Latin America (☎ 0181-747-3108 020-8747-3108 after April 1999), 16 Devonshire Rd., Chiswick, London W4 2HD, takes smallish groups to Latin America and specializes in tours for one or two people. Explore Worldwide (☎ 01252-344161, info@explore.co.uk), 1 Frederick St, Aldershot, Hants GU11 1LQ, is also a Latin America specialist.

OTT Expeditions (☎ 0114-258-8508, 258-8532, fax 255-1603, ottexpeditions.co.uk), Southwest Centre, Suite 5b, Troutbeck Road, Sheffield S7 2QA, is primarily a mountaineering company, which arranges 20-day ascents to Aconcagua (a nontechnical climb with a gradual approach and extended acclimatization period; prices are around £2395 including airfare from London) and other high Andean peaks. It also does three-week trekking excursions in Patagonia, including Torres del Paine, for £1995 including airfare.

Australia

In Australia, try World Expeditions, which has three offices: 441 Kent St, Sydney, NSW 2000 (☎ 02-9264-3366, fax 9261-1974, enquiries@worldexpeditions.com.au); 1-393 Little Bourke St, Melbourne, Victoria 3000 (☎ 03-9670-8400, fax 9670-7474, travel@worldexpeditions.com.au); and Shop 2, 36 Agnes St, Fortitude Valley (Brisbane) 4006 (☎ 07-3216-0823, fax 07 3216 0827, adventure@worldexpeditions.com.au).

Peregrine Bird Tours (☎ 03-9727-3343), 2 Drysdale Place, Mooroolbark, Victoria 3138, often schedules trips to Argentina. Peregrine Adventures (not affiliated with Peregrine Bird Tours), 258 Lonsdale St, Melbourne, Victoria 3000 (☎ 03-9662-2800, fax 9662-2422), also sometimes runs tours.

WARNING

The information in this chapter is particularly prone to change: Prices for international travel are volatile, routes are introduced and cancelled, airlines go out of business, schedules change, special deals come and go, and rules and visa requirements are amended. Airlines and governments seem to take a perverse pleasure in making price structures and regulations as complicated as possible. You should check directly with the airline or a travel agent to make sure you understand how a fare (and ticket you may buy) works. In addition, the travel industry is highly competitive, and there are many lurks and perks.

The upshot of this is that you should get opinions, quotes, and advice from as many airlines and travel agents as possible before you part with your cash. The details given in the chapter should be regarded as pointers and are not a substitute for your own careful, up-to-date research.

Getting Around

AIR

Argentine air traffic, routes, and fares have undergone major transformations since the privatization of Aerolíneas Argentinas, which handles domestic as well as international routes, and Austral, which handles domestic routes only. These two airlines charge identical fares and have the most extensive services, but some existing secondary airlines have expanded their routes, and others have come into existence. Both secondary and new airlines have undercut the very high fare structure of the established carriers. Apparently in response, Aerolíneas and Austral have introduced a supplementary fare system, which, with some restrictions, offers cheaper alternatives.

Perhaps the single greatest shortcoming of the air transport system is that many major cities have connections only through Buenos Aires, though short-haul airlines such as Southern Winds have begun to link provincial destinations without passing through the capital. Still, to fly the 950km from Salta to Mendoza by Aerolíneas or Austral, for example, one must actually travel a total of 2250km, by first flying to Buenos Aires (1270km) and then making the 980km connection to Mendoza.

Línea Aéreas Privadas Argentinas (LAPA) competes with Aerolíneas and Austral on many routes, though it has fewer planes and a smaller total capacity. Dinar Líneas Aéreas flies to Córdoba, Mendoza, Tucumán and Salta in the northwest, Mar del Plata, and Comodoro Rivadavia.

Líneas Aéreas del Estado (LADE), the air force's passenger service, flies mostly to Patagonian destinations, but reduced state subsidies have resulted in greatly diminished services. Recently acquired by the Brazilian airline Vasp, Transportes Aéreos Neuquén (TAN), the Neuquén provincial airline, has fairly extensive schedules from Mendoza in the north to Bariloche and Comodoro Rivadavia in the south. But other Patagonian carriers, most notably Kaikén Líneas Aéreas in Santa Cruz and Tierra del Fuego provinces, have smaller and slower planes. The only non-Patagonian carrier of this sort is Líneas Aéreas de Entre Ríos (LAER), which connects Paraná, Santa Fe, and other cities of the Littoral with Buenos Aires and the Atlantic beach resorts of Buenos Aires province.

Note that in the summer and around holidays, all Patagonian flights may be heavily booked, and it is advisable to make reservations as far in advance as possible. Flying with LADE or TAN is sometimes cheaper than covering the same distance by bus, but demand is heavy and flights are often booked (usually overbooked) well in advance. With polite insistence and a convincing story, you can often get a seat on a LADE flight in town, but in desperation do not hesitate to go to the airport, where you may well find a plane with empty seats.

Fares

The cost of flying in Argentina has fluctuated in recent years, partly because of increased competition for the former state-owned carriers Aerolíneas Argentinas and Austral; consult the accompanying map for the most recent standard airfare structure, which indicates the least and most expensive fares for particular routes. One low-cost alternative on some airlines is *banda negativa*, in which limited seats on a selected list of flights every month are available for discounts of 40% or so. Often, though not always, these are night flights and require advance purchase, but they are excellent bargains. There are also an increasing number of one-way and roundtrip excursion fares within the country, requiring 14 to 29 days advance purchase; these change frequently and are too numerous to list.

Air Passes

Aerolíneas Argentinas' 'Visit Argentina' fare, also valid on Austral, lets you fly anywhere served by either airline so long as you

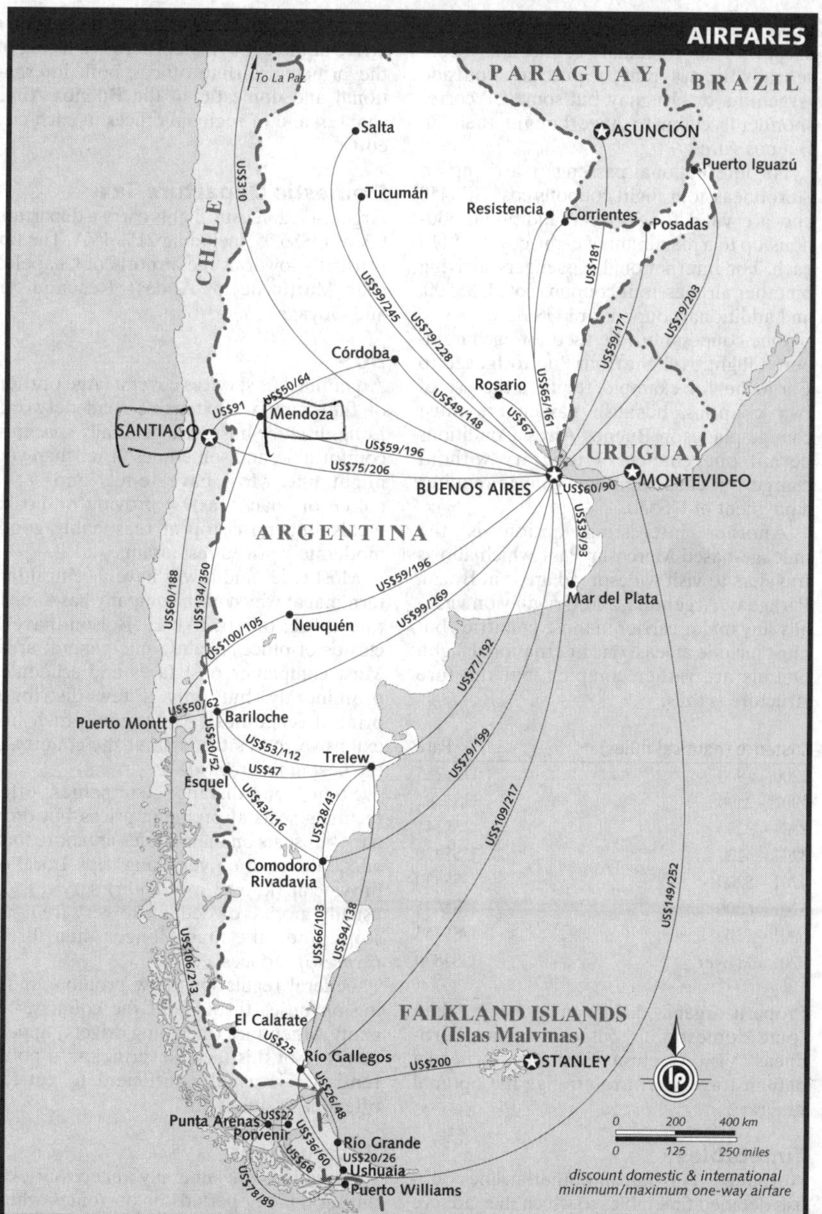
AIRFARES
To La Paz
PARAGUAY
BRAZIL
ASUNCIÓN
Salta
Puerto Iguazú
Tucumán
Resistencia
Corrientes
Posadas
CHILE
US$310
US$99/245
US$79/228
US$181
US$59/171
US$79/203
Córdoba
US$50/64
Rosario
US$65/161
US$91
Mendoza
US$49/148
US$67
SANTIAGO
US$59/196
US$75/206
URUGUAY
MONTEVIDEO
BUENOS AIRES
US$60/90
US$39/93
ARGENTINA
US$59/196
Mar del Plata
US$60/188
US$134/350
US$100/105
Neuquén
US$99/269
US$77/192
US$50/62
Puerto Montt
Bariloche
US$20/52
US$53/112
Trelew
US$79/199
US$47
Esquel
US$43/116
US$28/43
US$109/217
Comodoro Rivadavia
US$149/252
US$106/213
US$66/103
US$94/138
FALKLAND ISLANDS (Islas Malvinas)
El Calafate
US$25
Río Gallegos
US$200
STANLEY
US$26/48
Punta Arenas
US$22
Porvenir
US$36/60
Río Grande
US$20/26
US$66
Ushuaia
US$78/89
Puerto Williams
0 200 400 km
0 125 250 miles
discount domestic & international minimum/maximum one-way airfare

make no more than one stop in any city except for an immediate connection. Theoretically, the pass must be purchased outside Argentina or Uruguay, but some LP correspondents claim to have bought them in Buenos Aires.

For international passengers arriving on Aerolíneas, four flight coupons cost US$450 and are valid for 30 days; additional coupons, up to a maximum of eight, cost US$110 each. For international passengers arriving on other airlines, four coupons cost US$500, and additional coupons are US$130.

One coupon must be used for each numbered flight. A flight from Puerto Iguazú to Bariloche, for example, requires the use of two coupons, because passengers must change planes in Buenos Aires. Conditions permit one change of itinerary without charge, but each additional change requires a payment of US$50.

Another interesting option is the mileage-based Mercosur Pass, which allows travelers to visit widespread areas in Brazil, Paraguay, Argentina, and Uruguay on virtually any major carrier in those countries, but must include at least one international flight. Details are rather complex, but the fare structure is thus:

Distance (nautical miles)	Fare
1200 – 1900	US$225
1901 – 2500	US$285
2501 – 3200	US$345
3201 – 4200	US$420
4201 – 5200	US$530
5201 – 6200	US$645
6201 – 7200	US$755
7201 and over	US$870

Properly organized, this can be cheaper than some domestic air passes, such as Aerolíneas' 'Visit Argentina Pass', but you need a patient travel agent to arrange the optimal itinerary.

Timetables

Aerolíneas, Austral, and other airlines publish detailed timetables to which they adhere very closely. LADE will sometimes leave early if the flight is full or nearly full, so don't arrive at the airport late. There is a listing of the principal airline offices, both international and domestic, in the Buenos Aires chapter, and of regional offices in each city entry.

Domestic Departure Tax

Argentine domestic flights carry a departure tax of US$6.05, including 21% IVA. The tax is usually lower at the airports of Chapelco (San Martín de los Andes), Reconquista, and Goya.

BUS

Argentine bus services cover a large portion of the country's extensive road network. Long-distance buses are generally spacious, comfortable, and sometimes faster than you might like. Most have toilets and serve coffee or snacks; a few provide on-board meals, but most stop at reasonably good, moderately priced restaurants.

Most cities and towns have a central bus terminal at which each company has a separate office; others, like El Bolsón, have a cluster of offices in the same general area. Most companies post fares and schedules prominently, but only a few distribute printed schedules (Andesmar, which has extensive routes throughout the country, is the best in this regard).

Some long-distance companies offer reclining seats at premium prices, but ordinary bus seats on main routes are more than adequate, even on very long trips. Local or provincial (known as *común*) services are usually more crowded, make very frequent stops, and take much longer than direct *(expreso)* services.

Federal regulations now prohibit smoking on buses throughout the country, but many Argentines (including drivers) appear unaware of this fact. Nevertheless, a polite reminder is usually sufficient to get the offender to stub it out.

Reservations

Reservations are generally unnecessary, but during holiday periods or on routes where seats are limited, it's a good idea to buy your ticket as far in advance as possible. Christmas, New Year's, and Easter are obvious times, but do not overlook the winter holidays around Independence Day (July 9), when public transportation can also be very crowded.

Usually a trip to the bus terminal the day before you travel will suffice. The major exceptions are the infrequent international services on relatively remote routes, such as Salta to Calama and Antofagasta (Chile) or Comodoro Rivadavia (Chubut) to Coihaique (Chile). Purchase tickets for these and other infrequent routes as early as possible.

Costs

Bus fares are considerably costlier than in the Andean countries and somewhat more expensive than in Chile. The Dirección Nacional de Transportes has fixed a standard rate of about US$0.036 per kilometer, but a good rule of thumb is US$3 per hour of journey. Bus services, however, are private rather than state-operated, and fares respond quickly to market conditions and inflation.

Sample bus fares from Buenos Aires include:

Destination	Fare
Rosario	US$15
Mar del Plata	US$25
Santa Fe/Paraná	US$26
Bahía Blanca	US$32
Córdoba	US$30
Mendoza	US$40
Puerto Iguazú	US$45
Puerto Madryn	US$64
Salta	US$64
Bariloche	US$80
Río Gallego	US$107

Promotional fares are sometimes available, so inquire at several companies before buying your ticket. Depending on the company, university students and teachers sometimes receive 20% discounts on intercity bus fares, though this practice is less common than in the past. It's helpful to have student or university ID, which need not be current, but often just asking for the discount will be sufficient. Credit cards are usually not accepted for discount fares.

TRAIN

Private operators have assumed control of the profitable freight service on the formerly state-owned railways, but have shown little interest in providing passenger service except on commuter lines in and around Buenos Aires. The provinces of Buenos Aires, Río Negro, Chubut, Tucumán, and La Pampa continue to provide much-reduced passenger service.

Train trips are often longer than bus trips and subject to frequent delays, breakdowns, and strikes. If the railroads go on strike, you may find that your ticket is useless, although you should be able to get a refund.

Routes

In Buenos Aires, the Mitre, Belgrano, and San Martín lines operate from Estación Retiro; the Roca line from Estación Constitución; the Urquiza line from Estación Federico Lacroze; and the Sarmiento line from Estación Once. From Retiro, Constitución, and Once, there are suburban commuter services as well as intercity services. All four stations are served by the underground (Subte).

Operated by the province of Buenos Aires, the Ferrocarril Roca serves the Atlantic beach resort of Mar del Plata and other destinations in Buenos Aires province. The province of Río Negro operates the Roca line from its coastal capital of Viedma to Bariloche. From Esquel, the province of Chubut runs an attenuated version of the Roca's picturesque narrow-gauge spur as far as El Maitén.

Operated by the province of Tucumán, the Ferrocarril Mitre goes to Rosario, Santiago del Estero, and Tucumán. The Ferrocarril Sarmiento, though primarily a commuter line, still links the capital to Santa Rosa in La Pampa province. The Belgrano, San Martín, and Urquiza lines are now primarily commuter railways for Gran Buenos Aires, but the Urquiza and Belgrano also have some tourist excursions in Buenos Aires province.

Classes

There are four classes of passenger service, not all of which are available on every train. *Coche cama* or *dormitorio*, a sleeper compartment, is the costliest but most comfortable on long journeys such as Constitución-Bariloche. *Pullman* is considerably cheaper, with air-conditioning and reclining seats somewhat larger than those in *primera* (1st class). Primera is very acceptable in almost all circumstances, especially since the price difference is minimal compared to that of *turista* (tourist, or 2nd class), with its rigid bench seats.

For trips longer than a few hours, and especially on overnight trips, avoid turista class. There may be slight variations on all these categories.

Reservations

Because they are cheaper than buses, trains can be very crowded. During holiday periods such as Christmas and around Independence Day (July 9), it is very important to buy tickets as far in advance as possible. At most major stations, ticket purchases are now computerized and tickets will show date of travel *(fecha)*, departure time *(sale)*, carriage number *(coche)*, and seat *(asiento)*. When traveling with friends or family, Argentines often ignore seat assignments, but do not hesitate to insist on your proper seat or even call the conductor to straighten out any problems.

Costs

Argentine train fares are still lower than bus fares on comparable routes, but reduced state subsidies have meant increased prices. The minimum train fare to Mar del Plata from Buenos Aires is around US$16, for instance, while the usual bus fare is US$25 (the latter is more comfortable than the least expensive class of train, however).

CAR & MOTORCYCLE

Because Argentina is so large, many parts are easily accessible only by motor vehicle despite the country's extensive public transport system. Especially in Patagonia, where distances are great and buses can be infrequent, you cannot easily stop for something interesting at the side of the road and then continue on your merry way by public transport.

Unfortunately, operating a car is expensive. Although Argentina is self-sufficient in oil, the price of *nafta* (petrol) has risen to world levels at about US$0.80 per liter for *común* (regular) and US$1 for *super*, although *gas-oil* (diesel fuel) is only about one-third of that. Unleaded fuel is now widely available, but off the beaten track it's a good idea to carry extra.

Tolls are comparable to those in North America or Australia, pushing costs even higher unless shared by several people. In some areas, most notably Buenos Aires province, tolls on privatized highways are very high – as much as US$4 per 100km.

Formally, you must have an International or Inter-American Driving Permit to supplement your national or state driver's license. In practice, police rarely examine these documents closely and generally ignore the latter. They do not ignore automobile registration, insurance, and tax documents, which must be up to date. Except in Buenos Aires, security problems are few, and you should not drive in Buenos Aires anyway.

Although motorbikes have become fashionable among some Argentines, they are very expensive, and there are apparently no motorcycle rental agencies in Argentina.

Certain warning signs on the road that are worth heeding include:

bache	pothole
cruce ferrocarril	railroad crossing
guardaganado	cattle guard
vado	dip

Road Rules & Hazards

Once, in the province of Buenos Aires, an Argentine driver passed us at very high speed *on the left side* of a traffic island separating one-way lanes at a major T-intersection. In another instance, in the province of Salta, an enormous truck blithely ignored a red light to pass us at an intersection where dozens of schoolgirls were crossing the highway on their way home for lunch. Yet another time, after dark in the province of Neuquén, a car traveling in excess of 150km per hour *without headlights* passed and nearly collided with a bus headed in the opposite direction.

These incidents are not unusual. Anyone considering driving in Argentina should know that Argentine drivers are reckless, aggressive, and even willfully dangerous, ignoring speed limits, road signs, and even traffic signals. Traffic accidents are the main cause of death for Argentines between the ages of five and 35; in 1994, Argentina's traffic fatality rate of 1200 per million vehicles was about five times that in Italy (241 per million) or the USA (229 per million). In 1997, more than 11,000 Argentines died on the highways. The Argentine television network Telefé once referred to the highway slaughter as the 'Guerra del Tránsito' (Traffic War).

Theoretically, most Argentine highways have a speed limit of 80km/h, though some have been raised to 100km/h or more, but hardly anybody pays attention to these or any other regulations. Tailgating is another serious hazard – it is not unusual to see half a dozen cars a meter or less apart, waiting for their chance to overtake a truck, which itself may be exceeding the speed limit.

During the Pampas harvest season, pay particular attention to slow-moving farm machinery, which, though not a hazard in its own right, brings out the worst in impatient Argentine motorists. Night driving is inadvisable; in some regions animals may roam on the road, but more often, many drivers seem to believe that they can see in the dark and, consequently, do not bother to use their headlights.

Astonishingly, in a country where nearly everyone drives dangerously fast even on very bad roads, a traffic law that went into effect in 1995 *raises* speed limits to 120km/h on highways and 130km/h on freeways. Under the same law, drivers must carry their title document (*tarjeta verde* or green card; for foreign vehicles, customs permission is the acceptable substitute), emergency reflectors (*valizas*), and one-kilo fire extinguishers. Headrests are also required for the driver and each passenger, and motorcycle helmets are now obligatory, though they are rarely used, and the law rarely enforced.

You will rarely see police patrolling the highways, where high-speed, head-on crashes are common, but you will meet them at major intersections and roadside checkpoints where they conduct meticulous document and equipment checks. A notoriously bad spot is the intersection of RN 9 and RN 14 at Zárate, in Buenos Aires province. Provincial borders are also sites for these annoying inspections; especially irritating are the opposite ends of the tunnel beneath the Río Paraná, which connects the towns of Santa Fe (Santa Fe province) and Paraná (Entre Ríos province).

If the police ask, for instance, to check your turn signals (which almost no Argentine bothers to use), brake lights, or hand brake, it may well be a warning of corruption in progress. Equipment violations ostensibly carry heavy fines – one Entre Ríos policewoman insisted my faulty brake light would cost me a US$300 fine – but such checks are most commonly pretexts for graft. The police may claim that you must pay the fine at a local bank, which may not be open until the following day, or if it's on a weekend, until Monday. If you are uncertain about your rights, state in a very matter-of-fact manner your intention to contact your embassy or consulate, or feign such complete ignorance of Spanish that you're more trouble than the police think it's worth. Offer a *coima* (bribe) only if you are confident that it is 'appropriate' and unavoidable.

Rental

International rental agencies like Hertz, Avis, and AI have offices in Buenos Aires and in major cities and other tourist areas throughout Argentina. To rent a car, you must have a valid driver's license and be at least 21 years of age; some agencies may not rent to anyone younger than 25. It may also be necessary to present a credit card such as MasterCard or Visa.

Even at minor agencies, rental charges are now very high. The cheapest and smallest vehicles go for about US$27 per day plus US$0.27 per kilometer (you can sometimes negotiate a lower rate by paying in cash rather than by credit card); rates are even higher in Patagonia. When you factor in the cost of insurance and gasoline, operating a vehicle becomes very pricey indeed, unless several people share expenses. Although unlimited-mileage deals do exist, they usually only apply to weekly or longer periods and are very expensive. One potentially worthwhile tactic is to make a reservation with one of the major international agencies in your home country, which can sometimes guarantee lower rates.

If you opt for camping – feasible in or near most cities as well as the countryside – rather than staying in hotels, the money you save may offset a good part of the rental cost.

Purchase

If you are spending several months in Argentina, purchasing a car is an alternative worth exploring, but it has both advantages and disadvantages. On the one hand, it is more flexible than public transport and is likely to be cheaper than rentals, which can easily reach US$100 per day. If you resell it at the end of your stay, it may turn out even more economical. On the other hand, any used car can be a risk, especially on Patagonia's rugged backroads.

If you purchase a car, you must deal with the exasperating Argentine bureaucracy. You must have the title *(tarjeta verde* or green card), and license tax payments must be up-to-date. As a foreigner, you may find it useful to carry a notarized document authorizing your use of the car, since the bureaucracy moves too slowly to change the title easily. In any event, Argentines rarely do so because of the expense involved – even vehicles 30 years old or more often bear the original purchaser's name.

As a foreigner you may own a vehicle in Argentina, but, in theory at least, you may not take it out of the country even with a notarized authorization – although certain border crossings, such as Puerto Iguazú, appear to be more flexible. On the other hand, at Gualeguaychú in Entre Ríos province, Argentine customs were adamant in refusing permission for temporary export even with the legal owner's permission. Contact your consulate for assistance and advice, but hardly anyone can prevail against a truly determined customs official.

Argentina's domestic automobile industry has left a reserve of serviceable used cars in the country. The most popular models are Peugeot 404s and Ford Falcons, for which parts are readily available, but do not expect to find a dependable used car for less than about US$3000. Prices will be higher for a *gasolero*, a vehicle that uses cheaper diesel fuel. There is probably a better stock of used cars, at more reasonable prices, in Chile.

Insurance

Liability insurance is obligatory in Argentina, and police may ask to see proof of insurance at checkpoints. Fortunately, unlike many services in Argentina, it is reasonably priced; a four-month liability policy with US$1 million in coverage costs as little as US$100 (paid in cash), and is also valid, with slightly reduced coverage, in the neighboring countries of Chile, Bolivia, Paraguay, Brazil, and Uruguay. Since Chilean companies, for example, cannot provide such extensive coverage outside their own borders, foreign motorists may find it worthwhile to cross from Santiago to Mendoza to arrange a policy.

Among reputable Argentine insurers are Seguros Rivadavia and the Automóvil Club Argentino (ACA).

Automóvil Club Argentino

If you drive in Argentina, especially with your own car, it may be worthwhile to become a member of the Automóvil Club Argentino (ACA), which has offices, service stations, and garages throughout the country, offering free road service and towing in and around major cities. ACA also recognizes members of its overseas affiliates, such as the American Automobile Association (AAA), as equivalent to its own members and grants them the same privileges, including discounts on maps, accommodations, camping, tours, and other services. Membership costs about US$30 per month, which is more expensive than most of its overseas counterparts.

ACA's head office (☎ 802-6061) is at Av del Libertador 1850, Palermo, in Buenos Aires. ACA has offices in every major city.

Shipping a Vehicle

Chile is probably the best country on the continent for shipping a vehicle from overseas, though the situation in Argentina is improving. To get the vehicle out of customs, it typically involves routine paperwork. If the car is more than a few days in customs, however, storage charges can add up quickly.

To find a reliable shipper, check the yellow pages of your local phone directory under Automobile Transporters. Most transporters are accustomed to arranging shipments between North America and Europe, rather than from North America or Europe to South America, so it may take some of them time to work out details.

From the west coast of North America, one possibility is McClary, Swift & Co (☎ 650-872-2121, fax 872-3465), 360 Swift Ave, South San Francisco, CA 94080.

In Europe, try A Hartrodt Nederland (☎ 031-180-486222, fax 414353), Rietdekkerstraat 8, 2284-BM Ridderkerk, Netherlands. The Argentine representative is A Hartrodt SPL (☎ 01-326-2830, fax 322-1374), Av Corrientes 436, Oficina 163, Buenos Aires. Motorcyclists have used Aerolíneas Argentinas air freight to ship their vehicles, but this is far more expensive than sea freight.

When shipping a vehicle into Argentina or Chile, do not leave anything whatsoever of value in the vehicle if at all possible. Theft of tools in particular is very common.

BICYCLE

Bicycling is an interesting, inexpensive alternative for traveling around Argentina – if you camp, it could make your trip nearly as cheap as in the Andean countries.

There are many good routes for bicycling, especially around the Patagonian lake district and in the Andean Northwest – the highway from Tucumán to Tafí del Valle, the direct road from Salta to Jujuy, and the Quebrada de Cafayate would be exceptionally beautiful rides on generally good surfaces.

While many Argentines use bikes for transportation, bicycling is an increasingly popular recreational activity. Many towns do have bike shops, but high-quality bikes are expensive and repair parts can be hard to come by. Bicycle rentals (primarily mountain bikes) are available in Mendoza, Bariloche, and other towns in the lake district, where recreation is an important industry. Racing bicycles are suitable for some paved roads, but these are often narrow; a *todo terreno* (mountain bike) would be safer and more convenient, allowing you to use the unpaved shoulder and the very extensive network of graveled roads throughout the country. Argentine bicycles are improving in quality but are still not equal to their counterparts in Europe or the USA.

There are two major drawbacks to bicycling in Argentina. One is the wind, which in Patagonia can slow your progress to a crawl. The other is Argentine motorists with total disregard of anyone but themselves. On many of the country's straight, narrow, two-lane highways, they can be a serious hazard to bicyclists, but LP reader Paul Arundale, who has cycled extensively through the Southern Cone, suggests less-traveled secondary roads as excellent alternatives:

> Argentina is a wonderful country for cycling, as it is covered by a network of unsurfaced smooth earth or rough stone roads. This means that you can cycle anywhere in the country, even out of Buenos Aires and other large cities, without having to compete for road space with the speedy traffic on the main roads, as long as you are prepared with a good map and plenty of food and water.
>
> On these unsurfaced roads traffic is maybe one or two pickup trucks per day and, without exception, overtaking vehicles move completely across to the left-hand side of the road, which is not the case on main roads. There are several unsurfaced routes crossing the Andes into Chile, such as the Caracoles to Cochrane road in the south and the Bardas Blancas to Talca and the Jáchal to Vicuña routes either side of Santiago, which offer ideal, traffic-free cycling for the well prepared. There are

few fences near these roads, and a tent can be pitched anywhere.

Readers seeking more information on cycling in South America can find it in Walter Sienko's *Latin America by Bike*.

HITCHHIKING

Hitchhiking is never entirely safe in any country in the world, and we don't recommend it. Travelers who decide to hitch should understand that they are taking a small but potentially serious risk. People who do choose to hitch will be safer if they travel in pairs and let someone know where they are planning to go.

Along with Chile, Argentina is probably the best country for hitching in all of South America. The major drawback is that Argentine vehicles are often stuffed with families and children, but truckers will frequently pick up backpackers. At the *servicentros* at the outskirts of large Argentine cities, where truckers gas up their vehicles, it is often worthwhile soliciting a ride.

Women can and do hitchhike alone, but should exercise caution and especially avoid getting into a car with more than one man. In Patagonia, where distances are great and vehicles few, hitchers should expect long waits and carry warm, windproof clothing. A water bottle is also a good idea, especially in the desert north. Also carry some snack food.

There are a few routes along which hitching is undesirable. RN 40, still carrying a small (though increasing) amount of traffic from El Calafate to Perito Moreno and Río Mayo, is a challenge to your patience and the lack of services along the way is a serious drawback. The scenic route from Tucumán to Cafayate is very difficult past Tafí del Valle. The Andean crossing from Salta to Antofagasta, Chile, is utterly futile.

BOAT

Opportunities for boat or river travel in Argentina are limited, except for regular international services (see the Getting There & Away chapter). There is a passenger ferry from Rosario, Santa Fe province, across the Río Paraná to Victoria, Entre Ríos. There are also numerous boat excursions around the Delta of the Río de la Plata from the Buenos Aires suburb of Tigre. Every winter, there is a river cruise up the Paraná to Asunción, Paraguay; ask for details at travel agencies in the capital.

LOCAL TRANSPORT

To/From the Airport

In most Argentine cities, each airline has a minibus operating in tandem with the flight schedule; sometimes Aerolíneas Argentinas and Austral combine their operations. There is also usually a city bus which stops at the airport.

In Buenos Aires, there is a variety of ways to get to either the domestic airport Aeroparque or the international airport at Ezeiza. See the Buenos Aires chapter for details.

Bus

Even small Argentine cities have extensive public transportation networks, usually bus systems. Except when conducting 'work-to-rule' stoppages, Buenos Aires' bus drivers go for speed before safety, and there have been serious accidents in which buses have run over pedestrians on the sidewalk as well as on the street.

Buses are clearly numbered and usually carry a placard indicating their final destination. Since many identically numbered buses serve slightly different routes, pay attention to these placards. When you board a bus, tell the driver your final destination and he will indicate the fare; most buses now have automatic fare machines that issue the ticket (do not lose this ticket, which may be checked en route) and make change. In some cities *cospeles* (tokens) or magnetic tickets have supplanted coins.

Train

Despite reductions in long-distance services, there remains an extensive system of commuter trains from Constitución, Retiro, Once, and Lacroze stations to the suburbs of Gran Buenos Aires. These are very inexpensive and cheaper than buses over the comparable routes.

Underground

Buenos Aires is the only Argentine city with a subway system. Presently undergoing renovation and extension into some suburban barrios, it's the quickest way of getting around the city center. For details, see the Buenos Aires chapter.

Taxi & Remise

Like New Yorkers, the porteños of Buenos Aires make frequent use of taxis, which are digitally metered and reasonably priced. Outside Buenos Aires, meters are common but not universal, and it may be necessary to agree upon a fare in advance. Drivers are generally polite and honest, but there are exceptions; be sure the meter is set at zero. It is customary to round off the fare as a tip.

In areas like Patagonia, where public transportation can be scarce, it's possible to hire a cab with a driver for the day to visit places off the beaten track. If you bargain, this can actually be cheaper than a rental car, but negotiate the fee in advance.

Remises are radio taxis without meters that generally offer fixed fares within a given zone. They are an increasingly popular form of transportation and are slightly cheaper than taxis. Unlike taxis, they may not cruise the city in search of fares, but hotels and restaurants will gladly phone them for you.

ORGANIZED TOURS

Movi Track (☎/fax 087-316749, movitrack@arnet.com.ar), Buenos Aires 68, Oficina 1B, 4400 Salta, operates comfortable backroads excursions through northern Argentina and Chile in their custom-designed Movi Track (available for charters as well). Owners Frank and Heike Neumann speak excellent English. Movi Track's Buenos Aires agent is Kraft Travel Service (☎/fax 793-4062), E Lamarca 343, 1° Piso, No 17, 1640 Martínez, Provincia de Buenos Aires.

In Neuquén province, the Anglo-Argentine Estancia Huechahue, in a sheltered valley on the Río Aluminé, about 30km east of Junín de los Andes, offers all-inclusive riding and trekking holidays in pleasant surroundings both there and in Parque Nacional Lanín. Accommodations are very comfortable, amid apple orchards and tranquil forest plantations. For nonriding companions there are walking, bird watching, Indian history, and the activities of a working estancia.

The basic daily price of $245 per person includes transportation between Huechahue and San Martín de los Andes plus full board and beverages (the latter with minor exceptions). For details, contact Jane Williams (jane@satlink.com) for reservations, far in advance of the trip.

Buenos Aires

In the early 1980s, the Radical government of President Raúl Alfonsín proposed moving the seat of government to the small northern Patagonian city of Viedma, but powerful opposition soon forced him to abandon the plan. His failure vividly illustrated the persistent dominance of Buenos Aires; the relatively small Capital Federal (Federal District) and Gran Buenos Aires (Greater Buenos Aires), which includes nearby suburbs in Buenos Aires province, are home to nearly 40% of Argentina's 33 million citizens. Almost all Argentines admit that this concentration of political and economic power is undesirable, but the residents of large and important cities such as Córdoba and Rosario most vigorously criticize the capital's primacy.

HISTORY

Buenos Aires dates from 1536, when Spanish explorer Pedro de Mendoza camped on a bluff above the Río de la Plata, possibly at the site of present-day Parque Lezama. Mendoza's oversized expedition, comprising 16 ships and nearly 1600 men, arrived too late in summer to plant crops, and the few Querandí Indians reacted violently when the Spaniards forced them to seek food. Scant provisions and incessant Indian resistance led some members of the expedition to sail up the Paraná, where they founded the city of Asunción among the more sedentary and obliging Guaraní peoples. Within five years, the Spaniards had completely abandoned Buenos Aires to the Querandí.

More than four decades passed before the Spaniards of Asunción, led by Juan de Garay, reestablished themselves on the west bank of the Río de la Plata. Even then, at the end of a tenuous supply line stretching from Madrid via Panama and Lima, Buenos Aires was clearly subordinate to Asunción; the city survived but did not flourish. Garay himself died at the hands of the Querandí only three years later.

Over the next two centuries, Buenos Aires grew slowly but steadily on the basis of the enormous herds of feral cattle and horses that began to proliferate when the first Spaniards abandoned them on the Pampas. As local frustration with Spain's mercantile restrictions grew, merchants began to smuggle contraband from Portuguese and British vessels. In 1776 Buenos Aires' promotion to capital of the new Viceroyalty of the River Plate, which included the famous silver district of Potosí, was palpable recognition that the adolescent city had outgrown Spain's parental control.

In the late colonial history of Buenos Aires and the country, the British invasions of 1806 and 1807 were a major turning point. After first seeming to cooperate with British forces, criollo forces repelled them. Only three years later influential criollos, on the pretext that Spain's legitimate government had fallen, confronted and deposed Viceroy Baltasar Hidalgo de Cisneros. As described by American diplomat Caesar Rodney, the architects of the revolution and the people of the city showed remarkable restraint and maturity:

> At some periods of the revolution, when the bands of authority were relaxed, the administration actually devolved into the hands of the inhabitants of the city. Hence, it might have been imagined, endless tumult and disorder would have sprung up, leading directly to pillage and bloodshed. Yet no such disturbances ever took place; all remained quiet. . . . The people have in no instance demanded victims to satisfy their vengeance; on the contrary, they have sometimes, by the influence of public opinion, moderated the rigor with which their rulers were disposed to punish the guilty.

Six years later, in Tucumán, the United Provinces of the River Plate declared independence but failed to resolve the conflict between two elite sectors: the landowners of the interior, concerned about preserving their economic privileges, and the residents of Buenos Aires (not yet the capital), who maintained an outward orientation toward overseas commerce and European ideas. After more than a decade of violence and uncertainty, Federalist leader Juan Manuel de Rosas asserted his authority over Buenos Aires.

When Charles Darwin visited Buenos Aires in 1833, shortly after the ruthless Rosas took power, he was impressed that the city of 60,000 was:

> large; and I should think one of the most regular in the world. Every street is at right angles to the one it crosses, and the parallel ones being equidistant, the houses are collected into solid squares of equal dimensions, which are called quadras. On the other hand the houses themselves are hollow squares; all the rooms opening into a neat little courtyard. They are generally only one story high, with flat roofs, which are fitted with seats, and are much frequented by the inhabitants in summer. In the center of the town is the plaza, where the public offices, fortress, cathedral . . . stand. Here also, the old viceroys, before the revolution had their palaces. The general assemblage of buildings possesses considerable architectural beauty, although none individually can boast of any.

Rosas' reign lasted nearly another three decades, as Buenos Aires' influence grew – paradoxically so in the face of the dictator's (apparently) opportunistic Federalist convictions. His overthrow opened the city to European immigration, and the population grew from 90,000 in 1854, to 177,000 in 1869, to 670,000 in 1895. By the turn of the century, Latin America's largest city had more than a million inhabitants.

In the 1880s, when the city became the official federal capital, indignant provincial authorities moved their offices to a new capital at La Plata. Still, as agricultural exports boomed, imports flowed into the country, and a new port was built, Buenos Aires became even more important. According to British diplomat James Bryce, who visited the capital at the turn of the 19th century, none of the leaders of Glasgow, Manchester, or Chicago 'shewed greater enterprise and bolder conceptions than did the men of Buenos Ayres when on this exposed and shallow coast they made alongside their city a great ocean harbour.'

Immigration and growth brought problems of course, as families crowded into substandard housing, merchants and manufacturers kept wages low, and labor became increasingly militant. In 1919, under pressure from landowners and other elite sectors, President Hipólito Yrigoyen's Radical government ordered the army to suppress a metalworkers' strike in what became known as La Semana Trágica (the Tragic Week), setting an unfortunate precedent for the coming decades.

In the 1930s, ambitious municipal governments undertook a massive downtown modernization program, as broad avenues like Santa Fe, Córdoba, and Corrientes obliterated narrow colonial streets. Since WWII, sprawling Gran Buenos Aires has absorbed many once-distant suburbs. Smaller in population than Mexico City or São Paulo, Buenos Aires remains Argentina's dominant economic, political, and cultural center. But a city that once prided itself on its European sophistication and livability now shares the same problems as other Latin American megacities – pollution, noise, decaying infrastructure, declining public services, unemployment and underemployment, and spreading shantytowns.

Not all signs are negative. Since the restoration of democracy in 1984, Buenos Aires has regained its former vivacity – political and public dialogue are freewheeling, the publishing industry has rebounded, and the arts and music flourish within the limits of economic reality. Fewer foolish public-works projects, like the motorway to Ezeiza Airport, are being built. Buenos Aires has still seen better days, but continues to offer the visitor a rich and unique urban experience.

ORIENTATION

At first glance, Buenos Aires appears as massive and imposing as New York or London, but a brief orientation suffices for exploring the city's compact, regular center and the most accessible *barrios* (neighborhoods) on foot. On brutally hot and humid summer days, bus, underground, and taxi services are good alternatives.

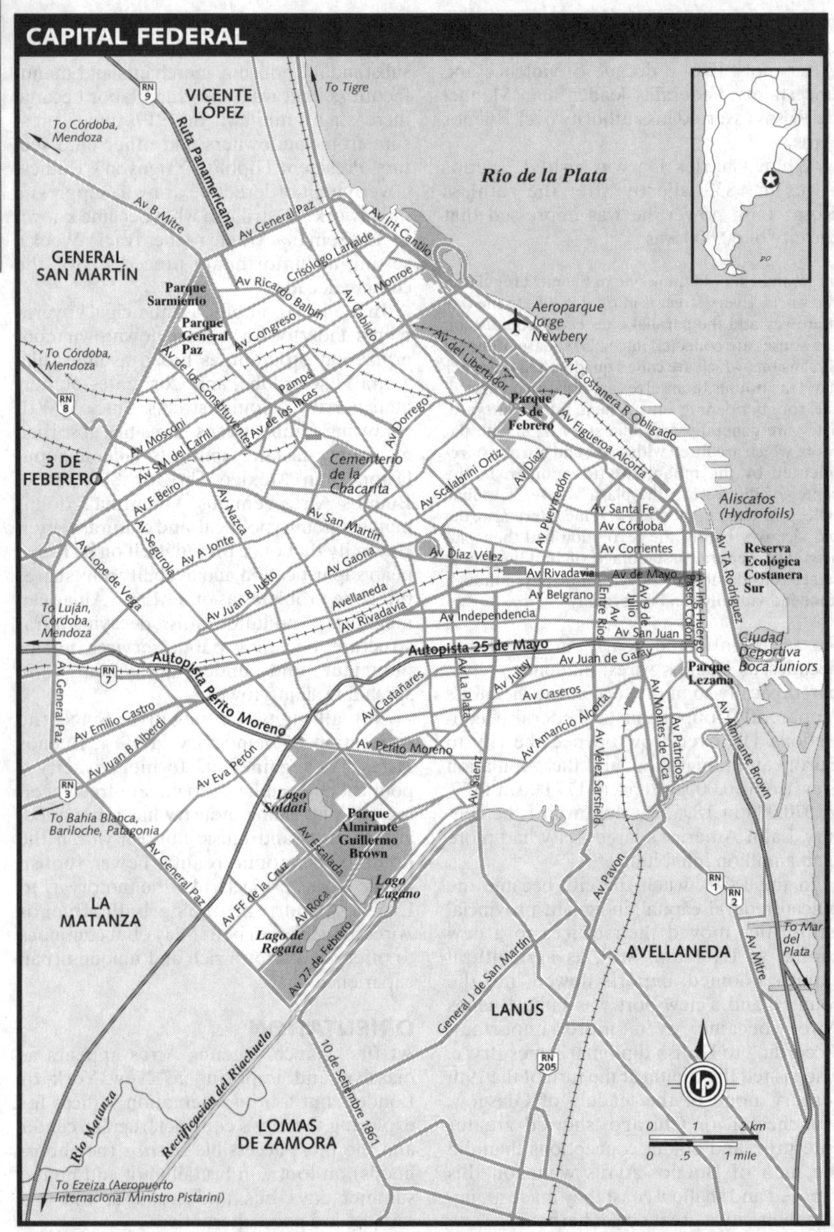
CAPITAL FEDERAL
Río de la Plata
VICENTE LÓPEZ
To Tigre
To Córdoba, Mendoza
Ruta Panamericana
Av B Mitre
Av General Paz
Av Int Cantilo
GENERAL SAN MARTÍN
Crisólogo Larralde
Monroe
Av Ricardo Balbín
Av Cabildo
Parque Sarmiento
Parque General Paz
Av Congreso
Aeroparque Jorge Newbery
Av del Libertador
Av Costanera R Obligado
Pampa
Av de los Constituyentes
Av de los Incas
Av Dorrego
Parque 3 de Febrero
Av Figueroa Alcorta
RN 8
Av Mosconi
Av SM del Carril
Cementerio de la Chacarita
Av Scalabrini Ortiz
Av Díaz
3 DE FEBERERO
Av F Beiro
Av Nazca
Av Pueyrredón
Aliscafos (Hydrofoils)
Av Santa Fe
Av Córdoba
Av Corrientes
Av San Martín
Av Segurola
Av A Jonte
Av Lope de Vega
Av Gaona
Av Díaz Vélez
Av Rivadavia
Av de Mayo
Reserva Ecológica Costanera Sur
Av TA Rodríguez
Av Belgrano
Av Juan B Justo
Avellaneda
Av Rivadavia
Av Independencia
Av Entre Ríos
Av 9 de Julio
Av Ing Huergo
Paseo Colón
To Luján, Córdoba, Mendoza
Av San Juan
Ciudad Deportiva Boca Juniors
Autopista 25 de Mayo
Av Juan de Garay
Av General Paz
RN 7
Autopista Perito Moreno
Av Castañares
Av La Plata
Av Jujuy
Parque Lezama
Av Caseros
Av Emilio Castro
Av Amancio Alcorta
Av Montes de Oca
Av Patricios
Av Almirante Brown
Av Juan B Alberdi
Av Eva Perón
Av Perito Moreno
Av Sáenz
Av Vélez Sarsfield
RN 3
To Bahía Blanca, Bariloche, Patagonia
Lago Soldati
Parque Almirante Guillermo Brown
Av Escalada
Av General Paz
Av FF de la Cruz
Lago Lugano
Av Pavon
RN 1
RN 2
LA MATANZA
Av Roca
Lago de Regata
Av 27 de Febrero
To Mar del Plata
AVELLANEDA
Av Mitre
General J de San Martín
LANÚS
RN 205
10 de Setiembre 1861
Rectificación del Riachuelo
Río Matanza
LOMAS DE ZAMORA
0 1 2 km
0 .5 1 mile
To Ezeiza (Aeropuerto Internacional Ministro Pistarini)

The traditional focus of activity is the Plaza de Mayo, where hundreds of thousands have rallied to cheer Perón or jeer Galtieri. Both the Catedral Metropolitana and remaining portions of the original Cabildo are also here, at the east end of Av de Mayo. At the west end is the Plaza del Congreso and the stately Congreso building, now undergoing a facelift after years of neglect. Street names change on each side of Av Rivadavia.

A pedestrian's nightmare, the broad Av 9 de Julio forms a second north-south axis, simultaneously encompassing Cerrito and Carlos Pellegrini north of Rivadavia, and Lima and Bernardo de Irigoyen south of Av de Mayo. It runs from Plaza Constitución in the south to Av del Libertador, which leads to the city's exclusive northern suburbs and their spacious parks.

One of the most popular tourist zones is the Microcentro, an area north of Av de Mayo and east of 9 de Julio that includes the Florida and Lavalle *peatonales* (pedestrian malls), Plaza San Martín, and the important commercial and entertainment areas along Avs Corrientes, Córdoba, and Santa Fe. Florida is a peatonal for its entire length, from Plaza San Martín to Diagonal Roque Sáenz Peña, and the Lavalle peatonal from Carlos Pellegrini has recently been extended beyond San Martín to Av Alem.

Beyond Av Santa Fe are the chic neighborhoods of Recoleta and Palermo. North of downtown, the residential areas of Retiro and Recoleta are informally known as Barrio Norte. South of the Plaza de Mayo are colorful, working-class San Telmo and La Boca.

Along the river, Av Costanera Rafael Obligado, more commonly known as 'La Costanera,' is a strip of restaurants and dance clubs, with occasional green spaces, which provide porteños' only real riverside access. Its major architectural landmark, the vaguely Tudor-style Club de Pescadores (Fishermen's Club), dates from 1937 and sits at the end of a 150m pier.

Street numbering is straightforward. Numbers on east-west streets start from zero near the waterfront, while those on north-south streets climb on each side of Av Rivadavia. Only outside the immediate downtown area does numbering become more complicated.

Maps The municipal Dirección de Turismo distributes a free *Plano Turístico*, which includes most of the central barrios and an up-to-date Subte (subway) diagram. The downtown area, however, is cluttered by three-dimensional representations of certain buildings and other features, to the detriment of its usability.

Metrovías, the private operator of the Subte, publishes a very good pocket-size map of the area it serves, within which most of the capital's tourist attractions fall. Available free from most public information offices, it's the most convenient single map to carry around.

Covering a smaller area on a larger scale, Guías Taylor's *Plano Turístico de la Ciudad de Buenos Aires* focuses on the Microcentro and San Telmo, Recoleta, La Boca, and Palermo barrios. Widely available from kiosks along Florida, it also contains a useful Subte diagram, but oversized symbols for some landmarks detract from the map's readability. A smaller bilingual version is available free from public information offices. Another common giveaway called *The Golden Map Buenos Aires* has similar virtues and shortcomings.

For visitors spending some time in Buenos Aires, the best resources are Lumi Transportes' *Capital Federal* and *Capital Federal y Gran Buenos Aires*, both in compact ring-binder format, with all city streets and bus routes indexed. A similar worthwhile acquisition is the *Guía Peuser*.

INFORMATION

Tourist Offices

The Dirección Nacional de Turismo (☎ 4312-2232), Av Santa Fe 883, is open weekdays 9 am to 5 pm; there's also a branch (☎ 4480-0224) at Aeropuerto Internacional Ezeiza. Both have knowledgeable English-speaking staff.

More convenient for most purposes is the municipal tourist kiosk at the intersection of

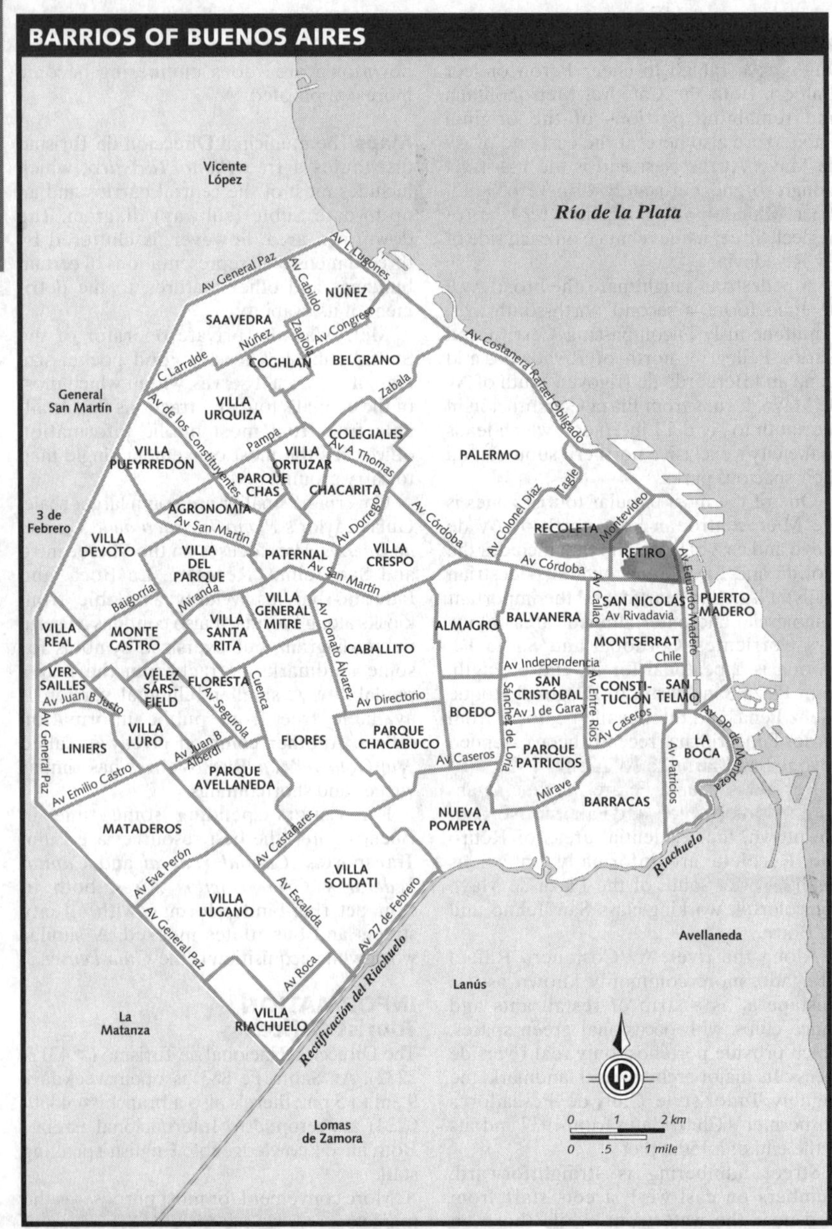
BARRIOS OF BUENOS AIRES
Río de la Plata
Vicente López
General San Martín
3 de Febrero
La Matanza
Lomas de Zamora
Lanús
Avellaneda
NÚÑEZ
SAAVEDRA
COGHLAN
BELGRANO
VILLA URQUIZA
COLEGIALES
VILLA PUEYRREDÓN
VILLA ORTUZAR
PARQUE CHAS
CHACARITA
PALERMO
AGRONOMÍA
RECOLETA
RETIRO
VILLA DEVOTO
VILLA DEL PARQUE
PATERNAL
VILLA CRESPO
SAN NICOLÁS
PUERTO MADERO
VILLA REAL
MONTE CASTRO
VILLA SANTA RITA
VILLA GENERAL MITRE
ALMAGRO
BALVANERA
MONTSERRAT
CABALLITO
VERSAILLES
VÉLEZ SÁRSFIELD
FLORESTA
SAN CRISTÓBAL
CONSTITUCIÓN
SAN TELMO
VILLA LURO
BOEDO
LINIERS
FLORES
PARQUE CHACABUCO
PARQUE PATRICIOS
LA BOCA
PARQUE AVELLANEDA
BARRACAS
MATADEROS
NUEVA POMPEYA
VILLA SOLDATI
VILLA LUGANO
VILLA RIACHUELO
Av General Paz
Av L Lugones
Av Cabildo
Zapiola
Av Congreso
Núñez
C Larralde
Av Costanera Rafael Obligado
Zabala
Av de los Constituyentes
Pampa
Av A Thomas
Tagle
Montevideo
Av Colonel Díaz
Av Córdoba
Av Dorrego
Av San Martín
Av Callao
Av Eduardo Madero
Av Rivadavia
Baigorria
Miranda
Av Donato Álvarez
Chile
Av Independencia
Cuenca
Av Directorio
Av Juan B Justo
Av Segurola
Sánchez de Loria
Av J de Garay
Av Entre Ríos
Av Caseros
Av DP de Mendoza
Av Juan B Alberdi
Av Emilio Castro
Av Patricios
Mirave
Riachuelo
Av Castañares
Av Eva Perón
Av Escalada
Av 27 de Febrero
Rectificación del Riachuelo
Av Roca
0 1 2 km
0 .5 1 mile

the Florida peatonal and Diagonal Roque Sáenz Peña (open 10 am to 6 pm weekdays, 2 to 6 pm weekends and holidays) and the office in the Galerías Pacífico, at Av Córdoba and Florida (open weekdays 10 am to 4 pm, Saturday 11 am to 6 pm). Both distribute excellent pocket-size maps in English and Spanish, as well as other brochures.

For more detailed information on the city, visit the Dirección General de Turismo de la Municipalidad de Buenos Aires (☎ 4476-3612, 4371-1496), in the Centro Cultural San Martín, 5th floor, Sarmiento 1551. This office sometimes organizes free weekend guided walks of certain barrios and also distributes a new series of brochures on walks and tours in barrios beyond the usual tourist circuit.

Immigration

The Dirección Nacional de Migraciones (☎ 4312-3288) is at Antártida Argentina 1335, just beyond Dársena Norte.

Money

While the convertibility law has reduced the need to change money, dozens of exchange houses still line San Martín, Argentina's equivalent of Wall St or the City of London, south of Av Corrientes. There are many more to the north of Corrientes, along Corrientes itself, and on the Florida peatonal. Cambio hours are generally 9 am to 6 pm weekdays, but a few open Saturday morning.

The only real reason to use cambios, however, is to cash traveler's checks, which are easier to change here than elsewhere in the country, or to exchange currencies other than US dollars. American Express, Arenales 707 near Plaza San Martín, changes its own traveler's checks without commission.

An ATM card is a far better alternative. Downtown ATMs are so abundant that it would be superfluous to mention any in particular. Holders of MasterCard and Visa can also get cash advances at most downtown banks between 10 am and 4 pm.

Lost or Stolen Credit Cards The following local representatives of major international banking institutions can aid travelers in replacing lost or stolen credit cards and/or traveler's checks:

American Express
(☎ 4312-1661)
Arenales 707

Diners Club
(☎ 4379-4545)
Carlos Pellegrini 1023

MasterCard
(☎ 4331-2088)
Perú 143

Visa
(☎ 4379-3300)
Corrientes 1437, 3rd floor

Post

Public The Correo Central, a distinctive beaux arts building at Sarmiento 189, occupies an entire block along Av Leandro Alem between Av Corrientes and Sarmiento. Open weekdays 9 am to 7:30 pm, it's the only post office that deals with international express mail. It does not accept US dollars. For international parcels weighing more than 1kg, visit the Correo Internacional, on Antártida Argentina, near Retiro Station. Hours are weekdays 11 am to 5 pm.

Private Private international and national services are more dependable than Correo Argentino (formerly Encotel) but also more expensive. Federal Express (☎ 4393-6054) is at Maipú 753. DHL International (☎ 4347-0600) is at Moreno 967.

Telephones

Argentina's two phone companies, Telecom and Telefónica, have split the city down the middle at Av Córdoba. Theoretically, everything north belongs to Telecom, while everything south is the responsibility of Telefónica, but occasionally there's a bit of overlap. Most public telephones work, though they are usually located on noisy corners.

To make a local call, purchase *cospeles* (tokens) or a more convenient *tarjeta magnética* (phone card) from almost any kiosk or newsstand, or from street vendors; there are two kinds of cospeles, one for local calls and one for long-distance. Should you get through, you will only be able to speak for about two minutes, so carry a pocketful of cospeles.

Long-distance offices are usually very busy, especially during evening (10 pm to 8 am) and weekend discount hours, when overseas calls are most economical. Telefónica's most convenient and efficient office, open 24 hours, is at Corrientes 701, where direct links with operators in North America, Japan, Europe, and neighboring countries simplify overseas collect or credit-card calls (see Facts for the Visitor for a list of operator services). Otherwise, an attendant will give you a priority number and, when that number is called, a cashier will give you a ticket for a booth; once in the booth, you can either dial directly or request operator assistance. When you finish your call, pay the cashier.

Telecom has a comparable office at Av Córdoba 379 in Retiro, but it keeps shorter hours, 9 am to 11 pm only. Many *locutorios* (long-distance offices) have sprung up around central Buenos Aires, so it's usually not necessary to make a long detour simply to place a long distance or overseas call, or to send or receive a fax. However, few locutorios care to handle collect or credit-card calls, which must be placed at Telecom or Telefónica offices, or from a private telephone.

Buenos Aires' area code is ☎ 011.

Telegrams, Telex & Fax

International telegrams, telexes, and faxes can be sent from Encotel, which is still a state monopoly, at Corrientes 711, next door to the main Telefónica office.

Email & Internet Access

Online services, including Internet cafés, are becoming more and more common in Buenos Aires, but they are still expensive compared with those in the US or Europe. The 2600 Internet Café (☎ 4807-4929), Scalabrini Ortiz 3191 in Palermo, charges US$8 per hour; it's open Monday to Thursday 11 am to midnight, Friday and Saturday 11 am to 1:30 am, and Sunday 6 pm to midnight. Other possibilities include the Leru Bar (☎ 4383-4940), at Rivadavia 1475 in San Nicolás (Congreso), and the Cybercafé (☎ 4775-9440), at Maure 1886 in Palermo, on the border of Belgrano.

Two Palermo shopping centers also have Internet cafés. At the Web Café (☎ 4827-8000), in the Alto Palermo Shopping at Díaz and Arenales, the US$11 hourly charge includes coffee and a snack. Cybermanía (☎ 4804-9666), at the Gazebo Paseo Alcorta, Av Figueroa Alcorta and Salguero, has two computers only.

Travel Agencies

Asatej (☎ 4311-6953, fax 4311-6840), the Argentine affiliate of STA Travel, has its main offices on the 3rd floor, Oficina 319B, at Florida 835. Open weekdays 9 am to 6 pm, it has the cheapest airfares available (the US$159 roundtrip to Santiago, Chile, is only slightly more than the equivalent bus fare, though airport taxes are additional). Asatej also publishes a brochure of discount offers at hotels, restaurants, and other businesses throughout the country for holders of international student cards.

Another youth- and student-oriented travel agency is the Asociación Argentina de Albergues de la Juventud (☎/fax 4476-1001), 2nd floor, Oficina 6, Talcahuano 214 in San Nicolás. It issues hostel memberships and international student cards, and has a message board for travelers (mostly young Argentines) seeking companions for extended trips.

American Express (☎ 4312-0900, fax 4315-1866), Arenales 707 north of Plaza San Martín, cashes its own traveler's checks without additional commission and offers many other services. Reader-recommended Swan Turismo (☎/fax 4816-2080), Cerrito 822, 9th floor, will help renegotiate air passes and make connections with LADE or other airlines for which timetables are not easily available outside the country.

Photography

Kinefot (☎ 4374-7445), Talcahuano 248 in San Nicolás (Congreso), has fast, high-quality developing of E-6 slide film, but is not cheap. For prints, try Le Lab (☎ 4322-2785), at Viamonte 624, or Laboclick, at Esmeralda 444.

For minor camera repairs, visit Gerardo Föhse (☎ 4311-1139), Florida 835, Local 37. For fast, reliable service on more complex problems, contact José Norres (☎ 4373-0963), 4th floor, Oficina 403, Lavalle 1569.

Bookstores

Buenos Aires' landmark bookstore El Ateneo (☎ 4325-6801), Florida 340, has a large selection of travel books, including LP guides, but foreign language books are expensive. Librería ABC, at Córdoba 685, has similar stock.

For the most complete selection of guidebooks, including nearly every LP title in print, visit Librerías Turísticas (☎ 4963-2866, ☎/fax 4962-5547), at Paraguay 2457 (Subte: Pueyrredón, Línea D), near Barrio Norte. Its prices are also the most reasonable for foreign-language guidebooks.

Visiting academics and curiosity seekers should explore the basement stacks at Librería Platero (☎ 4382-2215), Talcahuano 485, which stocks a remarkable selection of new and out-of-print books about Argentina and Latin America. The staff is knowledgeable in almost every field of interest and efficient in packaging and sending books overseas. Another shop with similar stock is Aquilanti (☎ 4952-4546), Rincón 79 in the Congreso area.

French speakers can find a wide selection of reading material at Oficina del Libro Francés, with locations at Esmeralda 861 (☎ 4311-0363) and Talcahuano 342, 2nd floor (☎ 4374-4747).

Several street markets have good selections of used books, including those at Plaza Lavalle near Librería Platero; Av Santa Fe outside the Palermo Subte station; and outside the Primera Junta Subte station (end of the line for Línea A).

Libraries

The Biblioteca Nacional (National Library, ☎ 4806-9764), at Agüero 2502 in Recoleta, is open Monday to Saturday 8 am to 9 pm, Sunday 11 am to 7 pm. The US Information Agency has moved its excellent Biblioteca Lincoln, which carries *The New York Times*, the *Washington Post*, and English-language magazines, to the Instituto Cultural Argentino-Norteamericano (☎ 4322-3855, 4322-4557), Maipú 672.

Cultural Centers

One of Buenos Aires' finest cultural resources is the high-rise Centro Cultural San Martín (☎ 4374-1251), with free or inexpensive galleries, live theater, and lectures. Most visitors enter from Av Corrientes, between Paraná and Montevideo, but the official address is Sarmiento 1551, where its Plaza Cubierta is a shaded alcove with rotating exhibitions of outdoor sculptures and occasional free concerts on summer evenings and weekends. Films are shown at its Sala Leopoldo Lugones (visited by more than 80,000 moviegoers in 1999), while photographers display their work at the basement Fotogalería. Ask at the front desk for a monthly list of events or check the boards outside the Corrientes entrance.

At Junín 1930 in Recoleta, the Centro Cultural Ciudad de Buenos Aires (☎ 4803-1041) also offers free or inexpensive events, such as art exhibitions and outdoor films on summer evenings. At the southeast corner of the Galerías Pacífico, at the corner of Viamonte and San Martín, the new Centro Cultural Borges (☎ 4319-5359) features art exhibits. It's open Monday to Thursday 10 am to 9 pm, Friday to Sunday 10 am to 10 pm. Admission is US$2.

There are also several foreign cultural centers in and around the Microcentro, such as the Instituto Cultural Argentino-Norteamericano (☎ 4322-3855, 4322-4557), at Maipú 672; the Alianza Francesa (☎ 4322-0068), Av Córdoba 936; the Instituto Goethe (☎ 4315-3327), 1st floor, Av Corrientes 319; and the Asociación Argentina de Cultura Inglesa/British Arts Centre (☎ 4393-6941), Suipacha 1333.

Laundry

In recent years, Laundromats have become much more common in Buenos Aires, but they tend to be more expensive than their equivalent in the USA or Europe – figure about US$6 to US$8 per load, washed, dried, and folded. Some inexpensive hotels have spots where you can wash your own clothes and hang them to dry. In some places maid service will be reasonable, but agree on charges in advance.

Medical Services

Buenos Aires' Hospital Municipal Juan Fernández (☎ 4801-5555) is at Av Cerviño 3356 in Palermo, but there are many others, including the highly regarded British Hospital (☎ 4304-1081), at Perdriel 74 in Barracas, a few blocks southwest of the Constitución train station. The reader-recommended Hospital Alemán (☎ 4821-1700) is a private facility at Av Pueyrredón 1640, Recoleta.

Dangers & Annoyances

Personal security is a lesser concern in Buenos Aires than in most other Latin American cities, but travelers cannot afford to be complacent – pickpockets, purse-snatchers, and the like certainly exist. Watch for common diversions such as the 'inadvertent' collision that results in ice cream or some similar substance being spilled on an unsuspecting visitor, who loses precious personal possessions while distracted by the apologetic perpetrator working in concert with a thief (one eloquent LP reader has referred to them as 'mustard artists').

One high-profile crime that has drawn attention in recent years has been robberies of upscale restaurants by well-dressed gunmen, who, after dining, hold up the restaurant and its clientele; if this worries you, it's better to take just the money you need for a night on the town.

WAYNE BERNHARDSON

Madres de la Plaza de Mayo

While such crimes get great publicity, you're more likely to be a traffic victim – porteño (an inhabitant of Buenos Aires) drivers, like most Argentines, jump the gun when the red light is about to turn green; pedestrians should not insist on the right-of-way. Other troublesome and potentially deadly hazards include potholes and loose tiles on city sidewalks, which can also be very slippery when wet – people have died after falling and striking their heads. Fireworks are a serious concern around New Year's and other holidays.

THINGS TO SEE & DO

Most porteños 'belong' to a *barrio* (borough or neighborhood) where they have spent almost all their lives. Tourists rarely explore most of these, but five fairly central ones and the outlying barrio of Belgrano contain most of the capital's major attractions. The boundaries indicated below are more convenient than precise and sometimes even overlap, but they should orient you to the most important public buildings, parks, and museums. Note that most museums charge about US$1 admission but are usually free on Wednesday or Thursday.

Plaza de Mayo & the Microcentro

In 1580, Juan de Garay refounded Buenos Aires just north of Pedro de Mendoza's encampment near present-day Parque Lezama. In accordance with Spanish law, he laid out the large Plaza del Fuerte (Fortress Plaza), later called Plaza del Mercado (Market Plaza), then Plaza de la Victoria, after the victories over the British invaders in 1806 and 1807. It acquired its present name of **Plaza de Mayo** after the month in which the Revolution of 1810 occurred.

Major colonial buildings here included the **Cabildo**, part of which still exists, and a church at a site now occupied by the **Catedral Metropolitana**; within the cathedral is the tomb of the repatriated San Martín, who died in France. In the center of the plaza, the

Pirámide de Mayo is a small obelisk covering an earlier monument, around which the Madres de la Plaza de Mayo still march every Thursday afternoon in their unrelenting campaign for a full accounting of Dirty War atrocities.

At the east end of the plaza, the **Casa Rosada** (presidential palace), begun during Sarmiento's presidency, occupies a site where colonial riverbank fortifications once stood – today it is more than a kilometer inland because of landfill. From its balcony, Juan Perón, General Leopoldo Galtieri, Raúl Alfonsín, and other Argentine politicians have convened throngs of impassioned Argentines when they felt it necessary to show public support. In 1955, naval aircraft strafed the Casa Rosada and other downtown buildings in the so-called Revolución Libertadora, which toppled Perón.

Most other public buildings in the area belong to the 19th century, when Av de Mayo first connected the Casa Rosada to the **Plaza del Congreso** and the **Palacio del Congreso** – obliterating part of the historic and dignified Cabildo in the process. The visiting British diplomat Bryce, though, found these developments symbols of progress:

> One great thoroughfare, the Avenida de Mayo, traverses the center of the city from the large plaza in which the government buildings stand to the still larger and very handsome plaza which is adorned by the palace of the legislature. Fortunately it is wide, and being well planted with trees it is altogether a noble street, statelier than Piccadilly in London, or Unter den Linden in Berlin, or Pennsylvania Avenue in Washington. . . .
>
> The streets are well kept; everything is fresh and bright. The most striking new buildings besides those of the new Legislative Chambers, with their tall and handsome dome, are the Opera-house, the interior of which equals any in Europe, and the Jockey Club, whose scale and elaborate appointments surpass even the club-houses of New York.

Modern Buenos Aires' faded elegance and failure to keep pace with European and North American capitals might surprise Bryce today, but visitors can still glimpse the city's 'belle epoque,' even though the focus of downtown activities has moved north along streets such as Florida, Lavalle, and Avs Corrientes, Córdoba, and Santa Fe.

In the early part of the century Florida, then closed to motor vehicles between noon and 1:30 pm, was the capital's most fashionable shopping street – a status since lost to Av Santa Fe. Today both Florida and perpendicular Lavalle are pedestrian malls. Demolition of older buildings created the broad avenues of Corrientes (the theater district), Córdoba, and Santa Fe. The even broader Av 9 de Julio, with its famous **Obelisco** at the intersection with Corrientes, is a pedestrian's worst nightmare, but fortunately a tunnel runs beneath it. Two blocks north of the Obelisco, the **Teatro Colón** is Buenos Aires' major architectural and cultural landmark.

At the north end of downtown, just beyond **Plaza Liberador General San Martín** and its magnificent *ombú* tree, is the famous **Torre de los Ingleses**, a Big Ben clone testifying to the partial truth of the common aphorism that 'an Argentine is an Italian who speaks Spanish, wishes he were English, and behaves as if he were French.' Ironically, since the 1982 Falklands War the plaza in which it stands, opposite Retiro Station, is now the **Plaza Fuerza Aérea Argentina** (Air Force Plaza).

Museo del Cabildo Modern construction has twice truncated the Cabildo, which dates from the mid-18th century, but there remains a representative sample of the arches that once spanned the Plaza de Mayo. The two-story building itself is more interesting than the scanty exhibits, which include mementos of the early 19th-century British invasions, some modern paintings in colonial- and independence-era styles, religious art from missions of the Jesuits and other orders, and fascinating early photographs of the plaza.

At Bolívar 65, the museum (☎ 4334-1782) is open Tuesday to Friday 12:30 to 7 pm, Sunday 3 to 7 pm. Admission is US$1. Guided tours take place at 4:30 pm.

Catedral Metropolitana Also on the Plaza de Mayo, the cathedral (built on the

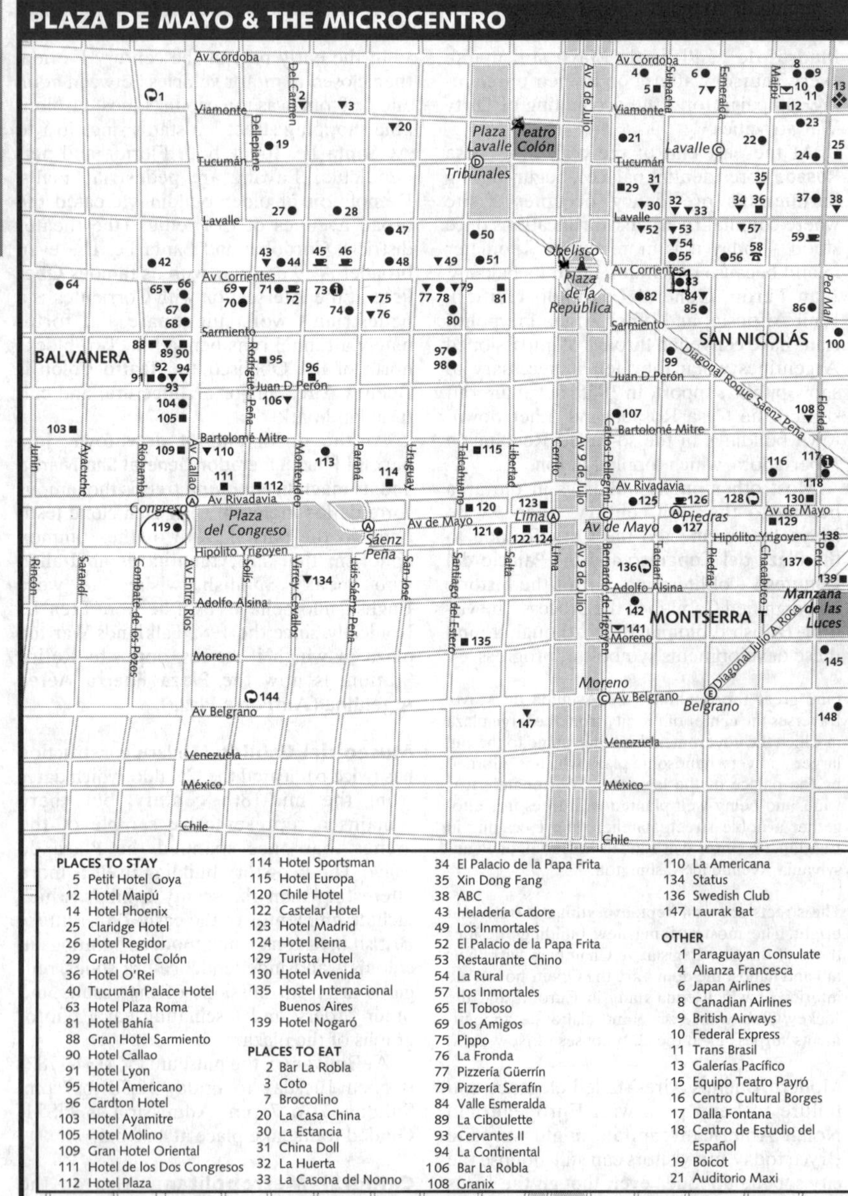
PLAZA DE MAYO & THE MICROCENTRO
Av Córdoba
Viamonte
Tucumán
Lavalle
Av Corrientes
Sarmiento
Juan D Perón
Bartolomé Mitre
Av Rivadavia
Av de Mayo
Hipólito Yrigoyen
Adolfo Alsina
Moreno
Av Belgrano
Venezuela
México
Chile
Del Carmen
Delfepiane
Rodríguez Peña
Junín
Ayacucho
Riobamba
Av Callao
Montevideo
Paraná
Uruguay
Talcahuano
Libertad
Cerrito
Carlos Pellegrini
Av 9 de Julio
Suipacha
Esmeralda
Maipú
Florida
Ped Mall
Rincón
Sarandí
Combate de los Pozos
Av Entre Ríos
Solís
Virrey Cevallos
Luis Sáenz Peña
San José
Santiago del Estero
Salta
Lima
Bernardo de Irigoyen
Tacuarí
Piedras
Chacabuco
Perú
Diagonal Roque Sáenz Peña
Diagonal Julio A Roca
Plaza Lavalle
Teatro Colón
Tribunales
Obelisco
Plaza de la República
Lavalle
SAN NICOLÁS
BALVANERA
MONTSERRA T
Congreso
Plaza del Congreso
Sáenz Peña
Lima
Av de Mayo
Piedras
Moreno
Belgrano
Manzana de las Luces
PLACES TO STAY
5 Petit Hotel Goya
12 Hotel Maipú
14 Hotel Phoenix
25 Claridge Hotel
26 Hotel Regidor
29 Gran Hotel Colón
36 Hotel O'Rei
40 Tucumán Palace Hotel
63 Hotel Plaza Roma
81 Hotel Bahía
88 Gran Hotel Sarmiento
90 Hotel Callao
91 Hotel Lyon
95 Hotel Americano
96 Cardton Hotel
103 Hotel Ayamitre
105 Hotel Molino
109 Gran Hotel Oriental
111 Hotel de los Dos Congresos
112 Hotel Plaza
114 Hotel Sportsman
115 Hotel Europa
120 Chile Hotel
122 Castelar Hotel
123 Hotel Madrid
124 Hotel Reina
129 Turista Hotel
130 Hotel Avenida
135 Hostel Internacional Buenos Aires
139 Hotel Nogaró
PLACES TO EAT
2 Bar La Robla
3 Coto
7 Broccolino
20 La Casa China
30 La Estancia
31 China Doll
32 La Huerta
33 La Casona del Nonno
34 El Palacio de la Papa Frita
35 Xin Dong Fang
38 ABC
43 Heladería Cadore
49 Los Inmortales
52 El Palacio de la Papa Frita
53 Restaurante Chino
54 La Rural
57 Los Inmortales
65 El Toboso
69 Los Amigos
75 Pippo
76 La Fronda
77 Pizzería Güerrín
79 Pizzería Serafín
84 Valle Esmeralda
89 La Ciboulette
93 Cervantes II
94 La Continental
106 Bar La Robla
108 Granix
110 La Americana
134 Status
136 Swedish Club
147 Laurak Bat
OTHER
1 Paraguayan Consulate
4 Alianza Francesa
6 Japan Airlines
8 Canadian Airlines
9 British Airways
10 Federal Express
11 Trans Brasil
13 Galerías Pacífico
15 Equipo Teatro Payró
16 Centro Cultural Borges
17 Dalla Fontana
18 Centro de Estudio del Español
19 Boicot
21 Auditorio Maxi

PLAZA DE MAYO & THE MICROCENTRO

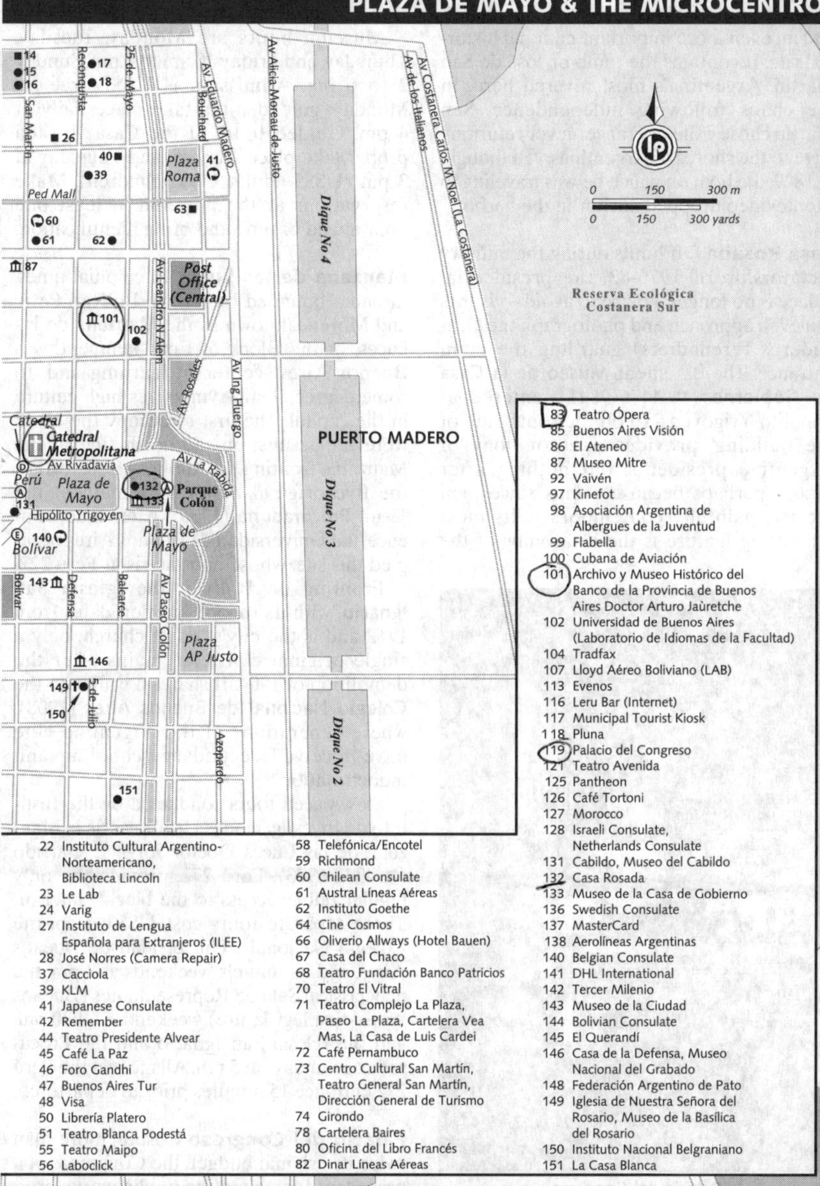

site of the original colonial church but not finished until 1827) is a religious landmark and an even more important national historical site. It contains the tomb of José de San Martín, Argentina's most revered hero. In the chaos following independence, San Martín chose exile in France, never returning alive to the shores of Argentina even though, in 1829, the boat on which he was traveling to Montevideo dropped anchor in the harbor.

Casa Rosada Off limits during the military dictatorship of 1976-83, the presidential palace is no longer a place to avoid – visitors can even approach and photograph the Granaderos (grenadiers) guarding the main entrance. The basement **Museo de la Casa de Gobierno** (☎ 4476-9841), entered at Hipólito Yrigoyen 219 on the south side of the building, provides a chronology of Argentine presidents, but nothing after 1966 – perhaps because events since then are too painfully contemporary. Its most interesting feature is the catacombs of the Fuerte Viejo, a colonial ruin dating from the 18th century.

ROBERT FRERCK

Palacio del Congreso

Museum hours are Monday, Tuesday, Thursday, and Friday 10 am to 6 pm, Sunday 2 to 6 pm. Admission is US$1, free on Monday; guided tours take place daily at 4 pm. Guided tours of the Casa Rosada proper take place Tuesday and Thursday at 3 pm (US$5 adults, US$2 children). Make reservations at the museum at least one hour ahead of time and bring identification.

Manzana de las Luces In colonial times, the area bounded by Alsina, Bolívar, Perú, and Moreno, known as the **Manzana de las Luces**, or the Block of Enlightenment, was Buenos Aires' center of learning and, to some degree, it still symbolizes high culture in the capital. The first to occupy the block were the Jesuits; on the north side of the Manzana, fronting on Adolfo Alsina, two of the five original buildings remain of the Jesuit **Procuraduría** (1730). After independence, the Universidad de Buenos Aires occupied this site, whose entrance is at Perú 222.

Fronting on Bolívar, the **Iglesia San Ignacio**, with its rococo interior, dates from 1712 and is the city's oldest church; only a single original cloister remains after the demolition of 1904. It shares a wall with the **Colegio Nacional de Buenos Aires** (1908), where generations of the Argentine elite have received secondary schooling and indoctrination.

Slow-paced tours conducted by the Instituto de Investigaciones Históricas de la Manzana de las Luces Doctor Jorge E Garrido (☎ 4342-6973), Perú 272, provide the only regular public access to the block's interior. Three separate tours cost US$3 each: the Colegio Nacional , Universidad de Buenos Aires, and its tunnels weekends at 3 pm; the neoclassical Sala de Representantes (Buenos Aires' first legislature) weekends at 4:30 pm; and the Iglesia San Ignacio and the Procuraduría Sundays at 5 pm. All meet at the Perú 272 entrance 15 minutes prior to departure.

Palacio del Congreso Costing more than twice its original budget, the Congreso set a precedent for Argentine public-works projects. Modeled on the Capitol Building in Washington, DC, and completed in 1906, it faces the Plaza del Congreso, where the **Monumento a los Dos Congresos** honors the congresses of 1810 in Buenos Aires and 1816 in Tucumán that led to Argentine independence. The monument's enormous granite steps symbolize the high Andes, and the fountain at its base represents the Atlantic Ocean, but the hordes of pigeons that stain the monument and foul its waters are poor surrogates for the Andean condor.

Museo Mitre Bartolomé Mitre was a soldier, journalist, and Argentina's first legitimate president under the Constitution of 1853, although he spent much of his 1862-8 term leading the country's armies against Paraguay. After leaving office, he founded the influential daily *La Nación*, which is still a porteño institution.

At San Martín 366, the Museo Mitre (☎ 4394-8240) is a sprawling colonial edifice (plus additions) where Mitre resided with his family – a good reflection of 19th-century upper-class life. Hours are weekdays 1 to 6:30 pm. Admission is US$1.

ROBERT FRERCK

Teatro Colón

Teatro Colón Ever since its opening in 1908 with a presentation of *Aïda*, this elaborate world-class facility for opera, ballet, and classical music has impressed visitors. In the lobby is a small but popular museum, with exhibits of costumes, instruments, and photographs of performers and performances.

Very worthwhile guided tours (US$5) take place hourly between 11 am and 3 pm weekdays, 9 am and noon on Saturday; there may also be a free tour at 3 pm on Thursday. They are given in Spanish, English, German, French, Portuguese, and even Danish, but only Spanish and English tours are always available. No tours take place in January.

On the tour, visitors see the theater from the basement workshops (which employ more than 400 skilled carpenters, sculptors, wigmakers, costume designers, and other *técnicos)* to the rehearsal rooms and the stage and seating areas. Note especially the *maquetas*, scale models used by the sculptors to help prepare the massive stage sets (the enormous pillars, statues, and other stage props are made of painted lightweight Styrofoam).

Occupying an entire block bounded by Libertad, Tucumán, Viamonte, and Cerrito (Av 9 de Julio), the imposing seven-story Teatro Colón (☎ 4382-6632) seats 2500 spectators and has standing room for another thousand. The main entrance is on Libertad, opposite Plaza Lavalle; for tours, enter from the Viamonte side.

Other Downtown Museums The well-organized **Archivo y Museo Histórico del Banco de la Provincia de Buenos Aires Doctor Arturo Jaúretche** (☎ 4331-1775), Sarmiento 362, is a superb introduction to Argentine economic and financial history from viceregal times to the present. It's open weekdays 10 am to 6 pm, Sunday 2 to 6 pm; admission is free.

At the **Museo Nacional del Teatro** (☎ 4815-8883, interno 195), in the Teatro Cervantes at Córdoba 1199 opposite Plaza Lavalle, exhibits include a gaucho suit worn by Gardel for his Hollywood film *El Día Que Me Quieras*. Also on display is the bandoneón belonging to Paquita Bernardo (the first Argentine musician to play the accordion-like instrument), who died of tuberculosis in 1925 at the age of 25. Hours are noon to 7 pm weekdays; admission is free.

The **Museo de la Ciudad** (☎ 4331-9855), on the 1st floor at Alsina 412, has both permanent and temporary exhibitions on porteño life and history. It's open weekdays 11 am to 7 pm, weekends 3 to 7 pm; admission is US$1, but is free on Wednesday.

Gutted by fire during the 1955 Revolución Libertadora against Perón, the late 18th-century **Museo de la Basílica del Rosario** in the Iglesia de Nuestra Señora del Rosario, at the corner of Defensa and Belgrano, contains relics of the British invasions and wars of independence. Hours are 9 am to 1 pm and 4:30 to 8:30 pm daily; guided tours take place at 3 pm Sunday. Alongside it, an eternal flame burns at the **Instituto Nacional Belgraniano**, which lionizes Argentina's second-greatest hero.

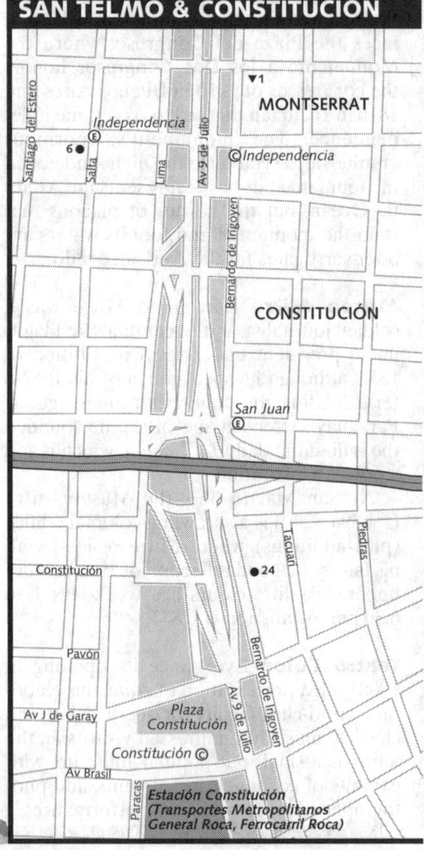

San Telmo

South of the Plaza de Mayo, San Telmo is an artist's quarter where bohemians find large spaces at low rents, but it's also the site of high-density slum housing in *conventillos* (tenements) once built as single-family housing for the capital's elite.

San Telmo is also famous for the rugged street fighting that took place when British troops invaded the city in 1806 and occupied it until the following year, when covert porteño resistance gave way to open counterattack. As British forces advanced up narrow Calle Defensa, an impromptu militia, supported by women and slaves pouring cauldrons of boiling oil and water from the rooftops and firing cannons from the balconies of the house at **Defensa 372**, routed the British back to their ships. Victory gave the porteños confidence in their ability to stand apart from Spain, though independence had to wait another decade.

At Defensa and Humberto Primo, **Plaza Dorrego** is the site of the famous Sunday flea market, the Feria de San Telmo. A few blocks south, at Defensa and Brasil, **Parque Lezama** is the presumptive site of Pedro de Mendoza's original foundation of the city.

After yellow fever hit the once-fashionable area in the late 19th century, the porteño elite evacuated to higher ground west and north of the present-day Microcentro. As immigrants poured into Argen-

tina, many older houses became conventillos housing European families in cramped, divided quarters with inadequate sanitary facilities. These conditions still exist – look for crumbling older houses with laundry on the balconies; a good example is the sprawling edifice at the corner of Balcarce 1170 and Humberto Primo.

Museo Histórico Nacional Appropriately located in Parque Lezama, this historical museum offers a panorama of the Argentine experience from its shaky beginnings to the present. The paintings in its Sala de la Conquista depicting the Spanish domination of wealthy, civilized Peru and Columbus' triumphant return to Spain contrast sharply with those of the Mendoza expedition's struggle on the shores of the Río de la Plata. There is also a map of Juan de Garay's second founding of the city four decades later.

In the Sala de la Independencia and other rooms are portraits of major figures, including Simón Bolívar, his ally and rival San Martín, both as a youth and disillusioned in old age, and Rosas and his scowling enemy Sarmiento. There are also portrayals of the

British invasions of 1806 and 1807, and of late 19th-century porteño life.

At Defensa 1600, the Museo Histórico (☎ 4307-1182) is theoretically open daily except Monday, 2 to 6 pm, but seems frequently closed for repairs. Admission is free.

Other San Telmo Museums The restored 19th-century Casa de la Defensa, at Defensa 372, may retain some elements of the historic structure despite an ill-advised 1970s remodeling. It houses the **Museo Nacional del Grabado** (☎ 4345-5300), a collection of mostly contemporary woodcuts and engravings. It's open daily except Saturday, 2 to 6 pm; admission is US$2 and usually includes a sample woodcut print.

Housed in a recycled tobacco warehouse at Av San Juan 350, the **Museo de Arte Moderno** (☎ 4361-1121) has become one of San Telmo's highlights for its collection of figurative art, as well as special exhibitions and film and video events. It's open Tuesday to Friday 10 am to 8 pm, weekends and holidays 11 am to 8 pm. Admission is US$1, but is free on Wednesday. The museum closes the entire month of January.

Well worth seeing is the private **Helft Collection** of modern Argentine art; there are no regularly scheduled hours, but guided tours (☎ 4307-9175) are available on request in Spanish, English, French, German, Italian, and Hungarian; reservations are essential.

ROBERT FRERCK

Twelve tails follow one *paseaperro* through a Recoleta park

La Boca

Literally Buenos Aires' most colorful barrio, La Boca was settled and built up by Italian immigrants along the **Riachuelo**, a small waterway lined by meatpacking plants and warehouses that separates Buenos Aires proper from the industrial suburb of Avellaneda. Part of La Boca's color comes from brightly painted houses of the **Caminito**, a favorite pedestrian walkway, which was once a rail terminus and takes its name from a popular tango. The rest comes from petroleum and industrial wastes tinting the waters of the Riachuelo, where rusting hulks and dredges lie offshore, and rowers strain to take passengers who prefer not to walk across the high girder bridge to Avellaneda.

It would probably be easier to refine the oily Riachuelo into diesel fuel than to clean it up, but María Julia Alsogaray, President Menem's environment secretary, has pledged to swim in it when a highly publicized cleanup campaign ends. By then she may well be hobbling in old age on a polluted watercourse solid enough to support her. (To be fair, some of the harbor's most hazardous eyesore rustbuckets have been removed.) At present, when rains are heavy and tides are high, floodwaters submerge much of the surrounding area.

Areas like La Boca were once places where immigrants could find a foothold in the country, but they were less than idyllic. Bryce, visiting at the turn of the 19th century, described them as:

> a waste of scattered shanties . . . dirty and squalid, with corrugated iron roofs, their wooden boards gaping like rents in tattered clothes. These are inhabited by the newest and poorest of immigrants from southern Italy and southern Spain, a large and not very desirable element among whom anarchism is rife.

In fact, French Basques preceded the Italians in La Boca. Today the area is partly an artists' colony, the legacy of the late painter Benito Quinquela Martín, but it's still a flourishing working-class neighborhood. The symbol of community solidarity is the Boca Juniors soccer team, once the club of disgraced superstar Diego Maradona; their stadium, **La Bombonera**, is at the corner of Brandsen and Del Valle Iberlucea.

Tourists also come to La Boca to savor the atmosphere of **Calle Necochea**, lined with pizzerias and garish cantinas. When these places were still brothels, the tango was not the respectable, middle-class phenomenon it is today.

The No 86 bus from Congreso is the easiest route to La Boca, although Nos 20, 25, 29, 33, 46, 53, 64, and 97 also stop in the vicinity of the Caminito.

Museo Nacional de Bellas Artes de La Boca Once the home and studio of Benito Quinquela Martín, La Boca's fine-arts museum exhibits his work and that of other 20th-century Argentine artists. At Pedro de Mendoza 1835, the museum (☎ 4301-1080) is open weekdays 10 am to 6 pm, weekends 11 am to 8 pm. Admission is free.

Recoleta & Barrio Norte

Northwest of downtown, fashionable Recoleta takes its name from the Franciscan convent that dates from 1716, but it is best known for the **Cementerio de la Recoleta** (Recoleta Cemetery), an astonishing necropolis where, in death as in life, generations of the Argentine elite repose in ornate splendor.

Alongside the cemetery, the **Iglesia de Nuestra Señora de Pilar**, a colonial church consecrated in 1732, is a national historical monument; adjacent to it is the important **Centro Cultural Ciudad de Buenos Aires**. Within easy walking distance are the **Museo Nacional de Bellas Artes** and the **Centro Municipal de Exposiciones**, which hosts book fairs and other cultural events.

Recoleta was among the areas to which the upper-class porteños of San Telmo relocated after yellow-fever outbreaks in the 1870s. It has many attractive public gardens and open spaces, including **Plaza Alvear**, **Plaza Francia** (where the capital's largest crafts fair takes place on Sunday), and several other parks stretching into the barrios of Palermo and Belgrano. One of the area's most characteristic and entertaining sights are its *paseaperros* (professional dog walkers) strolling with a dozen or more canines on leash.

Biblioteca Nacional After a decade of construction problems and delays, this ultramodern Proceso-era library opened just a few years ago, but the plaster is already cracking on some of the landscaped outdoor terraces. Prominent Argentine and Latin American literary figures of the stature of Ernesto Sábato frequently lecture at the facility. Open weekdays 10 am to 9 pm, the library (☎ 4806-4729) is at Agüero 2510.

Museo Nacional de Bellas Artes Unquestionably the country's most important art museum, Bellas Artes (Fine Arts Museum; ☎ 4803-0802) houses works by European masters like Renoir, Rodin, Monet, Toulouse-Lautrec, and van Gogh, as well as 19th- and 20th-century Argentine artists. At Av del Libertador 1473, it's open daily except Monday 12:30 to 7:30 pm; on Saturday it opens at 9:30 am. Admission is free.

Museo Municipal de Arte Hispanoamericano Isaac Fernández Blanco Containing an exceptional collection of colonial art, including silverwork, painting, costumes, and antiques, this museum (☎ 4327-0272) occupies the colonial-style Palacio Noel, set among attractive gardens at Suipacha 1422. Hours are 2 to 7 pm daily except Monday, but it shuts down completely in January and February. Museum admission is US$1, free on Thursday.

Museo de Motivos Argentinos José Hernández Named for the author of the gaucho epic *Martín Fierro*, this museum (☎ 4802-9967) really should be called Museo Carlos Daws after the Anglo-Argentine who donated most of the Argentine folk art on display. The artwork dates from prehistory through the colonial period to the present. Hours are weekdays 8 am to 7 pm and weekends 3 to 7 pm. The museum is at Av del Libertador 2373. Admission is US$1, free on Wednesday. It's closed the entire month of February.

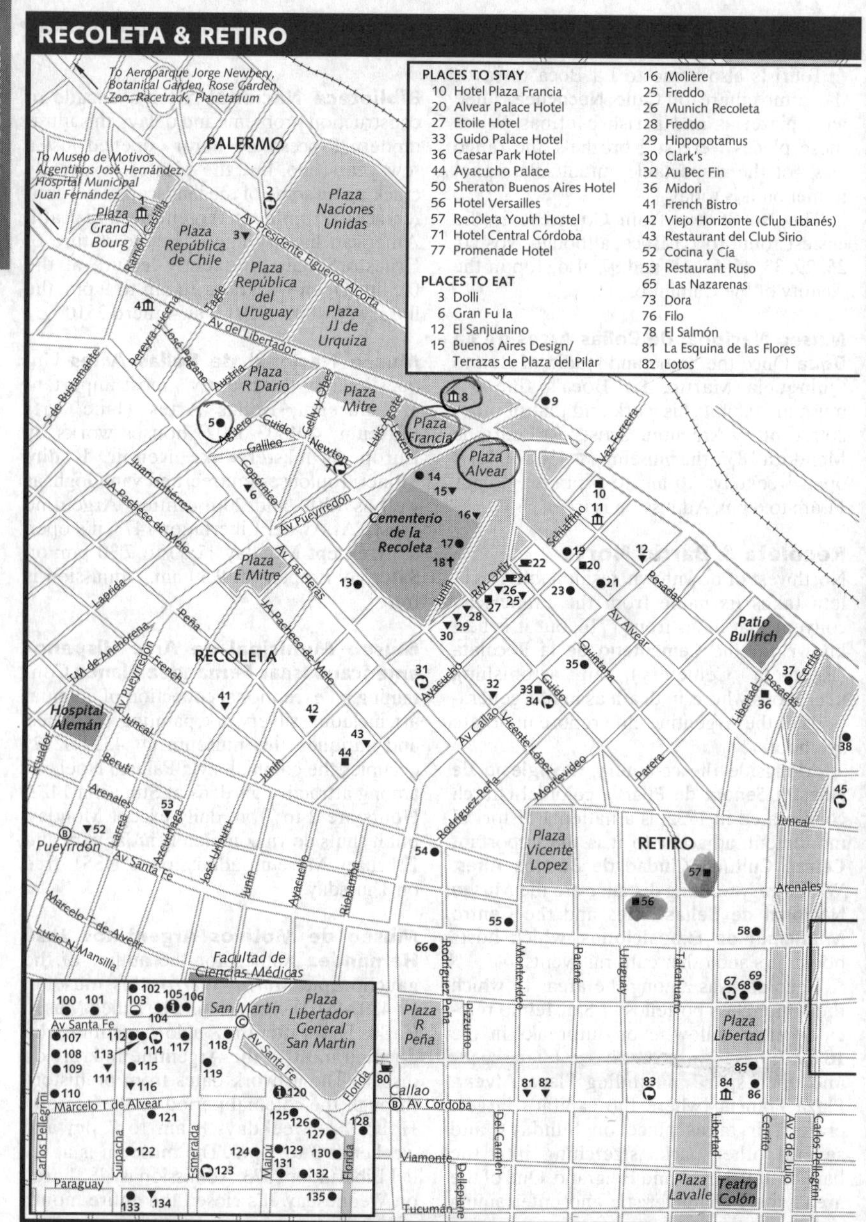
RECOLETA & RETIRO
PLACES TO STAY
10 Hotel Plaza Francia
20 Alvear Palace Hotel
27 Etoile Hotel
33 Guido Palace Hotel
36 Caesar Park Hotel
44 Ayacucho Palace
50 Sheraton Buenos Aires Hotel
56 Hotel Versailles
57 Recoleta Youth Hostel
71 Hotel Central Córdoba
77 Promenade Hotel
PLACES TO EAT
3 Dolli
6 Gran Fu la
12 El Sanjuanino
15 Buenos Aires Design/ Terrazas de Plaza del Pilar
16 Molière
25 Freddo
26 Munich Recoleta
28 Freddo
29 Hippopotamus
30 Clark's
32 Au Bec Fin
36 Midori
41 French Bistro
42 Viejo Horizonte (Club Libanés)
43 Restaurant del Club Sirio
52 Cocina y Cía
53 Restaurant Ruso
65 Las Nazarenas
73 Dora
76 Filo
78 El Salmón
81 La Esquina de las Flores
82 Lotos
To Aeroparque Jorge Newbery, Botanical Garden, Rose Garden, Zoo, Racetrack, Planetarium
To Museo de Motivos Argentinos José Hernández, Hospital Municipal Juan Fernández
PALERMO
RECOLETA
RETIRO
Plaza Grand Bourg
Plaza República de Chile
Plaza Naciones Unidas
Plaza República del Uruguay
Plaza JJ de Urquiza
Plaza R Darío
Plaza Mitre
Plaza Francia
Plaza Alvear
Cementerio de la Recoleta
Plaza E Mitre
Hospital Alemán
Patio Bullrich
Plaza Vicente Lopez
Facultad de Ciencias Médicas
San Martín
Plaza Libertador General San Martín
Plaza R Peña
Plaza Libertad
Plaza Lavalle
Teatro Colón
Pueyrredón
Callao
Av Córdoba
Av Presidente Figueroa Alcorta
Av del Libertador
Av Pueyrredón
Av Las Heras
Av Santa Fe
Av Alvear
Av Callao
Av 9 de Julio
Ramón Castilla
Tagle
Pereyra Lucena
José Pagano
Austria
S de Bustamante
Agüero
Guido
Galileo
Gelly y Obes
Newton
Luis Agote
Levene
Copérnico
Juan Gutiérrez
JA Pacheco de Melo
Vaz Ferreira
Schiaffino
Posadas
Junín
RM Ortiz
Quintana
Ayacucho
Vicente López
Montevideo
Rodríguez Peña
Parera
Laprida
TM de Anchorena
Peña
French
Juncal
Beruti
Arenales
Ecuador
Larrea
Azcuénaga
José Uriburu
Riobamba
Marcelo T de Alvear
Lucio N Mansilla
Paraná
Uruguay
Talcahuano
Libertad
Cerrito
Carlos Pellegrini
Pizzurno
Del Carmen
Viamonte
Tucumán
Delleplane
Suipacha
Esmeralda
Maipú
Florida
Paraguay

RECOLETA & RETIRO

87 La Chacra
97 Alimentari
111 Los Chilenos
116 Payanca
134 Yinyang

OTHER
1 Museo del Instituto Nacional Sanmartiniano
2 Canadian Consulate
4 Museo Nacional de Arte Decorativo, Museo de Arte Oriental
5 Biblioteca Nacional
7 UK Consulate
8 Museo Nacional de Bellas Artes
9 Centro Municipal de Exposiciones
11 Salas Nacionales de Cultura
13 Caño 14
14 Hard Rock Café
17 Centro Cultural Ciudad de Buenos Aires
18 Iglesia de Nuestra Señora de Pilar
19 López Taibo
21 Guido Mocasines
22 Café de la Paix
23 Perugia
24 La Biela
31 Uruguayan Consulate
34 Spanish Consulate
35 Shampoo
37 Zurbarán
38 Instituto Nacional de Enseñanza Superior en Lenguas Vivas
39 Museo Municipal de Arte Hispanoamericano Isaac Fernández Blanco
40 Post Office (International)
45 Brazilian Consulate
46 Irish Consulate
47 Asociación Argentina de Cultura Inglesa/British Arts Centre
48 Aerolíneas Argentinas
49 Torre de los Ingleses
51 Dirección Nacional de Migraciones
54 Guido Mocasines
55 Rossi y Carusso
58 TAP (Air Portugal)
59 Aguilar
60 Vermeer
61 Rubbers
62 American Express
63 Austral Líneas Aéreas
64 Hertz
66 Contramano
67 Italian Consulate
68 Teatro Coliseo
69 Transportes Aéreos de Mercosur (TAM)
70 Dollar
72 Danish Consulate
74 United Airlines
75 Welcome Marroquinería
79 Kelly's Regionales
80 Clásica y Moderna
83 Peruvian Consulate
84 Teatro Cervantes/Museo Nacional del Teatro
85 Localiza
86 Swan Turismo
88 Buquebus
89 Oficina del Libro Francés
90 Korean Air, Mexicana
91 National
92 Ferrytur
93 Librería ABC
94 Southern Winds
95 Asatej/Gerardo Föhse Camera Repair
96 Rancho Grande
98 Bárbaro
99 Telecom
100 Casa de Misiones
101 Casa de Jujuy
102 Alitalia, Malaysia Airlines
103 San Martín Bus
104 American Airlines
105 Dirección Nacional de Turismo
106 Budget
107 Experiment
108 Avianca, Iberia
109 LAPA
110 Diners Club
112 South African Airways
113 Vasp
114 French/Swiss Consulates, Swissair
115 Ecuatoriana
117 Aeroflot
118 Manuel Tienda León
119 Andesmar
120 Parques Nacionales
121 Econo
122 Enigma
123 Norwegian Consulate
124 Lihué Expediciones
125 AI (Car Rental)
126 Federico Klem, Lufthansa
127 Buenos Aires Así
128 Ruth Benzacar
129 Líneas Aéreas de Entre Ríos (LAER)
130 LanChile
131 Che Bandoneón
132 Historical Tours
133 Unirent
135 Air France

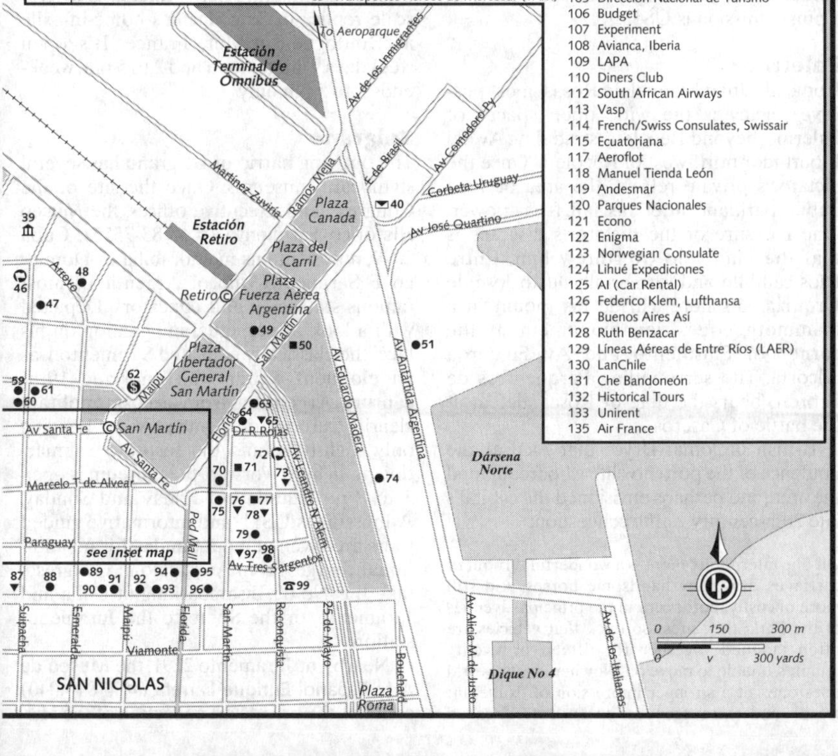

Other Recoleta Museums Housed in the Palais de Glace at Posadas 1725, the **Salas Nacionales de Cultura** (☎ 4804-4324) offers rotating cultural, artistic, and historical exhibitions. Once a skating rink, the unusual circular building is open weekdays 1 to 8 pm, weekends 3 to 8 pm. Admission varies depending on the program.

The **Museo Nacional de Arte Decorativo** (National Museum of Decorative Arts; ☎ 4806-8306) and the **Museo de Arte Oriental** (Museum of Oriental Art; ☎ 4801-5988) share the Palacio Errázuriz, a stunning beaux arts building at Av Libertador 1902. The former is open weekdays 2 to 8 pm, weekends 11 to 7 pm, with guided tours weekdays at 5 pm, weekends at 5 and 6 pm; admission is US$5. The latter, which was undergoing repairs at the time of writing, is open Tuesday to Sunday 3 to 7 pm, with guided tours Wednesday through Friday at 5 pm; admission is US$3.

Palermo

Ironically, Juan Manuel de Rosas' most positive legacy is the wide open spaces of Palermo, beyond Recoleta, straddling Av del Libertador northwest of Recoleta. Once the dictator's private retreat, the area became public parkland after his fall from power. One measure of the dictator's disgrace is that the man who overthrew him, Entre Ríos caudillo and former ally Justo José de Urquiza, sits here astride his mount in a mammoth equestrian monument at the corner of Sarmiento and Av Figueroa Alcorta. The surrounding Parque Tres de Febrero bears the date of Rosas' defeat at the battle of Caseros.

British diplomat Bryce marveled at the opulence of the porteño elite who frequented the area, and perhaps envisioned the capital's late 20th-century traffic congestion:

> On fine afternoons, there is a wonderful turnout of carriages drawn by handsome horses, and still more of costly motor cars, in the principal avenues of the Park; they press so thick that vehicles are often jammed together for fifteen or twenty minutes, unable to move on. Nowhere in the world does one get a stronger impression of exuberant wealth and extravagance. The Park itself, called Palermo, lies on the edge of the city towards the river, and is approached by a well-designed and well-planted avenue.

Now a major recreational resource for all porteños, Palermo contains the city's **Jardín Botánico Carlos Thays** (the botanical gardens, infested with feral cats), **Jardín Zoológico** (zoo), **Rosedal** (rose garden), **Campo de Polo** (polo grounds), **Hipódromo** (racetrack), and **Planetarium**.

As you might guess, some of these uses were not really for the masses, but elite sectors of society no longer have the park to themselves.

Museo del Instituto Nacional Sanmartiniano In Barrio Parque, occupying the small Plaza Grand Bourg at the junction of Aguado, Elizalde, and Castilla, this temple of undiscriminating hero worship is a 1:75-scale replica of San Martín's home-in-exile at Boulogne-Sur-Mer, France. It's open weekdays 9 am to noon and 2 to 5 pm, weekends 2 to 5 pm only.

Belgrano

The outlying barrio of Belgrano has several significant museums. Once the site of the Congreso and executive offices, the **Museo Histórico Sarmiento** (☎ 4783-7555), Cuba 2079, now contains memorabilia of Domingo F Sarmiento, one of Argentina's most famous statesmen and educators. Depicted with a look of perpetual indignation on his face, the classically educated Sarmiento was an eloquent writer who analyzed 19th-century Argentina from a cosmopolitan, clearly Eurocentric point of view. Lagging only slightly behind the Instituto Sanmartiniano in hero worship, the museum is open 3 to 8 pm Tuesday to Friday and Sunday. Admission is US$1, and informative guided tours are given at 4 pm Sunday for no additional charge. From Av Callao in Congreso, take bus No 60, disembarking at Cuba and Juramento, or the Subte to the Juramento station.

Nearby, at Juramento 2291, the **Museo de Arte Español Enrique Larreta** (☎ 4784-4040) contains the private art collection of the Hispanophile novelist. It's open Monday, Tuesday, and Friday 2 to 7:45 pm, Sunday and holidays 3 to 7:45 pm. Guided tours take place Sunday at 4 and 6 pm. Admission is US$1, but is free Tuesday. It's usually closed the entire month of January.

A few blocks away, the **Museo Casa de Yrurtia** (☎ 4781-0385), at O'Higgins 2390, belonged to sculptor Rogelio Yrurtia (probably the country's greatest), who designed the building in Mudejar style. Hours are Tuesday to Friday 3 am to 7:30 pm, weekends 4 to 8 pm. Admission is US$1. Informative guided tours take place at 4:30 pm Saturday afternoon for no extra charge; guides can be a bit pedantic toward visitors who they suspect know little Spanish.

The **Museo Libero Badii** (☎ 4784-8650), on the Barrancas de Belgrano at 11 de Setiembre 1990, contains the unconventional sculptures of one of Argentina's foremost modern artists. It's theoretically open Tuesday to Friday 10 am to 6 pm, weekends 3 to 7 pm, but the Fundación Banco de Crédito Argentino, which owns it, keeps irregular hours and usually locks the building – try standing around looking lost at the entrance. Admission is free.

LANGUAGE COURSES

For general information and advice on language courses, see the Facts for the Visitor chapter.

The Instituto de Lengua Española para Extranjeros (ILEE; ☎/fax 4375-0730, www.studyabroad.com/ilee), Oficina C, 7th floor, Lavalle 1619, has conversation-based courses at basic, intermediate, and advanced levels. Private classes cost US$17 per hour, and group lessons (no more than four students) are US$12 an hour; specialized instruction in areas such as Latin American literature and commercial Spanish costs US$30 per hour. The institute can also help arrange accommodations in a private home for around US$400 to US$500 per month single, US$600 per month double.

Another alternative is the Instituto Nacional de Enseñanza Superior en Lenguas Vivas (☎ 4393-7351), Carlos Pellegrini 1515, where monthlong intensive courses, with four hours of instruction daily at a basic, intermediate, or advanced level, cost $450. Three-month courses, with four hours of instruction weekly, cost US$50 per month.

The Centro de Estudio del Español (☎/fax 4315-1156, martinduh@act.net.ar), Reconquista 719, 11°E, offers four-week courses with two hours of daily instruction for US$320 plus US$20 in course materials. Shorter courses cost US$11 per hour plus materials. Individual tutoring costs US$17 hourly.

Tradfax (☎ 4373-5581, fax 4373-6074, royal@einstein.com.ar), Av Callao 194, 2nd floor, offers three-hour daily classes in general Spanish for US$180 per week. Commercial Spanish classes cost about US$30 more per week, and individual classes cost US$18 per hour. The organization also arranges lodging in nearby hotels from US$210 per week single, US$245 per week double.

The Universidad de Buenos Aires (UBA; ☎ 4343-1196, fax 4343-2733), 25 de Mayo 221, offers good instruction at its Laboratorio de Idiomas de la Facultad, but only for a few hours weekly; this is suitable if you're staying for an extended period in the city, but it's not very efficient if your visit will be relatively brief.

There are also many private tutors within the city, charging in the range of US$18 to US$22 per hour, such as English-speaking Dori Lieberman (☎/fax 4361-4843, dorotea@gramar.filo.uba.ar).

ORGANIZED TOURS

Many agencies offer half- and full-day city tours, but unless your time is very limited try to get around on your own. The Dirección General de Turismo (☎ 4371-1496, 4476-3612), on the 5th floor of the Centro Cultural San Martín at Sarmiento 1551, has suspended its free and very worthwhile (though often crowded) weekend guided tours (in Spanish only) of city barrios. It's worth contacting them, though, to see whether they resume their theme-oriented explorations of areas such as San Telmo, Palermo's parks and lakes, and Parque Lezama.

Life & Death in Recoleta & Chacarita

Death is the great equalizer, except in Buenos Aires. When the arteries harden after decades of dining at Au Bec Fin and finishing up with coffee and dessert at La Biela or Café de la Paix, the wealthy and powerful of Buenos Aires move ceremoniously across the street to Recoleta Cemetery, joining their forefathers in a place they have visited religiously all their lives. Perhaps no other place says more about Argentina and Argentine society.

According to Argentine novelist Tomás Eloy Martínez, Argentines are 'cadaver cultists' who honor their most revered national figures not on the date of their birth but of their death. Nowhere is this obsession with mortality and corruption more evident than at Recoleta Cemetery, where generations of the elite repose in the grandeur of ostentatious mausoleums – it is a common saying (and only a slight exaggeration) that 'it is cheaper to live extravagantly all your life than to be buried in Recoleta.'

Traditionally, money alone is not enough: You must have a surname like Anchorena, Alvear, Aramburu, Avellaneda, Mitre, Martínez de Hoz, or Sarmiento. The remains of Evita Perón, secured in a subterranean vault, are an exception that infuriates the presumptive aristocracy.

One reason for this is that the dead often play a peculiar, and more than just symbolic, role in Argentine politics. Evita rests in Recoleta only after her embalmed body's odyssey from South America to an obscure cemetery in Milan to her exiled husband's house in Madrid, finally returning to Buenos Aires (embalming is uncommon in Argentina). The man responsible for her 'kidnapping' was General Pedro Aramburu, a bitter political enemy of the Peróns who reportedly sought the Vatican's help in sequestering the cadaver after Perón's overthrow in 1955.

Aramburu himself was held for 'ransom' by the left-wing Peronist Montoneros *after* his assassination in 1970. Only when the military government of General Alejandro Lanusse ensured Evita's return to Perón in Madrid did Aramburu's body reappear to be entombed in Recoleta, now only a few short 'blocks' from Evita. To locate Evita's grave, ask directions to the relatively modest tomb of the 'Familia Duarte' (her maiden name).

Outside Recoleta's walls, the gourmet corridor of Calles RM Ortiz and Junín, along with a string of *albergues transitorios* (hotels that rent by the hour) on Calle Azcuénaga, raises interesting questions about the connections between food, sex, and death in Argentina.

ROBERT FRERCK

Juan Perón himself lies across town, in the much less exclusive graveyard of Chacarita, which opened in the 1870s to accommodate the yellow-fever victims of San Telmo and La Boca.

Although more democratic in its conception, Chacarita's most elaborate tombs match Recoleta's finest. One of the most visited belongs to Carlos

Life & Death in Recoleta & Chacarita

Gardel, the famous tango singer. Plaques from around the world cover the base of his life-size statue, many thanking him for favors granted. Like Evita, Juan Perón, and others, Gardel is a quasi-saint toward whom countless Argentines feel an almost religious devotion. The steady procession of pilgrims exposes the pervasiveness of spiritualism in a country that prides itself on European sophistication.

One of the best places to witness this phenomenon is the Chacarita tomb of Madre María Salomé, a disciple of the famous healer Pancho Sierra. Every day, but especially on the second day of each month (she died on October 2, 1928), adherents of her cult leave floral tributes – white carnations are the favorite – and lay their hands on her sepulcher in spellbound supplication. The anniversary of Gardel's death, June 26, 1935, is another major occasion, as pilgrims jam the cemetery's streets.

SANDRA BAO

Organized tours regularly visit Recoleta Cemetery, open daily 7 am to 6 pm, on Calle Junín across from Plaza Alvear, but most visitors wander about on their own. There are free guided tours (☎ 4803-1594) at 2:30 pm the last Sunday of each month.

To visit Chacarita, which attracts fewer visitors than Recoleta, take Línea B of the Subte to the end of the line at Federico Lacroze, from which it is a short walk (see the Capital Federal map). Look for the tomb of 'Tomás Perón,' but do not miss those of Gardel, Madre María, poet Alfonsina Storni, aviator Jorge Newbery, tango musician Aníbal 'Pichuco' Troilo, and comedian Luis Sandrini. Hours are identical to Recoleta's.

Around the corner from Chacarita, alongside each other on Av Elcano, the Cementerio Alemán (German Cemetery) and the Cementerio Británico (British Cemetery) are far less extravagant than either Recoleta or Chacarita, but have their own points of interest. The Cementerio Alemán contains a monument to Germany's WWII dead, though the symbolism is imperial rather than Hitlerian. The Británico is both more and less than its name suggests – there may be more Irish, Jewish, Armenian, Greek, and other immigrant tombs than there are tombs with truly British surnames. Perhaps the most notable headstone is that of Tierra del Fuego pioneer Lucas Bridges, author of the classic *The Uttermost Part of the Earth*, who died on board ship from Ushuaia to Buenos Aires.

Buenos Aires Tur (☎ 4371-2304), Lavalle 1444, Oficina 16, offers bus tours (US$14) that visit locations in Palermo, Recoleta, the Microcentro, San Telmo, and La Boca, as well as weekday afternoon visits to Tigre and the Delta via the Tren de la Costa (US$32). Buenos Aires Visión (☎ 4394-2986), Esmeralda 356, 6th floor, in the Microcentro, has similar itineraries and also arranges excursions to La Plata.

Buenos Aires Así (☎ 4315-1460), Marcelo T de Alvear 624, 2nd floor, has some more unconventional offerings, including a series of cultural-historical walking tours (US$16 to US$25). Historical Tours (☎ 4311-1019, histours@commet.com.ar), downstairs at Paraguay 647, focuses on theme-oriented tours on topics like immigration (visiting La Boca, San Telmo, and Puerto Madero, US$35) and Evita Perón (Argentina in the 1940s, US$30), among others, and has multilingual guides. Lihué Expediciones (☎ 4311-9610), Maipú 926, 1st floor, offers literary walking tours, following the footsteps of Borges and other porteño authors.

SPECIAL EVENTS

If you're in Buenos Aires for more than a very brief stay, see the municipal Dirección General de Turismo for its annual booklet listing special events in the city; one section of the booklet covers January through June, while the other covers from July through December.

For short-term visitors, Turismo's quarterly brochure of activities, which includes current exhibits, concerts, and other items, is a valuable resource.

Restricted to a small area on Av 9 de Julio between Bolívar and Av de Mayo, Buenos Aires' official and flagrantly commercial Carnaval is a very modest celebration by Brazilian standards (even Montevideo's is more impressive). Taking place on weekends only, most festivities in this slow-moving event consist of spraying passersby with canned foam, which, fortunately, leaves no permanent stains on clothing. However, visiting *comparsas* (troupes) from Carnaval hotbeds like Corrientes and Gualeguaychú, are worth seeing.

In late March, horse lovers flock to Palermo for the Exposición de Otoño de la Asociación Criadores de Caballos Criollos, showcasing Argentine-bred equines. It takes place at the Predio Ferial de la Sociedad Rural Argentina, on Av Sarmiento (Subte: Plaza Italia).

During the first three weeks of April, the Feria del Libro (book fair) attracts more than a million readers to the sprawling Centro Municipal de Exposiciones (☎ 4374-1251, interno 208), at Av Figueroa Alcorta and Av Pueyrredón in Recoleta. Admission costs about US$5, but many bookstores give away tickets.

Though porteño motorists seem to be constantly in training for the Gran Prix Fórmula 1, the capital's major auto race officially takes place in early to mid-April at the Autódromo Municipal Oscar Gálvez (☎ 4638-1995), on the outskirts of the city at Av General Paz and Av Coronel Roca in the barrio of Villa Riachuelo.

For the local art community, the counterpart to the Feria del Libro is mid-May's Feria de Galerías Arte BA, a rapidly growing event that now features more than 80 different galleries at the Centro Municipal de Exposiciones.

June 24 is the Día de la Muerte de Carlos Gardel, the anniversary of Gardel's death in a plane crash in Medellín, Colombia. Numerous tango events during the week bookend pilgrimages to the singer's tomb at Chacarita Cemetery.

Winter's biggest celebration is July's Exposición Internacional de Ganadería, Agricultura y Pesca, the annual agricultural exhibition organized by the Sociedad Rural Argentina (☎ 4326-5095). Like the horse-breeders' fair (see above), it takes place at the Predio Ferial in Palermo.

Though not a formal holiday, November 11 is the Día de San Martín de Tours, the capital's patron saint. In late November, runners can try the Maratón Internacional de la Argentina (☎ 4753-9040, interno 248), which draws up to 15,000 participants. It starts at

8 am in the 3800 block of Av Figueroa Alcorta.

It's not a formal holiday either, but Día del Tango commemorates Gardel's December 11 birth date. There are many tango events around this time, and the singer's tomb at Chacarita draws further crowds of pilgrims.

The spring polo season culminates in December's Campeonato Abierto Argentino de Polo (Argentine Open Polo Championship), taking place at Palermo's Campo Argentino de Polo (☎ 4774-4517), at Av del Libertador and Dorrego. Around the same time, the gaucho sport of pato holds its Campeonato Argentino Abierto de Pato (Argentine Open Pato Championship); for details, contact the Federación Argentino de Pato (☎ 4331-0222), Av Belgrano 530, 5th floor.

PLACES TO STAY

Buenos Aires has a wide variety of accommodations, ranging from youth hostels and down-in-the-mouth *hospedajes* to simple family-oriented hotels to five-star luxury lodgings of jet-set stature. Given elevated service-sector prices, there are very few outstanding values, but affordable, acceptable accommodations are still available.

Budget accommodations tend to be well past their prime but are not necessarily bad, and many mid-range hotels are either showing their age or have been cheaply remodeled (this is even true of some top-end accommodations). There are, however, some decent values in all categories, and a number of places still offer discounts up to 15% for payment in cash.

In ascending order of desirability, the budget areas are Constitución and Barracas near the southern train station (abundant options) San Telmo (limited but growing), the Microcentro (limited), and Av de Mayo and the Congreso area (abundant), but all these areas have both very good and very bad places. San Telmo is the most interesting zone, followed by Congreso for its access to the nightlife of Corrientes and Santa Fe. Both the Microcentro and Congreso have decent mid-range accommodations.

In areas such as Retiro, Recoleta, and Barrio Norte, top-end accommodations are the rule; budget travelers will find few alternatives, though some mid-range places exist. The Microcentro and Congreso also have additional top-end hotels.

Note that the letter following the name of an establishment indicates which map it appears on: **M** for Plaza de Mayo & the Microcentro, **R** for Recoleta & Retiro, and **S** for San Telmo & Constitution. If there is no letter, that means the hotel is beyond the map extents.

Places to Stay – Budget

Hostels Buenos Aires offers a choice of several hostels, both official and unofficial, all of them pretty good but some better than others.

In a rambling but charming building near Constitución station, easily reached by Subte, the official ***Albergue Juvenil*** *(S; ☎ 4394-9112, Brasil 675)* has 90 beds, a TV lounge, and a pleasant outdoor patio, but can be noisy when groups from the provinces visit the capital – avoid winter holidays in particular. Prices are US$10 per person, including breakfast but without kitchen privileges. The staff are helpful and friendly, but the hostel sometimes closes between noon and 6 pm. HI/AYH membership is obligatory.

Not affiliated with Hostelling International, ***El Hostal de San Telmo*** *(S; ☎ 4300-6899, fax 44300-9028, elhostal@satlink.com, Carlos Calvo 614)* is an outstanding facility for US$10 per person in three- and four-bed rooms. Rooms near and directly above the common areas, though, can be a bit noisy. Kitchen access, laundry service, cable TV, and email are available.

Budget accommodation is hard to find in Barrio Norte, but the recently opened ***Recoleta Youth Hostel*** *(R; ☎ 4812-4419, fax 4815-6622, mpa@interserver.com.ar, Libertad 1218)*, not yet officially affiliated with Hostelling International, occupies a recycled mansion. With unquestionably the best location of any hostel in town, it charges US$10 per person.

Another HI-affiliated facility, due to open in early 1999, is the 100-bed ***Hostel Internacional Buenos Aires*** *(☎ 4381-9760, Moreno 1273)* in the Congreso area. Rates should be comparable to other hostels in the capital.

Hotels Close to Plaza Dorrego, dilapidated but passable ***Residencial Carly*** *(S; ☎ 4361-7710, Humberto Primo 464)* has singles for US$10 with shared bath, singles/doubles for US$12/14 with private bath plus kitchen access. The staff is lackadaisical and there are noisy kids, but at these prices you can't expect too much.

At amiable, well-kept ***Hotel Zavalia*** *(S; ☎ 4362-1990, Juan de Garay 474)*, near Parque Lezama, rooms with shared bath cost only US$10/15, while those with private bath cost US$15/20. Rooms vary in quality (some have large balconies), but the main drawback is that families with children can make it noisy at times.

Hotel Bolívar *(S; ☎ 4361-5105, Bolívar 886)* is San Telmo's budget favorite. Several rooms have sunny balconies for US$15/22 with private bath. Popular with LP readers, ***Hotel Victoria*** *(S; ☎ 4361-2135, Chacabuco 726)*, in San Telmo, has very good ground-floor rooms, though some are a bit musty, for US$15/25 with private bath, kitchen access, laundry facilities, and an attractive patio.

Congreso is a good area for inexpensive lodging of decent quality. Not to be confused with Retiro's exclusive Marriott Plaza Hotel, the ramshackle but passable ***Hotel Plaza*** *(M; ☎ 4371-9747, Rivadavia 1689)* rents tiny singles with shared bath for US$12/15 and charges only slightly more, US$15/20, with private bath. Somc English is spoken at ***Hotel Bahía*** *(M; ☎ 4382-1780, Av Corrientes 1212)*, where rates are US$20 double; they may give a 10% discount to those with a student card. There's at least one credible report of theft from guest rooms, so watch your belongings.

Hotel Sportsman *(M; ☎ 4381-8021, Rivadavia 1425)*, in a pleasant older building, is popular despite its indifferent staff and some sagging mattresses. Rooms go for US$12/20 with shared bath, US$20/30 with private bath (10% less with student ID); the former are a better value.

Greatly improved ***Gran Hotel Oriental*** *(M; ☎ 4952-3371, Bartolomé Mitre 1840)* charges US$18/20 with shared bath, US$24/28 with private bath, both with breakfast. Some rooms have balconies but get street noise; interior rooms are quieter.

Central, friendly ***Hotel Maipú*** *(M; ☎ 4322-5142, Maipú 735)*, in a handsome but deteriorating building in the Microcentro, has simple, clean, and pleasant rooms, some with balconies, for US$19/24 single/double with shared bath, US$22/29 with private bath. Some internal rooms are dark, and in damp winter weather they can be musty.

Hotel O'Rei *(M; ☎ 4393-7186, Lavalle 733)*, near Florida, is one of the best-located budget hotels, but rooms fronting directly onto Lavalle can be noisy. Several readers have griped about grumpy management, but others have no complaints. Rooms with shared bath cost US$19/25, with private bath US$22/30. Ask for discounts on longer-term stays.

Some travelers have enjoyed the once-elegant ***Hotel Reina*** *(M; ☎ 4383-2264, Av de Mayo 1120)*, where singles/doubles with shared bath and breakfast cost US$20/30 (20% less for students), but some singles have been created with improvised partitions and are very small. Rates with private bath are US$25/37.

Still a decent value is friendly ***Gran Hotel Sarmiento*** *(M; ☎ 4374-8069, Sarmiento 1892)*, on a quiet block. Simple, tidy rooms (some of them cramped) with private bath cost US$25/35. Under the same management as the Sportsman, the slightly better ***Hotel Europa*** *(M; ☎ 4381-9629, Bartolomé Mitre 1294)* has rooms with private bath for US$26/35, 10% less with for students.

Friendly but ramshackle ***Hotel Versailles*** *(R; ☎ 4811-5214, Arenales 1364)* has spacious rooms and an excellent Barrio Norte location, but it's worn and past its peak for US$25/35 without breakfast.

Places to Stay – Mid-Range

In Congreso, the family-style ***Cardton Hotel*** *(M; ☎/fax 4382-1697, Juan D Perón 1559)*, an older mansion in good repair, is an excellent value starting at US$30/35 with cable TV. Under the same management and slightly more expensive at US$40/50 is the remodeled and recommended ***Hotel Americano*** *(M; ☎ 4382-4223, fax 4382-4229, Rodríguez Peña 265)*, nearby in Congreso.

Modest ***Hotel Central Córdoba*** *(R; ☎ 4311-1175, fax 4315-6860, San Martín 1021)* is friendly, pleasant, quiet, clean, and central, but also well-worn; some rooms are small, though charitable visitors might call them cozy. Rates are US$35/45 with private bath, phone, and TV, but without breakfast.

Many of the abundant mid-range hotels around Av de Mayo are worn – though not dirty – or cheaply remodeled. Among the best values here is the ***Chile Hotel*** *(M; ☎/fax 4383-7112, Av de Mayo 1297)*, an art nouveau landmark, where rooms with private bath and a good breakfast cost US$35/50. Although the street noise is considerable, corner rooms have huge balconies with choice views of the Congreso Nacional and the Casa Rosada.

Correspondents offer mixed reviews of ***Hotel Avenida*** *(M; ☎ 4331-4341, Av de Mayo 623)*, two blocks west of Plaza de Mayo, where rooms with private bath and breakfast cost US$38/48. Several consider its bright, spacious, and air-conditioned rooms a lesser value than other cheaper places – perhaps because the staff are less cheerful than the rooms – but recent reports suggest improvement. For about US$35/45 without breakfast, 10% less with a student discount, the ***Turista Hotel*** *(M; ☎ 4331-2281, Av de Mayo 686)*, across the block, has some adherents but has also drawn negative commentary. It gets hot in summer, and the air-con is balky.

Once a budget hotel, well-kept ***Petit Hotel Goya*** *(M; ☎ 4322-9311, Suipacha 748)* is no longer cheap at US$40/50 (including breakfast if the hotel bill is paid in cash), but it's friendly, spotless, central, quiet, and comfortable. Near Plaza del Congreso, the remodeled ***Hotel de los Dos Congresos*** *(M; ☎ 4372-0466, Rivadavia 1777)*, formerly Hotel Mar del Plata, charges US$40/52 with private bath, air-con, cable TV, and other amenities, but without breakfast. Further renovations may increase rates.

In a quiet building on a noisy street, the very clean, recommended ***Hotel Ayamitre*** *(M; ☎/fax 4953-1655, Ayacucho 106)* has rooms with TV, phone, and air-con for US$40/50 with breakfast. Rates also start around US$40/50 at the ***Tucumán Palace Hotel*** *(M; ☎ 4311-2298, fax 4311-2296, Tucumán 384)*, which has drawn some criticism for 'deferred maintenance.'

Several other hotels in the US$40/50 range include friendly ***Hotel Madrid*** *(M; ☎/fax 4381-9021, Av de Mayo 1135)*, with cable TV and breakfast, and ***Hotel Callao*** *(M; ☎ 4372-3534 Av Callao 292)*, in an interesting building.

Hotel Molino *(M; ☎/fax 4374-9112, Av Callao 164)* charges US$48/60 with air-con, private bath, and telephone, but some rooms are small and front onto this very busy, noisy block. At ***Hotel Plaza Roma*** *(M; ☎ 4314-0666, fax 4312-0839, Lavalle 110)*, near Puerto Madero, rooms with private bath and breakfast cost US$50/80.

At ***Hotel Regidor*** *(M; ☎ 4314-9516, Tucumán 451)*, the relatively spartan rooms with cable TV are an excellent value for US$55/65 with breakfast (about half the price of other four-star accommodations), but the staff can be snooty toward casually dressed visitors. For the same price but without breakfast, one correspondent praises the superbly located ***Hotel Promenade*** *(R; ☎ 4312-5681, fax 4311-5761, Marcelo T de Alvear 444)*, but another found its attractive lobby a misleading approach to 'grubby, grimy, and noisy' rooms above.

The otherwise dignified ***Guido Palace Hotel*** *(R; ☎ 4812-0341, fax 4812-0674, Guido 1780)*, in Recoleta, has an attractive 5th-floor patio, but the walls are scuffed and comforts few considering the US$60/70 price without breakfast. Prices have risen to US$64/81 at the ***Ayacucho Palace*** *(R; ☎ 4806-0611, fax 4806-1815, Ayacucho 1408)*, in a stylish French building close to Recoleta, but there's a US$5 per room discount for cash payment.

Charming, friendly ***Hotel Lyon*** *(M; ☎ 4372-0100, fax 4814-4252, Riobamba 251)* has spacious, well-maintained suites with private bath, cable TV, telephone, and other conveniences for US$68/80. Even larger ones cost only a little more, making it an outstanding value for a family or group.

Owners of ***Hotel Phoenix*** *(M; ☎ 4312-4845, fax 4311-2846, San Martín 780)*, an architectural gem, have made substantial investments to restore the splendor of the days when it hosted the Prince of Wales. Its 60 rooms now sport modern conveniences without diminishing the appeal of the original antiques, but improvements have come at a price – what was once a relatively inexpensive hotel now costs US$69/80, including a varied, abundant breakfast. There's a 10% discount for payment in cash.

Places to Stay – Top End

Top-end hotels almost invariably quote prices in dollars but do accept Argentine currency; all of them take credit cards. The prices below are rack rates, but guests making advance reservations can often obtain better deals.

Congreso is more a mid-range than an upscale area, but the four-star ***Castelar Hotel*** *(M; ☎ 4383-5000, fax 4383-8388, castelar@hotelnet.com.ar, Av de Mayo 1152)*, in a magnificent building, is one of the best top-end values for US$89/95 – only slightly dearer than some truly mediocre mid-range places.

Though it's a bit tattered by four-star standards, ***Hotel Nogaró*** *(M; ☎ 4331-0091, fax 4331-6791, Diagonal Presidente Julio A Roca 562)* offers a 15% cash discount that makes rooms starting at US$124/145 a little more palatable. Among its more appealing features is the good natural light in most rooms, not always common in the densely built downtown.

For US$140/152, few places match the old-world charm of ***Hotel Plaza Francia*** *(R; ☎/fax 4804-9631, Eduardo Schiaffino 2189)*. It's close to Recoleta Cemetery, restaurants, and museums.

Gran Hotel Colón *(M; ☎ 4320-3500, fax 4320-3507, Carlos Pellegrini 507)* charges US$160/185 for comfortable rooms with verdant (thanks to large potted plants) balconies, which overlook the Obelisco near one of the capital's most famous (and noisiest!) intersections, Av 9 de Julio and Av Corrientes.

If you plan to eat so much that walking back to your hotel might be an effort, consider five-star ***Etoile Hotel*** *(R; ☎ 4805-2626, fax 4805-3613, hotel@etoile.com.ar, RM Ortiz 1835)*, a high-rise located right on Recoleta's restaurant row. Standard suites start at US$200 per night, not including the whopping 21% IVA, and reach US$290 per night plus IVA for the Diplomatic Suite, but there's a 10% discount for Internet reservations.

Conveniently central, the venerable ***Claridge Hotel*** *(M; ☎ 4314-7700, fax 4314-8022, Tucumán 535)* is one of downtown's best. Rates are US$290 for very comfortable rooms with cable TV and other amenities. Opposite the Plaza Fuerza Aérea, the soaring towers of the modern ***Sheraton Buenos Aires Hotel*** *(R; ☎ 4318-9000, fax 4318-9353, San Martín 1225)* are less central and convenient, and much less personable, but it's close to the new gourmet ghetto at Puerto Madero. Singles/doubles cost US$275/295 plus IVA.

One of the area's newest luxury lodgings, frequented by visiting entertainers, is the ***Caesar Park Hotel*** *(R; ☎ 4819-1296, fax 4819-1299, hotel@caesar.com.ar, Posadas 1232)*, a soaring brick construction. 'Superior' singles/doubles cost US$270 plus IVA, while 'deluxe' rooms go for US$310, both including a buffet breakfast. The Caesar Park also has nonsmoking rooms, unusual in Argentina.

At the elegant ***Alvear Palace Hotel*** *(R; ☎ 4808-2100, fax 4804-0034, Av Alvear 1891)* doubles can reach US$350 and upward; another US$50 gets you a suite (most of which have spas). Since opening in 1928, it has been one of few places to maintain its standards through all the country's hard times.

PLACES TO EAT

Food in Buenos Aires ranges from the cheap and simple to the costly and sophisticated. Decent fixed-price meals are available for US$5 or less, but side orders, like chips and soft drinks, can drive a la carte prices up rapidly. Chinese *tenedor libre* (all-you-can-eat) restaurants provide the most food for the least money – as little as US$4 – but quality varies considerably.

In run-of-the-mill restaurants, standard fare is basic pasta like ravioli and gnocchi, short orders like milanesa, and the more economical cuts of beef, along with fried potatoes, green salad, and dessert; for just a little more, you can find the same sort of food but with better ingredients. More cosmopolitan meals are available at the capital's high-class restaurants, but these can be very costly. One place to catch up on the latest in haute cuisine is the 'Good Living' section in the Sunday *Buenos Aires Herald*, where Dereck Foster also offers the latest on Argentine wines, but by his criteria 'inexpensive' meals can easily cost US$15.

Porteños depend on cafés for hot and cold drinks, meals, socializing, and entertainment, and certain cafés meet all these needs, while others fill only a few. Some cafés are also bookstores. See Cafés in the Entertainment section for more about these.

Plaza de Mayo & the Microcentro

Argentine fast-food restaurants are generally inferior to standard inexpensive eateries, but there are exceptions. The ***Patio de Comidas***, on the lower level of the Galerías Pacífico on the Florida peatonal, has a number of moderately priced (about US$5 to US$7 or so) fast-food versions of some very good restaurants, including ***Sensu*** for Japanese, ***Romanaccio*** for pizza and pasta, and ***Freddo*** for ice cream. Since all have common seating, it's a good choice for groups unable to agree on where to eat.

The best bargain in town, the cafeteria at supermarket ***Coto*** *(Viamonte 1571)* offers a variety of very inexpensive (US$3 or less) meals of good quality; there's zero atmosphere or maybe lots of it from another point of view – the entire main floor is blissfully tobacco-free. The indigenous ***Pumper Nic***, a McDonald's clone, has many locations throughout the city. In quality, however, it falls just short of *vomitivo*.

Let Them Eat Beef

When Charles Darwin rode across the province of Buenos Aires in the 1830s, he could not contain his astonishment at the gauchos' diet, which he himself followed out of necessity:

> I had now been several days without tasting any thing besides meat: I did not at all dislike this new regimen; but I felt as if it would only have agreed with me with hard exercise. I have heard that patients in England, when desired to confine themselves exclusively to an animal diet, even with the hope of life before their eyes, have scarce been able to endure it. Yet the Gaucho in the Pampas, for months together, touches nothing but beef. . . . It is, perhaps, from their meat regimen that the Gauchos, like other carnivorous animals, can abstain long from food. I was told that at Tandeel, some troops voluntarily pursued a party of Indians for three days, without eating or drinking.

Many Argentines recognize that a diet so reliant on beef is unhealthy, but sedentary porteños continue to ingest it in large quantities. Visitors who don't make it a way of life can probably indulge themselves on the succulent grilled meat, often stretched on a vertical spit over red-hot coals in the picture windows of the city's most prestigious restaurants.

There are countless cheap but ordinary downtown *parrillas* (restaurant specializing in grilled dishes). Traditionally, one of the most popular and economical is ***Pippo*** *(☎ 4374-6365, Paraná 356)*. ***Cervantes II*** *(☎ 4372-8869, Perón 1883)* serves enormous portions of standard Argentine fare at low prices, but is often so crowded that you may wish to take out your food; alternatively go late for lunch or early for dinner. They enforce the nonsmoking section only if someone complains, however.

Mobbed at lunch, ***El Toboso*** *(☎ 4476-0519, Corrientes 1848)* is a decent, moderately priced parrilla with other daily specials, but very expensive drinks (US$2.50 for mineral water) drive up the prices. The pâté with bread is a nice touch not found at other similar places.

A good, popular, and moderately priced chain is ***El Palacio de la Papa Frita*** *(☎ 4393-5849, Lavalle 735, ☎ 4322-1559, Lavalle 954, ☎ 4326-8063, Corrientes 1612)*.

If you visit only one parrilla in Buenos Aires, ignore the rent-a-gauchos at ***La Estancia*** *(☎ 4326-0330, Lavalle 941)* and focus on its excellent food at moderate prices. Another option is ***La Rural*** *(☎ 4322-2654, Suipacha 453)*.

Though Argentina's abundance of Italian surnames might suggest otherwise, most so-called Italian food is actually hybrid Italian-Argentine, stressing pizza and pasta. Exceptions to this rule tend to be pricey, but ***La Casona del Nonno*** *(☎ 4322-9352, Lavalle 827)* has good lunch specials for US$4 and a separate, well-ventilated nonsmoking section upstairs.

Broccolino *(☎ 4322-7652, Esmeralda 776)* is one of Buenos Aires' best Italian values. It offers a bewildering variety of pasta sauces, along with a friendly and highly professional English-speaking staff, and also has a nonsmoking section.

Unsung ***Pizzería Güerrín*** *(Corrientes 1372)* sells very inexpensive slices of superb fugazza, fugazzeta, and other specialties plus excellent empanadas, cold lager beer to wash it all down, and many appealing desserts. It's cheaper to buy at the counter and eat standing up, but there's a much greater variety of toppings if you decide to be seated and served or to order an entire pizza to take out.

Nearby, traditionally excellent ***Pizzería Serafín*** *(Corrientes 1328)* is well worth a visit – their chicken empanadas are always good. At the corner of Callao and Mitre since 1936, ***La Americana*** also has very fine pizza and exceptional empanadas, but the best chicken empanadas (usually breast meat) are at ***La Continental*** *(Av Callao 202)*.

For a taste of nostalgia, visit the original branch of ***Los Inmortales*** *(☎ 4326-5303, Corrientes 1369)*, beneath the conspicuous billboard of Carlos Gardel, to peruse the historic photographs of Gardel and his contemporaries. There is also a branch at Lavalle 746 *(☎ 4322-5493)*.

Since 1929 ***ABC*** *(☎ 4393-3992, Lavalle 545)* has been a lunchtime classic for Middle European specialties, like goulash. ***Laurak Bat*** *(☎ 4381-0682, Av Belgrano 1174)*, part of the Centro Cultural Vasco, has been in the same place since 1877. For dessert, try their *natillas*, a tasty custard.

Although it's part of a chain, ***Bar La Robla*** *(☎ 4811-4484, Viamonte 1615)* prepares excellent seafood and standard Argentine dishes that are far from monotonous and moderately priced. Its US$3.50 lunch specials, including an appetizer and a small glass of clericó, are an excellent value. Service is superb, the environment pleasant, and there's a small but effectively segregated tobacco-free area. Another branch is at Montevideo 194 *(☎ 4381-3435)*.

One of the most memorable bilingual menus came from a Chinese restaurant, where an unusually creative mistranslation turned Spanish 'camarones a la plancha' (grilled shrimp) into English 'ironed shrimp.' Despite this vivid image, most Asian food is unremarkable Cantonese, but the tenedor libre restaurants, as cheap as US$4, are a good budget option – if you choose wisely. Most places have a salad bar with excellent ingredients and also offer a variety of Argentine standards, but they do tack on a US$1 surcharge if you don't order anything to drink; mineral water, soft drinks, and beer are where they make their profit.

There is little difference among them, but try ***Restaurante Chino*** *(Suipacha 477)*, ***China Doll*** *(Suipacha 544)*, ***La Fronda*** *(Paraná 342)*, and ***Los Amigos*** *(Rodríguez Peña 384)*. For better quality Chinese food, visit ***La Casa China*** *(☎ 4371-1352, Viamonte 1476)* or ***Xin Dong Fang*** *(Maipú 512)*.

La Casa de Orihuela *(☎ 4951-6930, Alsina 2163)*, in Congreso, serves exception-

ROBERT FRERCK

Tango in San Telmo, Buenos Aires

ROBERT FRERCK

Café La Biela, Recoleta, Buenos Aires

ROBERT FRIED

Tango musicians in La Boca, Buenos Aires

WAYNE BERNHARDSON

Cementerio de la Recoleta, Buenos Aires

DAVID R FRAZIER

El Obelisco, Plaza de la República, Av 9 de Julio – Buenos Aires

ally well-prepared Peruvian and regional dishes. Its US$6 fixed-price lunch is one of the city's best values, well worth a detour from other parts of town. The decor is pleasing, and the service cheerful and efficient. Also in Congreso, the modest but friendly ***Status*** *(☎ 4382-8531, Virrey Cevallos 178)* is a hangout for the capital's Peruvian community. Its large portions and reasonable prices make it worth a stop if you're nearby.

Since the mid-1980s, the carnivorous capital has enjoyed a vegetarian boom, and most vegetarian restaurants have the additional appeal of being nonsmoking, including the self-service tenedor libre ***La Ciboulette*** *(☎ 4373-2178, Sarmiento 1802)* for US$8. Reader endorsements for vegetarian restaurants include ***La Huerta*** *(Lavalle 893)*, ***Valle Esmeralda*** *(☎ 4394-9266, Esmeralda 370)*, with tenedor libre for US$6, and ***Granix*** *(Florida 126)*.

An open secret is the popular smorgasbord at the ***Swedish Club*** *(☎ 4334-1703, Tacuarí 143, 5th floor)*. Theoretically open to members only, it now takes place every Wednesday, but you can 'request' an invitation by phone. They're particularly enthusiastic if you have a Swedish surname, but the US$26 price tag makes it a special event for most people.

For ice-cream lovers, Buenos Aires is paradise. Our favorite, distinguished by the outline map of Italy above its otherwise unpretentious storefront, is ***Heladería Cadore***, at Av Corrientes and Rodríguez Peña. Chocoholics should not miss their exquisite chocolate *amargo* (semisweet) or chocolate *blanco* (white), and the *mousse de limón* also merits special mention.

San Telmo

A good, inexpensive choice in San Telmo is ***Jerónimo*** *(☎ 4300-2624, Estados Unidos 407)*, where entrées cost between US$3 and US$5 and desserts are about US$1.50. Diners form long lines outside ***DesNivel*** *(Defensa 855)* for their reasonably priced home-style pasta and parrillada.

Reader- and author-endorsed ***Pizzaría Las Marías II*** *(Bolívar 964-966)* is an unpretentious, outstanding pizzeria with friendly and efficient staff; try the *veneciana de pollo*. The ***Taberna Baska*** *(☎ 4383-0903, Chile 980)* serves Basque food.

It's stretching it a bit to call ***Nicole de Marseille*** *(☎ 4362-2340, Defensa 714)* a French restaurant, or even to call it Franco-Argentine, but its three-course weekday lunches for US$6 are a good value, with a wide choice of entrées and desserts. On the fringes of San Telmo, spicy cuisine from Jujuy is the specialty at friendly ***La Carretería*** *(Brasil 656)*, across from the main Hostelling International facility.

Part of the Casal de Catalunya cultural center, ***Hostal del Canigó*** *(☎ 4304-5250, 4300-5252, Chacabuco 863)* serves Catalonian specialties, like *pollo a la punxa* (chicken with calamari), along with Spanish and Argentine dishes. Prices are moderate, the large lunch portions include a complimentary glass of sherry, and the dining room woodwork and tilework lend it wonderful atmosphere.

In a restored colonial house near Plaza Dorrego, ***La Casa de Esteban de Luca*** *(☎ 4361-4338, Defensa 1000)* has very fine food at moderate prices. ***El Virrey de San Telmo*** *(☎ 4361-0331, Humberto Primo 499)* offers an international menu. ***La Scala de San Telmo*** *(☎ 4362-1187, Pasaje JM Giuffra 371)* serves a mid-range to upscale international menu to the accompaniment of live classical music.

Recoleta & Barrio Norte

At the Buenos Aires Design/Terrazas de Plaza del Pilar complex (☎ 4806-1111, ask for the individual restaurant extension unless otherwise indicated below), a food mall alongside the Centro Cultural Recoleta, choices range from relatively cheap fast-food to elaborate and sophisticated fare. The official address is at Av Pueyrredón 2501, but it's more easily accessible from the Junín entrance. All locales have both indoor and outdoor seating.

One of the best values here is ***Munich del Pilar*** *(☎ 4806-0149)*, where a US$10 weekday *menú ejecutivo* offers a choice of meat, chicken, or pasta entrées and includes drinks. ***Molière*** (R), closest to the Centro

Cultural, serves an excellent grilled salmon with appetizer and a large glass of house wine for US$15; service is well intentioned but erratic.

Several others in the complex are worth checking out: ***Café Champs Elysée*** *(☎ 4806-0098)*, more a confitería, known for tantalizing desserts; ***Caruso*** *(☎ 4806-3299)*, a pricey trattoria; ***Campos del Pilar*** *(☎ 4806-1111, interno 1276)*, a parrilla; ***Café Rex***, with cinematic décor; ***Mumy's***, serving pricey hamburgers as well as several reasonable combination plates; and ***Romanaccio***, good for pizza and pasta.

A step up from most all-you-can-eats is ***Gran Fu La*** *(☎ 4803-5522, Las Heras 2379)*, in Palermo, a few blocks from Recoleta Cemetery. The US$10 price tag for lunch or dinner reflects its higher quality and selection, including items like prawns, not normally on the menu elsewhere, and spicy a la carte dishes that most Argentines shy away from. ***Cocina y Cía*** *(☎ 4823-4431, Av Santa Fe 2461)* is a tenedor libre with varied food of excellent quality, including parrillada and vegetarian fare, for US$6; drinks, however, are pretty expensive.

El Sanjuanino *(☎ 4804-2909, Posadas 1515)* serves regional versions of Argentine dishes such as empanadas, locro, and sweets, and also delivers within the immediate area. Popular for lunch, moderately priced ***Payanca*** *(☎ 4312-5209, Suipacha 1015)* features spicy northern Argentine cuisine from the province of Salta.

Restaurant Ruso *(☎ 4805-7079, Azcuénaga 1562)*, in Barrio Norte, specializes in Russian food at reasonable prices (at least by Barrio Norte standards) of around US$8 to US$10 for lunch, US$15 for dinner. The engaging ***French Bistro*** *(☎ 4806-9331, French 2301)* is a pricey Continental restaurant at the corner of Azcuénaga, but selective diners can probably eat at mid-range prices.

One of the capital's most enduring vegetarian alternatives and also something of a cultural center, ***La Esquina de las Flores*** *(☎ 4813-3630, Av Córdoba 1587)* has moved its restaurant from the nearby corner of Montevideo to the upstairs of its health-food store. Daily fixed-price specials cost US$10 (US$6 for children), but there are less expensive a la carte choices as well. Another nearby vegetarian alternative is ***Lotos*** *(Av Córdoba 1577)*.

If price is no object, check out Recoleta institutions such as ***Munich Recoleta*** *(☎ 4804-4469, RM Ortiz 1871)* or nearby ***Clark's*** *(☎ 4801-9502, Junín 1777)*. Fixed-price lunches or dinners are in the US$20 to US$30 range, but a la carte meals can be much dearer. Acknowledged as one of Buenos Aires' best restaurants, ***Au Bec Fin*** *(☎ 4801-6894, Vicente López 1825)*, in Recoleta, has prices to match.

Renowned for its good value, the ***Restaurant del Club Sirio***, *(☎ 4806-5764, JA Pacheco de Melo 1902)*, in Barrio Norte/Recoleta, has tenedor libre Monday to Saturday evenings for US$18. ***Viejo Horizonte*** *(☎ 4806-0553, Junín 1460)*, part of the Club Libanés, serves Middle Eastern food.

Japanese food is becoming more common, with places such as the expensive ***Midori*** *(☎ 4814-5151, Posadas 1252)*, in the Caesar Park Hotel. Figure about US$20 and upward for lunch or dinner.

Crowded ***Alimentari*** *(☎ 4313-9382, San Martín 899)* has outstanding medialunas for breakfast, but try also ***Yinyang*** *(☎ 4311-3788, Paraguay 858)*, a macrobiotic restaurant.

The parrilla ***Dora*** *(☎ 4311-2891, Av Alem 1016)* is popular in part for its massive portions; menu prices look steep, but most dishes suffice for two people – the imposing half portion of *bife de chorizo* (US$9) weighs nearly half a kilo. LP correspondents have also praised its seafood and pasta, as well as 'incredible' desserts (which *are* expensive).

Nearby ***El Salmón*** *(☎ 4313-1731, Reconquista 968)* has a similar and slightly cheaper menu. Other highly regarded but pricier parrillas are ***La Chacra*** *(☎ 4322-1409, Av Córdoba 941)* and ***Las Nazarenas*** *(☎ 4312-5559, Reconquista 1132)*. If you can't cross the Andes, there's passable Chilean seafood and other national dishes at ***Los Chilenos*** *(☎ 4328-3123, Suipacha 1042)*.

Filo *(☎ 4311-0312, San Martín 975)* is a lively pizza-and-pasta place with a frequently changing menu. It has friendly service and great decor, but prices are not for the financially challenged.

For ice cream, try ***Freddo***, at Ayacucho and Quintana and at Ortiz and Guido.

Outer Barrios

Fiori y Canto *(☎ 4963-3250, Av Córdoba 3547)*, on the edge of Palermo Viejo, is an attractive combination of pizzeria, parrilla, and pasta restaurant, with particularly delicious homemade bread. ***La Cátedra*** *(☎ 4774-9859, Cerviño 4699)*, in Palermo (Subte: Plaza Italia), serves an excellent three-course lunch, including a small bottle of wine and coffee, for US$12 weekdays. A la carte prices are significantly higher, though it has a US$7 salad bar.

Franco-Argentine ***Dolli*** *(R; ☎ 4806-3366, Av Figueroa Alcorta 3004)*, at the corner of Tagle in Palermo, is one of Buenos Aires' landmark restaurants. Its prices are high, but not outrageous given the quality. Near Aeroparque, on the Costanera Av Rafael Obligado at Pampa, try the popular parrilla ***Los Años Locos*** *(☎ 4783-5126)*.

In Belgrano, ***L'Altro Cesare*** *(☎ 4781-7365, Monroe 2248)* is a very fine Italian restaurant with outstanding service and some innovative dishes – try the *canelones con humita* (maize-filled cannelloni; US$8) and for dessert, the very light chocolate mousse (US$5). There's also a US$5 tenedor libre special, and most pasta dishes are reasonable, though some of the more unusual sauces cost extra, making it expensive for diners who are not selective. The small non-smoking area is not really adequate.

Belgrano has a remarkable selection of ice-cream parlors, all deserving of a visit. The local branch of ***Freddo*** is at the corner of Juramento and Arcos. ***Heladería Chungo*** *(Virrey del Pino 2500)*, in Colegiales, is worth a detour in itself. ***Furchi*** *(Av Cabildo 1506)* serves Italian-style gelato. Also outstanding is ***Heladería Gruta*** *(☎ 4784-8417, Sucre 2356)*.

ENTERTAINMENT

Carteleras along Av Corrientes sell heavily discounted tickets for entertainment events, including movies, theater, and tango shows; most tango shows aren't worth US$40, but for half that they're worth considering. Since the number of discount tickets may be limited, buy them as far in advance as possible. It's always worth trying, though, so if you want to see a movie on short notice just phone or drop by to see what's available – the most recently released hits are unlikely to be among the options.

Cartelera Vea Más (☎ 4372-7285, 4372-7314, interno 219), Corrientes 1660 at Local 19 in the Paseo La Plaza complex (M), is open daily 10 am to 11 pm. Although the street address is on Corrientes, this cubbyhole office is more easily accessible from Sarmiento, one block south. Three blocks east, Cartelera Baires (M; ☎ 4372-5058), Corrientes 1372 at Local 25 in the Galería Teatro Lorange, is open Monday to Thursday 10 am to 10:30 pm, Friday and Saturday 10 am to midnight, and Sunday 2 to 10:30 pm.

Many porteño dailies have detailed entertainment supplements, including *La Nación* (Thursday), *Ámbito Financiero*, the *Buenos Aires Herald*'s expanded 'getOut!' and *Clarín* (all published on Friday), *Argentinisches Tageblatt* (Saturday), and *Página 12* (Sunday). Another good source for entertainment listings is the monthly freebie *Magazine Plus*, widely available around town.

Cafés & Confiterías

Café society is a major force in the life of Argentines in general and porteños in particular – they spend hours solving their own problems, the country's, and the world's over a chessboard and a cheap *cortado* (coffee).

Founded in 1858, the legendary ***Café Tortoni*** *(M; ☎ 4342-4328, Av de Mayo 829)* has occupied its present site since 1893. Oozing 19th-century atmosphere from the woodwork and billiard tables, it presents a greater variety of live entertainment than it once did, including both tango and traditional jazz, in a number of rooms. If you're looking for a chess match or following the footsteps of Borges, try the very traditional (since 1917) ***Richmond*** *(M; ☎ 4322-1341, Florida 468)*.

Av Corrientes is a favorite hangout for porteño intellectuals. Traditionally famous for nonconformist atmosphere is the once-spartan ***Café La Paz*** *(M; Av Corrientes 1599)*. After briefly closing in 1997, it reopened as a brighter and superficially more inviting place, with a more expensive and extensive food menu, but whether it can preserve its bohemian legacy is open to question. ***Café Pernambuco*** *(M; Av Corrientes 1680)* still has a good atmosphere for a cup of coffee or glass of wine.

Some of the porteño elite while away the hours on caffeine from ***La Biela*** *(R; ☎ 4804-0432, Quintana 598)*, across from the Cementerio de la Recoleta. The rest exercise their purebred dogs nearby, so watch your step in crossing the street to ***Café de la Paix*** *(R; ☎ 4804-6820, Quintana 595)*.

Some cafés serve as multipurpose bookstores, theaters, and nightclubs. The ***Foro Gandhi*** *(M; ☎ 4374-7501, Av Corrientes 1551)* is an arts-oriented coffeehouse offering live tango music and foreign film cycles at bargain prices.

It's been at the same Barrio Norte location since 1938, but only in the last decade has ***Clásica y Moderna*** *(R; ☎ 4812-8707, Av Callao 892)* become the intimate, sophisticated bookstore-café it is today. Besides offering live performances of folk, jazz, and popular music, it serves mid-range to upscale meals and even stocks the day's newspapers for patrons' convenience.

Dance Clubs

Dance clubs tend to the exclusive and expensive, with cover charges (usually including one drink) of US$15 to US$30 and upward. ***Morocco*** *(M; ☎ 4342-6046, Hipólito Yrigoyen 851)* is a favorite haunt of Argentine and other Spanish-speaking pop stars, but some porteños argue it's not what it used to be. If you still have some energy when it closes its doors, the nearby ***Pantheon*** *(M; Av de Mayo 948)* opens at 6 am Sunday morning.

On the boundary between Retiro and Recoleta is ***Shampoo*** *(R; ☎ 4813-4427, Av Quintana 362)*. ***Hippopotamus*** *(M; ☎ 4802-0500, Junín 1787)*, part of its namesake restaurant, is a Recoleta institution. Palermo clubs include the well-established ***Trump's*** *(☎ 4801-9866, Bulnes 2772)* and ***Metrópolis*** *(Av Santa Fe 4389)*. Recent readers' recommendations include the dressy ***Buenos Aires News*** *(☎ 4778-1500)*, a complex at Av del Libertador and Av Infanta Isabel, where the doormen can get picky about whom they condescend to admit.

Theater

Live theater enjoys great popularity. Av Corrientes, between 9 de Julio and Callao, is the capital's Broadway or West End, but there are many other venues. The city's major formal theater facility is the ***Teatro General San Martín*** *(M; ☎ 4374-8611, Av Corrientes 1530)*, where more than a quarter million people attended shows in its three main theaters in 1997.

Other key theaters include: the ***Teatro Nacional Cervantes*** *(☎ 4816-4224, Libertad 815)*, near Plaza Lavalle, ***Teatro Maipo*** *(M; ☎ 4322-4882, Suipacha 443)*, ***Teatro Presidente Alvear*** *(M; ☎ 4374-6076, Av Corrientes 1659)*, ***Teatro Blanca Podestá*** *(M; ☎ 4382-2592, Av Corrientes 1283)*, the uniquely designed ***Teatro Complejo La Plaza*** *(M; ☎ 4370-5350, Av Corrientes 1660)*, and the ***Teatro Avenida*** *(M; ☎ 4381-3193, Av de Mayo 1212)*.

The ***Teatro Fundación Banco Patricios*** *(☎ 4373-3776, Av Callao 312)* underwrites unconventional theater in remodeled facilities. The intimate ***Teatro El Vitral*** *(M; ☎ 4371-0948, Rodríguez Peña 344)* has three small venues seating about 40 people each. Another intimate theater venue/company is the ***Equipo Teatro Payró*** *(M; ☎ 4312-5922, San Martín 766)*.

Rock & Blues

El Samovar de Rasputín *(☎ 4302-3190, Del Valle Iberlucea 1251)*, in La Boca, presents blues and rock bands on weekends, from 11:30 pm. Admission is US$5. Another possibility is the ***Blues Special Club*** *(S; Almirante Brown 102)*, opposite Parque Lezama in La Boca, just across from San Telmo boundary.

In San Telmo proper, ***La Casa del Pueblo*** *(S; Defensa 740)* also features rock and roll bands. ***Coco Bahiano*** *(S; Balcarce 958)* is a reggae club. In nearby Constitución, try ***Cemento*** *(Estados Unidos 1200)*.

The Recoleta branch of the ***Hard Rock Café*** *(R; ☎ 4807-7625)*, at the junction of Pueyrredón and Azcuénaga, has live music, mostly but not exclusively cover bands, on weekends. It's open noon to 3 am daily and offers a 15% student discount.

Oh My God *(R; ☎ 4775-5238, Migueletes 1241)*, in Palermo, has live rock with a US$5 cover charge Friday and Saturday nights. ***La Casona del Conde*** *(☎ 4862-5215, Honduras 3852)*, in Palermo Viejo, features groups like the female a cappella unit Las Blacanblus.

Dr Jekyll *(☎ 4788-2411, Monroe 2315)*, in Belgrano, features porteño bands, like ska specialists Los Cafres, but the music varies depending on the night – there are even tango classes.

Jazz

Informal enough that patrons discard their peanut shells on the floor, ***Bárbaro*** *(R; ☎ 4311-6856, Tres Sargentos 415)*, in Retiro, employs groups like La Porteña Jazz Band, which also plays Café Tortoni. For contemporary jazz, try the Congreso venues of ***Girondo*** *(M; ☎ 4371-8838, Paraná 328)*, just off Av Corrientes, and ***Evenos*** *(M; ☎ 4381-7776, Mitre 1552)*, which also attracts popular artists of the stature of Charly García.

Oliverio Allways *(M; ☎ 4372-6906, Av Callao 360)*, in the Hotel Bauen in Balvanera, has live jazz and blues. ***Remember*** *(M; ☎ 4953-0638, Av Corrientes 1983)* is an informal pub that showcases jazz plus occasional blues and live theater.

Tango

Tango is experiencing a major boom on both the amateur and professional levels, and among all ages. One of the best sources on local trends is the free bimonthly newsletter ***Buenos Aires Tango***, which is widely distributed around town and full of ads for both shows and lessons.

Finding spontaneous tango is not easy, but you'll have the best luck at San Telmo's Sunday flea market on Plaza Dorrego, where very professional dancers entertain tourists without pandering to them. Other than that, plenty of clubs in San Telmo, Barracas, and La Boca portray Argentina's most famous cultural export for prices up to US$40 per show or more, depending whether dinner is included.

At the lower end of the scale, the cover for shows at ***Bar Sur*** *(S; ☎ 4362-6086, Estados Unidos 299)*, in San Telmo, is US$15, which includes unlimited pizza but not the fairly expensive drinks; it's open Monday to Saturday. The more central ***La Casa de Luis Cardei*** *(☎ 4373-8781, Av Corrientes 1660)*, in the Paseo La Plaza complex (M), has Friday and Saturday night shows for US$22.

Café Homero *(☎ 4773-1979, Cabrera 4946)*, a neighborhood tanguería in Palermo Viejo, has no cover charge but does enforce a US$30 minimum-consumption rule. Shows take place Thursday to Saturday at 11 pm. Nearby ***Club del Vino*** *(☎ 4833-0050, Cabrera 4737)* has a US$15 cover Friday night at 10 pm and a US$30 cover Saturday night at 9:30 pm.

Several nightspots in the Balvanera neighborhood of Abasto – Carlos Gardel's old haunts – are also good choices. ***Club Almagro*** *(☎ 4774-7454, Medrano 522)*, in the Almagro barrio, has very reasonably priced tango shows, which, unlike the big-budget extravaganzas, invite audience participation. Other Abasto venues include ***Babilonia*** *(☎ 4862-0683, Guardia Vieja 3360)*, just west of the Mercado de Abasto, a cultural center that also offers alternative theater and a tapas bar, and ***Fernandezes*** *(☎ 4866-4129)*, at Guardia Vieja and Billinghurst in Almagro.

At the same site since 1920, but remodeled in 1992, ***El Querandí*** *(M; ☎ 4345-0331, Perú 302)*, in Montserrat, offers dinner and a show at 8:30 nightly except Sunday for US$55 (the show starts at 10:30 pm). The classic tanguería ***Caño 14*** *(R; ☎ 4803-3660, Vicente López 2134)* has moved from its old San Telmo venue to Recoleta. In the outer barrio of Nueva Pompeya, ***El Chino*** *(Beazley 3565)*, a former warehouse near Av Amancio Alcorta, has become one of the capital's 'in' tango places, open from 11:30 pm Friday and Saturday night.

Its publicity brochure demonstrates the pitfalls of employing a translator with no qualifications beyond ownership of a bilingual dictionary, but ***Casa Blanca*** *(M; ☎ 4331-4621, Balcarce 668)* really appears to glory in hosting disgraced heads of state (Brazil's Fernando Collor de Mello and Mexico's Carlos Salinas de Gortari) and dropping the names of show-biz patrons (Omar Sharif, Oliver Stone, Mick Jagger, Eric Clapton). It does present some of the biggest names in tango, though; regular shows take place weekdays at 10 pm, Saturday at 9 and 11 pm. Ask about the 30% student discount.

Classical Music

The ***Teatro Colón*** *(M; ☎ 4382-0554, Libertad 621)* is Buenos Aires' landmark classical music venue, having hosted figures as prominent as Enrico Caruso, Placido Domingo, Luciano Pavarotti, and Arturo Toscanini.

The regular season for opera and classical music runs from March through November

Gardel & the Tango

In June 1935, a Cuban woman committed suicide in Havana, while a woman in New York and another in Puerto Rico tried to poison themselves, all over the same man whom none of them had ever met. The man whose smiling photograph graced their rooms had himself just died in a plane crash in Medellín, Colombia. On his body's long odyssey to its final resting place in Argentina, Latin Americans thronged to pay him tribute in Colombia, New York, Rio de Janeiro, and Montevideo. Once in Buenos Aires, his body lay in state at Luna Park stadium before a horse-drawn carriage took him to Chacarita Cemetery. The man was tango singer Carlos Gardel, *El Zorzal Criollo*, the songbird of Buenos Aires.

Originating around 1880, only a decade before Gardel's birth, the tango was the vulgar dance and music of the capital's *arrabales*, or fringes, blending gaucho verse with Spanish and Italian music. Gardel created the *tango canción*, the tango-song, taking it out of the brothels and tenements to New York and Paris. Only after Gardel had won over audiences in North America and Europe did the Argentine elite deign to allow it into their salons.

It was no accident that the tango grew to popularity when it did. In the late 19th century, the *Gran Aldea* (Great Village) of Buenos Aires was becoming an immigrant city where frustrated and melancholic Europeans displaced gaucho rustics, who retreated gradually to the ever more distant countryside. The children of those immigrants would become the first generation of porteños, and the tango-song summarized the new urban experience.

Permeated with nostalgia for a disappearing way of life, the melancholic tango-song expressed the apprehensions and anxieties of individuals. Its themes ranged from mundane pastimes like horse racing and other popular diversions to more profound feelings about the changing landscape of neighborhood and community, the figure of the mother, betrayal by women, and friendship or other personal concerns. English musician Robert Fripp has compared therelation of Argentines and tango to that of North Americans and the blues.

The inevitable transformations of La Boca's 'Caminito' mirrored the changes in Gardel's own life:

but really hits its stride during the winter months of June through August.

The Orquesta Filarmónica de Buenos Aires, often featuring guest conductors from throughout Latin America, normally plays Monday evenings at 9 pm.

From May to September, the ***Mozarteum Argentina*** *(☎ 4811-3448)* presents free weekly chamber music concerts at midday; also contact the ***Teatro Ópera*** *(M; ☎ 4326-1225, Av Corrientes 860)* for details. The Orquesta de Cámara Mayo plays regularly at the ***Auditorio de Belgrano*** *(☎ 4783-1783)*, Av Cabildo and Virrey Loreto, and at various other venues through the city.

Other classical music venues in Buenos Aires include ***Teatro Avenida*** *(☎ 4381-0662, Av de Mayo 1212)*, in Montserrat, which specializes in ballet productions, and the ***Teatro Coliseo*** *(R; ☎ 4807-1277, MT del Alvear 1125)*, in Recoleta.

Tickets for classical performances range from about US$20 to US$70, but some venues offer series discounts.

Gardel & the Tango

Caminito que entonces estabas	Caminito of what you once were
bordeado de trébol y juncos en flor	bordered by clover and flowering rushes
una sombra ya pronto serás	a shadow you soon will be
una sombra, lo mismo que yo . . .	a shadow just like me . . .

Though born in France, Gardel came to epitomize the porteño. When he was three, his poor and single mother brought him to Buenos Aires, where he passed his formative years in a neighborhood near the Mercado de Abasto (a central produce market near which porteños now board the Subte at Estación Carlos Gardel). In his youth, he worked at a variety of menial jobs but also entertained neighbors with his singing. His performing career began after he befriended Uruguayan-born José Razzano. They formed the popular duo Gardel-Razzano, which lasted until Razzano lost his voice.

From 1917 onward, Gardel performed solo. His voice, his singing, and his charisma made him an immediate popular success in Argentina and other Latin American countries, although the Argentine elite still despised the music and what it stood for – the rise of a middle class that challenged its monopoly on power. Building on this popularity, Gardel sang regularly on the radio and soon became a recording star. To broaden his appeal, he traveled to Spain and France, where widespread acceptance finally made him palatable even to the elite sectors of Argentine society, which once were scandalized by the tango's humble origins and open sensuality. Later he began a film career that was cut short by his death.

In a sense, Gardel's early death rescued him from aging and placed him in an eternal present, allowing his iconic figure to dominate Argentine popular culture. One measure of his immortality is the common saying that 'Gardel sings better every day.' Photographs of Gardel, with his unmistakably charismatic smile, are everywhere – one photo lab in Buenos Aires sold more than 350,000 pictures in the first two decades after his death. The large, devoted community of his followers, known as *gardelianos*, cannot pass a day without listening to his songs or watching his films.

Daily, a steady procession of pilgrims visit his plaque-covered tomb in Chacarita Cemetery, where, often, a lighted cigarette rests in the hand of his life-size statue. On December 11, 1990, the centenary of his birth, it was smothered in floral tributes.

For an excellent account of Gardel's life in English, see Simon Collier's *The Life, Music and Times of Carlos Gardel*, a serious biography that refrains from the most romantic exaggerations of the singer's fanatical devotees.

Cinemas

Buenos Aires is famous for its cinemas, which play first-run films from around the world, but there is also an audience for unconventional and classic films. The main cinema districts are along the Lavalle peatonal, west of Florida, and on Corrientes and Santa Fe, all easy walking distance from downtown. The price of tickets has risen dramatically in recent years, but most cinemas offer half-price discounts on Wednesday and sometimes for the first afternoon showing daily; Wednesday showings can be mobbed, so go early.

The ***Sala Leopoldo Lugones*** *(☎ 4374-8611, Av Corrientes 1530)*, at the Teatro General San Martín, regularly offers thematic foreign film cycles as well as reprises of outstanding commercial films. In addition to current releases, the ***Auditorio Maxi*** *(M; ☎ 4326-1822, Carlos Pellegrini 657)* also does retrospectives and less commercial films. ***Cine Cosmos*** *(M; ☎ 4953-5405, Av Corrientes 2046)* shows similar fare.

Since Spanish translations of English-language film titles are often misleading, check the ***Buenos Aires Herald*** to be certain what's playing. Except for children's films and cartoon features, which are dubbed, foreign films almost always appear in the original language with Spanish subtitles.

Gay & Lesbian Venues

Gay visitors will find a cluster congenial bars and dance clubs in the Recoleta-Barrio Norte area, as well as others scattered throughout town, mostly but not exclusively in Retiro and Palermo. The main area is around Av Santa Fe and Pueyrredón in Barrio Norte, where it's often possible to get free or discount admission tickets.

In Recoleta (Barrio Norte), ***Contramano*** *(Rodríguez Peña 1082)* is one of the city's oldest gay venues, with a slightly older clientele (men only). Also in Barrio Norte, open Wednesday through Sunday, the gigantic ***Bunker*** *(Anchorena 1170)* is a techno-style club with a hefty cover charge and a mixed clientele. Nearby reader recommendations include ***Gasoil*** *(Anchorena 1179)* and ***Abaco*** *(Anchorena 1347)*.

In Retiro, there's the popular but claustrophobically small ***Enigma*** *(R; Suipacha 927)*, with mostly pop music Friday and Saturday only, and ***Experiment*** *(R; ☎ 4328-1019, Carlos Pellegrini 1085)*. ***Bach Bar*** *(Cabrera 4390)*, in Palermo Viejo, is a smaller, quieter, and more intimate venue; it's closed Monday.

The Congreso area also has several clubs, though they're not as close together as those in Barrio Norte. ***Tercer Milenio*** *(M; Alsina 934)*, open Friday only, has salsa and other Latin styles. ***Vaivén*** *(M; Perón 1871)*, between Av Callao and Riobamba in Congreso, a new and well-designed club for men only, hasn't really developed an identity yet, but it bears watching. Close to Barrio Norte, ***Boicot*** *(M; Pasaje Dellepiane 657)* is a lesbian club.

SPECTATOR SPORTS

Buenos Aires has the highest density of first-division soccer teams in the world – eight of the country's 20 teams are based in the capital, while another five are in nearby suburbs. For information on tickets and schedules, contact the clubs listed below; where two addresses and telephone numbers appear, the first is the club office, and the second is the stadium, where tickets are normally purchased. *Entradas populares* (standing room) costs around US$10, while *plateas* (fixed seats) cost $20 and upward.

Argentinos Juniors
(☎ 4582-8949)
Boyacá 2152
(☎ 4551-6887)
Punta Arenas 1271

Boca Juniors
(☎ 4362-2260)
Brandsen 805

Ferrocarril Oeste
(☎ 4431-9203)
Cucha Cucha 350
(☎ 4432-3989)
Martín de Gainza 244

River Plate
(☎ 4788-1200)
Av Presidente Figueroa Alcorta 7597

San Lorenzo de Almagro
(☎ 4923-9212)
Av Fernández de la Cruz 2403

(☎ 4918-3455)
Av Perito Moreno between Av Fernández de la Cruz and Varela

Vélez Sársfield
(☎ 4641-5663)
Av Juan B Justo 9200

SHOPPING

Compulsive shoppers adore Buenos Aires. The main shopping zones are downtown, along the Florida peatonal and the more fashionable and more expensive Av Santa Fe, although Recoleta is another worthwhile area. Ritzy one-stop shopping centers, some of them recycled, such as Florida's Galerías Pacífico (☎ 4311-6323), Recoleta's Patio Bullrich (☎ 4815-3501), and Palermo's Alto Palermo (☎ 4821-6030), have begun to take business away from the traditional commercial center.

For general leather goods, Welcome Marroquinería (☎ 4312-8911), Marcelo T de Alvear 500 in Retiro, has been a Buenos Aires institution since 1930. Among other leather shops, try Rossi y Carusso (☎ 4811-5357), at Av Santa Fe 1601 in Barrio Norte; Chiche Farrace, in the Galerías Pacífico; Dalla Fontana (☎ 4311-1229), at Reconquista 735; and El Sol (☎ 4480-9950), at Av Libertador 1096.

For women's footwear, try Perugia (☎ 4804-6340), at Av Alvear 1862 in Recoleta. Guido Mocasines, Rodríguez Peña 1290 in Barrio Norte, is widely acknowledged as the city's best traditional shoemaker; there's also a branch at Av Quintana 333 (☎ 4811-4567). López Taibo, Av Alvear 1902 in Recoleta, sells men's shoes. Flabella (☎ 4322-6036), Suipacha 263, specializes in shoes for tango dancers.

Several provincial tourist offices, especially those along Av Santa Fe and Av Callao, have small but worthwhile selections of regional crafts. Look especially at the Casa de Misiones (☎ 4393-1812), Av Santa Fe 989 in Retiro; the nearby Casa de Jujuy (☎ 4393-6096), at Av Santa Fe 967; and the Casa del Chaco (☎ 4372-5209), Av Callao 322 in Balvanera. Kelly's Regionales (☎ 4311-5712), Paraguay 431 in Retiro, has a huge stock from throughout the country.

For typical items such as silverwork and mate paraphernalia, check out Artesanías Argentinas (☎ 4812-2650), at Montevideo 1386 in Barrio Norte. Che Bandoneón (☎ 4312-7193), Paraguay 697 in Retiro, specializes in tango souvenirs. Rancho Grande (☎ 4311-7603), Av Córdoba 543, Local 63 in Retiro, sells gaucho souvenirs.

Among the several San Telmo area craftsworkers dealing in *filete,* the colorful line paintings so typical of the capital since the turn of the century, are Jorge Muscia (☎ 4361-5942), at Carlos Calvo 370; Martiniano Arce, at Perú 1089, 1st floor; and Mabel Matto, at Estados Unidos 510, 1st floor.

Art Galleries

Most of Buenos Aires' dozens of art galleries offer fairly conventional works, either European or consciously derivative of European traditions, but a handful of venues promote more locally based, innovative efforts. For an up-to-date listing of events and current exhibits, consult the monthly tabloid newsletter *Arte al Día* (☎ 4805-7672), available at galleries and museums throughout the city.

In modern Argentine art, the consistently best gallery is Ruth Benzacar (☎ 4313-8945), downstairs at Florida 1000 in Retiro, but other worthwhile places (all in Retiro) include: Federico Klem (☎ 4312-2058), downstairs at MT de Alvear 636; Rubbers (☎ 4393-6010), at Suipacha 1175; Vermeer (☎ 4394-3462), across the street at Suipacha 1168; Aguilar (☎ 4394-6900), nearby at Suipacha 1178; and Zurbarán (☎ 4815-1556), at Cerrito 1522. Under the railroad bridge in Palermo, Galería der Brücke (☎ 4775-2175), at Av Libertador 3883, also displays interesting work.

Markets & Ferias

One of the capital's most interesting shopping districts, San Telmo is known for its fascinating flea market, the Feria de San Telmo, which takes place Saturday and Sunday from 10 am to about 5 pm on Plaza Dorrego (refrain from touching items on display). Prices have risen considerably at the nearby gentrified antique shops, but there are good restaurants, and buskers, mimes, and tango dancers frequently perform unannounced.

Only a short walk from Plaza Dorrego, there is now a Sunday market in spacious Parque Lezama, at the corner of Brasil and Av Paseo Colón, which also gets a fair number of street performers. In La Boca, at the Riachuelo end of the Caminito, the Feria Artesanal Plazoleta Vuelta de Rocha takes place weekends and holidays from 10 am to 6 pm; there is also an artists' market on the Caminito itself, open daily 10 am to 6 pm.

Another popular artisans' market takes place Sunday in Recoleta's Plaza Intendente Alvear, at Av Pueyrredón and Av del Libertador. The Feria Artesanal Plaza General Manuel Belgrano, at Juramento and Cuba in Belgrano, takes place weekends and holidays from 10 am to 8 pm, but it gets better as the day goes on – not until 4 or 5 pm do legitimate craftsworkers finally outnumber kitsch peddlers.

In the southwestern barrio of Mataderos, at the corner of Av Lisandro de la Torre and Bragado, the Feria de Mataderos is a lively market frequented by gauchos, folksingers, and other performers, along with 200 merchants selling practical goods in a 'general store' atmosphere. It's open weekends 11 am to 7 pm; from downtown, take bus No 155 up Calle Tucumán.

GETTING THERE & AWAY

Because of space limitations, very detailed air and bus schedules do not appear below, but most newspapers, including the *Buenos Aires Herald,* publish schedules of international arrivals and departures; for domestic flight frequencies, consult the appropriate destination in other chapters. Bus services are very frequent to most major domestic destinations.

Air

International Many major international airlines have offices or representatives in Buenos Aires. Most of the following serve Ezeiza for long-distance international flights, but a few from neighboring countries use Aeroparque.

Aeroflot
(☎ 4312-5573) Av Santa Fe 822

Aerolíneas Argentinas
(☎ 4320-2000) Perú 2

Air France
(☎ 4317-4700) Paraguay 610, 14th floor

Alitalia
(☎ 4310-9999) Suipacha 1111, 28th floor

American Airlines
(☎ 4318-1111) Av Santa Fe 881

Avianca
(☎ 4394-5990) Carlos Pellegrini 1163, 4th floor

British Airways
(☎ 4320-6600) Av Córdoba 650

Canadian Airlines
(☎ 4322-3632) Av Córdoba 656

Cubana de Aviación
(☎ 4326-5291) Sarmiento 552, 11th floor

Ecuatoriana
(☎ 4311-3010) Suipacha 1065

Iberia
(☎ 4327-2739) Carlos Pellegrini 1163, 1st floor

Japan Airlines
(☎ 4393-1896) Av Córdoba 836, 11th floor

KLM
(☎ 4480-9470) Reconquista 559, 5th floor

Korean Air
(☎ 4311-9237) Av Córdoba 755

LanChile
(☎ 4316-2200) Florida 954

Transportes Aéreos de Mercosur (TAM)
(☎ 4816-1000) Cerrito 1026

Lloyd Aéreo Boliviano (LAB)
(☎ 4326-3595) Carlos Pellegrini 141

Lufthansa
(☎ 4319-0600) MT de Alvear 636

Malaysia Airlines
(☎ 4312-6971) Suipacha 1111, 14th floor

Mexicana
(☎ 4312-6152) Av Córdoba 755, 1st floor

Pluna
(☎ 4342-4420) Florida 1

South African Airways
(☎ 4311-8184) Av Santa Fe 794, 3rd floor

Swissair
(☎ 4319-0000) Av Santa Fe 846, 1st floor

TAP (Air Portugal)
(☎ 4811-0984) Cerrito 1136

TransBrasil
(☎ 4394-8424) Florida 780, 1st floor

United Airlines
(☎ 4316-0777) Av Eduardo Madero 900, 9th floor
Varig
(☎ 4329-9204) Florida 630
Vasp
(☎ 4311-2699) Av Santa Fe 784

Domestic & Regional Most domestic and some regional flights leave from Aeroparque Jorge Newbery, a short distance north of downtown, but a few use Ezeiza. To Uruguay, in particular, services from Aeroparque are cheaper and more convenient than the major international airlines at Ezeiza.

Aerolíneas Argentinas
(☎ 4320-2000) Perú 2; (☎ 4327-1941) Arroyo 807; (☎ 4783-2507), Av Cabildo 2900. Argentina's traditional flag carrier has extensive domestic and international routes.

Andesmar
(☎ 4312-1077), Esmeralda 1063, 1st floor. A recent startup subsidiary of a well-established bus company, this regional airline serves northern and western cities (Rosario, Córdoba, Mendoza, La Rioja, Tucumán, and Salta) and Buenos Aires provincial beach resorts (Villa Gesell, Mar del Plata, Miramar).

Austral Líneas Aéreas
(☎ 4317-3605), Av Alem 1134. Close partners Austral and Aerolíneas share an identical fare structure, both serving nearly every major Argentine city between Bolivia and the Beagle Channel.

Dinar Líneas Aéreas
(☎ 4326-0135), Diagonal Roque Sáenz Peña 933. Having recently expanded routes, this regional carrier still flies mostly to the northwestern Argentine destinations of Tucumán, Salta, and Jujuy, but also to Córdoba, Mendoza, Mar del Plata, and Comodoro Rivadavia.

Líneas Aéreas del Estado (LADE)
(☎ 4361-7071), Perú 714. The airline that seemingly refuses to die in the face of budget cutbacks and privatizations, the Air Force's passenger service goes to southern Buenos Aires province and Patagonian destinations exclusively.

Líneas Aéreas de Entre Ríos (LAER)
(☎ 4311-5237), Maipú 935. This provincial carrier flies to Mesopotamian destinations in Entre Ríos and Corrientes, and to Santa Fe, La Pampa, and coastal Buenos Aires province.

Líneas Aéreas Privadas Argentinas (LAPA)
(☎ 4819-5272), Carlos Pellegrini 1075. LAPA has acquired many new planes and expanded routes to compete with Aerolíneas and Austral. Its capacity is still smaller than its competitors, and flights are often booked far in advance, especially those with discount fares. It also provides regional services to Punta del Este, Uruguay.

Southern Winds
(☎ 4312-2811, fax 44313-5883), Florida 868, 13th floor. This Córdoba-based startup links the capital with Córdoba, Río Cuarto, Mendoza, Salta, and Tucumán.

Transporte Aéreo Costa Atlántica (TACA)
(☎ 4307-1956), Bernardo de Irigoyen 1370, 1st floor. TACA flies small planes to Atlantic coastal destinations, Mesopotamia, Puerto Iguazú, and Bariloche in summer.

Bus

Buenos Aires' massive Estación Terminal de Ómnibus (☎ 4310-0700) is at Av Antártida Argentina and Ramos Mejía in Retiro, a short distance from the Retiro train station. Its Centro de Informes y Reclamos (☎ 4313-9594), Oficina 29 on the 2nd floor, provides general bus information and also monitors taxis serving the terminal; direct any complaint about taxi drivers to them.

Each of Retiro's 100-plus bus companies has a desk resembling an airline ticket counter (some of them shared). Discounted tickets are less prevalent than in the past, but student and university identification can still sometimes yield a reduction of 20%, except on special promotions.

Space prohibits more than the following representative sample of information; for more detailed information, phone or visit the terminal. To the most popular destinations, departures are frequent and reservations are rarely necessary except during peak summer and winter holiday seasons, but purchasing your ticket a day ahead of time is still a good idea.

While the list below is regionally organized, services do not always fit into convenient categories. Many Patagonian carriers, for example, stop in the Pampas of Buenos Aires province, while some serving Cuyo also continue to Chile. Bus companies and their regional destinations are given first, followed by tables of destinations, price, and estimated length of the trip. Fares are subject to great variability, and it pays to shop around on competing lines.

International Destinations Bus companies with routes to other countries include the following:

Ahumada (☎ 4311-4835) – Santiago, Chile

Chevallier (☎ 4314-5555) – Santiago, Chile

Chevallier Paraguaya (☎ 4313-2349) – similar routes to La Internacional

El Rápido Internacional (☎ 4315-0804) – Lima, Peru

Expreso Río Paraná (☎ 4313-3143) – Asunción, Paraguay

Fénix Pullman Norte (☎ 4313-0134) – Santiago, Chile.

General Urquiza (☎ 4313-2771) – nightly service to Montevideo

La Internacional (☎ 4313-3167) – Asunción, Paraguay, via Formosa and Clorinda.

Nuestra Señora de la Asunción (☎ 4313-2325) – similar routes to La Internacional

Ormeño Internacional (☎ 4313-2259) – Lima, Peru

Pluma (☎ 4313-3901) – Brazilian destinations, including Foz do Iguaçu, Porto Alegre, Florianópolis, Camboriú, Curitiba, São Paulo, and Rio de Janeiro

Rápido Yguazú (☎ 4315-6981) – Paraguay and Brazilian routes

TAC (☎ 4313-3627) – Santiago, Chile

Destination	Fare	Duration
Asuncion	US$56 to US$73	20 hours
Camboriú	US$90	27 hours
Curitiba	US$95	35 hours
Florianópolis	US$85	26 hours
Foz do Iguaçu	US$60	19 hours
Lima, Peru	US$160	80 hours
Montevideo	US$25	8 hours
Porto Alegre	US$71	21 hours
Rio de Janeiro	US$117	48 hours
Santiago, Chile	US$60	21 hours
São Paulo	US$101	42 hours

Atlantic Coast & the Pampas The following companies go to points along the coast and in the Pampas.

Chevallier (☎ 4314-5555) – Rosario and points north

Costera Criolla/Don Otto (☎ 4313-2449) – Buenos Aires province, La Plata, Bahía Blanca, Mar del Plata, and Patagonia

El Cóndor/La Estrella (☎ 4313-1700) – Buenos Aires province, Bahía Blanca, Mar del Plata, and Patagonia

Empresa Antón (☎ 4313-3051) – Mar del Plata and other beach resorts

La Internacional (☎ 4313-3167) – Rosario and points north

Micromar (☎ 4313-3130) – Mar del Plata and other beach resorts

Río de la Plata (☎ 4313-3616) – Mar del Plata and other beach resorts

Destination	Fare	Duration
Bahía Blanca	US$30	10 hours
Mar del Plata	US$25	7 hours
Rosario	US$20	6 hours

Mesopotamia, Misiones & the Gran Chaco Try the following companies:

El Norte Bis (☎ 4315-1102) – Resistencia and intermediates

El Rápido Argentino (☎ 4315-2505) – Littoral cities of Santa Fe, Paraná, and Corrientes

Empresa Kurtz (☎ 4315-1215) – Posadas, Puerto Iguazú

Tata/Central El Rápido (☎ 4313-3844) – Gualeguaychú, Colón, and northerly destinations, passing Parque Nacional El Palmar

Expreso Singer (☎ 4313-3937) – Posadas, Puerto Iguazú

Flecha Bus (☎ 4315-2781) – Paraná

Destination	Fare	Duration
Corrientes	US$40	14 hours
Gualeguaychú	US$11	3 hours
Paraná	US$21	7 hours
Posadas	US$39	14 hours
Puerto Iguazú	US$48	21 hours
Resistencia	US$43	15 hours
Santa Fe	US$21	6 hours

Córdoba & the Andean Northwest Companies with routes to Córdoba and the Andean Northwest include:

Ablo (☎ 4313-2995) – Rosario, Córdoba and its Sierras, La Rioja

Atahualpa (☎ 4315-0601) – Salta, Jujuy, and La Quiaca

Cacorba (☎ 4313-2651) – Córdoba, Catamarca

Chevallier (☎ 4314-5555) – Rosario, Córdoba, Santiago del Estero, Catamarca, and points north

El Santiagueño (☎ 4313-2085) – Santiago del Estero

General Urquiza (☎ 4313-2771) – La Rioja via Santa Fe

La Estrella (☎ 4315-3058) – Termas de Río Hondo, Santiago del Estero, Tucumán

La Internacional (☎ 4313-3167) – Salta, Jujuy

La Veloz del Norte (☎ 4315-0800) – Salta and the Bolivian border at Pocitos

Sierras de Córdoba (☎ 4313-3040) – Sierras de Córdoba

Valle de Calamuchita (☎ 4313-2085) – Sierras de Córdoba

Destination	Fare	Duration
Catamarca	US$42 to US$54	16 hours
Córdoba	US$25 to US$30	10 hours
Jujuy	US$64 to US$80	22 hours
La Rioja	US$52 to US$62	17 hours
Pocitos (Bolivia)	US$83	26 hours
Salta	US$64 to US$86	22 hours
Santiago del Estero	US$45	14 hours
Termas de Río Hondo	US$42	15 hours
Tucumán	US$30 to US$69	15 hours

Cuyo To get to Cuyo, try any of the following companies:

Autotransportes San Juan (☎ 4313-9625) – San Luis, San Juan

Chevallier (☎ 4314-5555) – San Luis, Mendoza

Expreso Jocolí (☎ 4311-8283) – San Luis, Mendoza

Expreso Uspallata (☎ 4314-1258) – Mendoza and intermediates

TAC (☎ 4313-3627) – San Luis, Mendoza

Destination	Fare	Duration
Mendoza	US$45 to US$55	14 hours
San Juan	US$40 to US$60	16 hours
San Luis	US$40 to US$45	12 hours

Patagonia Bus companies with Patagonian routes include:

Centenario (☎ 4314-5264) – San Martín de los Andes

Chevallier (☎ 4314-5555) – Neuquén, Bariloche

Costera Criolla/Don Otto (☎ 4313-5997) – coastal Patagonia: Tandil, Bahía Blanca, Puerto Madryn, Comodoro Rivadavia, Río Gallegos

El Cóndor/La Estrella (☎ 4313-1700) – Neuquén, Bariloche, RN 3 as far as Comodoro Rivadavia

El Valle (☎ 4313-2441) – Bariloche

Empresa Pehuenche (☎ 4311-8283) – Santa Rosa de La Pampa, Neuquén

El Pingüino (☎ 4315-4438) – Río Gallegos and intermediates, with connections to Punta Arenas, Chile

La Puntual (☎ 4313-2441) – RN 3 as far as Comodoro Rivadavia

TAC (☎ 4313-3627) – Bariloche

Vía Bariloche (☎ 4315-3122) – Bariloche

Destination	Fare	Duration
Bahía Blanca	US$25 to US$30	10 hours
Bariloche	US$75 to US$85	23 hours
Carmen de Patagones/ Viedma	US$35 to US$45	13 hours
Comodoro Rivadavia	US$60 to US$75	24 hours
Neuquén	US$45 to 55	16 hours
Puerto Madryn	US$35 to US$57	21 hours
Río Gallegos	US$70 to US$100	40 hours
San Martín de los Andes	US$65 to US$75	23 hours
Santa Rosa	US$25	9 hours
Tandil	US$16	6 hours

Train

Privatization of Ferrocarriles Argentinos has greatly reduced long-distance rail services, but the provinces of Buenos Aires, Tucumán, and La Pampa continue to provide limited long-distance passenger service to and from the capital.

The Mitre line operates from Estación Retiro, the Roca line from Estación Constitución, and the Sarmiento line from Estación Once de Septiembre (popularly known as 'Once'). Administered by the provinces of Buenos Aires, Ferrobaires (☎ 4304-0035) operates the Ferrocarril Roca, serving the Atlantic beach resorts of Mar del Plata, Pinamar, and other destinations in Buenos Aires province. Operated by the province of Tucumán, Ferrocarriles Tucumán SA (Tufesa, ☎ 4313-8060) operates the Ferrocarril Mitre to Rosario, Santiago del Estero, and Tucumán. The Ferrocarril Sarmiento (☎ 4861-0041), though primarily a commuter line, still links the capital to Santa Rosa, in La Pampa province.

Mar del Plata In season, as many as eight trains daily go to Mar del Plata; the ticket office at Constitución is open 7 am to midnight. Fares are US$16 turista, US$22 primera, US$28 Pullman, and US$40 for Friday's super Pullman.

Bahía Blanca Ferrobaires trains to Bahía Blanca leave nightly at 9:10 pm; Monday, Wednesday, and Saturday they go via Pringles, while other days they go via Lamadrid.

Fares are US$15 turista, US$17 primera, US$22 Pullman, and US$30 coche cama, but Ferrobaires does not accept dollars or credit cards. The ticket office at Constitución is open weekdays 9 am to 7 pm and Saturday 9 am to 1 pm, as well as 6:30 to 7:30 am Wednesday and Sunday.

Tucumán *El Tucumano* goes to Tucumán Monday, Wednesday, and Friday at 4 pm, via Rosario and Santiago del Estero (La Banda). The ticket office at Retiro is open weekdays 10 am to 6 pm, Saturday 9:30 am to 1 pm. Fares based on turista/primera/Pullman classes are:

Rosario US$10/12/16
La Banda (Santiago del Estero) US$30/34/43
Tucumán US$35/40/50

Santa Rosa From Estación Once, the Ferrocarril Sarmiento (☎ 4317-4407) goes to Santa Rosa Monday, Wednesday, and Friday at 8 pm. Fares are US$13 turista, US$15 primera, US$20 Pullman.

Car

No sane person would recommend driving in Buenos Aires, though, for a price, the standard agencies will let you take your chances. Rates tend to be cheaper than elsewhere in the country, but a car is much less useful because of heavy congestion, difficult and expensive parking, and abundant public transport. Try one of the following rental companies:

AI
(☎ 4312-9475) MT de Alvear 678
Budget
(☎ 4311-9870) Av Santa Fe 869
Dollar
(☎ 4315-8800) MT de Alvear 523
Econo
(☎ 4315-8104) MT de Alvear 866
Hertz
(☎ 4312-1317) Ricardo Rojas 451
Localiza
(☎ 4816-3999) Paraguay 1122
National
(☎ 4314-0705) Av Córdoba 725, 1st floor
Unirent
(☎ 4315-0777) Paraguay 864

Boat

Buenos Aires has regular ferry and *aliscafo* (hydrofoil) services to Colonia from Dársena Norte, near downtown at the foot of Viamonte, or from Dársena Sur, Av Pedro de Mendoza 20 in La Boca. There is a US$10 departure tax from these terminals; this is now normally included in the fare, but ask to be sure.

Colonia At Av Córdoba 699, Ferrytur (☎ 4315-6800, ☎ 4314-2300 at Dársena Norte, 4300-1366 at Dársena Sur) makes two crossings to Colonia (2½ hours) every weekday, and one every Saturday and Sunday, with the ferry *Ciudad de Buenos Aires*. These depart weekdays at 8 am and 4:29 pm, weekends at 8:15 am only; regular fares are US$23 one-way, US$17 for children ages three to nine; there are also senior citizens' discounts. Day trips are available from US$31, including lunch and a city tour

Ferrytur's hydrofoil *Sea Cat* goes to Colonia (45 minutes) four times weekdays, three times daily on weekends for US$32 one-way, US$24 for children ages three to nine; fares may be higher on selected peak days and in summer. There are also US$50 day trips including lunch and a city tour.

Buquebus (☎ 4313-4444), Av Córdoba 867, has two daily ferry sailings to Colonia on the *Eladia Isabel*, at 12:30 am daily except Sunday and at 8:15 am daily; return times from Colonia are 4 am and 7 pm. Passenger fares are the same as Ferrytur's; slightly more expensive first-class service is also available. A Buquebus colectivo leaves the Av Córdoba office for Dársena Sur 1½ hours prior to every departure.

Buquebus also runs high-speed 'Buqueaviones' to Colonia seven times daily from Dársena Norte. Fares are identical to those of Ferrytur, and more expensive first-class service is also available.

Montevideo Ferrytur does bus-hydrofoil combinations to Montevideo (US$40, four hours), with four departures weekdays and three on weekends. Buquebus runs the 'Buqueaviones' to Montevideo (2½ hours) four times daily. Fares are US$52 turista, US$67 primera; children ages two to nine pay US$17.

Cacciola runs a bus-launch-bus service from Buenos Aires to Montevideo at 8:30 am and 4:30 pm daily via the riverside suburb of Tigre and the Uruguayan terminal at Carmelo. Fares are US$25 one-way, US$45 return for the eight-hour trip (ask about off-season promotions). Tickets are available at their downtown Buenos Aires office (☎ 4394-5520), at Florida 520, 1st floor, Oficina 113. In Tigrea they're at the Terminal Internacional(☎ 4749-0329), Lavalle 520.

Carmelo Cacciola (☎ 4749-0329), at Lavalle 520 in Tigre, goes daily to Carmelo, Uruguay, at 8:30 am and 4:30 pm for US$11; children pay US$9.35. Movilán/Delta… 4119) also goes to Carmelo, at… 3:30 pm. There is a US$5 departu… Tigre.

Nueva Palmira Also from Tigre, Línea Delta (☎ 4749-0537) goes to Nueva Palmira, Uruguay, daily at 7:30 am. Fares are US$15 one-way, US$26 return.

GETTING AROUND

To/From the Airport

Nearly all domestic flights and some to neighboring countries leave from Aeroparque Jorge Newbery (☎ 4771-2071), on the Costanera Av Rafael Obligado, a few kilometers north of downtown in Palermo. For international flights, Aeropuerto Internacional Ministro Pistarini (☎ 4480-0235), commonly known as 'Ezeiza,' is about 35 km south of downtown.

The cheapest transportation to Aeroparque Jorge Newbery is city bus: No 37C ('Ciudad Universitaria') from Plaza Italia in Palermo; No 45 northbound from Constitución, Plaza San Martín, or Retiro, as well as intermediate points; or No 160B from Av Las Heras or Plaza Italia (US$0.50). Buses for downtown leave from Av Costanera Rafael Obligado, just outside the terminal.

To Ezeiza, the cheapest alternative is bus No 86 (be sure it says 'Ezeiza,' since not all No 86 buses go to the airport at the end of the line), for US$1.20. It starts in La Boca and comes up Av de Mayo past Plaza del Congreso. The more comfortable 'Servicio Diferencial' (US$5) guarantees a seat. Theoretically neither allows very bulky luggage; normal backpacks and suitcases are OK, and for a judicious tip you should be able to take almost anything. Because of heavy traffic, figure 1½ to two hours to Ezeiza. Both leave from the Aerolíneas Argentinas terminal, a short walk from the international terminal, where all carriers except Aerolíneas arrive.

Manuel Tienda León (☎ 4314-3636, 4314-2577), Av Santa Fe 790, runs a comfortable and efficient service to Ezeiza (US$14 one-way, about 45 minutes depending on traffic) in buses and minibuses, depending on demand, and also offers hotel pickup.

Regular services start at 4 and 5 am, continuing every half hour until 11 pm. Hours for return services are 6:30 am to 9:30 pm. Manuel Tienda León service to Aeroparque (US$5) starts at 7:10 am and continues every half hourly to 10:10 pm. Return service starts at 7:50 am and stops at 10:50 pm.

San Martín Bus (☎ 4314-4747, smbus@starnet.net.ar), Av Santa Fe 887, has recently begun to provide slightly cheaper service (US$11 one-way), departing hourly between 5:15 am and 9:15 pm. It also offers door-to-door service in the downtown area, and offers a 10% discount for international student cardholders.

Taxis to Ezeiza cost about US$30 plus a US$2 surcharge for using the *autopista* (freeway), but they may end up being cheaper than Manuel Tienda León for a group of three or four – try negotiating with the driver. The Ministerio de Economía y Obras y Servicios Públicos issues a list of authorized taxi fares from Ezeiza.

Taxis to Aeroparque cost about US$6 from downtown.

Bus

Buenos Aires has a large, complex bus system serving the entire Capital Federal and Gran Buenos Aires. For novices, the best guides are the *Guía Peuser*, which details nearly 200 different routes and includes a foldout map, and the *Capital Federal y Gran Buenos Aires*, which comes in a slightly larger but more convenient wire-binder format. Both guides are for sale at most kiosks and bookstores.

Many porteños have memorized the system and can instantly tell you which bus to take and where to get off for a particular destination. Be sure to check the sign in the window for the buses' ultimate destinations, since they don't all travel to the end of the line.

Unlike the Subte, fares depend on distance – when you board, tell the driver where you're going and he will charge you accordingly. Most buses now have automatic ticket machines, which also make small change, but accept only coins. The minimum fare is around US$0.70.

BUENOS AIRES SUBTE

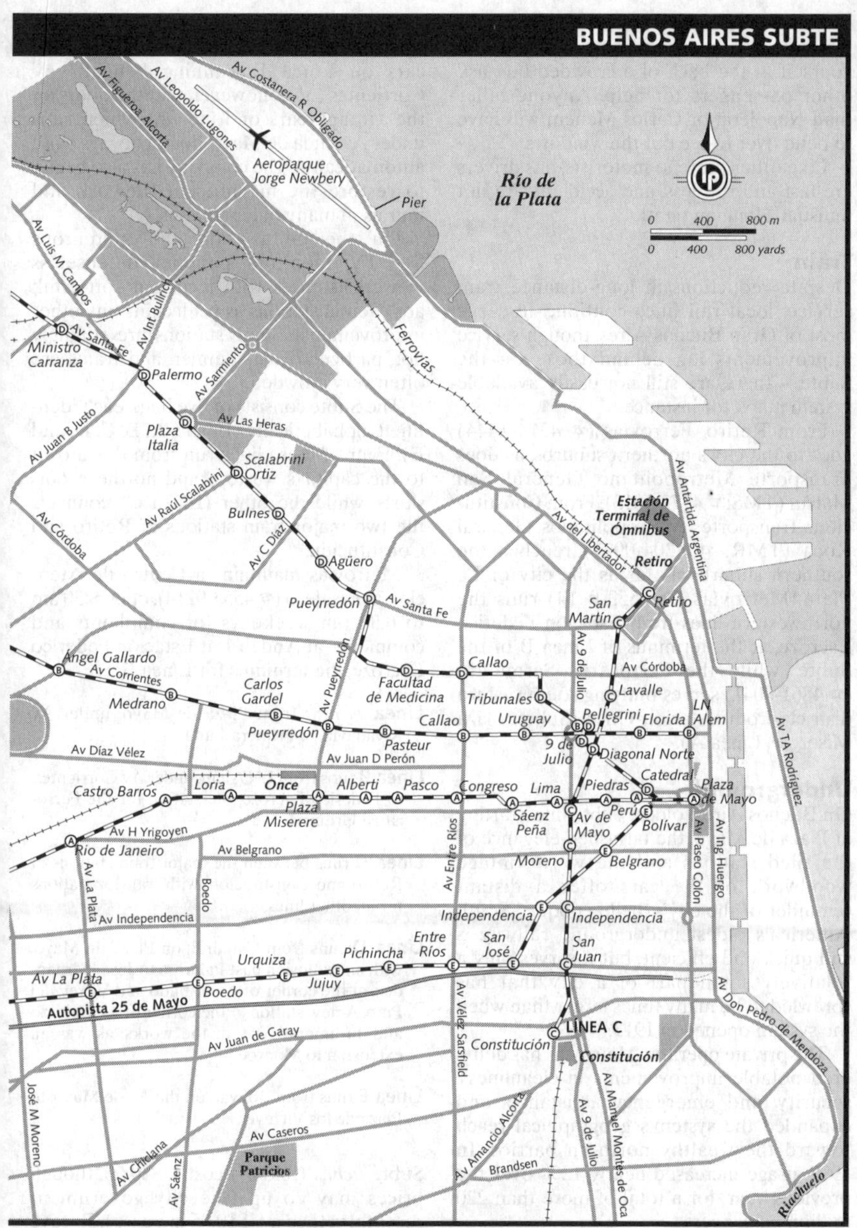

Drivers are usually polite enough to give warning of your stop. If not, or if you find yourself at the back of a crowded bus, ask other passengers for help. Anyone taller than Napoleon or Carlos Menem will have to bend over to see out the windows.

Like other porteño motorists, bus drivers are fast and ruthless, and accidents are not unusual. Hang on tight!

Train

Despite reductions in long-distance train service, local rail lines continue to serve most of Gran Buenos Aires, though service improvements lag behind those on the Subte – there are still not easily available system maps, for instance.

From Retiro, Ferrovías (☎ 4314-1444) goes to the city's northern suburbs, as does Transporte Metropolitano General San Martín (TMS; ☎ 4772-5013). From Constitución, Transportes Metropolitanos General Roca (TMR; ☎ 4304-0021) reaches the southern suburbs as far as the city of La Plata. Metrovías (☎ 4553-9214) runs the northwestern lines from Estación Federico Lacroze, at the terminus of Línea B of the Subte, while the Ferrocarril Sarmiento (☎ 4861-0041) serves outlying southwestern districts from Estación Once (Subte: Plaza Miserere, Línea A).

Underground

On Buenos Aires' oldest Subte line, starting at Plaza de Mayo, the tarnished elegance of the tiled stations and the worn vintage woodwork of the cars offer a distant reminder of the city's 'belle epoque.' South America's oldest underground railway is still quick and efficient, but it serves only a relatively small part of a city that has sprawled to be many times larger than when the system opened in 1913.

The private operator Metrovías has delivered notable improvements in cleanliness, security, and emergency assistance, and expanded the system's geographical reach toward the wealthy northern barrios. In 1997, usage increased nearly 12% over the previous year, for a total of more than 220 million passengers.

One of the first visible signs of progress was the introduction of comfortable new cars on Línea B, running beneath Av Corrientes (note, however, that the doors on the vintage cars of Línea A, which runs under Avenida de Mayo, do not always close automatically). The company has also begun to restore the magnificent tilework and murals in many older stations.

On the minus side, the ubiquitous SUBTV monitors pummel defenseless viewers/listeners with incessant soft-drink ads even in stations as yet lacking any other improvements. Some stations are stiflingly hot, particularly in summer, and trains are often very crowded.

The Subte consists of five lines, each identified alphabetically (Líneas A, B, C, D, and E). Four of these lines run from downtown to the capital's western and northern outskirts, while the other (Línea C) connects the two major train stations of Retiro and Constitución.

Metrovías maintains a Centro de Atención al Pasajero (☎ 4553-9214), open 8:30 am to 6:30 pm weekdays for complaints and comments, at Andén 1 at Estación Federico Lacroze, the terminus for Línea B.

Línea A runs from Plaza de Mayo, under Av Rivadavia, to Primera Junta.

Línea B runs from LN Alem, under Av Corrientes, to Federico Lacroze, the station for the Ferrocarril Urquiza.

Línea C runs between the major train stations of Retiro and Constitución, with transfer stations for all other lines.

Línea D runs from Catedral, on Plaza de Mayo, with an extension past Palermo to José Hernández, at the corner of Av Cabildo and Virrey del Pino. A new station at the corner of Av Cabildo and Juramento was in the works, as was an extension to Monroe.

Línea E runs from Bolívar, on the Av de Mayo, to Plaza de los Virreyes.

Subte *fichas* (tokens) cost US$0.50, though prices may go up (the city government recently vetoed a US$0.05 increase). To save time and hassle, buy a pocketful, since lines get backed up during rush hour and at other times. Trains operate 5 am to 10 pm except Sunday (8 am to 10 pm) and are frequent weekdays, though weekend waiting time can be considerable.

At a few stations, such as Alberdi, you can only go in one direction – in this case toward Primera Junta rather than Plaza de Mayo, so you may have to backtrack to reach your ultimate destination. At many stations, platforms are on opposite sides of the station, so make sure of your direction *before* passing through the turnstiles, or you'll have to exit and pay an additional fare.

Car

Because of heavy traffic, aggressive drivers, and parking problems, driving in Buenos Aires is inadvisable. Those choosing to drive should know that the area bounded by Av Leandro Alem, Av Córdoba, Av de Mayo, and Av 9 de Julio is off-limits to private motor vehicles, except buses, taxis, and delivery vans, weekdays between 7 am and 7 pm. Fines are stiff.

Taxi & Remise

Buenos Aires' numerous, reasonably priced taxis are conspicuous by their black-and-yellow paint jobs. All are now digitally metered; it costs about US$1 to drop the flag and another US$0.10 per 100 meters. Drivers are generally polite and honest, but there are exceptions; be sure the meter is set at zero. If you're carrying a large amount of luggage, there may be a small additional charge. Drivers do not expect a big tip, but it's customary to let them keep small change.

Remises are radio taxis without meters, which generally offer fixed fares within a given zone and are an increasingly popular form of transportation that is slightly cheaper than ordinary taxis. Unlike taxis, they may not cruise the city in search of fares. Most hotels and restaurants will gladly ring remises for you.

When it rains, demand is high and taxis can be hard to find, so you may have to wait out the storm in a confitería.

Around Buenos Aires

Just beyond the Capital Federal, Buenos Aires province offers several interesting and worthwhile attractions. The riverside suburb of Tigre, a popular retreat, is also the best base for exploring the Delta del Paraná, including historic Isla Martín García. It is also the departure point for passenger ferries across the river to Carmelo and Nueva Palmira, Uruguay (there is no vehicle ferry service).

TIGRE & THE DELTA DEL PARANÁ

Within commuting range of the capital, this suburb (population 290,000) at the confluence of the Río Luján and Río Tigre is a favorite weekend destination and the best departure point for exploring the Delta del Paraná and Isla Martín García. At the Estación Fluvial is the Dirección de Turismo (☎ 4512-4497).

One of Tigre's best attractions is the **Puerto de Frutos**, in the 1200 block of Av Cazón, where a major crafts fair takes place each weekend (though it's open every day 11 am to 7 pm). Its restaurant also serves tasty dishes. The **Museo de la Reconquista** (☎ 4749-0090), Liniers 818, was the house where Viceroy Liniers coordinated resistance to the British invasions of the early 19th century; it also deals with Delta history.

Tigre's counterpart to Disneyworld, but even tackier, is the **Parque de la Costa** (☎ 4732-6300), on Pereyra, open Wednesday to Sunday 11 am to midnight. Admission, with unlimited rides and games, is US$19 for adults, US$15 for children ages 9 to 12.

Places to Stay & Eat

Hotels are relatively few in the Delta, but try ***Hotel Laura*** *(☎ 4749-3898)*, on Canal Honda off the Paraná de las Palmas, for US$60 double with private bath weekdays, US$80 weekends. Though it has drawn some complaints for high prices and poor service, it also offers a US$15 Delta excursion. ***Hotel I'Marangatu*** *(☎ 4749-7350)*, on the Río San

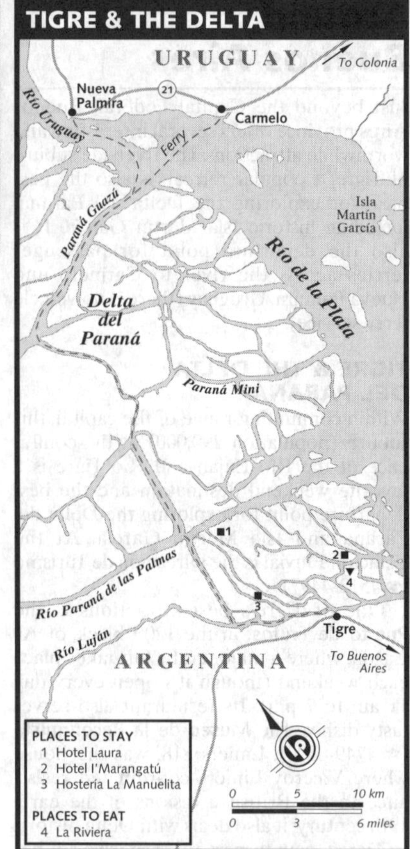

Antonio, charges US$80 during the week, US$100 on weekends. ***La Manuelita*** *(☎ 4749-0987)*, on the Río Carapachay, costs US$45 during the week, US$50 weekends.

In Tigre proper, the riverfront ***B&B Escauriza*** *(☎ 4749-2499, fax 4744-0938, Lavalle 557)* offers exactly what it says – homestyle lodging for US$35 per person with breakfast.

On the Río Tres Bocas, about 20 minutes from Tigre by launch, ***La Riviera*** *(☎ 4749-6177, 4749-5960)* is a popular restaurant offering good food and live music. It's frequented by gay clientele (but by no means exclusively).

Getting There & Away

Most but not all No 60 buses from Av Callao in Buenos Aires go to Tigre (US$1.70, 75 to 90 minutes, depending on traffic), but the Ferrocarril Mitre, leaving from platforms 1 or 2 at Estación Retiro, is probably quicker when traffic is heavy. It's also a bit cheaper (US$1.30).

For information on launches to and from Uruguay, see the Getting There & Away entry for Buenos Aires.

Getting Around

Catamaranes Interisleña (☎ 4731-0264) runs *lanchas colectivas* from Tigre's Estación Fluvial, Lavalle 419, to various Delta destinations for $5 per person round trip (children under age 8 go free). These will drop you off or pick you up at any riverside dock – just flag them down as you would a bus. Other companies with similar services, also at the Estación Fluvial, are Delta Argentino (☎ 4749-0537) and Lanchas Marsili (☎ 4413-4123).

ISLA MARTÍN GARCÍA

Navigating among the densely forested multiple channels of the Tigre and Paraná rivers,

WAYNE BERNHARDSON

Boats on the Delta del Paraná

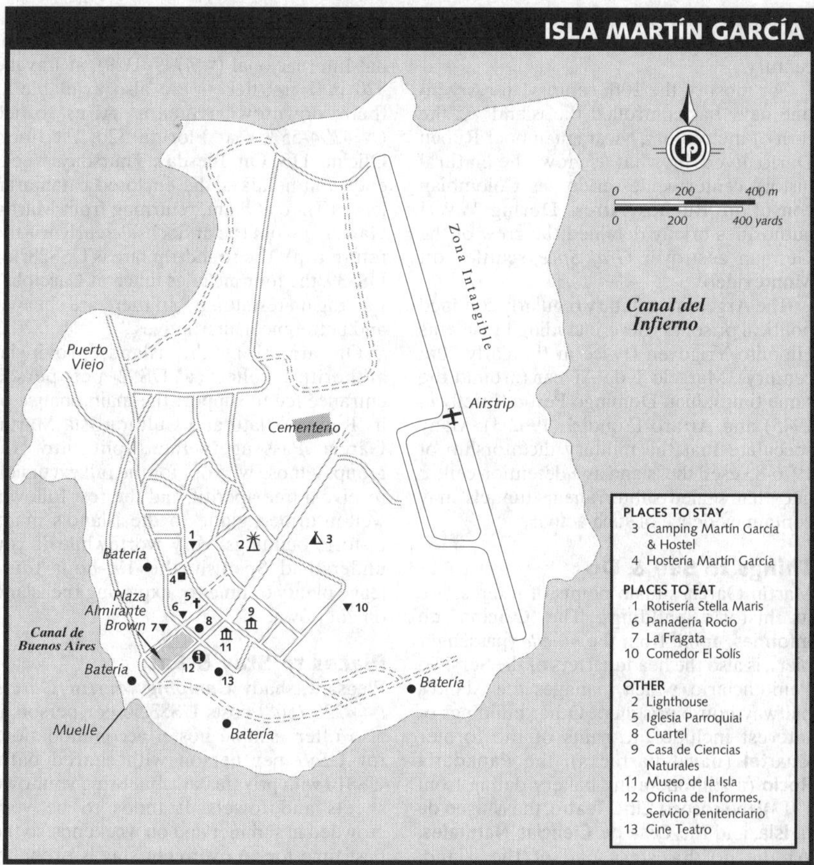

en route to historic Martín García, it's easy to imagine what ideal hideaways these were for colonial smugglers. Just off the Uruguayan Littoral, directly south of the city of Carmelo, the island is most famous – or infamous – as a prison camp. Four Argentine presidents have been held in custody here, and the Servicio Penitenciario of Buenos Aires province still uses it as a halfway house for prisoners near the end of their terms. At present, though, the island is more a combination of historical monument, tranquil nature reserve, and recreational retreat from the bustle of the federal capital.

History

In colonial times, Spain and Portugal contested possession of the island. Unlike the shifting sedimentary islands of the flood-prone delta, the bedrock of 180-hectare Martín García rises 27m above sea level; this high ground made it suitable for a fortress to guard the approach to the Uruguay and Paraná rivers. Irish Admiral Guillermo Brown gave the United Provinces of the River Plate their first major naval victory here in 1814, when a commando raid dislodged royalist troops who escaped to Montevideo. Both England and France took advantage of Argentine conflicts with Brazil to occupy the island in the early 19th century.

For most of the 20th century, the Argentine navy has controlled the island. At the turn of the century, Nicaraguan poet Rubén Darío lived in what is now the natural history center while serving as Colombian consul in Buenos Aires. During WWII authorities briefly detained the crew of the German destroyer *Graf Spee*, scuttled off Montevideo.

The Argentine military regularly confined political prisoners here, including Presidents Hipólito Yrigoyen (twice in the early 20th century), Marcelo T de Alvear (around the same time), Juan Domingo Perón (briefly in 1945) and Arturo Frondizi (1962-3). Many speculate that the military dictatorship of 1976-83 used the island as a detention center and that sealed subterranean tunnels may contain evidence of such activity.

Things to See & Do

Martín García's main points of interest are its historic buildings. The **Oficina de Informes**, uphill from the *muelle* (passenger pier), is also the headquarters of the Servicio Penitenciario, which manages the island's halfway-house prisoners. Other buildings of interest include the ruins of the former **Cuartel** (naval barracks), the **Panadería Rocio** (a still-operating bakery dating from 1913), the rococo **Cine-Teatro**, the **Museo de la Isla**, and the **Casa de Ciencias Naturales**. At the northwestern end of the island, beyond a block of badly deteriorating and overgrown houses, the **Puerto Viejo** (old port) has fallen into disuse due to sediments that have clogged the anchorage. The **Cementerio** contains the headstones of many conscripts who died in an epidemic in the early 20th century.

The densely forested northern part of the island offers quiet, pleasant walks if you don't mind fending off the mosquitoes. South of the airstrip, the **Zona Intangible** is closed to casual hikers because of its botanical value and the fire hazard.

Comedor El Solís has a **swimming pool** open to the public.

Organized Tours

Guided tours depart from Cacciola's Terminal Internacional (☎ 4749-0329), at Lavalle 520 in Tigre; tickets are also available at their downtown Buenos Aires office (☎ 4394-5520), at Florida 520, 1st floor, Oficina 113. On Tuesday, Thursday, weekends and holidays, the enclosed catamaran leaves Tigre at 8 am, returning from Martín García at 4 pm (be at dockside early for the return trip). The roundtrip fare is US$28; for US$39, the tour includes lunch at Cacciola's La Fragata restaurant, but there are cheaper and better meal alternatives.

On arrival at the island, provincial authorities collect a US$2 per person entrance fee to support the maintenance of its Reserva Natural y Cultural Isla Martín García. Passengers then split into two groups – those who opt for the full excursion receive a free aperitif, and the rest follow a well-informed guide to the island's many historic buildings. Very worthwhile if you understand Spanish, the 1½-hour tours leave plenty of time for exploring the island on your own.

Places to Stay & Eat

Pleasant, shady ***Camping Martín García*** *(☎ 4728-1808)* costs US$3.50 per person; it also offers simple hostel accommodations for US$7 per person with shared bath, US$10 with private bath, but bring your own sheets and towels. It tends to be very crowded in summer and on weekends, so the best time for an overnight stay is probably on weekdays or just before or after the peak summer season. Reservations are essential.

Cacciola offers full-board overnight packages, including transportation, for US$89 per person at its ***Hostería Martín García***; additional nights cost US$50 per person.

Comedor El Solís, with a US$10 tenedor libre including tasty boga and dessert, is a better value than the expensive lunch at Cacciola's ***La Fragata***, which is included in the full excursion. Drinks at Solís are extra but not outrageous. ***Rotisería Stella Maris*** also has decent, simple meals and drinks. The ***Panadería Rocio*** is renowned for its fruitcakes.

Shopping

Artisanal goods available at shops on the island include mate gourds and wooden ships, along with the usual T-shirts and mugs manufactured elsewhere.

Getting There & Away

See the Organized Tours and Tigre sections for details on transport to and from the island. Visitors camping on the island who do not to take the guided tour pay only US$23 return.

The Pampas

Argentina's celebrated Pampas are almost unrelentingly flat except for their extensive coastline, several small mountain ranges, and the delta of the Río de la Plata. These features give variety to the country's agricultural heartland, which comprises the provinces of Buenos Aires, La Pampa, and major parts of Santa Fe and Córdoba. Within this area are a surprising number of visitor attractions.

Buenos Aires province contains several important cities, particularly its capital of La Plata and the Atlantic port of Bahía Blanca. The colonial city of Luján is one of South America's most important religious centers, while the interior town of San Antonio de Areco wears the emblem of Argentina's gaucho culture. Every summer, porteños flock to Atlantic coast beach towns, particularly Mar del Plata. In the southern part of the province, there is scenic mountain country at Tandil and Sierra de la Ventana.

Rosario, a vital port for Argentina's agricultural commodities, is situated up the Río Paraná in Santa Fe province and vies with Córdoba for the status of 'second city' in the republic. Rosario, though, is not even capital of its own province – the colonial city of Santa Fe remains the seat of political power.

History

The aboriginal inhabitants of the Pampas were Querandí hunter-gatherers, less numerous and more dispersed than the sedentary, civilized peoples of the Andean Northwest or even the semisedentary Guaraní of the upper Paraná basin. Although they lacked both the plow and the domestic draft animals to cultivate the fertile Pampas, the Querandí had no real need for them – their subsistence came from hunting guanaco and rhea with *boleadoras* (also known as *bolas)* which, skillfully thrown, became entangled in the animal's legs and made it easy prey. Hunting was a communal rather than individual activity, and so long as game remained abundant on the Pampas' boundless pastures, the hard labor of cultivation was pointless.

The Querandí resisted the Spanish presence, besieging early settlements and preventing them from establishing any foothold in the area for more than half a century. Even after the definitive founding of the city of Buenos Aires in 1580, settlement of the Pampas proceeded slowly, only in part because Spain's mercantile policy favored already populous Peru and constrained potential rivals to Lima's political and economic primacy.

In many ways, feral animals accomplished what Madrid's early colonial policy actually discouraged – the spontaneous Europeanization of the Pampas. When the Spaniards abandoned their first settlement at Buenos Aires for the pleasures of Paraguay, they also left behind cattle and horses, which multiplied prodigiously in their absence.

During the centuries and even millennia before the arrival of the Spaniards, aboriginal peoples had transformed the Pampas

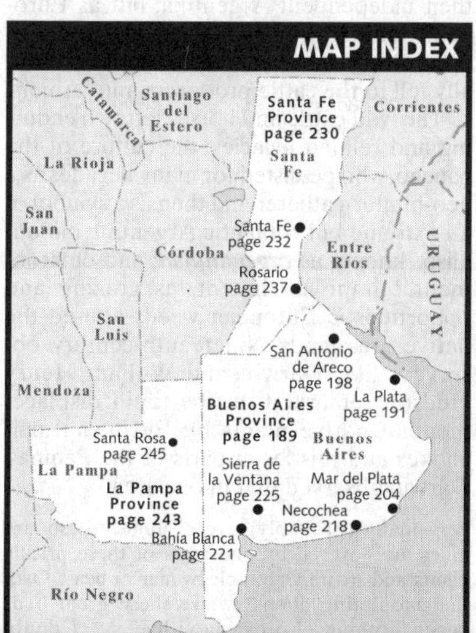

environment through hunting and, especially, through fire. Frequent burning, a hunting technique to flush out game, prevented reestablishment of *monte* (scrub forest) and directly benefited the grasses, which recuperated much more quickly. In turn, the new, succulent native grasses could support even more game.

Or more cattle. According to environmental historian Alfred Crosby, in 1619 (less than 40 years after the reestablishment of Buenos Aires), colonial officials informed Madrid that a harvest of 80,000 cattle per year for hides would not diminish the herds. One 18th-century visitor estimated the number of cattle south of modern Paraguay and north of the Río Negro at 48 million. Despite the impossibility of a truly accurate estimate, the numbers were obviously very great.

Horses were also numerous. Like the Plains Indians of North America, Araucanians on both sides of the Andes quickly learned to tame and ride them, which bolstered their resistance to the invasion of their territories into the late 19th century. On horseback they were even more formidable opponents against imperial Spain and then independent Argentina, but as European immigration increased, the Indians' options were fewer, and the Pampas eventually fell to the cattle producers and farmers.

The wild cattle and horses left two enduring and related legacies: the culture of the gaucho, who persisted for many decades as a neo-hunter-gatherer and then as a symbol of an extreme but romantic Argentine nationalism known as *argentinidad*; and environmental impoverishment, as grazing and opportunistic European weeds altered the native grasslands. Nineteenth-century observers like Darwin and William Henry Hudson remarked on the rapid displacement of native plants by European artichokes and thistles in parts of the Pampas. Darwin observed that in one area

> very many (probably several hundred) square miles are covered by one mass of these prickly plants, and are impenetrable by man or beast. Over the undulating plains, where these great beds occur, nothing else can now live . . . I doubt whether any case is on record of an invasion on so grand a scale of one plant over the aborigines.

Unpremeditated introductions of European biota, then, were at least as important as European force in undermining indigenous resistance and opening the frontier to overseas immigrants.

Upon Argentine independence, the country's doors opened fitfully to foreign commerce. The Pampas' *saladeros* (meat salting plant) yielded only hides, tallow, and salt beef, products with limited overseas markets. This trade, in turn, benefited the relatively few estancieros with the fortune to inherit or the foresight to grab large tracts of land. Some landowners did not survive the fall of Rosas, whose policies had encouraged the alienation of public lands for grazing establishments, but others prospered as Buenos Aires experienced a late-19th-century wool boom.

From shortly after mid-century the railroads, built largely with British capital, made it feasible to export wool and then beef, but the meat from rangy, unimproved criollo cattle did not appeal to British tastes. Improved breeds required more succulent feed, such as alfalfa, but the estancieros could not produce this on their enormous holdings with the skeletal labor force available to them. Consequently, their traditional opposition to immigration declined as they sought to attract tenant farmers to their holdings.

Although estancieros had no intention of relinquishing their lands, development of arable farming was an indirect benefit of the intensification of raising stock. Growing alfalfa required preparatory cultivation, so landowners rented their properties to *medieros* (sharecroppers), who raised wheat for four or five years before moving elsewhere, and thus landowners benefited both from their share of the wheat crop and from their new alfalfa fields. Still, shortly after the turn of the century, agricultural exports like maize, wheat, and linseed exceeded the value of livestock products such as hides, wool, and meat.

The Pampas are still famous for their beef, and estancias still dominate the

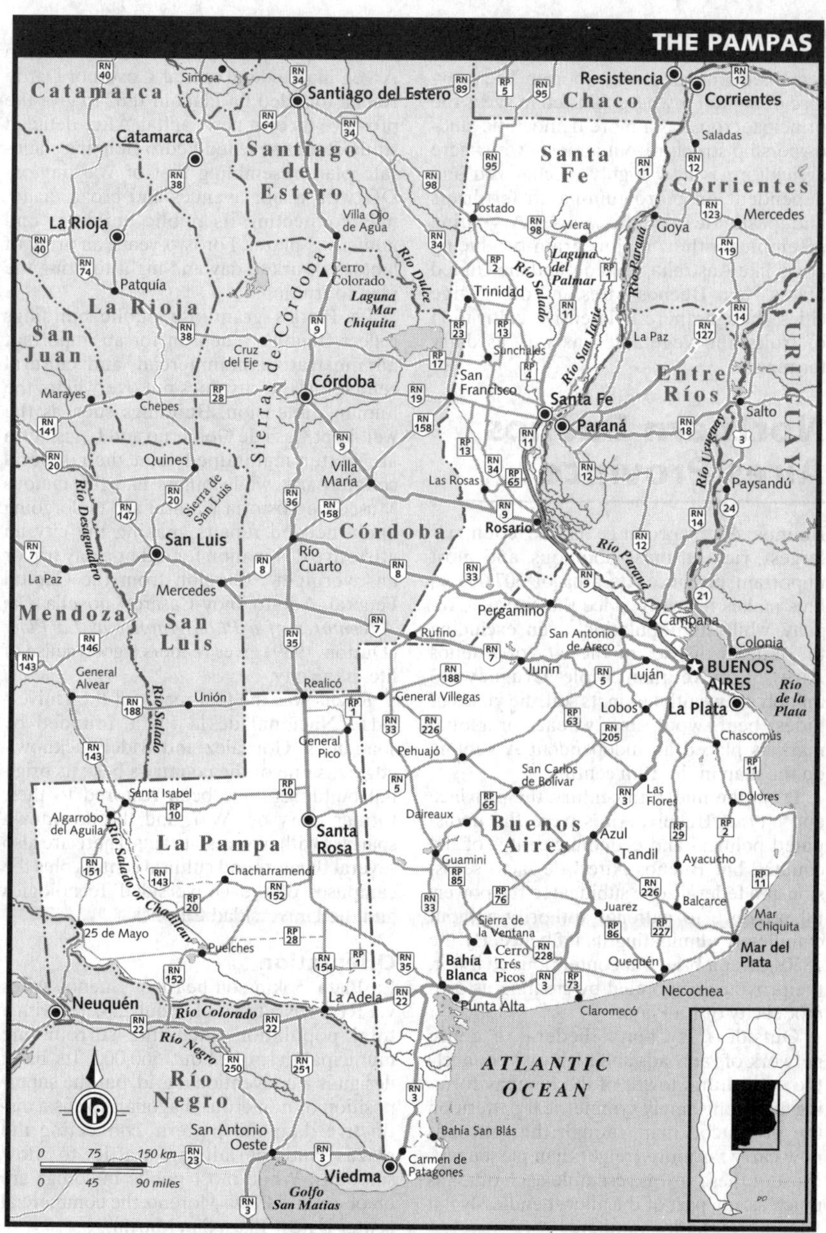
THE PAMPAS
Catamarca
Simoca
Santiago del Estero
Resistencia
Corrientes
Chaco
Catamarca
Santiago del Estero
Saladas
Santa Fe
Corrientes
La Rioja
Villa Ojo de Agua
Tostado
Vera
Goya
Mercedes
Cerro Colorado
Sierras de Córdoba
Río Dulce
Laguna del Palmar
Río Salado
Río Paraná
Patquía
Laguna Mar Chiquita
Trinidad
La Rioja
Río San Javier
La Paz
URUGUAY
San Juan
Cruz del Eje
Sunchales
Córdoba
San Francisco
Santa Fe
Entre Ríos
Marayes
Chepes
Paraná
Salto
Río Uruguay
Quines
Villa María
Las Rosas
Paysandú
Sierra de San Luis
Río Desaguadero
Córdoba
Rosario
San Luis
Río Cuarto
Río Paraná
La Paz
Mercedes
Pergamino
Campana
Mendoza
San Luis
Rufino
San Antonio de Areco
Colonia
Junín
Luján
BUENOS AIRES
General Alvear
Realicó
Río de la Plata
Unión
General Villegas
Lobos
La Plata
Río Salado
General Pico
Pehuajó
Chascomús
San Carlos de Bolívar
Santa Isabel
Las Flores
Dolores
Algarrobo del Aguila
Daireaux
Santa Rosa
Buenos Aires
Azul
La Pampa
Tandil
Ayacucho
Guamini
Chacharramendi
Río Salado or Chadileuvú
Juarez
Balcarce
Mar Chiquita
25 de Mayo
Sierra de la Ventana
Puelches
Cerro Três Picos
Mar del Plata
Quequén
Bahía Blanca
Necochea
Neuquén
La Adela
Punta Alta
Claromecó
Río Colorado
Río Negro
ATLANTIC OCEAN
Río Negro
San Antonio Oeste
Bahía San Blás
0 75 150 km
0 45 90 miles
Viedma
Carmen de Patagones
Golfo San Matias
RN 40
RN 34
RN 89
RP 5
RN 95
RN 12
RN 64
RN 34
RN 38
RN 95
RN 11
RN 12
RN 98
RN 123
RN 98
RN 40
RN 34
RN 119
RN 74
RP 2
RP 1
RN 11
RN 14
RN 38
RN 9
RN 23
RP 13
RN 127
RP 17
RP 4
RP 28
RN 19
RN 141
RN 158
RN 18
RN 9
RN 11
RP 13
RN 20
RN 34
RP 65
RN 12
RN 20
RN 36
RN 158
RN 147
RN 9
RN 14
RN 7
RN 8
RN 12
RN 8
RN 33
RN 9
RN 146
RN 35
RN 7
RN 143
RN 188
RN 5
RN 188
RP 1
RP 63
RN 205
RN 33
RN 226
RN 143
RP 11
RP 10
RN 5
RP 10
RP 65
RN 3
RP 29
RP 2
RN 151
RN 143
RN 152
RP 85
RN 226
RP 11
RP 20
RN 33
RP 76
RP 28
RP 86
RP 227
RN 154
RP 1
RN 35
RN 228
RN 152
RN 3
RP 73
RN 22
RN 22
RN 22
RN 250
RN 251
RN 3
RN 23
RN 3
RN 3

economy, but smaller landholdings have increased in number, and Argentina has remained a major grain exporter. The province of Santa Fe, where rain-fed maize is the principal crop, has a more democratic landownership structure, but almost everywhere agriculture is now highly mechanized and dependent on petroleum-based fertilizers and pesticides. In this sense, Argentina resembles other major grain-producing areas, like Australia, Canada, and the United States. Near Buenos Aires and other large cities, though, there is intensive cultivation of fruits and vegetables, as well as dairy farming.

Northern Buenos Aires Province

Buenos Aires province is the country's largest, richest, most populous, and most important province. Its area of 307,000 sq kms makes it nearly twice the size of Uruguay, while its population, even excluding the federal district of the city of Buenos Aires, is more than triple Uruguay's 3 million. Its wealth lies in its soil; the yields of hides, beef, wool, and wheat for global markets placed an independent Argentina on the map in the 19th century.

From the mid-19th century, the province and city of Buenos Aires were the undisputed political and economic center of the country, but Buenos Aires' de facto secession as a federal zone subjugated the powerful province to national authority without completely eliminating its influence. By the 1880s, after a brief but contentious civil war, the province responded by creating its own model city of La Plata.

Outside the Capital Federal, a dense network of railroads and highways connects the agricultural towns of the Pampas, forming an astonishingly symmetrical pattern on the provincial map, though the railroads now carry far more freight than passengers. Most of these towns resemble each other as much as any part of the almost endlessly flat Pampas resembles another.

LA PLATA

After the city of Buenos Aires became Argentina's federal capital, Governor Dardo Rocha founded La Plata in 1882 to give the province its own new capital. After detailed study, Rocha selected Pedro Benoit's elaborate plan, resembling that of Washington, DC, with major avenues and broad diagonals connecting its public buildings and numerous plazas. For two years, an army of laborers worked day and night to bring the plan to fruition.

La Plata's grandiose public buildings reflect Benoit's blueprint for an important administrative, commercial, and cultural center, but the city does not overwhelm the human dimension. Buildings such as the well-kept Casa de Gobierno and Legislatura are better maintained than their federal counterparts, while others like the famous Museo de Historia Natural are undergoing badly needed repairs, making the city an attractive destination for either a day trip or an overnight excursion from the Capital Federal. Adolfo Bioy Casares' novella *The Adventures of a Photographer in La Plata* (Dutton, 1989) gives readers a good sense of life in the city.

Rocha was the first rector of the Universidad Nacional de la Plata, founded by Joaquín V González and widely acknowledged as one of the country's best; its original buildings have been restored to their former glory on Av 7, and the downtown sparkles with new restaurants. There are also several theaters and cultural centers plus the campuses of the Universidad Tecnológica and the Universidad Católica.

Orientation

La Plata, 56km southeast of Buenos Aires via RP 14, is a town of about 225,000, with a total population, including surrounding municipalities, of about 560,000. Its basic design is a conventional grid, but the superposition of numerous diagonals forms a distinctive diamond pattern, connecting the plazas and permitting traffic to flow smoothly. While most public buildings are on or around Plaza Moreno, the commercial center is near Plaza San Martín.

BUENOS AIRES PROVINCE

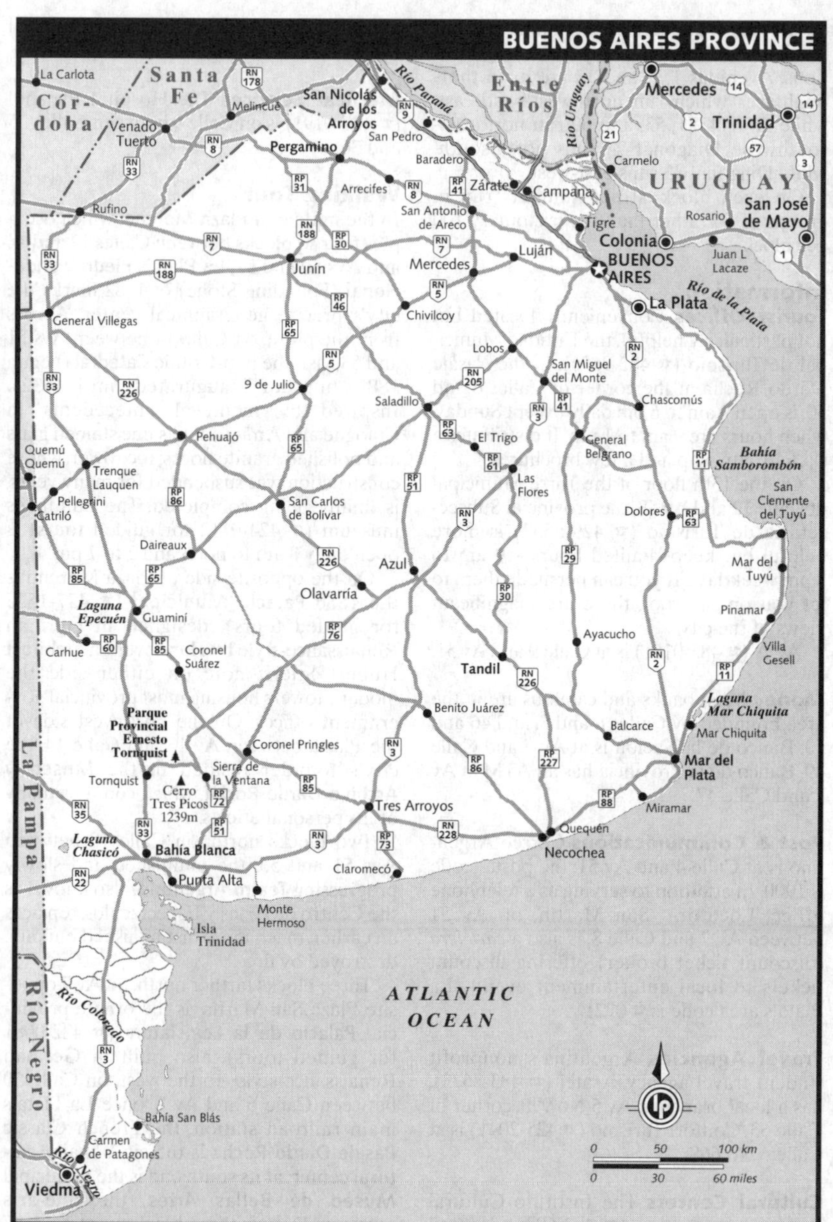

All streets are named and numbered, but residents use numbers only to identify locations. Avenidas 1, 7, and 13 are main thoroughfares which run northwest-southeast, while Avs 44, 51, 53, and 60 run northeast-southwest. Diagonal 74 runs north-south, while Diagonal 73 runs east-west.

On each block, street numbers run in groups of 50 rather than the customary 100 per block.

Information

Tourist Offices Conveniently located but not particularly helpful, the Entidad Municipal de Turismo (☎ 482-9656), in the Pasaje Dardo Rocha at the corner of Calles 6 and 50, is open 9 am to 6 pm daily except Sunday, when hours are 9 am to 1 pm. It distributes a sketchy city map and a few brochures.

On the 13th floor of the Torre Municipal at Calle 12 and Av 53, the provincial Subsecretaría de Turismo (☎ 429-5553) is more helpful but keeps limited hours – 9 am to 3 pm weekdays. If you can persuade them to let you on the roof, there are magnificent views of the city.

ACA (☎ 483-0161) is at Calle 9 and Av 51.

Money Most banks and cambios are in the area bounded by Calles 6 and 8, and 46 and 50. Banco de la Nación is at Av 7 and Calle 49. Banco de la Provincia has an ATM at Av 7 and Calle 47.

Post & Communications Correo Argentino is at Calle 4 and Av 51; the postal code is 1900. In addition to serving as a telephone office, Locutorio San Martín, on Av 51 between Av 7 and Calle 8, is also a *cartelera* (discount ticket broker) offering discount tickets to local entertainment events. La Plata's area code is ☎ 0221.

Travel Agencies Argentina's nonprofit student travel agency, Asatej (☎ 483-8673), has a local branch at Av 5 No 990, corner of Calle 53. Confort Turismo (☎ 425-2041) is at Calle 6 No 668.

Cultural Centers The Instituto Cultural Británico-Argentino (☎ 483-6035), located at Calle 12 No 869, hosts occasional cultural events and Friday night films.

Medical Services The Hospital Español (☎ 427-0191) is on Calle 9 between Calles 35 and 36.

Walking Tour

In the middle of **Plaza Moreno**, which occupies four sq blocks between Calles 12 and 14 and Avs 50 and 54, La Plata's **Piedra Fundacional** (Founding Stone) of 1882 marks the city's precise geographical center. Across from the plaza, on Calle 14 between Avs 51 and 53, visit the neo-Gothic **Catedral** (begun 1885, but not inaugurated until 1932). Inspired by medieval antecedents in Cologne and Amiens, it has fine stained glass and polished granite floors; the tower, whose construction was suspended for many years, is finally being completed. The building's museum (☎ 424-0112 for guided tours) is open daily 8 am to noon and 2 to 7 pm.

On the opposite side of Plaza Moreno is the 1886 **Palacio Municipal** (☎ 427-1535 for guided tours), designed in German Renaissance-style by Hannoverian architect Hubert Stiers; note on either side the modern towers housing most provincial government offices. On the northwest side of the Plaza, between Av 13 and Calle 14, the city's founder resided in the **Museo y Archivo Dardo Rocha**, which contains many of his personal effects.

Two blocks north, on Calle 10 between Avs 51 and 53, the unfinished and slowly progressing **Teatro Argentino**, also known as the Centro de Artes y Espectáculos, replaces an earlier, much more distinguished building destroyed by fire.

Three blocks farther north, on Av 7 opposite Plaza San Martín, is the ornate provincial **Palacio de la Legislatura** (☎ 422-0081 for guided tours), also built in German Renaissance-style. To the west, on Calle 50 between Calle 6 and Av 7, once La Plata's main railroad station, the French Classic **Pasaje Dardo Rocha** is the city's major cultural center; at its south end is the municipal **Museo de Bellas Artes**, the fine-arts museum. Detour three blocks west, to Av 7

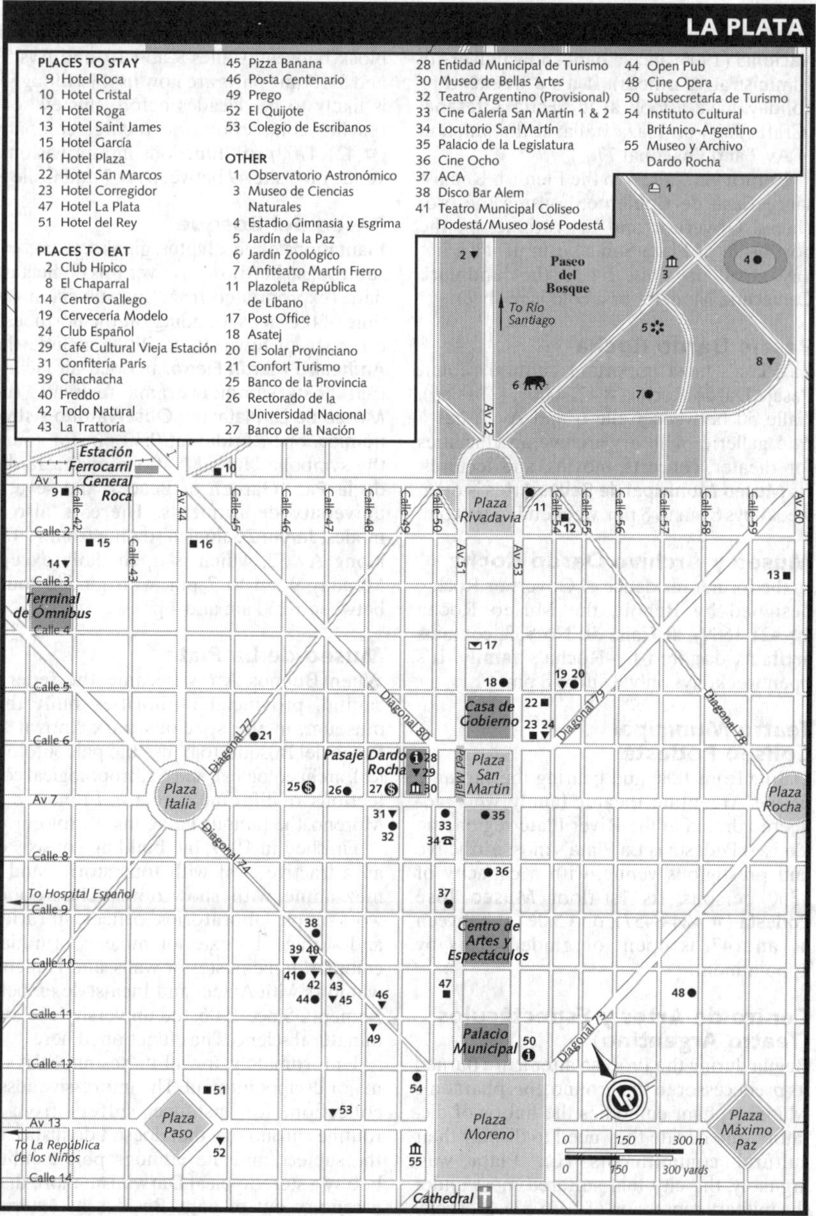
LA PLATA
PLACES TO STAY
9 Hotel Roca
10 Hotel Cristal
12 Hotel Roga
13 Hotel Saint James
15 Hotel García
16 Hotel Plaza
22 Hotel San Marcos
23 Hotel Corregidor
47 Hotel La Plata
51 Hotel del Rey
PLACES TO EAT
2 Club Hípico
8 El Chaparral
14 Centro Gallego
19 Cervecería Modelo
24 Club Español
29 Café Cultural Vieja Estación
31 Confitería París
39 Chachacha
40 Freddo
42 Todo Natural
43 La Trattoría
45 Pizza Banana
46 Posta Centenario
49 Prego
52 El Quijote
53 Colegio de Escribanos
OTHER
1 Observatorio Astronómico
3 Museo de Ciencias Naturales
4 Estadio Gimnasia y Esgrima
5 Jardín de la Paz
6 Jardín Zoológico
7 Anfiteatro Martín Fierro
11 Plazoleta República de Líbano
17 Post Office
18 Asatej
20 El Solar Provinciano
21 Confort Turismo
25 Banco de la Provincia
26 Rectorado de la Universidad Nacional
27 Banco de la Nación
28 Entidad Municipal de Turismo
30 Museo de Bellas Artes
32 Teatro Argentino (Provisional)
33 Cine Galería San Martín 1 & 2
34 Locutorio San Martín
35 Palacio de la Legislatura
36 Cine Ocho
37 ACA
38 Disco Bar Alem
41 Teatro Municipal Coliseo Podestá/Museo José Podestá
44 Open Pub
48 Cine Opera
50 Subsecretaría de Turismo
54 Instituto Cultural Británico-Argentino
55 Museo y Archivo Dardo Rocha
Paseo del Bosque
To Río Santiago
Estación Ferrocarril General Roca
Terminal de Omnibus
Plaza Rivadavia
Casa de Gobierno
Pasaje Dardo Rocha
Plaza San Martín
Ped Mall
Plaza Italia
Plaza Rocha
Centro de Artes y Espectáculos
Palacio Municipal
Plaza Paso
Plaza Moreno
Plaza Máximo Paz
Cathedral
To Hospital Español
To La República de los Niños
Av 1
Calle 2
Calle 3
Calle 4
Calle 5
Calle 6
Av 7
Calle 8
Calle 9
Calle 10
Calle 11
Calle 12
Av 13
Calle 14
Calle 42
Calle 43
Av 44
Calle 45
Calle 46
Calle 47
Calle 48
Calle 49
Calle 50
Av 51
Av 52
Av 53
Calle 54
Calle 55
Calle 56
Calle 57
Calle 58
Calle 59
Av 60
Diagonal 77
Diagonal 80
Diagonal 79
Diagonal 78
Diagonal 74
Diagonal 73
0 150 300 m
0 150 300 yards

between 47 and 48, to view the original buildings of the **Rectorado de la Universidad Nacional** (1905; once a bank, now university administrative offices). If it's a weekend or holiday, have a look at the **Feria Artesanal** (Crafts Fair) on Plaza Italia, at the junction of Av 7 and Diagonal 77.

Return via Calle 6 to the Flemish Renaissance **Casa de Gobierno**, housing the provincial Governor and his retinue, on the north side of Plaza San Martín. If it's a hot day, stroll up Calle 54 to the landmark **Cervecería Modelo** for a cold lager beer.

Pasaje Dardo Rocha

La Plata's most important cultural center, Pasaje Dardo Rocha (☎ 421-0061, 421-0066), Calle 50 between Calle 6 and Av 7, has a café, galleries, a library/archive, and facilities for theater, concerts, movies, and lectures. Its **Museo Municipal de Bellas Artes** is open weekdays 8 am to 8 pm, weekends 5 to 9 pm.

Museo y Archivo Dardo Rocha

In the former residence of Governor Rocha, designed by Benoit, the Museo Rocha (☎ 421-1689), at Calle 50 No 933, contains artifacts donated by Rocha's family. It's open weekdays only 8 am to 8 pm.

Teatro Municipal Coliseo Podestá

Dating from 1886 and bearing the surname of the Argentine theater family who pioneered drama in the River Plate region, the Coliseo Podestá is La Plata's most attractive and prestigious venue, with a capacity of 1360 persons. Its 1st-floor **Museo José Podestá** (☎ 424-8457), on Calle 10 between 46 and 47, is open for guided visits by appointment.

Centro de Artes y Espectáculos (Teatro Argentino)

Begun during the Proceso after a fire burned its predecessor to the ground, this pharaonic white elephant embodies the hubris of dictators who decide they need to display their cultural commitments (La Plata was, arguably, the city that suffered most under the military repression of 1976-83). Most city residents feel embarrassment about this oversized bunker, which occupies a full block between Calles 9 and 10, and Avs 51 and 53. Some parts are now usable, though it is likely to be decades before this eyesore reaches completion; the theater company (☎ 421-4700) still functions in a provisional venue on Calle 49 between Av 7 and Calle 8.

Paseo del Bosque

Plantations of eucalyptus, gingko, palm, and subtropical hardwoods cover this 60-hectare park (expropriated from an estancia at the time of the city's founding) at the northeastern edge of town. Its facilities include the **Anfiteatro Martín Fierro**, an open-air facility that hosts summer drama festivals; the **Museo de La Plata**; the **Observatorio Astronómico**, open Friday at 9:30 pm for tours; the symbolic United Nations of the **Jardín de la Paz** (Garden of Peace); and several university departments. There is also a modest **Jardín Zoológico** (dating from 1907), along Av 52, which is open daily except Monday 9 am to 7 pm, with guided tours between 10:30 am and 4 pm.

Museo de La Plata

When Buenos Aires became the federal capital, provincial authorities built this museum, in the spacious park known as Paseo del Bosque, to house the paleontological, archaeological, and anthropological collections of lifetime director Francisco P Moreno, the famous Patagonian explorer.

Finished in 1889, the building consists of an attractive oval with four stories and a mezzanine with showrooms, classrooms, workshops, laboratories, offices, libraries, and storage. Its exterior mixes Corinthian columns, Ionic posterior walls, and Hellenic windows with Aztec- and Inca-style embellishments. Since 1906, the university's school of natural sciences has functioned here.

Unfortunately, for all its resources, it's a major disappointment. The impressive fossil collection, for instance, suffers from a routine chronology that doesn't do justice to the subject, and the ethnographic exhibits betray a stereotypical Darwinism more than a century out of date. Besides its exterior repairs, the museum deserves a truly professional makeover of both the interior and its display materials.

At Paseo del Bosque 1900, the museum (☎ 425-7744) is open daily 10 am to 6 pm. Admission is US$3. Free guided tours are available 2 to 4 pm.

Places to Stay

Since visitors to La Plata are often government officials on per diem, hotels price their rooms accordingly. One of few budget hotels, ***Hotel Saint James*** *(☎ 421-8089, Calle 60 No 377)* charges US$20/30 single/double without breakfast. ***Hotel García***, Calle 2 No 525, is the only other real budget choice.

The friendly, remodeled ***Hotel Roca*** *(☎ 421-4916, Calle 42 No 309)* costs US$25/30 with shared bath, US$31/38 with private bath. ***Hotel Plaza*** *(☎ 421-0325, Av 44 No 358)*, near the train station, charges US$30/40 without breakfast but has a 3rd-floor budget double for US$30. Similar in price and standard, but better located, is one-star ***Hotel Roga*** *(☎ 421-9553, Calle 54 No 334)*, on a woodsy block where clean, comfortable rooms with private bath cost US$38/52.

At the top end are three-star lodgings like ***Hotel La Plata*** *(☎ /fax 422-9090, Av 51 No 783)*, near Plaza Moreno. The price of US$47/64 includes half-board, with a 10% discount for those who settle for breakfast only. ***Hotel Cristal*** *(☎ 424-1489, Av 1 No 620)* charges US$47/62, while ***Hotel San Marcos*** *(☎ 422-2249, Calle 54 No 523)* costs $54/73 and is conveniently close to the Cervecería Modelo.

Hotel del Rey *(☎ 424-1703, Plaza Paso 180)* is a new high-rise charging US$50/70. Four-star ***Hotel Corregidor*** *(☎ 425-6800, fax 425-6805, Calle 6 No 1026)* offers some luxuries for US$88/100.

Places to Eat

Among La Plata's traditional favorites are ***Club Everton***, on Calle 14 between Calles 63 and 64, and ***Club Matheu*** *(Calle 63 No 317)*, between Av 1 and Calle 2, both with limited but good menus at affordable prices. Pricier but very pleasant is the ***Club Hípico*** *(☎ 423-0937)*, in the Paseo del Bosque on Av 52.

For a good parrillada, try ***El Chaparral***, Av 60 and Calle 118 in the Paseo del Bosque, which has excellent *mollejas* (sweetbreads). On Plaza Paso, at the junction of Avs 13 and 44, ***El Quijote*** *(☎ 483-3653)* occupies a commonplace building but has delicious food, particularly the *ensalada de frutos de mar* (seafood salad). Local barristers advocate the ***Colegio de Escribanos***, Av 13 between Calles 47 and 48.

Chachacha *(☎ 422-5294, Calle 10 No 370)*, between 46 and 47, features an extensive choice of meat, chicken, and seafood crepes plus draft beer at moderate prices. ***Posta Centenario***, Diagonal 74 between 48 and 49, specializes in pork. The ***Centro Gallego*** *(Calle 42 No 373)* serves Spanish food, along with pasta and other *minutas* (short orders), as does the ***Club Español*** *(☎ 428-2033, Calle 6 No 1030)*. A popular Italian place is ***La Trattoría***, at Calle 47 and Diagonal 74; similar but more expensive is ***Prego*** *(Calle 11 No 805)*. ***Pizza Banana*** *(Calle 47 No 772)* is a branch of the popular Buenos Aires pizzeria.

Todo Natural, on Calle 47 between 10 and 11, is a good natural-foods market. The popular ice creamery ***Freddo*** has an outlet at Calles 47 and 10. For an espresso and a breath of fresh air, try the totally smoke-free ***Confitería París***, at the corner of Av 7 and Calle 49. The ***Café Cultural Vieja Estación*** is part of the Pasaje Dardo Rocha, opposite Plaza San Martín.

The quintessential La Plata experience is the 85-year-old ***Cervecería Modelo***, or simply La Modelo, at the corner of Calles 5 and 54. On a warm summer night, you can pass hours at their sidewalk tables, downing excellent *cerveza tirada* (lager beer) and complimentary peanuts; for something more substantial, try a *lomito* (beef sandwich) with chips. In winter there is plenty of space inside.

Entertainment

Cine Ocho *(☎ 482-5554, Calle 8 No 981)*, between Avs 51 and 53, has three screens. The ***Cine San Martín*** *(☎ 483-9947, Calle 7*

No 923), between 50 and 51, has two screens, while ***Cine Opera*** *(☎ 422-6502, Calle 58 No 770)*, between 10 and 11, has only one.

The ***Open Pub*** *(Calle 47 No 787)* is a live rock venue. Try also ***Disco Bar Alem*** *(Calle 47 No 717)* or ***El Solar Provinciano*** *(☎ 483-8811, Calle 5 No 1076)* for live music and/or dancing.

Spectator Sports

Gimnasia y Esgrima La Plata (☎ 422-8620), the local soccer club, has offices at Calle 4 No 979, but the team plays at the Estadio Gimnasia y Esgrima (☎ 424-0070) at the intersection of Calles 60 and 118 in the Paseo del Bosque. Buy tickets at the stadium, but always call first.

Getting There & Away

Bus The bus terminal (☎ 421-0992) is at Calles 4 and 42. Río de la Plata (☎ 422-9856) has buses every half-hour to Once, Constitución, and Retiro stations in Buenos Aires (US$2) and also offers a beach service to Pinamar and Villa Gesell.

Long-distance carriers include Costera Criolla (☎ 423-2808), which serves Mar del Plata, Miramar, Necochea, and Tandil. El Rápido Argentino (☎ 423-1616) goes to most provincial beach towns, from Mar de Ajó in the north to Necochea in the south. El Cóndor/La Estrella (☎ 423-2745) goes direct to Mar del Plata and to Bahía Blanca via Olavarría and Sierra de la Ventana. Río Paraná (☎ 424-2036) goes to Bahía Blanca and Carmen de Patagones.

Pampa (☎ 424-3064) runs to Tandil and Necochea, and Liniers (☎ 483-9147) goes daily to Santa Rosa, La Pampa province. General Urquiza (☎ 425-9292) goes to Córdoba and its Sierras. TAC (☎ 425-6943) goes daily to Mendoza via San Luis; at the same office, El Santiagueño goes to Santiago del Estero via Rosario, while Flecha Bus goes to Concordia. Empresa Tala (☎ 424-3064) has buses to Paso de los Libres and Corrientes. La Unión (☎ 424-0940) goes to Termas de Río Hondo.

Train Featuring a striking art nouveau dome and wrought-iron awnings, La Plata's turn-of-the-century Estación Ferrocarril General Roca (☎ 421-9377, 421-2575), at Av 1 and Calle 44, has undergone a much-needed modernization and repainting. Transportes Metropolitana SA General Roca (TMR) has 37 weekday trains to Constitución in Buenos Aires (1-1/2 hours, US$1.50), slightly fewer on Saturday, Sunday, and holidays. The last train leaves around 11 pm, but they start up again between 3 and 4 am. City buses serve the station.

AROUND LA PLATA

La República de los Niños

Evita Perón herself sponsored this 52-hectare scale-model city, completed shortly before her death in 1952, for the education and enjoyment of children. From its Plaza de la Amistad (Friendship Plaza), a steam train circles this architectural hodgepodge of medieval European and Islamic styles, with motifs from Grimms' and Andersen's fairy tales.

Like most public-works projects of its era, it's showing its age, but it's worth a visit if you have crabby kids to appease. Otherwise it's sort of a bargain-basement Disneyland.

República de los Niños (☎ 484-0194) is on Camino General Belgrano Km 7 and Calle 501, north of La Plata in the suburb of Manuel Gonnet. From Av 7 in La Plata, take bus No 518 or 273; note that not all No 273 buses go all the way. From Av 13 and 129, take bus No 338.

Admission is US$3, which includes the aquarium and *granja* (farm), but the train ride and doll museum cost extra. Children under 7 are free. Hours are 10 am to 6 pm Tuesday to Sunday.

Río Santiago

Ghost factories like the Swift meat-packing plant, which employed 24,000 workers at its peak, haunt the port of Río Santiago, at the end of the Roca line past La Plata. Infrequent trains are usually packed with soldiers coming from and going to the military academy there, so city bus No 214 (Berisso) is more frequent and dependable.

From the Río Santiago train station, it's also possible to take a boat to the picturesque **Isla Paulino**, which is rarely visited by tourists. Its inhabitants cultivate grapes in the highly regarded *viñedos de la costa* (coastal vineyards).

LUJÁN

Buenos Aires' second founder, Don Juan de Garay, granted the lands around the Río Luján to Spanish pioneers, but incessant Querandí raids and the distance from Buenos Aires deterred settlement until the 17th century, when this settlement along the Río Luján became an important stop on the cart road west.

Legend claims that, in 1630, a wagon containing a painting of the Virgin, en route from Brazil to a Portuguese farmer, would not budge until the gauchos removed the painting. Clearing the site, the image's devoted owner built a chapel where the Virgin had chosen to stay, about 5km from present-day Luján. Taking the name of La Virgen de Luján, the image became Argentina's patron saint, but she now occupies the French Gothic basilica, one of the city's two main tourist attractions. The other is a colonial historical museum complex.

Orientation

On the east bank of its namesake river, Luján (population 39,000) is only 65km from Buenos Aires via RN 7, so many people come from the federal capital for the day. Most places of interest, as well as hotels, are near the basilica, but Plaza Colón, five blocks southeast via Calle San Martín, is another major activity center.

Information

Tourist Offices There's an information kiosk at the corner of Lavalle and 9 de Julio, but it's open erratically. Luján's Comisión de Promoción Turística (☎ 420453, 433500) in the Edificio La Cúpula, at the west end of Lavalle, is more reliably open and better supplied with information and brochures. Hours are 8 am to 2 pm weekdays.

Post & Communications Correo Argentino is at Mitre 575; Luján's postal code is 6700. The area code is ☎ 02323.

WAYNE BERNHARDSON

Pilgrims honor the 'Virgencita' at the Basílica Nuestra Señora de Luján.

Basílica Nuestra Señora de Luján

Every year 4 million pilgrims from throughout Argentina visit Luján to honor the Virgin for her intercession in matters of peace, health, forgiveness, and consolation. The terminus of their journeys is this imposing basilica, where the 'Virgencita' (she is known by the affectionate diminutive) occupies a *camarín* (chamber) behind the main altar. Devotees have covered the stairs with plaques acknowledging her favors.

Every October since the Dirty War, a massive Peregrinación de la Juventud (Youth Pilgrimage) originates in Buenos Aires' Once Station, 62km away. In the days of the military dictatorship, when any mass demonstration was forbidden, this 18-hour walk had tremendous symbolic importance, but since the restoration of democracy it has become more exclusively devotional. The other large gathering of believers takes place May 8, the Virgin's day.

Within the basilica, visitors will find Gaelic inscriptions, Irish surnames, and a window dedicated to St Patrick. Near the basilica, whose towers rise 106m above the pampas, the **Museo Devocional** houses *exvotos* (gifts) to the Virgin, including objects of silver, wood, and wax, musical instruments, and icons from all over the world. It's open Tuesday to Friday 1 to 6 pm, weekends 10 am to 6 pm.

Complejo Museográfico Enrique Udaondo

Occupying three full hectares bounded by Calles Lezica y Torrezuri, Lavalle, San Martín, and Parque Ameghino, this museum complex includes the 30 rooms of the **Museo Colonial e Histórico**, housed in colonial buildings such as the **Cabildo** and the so-called **Casa del Virrey** (no viceroy ever lived there). Exhibits cover the area's history from pre-Columbian times but stop abruptly in the mid-20th century.

The **Museo de Transporte** has four showrooms with a remarkable collection of colonial and later horse carts, the first steam locomotive to serve the city from Buenos Aires, and a patio with a windmill and a horse-powered mill. The most offbeat exhibit is the stuffed remains of Mancha and Gato, the Argentine criollo horses ridden by Swiss adventurer AF Tschiffely from Buenos Aires to Washington, DC, in the late 1920s.

The complex (☎ 420245) is open Wednesday to Sunday 12:15 to 5:30 pm; admission is US$1. The combined library-archive is open weekdays 9:30 am to 6 pm, but closes in January.

Places to Stay

Camping For about US$4 per person per day, ***Camping El Triángulo*** *(☎ 430116)*, on RN 7 (Av Carlos Pellegrini) across the Río Luján, is basic and imperfectly maintained, but has plenty of shade and is OK for a night. There is another more expensive campground along the river near the Dirección Municipal de Turismo at Edificio La Cúpula. Informally, pilgrims camp just about anywhere they feel like it.

Hospedajes & Hotels Several budget hotels cater to the pilgrims who come throughout the year. Opposite the bus terminal, ***Hospedaje Royal*** *(☎ 421295, 9 de Julio 696)* has small rooms at US$20/28 single/double. Rates are US$30 double at ***Hotel Victoria*** *(☎ 420582, Lavalle 136)*, but without breakfast. On the northern side of the basilica, the friendly ***Hotel Carena*** *(☎ 423828, Lavalle 114)* charges US$30 single or double with private bath. Also nearby is dark and threadbare but clean and friendly ***Hotel Venecia*** *(Almirante Brown 100)*, which has small rooms with private baths and fans for US$20/25.

South of the basilica, the once-elegant ***Hotel de la Paz*** *(☎ 424034, 9 de Julio 1054)* has friendly ownership and acceptable rooms at US$35/40 with breakfast. The unlikeliest hotel name in this major devotional center belongs to ***Hotel Eros*** *(☎ 420797, San Martín 129)*. Very clean, small rooms, but without exterior windows, cost US$42/50 with private bath.

Probably the best in town is the new ***Hotel Hoxón*** *(☎ 429970, 9 de Julio 769)*, where rates start at US$58 double including breakfast and pool access.

Places to Eat

There's a cluster of cheap, fixed-menu restaurants near the basilica along Av Nuestra Señora de Luján, where very aggressive waiters nearly yank tourists off the sidewalk. These places are pretty much interchangeable, but most of them are pretty good values.

Half a block off the avenue ***Berlín*** *(San Martín 135)* serves Germanic specialties. Off the central Plaza Colón, the quiet ***Don Chiquito*** *(Colón 964)* has excellent but pricey Argentine food. Along the river, to the north of the basilica, ***El Colonial*** *(☎ 425226)* is a step above most other restaurants in town.

Undoubtedly the best in town, ***L'Eau Vive*** *(☎ 421774, Constitución 2112)*, between Entre Ríos and Doctor Luppi, is a superb

French restaurant run by Carmelite nuns from around the world. The US$11 mid-day menu is great value, but note the limited hours: noon to 2:15 pm for lunch, 8 to 10 pm for dinner (a very early closing hour for Argentines). The service is friendly and attentive, and the atmosphere is 100% tobacco-free.

Entertainment

There's a bit more to do than just worship in Luján. The ***Old Swan Pub*** *(☎ 433346, San Martín 546)* features salsa and merengue on Wednesday night, tango on Thursday night. For movies, try ***Cine Nuevo Numancia 1*** *(☎ 430860, San Martín 398)* or nearby ***Cine Nuevo Numancia 2*** *(☎ 430860, Italia 967)*.

Getting There & Away

Bus Luján's Estación Terminal de Ómnibus (☎ 20032, 20040) is on Av de Nuestra Señora del Rosario between Almirante Brown and Dr Reat, three blocks north of the basilica. Transporte Luján (Línea 52) leaves from Plaza Miserere (Estación Once) in Buenos Aires, while Transportes Atlántida (Línea 57) connects Luján with Palermo. Talsa also leaves frequently from Once (US$3).

There are also long-distance services. Empresa Argentina/El Rápido (☎ 430073) both serve Mar del Plata (US$26). La Estrella (☎ 420032 interno 23) goes to San Juan (US$51) and San Rafael, with connections to Mendoza, for US$48. General Urquiza (☎ 430073) goes to Rosario (US$14) and Córdoba (US$36).

Expreso Río Paraná (☎ 420044) and Ciudad de Posadas (☎ 433350) run up the Mesopotamian provinces.

Train The Ferrocarril Sarmiento (☎ 420439), at Av España and Belgrano, still runs trains to and from Estación Once (Plaza Miserere Subte) in Buenos Aires.

SAN ANTONIO DE ARECO

Dating from the early 18th-century construction of a chapel in honor of San Antonio de Padua (but named to reflect the river on which it's situated), this serene village is the symbolic center of Argentina's vestigial gaucho culture and host to the country's biggest gaucho festivity, Día de la Tradición, in November. Nestled in the verdant pampas of northern Buenos Aires province, it was the setting for Ricardo Güiraldes' famous novel *Don Segundo Sombra* (1927). Güiraldes' nephew Adolfo played the role of Don Segundo in director Miguel Antín's film version (1969), in which many locals served as extras.

Unlike most Argentine cities, San Antonio's street life centers not around the plaza but on the main commercial street of Alsina, where there's a wealth of quality artisanal goods – this is one of the best places in the country for typical souvenirs. While it's a popular weekend getaway for porteños, weekdays can be very quiet and Monday is utterly dead except when roaring motor scooters decimate the town's normally bucolic ambience (San Antonio's narrow streets are notorious echo chambers). At least the cobbled streets around Plaza Ruiz de Avellano help slow the traffic.

Orientation

San Antonio is on the south bank of Río Areco, 113km west of Buenos Aires via RN 8, which continues west to Pergamino, Río Cuarto, and Mercedes before meeting RN 7 to San Luis and Mendoza. At the eastern approach to town, RP 41 heads toward RN 9, Rosario, and points north.

East of the river, San Antonio has a very regular grid whose formal focus is Plaza Ruiz de Arellano, bounded by Lavalle, Ruiz de Arellano, B Mitre, and V Alsina (the main commercial drag). Street names change on each side of Arellano. Several points of interest are on or across the river, while San Antonio's numerous artisans are scattered around the downtown area.

Information

Tourist Offices San Antonio's Dirección de Turismo (☎ 43165), on Castex between Arellano and Zapiola, is open 8:30 am to 5:30 pm weekdays, 9:30 am to 5:30 pm weekends, and provides a useful pocket-size guide, updated monthly, with a map and other useful information. It also distributes

SAN ANTONIO DE ARECO

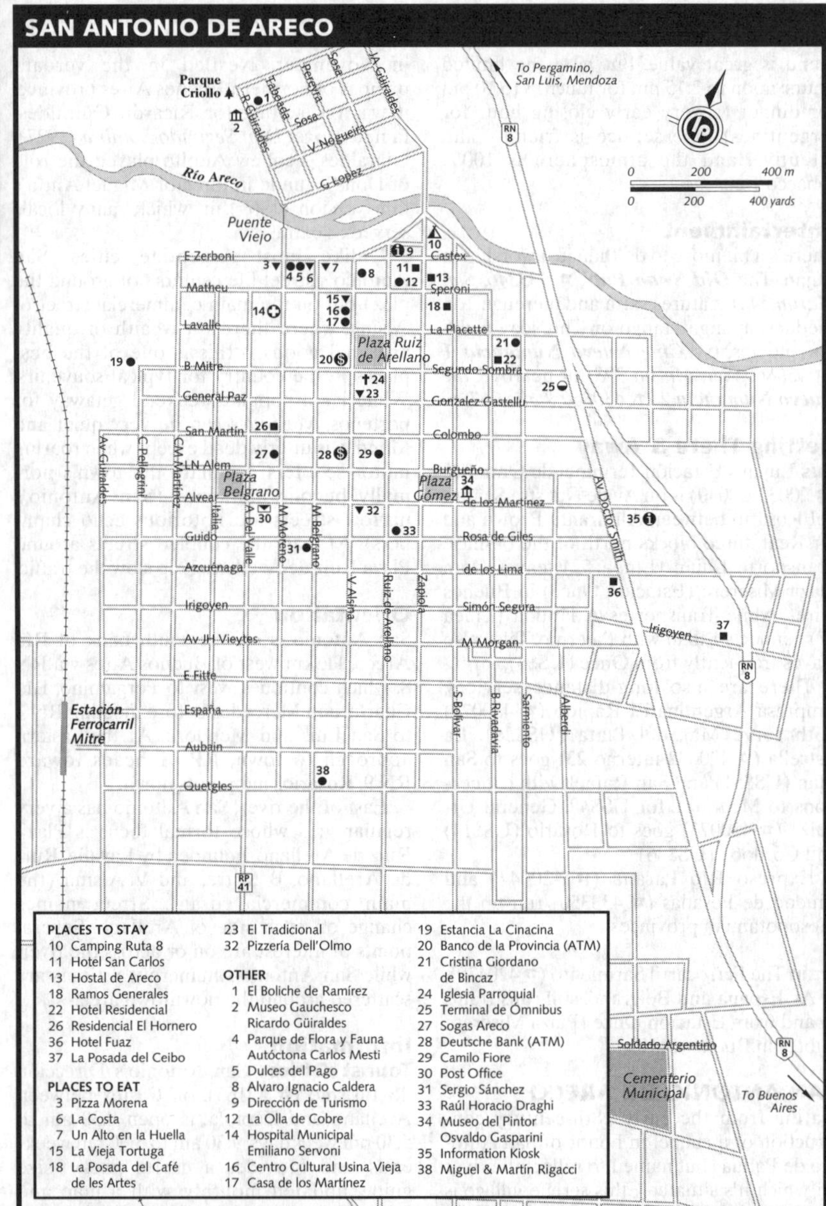

PLACES TO STAY
- 10 Camping Ruta 8
- 11 Hotel San Carlos
- 13 Hostal de Areco
- 18 Ramos Generales
- 22 Hotel Residencial
- 26 Residencial El Hornero
- 36 Hotel Fuaz
- 37 La Posada del Ceibo

PLACES TO EAT
- 3 Pizza Morena
- 6 La Costa
- 7 Un Alto en la Huella
- 15 La Vieja Tortuga
- 18 La Posada del Café de les Artes
- 23 El Tradicional
- 32 Pizzería Dell'Olmo

OTHER
- 1 El Boliche de Ramírez
- 2 Museo Gauchesco Ricardo Güiraldes
- 4 Parque de Flora y Fauna Autóctona Carlos Mesti
- 5 Dulces del Pago
- 8 Alvaro Ignacio Caldera
- 9 Dirección de Turismo
- 12 La Olla de Cobre
- 14 Hospital Municipal Emiliano Servoni
- 16 Centro Cultural Usina Vieja
- 17 Casa de los Martínez
- 19 Estancia La Cinacina
- 20 Banco de la Provincia (ATM)
- 21 Cristina Giordano de Bincaz
- 24 Iglesia Parroquial
- 25 Terminal de Ómnibus
- 27 Sogas Areco
- 28 Deutsche Bank (ATM)
- 29 Camilo Fiore
- 30 Post Office
- 31 Sergio Sánchez
- 33 Raúl Horacio Draghi
- 34 Museo del Pintor Osvaldo Gasparini
- 35 Information Kiosk
- 38 Miguel & Martín Rigacci

Pregón Turismo, a tabloid-size publication that provides more detailed material on San Antonio's attractions.

There's a small information kiosk, open only sporadically, on Calle de los Martínez near the junction with RN8.

Money Deutsche Bank has an ATM on Alsina between San Martín and Alem, while Banco de la Provincia has one on Mitre near Alsina.

Post & Communications Correo Argentino is at Alvear and Av Del Valle; the postal code is 2760. There are several downtown locutorios on Alsina; San Antonio's area code is 02326.

Medical Services The Hospital Municipal Emiliano Servoni (☎ 42391) is at Lavalle and Moreno.

Walking Tour

In the early 18th century **Plaza Ruiz de Arellano** was the site of the corrals of the town's founding estanciero; in its center, the **Monumento a Vieytes** honors locally born Juan Hipólito Vieytes, a figure in the early independence movement.

Historic buildings around the plaza include the **Iglesia Parroquial** (Parish Church) and the **Casa de los Martínez** (site of the main house of the original Ruiz de Arellano estancia). The **Centro Cultural Usina Vieja**, half a block north of the plaza, deserves a visit.

At the corner of E Zerboni and M Moreno, the **Parque de Flora y Fauna Autóctona Carlos Mesti** is San Antonio's modest zoo, open daily 9 am to noon and 2 to 7 pm; admission is US$1. Just to the north, conspicuously featured in the film version of *Don Segundo Sombra*, the **Puente Viejo** (1857) across the Río Areco follows the original cart road to northern Argentina. Once a toll crossing, it's now a pedestrian bridge leading to the **Parque Criollo y Museo Gauchesco Ricardo Güiraldes**, San Antonio's major visitor attraction.

The elderly painter Osvaldo Gasparini and his son Luis operate the **Museo Gauchesco del Pintor Gasparini** (☎ 43930), at the corner of Av del los Martínez and Bolívar, south of the square. Containing personal effects of Güiraldes as well as the owners' gauchesco artwork, it's open 8 am to 8 pm daily. Admission is free.

Ricardo Güiraldes and Segundo Ramírez (the real-life role model for Don Segundo Sombra) both lie in the **Cementerio Municipal** farther south, at the junction of RN 8 and Soldado Argentino.

Parque Criollo y Museo Gauchesco Ricardo Güiraldes

Inaugurated by the provincial government in 1938, a decade after Güiraldes' death, this elaborate museum is, on one level, a spurious 'Gaucholand' of restored and/or fabricated buildings idealizing and fossilizing the history of the Pampas. On the other hand, the contents are genuine and the complex's 90 hectares also provide an unalloyed introduction to the gaucho as a modern cultural phenomenon, allowing visitors to sense the degree to which his consciousness has permeated contemporary Argentine society.

The complex's centerpiece is the **Casa del Museo**, a 20th-century reproduction of an 18th-century *casco* (the large house of an estancia), which includes a Sala de los Escritores on gaucho literature (including the desk and chair of Walter Owen, who translated the gauchesco classic, *Martín Fierro*, into English); a Sala Pieza de Estanciero with a wooden bed belonging to Juan Manuel de Rosas (the ultimate rural

KEN LAFFAL

Cowboys on the plains

ARGENTINA

The Rise & Romance of the Gaucho

No one could have predicted the rise to respectability of that accidental icon, the Argentine gaucho. Dressed in baggy *bombacha*, the modern gaucho, with a leather *rastra* round his waist and a sharp *facón* in his belt, is the idealized version of a complex historical figure. Directly or indirectly, to most Argentines and foreigners, he is a latter-day version of the romantic characters portrayed in José Hernández' epic poem *Martín Fierro* and Ricardo Güiraldes' novel *Don Segundo Sombra*. Like his counterpart, the North American cowboy, he has received elaborate cinematic treatment. Ironically, only when he became a sanitized anachronism did he achieve celebrity.

Without the rich pastures of the Pampas and the cattle and horses that multiplied on them, the gaucho could never have flourished. In a sense, he replaced the Pampas Indian; usually a mestizo, he hunted burgeoning herds of cattle just as the Querandí Indians did the guanaco and rhea. As long as cattle were many, people few, and beef, hides, and tallow of some commercial value, his subsistence and independence were assured. This achieved, he could amuse himself gambling and drinking in the saloon, or *pulpería*. Nineteenth-century observers like Domingo Sarmiento thought the gaucho indolent but grudgingly acknowledged that he led a good life:

> Country life, then, has developed all the physical but none of the intellectual powers of the gaucho. His moral character is of the quality to be expected from his habit of triumphing over the forces of nature; it is strong, haughty and energetic. Without instruction, and indeed without need of any, without means of support as without wants, he is happy in the midst of his poverty and privations, which are not such to one who never knew nor wished for greater pleasures than are his already.

landowner); and a Sala del Gaucho with horsegear and various works of gauchesco art. Two rooms are dedicated to Güiraldes himself, another to his wife, Adelina del Carril de Güiraldes, and yet another to his painter cousin Alberto.

More authentic, or at least more venerable, than the Casa del Museo is the **Pulpería La Blanqueada**, a mid-19th-century building with a credible re-creation of a rural tavern. Alongside the pulpería are **La Tahona**, an 1848 flour mill shipped here from the town of Mercedes, and the **Galpón y Cuarto de Sogas**, where the estancia might have stored its carriages. Nearby is **La Ermita de San Antonio**, a colonial-style chapel with some colonial artifacts.

North of the river on Camino Ricardo Güiraldes, reached via the Puente Viejo, the grounds and buildings of the Museo Gauchesco (☎ 42583) are open daily except Tuesday 11 am to 5 pm. Admission is US$2

The Rise & Romance of the Gaucho

Even as Sarmiento wrote, the gaucho's independent, self-sufficient way of life was in decline. Just as the gauchos had replaced the Pampas Indians, so large landowners squeezed out the gauchos. The primitive livestock economy gave way to saladeros, which made use of a wider variety of products – processed hides, tallow and salted or jerked beef.

For their saladeros, landowners needed labor; the gaucho, with his horseback skills, was a desirable if unwilling source of manpower, but landowners were not reluctant to use their influence to coerce him. Classifying the gaucho as a 'lawless' element, discriminatory laws soon required internal passports, and men without jobs could no longer travel freely over the Pampas. Punishment for 'vagrancy' was often military conscription. As sheep replaced cattle on the Pampas, land was fenced and marked, forcing the gaucho to the fringes or onto the estancias.

Unlike the frontier, the estancia was not a democracy, and the gaucho was no longer his own master, even though his livestock skills were still in seasonal demand. He became instead a hired hand for an institution whose physical aspects bespoke hierarchy. As European immigrants came to occupy many saladero jobs, which often were detested by real gauchos, friction arose between gaucho 'natives' and Italian 'gringos'. Despite resistance, the day of the free-roaming gaucho was over by the late 19th century.

Ironically, about this time, Argentina discovered the gaucho's virtues in what has become known as *literatura gauchescha* ('gauchesque' literature, or literature *about* as opposed to *by* the usually illiterate gauchos). *Martín Fierro* romanticized the life of the independent gaucho at the point at which he was disappearing, much like the open-range cowboy of the American West.

Hernández deplored both opportunistic strongmen like Juan Manuel de Rosas, who claimed to speak for the gaucho, and 'civilizers' like Sarmiento, who had no scruples about discarding the people of the countryside. The gaucho's fierce independence, so often depicted as lawlessness, became admirable, and Hernández almost single-handedly rehabilitated the gaucho's image as Argentines sought an identity in a country rapidly being transformed by immigration and economic modernization. Having fought alongside the gaucho, Hernández eloquently championed him in the public forums of his country and pleaded for his integration into the country's future, noting the positive gaucho values that even Sarmiento admitted: courtesy, independence, and generosity. By the time the gaucho's fate was decided, urban Argentines had elevated him to a mythical status, incorporating these values into their own ideology.

for adults, US$1 for retired persons; children under age 12 get in free.

Centro Cultural Usina Vieja

On Alsina between Matheu and Lavalle, dating from 1901, the Centro Cultural Usina Vieja is a recycled power plant designated an industrial archaeological monument by UNESCO in 1978. Its exhibits and presentations have improved greatly in the past several years – copies of Florencio Molina Campos' amusing caricatures of gaucho life, for instance, are now professionally mounted, and there are excellent metal sculptures by the local artist Perera, most notably *La Cautiva*. Work by local artisans is also on display. Admission is free; hours are 8 am to 1 pm weekdays, 10 am to 5 pm weekends.

Estancia La Cinacina

For a day in the country, countless porteños choose Estancia La Cinacina, where US$30 buys an all-you-can-eat asado, entertainment in the form of folkloric music and dance, a tour of the estancia's museum, and horseback riding. La Cinacina (☎ 42045), at Mitre 9 only six blocks from Plaza Ruiz de Arellano, is less crowded and more comfortable on weekdays. Its Buenos Aires representative is Empresa Que La Opera (☎ 4342-1986, 4342-2841), Mitre 734, 10º B; tours including transportation from the capital cost US$60.

Special Events

Lasting a week in November, the Fiesta de la Tradición (dating from 1906) celebrates San Antonio's gaucho past – by presidential decree, San Antonio is the 'sede provincial de la tradición' (provincial site of tradition). The actual Día de la Tradición is November 10, but celebrations are moved to the following Sunday for convenience. Attractions include lectures, artisanal exhibits, guided tours of historic sites, displays of horsemanship, folk dancing, and the like. If visiting San Antonio during the festival, make reservations far in advance for the limited accommodations.

June 13 is the Día del Santo Patrono (Patron Saint's Day).

Places to Stay

San Antonio has decent but very limited accommodations; prices for lodging may rise on weekends, when reservations are advisable (the rates below are weekend rates). Reservations are imperative during November's Fiesta de la Tradición. At peak times, check the tourist office for information on B&B accommodation.

For US$5 per person, the spacious, shady riverside ***Camping Ruta 8*** has clean toilets and hot showers (from 4 pm to midnight only), but is prone to flooding when rains are heavy. The cheapest regular accommodations (by no means bad) are at conveniently located ***Hotel San Carlos*** *(☎ 43106)* at Zapiola and Castex, which charges US$30 double without breakfast. ***Hotel Residencial*** *(☎ 42166)*, Segundo Sombra and Rivadavia, is comparably priced and offers 15% student discounts.

Residencial El Hornero *(☎ 42733, Moreno 250)*, at San Martín, costs US$45 without breakfast, while ***Hotel Fuaz*** *(☎ 42487, Av Doctor Smith 488)* costs US$60 with breakfast. ***Ramos Generales*** *(☎ 456376, Bolívar 66)* offers excellent accommodations for US$50 double.

Another good value is ***La Posada del Ceibo*** *(☎ 44614)*, on Irigoyen between RN 8 and Av Smith, which charges US$55 double with breakfast. San Antonio's most attractive accommodations are at ***Hostal de Areco*** *(☎ 44063, Zapiola 25)*, which charges US$70 with breakfast.

Places to Eat

San Antonio has fewer eateries than one might expect, though the situation is improving. For homemade meals, try ***El Tradicional*** *(Alsina 173)*; otherwise, the only halfway appealing place downtown is ***Pizzería Dell'Olmo*** *(☎ 42506, Alsina 365)*.

Un Alto en la Huella *(☎ 455595)*, a parrilla at Belgrano and Zerboni, has decent *tenedor libre* (all-you-can-eat menu) for about US$7, while ***La Costa***, across the street, is slightly more expensive. Two good new choices are ***Pizza Morena*** *(☎ 456391)*, at the corner of Zerboni and Moreno (good sidewalk seating), and ***La Vieja Tortuga*** *(☎ 456080, Alsina 60)*, alongside the Centro Cultural Usina Vieja. The latter has live folkloric music Saturday at 10 pm.

Decorated as a turn-of-the-century general store almost to the point of self-parody, ***La Posada del Café de las Artes*** *(☎ 456376, Bolívar 66)*, part of the Ramos Generales complex, nevertheless has good homemade pasta and the like (hold the salt, though) at reasonable prices.

Shopping

San Antonio's artisans are known throughout the country, with many of their disciples practicing their trades in other cities and provinces. Mate paraphernalia, *rastras* (silver-studded belts), and *facones* (long-bladed knives) produced by skilled silversmiths are among the most typical items. Internationally known Raúl Horacio Draghi (☎ 44207), Guido 391, also works in leather.

Other top silversmiths include Miguel & Martín Rigacci (☎ 44016), Av Quetgles 333; Sergio Sánchez (☎ 42988), at Belgrano and Guido; and Alvaro Ignacio Caldera (☎ 42599), Alsina 17.

For horsegear and gaucho clothing, check out Sogas Areco (☎ 43797), Moreno 280, and Camilo Fiore, Arellano 266. Cristina Giordano de Bincaz (☎ 42829), Sarmiento 112, sells weavings. El Boliche de Ramírez, on Güiraldes opposite the Museo Gauchesco, carries a bit of everything.

For artisanal chocolates, try La Olla de Cobre (☎ 43105), Speroni 433. In addition to its restaurant, Ramos Generales, Bolívar 66, also produces homemade sweets, cheeses, and salami. Dulces del Pago (☎ 44751), Zerboni 136, makes a variety of tasty fruit preserves.

Getting There & Away

San Antonio's bus terminal (☎ 456387) is at Av Doctor Smith and General Paz. Frequent buses from Buenos Aires take 1½ hours (US$3.50). TAC and Sierras de Córdoba provide long-distance services between Buenos Aires and the provinces of Cuyo (San Luis, Mendoza, and San Juan) and Córdoba.

AROUND SAN ANTONIO DE ARECO

Surrounding San Antonio de Areco are a number of estancias offering overnight accommodations in the range of US$125 per person plus IVA, including full board; activities such as horseback riding, polo, and the like usually cost extra. Director María Luisa Bemberg shot part of her historical drama *Camila* at **Estancia La Bamba** (visit the San Antonio tourist office for details on accommodations and tours).

Unquestionably the most historic of nearby estancias is the Güiraldes family's **Estancia La Porteña** (☎ 011-4322-6023/5694 in Buenos Aires), which dates from 1850 and has a garden designed by renowned French architect Charles Thays, responsible for major public parks including Buenos Aires' Jardín Botánico. The **Estancia El Ombú** (☎ 492080; 011-4793-2454 in Buenos Aires) belonged to General Pablo Ricchieri, who first inflicted universal military conscription on the country.

Atlantic Coast Beaches

For porteños and others from Buenos Aires province, summer means the beach, and the beach means the Atlantic coast in general and Mar del Plata in particular. Every summer millions of Argentines take a holiday from their friends, families, and coworkers, only to run into them on the beaches. Those who can't make it in person participate vicariously in the beach scene every afternoon via nationwide TV.

Beach access is unrestricted, but *balnearios* (bathing resorts) are privately run, so access to toilets and showers is limited to those who rent tents. Legally, balnearios must have lifeguards, medical services, toilets, and showers. Most also have confiterías, paddleball courts (a current fad in Argentina), and even shops.

Even by Argentine standards, prices are hard to pin down, since they rise every two weeks from December 15 to February 15, and then decline slowly until the end of March, when most hotels and residenciales close. Those that stay open year-round lower their prices considerably, though Semana Santa (Holy Week) is an excuse to raise them briefly.

North of Mar del Plata to Cabo San Antonio, gentle dunes rise behind the generally narrow beaches of the province. Southwest from Mardel to Miramar, steep bluffs highlight the changing coastline, although access is still good for bathing. Beyond Miramar, toward Monte Hermoso, the broad sandy beaches delight bathers, fishing enthusiasts, and windsurfers.

MAR DEL PLATA

When Juan de Garay, founder of Buenos Aires, sailed along the Atlantic coast in 1581, he described the shoreline around present-day Mar del Plata as '*muy galana*' (very

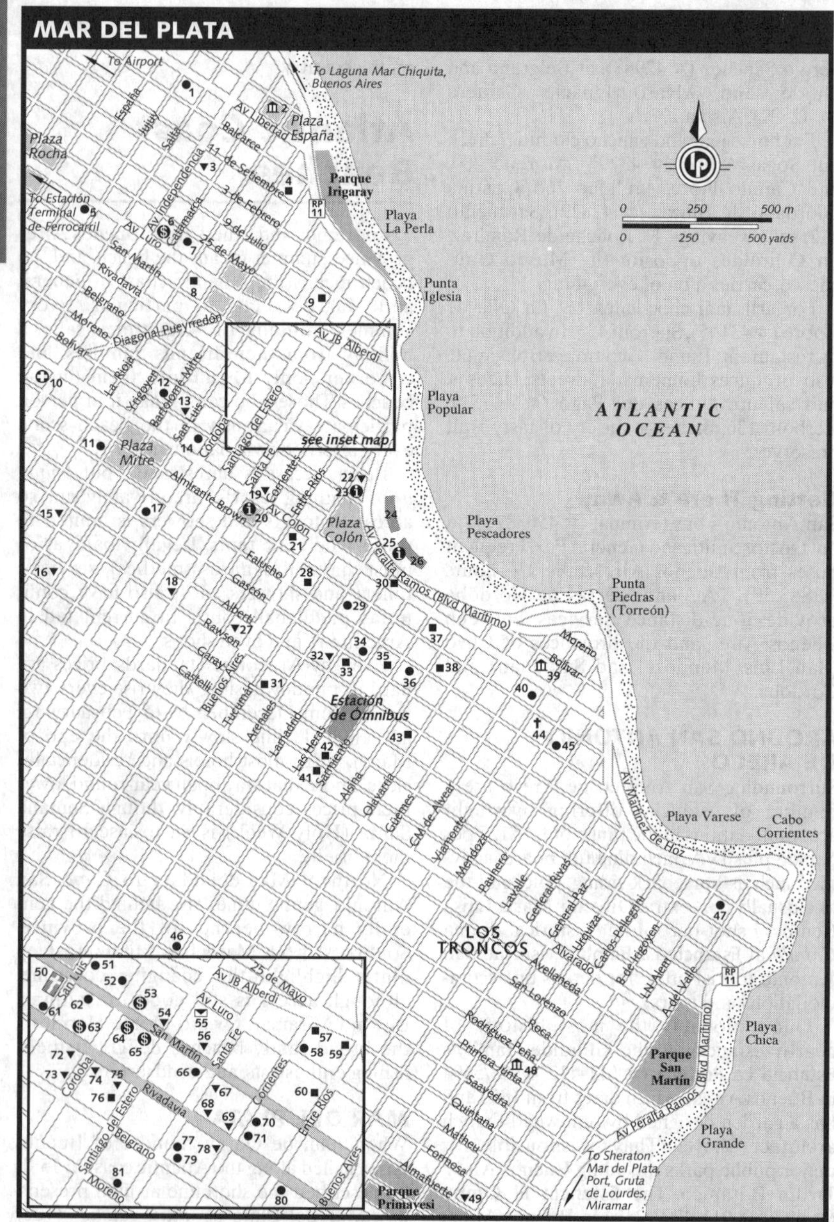
MAR DEL PLATA
To Airport
To Laguna Mar Chiquita, Buenos Aires
Plaza Rocha
To Estación Terminal de Ferrocarril
Plaza España
Parque Irigaray
Playa La Perla
Punta Iglesia
Playa Popular
ATLANTIC OCEAN
see inset map
Plaza Mitre
Plaza Colón
Playa Pescadores
Punta Piedras (Torreón)
Estación de Ómnibus
Playa Varese
Cabo Corrientes
LOS TRONCOS
Parque San Martín
Playa Chica
Playa Grande
Parque Primavesi
To Sheraton Mar del Plata, Port, Gruta de Lourdes, Miramar
0 250 500 m
0 250 500 yards
España
Jujuy
Salta
Av Libertad
Balcarce
Av Independencia
11 de Setiembre
3 de Febrero
9 de Julio
25 de Mayo
Catamarca
Av Luro
San Martín
Rivadavia
Belgrano
Moreno
Bolívar
Diagonal Pueyrredón
La Rioja
Yrigoyen
Bartolomé Mitre
San Luis
Córdoba
Santiago del Estero
Santa Fe
Corrientes
Entre Ríos
Av JB Alberdi
Av Colón
Almirante Brown
Falucho
Gascón
Alberti
Rawson
Garay
Castelli
Buenos Aires
Tucumán
Arenales
Lamadrid
Las Heras
Sarmiento
Alsina
Olavarría
Güemes
CM de Alvear
Viamonte
Mendoza
Paunero
Lavalle
General Rivas
General Paz
Urquiza
Alvarado
Carlos Pellegrini
B de Irigoyen
Avellaneda
LN Alem
A del Valle
San Lorenzo
Roca
Rodríguez Peña
Primera Junta
Saavedra
Quintana
Matheu
Formosa
Almafuerte
Av Peralta Ramos (Blvd Marítimo)
Av Martínez de Hoz
Moreno
Bolívar
RP 11

MAR DEL PLATA

PLACES TO STAY
4 Hotel Traful
8 Hotel España
9 Hotel Bologna
21 Hotel Benedetti
26 Gran Hotel Provincial
28 Hospedaje San Miguel
30 Hotel Hermitage
31 Albergue Juvenil, Hotel Pergamino
33 Hospedaje Lamadrid
35 Hotel Aguila Blanca
37 Hotel Nava
38 Hotel Alsina
41 Hostería La Madrileña
42 Gran Hotel Pelayo
43 Hospedaje Colonial
57 Hotel Presidente
59 Gran Hotel Iruña
60 Hotel Astor
76 Hostería Niza

PLACES TO EAT
3 Trattoría Napolitana
13 Teresa
15 Il Gato
16 Trenque Lauquen
18 La Biblioteca
19 Montecatini
22 La Estancia de Don Pepito
27 La Strada
32 Joe
49 La Marca
54 La Casona
56 Finca del Sol
67 La Casona
68 Manolo
69 Venezia
72 Ambos Mundos
73 El Palacio del Bife
74 La Casona
75 Empanadas del Tucumán
78 Strega

OTHER
1 Casa de Salta
2 Museo Municipal de Ciencias Naturales Lorenzo Scaglia
5 Cine Atlantic
6 Cambio Jonestur
7 Centro Cultural General Pueyrredón
10 Centro de Salud No 1
11 Teatro Municipal Colón
12 Krackers (Internet Access)
14 Budget
17 Sociedad de Cultura Inglesa
20 ACA
23 Ente Municipal de Turismo (Emtur)
24 Casino
25 Subsecretaría de Turismo
29 Locutorio Arenales
34 Lave-Quick
36 Laverap
39 Museo Municipal de Arte Juan Carlos Castagnino (Villa Ortiz Basualdo)
40 Villa Normandy
44 Iglesia Stella Maris
45 Torre Tanque
46 Centro Cultural Villa Victoria
47 Patur (Car Rental)
48 Chalet Los Troncos
50 Catedral de San Pedro
51 Oti Internacional (Amex)
52 Cine Ambassador
53 Banco de la Provincia
55 Post Office
58 Cine Teatro América, Cine Atlas
61 Exposición Cultural Arte y Nácar
62 LAPA
63 Cambio La Moneta
64 Banco de la Nación
65 Cambio Jonestur
66 Cine/Teatro Regina
70 Teatro Corrientes
71 Librería Galerna
77 Cartelera Baires
79 Teatro Santa Fe
80 Cine/Teatro Enrique Carreras
81 Aerolíneas Argentinas, Austral, Southern Winds

pleasing), but Europeans were slow to occupy the area. Nearly two centuries later, in 1747, Jesuit missionaries tried to evangelize the southern Pampas Indians, but the only reminder of their efforts is the body of water known as Laguna de los Padres.

More than a century later, Portuguese investors established El Puerto de Laguna de los Padres, with a pier and a saladero. Beset by economic problems in the 1860s, they sold out to Patricio Peralta Ramos, who founded Mar del Plata proper in 1874. Peralta Ramos helped develop the area as a commercial and industrial center, and later as a beach resort. By the turn of the century, many upper-class porteño families owned summer houses, some of which still grace Barrio Los Troncos.

Since the 1960s, middle-class porteño beachgoers outnumber locals three to one in summer. Multitudinous skyscrapers have risen because local authorities have failed to enforce building codes, leaving many beaches in the shade much of the day. As the 'Pearl of the Atlantic' has lost exclusivity, its architectural character and its calm, the Argentine elite have sought refuge in resorts such as nearby Pinamar or Punta del Este (Uruguay). Still, Mardel (as it is popularly known) remains the most successful Argentine beach town; its large population and well-developed infrastructure are able to support events like 1995's Panamerican Games.

Mar del Plata still has many appealing qualities, but unless you can relax amid thousands of gregarious vacationers, you may prefer spring or autumn, when prices are lower and the area's natural attractions are easier to enjoy.

Orientation

Mar del Plata (population 569,000), 400km south of Buenos Aires via RP 2, sprawls along 8km of beaches, though most points of interest are in the downtown area, bounded by Av JB Justo (running roughly west from the port), Av Independencia (running roughly northeast-southwest), and the ocean. On street signs, the coastal road is called Av Peralta Ramos, but most people refer to it as Blvd Marítimo. The downtown segments of San Martín and Rivadavia are both pedestrian malls.

Information

Tourist Offices At Blvd Marítimo 2267, opposite the casino, Mardel's Ente Municipal de Turismo (Emtur; ☎ 495-1777, emtur@mardelplata.com.ar) usually has an English-speaker on duty. Since the city gets so crowded in summer, the staff cope with tourists in assembly-line fashion, but it has good maps, informative brochures, a monthly activities calendar, and an efficient computerized information system. Hours are 8 am to 10 pm daily from mid-December to Semana Santa, 8 am to 8 pm the rest of the year. In summer only, Emtur has a branch at the bus terminal.

Opposite Plaza Colón, the provincial Subsecretaría de Turismo (☎ 495-5340), Local 60 in the Rambla del Hotel Provincial, Blvd Marítimo 2500, is less helpful. It's open weekdays 9 am to 8 pm, weekends 9 am to 1 pm and 4 to 8 pm.

ACA (☎ 491-2096) is at Av Colón 1450.

Money There are several cambios along San Martín and Rivadavia, including Jonestur, at San Martín 2574 and at Av Luro 3191; and La Moneta, at Rivadavia 2623. Banco de la Provincia is at San Martín 2563, and Banco de la Nación at San Martín 2594. There are many ATMs, mostly on Av Independencia.

Post & Communications Correo Argentino is at Av Luro 2460; the postal code is 7600. Locutorio Arenales, Arenales 2344, is one of many places offering phone and fax services. Mar del Plata's area code is ☎ 0223.

For Internet access, try the cybercafé *Krackers*, at Bartolmé Mitre 2069.

Travel Agencies Oti International (☎ 494-5414), San Luis 1632, is the AmEx representative.

Cultural Centers The Centro Cultural General Pueyrredón (☎ 493-6767), at Catamarca and 25 de Mayo, offers a variety of activities ranging from film screenings and theater to popular music, jazz, folklore, tango, and the like.

The Sociedad de Cultura Inglesa (☎ 495-6513), San Luis 2498, has a library with newspapers, magazines, and books in English, as well as occasional films and lectures.

Laundry There are many downtown laundries, including Laverap, at Falucho 1572, and Lava-Quick, at Las Heras 2471.

Medical Services Centro de Salud Municipal No 1 (☎ 495-0568) is at Av Colón 3294. The Hospital Regional (☎ 477-0262) is at JB Justo 6700.

Walking Tour

A stroll past some of Mar del Plata's mansions leaves vivid impressions of the city's upper-class origins and relatively recent past, when it was still the playground of wealthy Argentines. Built in 1920, **Villa Normandy**, Viamonte 2213, is one of few examples of the French style that survived the renovation craze of the 1950s; it is now the Italian consulate. On the hilltop, the neo-Gothic **Iglesia Stella Maris** (1910), at Brown 1054, features an impressive marble altar; its virgin is the patron saint of local fishermen. On the highest point of this hill, at Falucho 993, there are impressive views from the 88m **Torre Tanque** (1943; ☎ 451-1486).

After descending Viamonte to Rodríguez Peña, walk toward the ocean to the **Chalet Los Troncos** (1938), Urquiza 3454, which lent its name to this distinguished neighborhood. The timber of the gate and fence are quebracho and lapacho hardwoods from Salta province. Lining Calles Urquiza, Quintana, Lavalle, Rodríguez Peña, Rivas, and Almafuerte are examples of more recent but equally elite design. To return to the center, try the longer route along Av Peralta Ramos, which offers expansive views from **Cabo Corrientes**.

Museo Municipal de Arte Juan Carlos Castagnino

Once the summer residence of a prominent Argentine family, now the local fine-arts museum, the Villa Ortiz Basualdo (1909) resembles a Loire Valley castle. Its Belgian interior exhibits paintings, drawings, photographs, and sculptures by Argentine artists.

At Av Colón 1189, the museum (☎ 486-1636) is open daily 5 to 10 pm. Admission is free. Bus Nos 221, 581, 592, and 593 all go there.

Museo Archivo Histórico Municipal Roberto T Barili

In the Villa Emilio Mitre (1930), yet another summer residence of the Argentine oligarchy, a superb collection of turn-of-the-century photographs, along with other exhibits, recalls Mardel's colorful past. It also chronicles the demolitions that made room for the tacky high-rises that now blight the shoreline.

At Lamadrid 3870, the museum (☎ 495-1200) is open daily 2 to 6 pm; admission is free. Bus Nos 523, 524, and 591 go there.

Museo Municipal de Ciencias Naturales Lorenzo Scaglia

Paleontological, archaeological, geological, and zoological exhibits are on display in this museum, whose ground-floor aquarium features local fresh- and saltwater species. At Libertad 3099, on Plaza España, the museum (☎ 473-8791) is open 8:30 am to 12:30 pm and 2 to 8 pm weekdays, 3 to 8 pm weekends. Admission is free.

Banquina de Pescadores

Mar del Plata is one of the country's most important fishing ports and seafood-processing centers. At the port's picturesque wharf, fishermen and stevedores follow their routine on and around kaleidoscopically colored wooden boats, monitored by sea lions who have established a large colony – mostly male – along one side of the pier. In summer, their population declines as they leave to mate in mixed colonies at Isla de Lobos (near Punta del Este, Uruguay) and Península Valdés, Chubut.

In the early morning, unfazed by the chilly sea breeze, the fishermen load their nets and crates before spending the day at sea, escorted by the lions. At about 5 pm, the pier gets noisy and hectic as the returning fishermen sort and box the fish, bargain for the best price, and tidy up their boats and tools. The sea lions return to seek or fight over a resting spot.

There are excellent opportunities for photography – separated by a fence, you can approach within a meter of the lions, then close the day in one of the port complex's great restaurants or, more cheaply, in one of the standing-room seafood cafeterias. Local bus Nos 221, 511, 522, 551, 561, 562, and 593 go to the wharf from downtown.

A related attraction is the tribute to Mar del Plata's fishing community in the **Museo del Hombre del Puerto Cleto Ciocchini**, named for a local painter whose works are on display here. At Padre Dutto 383, about eight blocks north of the port, the museum (☎ 480-1228) is open Thursday to Saturday 5 to 7 pm only; admission is US$2.

Gruta de Lourdes

Luxuriant foliage covers this replica of the famous French grotto, which contains an image of Nuestra Señora de Lourdes, and a trail with the stations of the cross, which includes kitschy scale models of Bethlehem and Jerusalem, with a waterfalls, a sound and light show, and mobile figures.

Only 10 blocks from the port, at Magallanes 4100, Gruta de Lourdes (☎ 480-3072) is open daily 9 am to 8 pm; admission is free. From the port, walk along 12 de Octubre, the main commercial street in the area, to the 4100 block; Magallanes is the next block east. Bus No 522 also goes there.

Exposición Cultural Arte y Nácar

Many travelers have remarked favorably on this museum, which houses collector

Benjamín Sisterna's impressive assortment of 52,000 shells, representing 6000 different species from around the world. At San Luis 1771, the museum (☎ 491-5141) is open Monday through Saturday 4 to 8 pm; admission is free.

Catedral de San Pedro

At San Martín and San Luis, this turn-of-the-century neo-Gothic building features gorgeous stained glass, an impressive central chandelier from France, English-tile floors, and a ceiling of tiles from other European countries.

Centro Cultural Villa Victoria

During the 1920s and 1930s Victoria Ocampo, founder of the literary journal *Sur*, hosted literary salons of prominent intellectuals from around the world at her home, a prime example of Norwegian-built prefabs imported during Mar del Plata's 'belle epoque.' Among her guests were Jorge Luis Borges, Gabriela Mistral, Igor Stravinsky, and Rabindranath Tagore.

Ocampo donated the house to UNESCO in 1973, but eight years later the Municipalidad acquired it as a museum and cultural center. At Matheu 1851, Villa Victoria (☎ 492-0569) is open daily 10 am to 1 pm and 5 to 9:30 pm. Admission is US$2.

Mar del Plata Aquarium

Essentially an overpriced (US$15 adults, US$12 children) trained-seal show, this facility (☎ 467-0700), at Av Martínez de Hoz 5600 in Punta Mogotes, is open daily from 10 am to midnight in summer, 10 am to 10:30 pm in March, 9:30 am to 7 pm April to September, and 9:30 am to 8 pm October to November. Bus Nos 221, 511, 581, and 717 go there.

Organized Tours

Emtur conducts free organized tours *(Paseos para Gente Inquieta)* of city sights such as the Banquina de Pescadores and Centro Cultural Victoria Ocampo (in the Villa Victoria); register one day in advance at the Emtur office on Blvd Marítimo.

Combi-Tur (☎ 493-0732) has more extensive, less specialized excursions leaving from Plaza Colón, at Colón and Arenales. These include a city tour (US$7) and Laguna de los Padres (US$10), both departing daily at 3:30 pm.

The 30m *Crucero Anamora* (☎ 489-0310) offers one-hour harbor tours (US$10) several times daily from Dársena B at the port. Turimar (☎ 484-1450) has rather shorter weekend excursions, also departing from Dársena B.

Special Events

Mar del Plata's elaborate tourist infrastructure guarantees a wide variety of special events throughout the year. On February 10, the date in 1874 when Buenos Aires provincial governor Mariano Acosta authorized the city's creation, Mardel celebrates Fundación de la Ciudad.

Started in 1950, though interrupted for decades by Argentina's political and economic woes, Mardel's Festival Internacional de Cine (International Film Festival) takes place in November. Participants come from a variety of countries from around the world.

From December through March, there are many national golf, tennis, and polo tournaments and sailing regattas.

Places to Stay

It's worth reiterating that prices climb considerably from month to month during summer and fall in the off-season, when many of Mardel's 700 hotels and residenciales close their doors. Unless indicated otherwise, prices are from early high season. The least expensive accommodations are near the bus terminal.

Places to Stay – Budget

Camping South of town along RP 11 are several campgrounds, all very crowded in summer. Rates run around US$16 for up to four persons. Rápido del Sud buses to Miramar stop at each one.

Among the choices are ***Camping El Faro*** *(☎ 467-1168)*, at Playa del Faro, which can be reached by bus Nos 221 and 511; ***Camping Los Horneros*** *(☎ 469-9260)*, 15km south of the Punta Mogotes lighthouse; and

Camping Las Brusquitas, which is 39km south of the lighthouse.

Hostels A few blocks from the bus terminal, the AAJ-affiliated ***Albergue Juvenil*** *(☎ 495-7927, Tucumán 2728)* occupies a wing of Hotel Pergamino. Four-bedded rooms with shared bath cost US$12 per person without breakfast, US$13 with breakfast. Regular hotel accommodation, only slightly dearer, is a better value.

Hospedajes & Hosterías Two blocks from the terminal, ***Hospedaje Lamadrid*** *(☎ 495-5456, Lamadrid 2518)* has decent rooms for US$10 per person off-season, but it's pricier in summer. ***Hostería La Madrileña*** *(☎ 451-2072, Sarmiento 2957)* has clean, modest doubles with private bath for US$24. Also near the terminal is ***Hospedaje Colonial*** *(☎ 451-1039, Olavarría 2663)*.

Hotel Nava *(☎ 451-7611, Sarmiento 2258)* is a beautiful colonial-style house with friendly owners. A room for four with a huge, clean, shared bath is about US$15 per person with breakfast. ***Gran Hotel Pelayo*** *(☎ 451-2533, Sarmiento 2899)*, is good value at US$15 per person with breakfast.

Also try reader-recommended ***Hospedaje San Miguel*** *(☎ 495-7226, Tucumán 2383)*. Centrally located ***Hostería Niza*** *(☎ 495-1695, Santiago del Estero 1843)*, run by three sisters, is an excellent value for US$15 per person (only US$10 off-season) with breakfast and private bath.

Places to Stay – Mid-Range

At these one- and two-star hotels, prices range from US$30 to US$40 per person. At the lower end is ***Hotel Alsina*** *(☎ 451-4465, Alsina 2368)*, where off-season rates are as low as US$15 per person with breakfast. ***Hotel Aguila Blanca*** *(☎ 451-3810, Sarmiento 2455)*, is only slightly more expensive.

Costlier two-star hotels include ***Hotel España*** *(☎ 495-0526, Av Luro 2964)*, which charges US$38 double off-season with breakfast; ***Hotel Bologna*** *(☎ 494-3369, fax 493-8018, 9 de Julio 2542)*, for US$40 double off-season with breakfast; and modern ***Hotel Traful*** *(☎ 493-6650, fax 495-7034, Yrigoyen 1190)*, for US$30/50 single/double off-season, US$70 double in summer.

Places to Stay – Top End

In the high season, rooms in this category start around US$75 and can range well upward of US$100 per person. At the lower end of the price range, ***Hotel Astor*** *(☎ 492-1616, Entre Ríos 1649)* charges US$54/84 with breakfast, US$65/100 with half-board. ***Hotel Benedetti*** *(☎ 493-0031, Colón 2198)* costs US$80 double, while ***Hotel Presidente*** *(☎ 491-0236, Corrientes 1516)* charges US$92 for 'standard' rooms, US$101 for 'superior' rooms, including a buffet breakfast. ***Gran Hotel Iruña*** *(☎ 491-1060, fax 491-1183, Alberdi 2270)* costs US$104 double (US$119 with an ocean view).

Hotel Hermitage *(☎ 490-8116, Blvd Marítimo 2657)* is usually frequented by Argentine showbiz figures. The traditional luxury choice is the massive ***Gran Hotel Provincial*** *(☎ 491-5949, Blvd Marítimo 2300)*, which was once a training school for hotel workers. It offers spacious rooms, a famous casino, a restaurant, and a commercial gallery. There is also, however, the newer ***Sheraton Mar del Plata*** *(☎ 499-9000, Alem 4221)*, in Playa Grande, where rates start at US$155 but rise to $325 for beach views and even higher for suites.

Places to Eat

Although Mar del Plata's numerous restaurants, pizzerias, and snack bars usually hire extra help between December and March, they often struggle to keep up with impatient crowds, and there are always long lines. Food is generally good, and seafood at the restaurants in the Nuevo Complejo Comercial Puerto (the renovated old port) is invariably excellent, though costly – try for one ***La Caracola*** *(☎ 480-9113)*, at Local 6 of the complex. Around the bus terminal you can find very cheap *minutas*, or sandwiches.

At the corner of Av Colón and Corrientes, crowded ***Montecatini*** has cheap, standard Argentine food. In the same category, try ***Il Gato*** *(☎ 495-5309, Yrigoyen 2699)*, the tenedor libre ***Don Mateo*** *(☎ 493-3633, Santa Fe 2633)*, or ***Ambos Mundos*** *(☎ 495-0450, Rivadavia 2644)*; the latter serves abundant minutas and good *puchero de gallina* (chicken stew) at moderate prices. ***La Cantina de Armando*** *(☎ 472-5708, San Lorenzo 3101)* is also reasonable.

Of course there are many parrillas. ***La Estancia de Don Pepito*** *(☎ 495-0471, Blvd Marítimo 2235)*, across from the casino, serves large, moderately priced portions of pasta, parrillada, and seafood; look for discount coupons on flyers at the tourist office and around town. Although a bit expensive, ***Trenque Lauquen*** *(☎ 493-7149, Mitre 2807)* is excellent. ***La Marca*** *(☎ 451-8072, Almafuerte 253)* and ***El Palacio del Bife***, on Córdoba between Rivadavia and Belgrano, are similar.

Italian cuisine is popular among the beachgoers. A small, moderate place with good dishes is ***Teresa*** *(☎ 429-360, San Luis 2081)*. ***Trattoría Napolitana*** *(☎ 495-3850, 3 de Febrero 3158)* has costly but excellent food, while ***La Strada*** *(☎ 495-8992, Entre Ríos 2642)* is more moderate in price.

There are many pizzerias, which also sell good lager beer. ***Joe***, at Lamadrid and Alberti, serves superb pizza and calzones. ***Manolo*** *(☎ 494-5671, Rivadavia 2371)* has a variety of tasty pizzas. Try also ***Strega*** *(☎ 493-6183, Rivadavia 2320)* or the chain ***La Casona***, with branches at Rivadavia 2598 *(☎ 493-8943)*, at Santa Fe 1752 *(☎ 495-4266)*, and at the corner of San Martín and Santiago del Estero.

Finca del Sol *(San Martín 2563)* is a vegetarian tenedor libre charging US$6. ***Empanadas del Tucumán*** *(☎ 494-6266)*, on Santiago del Estero near Belgrano, serves outstanding spicy empanadas.

Venezia, at the corner of Rivadavia and Corrientes, is good for ice cream and coffee.

Argentines devour *alfajores* (biscuit sandwiches filled with chocolate, dulce de leche, or fruit) for afternoon tea or mate, but they can be sickly sweet. Havanna is a very popular brand, available at most groceries and many downtown shops.

Entertainment

As in Buenos Aires, there are carteleras that offer half-price tickets to movies and theater presentations. The Mardel branch of Cartelera Baires is at Santa Fe 1844, Local 33.

Cinema There are several first-run cinemas downtown, some of which double as theaters (designated here as cine teatros). Among them are the ***Cine Ambassador*** *(☎ 495-7271, Córdoba 1673)*, the ***Cine Teatro América*** *(☎ 494-3240, Av Luro 2289)*, the ***Cine Atlas*** *(☎ 494-3240, Av Luro 2289)*, the ***Cine Teatro Atlantic*** *(☎ 473-0206, Av Luro 3426)*, and the ***Cine Teatro Enrique Carreras*** *(☎ 494-2753, Entre Ríos 1828)*.

Theater When Buenos Aires shuts down in January, many shows come from the capital to Mar del Plata. Theaters mostly cater to vacationers by showing comedies that range from *café concert* (stand-up comedy) to vulgar but popular burlesque. Those which double as cinemas appear above.

The ***Teatro Auditorium*** *(☎ 495-7011, Blvd Marítimo 2280)*, part of the casino complex, offers musical theater with quality actors from the capital. Other venues include the ***Teatro Municipal Colón*** *(☎ 499-6210, Yrigoyen 1665)*, ***Teatro Corrientes*** *(☎ 493-7918, Corrientes 1766)*, and ***Teatro Santa Fe*** *(☎ 491-9728, Santa Fe 1854)*.

Dance Clubs After leisurely afternoons at the beach, Argentines stay up all night dancing and socializing. Mar del Plata has lots to offer partygoers along Av Constitución, fittingly nicknamed 'Avenida del Ruido' (Avenue of Noise), where dance clubs line both sides of the street. Among the current favorites are ***Chocolate*** *(☎ 479-4488, Constitución 4445)*, ***Azúcar*** *(☎ 479-8531, Constitución 4478)*, ***Sunset*** *(☎ 479-0989, Constitución 5046)*, ***Aquelarre*** *(☎ 479-2068, Constitución 5400)*, ***Go!*** *(☎ 479-6666, Constitución 5780)*, ***Sobremonte*** *(☎ 479-2600, Constitución 6690)*, and ***Coyote*** *(Constitución 6692)*. Bus No 551 runs all night.

Folk & Traditional Music Mardel has two peñas toward the north end of town: ***Casa del Folklore*** *(☎ 472-3955, San Juan 2543)* and ***Casa de Salta*** *(Libertad 3398)*.

Casinos Unlike its flashier counterparts in Las Vegas or Reno, the ***Casino Central*** *(☎ 495-7011)*, on Av Marítimo, is an elegant, black-tie venue at night, but less formal during the daytime. It's busy all day, especially after midnight.

Shopping

The Feria de los Artesanos takes place on Plaza San Martín every afternoon. There's also a Mercado de Pulgas (Flea Market) on Plaza Rocha, 20 de Setiembre between San Martín and Av Luro, seven blocks northwest of Plaza San Martín.

Mar del Plata is famous for sweaters and jackets. Shops along Av JB Justo, nicknamed 'Avenida del Pullover,' have competitive, near-wholesale prices. To go shopping there, take bus No 561 or 562. A multitude of boutiques along San Martín and Rivadavia cater to the fashion-conscious.

For books try Librería Galerna, on Corrientes between San Martín and Rivadavia.

Getting There & Away

Air Aerolíneas Argentinas and Austral share offices (☎ 496-0101, 479-2787, fax 493-2432), at Moreno 2442, and have several daily flights to Buenos Aires (US$99). LAPA (☎ 492-2112), Local 63 in the Galería de las Américas at San Martín 2648, flies to Aeroparque in Buenos Aires (US$43 to US$85) at least four times daily, and to Córdoba (US$89 to US$159) Friday and Sunday. Dinar Líneas Aéreas (☎ 494-2301), San Martín 2574, Local 36, flies Sunday to Aeroparque and Comodoro Rivadavia.

Southern Winds (☎ 493-2121), in the Hotel Provincial at Blvd Marítimo and Arenales, flies daily to Rosario (US$119 to US$139) and Córdoba (US$119 to US$139), weekdays to Mendoza (US$129 to US$169), Tucumán (US$159 to US$179), and Salta (US$179 to US$199), and Sunday to Neuquén (US$119 to US$139) and Bariloche (US$189 to US$209).

LADE (☎ 493-8220), Local 5 in the casino at Blvd Marítimo 2300, offers flights on Monday to Bahía Blanca (US$40), Viedma (US$57), Puerto Madryn (US$80), and Trelew (US$88); on Tuesday to Buenos Aires (US$38 to US$49); Wednesday to Neuquén (US$76 to US$99) and Bariloche (US$100 to US$130); Thursday to Bahía Blanca, Viedma, Neuquén, San Martín de los Andes (US$95), and Bariloche; and Friday to Buenos Aires.

Bus Mardel's busy Estación de Ómnibus (☎ 451-5406) is very central at Alberti 1602.

Among them, El Cóndor (☎ 451-2110), Costera Criolla (☎ 451-1759), Micromar (☎ 451-4893), Santa Fe (☎ 451-7042), and Dom Car (☎ 451-5932) run many buses to Buenos Aires; the latter two are the cheapest. El Cóndor also goes to La Plata, and Costera Criolla to La Plata and Bariloche. El Rápido (☎ 451-0600) goes to Balcarce, Tandil, and Santa Rosa (La Pampa), and to Neuquén and Bariloche.

Costamar (☎ 451-2843) serves nearby coastal destinations along RP 11 as far as Mar del Tuyú, including Villa Gesell and Pinamar. Rápido del Sud (☎ 451-0860) goes west to nearby Miramar. Autotransportes San Juan (☎ 451-1252) goes to San Juan.

TAC (☎ 454-0014) travels to Mendoza and other northern destinations, and to the Mesopotamian cities of Corrientes and Resistencia. Zenit (☎ 486-0512) goes to the Littoral cities of Santa Fe and Paraná. Empresa Argentina (☎ 451-0666) goes to Rosario, and Expreso Córdoba-Mar del Plata (☎ 451-8733) serves Córdoba, Santiago del Estero, and Tucumán.

Empresa Pampa (☎ 451-8478) goes to Necochea and Bahía Blanca, with connections to Patagonia. Transportadora Patagónica (☎ 493-5271) has southbound services to Viedma, Puerto Madryn, Trelew, Comodoro Rivadavia, and Río Gallegos.

Typical fares are: Miramar (US$3, one hour), Balcarce (US$4.25, one hour), Villa Gesell (US$7, 1½ hours), Necochea (US$9.50, two hours), Tandil (US$12, 2½ hours), La Plata (US$25, five hours), Buenos Aires (US$26 to US$33, seven hours), Bahía Blanca (US$31, seven hours), Neuquén (US$40), Viedma (US$45), Rosario (US$47), Córdoba (US$50), Santiago del Estero

(US$50), Santa Fe (US$55), Paraná (US$57), Tucumán (US$60), Bariloche, (US$65, 19 hours), Corrientes (US$67), Resistencia (US$68), Puerto Madryn (US$72), Trelew (US$73), Mendoza (US$75), Comodoro Rivadavia (US$94), and Río Gallegos (US$125).

Train The Estación Terminal de Ferrocarril (☎ 475-6076) is at Av Luro and Italia, about 20 blocks from the beach, and open 6 am to midnight daily. At the bus terminal, Ferrobaires (☎ 451-2501) is open 8 am to 8 pm Monday to Saturday, 10 am to 6 pm Sunday.

In summer the tourist train El Marplatense travels seven times daily (eight Sunday) to Buenos Aires. Reservations should be made far in advance, since it's usually booked solid through the season. One-way fares are turista US$16, primera US$22, Pullman US$28, and the Sunday super Pullman US$40.

Getting Around

Despite Mardel's sprawl, frequent buses reach just about every place in town. For information on local destinations, the tourist office can help.

To/From the Airport Aeropuerto Félix U Camet is at RN 2 Km 396, 10km north of the city. Bus No 542 leaves from the corner of Blvd Marítimo and Belgrano. Aerolíneas Argentinas (☎ 478-3314) has minibus service for US$3.50. A taxi or remise costs about US$8 to US$10 per person.

Car At the airport, try Avis (☎ 470-2100, fax 470-2582). Budget (☎ 495-6579) is downtown at Bolívar 2628. The cheapest is probably the local agency Patur (☎ 486-2646), Gascón 164, which has unlimited mileage deals with taxes included and discounts for multiday rentals.

AROUND MAR DEL PLATA

Mar Chiquita

Along RP 11, 34km north of Mar del Plata, the peaceful resort of Mar Chiquita is a paradise for swimming, fishing, and windsurfing (there's a December windsurf regatta). Fed by creeks from the Sierras de Tandil and sheltered by a chain of sand dunes, its namesake estuary, Laguna Mar Chiquita, alternately drains into the ocean or absorbs seawater, depending on the tides.

In the nearby community of Santa Clara del Mar, at Niza 1065, the **Museo Paleontológico Pachamama** features paleoecological, botanical, zoological, and archaeological exhibits. From Mar del Plata's casino, Bus Rápido del Sud goes eight times daily to Mar Chiquita, where there are several campgrounds and hotels, including ***Camping Playa Dorada*** *(☎ 493-9607)*.

Museo del Automovilismo Juan Manuel Fangio

Named for Argentina's most famous race car driver, one of the country's finest museums preserves a multimillion-dollar collection of classic and racing cars in his birthplace of Balcarce, 60km northwest of Mar del Plata via RN 226. While it stresses the worldwide exploits of Fangio and his contemporaries, it is not just for racing fanatics, as it also makes an effort to put automotive history into context, with parallel timelines and photographs of global events. Appropriately, visitors ascend a curving ramp in the form of a highway to the various levels.

Fangio, who died in 1995 at the age of 84, is the subject of Stirling Moss and Doug Nye's biographical tribute *Fangio: a Pirelli Album* (Motorbooks International). There is also shop with Fangio souvenirs.

At the corner of Dardo Rocha and Mitre, the museum (☎ 0266-430758) occupies an turn-of-the century building whose recycled interior offers 5000 sq m of display space. Despite an admission price of US$6 (US$2 children), no one can call this well-organized museum a rip-off. Hours are 11 am to 6 pm daily. El Rápido runs frequent buses from Mar del Plata (US$4.25).

VILLA GESELL

In the 1930s, merchant, inventor, and nature-lover Carlos Gesell designed this resort of zigzag streets lined with acacias, poplars, oaks, and pines to stabilize its shifting dunes. Gesell, with a permanent population of only about 18,500, is a popular destination, though middle- and working-class people shy away because of its perceived exclusivity. Still, backpackers and campers can pursue both traditional beach activities and less orthodox ones, like horseback riding.

Orientation

Villa Gesell is 100km northeast of Mar del Plata via RP 11 and about 360km south of Buenos Aires via RP 11, the scenic but dangerous coastal highway. Avenida 3, the only paved road, parallels the beach and runs from Av Buenos Aires, at the edge of the Barrio Norte suburb, south to the bus terminal and most of the campgrounds.

With few exceptions, streets are numbered rather than named. Outside Barrio Norte, the town center consists of 10 east-west alamedas and 145 north-south paseos. Barrio Norte lies between the beach in the east and Circunvalación in the west, and between Av Buenos Aires in the south and Calles 307 and 312 in the north.

Avenida 3 is Gesell's shopping and entertainment center, with teahouses, fine bakeries, and high-class restaurants plus artisan shops, boutiques, and video arcades. Everything is within walking distance, and the density of hotels and restaurants would probably dismay the city's founder.

Information

Tourist Offices The Secretaría de Turismo (☎ 458596), on Av Buenos Aires between RP 11 and Circunvalación at the northwestern approach to town, has friendly staff but poor maps. There's another office in the Municipalidad (☎ 462201), at Av 3 No 820, plus several booths throughout the city with information on accommodations, places to eat, and bus schedules.

ACA (☎ 462-273) is on Av 3, between Paseos 112 and 113.

Post & Communications Correo Argentino is on Av 3 between Paseos 105 and 106. The postal code is 7165. Villa Gesell's telephone code is ☎ 02255.

Medical Services Hospital Municipal Arturo Illía (☎ 462618) is located at Calle 123 and Av 8.

Things to See & Do

The **Museo Histórico Municipal** (☎ 468456), at Alameda 202 and Calle 302, has guided tours daily between 9 am and 1 pm, and 4 and 9 pm.

At the **Muelle de Pesca**, at Playa and Paseo 129, the 15m pier offers year-round fishing for mackerel, rays, shark, and other varieties.

Riding is a popular activity at places like the **Escuela de Equitación San Jorge** (☎ 454446), at Circunvalación and Paseo 102, where you can rent horses independently or take guided excursions. Local golfers frequent the **Club de Golf** (☎ 454983), at RP 11 and Av Buenos Aires.

Organized Tours

El Trencito de Villa Gesell (☎ 468354), actually a bus, leaves from Plaza Carlos Gesell at variable times for a two-hour excursion past the Casa de Don Carlos Gesell, the pine forest, the amphitheater, the pioneer houses, the pier, and the bus terminal. It costs US$5 per person, but children under five ride free.

Turismo Aventura Edy (☎ 462558, 466797) runs trips to Faro Querandí, the local lighthouse, carrying up to 10 passengers in 4WD jeeps on a 30km trip over dunes, with stops along the way for photography, swimming, and exploring. The lighthouse itself, one of the highest and most inaccessible in the country, soars impressively above the surrounding dense forest. Four-hour trips, leaving daily at 9 am and 3 pm, cost US$15 per adult, US$10 per child.

Places to Stay

Listings below constitute only a fraction of Villa Gesell's 200-plus hotels, hosterías, hospedajes, aparthotels, and the like; only a handful are open all year. There's really no such a thing as an inexpensive, basic hospedaje with shared bath – most places include private bath and even a telephone. For the most up-to-date price information and to make reservations, contact Casa de Villa Gesell in Buenos Aires.

Places to Stay – Budget

Camping Gesell's dozen campgrounds usually charge a four-person minimum at US$5 to US$8 per person. Most close at the end of March, but three clustered at the south end of town on Av 3 are open all year: ***Camping Casablanca*** *(☎ 470771)*, ***Camping Mar Dorado*** *(☎ 470963)*, and ***Camping Monte Bubi*** *(☎ 470732)*.

Hospedajes & Hotels Figure about US$30 for singles/doubles with breakfast in places like ***Hospedaje Aguas Verdes*** *(☎ 462040)*, Av 5 between Paseos 104 and 105, and ***Hospedaje Sarimar***, Av 3 between Paseos 117 and 118. Sprawling ***Hospedaje Inti Huasi*** *(☎ 468365)*, Alameda 202 at Av Buenos Aires, has 54 rooms with private bath.

Hospedajes open all year include ***Hospedaje Villa Gesell*** *(☎ 462053, Av 3 No 812)* and ***Hospedaje Marino*** *(☎ 462436)*, at Av 1 and Paseo 112. Tiny ***Hospedaje Viya*** *(☎ 462757)* is on Av 5 between Paseos 105 and 106. ***Hospedaje Antonio*** *(☎ 462246)*, Av 4 between Paseos 104 and 106, has some rooms with shared bath and others with private bath.

Among slightly more expensive one-star hotels, both ***Hotel Aldea Marina*** *(☎ 462835)*, Av 3 between Paseos 114 and 115, and ***Hotel Demi*** *(☎ 462658)*, Av 3 and Paseo 111, remain open all year. Prices run around US$40.

Places to Stay – Mid-Range

There are several two-star hotels, starting around US$50, but only four are open all year: ***Hotel Bellavista*** *(☎ 462293)*, Paseo 114 between Avs 1 and 3, ***Hotel El Cisne*** *(☎ 463456, Av 4 No 330)*, between Paseos 102 and 104, ***Hotel La Posada de la Villa*** *(☎ 464855)*, Paseo 125 between Avs 1 and 2, and ***Hotel Romina*** *(☎ 476074)*, at Av 1 and Paseo 140.

Places to Stay – Top End

The most expensive hotels start around US$80 double and rise to US$170. Try ***Hotel Coliseo*** *(☎ 463420, fax 462955)*, at Av 1 and Paseo 107, or ***Hotel Terrazas Club*** *(☎/fax 463214)*, Av 2 between Paseos 104 and 105, both of which have swimming pools; or ***Hotel Gran Internacional*** *(☎ 468672)*, Paseo 103, between Av 1 and Paseo Costanero.

Places to Eat

Villa Gesell has a wide variety of restaurants, mostly along Av 3, catering to all tastes and budgets. ***La Jirafa Azul*** *(☎ 462431)*, on Av 3 between Av Buenos Aires and Paseo 102, has long had a reputation for serving a menu of good and cheap standards. Owner-operated ***Cantina Arturito*** *(☎ 463037, Av 3 No 186)*, between Paseos 126 and 127, serves large portions of exquisite homemade pasta, as well as shellfish and home-cured ham, at medium to expensive prices. For tasty seafood, try also ***El Comedor***, Av 3 between Paseos 108 and 109, which has good but not cheap paella.

For sandwiches and hamburgers plus superb service from the owners, try ***Sangucheto***, Paseo 104 between Avs 3 and 4. Also good and family-attended, with some health food and drinks, is ***La Martona***, Paseo 106 near Avs 3.

Entertainment

Music The European country-style Playa Hotel, Alameda 205 and Calle 304 in Barrio Norte, established Villa Gesell as a vacation resort, and every summer, the Sociedad Camping Musical organizes chamber music concerts in its auditorium. Other musical events, such as the Encuentros Corales (a gathering of choirs from around the country) take place at the town's Anfiteatro del Pinar (amphitheater), Av 10 and Paseo 102.

Theater The ***Casa de la Cultura*** *(☎ 462513)*, Av 3 and Paseo 109, offers live theatrical productions in summer.

Cinema Villa Gesell has three cinemas: the ***Cine Atlantic*** *(☎ 462323, Paseo 105)*, between Avs 2 and 3; the ***Cine Teatro Atlas***

(☎ 462969, Paseo 108), between Avs 3 and 4; and the two-screen ***Cine San Martín*** *(☎ 462206, 462372, Paseo 105)*, between Avs 2 and 3.

Dance Clubs Dance clubs include ***Dixit***, on Paseo 106 between Avs 3 and 4; ***Le Brique***, on Av 3 between Av Buenos Aires and Av 1; ***Chamaco***, on Av 2 between Paseos 102 and 104; and ***Sabash*** on Paseo 103 between Costanera and Av 1.

Shopping

The Feria Artesanal, Regional y Artística takes place daily on Av 3, between Paseos 112 and 113, from mid-December through mid-March and during Semana Santa and winter weekends and holidays.

Getting There & Away

Air Aerolíneas Argentinas (☎ 468228), at Av Buenos Aires and Av 10 in town, has flights between Buenos Aires and Villa Gesell (US$125) daily during the summer. LAPA (☎ 458219), Av Buenos Aires and Alameda 211, has daily flights (US$39 to US$85) as well. Líneas Aéreas Entre Ríos (Laer; ☎ 468169), Av Buenos Aires between Paseos 205 and 206, flies to and from Buenos Aires (US$63) 15 times weekly.

Bus The main Terminal de Ómnibus (☎ 476058) is at Av 3 and Paseo 140, on the south side of town. Some long-distance buses stop at the Mini Terminal (☎ 462340) on Av 4, between Paseos 104 and 105.

Empresa Río de la Plata (☎ 462224), a block from the Mini Terminal, has several direct buses daily to Buenos Aires (seven hours) in summer, as do Rápido Argentino (☎ 476344) and Antón (☎ 462315), Paseo 108 between Avs 3 and 4. Fares are around US$20.

PINAMAR

Son of a well-known elite Argentine family, architect Jorge Bunge founded and designed the sophisticated resort of Pinamar in 1944 as an elegant refuge for upper-class porteños. Its beautiful beaches, extensive forests, sandy streets, luxury homes and hotels, chic shops, and posh restaurants have made Pinamar the 'in' place for Argentines who needn't work for a living.

Bathed by a tropical current from Brazil, its waters are pleasantly warm and its clean beaches slope gradually into a sea abundant with fish. The adjacent resorts of Ostende and Valería del Mar differ little but offer more moderate prices. Cariló, also nearby, has an country-club atmosphere but merits a visit for those wishing to glean insights into upper-class Argentine life. Do not let the security gates deter you from entering, although you will probably be asked to leave your name.

Pinamar acquired notoriety in early 1997 with the still-unresolved murder of photojournalist José Luis Cabezas, which was linked to bodyguards of shady businessman Alberto Yabrán, who had investments in Pinamar and committed suicide barely a year later. After Buenos Aires provincial governor Eduardo Duhalde declined to vacation in Pinamar because of the Cabezas case, the town's tourist secretary had to plead in the press for Argentines not to change their vacation plans.

Orientation

Pinamar (population 12,000), 120km north of Mar del Plata via RP 11 and 320km southeast of Buenos Aires via RN 2, was planned around an axis formed by Av Libertador, parallel to the beach, and Av Bunge, perpendicular to the beach. On either side of Bunge, the streets in the original plan form two large fans, making orientation tricky at first, but the newer parts of town follow a conventional grid.

Pinamar's commercial area is compact, since residents are zealous about zoning codes. Most shops, restaurants, and hotels are on or within a few blocks of Av Bunge, the main thoroughfare.

Information

Tourist Offices The busy Secretaría de Turismo (☎ 491680), Av Bunge 654 at Libertador, has a good pocket-size map with useful descriptions of Pinamar, Valería, Ostende, and Cariló. ACA (☎ 482744) is at Del Cazón 1365.

Post & Communications Correo Argentino is at Jasón 524; the postal code is 7167. The telephone office is at Jasón and Shaw; Pinamar's area code is ☎ 02254.

Medical Services The Hospital Comunitario (☎ 482390) is at Shaw 250.

Things to See & Do

Pinamar is another outdoors center where, besides sunbathing and swimming, people also enjoy other water sports, including surfing, windsurfing, water-skiing, kayaking, and, of course, fishing. Also popular are golf, horseback riding, tennis, paddleball, and hiking in the woods. Unfortunately, roaring dune buggies, both on the beach and even along nature trails, are also popular.

Places to Stay

Pinamar lacks real budget accommodations – prices are notably higher than in Gesell – but there is a youth hostel in nearby Ostende. There's also a handful of hospedajes, along with plenty of hotels, motels, and hosterías that are invariably full during the season, so reservations are a must. Prices below are for summer, but off-season rates are up to 40% lower.

Places to Stay – Budget

Camping Three campgrounds, charging around US$18 per site, serve the area between Ostende and Pinamar. ***Autocamping Moby Dick*** *(☎ 486045)*, on Av Víctor Hugo and Tuyú in Ostende, has a dense tree canopy. ***Camping Saint Tropez*** *(☎ 482998)*, at Quintana and Nuestras Malvinas in Mar de Ostende, has a good beachfront location, but is small. ***Camping Ostende*** *(☎ 486277)* is on Cairo and Av La Plata in Ostende.

Hostels The beachfront ***Albergue Estudiantil*** *(☎ 482908)*, at Nuestras Malvinas and Sarmiento in Ostende, is a friendly place, offering 85 beds at dormitory rates of $12 per person.

Hospedajes & Hotels Hospedajes start around US$40 double at ***Hospedaje Valle Fértil*** *(☎ 484799, Del Cangrejo 1110)*, rising to US$45 at ***Hospedaje Las Acacias*** *(☎ 485175, Del Cangrejo 1358)*, and US$55 at ***Hospedaje Rose Marie*** *(☎ 482522, Las Medusas 1381)*.

One-star ***Hotel Yacanto*** *(☎ 482367, Rivadavia 509)* costs US$63 double. ***Hotel Berlín*** *(☎ 482320, Rivadavia 326)* charges US$60/70 single/double.

Places to Stay – Mid-Range

Mid-range accommodations start around US$79 at ***Posada del Centro*** *(☎ 482241, Av Constitución 556)*. ***Hotel San Marco*** *(☎ 482424, Del Mejillón 1089)* is slightly dearer. Under the same management as Posada del Centro, ***Hotel La Posada*** *(☎ 482267, Del Tuyú 98)* includes continental breakfast in its pleasant surrounding garden for US$90.

Places to Stay – Top End

Hotel Sardegna *(☎ 482760, Jasón 840)*, ***Hotel La Golondrina*** *(☎ 482240, Av Constitución 590)*, and ***Hotel Riviera*** *(☎ 482334, Del Tuyú 51)* all charge in the US$100 range. Similarly priced ***Hotel El Bufón del Rey*** *(☎ 482323, Delfines 81)* has an intriguing French sculpture of a jester with twins in his arms that allegedly helps infertile couples. The owners welcome visits from nonguests. Weekly rates are around US$450.

The most expensive in this group are the four-star, ultramodern ***Hotel del Bosque*** *(☎ 482480, Av Bunge 1550)*, for US$148, and ***Hotel Algeciras*** *(☎ 485550, Av Libertador 75)*, where doubles run US$188.

Places to Eat

From the local rotisseries to the most exclusive restaurants, Pinamar food is superb but costly. ***Con Estilo Criollo*** *(☎ 490818)*, Av Bunge and Marco Polo, serves great pork and *chivito a la parrilla* (grilled kid goat).

Mamma Liberata, Av Bunge and Simbad el Marino, and ***Club Italiano*** *(☎ 484455)*, Eneas and Cazón, offer tasty pasta. ***Paxapoga*** *(☎ 484985)*, Avs Bunge and Libertador, is a parrilla and pasta place open all year.

German cooking, mostly breads and cakes, can be found at ***Tante*** *(☎ 482735, De las Artes 35)*. ***El Vivero*** *(☎ 495240)*, Avs Bunge and Libertador, is an enormous but high-quality vegetarian restaurant.

For ice cream, there's ***Freddo*** at the corner of Av Bunge and Simbad El Marino.

Getting There & Away

Air Aerolíneas Argentinas (☎ 483663) is at Av Bunge 799, as is Alameda Tur (☎ 481965), the agent for LAPA and Laer. For schedules, see the Villa Gesell entry.

Bus The Terminal de Ómnibus is on Shaw between Del Pejerrey and Del Lenguado. Empresas Antón (☎ 482378) and Río de la Plata (☎ 482247) serve Buenos Aires, as do Expreso Paraná (☎ 485068) and Central Argentino (☎ 482885). Costamar (☎ 482885) connects the beaches.

Train Trains run to Pinamar's Estación Divisadero (☎ 497973) in January and February only. Get tickets to Constitución (Buenos Aires) at the bus terminal.

SAN CLEMENTE DEL TUYÚ

San Clemente del Tuyú (population 9800), 320km southeast of Buenos Aires, is one of 11 localities forming the Partido de la Costa, the closest beach resort area to the capital. Only a few kilometers from Punta Rasa, the southern tip of Bahía Samborombón, its beaches are less attractive than those further south, but its location near Cabo San Antonio puts it on the flyway for migratory birds from as far away as Alaska and Canada.

Punta Rasa's **Estación Biológica de la Fundación Vida Silvestre** is both a good fishing area (for corvina negra) and an interesting area for birders. Ask for information at San Clemente's Oficina de Turismo (☎ 0252-421478), Calle 2 No 2090.

Places to Stay & Eat

Several campgrounds at the entrance to town charge about US$3 per person and US$3 per tent. San Clemente also has a number of reasonably priced, comfortable hotels with high-season prices around US$15 to US$22 per person. ***Hotel Riviera*** *(☎ 421679, Calle 21 No 312)* and ***Hospedaje Quinta Av*** *(☎ 421035, Calle 5 No 1561)* are both good values in this category.

Restaurant Oraya, Calle 1 between Avs 13 and 14, has reasonable prices and an excellent *pollo al ajillo* (garlic chicken). ***La Quebrada***, Calle 1 between Avs 13 and 22, is a cheap, basic family-oriented parrilla. ***Pizzería Gugupa***, Calle 1 No 2426, has tasty pizza.

Getting There & Away

Frequent buses connect San Clemente with Buenos Aires from the Parador de Ómnibus (☎ 421340) at Calle 10 and Av San Martín. There are also buses on down the coast toward Pinamar, Villa Gesell, and Mar del Plata.

NECOCHEA

From Cabo Corrientes in Mar del Plata, car-clogged RN 11 follows dramatic headlands southwest beyond the summer presidential residence at **Chapadmalal** and holiday complexes belonging to different trade unions (a legacy of Peronism) and passing the family resort of **Miramar**, 45km southwest. Another 80km west via RP 88, Necochea (population 79,000) is a tranquil family favorite on the Río Quequén Grande, 500km south of Buenos Aires. Notable for wide, sandy beaches, dunes, and a casino, the town counts many Danes among its permanent population.

Orientation

The south-flowing Quequén Grande divides the city in half. East of the river, all streets are numbered 500 and above; west of the river street numbers run from 2 to the low 100s in the center. Even-numbered streets run parallel to the sea, and odd numbered streets run perpendicular. Bridges at Calle 46 (Yrigoyen) and Calle 10 (Av República Oriental del Uruguay) connect the two areas.

The focus of tourist activity is the regular grid between Av 10 (República Oriental del Uruguay) and the beach, a pedestrian-friendly area surrounded by Parque Provincial Miguel Lillo. Calle 83 (Alfredo Butti) is its main commercial street.

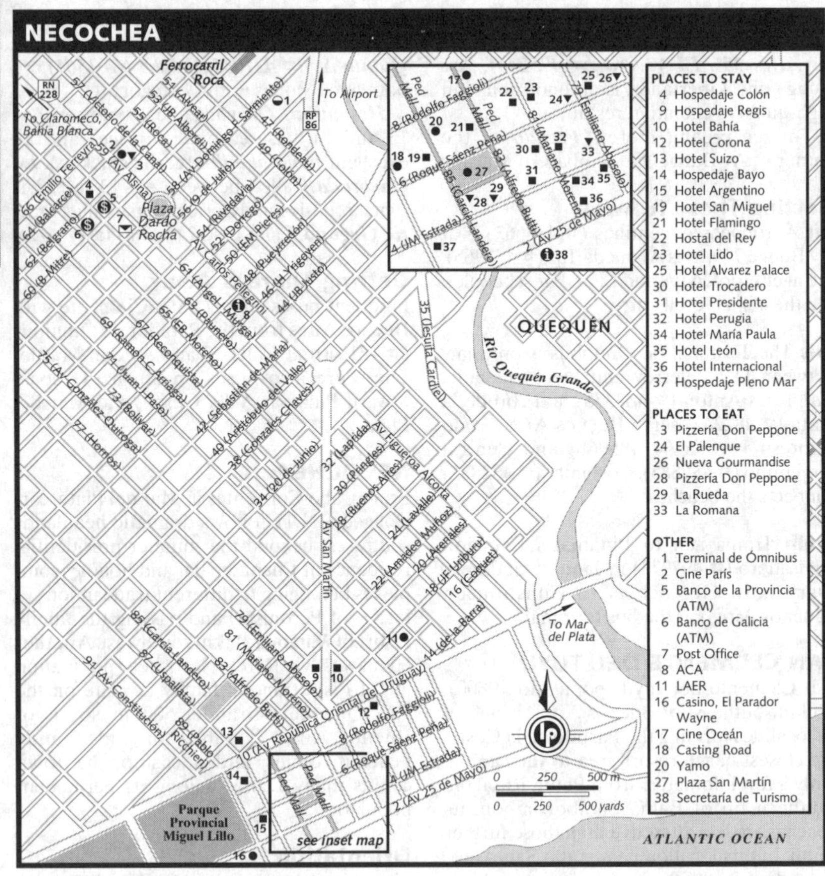

Avenida 59 (Alsina), also RN 228, changes names several times: North of Av 58 (Sarmiento) and Plaza Dardo Rocha, it is Alsina; south of Av 58 it is Av Carlos Pellegrini as far as Diagonal San Martín, where it becomes Av Figueroa Alcorta.

Information

Tourist Offices The Secretaría de Turismo (☎ 425983, 430158), right on the beach at Av 2 (25 de Mayo) and Calle 83 (Butti), is open 8 am to 8 pm daily. ACA (☎ 422106) is at Av 59 No 2073.

Money There are ATMs at Banco de Galicia, Calle 60 (Mitre) 3164, and Banco de la Provincia, Calle 60 (Mitre) 3000.

Post & Communications Correo Argentino is at Av 58 (Sarmiento) and Calle 63 (Paunero); the postal code is 7630. There are several locutorios along Av 59 (Pellegrini) and Av 75 (González Quiroga); Necochea's area code is ☎ 02262.

Medical Services The Hospital Municipal (☎ 422405) is on Av 59 (Alsina) at the northern approach to town, between Calles 100 and 104.

Dangers & Annoyances Sunbathers on the beach have been run over by four-wheel motorcycles.

Things to See & Do

The dense pine woods of **Parque Provincial Miguel Lillo**, a large greenbelt along the beach, are widely used for bicycling, horseback riding, hiking, and picnicking. Publicity brochures assert that the **Casino** is 'irresistible.'

The Río Quequén Grande, rich in rainbow trout and mackerel, also allows for adventurous canoeing, particularly around the falls at Saltos del Quequén. At the village of **Quequén** at the river's mouth, several stranded shipwrecks offer good opportunities for exploration and photography below sculpted cliffs. The **faro** (lighthouse) is another local attraction.

Places to Stay – Budget

Accommodations in Necochea are far more reasonable than in Mar del Plata, Villa Gesell, or Pinamar, but prices can rise above the levels indicated if the tourist season is busy.

Camping In Parque Lillo, ***Camping Americano*** *(☎ 435832)*, at Av 2 and Calle 101, costs around US$5 per person.

Hospedajes & Hotels Most accommodations are close to the beach. The most reasonable are hospedajes in the US$10 per person range, such as ***Hospedaje Regis*** *(☎ 425870, Av San Martín 726)*, ***Hospedaje Bayo*** *(☎ 423334, Calle 87 No 338)*, ***Hospedaje Colón*** *(☎ 424825, Calle 62 No 3034)*, and ***Hospedaje Pleno Mar*** *(☎ 422674, Calle 87 No 250)*.

One-star hotels start around US$12 per person – try the simple but clean and quiet ***Hotel Alvarez Palace*** *(☎ 423667, Av 79 No 304)*. Other possibilities include ***Hotel Lido*** *(☎ 423508, Calle 81 No 328)*, ***Hotel María Paula*** *(☎ 423903, Calle 4 No 3927)*, and ***Hotel Suizo*** *(☎ 424008, Calle 22 No 4235)*.

For US$9 per person with breakfast, large bathrooms, and abundant closet space, cheerful ***Hostal del Rey*** *(☎ 425170, Calle 81 (Moreno))*, between Calles 6 and 8 is an off-season bargain, but would be a good deal even at twice the price in summer.

Places to Stay – Mid-Range

Prices start around US$15 to US$25 per person at the numerous two-star hotels, such as ***Hotel Argentino*** *(☎ 423661, Calle 87 No 293)*, ***Hotel Trocadero*** *(☎ 422589, Calle 81 No 279)*, ***Hotel Flamingo*** *(☎ 420049, Calle 83 No 333)*, and ***Hotel Internacional*** *(☎ 424587, Calle 81 No 232)*.

Places to Stay – Top End

Charging about US$25 to US$30 per person are three-star hotels such as ***Hotel León*** *(☎ 424800, Av 79 No 229)*, ***Hotel Perugia*** *(☎ 422020, Calle 81 No 288)*, ***Hotel San Miguel*** *(☎ 425155, Calle 85 No 301)*, ***Hotel Corona*** *(☎ 422646, Av 75 No 371)*, and ***Hotel Bahía*** *(☎ 423353, Av San Martín 731)*.

Necochea's best, four-star ***Hotel Presidente*** *(☎ 423800, Calle 4 No 4040)* charges US$45 per person.

Places to Eat

La Romana, on Av 79 between Calles 4 and 6, is a great value with tenedor libre pasta for only US$4.50. ***El Palenque***, Av 79 and Calle 6, has good parrillada and reasonable prices.

Pizzería Don Peppone *(☎ 431364)*, on the Peatonal 85 at Av 4, offers good prices, fast service, and excellent quality; there's another branch *(☎ 426390)* at Av 59 No 2828. Popular even in the off-season, ***La Rueda*** *(☎ 421215, Calle 4 No 4144)* serves excellent competitively priced parrillada, seafood, and Italian cuisine.

Entertainment

Cine París *(☎ 422273, Av 59 No 2854)* shows first-run movies. Also try ***Cine Oceán*** *(☎ 435672, Calle 83 No 450)*. There are several downtown dance clubs, including ***Yamo***, on Calle 85 between Calles 6 and 8, ***El Parador Wayne***, at Av 2 and Calle 91, and ***Casting Road***, Calle 87 between 4 and 6.

Getting There & Away

Air Aeropuerto Necochea (☎ 425826), 12km north of town on RP 86, has flights to Buenos Aires' Aeroparque eight times weekly in summer with Laer (☎ 428517, 1556-2792 cellular), Calle 16 No 3428.

Bus The Terminal de Ómnibus (☎ 422470) is on Av 58 (Sarmiento) between Calle 47 (Rondeau) and Av 45 (Jesuita Cardiel), near the river. Both El Cóndor (☎ 422120) and Costera Criolla (☎ 425553) have several buses daily to Buenos Aires ($25, seven hours). Empresa Córdoba Mar del Plata (☎ 422470) serves the interior, and there are often special services by other carriers in summer. El Rápido (☎ 422470) connects Necochea with Mar del Plata, Bariloche, Tandil, and Santa Rosa. Autotransportes San Juan goes three times weekly to San Juan via Santa Rosa.

Train The Ferrocarril Roca (☎ 450028) has trains between nearby Quequén and Constitución (Buenos Aires), via Tandil, three times weekly in each direction.

Southern Buenos Aires Province

In only two parts of Buenos Aires province does granitic bedrock tower above the deep sediments of the Pampas. Trending from northwest to southeast, the low mountain ranges of Tandilia and Ventania disrupt the monotony of the otherwise endlessly flat terrain. The easterly Sierras de Tandil are low, rounded hills whose peaks, not exceeding 500m, take the names of the counties they cross – Olavarría, Azul, Tandil, and Balcarce. The westerly Sierra de la Ventana, its jagged peaks reaching above 1300m in places, is more scenic and attracts hikers and climbers. Between the two ranges is a generally level area that slopes only gradually toward the bluffs and sandy beaches of the Atlantic coast, between Mar del Plata and Claromecó. The area's most important city is the port of Bahía Blanca.

BAHÍA BLANCA

In an early effort to establish military control on the periphery of the Pampas, Colonel Ramón Estomba situated the pompously named Fortaleza Protectora Argentina at the natural harbor of Bahía Blanca in 1828. In 1884 the railway connected the area with Buenos Aires, but another 11 years passed before Bahía Blanca officially became a city.

Only in this century has this port city flourished in commerce and industry, primarily through agriculture and petrochemicals. Its location makes it the southern gateway to Buenos Aires province, as well as the Atlantic outlet for produce from the Río Negro Valley, and the coastal approach to Patagonia.

The presence of the military continues to play a major role – Bahía Blanca is home to Puerto Belgrano, South America's largest naval base, as well as to army and air force bases, and some Argentines consider it the most reactionary, or at least conservative, city in the country. When political pressure forced closure of the ESMA or Naval Mechanics' School, a notorious Buenos Aires torture center during the Proceso, President Carlos Menem ordered its relocation to Bahía Blanca.

On the other hand, while Bahía Blanca is more an important crossroads than a tourist destination per se, the wildly idiosyncratic museum in the suburb of Puerto Ingeniero White is reason enough for a stopover. Bahía Blanca is also home to the prestigious Universidad Nacional del Sur.

Orientation

Bahía Blanca (population 283,000) is located 653km southwest of Buenos Aires via RN 3, 530km east of Neuquén via RN 22, and 278km north of Viedma via RN 3. Plaza Rivadavia is the center of the town's grid. Street names change on either side of the plaza along Av Colón and Hipólito Yrigoyen.

Information

Tourist Offices Bahía Blanca's Oficina de Información Turística (☎ 455-1110), at Alsina 45 across from Plaza Rivadavia, is

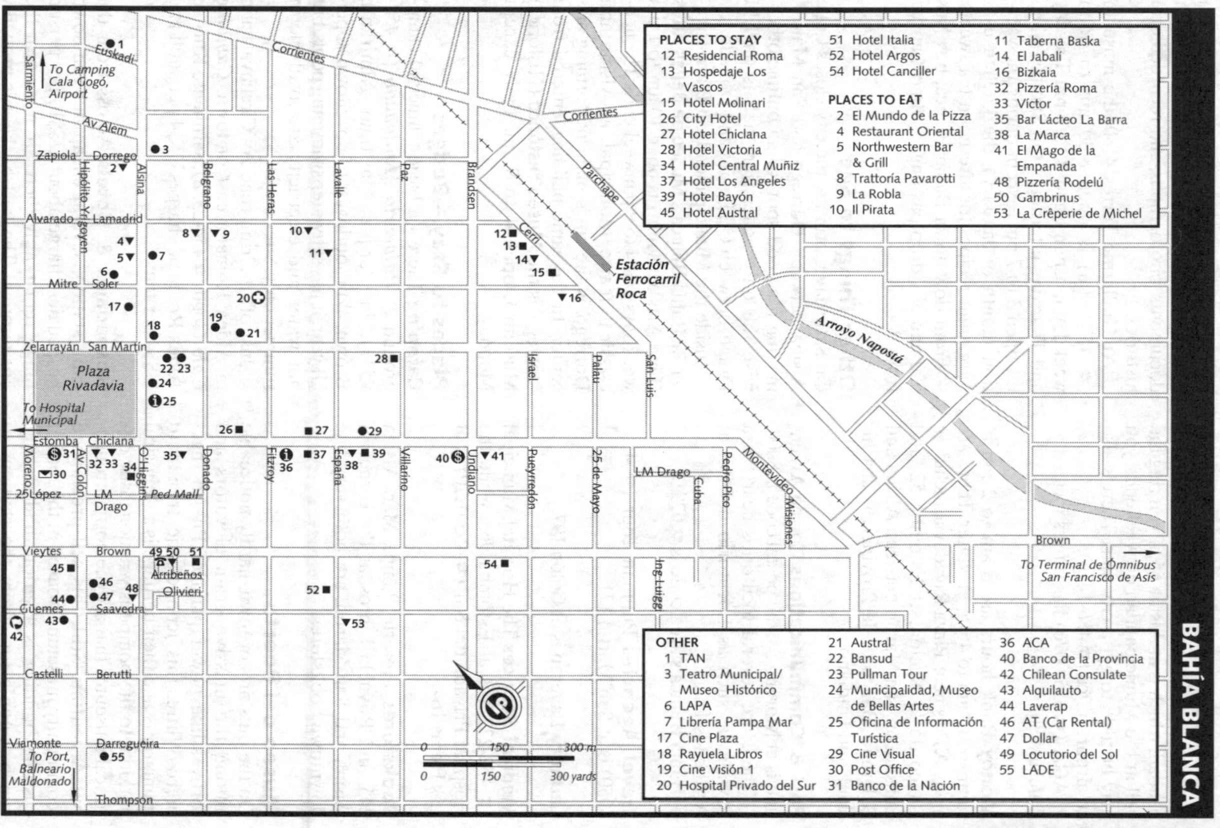
BAHÍA BLANCA
PLACES TO STAY
12 Residencial Roma
13 Hospedaje Los Vascos
15 Hotel Molinari
26 City Hotel
27 Hotel Chiclana
28 Hotel Victoria
34 Hotel Central Muñiz
37 Hotel Los Angeles
39 Hotel Bayón
45 Hotel Austral
51 Hotel Italia
52 Hotel Argos
54 Hotel Canciller
PLACES TO EAT
2 El Mundo de la Pizza
4 Restaurant Oriental
5 Northwestern Bar & Grill
8 Trattoría Pavarotti
9 La Robla
10 Il Pirata
11 Taberna Baska
14 El Jabalí
16 Bizkaia
32 Pizzería Roma
33 Víctor
35 Bar Lácteo La Barra
38 La Marca
41 El Mago de la Empanada
48 Pizzería Rodelú
50 Gambrinus
53 La Crêperie de Michel
OTHER
1 TAN
3 Teatro Municipal/ Museo Histórico
6 LAPA
7 Librería Pampa Mar
17 Cine Plaza
18 Rayuela Libros
19 Cine Visión 1
20 Hospital Privado del Sur
21 Austral
22 Bansud
23 Pullman Tour
24 Municipalidad, Museo de Bellas Artes
25 Oficina de Información Turística
29 Cine Visual
30 Post Office
31 Banco de la Nación
36 ACA
40 Banco de la Provincia
42 Chilean Consulate
43 Alquilauto
44 Laverap
46 AT (Car Rental)
47 Dollar
49 Locutorio del Sol
55 LADE
To Camping Cala Gogó, Airport
To Hospital Municipal
To Port, Balneario Maldonado
To Terminal de Ómnibus San Francisco de Asís
Estación Ferrocarril Roca
Arroyo Napostá
Plaza Rivadavia
Ped Mall
Euskadi
Corrientes
Av Alem
Sarmiento
Zapiola
Dorrego
Alsina
Hipólito Yrigoyen
Alvarado
Lamadrid
Mitre
Soler
Zelarrayán
San Martín
Estomba
Chiclana
Moreno
Av Colón
O'Higgins
López
LM Drago
Vieytes
Brown
Arribeños
Olivieri
Güemes
Saavedra
Castelli
Berutti
Viamonte
Darregueira
Thompson
Belgrano
Las Heras
Lavalle
Paz
Brandsen
Donado
Fitzroy
España
Villarino
Undiano
Pueyrredón
25 de Mayo
Pedro Pico
Cuba
Ing Luiggi
Montevideo
Misiones
Israel
Palau
San Luis
Cerri
Parchape
0 150 300 m
0 150 300 yards

open weekdays 8 am to 1:30 pm, Saturday 10 am to 1 pm. It is next door to the Municipalidad, which is at Alsina 65; if you ring the bell at the Municipalidad on weekends, you may be able to get a city map. There's also an airport office (☎ 486-1456).

ACA (☎ 455-0076) has offices located at Chiclana 305.

Money Bank hours are 8 am to 2 pm in summer, 10 am to 4 pm in winter. There are many ATMs near Plaza Rivadavia, including Banco de la Nación, at Estomba 52, and Bansud, on San Martín between Alsina and Belgrano. Banco de la Provincia is at Chiclana and Undiano.

Post & Communications Correo Argentino is at Moreno 34; the postal code is 8000.

There are several locutorios near Plaza Rivadavia, such as Locutorio del Sol at Arribeños 112.

Bahía Blanca's area code is ☎ 0291.

Travel Agencies Pullman Tour (☎ 455-4950) is at San Martín 171.

Laundry Laverap is at Colón 197.

Medical Services The Hospital Municipal (☎ 452-2222) is at Estomba 968, while the Hospital Privado del Sur (☎ 455-0270) is at Las Heras 164.

Bookstores Librería Pampa Mar, Alsina 245, and Rayuela Libros, at the corner of Alsina and San Martín, are both very fine downtown bookstores.

Museo del Puerto

On the outskirts of town, hardly noticeable among the massive grain elevators and fortress-like power plant of Puerto Ingeniero White, this iconoclastic tribute to immigrants and their heritage is a whimsical antidote to the pompously nationalistic historical museums that are the norm throughout Argentina. Still, this self-proclaimed 'community museum,' housed in the former customs building, is a serious undertaking, run by people for whom the rhythms of everyday life are more significant than San Martín's birthday. It includes an archive with documents, photographs, and recorded oral histories.

At Guillermo Torres 4180, the museum (☎ 457-3006) is open 8:30 am to noon weekday mornings and 4 to 7 pm Tuesday and Thursday afternoon. On Sunday, when it's open 3 to 7 pm (except during the vacation month of January), the kitchen uses immigrant recipes for afternoon tea sweets.

From downtown Bahía Blanca, bus Nos 500 and 501 drop passengers almost at the front door.

Other Things to See

On Saturday mornings, the city closes Calle Alsina between Dorrego and San Martín, making it a good spot for an outing; otherwise the only pedestrian mall is on LM Drago, between O'Higgins and Donado.

Inside the Municipalidad, on Plaza Rivadavia, Bahía Blanca's **Museo de Bellas Artes** (Fine Arts Museum) is open 10 am to 1 pm weekdays and 4 to 8 pm weekends. The neoclassical **Teatro Municipal**, at Alsina and Dorrego, is the city's main performing arts center. In the same building, entered from Dorrego, is the **Museo Histórico** (Historical Museum), open 4 to 9 pm daily except Monday.

Places to Stay – Budget

Camping There's a basic municipal campground at ***Balneario Maldonado*** *(☎ 452-9511)*, in Parque Marítimo Almirante Brown, 4km southwest of downtown. Open all year, it has saltwater swimming pools, but hot water and electricity are available in summer only. Sites are US$5.

Just off the ring road Av Circunvalación in Aldea Romana east of town, ***Camping Cala Gogó*** *(☎ 454-2388)*, Sarmiento Km 4 in Aldea Romana, charges US$4 per adult and US$4 per tent.

Hospedajes & Hotels Across from the train station, several cheap but run-down hospedajes charge about US$10 per person range; remarkably, there are none near the bus terminal. The best of these is probably simple but clean and friendly ***Residencial Roma*** *(☎ 453-8500, Cerri 759)*. There's also ***Hotel Molinari*** *(☎ 452-2871, Cerri 717)* and ***Hospedaje Los Vascos*** *(☎ 452-9290, Cerri 747)*. Four blocks away is ***Hotel Victoria*** *(☎ 452-0522, General Paz 84)*.

On Chiclana, closer to Plaza Rivadavia, accommodations are better and slightly pricier. ***Hotel Bayón*** *(☎ 452-2504, Chiclana 487)*, charges about US$12/22 single/double with shared bath, US$16/28 with private bath. Comparable ***Hotel Los Angeles***, Chiclana 367, is very clean.

Places to Stay – Mid-range

Though undistinguished, friendly ***Hotel Canciller*** *(☎ 453-8270, Brown 667)* has small but spotless singles with phone, parking, cable TV, and breakfast for US$20 with shared bath, US$30 with private bath. At ***City Hotel*** *(☎ 453-0176, Chiclana 228)* rates start at US$27/36 and rise to US$34/42 for rooms with TV, telephone, air-con, and private bath.

Friendly ***Hotel Central Muñiz*** *(☎ 456-0060, O'Higgins 23)* has rooms with private bath starting at US$32/43. ***Hotel Chiclana*** *(☎ 453-0436, Chiclana 370)* costs US$33/40 with breakfast and TV. Pleasant ***Hotel Italia*** *(☎ 456-2700, Brown 181)* has nice rooms with bath for US$40/50 and a good restaurant on the premises.

Places to Stay – Top End

Prices and standards are similar at Bahía Blanca's three-star, top-end hotels. ***Hotel Austral*** *(☎ 456-1700, Av Colón 159)* has comfortable rooms with TV and telephone ranging from US$55/62 to US$89/95. The comparable ***Hotel Argos*** *(☎ 455-0404, España 149)* is slightly cheaper.

Places to Eat

At breakfast, try ***Bar Lácteo La Barra*** *(Chiclana 155)* for fresh juices and tasty grilled sandwiches. For take-out empanadas, there's ***El Mago de la Empanada*** *(☎ 456-5393)*, on Undiano near Chiclana.

Food is plain but abundant and inexpensive at ***El Jabalí*** *(☎ 452-8463, Av Cerri 757)*. There are many parrillas, including ***Víctor*** *(☎ 452-3814, Chiclana 83)*, which also serves seafood, and ***La Marca*** *(☎ 456-3807, Chiclana 417)*. Try also the ***Northwestern Bar & Grill*** *(Alsina 240)*.

Plaza Rivadavia features modest eateries like ***Pizzería Roma*** *(☎ 452-8306, Chiclana 17)*. Other good pizzerias include ***El Mundo de la Pizza*** *(☎ 454-5054, Dorrego 55)*, ***Il Pirata*** *(Lamadrid 360)*, and ***Pizzería Rodelú*** *(☎ 455-1332)*, at O'Higgins and Saavedra.

A local institution for more than a century, ***Gambrinus*** *(☎ 452-2380, Arribeños 164)* is a *chopperia* (a beer joint with food) with lively atmosphere, friendly service, and some imaginative dishes (try chicken in corn-and-artichoke sauce). Moderately priced ***Trattoria Pavarotti*** *(☎ 451-4874, Belgrano 272)* is another good choice, serving varied three-course lunches for US$8; the service seems faster for those ordering a la carte.

Taberna Baska *(☎ 452-1788, Lavalle 284)* serves appetizing, reasonably priced Spanish food. ***Restaurant Oriental***, Alsina 280, is a Chinese tenedor libre charging US$7. Local residents also recommend ***La Robla*** *(☎ 455-1307, Belgrano 251)* and ***Bizkaia*** *(☎ 452-0191, Soler 769)*, near Av Cerri. French-run ***La Crêperie de Michel*** *(☎ 454-0725, España 220)* has an excellent reputation.

Entertainment

For first-run movies, check out ***Cine Visual*** *(☎ 451-8503, Chiclana 452)*, ***Cine Plaza*** *(☎ 453-3289, Alsina 166)*, or ***Cine Visión 1*** *(Belgrano 137)*.

Shopping

On weekends there's a *feria de artesanos* (artisans' market) on Plaza Rivadavia, opposite the Municipalidad.

Getting There & Away

Air Austral (☎ 451-9938, 486-0299), San Martín 298, has three flights to Buenos Aires (US$124) on weekdays, two on weekends, and it serves Santa Rosa (US$78) daily except Saturday.

LAPA (☎ 456-4522), Soler 68, flies twice daily to Buenos Aires' Aeroparque (US$39 to US$105) except Sunday (one flight) and daily to Río Gallegos (US$97 to US$163) and Río Grande (US$125 to US$207). TAN (☎ 451-1305), Euskadi 46, flies six times weekly to Neuquén (US$50 to US$63) and Sunday to Bariloche (US$100 to US$114).

LADE (☎ 452-1063), Darregueira 21, flies Thursday to Viedma (US$25), Neuquén (US$41), San Martín de los Andes (US$78), and Bariloche (US$81), and Friday to Viedma, Puerto Madryn (US$50), and Trelew (US$57).

Bus A key transport node for southern Buenos Aires province and points south, Bahía Blanca's Terminal de Ómnibus San Francisco de Asís (☎ 481-8121), Brown 1700, is about 2km east of Plaza Rivadavia.

Costera Criolla (☎ 452-1075), La Estrella (☎ 481-4846), Plusmar (☎ 481-9556), TAC (☎ 481-9626), Centenario (☎ 481-9660), Jetcar (☎ 482-1558), Ñandú del Sur (☎ 481-8888), and El Cóndor (☎ 482-4846) serve Buenos Aires many times daily. La Estrella also goes to La Plata and Comodoro Rivadavia, and daily except Saturday at 6 am and 8:40 pm to Sierra de la Ventana. Expreso Cabildo (☎ 481-7363) goes to Sierra de la Ventana weekdays at 8:20 pm and Saturday and 1:30 pm.

Pampa (☎ 424121) goes to Necochea and Mar del Plata. Río Paraná (☎ 482-1306) goes to Tandil, La Plata, Buenos Aires, and northern destinations.

TUP (☎ 432140) and TUS (☎ 481-7177) have buses to Córdoba. Andesmar (☎ 481-5462) runs extensive routes toward Cuyo (connecting to Chile) and Patagonia. Ticsa (☎ 481-6303) serves San Luis and San Juan daily, as does Autotransportes San Juan.

Via Bariloche/El Valle (☎ 482-0134) travels to Neuquén and Zapala in Patagonia, via the Río Negro valley, four times daily, and to San Martín de los Andes and Bariloche. La Acción (☎ 482-6152) goes to Buenos Aires, Viedma, and Neuquén. La Unión del Sud (☎ 482-1012) goes to Buenos Aires, Zapala, and Neuquén. Centenario also goes to Zapala and Neuquén, with connections to southern Chile. TAC also goes to Bariloche.

Don Otto (☎ 481-8585) has buses to coastal Patagonian cities daily at 8 am, and to Río Gallegos on Wednesday. La Puntual (☎ 482-1146) goes as far as Comodoro Rivadavia, also stopping in Viedma, Puerto Madryn, and Trelew. El Pingüino goes to Río Gallegos and intermediates.

Sample fares and times include Mar del Plata (US$21, seven hours), La Plata (US$23, nine hours), Buenos Aires (US$25, 10 hours), Neuquén (US$30, 10 hours), Bariloche (US$41, 14 hours), Trelew (US$42, 12 hours), Comodoro Rivadavia (US$47, 15 hours), and Río Gallegos (26 hours, US$78).

Train From the once-grand but now rundown Estación Ferrocarril Roca (☎ 452-1168), Av Cerri 750, Ferrobaires goes to Constitución Monday, Wednesday, Friday, and Saturday at 7:35 pm (via Lamadrid); and Tuesday, Thursday, and Sunday at 8 pm (via Pringles). Fares are US$15 turista, US$17 primera, US$22 Pullman, and US$30 coche cama.

Getting Around

To/From the Airport Aeropuerto Comandante Espora (☎ 452-1665) is 15km east of town on the naval base, RN 3 Norte Km 674. Austral provides its own transport (US$3) to the airport.

Bus Local buses cost US$0.70; buy magnetic cards from kiosks. Bus Nos 505, 512, 514, 516, and 517 serve the terminal from downtown. Bus No 505 goes out Av Colón to Balneario Maldonado.

Car Try AT (☎ 454-3944), at Colón 180; Alquilauto (☎ 452-4444), at Güemes 14; or Dollar (☎ 456-2526), at Colón 194.

SIERRA DE LA VENTANA

Just north of Bahía Blanca, this charming, slow-paced village, resembling the Sierras de Córdoba, is popular with Argentines but underappreciated by foreigners. Its more conventional facilities include a casino, golf links, and swimming pools, but it also offers hiking, climbing, riding, bicycling, kayaking, and fishing. There are comfortable, if

DAVID R FRAZIER

Buenos Aires parrilla

ROBERT FRERCK

Mate break, La Pampa province

SYLVIA STEVENS

Quechua woman at market in northwestern Argentina

WAYNE BERNHARDSON

La Plata's cathedral, Buenos Aires province

WAYNE BERNHARDSON

Ruins, San Ignacio Miní, Misiones province

WAYNE BERNHARDSON

La República de los Niños, Buenos Aires province

limited, accommodations and good food (don't overlook the local chocolates).

Orientation

Sierra de la Ventana refers both to the mountain range and to this town, 125km north of Bahía Blanca via RN 33 to Tornquist, and then RP 76. It is 602km from Buenos Aires via RN 3 to Azul, RN 226 to Olavarría, and RP 76.

The Río Sauce Grande divides the village into two sectors: Sierra de la Ventana proper (Villa Tivoli), with government offices and businesses, and the residential barrio of Villa Arcadia. Av San Martín is the main street, with most services near the train station.

Information

Tourist Offices Alongside the train station at Roca 15, the Oficina de Turismo y Delegación Municipal (☎ 491-5303) has a useful packet of maps and flyers. It's open daily 8 am to 8 pm, 7 am to 1 pm and 3 to 9 pm in summer.

Money Banco de la Provincia, San Martín 260, has no ATM.

Post & Communications Correo Argentino is at Av Roca and Alberdi; the postal code is 8168. Locutorio Televentana is at Av San Martín 291; the area code is ☎ 0291.

Laundry Laverap is on Güemes near San Martín.

Places to Stay – Budget

Camping There are several free ***campsites*** along the Río Sauce Grande, with access to toilets and showers at the nearby municipal swimming pool (US$2.50). If you prefer an organized campground, try ***Camping El Paraíso*** *(☎ 491-5299)*, on Diego Meyer, which has good facilities for US$5 per adult, US$2 per child.

Hostel In Villa Arcadia, at the east end of Coronel Suárez, the ***Ymcapolis*** *(☎ 491-5004)* provides hostel accommodations in a stylish old building for US$10 per person.

Hospedajes & Hotels Sierra de la Ventana's moderately priced accommodations include ***Hospedaje La Perlita*** *(☎ 491-5020)*, Islas Malvinas and Pasaje 3, charging

US$15 per person. For the same price, ***Hotel Anay-Ruca*** *(☎ 491-5191)*, E Rayes and Punta Alta in Villa Arcadia, includes breakfast.

Places to Stay – Mid-Range

ACA's ***Motel Maitén*** *(☎ 491-5073, Iguazú 93)*, at Mercedes, is good value at US$19 per person for members and US$23 for nonmembers; rates include breakfast. ***Residencial Carlitos*** *(☎ 491-5011)*, at Coronel Suárez and Punta Alta in Villa Arcadia, costs US$21 per person with breakfast. ***Hotel Atero*** *(☎ 491-5002)*, Av San Martín and Güemes, has singles for US$23 including breakfast.

Hotel Pillahuinco *(☎ 491-5024)*, on Rayes between Punta Alta and Pillahuinco in Villa Arcadia, has rooms for US$27/50 single/double with breakfast; other meals are also available.

Places to Stay – Top End

Hotel Silver Golf *(☎ 491-5079)*, at Barrio Parque Golf, costs US$30 with half-board. The most expensive accommodations are at ***Hotel Provincial*** *(☎ 491-5025)*, on Drago between Bahía Blanca and Islas Malvinas, which charges US$65/110 with half-board.

Places to Eat

Besides hotel restaurants, try ***Posada La Espadaña***, on RP 76 (1km from the village), and ***Rali-Hue***, a parrilla on Av San Martín between Bahía Blanca and Islas Malvinas. ***Ser*** *(☎ 491-5055)*, on Güemes just off the main drag, has large portions of good pizza and pasta, but drinks are expensive. ***El Establo***, on San Martín between Islas Malvinas and Av Roca, is a decent pizzeria that also serves fixed-price lunches.

Getting There & Away

Sierra de la Ventana's modest Terminal de Ómnibus (☎ 491-5091) is at Av Roca 80. La Estrella has nightly buses to Buenos Aires (US$25, 7½ hours) at 10:30 pm and an 8 am service to La Plata. Expreso Cabildo runs buses to Bahía Blanca, via Tornquist, at 6:45 am and 7 pm daily.

Getting Around

Expreso de la Sierra (☎ 491-5180) runs twice daily between Sierra de la Ventana and Tornquist, stopping at Saldungaray, Villa Ventana, and Abra de la Ventana. Weekday departures are at 6:45 am and 4:30 pm, weekend departures at 8:30 am and 4 pm. Returns from Tornquist are at 12:30 and 7:30 pm daily.

AROUND SIERRA DE LA VENTANA

For activities in and around Sierra de la Ventana, including trekking and climbing, contact Geoturs (☎ 491-5355), Av San Martín 193, which organizes hikes of Cerro Tres Picos and other excursions.

Cerro Tres Picos

The 1239m Cerro Tres Picos, 7km northwest of Sierra de la Ventana, is a fine choice for a backpack trip. Since this is the private property of Estancia Cerros Colorados, there is a US$4 admission charge. Those making a day hike must begin by 9 am; overnighters can start as late as 2 pm.

Villa Ventana

About 17km northwest of Sierra de la Ventana, this genial village offers shady lanes, a riverside balneario with a municipal campground, and an excellent teahouse, El Rincón de la Villa (☎ 02919-410111), which alone justifies a stop if you're nearby.

Parque Provincial Ernesto Tornquist

Imposing wrought-iron gates mark the entrance to this scenic 6700-hectare park, which once belonged to the Tornquists, a banking family that donated the lands to the province. Its high point is the two-hour hike to 1136m **Cerro de la Ventana**, which offers dramatic views of surrounding hills and the distant Pampas. Other worthwhile sights are the Indian caves at **Las Cuevas del Toro de Corpus Cristi** and the gorge at **Garganta Olvidada**.

From 8 am to 6 pm, rangers in the trailer at the Cerro de la Ventana trailhead collect a US$1 entry fee and routinely deny permission to climb after 1 pm on this occasionally steep, but short, well-marked, and otherwise easy hike. Insistent hikers can get permission by signing a waiver; in fact, a later start is better because you'll have the view to yourself instead of sharing it with dozens of porteño tobacco addicts who manage to huff and puff their way to the crest of what is probably the country's most-climbed peak (some might find it easier if they left their spray paint cans behind).

At the main entrance, there's an informative **Centro de Visitantes** (☎ 02919-410039), open 8 am to 1 pm and 2 to 6:30 pm daily, with a well-organized display on local ecology enhanced by audiovisuals. The **Corral de Recrías** contains local fauna, mostly deer and guanaco, and there's also a forestry station. In summer there are five-hour ranger-guided walks to the gorge at **Garganta del Diablo** (Devil's Throat) daily except Tuesday and Thursday at 9 am.

At the Cerro de la Ventana trailhead, the friendly ***Campamento Base*** *(☎ 02919-410067)* has shaded campsites, with clean baths and excellent hot showers for US$5 per person. ***Hotel El Mirador*** *(☎ 02919-441338)*, on RP 76 near Cerro de la Ventana, has singles/doubles at US$30/49 with breakfast.

TANDIL

On a plain nearly enveloped by a horseshoe-shaped range of hills, the city of Tandil arose from Fuerte Independencia, a military outpost established in 1823 by Martín Rodríguez. In the early 1870s, one of the most notorious incidents in provincial history began here when a group of renegade gauchos, followers of the eccentric healer Gerónimo de Solané (popularly known as Tata Dios) gathered at nearby Cerro La Movediza to distribute weapons before going on a murderous rampage against European settlers and recent immigrants. A few years later, Francisco Fernández dramatized the incident in his play *Solané*.

Today Tandil (population 96,500) offers services for an important agricultural and dairy zone and is a center for manufacturing cement and limestone, but it's probably also the most scenically diverse city in the Pampas, and a hub for climbing and mountain biking. It traditionally attracts masses of visitors at Easter to see Calvario, a hill ostensibly resembling the site of Christ's crucifixion at Golgotha, but the town's cobbled downtown streets and leisurely pace lend it charm at any season. The Universidad del Centro de la Provincia de Buenos Aires is known for its agronomy and computer science departments.

Orientation

Tandil is 384km south of Buenos Aires via RN 3 and RN 226, and 170km northwest of Mar del Plata via RN 226. The downtown area is bounded by Avs Rivadavia to the west, Avellaneda to the south, Buzón to the east, and del Valle to the north. Street names change at the intersections of Avellaneda/Estrada and Rivadavia/Dorrego. The main commercial streets are Rodríguez and 9 de Julio, while the principal center of social activity is Plaza Independencia, a two-block area bounded by Rodríguez, Belgrano, Chacabuco, and Pinto.

Information

Tourist Offices The Dirección Municipal de Turismo (☎ 432073), 9 de Julio 555, distributes a good city map and useful brochures.

ACA (☎ 425463) is at Rodríguez 399.

Post & Communications Correo Argentino is at 9 de Julio 455; Tandil's postal code is 7000. The most central locutorio is Telefónica Centro, 9 de Julio 898.

The area code is ☎ 02293.

Travel Agencies Drop by Barbini Turismo (☎ 428612), Maipú 1375, to arrange tours and activities in and around Tandil.

Medical Services Hospital Municipal Ramón Santamarina (☎ 422010) is at Paz 406.

Things to See & Do

Tandil's historic **Museo Tradicionalista Fuerte Independencia**, 4 de Abril 845, is open Tuesday to Sunday 4 to 8 pm. The **Museo de Bellas Artes**, Chacabuco 367, is open Tuesday to Sunday 5 to 8 pm.

The easy walk to **Parque Independencia** from the southwestern edge of downtown offers good views of the city, particularly at night. The **Dique del Fuerte**, only 12 blocks south of Plaza Independencia, is a huge reservoir where the Balneario Municipal operates three swimming pools.

At the north edge of town, where Tata Dios gathered his supporters over a century ago, a 300-ton boulder teetered precariously atop **Cerro La Movediza** for many years before falling, and the site still attracts visitors. Take bus No 503 (blue).

Places to Stay

Camping On Av San Gabriel, beyond the Dique del Fuerte, clean, shady ***Camping Municipal Pinar de la Sierra*** *(☎ 425370)* charges US$8 per site (up to four people) and has a grocery and hot showers. Some but not all No 500 (yellow) buses go there – ask the driver.

Hospedajes & Hotels Friendly, modest, and tidy ***Hotel Kaikú*** *(☎ 423114, Mitre 902)* is good value at US$10/14 single/double with breakfast. Basic ***Hotel Cristal*** *(☎ 443970, Rodríguez 871)* is also cheap at US$10 per person. The congenial ***Hospedaje Savoy*** *(☎ 425602)*, an old-fashioned family hotel at Alem and Mitre, has a confitería for breakfast or snacks; rates are US$12/20 for rooms with private bath.

Hotel Austral *(☎ 425606, 9 de Julio 725)* charges US$25 per person with private bath and breakfast. Across from Plaza Independencia, the very pleasant ***Plaza Hotel*** *(☎ 427160, General Pinto 438)* costs US$70/90 with breakfast; its confitería serves the best coffee in town.

The lone gaucho.

Places to Eat

Probably the cheapest place to eat is the ***Comedor Universitario***, a student diner in a stone house at the corner of Maipú and Fuerte Independencia, just south of Plaza Independencia.

For tasty *pollo a la piedra* (grilled chicken) try ***El Nuevo Don José*** *(☎ 424970, Monseñor De Andrea 269)*. ***El Estribo*** *(☎ 425943, San Martín 750)* has savory pork. At ***La Farola***, Pinto 680, the dish to order is *pejerrey*, a tasty mackerel. For parrillada, go to the ***Grill Argentino*** *(☎ 448666, Rodríguez 552)*. The restaurant at ***Plaza Hotel*** (see Places to Stay) is also highly regarded.

Shopping

La Yunta (☎ 437255), Sarmiento 613, stocks an impressive selection of horsegear, leather goods, and other gaucho souvenirs.

Getting There & Away

Air Laer (☎ 429213), Hipólito Yrigoyen 714, flies six times weekly to Aeroparque in Buenos Aires and to Necochea.

Bus Tandil's Terminal de Ómnibus (☎ 425585), Av Buzón and Portugal, has an on-site casino. La Estrella (☎ 426018) and Río Paraná (☎ 424812) go to Buenos Aires three times daily. Río Paraná also goes to coastal destinations from Bahía Blanca to Pinamar and Villa Gesell.

El Rápido (☎ 442780) travels to Mar del Plata every two hours, and also heads west to Santa Rosa, La Pampa. Costera Criolla (☎ 425970) goes to La Plata and Buenos Aires; Pampa (☎ 424249) goes to La Plata and Necochea.

TAC (☎ 425275) serves the west to Mendoza, as does Autotransportes San Juan, in the same office, which continues the city of San Juan. Others in the same office include Tirsa to Rosario and Expreso Córdoba-Mar del Plata. Empresa Jocolí

(☎ 424249) provides additional services between Mendoza and Mar del Plata.

Getting Around

Bus Tandil's excellent public transportation system reaches every important sight. Bus No 500 (yellow) goes to Dique del Fuerte and the municipal campground. No 501 (red) goes to the bus terminal, and No 503 (blue) goes to Cerro La Movediza, the university, and the bus terminal.

Car Localiza (☎ 434002) is at Av España 555.

AROUND TANDIL

Estancia Acelain

Built in 1924 with local stone, the opulent casco of Hispanophile writer Enrique Larreta features furnishings and ornaments, which, following Larreta's love for the old country, were brought from Spain. Surrounded by dense woods, the estancia also features a natural lagoon with good mackerel fishing.

Larreta (1875-1961), whose erudite historical novels made him famous, used Acelain as a country retreat from his Buenos Aires house in the barrio of Belgrano; the house is now a museum. The chapel has stained-glass windows imported from Germany.

One of many wealthy estancias in Buenos Aires province, Estancia Acelain (☎ 0293-420064), reached from RN 226 Km 205 between Tandil and Azul, is open to the public.

Santa Fe Province

Along with Buenos Aires province to the south, Santa Fe is the heartland of the Humid Pampas, an agricultural area of phenomenal fertility, even though its northernmost areas are part of the drier, less-fertile Chaco. Many groups of Indians, including the Toba and Mocoví, resisted and disrupted early Spanish settlements here.

Marginal during colonial times, Santa Fe grew dramatically after independence, especially with expansion of the railroads. Unlike the province of Entre Ríos, a virtual island on the opposite bank of the Paraná, Santa Fe benefited from better overland communications to Buenos Aires and the cities to the north and northwest.

Although caudillos like Estanislao López and other large estancieros controlled the province, they put up minimal resistance to small farmers because Indians deterred the expansion of the estancias. Landowners believed agricultural colonization would benefit them by reducing both the Indian threat and their burden of taxes. In the second half of the 19th century, according to historian David Rock, land under cultivation increased from almost nil to 1.5 million hectares, mostly in family farms, a dramatic contrast to the latifundios of Buenos Aires province.

Agricultural expansion spurred the growth of Rosario, a port city that soon surpassed the provincial capital of Santa Fe in size and importance. In southern Santa Fe, wheat cultivation helped double the province's population between 1895 and the outbreak of WWI. As the industrial and agricultural significance of Córdoba grew, so did that of Rosario, Córdoba's link to overseas.

About 4000 Mocoví Indians remain dispersed throughout the province. The largest concentration is in Recreo, a small village of sharecroppers and artisans 17km north of Santa Fe, but there are additional communities in Helvecia and San Javier, to the northeast of Santa Fe.

SANTA FE

In 1573 Juan de Garay, on an expedition from Asunción, founded Santa Fe de la Vera Cruz on the Río San Javier, a secondary tributary of the Paraná. In the mid-17th century, though, the Spaniards wearied of constant Indian raids, floods, and isolation, so the local *cabildo* (town council) moved the city, stock and block, southward to its present site near the confluence of the Río Salado and the main channel of the Paraná. Although the city was rebuilt on the exact urban plan of abandoned Santa Fe La Vieja, a neo-Parisian building boom in the 19th century and more recent construction have

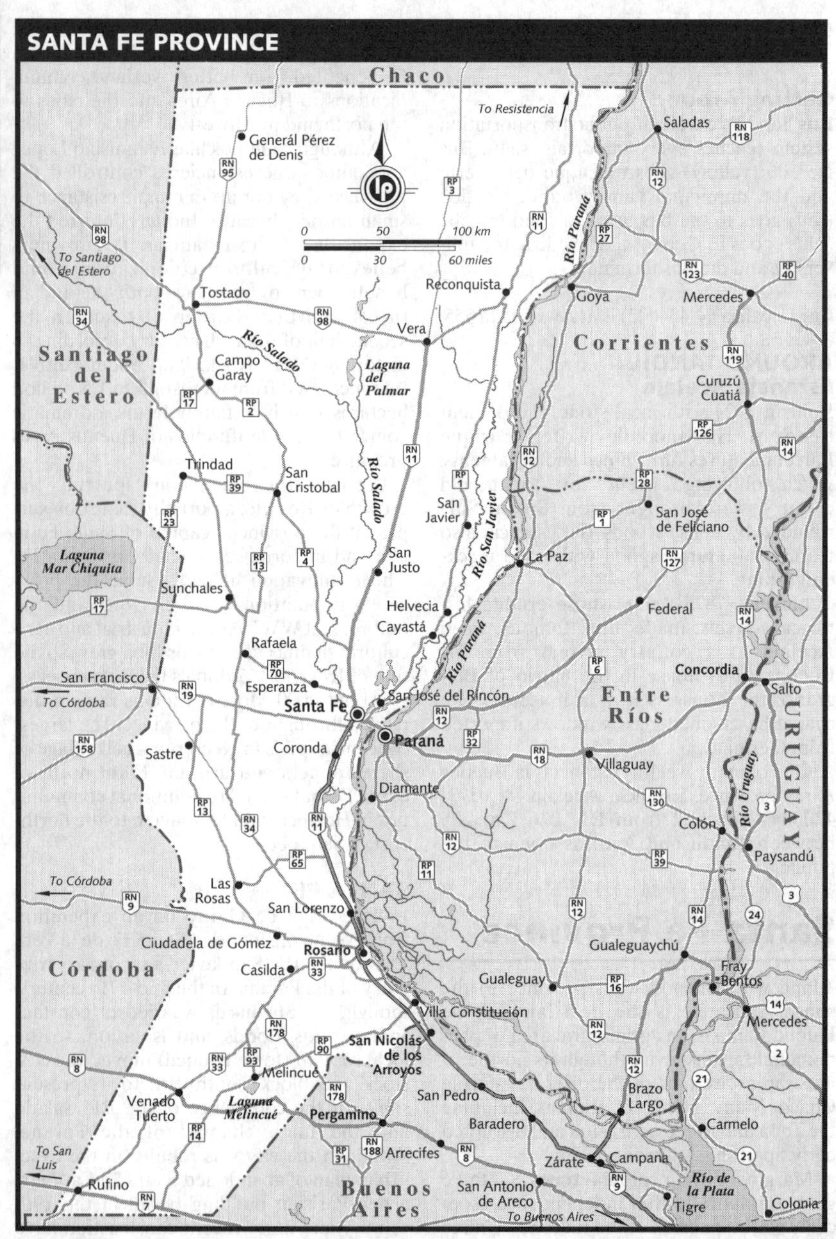
SANTA FE PROVINCE
Chaco
To Resistencia
Saladas
Generál Pérez de Denis
0 50 100 km
0 30 60 miles
To Santiago del Estero
Reconquista
Goya
Mercedes
Tostado
Vera
Río Salado
Laguna del Palmar
Corrientes
Santiago del Estero
Campo Garay
Curuzú Cuatiá
Río Paraná
Trindad
San Cristobal
Río Salado
San Javier
Río San Javier
San José de Feliciano
Laguna Mar Chiquita
San Justo
La Paz
Sunchales
Helvecia
Federal
Cayastá
Rafaela
Río Paraná
Concordia
San Francisco
Esperanza
San José del Rincón
Salto
To Córdoba
Santa Fe
Entre Ríos
URUGUAY
Paraná
Sastre
Coronda
Villaguay
Diamante
Río Uruguay
Colón
Paysandú
To Córdoba
Las Rosas
San Lorenzo
Ciudadela de Gómez
Gualeguaychú
Rosario
Córdoba
Casilda
Gualeguay
Fray Bentos
Villa Constitución
Mercedes
San Nicolás de los Arroyos
Melincué
Venado Tuerto
Laguna Melincué
San Pedro
Brazo Largo
Pergamino
Baradero
Carmelo
To San Luis
Arrecifes
Zárate
Campana
Río de la Plata
Rufino
Buenos Aires
San Antonio de Areco
To Buenos Aires
Tigre
Colonia

left only isolated colonial buildings. Those that remain are well worth seeing.

Although still capital of its province, Santa Fe's population of about 385,000 leaves it second in economic power to burgeoning Rosario. Still, the capital is an important agro-industrial center for shipping and processing regional produce, and building and distributing farm machinery.

Upstream river events dramatically affect the city. In 1964 Laguna Setúbal desiccated because of drought in the upper Paraná basin; in 1983 the river rose to 9.2m, well above its stable level of 4.2m, and destroyed the bridge that connected the city with El Rincón and Paraná, across the river in Entre Ríos. A new bridge links these areas, but the twisted Puente Colgante (Hanging Bridge) testifies to the river's power.

Beyond the city, the river has fostered a little-known but intriguing way of life among the people of 'suburban' villages, such as Alto Verde. When the river rises, these fisherfolk evacuate their houses for temporary refuge in the city, but when the floods recede they rebuild their houses on the same spot. The *baqueanos* (backcountry trackers) of the islands know the marshes and dense forests of the middle Paraná as well as porteños know the corner of Florida and Corrientes.

Orientation

Tributaries of the Paraná surround Santa Fe, but the main channel flows about 10km east. An access canal connects the port of Santa Fe with the Río Colastiné and the Paraná. The Río Salado meanders to the west, while Laguna Setúbal, a wide, shallow section of the Río Saladillo, borders it on the east.

RN 11 links Santa Fe with Rosario (167km) and Buenos Aires (475km) to the south and with Resistencia (544km) and Asunción, Paraguay, to the north. Between Rosario and Santa Fe, the faster *autopista* (freeway) A-008 parallels the ordinary route. To the east, RN 168 connects Santa Fe with its twin city of Paraná (25km), Entre Ríos province, although the Uranga Sylvestre Begnis tunnel beneath the main channel of the Paraná is maintained by both provinces.

All of the city's remaining colonial buildings are within a short walk of Plaza 25 de Mayo, the town's functional center. Avenida San Martín, north of the plaza, is the major commercial street; between Juan de Garay and Eva Perón, it's an attractive *peatonal* (pedestrian mall).

Information

Tourist Offices In the bus terminal at Belgrano 2910, Santa Fe's motivated, well-informed Dirección Municipal de Turismo (☎ 457-4123) has loads of brochures and detailed information in loose-leaf binders. It's open daily 7 am to 1 pm and 2 to 8 pm.

At the southern highway approach to town, the Boca del Tigre office (☎ 457-1812) is open weekdays 7 am to 1 pm and 2 to 8 pm, Saturday 8 am to 8 pm. The office at the Paseo del Restaurador (☎ 457-1881), north of downtown at Blvd Zavalla and JJ Paso, keeps the same hours.

ACA (☎ 455-3862) is at Av Rivadavia 3101, near Suipacha, with a second branch (☎ 455-4142) at Pellegrini and Av San Martín.

Money Tourfe, San Martín 2500, collects 3% commission on traveler's checks. Several ATMs are along the San Martín peatonal.

Post & Communications Correo Argentino is at Av 27 de Febrero 2331, near Mendoza; the postal code is 3000. Telecom long-distance telephone services are upstairs at the bus terminal.

Santa Fe's area code is ☎ 0242.

Travel Agencies Vacaciones Felices (☎ 456-1608), Mendoza 2615, is the local AmEx representative.

Bookstores Librería Colmegna, San Martín 2546, has a good selection of Argentine history and literature.

Laundry Lavamax is on 9 de Julio between Salta and Lisandro de la Torre. Lavadero Junín II is at Rivadavia 2834.

Medical Services Hospital Provincial José María Cullen (☎ 459-9719, 455-8770) is at

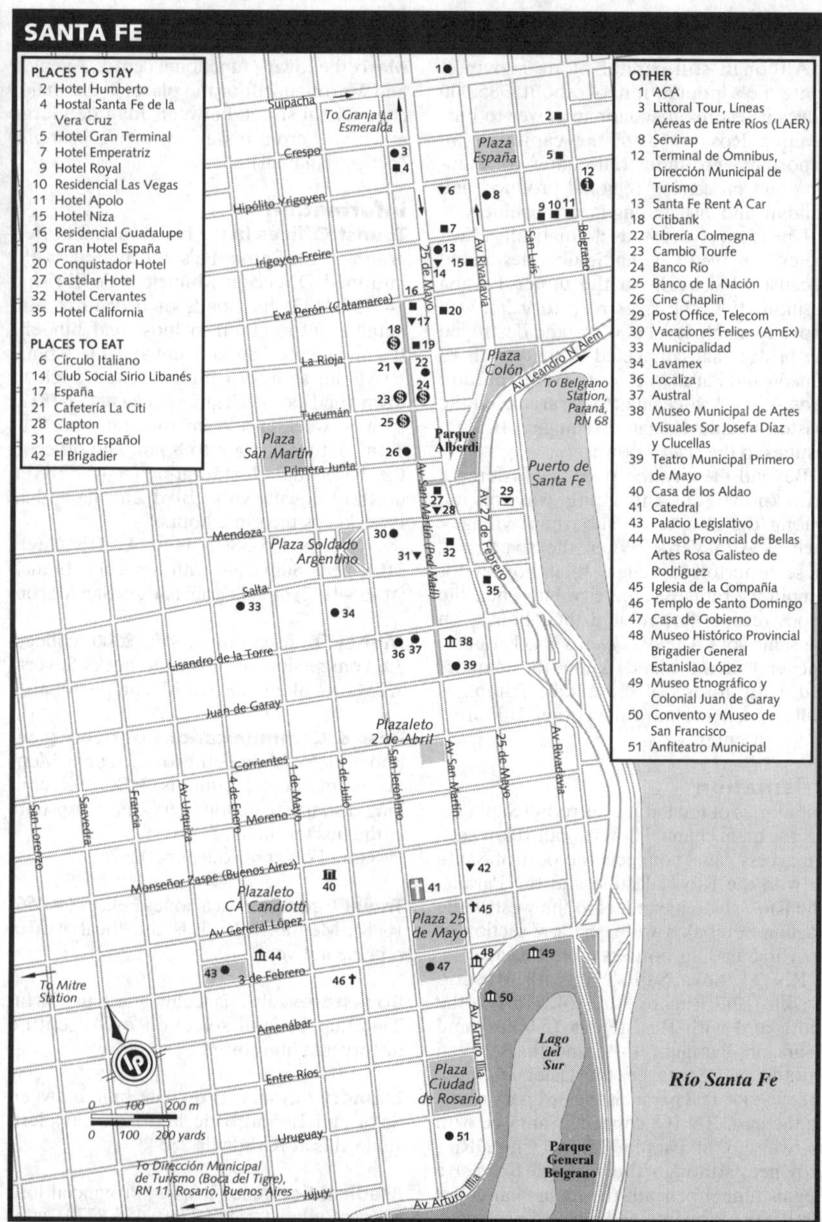
SANTA FE
PLACES TO STAY
2 Hotel Humberto
4 Hostal Santa Fe de la Vera Cruz
5 Hotel Gran Terminal
7 Hotel Emperatriz
9 Hotel Royal
10 Residencial Las Vegas
11 Hotel Apolo
15 Hotel Niza
16 Residencial Guadalupe
19 Gran Hotel España
20 Conquistador Hotel
27 Castelar Hotel
32 Hotel Cervantes
35 Hotel California
PLACES TO EAT
6 Circulo Italiano
14 Club Social Sirio Libanés
17 España
21 Cafetería La Citi
28 Clapton
31 Centro Español
42 El Brigadier
OTHER
1 ACA
3 Littoral Tour, Líneas Aéreas de Entre Ríos (LAER)
8 Servirap
12 Terminal de Ómnibus, Dirección Municipal de Turismo
13 Santa Fe Rent A Car
18 Citibank
22 Librería Colmegna
23 Cambio Tourfe
24 Banco Río
25 Banco de la Nación
26 Cine Chaplin
29 Post Office, Telecom
30 Vacaciones Felices (AmEx)
33 Municipalidad
34 Lavamex
36 Localiza
37 Austral
38 Museo Municipal de Artes Visuales Sor Josefa Díaz y Clucellas
39 Teatro Municipal Primero de Mayo
40 Casa de los Aldao
41 Catedral
43 Palacio Legislativo
44 Museo Provincial de Bellas Artes Rosa Galisteo de Rodriguez
45 Iglesia de la Compañía
46 Templo de Santo Domingo
47 Casa de Gobierno
48 Museo Histórico Provincial Brigadier General Estanislao López
49 Museo Etnográfico y Colonial Juan de Garay
50 Convento y Museo de San Francisco
51 Anfiteatro Municipal
Suipacha
To Granja La Esmeralda
Crespo
Hipólito Yrigoyen
Irigoyen Freire
Eva Perón (Catamarca)
La Rioja
Tucumán
Primera Junta
Mendoza
Salta
Lisandro de la Torre
Juan de Garay
Corrientes
Moreno
Monseñor Zaspe (Buenos Aires)
Av General López
3 de Febrero
Amenábar
Entre Ríos
Uruguay
Jujuy
Plaza España
Plaza Colón
Parque Alberdi
Plaza San Martín
Plaza Soldado Argentino
Plazaleto 2 de Abril
Plazaleto CA Candiotti
Plaza 25 de Mayo
Plaza Ciudad de Rosario
Puerto de Santa Fe
Lago del Sur
Parque General Belgrano
Río Santa Fe
San Luis
Belgrano
Av Rivadavia
25 de Mayo
Av San Martín (Ped Mall)
Av 27 de Febrero
Av Leandro N Alem
To Belgrano Station, Paraná, RN 68
San Lorenzo
Saavedra
Francia
Av Urquiza
4 de Enero
1 de Mayo
9 de Julio
San Jerónimo
Av San Martín
Av Arturo Illia
To Mitre Station
To Dirección Municipal de Turismo (Boca del Tigre), RN 11, Rosario, Buenos Aires
0 100 200 m
0 100 200 yards

Lisandro de la Torre and Freire, west of downtown.

Convento y Museo de San Francisco

Built in 1680, Santa Fe's principal historical landmark has walls more than a meter thick, supporting a roof whose Paraguayan cedar and hardwood beams are held together by fittings and wooden spikes rather than nails. The handworked doors are original, and the baroque pulpit is laminated in gold.

Like many other colonial churches, the building's floor plan duplicates the Holy Cross. Parts of the interior patio are open to the public, however, the cloisters beyond are off limits.

Besides these architectural features, the church holds many works of colonial art. Note also the tomb of Padre Magallanes, who was killed by a jaguar, which, driven from the shores of the Paraná during the floods of 1825, took refuge in the church.

The church also contains the coffins of the Santa Fe caudillo Estanislao López and his wife.

Adjacent to the church is a **historical museum** covering topics both sacred and secular from colonial and republican times. Its Sala de los Constituyentes displays wax figures of the representatives to the assembly that wrote the Argentine Constitution of 1853.

At Amenábar 2257, the Convento y Museo (☎ 459-3303) is open daily 9 am to noon and 4 to 7 pm.

Museo Histórico Provincial Brigadier General Estanislao López

In a moist but well-preserved late 17th-century building, this museum contains permanent exhibits on the 19th-century civil wars, provincial governors (and caudillos), period furnishings, and religious art plus a room with changing displays on more contemporary themes.

At San Martín 1490, the museum (☎ 459-3760) is open weekdays 8 am to noon and 4 to 7 pm, weekends 3 to 6 pm.

Museo Etnográfico y Colonial Juan de Garay

The most interesting single item in this museum is a scale model of the original settlement of Santa Fe La Vieja. It has an excellent collection of Spanish colonial artifacts from excavations at the former settlement site, near present-day Cayastá, and displays of indigenous basketry, Spanish ceramics, and coins. The staff are very patient and helpful in explaining details.

At 25 de Mayo 1470, the museum (☎ 459-5857) is open Tuesday to Friday 9 am to noon and 3 to 7 pm, Sunday and holidays 8:30 am to 12:30 pm and 4 to 7 pm. Admission is free, but they ask for donations.

Granja La Esmeralda

On the northern outskirts of Santa Fe, this experimental farm also contains a worthwhile zoo that concentrates on provincial native fauna, mostly in spacious enclosures. The most impressive specimens are tropical birds, such as toucans, big cats (pumas and jaguars), and the giant anteater.

Admission is US$0.50; hours are from 8 am to 7 pm. Bus No 10 bis, which crosses the San Martín peatonal, goes to the Granja.

Other Things to See

Santa Fe is one of Argentina's oldest cities, but the 20th century has changed its face considerably – in 1909, for example, the French Renaissance **Casa de Gobierno** (Government House) replaced the demolished colonial cabildo on Plaza 25 de Mayo. Four blocks west is the **Palacio Legislativo**, on 3 de Febrero, between 4 de Enero and Urquiza.

Many remaining colonial buildings are museums, although several revered churches still serve their original purpose. The exterior simplicity of the Jesuit **Iglesia de la Compañía**, on the east side of Plaza 25 de Mayo, masks an ornate interior. Dating from 1696, it's the province's best-preserved colonial church.

The **Templo de Santo Domingo**, at 3 de Febrero and 9 de Julio, dates from the mid-17th century but has undergone several modifications. Its interior is Ionic, while the exterior is a combination of Ionian and

Roman styles; atop stands a pair of symmetrically placed bell towers and a dome.

The **Casa de los Aldao**, Monseñor Zaspe (Buenos Aires) 2845, is a restored two-story, early-18th-century house (☎ 459-3222). Like others of its time, it has a tile roof, balconies, and meter-thick walls. Hours are 8 am to noon and 4 to 7 pm weekdays.

The **Museo Provincial de Bellas Artes Rosa Galisteo de Rodríguez** (☎ 459-6142), 4 de Enero 1510, is the provincial fine-arts museum. It's open Tuesday to Friday 10 am to noon and 4 to 8 pm, weekends 4 to 9 pm. There's also the **Museo Municipal de Artes Visuales Sor Josefa Díaz y Clucellas** (☎ 459-9696), San Martín 2068, open weekdays 8:30 am to 12:30 pm and 3:30 to 8 pm, Saturday 9:30 am to 12:30 pm and 5 to 8 pm, and Sunday 5 to 8 pm.

Places to Stay – Budget

Several inexpensive accommodations are exactly opposite the bus terminal or nearby. The absolute cheapest is ***Residencial Las Vegas*** *(Irigoyen Freire 2246)*, where singles/doubles cost only US$10/16. ***Hotel Alfil*** *(☎ 453-5044, Belgrano 2859)* has air-con rooms for US$10/15 with shared bath, US$13/20 with private bath.

Residencial Guadalupe *(☎ 452-1289, Eva Perón 2575)* is slightly dearer at US$12/18. At ***Hotel Gran Terminal*** *(☎ 453-2057, Hipólito Yrigoyen 2222)*, rooms with shared bath cost US$15/22, and those with private bath cost US$20/32. ***Hotel Royal*** *(☎ 452-7359, Irigoyen Freire 2256)* is slightly cheaper.

Hotel Apolo *(☎ 452-7984, Belgrano 2821)* is clean but dark for US$15/28 shared bath, US$22/38 private bath. ***Hotel Humberto*** *(☎ 455-0409, Crespo 2222)* charges US$18/25.

There are a few budget choices closer to downtown. Modern, undistinguished ***Hotel California*** *(☎ 452-3988, 25 de Mayo 2190)* is very friendly. It has a dozen rooms, all with private bath, for US$17/25. ***Hotel Cervantes*** *(☎ 452-9886, 25 de Mayo 2277)* charges US$20/30.

Places to Stay – Mid-Range

Perhaps the town's best value, ***Hotel Emperatriz*** *(☎ 453-0061, Irigoyen Freire 2440)* occupies a remodeled private house once owned by an elite local family. It's quiet, friendly, and dignified for US$25/35 with private bath. Another good choice is ***Hotel Niza*** *(☎ 452-2047, Rivadavia 2755)*, where rooms with private bath, air-con, and telephone cost US$26/40. The large, impersonal, and rather noisy ***Castelar Hotel*** *(☎ 452-0141, 25 de Mayo 2349)* charges US$35/46; some of the larger rooms are slightly more expensive.

Places to Stay – Top End

At unpretentious ***Gran Hotel España*** *(☎ 455-5745, 25 de Mayo 2647)*, rates start at US$53/61. If you have money to burn, the owners of the Gran Hotel España will happily accept it across the street at the ***Conquistador Hotel*** *(☎ 455-1195, 25 de Mayo 2676)*, which is more modern but no better at US$73/93. Slightly dearer, and probably superior, is ***Hostal Santa Fe de la Vera Cruz*** *(☎ 455-1740, Av San Martín 2954)*, where rates are US$77/89.

Places to Eat

On Belgrano, across from the bus terminal, several very good, inexpensive places serve Argentine staples, such as empanadas, pizza, and parrillada. At La Rioja 2609, try ***Cafetería La Citi*** for coffee and sandwiches. ***Clapton*** *(☎ 453-2236, San Martín 2300)* also has good sandwiches and lunches. ***El Brigadier*** *(☎ 458-1607, San Martín 1607)* is a cheap parrilla.

The ***Círculo Italiano*** *(☎ 452-0628, Hipólito Yrigoyen 2457)* prepares good, moderately priced lunch specials. The ***Club Social Sirio Libanés***, on San Martín between Irigoyen Freire and Eva Perón, serves Middle Eastern fare.

For a downtown splurge, try ***España*** *(☎ 455-6481, Av San Martín 2642)*. The ***Centro Español*** *(☎ 456-9968, San Martín 2219)* has a classy Spanish restaurant.

North of downtown, ***Las Leñas*** *(☎ 456-9947, San Luis 3499)* is a good but pricey parrilla. ***Carlucci*** *(☎ 453-5176, Av Freire 2350)* has fine Italian food.

Tourists and locals both flock to riverside ***El Quincho de Chiquito*** *(☎ 460-2608)*, some distance north of downtown at Brown and Obispo Vieytes. Because of its size, service is pretty impersonal, but it still serves outstanding grilled river fish, such as boga and sábalo, and exceptional hors d'oeuvres, like fish empanadas. In practice, if not in theory, it's all you can eat for about US$10 to US$15 plus drinks. Take bus No 16 on Av Gálvez, which parallels Suipacha four blocks to the north.

Not far away, ***El Quincho de don Pito*** *(☎ 0270-451576, Riobamba 7499)* has similar tenedor libre fare and a US$7.50 lunch menu.

Entertainment

Cinema *Cine Chaplin (☎ 452-6856)*, at the back of a gallery on San Martín between Tucumán and Primera Junta, shows recent films.

Theater Designed in the French Renaissance style so common in turn-of-the-century Argentina, the ***Teatro Municipal Primero de Mayo*** *(☎ 457-1883, Av San Martín 2020)* offers performance of drama and dance.

Getting There & Away

Air Austral (☎ 459-8400), Lisandro de la Torre 2633, has 25 weekly nonstops to Buenos Aires (US$81). Litoral Tur (☎ 499-5414), San Martín 2984, is the representative of Líneas Aéreas de Entre Ríos (Laer), which flies daily except Sunday to Buenos Aires' Aeroparque (US$65).

Bus The Oficina de Informes (☎ 454-7124) at the Estación Terminal de Ómnibus, Belgrano 2940, is open 6 am to 10 pm; it posts all fares for destinations throughout the country, so it's unnecessary to run from window to window for comparison.

Etacer (☎ 452-0941) crosses the river to Paraná at least hourly all day and night.

El Rápido (☎ 453-4965), La Internacional (☎ 452-6346), and Micro Ejecutivo (☎ 455-8222) all go to Rosario and Buenos Aires. At the same window as Micro Ejecutivo, Zenit goes to Mar del Plata.

Empresa Kurtz (☎ 453-0306) goes to Resistencia, Corrientes, and Posadas, continuing to Puerto Iguazú. El Norte Bis (☎ 452-9725) serves Corrientes. Expreso Singer (☎ 453-0306) stops in Santa Fe en route between Córdoba and Posadas. Puerto Tirol (☎ 455-7013) serves Buenos Aires, Corrientes, and Formosa.

El Turista (☎ 455-8696) has inexpensive services to Córdoba and its sierras, as does El Serrano (☎ 455-3524). El Práctico (☎ 456-4000) goes to Córdoba and Villa Carlos Paz. TAC (☎ 453-0306) goes to Mendoza and other Cuyo destinations.

Several carriers serve Patagonian destinations, including Alto Valle (☎ 456-1251) to Neuquén and Tirsa (☎ 453-9690) to Bariloche. To Bahía Blanca, the coastal gateway to Patagonia, try TUS (☎ 455-7013) or Central Argentino (☎ 453-0306).

Penha (☎ 453-9690) has international services to Porto Alegre and Florianópolis, Brazil. Other Brazilian carriers include Norosur (☎ 455-7013) and Pluma (☎ 453-0306). Godoy (☎ 452-6346) goes to Asunción, Paraguay (US$41 to US$57, 13 hours). Cora (☎ 455-7013) goes to Montevideo, Uruguay (US$45, 12 hours).

Typical fares include Paraná (US$3, one hour), Rosario (US$10, two hours), Córdoba (US$18, seven hours), Corrientes (US$21, 10 hours), Gualeguaychú (US$21), Resistencia (US$26), Buenos Aires (US$26, six hours), Posadas (US$30, 12 hours), San Luis (US$31), Santiago del Estero (US$33), Mendoza (US$35 to US$40, 13 hours), Roque Sáenz Peña (US$35), Puerto Iguazú (US$40, 16 hours), Tucumán (US$42), Mar del Plata (US$47, 13 hours), Porto Alegre, Brazil (US$51), Salta (US$57), Neuquén (US$65, 16 hours), São Paulo, Brazil (US$82), Rio de Janeiro, Brazil (US$92), Bariloche (US$95).

Getting Around

To/From the Airport For US$0.75, city bus A (yellow) goes to Aeropuerto Sauce Viejo (☎ 457-0642), which is 7km south of town on RN 11.

Car Localiza (☎ 459-5666) is at Lisandro de la Torre 2665. Santa Fe Rent A Car (☎ 452-1001) is at 25 de Mayo 2786.

River For a view of the river, the 200-passenger *Cirinda* (☎ 459-5336) makes weekend and holiday excursions for US$6 adults, US$4 children.

AROUND SANTA FE

Alto Verde

Shaded by enormous willows and other trees, Alto Verde is a picturesque fishing village on Isla Sirgadero, accessible only by canoe for most of the year. In really wet years, when the Paraná floods and destroys their houses, fishing families abandon the island for Santa Fe, returning and rebuilding when the flood waters recede. To reach the village, catch a launch from Puerto del Piojo, in the port complex at the east end of Calle Mendoza in Santa Fe.

San José del Rincón

Many Santafesinos maintain weekend homes at San José del Rincón, whose shady earthen roads still offer a few colonial buildings and an excellent **Museo de la Costa** (Museum of the Coast), open 8 am to noon and 4 to 8 pm daily. Local gardeners cultivate ornamentals, such as gladiolus bulbs, which are for sale in the city, and camping and fishing are popular pastimes.

No 19 Servitur buses from Santa Fe go directly to Rincón.

Cayastá

The Río San Javier has eroded away part of Cayastá, the original site of Santa Fe La Vieja, including half of the Plaza de Armas, but excavations have revealed the sites of the cabildo and the Santo Domingo, San Francisco, and Merced churches. Authorities have erected protective structures to guard the remains of these buildings. For educational purposes, they have also reconstructed a typical period house with furnishings.

Excavations have also uncovered numerous colonial artifacts, some of them exhibited in the nearby **Museo de la Colonización y Población del Virreyanto de la Plata** (☎ 02405-493056) and others in the Museo Etnográfico in present-day Santa Fe. Hours are 8 am to 6 pm weekdays and 10 am to noon and 2 to 6 pm weekends, but you can usually talk your way onto the grounds even when it's closed.

Cayastá is 78km northeast of Santa Fe on RP 1. About 2km north of the ruins on RP 1, ***Comedor Cayastá*** is excellent value, offering full meals with salad and dessert for US$5 or less; service is friendly and attentive. There is regular bus service from the capital.

ROSARIO

Rosario's first European inhabitants settled here informally around 1720 without sanction from the Spanish Crown, but after independence, Rosario quickly superseded Santa Fe as the province's economic powerhouse and it is now, arguably, the republic's second city (a status disputed by Córdoba). Still the provincial capital retains political primacy, to the irritation of Rosarinos.

Argentina's first trunk railway connected Rosario with Córdoba and, later, with Mendoza and Tucumán. The Central Argentine Land Company, an adjunct of the railroad, was responsible for bringing in agricultural colonists from Europe for whom Rosario was a port of entry. Between 1869 and 1914 Rosario's population multiplied nearly tenfold to 223,000, easily overtaking the capital in numbers.

Rosario (population 980,000) is a 19th-century city with no colonial pretensions, but its many French Renaissance buildings are typical of turn-of-the-century Argentine architecture. Some call it the 'Chicago of Argentina' because of its industrial importance and role in exporting the produce of a large agricultural heartland – despite its distance up the Paraná, the port can accommodate ocean-going vessels as easily as Buenos Aires. Its waterfront access, where many new restaurants grace the older buildings along the costanera, is a feature nearly absent in Buenos Aires.

Many visitors are nationalistic Argentines who cherish Rosario as 'Cuna de la Bandera' (Cradle of the Flag), but the city is also the official birthplace of the legendary guerrilla leader Ernesto 'Che' Guevara. In a recent development that would disgust Che, US-based General Motors opened a factory

ROSARIO

PLACES TO STAY
15 Savoy Hotel
16 Hotel República
24 Hotel Libertador
35 Nuevo Hotel Europeo
46 Hotel Litoral
47 Hotel Normandie
50 Romijor Hotel
51 Hotel Monumento
52 Hotel Buenos Aires
54 Residencial Mendoza
55 Residencial La Viña
57 Benidorm Hotel
60 Hotel Bahía

PLACES TO EAT
8 Bajo Cero
14 Café de La Paz
22 Miscellanea
26 Rincón Vegetariano
29 Hans
30 Pico Fino
58 Rich
61 El Sol
62 Centro Gallego

OTHER
1 Fidel Unplugged Bar
2 Fénix Bar
3 Centro de Expresiones Contemporáreas
4 Ernesto 'Che' Guevara's Former Home
5 Berlín Ciber Café
6 Zeppelín Bar
7 Teatro Municipal
9 Risk Co.
10 Aerolíneas Argentinas, Austral
11 Localiza
12 Startel
13 Cine Atlas
17 Mercado de Pulgas del Bajo
18 Museo de Arte Decorativo Firma y Odilio Estévez
19 Ente Turístico Rosario (Etur)
20 Museo Provincial de Ciencias Naturales Doctor Angel Gallardo
21 Biblioteca Argentina J Alvarez
23 Plaza Pringles
25 Asatej
27 Stratford Bookshop
28 Southern Winds
31 Exprinter
32 Catedral
33 Monumento Nacional a la Bandera
34 Varig
36 Rosario Central
37 Grupo 3 de Turismo (AmEx)
38 Andesmar
39 Cine Heraldo
40 Banco Nazionale del Lavoro
41 Cine Monumental
42 Post Office
43 Laverap
44 Estación Fluvial, Museo del Paraná y las Islas
45 Local Bus Terminal
48 Centro Cultural Rivadavia
49 Telecom
53 Raíces
56 Teatro Vivencias
59 Cine Gran Rex
63 Teatro El Círculo
64 Museo Barnes de Arte Sacro
65 ACA
66 Museo de la Ciudad
67 Museo Municipal de Bellas Artes Juan B Castagnino
68 Museo Histórico Provincial Doctor Julio Marc

Río Paraná
To RN 11, Santa Fe
Rosario Norte (Main Railway Station)
Isla del Espinillo
Entre Ríos
Santa Fe
To Long Distance Bus Terminal, RN 9, Airport, Córdoba
Plaza San Martín
Plaza 25 de Mayo
Plaza Sarmiento
Parque de la Bandera
Parque Independencia
Hipodromo
(Ped Mall)
Salta
Catamarca
Tucumán
Urquiza
San Lorenzo
Santa Fe
Córdoba
Rioja
San Luis
San Juan
Mendoza
3 de Febrero
9 de Julio
Av del Huerto
Av Belgrano
Av de la Libertad
Santiago
Alvear
Blvd Oroño
Balcarce
Moreno
Dorrego
Italia
España
Roca
Paraguay
Av Corrientes
Entre Ríos
Mitre
Sarmiento
San Martín
Maipú
Laprida
Buenos Aires
25 de Diciembre
1 de Mayo
LN Alem
Ayacucho
Colón
Necochea
Av Int Morcillo
Av Carlos Pellegrini
E Zeballos
Montevideo
Cochabamba
Pasco
Ituzaingó
Cerrito
Rio Bamba
To Camping 26 de Noviembre
To Complejo Municipal Astronómico Educativo Rosario, Parque Urquiza
To RN 178, Pergamino, Hospital Clemente Alvarez
To RN 9, Buenos Aires, Córdoba
0 250 500m
0 250 500 yards

to produce 84,000 Chevrolet Corsas per annum. Rosario is also home to many creative artists, including musicians Fito Páez and León Gieco, and has an active music scene.

Orientation

On a bluff above the west bank of the main channel of the Rio Paraná, Rosario is 320km upstream from Buenos Aires; its size and port status make it a major transport node. RN 9, the main route to Córdoba, is also the major freeway connecting Rosario with Buenos Aires. Heading north to Santa Fe are RN 11 and its parallel freeway, A-008, while RN 178 goes south to the prosperous farm zone around Pergamino, in Buenos Aires province, and RN 33 heads southwest to Venado Tuerto. Motorists can bypass the city on Av Circunvulación.

Rosario displays a very regular grid pattern except where the curvature of the bluffs above the river channel dictates otherwise – much of this area is open space, with excellent river views and access. Traditionally, the focus of urban activities is Plaza 25 de Mayo, but the pedestrian streets of San Martín and Córdoba mark the commercial center. Downtown's shady plazas offer relief from the heat, while beyond downtown the streets are tree-shaded and many new plantings are signs of municipal vigor. There are some 70 sq blocks of open space in Parque Independencia, southwest of downtown.

Information

Tourist Offices The Ente Turístico Rosario (Etur; ☎ 480-2230, fax 480-2237, etur@rosario.gov.ar), on the waterfront at Av Belgrano and Buenos Aires, is open 8 am to 8 pm weekdays, 9 am to 8 pm weekends. It has a computerized information system and also offers weekend walking tours of the city.

ACA (☎ 448-4410) is at Blvd Oroño and 3 de Febrero.

Money Cambios along San Martín and Córdoba change cash and traveler's checks, the latter with the usual discount and commission. Try Exprinter at Córdoba 960. There are also many ATMs.

Post & Communications Correo Argentino is at Córdoba 721; the postal code is 2000. Among the many locurorios, Startel is at Mitre 680. Rosario's area code is ☎ 0241.

The Berlín Ciber Café, Tucumán 1289, has Internet access and live music as well. There is also Internet access at Biblioteca Argentina J Alvarez, Roca 651, from 2 to 8 pm daily.

Travel Agencies Grupo 3 de Turismo (☎ 449-1783), Córdoba 1147, is the AmEx representative. The nonprofit student travel agency Asatej (☎ 425-3798) is at Corrientes 653, 6th floor.

Cultural Centers The Centro Cultural Rivadavia (☎ 480-2401), Av San Martín 1080, is a good place to find out what's happening in town. It shows free or inexpensive films, and hosts dance and theater events. Its galleries provide a showcase for the local arts community.

The Centro de Expresiones Contemporáreas (☎ 480-2243), Av Belgrano and Bajada Sargento Cabral, consists of recycled historical buildings now providing spaces for special exhibitions; there is sometimes an admission charge.

Bookstores Stratford Bookshop (☎ 424-1822), on Mitre between Santa Fe and Córdoba, sells English-language books.

Laundry Laverap is at Rioja 607.

Medical Services Hospital Clemente Alvarez (☎ 480-2111) is at Rueda 1110.

Monumento Nacional a la Bandera

Manuel Belgrano, who designed the eloquently simple Argentine flag, rests in a crypt beneath a colossal 78m tower in architect Angel Guido's boat-shaped monument, a conspicuously overbearing manifestation of patriotic hubris even by the standards of a country known for the crudest nationalism. The monument's single redeeming attribute is the view of the Paraná waterfront from its location at the foot of Av Córdoba.

Heroic sculptures by Alfredo Bigatti and José Fioravanti and bas-reliefs by Eduardo Barnes symbolically represent the regions of the country and various patriotic figures. Its museum (☎ 480-2238), containing the original flag embroidered by Catalina de Vidal, is open daily 9 am to 7 pm. On Wednesday at 8:15 am, there's a flag ceremony with a military band.

Every June, Rosario celebrates La Semana de la Bandera (Flag Week), climaxed by ceremonies on June 20, the anniversary of Belgrano's death.

Museo del Paraná y Las Islas

Thanks to the romantic but engaging murals of local painter Raúl Domínguez, this museum on the 1st floor of the waterfront Estación Fluvial, Av Belgrano and Rioja, is a far more worthwhile sight than the pretentious Monumento a la Bandera. Life on the river – flora, fauna, and people – is the focus of paintings like *Recorrido del Paraná* (Exploring the Paraná), *Cortador de Paja* (Thatch Cutter), *El Paraná y Sus Leyendas* (The Paraná and Its Legends), *El Nutriero* (The Otter Trapper), *Creciente* (In Flood), *Bajante* (In Drought), and others.

While the museum proper is undergoing restoration and is open erratically, the murals can be seen whenever the building is open, generally on weekends.

Other Things to See & Do

The **Museo Histórico Provincial Doctor Julio Marc** (☎ 421-9678), in Parque Independencia, contains some pre-Colombian and colonial exhibits, but concentrates on postindependence materials. It's open weekdays 9 am to 6 pm, weekends 3 to 8 pm. The municipal **Museo de la Ciudad** (☎ 480-2524), Blvd Oroño 2350, is open weekdays from 10 am to 1 pm, weekends 5 to 8 pm.

The fine-arts **Museo Municipal de Bellas Artes Juan B Castagnino** (☎ 480-2542), at Avs Pellegrini and Oroño, is open Tuesday to Friday 4 to 10 pm. It houses a permanent collection of European and Argentine art, with occasional contemporary exhibitions. The **Museo Barnes de Arte Sacro** (☎ 448-3784), Laprida 1235, exhibits sculptures from the man responsible for parts of the Argentine flag monument. It's open Thursday 4 to 6 pm.

There are wider-ranging collections at the **Museo de Arte Decorativo Firma y Odilio Estévez** (☎ 480-2547), Santa Fe 748. It's open Friday, Saturday, and Sunday 4 to 8 pm.

Visitors interested in the environment and wildlife can visit the **Museo Provincial de Ciencias Naturales Doctor Angel Gallardo** (☎ 425-7969), at Moreno 758 near Plaza San Martín. It's open Tuesday to Friday 9 am to 12:30 pm and Tuesday, Friday, and Sunday 3 to 6 pm.

Those interested in more distant environments can visit the planetarium at the **Complejo Municipal Astronómico Educativo Rosario** (Municipal Observatory; ☎ 480-2554) in Parque Urquiza, which has shows Saturday and Sunday from 5 to 6 pm. Friday, Saturday, and Sunday, from 9 to 10 pm, visitors can view the austral skies through its 2250mm refractor telescope and 4500mm reflecting telescope.

Though not on the formal tourist circuits, the apartment building at Entre Ríos 480, designed by famed architect Alejandro Bustillo, was where Ernesto Guevara Lynch and Celia de la Serna resided in 1928 after the birth of their son, Ernesto Guevara de la Serna, popularly known as 'Che.' According to biographer Jon Anderson, young Ernesto's birth certificate was falsified (he was born more than a month before the official date of June 14), but this was certainly **Che's first home**, however briefly.

River Excursions

Weekends and holidays, the *Ciudad de Rosario I* (☎ 425-7895) cruises the Paraná at 4 and 6:30 pm from the Estación Fluvial.

Special Events

Besides La Semana de la Bandera (see Monumento Nacional a la Bandera), Rosario holds its own Semana de Rosario in the first week of October and the national Encuentro de las Colectividades, a tribute to the country's immigrants, in November.

Places to Stay – Budget

Camping A campground called ***Camping 26 de Noviembre*** is in the Ciudad Universitaria at the south end of Av Belgrano, near Blvd 27 de Febrero. Anyone wishing to camp here must ask permission in person from the Asociación del Personal de la Universidad Nacional de Rosario, Córdoba 1900.

Hotels Friendly, inexpensive ***Hotel Normandie*** *(☎ 424-0381, Mitre 1030)* has singles/doubles for US$18/28 with private bath and breakfast, slightly less for rooms with shared bath. Comparably priced is ***Hotel Bahía*** *(Maipú 1254)*.

Centrally located ***Residencial La Viña*** *(☎ 421-4549, 3 de Febrero 1244)* is a good value for US$20/25. ***Hotel Litoral*** *(☎ 421-1426, Entre Ríos 1043)* across from noisy Plaza Sarmiento, has attractive balconies opening out from many of its rooms, which cost US$22/32. For about the same price, ***Residencial Mendoza*** *(☎ 424-6544, Mendoza 1246)* includes breakfast. Fans are provided, but air-con is extra.

Near the long-distance bus terminal, ***Hotel Gran Confort*** *(☎ 438-0486, Pasaje Quintanilla 657)* has rooms with private bath for US$20/30. Across the street, ***Hotel Residencial*** *(☎ 437-3413, Pasaje Quintanilla 628)* has good singles without TV for US$19; singles/doubles with TV go for US$22/29.

Places to Stay – Mid-Range

Romijor Hotel *(☎ 421-7276, Laprida 1050)* has quiet patio rooms for US$27/40. Directly across from the long-distance bus terminal, modern ***Hotel Embajador*** *(☎ 438-4188, Santa Fe 3554)* charges US$30/42. The ***Savoy Hotel*** *(☎ 448-0071, San Lorenzo 1022)* maintains a shabby dignity for about US$30/45.

At the ***Benidorm Hotel*** *(☎ 421-9368, San Juan 1049)*, rates are US$35/50 with private bath. The dark but friendly ***Hotel Monumento*** *(☎ 440-6446, Buenos Aires 1020)* is comparable at US$35/45.

Places to Stay – Top End

Top of the line places, such as ***Nuevo Hotel Europeo*** *(☎ 424-0382, San Luis 1364)* start at about US$69/80. ***Hotel República*** *(☎ 424-8580, San Lorenzo 955)* charges US$75/90. The best in town is ***Hotel Libertador*** *(☎ 424-1005)*, at Córdoba and Corrientes, which charges US$83/99.

Places to Eat

Probably the best value in town is ***Pico Fino*** *(San Martín 783)*, which offers a varied menu of Argentine and international food, outstanding service, and very reasonable prices. They'll even make half-pizzas (four portions), and the fresh-squeezed orange juice for less than US$2 is an outstanding value.

The ***Centro Gallego*** *(Buenos Aires 1137)* serves fixed-price all-you-can-eat meals, while ***Hans*** *(☎ 421-6931, Mitre 777)* is also economical. For noncarnivores, ***Rincón Vegetariano*** *(Mitre 720)* is a meatless alternative. ***El Sol*** *(Laprida 1121)* is a Chinese tenedor libre.

Miscellanea *(Roca 655)* is a very popular bar/restaurant. ***Confitería La Esquina*** *(Sarmiento 598)* also draws big crowds. ***Rich*** *(☎ 440-8657, San Juan 1031)* is fine for Italian food, and don't overlook the rotisería alongside.

Rosario's classic eatery is the venerable ***Sunderland Bar*** *(☎ 482-3663, Av Belgrano Sur 2210)* with excellent service, superb food at reasonable prices, and great atmosphere; desserts are expensive, though.

Bajo Cero *(☎ 425-1538)*, at the corner of Santa Fe and Roca, has a huge selection of ice-cream flavors.

Entertainment

Cinema The four-screen ***Cine Monumental*** *(☎ 421-6289, San Martín 999)*, the ***Cine Gran Rex*** *(☎ 421-3805, San Martín 1139)*, the ***Cine Heraldo*** *(☎ 426-4686, San Martín 866)*, and the ***Cine Atlas*** *(☎ 426-0252, Mitre 643)* show first-run movies.

Bars Rosario's lively bar scene, concentrated in the area bounded by Av Belgrano, Av Corrientes, and Santa Fe, is a good area for live music. Try the ***Fidel Unplugged Bar*** *(Sarmiento 384)* for its Thursday night jam sessions, the ***Zeppelín Bar***, at the corner of Av Belgrano and Tucumán, or the ***Fénix***

Bar, at the corner of San Martín and Tucumán. The ***Berlín Ciber Café*** *(Tucumán 1289)* also offers live music.

Risk Co., on Santa Fe between Roca and Paraguay, is a modernistic multiscreen sports bar.

The ***Sunderland Bar*** *(Av Belgrano Sur 2210)* tends to feature bigger popular music acts, like Andrés Calamaro, but is also a great place just for a brew.

Theater The ***Teatro El Círculo*** *(☎ 448-3784)*, at the corner of Laprida and Mendoza, is one of the city's main performing arts theaters. ***Teatro Vivencias*** *(☎ 421-7045, Mendoza 1171)* is an alternative theater venue.

Spectator Sports

Rosario has two first-division soccer teams. **Newell's Old Boys** (☎ 421-1180) has offices and plays at Estadio Parque Independencia. **Rosario Central** (☎ 421-0000) has offices at Mitre 857, but its stadium (☎ 438-9595) is at Blvd Avellaneda and Av Génova; tickets are also sold at the stadium. Always call to check on game times.

Shopping

The Mercado de Pulgas del Bajo is a picturesque flea market that takes place weekend and holiday afternoons at Av Belgrano and Buenos Aires.

Raíces, at the corner of Mendoza and Entre Ríos, sells a wide selection of indigenous crafts from throughout the country.

Getting There & Away

Air Aerolíneas Argentinas and Austral (☎ 448-0372) share offices at Santa Fe 1412. Aerolíneas has 11 weekly flights to Aeroparque in Buenos Aires (US$67), and Austral has 23.

Southern Winds (☎ 425-3808), Mitre 737, flies daily to Córdoba (US$59 to US$79) and Tucumán (US$119 to US$139), continuing daily to Neuquén (US$139 to US$169), most days to Salta (US$139 to US$159), daily except Sunday to Mar del Plata (US$119 to US$139), and twice weekly to Bariloche (US$189 to US$199).

Andesmar (☎ 424-8070), Rioja 1198, flies 11 times weekly to Córdoba (US$39 to US$63); weekdays to Buenos Aires (US$49 to US$67), Mendoza (US$87 to US$119), and Tucumán (US$53 to US$77); and Tuesday, Wednesday, and Thursday to La Rioja (US$85 to US$98).

Rosario's only international service is three times weekly to São Paulo and Belo Horizonte with Varig (☎ 425-6262), Corrientes 729, 7th floor.

Bus The Estación Mariano Moreno (☎ 437-2384/5/6) is at Cafferata 702, near Santa Fe. From downtown Calle San Juan, take bus No 101.

Urquiza (☎ 430-2298) goes to Buenos Aires frequently, to La Plata (eight per day), and to Mar del Plata (three per day). Ablo/Costera Criolla (☎ 439-7186) goes to Mar del Plata, Bahía Blanca, and Comodoro Rivadavia, and passes through Rosario en route from Buenos Aires to Córdoba and La Rioja.

Empresa Argentina (☎ 439-4398) goes to La Plata and Mar del Plata; Tirsa (☎ 439-0842) goes to Mar del Plata and Bariloche; and Zenit (☎ 430-9333) goes to Mar del Plata and other coastal destinations.

Chevallier (☎ 438-6034) has services southeast to Buenos Aires, west to Córdoba, southwest to Neuquén and Bariloche, north to Tucumán, and northeast to Corrientes. El Rápido/Tata (☎ 439-8493) connects Buenos Aires, Rosario, Santa Fe, Santiago del Estero, and Corrientes.

La Estrella (☎ 430-6194) goes to Santiago del Estero and Tucumán. La Veloz del Norte (☎ 437-0466) serves Santiago del Estero, Tucumán, and Salta.

TAC (☎ 438-9706) has buses to Córdoba, Mendoza, and Buenos Aires. Cacorba Córdoba (☎ 438-0038) also serves Córdoba and its Sierras, and Cuyo.

Ciudad de Gualeguay (☎ 439-0538) goes twice daily to Paraná and Gualeguaychú. Flecha Bus (☎ 430-9333) goes to Paraná, Corrientes, and other Mesopotamian destinations. Kurtz (☎ 437-0393) and El Norte Bis (☎ 439-4131) go to Resistencia, Corrientes, Posadas, and Puerto Iguazú.

International services include: La Internacional (☎ 438-8748) to Asunción and Ciudad del Este (Paraguay); Pluma (☎ 437-3152) to Porto Alegre and Rio de Janeiro (Brazil); Cora (☎ 438-0038) and El Rápido Internacional (☎ 430-7865) to Montevideo (Uruguay). Encon (☎ 439-0698) goes to Montevideo, Piriápolis, and Punta del Este.

Typical destinations include Buenos Aires (US$15, four hours), Córdoba (US$20, six hours), La Plata (US$22, six hours), San Luis (US$25), Mendoza (US$30), Resistencia (US$30, 10 hours), Asunción (US$40 to US$56, 12 hours), Montevideo (US$51, 10 hours), Salta (US$65, 17 hours), and Bariloche (US$76, 23 hours).

Train From Estación Rosario Norte (☎ 439-2429), Av del Valle 2700, northbound services to Santiago del Estero (La Banda; US$15 to US$18) and Tucumán (US$17 to US$25) leave Tuesday and Saturday at 2:58 am. Southbound services to Retiro (US$8 to US$12) leave weekdays at 8:19 am. Take bus No 120 from San Juan and Mitre to the station.

Getting Around

To/From the Airport Aerolíneas Argentinas runs its own buses to Aeropuerto Fisherton (☎ 456-7997), 8km west of town. Public buses to Fisherton go only within about 1km of the airport.

A taxi or remise costs about US$12.

Bus From the local bus station on Plaza Sarmiento, the city's extensive system goes virtually everywhere.

Car Localiza (☎ 439-1336) has an office at San Lorenzo 1286.

La Pampa Province

For most Argentines, La Pampa is like the Great Plains or the prairies for Americans and Canadians – a place you cross to get somewhere else. Primarily an agricultural zone, it was settled after Buenos Aires province because Indian resistance deterred European incursions for longer, and because its erratic rainfall made agriculture more unpredictable than in the easterly Humid Pampas. It borders six other provinces: Río Negro, Neuquén, Mendoza, San Luis, Córdoba, and Buenos Aires.

No one would visit Argentina just to see La Pampa, though its capital city of Santa Rosa is an attractive administrative and service center, but its little-known Parque Nacional Lihué Calel more than justifies a detour from the standard routes to and from Patagonia. Travelers returning from Neuquén to Buenos Aires will find its tranquil granitic peaks a very interesting alternative.

Despite the monotony implied by its name, La Pampa offers a variety of environments, including rolling hills with native *caldén* forests, desert zones with saline lakes, which support flamingos and other birds, and extensive native grasslands.

SANTA ROSA

In the midst of the Pampas, 600km southwest of Buenos Aires, Santa Rosa was not legally founded until 1892. French, Spanish, and Italian immigrants arrived with the expansion of the railroads at the turn of the 19th century, but one measure of its continuing isolation and insignificance was that, until 1951, the surrounding area remained a territory rather than a province. It is now a clean and pleasant city with a population of about 82,000.

Orientation

Santa Rosa is only 80km from the Buenos Aires provincial border on RN 5, which is paved all the way from the Federal Capital. RN 35 goes north to Córdoba and southeast to Bahía Blanca.

North of Av España, the city consists of a standard grid centered on the spotless but nearly shadeless Plaza San Martín, the site of the rather ugly modernistic Catedral. Most businesses are on the plaza and its surrounding streets, though a more recent focus of activity is the modern Centro Cívico, seven blocks east on Av Pedro Luro.

One km west, Laguna Don Tomás is a major recreational resource for city residents. In the quadrant southwest of the Av España-Av Pedro Luro junction, streets trend northwest to southeast, rather than north to south.

Information

Tourist Offices The enthusiastically helpful Dirección Provincial de Turismo (☎ 425060) is at Av Pedro Luro and Av San Martín, across from the bus terminal. The English-speaking staff have maps and brochures, and the building's Mercado Artesanal has an interesting selection of local handicrafts. Hours are weekdays 7 am to 1:30 pm and 5 to 9 pm, weekends 9 am to noon and 5 to 9 pm.

The Municipalidad maintains a Centro de Información Turística at the bus terminal, open 24 hours. ACA (☎ 422435) is at Av San Martín 102, at the corner of Coronel Gil.

Money Several banks will change money, though not traveler's checks. Banco de la Nación is at Av Roca 1, on Plaza San Martín. Banco de La Pampa has an ATM on Av Luro, alongside the provincial tourist office, and another at Pellegrini 255.

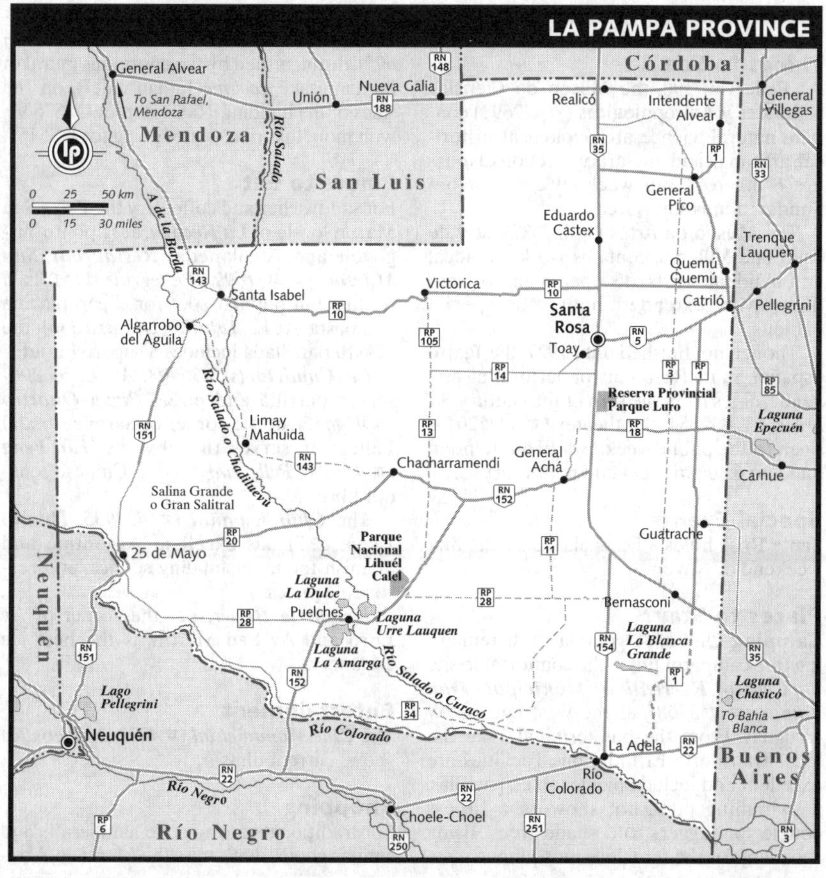

Post & Communications Correo Argentino is at Hilario Lagos 258; Santa Rosa's postal code is 6300. Telefónica Centro is a locutorio on Avellaneda near Quintana; the area code is 02954.

Travel Agencies Downtown travel agencies include Swiss Travel (☎ 425952), at Pellegrini 219, and Vega Viajes (☎ 433415), at Garibaldi 426.

Medical Services Hospital Lucio Molas (☎ 455000) is at Raúl P Diaz and Pilcomayo, 2km north of downtown.

Laundry Laverap is at Rivadavia 253.

Things to See

At Pellegrini 190, the **Museo de Ciencias Naturales y Antropológicas** (☎ 422693) contains natural science, archaeological, historical, artisanal, and fine-arts collections. Hours are 8 am to 1 pm weekdays, 6 to 9 pm Sunday; admission is free.

The **Museo de Artes** (☎ 427332), at 9 de Julio and Villegas, contains works by local and national artists. It's open 8 am to 1 pm daily, with extended hours for special exhibits.

Though not finished until 1927, the **Teatro Español**, Santa Rosa's major performing arts venue, dates from the turn of the century. At Hilario Lagos 54, the theater (☎ 424520) is open to the public weekdays 10 am to noon and 4 to 6:30 pm; weekend hours vary.

Special Events

Santa Rosa holds a Festival de Jazz the first weekend of November.

Places to Stay

Camping One of Argentina's last remaining free campgrounds is the comfortable site at ***Centro Recreativo Municipal Don Tomás*** *(☎ 455368)*, at the west end of Av Uruguay. From the bus terminal, take the local Transporte El Indio bus. Facilities are excellent and include picnic tables, parrillas, a swimming pool, hot showers, a fitness course for joggers, and shade trees. Bring repellent for the ferocious mosquitoes.

Hospedajes, Hosterías & Hotels Except for camping, really cheap accommodations are scarce. The most reasonable is ***Hospedaje Mitre*** *(☎ 425432, Emilio Mitre 74)*, a short walk from the bus terminal. Singles/doubles are US$15/27 with shared bath, US$21/34 with private bath. Rates are marginally cheaper at ***Hostería Santa Rosa*** *(☎ 423868, Hipólito Yrigoyen 696)*.

At ***Hostería Río Atuel*** *(☎ 422597, Av Pedro Luro 356)*, conveniently across from the bus terminal, rooms with private bath are US$28/42. The central ***Hotel San Martín*** *(☎ 422549, Alsina 101)* has rooms with private bath for US$29/49.

The uncontested top of the line is the highrise ***Hotel Calfucurá*** *(☎ 423608, San Martín 695)*, distinguished by the enormous mural of its namesake *cacique*(Indian chief), on the sides of the building. Rates start at US$76/97, with more luxurious suites going for US$155.

Places to Eat

For sandwiches and coffee, try the Plaza San Martín locale of ***La Recova***, at Hipólito Yrigoyen and Avellaneda. ***Restaurant San Martín*** *(☎ 431099, Pellegrini 115)* is a routine but popular spot for cheap parrilla and pasta. At ***La Tablita*** *(Urquiza 336)*, the US$10 parrillada includes a superb buffet.

La Candela *(☎ 436993, Av Luro 290)* serves parrilla and pizza. ***Pizza Quattro*** *(☎ 434457)*, at the corner of Sarmiento and Pellegrini, serves the obvious. ***Tai Feng*** *(☎ 453488, Pellegrini 43)* is a Chinese tenedor libre.

The ***Club Español*** *(☎ 423935, Hilario Lagos 237)* has excellent Argentine and Spanish food, outstanding service, and reasonable prices.

Heladería Roberts, at the corner of Av Luro and Av San Martín, is the best ice creamery.

Entertainment

The ***Cine Monumental*** *(☎ 422342, Lagos 70)* shows current films.

Shopping

For traditional gaucho-style handicrafts and similar goods, don't miss the Mercado Artesanal in the tourist office; note the horse gear, silverwork, woolen goods, and wood carvings from caldén trees, which cover large extents of the province. Also check out the tremendous selection at El Matrero, Pellegrini 86, and Artesanías Argentinas, at Av Luro 430.

Getting There & Away

Air Austral (☎ 433076), Rivadavia 258, flies Sunday through Friday to Bahía Blanca (US$78), where there are onward connections to other cities.

Bus The Estación Terminal de Ómnibus (☎ 422952, 422249) is at the Centro Cívico, Av Pedro Luro 365.

Buenos Aires buses are numerous with Chevallier (☎ 427056), Empresa Pehuenche (☎ 422952), El Zorzal (☎ 435212), TAC (☎ 437779), and others. El Rápido (☎ 431113) serves Mar del Plata, and TUS (☎ 432140) has services to the Mesopotamian littoral. Liniers (☎ 427056) goes to La Plata.

Chevallier offers one or two services daily to San Martín de los Andes and Bariloche. It also goes to Rosario and has the only

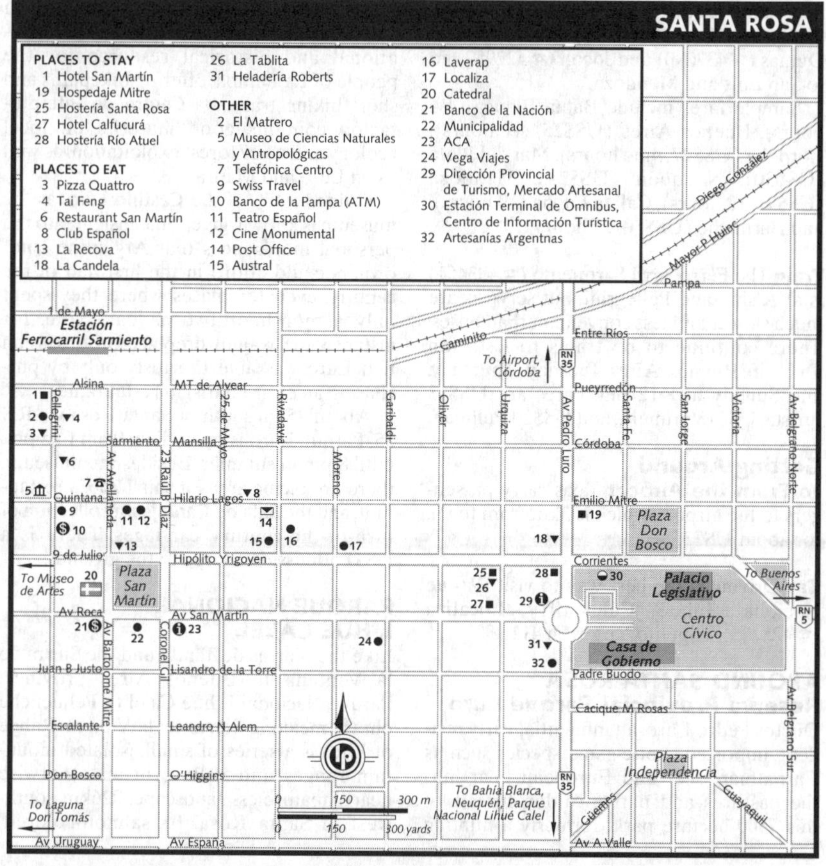

regular service passing Parque Nacional Lihué Calel (US$22), departing Wednesday at midnight en route to Neuquén. Other carriers serving Neuquén include Alto Valle (☎ 422952), Empresa Pehuenche, and La Estrella (☎ 422952).

TAC (☎ 437779) goes primarily to Mendoza, but also has extensive routes from Jujuy to Río Gallegos. TUP (☎ 432140) goes to Comodoro Rivadavia and Caleta Olivia.

Autortransporte San Juan (☎ 422742) connects Santa Rosa with the Cuyo provinces and Buenos Aires coastal destinations. Andesmar (☎ 432841) offers buses between Mendoza and Bahía Blanca, and buses between Mendoza and Caleta Olivia via Santa Rosa. Ticsa (☎ 422952) serves San Juan. Dumas (☎ 437090) and Jocoli (☎ 422952) go to San Luis and Mendoza.

Sample fares include Bahía Blanca (4½ hours), Buenos Aires (US$25, six hours), Córdoba (US$27, nine hours), Mar del Plata (US$30), Neuquén (US$24), Mendoza (US$41, 12 hours), Caleta Olivia (19 hours), and Bariloche (US$50, 21 hours).

Train The Ferrocarril Sarmiento (☎ 433451) is at Alsina and Pellegrini, but services are much slower and less convenient than buses. There continue to be trains to Estación Once in Buenos Aires Tuesday, Thursday, and Sunday at 8:12 pm. Fares are US$13 turista, US$15 primera, and US$20 Pullman.

Getting Around

To/From the Airport Taxis carry passengers to the airport, which is 3km from town, for about US$3.

Car Driving is the best way to visit Parque Nacional Lihué Calel. Try Localiza (☎ 425773), Hipólito Yrigoyen 411.

AROUND SANTA ROSA

Reserva Provincial Parque Luro

Doctor Pedro Luro, an influential early resident, imported exotic game species such as Carpathian deer and European boar into the pastures and native caldén forests of this 7500-hectare park, formerly a hunting preserve. Luro also built an enormous French-style mansion (now a museum) to accommodate foreign hunters.

With the decline of sport hunting by the European aristocracy during and after WWI, followed by the Great Depression, Luro went bankrupt, and his heirs had to sell the preserve, which fell into disrepair; animals escaped through holes in the fences, and some suffered depredations by poachers (which continue to this day). During and after WWII, Luro's successor Antonio Maura exploited its forests for firewood and charcoal, grazed cattle and sheep, and bred polo ponies.

Since its acquisition by the province in 1965, Parque Luro has served as a recreational and historical resource for the people of La Pampa, offering bikepaths and short hiking trails. Its **Centro de Interpretación** contains good material on local ecology and early forest exploitation, as well as on Luro and Maura.

Guided tours of the **Castillo Luro**, as the museum is known, give some insight into the personal indulgences that Argentine landowners could afford in the first half of the century, even for places where they spent only a month or two a year. Note, for instance, the walnut fireplace, an obsession that Luro was able to satisfy only by purchasing an entire Parisian restaurant.

About 35km south of Santa Rosa via RN 35, Parque Luro is open daily 9 am to 5 pm, until 8 pm in summer. Besides the museum, there are picnic areas, a small zoo, a restaurant, and the **Sala de Caruajes**, a collection of turn-of-the-century carriages. There is a US$1 admission charge to the grounds.

PARQUE NACIONAL LIHUÉ CALEL

Like the Sierras de Tandil and the Sierra de la Ventana in Buenos Aires province, Parque Nacional Lihué Calel (a Pehuenche phrase meaning Sierra de la Vida or Range of Life) is a series of small, isolated mountain ranges and valleys in an otherwise nearly featureless landscape, 226km southwest of Santa Rosa. Its salmon-colored, exfoliating granites (resembling parts of Joshua Tree National Monument in California's Mojave Desert) do not exceed 600m but still offer a variety of subtle environments, which change with the season and even with the day, providing a refuge from the monotony of the Pampas.

Though desertic Lihué Calel receives only about 400mm of rainfall per annum, water is an important factor in the landscape. Sudden storms can bring flash floods or create impressive ephemeral waterfalls over the nicks in the granite near the visitor center. Even when the sky is cloudless, the subterranean streams in the valleys nourish the monte, a scrub forest with a surprising variety of plant species. Within the park's 10,000 hectares exist 345 species of plants, nearly half the total found in the entire province.

In this thinly populated area survives wildlife that is now extinct in the Humid Pampas farther east – the author once saw a puma *(Felis concolor)* in the park campground, although the large cats are not common. Other cats are likelier to be seen, including Geoffroy's cat *(Felis geoffroyi)* and the yaguarundi *(Felis yagouaroundi)*, but the most common predator is the Patagonian fox. Also remaining are other large mammals such as the guanaco *(Lama guanicoe)*, more common on the Patagonian steppe, and smaller species like the *mara* or Patagonian hare *(Dolichotis patagonicum)* and *vizcacha (Lagostomus maximus)*, a wild relative of the domestic chinchilla.

The varied bird life includes the rhea or *ñandú (Rhea americana)* and many birds of prey, including the *carancho* or crested caracara *(Polyborus plancus)*. Although you are not likely to encounter them, be aware of the highly poisonous pit vipers commonly known as *yarará (Bothrops spp)*.

Until General Roca's so-called Conquista del Desierto (Conquest of the Desert), Araucanian Indians successfully defended the area against European invasion. Archaeological evidence, including petroglyphs, recalls their presence and of that of their ancestors. Lihué Calel was the last refuge of the Araucanian cacique (leader) Namuncurá, who eluded Argentine forces for several years before finally surrendering.

Things to See & Do

From the park campground, an excellent signed nature trail follows an intermittent stream through a dense thorn forest of caldén *(Prosopis caldenia)*, a local species of a common worldwide genus, and other typical trees. This trail leads to a petroglyph site, unfortunately vandalized since 1927. The exceptionally friendly and knowledgeable rangers accompany visitors if their schedule permits.

During and after rainstorms, the granite boulders on the upper-stream course briefly form spectacular waterfalls. There is a marked trail to the 589m peak, which bears the unwieldy name of **Cerro de la Sociedad Científica Argentina**, and the climb is gradual enough in any direction that you can choose your route. Watch for flowering cacti such as *Trichocereus candicans* between the boulders, but be advised that the granite is very slippery when wet. From the summit, there are outstanding views of the entire Sierra and its surrounding marshes and salt lakes, such as Laguna Urre Lauquen to the southwest.

If you have time or a vehicle, visit **Viejo Casco**, the big house of the former Estancia Santa María before the provincial government expropriated the land; it was later transferred to the national park system. It's possible to make a circuit via the **Valle de las Pinturas**, where there are more, undamaged petroglyphs. Ask rangers for directions.

Places to Stay

Near the visitor center is a very comfortable ***campground*** with shade trees, picnic tables, firepits, clean toilets, cold showers (summer weather is hot enough for them to be acceptable), and electricity until 11 pm. Nearby you're likely to see foxes, vizcachas, and many, many birds. There is no charge, but bring food – the nearest available supplies are at the town of Puelches, 35km south.

On the highway, it is possible to stay at

the ***ACA Hostería*** (☎ *02952-436101*), which charges US$20/30 single/double and also has a restaurant.

Getting There & Away

Most buses between Santa Rosa and Neuquén now use RP 20; the only remaining regular bus service using RN 152 from Santa Rosa to Chelforó (on RN 22 in Río Negro province) is Chevallier's weekly service to Neuquén at midnight Wednesday, which drops passengers at Lihué Calel in the predawn hours for US$22.

Sacra (☎ 428903), Av Luro 1340 in Santa Rosa, provides minibus service to and from the town of Puelches (US$12) Monday, Wednesday, and Friday at 6 am, passing through Lihué Calel en route. The only other alternative is to take a bus to the RP 152 junction at El Carancho and hitch south from there.

Argentine Mesopotamia

Mesopotamia is that part of Argentina between the Paraná and Uruguay Rivers, comprising the provinces of Entre Ríos, Corrientes, and Misiones. Historically, the rivers' winding channels and sandbars made navigation difficult above present-day Rosario (Santa Fe province), while their breadth made cross-river communications equally awkward. In effect, Mesopotamia was an island. The area between and along the rivers is commonly known as the Littoral.

Subtropical Misiones, northeast of Corrientes, is a political geographic peninsula between the Paraná and the Uruguay, nearly surrounded by the countries of Paraguay and Brazil. Its most spectacular attraction is the awesome series of waterfalls collectively known as the Cataratas del Iguazú, the setting for the outstanding Hollywood film *The Mission*. Corrientes borders both Brazil and Uruguay to the east, and the provinces of Chaco and Santa Fe to the west.

History

In history and geography, Mesopotamia differs greatly from the Argentine heartland. Nomadic hunter-gatherers populated the temperate Pampas when Europeans first arrived, but the Guaraní peoples, from northern Entre Ríos through Corrientes and into Paraguay and Brazil, were semisedentary agriculturalists, raising sweet potatoes, maize, manioc, and beans. Riverine fish also played an important dietary role.

Rumors of wealthy Indian civilizations first drew Europeans to the region. Pedro de Mendoza led the earliest expedition to the Río de la Plata, the estuary formed by the two rivers, but his founding of Buenos Aires in 1536 proved ephemeral when Querandí Indians drove out his sick, starved, and ill-prepared crew, delaying the city's reestablishment for nearly half a century. The following year, Mendoza's lieutenant Juan de Ayolas established an upper Paraná beachhead at Asunción, where the Spaniards could obtain food and supplies from the friendlier Guaraní. Settlement thus proceeded southward from Asunción rather than northward from Buenos Aires. Corrientes was founded in 1588, Santa Fe about the same time. For further information on early Spanish settlement in the upper Paraná, see the Paraguay chapters.

Jesuit missionaries helped colonize the upper Uruguay and Paraná, concentrating the native Guaraní populations in settlements and at least approaching the Spanish ideal of reciprocal rights and responsibilities in dealing with native peoples. To be sure, the Jesuits exploited native labor on their *yerba mate* (Paraguayan tea) plantations, but they also conscientiously taught the Spanish language, Catholic religion, and

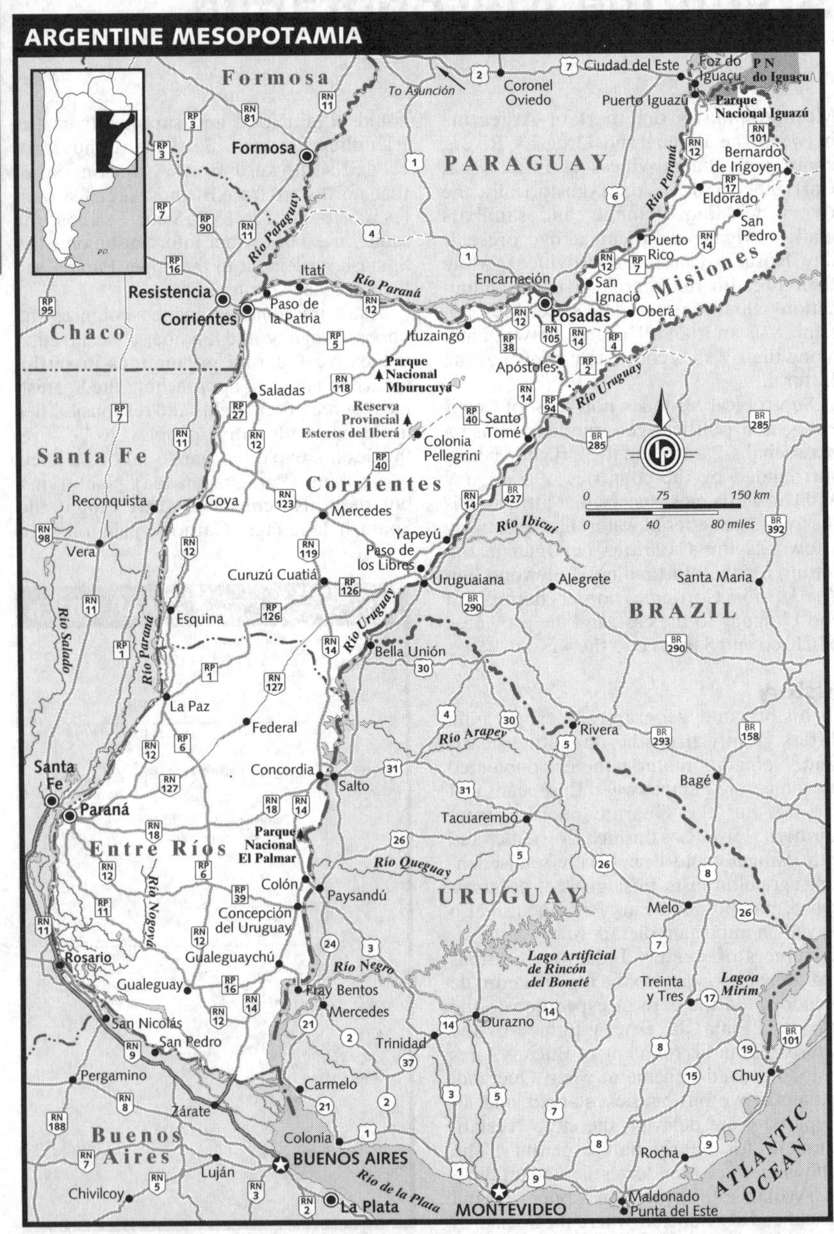
ARGENTINE MESOPOTAMIA
Formosa
PARAGUAY
Chaco
Santa Fe
Corrientes
Misiones
Entre Ríos
Buenos Aires
BRAZIL
URUGUAY
ATLANTIC OCEAN
To Asunción
Ciudad del Este
Foz do Iguaçu
PN do Iguaçu
Coronel Oviedo
Puerto Iguazú
Parque Nacional Iguazú
Bernardo de Irigoyen
Eldorado
San Pedro
Puerto Rico
San Ignacio
Oberá
Encarnación
Posadas
Apóstoles
Formosa
Resistencia
Corrientes
Itatí
Paso de la Patria
Ituzaingó
Parque Nacional Mburucuyá
Saladas
Reserva Provincial Esteros del Iberá
Colonia Pellegrini
Santo Tomé
Reconquista
Goya
Mercedes
Yapeyú
Paso de los Libres
Vera
Curuzú Cuatiá
Uruguaiana
Alegrete
Santa Maria
Esquina
Bella Unión
La Paz
Federal
Rivera
Concordia
Salto
Bagé
Santa Fe
Paraná
Tacuarembó
Parque Nacional El Palmar
Colón
Paysandú
Concepción del Uruguay
Melo
Rosario
Gualeguaychú
Gualeguay
Fray Bentos
Mercedes
Treinta y Tres
Lagoa Mirím
San Nicolás
San Pedro
Durazno
Trinidad
Pergamino
Carmelo
Zárate
Chuy
Colonia
BUENOS AIRES
Luján
Chivilcoy
La Plata
MONTEVIDEO
Rocha
Maldonado
Punta del Este
Río Paraguay
Río Paraná
Río Uruguay
Río Ibicuí
Río Salado
Río Nogoyá
Río Arapey
Río Queguay
Río Negro
Río de la Plata
Lago Artificial de Rincón del Boneté
0 75 150 km
0 40 80 miles

other European customs to their charges. Portuguese slavers' and secular Spaniards' jealousy of the missions' economic success and their monopolization of the Indian labor force led to the Jesuits' expulsion and the disintegration of mission communities, but their ruins, which today attract many visitors to Misiones province, are monuments to an extraordinary history. The presence of the Guaraní is reflected in many place names and linguistic survivals, such as the common usage of the word *gurí*, meaning 'child,' by the general populace. Perhaps 15,000 Guaraní remain in the region.

Entre Ríos Province

This province's name literally describes its location between two major waterways. Covered by rolling grasslands, with gallery forests lining its riverbanks, Entre Ríos has always supported livestock enterprises, but it's also an important agricultural area. Fiercely independent from Buenos Aires, at one time even declaring itself independent, it ironically became a Unitarist stronghold after dictator Juan Manuel de Rosas took power there. Local caudillo Justo José Urquiza, commanding an army of provincial loyalists, Unitarists, Brazilians, and Uruguayans, was largely responsible for Rosas' demise and the eventual adoption of Argentina's modern constitution.

The provincial economy formerly resembled that of Buenos Aires. Large landowners, including Urquiza, controlled extensive cattle estancias. Like their Buenos Aires counterparts, these estancias salted their beef and prepared hides for export at riverside locations. By the 1880s, colonization schemes managed to settle 15,000 European immigrant farmers in the province, including Russo-Germans south of Paraná and Russian Jews near Basavilbaso west of Concepción.

In the early 20th century, improved cattle breeds began to displace Entre Ríos' native criollo types. Poor rail connections with Buenos Aires, not established until 1908 and even then via ferry rather than bridges, retarded economic modernization. Locally built meat freezer plants brought greater prosperity, but construction of the Zárate-Brazo Largo bridge across the Río de la Plata delta enabled the livestock processing industry to move south to Buenos Aires province.

For visitors, Entre Ríos' principal attractions are the rivers and their recreational opportunities. These include camping and fishing in winter, spring, and autumn, when the weather is not oppressively hot. Parque Nacional El Palmar, established to protect the region's declining native palm forests, is only a few hours north of Buenos Aires on the Río Uruguay. There are several bridges across the river to the neighboring republic of Uruguay.

PARANÁ

One of Mesopotamia's oldest cities, Paraná is also the provincial capital. Although it has no official founding date, most residents associate it with the establishment of the Parroquia (Parish) del Rosario de la Bajada in 1730. From 1853 to 1861, it was capital of the short-lived Argentine Confederation, but soon lost political primacy to Buenos Aires. In April 1994 it hosted the Convención Constituyente, which rewrote the Argentine constitution to permit President Carlos Menem to run for reelection.

Paraná is a pleasant, modern city (population 230,000) whose major attraction is the river itself, accented by large public parks and campgrounds. The most important public buildings date from the 19th century. Paraná and neighboring Santa Fe, across the river, take pride in having built the subfluvial Uranga Silvestre Begnis tunnel, which connects the two cities, despite initial apathy and, later, active opposition from the federal government. The city is an unusual hotbed of interest in North American softball, having hosted national and international tournaments, including the 1995 Panamerican Games.

Orientation

Paraná sits on a high bluff on the east bank of the Río Paraná, 500km north of Buenos Aires via RN 9 to Rosario and RN 11 to

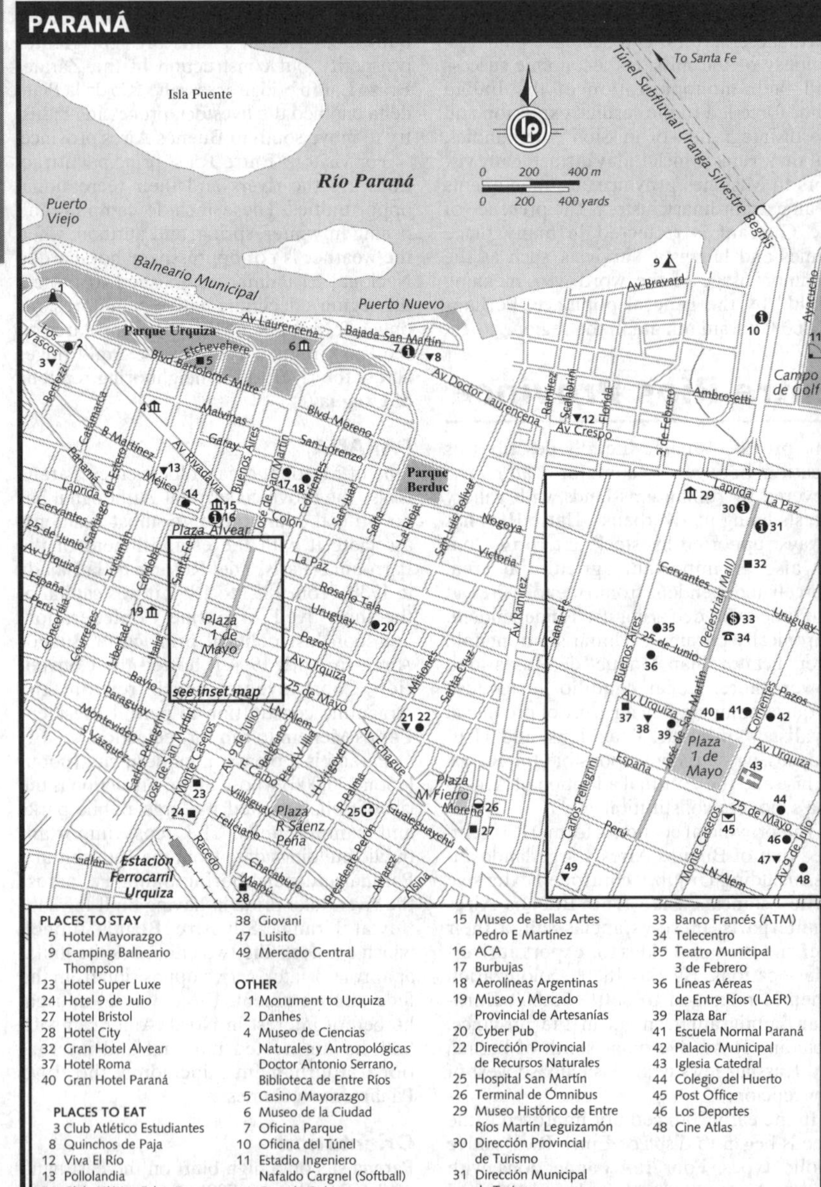
PARANÁ
Isla Puente
Río Paraná
Puerto Viejo
0 200 400 m
0 200 400 yards
To Santa Fe
Túnel Subfluvial Uranga Silvestre Begnis
Balneario Municipal
Puerto Nuevo
Av Bravard
Ayacucho
Campo de Golf
Parque Urquiza
Los Vascos
Bertozzi
Echevehere
Blvd Bartolomé Mitre
Av Laurencena
Bajada San Martín
Av Doctor Laurencena
Ramírez
Scalabrini
Florida
3 de Febrero
Ambrosetti
Av Crespo
Malvinas
Blvd Moreno
Catamarca
B Martínez
Garay
San Lorenzo
Av Rivadavia
Buenos Aires
José de San Martín
Corrientes
Parque Berduc
Panamá
Mejico
Laprida
Santiago del Estero
Cervantes
25 de Junio
Av Urquiza
España
Perú
Tucumán
Córdoba
Santa Fe
Plaza Alvear
Colón
San Juan
Salta
La Rioja
San Luis Bolívar
Nogoya
Victoria
La Paz
Rosario Tala
Uruguay
Pazos
Plaza 1 de Mayo
see inset map
Concordia
Gourreges
Libertad
Italia
Bavio
Paraguay
Montevideo
S Vázquez
Carlos Pellegrini
José de San Martín
Monte Caseros
Av 9 de Julio
F Carbo
Belgrano
Pte AV Illia
H Yrigoyen
P Palma
LN Alem
Av Echagüe
25 de Mayo
Misiones
Santa Cruz
Av Ramírez
Plaza M Fierro
Moreno
Gualeguaychú
Villaguay
Plaza R Saenz Peña
Feliciano
Chacabuco
Maipú
Racedo
Presidente Perón
Alvarez
Alsina
Galán
Estación Ferrocarril Urquiza
Laprida
La Paz
Cervantes
Uruguay
25 de Junio
Buenos Aires
José de San Martín (Pedestrian Mall)
Corrientes
Pazos
Av Urquiza
Plaza 1 de Mayo
España
Perú
Carlos Pellegrini
Monte Caseros
25 de Mayo
Av 9 de Julio
LN Alem
PLACES TO STAY
5 Hotel Mayorazgo
9 Camping Balneario Thompson
23 Hotel Super Luxe
24 Hotel 9 de Julio
27 Hotel Bristol
28 Hotel City
32 Gran Hotel Alvear
37 Hotel Roma
40 Gran Hotel Paraná
PLACES TO EAT
3 Club Atlético Estudiantes
8 Quinchos de Paja
12 Viva El Río
13 Pollolandia
21 Club Atlético Echagüe
38 Giovani
47 Luisito
49 Mercado Central
OTHER
1 Monument to Urquiza
2 Danhes
4 Museo de Ciencias Naturales y Antropológicas Doctor Antonio Serrano, Biblioteca de Entre Ríos
5 Casino Mayorazgo
6 Museo de la Ciudad
7 Oficina Parque
10 Oficina del Túnel
11 Estadio Ingeniero Nafaldo Cargnel (Softball)
14 Casa de Gobierno
15 Museo de Bellas Artes Pedro E Martínez
16 ACA
17 Burbujas
18 Aerolíneas Argentinas
19 Museo y Mercado Provincial de Artesanías
20 Cyber Pub
22 Dirección Provincial de Recursos Naturales
25 Hospital San Martín
26 Terminal de Ómnibus
29 Museo Histórico de Entre Ríos Martín Leguizamón
30 Dirección Provincial de Turismo
31 Dirección Municipal de Turismo
33 Banco Francés (ATM)
34 Telecentro
35 Teatro Municipal 3 de Febrero
36 Líneas Aéreas de Entre Ríos (LAER)
39 Plaza Bar
41 Escuela Normal Paraná
42 Palacio Municipal
43 Iglesia Catedral
44 Colegio del Huerto
45 Post Office
46 Los Deportes
48 Cine Atlas

Santa Fe; approaches through southern Entre Ríos are shorter but slower because of substandard roads. Its city plan is more irregular than most Argentine cities, with numerous diagonals, curving boulevards, and complex intersections. Plaza 1 de Mayo is the town center; on Saturday mornings, virtually the entire town congregates for a *paseo* (outing) down the peatonal José de San Martín.

Except for San Martín, street names change on all sides of the plaza. At the north end of San Martín, Parque Urquiza extends more than a kilometer along the riverfront and the bluffs above it. Many other attractive parks and plazas are scattered throughout the city.

Information

Tourist Offices The Dirección Municipal de Turismo (☎ 420-1805 interno 27) is on San Martín near the corner of La Paz; daily hours are from 8 am to 8 pm. There are branches at the bus terminal, at the Oficina Parque (☎ 420-1837) on the riverfront at Bajada San Martín and Av Laurencena, and at the Oficina del Túnel (☎ 420-1803), at the tunnel outlet, as you enter Paraná from Santa Fe.

The Dirección Provincial de Turismo (☎ 422-3384) is at Laprida 5.

ACA (☎ 431-1319) is at Buenos Aires 333.

Money There are many ATMs – try Banco Francés at San Martín 763 or Banco Galicia on San Martín near Perú.

Post & Communications Correo Argentino is at 25 de Mayo and Monte Caseros; the postal code is 3100. There's a Telecentro on San Martín between Uruguay and Pazos. Paraná's area code is ☎ 0343.

The Cyber Pub, at the corner of La Rioja and Uruguay, has Internet access.

Laundry Burbujas is on Nogoya between San Martín and Corrientes.

Medical Services Hospital San Martín (☎ 423-3707) is at Presidente Perón 450, near Gualeguaychú.

Dangers & Annoyances Beware *jejenes*, annoying biting insects, along the river in summer.

Walking Tour

Walkers can see most of Paraná's key buildings in a short stroll starting at Plaza 1 de Mayo, where the post office occupies the erstwhile site of General Urquiza's residence. The **Iglesia Catedral** (Cathedral) has been on the plaza since 1730, though the current building dates only from 1885; its museum is open 5 to 7 pm daily. When Paraná was capital of the Argentine Confederation, the Senate deliberated at the present **Colegio del Huerto**, behind the Catedral at 9 de Julio and 25 de Mayo.

Just north of the cathedral, at Corrientes and Av Urquiza, are the **Palacio Municipal** (1889) and the **Escuela Normal Paraná** (Paraná Normal School), founded by the famous educator and President Domingo F Sarmiento. Across San Martín, at 25 de Junio 60, is the **Teatro Municipal 3 de Febrero** (1908). At the north end of the San Martín peatonal, several museums cluster around **Plaza Alvear**. A block west, bounded by Córdoba, Laprida, and Santa Fe, the **Centro Cívico** contains the provincial **Casa de Gobierno** and other government offices. Farther west, along the diagonal Av Rivadavia, is the **Biblioteca de Entre Ríos**, the provincial library.

You can continue to **Parque Urquiza**, walk the length of the park, and double back at the foot of San Martín to return to Plaza 1 de Mayo. The park has a number of significant monuments, including the **Monumento a Urquiza**, and also features the **Museo de la Ciudad**, at the corner of Av Laurencena and San Martín.

Museums

On the costanera Av Laurencena in Parque Urquiza, the **Museo de la Ciudad** (☎ 420-1838) focuses on Paraná's urban past and surroundings. It's open daily except Monday 4 to 8 pm, Tuesday to Friday 8 am to noon, and Saturday 9 am to noon; winter hours are slightly shorter and earlier. Admission is free.

Flaunting local pride, the modern **Museo Histórico de Entre Ríos Martín Leguizamón** (☎ 431-2735), on Plaza Alvear at Laprida and Buenos Aires, contains well-arranged displays of 19th-century artifacts of provincial life, along with outstanding portrait collections. The knowledgeable but patronizing guides, though, go to rhetorical extremes in emphasizing the role of provincial caudillos in Argentine history. The museum is open 8 am to 1 pm and 3 to 8 pm weekdays, 9 am to noon weekends, and 5 to 8 pm Saturday. Winter hours are similar but it's closed Saturday mornings. There is a small admission fee.

Oil paintings, illustrations, and sculptures by provincial artists are the focus of the subterranean **Museo de Bellas Artes Pedro E Martínez**, just off Plaza Alvear at Buenos Aires 355. The museum (☎ 431-1527) is open Tuesday to Friday 8 am to 1 pm and 3 to 8 pm, Saturday 9 am to noon and 5 to 8 pm, Sunday and Monday 4 to 8 pm. In winter, when it's open Sunday and Monday mornings instead of afternoons, hours are slightly shorter.

Promoting handicrafts from throughout the province, the **Museo y Mercado Provincial de Artesanías** is a combined crafts center and museum displaying a variety of media including wood, ceramics, leather, metal, bone, and iron. At Av Urquiza 1239, the museum (☎ 422-4540) is open 8 am to noon and 4 to 8 pm weekdays, 8 am to 1 pm Saturday; the winter opening hour is 7 am.

Natural history and archaeological specimens are the focus of the partially remodeled **Museo de Ciencias Naturales y Antropológicas Doctor Antonio Serrano**, near Parque Urquiza. At Av Rivadavia 462, the museum (☎ 431-2635) is open weekdays 8 am to noon and 2 to 6:30 pm, Saturday 9:30 am to 12:30 pm and 2:30 to 6:30 pm, Sunday 8:30 am to 12:30 pm. Winter hours are slightly shorter but start earlier.

Túnel Subfluvial Uranga Silvestre Begnis

Until this tunnel beneath the Río Paraná opened in 1969, the provincial capitals of Paraná and Santa Fe had to rely on ferryboats for interurban transport – the federal government, then building a bridge between Buenos Aires province and southern Entre Ríos, refused even to allow the two provinces to build a bridge, a right constitutionally reserved to Buenos Aires. This forced the provinces into a more difficult and costly (US$60 million) alternative, the 2.4km tunnel beneath the Paraná's main channel. On its 25th anniversary in 1994, the tunnel was renamed to honor former Entre Ríos governor Raúl Lucio Uranga and former Santa Fe governor Carlos Silvestre Begnis, who tenaciously promoted the project despite federal opposition.

Free of charge, hourly guided tours (☎ 424-3622) of the tunnel include a film and visit to the control center; any bus to Santa Fe will drop you at the tunnel entrance. Daily hours are 8 am to 6 pm all year.

Motorists should be aware of irritating document checks from the provincial police at each end of the tunnel. The passenger vehicle toll is US$2.

Activities

Fishing River fishing is a popular local pastime, and tasty local game species like boga, sábalo, dorado, and surubí reach considerable size. Licenses are available through the Dirección Provincial de Recursos Naturales (☎ 431-6773) at 25 de Mayo 565.

Water Sports Boating, water-skiing, windsurfing, and swimming are popular pastimes for much of the year. Sporting goods are available at Los Deportes (☎ 421-3991), 9 de Julio 178.

River Excursions From the Puerto Nuevo at Costanera and Vélez Sarsfield, the Paraná Rowing Club (☎ 431-2048) conducts hour-long river excursions (US$3) at 3:30 and 5 pm Friday, Saturday, and Sunday.

Special Events

Every January, Paraná hosts the Fiesta Provincial de Música y Artesanía Entrerriana, featuring regional folk music. In October, the Fiesta Provincial La Raya y La Hermandad acknowledges immigrants' contributions to provincial development.

Perhaps the most unusual event is February's recently revived Maratón Internacional Hernandárias-Paraná, an 88km swim that attracts contestants from around the world. It is part of Paraná's annual Fiesta del Río.

At Diamante, 44km south of Paraná, the January Fiesta Nacional de Jineteada y Folklore celebrates gaucho culture and music. Diamante also is the site of February's Fiesta Provincial del Pescador (Provincial Fisherman's Festival).

Places to Stay – Budget

Camping The closest campground to downtown and to Parque Urquiza is shady ***Camping Balneario Thompson*** *(☎ 420-1583)*, which can be noisy on weekends when locals gather for all-night asados. Sites cost US$4 per tent plus US$1 per person and per vehicle. The cold showers are not a problem in the summer, but they aren't that enjoyable during more changeable spring and autumn weather (it can also flood). Buses Nos 1 and 6, with the sign 'Thompson,' connect the campground with downtown.

There are other good campgrounds at ***Toma Vieja*** *(☎ 420-1821)*, the old waterworks, a few kilometers outside town but accessible by bus No 5; and at ***Los Arenales*** *(☎ 434-8144)*, reached by bus No 1 (red). Prices are US$8 per site.

Hotels Compared to Santa Fe, accommodations in Paraná are fairly limited in all categories and not particularly cheap. The best budget choice is ***Hotel City*** *(☎ 431-0086, Blvd Racedo 231)*, directly opposite the train station, with a wonderful patio garden and cool rooms with high ceilings. Singles/doubles are US$20/31 with private bath, slightly less with shared bath; unlike other budget places, it accepts credit cards.

Prices are similar at ***Hotel 9 de Julio*** *(☎ 431-3047, 9 de Julio 674)*, half a block from the train station, and at downtown ***Hotel Roma*** *(☎ 431-2247, Urquiza 1061)*.

Places to Stay – Mid-Range

Hotel Bristol *(☎ 431-3961, Alsina 221)*, near the bus terminal, is more expensive at US$25/35, but clean and attractive. The modern but drab ***Hotel Super Luxe*** *(☎ 423-2835, Villaguay 162)* has rooms with private bath at US$26/42. ***Gran Hotel Alvear*** *(☎ 422-0000, San Martín 637)* charges US$44/61.

Places to Stay – Top End

Gran Hotel Paraná *(☎ 422-3900, Urquiza 976)*, on Plaza 1 de Mayo, has rooms with private bath and many other conveniences from about US$50/72 to US$67/99, but the new kid on the block is the five-star ***Hotel Mayorazgo*** *(☎ 423-0333)*, in Parque Urquiza at Etchevehere and Miranda, where singles/doubles with full buffet breakfast cost US$120/150.

Places to Eat

A good place to stock up on food is the ***Mercado Central***, at Pellegrini and Bavio. River fish is the local specialty, though; try ***Pollolandia*** *(☎ 421-3671, Tucumán 418)* for a bargain on tasty grilled boga.

One of Paraná's traditional favorites is ***Luisito*** *(☎ 431-6912, 9 de Julio 140)*. ***Don Charras*** *(☎ 434-49760, Av Raúl Uranga 1127)*, near the junction to the tunnel, is a highly regarded parrilla. Another exteemed parrilla is ***Giovani*** *(☎ 423-0527, Av Urquiza 1045)*.

Other recommended restaurants include ***Viva El Río*** *(☎ 431-9411, Av Crespo 71)*, ***Quinchos de Paja*** *(☎ 423-1845)*, on Salta between Av Laurencena and Bajada San Martín, ***Club Atlético Echagüe*** *(☎ 431-2099, 25 de Mayo 555)*, and ***Club Atlético Estudiantes*** *(☎ 431-2390)* at Los Vascos and Bertozzi.

Costa Azul *(Alvear 641)* has ice cream and a very welcome water cooler.

Entertainment

Theater The municipal ***Teatro 3 de Febrero*** *(☎ 420-1800, 25 de Junio 60)* puts on exhibitions of local art, inexpensive films, and other activities.

Cinema The ***Cine Atlas*** is on Av 9 de Julio between 25 de Mayo and Alem.

Casinos If you have money to spare, you can gamble at the ***Casino Mayorazgo*** on Etchevehere in Parque Urquiza, in the hotel of the same name, but remember that the Spanish word for slot machine is *tragamonedas* (coin-swallower). Winter hours are 9 pm to 3 am, summer hours 9:30 pm to 3:30 am.

Dance Clubs Nightspots worth checking out are the ***Plaza Bar*** on Urquiza, next to the former Plaza Hotel, ***Escándolo*** on Av Estrada, west of the Puerto Viejo, and ***Danhes***, near the Urquiza monument at the west end of Av Rivadavia.

Spectator Sports

Popular since the 1960s, softball gives Paraná the look of a small town in the US Midwest on summer weekends, from the number of children and teenagers walking around town in uniform. Both youth and adult leagues play on the city's eight fields, three of which are lit at night. Both slow- and fast-pitch versions are popular; the level of play varies, but can be excellent.

In 1995 the city hosted the men's and women's Panamerican Games softball championships at its Estadio Ingeniero Nafaldo Cargnel, near the entrance to the tunnel to Santa Fe. Games take place almost every night at the stadium, with free admission except for special events like regional or national championships.

Getting There & Away

Air Aerolíneas Argentinas (☎ 423-2425) has offices at Corrientes 563, but flights leave from Santa Fe's Aeropuerto Sauce Viejo. See Getting There & Away for Santa Fe, in the Pampas chapter, for details.

Líneas Aéreas de Entre Ríos (Laer: ☎ 423-0347), with an office at 25 de Junio 77, flies from Paraná to Buenos Aires' Aeroparque (US$65) an average of four times daily. It operates its own minibus service to Aeropuerto Ciudad de Paraná, just outside the city limits.

Bus The Terminal de Ómnibus (☎ 422-1282) is on Av Ramírez between Posadas and Moreno, opposite Plaza Martín Fierro. Paraná is a center for provincial bus services, but Santa Fe is more convenient for long-distance trips. About every hour throughout the day and night, Etacer buses (☎ 431-6809) leave for Santa Fe (US$2).

There are about 20 buses daily to Buenos Aires with El Rápido (☎ 423-2080), Flecha Bus (☎ 422-5577), Basa (☎ 431-6872), San José (☎ 431-3581), and Norosur (☎ 431-6981), passing through Santa Fe and Rosario. Other Rosario carriers include Ciudad de Paraná (☎ 422-2100), Ciudad de Gualeguay (☎ 431-2009), ETA (☎ 431-5414), and Paccot.

To Puerto Iguazú and intermediates, there are four buses daily with Singer, Litoral, and Crucero del Norte. TAC goes to Corrientes and Resistencia, in the Chaco.

Zenit, Flecha Bus, Basa, and Norosur have service to Mar del Plata, while Flecha Bus goes twice daily to La Plata. Central Argentino, TUS, and Ñandú del Sur go to Bahía Blanca. Alto Valle goes to Neuquén.

There are at least a dozen buses daily to Córdoba with Ciudad de Paraná, Crucero del Norte, El Litoral, Singer, Basa, El Turista, El Serrano, and with TAC, which continues to Mendoza.

International carriers include Cora (☎ 431-5439), which goes to Montevideo, Uruguay, four times weekly, and Singer, which travels to Porto Alegre, Brazil.

Fares and times are very similar to those from Santa Fe; add or subtract about half and US$2 depending on whether you're passing through there or not.

LA PAZ

On the east bank of the Paraná, about 160km northwest of the provincial capital, La Paz is known for excellent fishing and good camping. In February it celebrates the **Fiesta Nacional de Pesca Variada de Río** (National River Fishing Festival). It also has a regional museum.

The tourist office (☎ 422389) is at Echagüe 787. La Paz's postal code is 3190, while the area code is ☎ 03437. For modest accommodations, try the basic and rather cramped ***Residencial Las Dos M*** *(☎ 421303, Urquiza 825)*, where singles/doubles cost US$12/20. For more comfort there's ***Hotel Milton*** *(☎ 422232)* at Italia 1029 for US$28/40, with a small surcharge for credit cards.

GUALEGUAYCHÚ

Founded in 1783 by Tomás de Rocamora, Gualeguaychú (population 68,000) is the first substantial town encountered by travelers arriving in Entre Ríos from Buenos Aires. While not a major destination for most foreigners, it has considerable historical interest, offers good river recreation, holds one of Argentina's best carnivals, and leads to the most southerly bridge crossing into Uruguay.

Orientation

Some 220km north of Buenos Aires and 13km east of RN 14, Gualeguaychú sits on the east bank of its namesake river, a tributary of the Uruguay. Plaza San Martín, occupying four square blocks, is the center of its very regular grid pattern. RN 136 bypasses

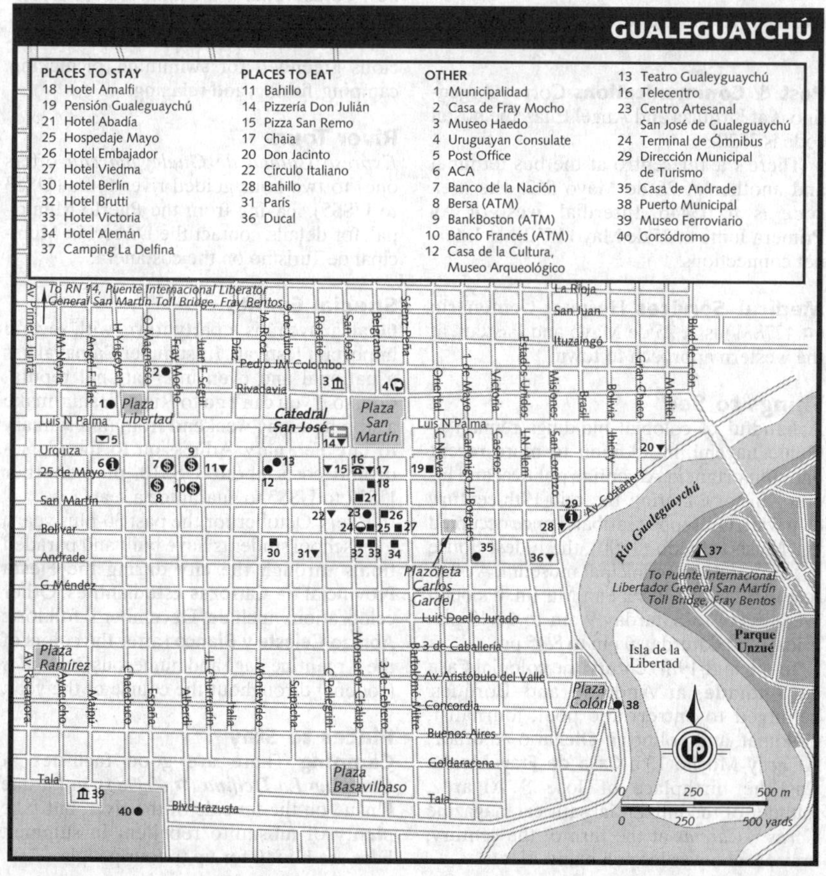

the city center en route to the Puente Internacional General Libertador San Martín, a toll bridge leading to the Uruguayan city of Fray Bentos.

Information

Tourist Offices The Dirección Municipal de Turismo (☎ 422900) is on Av Costanera near the bridge across the Río Gualeguaychú. It's open 8 am to 10 pm in summer, 8 am to 8 pm in winter, and has good brochures and a list of accommodations, but poor-quality maps. ACA (☎ 426088) is at Urquiza and Chacabuco.

Money There are several banks, mostly with ATMs, along Av 25 de Mayo.

Post & Communications Correo Argentino is at Urquiza and Ángel Elías; the postal code is 2820.

There's a Telecentro at the bus terminal and another at 25 de Mayo 562. The area code is ☎ 03446. Interdial, west of Av Primera Junta at 25 de Mayo 1550, has Internet connections.

Medical Services Hospital Centenario (☎ 427831) is at 25 de Mayo and Pasteur, at the western approach to town.

Things to See

A handful of colonial buildings remain in Gualeguaychú, in addition to more recent ones important in Argentine political and literary history. During the mid-19th-century civil wars, Giuseppe Garibaldi once occupied the **Museo Haedo** (1800), the oldest house in town and the municipal museum. At San José 105 just off Plaza San Martín, it's open Wednesday to Saturday 9 am to 11:45 pm, Friday and Saturday 6 pm to 8:45 pm.

In the mid-19th century, the colonial **Casa de Andrade**, at Andrade and Borques, belonged to entrerriano poet, journalist, diplomat, and politician Olegario Andrade. At Fray Mocho 135, **Casa de Fray Mocho** was the birthplace of José S Álvarez, founder of the influential satirical magazine *Caras y Caretas* at the turn of the century; Fray Mocho was his pen name.

Dating from 1920, the unusual **Casa de la Cultura**, 25 de Mayo 734, has occasional public exhibitions and contains the city's **Museo Arqueológico**, open Monday through Saturday 6 to 9 pm. The **Teatro Gualeyguaychú** *(☎ 431757, Urquiza 705)*, inaugurated in 1914 with a performance of *Aïda*, still hosts symphony, ballet, and theater.

At the former Estación Ferrocarril Urquiza, at the south end of Maipú, the **Museo Ferroviario** is an open-air exhibit of steam locomotives, dining cars, and other hardware from provincial rail history. Alongside the station, on Blvd Irazusta, the new **Corsódromo** is the main site for Gualeguaychú's lively Carnaval.

Across the river, **Parque Unzué** is a spacious greenbelt for swimming, picnicking, camping, fishing, and relaxing.

River Tours

Expreso Ciudad de Gualeyguaychú offers one- to two-hour guided river tours (US$3 to US$5), leaving from the Puerto Municipal; for details, contact the Dirección Municipal de Turismo on the costanera.

Special Events

Gualeguaychú is a party town, with several important festivals. Its summer **Carnaval** has a national and even international reputation, so if you can't go to Rio or Bahía, make a stop here any weekend from mid-January to late February. Admission to the Corsódromo costs about US$10, plus another US$2 to US$3 to guarantee a seat.

Every October for the past 30-plus years, high school students have built and paraded floats through the city during the **Fiesta Provincial de Carrozas Estudiantiles**. Other celebrations include December's folkloric **Abrazo Celeste y Blanco** (after the colors of the Argentine flag) and numerous *jineteadas* (rodeos) throughout the course of the year.

Places to Stay

Camping There are good facilities at ***Camping La Delfina*** *(☎ 423984)*, in Parque Unzué on the far side of the river, but take plenty of mosquito repellent in summer. Fees are US$10 for up to four people.

Hospedajes & Hotels Most reasonably priced hotels are near the bus station. The cheapest is clean, friendly ***Pensión Gualeguaychú*** *(25 de Mayo 456)*, where rooms with shared bath are US$10 per person.

Hotel Amalfi *(☎ 425677, 25 de Mayo 579)* charges US$15/20 single/double with shared bath, US$20/30 with private bath. At ***Hospedaje Mayo*** *(☎ 427661, Bolívar 550)*, rates with private bath are US$15/20. In the same range is ***Hotel Alemán*** *(☎ 426153, Bolívar 535)*, whose rates are US$15 per person with shared bath, US$20 per person with private bath.

Hotel Victoria *(☎ 426469, Bolívar 565)* costs US$20/34. Both ***Hotel Brutti*** *(☎ 426048, Bolívar 571)* and ***Hotel Abadía*** *(☎ 427675, San Martín 588)* charge US$20/35 with private bath and breakfast.

Hotel Viedma *(☎ 424262, Bolívar 530)* costs US$40/64, while ***Hotel Berlín*** *(☎ 425111, Bolívar 733)* has rooms for US$45/65 with breakfast.

Closest to luxury is three-star ***Hotel Embajador*** *(☎ 424414)*, at San Martín and 3 de Febrero, which also has a casino. Weekday rates are only slightly higher than the Berlín, and breakfast is included, but on the weekend, rates rise to US$85/90.

Places to Eat

Most better restaurants are along the costanera, such as ***Ducal*** *(☎ 427602)* at the corner of Andrade (good fish), but try also the ***Círculo Italiano*** *(☎ 422155, San Martín 647)* or ***París*** *(☎ 423850, Pellegrini 180)*. For pizza, try ***Pizzería Don Julián*** *(☎ 425112, Urquiza 607)* or ***Pizza San Remo*** *(☎ 426891, 25 de Mayo 634)*.

Chaia, at 25 de Mayo and 3 de Febrero, is a parrilla. ***Don Jacinto*** *(☎ 429222)*, at Urquiza and Montiel, is an upscale seafood alternative.

For ice cream, ***Bahillo*** has branches alongside the tourist office on Av Costanera, and at the corner of Díaz and 25 de Mayo.

Shopping

For crafts, visit the Centro Artesanal San José de Gualeguaychú on San Martín near Monseñor Chalup.

Getting There & Away

The run-down Terminal de Ómnibus (☎ 427987), very central at Bolívar and Monseñor Chalup, is likely to move in the near future.

Buenos Aires has frequent services by San José (☎ 428412), Flecha Bus (☎ 424070), El Tata (☎ 424349), Nuevo Expreso, and El Rápido.

Ciudad de Gualeguay (☎ 424061) has five buses daily to Paraná via Victoria, three daily to Santa Fe and Rosario. San José also goes to Paraná. Three times weekly, El Litoral offers service to Córdoba by way of Santa Fe.

Nuevo Expreso Gualeguaychú (☎ 423822) runs up the littoral to Colón, Concordia, Corrientes, and Resistencia. Jovi Bus goes to Concepción, Colón and Concordia at 5 am and 4:25 pm daily.

At noon and 7 pm, daily except Sunday, Ciudad de Gualeguay goes to Fray Bentos, Uruguay, continuing to Mercedes. Cauvi (☎ 424-3449) has direct service to Montevideo at 12:30 am, but connections are more frequent in Mercedes.

Sample fares include Fray Bentos (US$4, one hour), Mercedes, Uruguay (US$5, 1½ hours), Buenos Aires (US$20, three hours), Paraná (US$20, six hours), and Córdoba (US$40, 11 hours).

CONCEPCIÓN

Concepción del Uruguay (population 57,600) is a crossroads town whose tourist services make it a suitable stopover for travelers on long trips north. It is on the Río Uruguay east of the junction of RN 14 from Buenos Aires and RP 39 to Paraná, and midway between Gualeguaychú and Parque Nacional El Palmar.

The region's primary attraction is the Palacio San José, General Urquiza's palatial residence, which is located 30km west of town. This is where Urquiza was assassinated by the forces of his rival, Ricardo López Jordán.

The Subsecretaría Municipal de Turismo (☎ 425820), 9 de Julio 844, is open 8 am to 8 pm daily, but even later in summer. Concepción's area code is ☎ 03442.

Places to Stay & Eat

There are campgrounds at the ***Balneario Municipal Itapé*** *(☎ 427852)* at the south end of Av 3 de Febrero and at ***Banco Pelay*** *(☎ 424003)* north of town. Both charge around US$8 for two persons.

Less than two blocks south of the central Plaza General Francisco Ramírez, the convenient ***Residencial Centro*** *(☎ 427429, Mariano Moreno 130)* charges US$15/25 single/double, while the nearby ***Residencial La Posada*** *(☎ 425461, Mariano Moreno 166)* costs US$15/28.

The ***Grand Hotel*** *(☎ 425586, Eva Perón 114)*, which is north of the plaza, charges from US$36/53 to US$50/60 for two-star facilities.

There are several restaurants just north of the Plaza, including ***Vieja Esquina*** *(☎ 431633)* and ***La Delfina*** *(☎ 429468)*, both at Eva Perón and Rocamora. ***La Salamanca*** *(☎ 432715)*, on the Costanera Norte, is also worth a look.

Getting There & Away

The Terminal de Ómnibus (☎ 422352) is at General Galarza and Blvd Constituyentes, 10 blocks west of the Plaza.

There are seven buses daily to Buenos Aires with Tata (☎ 427117), which also goes to Paso de los Libres at 10 am and 11 pm, continuing to Corrientes and Roque Sáenz Peña.

Jovi Bus (☎ 422590) goes to Colón and Concordia at 6:10 am and 5:30 pm, and to Gualeguaychú at 11:15 am and 9:15 pm. Empresa San José goes to Paraná five times daily between 12:45 am and 6:15 pm.

Paccot goes to Paysandú, Uruguay (US$3.50), at 5:30 pm daily except Sunday.

Sample fares include Buenos Aires (US$16, four hours), Corrientes (US$26), and Roque Sáenz Peña (US$40).

PALACIO SAN JOSÉ

Topped by twin towers and surrounded by elegant gardens, Justo José Urquiza's palatial pink palace may have been his way of saying that his power was as great as that of his arch-rival Rosas in Buenos Aires. Allies like Sarmiento and Mitre ate at Urquiza's 8.5m dining room table, enjoying meals cooked over the massive octagonal stove, and slept in the palatial bedrooms. Urquiza's wife, 25 years his junior, turned the bedroom where López Jordán murdered her husband into a permanent shrine.

Hours at the palace (☎ 03442-495020) are 9 am to 1 pm and 2 to 5:30 pm daily. Admission is US$2 for adults, US$1 for kids. There's a passable comedor on the grounds, but no accommodation nearby.

Getting There & Away

You can reach the Palacio, 30km west of Concepción via RP 39, by taking the 1:15 pm Empresa San José bus from Concepción to Paraná and getting off at the junction, where it's a half-hour walk to the grounds. Enough people visit the site that you should be able to ask for a lift back to town.

COLÓN

One of three main Entre Ríos border crossings, Colón (population 16,400) sits on the west bank of the Río Uruguay, connected to the Uruguayan city of Paysandú by the Puente Internacional General Artigas.

Founded in 1863, Colón has an attractive waterfront lined with many impressive older buildings, but flooding in recent years, caused by upstream dam discharges, has wiped out several fine beaches. In mid-February, the city hosts the Fiesta Nacional de la Artesanía, a long-running crafts fair held in Parque Quirós that features live folkoric entertainment by nationally known artists.

Four km northwest of Colón is the **Molino Forclaz**, the area's first flour mill. It's also worth visiting the nearby village of **Colonia San José**, 8km west, where in 1857 European pioneers established the country's second agricultural colony; an interesting regional museum displays period tools and memorabilia.

Open 8 am to 9 pm daily, the Subsecretaría de Turismo (☎ 421996) occupies the former Aduana (Customs Building), built by Urquiza at Emilio Gouchon and Av Costanera Gobernador Quirós. Correo Argentino is at Artigas and 12 de Abril; Colón's postal code is 3280. The area code is ☎ 03447.

Places to Stay & Eat

The ***Camping Municipal Norte*** *(☎ 421917)* and the ***Camping Municipal Inkier*** *(☎ 1564-3159, cellular)*, at the north end of town, both charge US$8 double per site. Otherwise, try the inexpensive ***Hospedaje Bolívar*** *(☎ 422721, Bolívar 577)* for US$10 per person, or ***Residencial Ver-wei*** *(☎ 421579, 25 de Mayo 10)* for US$22/30 single/double. ***Hotel Holimasú*** *(☎ 421305, Belgrano 28)*, on Plaza San Martín, is a step up for US$33/42 (ask for cash discount).

For eats, there's the tenedor libre ***Amicci*** *(☎ 422418)* at Alem and Urquiza for about US$6, or the river fish at ***El Viejo Almacén*** *(☎ 422216)*, Urquiza and Paso.

Getting There & Away

Colón's Terminal de Ómnibus (☎ 421716) is at Rocamora and 9 de Julio. The many north-south buses that stop here also pass the entrance to Parque Nacional El Palmar.

Paccot goes to Paysandú, Uruguay (US$2.50), Monday through Saturday at 9 am and 1:45 and 6:30 pm, Sunday at 9 pm only.

PARQUE NACIONAL EL PALMAR

In the 19th century, the native yatay palm covered large parts of Entre Ríos, Uruguay, and southern Brazil, but the intensification of agriculture, ranching, and forestry throughout the region destroyed much of the palm savannas and inhibited the species' reproduction. On the west bank of the Río Uruguay, midway between Colón and Concordia, 8500-hectare Parque Nacional El Palmar preserves the last extensive stands of *Syagrus yatay* on the Argentine littoral. The state acquired this former cattle estancia, now one of the Argentine park system's most visited units, in 1966.

Most of the remaining palms in El Palmar are relics, some more than two centuries old, but under protection from grazing and fire they have once again begun to reproduce. Reaching a maximum height of about 18m, with a trunk diameter of 40cm, the larger specimens clustered throughout the park

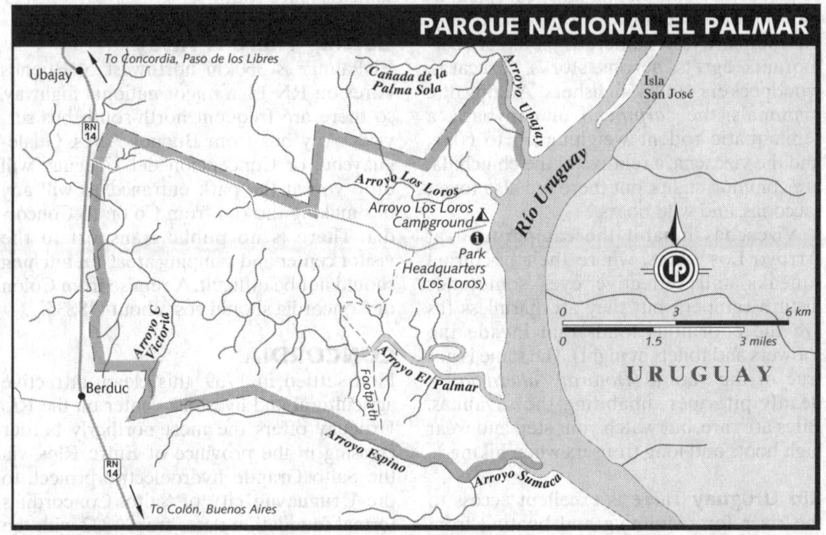

accentuate a striking and soothing subtropical landscape that lends itself to photography. The grasslands and the gallery forests along the river and creeks shelter much wildlife, including birds, mammals, and reptiles.

The park is remarkably tranquil and undeveloped, despite its proximity to population centers, so most activities are oriented toward the park's natural attractions. Park admission, collected at the entrance on RN 14, is US$5 per person.

Things to See & Do

Centro de Interpretación Across from the Arroyo Los Loros campground, the visitor center (☎ 03447-493031) is open 9 am to 8 pm daily. It has displays on natural history, including a small herpetarium (reptile house), and offers slide shows in the evening. There is a confitería next door at which you can get food and drink. The *intendencia* (park administration) was once the casco of the estancia.

Wildlife Viewing To view wildlife, go for walks along the watercourses or through the palm savannas, preferably in early morning or just before sunset. The most conspicuous bird is the *ñandú* or rhea *(Rhea americana)*, but there are also numerous parakeets, cormorants, egrets, herons, storks, caracaras, woodpeckers, and kingfishers. Among the mammals, the *carpincho* or capybara, a semiaquatic rodent weighing up to 60kg, and the vizcacha, a relative of the chinchilla, are common sights, but there are also foxes, raccoons, and wild boars.

Vizcachas inhabit the campground at Arroyo Los Loros, where their nocturnal squeaks and reflective eyes sometimes disturb campers, but they are harmless (as are the enormous toads that invade the showers and toilets at night). The same is not true of the yarará *(Bothrops alternata)*, a deadly pit viper inhabiting the savannas. Bites are rare, but watch your step and wear high boots and long trousers when hiking.

Río Uruguay There is excellent access to the river for swimming and boating from the campground, as well as a series of short hiking trails comprising **El Paseo de la Glorieta**. You can rent canoes at the campground store.

Arroyo Los Loros A short distance by gravel road from the campground, this is a good place to observe wildlife.

Arroyo El Palmar Five km from Los Loros is Arroyo El Palmar, a pleasant stream with a beautiful swimming hole, accessible by a good gravel road. It's a fine place to see birds and, crossing the ruined bridge, visitors can walk for several kilometers along a palm-lined road now being reclaimed by savanna grasses.

Places to Stay

Fortunately, there are no hotels in the park and the only option is to camp at ***Los Loros*** *(☎ 03447-493031)*, which has shady level sites, hot showers, a store, and a confitería. Campers pay a one-time fee of US$3 to US$4 per tent as well as US$4 per person per day. The nearest hotels are in the cities of Concordia, about 50km north of the park entrance on RN 14, and Colón, about the same distance south.

Getting There & Away

El Palmar is 360km northwest of Buenos Aires on RN 14, a major national highway, so there are frequent north-south bus services. Any bus from Buenos Aires, Gualeguaychú, or Concepción del Uruguay will drop you at the park entrance, as will any bus making the run from Colón to Concordia. There is no public transport to the visitor center and camping area, but hitching should not be difficult. A remise from Colón or Concordia should cost about US$35.

CONCORDIA

First settled in 1769, this clean, attractive agricultural and livestock center on the Río Uruguay offers the most northerly border crossing in the province of Entre Ríos, via the Salto Grande hydroelectric project, to the Uruguayan city of Salto. Concordia's formal foundation dates from 1832 with the construction of its Catedral San Antonio de

Padua. Visitors come for its riverside beaches and fishing.

Orientation

Concordia (population 123,500) is 431km north of Buenos Aires and 65km north of Parque Nacional El Palmar via RN 14. Its grid centers on Plaza 25 de Mayo; street names change one block west, on each side of Entre Ríos, which is a popular north-south peatonal between Bernardo de Irigoyen and Urdinarraín (do not confuse east-west Bernardo de Irigoyen for the north-south thoroughfare Av Hipólito Yrigoyen, one block east of the Plaza, which leads to the bus terminal).

Information

Tourist Offices The municipal Secretaría de Turismo (☎ 421-2137, 421-3905), Mitre 64, is open daily 7 am to 10 pm.

ACA (☎ 421-6544) is at Pellegrini and Corrientes.

Money There are several banks with ATMs in the vicinity of Plaza 25 de Mayo.

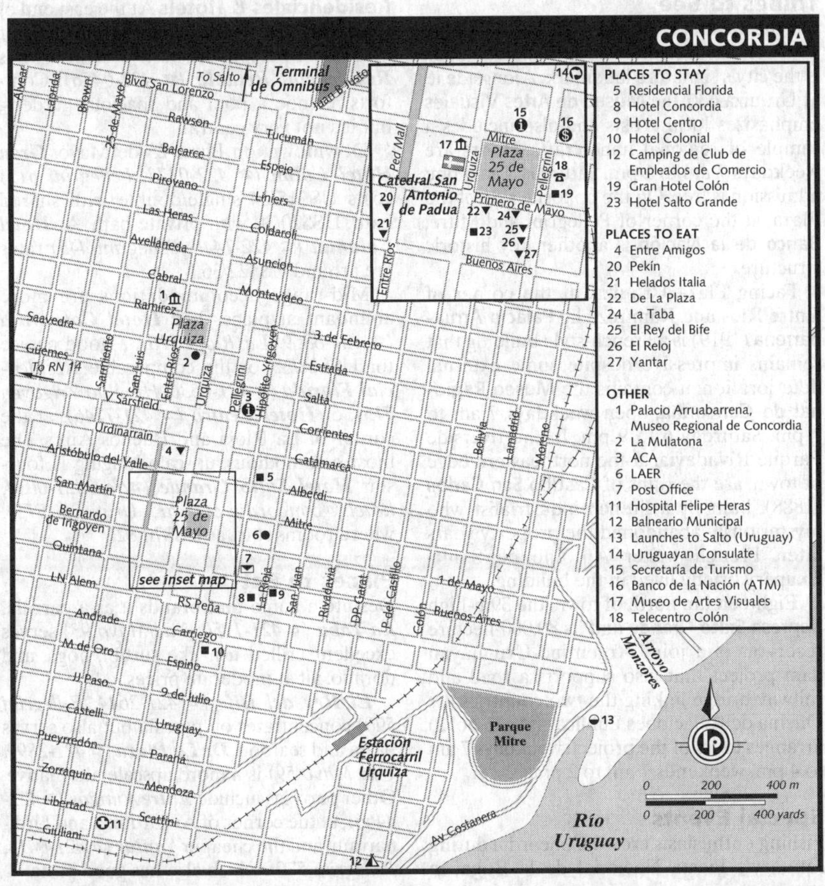

Post & Communications Correo Argentino is on Hipólito Yrigoyen between 1 de Mayo and Buenos Aires; the postal code is 3200.

Telecentro Colón is on Pellegrini between Mitre and Primero de Mayo. Concordia's area code is ☎ 0345.

Medical Services Hospital Felipe Heras (☎ 421-2580) is at Entre Ríos 135.

Laundry La Mulatona (☎ 421-1517) is at Saavedra 43.

Things to See

On the west side of Plaza 25 de Mayo, the 19th-century **Catedral San Antonio de Padua** is the city's signature landmark. Alongside it, at Urquiza 636, the **Museo de Artes Visuales** emphasizes local artists and also includes a sample of regional handicrafts. Hours are weekdays 7 am to 1 pm, Saturday 7 to 9 pm; admission is free. On the opposite side of the Plaza, at the corner of Pellegrini and Mitre, **Banco de la Nación** is another key historic structure.

Facing Plaza Urquiza, at the corner of Entre Ríos and Ramírez, the **Palacio Arruabarrena** (1919) is a French-style building that remains impressive despite some external deterioration; it contains the **Museo Regional de Concordia**, open weekdays 7 am to 1 pm, Saturday 6 to 9 pm. In the riverside Parque Rivadavia, at the northeastern edge of town, are the ruins of **Castillo San Carlos** (1888), built by a French industrialist who mysteriously abandoned the property years later. French writer Antoine de Saint-Exupéry briefly lived in the building.

Eighteen km north of town, the 39m-high **Represa Salto Grande** and its 80,000-hectare reservoir is a joint Argentine-Uruguayan dam project that also supports a road and railway bridge linking the two countries. Its Oficina de Relaciones Públicas (☎ 421-6612) arranges tours of the project, weekdays 7 am to 4 pm, weekends 7 am to 2 pm.

Special Events

Fishing enthusiasts crowd Concordia during January's Fiesta Nacional de la Boga, in search of the region's tastiest river fish. The city holds its Fiesta Nacional de Citricultura (National Citrus Festival) the first week in December.

Places to Stay

Camping The most convenient camping place, also close to the port for crossings to Salto, is the ***Camping de Club de Empleados de Comercio*** *(☎ 422-0080)* at the Balneario Municipal at the foot of San Juan, beyond the railroad tracks. Rates are US$8 per site.

Residenciales & Hotels At the east end of Coldaroli near the beach at Playa Nebel, for US$15 per person, the best value in town is ***Residencial Betanía*** *(☎ 431-0456)*. Comforts include a pool and spacious gardens, but it's not very central.

Downtown, on Plaza 25 de Mayo, ***Gran Hotel Colón*** *(☎ 422-0373, Pellegrini 611)* costs US$15/24 single/double with shared bath, US$20/30 with private bath. At ***Hotel Colonial*** *(☎ 422-1448, Pellegrini 443)* rates are around US$22/36.

Mid-range accommodations are more abundant at places like ***Hotel Concordia*** *(☎ 421-6869, La Rioja 516)*, a good choice for US$28/35, or the comparable ***Residencial Florida*** *(☎ 421-6536, Hipólito Yrigoyen 715)*, or ***Hotel Centro*** *(☎ 421-7746)*, at the corner of La Rioja and Buenos Aires. The most commodious, upscale lodging is four-star ***Hotel Salto Grande*** *(☎/fax 421-0034, hotels@concordia.com.ar; Urquiza 575)*, where rooms start at US$70/82.

Places to Eat

Despite a name that brands it as a parrilla, ***La Taba*** *(☎ 421-1150, 1 de Mayo 93)* serves excellent grilled fish like surubí, boga, and dorado, all at moderate prices.

El Rey del Bife *(☎ 421-2644, Pellegrini 590)* concentrates on parrilla but also serves pasta and seafood. ***De La Plaza*** *(☎ 421-2899, 1 de Mayo 59)* is a more upscale alternative. Other parrillas include ***Entre Amigos*** *(☎ 422-4466)*, at the corner of Av Urquiza and Urdinarraín, and the cheaper ***Yantar*** *(☎ 421-0414, Pellegrini 570)*, which also has good pasta.

El Reloj, on Pellegrini between Primero de Mayo and Buenos Aires, is a pizzería with good ambience. ***Pekín***, on Entre Ríos between Bernardo de Irigoyen and Quintana, is a Chinese tenedor libre in the US$6 to US$7 range.

For ice cream, try ***Helados Italia*** on Entre Ríos between Bernardo de Irigoyen and Quintana.

Getting There & Away

Air Laer (☎ 421-1551), La Rioja 620, has 13 weekly flights to Aeroparque in Buenos Aires (US$65) and flies eight times weekly to Paso de los Libres (US$21).

Bus The Terminal de Ómnibus (☎ 421-7235) occupies the triangle formed by Blvd San Lorenzo, Hipólito Yrigoyen, and the diagonal Juan B Justo.

Buses to Salto, Uruguay (US$3, 45 minutes), operate daily except Sunday. Chadre (☎ 421-4157) leaves at noon and 6 pm, returning at 8 am and 2 pm, while Flecha Bus (☎ 421-4182) leaves at 11:30 am and 6:30 pm, returning at 2 and 8:30 pm.

Long-distance buses between Buenos Aires and the provinces of Corrientes and Misiones resemble those passing through Gualeguaychú, Concepción, and Colón. Flecha Bus has five buses daily to the capital (US$23, six hours), while Tata (☎ 421-5880) and Itapé (☎ 421-5800) provide additional services. Flecha Bus has additional direct service to La Plata. Singer (☎ 4212594) and El Norte Bis (☎ 421-5800) go to northern Mesopotamian destinations. Jovi Bus (☎ 421-9981) serves destinations within Entre Ríos.

Boat From the port past the east end of Carriego, launches cross the river to Salto weekdays at 8:45 and 10 am, noon, and 2:30 and 6:30 pm. Saturday and holiday crossings are at 8:45 am, noon, and 2:30 and 6 pm, while Sunday crossings are at 8:30 am only, returning at 6 pm. The 15-minute trip costs US$4 for adults, US$2 for children.

Getting Around

To/From the Airport Aeropuerto Comodoro Pierrestegui (☎ 425-1001) is 14km north of town via Av Monseñor Rosch. A remise costs about US$8.

Corrientes Province

Like Entre Ríos, Corrientes traditionally has been an isolated province whose inhabitants proclaim a strong regional identity. Southern Corrientes' low, rolling terrain, with its productive agriculture, closely resembles Entre Ríos. The alluvial grasslands of the north, though, support mostly livestock except where interrupted by marshes like the Esteros del Iberá, whose wildlife is comparable to that of Brazil's better known Pantanal. Gallery forests are common along the many watercourses, but plantations of exotic conifers also flourish in the warm, humid climate. Winter and early spring are the best times for a visit because summer can be oppressively hot.

During colonial times, settlement in Corrientes advanced southward from Paraguay. Indian resistance discouraged a permanent Spanish presence until 1588, with the founding of the city of Corrientes. Jesuit priests were the region's most effective colonizers until their expulsion from South America in 1767; their most southerly mission, at Yapeyú on the Río Uruguay, was also the birthplace of Argentina's greatest hero, José de San Martín.

Since independence, Corrientes' economy has relied on livestock, first cattle and, more recently, sheep. The province's distance from markets discouraged attempts to improve its cattle breeds until well into the 20th century. In recent years, forestry and timber processing have become important industries. Efforts at encouraging provincial industry through large-scale energy developments like the trouble-plagued hydroelectric project at Yacyretá have so far seen limited success.

For visitors, the Río Paraná and its fishery are the province's traditional attraction, but Iberá is truly extraordinary. Both the city and province of Corrientes also hold the country's most notable celebrations of Carnaval. The city has many historic buildings dating to colonial times.

CORRIENTES

Founded just below the confluence of the Río Paraná and the Río Paraguay by Spaniards moving south from Asunción in 1588, the provincial capital of Corrientes is one of Argentina's oldest and most historic cities. Originally called Vera de los Siete Corrientes, after its founder Juan Torres de Vera y Aragón and the shifting currents of the Paraná, it suffered repeated Indian uprisings before establishing itself permanently. In the early 19th century, it was part of the short-lived 'República de Entre Ríos.' On the opposite bank of the Paraná is Resistencia, capital of Chaco province.

Corrientes (population 333,600) was the setting for Graham Greene's novel *The Honorary Consul*, later made into a bad Hollywood film.

Orientation

Overland connections from Buenos Aires, 1025km south via RN 12 and other roads, are good. Corrientes' regular grid centers on Plaza 25 de Mayo, though major public buildings are more spread out than in most Argentine cities. There are several other important plazas, including Plaza La Cruz and Plaza JB Cabral. Between Salta and San Lorenzo, Calle Junín is a peatonal along which most commercial activities are concentrated.

Calle Junín and most other areas of interest to the visitor are within a triangle formed by three main streets: Av Costanera General San Martín (which changes names to Plácido Martínez at its eastern end), north-south Av España, and Av 3 de Abril, a westward extension of Av Gobernador Ferré, which leads to the Puente General Manuel Belgrano to Resistencia. To the east, RN 12 parallels the Paraná to Ituzaingó and to Posadas, the capital of Misiones province.

Information

Tourist Offices Much improved over recent years, the friendly and helpful Dirección Provincial de Turismo (☎ 427200, 424565) is at 25 de Mayo 1330. It's open weekdays 7 am to 1 pm and 3 to 9 pm, weekends 8 am to noon and 4 to 8 pm. The Dirección Municipal de Turismo maintains an office in Parque Cambacuá (☎ 423779) at Pellegrini 542.

ACA (☎ 422844) is at 25 de Mayo and Mendoza.

Money Cambio El Dorado is at 9 de Julio 1341. There are also several banks with ATMs on and around 9 de Julio.

Post & Communications Correo Argentino is at the corner of San Juan and San Martín; the postal code is 3400. There are Telecentros at the corner of Santa Fe and Junín, at Pellegrini 1239, and at Av Costanera 924; Corrientes' area code is ☎ 03783.

Cultural Centers The Teatro Oficial Juan de Vera (☎ 427743), honoring the city's colonial founder, offers classical music concerts and other cultural events at San Juan 637.

Travel Agencies Quo Vadis (☎ 423096, fax 421958), Pellegrini 1140, is the AmEx representative.

For less conventional services such as trips to Parque Nacional Mburucuyá, contact 4WD Empresa de Viajes de Turismo (☎/fax 433269), Junín 1062, Local 18.

Medical Services The Hospital Escuela San Martín (☎ 420697, 421371) is at Av 3 de Abril 1251.

Walking Tour

In Corrientes' stifling summer heat, early-morning or late-afternoon hours are best for sightseeing. A good starting point is the **Convento de San Francisco**, Mendoza 450, a colonial church beautifully restored in 1939. Dating from the city's founding, it has a museum (☎ 422936) open 8 am to noon and 5 to 9 pm weekdays.

From the Convento, walk west along Plácido Martínez, detouring up Calle San Juan to view the innovative **historical murals** (see below) before strolling along the tree-lined Av Costanera, past the small but interesting **Jardín Zoológico**. Beyond the zoo are excellent views of the **Puente Belgrano**, the bridge crossing the Paraná to Resistencia.

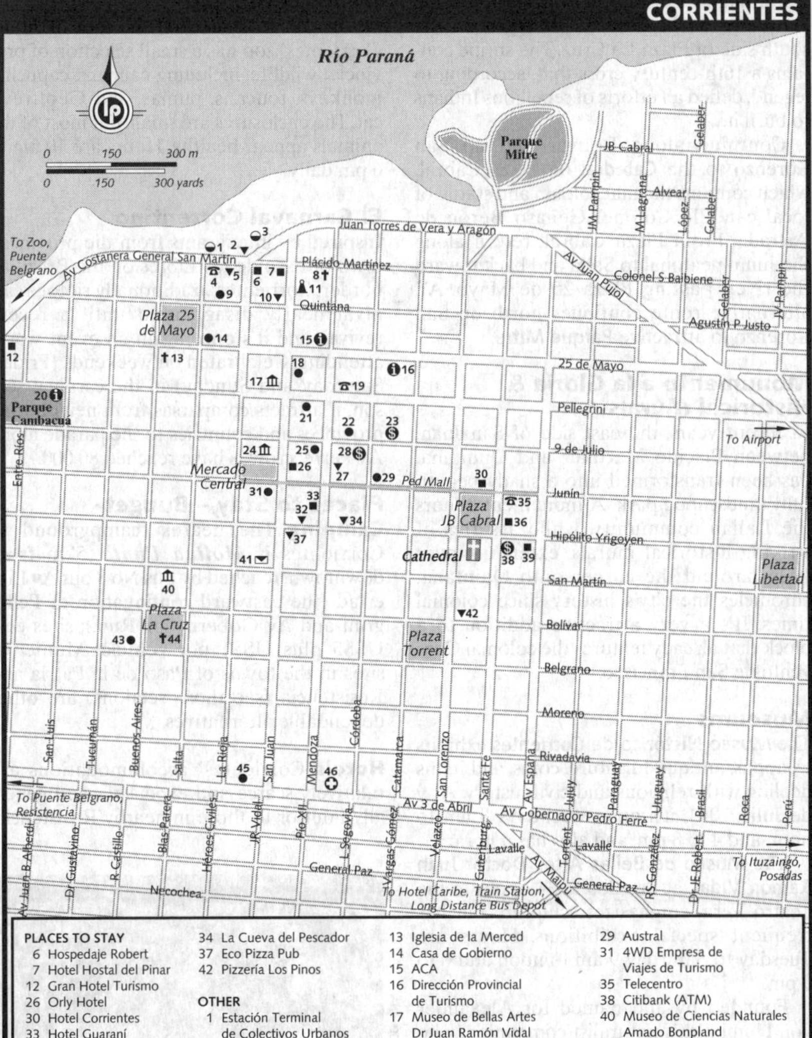

PLACES TO STAY
- 6 Hospedaje Robert
- 7 Hotel Hostal del Pinar
- 12 Gran Hotel Turismo
- 26 Orly Hotel
- 30 Hotel Corrientes
- 33 Hotel Guaraní
- 36 Hotel San Martín
- 39 Hotel Sosa

PLACES TO EAT
- 2 Pamper Pizzería
- 5 Heladería Trieste
- 10 Heladería Trieste
- 27 Las Espuelas
- 32 Heladería La Terraza
- 34 La Cueva del Pescador
- 37 Eco Pizza Pub
- 42 Pizzería Los Pinos

OTHER
- 1 Estación Terminal de Colectivos Urbanos
- 3 Resistencia-Corrientes Bus Depot
- 4 Telecentro
- 8 Convento de San Francisco, Museo Franciscano
- 9 Museo de Artesanía Folklórica
- 11 Monumento a la Gloria, Historical Murals
- 13 Iglesia de la Merced
- 14 Casa de Gobierno
- 15 ACA
- 16 Dirección Provincial de Turismo
- 17 Museo de Bellas Artes Dr Juan Ramón Vidal
- 18 Teatro Oficial Juan de Vera
- 19 Telecentro
- 20 Dirección Municipal de Turismo
- 21 Quo Vadis
- 22 LAPA
- 23 Cambio El Dorado
- 24 Museo Histórico de Corrientes
- 25 Cine Colón
- 28 Banco de la Nación (ATM)
- 29 Austral
- 31 4WD Empresa de Viajes de Turismo
- 35 Telecentro
- 38 Citibank (ATM)
- 40 Museo de Ciencias Naturales Amado Bonpland
- 41 Post Office
- 43 Zoca Pub
- 44 Iglesia de la Cruz/Santuario de la Cruz del Milagro
- 45 Localiza
- 46 Hospital Escuela San Martín

Returning by Edison and Bolívar, stop at the **Santuario de la Cruz del Milagro** on the south side of Plaza La Cruz. The shrine contains a 16th-century cross that, according to legend, defied all efforts of rebellious Indians to burn it.

Continue along Bolívar and up San Lorenzo to the **Catedral** on Plaza Cabral, which contains the mausoleum and statue of local caudillo Colonel Genaro Berón de Astrada. From Plaza Cabral, return along the Junín peatonal to Salta and back toward the river, passing Plaza 25 de Mayo. An alternative route continues north on San Lorenzo to attractive **Parque Mitre**.

Monumento a la Gloria & Historical Murals

In recent years, the east side of San Juan, between Plácido Martínez and Quintana, has been transformed into a shady beautifully landscaped park. A monument honors the Italian community, while a series of striking historical murals, extending over 100m around the corner onto Quintana, chronicles the city's history since colonial times. It's a very attractive addition to a block that already features the colonial Convento de San Francisco.

Museums

The **Museo Histórico de Corrientes** exhibits weapons, antique furniture, coins, and items dealing with religious and civil history. At 9 de Julio 1044, it's open weekdays 8 am to noon and 4 to 8 pm, and also has a library.

The **Museo de Bellas Artes Doctor Juan Ramón Vidal**, at San Juan 634 opposite the Teatro Vera, emphasizes sculpture but has frequent special exhibitions. Hours are Tuesday to Saturday 9 am to noon and 6 to 9 pm.

Founded by and named for Alexander von Humboldt's naturalist companion, who spent much of his life in the province and is buried at Paso de los Libres, the **Museo de Ciencias Naturales Amado Bonpland**, undergoing renovation at San Martín 850, has some good fossils but is otherwise unexceptional. It's open weekdays 9 am to noon and 4 to 9 pm.

Jardín Zoológico

On the Av Costanera at the foot of Junín, Corrientes' zoo has a small selection of provincial wildlife, including caimans, capuchin monkeys, toucans, pumas, and Geoffrey's cat. The enclosures are small, but most of the animals appear healthy. Hours are 10 am to 6 pm daily.

El Carnaval Correntino

Inspired by immigrants from the provincial town of Paso de los Libres on the Brazilian border, Corrientes' traditionally riotous carnival nearly disappeared until a recent revival, and it's once again an event worth attending. Celebrated on weekends (Friday, Saturday, and Sunday) in the carnival season, it attracts comparsas from neighboring provinces and countries to the parade along Av Ferré; crowds have reached 80,000.

Places to Stay – Budget

Camping The nearest campground to Corrientes is ***Molina Punta***, 5km from downtown, reached by bus No 8 out Av Libertad (the eastward continuation of Pellegrini and Av Gobernador Ruiz); sites cost US$5 plus US$1 per vehicle. Municipal sites in the towns of Paso de la Patria and Resistencia (see those sections) are other dependable alternatives.

Hotels Corrientes' accommodations are relatively scarce and expensive, and generally inferior to those in nearby Resistencia.

SECRETARÍA DE TURISMO ARGENTINA

Corrientes Gauchos

During Carnaval, however, the provincial tourist office maintains a list of casas de familia where lodging generally ranges from US$10 to US$20 per person.

Regular budget choices include ***Hospedaje Robert*** *(La Rioja 415)* (no phone) and ***Residencial Necochea*** *(Héroes Civiles 1898)* (no phone), on the southward extension of La Rioja. Rates are around US$18/30 single/double with shared bath. ***Hotel Caribe*** *(☎ 442197, Maipú 2590)*, close to the bus terminal, charges US$25/35 with private bath.

Run-down but friendly ***Hotel Sosa*** *(☎ 466747, Yrigoyen 1676)*, half a block from Plaza Cabral, charges US$31/35 but there's a substantial discount for cash.

Places to Stay – Mid-Range

On Plaza Cabral, ***Hotel Corrientes*** *(☎ 421344, Junín 1549)* charges US$35/48. Having undergone a major facelift, the ***Orly Hotel*** *(☎ 427388, San Juan 867)* charges about US$41/50 for rooms that are spotlessly clean. ***Hotel San Martín*** *(☎ 421314, Santa Fe 955)* is comparably priced at US$46/57.

The ***Gran Hotel Turismo*** *(☎ 433174, Entre Ríos 650)* is in parklike grounds with a swimming pool, restaurant, and bar. It's on the Av Costanera General San Martín (don't be fooled by the street address), and is a good value at US$48/58.

Places to Stay – Top End

Rates at ***Hotel Guaraní*** *(☎ 433800, fax 424620, Mendoza 970)* start at US$38/58, but most rooms are in the US$60/75 range. At the four-star, high-rise ***Hotel Hostal del Pinar*** *(☎ 436100, Plácido Martínez 1098)*, on the riverfront, rooms with private bath and breakfast are about US$46/67.

Places to Eat

The Junín peatonal has many cafés and confiterías, but shuts down during the midday heat. For cheap eats, look in and around the ***Mercado Central*** (Central Market) on Junín between La Rioja and San Juan.

Pizzería Los Pinos, at Bolívar and San Lorenzo, is a good fast-food choice, but the lively and slightly more expensive ***Eco Pizza Pub*** *(☎ 425900, Hipólito Yrigoyen 1108)* has better food. ***Pamper Pizzería***, at the corner of Av Costanera and La Rioja, is another pizza alternative.

Las Espuelas *(Mendoza 847)* is an outstanding parrilla, but prices have risen enough that it's not quite the value it once was. At lunchtime, you may wish to take advantage of its air conditioning, but the outdoor patio can be pleasant for dinner. Prices are high but not outrageous at ***La Cueva del Pescador*** *(☎ 422511, Hipólito Yrigoyen 1255)*, a very fine fish restaurant with good atmosphere.

Heladería Trieste, with locations at the corner of San Juan and Quintana and on Av Costanera near La Rioja, has superb ice cream and a very welcome water cooler. Another possibility is ***Heladería La Terraza*** *(☎ 423219, Hipólito Yrigoyen 1135)*.

Entertainment

The three-screen ***Cine Colón*** *(☎ 431956)*, on 9 de Julio between San Juan and Mendoza, shows current films.

The ***Zoca Pub***, at Buenos Aires and Belgrano, has live rock & roll.

Shopping

Local crafts are available at the Museo de Artesanía Folklórica, in a colonial house at Quintana 905. Hours are weekdays except Tuesday (when it's closed) from 7:30 am to 12:30 pm and 2 to 6 pm, and Saturday 9 am to noon and 3 to 6 pm.

Getting There & Away

Air Austral (☎ 423918), Junín 1301, flies twice daily to Buenos Aires (US$161) except Sunday (once only). They fly Sunday to Posadas (US$62), and there are also flights from nearby Resistencia, with both Austral and Aerolíneas Argentinas.

LAPA (☎ 431628), 9 de Julio 1261, flies 10 times weekly to Buenos Aires' Aeroparque (US$59 to US$79).

Bus Resistencia has better long-distance bus connections, especially to the west and northwest. Buses to Resistencia (US$2) leave from the local bus terminal, on Av Costanera General San Martín at La Rioja, at frequent intervals throughout the day. Albizzatti (☎ 442850) goes to provincial destinations like Goya and Esquina.

There are at least four buses daily to Buenos Aires, some via Paraná, Santa Fe, and Rosario and others via Entre Ríos, with Chevallier (☎ 442180), Flecha Bus (☎ 442108), El Zonda (☎ 442150) and Tata/El Rápido (☎ 463227), which also goes to Córdoba. Itatí (☎ 460279) is another important Buenos Aires and regional carrier.

Expreso Ciudad de Posadas (☎ 442183) and Kurtz (☎ 463590) have regular runs to Posadas, capital of Misiones province, where there are connections to the former Jesuit missions and to Puerto Iguazú. El Zonda links Corrientes with Posadas and Puerto Iguazú, and also crosses the Chaco to Tucumán. Puerto Tirol (☎ 442158) serves the western bank of the Paraná, with routes running from Formosa south to Buenos Aires.

Tata/El Rápido also goes to Paso de los Libres, on the Brazilian border, via the interior city of Mercedes, for access to the Esteros del Iberá. Empresa Tala (☎ 446384) goes to a wide variety of destinations both domestic (Formosa, Concordia, Buenos Aires, La Plata) and foreign (Uruguaiana, Brazil; and Asunción, Paraguay). Co-Bra (☎ 446416) offers direct service to Brazil.

Typical fares include Posadas (US$18, 4½ hours), Rosario (US$30, 10 hours), Puerto Iguazú (US$35, 10 hours), and Buenos Aires (US$35 to US$50, 12 hours).

Getting Around

To/From the Airport Local bus No 8 goes to Corrientes' Aeropuerto Doctor Fernando Piragine Niveyro (☎ 431628), about 10km east of town on RN 12. Austral runs a minibus to Resistencia to coincide with flight schedules.

Bus The long-distance bus terminal, the Estación Terminal de Transporte Gobernador Benjamín S González (☎ 442149) is on Av Maipú. From the local bus station on Av Costanera, take bus No 6.

Car Localiza (☎ 426270) is at Av 3 de Abril 1047.

PASO DE LA PATRIA

Superb sport fishing has made this flood-prone riverside resort of unpaved streets, 30km northeast of Corrientes at the confluence of the Paraguay and Paraná, an international destination for knowledgeable anglers. High season is July to September; early October to early March is the closed season.

Information

The Dirección de Turismo (☎ 494007) is at 25 de Mayo 518. Paso de la Patria's postal code is 3904, while the area code is ☎ 03783.

Fiesta Internacional del Dorado

The highlight of this annual festival, held in mid-August, is a four-day competition for the largest specimens of the carnivorous dorado *(Salminus maxiliosus)*, known as the 'tiger of the Paraná' for its fighting nature. The dorado weighs up to 25kg, and the minimum allowable catch size is 75cm. Entry costs around US$60 per person. Besides the dorado, local sport species include the surubí (weighing up to 70kg), the tasty boga, sábalo, pejerrey, pacú, patí, manduví, manduve, mangrullo, chafalote, and armado. Methods include trolling, spinning, and fly casting. Night fishing is possible.

Places to Stay

Several campgrounds charge about US$5 to US$6 per tent per day, plus US$3 per vehicle, with all facilities. Many correntinos have weekend houses here and often rent them to visitors. Prices for a two-bedroom house start at around US$60 per day for up to six persons. For more information, contact the tourist office.

One alternative for local accommodations is ***Le Apart Hotel*** *(☎ 494174, 25 de Mayo 1201)*, which charges US$120 per day with breakfast for up to four persons.

Getting There & Away

There is frequent bus service to and from Corrientes.

MERCEDES

At the junction of RN 123 and RN 119, 120km northwest of Paso de los Libres,

Mercedes is the main gateway to the spectacular wetlands wildlife of the Esteros del Iberá. It is also home to the shrine to the Gaucho Antonio Gil, an enormously popular religious phenomenon (see The Gaucho Antonio Gil).

Correo Argentino is at the corner of Rivadavia and Martínez; the postal code is 3470. Mercedes' area code is ☎ 03773.

Places to Stay & Eat

At the Antonio Gil shrine, 9km west of town, there is inexpensive camping, but the ***Camping Municipal*** in Parque Tressens, at the east end of town, presently lies flooded under the waters of the Arroyo las Garzas.

Hotel Santa Rita *(☎ 420128, Dr Rivas 1180)* charges US$15 per person. Dark, rundown ***Hotel Plaza*** *(San Martín 698)*, at the corner of Plaza 25 de Mayo, costs US$18/32 single/double. ***Hotel Victoria*** *(☎ 420330)*, two blocks from the bus terminal at Juan Pujol and José María Gómez, is a better choice for US$26/46.

At the corner of Sarmiento and Pujol, also on Plaza 25 de Mayo, ***La Casa de Chipola*** is a standard parrilla with moderate prices and good, friendly service.

Getting There & Away

The Terminal Hipólito Yrigoyen is at San Martín and Alfredo Perreyra. Co-Bra has twice-daily buses to and from Paso de los Libres, but there are also buses passing through with Gauchot (to and from Corrientes), Central El Rápido, Ruta Atlántica, Paula Tours, El Crucero, and Águila Dorada.

Itatí buses to Colonia Pellegrini (two hours, US$8), in the Esteros del Iberá, leave Monday at 5 am and 2 pm, Tuesday through Friday at 2 pm, and Saturday at 10 am.

Gaucho Antonio Gil

Second only to the Difunta Correa (see the Cuyo chapter) as an object of popular devotion in Argentina, the Gaucho Antonio Gil was a Robin Hood figure whose shrine just outside Mercedes, in Corrientes province, attracts tens of thousands of pilgrims every year. Unlike the Difunta Correa, who probably never existed, Antonio Gil was a real historical figure, a 19th-century conscript who deserted the army of Colonel Juan de la Cruz Salazar and spent several years on the run, supported by the poor of the Corrientes countryside. Finally captured and reportedly hanged from an espinillo tree that still stands near his crypt, even as a judicial pardon awaited him in the town of Goya, Gil became a legend that soon spread beyond the province and Mesopotamia.

Like the Difunta Correa shrine, Antonio Gil's last resting place is the site of chapels and storehouses holding thousands of ex-votos brought by believers in miracles (among them, Corrientes' Mandiyú soccer team – although while Gil's intercession may have gotten them into the first division, it couldn't keep them there). Though less common than those of the Difunta Correa, Gaucho Gil roadside sites are even more conspicuous for their dozens of bright red flags flying in the breeze. January 8, the date of Gil's death, attracts the most pilgrims to the Mercedes site.

ESTEROS DEL IBERÁ

Esteros del Iberá, a wetlands wilderness covering 13,000 sq km in the north-central part of the province (14% of its entire territory), is a wildlife cornucopia comparable – if not superior – to Brazil's Pantanal do Mato Grosso. Aquatic plants and grasses, including 'floating islands,' dominate the marsh vegetation, while trees are relatively few. The most notable wildlife species are reptiles like the caiman, mammals like the maned wolf, howler monkey, neotropical otter, capybara, and pampas and swamp deer, and more than 350 bird species.

For independent travelers, the settlement of Colonia Pellegrini, 120km northwest of Mercedes on Laguna Iberá, is the easiest place to organize trips into the marshes. Much but not all of the wildlife is nocturnal.

Launch tours, costing about US$20 per hour for up to five persons, are a bargain for what they offer.

The best place to purchase supplies is the town of Mercedes, 107km southwest of Colonia Pellegrini, though some groceries are available in Pellegrini itself.

Organized Tours

Since the logistics of visiting the Esteros are awkward, organized tours can be a good alternative. Estancia Capi-Vari (☎/fax 03773-420180), Beltrán 190 in Mercedes, arranges stays on an estancia at the southwestern corner of the reserve.

Both the Estancia San Gará and the Posada Aguapé offer trips into the wetlands. See Places to Stay, below.

Places to Stay

Camping is possible at Colonia Pellegrini for about US$2 per person. The peaceful, rustic but comfortable ***Hostería Ñandé Retá*** *(☎ 03773-421741, ☎/fax 03773-420155 in Mercedes; ☎ 03773-15-629536 cellular)* is a bargain for US$42 per person with full board. They also arrange transport from Mercedes and offer tours on site.

More luxurious is the colonial-style ***Posada Aguapé*** *(☎ 0376-492-9759 in Corrientes; ☎ 011-4742-3015 in Buenos Aires; aguape@interserver.com.ar)*; by mail, contact María Paz Galmarini, Coronel Obarrio 1038, 1642 San Isidro, Provincia de Buenos Aires. Rates run from US$95 to US$120 per day with full board.

On the north side of the Esteros, Estancia San Gará *(☎ 03752-427217 in Posadas, 03786-420041 in Ituzaingó)*, which offers weekend trips into the wetlands, has rooms for US$80 per person per day with meals (US$50 with dormitory accommodations). It's at RN 12, Km 1237.

Getting There & Away

Colonia Pellegrini, 107km northeast of Mercedes via RP 40, is the best center for visiting the Esteros. There is frequent public transportation between Paso de Los Libres and Corrientes to Mercedes, where Itatí buses to Colonia Pellegrini (two hours) leave Monday at 5 am and 2 pm, Tuesday through Friday at 2 pm, and Saturday at 10 am. They return to Mercedes at 6 am Monday through Saturday, and also at 1 pm Saturday.

PASO DE LOS LIBRES

Brazilian influence made Paso de los Libres, a town of 39,000 on the Río Uruguay, the 'Cradle of the Carnaval of Corrientes.' About 700km north of Buenos Aires and 370km south of Posadas on RN 14, it has the most convenient international border crossing in the province, to the much larger Brazilian city of Uruguaiana on the opposite bank of the river. Brazilians come here to load up on consumer trinkets.

Orientation

On the west bank of the Uruguay, Paso de los Libres has a standard rectangular grid, centered on Plaza Independencia. The principal commercial street is Av Colón, one block west. Most points of interest are nearby, but the international bridge to Uruguaiana is about 10 blocks southwest.

Information

There's no tourist office, but try the ACA station near the border complex.

Post & Communications Correo Argentino is at General Madariaga and Juan Sitja Min; the postal code is 3230. Telecentro Mercosur is at Colón 975; the area code is ☎ 03772.

Money Libres Cambio is at Av Colón 901.

Medical Services Hospital San José (☎ 421404) is on Calle T Alisio, on the east side of Plaza España.

Bonpland's Tomb

Paso de los Libres is the final resting place of Amado (Aimé) Bonpland, the famous naturalist and travel companion of Alexander von Humboldt on the latter's epic South American journey in the early 19th century. Bonpland eventually settled in Corrientes,

where he founded the province's first natural history museum.

The frequently visited tomb is in the Cementerio de la Santa Cruz, just beyond the bus station, about 10 blocks west of downtown via Av San Martín. Ask the attendant for directions to 'El sabio Bonpland.'

Places to Stay & Eat

The cheapest lodging is ***Residencial Colón Hotel*** *(Av Colón 1065)*, which charges US$15 per person with private bath. Comfortable ***Hotel Iberá*** *(☎ 421848, Coronel López 1091)* has rooms with bath and very welcome air-con for US$25/35 for singles/doubles. High-rise ***Hotel Alejandro Primo*** *(☎ 424101, Pago Largo 1156)* is the best in town for US$55/80.

ACA has a mediocre restaurant near the border complex, but try also ***La Victoria*** *(☎ 421577, Colón 585)*.

Getting There & Away

Air Laer (☎ 422395), Colón 1028, flies to Concordia (US$21) and Buenos Aires (US$86) eight times weekly. There's a larger airport on the Brazilian side.

Bus The Terminal de Ómnibus (☎ 421608) is at Av San Martín and Santiago del Estero. Provincial bus services run three times daily to Corrientes, twice daily to Goya, and twice daily to Santo Tomé via Yapeyú.

Expreso Singer (☎ 424716) and Crucero del Norte (☎ 425171) pass through Paso de Los Libres three times daily en route between Buenos Aires and Posadas (six hours). Flecha Bus (☎ 425088) goes to Buenos Aires and to Camboriú, Brazil. Tala goes daily to La Plata.

There are also daily buses to Paraná and Santa Fe, and daily service to Rosario except Thursday. Daily, except Thursday, Paso de los Libres is a stopover between Córdoba and Puerto Iguazú.

YAPEYÚ

Founded in 1626, this southernmost Jesuit mission once had a population of more than 8000 Guaraní Indians, who tended as many as 80,000 cattle. After the order's expulsion in 1767, the Indians dispersed and the mission fell into ruins. In 1778, José de San Martín, Argentina's greatest national hero, was born in a modest dwelling whose ruins still exist in a protected site. Many houses in this placid riverside village of 1200 people are built of red sandstone blocks salvaged from the mission buildings.

On the west bank of the Río Uruguay, Yapeyú is 55km north of Paso de Los Libres and 6km southeast of RN 14. Everything in town is within easy walking distance of the central plaza. The area code is ☎ 03772.

Things to See

On the south side of Plaza San Martín, the **Museo de Cultura Jesuítica** consists of several modern kiosks, built on the foundations of mission buildings, whose photographic displays are a good introduction to the mission zone. A sundial and a few other mission relics are also here.

In 1938 Argentina's federal government completed a pretentious temple that shelters and encloses the **Casa de San Martín**, the Liberator's modest birthplace. The interior is covered with tributary plaques, including a prominent one from once de facto president General Jorge Rafael Videla – a Dirty War criminal who was given a life sentence, pardoned later by Menem, and is now being reinvestigated for kidnapping of children – attesting to his 'most profound faith' in San Martín's ideals of liberty.

Next door to San Martín's birthplace, in a house dating from Jesuit times, the **Museo Sanmartiniano** contains a number of artifacts and documents from San Martín and his family (as of early 1998, the museum was temporarily relocated to the Granaderos regiment at the south end of Av del Libertador). Opening hours are erratic.

Places to Stay & Eat

Yapeyú has limited accommodations. The ***Camping Municipal*** near the river charges US$5 with hot showers, but insects can be abundant and the most low-lying parts can flood in heavy rain – choose your tent site carefully.

Hotel San Martín *(Sargento Cabral 712)*, on the plaza, is bright and cheerful for $15/20 single/double. ***El Parador Yapeyú*** *(☎ 493056)*, at the entrance to town, has bungalows for US$30/40.

Restaurant Bicentenario has well-prepared food, reasonable prices, and friendly, attentive service. ***Comedor El Paraíso***, next to Hotel San Martín, serves passable meals as well.

Getting There & Away

The small bus station is at Av del Libertador and Chacabuco. Singer stops three times daily en route between Paso de los Libres and Posadas.

SANTO TOMÉ

Another stop on the Jesuit mission circuit, with some fine subtropical architecture, Santo Tomé (population 20,300) is 140km north of Yapeyú via RN 14. Its **Museo Histórico Regional**, Navajas 844, is open weekdays 8 to 11 am and 5 to 7 pm, and also has a library. It's possible to cross to the Brazilian town of São Borja, which also has Jesuit ruins, via a new bridge across the Río Uruguay.

The ***Hotel ACA*** *(☎ 0756-20162)*, at Patricio Bertrán and Belgrano, has good accommodations, and there are several campgrounds along Av San Martín. Singer goes three times daily to Posadas.

Misiones Province

On the political geographic map of Argentina, Misiones is the peninsula surrounded by the ocean of Brazil and Paraguay. Its outstanding natural feature is the Cataratas del Iguazú (Iguazú Falls) on the upper Paraná, one of South America's greatest natural attractions, but the cultural landscape of ruined Jesuit missions also draws large numbers of visitors.

Unlike the rest of Argentine Mesopotamia, Misiones is mountainous. The Sierra Central, separating the watersheds of the two major rivers, reaches up to 800m, although it only rarely exceeds 500m. The natural vegetation is mostly subtropical forest, though some large stands of native araucaria pines remain; however, the forest cover in the province declined from 2.5 million hectares to 1.1 million hectares between 1914 and 1983.

Economically, Misiones is the country's largest producer of *yerba mate*, the staple drink of Argentines and of many Uruguayans, Paraguayans, and Brazilians. Most yerba plantations are just east of the provincial capital of Posadas, but the central uplands also support large tea monocultures. In recent years plantation forestry has become important, with northern hemisphere pines replacing native araucarias.

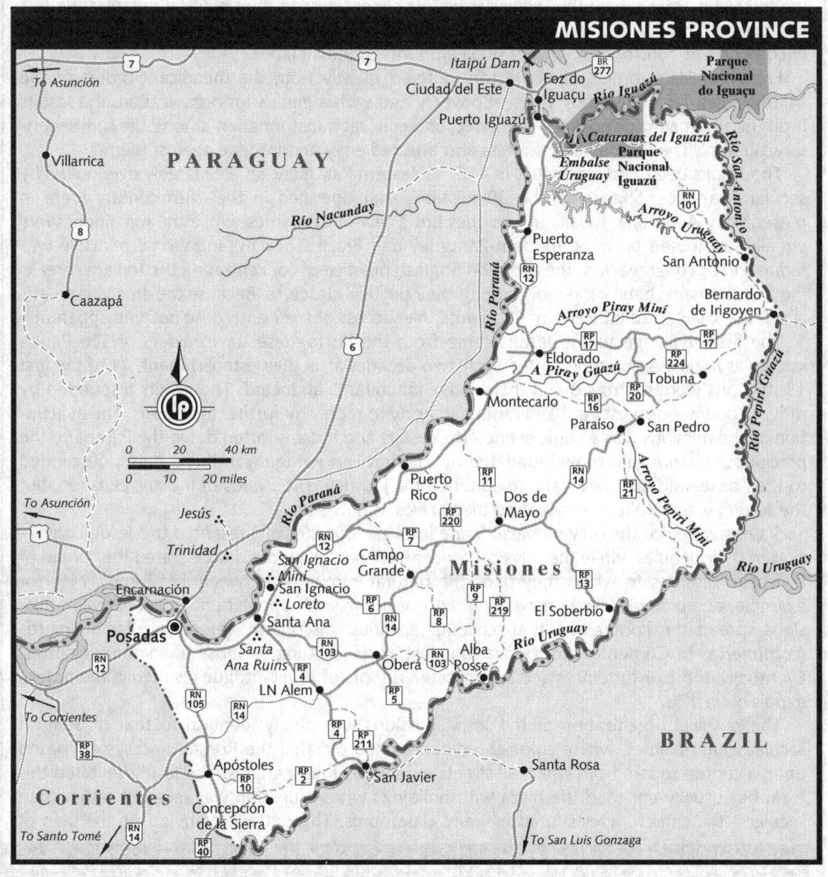

History

Misiones is famous for the Jesuit settlements *(reducciones* or *congregaciones)*that gave their name to the province (see boxed text). From 1607, after finding the nomadic Indians of the Chaco poor candidates for missionary instruction, the Jesuits established 30 missions among the semisedentary Guaraní in

The Jesuit Missions

After the Spaniards realized that America was not a storehouse of precious metals, they sought their wealth through the *encomienda*, a grant of native labor that also assigned them the responsibility of catechizing 'their' Indians and teaching them Spanish. Although Spaniards rarely lived up to their part of the bargain, the encomienda successfully overcame problems of economic organization in settled, densely populated areas like Mexico and Peru – at least until the Indians died out from smallpox and other introduced diseases. But the encomienda was ineffective in areas where the Indians were less sedentary and their political organization less centralized. This was the case on the upper Paraná of Paraguay and Argentina, where Spanish encomenderos controlled only very small amounts of Indian labor.

Enter the Jesuit order, whose history differed greatly from the mendicant orders of the Middle Ages. Unhindered by vows of poverty and with a genius for organization, the Jesuits brought about a major political, economic, and cultural transformation among the semisedentary Guaraní. Their remarkable success also aroused envy and intrigue against them.

The Jesuits began their activities in 1607 in eastern Paraguay, an area largely overlooked by secular Spaniards. Sixteen of the 30 missions that operated in the 18th century were in present-day Argentina, mostly in Misiones but a few in Corrientes, while the remainder were equally distributed between modern Paraguay and Brazil. Their organizational principle was *reducción* or *congregación*, the common Spanish practice of concentrating the Indians, breaking their nomadic habits and reorganizing their political structure. Because the area was so isolated, the Jesuits had little competition until the success of their enterprise became apparent.

The first challenge to the Jesuits came from the Portuguese slave raiders of São Paulo, known as *paulistas* or *bandeirantes*. Only two decades after their establishment, 11 of the first 13 missions were destroyed and their native inhabitants abducted. The Jesuits responded by moving operations westward and raising an army to repel any further incursions. The evacuation of the missions was an epic event – the Jesuits and Indians rafted down the Paraná to the precipitous Guairá Falls (now inundated by the Brazilian-Paraguayan Itaipú dam), descended to their base, and built new rafts to continue the journey. Thousands of Indians perished, but the Jesuits successfully re-established themselves at new sites.

Slavers were not the only menace. Some local *caciques* (chiefs) resented the Jesuit conversion of their peoples, while the physical concentration of the Indians accelerated the spread of European diseases to which they had little natural immunity. Between 1717 and 1719, for example, an epidemic killed off nearly a sixth of the mission population. Travel between missions spread the contagion. In succeeding decades, discontent among secular Spaniards *(comuneros)* in Corrientes led to invasions just as devastating as those of the bandeirantes. Eventually, these disturbances and exaggerated rumors of Jesuit intrigue resulted in the order's expulsion in 1767.

The physical organization of the Jesuit missions was nearly identical to that of Spanish secular municipalities, where colonial ordinances had dictated the Roman grid system based upon a central square from which all streets extended at right angles. The Jesuits imitated this form but usually enclosed the plaza with buildings whose function was religious rather than secular – the church, priests' quarters, and classrooms. This pattern is obvious in the plan of

the upper Paraná, in present-day Argentina, Brazil, and Paraguay. Perhaps as many as 100,000 Indians lived in these settlements, which resembled other Spanish municipalities but operated with a political and economic autonomy that made them the envy of other Iberian settlers, who resented the missions' wealth and their monopoly on the

The Jesuit Missions

San Ignacio Miní, the best restored of the Argentine missions. Often earthworks or a trench surrounded the settlement for purposes of defense.

The mission economy was largely agricultural and diversified. The Indians raised their own subsistence crops (maize, sweet potatoes, and cassava) but also labored on communal fields. *Yerba mate* was the most important plantation crop, but cotton, citrus, and tobacco were also significant. Within the settlement itself, intensive vegetable gardening yielded carrots, tomatoes, beans, peas, radishes, and beets. Outside the settlement, native herders tended the mission's numerous livestock. When the Jesuits were expelled, San Ignacio Miní had a population of 3200 but possessed 10 times that many cattle and more than twice that many sheep and goats.

Life on the reducción was probably less idyllic than portrayed in the film *The Mission*, but the labor was certainly less odious than elsewhere. The Jesuits closely regulated many aspects of everyday life such as education and dress, but their exuberant approach to work made mission residence sufficiently attractive that many Indians willingly chose it over the grim certainties of the encomienda. With the aid of skilled German priests, the Guaraní learned crafts and trades like weaving, baking, carpentry, cabinetmaking, and even the design of musical instruments. Unfortunately, these skills were useless to them in the post-mission world.

Indian labor that made that wealth possible. The missions competed with secular producers in the cultivation and sale of *yerba mate*, then the region's only important commodity.

The Jesuits' high degree of organization is evident in ruins like San Ignacio Miní, with its enormous plaza, imposing church, and extensive outbuildings. Unlike most secular Spaniards and many other monastic orders, they took their obligation to instruct indigenous peoples in the Spanish language and Catholic religion seriously, but they also taught music, literature, and the arts. Much of the elaborate sandstone statuary that embellishes the ruins is the work of Guaraní sculptors.

Long before expulsion, the missions had begun to suffer *malocas* (Portuguese slave raids) and other setbacks – despite their good intentions, the Jesuits' concentration of Indians in fixed settlements made them more vulnerable to epidemics like smallpox. In the political vacuum after 1767, mission communities disintegrated rapidly and much of the area lapsed into virtual wilderness. Densely forested areas became a refuge for Indians lacking the protection of the missions but unwilling to submit to the demands of secular Spaniards.

During the 19th century, Argentina, Brazil, and Paraguay contested the territory, but after the War of the Triple Alliance (1865 – 1870) between Paraguay on the one hand and Argentina, Uruguay, and Brazil on the other, Argentina took definitive control. Precise boundaries were not yet finalized, but European colonization proceeding from Corrientes by the mid-19th century soon intensified. Exploitation of wild *yerba mate* spurred settlement but resulted in large concessions of land to a very few individuals and companies. The federal government confiscated many of these holdings when their owners failed to survey and carry out improvements and, soon after, actively encouraged small-scale agricultural settlement.

SECRETARÍA DE TURISMO ARGENTINA

Iguazú Falls

By the turn of the century, colonists represented many nationalities: Poles, Brazilians, Argentines, Paraguayans, Italians, Russians, Germans, Spaniards, French, Swedish, unspecified Asians, Swiss, Arabs, Danes, British, Greeks, and North Americans. The most successful were the German colonists around Eldorado on the upper Paraná, but the entire province preserves a polyglot heritage acknowledged by all its residents. The father of Cuban-Argentine revolutionary Che Guevara ran an unsuccessful *yerba mate* plantation at Puerto Caraguatay, near Montecarlo, where Che spent part of his infancy.

The most ironic episode in provincial history never came to pass. During the depression of the 1930s, British officials in the Falkland Islands briefly considered relocating Islanders to a colonization project at Victoria, near Eldorado, but gave up the project on the rationale that Falklanders were not suited for the humid subtropics. In the 1950s, Japanese immigrants settled successfully in the province, but most recently there has been a further influx of Brazilians. Besides agriculture, forestry, and some mining, tourism is now a major factor in the provincial economy.

For a superb account of the environment and colonization in Misiones from colonial times to the present, see Robert Eidt's *Pioneer Settlement in Northeast Argentina* (University of Wisconsin, 1971). For the history of the Jesuit mission era, see Nicholas P Cushner's *Jesuit Ranches and the Agrarian Development of Colonial Argentina, 1650 – 1767* (Albany, SUNY Press, 1982).

Visitors who read Spanish well may wish to acquire the *Guía Turística de Misiones* (Posadas: Editora y Difusora de Guías SRL, 1994), which focuses on the province and has gone through 13 editions.

POSADAS

Named for Gervasio Antonio de Posadas, who decreed the creation of Entre Ríos and Corrientes while briefly holding the position of Director of the Provincias Unidas in 1814, the city of Posadas is Misiones' provincial capital and commercial center. As part of Corrientes province, Posadas first developed after the War of the Triple Alliance because of its strategic location. When the federal government made Misiones a separate territory in the 1880s, Corrientes reluctantly surrendered Posadas, which became the territorial capital and the gateway to the pioneer agricultural communities of interior Misiones. In 1912, the Urquiza railway connected the city with Buenos Aires.

Despite its recent pioneer past, Posadas is a modern city of 250,000 whose plentiful shade trees mitigate the summer heat and humidity. For most travelers, it's a brief stopover en route to Paraguay or Iguazú, but no one should miss the restored Jesuit missions at San Ignacio Miní, about 50km east, or at Trinidad on the Paraguayan side of the border. The city is losing some of its low-lying areas to flooding from the Yacyretá hydroelectric project, a different sort of monument.

Orientation

Posadas is on the south bank of the upper Río Paraná, 1310km north of Buenos Aires by RN 14, 310km east of Corrientes via RN 12, and 300km southwest of Puerto Iguazú, also via RN 12. Since April 1990, a handsome international bridge has linked Posadas with the Paraguayan city of Encarnación, across the river, but launches still operate between the port areas of the two cities.

Plaza 9 de Julio is the center of Posadas' standard grid. The city center, 14 blocks square, is circumscribed by four major thoroughfares: Av Corrientes in the west, Av Guacurarí in the north, Av Roque Sáenz Peña on the east, and Av Mitre to the south. Av Mitre leads east to the international bridge.

Theoretically, all streets in the city center have been renumbered, but new and old systems continue to exist side by side, creating great confusion to nonresidents, since most locals use the old system. Wherever possible, the information below refers to unambiguous locations rather than street numbers; if street numbers are given, the new number appears first with the old number in parentheses.

Information

Tourist Offices The well-organized, well-informed provincial Secretaría de Turismo (☎ 447540/1, 800-555-0297 toll-free; turismo@electromisiones.com.ar) is at Colón 1985 (formerly 393) between Córdoba and La Rioja. Offering numerous maps and brochures, it's open 8 am to 8 pm weekdays, 8 am to noon and 4:30 to 8 pm weekends and holidays.

ACA (☎ 436955) is at Córdoba and Colón.

Money Cambios Mazza, on Bolívar between San Lorenzo and Colón, changes traveler's checks. Banco Nazionale del Lavoro has an ATM on Bolívar, at the southeastern corner of Plaza 9 de Julio, but there are several others downtown.

Post & Communications Correo Argentino is at Bolívar and Ayacucho; the postal code is 3300. Telecentro Bolívar is at the corner of Bolívar and Colón; Posadas' area code is ☎ 03752.

Travel Agencies Express Travel (☎ 437687), Félix de Azara 2097, is the AmEx representative.

Bookstores Liverpool Libros, at Ayacucho and La Rioja, has English-language books.

Medical Services Hospital General R Madariaga (☎ 447775) is about 1km south of downtown, at Av López Torres 1177.

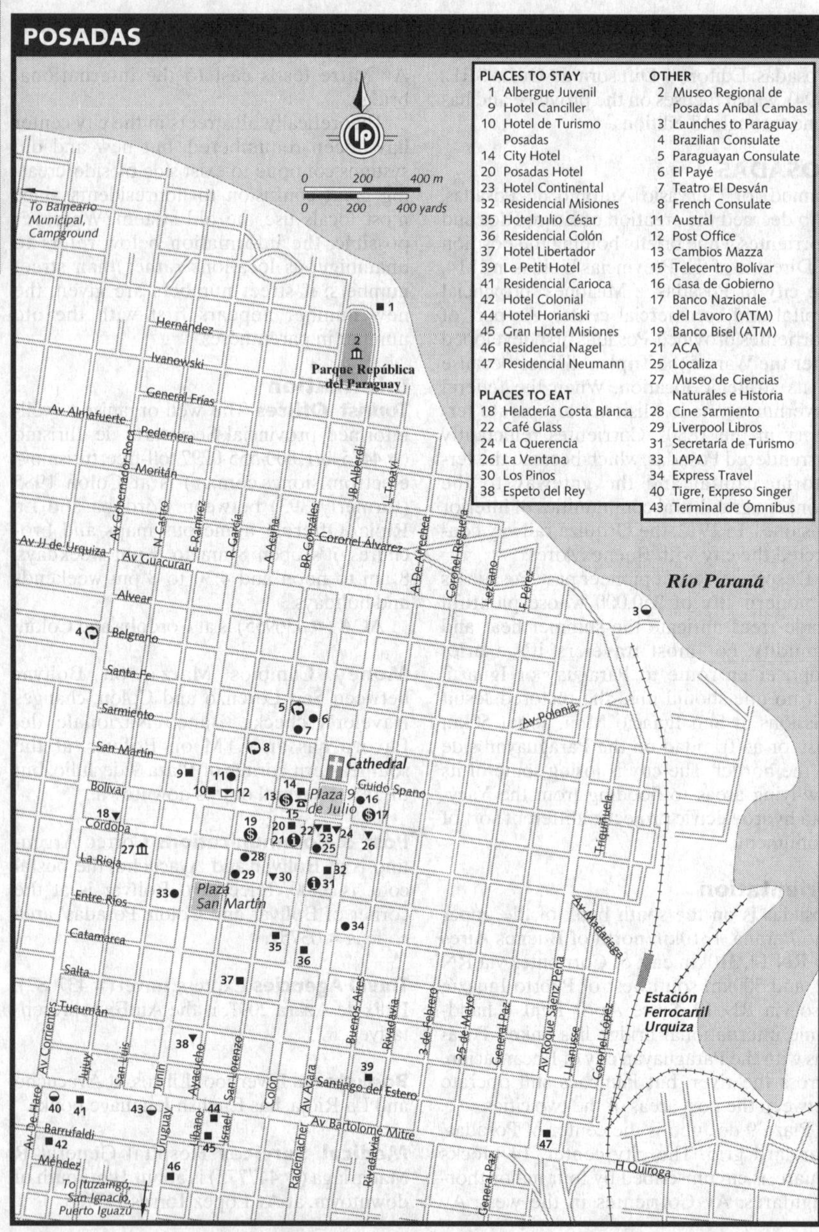
POSADAS
PLACES TO STAY
1 Albergue Juvenil
9 Hotel Canciller
10 Hotel de Turismo Posadas
14 City Hotel
20 Posadas Hotel
23 Hotel Continental
32 Residencial Misiones
35 Hotel Julio César
36 Residencial Colón
37 Hotel Libertador
39 Le Petit Hotel
41 Residencial Carioca
42 Hotel Colonial
44 Hotel Horianski
45 Gran Hotel Misiones
46 Residencial Nagel
47 Residencial Neumann
PLACES TO EAT
18 Heladería Costa Blanca
22 Café Glass
24 La Querencia
26 La Ventana
30 Los Pinos
38 Espeto del Rey
OTHER
2 Museo Regional de Posadas Aníbal Cambas
3 Launches to Paraguay
4 Brazilian Consulate
5 Paraguayan Consulate
6 El Payé
7 Teatro El Desván
8 French Consulate
11 Austral
12 Post Office
13 Cambios Mazza
15 Telecentro Bolívar
16 Casa de Gobierno
17 Banco Nazionale del Lavoro (ATM)
19 Banco Bisel (ATM)
21 ACA
25 Localiza
27 Museo de Ciencias Naturales e Historia
28 Cine Sarmiento
29 Liverpool Libros
31 Secretaría de Turismo
33 LAPA
34 Express Travel
40 Tigre, Expreso Singer
43 Terminal de Ómnibus
0 200 400 m
0 200 400 yards
To Balneario Municipal, Campground
Parque República del Paraguay
Río Paraná
Cathedral
Plaza 9 de Julio
Plaza San Martín
Estación Ferrocarril Urquiza
To Ituzaingó, San Ignacio, Puerto Iguazú
Hernández
Ivanowski
General Frías
Av Almafuerte
Pedernera
Moritán
Av JJ de Urquiza
Av Guacurarí
Coronel Álvarez
Alvear
Belgrano
Santa Fe
Sarmiento
San Martín
Bolívar
Guido Spano
Córdoba
La Rioja
Entre Ríos
Catamarca
Salta
Tucumán
Santiago del Estero
Av Bartolomé Mitre
Barrufaldi
Méndez
H Quiroga
Av Polonia
Av Madariaga
Av Gobernador Roca
N Castro
E Ramírez
R García
A Acuña
BR González
JB Alberdi
L Trealvi
A De Arrechea
Coronel Reguera
Lezcano
F Pérez
Triquiñuela
Av Corrientes
Av De Haro
Jujuy
San Luis
Junín
Uruguay
Ayacucho
Líbano
Israel
San Lorenzo
Colón
Av Azara
Rademacher
Buenos Aires
Rivadavia
Rivadavia
3 de Febrero
25 de Mayo
General Paz
General Paz
Av Roque Sáenz Peña
J Lanusse
Coronel López

Museums
The natural-history section of the **Museo de Ciencias Naturales e Historia**, on San Luis between Córdoba and La Rioja, focuses on fauna and the geology and mineralogy of the province; it also has an excellent serpentarium (every July morning at 10 am there is a demonstration of venom extraction), an aviary, and an aquarium. Its historical section stresses prehistory, the Jesuit missions, and modern colonization. Weekday hours are 7 am to noon and 2 to 7 pm, while weekend hours are 9 am to noon.

At the north end of Alberdi in Parque República de Paraguay, the **Museo Regional de Posadas Aníbal Cambas** has an interesting collection of stuffed natural-history specimens, ethnographic artifacts and historical relics. Hours are 7 am to 7 pm weekdays.

Places to Stay – Budget
Camping The campground at the riverside Balneario Municipal is cramped, noisy, and overpriced at US$7 per site; locals overrun the place on weekends in particular, so sleep is impossible. It's not recommended, but there's no nearby alternative.

Hostels For US$8 per night, there are hostel accommodations at the AAJ-affiliated ***Albergue Juvenil*** *(☎ 423700)* at the Anfiteatro MA Ramírez, on the riverfront at the north end of Alberdi. Like the campground, however, its standards are not up to snuff.

Residenciales & Hotels Posadas offers a small selection of cheap accommodations, though there are better values across the river in Encarnación, Paraguay. ***Residencial Misiones*** *(☎ 430133)*, on Av Azara between La Rioja and Córdoba, costs only US$15/25 single/double with private bath, but some visitors have questioned its standards. A good, comparably priced choice is ***Residencial Neumann*** *(☎ 424675, Roque Sáenz Peña 665)*, between Mitre and Santiago del Estero. ***Residencial Nagel*** *(☎ 425656, Pedro Méndez 2148)* at Uruguay, charges US$16 per person.

Places to Stay – Mid-Range
Mid-range accommodations are generally a better value, starting with the outstanding ***Hotel Colonial*** *(☎ 436149, Barrufaldi 2419)*, near the Singer/Tigre bus terminal, for US$22/36 for singles/doubles. The slightly dearer (US$25/35) but equally desirable ***Le Petit Hotel*** *(☎ 436031, lepetit@electromisiones.com.ar, Santiago del Estero 1635)*, between Rivadavia and Buenos Aires, is more central.

Reservations are advisable at both of those very popular places, but not at the distinctly unfriendly but otherwise passable ***Residencial Colón*** *(☎ 425085, Colón 2169 (formerly 485))*. Despite its impersonal appearance, the high-rise ***Hotel de Turismo Posadas*** *(☎ 437401)*, at Bolívar and Junín, is much friendlier and its balconies have excellent river views; rates are US$25/38.

Others in this range include ***Hotel Horianski*** *(☎ 422673)* at Av Mitre and Líbano for US$22/34; the ***City Hotel*** *(☎ 433901)* on Colón opposite Plaza 9 de Julio, for US$23/35; and the ***Residencial Carioca*** *(☎ 424113, Av Mitre 58)*, near the Singer bus terminal, which has rooms for US$25/34.

For US$30/40 with breakfast, ***Gran Hotel Misiones*** *(☎ 422777)*, on Líbano at Barrufaldi near the main bus terminal, also has a restaurant. ***Hotel Canciller*** *(☎ 431602, Junín 258)* at San Martín, charges US$31/45 with private bath but without breakfast.

Places to Stay – Top End
Hotel Libertador *(☎ 436901, San Lorenzo 2208)*, between Catamarca and Salta, charges US$50/60 for singles/doubles with breakfast. ***Hotel Continental*** *(☎ 427045, Bolívar 314)*, opposite Plaza 9 de Julio, charges US$50/68 with similar services.

At the top-of-the-line ***Posadas Hotel*** *(☎ 440888, Bolívar 1949)*, between Colón and San Lorenzo, rates are US$59/69. The city's only four-star facility, ***Hotel Julio César*** *(☎ 427930, Entre Ríos 1951)*, between San Lorenzo and Colón, charges US$72/88.

Places to Eat
There are many interchangeable, inexpensive eateries along San Lorenzo west of the

plaza, but parrillas are the standard, with several excellent ones. The spiffiest is ***La Querencia*** *(☎ 437117)* on Bolívar, across from Plaza 9 de Julio. ***La Ventana*** *(☎ 437581, Bolívar 1725 (formerly 580))*, between Av Azara and Buenos Aires, has a varied menu with large portions and reasonable prices – at least for some items.

Espeto del Rey, at Tucumán and Ayacucho, has moderately priced lunches in addition to its roasted chicken specialty. ***Los Pinos*** *(☎ 427252)*, at the corner of San Lorenzo and La Rioja, is one of Posadas' better pizzerias.

Café Glass, at the corner of Bolívar and Colón, is a good breakfast spot. For ice cream, try ***Costa Blanca*** at Jujuy and Córdoba.

Entertainment

Cine Sarmiento, on Córdoba between San Lorenzo and Ayacucho, shows current films. ***Teatro El Desván***, a theater company on Sarmiento between Colón and San Lorenzo, offers works by major Spanish-language playwrights like Federico García Lorca, and also has a children's theater.

Shopping

Posadas has a good selection of artisanal products. Try La Barraca, next door to Teatro El Desván, or El Payé, around the corner on Colón, where there's a good selection of *mate* paraphernalia (gourds and bombillas), basketry, wood carvings, and ceramics.

Getting There & Away

Air Austral (☎ 432889, 435031), at Ayacucho 264 and San Martín, flies 17 times weekly to Buenos Aires' Aeroparque (US$129 to US$171).

LAPA (☎ 440300), Junín 2054, flies twice daily to Aeroparque (US$59 to US$149) and Sunday to Puerto Iguazú (US$20 to US$42).

Bus The main Terminal de Ómnibus (☎ 425800) has moved to Ruta 12 and Av Santa Catalina, reachable from downtown by bus Nos 8, 15, and 21.

Buses to Encarnación, Paraguay, leave every 20 minutes from the corner of Mitre and Junín, opposite the main terminal, and pass through downtown via Ayacucho, San Martín and Av Roque Sáenz Peña. With border formalities, the trip can take an hour, but is often quicker; fares are US$1 *común*, US$2 *servicio diferencial* (with air-con).

To Puerto Iguazú, Martignoni (☎ 434924) and Tigre buses take 5½ hours express but much longer on the milk run. Tigre's earliest bus to San Ignacio Miní that departs at a reasonable hour leaves at 6:10 am; departures are hourly thereafter. There are numerous buses to Oberá with Singer and other companies.

Singer has daily service to Buenos Aires and intermediate points, between Resistencia and Puerto Iguazú, and to Santa Fe and Córdoba. Other Buenos Aires carriers include El Crucero (☎ 420426), Río Paraná (☎ 427008), Empresa Kurtz (☎ 421646), Metro Bus Klein (☎ 428165), Expreso Vía Bariloche (☎ 435788), and Empresa Tigre Iguazú (☎ 426210). Ciudad de Posadas (☎ 424331), El Norte Bis (☎ 422393), and Kurtz all go to Rosario.

El Crucero, Martignoni, and Kurtz all run buses to Corrientes and Resistencia, connecting across the Chaco to northwestern Argentina. Cotal (☎ 439924) has service to Mendoza via Santiago del Estero, Catamarca, La Rioja, and San Juan. La Estrella (☎ 424404) and La Nueva Estrella (☎ 421834) both go to Tucumán.

Singer also has international services daily to Asunción all year and three times weekly to Porto Alegre, Brazil in summer. Nuestra Señora de la Asunción (☎ 424404) also does the Asunción route. Penha (☎ 439924) goes to São Paulo at 5 am daily via Curitiba.

Typical fares include Corrientes (US$18, 4½ hours), Resistencia (US$20, five hours), Asunción (5½ hours), Puerto Iguazú (5½ hours, US$20), Buenos Aires (US$30, 14 hours; US$55 in *coche cama* sleepers), Porto Alegre (12 hours), Santa Fe (14 hours), Rosario (16 hours), Tucumán (18 hours), Córdoba (US$41, 17½ hours), Santiago del Estero (18½ hours), São Paulo (24 hours), and Mendoza (34½ hours).

Boat Launches across the Paraná to Encarnación (US$1) continue to operate from the dock at the east end of Av Guacurarí, although they may cease as the rising reservoir behind Yacyretá Dam floods low-lying parts of the two cities.

Getting Around

To/From the Airport Austral runs its own minibus to Aeropuerto Internacional Posadas, 12km southwest of town via RN 12, but the No 8 bus also goes there from San Lorenzo between La Rioja and Entre Ríos. A remise costs about US$10.

Car Localiza (☎ 430901) is at Colón 1933, between Bolívar and Córdoba.

AROUND POSADAS

Yacyretá Dam

A vivid lesson in foreign debt, this gigantic hydroelectric project is actually in Corrientes province near the town of Ituzaingó, but is more accessible from Posadas. At Ituzaingó, 1½ hours from Posadas by bus, the Argentine-Paraguayan Entidad Binacional Yacyretá has delegated the task of explaining away the Yacyretá debacle to Engel Barrea. His tours (US$3.50 per person) of the project leave from the Centro Cultural Ituzaingó (☎ 03786-420008) at 10 and 11 am, and at 3, 4, and 5 pm. The Centro Cultural also has a first-run movie theater with free or inexpensive showings.

A museum displays artifacts unearthed in the process of construction and a scale model of the project, and you can also see the enormous city built to house the dam workers. Guides are well rehearsed, but the bus rarely slows and never stops for photographs. For a more complete analysis of the Yacyretá debacle, see Gustavo Lins Ribeiro's *Transnational Capitalism and Hydropolitics in Argentina: the Yacyretá High Dam* (Gainesville: University Press of Florida, 1994).

Visitors opting to stay overnight might try moderately priced ***Hotel Géminis*** *(☎ 420324, Corrientes 943)* or the more elaborate ***Hotel Yaciretá*** *(☎ 420577)* at Buenos Aires and Loreto. Empresa Ciudad de Posadas

Megawatts for Megabucks

Upon its completion in 1997, Yacyretá Dam formed a monstrous reservoir of 1800 sq km that submerged the Paraná more than 200km upstream, inundated low-lying areas of Posadas and Encarnación, required the relocation of nearly 40,000 people, and connected Ituzaingó with the Paraguayan city of Ayolas in a new border crossing. Presumably it will provide energy for industrial development in Argentina's northern provinces, increasing Argentine and Paraguayan electricity supplies by 50%. At last check, its four functioning turbines were generating 2.8 million megawatts of power, and water was lapping at the sidewalks of the older parts of Encarnación. The remaining 16 turbines are due to come on over the next several years.

While the stated rationale for development of Yacyretá was energy demand, informed analysts believe that geopolitics played a more important role in Juan Perón's last government, which proposed the project in 1973. Current Argentine President Carlos Menem himself once called the project 'a monument to corruption' that may cost eight times the original estimate of US$1.5 billion (thousand million); it presently stands at US$8.5 billion. Despite Menem's original, publicly stated intention of stopping the project, his government solicited further loans to continue construction and has resisted compensating Paraguay for the relocation of those displaced by the rising waters (it will flood five times as much Paraguayan as Argentine territory). There are attempts to privatize the project in order to get buyers to assume the debt, with the incentive of permitting sales to Brazil, but this would do away with a proposed 15% reduction in the domestic price of electricity in Argentina.

(☎ 420111) and Singer link Ituzaingó with Corrientes and Posadas.

Santa Ana

With help from Germany and Italy, the Misiones provincial government is excavating and restoring Jesuit ruins at sites like Santa Ana (founded 1633), where luxuriant rain forest and strangler figs have long covered a settlement that once housed 2000 Guaraní neophytes. New *centros de apoyo* (support centers) house researchers and restoration workers and offer tourist services. The standing walls have been cleared at the temple of Santa Ana, which must have been magnificent even though none of its decorative embellishments remain. Incongruously adjacent to the temple is an abandoned 20th-century cemetery that would be an ideal location for a zombie or vampire movie – including open coffins.

Admission to Santa Ana, now administered by the Fondo de Investigación de la Cultura Jesuítica-Guaraní, costs US$1. Hours are 7 am to 6 pm daily. There is a café on site for light meals. Buses from Posadas will drop passengers at the clearly marked turnoff Km 43 along RN 12, where it's a 1km walk to the ruins.

Loreto

Founded in 1632 by Padre Antonio Ruiz de Montoya, Loreto saw the first book published in what is now Argentina in the year 1700; *Martirologio Romano* (Roman Martirology) was later translated into Guaraní. Though the restoration work is in an earlier stage here than at Santa Ana, plaques quoting descriptions of the buildings by early Jesuit fathers contribute to the atmosphere.

Like Santa Ana, Loreto has a centro de apoyo with a café and there is even ***accommodation*** (US$15 for a three-bed room, with kitchen facilities) open to tourists. Buses from Posadas stop at Km 48 along RN 12, but the distance from the highway is greater than at Santa Ana. Admission to the ruins, also administered by the Fondo de Investigación de la Cultura Jesuítica-Guaraní, costs US$1.

SAN IGNACIO & SAN IGNACIO MINÍ

Visitors can see the ruins of San Ignacio Miní, the former reducción, on a day trip from Posadas, but lodging in the village of San Ignacio (population 5000) allows more time to explore and appreciate them. Other sights include the house of Uruguayan writer Horacio Quiroga and the provincial museum. Everything in town is within easy walking distance.

San Ignacio is 56km northeast of Posadas via RN 12. From the highway junction, the broad Av Sarmiento leads about 1km to Calle Rivadavia, which leads six blocks north to the ruins. San Ignacio's area code is ☎ 03752.

San Ignacio Miní

San Ignacio Guazú, founded in 1609 but abandoned after repeated attacks by Brazilian slavers, was the forerunner of San Ignacio Miní, which was founded in 1632 on the Río Yabebiry and later shifted to its present site until its abandonment in 1767. Its ruins, rediscovered in 1897 and restored after 1943, belong to a style known as 'Guaraní baroque.' At its peak, in 1733, the mission had a Guaraní population of nearly 4000.

Designed by Italian Jesuit architect Juan Brasanelli, the enormous red sandstone church, 74m long and 24m wide with walls 2m thick at the base, was the focal point of the settlement. Adjacent to the tile-roofed church, which was embellished with bas-relief sculptures by Guaraní artists, were the cemetery and the priests' cloisters. In the same complex were classrooms, a kitchen, a dining room, and workshops. On all sides of the Plaza de Armas were the Indians' living quarters.

Unfortunately, at least from an aesthetic viewpoint, authorities have had to erect scaffolding to keep some of the walls from collapsing; while this is understandable for practical reasons, it disrupts the visual unity of the ruins. For photography, focus instead on the details, especially the elaborately carved doorways.

Admission to the ruins, which are open 7 am to 7 pm daily, is US$2.50; the nightly

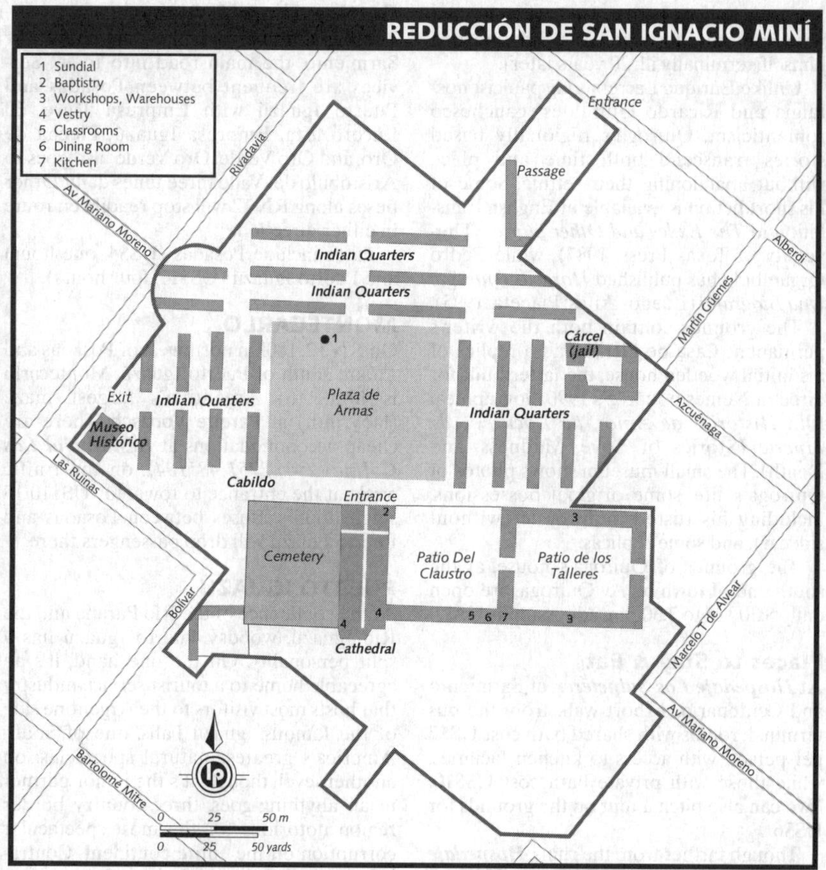

Luz y Sonido (Light and Sound) costs an extra US$2.50. The entrance has moved to the north side on Calle Alberdi, where visitors pass through very good historical displays in the **Centro de Interpretación Regional** before emerging onto the grounds.

Museo Provincial Miguel Nadasdy

On Av Sarmiento near the turnoff to the ruins, this museum displays the archaeological and ethnological collections of a dedicated Romanian immigrant. Focus on the exhibits, which include stone tools, a complete dugout canoe, and 19th-century weapons, and try to overlook the bizarre theories of local prehistory. Opening hours are 7:30 am to noon and 3:30 to 7 pm daily.

Casa de Horacio Quiroga

Uruguayan-born of Argentine parents, Quiroga was a poet and novelist who also dabbled in other activities, taking some of the earliest photographs of the rediscovered ruins at San Ignacio Miní and farming cotton (unsuccessfully) in the Chaco. He lived in

San Ignacio from 1910 to 1917, when his first wife committed suicide (as did Quiroga himself, terminally ill, 20 years later).

Unlike Enrique Larreta's Hispanicist nostalgia and Ricardo Güiraldes' gauchesco romanticism, Quiroga's regionally based stories transcend both time and place without abandoning their setting. Some of his short fiction is available in English translation in *The Exiles and Other Stories* (University of Texas Press, 1987), while Pedro Orgambide has published *Horacio Quiroga: Una Biografía* (Buenos Aires: Planeta, 1995).

The grounds contain both the writer's permanent **Casa de Piedra** and a replica of his initial wooden house, the latter built for director Nemesio Juárez's 1996 biographical film *Historias de Amor, de Locura y de Muerte* (Stories of Love, Madness, and Death). The small museum shows photos of Quiroga's life, some original possessions, including his rusted motorcycle (without sidecar), and some replicas.

The grounds of Quiroga's house, at the south end of town on Av Quiroga, are open daily 8:30 am to 7:30 pm; admission is US$2.

Places to Stay & Eat

At ***Hospedaje Los Salpeterer***, at Sarmiento and Centenario, a short walk from the bus terminal, rooms with shared bath cost US$7 per person with access to kitchen facilities, while those with private bath cost US$10. Two can also pitch a tent on the grounds for US$6.

Though farther from the ruins, ***Hospedaje El Descanso*** *(☎ 470207, Pellegrini 270)* is a real find, with spartan but spotless rooms and friendly German-speaking management; singles cost US$6 with shared bath, while doubles with private bath cost US$15. Highly recommended ***Hotel San Ignacio*** *(☎ 470047, Sarmiento 823)* has singles/doubles with bath for about US$20/30.

There are several places to eat near the exit to the ruins on Rivadavia, where ***Coco*** has first-rate, home-style dinners starting at US$4, with attentive service; ***La Casa Azul*** is more an assembly line comedor. ***Don Valentín***, near the Alberdi entrance to the ruins, is also very good.

Getting There & Away

The bus terminal is at the west end of Av Sarmiento, the main road into town. Services are frequent between Posadas and Puerto Iguazú with Empresa Tigre, El Lucero, Eta, Empresa Iguazú, Flecha de Oro, and Oro Verde. Oro Verde also goes to Aristóbulo del Valle three times daily. Other buses along RN 12 will stop readily en route in either direction.

Fares include Posadas (US$4, one hour) and Puerto Iguazú (US$17, four hours).

MONTECARLO

On RN 12, 180km northwest of Posadas and 110km south of Puerto Iguazú, Montecarlo is home to Argentina's largest maze (labyrinth) at **Parque Vortisch**. There are cheap accommodations at ***Residencial Las Colinas*** *(☎ 03751-481104)*, on the traffic circle at the entrance to town, for US$10/15 single/double. Buses between Posadas and Puerto Iguazú will drop passengers there.

PUERTO IGUAZÚ

At the confluence of the Río Paraná and the Río Iguazú, woodsy Puerto Iguazú has a split personality. On the one hand, it's an agreeable home to a tourist service industry that hosts most visitors to the Argentine side of the famous Iguazú Falls, one of South America's greatest natural spectacles; on another level, though, it's the junior partner in an anything-goes, three-country border region notorious for the most spectacular corruption on the entire continent. Contraband of all sorts, including drugs, guns, money, and people, including presumed terrorists, passes almost without hindrance into and back from Brazil and Paraguay.

That said, for tourists and travelers Puerto Iguazú (population 36,000) in particular is far less hazardous than Foz do Iguaçu (Brazil) and Ciudad del Este (Paraguay), and even those cities are reasonably safe for savvy travelers. Despite the area's popularity, Puerto Iguazú prices for food and accommodations are surprisingly reasonable. Some visitors stay at Foz, on the Brazilian side, but certain nationalities (including Americans and Australians) need a visa to do so.

Travelers interested in the seamier side of the triple-border area who know Spanish should look for Argentine journalist Hernán López Echagüe's best-selling *La Frontera: Viaje al Misterioso Triángulo de Brasil, Argentina y Paraguay* (Buenos Aires, Planeta, 1997).

Orientation

Some 300km northeast of Posadas via paved RN 12, Puerto Iguazú has an irregular city plan, but is small enough to find your way around easily. The main drag is the diagonal Av Victoria Aguirre, which enters town in the southeast, but most services are just north of Av Victoria Aguirre in a rabbit warren of streets that cross each other at odd angles.

From the Hito Argentino, a small obelisk marking Argentine territory at the confluence of the Paraná and Iguazú at the west end of Av Tres Fronteras, you can see both Brazil and Paraguay (which have similar markers on their sides of the confluence).

Information

Tourist Offices The Secretaría de Turismo (☎ 420800), Av Victoria Aguirre 311, is open weekdays 8 am to 1 pm, weekends 8 am to noon, and daily 4 to 8 pm.

ACA (☎ 420165) is on the highway to the park, just beyond Camping El Pindo.

Money Banco de Misiones has an ATM at Av Victoria Aguirre 330.

Post & Communications Correo Argentino is at Av San Martín 780; the postal code is 3370. Telecentro Cataratas is on Av Victoria Aguirre between Los Cedros and Aguay; Puerto Iguazú's area code is ☎ 03757.

The Las Vegas Coffee Shop (☎ 422962), on Aguirre near Bonpland, offers Internet access.

Travel Agencies Turismo Operativo Misionero (☎ 421240), Mariano Moreno 58, arranges trips to less-frequented areas of Parque Nacional Iguazú and to less-frequented destinations like Esteros del Iberá.

Medical Services Hospital Marta Teodora Shwartz (☎ 420288) is at Av Victoria Aguirre and Ushuaia.

Dangers & Annoyances Motorists should note that car theft is common in the triple-border area, though carjacking is unusual on the Argentine side. It's a good idea to have antitheft devices and secure parking at night.

Time Note that Argentina is sometimes an hour behind Brazil, which means that 7 am in Brazil is 6 am in Argentina.

Organized Tours

Many local operators offer day tours to the Brazilian side of the falls. For about US$25, these include a meal and a trip to Itaipú dam and Ciudad del Este in Paraguay. One reader recommendation is Turismo Cuenca del Plata (☎ 420338), on Paulino Amarante near Hostería Los Helechos.

Places to Stay

Both Puerto Iguazú and Foz do Iguaçu have many suitable places to stay in all price ranges. Foz usually tends to be a bit cheaper and Brazilian food may be a welcome change for anyone tired of beef, but the accommodations here are a better value than in other parts of Argentina. The relative absence of street crime in Puerto Iguazú may tip the balance for some travelers.

Note that higher prices may prevail during Semana Santa and during Argentine winter holidays in July, and occasionally in January if demand is heavy.

Places to Stay – Budget

Camping At Km 3½ of RN 12 on the edge of town, ***Camping El Pindo*** charges US$3 per person and US$3 per vehicle. ***Camping Americano*** *(☎ 420820)*, at Km 5, charges US$4 per person and US$4 per tent; some visitors have complained of dirtiness at the latter.

Hostels Hostelling International has two local affiliates. ***Residencial Uno*** *(☎ 420529, Fray Luis Beltrán 116)* charges US$10 with breakfast and has the better hostel atmosphere, while the slightly more expensive ***Residencial La Cabaña*** *(☎ 420564, Av Tres Fronteras 434)* is more like a motel – more privacy but less contact with other travelers.

Residenciales, Hosterías & Hotels For US$12/22 or even less off-season, tidy ***Residencial Río Selva*** *(☎ 421555, San Lorenzo 140)* also has a pool. ***Hostería San Fernando*** *(☎ 421429)*, at Av Córdoba 693 opposite the bus terminal, has shown improvement for US$15/22. Comparably priced ***Residencial Paquita*** *(☎ 420434, Av Córdoba 158)* adds a US$3 surcharge for air-con.

Shady ***Hostería Los Helechos*** *(☎ 420338, Paulino Amarante 76)* is superb value for US$15/25, though dearer in high season at around US$20/30. ***Residencial Arco Iris*** *(☎ 420636, Curupy 152)* is very popular with travelers for US$15/20 single/double with private bath, even less off-season.

Residencial King *(☎ 420360, Av Victoria Aguirre 209)* has attractive grounds and a swimming pool for US$15/20 with shared bath, US$20/25 with private bath. ***Residencial Tierra Colorada*** *(☎ 420649, El Oro 265)* charges identical rates.

Farther out, ***Residencial La Cabaña*** *(☎ 420564, Av Tres Fronteras 434)* is quieter at US$15/20 in low season, US$20/30 in peak season; spacious rooms with private bath are a bit dark and worn, but also have air-con. ***Hotel Paraná*** *(☎ 422206, Av Brasil 24)* is another budget choice for US$18/30.

Places to Stay – Mid-Range

The declining ***Hotel Libertador*** *(☎ 420570, Bonpland 475)* has lost some of its former prestige. Rates are US$25/35 in low season, US$36/48 in high season. In the same category is ***Hotel Alexander*** *(☎ 420249, Av Córdoba 222)*. The perennial favorite ***Hotel***

Saint George *(☎ 420633, Av Córdoba 148)* costs US$30/35 in low season, US$35/50 in high season, and also has a swimming pool.

Places to Stay – Top End

Overlooking the confluence, ***Hotel Esturión*** *(☎ 420020, fax 420414, Av Tres Fronteras 650)* charges US$110 double with breakfast. For just a little more, about US$112/135, indulge yourself at the hideously ill-sited ***Hotel Internacional Iguazú*** *(☎ 420296, fax 420311)*, near the visitor center at Parque Nacional Iguazú. Rooms with a view of the falls cost US$147/177, however. If you have a package tour with full board, obtain meal coupons before dining or you may end up paying extra.

Places to Eat

There are many places to eat, but there's also rapid turnover. For the cheapest eats, stroll around the triangle formed by Av Brasil, Perito Moreno, and Ingeniero Eppens. One reader recommends the Saturday fruit market at Córdoba and Félix de Azara.

The ***Fechoría Bar*** *(☎ 420182, Eppens 294)* near Brasil, is a good breakfast choice. ***Blanco Paraíso*** is a lively confitería on Aguirre near Brazil.

El Criollito, on Av Tres Fronteras just west of the Plaza, has a superb Argentine menu, relaxed atmosphere, outstanding service and sidewalk seating. ***La Rueda*** *(☎ 422531, Av Córdoba 28)* serves excellent grilled surubí for around US$7, but portions are relatively small and the vegetables badly overcooked.

Recommended parrillas include ***Tomás*** *(☎ 420850)*, at the bus terminal, ***Charo*** *(☎ 421529, Córdoba 106)*, and ***El Tío Querido*** *(☎ 420750)*, on Bonpland alongside Hotel Libertador.

It's drawn mixed comment, but ***La Esquina*** *(☎ 420633, Av Córdoba 148)*, in the Hotel St George, remains a personal favorite, though it's increasingly pricey.

For pizza, try the popular, traditional ***Pizza Pizuela*** *(☎ 423142, Av Victoria Aguirre 233)* or ***Pizza Color***, Av Córdoba and Paulino Amarante.

Entertainment

Puerto Iguazú is surprisingly weak on night life, but try ***Peña Atahualpa***, on Eppens between Av Brasil and Bonpland, for live music.

Getting There & Away

Air Aerolíneas Argentinas (☎ 420168), Aguirre 295, flies three or four times daily to Buenos Aires (Aeroparque) for US$109 to US$203, and Monday, Wednesday, and Friday to Rio de Janeiro.

LAPA (☎ 420390), Perito Moreno 184, Local 2, flies to Aeroparque (US$79 to US$169) daily except Sunday, when it has two flights.

There are international services, as well as Brazilian domestic services, across the border in Foz do Iguaçu. Ciudad del Este, Paraguay, also has an increasing number of flights.

Bus The Terminal de Ómnibus (☎ 420854) is at Avs Córdoba and Misiones. Services to and from Posadas are numerous with Cotal, Flecha de Oro, Horianski, Kurtz, Kruse, Martignoni, Aristóbulo del Valle, Empresa Iguazú, Expreso Singer (☎ 422891), and Expreso Tigre Yguazú (☎ 420854).

Expreso Singer also continues to Corrientes and Resistencia, has provincial services to the immigrant-dominated sierra town of Oberá, and offers direct service to Córdoba, Buenos Aires, and La Plata. El Litoral goes to Córdoba, Paraná, Santa Fe, and Buenos Aires.

Other companies, some with slightly cheaper service to the capital, include Crucero del Norte (☎ 420291), Klein, Kurtz, and Vía Bariloche, which continues to Bariloche (with a nearly 10-hour layover). Expreso Ciudad de Posadas (☎ 420854) goes nightly at 10 pm, connecting to Corrientes and Resistencia and across the Chaco to Salta and Jujuy.

La Estrella goes daily to Resistencia, Santiago del Estero, Termas de Río Hondo, Tucumán, Salta, and Jujuy. They also go to Buenos Aires at 1 and 5:30 pm and to Rosario at 10 am via Paso de los Libres, Paraná, and Santa Fe.

Cotal has direct service to Mendoza, a 40-hour marathon via Santiago del Estero and San Juan.

Sample fares include Posadas (US$20, 5½ hours), Resistencia (US$38, 10½ hours), and Buenos Aires (US$45, 22 hours).

Getting Around

To/From the Airport Expreso Aristóbulo del Valle (☎ 420348, 420490), Entre Ríos 239, charges US$3 to the airport and will pick up passengers at hotels; phone for reservations. A remise will run around US$15.

Bus From the bus terminal, 18 El Práctico buses daily leave to Parque Nacional Iguazú (US$2) between 6:40 am and 7:25 pm, returning between 7:30 am and 8:15 pm – catch an early one to avoid the heat and the tour buses that swarm around the falls about 11 am, when noisy Brazilian helicopters also begin their flights.

Frequent buses with Itaipú, Pluma, Tres Fronteras, Risa, and El Práctico cross to Foz do Iguaçu (US$2) and to Ciudad del Este, Paraguay from the bus terminal.

Car Try AI (☎ 422521) at Hotel Esturión, Av Tres Fronteras 650.

Taxi For groups of three or more hoping to see both sides of the falls as well as Ciudad del Este and the Itaipú hydroelectric project, a shared cab or remise can be a good idea; figure about US$80 for a full day's sightseeing. Contact the Asociación de Trabajadores de Taxis (☎ 420282), Rolón Hermanos (☎ 420331), or simply approach a driver.

PARQUE NACIONAL IGUAZÚ

Near the visitor center at Parque Nacional Iguazú, a plaque credits Álvar Núñez Cabeza de Vaca with the discovery of the awesome Iguazú Falls in 1541 – but he was

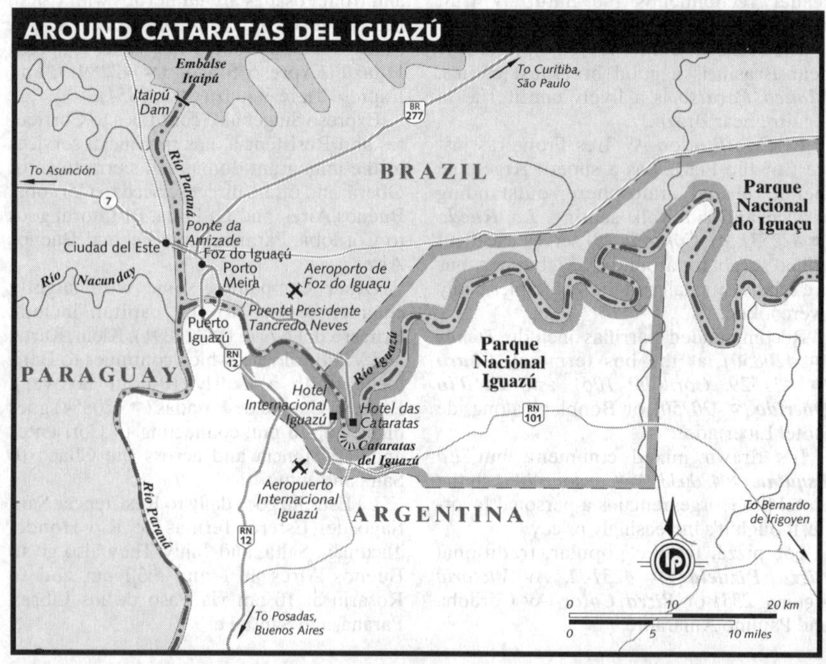

SARAH J HAWKINS

Catwalk at Iguazú Falls.

merely the first European to view them. For the Guaraní Indians of the region and their predecessors, these impressive falls had been the source of legend for millennia.

According to Guaraní tradition, the falls originated when an Indian warrior named Caroba incurred the wrath of a forest god by escaping downriver in a canoe with a young girl named Naipur, with whom the god had become infatuated. Enraged, the god caused the riverbed to collapse in front of the lovers, producing a line of precipitous falls over which Naipur fell and, at their base, turned into a rock. Caroba survived as a tree overlooking his fallen lover.

The geological origins of the falls are simpler and more prosaic. In southern Brazil, the Río Iguazú passes over a basaltic plateau that ends abruptly just east of the confluence with the Paraná. Where the lava flow stopped, at least 5000 cubic meters of water per second plunges more than 70m into sedimentary terrain below – during floods, the volume can be many times greater. Before reaching the falls, the river divides into many channels with hidden reefs, rocks, and islands separating the many visually distinctive falls that together form the famous *cataratas*. In total, the falls are more than 2km across.

You can see many of the falls up close via a system of *pasarelas* (catwalks), which offer unmatchable views. The most awesome is the semicircular Garganta del Diablo (Devil's Throat), a deafening and dampening but indispensable part of the experience.

Parque Nacional Iguazú occupies a total area of about 55,000 hectares, of which 6000 hectares constitute a Reserva Nacional, allowing commercial development in the immediate area of the falls. Above the falls, the river itself is suitable for canoeing, kayaking, and other water sports.

Other attractions are well worth seeing, including substantial areas of subtropical rain forest, with unique flora and fauna – there are thousands of species of insects, hundreds of species of birds, and many mammals and reptiles. The park is under threat, however, from Brazil's upstream dam at Caxias, whose filling could reduce the flow over the falls by more than 80% between September and November.

Information

Buses from Puerto Iguazú drop passengers at the Centro de Informes (☎ 03757-420180), near the Hotel Internacional, where there's a small museum. There's also a gift shop, bar, photo developing and many other services, including restaurants and snack bars.

Dangers & Annoyances

As Cabeza de Vaca noted, the Río Iguazú's currents are indeed strong and swift; more than one tourist has been swept downriver and drowned in the area of Isla San Martín. It should go without saying that no one should get too close to the falls proper – no one has ever gone over the Cataratas, in a barrel or otherwise, and lived to tell about it.

Parque Nacional Iguazú's orderly trails and large numbers of visitors can give a false sense of security, but park wildlife is potentially dangerous – in 1997, a jaguar killed the infant son of a park ranger. While this is not cause for hysteria, visitors should respect the big cats in particular and, if you encounter one, do not panic. Speak calmly but loudly, do not run or turn your back on the animal, and do everything possible to appear bigger than you are, by waving your arms or clothing for example.

Human predators may abscond with your personal belongings, so watch your things while hiking. This is not exactly epidemic, but it's not unheard of either.

Cataratas del Iguazú

Before seeing the falls themselves, have a quick look around the visitor center museum where, depending on the budget, there may be informational brochures. The tower near the visitor center offers a good overall view, but walking around is the best way to see the falls. Plan your hikes before or after the mid-morning influx of tour buses. At midday, you can take a break from the heat at the restaurant and confitería here.

Formerly, an interconnected series of catwalks led to all the falls from the visitor center, but floods have destroyed many of them and isolated those that go to **Garganta del Diablo**, the single most impressive cascade.

You can see most of the falls by roaming at will on the trails and catwalks around the visitor center; descending to the river, you can take a launch across to **Isla Grande San Martín**, whose cost is now included in the park entry fee. Although the trip takes only a few minutes, the island offers views not available elsewhere and insulates you from the masses on the mainland. Swimming and picnicking are possible, but do not venture too far off the beach.

After returning to the mainland, you can catch a bus or taxi to Puerto Canoas (hourly buses cost US$1 for the 4km ride), where a US$4 launch takes you to the remains of the pasarela to the Garganta del Diablo overlook. At Ñandú, there is a confitería and, a bit farther on, a free rudimentary campground with pit toilets but no water. Beyond the confitería, the road may not be passable to ordinary cars after heavy rain.

Of all the sights on earth, the Garganta del Diablo must come closest to the experience of sailing off the edge of a flat earth imagined by early European sailors. On three sides, the deafening cascade plunges to a murky destination; the vapors soaking the viewer blur the base of the falls. It is difficult to abandon a site of such menacing attraction, where you can still sense the awe that the region's native peoples must have felt. Faced with this spectacle, though, early Spaniards showed only a practical indifference; Cabeza de Vaca reported that

> the current of the Yguazú was so strong that the canoes were carried furiously down the river, for near this spot there is a considerable fall, and the noise made by the water leaping down some high rocks into a chasm may be heard a great distance off, and the spray rises two spears high and more over the fall. It was necessary, therefore, to take the canoes out of the water and carry them by hand past the cataract for half a league with great labor.

Similar contemporary attitudes may have resulted in the use of the word 'Iguazú' in a common line of Argentine toilet bowls, but at least since 1943, when the federal government incorporated the area into its national park system, hundreds of thousands of visitors have felt much greater emotion than the Spanish explorers. Still, relatively few venture beyond the immediate area of the falls to appreciate the park's forest scenery and wildlife.

Flora & Fauna

Despite pressures for development and deforestation, Parque Nacional Iguazú presents a nearly pristine area of subtropical rain forest, with more than 2000 identified plant species, countless insects, 400 species of birds, and many mammals and reptiles. High temperatures, rainfall, and humidity encourage a diverse habitat.

Resembling the tropical Amazonian rain forest to the north, the forests of Misiones consist of multiple levels, the highest a closed canopy more than 30m high. Beneath the canopy are several additional levels of trees, plus a dense ground-level growth of shrubs and herbaceous plants. One of the most interesting species is the *guapoy* or strangler fig *(Ficus monckii)*, an epiphyte that uses a large tree for support until it finally asphyxiates its host. This species covers the ruins of many abandoned Jesuit mission buildings elsewhere in the province.

Other epiphytes exploit their hosts without harming them. Orchids use the limbs of large trees like the lapacho *(Tabebuia ipe)* or *palo rosa (Aspidosperma polyneuron)* for support only, absorbing essential nutrients from rainfall or the atmosphere. At lower levels in the forest, you will find wild specimens of yerba mate

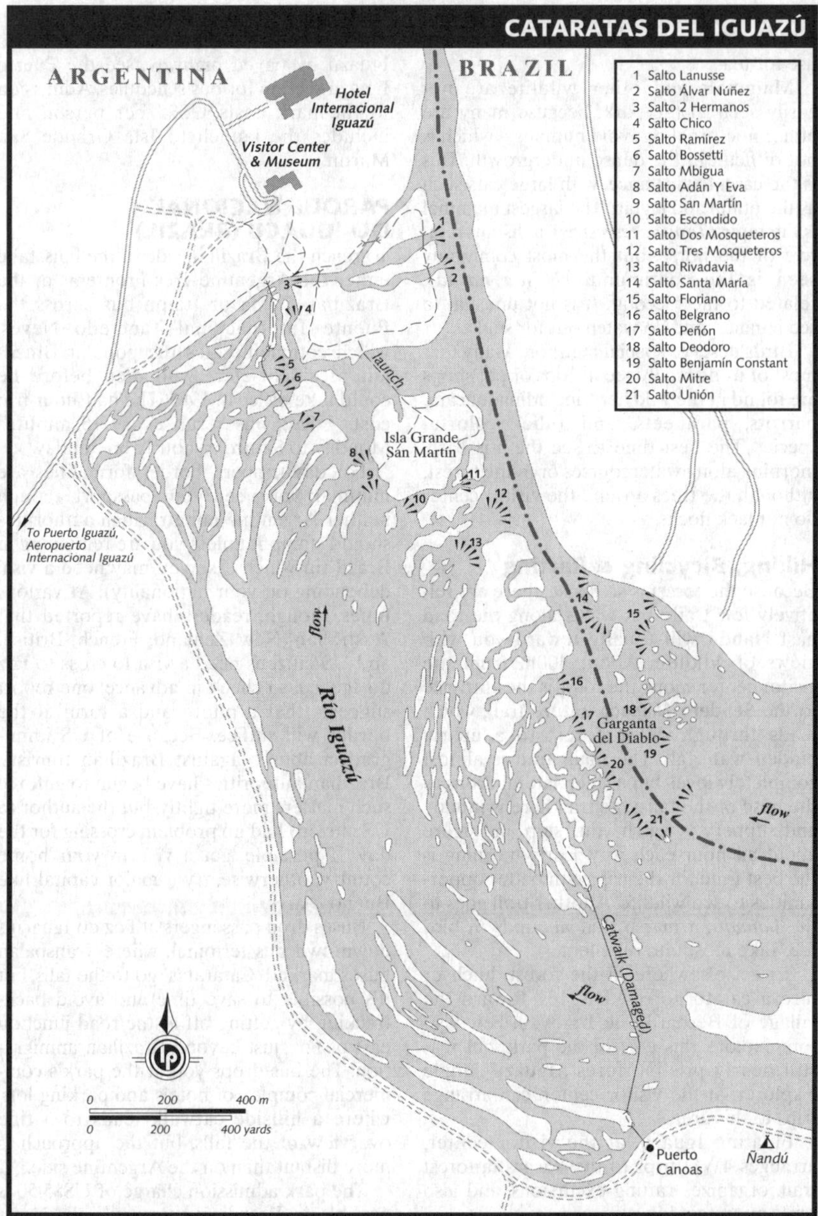

CATARATAS DEL IGUAZÚ
ARGENTINA
BRAZIL
Hotel Internacional Iguazú
Visitor Center & Museum
1 Salto Lanusse
2 Salto Álvar Núñez
3 Salto 2 Hermanos
4 Salto Chico
5 Salto Ramírez
6 Salto Bossetti
7 Salto Mbigua
8 Salto Adán Y Eva
9 Salto San Martín
10 Salto Escondido
11 Salto Dos Mosqueteros
12 Salto Tres Mosqueteros
13 Salto Rivadavia
14 Salto Santa María
15 Salto Floriano
16 Salto Belgrano
17 Salto Peñón
18 Salto Deodoro
19 Salto Benjamín Constant
20 Salto Mitre
21 Salto Unión
launch
Isla Grande San Martín
To Puerto Iguazú, Aeropuerto Internacional Iguazú
flow
Río Iguazú
Garganta del Diablo
flow
Catwalk (Damaged)
flow
0 200 400 m
0 200 400 yards
Puerto Canoas
Ñandú

(Ilex paraguariensis), which Argentines and other residents of the Río de la Plata region use for tea.

Mammals and other wildlife are not easily seen in the park, because many are either nocturnal or avoid humans – which is not difficult in the dense undergrowth. This is the case, for instance, with large cats such as the puma and jaguar. The largest mammal is the tapir *(Tapirus terrestris)*, a distant relative of the horse, but the most commonly seen is the coatimundi *(Nasua nasua)*, related to the raccoon. It is not unusual to see iguanas, and do watch out for snakes.

Birds deserve special mention. Many that most of us normally see in zoos or pet shops are found in the wild here, including toucans, parrots, parakeets, and other colorful species. The best time to see them is early morning along watercourses or in the forest, although the trees around the visitor center do not lack flocks.

Hiking, Bicycling & Rafting

Because the forest is so dense, there are relatively few trails, but walks along the road past Ñandú will usually reward you with views of wildlife. About 400m from the visitor center, along the road, is the entrance to the **Sendero Macuco** nature trail, which leads through dense forest to a nearly hidden waterfall. The main trail is almost completely level, but a steep lateral drops to the base of the falls; the trail here is muddy and slippery – watch your step and figure about an hour each way. Early morning is the best time for the trip, with better opportunities to see wildlife. Another trail goes to the *bañado*, a marsh that abounds in bird life. Take mosquito repellent.

To get elsewhere in the forest, hitch or hire a car to go out RN 101 toward the village of Bernardo de Irigoyen. Few visitors explore this part of the park, but it is still nearly pristine forest. Iguazú Jungle Explorer, at the visitor center, can arrange trips to this area.

Floating Iguazú, at the visitor center, arranges 4WD trips to the Yacaratia forest trail, organizes rafting excursions, and also rents mountain bikes.

Getting There & Away

The Cataratas are 20km northeast of Puerto Iguazú by paved highway; see the Puerto Iguazú section for bus schedules. Admission to the park costs US$5 per person and includes the launch to Isla Grande San Martín.

PARQUE NACIONAL DO IGUAÇU (BRAZIL)

To reach the Brazilian side of the falls, take either the Argentine Tres Fronteras or the Brazilian Pluna or Itaipú bus across the Puente Internacional Tancredo Neves, which commemorates the popular Brazilian president-elect who died before he could take office in 1985. The half-hour trip costs US$2; buses run every 15 minutes Monday to Saturday, hourly on Sunday.

For day-trippers, border formalities are minimal; you need your passport, though neither Argentine nor Brazilian authorities should stamp it unless you are remaining in Brazil (in which case you may need a visa, depending on your nationality). At various times, though, readers have reported that Australian, New Zealand, French, British, and US citizens need a visa to cross to Foz do Iguaçu, so check in advance; one report suggests that a photo and a form at the border will suffice. Because of US immigration abuses against Brazilian tourists, Brazilian authorities have begun to enforce such matters more tightly, but the author (a US citizen) had no problem crossing for the day. If possible, get a visa in your home country; otherwise, try a major capital like Buenos Aires.

Buses drop passengers at Foz do Iguaçu's downtown bus terminal, where Transbalan buses marked 'Cataratas' go to the falls, but it's possible to save time and avoid backtracking by getting off at the road junction east of Foz, just beyond Brazilian immigration. The bus drops you at the park's commercial complex of hotels and parking lots, where a hillside catwalk leads to a fine overview of the falls, but the approach is more distant than on the Argentine side.

The park admission charge of US$5.50 is payable in Brazilian currency only; hours are 8 am to 6 pm daily. Argentine officials continue to protest that low-flying Brazilian helicopters, which offer aerial views of the falls for US$60, have disturbed wildlife, including nesting birds.

FOZ DO IGUAÇU (BRAZIL)

Having ballooned, thanks to the Itaipú hydroelectric scheme, from a modest town of 34,000 in 1970 to a sprawling city of 220,000 today, frenzied Foz do Iguaçu suffers from considerable street crime, particularly at night. At the same time, its high-rise buildings and relatively sparse greenery contribute to an urban heat island effect that makes its streets less comfortable than those of woodsy Puerto Iguazú.

Orientation

Foz do Iguaçu is at the confluence of the Iguaçu and Paraná Rivers, 630km south of Curitiba by BR-277. The Ponte Presidente Tancredo Neves links the city to Puerto Iguazú, Argentina, across the Río Iguaçú, while the Ponte da Amizade connects it to Ciudad del Este, Paraguay, across the Paraná.

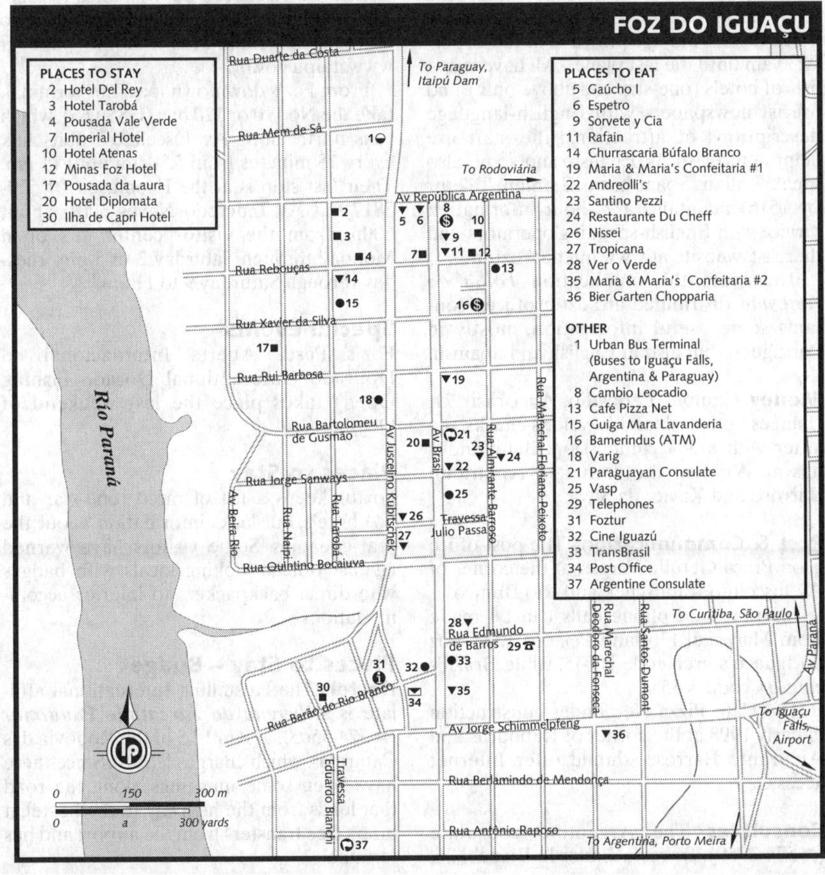

Fifteen km upstream is Itaipú, the world's largest hydroelectric project.

Foz do Iguaçu has a compact center with a fairly regular grid, presenting no great difficulties of orientation. Av das Cataratas, at the southwest edge of town, leads 20km to the world-famous falls via BR-469 and toward the Argentine border. Westbound BR-277 leads to Ciudad del Este.

Information

Tourist Offices Foztur maintains city information booths at Rua Rio Branco and Av Juscelino Kubitschek (☎ 574-2196, foztur@fnn.net; open 8 am to 10 pm), at the Rodoviária (long-distance bus terminal; ☎ 522-2633, 6 am to 6 pm), and at the airport (9:30 am until the last plane). All have maps, lists of hotels (one-star and above only), and tourist newspapers with English-language descriptions of attractions; the staff are helpful, most speak English, and some also speak Italian, Spanish, or German. Teletur (☎ 1516) maintains a 24-hour information service with English-speaking operators, and there's a website at www.fnn.net/foztur/.

The bimonthly publication *Folha da Amizade*, distributed at Foztur offices, contains some useful information, mostly in Portuguese but also in English and Spanish.

Money Cambio Leocadio, Av Brasil 71, changes both cash and traveler's checks, the latter with a 3% commission. Bamerindus has an ATM at the corner of Almirante Barroso and Xavier da Silva.

Post & Communications The post office is on Praça Getúlio Vargas, at the corner of Av Juscelino Kubitschek and Rio Branco.

International phone calls can be made from Marechal Floriano Peixoto 1222. Foz do Iguaçu's area code is 045, while Brazil's country code is 55.

The Café Pizza Net, under construction in early 1998 at the corner of Rebouças and Almirante Barroso, should offer Internet access.

Consulates The Argentine consulate (☎ 574-2969), Travessa Eduardo Bianchi 26, is open weekdays 9:30 am to 2 pm. Paraguay's consulate (☎ 523-2898), Bartolomeu de Gusmão 738, is open weekdays 8:30 am to 4:30 pm.

Laundry Guiga Mara Lavanderia is at Rua Tarobá 834.

Usina Hidrelétrica Itaipu

Free guided tours of the Brazilian side of the Itaipu hydroelectric project take place at 8, 9, and 10 am, and 2, 3, and 4 pm; for details on the project, see the Ciudad del Este section in the Eastern Paraguay chapter. The Centro de Recepcão de Visitantes (☎ 520-6398), 10km north of Foz at Av Tancredo Neves 6702, maintains a home page at www.itaipu.gov.br.

From Foz's downtown local bus terminal, take the No 110 or 120 bus (US$0.65), which runs north along Av Juscelino Kubitschek every 15 minutes from 5:30 am until 11 pm. Their last stop is at the Ecomuseu (☎ 520-5817), at Av Tancredo Neves 6001, about 600m from the visitor center; it's open Monday through Saturday 2 to 5 pm, Tuesday through Saturday 9 to 11 am.

Special Events

Foz's Pesca Aberta Internacional ao Dourado (International Dorado Fishing Open) takes place the last weekend of October.

Places to Stay

Foztur keeps a list of rated (one-star and up) hotels, but lacks information about the real cheapies. Some visitors have warned against official-looking locals with badges who direct backpackers to inferior accommodations.

Places to Stay – Budget

Hostels The Hostelling International affiliate is ***Albergue da Juventude Paudimar*** *(☎ 574-5503)*, at Km 12.5 of the Rodovia das Cataratas, which charges US$10. Since there have been some muggings along the road that leads from the highway to the hostel, it offers free transfers from the airport and bus terminal.

Hotels ***Hotel Atenas*** *(Almirante Barroso 2215)* is the cheapest in town for US$7/12 with shared bath. For US$9 per person with breakfast, though, the best budget choice is clean, safe, and friendly ***Pousada da Laura*** *(☎ 572-3628, Naipi 671)*; look carefully for the sign at this inconspicuous location.

Pousada Vale Verde *(☎ 574-2925, Rebouças 335)*, the former youth hostel, has drawn readers' complaints about the paper-thin walls and lack of privacy, but the lady who runs the place is helpful. Rates are US$9 per person without breakfast, but for an extra US$1 you can eat it in the café out front.

The ***Minas Foz Hotel*** *(☎ 574-5208, Rua Rebouças 809)* has *apartamentos* (rooms with private bath) for US$10/14 single/double without breakfast. The ***Imperial Hotel*** *(☎ 523-1299, Av Brasil 168)* is a reasonable choice, with apartamentos for US$15/25, but the front rooms have a tendency to get noisy.

Places to Stay – Mid-Range

Hotel Del Rey *(☎ 523-2027, Rua Tarobá 1020)* and the next-door ***Hotel Tarobá*** *(☎ 574-3890, Rua Tarobá 1048)* both charge US$30 double; the former has a pool and larger rooms. At ***Ilha de Capri Hotel*** *(☎ 523-1685, Rio Branco 409)* singles/doubles go for US$28/40. It's close to a few eateries, and has a pool and good breakfasts. For US$30/40, ***Hotel Diplomata*** *(☎ 523-1615, Av Brasil 678)* also has a pool.

Places to Stay – Top End

At the top end, the classiest place to stay is the ***Hotel das Cataratas*** *(☎ 523-2266)*, right at the falls. Singles/doubles cost US$190/220.

Places to Eat

For baked goods, sandwiches, and hot chocolate, reader-recommended ***Maria's and Maria Confeitaria*** *(☎ 574-5472, Av Brasil 505; ☎ 523-5472, Av Brasil 1285)* has two locations. ***Tropicana*** *(Av Juscelino Kubitschek 198)* is a student hangout that gets pretty lively. A short block north, ***Nissei*** is an expensive Japanese restaurant that, however, has nightly specials for US$5. ***Santino Pezzi***, on Almirante Barroso between Jorge Sanways and Bartolomé de Gusmão, serves good pasta dishes from US$8.

Vegetarians can munch on the US$5.50 buffet at ***Ver o Verde*** *(☎ 574-5647, Edmundo de Barros 111)* from 11 am to 3 pm. ***Rafain*** *(☎ 523-2233)*, at the corner of Av Brasil and Rebouças, has a wider buffet menu. ***Andreolli's*** *(Jorge Sanways 681)* has even more choices, including meat, and is cheaper.

Foz has many *churrascarias*, the Brazilian counterpart to the Argentine parrilla. Among them are the upscale ***Búfalo Branco*** *(☎ 574-5115, Rebouças 530)* and the more modest ***Espetro*** and ***Gaúcho I***, alongside each other on Av Republica Argentina between Av Juscelino Kubitschek and Av Brasil.

The ***Bier Garten Chopparia*** *(☎ 523-3700)*, at Av Jorge Schimmelpfeng and Marechal Deodoro da Fonseca, serves a good variety of pizza, steaks, and chops. It's in a pleasant setting, and gets crowded at night. For seafood, ***Restaurante Du Cheff*** *(☎ 523-1611, Almirante Barroso 683)* is expensive but excellent.

Sorvete y Cia, on Av Brasil between Av Republica Argentina and Rebouças, is an ice-cream buffet that charges by weight (Brazilian ice creameries serve a wider variety of tasty tropical fruit flavors than their Argentine counterparts).

Entertainment

The ***Cine Iguazú***, at the corner of Rua Rio Branco and Av Brasil, shows current films.

Getting There & Away

Air TransBrasil (☎ 574-3836), Av Brasil 1225, has twice-weekly flights to Córdoba (Argentina), but most flights are domestic services to Rio de Janeiro, São Paulo, and intermediate points with Vasp (☎ 523-2212), Av Brasil 845, and Varig (☎ 523-2111), Av Juscelino Kubitschek 463.

Bus From Foz do Iguaçu, there are 14 buses daily to Curitiba (US$33, 9½ hours) via BR-277, eight to São Paulo (US$42, 14 hours), and six to Rio (US$54, 21 hours).

Getting Around

To/From the Airport For US$0.65, catch the 'Parque Nacional' bus (from the urban bus terminal), which runs every 20 minutes from 5:30 am until 7 pm, then hourly until midnight; the trip takes 30 minutes. A taxi costs US$20.

To/From the Bus Terminal All long-distance buses arrive and depart from the Rodoviária (☎ 522-2950), 6km from downtown on Av Costa e Silva. To get downtown, walk downhill to the local bus stop and catch any 'Centro' bus. They start at 5:30 am and run every 15 minutes until 1:15 am.

Bus All local buses leave from the urban bus terminal on Av Juscelino Kubitschek just north of Av Republica Argentina. On weekdays the first 'Cataratas' bus to the Brazilian side of the falls (US$1) leaves the terminal at 8 am and runs hourly until 6 pm in winter, 7 pm in summer; the last one leaves the falls at 7 pm in winter and 8 am in summer, after which cabs charge extortionist rates to return to Foz. At the park entrance, the bus waits while you pay the US$5.50 entry fee (in Brazilian currency only). On weekends and public holidays, the first bus leaves the terminal at 8 am, the second at 10 am; thereafter buses leave every 40 minutes until 6 pm.

Buses to Puerto Iguazú (US$1 to US$2) start at 7 am and run every 15 minutes (every 50 minutes on Sunday) until 8:50 pm. Buses for Ciudad del Este begin running at 7 am and leave every 10 minutes.

The Gran Chaco

The Gran Chaco is a lowland of savannas and thorn forests extending from about 30° south latitude into Paraguay, eastern Bolivia, and western Brazil. Together, Chaco and Formosa provinces comprise most of the Argentine Chaco, though parts of the region also fall within the boundaries of the western provinces of Salta and Santiago del Estero and on the northern edges of Santa Fe and Córdoba. Summer is brutally hot; in winter there are occasional frosts. Rainfall is high in the eastern border with Corrientes, but low toward the west, where irrigation is essential for agriculture.

Traditionally, the region's economy relies on agriculture and forestry, particularly exploitation of *Quebrachia lorentzii*, whose common name *quebracho* (axe-breaker) derives from its rock-hard wood. The quebracho was once an unsurpassed source of natural tannin for leather processing, while the related *quebracho colorado* served for timber, firewood, and charcoal. Presently, the region is suffering accelerated forest clearance for rain-fed agriculture, as cotton and oil crops, especially sunflowers, become more important. Petroleum exploration is proceeding in the area north of Castelli, along the border between the two provinces.

The mostly roadless western half of Chaco province is popularly known as El Impenetrable. Except between the main cities of the eastern Chaco, such as Resistencia and Formosa, roads can be very bad and communications difficult. Crossing the northern Chaco, in Formosa province, can be particularly challenging; while paved RN 81 continues to advance westward, reaching the town of Las Lomitas 60km west of Estanislao del Campo, the rainy winter can still present problems, and travelers should anticipate delays.

History

In colonial times, Europeans avoided the hot, desolate Chaco, whose few hunter-gatherer peoples resisted colonization and were not numerous enough to justify their pacification for encomiendas. Today, about 20,000 Guaycurú (Toba, Mocoví) and Mataco peoples remain in both the region's interior and urban areas.

The earliest Spanish settlement was probably Concepción del Bermejo (75km north of present-day Roque Sáenz Peña), which was founded in 1585 but abandoned in 1632 due to Indian resistance and rediscovered only recently. After the mid-18th century, Jesuit missionaries had some success among the Abipone people, but their expulsion from the Americas in 1767 again delayed European settlement.

Permanent settlement came much later. Oppressive summer heat, Indian resistance, and poisonous snakes discouraged exploration of the dense thorn forests until the mid-19th century, when woodcutters from Corrientes entered the region's forests to exploit the valuable quebracho. This eventually opened the region to agricultural expansion, which has primarily taken the form of cotton and cattle production.

Colonization proceeded from the province and city of Corrientes but was not really permanent until 1872. Resistencia, founded in 1750 as the Jesuit reducción of San Fernando del Río Negro, was the jumping-off point for woodcutters. The two railroads built across the Chaco have made it easier to

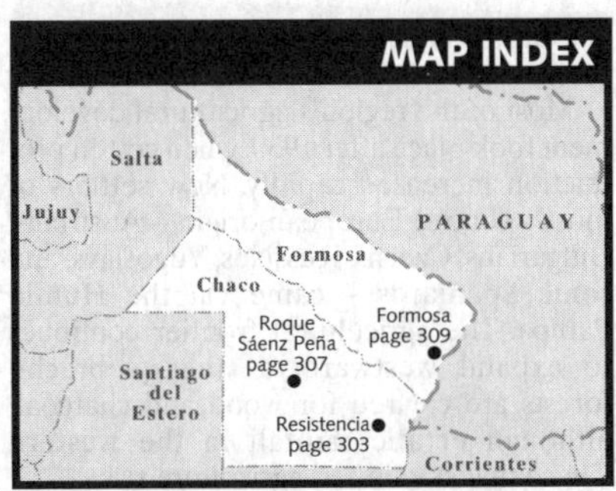

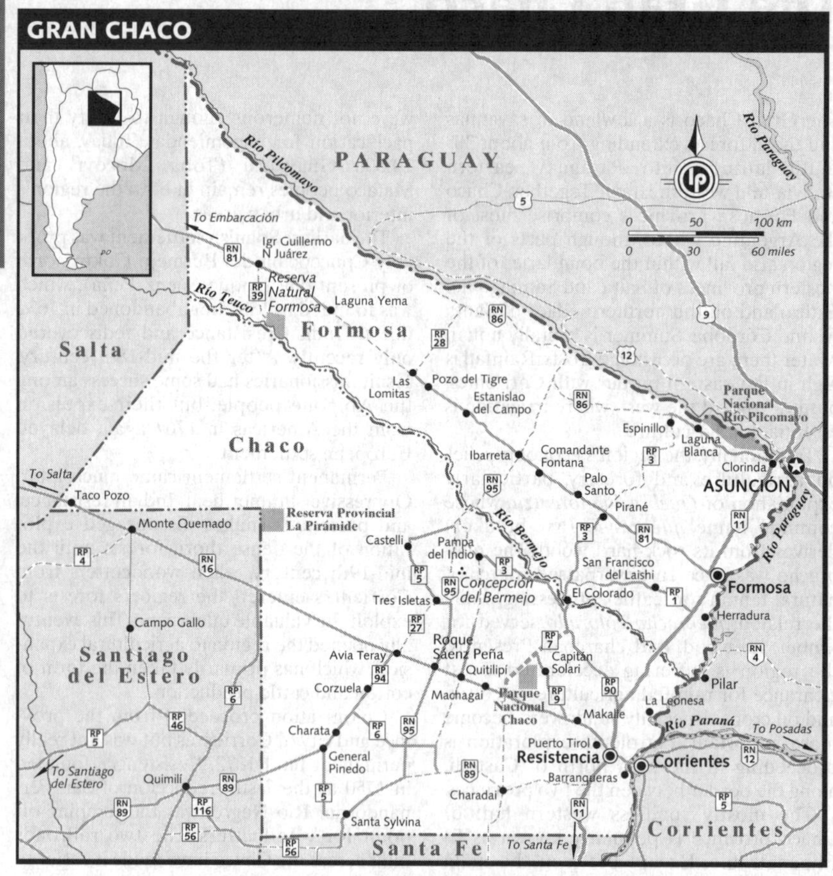

GRAN CHACO

get logs to Resistencia and Formosa, where there is sufficient water to process the tannin.

Most of the region's agricultural development took place after 1930, when cotton production increased rapidly. New settlers of mostly central European origin – Austrians, Bulgarians, Czechs, Russians, Yugoslavs, and some Spaniards – came via the Humid Pampa. The agricultural frontier continues to expand westward, as the quebracho forests are cleared for wood and charcoal, although erratic rainfall in the western Chaco makes rain-fed agriculture risky.

RESISTENCIA

First settled in 1750, the capital of Chaco province grew rapidly with development of the tannin industry and subsequent agricultural progress. Surprisingly, for an erstwhile frontier town, it is proudest of its fine-arts tradition and prefers to be known as the 'city of sculptures' or 'the open-air museum' for the many statues, often very unconventional, in virtually every public space.

Probably the frontier tradition of wood carving helped establish this unique cultural oasis; there is also an important university, as well as several cultural centers and many museums. Local sculptors are nothing if not adaptable – in 1998, contestants from this brutally hot and humid city won a prize for the best ice sculpture in the 1998 Winter Olympics at Sapporo, Japan.

Orientation

Linked to Corrientes by the Belgrano bridge across the Paraná, Resistencia (population 268,000) is not directly on the river; an eastbound road connects it to the small port of Barranqueras. It is 1019km north of Buenos Aires on RN 11 via Rosario and Santa Fe.

Refurbished Plaza 25 de Mayo, occupying four square blocks and featuring eight new fountains, is the focus of the city center. Street names change on each side of the plaza. Av Sarmiento is the main access route from RN 16, which leads east to the Belgrano bridge and west to Roque Sáenz Peña, continuing across the Chaco to Salta and Santiago del Estero. Av 25 de Mayo leads northwest from the plaza to RN 11, which also goes north to Formosa and the Paraguayan border at Clorinda.

Information

Tourist Offices The Dirección Provincial de Turismo (☎ 423547) is at Santa Fe 178. Hours are weekdays 7:30 am to 1 pm and 3 to 7:30 pm. There's also a new tourist kiosk (☎ 458289) at Roca on Plaza 25 de Mayo, open 8 am to 9 pm weekdays and 9 am to midnight weekends.

ACA (☎ 470507) is at Av 9 de Julio and Av Italia, three blocks from Plaza 25 de Mayo.

Money Cambio El Dorado, Jose María Paz 36, changes traveler's checks at reasonable rates. There are several ATMs in and around Plaza 25 de Mayo.

Post & Communications Correo Argentino faces Plaza 25 de Mayo at Sarmiento and Yrigoyen; the postal code is 3500.

There's a Telecentro at JB Justo 136, and a bigger one at the corner of Arturo Illia and Colón.

Resistencia's area code is ☎ 03722.

Travel Agencies Among the best established travel agencies are Viajes Firenze (☎ 433333), at JB Justo 148, and Sin Fronteras (☎ 431055), at Necochea 70.

Cultural Centers The Centro Cultural Leopoldo Marechal, Pellegrini 272, has regular art exhibitions and performances; it's open weekdays 9 am to noon and 7 to 9 pm. The Centro Cultural Nordeste (☎ 422649), Arturo Illia 353, has similar facilities.

Laundry Laverap has facilities at Vedia 23 (☎ 424223) and at Vedia 319 (☎ 445833).

Medical Services Hospital Ferrando (☎ 425050) is at Av 9 de Julio 1101, near Mena.

Sculptures

There's insufficient space to detail the number of sculptures in city parks and on the sidewalks, but the tourist office distributes a map with their locations, which makes a good introduction to the city (walk around early in the morning, before the suffocating summer heat). The best starting point is the new **Parque de las Esculturas Aldo y Efraín Boglietti**, at Avs Laprida and Sarmiento, a 2500-sq-meter area alongside the old French railroad station (see Museo de Ciencias Naturales).

The **Museo Provincial de Bellas Artes René Brusan**, which concentrates on sculpture, is at Mitre 163; it's open Tuesday to Friday 8 am to noon and 6 to 8:30 pm. Another center for Resistencia's arts community is the **Taller de Artes Visuales**, Arturo Illia 353, open weekdays 9 to 11:30 am and 4 to 7 pm.

El Fogón de los Arrieros

Famous for an eclectic collection of art objects from around the Chaco, Argentina, and the world, as well as a popular bar, this privately owned museum (☎ 426418) was the driving force behind Resistencia's progressive displays of public art; it also features the wood carvings of local artist Juan de Dios Mena. At Brown 350, El Fogón (☎ 426418) is open 9 to 11 pm daily.

Museo Policial

The provincial police museum features the usual grisly photos of auto accidents, tales of crimes of passion, and tedious drug-war rhetoric, but it redeems itself with absorbing accounts of *cuatrerismo* (cattle rustling, still widespread in the province) and social banditry (including the remarkable tale of two 1960s outlaws who, after killing a policeman, lived for five years on the run, helped by the *humildes* (poor rural people) of the province.

At Roca 233, the museum is open 8 am to noon and 4 to 8 pm weekdays. Police officers accompany visitors on guided tours.

Museo Regional de Antropología Juan Alfredo Martinet

Archaeology, rather than the much broader field of anthropology, is the focus of this museum at the Universidad Nacional del Noreste. There are ethnographic exhibits as well, but uncritical acceptance of Argentine scholar Ángel Rosenblat's long-outdated estimates for the aboriginal population of the Americas at European contact illustrates the difficulties provincial universities face in keeping up with recent research. At Av Las Heras 727, the museum is open weekdays 8 am to noon and 4 to 9 pm; admission is free.

Museo Histórico Regional Ichoalay

Named for a cacique who negotiated a peace settlement with the Spanish governor of Corrientes in 1750, the poorly organized provincial history museum features ethnographic materials relating to Chaco Indians and exhibits on European colonization. Within a school at Donovan 425, opposite Plaza 9 de Julio, it's supposedly open weekdays 8 am to noon and 2 to 5:30 pm, but visitors may have to track down the staff for access.

Museo de Ciencias Naturales

Recently relocated to the former Estación Ferrocarril Francés (French Railroad Station) on Laprida near Pellegrini (note the 1882 Hardy locomotive outside), this museum has a good collection of stuffed birds of the region but is otherwise unexceptional, although it has a friendly and dedicated staff. It's open weekdays 8 am to noon.

Other Museums

Well behind schedule, a new **Museo de la Escultura en Madera** (Museum of Wood Sculptures) is still due to open at some future date near the Domo del Centenario, a performing arts amphitheater in Parque 2 de Febrero, north of downtown. The **Museo del Hombre Chaqueño** (Museum of Chaco Man; ☎ 426112), Arturo Illia 655, focuses on the colonization of the Chaco.

Centro de Ofidiología Resistencia

Reptile-lovers will enjoy a visit to this regional snake research center, which offers good audiovisual programs. At Santiago del Estero 488, the center (☎ 422867) is open daily after 6:30 pm, but phone ahead.

Barrio Toba

About 1500 Toba Indians inhabit this modern government reducción, which appears cohesive and well-kept, if impersonal. At its **Cooperativa de Artesanos**, some of the ceramics are very cheap and gaudy, but the *yiscas* (string bags) and other goods show traditional skills. To reach the barrio, take bus No 7 from Plaza 25 de Mayo.

Special Events

The third week of July, Resistencia's Plaza 25 de Mayo hosts the Concurso Nacional e Internacional de Escultura y Madera, a competition in which the participants have seven days to carve a trunk of urunday (a native tree) into a work of art. For more information, contact the Fundación Urunday (☎ 436694), Av San Martín 465.

In August, the Exposición de Ganadería showcases the region's best livestock.

Places to Stay – Budget

Camping Fifteen blocks from downtown, ***Camping Parque 2 de Febrero*** *(Av Avalos 1100)* has good facilities, including shade, but can get crowded and noisy in high season –

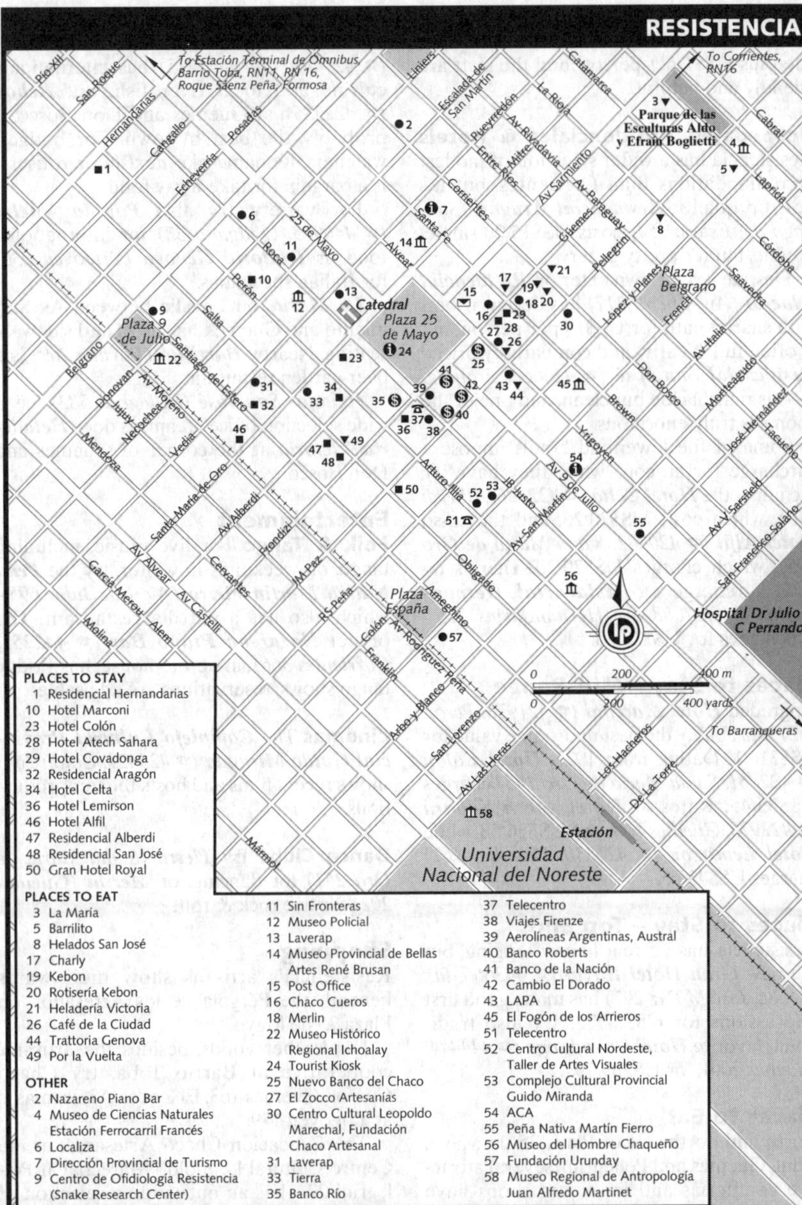

RESISTENCIA
To Estación Terminal de Omnibus, Barrio Toba, RN11, RN 16, Roque Sáenz Peña, Formosa
To Corrientes, RN16
Parque de las Esculturas Aldo y Efraín Boglietti
Plaza Belgrano
Catedral
Plaza 25 de Mayo
Plaza 9 de Julio
Plaza España
Hospital Dr Julio C Perrando
To Barranqueras
Estación
Universidad Nacional del Noreste
0 200 400 m
0 200 400 yards
PLACES TO STAY
1 Residencial Hernandarias
10 Hotel Marconi
23 Hotel Colón
28 Hotel Atech Sahara
29 Hotel Covadonga
32 Residencial Aragón
34 Hotel Celta
36 Hotel Lemirson
46 Hotel Alfil
47 Residencial Alberdi
48 Residencial San José
50 Gran Hotel Royal
PLACES TO EAT
3 La María
5 Barrilito
8 Helados San José
17 Charly
19 Kebon
20 Rotisería Kebon
21 Heladería Victoria
26 Café de la Ciudad
44 Trattoria Genova
49 Por la Vuelta
OTHER
2 Nazareno Piano Bar
4 Museo de Ciencias Naturales Estación Ferrocarril Francés
6 Localiza
7 Dirección Provincial de Turismo
9 Centro de Ofidiología Resistencia (Snake Research Center)
11 Sin Fronteras
12 Museo Policial
13 Laverap
14 Museo Provincial de Bellas Artes René Brusan
15 Post Office
16 Chaco Cueros
18 Merlin
22 Museo Histórico Regional Ichoalay
24 Tourist Kiosk
25 Nuevo Banco del Chaco
27 El Zocco Artesanías
30 Centro Cultural Leopoldo Marechal, Fundación Chaco Artesanal
31 Laverap
33 Tierra
35 Banco Río
37 Telecentro
38 Viajes Firenze
39 Aerolíneas Argentinas, Austral
40 Banco Roberts
41 Banco de la Nación
42 Cambio El Dorado
43 LAPA
45 El Fogón de los Arrieros
51 Telecentro
52 Centro Cultural Nordeste, Taller de Artes Visuales
53 Complejo Cultural Provincial Guido Miranda
54 ACA
55 Peña Nativa Martín Fierro
56 Museo del Hombre Chaqueño
57 Fundación Urunday
58 Museo Regional de Antropología Juan Alfredo Martinet

not least because of the dance clubs across Av Avalos. Fees are reasonable at US$4 per site plus US$1 per person, and the staff are friendly and helpful.

Hospedajes, Residenciales & Hotels

Resistencia has a wider selection of modest accommodations than Corrientes, but it's not top quality. ***Residencial Aragón*** *(Santiago del Estero 154)* costs US$15/20 single/double, but it's pretty dreary.

Despite a run-down exterior, ***Residencial Alberdi*** *(Av Alberdi 317)* has decent rooms with shared bath for US$18 per person, but is often full. Nearby and comparably priced ***Residencial San José*** *(☎ 426062, Frondizi 304)* is ramshackle but clean, and one of the rooms is truly enormous.

Some of the lower-end hotels impose a surcharge for air-con (when they have it), including the ***Hotel Celta*** *(☎ 422986, Alberdi 210)*, which costs US$20/25, and the so-so ***Hotel Alfil*** *(☎ 420882, Santa María de Oro 495)*, which charges US$20/30. There's no such surcharge at ***Residencial Hernandarias*** *(☎ 427088, Av Hernandarias 215)*, which goes for US$23/35.

Places to Stay – Mid-Range

Upgraded ***Hotel Marconi*** *(☎ 421978, Perón 352)* is probably the best mid-range value for US$31/41. Dating from 1927, ***Hotel Colón*** *(☎ 422861, Santa María de Oro 143)* charges US$35/45. Rates at ***Hotel Atech Sahara*** *(☎ 422970, Güemes 160)* are US$36/58, while ***Hotel Lemirson*** *(☎ 421330, Frondizi 167)* charges US$43/65.

Places to Stay – Top End

Resistencia has no real luxury lodging, but the new ***Gran Hotel Royal*** *(☎ 443666, fax 424586, José M Paz 297)* has made good first impressions for US$62/72. Try also traditional favorite ***Hotel Covadonga*** *(☎ 444444, Güemes 200)*, for US$69/79.

Places to Eat

North and northwest of Plaza 25 de Mayo, along Güemes and Pellegrini, several attractive confiterías and ice-cream shops have rejuvenated this part of town. Try, for instance, ***Café de la Ciudad*** *(☎ 420214, Pellegrini 109)*, formerly a sleazy bar. ***Charly*** *(☎ 429491, Güemes 215)* has international cuisine and local river fish, but ***Kebon*** *(☎ 422385)*, at Güemes and Don Bosco, is probably the best in town. For budget-watchers, its namesake next-door rotisería is a bargain for take-away food.

For variety, try also ***Por la Vuelta*** *(☎ 440985, Obligado 33)* for international food or ***Trattoria Genova*** *(Yrigoyen 236)* for Italian specialties.

La María, on Lavalle between Av Sarmiento and Güemes, has pizza and sidewalk seating. Nearby ***Barrilito*** *(Lavalle 269)* is a beer-garden restaurant.

Helados San José *(Pellegrini 582)* has a wide selection of ice cream, as does ***Heladería Victoria*** at the corner of Güemes and Don Bosco.

Entertainment

Folk & Tango For live music, including tango, on weekends in winter, try the ***Peña Nativa Martín Fierro*** *(Av 9 de Julio 695)*, which also has a parrilla restaurant. The pricier ***Nazareno Piano Bar*** *(☎ 442251, Corrientes 366)*, in an old house, has Friday tango shows; reservations are advisable.

Cinemas The ***Complejo Cultural Provincial Guido Miranda*** *(☎ 425421, Colón 164)* shows recent films and hosts theater productions.

Dance Clubs Try ***Tierra*** *(Santa María de Oro 251)* for dancing, or ***Merlin*** *(Güemes 202)* for live rock & roll.

Shopping

Resistencia's artisans show their wares beneath the Pérgola de los Artesanos, on Plaza 25 de Mayo.

For leather goods, besides the artisans' cooperative at Barrio Toba, try Chaco Cueros, Güemes 163. El Zocco Artesanías is at Yrigoyen 179.

The Fundación Chaco Artesanal, in the Centro Cultural Leopoldo Marechal at Pellegrini 272, has an outstanding selection of crafts.

Getting There & Away

Air Aerolíneas Argentinas (☎ 445553) and Austral (☎ 446800) share offices at Frondizi 99, but only Austral has flights from Resistencia, twice daily to Buenos Aires' Aeroparque (US$161) except Sunday, when there's only one flight. LAPA (☎ 430201), Pellegrini 100, flies daily to Aeroparque (US$59 to US$129).

Bus Resistencia is an important hub of bus travel for destinations in all directions; its still sparkling Estación Terminal de Ómnibus (☎ 461098), at Av MacLean and Islas Malvinas, replaced the dilapidated downtown terminal several years ago. Godoy Resistencia buses make the rounds between Corrientes and Resistencia at frequent intervals throughout the day.

Buses to Buenos Aires and intermediate points are numerous with La Internacional (☎ 460901), La Estrella (☎ 460905), El Tala (☎ 461104), Puerto Tirol (☎ 460904), Ciudad de Posadas (☎ 460931), El Norte Bis (☎ 460908), El Pulqui (☎ 460113), El Gauchito de Río Hondo (☎ 464182), Caraza (☎ 464772), El Cometa (☎ 464148), and Empresa Domínguez (☎ 461101).

Empresa Martignoni (☎ 460907), Singer (☎ 460907), Kurtz (☎ 438804), El Cometa (☎ 464182), and Ciudad de Posadas all go to Posadas, with all but El Cometa continuing to Puerto Iguazú.

Northbound service to Formosa and the Paraguayan border is frequent with Puerto Tirol, El Tala, Godoy SRL (☎ 460902), and Cacorba. Godoy SRL has two early morning buses to Asunción (Paraguay), while El Tala has one and Empresa Yacyretá another. Godoy also goes to Naick-Neck and Laguna Blanca, near Parque Nacional Pilcomayo.

Ciudad de Gualeguaychú (☎ 460907) goes twice daily to Gualeguaychú via Mercedes, Concordia, and other intermediate points. El Pulqui, El Norte Bis, and Puerto Tirol all have early evening service to Rosario via Santa Fe. El Tala goes to La Plata at 6 pm daily, while San Cristóbal goes slightly earlier. Ciudad de Posadas goes to Mar del Plata Monday and Thursday at midday.

La Estrella, Cacorba (☎ 463528), and El Pulqui cross the Chaco to Córdoba at least daily among them. La Estrella also goes twice nightly to Tucumán, while La Nueva Estrella (☎ 460907) goes once. La Estrella connects with Roque Sáenz Peña and also goes to the village of Capitán Solari, near Parque Nacional Chaco, four times daily. La Veloz del Norte (☎ 464464) crosses the Chaco to Salta and Jujuy daily at 5 pm, while Central Sáenz Peña (☎ 460907), also departing at 5 pm, goes only as far as Salta.

TAC (☎ 461103) goes nightly at 9 pm to the Cuyo destinations of San Juan and Mendoza, via La Rioja and Catamarca. Cotal does the same route Tuesday, Thursday, and Sunday at 12:40 am.

Samples fares include Puerto Iguazú (US$38, 10½ hours), Salta (US$32 to US$42, 13 hours) and Buenos Aires (US$43, 15 hours).

Getting Around

To/From the Airport Aeropuerto San Martín is 6km south of town on RN 11; take bus No 3 (black letters) from the post office on Plaza 25 de Mayo.

To/From the Bus Station Take bus No 3 or No 10 from the Casa de Gobierno (near the post office) on Plaza 25 de Mayo.

Car Localiza (☎ 439255) is at Roca 460.

PARQUE NACIONAL CHACO

Preserving several diverse ecosystems reflecting subtle differences in relief, soils, and rainfall, this very accessible but little-known park protects 15,000 hectares of the humid eastern Chaco. It is 115km northwest of Resistencia via RN 16 and RP 9.

Ecologically, Parque Nacional Chaco falls within the 'estuarine and gallery forest' subregion of the Gran Chaco, but the park encompasses a variety of marshes, open grasslands, palm savannas, scrub forest, and denser gallery forests. The most widespread ecosystem is the *monte fuerte*, where mature specimens of quebracho, algarrobo, and lapacho reach above 20m, while lower stories of immature trees and shrubs provide a variety of habitats at distinct elevations.

Scrub forests form a transitional environment to seasonally inundated savanna grasslands, punctuated by *caranday* and *pindó* palms. More open grasslands have traditionally been maintained by human activities, including grazing and associated fires, but these are disappearing. Marshes and gallery forests cover the smallest areas, but they are biologically the most productive. The meandering Río Negro has left several shallow oxbow lakes where dense aquatic vegetation flourishes.

Mammals are few and rarely seen, but birds are abundant, including the rhea, jabirú stork, roseate spoonbill, cormorants, common caracaras, and other less conspicuous species. The most abundant and widely distributed insect species is the mosquito, so plan your trip during the relatively dry, cool winter and bring insect repellent.

Information

The Administración (☎ 03725-496190) now collects a US$2 admission charge at the park entrance. Park service personnel are extremely hospitable and will accompany visitors if their duties permit.

The Ñandú, or rhea, resembles a small ostrich.

Activities

Hiking and bird watching are the principal activities, best done in early morning or around sunset. Some inundated areas are accessible only while horseback riding; inquire about horses and guides in Capitán Solari, 6km east of the park.

Places to Stay & Eat

At Capitán Solari, you may find basic accommodations, but ***camping*** is the only alternative at the park itself. Fortunately, there are numerous shaded sites with clean showers (cold water only) and toilets, despite many ants and other harmless *bichos* (critters). A tent or other shelter is essential. There are fire pits, picnic tables, plenty of wood lying around for fuel, and no fees, but beware of Panchi, the rangers' pet monkey, who will steal anything not tied down.

Weekends can be crowded with visitors from Resistencia, but at other times you may have the park to yourself. Sometimes on weekends a concessionaire from Resistencia sells meals, but it's better to bring everything you need from Resistencia or Capitán Solari.

Getting There & Away

Capitán Solari is 2½ hours from Resistencia by bus; La Estrella has four buses daily, at 6:30 am and 12:30, 5:30, and 8 pm; return buses from Capitán Solari to Resistencia leave at 5:30 and 11:30 am and 5 pm.

From Capitán Solari, you will have to walk or catch a lift to the park entrance; the road may be impassable for motor vehicles in wet weather. If possible, avoid walking in the midday heat.

ROQUE SÁENZ PEÑA

Properly speaking, this city of 70,000 people, 168km west of Resistencia, goes by the cumbersome name of Presidencia Roque Sáenz Peña, after the term of the Argentine leader responsible for the adoption of electoral reform and universal male suffrage in 1912.

Primarily a service center for cotton and sunflower growers, Roque Sáenz Peña's main visitor attraction, especially in winter,

is its thermal baths, fortuitously discovered by drillers seeking potable water in 1937. The city is brutally hot in summer and, except around the plazas, almost treeless. Several immigrant communities have their own clubs, including Italians, Yugoslavs, and Bulgarians. The city, which also has one of the country's better zoos, is the gateway to the 'Impenetrable' of the central Chaco.

Orientation

Roque Sáenz Peña straddles RN 16, which connects Resistencia with Salta. Its regular grid plan centers on willow-shaded Plaza San Martín; Av San Martín is the principal commercial street.

Information

Tourist Offices The Oficina Municipal de Turismo (☎ 422135) is at Av San Martín and 9 de Julio. ACA (☎ 420471) is at Rivadavia and 25 de Mayo.

Money For currency exchange, try Banco Nordecoop, 25 de Mayo 464, or Banco de la Nación, Av San Martín 301.

Post & Communications Correo Argentino is at Belgrano 602, corner of Mitre; the postal code is 3700. There's a locutorio at Av San Martín 919; the area code is ☎ 03732.

Travel Agencies Tobas Tour (☎ 421723) is at 9 de Julio 479.

Medical Services Hospital 4 de Junio (☎ 421404) is at Las Malvinas 1350.

Termas de Sáenz Peña

Consciously developed for tourism, this complex of saunas, mineral baths, and Turkish baths also offers massage, a spa, physical therapy, and other services. In summer, you may notice little difference between air and water temperature, which is about 45°C.

At Brown 541 between Av San Martín and Mariano Moreno, the complex is open weekdays 7 am to noon and 3:30 to 10 pm, Saturday 2:30 to 9 pm. Thermal baths cost US$5, Turkish baths US$7, and saunas US$12 per person.

Parque Zoológico y Complejo Ecológico

At the junction of RN 16 and Ruta 95, 3km east of downtown, this spacious and nationally renowned zoo and botanical garden emphasizes regionally important birds and mammals rather than ecological exotics. Featured species are tapir and jaguar.

The zoo (☎ 422145) has two large artificial lakes frequented by migratory waterfowl. Bus No 2 goes from downtown to the zoo, which is within reasonable walking distance if it's not too hot. Admission is US$0.50 per adult plus US$1 per vehicle; kids get in free. Hours are 7 am to 7 pm daily.

Special Events

In May, Roque Sáenz Peña hosts the Fiesta Nacional del Algodón (National Cotton Festival). Chaco province grows nearly two-thirds of the country's total cotton crop.

Places to Stay

Camping The former municipal site along the eastern approach to town just north of RN 16, ***Camping El Descanso*** charges US$6 per site. It has good, shady facilities, but can be very noisy on weekends. Bus No 1 from downtown goes there.

Residenciales & Hotels The best bargain is ***Residencial El Colono*** *(☎ 422338, Av San Martín 755)*, where singles with shared bath are US$10; it also has a good restaurant with sidewalk seating. ***Hotel Asturias*** *(☎ 420210, Belgrano 402)* charges about US$15 per person for rooms without air-con, US$30/35 for singles/doubles with air-con. The new ***Hotel Internacional*** *(☎ 421140, Urquiza 289)* is a good value at US$20/30.

At ***Hotel Orel*** *(☎ 420101, Av San Martín 131)* and ***Hotel Augustus*** *(☎ 422068, Belgrano 483)* rates are around US$22/30 with shared bath, US$29/40 with private bath; the Augustus tacks on 50% for air-con. Four-star ***Hotel Gualok*** *(☎ 420521, Av San Martín 1198)*, part of the thermal baths complex, charges US$51/70 and also has a restaurant.

Places to Eat

Besides the hotel restaurants there are numerous restaurants and confiterías along Av San Martín. Also try ***Pizzería Roma***, an appealing place at Av Mitre and Mariano Moreno, and ***La Candela***, at the corner of Brown and Mariano Moreno.

Getting There & Away

The bus terminal (☎ 420280) is east of downtown, on Petris between Avellaneda and López y Planes; take bus No 1 from Av Mitre.

La Internacional (☎ 425340) and El Tata (☎ 425321) both go to Buenos Aires (US$53, 17 hours). Ciudad de Sáenz Peña (☎ 420222) and La Estrella (☎ 421553) both go to Resistencia (US$10, two hours), while Ciudad de Sáenz Peña serves many other provincial destinations. Many trans-Chaco services from Resistencia pick up passengers here as well.

FORMOSA

Much like North American teenagers in their automobiles, the adolescents of Formosa, capital of its namesake province, race up and down the main drag (Av Doctor Luis

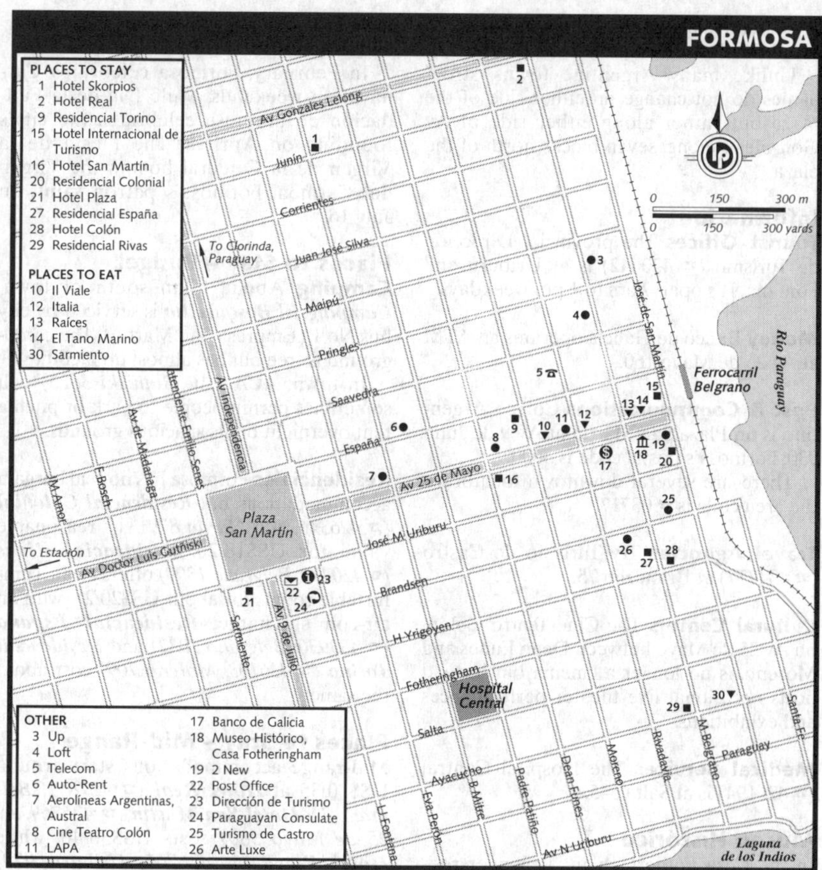

Gutñiski) of this steamingly hot city in platoons of underpowered motor scooters. Like Resistencia, however, Formosa's numerous sculptures – not just monuments – evince a serious cultural commitment. The city may also have the highest density of ice creameries in the country.

Orientation

Formosa (population 203,000) is 169km north of Resistencia and 113km south of Clorinda, on the border with Paraguay, via RN 11. It is also possible, though still not easy, to cross the northern Chaco via RN 81 and continue to Bolivia. The Ferrocarril Belgrano no longer carries passengers across the Chaco to Embarcación.

Av Doctor Luis Gutñiski, as RN 11 is known through town, heads eastward to Plaza San Martín, a four-block public park beyond which Av 25 de Mayo, the heart of the city, continues to the shores of the Río Paraguay.

From the north side of Plaza San Martín, Av Independencia is RN 11, heading north to Clorinda and Paraguay, although the

Av Circunvalación does allow motorists to avoid the downtown area.

Unlike many Argentine towns, street names do not change on either side of the plaza but rather along either side of Av Gonzales Lelong, seven blocks north of the plaza.

Information

Tourist Offices The provincial Dirección de Turismo (☎ 420442) is at Uriburu and Fontana. It's open 7 am to 1 pm weekdays.

Money Banco de Galicia operates an ATM at Av 25 de Mayo 160.

Post & Communications Correo Argentino is on Plaza San Martín at Av 9 de Julio 930; Formosa's postal code is 3600.

There are several downtown locutorios; the area code is ☎ 03717.

Travel Agencies Try Turismo de Castro (☎ 434777) at Brandzen 75.

Cultural Centers The Cine Teatro Colón, on Av 25 de Mayo between Dean Funes and Moreno, is no longer a cinema but instead hosts occasional live theater performances and exhibitions.

Medical Services The Hospital Central (☎ 426194) is at Salta 545.

Museo Histórico

In the Casa Fotheringham, a pioneer residence that was the province's first Casa de Gobierno, the municipal historical museum focuses on the foundation and development of Formosa (part of the Paraguayan Chaco until the 19th-century War of the Triple Alliance). It's at the corner of Belgrano and Av 25 de Mayo.

Special Events

Formosa's annual Fiesta del Río, lasting a week in mid-November, features an impressive nocturnal religious procession in which 150 boats from Corrientes sail up the Río Paraguay. There are also sports competitions, including swimming, kayaking, windsurfing, and sailing.

In February, Formosa celebrates Carnaval on weekends, while Día de la Fundación de Formosa celebrates the city's founding on April 8. The Fiesta de la Virgen de la Catedral honors the Virgen del Carmen, Formosa's patron saint, on July 16.

Places to Stay – Budget

Camping About 15km south of town, ***Camping El Bosquecillo*** is serviced by city bus No 1 (Empresa San Martín). The campground is free but has almost no facilities.

In town, ***ACA*** *(Av Gutñiski 3025)* will sometimes permit people to park or pitch a tent overnight on its spacious grounds.

Residenciales Formosa has no real bargain accommodations, but ***Residencial Colonial*** *(☎ 426346, San Martín 879)* is a reasonable value for US$18/20. ***Residencial Rivas*** *(☎ 420499, Belgrano 1399)* offers clean, comfortable rooms for about US$20/25, with an air-con surcharge. ***Residencial España*** *(☎ 433930, Belgrano 1032)* and ***Residencial Torino*** *(☎ 426103, Moreno 709)* cost about the same.

Places to Stay – Mid-Range

Mid-range accommodations start around US$30/35 at ***Hotel Real*** *(☎ 427851, Belgrano 1)*. ***Hotel San Martín*** *(☎ 426769, Av 25 de Mayo 380)* costs US$30/40, while ***Hotel Plaza*** *(☎ 426767, Uriburu 920)* charges US$32/55. ***Hotel Colón*** *(☎ 420719, Belgrano 1068)* costs US$38/55. Rates at ***Hotel Skorpios*** *(☎ 420894, Mitre 98)* are US$45/50.

Places to Stay – Top End

Both the ***Hotel Colón*** and ***Hotel Plaza*** have somewhat costlier, more comfortable rooms in the US$48/55 range, but the modernistic ***Hotel Internacional de Turismo*** *(☎ 430935, San Martín 759)* is the most impressive in town. 'Executive' singles/doubles cost US$71/89, though there are also some rooms around US$50.

Places to Eat

Both ***Raíces*** *(☎ 427058, Av 25 de Mayo 65)* and ***El Tano Marino*** *(☎ 420628, Av 25 de Mayo 55)*, next door, offer good, reasonably priced meals in pleasant surroundings. ***Italia*** *(Rivadavia 792)* serves pizza and pasta, while ***Il Viale*** *(Av 25 de Mayo 275)* is a confitería. ***Sarmiento*** *(San Martín 1338)* serves beef and seafood.

Entertainment

Formosa's several dance clubs all have English names: ***2 New*** *(Av 25 de Mayo 18)*, ***Loft*** *(Belgrano 545)*, and ***Up*** *(Belgrano 636)*.

Shopping

Arte Luxe, Brandzen 104, has Formosa's best selection of crafts.

Getting There & Away

Air Austral (☎ 429392), Av 25 de Mayo 603, flies daily to Buenos Aires' Aeroparque (US$180).

LAPA (☎ 435979), Av 25 de Mayo 215, flies daily except Sunday to Corrientes (US$13 to US$23), a flight that continues to Aeroparque (US$59 to US$149).

Bus Formosa's modern Estación Terminal de Ómnibus is on Av Gutñiski and Antártida Argentina, 15 blocks west of Plaza San Martín. Godoy SRL (☎ 430816, 433330) goes to Clorinda (on the Paraguayan border), Resistencia, and Buenos Aires (US$50, 18 hours). Puerto Tirol (☎ 433320) has frequent service to Resistencia and Corrientes, with daily service to Buenos Aires. El Norte Bis (☎ 433500) passes through Formosa each day en route from Clorinda to Buenos Aires. El Tala (☎ 433353) goes each day to La Plata via Resistencia, Corrientes, and Buenos Aires.

Cacorba (☎ 433488) serves Córdoba five times weekly. Empresa Giroldi (☎ 431700) crosses the northern Chaco as far as Embarcación, in the province of Salta, where connections to Bolivia are possible.

Navarro (☎ 423598), at the corner of Alberdi and Corrientes, runs buses to Clorinda and Laguna Naick-Neck (Parque Nacional Río Pilcomayo) daily at 5:30 am and 2 and 8 pm.

Getting Around

Aeropuerto El Pucú is only 4km south of town along RN 11, so cabs are an inexpensive alternative. For car rental, try Auto-Rent (☎ 431721), at España 557.

CLORINDA

Notorious for fierce customs checks, squalid Clorinda (population 45,000) is the border crossing to Asunción, Paraguay, via the Puente Internacional San Ignacio de Loyola. Some officials at Puerto Falcón on the Paraguayan side are flagrantly corrupt, even offering to buy tourist vehicles themselves. Godoy SRL (☎ 421110) crosses the border at regular intervals from Clorinda's bus station at San Martín and Paraguay, where Navarro buses to Parque Nacional Río Pilcomayo also depart. The postal code is 3610, the area code ☎ 03718.

Formosa is a more agreeable place to stay, but if you're stuck, there's inexpensive lodging for about US$13/20 at ***Residencial Ortega*** *(☎ 421593, Libertad 1213)* and at the ***Hotel San Martín*** *(☎ 421211, 12 de Octubre 1150)*.

PARQUE NACIONAL RÍO PILCOMAYO

West of Clorinda, the wildlife-rich marshlands of 60,000-hectare Parque Nacional Río Pilcomayo, resembling Parque Nacional Chaco in its ecology and environments, hug the Paraguayan border. Its outstanding feature is shallow, shimmering **Laguna Blanca**, where, at sunset, yacarés lurk on the lake surface. Other wildlife (except for birds) is likelier to be heard than seen among the dense aquatic vegetation.

From the park's campground, a wooden *pasarela* (walkway) leads to the lakeshore, where there is a platform overlook about 5m high, plus three lake-level platforms for swimming and sunbathing (the water is barely a meter deep). It's especially tranquil and appealing late in the day – after picnickers and day-trippers have returned to

Clorinda and Formosa – but carry plenty of mosquito repellent.

Places to Stay & Eat

The free ***camping*** facilities are seldom used except on weekends; automobiles cannot enter the campground proper but must park nearby. There are showers in the bathrooms, but the water is saline and most people prefer the lake, which offers relief from the heat. Just outside the park entrance, a small **shop** sells basic food and cold drinks, including beer.

At the town of Laguna Blanca, 11km beyond the turnoff, accommodations are available at ***Hotel Guaraní*** *(☎ 03718-470024)*, at San Martín and Sargento Cabral.

Getting There & Away

Navarro runs buses from Formosa and Clorinda along RN 86 to Laguna Naick-Neck, where there is a well-marked turnoff to the ranger station at Laguna Blanca.

From the turnoff, however, you will have to hike or try to hitch the remaining 5km to Laguna Blanca.

Córdoba

Córdoba, a transitional province between the Andes and the Pampas, is popular with Argentine tourists but less frequented by foreigners. Excluding Patagonia, it lies in the virtual center of the country, bounded by the Andean provinces to the northwest, Cuyo to the southwest, Gran Chaco to the northeast, and the Pampas to the southeast. Most of the province is agricultural, but its major attractions are the capital city of Córdoba and its scenic mountain hinterland, the Sierras de Córdoba. Many of the province's features appeal to conventional tastes, but newly paved roads have improved accessibility to opportunities off the beaten track. Historical attractions are abundant and diverse.

The city of Córdoba once rivaled Buenos Aires for political, economic, and cultural supremacy. From the early 17th century, when Buenos Aires languished at the end of Spain's circuitous mercantile supply route, Córdoba's churches and universities were among Latin America's finest. Today it remains one of Argentina's key industrial centers, especially as the heart of the automotive industry.

The geologically complex Sierras, consisting of three longitudinal ranges reaching as high as 2800m, stretch 500km from north to south, separating the Pampas from the Andes. Giving birth to several east-flowing rivers, prosaically named Primero (First), Segundo (Second), Tercero (Third), and Cuarto (Fourth), the Sierras offer literally hundreds of small towns and even tinier villages. In the northeast of the province, the Río Primero drains into the Laguna Mar Chiquita, a shallow, inland sea.

The Sierras' attractions range from reservoirs, artificial sandy beaches, noisy dance clubs, and the gaudy casinos of tacky resorts like Villa Carlos Paz to more sedate places such as Cosquín and Candonga. Outside the peak summer season, prices for accommodations can be much lower and bargaining is possible, but many places close by the end of March. The Sierras' dense network of roads, many well paved but others graveled, make them good candidates for bicycle touring – Argentine drivers here seem a bit less ruthless than elsewhere in the country. A mountain bike is still the best choice, but a touring bike would suffice if you plan your itinerary well.

History

Before the arrival of the Spaniards, sedentary Comechingones Indians occupied the area around Córdoba. Like their counterparts farther north, they were maize cultivators, but they also herded llamas and gathered fruit from the algarrobo tree. Proficient warriors, they effectively resisted the Spanish for a brief period – by one account, they shot a Spaniard so full of arrows that he 'looked like San Sebastián,' a famous Christian martyr.

The Spaniards also found that the local Indians lacked the hierarchical political structure that had facilitated efforts to bring other tribes under the encomienda system:

> It is notorious that no village which has a cacique is the subject of another cacique or pueblo. These people are in such anarchy that in all the encomiendas which exist or are being established each pueblo and cacique is mentioned by itself even if there are only two Indians.

Jerónimo Luis de Cabrera founded the city of Córdoba in 1573. It quickly became the

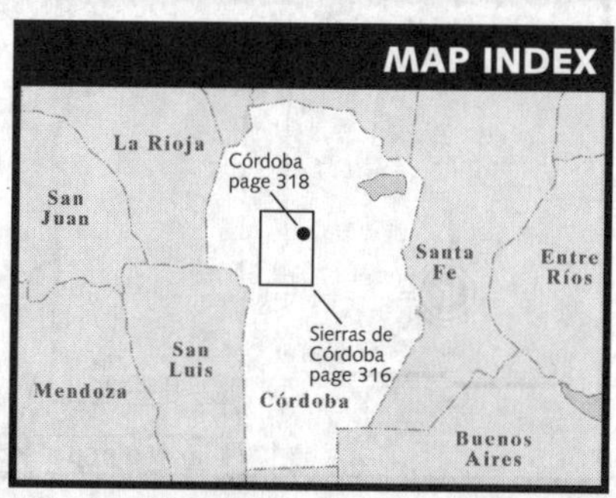

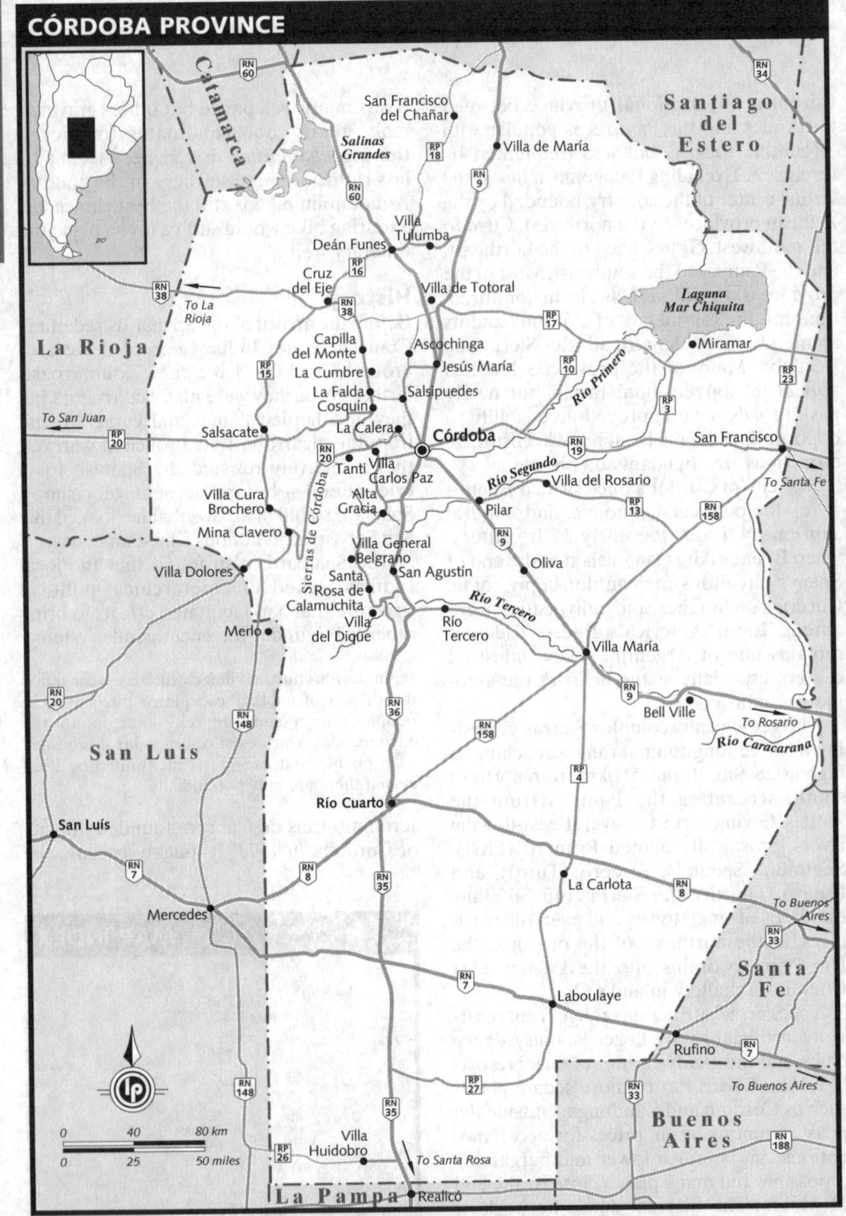
CÓRDOBA PROVINCE
Catamarca
Santiago del Estero
La Rioja
San Luis
Santa Fe
Buenos Aires
La Pampa
Salinas Grandes
Laguna Mar Chiquita
Sierras de Córdoba
Río Primero
Río Segundo
Río Tercero
Río Caracarana
San Francisco del Chañar
Villa de María
Villa Tulumba
Deán Funes
Cruz del Eje
Villa de Totoral
Capilla del Monte
Ascochinga
Jesús María
La Cumbre
La Falda
Salsipuedes
Cosquín
Salsacate
La Calera
Córdoba
Tanti
Villa Carlos Paz
Alta Gracia
Villa Cura Brochero
Mina Clavero
Villa Dolores
Villa General Belgrano
San Agustín
Santa Rosa de Calamuchita
Villa del Dique
Merlo
Río Tercero
Pilar
Oliva
Villa del Rosario
Miramar
San Francisco
Villa María
Bell Ville
Río Cuarto
San Luís
Mercedes
La Carlota
Laboulaye
Rufino
Villa Huidobro
Realicó
To La Rioja
To San Juan
To Santa Fe
To Rosario
To Buenos Aires
To Buenos Aires
To Santa Rosa
RN 60
RN 34
RP 18
RN 9
RN 60
RP 16
RN 38
RN 38
RP 17
RP 10
RP 15
RP 23
RP 3
RP 20
RN 20
RN 19
RP 13
RN 158
RN 9
RN 9
RN 20
RN 148
RN 36
RN 158
RP 4
RN 7
RN 8
RN 35
RN 8
RN 33
RN 7
RN 7
RN 148
RP 27
RN 33
RN 35
RP 26
RN 188
0 40 80 km
0 25 50 miles

center for Spanish activities, with a strong missionary presence facilitated by its agricultural potential and the readily accessible construction materials. The well-intentioned Dominicans, Franciscans, and Jesuits failed to protect the native population, however. In the century after Córdoba's founding, the number of Indians in encomienda declined from more than 6000 to fewer than 500, due primarily to introduced diseases. Little evidence remains of their presence except in place names – the major mountain range southwest of the city is the Sierra de Comechingones.

Córdoba's ecclesiastical importance made it a center for education, fine arts, and architecture. Many impressive colonial monuments still grace the city center where, on weekends when the bustling auto traffic abates, travelers can still absorb the 17th-century ambience and visualize how Buenos Aires depended on its connections to the north. With the creation of the Viceroyalty of the River Plate, followed by Argentine independence, Córdoba underwent the same reorientation as the rest of the country, becoming subject to the economic whims of the port capital.

Still, Córdoba continued to assert its autonomy in many ways. Royalist forces from the city unsuccessfully resisted Buenos Aires in the early years of the wars of independence; under the cry 'Religion or Death,' Córdoba's conservative clergy were outspoken opponents of Unitarist intellectuals like Bernardino Rivadavia. Nevertheless, the city soon benefited from increased foreign trade, doubling its population between 1840 and 1860.

Things changed, as in the rest of Argentina, when European immigrants swarmed into the country in the late 19th century. Railway expansion in the 1870s stimulated the growth of the province – between 1882 and 1896, the number of agricultural colonies increased from just five to 176. Still, because of the phenomenal growth in Buenos Aires and the Pampas, Córdoba experienced a relative decline.

Eventually, the local establishment's political conservatism aroused so much dissatisfaction among the populace that, especially in the university, it spawned an aggressive reform movement that had a lasting impact both locally and nationally. In the late 1960s, university students and auto workers forged a coalition that nearly unseated the de facto military government of General Juan Carlos Onganía in an uprising known as the *cordobazo*. In the following years, many such insurrections, ignited by local conditions but growing increasingly broader and more radical in their aims, took place around the country.

Today, after the chaos of the 1970s and early 1980s, the region's economy has again declined as a result of the automobile industry's obsolete equipment and the general stagnation of the Argentine economy. There are signs of revival, however, as Fiat has reestablished itself in the provincial capital.

CÓRDOBA

With more than 1.3 million inhabitants, the provincial capital is one of Argentina's major cultural and industrial centers. At 400m above sea level at the foot of the Sierra Chica, the city has sprawled well north of the Río Primero (also known as the Suquía) and into the surrounding countryside. Its downtown is compact and readily explored on foot, while industrial zones occupy the southern suburbs.

Orientation

Córdoba is 710km northwest of Buenos Aires and 330km south of Santiago del Estero via RN 9. Plaza San Martín is its urban nucleus; most colonial attractions lie within a quadrant demarcated by Av Olmos to the north, Av Maipú to the east, Blvd Illia to the south, and Av General Paz to the west. The commercial center is just northwest of the plaza, where the main pedestrian malls, 25 de Mayo and Rivera Indarte, intersect each other. Obispo Trejo, just west of the plaza, has the finest concentration of colonial buildings.

Just south of downtown, Parque Sarmiento offers relief from the bustling, densely built downtown, but the largest open space is Parque General San Martín, on the

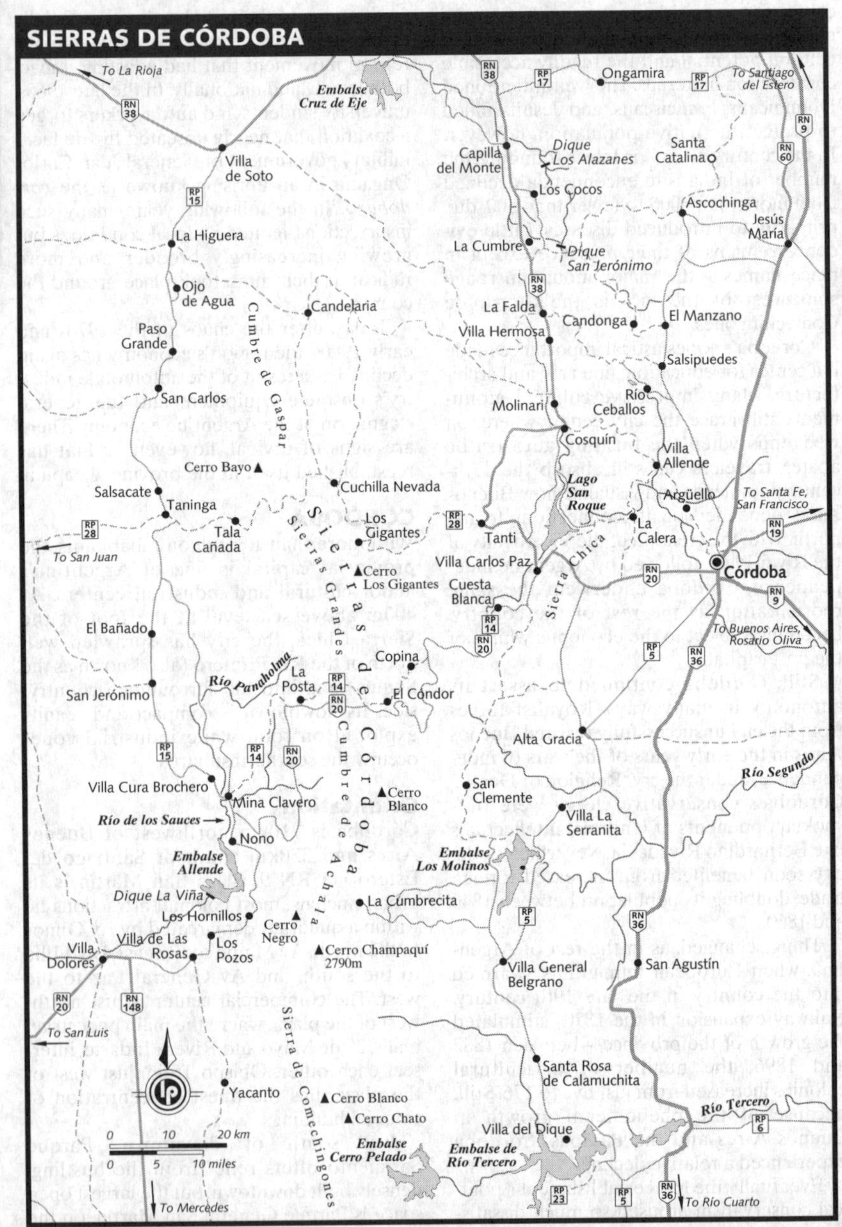
SIERRAS DE CÓRDOBA
To La Rioja
RN 38
Embalse Cruz de Eje
RN 38
RP 17
Ongamira
RP 17
To Santiago del Estero
RN 9
RN 60
Villa de Soto
Capilla del Monte
Dique Los Alazanes
Santa Catalina
RP 15
Los Cocos
Ascochinga
Jesús María
La Higuera
La Cumbre
Dique San Jerónimo
RN 38
Ojo de Agua
Candelaria
La Falda
Villa Hermosa
Candonga
El Manzano
Paso Grande
Cumbre de Gaspar
Salsipuedes
San Carlos
Molinari
Río Ceballos
Cosquín
Villa Allende
Cerro Bayo
Cuchilla Nevada
Lago San Roque
Argüello
To Santa Fe, San Francisco
Salsacate
Taninga
Los Gigantes
RP 28
Tanti
La Calera
RN 19
RP 28
Tala Cañada
Sierras de Córdoba
Sierras Grandes
Sierra Chica
To San Juan
Cerro Los Gigantes
Villa Carlos Paz
RN 20
Córdoba
Cuesta Blanca
RN 9
RP 14
El Bañado
RN 20
To Buenos Aires, Rosario Oliva
Copina
RP 5
RN 36
Río Panaholma
La Posta
RP 14
RN 20
El Cóndor
San Jerónimo
Cumbre de Achala
Alta Gracia
RP 15
RP 14
RN 20
Río Segundo
Villa Cura Brochero
Cerro Blanco
San Clemente
Mina Clavero
Villa La Serranita
Río de los Sauces
Nono
Embalse Allende
Embalse Los Molinos
Dique La Viña
La Cumbrecita
RP 5
RN 36
Los Hornillos
Cerro Negro
Villa Dolores
Villa de Las Rosas
Los Pozos
Cerro Champaquí 2790m
San Agustín
RN 20
RN 148
Sierra de Comechingones
Villa General Belgrano
To San Luis
Santa Rosa de Calamuchita
Yacanto
Cerro Blanco
Cerro Chato
Río Tercero
RP 6
0 10 20 km
0 5 10 miles
Villa del Dique
Embalse Cerro Pelado
Embalse de Río Tercero
RP 23
RP 5
RN 36
To Mercedes
To Río Cuarto

banks of the Suquía on the northwestern outskirts of town.

Information

Tourist Offices The provincial Subsecretaría de Turismo (☎ 421-4027) and the municipal Dirección de Turismo (☎ 433-1542) have information desks in the historic Casa Cabildo, at Independencia 30 on the west side of Plaza San Martín, but both pretty much take the attitude that 'we're here to hand out brochures, nothing more, nothing less.' Hours are weekdays 8 am to 9 pm, weekends 9 am to noon and 5 to 8 pm.

The Dirección de Turismo (☎ 422-5761) has an additional office at the Casa del Obispo Mercadillo, downstairs at Calle Rosario de Santa Fe 39 on the north side of the plaza, open weekday business hours only. The Subsecretaría (☎ 423-3248) has an office at Tucumán 360, open weekdays 8 am to 2 pm, and another (☎ 423-4169) at the bus terminal, Blvd Perón 380, open weekdays 7:30 am to 8:30 pm, weekends 8 am to 8 pm; if arriving by bus or at the nearby train station, look here for the latest hotel information. An additional office (☎ 481-1241) is at Aeropuerto Pajas Blancas, open weekdays 8 am to 8 pm.

ACA (☎ 421-4636) is at Av General Paz and Humberto Primo, eight blocks north of Plaza San Martín.

Money For changing cash or traveler's checks (the latter with a hefty commission), try Barujel at the corner of Rivadavia and 25 de Mayo. There are many ATMs downtown and at the bus station.

Post & Communications Correo Argentino is at Av General Paz 201; central Córdoba's postal code is 5000. There are Telecentros in many downtown locations, including Plaza San Martín, and at the bus station. Córdoba's area code is ☎ 0351.

Travel Agencies For tours around Córdoba, try Aeroturis (☎ 442-1872), Av Olmos 351. The AmEx representative is Grupo 3 de Turismo (☎ 428-3000), Rivadavia 26/28, Oficina 4. The nonprofit student travel agency Asatej (☎ 423-7421) is at Belgrano 194, Planta Alta.

Medical Services The Hospital de Urgencias (☎ 421-0243) is at Catamarca and Blvd Guzmán.

Historic Center

Downtown Córdoba is a treasure of colonial buildings and other historical monuments. Besides specific buildings detailed below, see also the restored 18th-century **Cabildo** on Plaza San Martín; the **Casa del Obispo Mercadillo**, with a colonial wrought-iron balcony at Rosario de Santa Fe 39; and the 18th-century **Iglesia de Santa Teresa y Convento de Carmelitas Descalzas de San José**, Independencia 122, which contains the **Museo de Arte Religioso Juan de Tejeda** (☎ 423-0175), open Wednesday through Saturday 9:30 am to 12:30 pm. Admission is from US$1.

The **Hospital San Roque**, at the corner of Santa Fe and Salta, dates from 1763, though most of the building is newer. Alongside it, the **Iglesia San Roque** (1764) retains more of its historical integrity. Later ecclesiastical landmarks include the **Basílica Nuestra Señora de la Merced** (built between 1826 and 1876), on Rivadavia between Av Olmos and 25 de Mayo, and the **Basílica de Santo Domingo** (1857-62), at the corner of Av General Paz and Deán Funes.

There are guided tours of the **Legislatura Provincial**, the provincial legislature, at the corner of the Rivera Indarte and Rosario de Santa Fe pedestrian malls, given at 11 am on weekdays.

Iglesia Catedral

Begun in 1577, the construction of Córdoba's cathedral dragged on for over two centuries under several architects, including Jesuits and Franciscans, and lacks any sense of architectural unity. Crowned by a Romanesque dome, it overlooks Plaza San Martín, at Independencia and 27 de Abril.

Interred within the cathedral are several notable figures in Argentine and regional history, including Gregorio Funes (a cleric and an important politician in the early

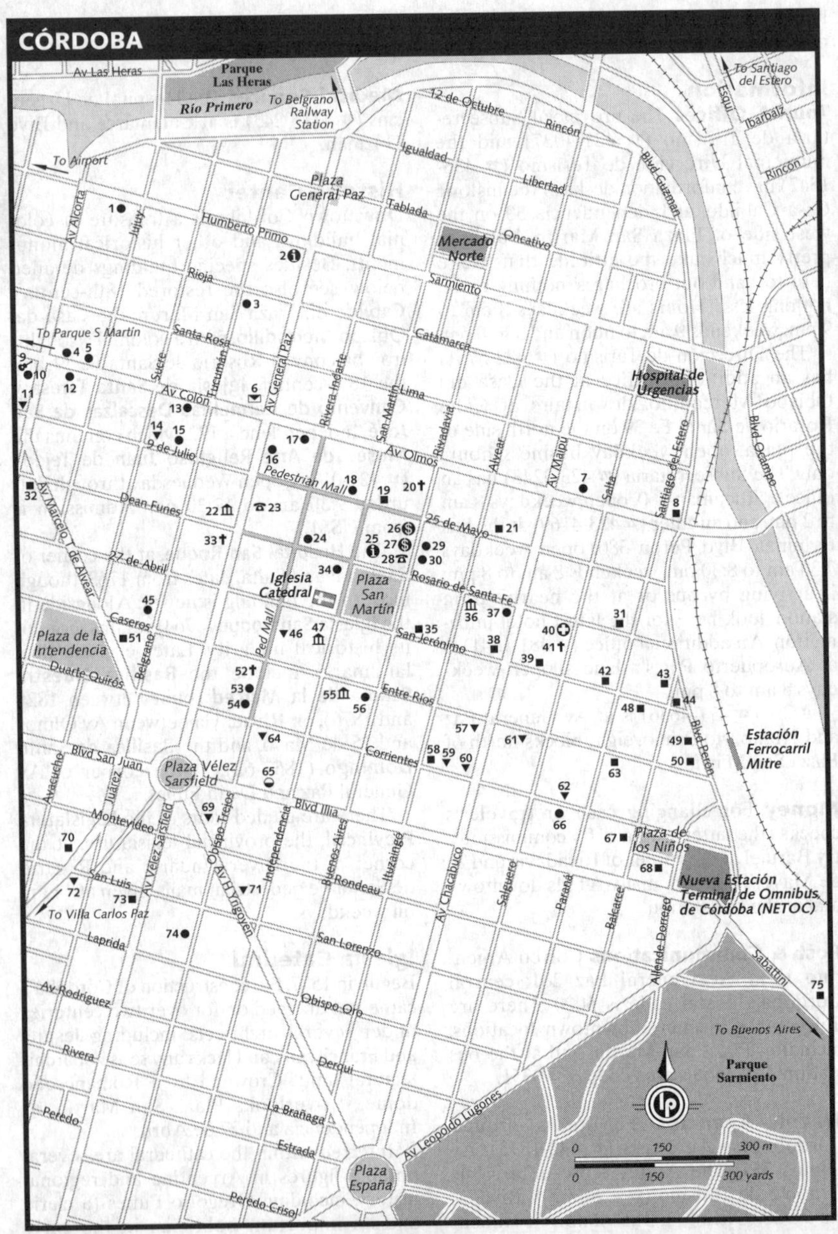
CÓRDOBA
Av Las Heras
Parque Las Heras
Río Primero
To Belgrano Railway Station
To Santiago del Estero
To Airport
Plaza General Paz
Mercado Norte
Hospital de Urgencias
To Parque S Martín
Iglesia Catedral
Plaza San Martín
Plaza de la Intendencia
Pedestrian Mall
Ped Mall
Plaza Vélez Sarsfield
Estación Ferrocarril Mitre
Plaza de los Niños
Nueva Estación Terminal de Omnibus de Córdoba (NETOC)
To Villa Carlos Paz
To Buenos Aires
Parque Sarmiento
Plaza España
12 de Octubre
Rincón
Igualdad
Libertad
Tablada
Oncativo
Sarmiento
Catamarca
Lima
Av Olmos
25 de Mayo
Rosario de Santa Fe
San Jerónimo
Entre Ríos
Corrientes
Blvd Illia
Rondeau
San Lorenzo
Obispo Oro
Derqui
La Brañaga
Estrada
Peredo Crisol
Humberto Primo
Rioja
Santa Rosa
Av Colón
9 de Julio
Dean Funes
27 de Abril
Caseros
Duarte Quirós
Blvd San Juan
Montevideo
San Luis
Laprida
Av Rodríguez
Rivera
Peredo
Av Alcorta
Jujuy
Sucre
Tucumán
Av General Paz
Rivera Indarte
San Martín
Rivadavia
Alvear
Av Maipú
Salta
Santiago del Estero
Blvd Guzmán
Blvd Ocampo
Esquiú
Ibarbalz
Av Marcelo T de Alvear
Belgrano
Avacuche
Juárez
Av Vélez Sarsfield
Obispo Trejo
Av H Yrigoyen
Independencia
Buenos Aires
Ituzaingó
Av Chacabuco
Salguero
Paraná
Balcarce
Allende Dorrego
Blvd Perón
Sabattini
Av Leopoldo Lugones
0 150 300 m
0 150 300 yards

independence period); General José María Paz (a military strategist and politician who fought as a young man in the wars of independence and, later, against Rosas and other Federalist caudillos); and Fray Mamerto Esquiú (a Catamarca-born Franciscan priest who strongly influenced Argentina's constitution of 1853).

Manzana de las Luces

Like Buenos Aires, Córdoba has its own 'Block of Enlightenment,' initially associated with the influential Jesuit order. Designed by the Flemish Padre Philippe Lemaire, the **Iglesia de La Compañía**, at Obispo Trejo and Caseros, dates from 1645 but was not completed until 1671, with the successful execution of Lemaire's plan for a timber roof in the form of an inverted ship's hull. It has a modest exterior and an ornate but tasteful interior, with an altarpiece carved of Paraguayan cedar.

In 1613, Fray Fernando de Trejo y Sanabria founded the Seminario Convictorio de San Javier, which, elevated to university status in 1622, was the forerunner of the **Universidad Nacional de Córdoba**, Obispo Trejo 242. The nearby **Colegio Nacional de Monserrat**, Obispo Trejo 294, dates from 1782, but has its origins in an earlier Jesuit institution. The building is considerably modified, but the interior cloisters are original.

Museo Histórico Provincial Marqués de Sobremonte

Claiming to be one of the country's most important historical museums, this 18th-century house once belonged to Rafael Núñez, the colonial governor of Córdoba and later Viceroy of the Río de la Plata. It has

CÓRDOBA

PLACES TO STAY
8 Hotel Waldorf
19 Hotel Garden
21 Hotel Claridge
31 Hotel Florida
32 Hotel Mediterráneo
35 Hotel Sussex
38 Hotel Felipe II
39 Hotel Dallas
42 Residencial Thanoa
43 Hotel Riviera
44 Hotel Viña de Italia
48 Corona Hotel
49 Residencial Central
50 Hotel Termini Roma
51 Panorama Hotel
58 Ducal Suites
63 Hospedaje Suzy
67 Residencial El Cielo
68 Bristol Hotel
70 Hotel de la Cañada
73 Hotel Gran Rex
75 Hotel Cesar Carman

PLACES TO EAT
11 Soppelsa
14 Estancia La María
46 Mandarina
57 Café Pause
59 Viejos Tiempos
60 Café Jameo
61 Minoliti
62 La Zete
64 La Candela
69 Guccio
71 Pizza Cero
72 Tenorio

OTHER
1 Localiza
2 ACA
3 Subsecretaría de Turismo
4 Southern Winds
5 Aerolíneas Argentinas, Austral
6 Post Office
7 Aeroturis
9 Córdoba Open Plaza
10 Lapa
12 Dinar
13 Cinerama
15 Regionales La Fama
16 Cine Gran Rex
17 TAN
18 Varig
20 Basílica Nuestra Señora de la Merced
22 Museo Doctor Genaro Pérez
23 Telecom
24 Legislatura Provincial
25 Dirección de Turismo (Casa del Obispo Mercadillo)
26 Cambio Barujel
27 Cambio Exprinter
28 Telecentro
29 Cine General Paz
30 Grupo 3 de Turismo (AmEx)
33 Basílica de Santo Domingo
34 Casa Cabildo (Subsecretaría de Turismo, Dirección de Turismo)
36 Museo Histórico Provincial Marqués de Sobremonte
37 Andesmar
40 Hospital San Roque
41 Iglesia San Roque
45 Asatej
47 Iglesia de Santa Teresa y Convento de Carmelitas Descalzas de San José, Museo de Arte Religioso Juan de Tejeda
52 Iglesia de la Compañía
53 Seminario Convictorio de San Javier, Universidad Nacional de Córdoba
54 Colegio Nacional de Monserrat
55 Museo de la Ciudad
56 Al Rent A Car (Hotel Dorá)
65 Minibuses to Villa Carlos Paz, Cosquín, Calamuchita, Villa General Paz
66 Avis
74 Club Andino de Córdoba

26 rooms and five interior patios, but its most notable feature is a wrought-iron balcony supported by carved wooden brackets. Exhibits include collections of religious paintings, Indian and gaucho weapons, musical instruments, leather and wooden trunks, furniture, and other miscellanea.

At Rosario de Santa Fé 218, the museum (☎ 433-1661) is open Tuesday to Saturday 9 am to 1 pm and 3 to 7 pm, Sunday 10 am to 1 pm, except during summer when it keeps only morning hours and is closed Sunday. Admission is US$1.

Art Museums

Not quite what its name implies, the **Museo de la Ciudad** (☎ 433-2721), Entre Ríos 40, features modern art; hours are weekdays 10 am to 1:30 pm and 4:30 to 9 pm.

The **Museo Doctor Genaro Pérez** (☎ 4331-5121), Av General Paz 33, specializes in three-dimensional arts, which are displayed in an unusual turn-of-the-century building known as the Palacio Garzón (named for its original owner). It's open Tuesday to Friday 9:30 am to 1:30 pm and 4:30 to 8:30 pm, weekends 10 am to 8 pm.

Climbing

For information on climbing or exploring the Sierras de Córdoba, contact the Club Andino de Córdoba, at Duarte Quirós 1591 or at Obispo Trejo 658. It's open Wednesday 8:30 to 11 pm and Saturdays 11 am to 1 pm.

Special Events

During the first three weeks of April, the city puts on a large crafts market (locally called 'FICA') at the city fairgrounds, on the town's north side near Chateau Carrera stadium.

Córdoba celebrates the founding of the city on July 6. Mid-September's Feria del Libro is a regional book fair, smaller than Buenos Aires' but still significant enough to draw literary figures of the stature of Eduardo Galeano; Córdoba is a notable regional publishing center.

Places to Stay – Budget

Camping The nearest site is in Parque General San Martín, 13km from downtown. City bus No 31 from Plaza San Martín goes as far as the Complejo Ferial, an exhibition and entertainment complex about 1km from the entrance, so you'll have to walk or hitch the last stretch.

The campground itself is spacious, but there's only limited shade. Showers and toilets could be cleaner and the water supply is unreliable, but it's passable. Charges are around US$4 per site.

Hospedajes, Residenciales & Hotels As usual, most economy lodging is near the bus terminal and the train station. Among the cheapest in town is ***Residencial Thanoa*** *(San Jerónimo 479)*. Quiet, friendly, and very basic but not too bad, it costs just US$10 per person with shared bath. For about the same price, family-oriented ***Residencial Central*** *(☎ 421-6667, Blvd Perón 150)* is shabby but very clean. Rooms with private bath cost US$25. Spotless ***Hospedaje Suzy*** *(Entre Ríos 528)* has singles (but no doubles) for just US$13 with shared bath. Try also the basic, comparably priced ***Residencial El Cielo*** *(Balcarce 324)*.

Not quite equal to its prestigious Buenos Aires namesake, ***Hotel Claridge*** *(☎ 421-5741, 25 de Mayo 218)* has balconied rooms with balky air-con on a quiet pedestrian street for US$14/25 for singles/doubles; interior rooms cost US$10 per person. Downtown ***Hotel Florida*** *(☎ 422-8373, Rosario de Santa Fé 459)* charges US$10/18 with shared bath, US$17/25 with private bath.

Places to Stay – Mid-Range

For US$20/30 for singles/doubles, clean and friendly but drab ***Bristol Hotel*** *(☎ 423-9950, fax 423-2216, Pasaje Corrientes 64)* is close to the bus terminal; the air-con is unreliable. The modern ***Hotel Termini Roma*** *(☎ 421-8721, Entre Ríos 687)* has rooms with private bath for US$20/28. Attractive, well-kept ***Hotel Garden*** *(☎ 421-4729, 25 de Mayo 35)* is a good value for US$23/40.

The ***Corona Hotel*** *(☎ 422-8789, San Jerónimo 574)* charges US$30/40, while the modern ***Hotel Gran Rex*** *(☎ 423-8659, Vélez Sarsfield 600)* costs US$30/46. Rates at ***Hotel Dallas*** *(☎ 421-6091, San Jerónimo 339)* are

Iguazú Falls, Misiones province

SARAH J HAWKINS

Parque Nacional El Palmar, Entre Ríos province

WAYNE BERNHARDSON

Sunflowers, the Gran Chaco

WAYNE BERNHARDSON

WAYNE BERNHARDSON

Parque Nacional Talampaya, La Rioja province

WAYNE BERNHARDSON

Iglesia San Francisco, Salta

WAYNE BERNHARDSON

Detail, Iglesia de San Francisco, Yavi, Jujuy province

US$42/53. ***Hotel Viña de Italia*** *(☎ 422-6589, San Jerónimo 611)* is modern but inviting at US$42/58. In a beautiful building, ***Hotel Sussex*** *(☎ 422-9070, San Jerónimo 125)* costs US$45/60. The ***Hotel Waldorf*** *(☎ 422-8051, Av Olmos 531)* is identically priced.

Places to Stay – Top End

Top-end accommodations start around US$55/66 at ***Hotel Riviera*** *(☎ 423-5303, Balcarce 74)*, close to the bus terminal. Reader-recommended ***Hotel Felipe II*** *(☎ 421-4752, San Jerónimo 279)* has quiet rooms for US$62/80.

A bit beyond downtown near San Luis is the stylish wood, brick, and concrete ***Hotel de la Cañada*** *(☎ 421-4649, Av Alvear 580)* for US$71/94. At ***Hotel Cesar Carman*** *(☎ 424-3825, Av Sabattini 459)*, on the east side of Parque Sarmiento, rates are US$73/90.

The spiffy new ***Ducal Suites*** *(☎ 426-8888, Corrientes 201)* charges US$75/85. ***Hotel Mediterráneo****(☎ 424-0086, Av Marcelo T de Alvear 10)* costs US$75/98, but offers weekend discounts. The ***Panorama Hotel*** *(☎ 420-4000, Marcelo T de Alvear 251)* costs US$91/116.

Places to Eat

The municipal ***Mercado Norte***, at Rivadavia and Oncativo, has excellent inexpensive eats – pizza, empanadas, and lager beer. Many other cheap eateries line Blvd Perón, near the train and bus terminals, and side streets such as San Jerónimo, where numerous video bars serve meals – the evening's shows are posted outside, taking precedence over the food.

Recommended cafés include ***Café Jameo*** *(Av Chacabuco 294)* and the hole-in-the wall ***Café Pause*** *(Av Chacabuco 216)*. ***Mandarina*** *(☎ 426-4909, Obispo Trejo 171)* has reasonable, fixed-price meals in pleasant but informal surroundings. ***La Candela***, on Corrientes near Obispo Trejos, is a student hangout featuring empanadas and *locro* (spicy meat and vegetable stew, typical in the Andean Northwest).

Córdoba has numerous quality pizzerias, including ***Viejos Tiempos***, on Corrientes between Ituzaingó and Av Chacabuco, ***Tenorio*** *(☎ 426-4482)*, at the corner of San Luis and Av Marcelo T de Alvear, and ***Pizza Cero*** (a branch of the Buenos Aires chain), on Av Hipólito Yrigoyen between Obispo Trejos and Independencia.

Minoliti *(Entre Ríos 358)* is a very good bargain-priced Italian restaurant. ***Guccio***, on Av Hipólito Yrigoyen near Obispo Trejos, is a more expensive Italian choice but offers a US$12 fixed-price lunch or dinner.

Estancia La María *(9 de Julio 364)* is a parrilla with its menu in French, German, English, and Italian. ***La Zete*** *(Corrientes 455)* serves Middle Eastern food.

Soppelsa, at the corner of Av Figueroa Alcorta and 9 de Julio, is one of the city's best ice creameries.

Entertainment

Cinemas Córdoba has numerous cinemas, including the ***Cine Gran Rex***, on Av General Paz between Av Olmos and 9 de Julio, the two-screen ***Cine General Paz***, on Rivadavia between 25 de Mayo and Rosario de Santa Fe, and the three-screen ***Cinerama***, on Av Colón between Sucre and Tucumán.

Dance Clubs The ***Córdoba Open Plaza*** *(Av Colón 600)* has live music until 4 am.

Spectator Sports

Córdoba's first-division soccer teams are Belgrano and Talleres de Córdoba. The ***Estadio Belgrano*** (☎ 480-0852) and offices are at Arturo Orgaz 510, while the ***Estadio Talleres de Córdoba*** is at General Ricchieri 1595; its offices (☎ 423-3576) are downtown at Rosario de Santa Fe 11.

Shopping

Regionales La Fama, 9 de Julio 336, has good alpaca woolens.

Getting There & Away

Air Aerolíneas Argentinas and Austral share offices (☎ 426-7600) at Av Colón 520. Aerolíneas has more than 40 flights weekly to Buenos Aires' Aeroparque (US$47 to US$148) and Ezeiza, and also a daily flight to Mendoza (US$64 to US$69). Austral has 60 to Aeroparque and 24 to Mendoza.

Córdoba's only international service is to Porto Alegre, Florianópolis, and São Paulo, Brazil, three times weekly with Varig (☎ 425-6262), 9 de Julio 40, 7th floor.

LAPA (☎ 426-3336), Av Figueroa Alcorta 181, flies four times daily to Aeroparque (US$49 to US$119). Dinar (☎ 426-2020), Av Colón 533, flies twice daily weekdays and once Saturday to Aeroparque (US$65 to US$125); the morning flight connects to Comodoro Rivadavia.

TAN (☎ 421-6458), Av Colón 119, 3rd floor, flies to San Juan (US$50 to US$70) Thursday, Saturday, and Sunday; and to Mendoza (US$39 to US$74) and Neuquén (US$69 to US$110) eight times weekly.

Southern Winds (☎ 424-7251), Av Colón 540, flies to Mendoza (US$59 to US$79) twice daily, to Tucumán (US$67 to US$89) and Salta (US$82 to US$109) twice daily weekdays and once daily weekends, and daily to Neuquén (US$89 to US$119). It also goes twice weekly to Aeroparque (US$74 to US$99), five time weekly to Bariloche (US$127 to US$169) and Mar del Plata (US$104 to US$139), and 18 times weekly to Rosario (US$59 to US$79).

Andesmar (☎ 421-7191), Av Chacabuco 80, flies twice daily to Rosario (US$39 to US$63), weekdays to Aeroparque (US$69 to US$93), 12 times weekly to Mendoza (US$49 to US$69) and Tucumán (US$53 to US$77), eight times weekly to Salta (US$76 to US$100), and three times weekly to La Rioja (US$35 to US$59).

Bus Rarely is a bus terminal an attraction in its own right, but the Nueva Estación Terminal de Ómnibus de Córdoba (NETOC; ☎ 423-4199, 423-0532), at Blvd Perón 300, deserves a visit even if you're not taking a bus trip. Facilities include a pharmacy, travel agency, post office, day-care center, photo lab, and first-aid station, plus two banks and ATMs, public telephones, and more than 40 shops, restaurants, and other utterly unexpected services – including hot showers.

Almost as an afterthought, dozens of bus companies serve local, provincial, national, and international destinations. Carriers to Rosario, Buenos Aires, and intermediate points include Betel (☎ 424-4140), Costera Criolla (☎ 422-6160), Ablo (☎ 424-7015), General Urquiza (☎ 421-0711), Chevallier (☎ 422-5898), and Cacorba (☎ 422-5973), which also serves Resistencia and Formosa five times weekly. General Urquiza continues to La Plata, while Chevallier (☎ 422-5898) also goes to Catamarca.

TUS/TUP (☎ 421-5240) serve Bahía Blanca, Tandil, Santa Rosa (La Pampa), and Bariloche (five times weekly; ask about student and retiree discounts). Empresa Córdoba Mar del Plata (☎ 422-6979) goes to Atlantic coastal resorts, as does Mar Chiquita (☎ 422-7222). Betel also goes to Mar del Plata.

Socasa (☎ 423-5469) goes to San Juan twice weekly, with a 20% discount on roundtrip fares. Autotransportes San Juan (☎ 422-1951) also goes to San Juan. Other Cuyo carriers include Expreso Uspallata (☎ 425-3066), TAC (☎ 423-7666), and Tas Choapa (☎ 425-6054), all with Chilean connections via their principal destination of Mendoza.

La Veloz del Norte (☎ 424-4627) goes to Salta and Orán, on the Bolivian border, while Panamericano (☎ 421-3971) and Atahualpa (☎ 421-8779) go to Tucumán and Salta, continuing to Bolivian border crossings at La Quiaca and Pocitos. El Tucumano (☎ 422-7416) has similar regional services.

La Estrella (☎ 422-6927) traverses the Chaco to Roque Sáenz Peña and Resistencia three times weekly, goes to the northwestern cities of Catamarca, Tucumán, Salta, and Jujuy and also to Patagonian destinations such as Neuquén. Other Patagonian carriers include Transportes Ko-Ko (☎ 423-5892) and Andesmar (☎ 422-1951).

El Serrano (☎ 422-9751) has buses to Santa Fe, Gualeguaychú, and Corrientes, while Ciudad de Paraná (☎ 422-9751) goes to Paraná and other Mesopotamian destinations. Expreso Encon (☎ 423-5150) goes to Paso de los Libres, on the Brazilian border, via Colón and Concordia. Expreso Singer (☎ 422-6273) offers through buses to Posadas and Puerto Iguazú.

El Práctico (☎ 422-5160) goes to Santa Fe and Villa Carlos Paz. Many companies serve

Córdoba's mountain hinterlands, including Sierras del Córdoba (☎ 421-0711), Sierras de Calamuchita (☎ 422-6080), and Transportes La Cumbre (☎ 424-7508).

Cora (☎ 425-4765) serves Montevideo four times weekly, with connections to Brazil. Penha (☎ 427-0400) has Brazilian services.

Sample fares include Mina Clavero (US$10, three hours), Catamarca (US$16, 5½ hours), Santiago del Estero (US$17, five hours), Santa Fe (US$18, seven hours), Paraná (US$20, eight hours), Tucumán (US$20, eight hours), Buenos Aires (US$20 to US$25, 10 hours), Mendoza (US$30, 10 hours), Posadas (US$41, 19½ hours), Salta (US$45, 12 hours), Asunción (US$46, 16 hours), Montevideo (US$47, 15 hours), and Bariloche (US$105, 22 hours).

Minibus Frequent minibuses to Villa Carlos Paz, Cosquín, Calamuchita, and Villa General Paz leave from Blvd Illia between Obispo Trejos and Independencia.

Train The tourist-oriented Tren de las Sierras (☎ 482-2252) goes Thursday and Friday at 9 am to Cosquín (US$5, two hours), La Falda, and Huerta Grande (US$8, 2½ hours), continuing Saturday and Sunday to La Cumbre and Capilla del Monte (US$10, 3¾ hours).

City buses Nos 51, 53, 54, and 56 go to the suburban station at Rodríguez del Busto and Manuel Cardeñoza in Barrio Alto Verde; the return train from Capilla del Monte leaves at 3:30 pm, from Huerta Grande at 4:23 pm.

Getting Around

To/From the Airport Aeropuerto Pajas Blancas (☎ 481-0696) is 15km north of town via Av Monseñor Pablo Cabrera. From the NETOC bus terminal, the Empresa Ciudad de Córdoba (☎ 424-0048) bus marked 'Salsipuedes' goes to the airport.

For US$3, Airport Kombis (☎ 470-1529) leaves from Hotel Sussex, San Jerónimo 125.

Bus City buses require cospeles (tokens), available for US$0.70 from kiosks.

Car For circuits in the Sierras de Córdoba, a car would be useful, though a bicycle would be an excellent alternative. Try AI (☎ 422-4867), at Hotel Dorá, Entre Ríos 78, or at the airport (☎ 481-7157); Localiza (☎ 423-6505), at Humberto Primo 531; or Avis (☎ 422-2483), at Corrientes 452.

LA CALERA

It's an easy day trip to La Calera's simple **Capilla Jesuítica** (1727), the restored and modernized Jesuit chapel just 18km northwest of downtown Córdoba. There are many ***parrillas***, a ***municipal campground***, and dozens of roadside stands selling regional specialties like salami and fresh bread for picnicking. Stop at places whose handmade signs proclaim *salami casero* and *pan casero*.

VILLA CARLOS PAZ

Only 36km west of Córdoba, on the shores of so-called Lago San Roque (in reality, a large reservoir), Villa Carlos Paz (permanent population 44,000) is a minor-league, freshwater Mar del Plata with more than 12,000 hotel spaces. Almost every Argentine household seems to have photos of family members riding the **Aerosilla Carlos Paz** (☎ 422254), a chairlift that has carried tens of thousands to the 953m summit of Cerro de la Cruz since 1955. Among the more bogus attractions are Golden City (a Wild West gunfighter village) and a paintball park.

Information

The well-organized Secretaría de Turismo (☎ 425059), at San Martín and Yrigoyen, is open 7 am to 11 pm in summer, 7 am to 9 pm the rest of the year; there's a branch office (☎ 421624) at the Estación Terminal de Ómnibus, San Martín 400. Both distribute useful maps and thorough guides to local services.

Correo Argentino is at Av San Martín 190; the postal code is 5152. There are several Telecentros along Av San Martín; the area code is ☎ 03541. ATMs are also numerous.

Places to Stay & Eat

Carlos Paz campgrounds charge around US$3 to US$6 per person, including ACA's

Centro Turístico *(☎ 422132)*, directly on the reservoir at Av San Martín and Nahuel Huapi, and ***Bahía del Gitano*** *(☎ 422947)*, at Azopardo and Artigas.

The local Hostelling International affiliate is ***Hostel Acapulco*** *(☎ 421929, fax 431030, acapulco@hostels.org.ar, La Paz 75)*, with beds for US$12, including kitchen privileges and a swimming pool. The two-star ***Hostería Alpenrose*** *(☎ 430095, Hipólito Yrigoyen 615)* charges around US$20 per person. Top-of-the-line ***Hotel Portal del Lago*** *(☎ 424931, portal@hotelnet.com.ar)*, at Av Gobernador Álvarez and Gobernador Carrera, costs US$98/139 single/double.

Mexican food is relatively uncommon in Argentina, but Villa Carlos Paz has the ***Guacamole Ranch*** *(☎ 432613, 9 de Julio 50)*, which also has live salsa entertainment. Otherwise, there are dozens of ***parrillas*** and ***pizzerias***.

Getting There & Away

Cotap (☎ 423699) has buses to Córdoba every 15 minutes from the Estación Terminal de Ómnibus, San Martín 400; some long-distance companies from Buenos Aires start and end their Córdoba routes here. Several companies head east toward the Cuyo provinces, including Uspallata, La Cumbre, TAC, and Jocolí.

COSQUÍN

Known for its Festival Nacional del Folklore (national folklore festival), held the last week of January for more than 30 years, Cosquín has added classical music and ballet performances to the mix. By most accounts, the festival has declined, but the surrounding countryside still makes the town (population 18,000) one of the more appealing destinations near the provincial capital, which is 63km away via RN 38. There are also many events during Semana Santa.

The Dirección Municipal de Turismo (☎ 451901), San Martín 560, is open weekdays 8 am to 9 pm, weekends 9 am to 6 pm. Cosquín's postal code is 5166; the area code is ☎ 03541. Cosquín also has its own web page (www.onenet.com.ar/cosquin).

East of town, 1260m **Cerro Pan de Azúcar** offers good views of the Sierras and, on a clear day, the city of Córdoba. Hitch or walk (buses are few) 5km to a saddle where a steep 25-minute climb to the summit will save you the US$7 for the *aerosilla* (chairlift). Also at the saddle is a confitería whose owner, a devotee of Carlos Gardel, has decorated his business with Gardel memorabilia and built a mammoth statue of the great man.

Places to Stay & Eat

At Santa María de la Punilla, just south of Cosquín, ***Camping Fiesta*** *(☎ 480577)* is the nearest campground. For good, inexpensive accommodations, starting at US$10 per person, try ***Hostería Mary*** *(☎ 452095, Bustos 545)*. ***Residencial Esteleta*** *(☎ 451473, Catamarca 138)* charges US$15/24 single/double, but is open summer only.

Owner-operated ***Petit Hotel*** *(☎ 451311, A Sabattini 739)* is very friendly and quiet, with an attractive patio with a parrilla for asados. Summer prices are US$27/37, but off-season rates may be half that. ***Hotel del Valle*** *(☎ 452802, San Martín 330)* costs US$40/50, while the ***Gran Sierras Hotel*** *(☎ 452120)* charges US$65/75.

For food, there's ***Pizzería Riviera*** *(☎ 451152)*, Av San Martín and Sabattini, and several parrillas, including ***San Marino***, Av San Martín 707.

Getting There & Away

Coscor, La Calera, and El Serranito run buses from Cosquín to Córdoba. There are direct services to Mendoza (14 hours) with La Cumbre daily at 9:15 am.

LA FALDA

At the base of the precipitous Sierra Chica, 78km from Córdoba, this woodsy town of 30,000 inhabitants may be the most pleasant resort in the immediate capital area. The narrow, zigzag road across the Sierra Chica to Salsipuedes, Río Ceballos, and back to Córdoba climbs to 1500m at Cerro El Cuadrado, but the best views are back to the west. There are no buses over this route, but there is enough auto traffic that hitching should be possible in high season and on weekends. Dedicated joggers can get an excellent workout.

Information

The Secretaría Municipal de Turismo (☎ 422764, lafalda@nt.com.ar), Av España 50, is open 7 am to 9 pm daily. It also has a web page (www.nt.com.ar/lafalda/).

Correo Argentino is at Av Argentina 199; La Falda's postal code is 5172. There's a locutorio at Diagonal San Martín 23; the area code is ☎ 03548.

Things to See

La Falda has two noteworthy museums. The **Museo de Trenes en Miniatura** (Miniature Train Museum; ☎ 423041), Las Murallas 200, is open 9:30 am to 8:30 pm daily in summer; the rest of the year, hours are 10 am to 12:30 pm and 3 to 7 pm, weekends and holidays only. Admission is US$5. The **Museo Arqueológico Ambato** (☎ 422217), Cuesta del Lago 1469, exhibits ceramics from the region. It's open 9:30 am to 1 pm and 3 to 9 pm daily; admission is US$1.

Places to Stay & Eat

Nearby Villa Hermosa's ***Balneario Siete Cascadas*** *(☎ 423869)* charges US$4 per person for camping; while you're there, check out the historical museum in the old train station.

Hospedaje San Remo *(☎ 422409, Av Argentina 108)* has singles/doubles for US$13/15. Recommended ***Hostería Marín*** *(☎ 422640, Güemes 134)* costs US$10 per person, US$12 with breakfast. ***Hotel Majestic*** *(☎ 422117, Capital Federal 140)* is also reasonably priced at US$15 per person. The ***Old Garden Residencial*** *(☎ 422842, Capital Federal 28)* has a pool and beautiful grounds but is notably more expensive at US$20 per person.

There are many parrillas and pizzerias along Av Edén, including ***La Parrilla de Raúl*** *(☎ 421128, Av Edén 1000)* and ***Nippur*** *(Av Edén 164)*.

Entertainment

The ***Cine Teatro Rex*** *(☎ 424784, 9 de Julio 186)* shows current movies.

Shopping

Avs Eden and España are the main shopping districts; try the woolens at Martex, Av España 446. At the former train station is the Feria Artesanal del Andén, open 6 pm to 1 am in summer and on long weekends such as Semana Santa.

Getting There & Away

The Estación Terminal de Ómnibus is at Güemes and RN 38. La Calera (☎ 422210) and El Serranito (☎ 422395) have buses to and from Córdoba (US$3.50). There are also long-distance services to Buenos Aires and intermediate points with Ablo (☎ 422466), Cacorba (☎ 422023), Chevallier (☎ 422417), and General Urquiza (☎ 422466); to San Juan and Mendoza with Empresa La Cumbre; and to Resistencia with La Estrella.

CANDONGA

Candonga's 18th-century Jesuit chapel is a minor masterpiece in a picturesque, isolated canyon. At one time it was part of the Jesuit Estancia Santa Gertrudis, whose overgrown ruins (including buildings, a large stone wall, and an aqueduct) can still be seen. Though there is no public transportation directly to the site, there is enough traffic that you should be able to hitch from El Manzano, 40km north of Córdoba (try Empresa Ciudad de Córdoba or Sierras de Córdoba).

A day trip is worthwhile, but there are good accommodations at ***Hostería Candonga*** *(☎ 0351-471-0683 in Córdoba for reservations)*. For US$35 per person you get room and full board, including well-prepared Argentine and regional specialties like *asado con cuero* (side of beef barbecued in its own hide), locro, empanadas, and homemade desserts. With half-board, rates are US$25 per person

JESÚS MARÍA

After losing their operating capital to pirates off the Brazilian coast, the Jesuits sold wine from Jesús María to support their university in colonial Córdoba. One of the finest Jesuit estancias, Jesús María enjoyed a diverse economy based on irrigated vineyards, orchards and croplands, livestock, and ancillary industries. Presently, the town of Jesús María (population 27,000), 51km north of Córdoba via RN 9, is home to the annual Fiesta Nacional de Doma y Folklore, a celebration of gaucho horsemanship and customs.

Set on superbly landscaped grounds, the church and convent now constitute the **Museo Jesuítico Nacional de Jesús María**, open weekdays 8 am to noon and 2 to 7 pm (from 3 pm in summer), weekends 2 to 6 pm (3 to 7 pm in summer) only; admission is US$1. The museum has good archaeological pieces from the Comechingones Indians, informative maps of the missionary trajectory, and well-restored (though dubiously authentic) rooms, including the kitchen and toilets, plus displays of art, coins, and 19th-century dishware.

Five km away, the colonial post house of **Sinsacate** was the site of a wake for the murdered La Rioja caudillo Facundo Quiroga in 1835. It's open 3 to 7 pm daily from mid-November to mid-March, 2 to 6 pm daily the rest of the year, but the caretaker is rarely punctual. Admission is US$1.

Ciudad de Córdoba and Cadol run buses between Córdoba and the town of Jesús María, which has limited accommodations and one notable restaurant, ***El Faro***.

SANTA CATALINA

Only about 12km north of Ascochinga, but more easily reached from Jesús María, this Jesuit estancia was perhaps the richest and most elaborate in the region. It is now in private hands, but open to visitors.

ALTA GRACIA

Only 35km southwest of Córdoba, the colonial mountain town of Alta Gracia is steeped in history – its illustrious residents range from Jesuit pioneers to Viceroy Santiago Liniers, Spanish composer and civil war refugee Manuel de Falla, and revolutionary Che Guevara (who spent his adolescence here). In the first half of the 20th century, the town (whose architecture closely resembles parts of Mar del Plata) was a summer retreat for the Argentine oligarchy, but it's not the social center it once was.

Information

The municipal Dirección de Turismo (☎ 423455) occupies an office in the Reloj Público, the clock tower at the corner of Av del Tajamar and Calle del Molino.

The post office is at the corner of Av Belgrano and Olmos; the postal code is 5186. There's a Telecentro at Av del Libertador 1909; the area code is ☎ 03547.

Things to See

From 1643 to 1762, Jesuit fathers built the **Iglesia Parroquial Nuestra Señora de la Merced** on the west side of the central Plaza Manuel Solares; directly south of the church, the colonial Jesuit workshops of **El Obraje** (1643) are now a public school.

Liniers, one of the last officials to occupy the post of Viceroy of the River Plate, was a hero for resisting the British invasion of Buenos Aires in 1806, but was executed for his loyalty to Spain and opposition to Argentine independence. Now buried in his native France, he resided in what is now the **Museo Histórico Nacional del Virrey Liniers**, alongside the church, open Tuesday to Friday 9 am to 1 pm, weekends and holidays 9:30 am to 12:30 pm and 5 to 8 pm. The US$2 admission includes an informative guided tour; it's free on Wednesday.

Directly north of the museum, across Av Belgrano, the **Tajamar** (1659) is a colonial dam used to store water to irrigate the Jesuit fields, now a public park. Some blocks west, on Av Vélez Sarsfield, squatters inhabit the crumbling **Sierras Hotel**, which, during Alta Gracia's social heyday, was the meeting

WAYNE BERNHARDSON

Former home of Che Guevara

place for the elite (including Che's relatives). Though the interior is nearly gutted, the exterior is almost intact and there are ostensible plans to refurbish this historic landmark.

From 1939 until his death in 1946, Falla lived in **Villa Los Espinillos**, now a museum at the corner of Carlos Pellegrini and Calle Manuel de Falla. It's open Tuesday to Saturday 9:30 am to 12:30 pm and daily except Monday 3 to 8 pm in January and February; the rest of the year, hours are daily except Monday 2 to 7 pm. Admission is US$1.

In the 1930s, the youthful Ernesto Guevara's family moved here because a doctor recommended the dry climate for his asthma. Though Che lived in several houses, the family's primary residence was **Villa Beatriz** (still a private home), at Avellaneda 501 in Villa Carlos Pellegrini. The **Museo de la Ciudad**, in the Casa de la Cultura on the south side of the plaza, has a photographic display on Che's life.

Places to Stay & Eat

Hostería Asturias *(☎ 423668, Vélez Sarsfield 127)*, in a fine old railroad building, charges only US$15/20 single/double with private bath, but is often full. Friendly ***Hotel Cavadonga*** *(☎ 423456, Presidente Quintana 285)*, opposite the old Sierras Hotel, is good value for US$18/23, with firm beds and private bath.

Trattoria Oro *(☎ 422933, España 18)*, opposite Plaza Manuel Solar, has a varied menu and excellent service; try the canelones de choclo, empanadas salteñas, and particularly delicious flan.

Getting There & Away

The Terminal de Ómnibus is at the corner of Av Sarmiento and Vélez Sarsfield. Colta (☎ 421920) has direct bus service to Buenos Aires (US$47, 13 hours), and there are many buses to Córdoba (45 minutes, US$2.50).

VILLA GENERAL BELGRANO

About 90km southwest of Córdoba via RP 5, Villa General Belgrano flaunts its Teutonic origins as a settlement of unrepatriated survivors from the sunken German battleship *Graf Spee* near Montevideo during WWII. The town's Oktoberfest is the *Fiesta Nacional de la Cerveza*, the first two weekends of October.

The Oficina de Informes (☎ 462215), on Plaza José Hernández, is open 9 am to 8 pm daily. The postal code is 5194; the area code is ☎ 03546.

Valle de Calamuchita buses serve Villa General Belgrano from Córdoba.

Places to Stay

Camping San José *(☎ 462496)* charges US$4 per person and US$3 per site. The AAAJ-affiliated youth hostel ***El Rincón*** *(☎ 461323)*, 600m from the bus terminal, charges only $8 per person with kitchen privileges.

Typical lodging includes ***Hotel Baviera*** *(☎ 461476, El Quebracho 21)*, for US$40/58 single/double, and ***Hotel Prater*** *(☎ 461167, El Quebracho 4)*, for US$29 per person (US$20 off-season). For more upscale lodging, try ***Hotel Edelweiss*** *(☎ 461284, edelweis@tecomnet.com.ar, Av Ojo de Agua 295)*, where rates range from US$51/64 to US$77/96 in high season, or comparably priced ***Hotel Bremen*** *(☎ 461133)* at RP 5, Km 741.

CANDELARIA

In this remote part of the Sierras, east of La Higuera, the thick walls and buttresses, ironclad algarrobo doors, and hideaways of the church and casco of this colonial estancia (1693) betray their defensive purpose in an area where Indian resistance was intense. Candelaria is about 220km northwest of Córdoba via RP 28 , the most direct road, but it's also accessible from RP 15, the Altas Cumbres route.

MINA CLAVERO

Mina Clavero's therapeutic mineral waters began to attract vacationers from Córdoba before the turn of the century, when Doña Anastasia Fabre de Merlo opened the first guesthouse on the advice of the 'gaucho priest' José Gabriel Brochero, who had gotten to know the area in the course of his evangelical activities. A century later, Mina Clavero is an important resort with hotels, campgrounds, restaurants, and vacation homes along the Río de los Sauces. Its limpid streams, rocky waterfalls, and idyllic mountain landscapes provide a relaxing escape for refugees from the faster-paced life of Córdoba and Buenos Aires.

Orientation

Mina Clavero is 170km southwest of Córdoba via RN 20, near its junction with RN 15, the splendid Nuevo Camino de las Altas Cumbres (Highway of the High Peaks). It sits at the confluence of Río de Los Sauces and Río Panaholma, in the Valle de Traslasierra between the eastern Sierras Grandes and Cumbre de Achala and the western Sierra de Pocho. At the confluence, the streams become the Río Mina Clavero, which divides the town.

Avenida San Martín is the main street of a relatively irregular town plan, but Mina Clavero's compactness makes orientation easy. Walking is the primary means of getting around.

Information

Tourist Offices The Dirección de Turismo (☎ 470171), Av San Martín 1464, is open 8 am to 10 pm daily.

Money Banco de la Nación, Av San Martín 898, and Banco de la Provincia, Av San Martín 1982, change US cash; the latter has an ATM.

Post & Communications Correo Argentino is at Av San Martín and Pampa de Achala; the postal code is 5889. Telecom has cabinas at Av San Martín 1022; the area code is ☎ 03544.

Medical Services The Hospital Vecinal (☎ 470285) is at Fleming 1332.

Places to Stay

Many accommodations close by the end of March, when the town almost rolls up the sidewalks. Unless otherwise indicated, rates are for high-season doubles, and off-season prices may be much lower (when single rates are easier to get). Hospedajes usually do not include breakfast, while other categories of accommodations do.

Places to Stay – Budget

Camping *Autocamping Río Abajo (☎ 471-0730)*, 3km south of town toward Nono, is the only campground open all year. It has shady riverside grounds, impeccable bathrooms, hot showers, and laundry facilities. Daily charges are US$4 per person per site, including vehicle and electricity.

Hosterías, Hospedajes & Hotels Budget accommodations, which are very decent, start around US$20 at ***Hospedaje Aire y Sol*** *(☎ 470979, Rivadavia 551)*. ***Hospedaje Franchino*** *(☎ 470395, Mitre 1454)* is slightly more expensive. Rooms at ***Hospedaje El Parral*** *(☎ 470005, Intendente Vila 1430)* cost around US$30.

Hostería Champaquí *(☎ 470393, Intendente Oviedo 1430)* is an excellent value for US$30 with breakfast. Others in this category include ***Hotel Milac Navira*** *(☎ 470278, Oviedo 1407)*, also with breakfast, and the reasonable ***Hotel Agüero*** *(☎ 470439, 12 de Octubre 1139)*.

Places to Stay – Mid-Range

Mid-range accommodations start around US$38 to US$40 at places like ***Hotel La Morenita*** *(☎ 470347, Urquiza 1142)*, ***Hotel Marengo*** *(☎ 470224, Av San Martín 518)*, and ***Hotel España*** *(☎ 470123, Av San Martín 1687)*. A bit more upscale is ***Hotel Aguirre*** *(☎ 470239, Av San Martín 1148)* for US$46.

Places to Stay – Top End

Hotel Rossetti *(☎ 470728, Mitre 1434)* charges US$70, and ***Hotel Molino Blanco*** *(☎ 470124, Urquiza 1366)* has rooms at US$75. The fancy ***Motel du Soleil*** *(☎ 470066)*, at Mitre and La Piedad at the entrance to town, has rooms at US$80 with breakfast.

Places to Eat

La Sombrilla, on Av Costanera by the river, has a good ***diente libre*** (all-you-can-eat) deal. ***Lo de Jorge*** *(☎ 470343)*, on Poeta Lugones, serves good, abundant parrillada at reasonable prices. ***La Mamita*** *(☎ 471063, Mitre 1600)* has tasty pasta.

Other choices include ***Di Solito*** *(San Martín 1234)* and ***Del Carmen***, at San Martín and Lugones, for pizza. There's also ***El Rincón de Jorge*** *(☎ 470652, Av Mitre 1198)*, opposite the bus terminal, for pizza, pasta, and parrillada.

Confitería Suiza, at Av San Martín and Intendente Vila, has authentic Swiss pastries.

Getting There & Away

The Terminal de Ómnibus is at Mitre 1191. Empresa El Petizo (☎ 470425) and Pampa de Achala have several daily buses to Córdoba and Villa Dolores; El Petizo also goes to Merlo and to Mendoza. TAC (☎ 470420) has daily service to Merlo, San Luis, Mendoza, and Buenos Aires. Uspallata goes twice daily and Jocolí once to San Luis and Mendoza. Chevallier (☎ 470433) goes daily to Buenos Aires (US$48, 17 hours).

AROUND MINA CLAVERO

Museo Rocsen

Operated by JJ Bouchon, an anthropologist, curator, and collector who first came to Argentina in 1950 as cultural attaché in the French embassy, this eclectic museum displays more than 11,000 pieces ranging from European furniture and Pacific seashells to Peruvian mummies and musical instruments. Though these materials might sound like an odd combination, the collection is so well presented that individual exhibits truly recreate the ambience of a rural rancho or German bedchamber. Particularly well done are the Rincón del Oligarca de Campo (Rural Landowner's Corner) and Rincón del Oligarca de Ciudad (Urban Elite Corner).

The museum is in the pastoral village of Nono, a onetime Indian settlement 9km south of Mina Clavero. Hours are 9 am to sunset daily; admission is US$4. The museum shop sells well-made ceramic reproductions of artifacts at reasonable prices.

VILLA DE LAS ROSAS

Charming Villa de las Rosas, 31km south of Mina Clavero, stands out among several small villages along the Altas Cumbres route since it provides the most direct route to the summit of 2790m **Cerro Champaquí**, the province's highest peak. The Oficina de Informes (☎ 03544-494303), on the plaza, is open 9 am to 1 pm and 3 to 7 pm daily; it can provide a list of mountain guides.

For accommodations, try ***Camping Guasmara***, which costs US$10 per site, or ***Hostería Las Rejas*** *(☎ 03544-494433)*, which charges US$17 per person. ***Los Horcones*** serves typical regional food

YACANTO

About 15km south of Villa de las Rosas is the village of Yacanto, site of the *Golf Club & Hotel Yacanto* (☎ 03544-482002), whose turn-of-the-century building and surrounding manicured parkland once belonged to the British railways. Hiking, tennis, and horseback riding are popular activities here, where businesspeople from Córdoba and Buenos Aires take a break from stressful city life. It's worth a visit even if you can't afford US$76/112 single/double with breakfast.

Cuyo

Settled from and originally part of colonial Chile, the Andean provinces of Mendoza and San Juan, plus adjacent San Luis, still retain a strong regional identity, and their substantial mestizo population distinguishes them from Buenos Aires and the Pampas. The formidable barrier of the Andes is the backdrop for one of Argentina's key agricultural regions, which produces grapes for wine, mostly for the internal market, rather than beef and grain for export; the term 'Cuyo' derives from the Huarpe Indian word *cuyum*, meaning 'sandy earth.'

Cuyo lies in the rain shadow of the massive Andean crest, where 6962m Cerro Aconcagua is the Americas' highest peak, but enough snowfall accumulates on the eastern slopes to sustain rivers that irrigate the extensive lowland vineyards, despite the dry climate. Because of these advantages, *mendocinos*, inhabitants of the province of Mendoza, call their home La Tierra de Sol y Buen Vino (Land of Sun and Good Wine).

With its varied terrain and gentle climate, Cuyo also offers outdoor recreation year-round. Possible summer activities include climbing, trekking, riding, rafting, kayaking, canoeing, fishing, waterskiing, hang gliding, windsurfing, and sailing. Downhill skiing is a popular, if costly, winter pastime. Many travelers visit Mendoza en route between Santiago, Chile, and Buenos Aires, but one should not overlook the other provinces, particularly San Juan, for off-the-beaten-track possibilities.

Mendoza Province

For most of its history Mendoza has been isolated from both the other Andean provinces and the distant Pampas. In large part this resulted from an accident of history – the settlement of Cuyo from Chile.

Like their counterparts farther north in Tucumán, Cuyo's Huarpe Indians practiced irrigated agriculture. Their population was large enough to encourage Spaniards to cross the 3850m Uspallata Pass from Santiago to found encomiendas, but the difficulty of traversing the mountains in winter stimulated economic independence and political initiative. Still, trans-Andean communications were the rule, with links to Lima via Santiago rather than northward to Tucumán and Bolivia. Because of its geographic isolation, Buenos Aires remained a remote backwater for nearly two centuries.

Irrigated vineyards first became important during colonial times, along with fattened cattle for the Santiago market, but isolation limited the region's prosperity – 17th-century Carmelite priest Antonio Vásquez de Espinosa observed that 'There are very good vineyards from which they make quantities of wine which they export in carts via Córdoba to Buenos Aires,' yet 'the people are very poor, with few possibilities and no help from headquarters, being so distant and remote.'

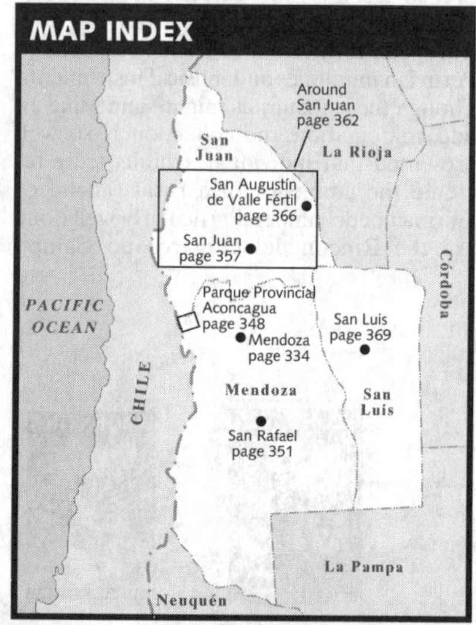

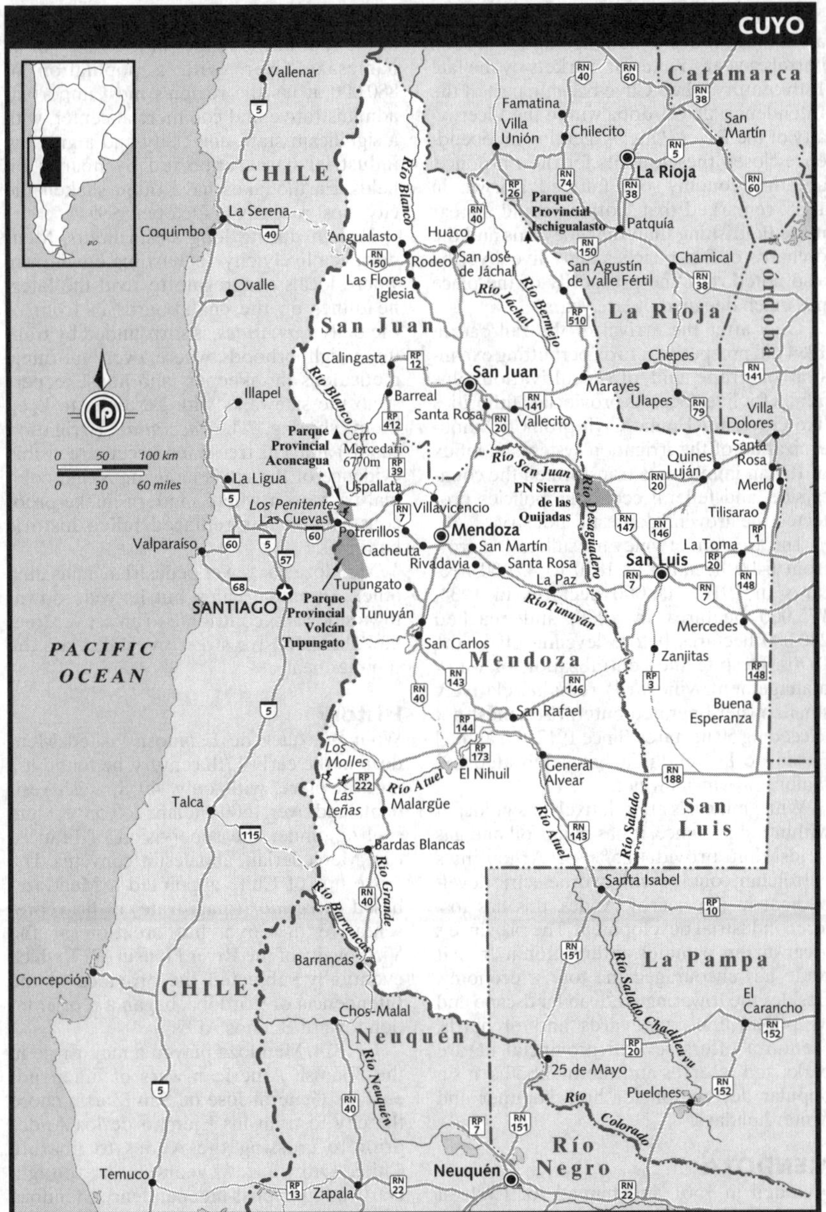
CUYO
Catamarca
La Rioja
Córdoba
San Juan
Mendoza
San Luis
La Pampa
Neuquén
Río Negro
CHILE
PACIFIC OCEAN
Vallenar
La Serena
Coquimbo
Ovalle
Illapel
La Ligua
Valparaíso
SANTIAGO
Talca
Concepción
Temuco
Famatina
Villa Unión
Chilecito
La Rioja
San Martín
Parque Provincial Ischigualasto
Patquía
Chamical
San Agustín de Valle Fértil
Angualasto
Huaco
Rodeo
San José de Jáchal
Las Flores
Iglesia
Calingasta
San Juan
Chepes
Marayes
Ulapes
Villa Dolores
Barreal
Santa Rosa
Vallecito
Parque Provincial Aconcagua
Cerro Mercedario 6770m
Uspallata
Los Penitentes
Las Cuevas
Villavicencio
Potrerillos
Mendoza
Cacheuta
San Martín
Rivadavia
Santa Rosa
La Paz
PN Sierra de las Quijadas
Quines
Luján
Merlo
Tilisarao
La Toma
San Luis
Mercedes
Zanjitas
Buena Esperanza
Tupungato
Parque Provincial Volcán Tupungato
Tunuyán
San Carlos
San Rafael
Los Molles
Las Leñas
El Nihuil
Malargüe
General Alvear
Bardas Blancas
Santa Isabel
Barrancas
Chos-Malal
El Carancho
25 de Mayo
Puelches
Neuquén
Zapala
Río Blanco
Río Jáchal
Río Bermejo
Río San Juan
Río Desaguadero
Río Tunuyán
Río Atuel
Río Salado
Río Grande
Río Barrancas
Río Neuquén
Río Salado Chadileuvu
Río Colorado
0 50 100 km
0 30 60 miles
ARGENTINA

Local vintners developed commerce across the Andes to Santiago and sold 7300 barrels a year to interior markets by the late 18th century, when Cuyo became part of the Intendencia de Córdoba within the Viceroyalty of the River Plate; Argentine independence closed these outlets for their producc, and the economy soon faltered. Darwin, in 1835, remarked that 'nothing could appear more flourishing than the vineyards and the orchards of figs, peaches and olives,' yet he also noted that 'the prosperity of the place has much declined of late years.'

Only after the arrival of the railroad in 1884 did prosperity return, permitting expansion of grape and olive cultivation plus alfalfa for livestock. As provincial authorities like Governor Emilio Civit promoted modernization of the irrigation system, an influx of Italian immigrants transformed the countryside, and federal economic policies protected the growing domestic industry.

The area under vineyard cultivation grew from 6400 hectares in 1890 to 45,000 hectares in 1910; 100,000 hectares in 1934, 175,000 hectares in 1960; and reached 240,000 hectares before leveling off in the 1970s. Despite the centralization of water management, vineyards remain relatively small, owner-operated enterprises, most not exceeding 50 hectares. Since 1913, the annual Fiesta de la Vendimia has celebrated the famous provincial wines.

While minerals are relatively insignificant within the province, it has major oil and gas fields that provide 25% of Argentina's petroleum; coupled with hydroelectric development in the nearby Andes, this has fostered industrial development. The province's location on a major international transit route has encouraged the tourist economy. Besides the towering Andean landscape and its poplar-lined vineyards and orchards, Mendoza offers several provincial nature parks and reserves and thermal baths. It's a popular destination for both summer and winter holidays.

MENDOZA

Founded in 1561 and named for Chilean Governor García Hurtado de Mendoza, the provincial capital sits 761m above sea level at the foot of the Andes in the valley of its namesake river. With a population of 880,000, it it's the region's most important administrative and commercial center, with a significant state university and a growing industrial base supported by nearby oil fields. Earthquakes have often shaken the city, most recently in October 1997.

Except during long siesta hours, Mendoza is a lively city. Its bustling downtown, where locals congregate to read the latest headlines on the chalkboards in front of the daily *Los Andes*, is surrounded by tranquil neighborhoods, where, every morning, meticulous shopkeepers and housekeepers swab the sidewalks with kerosene to keep them shining. The *acequias* (irrigation canals) along its tree-lined streets are visible evidence of the city's indigenous and colonial past, even where modern quake-proof construction has replaced fallen historic buildings.

Mendoza has fewer pedestrian malls than other Argentine cities, but its wide downtown sidewalks contribute to an active street life. The extensive street trees alleviate the summer heat.

History

When Vásquez de Espinosa visited Mendoza in the early 17th century, he found it a modest place, with only '40 Spanish residents and over 1500 Indians to convert and civilize,' under the supervision of Franciscan, Mercederian, and Jesuit convents. The Governor of Chile appointed a Mendoza-based *corregidor* (magistrate) as his representative in Cuyo, but creation of the Viceroyalty of the River Plate in 1777, which eventually subjected the province to the Intendencia of Córdoba, began a reorientation toward Buenos Aires.

In 1814, Mendoza played a major role in the Spanish American wars of independence, as General José de San Martín chose the city to train his Ejército de los Andes prior to crossing the Andes to liberate Chile. Only a few years later, though, Darwin found post-independence Mendoza depressing:

To my mind the town had a stupid, forlorn aspect. Neither the boasted alameda, nor the scenery, is at all comparable with that of Santiago; but to those who, coming from Buenos Aires, have just crossed the unvaried Pampas, the gardens and orchards must appear delightful.

Arrival of the railroad, along with the modernization of provincial irrigation works, returned Mendoza to prosperity. Today 80% of the country's wine comes from bodegas in and around the city, but construction of oil-fired and hydroelectric power plants has encouraged the development of petrochemicals and light industry, diversifying the city's economic base and related services, and thus promoting population growth. This has not been without cost: Expansion of the Universidad Nacional de Cuyo, for example, displaced squatters from the western outskirts of the city, north of Parque San Martín.

Orientation

Mendoza is 1040km west of Buenos Aires via RN 7 and 340km northwest of Santiago de Chile via the Los Libertadores border complex, whose trans-Andean tunnel has supplanted the higher Uspallata route.

Strictly speaking, the provincial capital proper is a relatively small area with a population of only about 130,000, but the inclusion of adjacent suburbs of Gran Mendoza (Greater Mendoza) in the departments of Las Heras (to the north), Guaymallén (to the east), and Godoy Cruz (to the south) along with nearby Maipú and Luján de Cuyo, swells the population to nearly 900,000.

Renovated Plaza Independencia occupies four square blocks in the city center; on its east side, the Cámara de Diputados (provincial legislature) is painted *celeste* (sky blue) and white, the Argentine national colors. On weekends open-air concerts and an artisans' market often take place on the plaza.

Two blocks from each of the corners of Plaza Independencia, four smaller plazas are arranged in a virtual orbit. Beautifully tiled, restored Plaza España deserves special mention.

Often on weekdays and zealously on Saturday, mendocinos socialize at the numerous sycamore-shaded confiterías on Av San Martín, which crosses the city from north to south. The poplar-lined Alameda, beginning at the 1700 block of San Martín, was a traditional site for 19th-century promenades. Avenida Las Heras, also shaded by sycamores, is the principal commercial street.

A good place to orient yourself is the Terraza Mirador, the rooftop terrace of the Municipalidad, 9 de Julio 500, which offers panoramic views of the city and surroundings. It's open to the public 8 am to 8 pm daily.

Information

Tourist Offices The Dirección Municipal de Turismo (☎ 449-5185, fax 438-1387) in the Municipalidad at 9 de Julio 500, is open 8:30 am to 1:30 pm weekdays. For most purposes, though, the municipal Centro de Información y Asistencia al Turismo (☎ 420-1333), on the broad Garibaldi sidewalk near Av San Martín, is the most convenient information source; open 9 am to 9 pm daily, it has good maps and detailed handouts, and there's usually an English speaker on hand. The best available map, sold here for US$7, is Guía Roja's *Todo Mendoza – Planos Gran Mendoza y Provincia*, which includes the capital and all its surrounding suburbs and has an index of street names. Another Centro de Información (☎ 429-6298) is at Las Heras and Mitre. There's also an Oficina de Informes (☎ 431-3001), open 7 am to 11 pm, in the bus terminal.

At Av San Martín 1143, the provincial Subsecretaría de Turismo (☎ 420-2800) is open weekdays 7 am to 9 pm. The friendly staff operate an excellent computerized information system, but most of them seem to be on automatic pilot, and dealing with them is like a voicemail encounter. They have good maps, but no other brochures.

ACA (☎ 420-2900) is at Av San Martín and Amigorena.

For information on the southern part of the province, contact the Casa de San Rafael (☎ 420-1475), Av Alem 308, and/or the Casa de Malargüe (☎ 425-9564), España 1075.

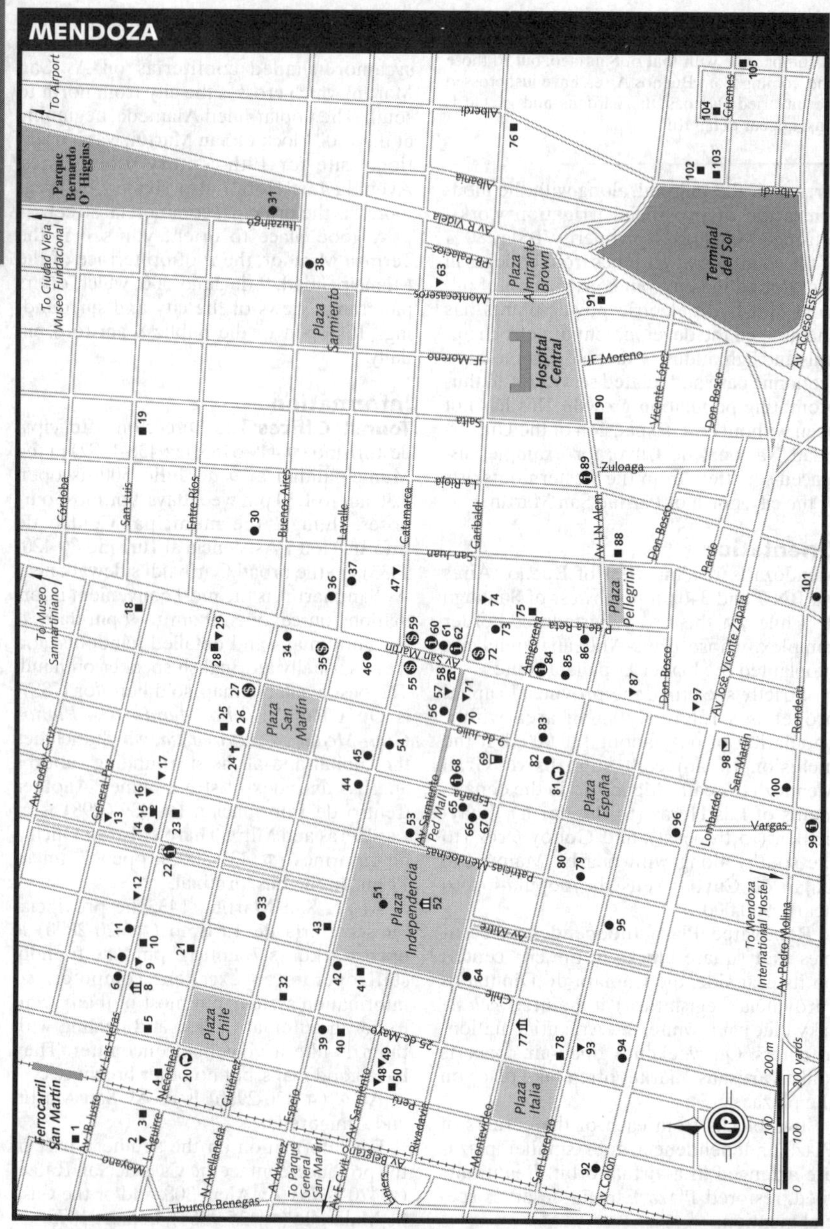
MENDOZA
To Airport
Parque Bernardo O' Higgins
To Ciudad Vieja Museo Fundacional
To Museo Sanmartiniano
Plaza Sarmiento
Plaza San Martín
Plaza Independencia
Plaza Chile
Plaza Italia
Plaza España
Plaza Pellegrini
Plaza Almirante Brown
Hospital Central
Terminal del Sol
Ferrocarril San Martín
To Parque General San Martín
To Mendoza International Hostel
Av Sarmiento Ped Mall
Av San Martín
Av Las Heras
Av Colón
Av Mitre
Av Acceso Este
Av JB Justo
Av Godoy Cruz
Av Belgrano
Av E Civit
Av Pedro Molina
Av José Vicente Zapata
Av LN Alem
Av R Videla
Córdoba
San Luis
Entre Ríos
Buenos Aires
Lavalle
Catamarca
Garibaldi
La Rioja
San Juan
Salta
JF Moreno
Montecaseros
PB Palacios
Alberdi
Albania
Ituzaingó
General Paz
Necochea
Gutiérrez
Espejo
25 de Mayo
Rivadavia
Montevideo
San Lorenzo
Chile
Patricias Mendocinas
España
9 de Julio
Amigorena
P de la Reta
Zuloaga
Vicente López
Don Bosco
Pardo
Rondeau
Lombardo
Vargas
Güemes
Tiburcio Benegas
N Avellaneda
A Álvarez
Perú
Vilters
L Aguirre
Moyano
200 m
200 yards

Immigration Migraciones (☎ 438-0569) is at Av España 1425.

Money Cambio Santiago, Av San Martín 1199, is one of the few places open on Saturday (until 8 pm); it takes a 2% commission on traveler's checks. Exprinter, another large but efficient cambio, is at Av San Martín 1198.

Two downtown banks are also architectural landmarks: the massive Banco Mendoza, at the corner of Gutiérrez and San Martín, and Banco de la Nación, at Necochea and 9 de Julio. There are many ATMs downtown.

Post & Communications Correo Argentino is at Avs San Martín and Colón; central Mendoza's postal code is 5500. There are many *locutorios*, such as Fonobar, Sarmiento 23 (where you can order a drink while you make your call). The area code is ☎ 0261.

Fifty, Colón 199, offers Internet access for US$6 per hour.

MENDOZA

PLACES TO STAY

1 Hotel Margal
3 Hotel Laerte
4 Hotel Vigo
5 Hotel Petit
10 Hotel Rincón Vasco
18 Hotel City
19 Hotel Escorial
21 Hotel Necochea
23 Hotel Balbi
25 Hotel El Torreón
28 Imperial Hotel
32 Hospedaje Mayo
40 Hotel Princess
41 Plaza Hotel
43 Hotel Argentino
50 Hotel Crillón
75 Gran Hotel Huentala
76 Residencial Eben-Ezer
78 Hotel Aconcagua
88 Hotel Galicia
90 Hotel Center
91 Residencial Savigliano
102 Hotel Terminal
103 Residencial Alexander
104 Residencial 402
105 Hospedaje Carmen

PLACES TO EAT

2 Centro Andaluz
9 Café Mediterráneo
12 Rincón de La Boca
13 Montecatini
15 Café La Avenida
16 La Marchigiana
17 Mercado Central
29 Trevi
47 Las Vías
48 La Florencia
49 Sarmiento
57 Soppelsa
63 Onda Verde
71 Il Tucco
74 La Nature
80 El Mesón Español
87 Asia
93 Línea Verde
97 Trattoria La Veneciana

OTHER

6 Empresa Jocolí
7 Esquí Mendoza Competición
8 Museo Popular Callejero
11 Turismo Mendoza
14 Las Viñas
20 Italian Consulate
22 Centro de Información y Asistencia al Turismo
24 Iglesia, Convento y Basílica de San Francisco
26 Migraciones
27 Banco de la Nación
30 Teatro Mendoza
31 Acuario Municipal
33 Localiza Rent A Car
34 Asatej
35 Banco de Mendoza
36 Cine Opera
37 Cine Teatro Universidad
38 Hertz
39 Instituto Dante Alighieri
42 Teatro Independencia
44 Turismo Maipú
45 Andesmar
46 Y Libros
51 Teatro Quintanilla
52 Museo de Arte Moderno
53 Cámara de Diputados
54 LanChile
55 Cambio Exprinter
56 Dinar
58 Fonobar
59 Cambio Santiago
60 Subsecretaría de Turismo
61 Mercado Artesanal
62 Centro de Información y Asistencia al Turismo
64 Instituto Cultural Argentino Norteamericano
65 Isc Viajes (AmEx)
66 Lapa, TAN
67 Kaikén Líneas Aéreas, Southern Winds
68 Casa de Malargüe
69 Café Soul
70 Aerolíneas Argentinas, Austral
72 Citibank (ATM)
73 Turismo Sepean
77 Museo del Pasado Cuyano
79 Club Andino Italiano/Centro Italiano
81 German Consulate
82 English House Bookstore
83 Aymará Turismo
84 ACA
85 García Santos Libros
86 Avis
89 Casa de San Rafael
92 Extreme
94 Laverap
95 La Lavandería
96 Fifty (Internet Access)
98 Post Office
99 Terraza Mirador/Dirección Municipal de Turismo, Microcine Municipal David Eisenchlas
100 English Lending Library
101 Iaim Instituto Cultural

Travel Agencies The student travel agency Asatej (☎/fax 429-0087, tstudent@satlink.com) is at San Martín 1366, Local 16. The AmEx representative is Isc Viajes (☎ 425-9259), Av España 1016.

Bookstores The English House Bookstore, 9 de Julio 916, has a good selection of reading material. García Santos Libros (☎ 429-2287), San Martín 921, has a good selection of Spanish language literature and books on Argentina, as does Y Libros (☎ 425-2822), Av San Martín 1252.

Libraries The English Lending Library (☎ 423-8396), Pedro Molina 61, loans English-language books on a fee basis depending on the number of books borrowed, starting at US$5 per month for one book per week. Hours are 8 am to 8 pm daily. The Instituto Argentino-Norteamericano (see Cultural Centers) also has a lending library.

Cultural Centers The Instituto Cultural Argentino Norteamericano (☎ 423-6367) is at Chile 987. The Alianza Francesa (☎ 423-4614) is at Chile 1754, and the Instituto Dante Alighieri (☎ 425-7613) at Espejo 638.

Laundry Laverap (☎ 423-9706) is at Colón 547; La Lavandería (☎ 429-4782) at San Lorenzo 352.

Medical Services Mendoza's Hospital Central (☎ 420-0600) is at José F Moreno and Alem. If you need an ambulance, call the Servicio Coordinado de Emergencia (☎ 428-0000).

Ruinas de San Francisco

Occupying an entire block in the Ciudad Vieja (Old Town) at the corner of Ituzaingó and Fray Luis Beltrán, these misnamed ruins belong to a Jesuit-built church/school that dates from 1638.

After the Jesuits were expelled in 1767, the Franciscans, whose own church was demolished in the 1782 earthquake, took over the buildings.

Museo Fundacional

One might call Mendoza's sparkling Museo Fundacional empty, but it would be more accurate to call it spacious, as the high-ceilinged structure on Plaza Pedro del Castillo protects excavations of the colonial Cabildo, destroyed by an earthquake in 1861, and of the slaughterhouse then built on the Cabildo's foundations. At that time, the city's geographical focus shifted west and south to its present location.

The museum starts at the beginning – the Big Bang – and works through all of human evolution as if the city of Mendoza were the climax of the process. Nevertheless, for all the subtle pretensions, it's one of few Argentine museums that acknowledges the indigenous Huarpes' role in the region's development and the region's contemporary mestizo culture. There are several good dioramas of the city at various stages of its development, a decent selection of historical photographs (most of them lamentably small), and ancient and modern artifacts.

Open Monday to Saturday 8 am to 8 pm, Sunday 3 to 10 pm, the air-conditioned facility (☎ 425-6927), at Alberdi and Videla Castillo, has a small confitería and a shop selling credible reproductions of archaeological pieces. Admission is US$1.50 for adults, US$1 for students.

Museo Popular Callejero

This innovative outdoor museum along Av Las Heras, between 25 de Mayo and Perú, consists of a series of encased dioramas depicting changes in one of Mendoza's major avenues since its 1830 creation as Callejón de las Maruleilas, in a dry watercourse. The dioramas depict typical scenes as it became Calle de la Circunvalación (1863), Calle de las Carretas (an informal, common name dating from 1880), Calle Las Heras (1882, after San Martín's contemporary and colleague, Gregorio de Las Heras), Calle del Ferrocarril (1885, for obvious reasons), Boulevard de las Palmeras (1908, for the palm trees planted along it), and Calle de los Inmigrantes (1912). Because it's on the street, it's open to viewing 24 hours a day.

Iglesia, Convento & Basílica de San Francisco

Many cuyanos consider this church's image of the Virgin of Cuyo, patron of San Martín's Ejército de los Andes (Army of the Andes), miraculous because it survived Mendoza's devastating 1968 earthquake. In the Virgin's semicircular *camarín* (chamber), visitors leave tributes to her and to San Martín. A mausoleum within the building holds the remains of San Martín's daughter, son-in-law, and granddaughter, which were repatriated from France in 1951.

At Necochea 201, the church is open to the public from Monday to Saturday 9 am to noon.

Museo Histórico General San Martín

José de San Martín's name graces parks, squares, and streets everywhere in Argentina, but the Libertador is especially dear to Mendoza, where he resided with his family and recruited and trained his army to cross into Chile. At Remedios Escalada de San Martín 1843, the museum (☎ 425-7947) is open 9 am to noon weekdays only.

Museo de Bellas Artes Emiliano Guiñazú (Casa de Fader)

Paintings and sculptures by Argentine artists, particularly Mendocinos, add flavor to this art museum (☎ 496-0224) in a distinguished historical residence in the suburb of Luján de Cuyo. From downtown, take bus No 200 to San Martín 3651.

Other Museums

At Montevideo 544, the historical **Museo del Pasado Cuyano** (☎ 423-6031) has collections of documents and period furniture. It opens weekday mornings 9 am to noon, and Tuesday and Friday afternoon, with guided tours at 11 am.

The **Museo Municipal de Arte Moderno** (☎ 425-7279), underground at Plaza Independencia, is a relatively small but well-organized facility with rotating exhibits. It's open Tuesday to Saturday 9 am to 1 pm and 4 to 9 pm, Sunday 4 to 9 pm only.

Acuario Municipal

Mendoza's municipal aquarium contains both local and exotic fish, the most interesting of which are species from the Río Paraná. At Ituzaingó and Buenos Aires, the aquarium (☎ 425-3824) is open 8:30 am to 8:30 pm daily. Admission is US$1.50.

Parque General San Martín

Originally forged for the Turkish Sultan Hamid II, the impressive gates to this 420-hectare park west of downtown came from England. Designed by architect Carlos Thays in 1897 and donated to the provincial government by two-time governor and later senator Emilio Civit, the park itself has 50,000 trees of about 700 different species and is popular for weekend family outings and other activities. The famous **Cerro de la Gloria** features a monument to San Martín's Ejército de los Andes for their liberation of Argentina, Chile, and Peru from the Spaniards. On clear days, views of the valley make the climb especially rewarding.

Within the park, several museums focus on archaeology, mineralogy, and natural history, including the **Museo de Ciencias Naturales y Antropológicas Juan Cornelio Moyano** (☎ 428-7666), the **Museo Domingo Faustino Sarmiento** (☎ 428-1133), and the **Museo Mineralógico Manuel Telechea** (☎ 424-1794). The **Museo Arqueológico de la Universidad Nacional de Cuyo** (☎ 449-4093), part of the Facultad de Filosofía y Letras, focuses on American archaeology.

Bus No 110 ('Favorita') from around Plaza Independencia or Plaza España goes to the park, continuing to the **Jardín Zoológico** (☎ 425-0130), in an impressive hillside setting. The zoo is open Tuesday to Sunday 9 am to 7 pm. From the park entrance, open-air buses called *bateas* carry visitors to the summit of Cerro de la Gloria.

Activities

Mendoza and its Andean hinterland constitute one of Argentina's major outdoor recreation areas, with several agencies organizing expeditions for climbers and trekkers, rafting trips on the Río Mendoza and other rivers, mule trips, and the like. Among these agencies are the following and their specialties:

Andesport (climbing, trekking, mule trips)
(☎ 424-1003)
Rufino Ortega 390

Aymará Turismo (mule trips, trekking, rafting)
(☎ 420-0607)
9 de Julio 933

Betancourt Rafting (rafting, mountain biking, parasailing)
(☎ 439-1949, betancourt@lanet.com.ar)
Ruta Panamericana & Río Cuevas, Godoy Cruz

Piuquén Viajes (mule trips, trekking across the Andes)
(☎ 425-3984)
Alvarez 332

Rumbo al Horizonte (climbing, skiing, expeditions, adventure courses)
(☎ 452-0641)
Caseros 1053, Godoy Cruz

Travesía (rafting, trekking)
(☎ 428-2677)
Reconquista 1080, Godoy Cruz

Travesías Andinas (mountain biking)
(☎ 429-0029, 424-0018)
Av San Martín 1998

Climbing & Mountaineering For the latest information, contact the Club Andinista Mendoza (☎ 431-9870), Fray Luis Beltrán 357, Guaymallén; the Club Andino Italiano (☎ 429-3973), in the Centro Italiano at Patricias Mendocinas 843; Fernando Grajales (☎/fax 429-3830), at José Francisco Mendoza 898, 5500 Mendoza; or Rudy Parra at Aconcagua Trek (☎/fax 431-7003), Güiraldes 246, Dorrego.

For climbing and hiking equipment, both rental and purchase, try Orviz (☎ 425-1281), Av JB Justo 550.

Cycling & Mountain Biking Both road cycling and, increasingly, mountain biking are popular activities in and around Mendoza. For bicycle-oriented events, see the Special Events entry.

Navegante EV&T (☎ 429-1615) runs 5½ hour, 25km mountain-bike tours every morning and afternoon in the *precordillera* (Andean foothills) of Mendoza (US$30), and also rents mountain bikes. Travesías Andinas runs full-day trips to Potrerillos (US$70) as well as shorter excursions.

Skiing For purchase and rental of ski equipment, try Esquí Mendoza Competición (☎ 425-2801), at Las Heras 583; Extreme (☎ 429-0733), at Colón 733; or Rezagos de Ejército (☎ 423-3791), at Mitre 2002.

White-Water Rafting The major rivers are the Mendoza and the Diamante, near San Rafael, with trips ranging from half-day excursions (US$30) to overnight (US$190) and three-day expeditions (US$350). In addition to the agencies mentioned above, readers have recommended Ríos Andinos (☎ 02685-404334), Adolfo Calle 965, Dorrego, Guaymallén.

Language Courses

IAIM Instituto Intercultural (☎ 429-0269, fax 424-8840, info@iaimnet.com.), Rondeau 277, offers Spanish-language instruction for foreigners.

Organized Tours

Get a route map of the Municipalidad's Bus Turístico (☎ 420-1333), whose well-versed guides (some of them English-speaking) offer the best possible orientation to the city for US$10. Good for 24 hours, the ticket allows you to board and reboard at any of several fixed stops throughout the city; the circuit begins at the corner of Garibaldi and Av San Martín and goes as far as the summit of Cerro de la Gloria. Hours are 10 am to 8 pm daily from January 1 to Semana Santa.

Several conventional travel agencies organize trips in and around town, including Turismo Mendoza (☎ 429-2013), at Las Heras 543; Turismo Sepean (☎ 420-4162), at Primitivo de la Reta 1088; Expreso Jocolí (☎ 423-0466), at Av Las Heras 601; and Turismo Maipú (☎ 429-4996), at Espejo 207. Among the possibilities are tours of the city (US$12), the wineries and Dique Cipoletti (US$13), Villavicencio (US$17), and the high cordillera around Potrerillos, Vallecitos, and Uspallata (US$28). More distant excursions, such as San Juan (US$29) and the Cañon del Atuel (US$39) as well as winter ski trips, are also possible.

Special Events

Mendoza's biggest annual event, the Fiesta Nacional de la Vendimia (Wine Harvest Festival), lasts about a week from late February to early March. It features a parade, with floats from each department of the province, on Av San Martín, as well numerous concerts and folkloric events, terminating with the coronation of the festival's queen in the Parque General San Martín amphitheater.

In February, the provincial equivalent of the Tour de France is the Vuelta Ciclística de Mendoza. In July and August, the Festival de la Nieve features ski competitions.

Places to Stay

Mendoza has abundant accommodations in all categories. The tourist booth at the bus terminal may help find good rooms at bargain prices, while the downtown office also keeps a list of casas de familia, offering accommodations from about US$10 to US$15 single. For March's Fiesta de la Vendimia, reservations are advisable.

Places to Stay – Budget

Camping Recently renovated, convenient ***Churrasqueras del Parque*** *(☎ 428-0511)*, in Parque General San Martín, has good facilities, but its popular restaurant means it can be noisy late at night, especially on weekends. Fees are US$2.50 per person, per tent, and per vehicle. Take bus No 50, 100, or 110 from downtown.

Bus No 110 continues to ***El Challao*** *(☎ 431-6085)*, 6km north of downtown, which charges US$7 for two persons and US$1 for each additional person. Woodsy ***Parque Suizo*** *(☎ 444-1991, 428-3915)*, 9km from downtown in Las Heras, charges US$12 per site for up to three persons. Each has clean, hot showers, laundry facilities, electricity, and a grocery.

Hostels Mendoza has three Hostelling International affiliates. Reasonably close to the tourist office, friendly ***Hostel Campo Base*** *(☎ 155-696036, campbase@hostels.org.ar, Mitre 946)*, between Montevideo and Rivadavia, is most popular with climbers but draws a wider clientele as well and has good common spaces. Rates are US$8 for hostel bunks; cabañas for couples are under construction. Email access is available.

Friendly but more central and comfortable, the ***Mendoza International Hostel*** *(☎ /fax 424-0018, www.hostelmendoza.net, España 343)* costs US$12 with breakfast. It also offers other meals, email access, entertainment, and organized tours.

The ***Hostel Guaymallén*** *(☎ 426-3300, Tirasso 2170)*, in Guaymallén, offers beds for US$8 without kitchen privileges, but it is less than central and most popular with large tour groups.

Residenciales & Hotels Mendoza's cheapest accommodations are just north of the bus terminal, on Güemes and nearby streets. For around US$10 per person, include funky, barely passable ***Residencial 402*** *(Güemes 402)* and ***Residencial Alexander*** *(☎ 431-0859, Güemes 294)*. ***Residencial Eben-Ezer*** *(☎ 431-2635, Alberdi 580)* is another cheapie near the bus terminal, as is recommended ***Hospedaje Carmen***, Güemes 519 (good hot water, friendly staff).

Across Av Videla from the bus terminal (take the pedestrian underpass), ***Residencial Savigliano*** *(☎ 423-7746, Pedro Palacios 944)* has drawn enthusiastic commentary for US$10 per person, with breakfast, shared bath, reasonable privacy, and access to cable TV. For about the same price in nearby Dorrego, try ***Hotel Mariani*** *(☎ 431-9932, Lamadrid 121)*, with private bath and breakfast, and ***Casa de Familia*** *(☎ 432-0645, Sobremonte 1084)*, with breakfast plus kitchen and laundry privileges.

Recommended ***Hotel Galicia*** *(☎ 420-2619, San Juan 881)* is central, clean, and friendly for US$12/20 single/double with shared bath, US$30 double with private bath. Equally central ***Hotel Vigo*** *(☎ 425-0208, Necochea 749)* is perhaps one of the best inexpensive hotels in town, a bit rundown but with a nice garden; singles/doubles are US$15/26.

Places to Stay – Mid-Range

Mid-range hotels start around US$20/29, including clean, pleasant ***Hotel Escorial*** *(☎ 425-4777, San Luis 263)* and ***Hotel San Remo*** *(☎ 423-4068, Av Godoy Cruz 477)*, north of downtown, for US$22/35. ***Hotel Center*** *(☎ 423-8270, Alem 547)*, near the bus terminal, is basic though no longer really cheap, with rooms for US$23/35.

Similarly priced ***Hotel Terminal*** *(☎ 431-3893, Alberdi 261)* is tidy and comfortable but rooms are rather small. For US$25/35, enthusiastically recommended ***Hotel Laerte*** *(☎ 423-0875, Leonidas Aguirre 19)* is modern but homey. Comparable ***Hotel Petit*** *(☎ 423-2099, Perú 1459)* is clean and friendly for US$25/35. Also recommended and the same price are the downtown ***Imperial Hotel*** *(☎ 423-4671, Las Heras 84)* and ***Hotel Margal*** *(☎ 425-2013, Av JB Justo 75)*. Slightly dearer at US$28/39, but still a good value, is ***Hospedaje Mayo*** *(☎ 425-4424, 25 de Mayo 1265)*.

Though some travelers may think ***Hotel Rincón Vasco*** *(☎ 423-3033, Las Heras 590)* a bit run-down, it is in an excellent location. Rooms are US$30/40, but try negotiating a cheaper rate for longer stays. ***Hotel City*** *(☎ 425-1343, General Paz 95)* charges US$30/39.

Slightly dearer mid-range places include recommended ***Hotel Argentino*** *(☎ 425-4000, Espejo 455)* for US$39/55; central, comfy ***Hotel Necochea*** *(☎ 425-3501, Necochea 541)* for US$40/42; and ***Hotel América*** *(☎ 425-6514, JB Justo 812)* for US$45/60.

Places to Stay – Top End

Hotels in this category start at about US$50/65, including a continental breakfast at ***Hotel El Torreón*** *(☎ 423-3900, España 1439)*. Two better values downtown, both close to Plaza Independencia and restaurants, are ***Hotel Crillón*** *(☎ 423-8963, Perú 1065)* for US$60/75 and ***Hotel Princess*** *(☎ 423-5669, 25 de Mayo 1168)* for US$70/90. ***Hotel Balbi*** *(☎ 438-0626, Las Heras 340)* charges US$69/89.

In a stylish neocolonial building, the highly recommended ***Plaza Hotel*** *(☎ 425-6300, Chile 1124)* dates from 1925; it's a good value at US$85/100. ***Hotel Aconcagua*** *(☎ 420-4455, San Lorenzo 545)* charges US$83/125, but has drawn criticism for noise, 'deferred maintenance,' and glacially sluggish checkouts. Rates at ***Gran Hotel Huentala*** *(☎ 420-0766, Primitivo de la Reta 1007)* are US$94/142.

Places to Eat

Many of Mendoza's varied restaurants, pizzerias, cafés, and snack bars are downtown, but diners should not hesitate to look elsewhere. Probably the best budget choice is the ***Mercado Central***, at Av Las Heras and Patricias Mendocinas, where a variety of stalls offer inexpensive pizza, empanadas, sandwiches, and groceries in general; its exceptional value and great atmosphere make it one of Mendoza's highlights.

Despite its Italian moniker, ***Boccadoro*** *(☎ 425-5056, Mitre 1976)* is a parrilla. Other possibilities include plain but cheap ***Arturito*** *(☎ 425-1489, Chile 1515)*, ***Sarmiento*** *(☎ 438-0824, Sarmiento 658)*, and ***La Florencia***, at Sarmiento and Perú.

Several places specialize in pasta, however, including traditional favorite ***Trattoria La Veneciana*** *(☎ 423-7737, Av San Martín 739)*, recommended ***Montecatini*** *(☎ 425-2111, General Paz 370)*, and ***Trevi*** *(☎ 423-3195, Las Heras 70)*, which has outstanding lasagna. The two locations of ***Il Tucco***, at Emilio Civit 556 near the entrance to Parque San Martín and at Sarmiento 68 *(☎ 420-2565)*, both have excellent food and moderate prices.

Mendoza's finest Italian restaurant is ***La Marchigiana*** *(☎ 423-0751, Patricias Mendocinas 1550)*, which draws celebrities (Brad Pitt dined here while filming *Seven Years in Tibet)*, but the gracious hostess welcomes everyone; though relatively expensive, it's worth the splurge. For inexpensive pizza, try ***Rincón de La Boca*** *(Las Heras 485)*, with good *fugazzeta* (cheese and onion pizza), hard to find in Mendoza, and *chopp* (draft or lager) plus friendly service and sidewalk seating.

The ***Centro Andaluz*** *(☎ 423-2971, Leonidas Aguirre 35)* has tasty paella. For typical Spanish food, ***El Mesón Español***

(☎ 429-5313, Montevideo 244) has moderate fixed-price meals. ***Café Mediterráneo*** *(Las Heras 596)* has interesting, moderately priced lunch specials. ***Praga*** *(Leonidas Aguirre 413)* has drawn praise from local residents.

The popular ***Asia*** *(San Martín 821)* is one of few *tenedor libre*, or all-you-can-eat, Chinese restaurants in town. For Middle Eastern cuisine, try ***Café La Avenida*** *(Las Heras 341)*. For regional specialties, long-time residents recommend ***El Retortuño*** *(☎ 431-6300)*, on Dorrego near Adolfo Calles in Guaymallén, which has live Latin American music on weekend evenings; take the 'Dorrego' trolley from downtown.

Vegetarians can find several choices, including wholesome, reasonably priced ***Onda Verde*** *(Montecaseros 1177)*, ***Línea Verde*** *(☎ 423-9806, San Lorenzo 550)*, which also has a takeaway rotisería, ***La Nature*** *(☎ 420-0882, Garibaldi 63)*, and ***Las Vías*** *(☎ 425-0053, Catamarca 76)*.

Café del Teatro, at the corner of Chile and Perú, is a hangout for the downtown theater crowd. For ice cream, try ***Soppelsa*** *(Sarmiento 57)*.

Entertainment

Dance Clubs Downtown discotheques include ***La Luz*** *(San Martín 300)*, ***Saudades*** *(☎ 438-0862)*, at San Martín and Barraquero, and, on the westward extension of Av Colón, ***Epicentro*** *(☎ 429-8414, Aristides Villanueva 256)*, which has a karaoke bar. There are many others in the suburb of Chacras de Coria, on Mendoza's southern outskirts, such as ***Aloha***, ***Campo de Vuelo***, and ***Runner***.

Cinema The ***Microcine Municipal Davíd Eisenchlas*** *(☎ 449-5100, 9 de Julio 500)*, in the basement of the Municipalidad, shows occasional art films. The only regular downtown cinema is ***Cine Opera*** *(☎ 429-3120, Lavalle 54)*, though ***Cine Teatro Universidad*** *(Lavalle 77)*, across the street, also shows films on occasion.

The remainder are suburban multiplexes: ***Cine Village Mendoza*** *(☎ 421-0700)*, at Mendoza Plaza Shopping in Guaymallén (take the T-Red bus from 9 de Julio), and the ***Cinemark*** *(☎ 439-5245, Panamericana 2650)*, at the Palmares Open Mall (take bus No 43 from Plaza Independencia). Mendoza also has a drive-in, ***Autocine El Cerro*** *(☎ 425-2015)*, on Av Champagnat just north of the Ciudad Universitaria – Joe Bob says to check it out.

Theater The ***Teatro Quintanilla*** *(☎ 423-2310)* is alongside the Museo de Arte Moderno, underground at Plaza Independencia. ***Teatro Independencia*** *(☎ 438-0644)* is nearby at the corner of Espejo and Chile. The Universidad Nacional del Cuyo hosts performances at ***Teatro Mendoza*** *(☎ 429-7279, San Juan 1427)*.

Bars Recommended ***Café Soul*** *(☎ 429-9652, Rivadavia 135)* has live music, including tango and flamenco from time to time. Another possibility is ***El Rincón del Poeta*** *(Alberdi 456)*, in the Ciudad Vieja.

Shopping

Friday, Saturday, and Sunday, the outdoor Plaza de las Artes market takes place on Plaza Independencia.

Open weekdays 8 am to 1 pm, the Mercado Artesanal (☎ 420-4239), downstairs at Av San Martín 1143, features provincial handicrafts, including vertical-loom weavings (Huarpe-style) from the northwest of the province and horizontal looms (Araucanian-style) from the south, woven baskets from Lagunas del Rosario, and braided, untanned-leather horse gear. Prices are reasonable, and the staff is knowledgeable and eager to talk about crafts and the artisans, who receive the proceeds directly.

Las Viñas (☎ 425-1520), Las Heras 399, has a wide selection of Argentine crafts.

Getting There & Away

Air Aerolíneas Argentinas (☎ 420-4185) and Austral share offices at Sarmiento 82, Aerolíneas flies three times daily to Buenos Aires' Aeroparque Jorge Newbury (US$57 to US$196) except on Saturday (two flights) and daily to the capital's Ezeiza via Córdoba. Austral has 24 flights weekly to Aeroparque.

LanChile (☎ 420-2890), Espejo 128, flies twice daily to Santiago de Chile, the only international flights from Mendoza.

Lapa (☎ 429-1061), España 1012, flies 20 times weekly to Aeroparque (US$59 to US$149); Monday, Wednesday, and Friday flights stop in San Juan (US$20 to US$35). TAN (☎ 434-0240), also at España 1012, has 20 flights weekly to Neuquén (US$85 to US$100), some via Chos Malal or Rincón de los Sauces; and daily flights to Córdoba (US$39 to US$74), some via San Juan (US$80 to US$90; yes, it would be cheaper to buy a ticket to Córdoba and get off in San Juan). Dinar (☎ 420-4520), Sarmiento 69, flies twice weekdays and once Saturday to Aeroparque (US$85 to US$179).

Andesmar (☎ 438-0654), Espejo 189, flies twice daily except Saturday to Córdoba (US$49 to US$69) and Tucumán (US$102 to US$149), weekdays to Rosario (US$87 to US$119), and at least daily (except Saturday) to Salta (US$125 to US$159).

Kaikén Líneas Aéreas (☎ 438-0243), at Rivadavia 209, flies daily except Sunday to Neuquén (US$100), Bariloche (US$140 to US$170), Comodoro Rivadavia (US$160 to US$260), Río Gallegos (US$215 to US$283), Río Grande (US$251 to US$320), and Ushuaia (US$265 to US$350). Southern Winds, at the same address, flies twice daily to Córdoba (US$59 to US$79), daily to Tucumán (US$119 to US$159), Salta (US$127 to US$169), Neuquén (US$104 to US$139), and Mar del Plata (US$127-US$169); and weekends to Bariloche (US$134 to US$179).

Bus Mendoza's sprawling Terminal del Sol (☎ 431-1299, 431-3001) is at Av Gobernador Videla and Av Acceso Este, in Guaymallén (which is really just across the street from downtown). Hot showers are available here for US$2.

Border Crossings Numerous companies cross the Andes to Santiago de Chile, Viña del Mar, and Valparaíso (US$20, eight hours) every day. Among them are Tur Bus (☎ 431-1008), Chile Bus (☎ 431-5596), El Rápido (☎ 431-4093), TAC (☎ 431-0518, 431-2687), Ahumada (☎ 431-6281), Tas Choapa (☎ 431-2140), O'Higgins (☎ 431-3199), Cata (☎ 431-0782), and Fénix (☎ 431-1800). The taxi colectivos with Coitram (☎ 431-1999) or Chiar (☎ 431-1736) take about seven hours (US$25, sometimes cheaper).

Several carriers have connections to Lima, Perú (72 hours), via Santiago, including El Rápido, Tas Choapa, and Ormeño (☎ 424-7692).

Empresa General Artigas (EGA; ☎ 431-7758) goes to Montevideo, Uruguay (22 hours), at 1:30 pm Sunday, with onward connections to Punta del Este and Brazil. El Rápido goes there at 8 pm Tuesday.

Long Distance To Buenos Aires, there are about 20 buses daily, with TAC, Chevallier, Central Argentino, Cata, El Rápido, Uspallata, and Jocolí. Four of these buses (with TAC, Central Argentino, and Chevallier) continue to La Plata. There are frequent services to Mar del Plata with TAC, Andesmar, El Rápido, Autotransportes San Juan Mar del Plata, and Jocolí.

There are more than 15 buses daily to Córdoba with TAC, Autotransportes San Juan, La Cumbre, Expreso Uspallata (via the Altas Cumbres route but, unfortunately, at night), Chevallier, Jocolí, and El Rápido. Uspallata goes twice daily to Mina Clavero, and TAC goes once. Uspallata, TAC, and Jocolí all go to Villa Carlos Paz, and La Cumbre goes to various destinations in the Sierras de Córdoba. TAC, Central Argentino, and El Rápido all go to Rosario. TAC has two buses daily to Santa Fe and Paraná, while Villa María (☎ 431-0585) has one.

There are about 15 buses daily to La Rioja and Catamarca with Andesmar, Bosio, La Estrella, Autotransportes Mendoza, TAC, and El Rápido. Andesmar, Autotransportes Mendoza, Bosio, La Estrella, TAC, and El Rápido combined send at least 10 buses daily to Tucumán, Salta, and Jujuy. Empresa Vallecito goes daily to Chilecito, La Rioja, at 7:30 pm.

La Estrella and Autotransportes Mendoza go to Santiago del Estero, the former with a change of bus in Tucumán, the latter in Catamarca. TAC and La Estrella cross the

Chaco daily to Resistencia and Corrientes, but the latter involves a long layover in Córdoba. La Estrella goes nightly at 8 pm to Posadas, connecting to Puerto Iguazú. Empresa Cotal (☎ 431-6933) has buses to Posadas and Puerto Iguazú three times weekly, via Santiago del Estero, Roque Sáenz Peña, Resistencia, and Corrientes.

Andesmar, Jocolí, and TAC all go to Santa Rosa, La Pampa, en route to the Atlantic beach resorts of Buenos Aires province. Andesmar goes twice daily and TAC once to Bahía Blanca. Bariloche is also served by a daily bus with Andesmar (7 pm) and TAC (8 pm), continuing to El Bolsón and Esquel. Andesmar goes to Puerto Madryn, Comodoro Rivadavia, and Caleta Olivia at 7 am and 7 pm daily; buses to Caleta Olivia continue to Río Gallegos. TAC has a 7:30 pm bus to Santa Rosa, La Pampa, which has an immediate connection to Río Gallegos.

To Neuquén, there are nine buses daily with Andesmar, Empresa Alto Valle, TAC, Empresa del Sur y Media Agua, and El Rápido. To San Martín de los Andes, TAC has nightly buses at 7 and 8:30 pm, the former with an hour layover in Cipoletti. Both stop in Zapala.

Sample fares include Córdoba (US$30, 10 hours), Chilecito (10½ hours), Villa Carlos Paz (US$29, 11 hours), La Falda (US$38, 12 hours), Santa Rosa (US$39, 12 hours), Neuquén (US$40, 13 hours), Tucumán (US$39, 14 hours), Buenos Aires (US$45-US$55, 14 hours), Zapala (US$48, 15-1/2 hours), Bahía Blanca (US$55, 16 hours), La Plata (US$50-US$55, 16 hours), Salta (US$52-61, 19 hours), San Martín de los Andes (US$67, 19½ hours), Jujuy (US$53, 20 hours), Bariloche (US$63, 20 hours), El Bolsón (21 hours), Puerto Madryn (US$73, 23 hours), Corrientes (US$69, 24 hours), Esquel (24 hours), Comodoro Rivadavia (US$94, 30 hours), Caleta Olivia (US$98, 32 hours), Posadas (34 hours), Puerto Iguazú (US$98, 36 hours), and Río Gallegos (US$129, 41 hours).

Provincial & Regional To Uspallata and Los Penitentes, for Parque Provincial Aconcagua, there are two buses daily with Expreso Uspallata (☎ 431-3309). Empresa Jocolí (☎ 431-4409) and Turismo Maipú (☎ 429-4976), at Espejo 207, each have a daily service, while several other companies have weekend service, including Turismo Mendoza (☎ 420-1701), at Las Heras 543; Mendoza Viajes (☎ 438-0480), at Paseo Sarmiento 129; and Turismo Luján (☎ 431-1685), at Las Heras 420.

Buses to San Juan are numerous with Andesmar (☎ 431-3953), Bosio (☎ 431-1115), Autotransportes Mendoza (☎ 431-4561), La Estrella (☎ 431-1324), TAC, Empresa Sur y Media Agua (☎ 431-2570), Autotransportes San Juan Mar del Plata (☎ 431-2840), and Empresa Vallecito (☎ 432-0935). There are also many to San Luis with TAC, Empresa Jocolí, Andesmar, Chevallier (☎ 431-0235), Autotransportes San Juan Mar del Plata, Expreso Uspallata, and Central Argentino (☎ 431-3112). Empresa Jocolí goes three times daily to the San Luis mountain resort of Merlo, Expreso Uspallata once.

La Cumbre (☎ 431-6887) has daily buses to the Difunta Correa Shrine in San Juan province at 7:30 pm, but weekend day trips are possible with TAC, Jocolí, Autotransportes Mendoza, and Empresa Vallecito. Vallecito goes daily at 7:30 pm to San Agustín del Valle Fértil. El Triunfo goes Friday at 8:30 pm and Sunday at 9 pm to Barreal and Calingasta, in western San Juan province. TAC and Empresa Sur y Media Agua go three times daily to Jáchal, north of San Juan.

Service is frequent to San Rafael and General Alvear with TAC, Expreso Uspallata, and Andesmar. To Malargüe, TAC has at least two direct buses daily and others with a change of bus in San Rafael. Transporte Viento Sur (☎ 429-1556), Av España 1112, has a 7 pm bus that arrives 2 am in Malargüe.

In ski season, several companies directly go to Las Leñas, including Turismo Mendoza, Autotransportes Mendoza, Expreso Uspallata and Turismo Luján, but the only daily services are with TAC (changing buses in San Rafael) and Mendoza Viajes, which leaves from Sarmiento and 9 de Julio rather than the terminal.

Typical fares include San Juan (US$10, two hours), Los Penitentes (US$9, four hours), Barreal (four hours), San Agustín del Valle Fértil (six hours), Las Leñas (US$15, 6½ hours), and Malargüe (US$20, seven hours).

Getting Around

Mendoza is more spread out than most Argentine cities, so you will need to walk or learn about the bus system to get around. Local buses and trolleys cost around US$0.55, more for longer distances such as the trip to the airport. A new system of magnetic fare cards, sold in multiples of this basic fare, has had a rocky beginning.

To/From the Airport Aeropuerto Internacional Plumerillo (☎ 448-7128) is 6km north of downtown on RN 40. Bus No 60 ('Aeropuerto') from Calle Salta goes straight to the terminal.

Bus The enormous, modern, and very busy Terminal del Sol (☎ 431-1299, 431-3001) is at Avs Gobernador Videla and Acceso Oeste in Guaymallén, just beyond the Mendoza city limits. The 'Villa Nueva' trolley from Lavalle, between Av San Martín and San Juan, goes there, but it's walking distance for many people.

Car Rental cars can be difficult to get at the airport, but it may be easier in town. Avis (☎ 429-6403) is at Primitivo de la Reta 914, Localiza (☎ 449-1492) at Gutiérrez 470, and Hertz (☎ 425-5666) at Buenos Aires 536.

AROUND MENDOZA

There are varied sights and recreational opportunities in and near Mendoza. Almost all of them are possible day trips, but some more distant ones would be more suitable for at least an overnight stay.

Wineries

Wineries in the province yield nearly 70% of the country's production; most of those near Mendoza offer tours and tasting. Southeast of downtown in Maipú, **Bodega La Colina de Oro** (☎ 497-6777), Ozamis 1040, is open weekdays 9 am to 7 pm, weekends 9 am to 11 pm. Take bus No 150 or 151 from downtown.

In Coquimbito, Maipú, **Bodega Peñaflor** (☎ 497-2388), on Mitre, is open weekdays 8 am to 4 pm. Bus Nos 170, 172, and 173 go there. Also in Coquimbito is **Bodega La Rural** (☎ 497-2013), on Montecaseros, whose Museo Francisco Rutini displays winemaking tools used by 19th-century pioneers, as well as colonial religious sculptures from the Cuyo region. Open weekdays 9 am to 6 pm, weekends 9 am to 11 am only, it produces the highly regarded San Felipe wines.

Bodega Santa Ana (☎ 421-1000), at Roca and Urquiza, Villa Nueva, Guaymallén, opens weekdays 8:30 am to 5 pm; take Bus No 200 ('Buena Nueva via Godoy Cruz'). **Bodega Escorihuela** (☎ 424-2744), Belgrano 1188 in Godoy Cruz, is open weekdays 9:30 am to 4:30 pm. Take bus 'T.'

Bodegas Chandon (☎ 490-0040), at Km 29 of RN 40 in Luján de Cuyo, south of Mendoza, has five guided tours every weekday between 9:30 am and 3:30 pm from April to January. In February and March, there's an additional 5 pm tour weekdays and three tours Saturday morning.

Calvario de la Carrodilla

A national monument since 1975, this church in Carrodilla, Godoy Cruz, houses an image of the Virgin of Carrodilla, the patron of vineyards, brought from Spain in 1778. A center of pilgrimage for Mendocinos and other Argentines, it also has samples of indigenous colonial sculpture. Reached by bus Nos 10 and 200, it is open weekdays 10 am to noon and 5 to 8 pm.

Cacheuta

About 40km west of Mendoza in the department of Luján de Cuyo, Cacheuta (altitude 1237m) is renowned for its medicinal thermal waters and agreeable microclimate. Since 1986, the facilities at ***Hotel Termas Cacheuta*** *(☎ 02624-482082, 0261-431-6085, fax 0261-431-6089 in Mendoza)* have undergone modernization, and singles/doubles now cost US$115/192 with full board. The rooms are pleasant but unexceptional for the price, which includes hot tubs, massage, mountain bikes, and recreation programs. The local mailing address is Rodríguez Peña 1412, Godoy Cruz, Mendoza; in Buenos Aires (☎ 011-4322-8340, fax 4322-5672), the mailing address is Tucumán 672. Nonguests may use the baths for US$10 per person.

Besides the hotel complex, there are also ***Camping Termas de Cacheuta***, at Km 39 of RN 7, and the well-regarded restaurant ***Mis Montañas***.

Potrerillos

Passing through a typical precordillera landscape along the Río Blanco, the main source of drinking water for the capital, westbound RN 7 leads to the Andean resort of Potrerillos (altitude 1351m), 45km from Mendoza. Bird watching is excellent in summer, but the area is also becoming a mecca for white-water rafting.

The ***Camping del ACA***, on RN 7 at Km 50, costs US$10 per site for members, US$12 for nonmembers. There are two hotels: the modest ***Hotel de Turismo*** and the luxurious ***Gran Hotel Potrerillos*** *(☎ 0261-423-3000)*, which charges US$78/84 with breakfast, US$96/120 with half-board, and US$114/156 with full board. The town also contains the restaurant ***Armando***.

Opposite the ACA campground, Argentina Rafting Expediciones (☎/fax 02624-482037, chemartin@cpsarg.com) arranges white-water rafting and kayaking on the Río Mendoza and the Diamante (near San Rafael), as well as trekking and mountain biking. River trips range from a 5km, half-hour Class II (US$10) to a 50km, five-hour Class III-IV descent over two days (US$120). Transfers from and to Mendoza cost an additional US$10.

Río Extremo Rafting (☎/fax 02624-482007, cellular 02611-5563-0986, 02611-5563-6558, rioextremo@lanet.losandes.com.ar), Av Los Cóndores s/n, or Güemes 785, Dpto 9, Godoy Cruz in Mendoza, also descends the Río Mendoza.

Termas Villavicencio

Mineral water from Villavicencio is now sold throughout the country, though early travelers were unimpressed with the area. In the 1820s, Francis Bond Head wrote that 'the post of Villavicencio, which in all the maps of South American looks so respectable, now consists of a solitary hut without a window, with a bullock's hide for a door, and with very little roof,' while a few years later Darwin found it a 'solitary hovel.' Neither could have anticipated the spectacular mountain setting would one day host the thermal baths resort of the *Gran Hotel de Villavicencio*, which has been closed for more than a decade because of legal entanglements. The hotel was due to reopen in 1995 but there's been no discernible movement since then.

Panoramic views make the *caracoles* (winding roads) to and beyond Villavicencio (altitude 1800m), 51km northwest of Mendoza on RP 52, an attraction in itself. There is free camping alongside ***Hostería Villavicencio***, which serves simple meals. Expreso Jocolí (☎ 0261-431-4409 in Mendoza), runs buses to Villavicencio Wednesday, Saturday, and Sunday.

Ski Resorts

While wine ages in the barrels, the soil lies barren, and the poplars stand leafless, the snow brings visitors to the province from Argentina and overseas.

Two ski areas, the nearest to Mendoza, are covered here; for fashionable Las Leñas and Los Molles, see the relevant information under Malargüe.

Vallecitos Ranging between 2900 and 3200m in the Cordón del Plata, only 80km southwest of Mendoza, Vallecitos is the area's smallest (only 88 hectares with six downhill runs) and least expensive ski resort. It's open July to early October; for more information, contact Valles del Plata (☎ 0261-431-2713) in Mendoza.

Most skiers stay in Mendoza since the resort is so close, but ***Hostería La Canaleta*** *(☎ 0261-431-2779)* has four-bunk rooms with private bath, a restaurant, and a snack bar. The cheapest accommodations are ***Refugio San Antonio***, which has rooms with shared bath and a restaurant.

Los Penitentes Both scenery and snow cover are excellent at Los Penitentes, 165km west of Mendoza via RN 7, which offers downhill and cross-country skiing at an altitude of 2580m. Lifts and accommodations are modern, and the maximum vertical drop on its 21 runs is more than 700m.

Hostería Los Penitentes has double and quadruple rooms with private bath, plus a restaurant and bar. Weekly rates during the ski season range from US$617 to US$671 singles, US$499 to US$542 doubles. For detailed information, contact the Los Penitentes office (☎ 0261-427-1641), Paso de los Andes 1615, Departamento C, Godoy Cruz.

Another resort hotel is four-star ***Hostería Ayelén*** *(☎ 0261-427-1123, fax 427-1283, ayelen@lanet.losandes.com.ar)*, which charges US$53/70 single/double in summer, US$88/114 in ski season. The postal address is Juan B Justo 1490, 5547 Godoy Cruz, Mendoza.

Five 'apart-hotels' (dormitory-style lodgings) in Los Penitentes also offer maid service, bar, and reception. For more modest accommodations at nearby Puente del Inca, contact Gregorio Yapurai (☎ 0261-430-5118 in Mendoza), who has ***cabañas*** with hot water, kitchen, and fridge for US$18 per person.

Confitería La Herradura is a skiers' hangout. A small ***market*** also keeps long hours.

Parque Provincial Volcán Tupungato

Serious climbers consider 6650m Tupungato a far more challenging and interesting climb than Aconcagua. The main approach is from the town of Tunuyán, 82km south of Mendoza via RN 40, where the Dirección de Turismo (☎ 02622-422193), at República de Siria and Alem, can provide information. Many of the same outfitters who arrange Aconcagua treks can also deal with Tupungato.

USPALLATA

The polychrome mountains surrounding this crossroads village, 1751m above sea level and 105km west of Mendoza via RN 7, so resembles highland central Asia that director Jean-Jacques Annaud used it as the location for the Brad Pitt epic *Seven Years in Tibet*. Uspallata is an excellent base for exploring the scenic sierras, but in the long run, the prosperity of its 3000 inhabitants may rest more on its becoming a *zona franca* (duty-free zone) because of its proximity to Valparaíso, Chile.

Information

Uspallata's tourist office, a kiosk alongside the YPF gas station, was vacant at last pass. There's a post office (postal code 5545) and a branch of Banco de Mendoza, but no ATM. Comunicación Alta Montaña, just north of the highway junction, provides phone services; Uspallata's area code is ☎ 02624.

Things to See & Do

A good rock-climbing area known as **Cerro Montura** is along RN 7 en route to Parque Provincial Aconcagua and Paso de los Libertadores, but farther up the valley the rock is too friable for safe climbing.

One km north of the highway junction, a signed lateral leads to ruins and a museum at the **Bóvedas Históricas Uspallata**, a metallurgical site since pre-Columbian times. There are dioramas of battles on General Gregorio de Las Heras' campaign across the Andes in support of San Martín. About 4km northeast of Uspallata on the Villavicencio road, in a volcanic outcrop known as **Cerro Tunduqueral**, is a faded but still visible set of petroglyphs, near a small monument to San Ceferino Namuncurá.

Mendoza-bound motorists should consider taking the **Caracoles de Villavicencio**, a good gravel road even more scenic than paved RN 7. Ignore the sign at Uspallata that restricts the descent *(bajada)* to 2 to 8 pm and the ascent *(subida)* to 7 am to noon; it's open to two-way traffic at all hours. About 3km past the entrance to the Caracoles is a memorial to Darwin, who discovered fossil *Araucaria* trees here; at present, their distribution is more southerly. At 3800m, 26km from Uspallata, the high point is the **Cruz del Paramillo**, a way station for the Virgin of Fátima, with expansive views of the Andean peaks to the west.

Places to Stay & Eat

Uspallata's poplar-shaded ***Camping Municipal*** *(☎ 420009)*, 500m north of the Villavicencio junction on RP 52, charges US$5.60 per site. The north end of the facilities, near the wood-fire-stoked hot showers, is much quieter and the best place to pitch a tent.

Hotel Viena *(☎ 420046, Av Las Heras 240)*, east of the highway junction, is a bargain at US$15 per person with private bath and cable TV. Closer to the junction, improved, friendly ***Hostería Los Cóndores*** *(☎ /fax 420002, 420303)* costs US$25/35 single/double. All rooms have cable TV, the bathrooms are huge, and it also has an onsite restaurant.

Built by the Confederación de Empleados de Comercio in the late 1940s, ***Hotel Uspallata*** *(☎ 420003)*, about 1km west of the junction, looks a bit shopworn since its Peronist glory days but still offers spacious grounds, tennis courts, a huge swimming pool, a bar, a bowling alley, pool tables, and a restaurant. For US$30/46 with breakfast, it remains one of the country's better values.

At the southern approach to town on RN 7, the highly recommended but still not outrageously expensive ***Hotel Valle Andino*** *(☎ 420033, 0261-425-8424 in Mendoza)* has an indoor pool. Rates are US$37 per person with breakfast, US$47 with half-board, and US$74 with full board. Facilities also include tennis courts, a game room, a reading room, and a TV lounge.

Several parrillas are the main dining alternatives. Behind the YPF station, ***Parrilla San Cayetano*** *(☎ 420049)* is a convenient stop offering decent food for travelers en route to and from Chile. South of the junction is ***El Rancho de Olmedo***; another longtime favorite, ***Dónde Pato*** has moved to roomy new quarters nearby. ***Café Tibet***, in a strip mall across the junction, capitalizes on Uspallata's cinematic notoriety.

Getting There & Away

From new offices just north of the junction, Expreso Uspallata runs three buses every weekday, four on weekends, between Mendoza (US$8) and Uspallata, as far as Puente del Inca. Buses between Mendoza and Santiago will carry passengers to and across the border, but are often full.

PARQUE PROVINCIAL ACONCAGUA

North of RN 7, nearly hugging the Chilean border, Parque Provincial Aconcagua protects 71,000 hectares of the wild high country surrounding South America's and the Western Hemisphere's highest summit, 6960m Cerro Aconcagua. Passing motorists can stop to enjoy the view of the peak from **Laguna Horcones**, a 2km walk from the parking lot just north of the highway, where there's a ranger available 8 am to 9 pm weekdays, 8 am to 8 pm Saturday. There are also rangers at the junction to Plaza Francia, about 5km north of Horcones; at Plaza de Mulas on the main route to the peak; at Las Leñas, on the Polish Glacier Route up the Río de las Vacas to the east; and at Plaza Argentina, the last major camping area along the Polish Glacier Route.

Cerro Aconcagua

Often called the 'roof of the Americas,' the volcanic andesite summit of Aconcagua covers a base of uplifted marine sediments. The origin of the name is unclear; one possibility is the Quechua term *Ackon-Cahuac*, meaning 'stone sentinel,' while another is the Mapuche phrase *Acon-Hue*, signifying 'that which comes from the other side.'

Italian-Swiss climber Mathias Zurbriggen made the first recorded ascent in 1897. Since then, the peak has become a favorite destination for climbers from around the world, even though it is technically less challenging than other nearby peaks, most notably Tupungato to the south. In 1985, the Club Andinista Mendoza's discovery of an Inca mummy at 5300m on the mountain's southwest face proved that the high peaks were a pre-Columbian funerary site.

Reaching the summit requires a commitment of at least 13 to 15 days, including acclimatization time; some climbers prefer the longer but more scenic, less crowded, but also more technical Polish route. Potential climbers should acquire RJ Seeker's climbing guide *Aconcagua* (Seattle, The

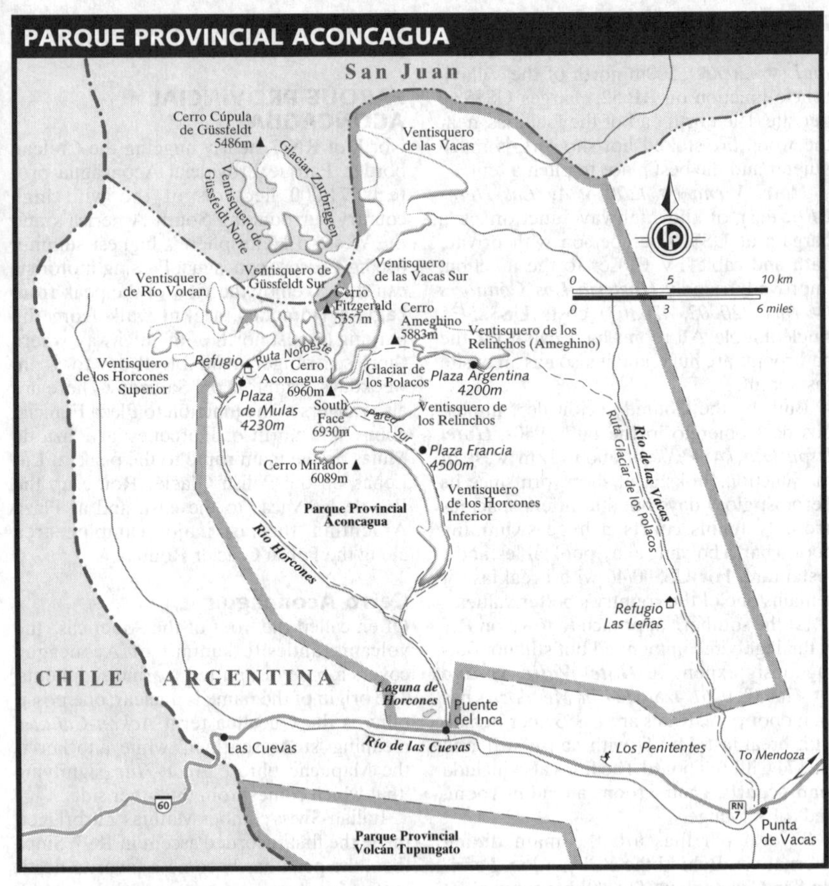

Mountaineers, 1994). There's less detailed information in the 3rd edition of Bradt Publications' *Backpacking in Chile & Argentina*. There is also an Internet information page (www.aconcagua.com.ar).

Nonclimbers can trek to ***base camps*** and ***refugios*** beneath the permanent snow line; note that tour operators and climbing guides set up seasonal tents at the best campsites en route to and at the base camps, so independent climbers and trekkers usually get the leftover spots. On the Northwest Route there is also a rather luxurious and expensive Hotel Plaza de Mulas (☎ radio-telephone 0261-425-7065).

Permits From December to March, permits are obligatory both for trekking and climbing in Parque Provincial Aconcagua; park rangers at Laguna Horcones will not permit visitors to proceed up the Quebrada de los Horcones without one. These permits, which cost US$30 for trekkers (seven days), US$80 for climbers (20 days) in December and February, and US$120 for climbers in January, are available only in Mendoza, at the Dirección de Recursos Naturales Renovables (☎ 0261-425-2090), Av Boulogne Sur Mer s/n, in Parque San Martín. The process is routine, and the office is open weekdays 8 am to 8 pm, weekends 8 am to noon. A shorter, three-day trekking permit is available for US$15 (US$20 in January) to Plaza Francia only, but its lack of flexibility makes it a poorer deal than the permit for the longer period. Argentine nationals pay half price at all times.

Routes There are three main routes up Cerro Aconcagua. The most popular one, approached by a 40km trail from Los Horcones, is the **Ruta Noroeste** (Northwest Route) from Plaza de Mulas, 4230m above sea level. The **Pared Sur** (South Face), approached from the base camp at Plaza Francia via a 36km trail from Los Horcones, is a demanding technical climb.

From Punta de Vacas, 15km southeast of Puente del Inca, the longer but more scenic **Ruta Glaciar de los Polacos** (Polish Glacier Route) first ascends the Río de las Vacas to the base camp at Plaza Argentina, a distance of 76km. Wiktor Ostrowski and others pioneered this route in 1934. Climbers on this route must carry ropes, screws, and ice axes, in addition to the usual tent, warm sleeping bag and clothing, and plastic boots. This route is more expensive because it requires the use of mules for a longer period.

Mules The cost of renting cargo mules, which can carry about 60kg each, has gone through the roof – the standard fee among outfitters is US$120 for the first mule from Puente del Inca to Plaza de Mulas, though two mules cost only US$160. A party of three should pay about US$240 to get their gear to the Polish Glacier Route base camp and back.

For mules, one alternative is Ricardo Jatib's Aconcagua Express (☎ 0261-444-5987). Another reliable muleteer is Fernando Grajales, operating from Hostería Puente del Inca from December through February. One party recommends Carlos Cuesta, who lives next to the cemetery at Puente del Inca.

Puente del Inca

One of Argentina's most striking natural wonders, this stone bridge over the Río Mendoza is 2720m above sea level and 177km from Mendoza. (The Río de las Cuevas just south of the park becomes the Río Mendoza just beyond Punta de Vacas.) From here trekkers and climbers can head north to the base of Aconcagua, south to the pinnacles of **Los Penitentes** (so-named because they resemble a line of monks), or even farther south to 6650m **Tupungato**, an impressive volcano that is partly covered by snow fields and glaciers and a more challenging technical climb than Aconcagua.

Camping Los Puquios is an inexpensive alternative for lodging, as is ***Albergue El Refugio***. The pleasant ***Hostería Puente del Inca*** *(☎ 02624-420222, 0261-438-0480 in Mendoza)* charges US$40/50 single/double with breakfast, though posted prices may be higher. Multibed rooms may be as low as US$25 per person with breakfast. It has a ***restaurant*** and may help arrange trekking

SECRETARÍA DE TURISMO ARGENTINA

Puente del Inca

WAYNE BERNHARDSON

Aconcagua Climbers' Cemetery

and mules. Dinner costs around US$15, but, writes one visitor, the food there 'tastes better *after* the climb.'

Cristo Redentor

Pounded by chilly but exhilarating winds, nearly 4000m above sea level on the Argentine-Chilean border, the rugged high Andes make an fitting backdrop for this famous monument, erected after a territorial dispute between the two countries was settled in 1902. The view is a must-see either with a tour or by private car (since the hairpin road to the top is no longer a border crossing into Chile), but the first autumn snowfall closes the route. At Las Cuevas, 10km before the border, travelers can stay at ***Hostería Las Cuevas***.

Organized Tours

Many of the adventure-travel agencies in and around Mendoza arrange excursions into the high mountains; for their names and addresses see Activities in the Mendoza section. It is also possible to arrange trips with overseas operators; for details, see the Organized Tours entry in the Getting There & Away chapter.

Aconcagua The most established operators are Fernando Grajales (☎ /fax 429-3830), José Francisco Mendoza 898, 5500 Mendoza, and Rudy Parra's Aconcagua Trek (☎ /fax 0261-431-7003), Güiraldes 246, 5519 Dorrego, in Mendoza.

Several guides from the Asociación de Guías de Montaña lead two-week trips to Aconcagua, among them Alejandro Randis (☎ 0261-496-3461), Daniel Pizarro (☎ 0261-423-0698), and Gabriel Cabrera of Rumbo al Horizonte (☎ 0261-452-0641). The trips leave from Mendoza by bus to Puente del Inca, then follow the Ruta Noroeste, partly on mule.

Pared Sur Operadores Mendoza (☎ 425-3334, 423-1883) at Las Heras 420, in Mendoza, has trips of three and six days from Puente del Inca, partly by horse or mule, usually contracted with Fernando Grajales (see Aconcagua above). Trips follow the route that climbers attempting the difficult south face of Aconcagua must traverse.

SAN RAFAEL

Founded as a military outpost, beneath a backdrop of scenic peaks far less frequented than those farther north, San Rafael (population 98,000) is now a modern commercial-industrial center. Like Mendoza, its clean sidewalks, tree-lined streets, and parks are a local pride. San Rafael's acequias are a reminder that, in the surrounding desert, the Río Atuel and the Río Diamante irrigate 60,000 hectares of vineyards producing nationally and internationally known wines by Suter, Bianchi, Lávaque, and others. The Atuel, in particular, is also a popular white-water rafting destination.

Orientation

San Rafael is 230km southeast of the city of Mendoza via RN 40 and RN 143 and 189km northeast of Malargüe via RN 40. The main thoroughfare is RN 143, known as Av Hipólito Yrigoyen west of Av El Libertador/Av San Martín, the city's main north-south axis. East of Libertador/San Martín, RN 143 is known as Av Bartolomé Mitre. Most areas of interest to visitors are northwest of the Yrigoyen-San Martín intersection.

Information

Tourist Offices The Coordinación Municipal de Turismo (☎ 424217, 0800-222-2555), Av Hipólito Yrigoyen 745, has helpful staff and useful brochures and maps. It's open 8 am to 8:30 pm daily (to 10 pm in summer).

Money Mundial Cambios is at Comandante Salas 25. Several banks along Yrigoyen have ATMs, including Banco de la Nación, at Yrigoyen 113.

Post & Communications Correo Argentino is at San Lorenzo and Barcala; the postal code is 5600. Among the many locutorios is Nueva Telefonía, at San Lorenzo 68; the area code is ☎ 02627.

Travel Agencies Among the agencies arranging local excursions is Buttini Hermanos (☎ 421413), Corrientes 495. Leufú (☎/fax 428164), Cabildo 1483, does rafting, mountain biking, and other activities.

Medical Services San Rafael's Hospital Teodoro J Schestakow (☎ 424290) is at Emilio Civit 151, at the corner of Corrientes.

Things to See

Worthwhile sights are **Parque Hipólito Yrigoyen**, at the west end of town, the **Catedral**, at Belgrano and Pellegrini on the north side of Plaza San Martín, and the **Museo de Historia Natural** (☎ 422121 interno 290), 6km from downtown on Isla Río Diamante, an island in the middle of the river.

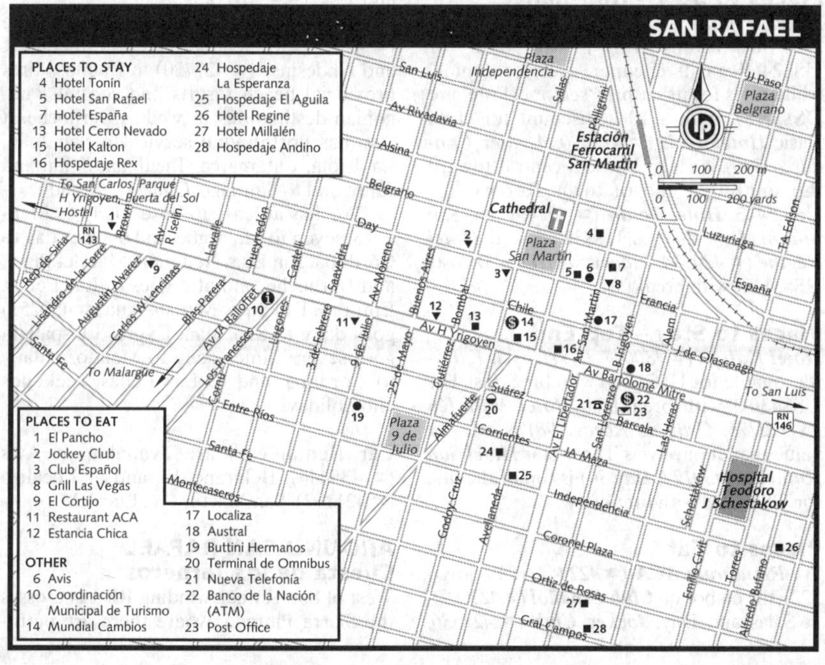

Places to Stay – Budget

Camping On Isla Río Diamante, 6km east of downtown, ***Camping El Parador*** *(☎ 427983)* charges US$5 per tent site.

Hostels The Hostelling International affiliate, ***Puesta del Sol Hostel*** *(☎ 434881, fax 430187, puestaso@hostels.org.ar, Deán Funes 998)* is about 1½km west of the tourist office and costs US$10.

Hospedajes & Hotels The best value in town is ***Hospedaje La Esperanza*** *(☎ 422382, Avellaneda 263)* for US$15/26 with shared bath, US$19/32 with private bath. Alternatives include ***Hospedaje El Aguila*** *(☎ 430886, Entre Ríos 88)* for US$15 per person, ***Hospedaje Rex*** *(☎ 422177, H Yrigoyen 56)* for US$19/29, ***Hospedaje Andino*** *(☎ 421877, General Campos 197)*, and ***Hotel Cerro Nevado*** *(☎ 428209, H Yrigoyen 376)* for US$22/34.

Places to Stay – Mid-Range

Hotel España *(☎ 424055, Av San Martín 270)* has rooms with private bath for US$24/40 in its cheaper 'sector colonial,' while rates for its cushier 'sector celeste' are US$35/57, with a 10% discount for cash. Basic ***Hotel Turis*** *(☎ 428090, Alvarez Condarco 340)* is clean but less central toward the southwest end of town. Rooms cost US$29/43. ***Hotel Tonín*** *(☎ 422499, Av San Martín 327)* charges US$31/50, and ***Hotel Regine*** *(☎ 430274, Independencia 623)* costs US$31/59 with breakfast.

Places to Stay – Top End

Hotel Kalton *(☎ 430047, H Yrigoyen 120)* is reasonable for US$36/64 with breakfast. For US$43/83 with breakfast, ***Hotel Millalén*** *(☎ 422776, Ortíz de Rosas 198)* is a lesser value than it once was. Three-star ***Hotel San Rafael*** *(☎ 430127, Day 30)* is top of the line for US$63/88 with breakfast.

Places to Eat

Try ***Restaurant ACA*** *(☎ 422444, H Yrigoyen 522)*; the elaborate ***Club Español*** *(☎ 422907)*, at Salas and Day; ***Jockey Club*** *(☎ 422336, Belgrano 338)*; or ***El Encuentro***, at Coronel Plaza (the eastward extension of Santa Fe) and Patricias Mendocinas. The local parrillas are on Av H Yrigoyen: ***El Cortijo*** *(☎ 423988) at No 999*, ***El Pancho*** at No 1110, and ***Estancia Chica*** at No 336. ***Grill Las Vegas*** *(☎ 421390, San Martín 226)* is a decent but unexceptional parrilla.

Getting There & Around

Air Austral (☎ 430036), Mitre 102, flies daily to Buenos Aires (US$119 to US$190) via San Juan.

Bus San Rafael's bus station is on Coronel Suárez between Avellaneda and Almafuerte. Most services from Mendoza to Buenos Aires province and points south pass through here, except for those directly to the federal capital. San Rafael does have direct nightly service to Buenos Aires (US$46, 13 hours) with La Estrella (☎ 422079), Expreso Uspallata (☎ 423169), and TAC (☎ 422209).

Other carriers include Alto Valle (☎ 423731) to Neuquén and intermediates, and Andesmar (☎ 427720) to Buenos Aires provincial beach resorts and coastal Patagonian destinations, as well as Bariloche. It also has northbound service to San Juan, La Rioja, Catamarca, Tucumán, Salta, and Jujuy, and to Santiago, Chile, via Mendoza.

TAC has at least 10 buses daily to Mendoza, seven to Malargüe, and one per day to Córdoba, San Luis, Neuquén, Mar del Plata, and Bariloche, and also goes to Las Leñas. Empresa Del Sur y Media Agua (☎ 430251) goes daily to San Juan. Expreso Uspallata goes several times daily to Mendoza, daily to Córdoba, and to Las Leñas weekends and holidays.

Car Rental cars are available at Avis (☎ 435444), Belgrano 17, and at Localiza (☎ 421197), San Martín 116, Local 28.

AROUND SAN RAFAEL

Cuesta de los Terneros

West of San Rafael, winding RP 144 crosses the Sierra Pintada, where there are petro-

SARAH J HAWKINS

Outside of El Calafate, on the way to the Moreno Glacier, Santa Cruz province

ANDREA BOONER

Circuito Grande, Río Negro province

ROBERT RATTNER

Gaucho, Las Pampas

SARAH J HAWKINS

Moreno Glacier, Santa Cruz province

WAYNE BERNHARDSON

Península Valdés, Chubut province

WAYNE BERNHARDSON

Parque Nacional Perito Moreno

glyphs on the **Cuesta de los Terneros**, 32km from the city.

Cañón del Atuel

South along the Río Atuel, RP 173 passes through a multicolored ravine that locals compare to Arizona's Grand Canyon of the Colorado, though much of Cañón del Atuel has been submerged by three hydroelectric dams. Nevertheless, there is white-water rafting on its upper reaches, and Portal del Atuel (☎ 02627-423583), at Km 35, does two-hour descents of the river.

El Nihuil, 79km from San Rafael, is one of the province's main water-sports centers. Its 9600-hectare reservoir, **Dique El Nihuil**, has a constant breeze that makes it suitable for windsurfing and sailing; other activities include swimming, canoeing, and fishing.

The ***Camping Club de Pescadores*** *(☎ 426087)* charges US$10 for tent sites, and rents four-person bungalows for US$80; it also has a restaurant and store. El Nihuil proper has several ***restaurants*** and a gas station.

TAC has buses from San Rafael at 6 am, 11 am, and 6:30 pm.

GENERAL ALVEAR

In the late 19th century, General Diego de Alvear acquired rich valley lands that originally belonged to the Mapuche cacique Goico and populated them with immigrants to form an agricultural colony, now a town of 24,000 on the banks of the Río Atuel and the southeastern gateway to Mendoza province. Among the products are fruits, vegetables, fodder, timber, olives, and wine – you can visit the wineries along the poplar-lined roads around town.

Orientation & Information

General Alvear is 90km east of San Rafael via RN 143. The main thoroughfares, Av Libertador and Av Alvear, divide the town into quadrants, with street names modified by directional indicators.

The tourist office (☎ 424594) at the bus terminal provides information. General Alvear's area code is ☎ 02625.

Places to Stay & Eat

Modest accommodations are available for US$20/35 at ***Hotel Grosso*** *(☎ 420392, Lange 31)*. ***Hotel Salamanca*** *(☎ 424141, Av Alvear Este 802)* costs US$20/36 and also has a restaurant. ***Hotel Buenos Aires*** *(☎ 422972, Lange 54)* charges US$25/44.

The ***Club Español*** *(☎ 422320)*, on Av Alvear Este, is probably the best restaurant.

Shopping

Wine is the thing to buy from wine shops or supermarkets. Wine shops include Vinería Blanco at Av San Martín 463, Vinería El Turista at Mitre 2576, and Vinería Favimar at Av San Martín 235.

Getting There & Away

Buses to and from San Rafael and Mendoza also pass through General Alvear.

MALARGÜE

Pehuenche Indians hunted and gathered in the valley of Malargüe, a term that derives from a Mapuche word meaning either 'Place of Rocky Mesas' or 'Place of Corrals.' Spanish conquistador Francisco de Villagra reached the area in 1551. As in most regions of the country, the 19th-century advance of European agricultural colonists displaced and dispossessed the original inhabitants. Today petroleum is the principal industry, followed by uranium-processing for the Comisión Nacional de Energía Atómica. Malargüe is also a center for outdoor activities.

Malargüe has a wealth of archaeological and paleontologic sites, but nearby cave paintings and petroglyphs are closed for study. Two fauna reserves, Payén and Laguna Llancanelo, are close by, and caving is possible at Caverna de las Brujas and Pozo de las Animas. Upscale Las Leñas offers excellent skiing in winter and hiking in summer.

Orientation & Information

Malargüe (population 18,500) is 189km southwest of San Rafael via paved RP 144 and RN 40, which becomes Av San Martín through town. The Dirección de Turismo y

Medio Ambiente (☎ 471659, 470148, 0800-666-8569) has new facilities at the northern end of town, directly on the highway.

Correo Argentino is at Adolfo Puebla and Saturnino Torres; Malargüe's postal code is 5613. There are several locutorios along Av San Martín; the area code is ☎ 02627. Banco de Mendoza has an ATM at Av San Martín and Ruibal.

Things to See

At the northern approach to town, Malargüe's **Parque de Ayer** is a shady, professionally landscaped park that also serves as something of an open-air museum for objects that won't fit into the regional museum. Just south of the park, the **Molino de Rufino Ortega** is a former flour mill built by the town's founder.

In the *casco*, or the 'big house' of Ortega's former estancia, just north of the park and south of the tourist office, the **Museo Regional Malargüe** (☎ 471659) is a collection of odds and ends that's more amusing than instructive. In summer, it is open Tuesday to Friday 8 am to 1 pm and 3 to 7 pm, weekends 9 am to noon and 4 to 8 pm; the rest of the year, hours are 10 am to 6 pm Tuesday to Sunday. Admission is free.

Places to Stay & Eat

Malargüe has abundant, reasonably priced accommodations, though prices rise during ski season. Open all year, ***Camping Municipal Malargüe*** *(☎ 470691)*, on Alfonso Capdevila at the north end of town, charges US$5 per site.

Hotel Bambi *(☎ 471237, Av San Martín 410)* is the cheapest in town at US$20/35 single/double with private bath. Plain but comfortable ***Hotel Turismo*** *(☎ 471042, Av San Martín 224)* costs US$24/35 with breakfast and private bath. The ***Hotel Rioma*** *(☎ 471065, Fray Inalicán 68)* costs US$25/38, while rates at ***Hotel Reyén*** *(☎ 471429, Av San Martín 938)* are US$30/45.

The best in town, well-regarded ***Hotel Portal del Valle*** *(☎ 471294)*, RN 40 s/n at the north end of town, costs US$50 per person with half-board.

La Posta *(☎ 471306, Av Roca 374)* serves local specialities such as *chivito* (barbecued goat) and trout.

Getting There & Away

Air There are flights to and from Buenos Aires in ski season only, leaving from the Aeródromo Malargüe (☎ 471600) at the south end of town. The Aerolíneas/Austral representative is Karen Travel (☎ 470342), Av San Martín 1056.

Bus The Terminal de Ómnibus is at the corner of Av General Roca and Aldao. To Mendoza, TAC (☎ 471286) has at least two direct buses daily plus others requiring a change of bus in San Rafael; Expreso Uspallata (☎ 470514) has one per day. Transporte Viento Sur (☎ 470486), San Martín 891, has 4 am and 7 pm buses to Mendoza (4½ hours, US$20).

There is summer service, once or twice weekly, from Malargüe across the 2500m Paso Pehuenche and down the spectacular canyon of the Río Maule to Talca, Chile.

Getting Around

For transport to Las Leñas ski resort (about US$10 roundtrip), contact Transportes Payún (☎ 471426), at Av Roca 416, Transporte San Martín (☎ 471710), at General Villegas 429, or Turilmalar (☎ 470812), which is also a travel agency at Av San Martín and Saturnino Torres.

AROUND MALARGÜE

Caverna de Las Brujas

Malargüe travel agencies arrange excursions (US$20 per person with an obligatory guide) to this limestone cave on Cerro Moncol, 72km south of Malargüe and 8km north of Bardas Blancas along RN 40. The nearby Bosques Petrificados de Llano Blanco, containing petrified Araucaria trees over 120 million years old, is 8km from Bardas Blancas via RN 40 and a 2km lateral.

Los Molles

Los Molles is a small, quiet resort along RP 222 in the transverse valley of the Río

Salado, 55km northwest of Malargüe. Single 1100m lifts carry skiers up the relatively gentle slopes, covering 90 hectares, while the thermal baths provide a local attraction. On the road to more exclusive Las Leñas, Los Molles' accommodations include the 155-room ***Hotel Lahuen-Co*** *(☎ 02627-499700)* and the ***Hotel Hualum*** *(☎ 02627-499701)*, but there are also a couple small ***guesthouses***. It is cheaper to stay here and ski at Las Leñas, but Los Molles lacks the larger resort's nightlife.

LAS LEÑAS

Designed primarily to attract wealthy foreigners, Las Leñas is Argentina's most self-consciously prestigious ski resort, but despite the glitter it's not totally out of the question for budget travelers. Since opening in 1983, it has attracted an international clientele who spend their days on the slopes and nights partying until the sun comes up.

Open mid-June to early October, with international competitions every year, Las Leñas is 445km south of Mendoza, 200km southwest of San Rafael, and only 70km from Malargüe, all via RN 40 and RP 222.

Its 33 runs cover 3300 hectares; the area has a base altitude of 2200m, but the slopes reach 3430m for a maximum drop of 1230m. One of the runs has lights and music twice a week, and there is a ski school with classes at several levels, taught in Spanish, English, French, German, Italian, and Portuguese.

Outside ski season, Las Leñas is also attempting to attract summer visitors who enjoy weeklong packages stressing activities such as windsurfing, mountain biking, horseback riding, and hiking. Rates start around US$620 per person, double occupancy, with full board at Hotel Piscis (see Places to Stay & Eat); slightly cheaper apart-hotels, lodging four to six persons per unit, also have access to facilities at the Piscis.

Arrange both winter and summer holidays through Badino Turismo (☎ 011-4326-1351, fax 4393-2568), Perón 725, 6th floor, in Buenos Aires. Las Leñas also has a home page (www.laslenas.com/).

Lift Tickets

Prices for lift tickets vary considerably throughout the ski season, which runs from mid-June to late September. Children's tickets are discounted about 30%. Half-day tickets range from US$18 in low season to US$32 in high season; there are corresponding rates for one-day (US$27 to US$42), three-day (US$80 to US$120), four-day (US$105 to US$160), one-week (US$160 to US$260), 15-day (US$285 to US$475), one-month (US$440 to US$525), and season (US$735) passes.

Lifts function 9 am to 5 pm daily. Rental equipment is readily available.

Ski Packages

Two hotels on or near the slopes offer ski packages that include seven nights' accommodations with unlimited skiing and half-board. Children ages four to 11 get a 20% discount, and children under four are free.

Depending on the time of the season, Hotel Piscis' weekly adult rates range from US$912 to US$2435 per person. Rates at Hotel Escorpio range from US$730 to US$1820, while those at Hotel Aries range from US$750 to US$1490.

In addition, apart-hotels offer similar packages without meals but do have kitchenettes. Rates range from US$360 to US$1365 per person. For more hotel information, see the Places to Stay & Eat entry.

Places to Stay & Eat

Las Leñas has a small village with three luxury hotels *(☎ 02627-471100 for all)*, the most extravagant of which is 99-room ***Hotel Piscis***, which has wood-burning stoves, a gymnasium, sauna facilities, a swimming pool, the restaurant ***Las Cuatro Estaciones***, a bar, a casino, and shops. The others are 47-room ***Hotel Escorpio*** and ***Hotel Aries***. There are also small ***self-catering apartments*** with two to six beds and shared bathrooms, restaurants like ***El Brasero*** and ***Johnny's***, and a ***supermarket***.

Budget travelers can stay more economically at Los Molles, 20km down the road, or at Malargüe, 70km away.

Getting There & Away

In season, there are charter flights from Buenos Aires to Malargüe for US$320 roundtrip, including transfers to and from Las Leñas. Airport transfers alone cost US$25 roundtrip to Malargüe, US$90 to San Rafael.

There is scheduled bus service in season from Mendoza, San Rafael, and Malargüe with several companies; for details, see the respective city entries.

San Juan Province

If you can disregard the desiccated carcasses of cattle and horses struck by trucks and buses along RN 40 between Mendoza and San Juan, consider stopping to purchase melons and brightly painted gourds arranged in eye-catching geometric patterns at the colorful roadside fruit stands that line the way. While not well known to most foreign travelers, the province offers some truly appealing cultural attractions and rarely visited backcountry.

The province is promoting the improvement of RN 150 over the Andes to La Serena and Coquimbo, Chile, in order to achieve a closer, mutually beneficial economic integration with its western neighbor. Although the 4765m Paso de Agua Negra is considerably higher than the heavily used Uspallata alternative near Mendoza, the drier climate means lower snowfall and theoretically better accessibility – though the Uspallata route is rarely closed for long. The promotion of mining for both precious and base metals, particularly in the departments of Calingasta and Iglesias along the Chilean border, may bring increased traffic to the area.

SAN JUAN

Despite its provincial capital status, modern construction, and wide, tree-lined avenues, San Juan retains the rhythm and cordiality of a small town. With an annual average of nine hours of sun daily, the city is nicknamed Residencia del Sol (Residence of the Sun). El zonda, the dry north wind, often brings withering heat and very high pressure, slowing the pace of local activities. As in Mendoza, the streets are empty during siesta hours, between noon and 4 pm.

Founded as San Juan de la Frontera in 1562 by Juan Jufré de Loaysa y Montesso, the desert city struggled in its early years – in the early 17th century, Vásquez de Espinosa remarked that its 24 Spanish residents were 'poverty stricken' and 'powerless' to convert the area's 800 Huarpe Indians. From colonial times to the present, San Juan has lagged behind larger and more influential Mendoza. Though surrounding vineyards and orchards have grown and improved, it has failed to attract supporting industries and lies off the region's principal transit routes.

A massive 1944 earthquake destroyed the city center, and Juan Perón's subsequent relief efforts are what first made him a national figure. Completely rebuilt since then, the downtown sparkles from the efforts of full-time custodians who sweep the sidewalks, and water and patrol the parks and plazas, shooing people off the manicured lawns. As in Mendoza, people swab the sidewalks with kerosene to keep them shining.

Orientation

San Juan is 170km north of Mendoza via RN 40, which passes through San Juan from north to south, and 1140km from Buenos Aires. Like most Argentine cities, San Juan's grid pattern makes orientation very easy; the addition of cardinal points to street addresses helps even more. East-west Av San Martín and north-south Calle Mendoza divide the city into quadrants. The functional center of town is south of Av San Martín.

Information

Tourist Offices The Ente Provincial de Turismo (Enprotur; ☎ 422-7219), Sarmiento 24 Sur, has a good map of the city and its surroundings plus useful information and brochures on the rest of the province, particularly Parque Provincial Ischigualasto (Valle de la Luna). Hours are 7 am to 9 pm weekdays, 9 am to 9 pm weekends; the satellite office at the bus terminal is open 7 am to 8 pm weekdays, 9 am to 1 pm weekends.

ACA (☎ 422-6625) is at 9 de Julio 802.

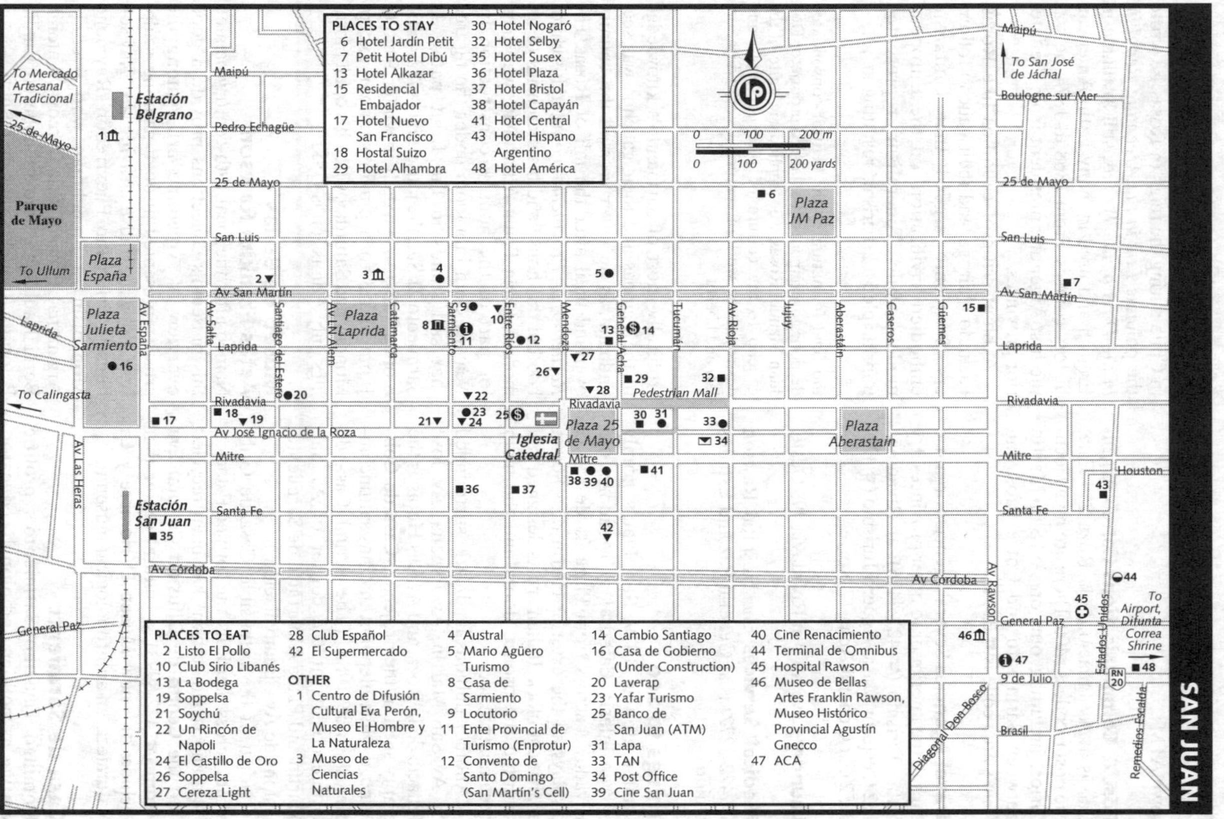
SAN JUAN
PLACES TO STAY
6 Hotel Jardín Petit
7 Petit Hotel Dibú
13 Hotel Alkazar
15 Residencial Embajador
17 Hotel Nuevo San Francisco
18 Hostal Suizo
29 Hotel Alhambra
30 Hotel Nogaró
32 Hotel Selby
35 Hotel Susex
36 Hotel Plaza
37 Hotel Bristol
38 Hotel Capayán
41 Hotel Central
43 Hotel Hispano Argentino
48 Hotel América
PLACES TO EAT
2 Listo El Pollo
10 Club Sirio Libanés
13 La Bodega
19 Soppelsa
21 Soychú
22 Un Rincón de Napoli
24 El Castillo de Oro
26 Soppelsa
27 Cereza Light
28 Club Español
42 El Supermercado
OTHER
1 Centro de Difusión Cultural Eva Perón, Museo El Hombre y La Naturaleza
3 Museo de Ciencias Naturales
4 Austral
5 Mario Agüero Turismo
8 Casa de Sarmiento
9 Locutorio
11 Ente Provincial de Turismo (Enprotur)
12 Convento de Santo Domingo (San Martín's Cell)
14 Cambio Santiago
16 Casa de Gobierno (Under Construction)
20 Laverap
23 Yafar Turismo
25 Banco de San Juan (ATM)
31 Lapa
33 TAN
34 Post Office
39 Cine San Juan
40 Cine Renacimiento
44 Terminal de Omnibus
45 Hospital Rawson
46 Museo de Bellas Artes Franklin Rawson, Museo Histórico Provincial Agustín Gnecco
47 ACA
Estación Belgrano
Estación San Juan
Parque de Mayo
Plaza España
Plaza Julieta Sarmiento
Plaza Laprida
Plaza 25 de Mayo
Iglesia Catedral
Plaza JM Paz
Plaza Aberastain
Pedestrian Mall
To Mercado Artesanal Tradicional
To Ullum
To Calingasta
To San José de Jáchal
To Airport, Difunta Correa Shrine
0 100 200 m
0 100 200 yards
Maipú
Pedro Echagüe
25 de Mayo
San Luis
Av San Martín
Laprida
Rivadavia
Av José Ignacio de la Roza
Mitre
Santa Fe
Av Córdoba
General Paz
Av Las Heras
Av España
Av Salta
Santiago del Estero
Av LN Alem
Catamarca
Sarmiento
Entre Ríos
Mendoza
General Acha
Tucumán
Av Rioja
Jujuy
Aberastain
Caseros
Güemes
Av Rawson
Boulogne sur Mer
Houston
Estados Unidos
9 de Julio
Brasil
Diagonal Don Bosco
Remedios Escalda
RN 20

Money Cambio Santiago is at General Acha 52 Sur, and there are several downtown ATMs.

Post & Communications Correo Argentino is at Av Ignacio de la Roza 259 Este; the postal code is 5400. There are many locutorios, including one on Av San Martín between Sarmiento and Entre Ríos; San Juan's area code is ☎ 0264.

Travel Agencies Several agencies organize trips to the interior or to other provinces. Try Yafar Turismo (☎ 421-4476), at Rivadavia 182 Oeste, or Mario Agüero Turismo (☎ 422-3652), at General Acha 17 Norte.

Laundry Laverap is at Rivadavia 498 Oeste.

Medical Services The Hospital Rawson (☎ 422-2272) is at General Paz and Estados Unidos.

Things to See

Inaugurated in 1979, San Juan's grimly barren **Iglesia Catedral**, at Mendoza and Rivadavia across from Plaza 25 de Mayo, displays all the exterior charm of a Soviet apartment block. Italian artists designed and sculpted the bronze doors and the main ornaments inside.

Another dubious landmark, surrounded by Av San Martín, Av España, Av Jose Ignacio de la Roza, and Av Las Heras, is the empty shell of the projected **Casa de Gobierno**, a white elephant that has sat uncompleted since 1985. (The actual Casa de Gobierno sits at the corner of Av San Martín and Paula Albarracín de Sarmiento, just inside Av Circunvalación.)

North of the ostensible Casa de Gobierno, across San Luis, the former Estación Belgrano (train station) has been recycled into the **Centro de Difusión Cultural Eva Perón** (☎ 422-8993), a cultural center that includes the new **Museo El Hombre y La Naturaleza**, an anthropological museum.

Casa de Sarmiento

Domingo Faustino Sarmiento's prolific writing as politician, diplomat, educator, and journalist made him a public figure both within and beyond Argentina. Exiled in Chile during the reign of Rosas, he wrote the polemic *Life in the Argentine Republic in the Days of the Tyrants*, still available in English and used in many Latin American history courses. From 1868 to 1874, he was the first Argentine president from the interior provinces.

A blunt critic of caudillos like Rosas, Facundo Quiroga, and their gaucho followers, Sarmiento argued that Unitarism embodied 'civilization' on the European model, while Federalism represented unprincipled 'barbarism,' resulting in ...

> the final formation of the central consolidated despotic government of the landed proprietor Don Juan Manuel Rosas, who applied the knife of the gaucho to the culture of Buenos Ayres, and destroyed the work of centuries – of civilisation, law and liberty.

Ironically, most of Sarmiento's knowledge of the Pampas and their gauchos was secondhand, as he never crossed the country overland until after the fall of Rosas. His *Recuerdos de Provincia* recounted his childhood in this house and his memories of his mother, Doña Paula Albarracín, who paid for part of the house's construction by weaving cloth in a loom under the fig tree that still stands in the front patio. At Sarmiento 21 Sur, the museum (☎ 422-4603) is open 9 am to 7 pm daily in winter, 9 am to 1 pm and 3 to 8 pm in summer except Monday and Saturday, when it's open mornings only. Admission is US$1.

Museo de Bellas Artes Franklin Rawson

Named after the local 19th-century painter, this museum's collections provide a good overview of Argentine art. Among the artists represented through painting, sculpture, drawing, and engraving are Rawson himself, Prilidiano Pueyrredón, Raymond Monvoisin (a Frenchman who lived in Argentina), Ernesto de la Cárcova, Antonio Berni, Raúl Soldi, Lino Spilimbergo, Emilio Petorutti, Raquel Forner, and others.

At General Paz 737 Este, the museum (☎ 422-8104) is open weekdays 9 am to 12:30 pm. Admission is free.

Museo Histórico Provincial Agustín Gnecco

In the same building as the Museo de Bellas Artes, this museum has a notable collection of historical material related to San Juan's colonial life and political development. It also has some archaeological artifacts and an exceptional coin collection assembled by the historian whose name it bears. Admission is free.

Convento de Santo Domingo

At Av San Martín and Entre Ríos, the present Dominican convent, constructed after the earthquake, lacks the grandeur of the 17th-century original, the order's richest in the territory. The only part of the old building to survive the quake was the cell occupied by San Martín, who during several brief visits in 1815, held meetings to solicit political and financial support for his Ejército de los Andes, one of whose local divisions liberated Coquimbo and La Serena, Chile. The original furnishings and some other materials are on display in the small museum at Laprida 96 Oeste, open Monday to Saturday 9 am to noon in summer, 9 am to 7 pm daily the rest of the year. Admission is free.

Museo de Ciencias Naturales

The San Juan natural sciences museum's most interesting specimen is the skeleton of the dinosaur *Herrerasaurus* from Ischigualasto, but most of the provincial minerals, fossils, and other exhibits here are so poorly organized and interpreted that the entire facility is marginal. At Av San Martín 315 Oriente, the museum (☎ 421-6774) is open 8 am to 1 pm and 3 to 8 pm weekdays, 9 am to noon Saturdays; free admission.

Mercado Artesanal Tradicional

Inaugurated in 1985 to promote local handicrafts, the market is in the Parque de Mayo, at 25 de Mayo and Urquiza, beneath the Auditorio Juan Victoria. Particularly attractive are the brightly colored *mantas* (shawls) of Jáchal, and the warm ponchos. Besides textiles, there is pottery, riding gear, and basketry, as well as traditional silver knife handles, *mate* gourds, and key chains. The market is open weekdays.

Wineries

For samples of the region's famed *blanco sanjuanino* (white wine) and champagne, visit **Antigua Bodega Chirino** (☎ 421-4327), Salta 782 Norte. Hours are 8:30 am to 12:30 pm daily, and 4:30 to 8:30 pm daily except Sunday.

In the eastern suburb of San Martín, **Bodega Peñaflor** (☎ 497-1031, 497-1060, ask for English-speaking Hugo Torres) manufactures the popular but mass-produced Termidor wines and also gives tours. Catch bus No 13 ('San Martín') on Av Córdoba.

Organized Tours

San Juan travel agencies (see Information) arrange trips to some of the province's better but less easily accessible visitor attractions, including Parque Provincial Ischigualasto (US$52), Calingasta/Barreal (US$35), Dique Ullum (US$16), and Jáchal/Pismanta (US$42).

Raphael Joliat (☎ 434-3014), a San Juan-based Swiss citizen, conducts backcountry vehicle tours for between US$70 and US$120 per person per day.

Places to Stay – Budget

Camping The municipal site, ***El Pinar Camping***, is on Av Benavídez Oeste, 6km from downtown. Reached by Empresa de la Marina buses, it has a small artificial lake, a swimming pool, and a forest plantation. Charges are US$3 per person and US$2 per tent. There are other sites west of the city, where Av San Martín becomes RP 14 to Dique Ullum and Parque Rivadavia. Take bus No 23 (Zonda) or No 29 (Ullum).

Pensions & Residenciales There are several convenient, inexpensive lodgings, some of which charge by the hour. Near the bus terminal, small rooms with shared bath at friendly ***Hotel Hispano Argentino***

(Estados Unidos 381 Sur) cost US$10 per person. Similar in standard is ***Hotel Susex*** *(España 348 Sur)*, for US$15 per person.

Residencial Embajador *(☎ 422-5520, Av Rawson 25 Sur)* has nice, clean rooms at US$15/25 single/double. Tidy ***Hotel Central*** *(☎ 422-3174, Mitre 131 Este)* is central but quiet, has firm beds, and costs US$19/36 with private bath. The new ***Petit Hotel Dibú*** *(☎ 420-1034)*, Av San Martín and Patricias Sanjuaninas, has spotless, spacious rooms with breakfast for US$20/36.

Places to Stay – Mid-Range

Mid-range hotels show more variation in price than in standards and services. All offer telephones, heating, air-con, and parking. Some have a restaurant or confitería.

The best values in this category are ***Hotel América*** *(☎ 421-4514, 9 de Julio 1052 Este)*, which charges US$25/36 with private bath, and ***Hotel Plaza*** *(☎ 422-5179, Sarmiento 344 Sur)*, where rates are US$29/38. Plain but spotless, ***Hotel Nuevo San Francisco*** *(☎ 427-2821, fax 422-3760, Av España 284 Sur)* is also friendly and comfy for US$30/34, US$34/42 with air-con.

Hotel Alhambra *(☎ 422-8280, General Acha 180 Sur)* has rooms for US$34/46; in the same range is ***Hotel Selby*** *(☎ 422-4777, Av Rioja 183 Sur)*. The attractive new ***Hostal Suizo*** *(☎ 422-4293, Av Salta 272 Sur)* charges US$35/40. ***Hotel Bristol*** *(☎ 422-2629, Entre Ríos 368 Sur)* and ***Hotel Jardín Petit*** *(☎ 421-1825, 25 de Mayo 345 Este)* both cost US$38/50.

Places to Stay – Top End

San Juan's costliest hotels are comfortable but less luxurious than those in Mendoza. ***Hotel Capayán*** *(☎ 422-5122, Mitre 31 Este)* costs US$41/55, while ***Hotel Nogaró*** *(☎ 422-7501, Ignacio de la Roza 132 Este)* charges US$54/69. At five-star ***Hotel Alkazar*** *(☎ 421-4965, Laprida 82 Este)* rates are US$98/120 with breakfast.

Places to Eat

One of San Juan's small pleasures are the numerous downtown *carritos* (carts) selling gulps of ice-cold, freshly squeezed orange juice for about US$0.60. Juices are also good at ***Cereza Light***, at Mendoza and Laprida.

The ***Club Sirio Libanés*** *(☎ 422-3841, Entre Ríos 33 Sur)* serves moderately priced Middle Eastern food in a very pleasant environment of beautifully conserved tiles and woodwork. The more somber ***Club Español*** *(☎ 422-3389, Rivadavia 32 Este)* has ordinary food and erratic service. ***La Bodega*** *(☎ 421-4965, Laprida 82 Este)*, in the Hotel Alkazar, is a sumptuous, expensive French restaurant. Near the outskirts of town, on Av Circunvalación near Av San Martín, ***Wiesbaden*** *(☎ 426-1869)*, on Av Circunvalación near Av San Martín, has good German food.

La Nonna María *(☎ 426-2277)*, west of downtown at Av San Martín and Perito Moreno, has excellent pasta. ***Pirandello*** *(☎ 426-0260, San Martín 3105 Oeste)* is an outstanding sandwich place. ***El Supermercado***, on General Acha between Santa Fe and Córdoba, is a traditional market with good paella. The vegetarian ***Soychú*** *(☎ 422-1939, Ignacio de la Roza 223 Oeste)* serves a highly recommended tenedor libre lunch.

Bigotes *(☎ 422-6665, Las Heras 647 Sur)* has tenedor libre beef, chicken, and salads for a reasonable price. For parrillada, try also ***Nahuel*** at Av Circunvalación and Salta, ***Las Leñas*** *(☎ 423-2100, Av San Martín 1670 Oeste)*, ***El Castillo de Oro*** *(☎ 427-3615, Av Ignacio de la Roza 199 Oeste)*, and ***Las Cubas*** *(☎ 423-4979)*, Av San Martín and Perito Moreno.

Un Rincón de Napoli *(Rivadavia 175 Oeste)* has a wide selection of pizzas and good beer; it's a bit dingy, but also prepares food to go. ***Listo El Pollo*** *(☎ 422-3512)*, at Av San Martín and Santiago del Estero, specializes in grilled chicken.

For ice cream, there are two branches of ***Soppelsa*** *(Av Ignacio de la Roza 639 Oeste, Mendoza 163 Sur)*.

Entertainment

San Juan has two downtown cinemas: the two-screen ***Cine San Juan*** *(☎ 423-3503, Mitre 41 Este)* and the ***Cine Renacimiento***, at the corner of Mitre and General Acha.

Shopping

At the entrance to the Ente Provincial de Turismo, the main tourist office at Sarmiento 24 Sur, artisanal pottery, crafts, wines, and dried fruits are for sale.

Getting There & Away

Air Austral (☎ 422-0205), Av San Martín 215 Oeste, flies twice daily to Aeroparque in Buenos Aires (US$75 to US$149) except Sunday (once only) and daily except Saturday to San Luis.

Lapa (☎ 421-6039), Av José Ignacio de la Roza 160, flies Monday, Wednesday, and Friday to Aeroparque (US$59 to US$149); and Tuesday, Thursday, Saturday, and Sunday to Mendoza (US$20 to US$35).

TAN (☎ 427-5875), Av José Ignacio de la Roza 288 Este, flies Tuesday, Thursday, and weekends to Córdoba (US$50 to US$70), and weekends to Mendoza (US$80 to US$90) and Neuquén (US$98 to US$115).

Bus The Terminal de Ómnibus (☎ 422-1604) is at Estados Unidos 492 Sur. There are international services to Santiago, Viña del Mar, and Valparaíso with Tas Choapa (☎ 421-4465), TAC (☎ 421-4108), La Estrella (☎ 422-1365), and Covalle Bus. All of these involve a change in Mendoza.

Autotransportes San Juan Mar del Plata (☎ 422-1105) has six buses daily to Buenos Aires and service to Mar del Plata on Tuesday, Friday, and Saturday. Chevallier (☎ 422-2871) goes to Córdoba, with a connection to Buenos Aires. Empresa Socasa (☎ 422-1120) has two buses daily to Córdoba, one via La Rioja. Buses 20 de Junio (☎ 422-1870) goes to Córdoba, via the scenic Altas Cumbres route, and to Pismanta.

TAC serves Mendoza, northern San Juan (Jáchal), Bariloche in the south, and San Luis, Merlo, and Paraná in the east. Empresa del Sur y Media Agua (☎ 422-3799) has frequent buses to Mendoza and daily service to Rosario and Neuquén. La Estrella has direct buses to Mendoza, La Rioja, Catamarca, and Tucumán.

Ticsa (☎ 421-4175) goes every afternoon to Bahía Blanca. Andesmar (☎ 422-2871) goes to beach resorts in Buenos Aires province and to Salta and Jujuy, where there are further services with Bosio (☎ 421-7745), Autotransportes Mendoza (☎ 421-7735), and El Rápido (☎ 421-4532).

Empresa Vallecito (☎ 422-1181) has a daily bus to Caucete, the Difunta Correa Shrine, and San Agustín del Valle Fértil; and a nightly bus to Chilecito at 10:15 pm. Among them, TAC, Empresa del Sur y Media Agua, and 20 de Julio have five buses daily to Jáchal.

Sample fares include Difunta Correa (US$3, one hour), Mendoza (US$10, two hours), Pismanta (US$14), San Luis (US$15), La Rioja (US$15, six hours), Córdoba (US$25, eight hours), Catamarca (US$26, eight hours), Santiago de Chile (US$30, nine hours), Rosario (US$30, 12 hours), Tucumán (US$33, 13 hours), Buenos Aires (US$40 to US$60, 16 hours), Neuquén (US$49, 15 hours), Salta (US$50, 17 hours), Bahía Blanca (US$69, 16 hours), Jujuy (US$55, 18½ hours), Mar del Plata (US$70), and Bariloche (US$72).

Getting Around

Aeropuerto Las Chacritas (☎ 425-0487) is 13km southeast of town on RN 20. A taxi or remise costs about US$10. For car rental, try Localiza (☎ 421-9494), at Av Rioja 1187 Sur.

AROUND SAN JUAN

Dique Ullum

Only 18km west of San Juan, this 3200-hectare reservoir is a center for nautical sports – swimming, fishing, kayaking, water-skiing, and windsurfing (though no rental equipment is available). Bus No 23 from Av Salta or No 29 from the terminal via Av Córdoba both go hourly to the dam outlet.

There's a good hike, however, from the outlet to the 1800m summit of **Cerro Tres Marías** in the Serranía de Marquesado on the south side of the reservoir. Get off the bus from San Juan at El Castillito/El Paredón del Dique resturant and climb the Stations-of-the-Cross Trail, then continue 1½ hours southwest over the dry hills to the summit. Take plenty of water, since it's very hot and exposed; early morning and late

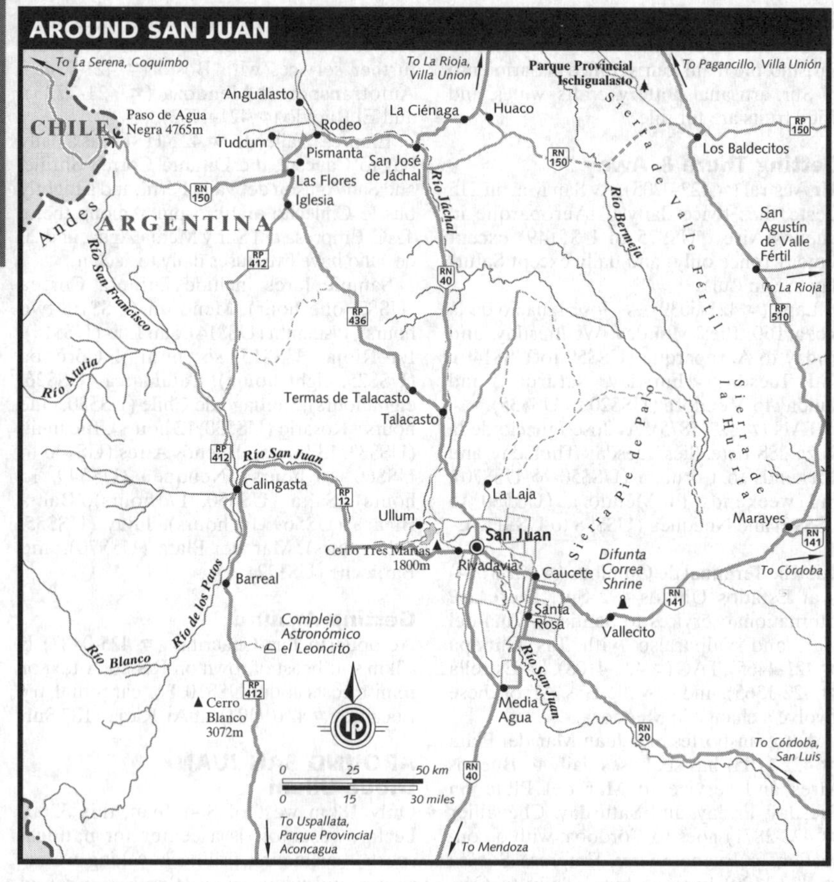

afternoon are the best times to enjoy the panoramic views.

Museo Arqueológico La Laja

Focusing on regional prehistory, this museum (part of the provincial university) has seven display rooms, organized chronologically from the Fortuna culture of 6500 BC to the Incas and their trans-Andean contemporaries, with mummies, basketry, tools of many different materials, sculptures, petroglyphs, and the remains of cultivated plants.

The Moorish-style building was once a hotel that featured thermal baths, which are still in use – after your visit, enjoy a hot soak for US$4. The museum grounds include reproductions of natural environments, farming systems, petroglyphs, and house types, all built to scale.

To reach the museum, 25km north of San Juan in the village of La Laja, take any bus No 20 ('Albardón') from Av Córdoba in San Juan. Buses at 8:20 and 10:30 am, and 1:15, 3:25, and 5 pm, go all the way; if you miss any of them, take any No 20 to Las Piedritas and hitch the last 5km with trucks or other vehicles going to the quarry across from the museum. The museum is open 9 am to 5:30 pm daily; admission is US$2.

Reserva Nacional El Leoncito

West of San Juan, RP 12 climbs the valley of the Río San Juan, between the Sierras del Tigre to the north and the Sierra del Tontal to the south, before arriving at the village of Calingasta and intersecting southbound RP 412, to Barreal and Uspallata (Mendoza province).

South of Barreal, 76,000-hectare Reserva Nacional El Leoncito occupies a former estancia that is typical of the Andean precordillera. The reserve is the site of two observatories, the **Complejo Astronómico El Leoncito** and the **Observatorio Astronómico Doctor Carlos U Cesco.**

Calingasta's modest ***Hotel Calingasta*** *(☎ 02648-421033)* charges US$15 per person; there's also a municipal ***campground***. Barreal's wider range of accommodations include ***Posada San Eduardo*** *(☎ 02648-441046)* for US$35/50 with breakfast, ***Hotel Barreal*** *(☎ 02648-441104)*, and a ***campground*** (US$8 per site). There are also several restaurants, including recommended ***Isidoro***. The El Triunfo bus to Mendoza leaves at 5:55 am Friday and 4:25 pm Sunday (US$11, four hours); there is also service from San Juan.

DIFUNTA CORREA SHRINE

At Vallecito, about 60km southeast of San Juan, the shrine of the Difunta Correa, a popular saint, is one of the most fascinating, offbeat cultural phenomena in all of Argentina. While patronizing and pejorative, Sarmiento's commentary on Argentine rural religion in the 19th century provides some idea of what to expect:

> To this, that is, to natural religion, is all religion reduced in the pastoral districts. Christianity exists, like the Spanish idioms, as a tradition which is perpetuated, but corrupted; coloured by gross superstitions and unaided by instruction, rites, or convictions.

Places to Stay & Eat

Unless you're a believer, the Difunta probably makes a better day trip than an overnight stay, but reasonably good accommodations are available at ***Hotel Difunta Correa*** for US$20/25 single/double, and there's one inexpensive ***hostería***. Pilgrims ***camp*** almost anywhere they feel like it.

There is good street food and two quinchos (thatched-roof, open-sided buildings) with minutas plus ***Comedor Don Roque***, which has terrific soup and empanadas on Sundays; it's on RN 20 at the entrance to the village.

Getting There & Away

Empresa Vallecito goes daily from San Juan to the shrine (US$3), but any other eastbound bus, toward La Rioja or Córdoba, will drop passengers at the entrance. On weekends, there are many excursions from Mendoza; see the Mendoza entry for details.

Another alternative is to take a bus to Caucete, midway between San Juan and Vallecito, and go to the offices of Fundación Cementerio Vallecito, where you can catch a lift with the water trucks that serve the shrine.

SAN JOSÉ DE JÁCHAL

Founded in 1751, surrounded by vineyards and olive groves, Jáchal (population 9700) is a charming village with a mix of older adobes and contemporary brick houses where weavers still make ponchos and blankets on 19th-century looms. Jachalleros, the local residents, are renowned for fidelity to indigenous and gaucho crafts traditions; in fact, Jáchal's reputation as the Cuna de la Tradición (Cradle of Tradition) is celebrated during November's Fiesta de la Tradición.

Across from the main plaza, the **Iglesia San José**, a national monument, houses the *Cristo Negro* (Black Christ) or *Señor de la Agonía* (Lord of Agony), a grisly leather image with articulated head and limbs, brought from Potosí in colonial times.

Places to Stay & Eat

There are several campgrounds in the vicinity. ***Hotel San Martín*** *(☎ 02647-420431)*, at

Difunta Correa

Legend has it that during the civil wars of the 1840s, Deolinda Correa followed the movements of her sickly conscript husband's battalion on foot through the deserts of San Juan, carrying food, water, and their baby son in her arms. When her meager supplies ran out, thirst, hunger, and exhaustion killed her, but when passing muleteers found them, the infant was still nursing at the dead woman's breast. There are many versions of this story, but the main points are the same, despite uncertainty that she ever even existed. Commemorating this apparent miracle, her shrine at Vallecito is widely believed to be the site of her death.

Difunta literally means 'defunct'; Correa is her surname. Technically she is not a saint but rather a 'soul,' a dead person who performs miracles and intercedes for people – the child's survival was the first of a series of miracles attributed to her. Since the 1940s, her shrine, originally a simple hilltop cross, has grown into a small village with its own gas station, school, post office, police station, and church. At 17 chapels or exhibit rooms, devotees leave *exvotos* (gifts) in exchange for supernatural favors. In addition, there are two hotels, several restaurants, a commercial gallery with souvenir shops, and offices for the nonprofit organization that administers the site.

A visit to the shrine is an unusual and worthwhile experience even for nonbelievers. The religious imagery and material manifestations resemble no other Christian shrine in Latin America – some people build and leave elaborate models of homes and cars obtained through her intercession. Pilgrims, locals, and even merchants are all eager to talk about the Difunta. It is perhaps the strongest popular belief system in a country that harbors a variety of unusual religious practices independent of Roman Catholicism, the official state religion, even if clearly related to it. They tell of miraculous cures, assistance at difficult childbirth, economic windfalls, and protection of travelers.

In fact, truckers are especially devoted. From La Quiaca, on the Bolivian border, to Ushuaia in Tierra del Fuego, you will see roadside shrines with images of the Difunta Correa, wax candles, small bank notes, and the unmistakable bottles of water left to quench her thirst. At some sites, there appears to be enough parts to build a car from scratch – do not mistake wheels, brake shoes and crankshafts for piles of trash – but refrain from taking anything away unless you really need it, since it is said that she also has a vengeful streak.

Despite lack of government support and Catholic Church's open antagonism, the shrine has grown as belief in the Difunta Correa has become more widespread. People visit the shrine all year round, but at Easter, May 1, and Christmas, up to 200,000 pilgrims descend on Vallecito. Weekends are busier and more interesting than weekdays.

Etchegaray and Florida, has clean singles/doubles for US$15/23 with shared bath, US$18/30 with private bath. Accommodations at ***Hotel Plaza*** (*☎ 02647-420431, San Juan 545*) are comparable for US$18/28 with shared bath, US$25/45 with private bath. ***El Chatito Flores***, half a block west of the plaza, has good but moderately priced meals.

Getting There & Away

The bus terminal is at the corner of San Juan and Obispo Zapata. Among them, TAC, Empresa del Sur y Media Agua, and 20 de Julio have five buses daily to San Juan, with the former two continuing to Mendoza.

AROUND SAN JOSÉ DE JÁCHAL

A day trip on RN 40 north of San Juan allows visitors to pass through a beautiful landscape, rich with folkloric traditions and rarely seen by foreigners. East of Jáchal, the road climbs the precipitous **Cuesta de Huaco**, with a view of Los Cauquenes dam, before arriving at the village of **Huaco**, whose 200-year-old Viejo Molino (Flour Mill) justifies the trip. It is the birthplace of poet Don Buenaventura Luna, who put the Jachallero culture in the map.

Backtracking to RN 150, you cross the **Cuesta del Viento** and pass through the tunnels of Rodeo to the west of Jáchal to the department of Iglesia, home of the precordillera thermal baths of **Pismanta**. The 42°C waters are recommended for rheumatic ailments, circulation, and general cleansing and relaxation. For US$58 per person with full board, ***Hotel Termas de Pismanta*** *(☎ 02647-497002)* has rooms with private bath and a swimming pool. Budget travelers can try ***Hospedaje La Olla*** *(☎ 02647-497003)* for US$8 per person.

RN 150 continues westwards to La Serena and Coquimbo, both in Chile, via the 4765m **Paso de Agua Negra**. South of Pismanta, RP 436 returns to RN 40 and San Juan. Another worthwhile stop is **Iglesia**, a small Andean town where people cultivate fruit (mostly apples), make goat and cow cheeses, and weave blankets, ponchos, and saddlebags.

SAN AGUSTÍN DE VALLE FÉRTIL

Founded in 1788, San Agustín de Valle Fértil (population 3000) is a cheerful village where people sit on the sidewalks on summer evenings greeting passersby, and there are as many bicycles as automobiles; even the usually aggressive Argentine motorist appears to appreciate the relaxed pace. Visitors to Parque Provincial Ischigualasto frequently stay at the town, which celebrates the anniversary of its founding on April 4.

Thanks to San Agustín's temperate climate and high rainfall, the colorful hills, rivers, exuberant flora, and varied fauna contrast dramatically with the desert landscapes of the rest of the province. The main economic activities are farming and animal husbandry, and mining of quartz, mica, and marble plus smaller quantities of granite, gold, and iron.

Orientation & Information

San Agustín lies among the Sierras Pampeanas, gentle sedimentary mountains cut by impressive canyons, 247km northeast of San Juan via RN 141 and RP 510, which continues to Ischigualasto and La Rioja. San Agustín is small enough that locals pay little attention to street names, so ask directions or use the LP map.

Open 7 am to 1 pm and 5 to 10 pm weekdays, 8 am to 1 pm only Saturday, the Dirección de Turismo (on General Acha directly across from the plaza) is exceptionally helpful with general information and can also help arrange car or mule excursions into the backcountry sierras and canyons. The private Cámara de Turismo maintains an office at the bus terminal.

The post office is at Laprida and Mendoza. Modern communications have been slow to reach San Agustín, but there's a public telephone alongside the tourist office; the area code is ☎ 02646. Telefónica also has a locutorio alongside the tourist office.

Things to See & Do

Spending a day by the Río Seco is pleasant and relaxing, whether fishing, sunbathing, or walking. About 300m across the river are the petroglyphs of **Piedra Pintada**; about 500m farther north are the **Morteros Indígenas** (Indian Mortars). At the north end of town, near the Escuela Agrotécnica, is the Diaguita archaeological site known as the **Meseta Ritual**.

The village of **La Majadita**, 7km from San Agustín by mule or cart, is only reachable during the winter dry season, since the road

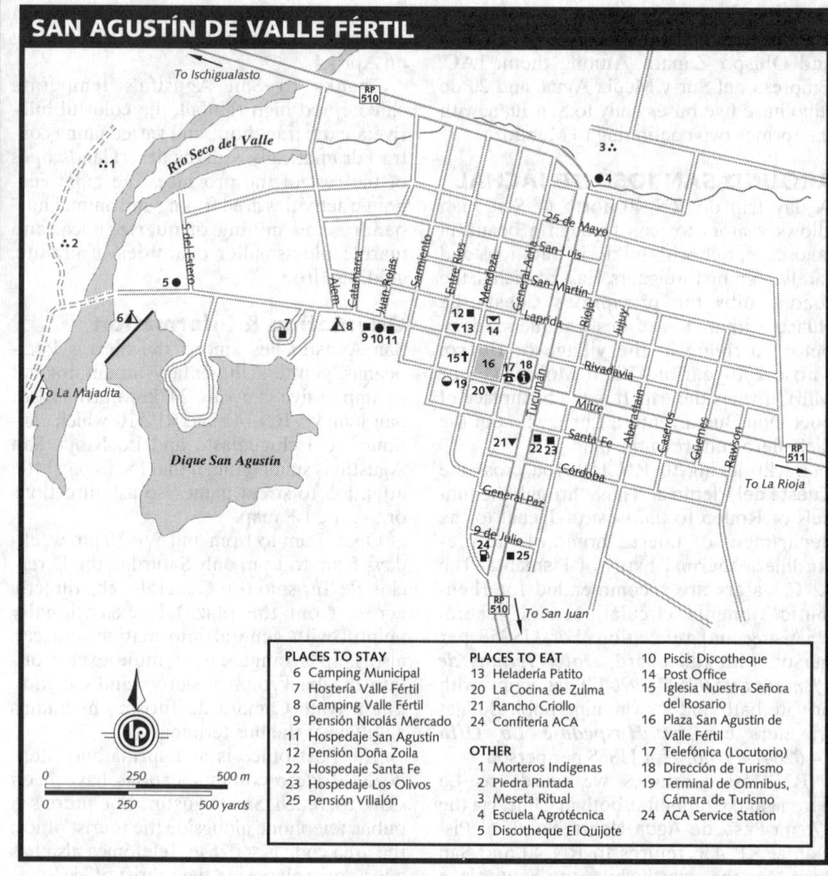

crosses the river several times. You can find lodging at a local rancho, where you can eat kid goat and goat cheese, and have fresh milk in the morning.

Places to Stay & Eat

No longer a bargain, the ***Camping Municipal*** charges US$8 per site. Shady ***Camping Valle Fértil***, the former ACA site, has better facilities for US$10, but try bargaining if it's not crowded. Given its popularity among Sanjuaninos, it gets very crowded during long weekends and holidays.

The cheapest and most pleasant places are private homes. Four families all charge about US$9/12 for singles/doubles with shared bath: ***Pensión Doña Zoila*** *(☎ 420147)*, ***Pensión Nicolás Mercado***, and ***Pensión Villalón*** *(☎ 420148)*. For US$10 per person, ***Hospedaje San Agustín*** *(☎ 420004)* has rooms with private bath and hot water plus a restaurant/confitería.

Similar in price, but with shared bath, is ***Hospedaje Los Olivos*** *(☎ 420115)*. At ***Hospedaje Santa Fe*** *(☎ 420012)*, rooms with shared bath cost US$10 to US$12 per person.

Recently reopened, the spectacularly sited ***Hostería Valle Fértil*** has great valley views and a good restaurant/confitería. Rates are US$45/60 with breakfast, US$56/82 with half-board, and US$67/104 with full board.

Besides the hotel restaurants, try ***La Cocina de Zulma*** and ***Rancho Criollo***, also a parrilla. ***Heladería Patito*** has palatable ice cream.

Entertainment

San Agustín has a couple of discos on Rivadavia, ***Piscis*** and ***El Quijote***.

Getting There & Away

The bus station is on Mitre between Entre Ríos and Mendoza. From San Juan (US$12, 4½ hours), take Empresa Vallecito buses, which leave at 6:30 pm nightly; to San Juan, buses leave at 5 pm. There are Monday and Friday buses to La Rioja (US$7), which can drop off passengers at the Ischigualasto turnoff.

Ask at the tourist office to arrange a private car to Parque Provincial Ischigualasto for about US$80; otherwise taxis cost about US$200.

PARQUE PROVINCIAL ISCHIGUALASTO

Over time the persistent action of water has exposed a wealth of fossils (some 180 million years old from the Triassic period) in Parque Provincial Ischigualasto, named for an early Paleo-Indian culture and comparable to North American national parks like Bryce Canyon or Zion. Its museum displays some of these fossils, including the carnivorous dinosaur *Herrerasaurus* (not unlike *Tyrannosaurus rex)*, the *Eoraptor lunensis* (the oldest-known predatory dinosaur), and good dioramas of the park's paleo-environments.

Colloquially known as one of South America's many *Valles de la Luna* (Valleys of the Moon), 63,000-hectare Ischigualasto is a desert valley between two sedimentary mountain ranges, the Cerros Colorados in the east and Cerro Los Rastros in the west. Over millennia, at every meander in the canyon, the waters of the nearly dry Río Ischigualasto have carved distinctive shapes in the monochrome clay, red sandstone, and volcanic ash. Predictably, some of the these forms have acquired popular names: including Cancha de Bochas (The Ball Court), El Submarino (The Submarine), and El Gusano (The Worm). The desert flora of algarrobo trees, shrubs, and cacti complement the eerie landforms.

From the visitor center, isolated 1748m **Cerro Morado** is a three- to four-hour walk gaining nearly 800m in elevation and yielding outstanding views of the surrounding area. Take plenty of drinking water and high energy snacks.

Places to Stay & Eat

Camping is permitted at the visitor center, which also has a confitería with simple meals (breakfast and lunch) and cold drinks; dried fruits and bottled olives from the province are also available. There are toilets and showers, but because water must be trucked in, don't count on them. There is no shade.

Getting There & Away

Ischigualasto is about 80km north of San Agustín via RP 510 and a paved lateral to the northwest. Given its size and isolation, the only practical way to visit the park is by vehicle. After you arrive at the visitor center and pay the US$5 entrance fee, one of the rangers will accompany your vehicle on a two-hour, 45km circuit through the park. Note that the park roads are unpaved and some can be impassable after rain, necessitating a shorter trip.

If you have no vehicle, ask the tourist office in San Agustín about hiring a car and driver there. Alternatively, contact Noli Sánchez or Jorge Gargiulo (☎ 02646-491100) at the park or through Triassic Tour (☎ 0264-423-0358), Hipólito Yrigoyen 294 Sur in San Juan; tour rates are about US$10 per person for a minimum of four people trip in a 10-passenger minibus.

The Empresa Vallecito bus from San Juan to La Rioja stops at the Los Baldecitos checkpoint on RP 510, but improved RN 150 from Jáchal is shorter and may supersede the former route.

San Luis Province

Popularly known as *La Puerta de Cuyo* (The Door to Cuyo), the province of San Luis draws many Argentine visitors, but very few foreigners visit the province's delightful hill country, a western extension of the Sierras de Córdoba. Its major attraction is the picturesque town of Merlo, but Parque Nacional Las Quijadas, in the northern part of the province, is a nature reserve and dinosaur site comparable to San Juan's Parque Provincial Ischigualasto.

Within Cuyo's strong regional identity, residents of the province resolutely assert their own singularity as *puntanos*. The provincial government publishes a tourist guide, in both Spanish and readable English, with a small but good atlas of the province; it's available at the Casa de San Luis in Buenos Aires or at the Dirección de Turismo in the city of San Luis.

SAN LUIS

Founded in 1594 and capital of its namesake province, San Luis is the eastern gateway to Cuyo. During the 1970s and 1980s, this lively city of 130,000 people grew and attracted industry through a program of industrial promotion and tax incentives.

Orientation

On the north bank of the Río Chorrillos, San Luis is 260km from Mendoza via RN 7, 456km from Córdoba via RN 148, and 850km from Buenos Aires via either RN 7 or RN 8.

The commercial center is along the parallel streets of San Martín and Rivadavia between Plaza Pringles in the north and Plaza Independencia in the south.

Information

Tourist Offices The Dirección Provincial de Turismo (☎ 423957, 0800-666-6176), open weekdays 8 am to 10 pm and weekends 8 am to 8 pm, is at the triangular intersection formed by Junín, San Martín, and Av Arturo Illia. Its flashy brochures are short on information, but the staff can provide more thorough material, including a hotel list with budget alternatives.

ACA (☎ 423188) is at Av Illia 401.

Money Alituris (☎ 423034), Colón 733, changes dollars and Chilean pesos weekdays 8 am to noon, Saturday 8:30 am to 12:30 pm. Several banks, mostly around Plaza Pringles, have ATMs.

Post & Communications The post office is at Arturo Illia and San Martín; the postal code is 5700. Locutorio San Martín is at San Martín 633; San Luis's area code is ☎ 02652.

Travel Agencies Besides Alituris (see Money), try Dasso Viajes (☎ 426616) at Rivadavia 615.

Medical Services The Hospital Regional (☎ 422627) is at Av República Oriental del Uruguay 150 (the eastward extension of Bolívar).

Things to See

Local materials, including provincial woods such as algarrobo for windows and frames and white marble for steps and columns, complement the French tiles of the 19th-century **Iglesia Catedral**, on Rivadavia across from Plaza Pringles.

On the north side of Plaza Independencia is the provincial **Casa de Gobierno**. Across the plaza, on the south side, the **Iglesia de Santo Domingo** and its convent date from the 1930s, but reproduce the Moorish style of the 17th-century building they replaced. Part of the old church is visible inside the **Archivo Histórico Provincial**, with striking algarrobo doors, around the corner on San Martín.

Dominican friars at the **Mercado Artesanal**, next to Iglesia de Santo Domingo on 25 de Mayo, sell gorgeous handmade wool rugs as well as ceramics, onyx crafts, and weavings from elsewhere in the province. It's open weekdays 7 am to 1 pm.

Places to Stay – Budget

***Residencial María Eugenia** (☎ 430361, 25 de Mayo 741)* has large, clean rooms with

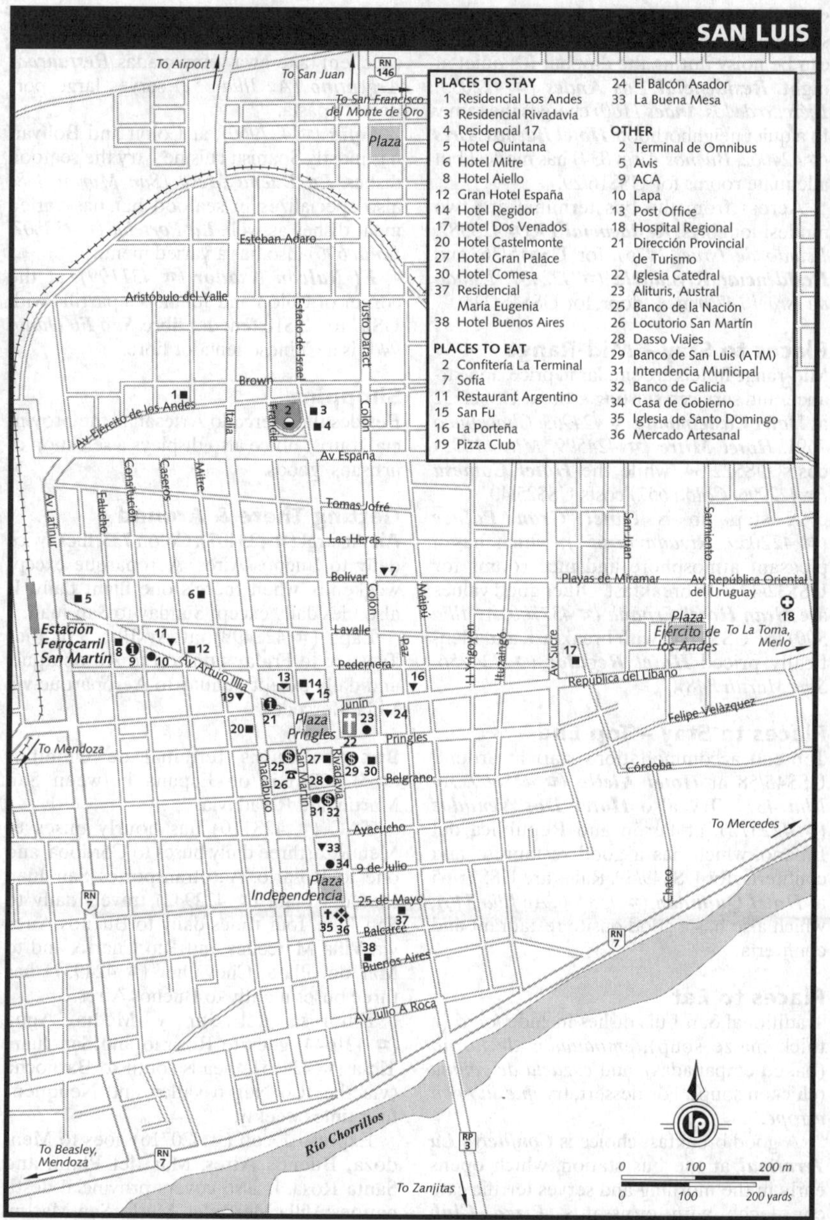
SAN LUIS
PLACES TO STAY
1 Residencial Los Andes
3 Residencial Rivadavia
4 Residencial 17
5 Hotel Quintana
6 Hotel Mitre
8 Hotel Aiello
12 Gran Hotel España
14 Hotel Regidor
17 Hotel Dos Venados
20 Hotel Castelmonte
27 Hotel Gran Palace
30 Hotel Comesa
37 Residencial María Eugenia
38 Hotel Buenos Aires
PLACES TO EAT
2 Confitería La Terminal
7 Sofía
11 Restaurant Argentino
15 San Fu
16 La Porteña
19 Pizza Club
24 El Balcón Asador
33 La Buena Mesa
OTHER
2 Terminal de Omnibus
5 Avis
9 ACA
10 Lapa
13 Post Office
18 Hospital Regional
21 Dirección Provincial de Turismo
22 Iglesia Catedral
23 Alituris, Austral
25 Banco de la Nación
26 Locutorio San Martín
28 Dasso Viajes
29 Banco de San Luis (ATM)
31 Intendencia Municipal
32 Banco de Galicia
34 Casa de Gobierno
35 Iglesia de Santo Domingo
36 Mercado Artesanal
To Airport
To San Juan
RN 146
To San Francisco del Monte de Oro
Plaza
Esteban Adaro
Aristóbulo del Valle
Estado de Israel
Justo Daract
Brown
Av Ejército de los Andes
Italia
Francia
Colón
Av España
Constitución
Caseros
Mitre
Falucho
Av Lafinur
Tomas Jofré
Las Heras
Bolívar
Lavalle
Pedernera
Junín
Pringles
Belgrano
Ayacucho
9 de Julio
25 de Mayo
Balcarce
Buenos Aires
Av Julio A Roca
Maipú
Paz
H Yrigoyen
Ituzaingó
Av Sucre
San Juan
Sarmiento
Chaco
Córdoba
Playas de Miramar
Av República Oriental del Uruguay
Plaza Ejército de los Andes
To La Toma, Merlo
República del Líbano
Felipe Velázquez
Estación Ferrocarril San Martín
Av Arturo Illia
Plaza Pringles
Chacabuco
San Martín
Rivadavia
Plaza Independencia
To Mendoza
To Mercedes
RN 7
Río Chorrillos
RP 3
To Beasley, Mendoza
To Zanjitas
0 100 200 m
0 100 200 yards

shared bath for US$15/25 single/double; since all rooms front onto an enclosed hall, it can be noisy during the day, but it's quiet at night. ***Residencial Los Andes*** *(☎ 422033, Ejército de los Andes 1180)* charges the same. In a quiet neighborhood, ***Hotel Buenos Aires*** *(☎ 424062, Buenos Aires 834)* has modest but adequate rooms for US$16/29.

Across from the bus terminal are two modest lodgings: ***Residencial 17*** *(☎ 423387, Estado de Israel 1476)*, for US$15/26, and ***Residencial Rivadavia*** *(☎ 422437, Estado de Israel 1470)*, next door, for US$18/22.

Places to Stay – Mid-Range

Mid-range hotels are similar in price, appearance, and services, starting around US$22/32 at ***Hotel Castelmonte*** *(☎ 424963, Chacabuco 769)*. ***Hotel Mitre*** *(☎ 424599, Mitre 1035)* costs US$22/34, while the ***Hotel Comesa*** *(☎ 422996, Colón 667)* costs US$25/40.

A step up is ***Hotel Gran Palace*** *(☎ 422059, Rivadavia 657)*, which has a pleasant atmosphere and nice rooms for US$32/47 with breakfast. Other good values are ***Gran Hotel España*** *(☎ 437700, Av Illia 300)* for US$34/46 with breakfast, and identically priced ***Hotel Regidor*** *(☎ 424756, San Martín 848)*.

Places to Stay – Top End

Top-end accommodations start at around US$45/58 at ***Hotel Aiello*** *(☎ 425609, Av Illia 431)*. Try also ***Hotel Dos Venados*** *(☎ 422312)*, at Perón and República del Líbano, which has a good restaurant and confitería, for US$49/59. Rates are US$55/65 at ***Hotel Quintana*** *(☎ 438400, Av Illia 546)*, which also has a good onsite restaurant and confitería.

Places to Eat

Traditional San Luis dishes include *locro* (a thick maize soup), *empanadas de horno* (baked empanadas), and *cazuela de gallina* (chicken soup). For dessert, try *quesillo con arrope*.

A good breakfast choice is ***Confitería La Terminal*** at the bus station, which opens early in the morning and serves terrific café con leche with croissants. ***Pizza Club*** *(☎ 441144, Av Illia 113)* has varied pizza toppings, good service and atmosphere, and excellent take-away empanadas. ***Restaurant Argentino*** *(Av Illia 352)* serves large portions of pasta.

Sofía *(☎ 427960)*, at Colón and Bolívar, has mostly Spanish cuisine – try the seafood dishes. ***La Buena Mesa*** *(San Martín 488)* also specializes in seafood but has varied meat dishes as well. ***La Porteña*** *(☎ 423807, Junín 696)* also has a varied menu.

El Balcón Asador *(☎ 431199)*, at the corner of Colón and Junín, is a parrilla with US$7 to US$10 tenedor libre. ***San Fu*** *(Junín 940)* is a Chinese tenedor libre.

Shopping

Besides the Mercado Artesanal, the provincial tourist office also displays a selection of artisans' goods.

Getting There & Around

Air Austral (☎ 423407), Colón 733, flies twice daily to Buenos Aires' Aeroparque except weekends, when there's one flight daily. It also flies daily except Sunday to San Juan.

Lapa (☎ 422499), at Av Illia 331, flies Tuesday to Friday nonstop to Aeroparque, and daily except Sunday to Aeroparque via Villa Mercedes.

Bus San Luis's Terminal de Ómnibus (☎ 424021) is on España between San Martín and Rivadavia.

TAC (☎ 423110) has hourly buses to Mendoza, three daily buses to Córdoba, and one to Rosario. Autotransportes San Juan Mar del Plata (☎ 422942) travels daily to San Juan, four times daily to Buenos Aires via Villa Mercedes and Río Cuarto, and to Mar del Plata. Chevallier (☎ 424937) has three buses nightly to Buenos Aires.

Empresa del Sur y Media Agua (☎ 421644) goes to Rosario and San Juan. Ticsa (☎ 424651) heads south to Bariloche (via the Río Negro valley and Neuquén) four times weekly.

Expreso Jocolí (☎ 420716) goes to Mendoza, Buenos Aires, Mar del Plata, and Santa Rosa. It also covers provincial destinations: Villa Mercedes, Merlo, San Martín,

Unión, Trapiche, Florida, and Pozo de los Funes. Transporte Ser (☎ 432009) goes three times daily to Merlo. Empresa Dasso (☎ 425386) travels to small provincial towns.

Sample fares include San Juan (US$15, four hours), Mendoza (US$16, three hours), Buenos Aires (US$40, 12 hours), Rosario (11 hours, US$33), Merlo (US$22), and Mar del Plata (US$50).

Car Avis (☎ 429548) has an office at Hotel Quintana, Av Illia 546.

PARQUE NACIONAL SIERRA DE LAS QUIJADAS

Resembling San Juan's Parque Provincial Ischigualasto, this rarely visited national park sets aside 150,000 hectares of red sandstone canyons and dry lake beds among the Sierra de las Quijadas, whose peaks reach 1200m at Cerro Portillo. The Universidad Nacional de San Luis and New York's Museum of Natural History are collaborating on paleontological excavations here and have discovered dinosaur tracks and fossils from the Lower Cretaceous, about 120 million years ago.

Despite the shortage of visitors, access to the park is excellent – buses from San Luis to San Juan will drop visitors just beyond the village of Hualtarán, about 110km northwest of San Luis via RN 147 (the highway to San Juan).

At this point, a 6km lateral leads west to a viewpoint overlooking the **Potrero de la Aguada**, a scenic depression beneath the peaks of the Sierras that collects the runoff from much of the park and is a prime wildlife area.

It's sometimes possible to catch a lift from the junction, where the park rangers have a house, to the overlook. Hiking possibilities are excellent, but the complex canyons require a tremendous sense of direction or, preferably, a local guide. Even experienced hikers should beware summer rains and flash floods, which make the canyons extremely dangerous.

There's a shady new ***campground***, free of charge, near the overlook, and a small store with groceries and drink, including very welcome ice-cold beer. For US$4, readers who know Spanish can acquire David Rivarola's thorough, self-published guide *El Parque Nacional Sierra de las Quijadas y sus Recursos Naturales*, either at the store or at the provincial tourist office in San Luis.

MERLO

Founded in 1797, the hill resort of Merlo struggles to retain the colonial atmosphere imparted by its church, plaza, and other buildings against a wave of modern construction. In the northeastern corner of the province, 900m above sea level on the western slope of the Sierras de Comenchingones, Merlo's mountainous locale and gentle climate make it a popular resort, but one much less frequented than the nearby Sierras de Córdoba. The permanent population is about 6700.

Orientation & Information

Merlo is 180km northeast of San Luis via RP 20 to La Toma and RN 148 to Santa Rosa del Conlara, where RP 5 leads directly east to Merlo. Downtown's activity center is Plaza Sobremonte, bounded by Coronel Mercau, Presidente Perón, Presbítero Becerra, and Juan de Videla, but most tourist services are two blocks south, along Av del Sol, which climbs eastward into the quiet foothills of El Rincón.

The municipal Oficina de Informes (☎ 476078), Coronel Mercau 605, has information on hotels and campgrounds, but little on activities. The Dirección Provincial de Turismo (☎ 476079), at the traffic circle junction of RP 5 and RP 1, is open 8 am to 8 pm daily (to 10 pm in summer).

Correo Argentino is at Coronel Mercau 579; the postal code is 5881. The Cooperativa Telefónica is at Juan de Videla 112; the area code is ☎ 02656.

Places to Stay

Merlo's abundant accommodations tend to be crowded in summer, around Semana Santa, and during winter holidays in July. At these peak times, rates indicated below can rise by a third or more.

Places to Stay – Budget

Camping In El Rincón, about 2km from the town center via Av del Sol, the shady and tidy ***Camping Don Juan*** *(☎ 475942)* has superb views of the Sierra; fees are US$5 per site. Empresa la Costa buses go there hourly.

Residenciales & Motels Merlo's cheapest lodging is downtown ***Residencial Oviedo***, *(☎ 475193, Coronel Mercau 799)*, where rooms with private bath cost US$10 per person. SMATA, the automobile workers' union, runs ***Motel Merlo*** *(☎ 475740, Av Dos Venados 1277)*, which has an exceptional setting and is open to the public if space is available. Rates are US$17/30 single/double with breakfast.

Try also ***Residencial Amancay*** *(☎ 475311, Av del Sol 500)* for US$30 double, but the best value in town is the ***Yana-Munay*** *(☎ 475055)*, an outstanding teahouse that also has a couple rooftop rooms with expansive views toward the west. On Av de los Césares in El Rincón, it costs US$15 per person with private bath and a superb breakfast.

Places to Stay – Mid-Range

Mid-range accommodations start around US$35 double with breakfast at places like ***Residencial Planetario*** *(☎ 475412)*, at Av del Sol and Marte. In the US$40 range are ***Hotel Contilo*** *(☎ 475293)*, at Los Tilos and P Conti, and ***Residencial Sierras Verdes*** *(☎ 475340, Av del Sol 458)*. ***Hotel Mirasierras*** *(☎ 475045)*, Av del Sol and Pedernera, and ***Motel Algarrobo*** *(☎ 475208, Av del Sol 1120)* both charge around US$50.

Places to Stay – Top End

Set among attractive gardens, ***Residencial Piscu Yaco*** *(☎ 475419, Pasaje los Teros 235)* costs US$70 double. Three-star ***Hotel Casablanca*** *(☎ 475084, Av del Sol 50)* charges US$80 double with breakfast, while ***Hotel Parque*** *(☎ 475110, Av del Sol 821)* costs US$55 per person with half-board.

Places to Eat

Most hotels, especially top-end ones, have restaurants that are open to the general public. There are many good choices along Av del Sol, such as the attractive parrilla ***La Estanzuela*** *(Av del Sol 2)*. For afternoon tea (the closer to sunset, the better), don't miss the hillside gardens at ***Yana-Munay*** teahouse *(☎ 475055)*, on Av de los Césares in El Rincón.

Getting There & Away

The Terminal de Ómnibus is at Coronel Pringles 530. Empresa Jocolí (☎ 475328) and TAC connect Merlo to Buenos Aires (US$45, 12 hours), while Chevallier, Jocolí (three times daily), Expreso Uspallata (☎ 476055), and TAC also link Merlo with San Luis and Mendoza (US$22, 6½ hours). Sierras Córdobesas (☎ 476043) heads north into Córdoba province, as do Casilda (☎ 476055) and El Petizo. Transporte Ser goes three times daily to San Luis.

The Andean Northwest

Argentina's most 'traditional' region, the Andean Northwest *(Noroeste Andino)* consists of the provinces of Jujuy, Salta, Tucumán, La Rioja, Catamarca, and Santiago del Estero, all of which had thriving cities when Buenos Aires was still an insignificant hinterland. The region's tangible pre-Hispanic and colonial past make the trip south from Peru and Bolivia to the Argentine heartland a journey through time as well as space. Even today, the northern provinces resemble the Andean countries as much or more than they do the cultural core of the Argentine Pampas, and substantial Quechua Indian communities exist as far south as Santiago del Estero.

In pre-Columbian times, the Noroeste was the most densely populated part of what is now Argentina, with perhaps two-thirds of the population. Several indigenous groups, most notably the Diaguita, practiced irrigated maize agriculture in the valleys of the eastern Andean foothills; they also cultivated complementary crops like potatoes, beans, squash, and quinoa (a native Andean grain) at different altitudes. While their numbers were smaller and their political organization less complex than the civilizations of Peru and Bolivia, they could mobilize enough labor to build agricultural terraces and military fortifications. Other groups included the Lules, southwest of present-day Salta, the Tonocote, around Santiago del Estero, and the Omaguaca of Jujuy.

Decades before the European invasion, the Incas began to expand their influence among the Diaguita and other southern Andean peoples; Vásquez de Espinosa wrote that 'they came to render obedience' to the Inca Viracocha, who sent 'delegates down there to take possession and to see that they were instructed and disciplined in his false religion.' The area remained peripheral to but oriented toward the agricultural Andean civilizations rather than toward the foragers of the Pampas; when Spaniards replaced the Inca at the apex of political authority, they benefited from and reinforced this orientation, founding cities as they advanced south.

The first Spaniard to visit the region was Diego de Almagro, whose expedition from Cuzco to Santiago, Chile, traced the eastern side of the Andes before crossing the heights of the Puna de Atacama. En route, Almagro and his men passed through present-day Jujuy and Salta, but it was decades before the Spaniards established permanent settlements in the region, known in colonial times as 'Tucumán.' The Spaniards hoped that Indian populations would be large enough for substantial encomiendas, but the area never matched Peru's wealth of labor and tribute.

The earliest Spanish city, founded in 1553, was Santiago del Estero, but Indians

MAP INDEX

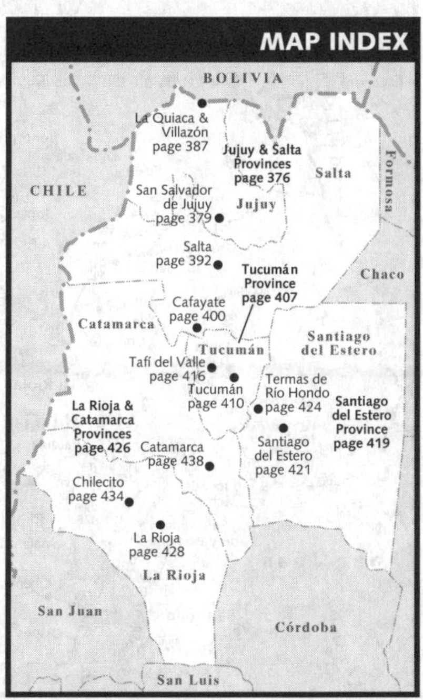

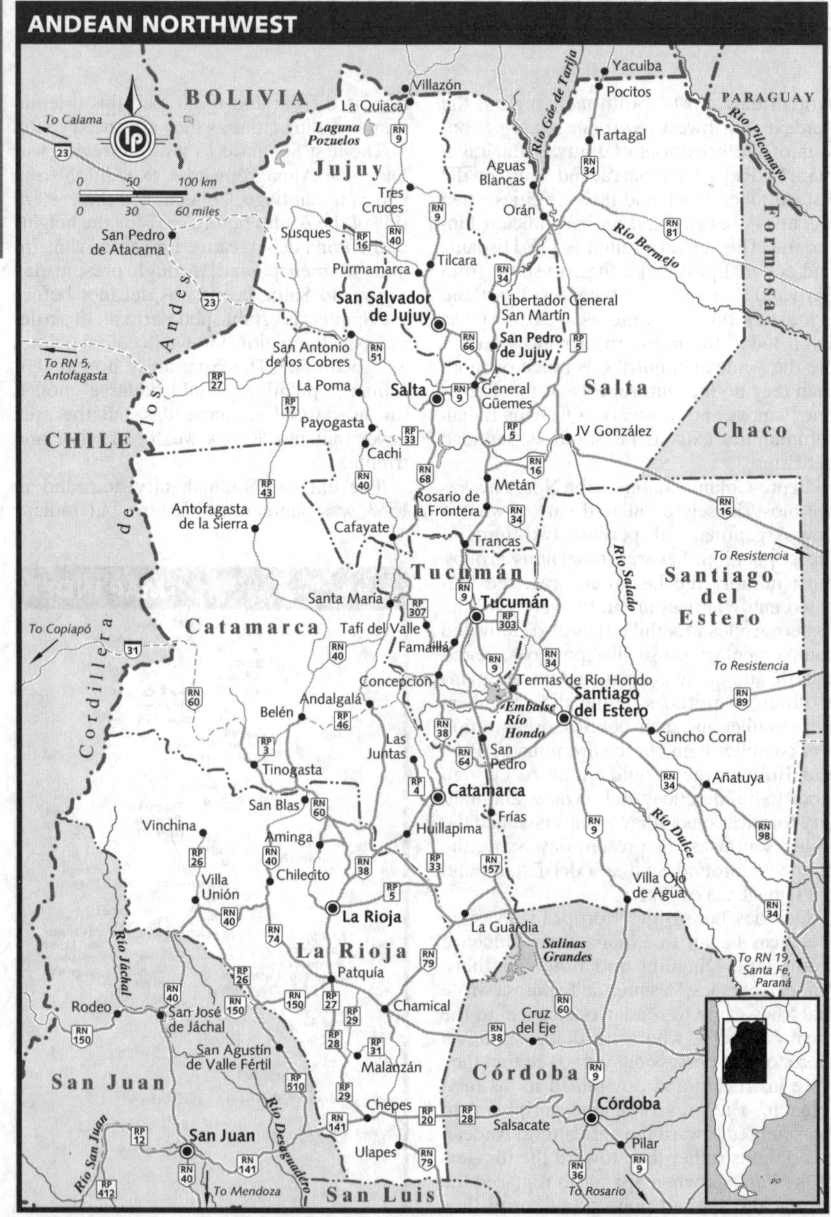
ANDEAN NORTHWEST
BOLIVIA
PARAGUAY
CHILE
Jujuy
Salta
Chaco
Formosa
Tucumán
Santiago del Estero
Catamarca
La Rioja
Córdoba
San Juan
San Luis
Cordillera de los Andes
0 50 100 km
0 30 60 miles
To Calama
To RN 5, Antofagasta
To Copiapó
To Resistencia
To Resistencia
To RN 19, Santa Fe, Paraná
To Mendoza
To Rosario
Villazón
La Quiaca
Laguna Pozuelos
Yacuiba
Pocitos
Tartagal
Aguas Blancas
Orán
Río Gde de Tarija
Río Pilcomayo
Río Bermejo
Tres Cruces
Susques
San Pedro de Atacama
Purmamarca
Tilcara
San Salvador de Jujuy
Libertador General San Martín
San Pedro de Jujuy
San Antonio de los Cobres
La Poma
Salta
General Güemes
Payogasta
Cachi
JV González
Metán
Rosario de la Frontera
Antofagasta de la Sierra
Cafayate
Trancas
Río Salado
Santa María
Tucumán
Tafí del Valle
Famaillá
Concepción
Termas de Río Hondo
Embalse Río Hondo
Santiago del Estero
Belén
Andalgalá
Las Juntas
San Pedro
Suncho Corral
Tinogasta
Catamarca
Añatuya
San Blas
Frías
Vinchina
Aminga
Huillapima
Río Dulce
Chilecito
Villa Unión
Villa Ojo de Agua
La Rioja
La Guardia
Salinas Grandes
Río Jáchal
Patquía
Rodeo
San José de Jáchal
Chamical
Cruz del Eje
San Agustín de Valle Fértil
Malanzán
Chepes
Córdoba
Salsacate
Río San Juan
Río Desaguadero
San Juan
Ulapes
Pilar
RN 9
RN 34
RN 81
RP 16
RN 40
RN 66
RP 5
RN 51
RP 27
RP 17
RP 33
RN 16
RN 68
RP 43
RN 307
RP 303
RN 60
RP 46
RN 38
RN 64
RP 3
RP 4
RN 89
RN 98
RP 26
RN 74
RN 79
RN 157
RN 150
RP 27
RP 29
RP 28
RP 31
RP 510
RN 141
RP 20
RP 12
RP 412
RN 141
RN 36
23
31

destroyed several others before the successful founding of San Miguel de Tucumán (1565), Córdoba (1573), Salta (1582), La Rioja (1591), and San Salvador de Jujuy (1592). The Cuyo region, including the cities of Mendoza and San Juan, was settled from Santiago, Chile – across the Andes – about the same time as Tucumán, while Catamarca was founded more than a century later.

These settlements were not impressive in their infancy; according to historian David Rock, the number of Spaniards in the region did not exceed 700 at the end of the 16th century. Still, they established the basic institutions and visible features of Spanish colonial rule that still survive in many modern Argentine cities: the *cabildo* (town council), the church, and the rectangular plaza surrounded by a cluster of public buildings. Spanish citizens received rights to Indian labor from the governor or the members of the cabildo, but as the Indians fell to European diseases and Spanish exploitation over the next century, encomiendas lost most of their value. In Santiago del Estero, for instance, 12,000 Indians labored under 48 encomiendas in 1582, while in 1673 the remaining 34 encomiendas controlled only 3358 Indians.

In colonial times, Tucumán was an economic satellite of the bonanza silver mine at Potosí, in present-day Bolivia. Spanish activities started with the provision of mules and the cultivation of cotton and production of textiles, but as the region recovered from 17th-century depression (due largely to labor shortages), sugar cane eventually dominated the economy. In part, the Spaniards had no alternative to this northward orientation, since the crown's mercantile policy decreed that commerce between Spain and the colonies had to be routed through Lima, by sea to Panama, across the isthmus to the Caribbean, and then across the Atlantic.

Only after the creation of the Viceroyalty of the River Plate in 1776 did this orientation change, as Buenos Aires slowly emerged from Lima's shadow. The opening of the Atlantic to legal shipping toward the end of the colonial period, followed by political independence, relegated Jujuy and Salta to economic marginality, but the adoption of a sugar monoculture reversed Tucumán's economic orientation and increased its importance in the new country. Completion of a railroad from Córdoba in 1874 spurred a threefold production in sugar by the end of the decade. By 1914, 100,000 hectares of sugar cane, mostly in Tucumán, were yielding 250,000 tons per annum, enough to satisfy domestic demand.

Sugar continues to dominate the provincial economy, occupying more than 60% of the total agricultural land and causing social, economic, and ecological problems. Large farms and factories characterize the industry, whose seasonal labor requirements during the winter *zafra* (harvest) mean high unemployment the rest of the year. Tobacco is a distant second, and citrus is locally significant, but attempts to further diversify the agricultural economy have had limited success despite some progress with soybeans.

Jujuy Province

Bounded by Bolivia to the north, Chile to the west, and Salta province to the south and east, Jujuy is a southern extension of the high Andean steppe *(altiplano)*, where soaring volcanic peaks tower over saline lakes *(salares)* above 4000m in the thinly populated west. To the east, a lower range of foothills gives way to deeply dissected river valleys like the Quebrada de Humahuaca, whose Río Grande has exposed spectacular desert landforms, before opening onto subtropical lowlands toward the Gran Chaco. Jujuy has several wildlife and fauna reserves, though access is generally not easy.

One of Argentina's smallest and poorest provinces, Jujuy is nevertheless rich in archaeological and cultural resources. While a handful of colonial remains surround Plaza Belgrano in San Salvador de Jujuy, most sites of interest are in the countryside, especially the villages of the Quebrada de Humahuaca.

The province's very name may be evidence of Inca influence – according to Inca noble Guamán Poma de Ayala, the region's

Inca-designated governors went by the Quechua title of *Xuxuyoc*, a word early European residents Hispanicized as 'Jujuy' (another explanation is that the Spaniards corrupted the name of the Río Xibi Xibi). In colonial times it gained a certain prosperity through sugar-cane cultivation under Jesuit missionaries and, well after independence, British investors. Tobacco is the second most important crop.

Like several other provinces, Jujuy has suffered considerably in the economic transition of the Menem administration, seeing a 30% decline in GDP since President Menem took office in 1990. Several times since, disgruntled state workers have vigorously protested unpaid salaries, and in one instance attempted to burn the provincial Casa de Gobierno to the ground.

Budget travelers approaching Jujuy from Bolivia are likely to find Argentine prices an unpleasant shock. Before panicking and dashing back across the border, look at alternatives for cheaper lodging, food, and transportation suggested in this chapter and elsewhere in the book. A handful of travelers arrive via the trans-Chaco highways from Resistencia or Formosa; for approaches from the south, see the entry for Salta below.

SAN SALVADOR DE JUJUY

At the southern end of the Quebrada de Humahuaca, where the valley broadens and the climate is perpetually springlike at 1200m, the Spaniards founded San Salvador de Jujuy in 1592 as the most northerly of their colonial cities in present-day Argentina. Now commonly known as 'Jujuy,' the town's proper name distinguished it as a Spanish settlement and also avoided confusion with nearby San Pedro de Jujuy.

In the early 17th century, according to Vásquez de Espinosa, Jujuy had about '100 Spanish residents, mostly muleteers, who freight flour, corn, cheese, and other foodstuffs to the Chichas and Lipes mines; they have mule and cattle ranches, and drive their stock to Potosí.' During the wars of independence, at the command of General Manuel Belgrano, residents evacuated the city to avoid falling into royalist hands;

August's weeklong celebration of the *éxodo jujeño* (Jujuy exodus) is the city's (and the province's) biggest annual event.

Orientation

At the mouth of the Quebrada de Humahuaca, Jujuy (population 200,000) sits above the flood plain of the Río Grande at its confluence with the smaller Río Xibi Xibi, 1650km from Buenos Aires. RN 9 leads north up the Quebrada de Humahuaca, while RN 66 leads southeast to a junction with RN 34, the main highway to Salta

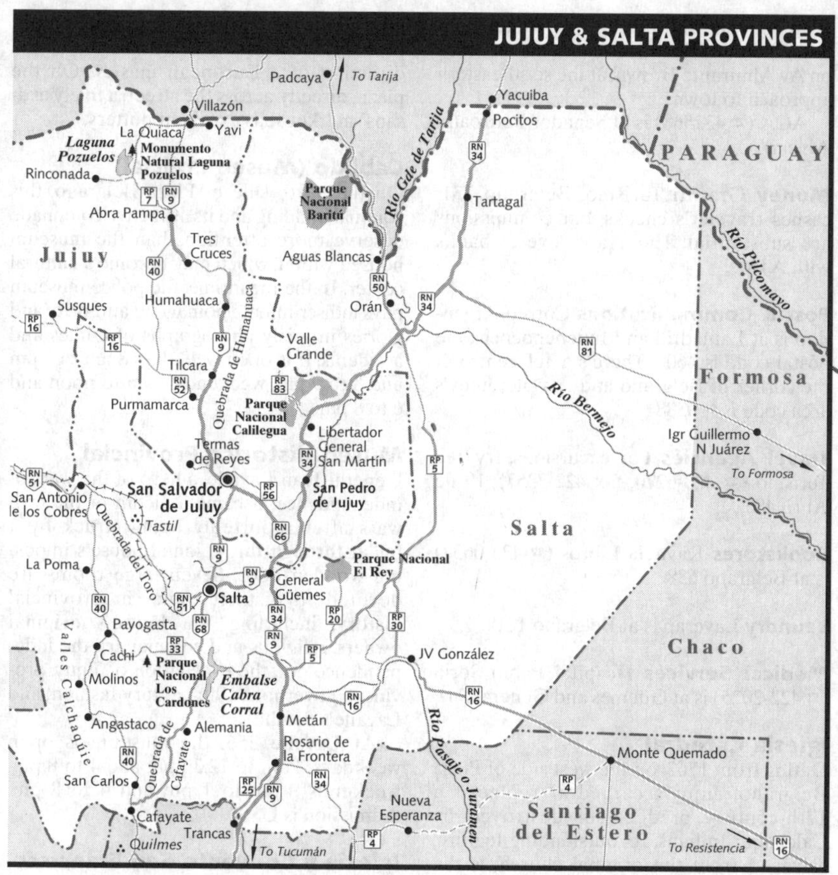

(though not the most direct). For motorists or cyclists, southbound RN 9 is a much shorter, though winding and narrow, alternative route to Salta.

Jujuy consists of two main parts: the old city, with a fairly regular grid pattern between the Río Grande and the Xibi Xibi, and a newer area south of the Xibi Xibi that sprawls up the nearby hills. Shantytowns crowd the flood plain of the Río Grande beneath the San Martín bridge, which leads to San Pedro de Jujuy by an attractive but little-used route.

The main public buildings are clustered around Plaza Belgrano. The 700 block of Belgrano (between Necochea and Lavalle), the main commercial street, is a pedestrian mall.

Information

Tourist Offices The Dirección Provincial de Turismo (☎ 422-1326) is at Belgrano 690. The staff vary in their attention to visitors but have an abundance of maps, brochures, and other materials. Hours are 7:30 am to 1 pm and 3 to 9 pm daily.

In summer and during July winter holidays, the municipalidad maintains an office on Av Almirante Brown, at the southeastern approach to town.

ACA (☎ 422568) is at Senador Pérez and Alvear.

Money Graffiti Turismo, Belgrano 731, cashes traveler's checks, but commissions are substantial. There are several banks with ATMs.

Post & Communications Correo Argentino is at Lamadrid and Independencia; the postal code is 4600. There's a Telecentro at the corner of Belgrano and Lavalle; Jujuy's area code is ☎ 0388.

Travel Agencies For excursions, try Tea Turismo (☎ 423-6270, fax 422-2357), 19 de Abril 485.

Bookstores Rayuela Libros (☎ 423-0658) is at Belgrano 638.

Laundry Laverap is at Belgrano 1214.

Medical Services Hospital Pablo Soria (☎ 422-2025) is at Güemes and General Paz.

Iglesia Catedral

Dating from 1763, on the west side of Plaza Belgrano, Jujuy's cathedral replaced a 17th-century predecessor destroyed by Calchaquí Indians. Its outstanding feature, salvaged from the original church, is the gold-laminated Spanish baroque pulpit, probably built by local artisans under the direction of a European master. On the plaza, directly across the street, a lively artisans' market sells excellent pottery.

WAYNE BERNHARDSON

Jujuy: The cathedral's gilt baroque pulpit

Cabildo (Museo Policial)

On the north side of Plaza Belgrano, this colonial building and its attractive colonnade deserve more attention than the museum housed within, which may become a cultural center. In the meantime, the police museum pays indiscriminate homage to authority and glories in grisly photographs of crimes and accidents. It is open weekdays 8 am to 1 pm and 3 to 9 pm, weekends 9 am to noon and 6 to 8 pm.

Museo Histórico Provincial

General Juan Lavalle, a hero of the wars of independence, became a victim of the civil wars after reportedly being struck by a bullet through this colonial house's imposing wooden door. Seven large rooms are devoted to distinct topics in provincial history, including the house's original owners, religious and colonial art, the independence era, the evacuation of Jujuy, provincial governors, 19th-century fashion, and Lavalle's death.

At Lavalle 256, the museum is open weekdays 7 am to 12:30 pm and 4 to 8 pm, weekends 9 am to 1 pm and 4 to 8 pm. Admission is US$1.

Iglesia y Convento San Francisco

While the Franciscan order has been in Jujuy since 1599, the current church and convent, the third at the corner of Belgrano and Lavalle, dates only from 1912. Nevertheless, its new **Museo Histórico Franciscano Jujuy** retains diverse relics from the early Franciscan presence, as well as a strong selection of colonial art from the Cuzco school. The museum is open 10 am to 1 pm and 7 to 10 pm daily; admission is free.

Iglesia Santa Bárbara

Paintings from the well-known Cuzco school decorate the walls of this colonial church at Lamadrid and San Martín.

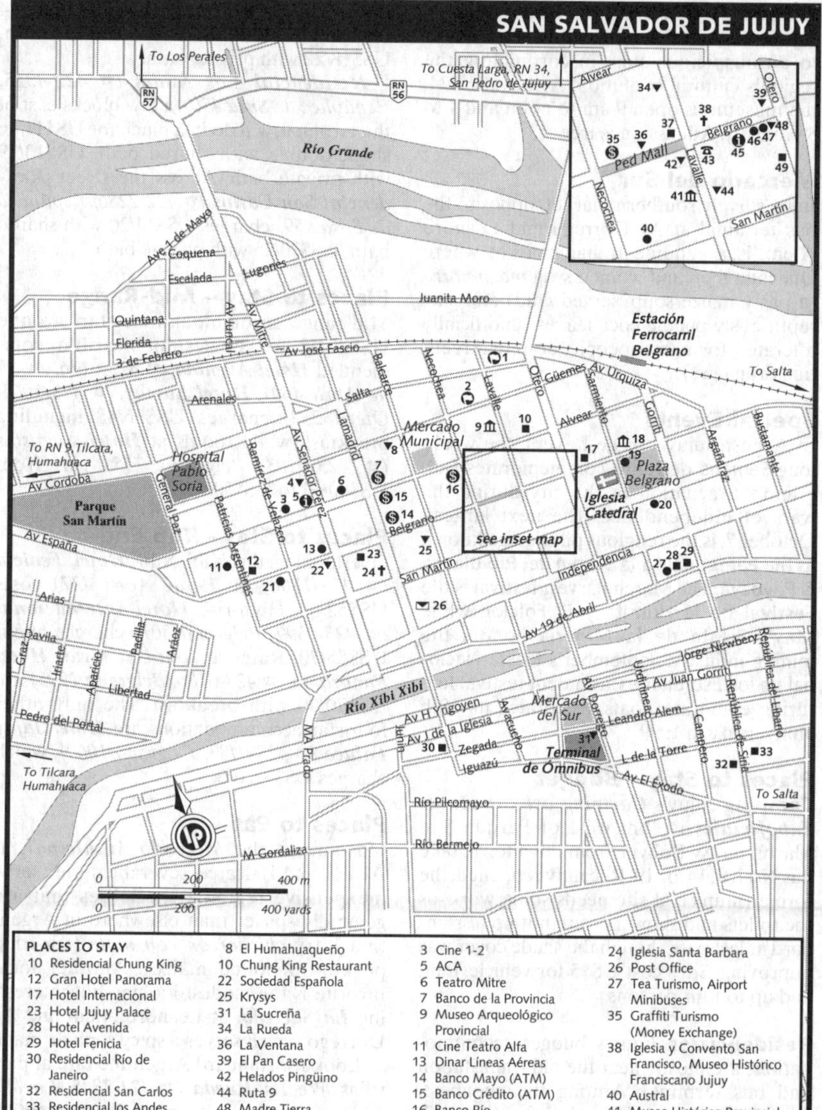

PLACES TO STAY
- 10 Residencial Chung King
- 12 Gran Hotel Panorama
- 17 Hotel Internacional
- 23 Hotel Jujuy Palace
- 28 Hotel Avenida
- 29 Hotel Fenicia
- 30 Residencial Río de Janeiro
- 32 Residencial San Carlos
- 33 Residencial los Andes
- 37 Hotel Augustus
- 49 Hotel Sumay

PLACES TO EAT
- 4 La Quebrada
- 8 El Humahuaqueño
- 10 Chung King Restaurant
- 22 Sociedad Española
- 25 Krysys
- 31 La Sucreña
- 34 La Rueda
- 36 La Ventana
- 39 El Pan Casero
- 42 Helados Pingüino
- 44 Ruta 9
- 48 Madre Tierra

OTHER
- 1 Italian Consulate
- 2 Bolivian Consulate, Lloyd Aéreo Boliviano
- 3 Cine 1-2
- 5 ACA
- 6 Teatro Mitre
- 7 Banco de la Provincia
- 9 Museo Arqueológico Provincial
- 11 Cine Teatro Alfa
- 13 Dinar Líneas Aéreas
- 14 Banco Mayo (ATM)
- 15 Banco Crédito (ATM)
- 16 Banco Río
- 18 Cabildo/Museo Policial
- 19 Mercado de Artesanos
- 20 Casa de Gobierno
- 21 Laverap
- 23 Avis
- 24 Iglesia Santa Barbara
- 26 Post Office
- 27 Tea Turismo, Airport Minibuses
- 35 Graffiti Turismo (Money Exchange)
- 38 Iglesia y Convento San Francisco, Museo Histórico Franciscano Jujuy
- 40 Austral
- 41 Museo Histórico Provincial
- 43 Telecentro
- 45 Dirección Provincial de Turismo
- 46 Rayuela Libros
- 47 LAPA

Museo Arqueológico Provincial

Jujuy's new archaeological museum is off to an auspicious start in chronicling the region's cultural evolution. At Lavalle 434, the museum is open 9 am to noon and 4 to 8 pm daily. Admission is free.

Mercado del Sur

Jujuy's lively southern market, opposite the bus terminal at Av Dorrego and Leandro Alem, is a genuine Indian market where Quechua men and women swig *mazamorra* (a pasty maize soup, served cold) and surreptitiously peddle coca leaves (unofficially tolerated for native people, despite Argentine drug laws).

Special Events

In August, Jujuy's biggest event, the weeklong **Semana de Jujuy**, commemorates Belgrano's evacuation of the city during the wars of independence. The next largest, October 7, is the religious pilgrimage known as the **Peregrinaje a la Virgen del Río Blanco & Paypaya**. The March harvest festival is the **Festival de la Humita y El Folclor**, while May's **Fiesta de la Minería** honors the mining industry. September's **Fiesta Nacional de los Estudiantes**, a student festival featuring elaborate floats, celebrates its 50th anniversary in 1999.

Places to Stay – Budget

Camping Jujuy's ***Camping del Círculo de Suboficiales*** is 3km west of Parque San Martín on Av Bolivia; from downtown, take bus No 1, 9, 14, or 19. Recently reopened, the former municipal site needs some work, as the toilets and showers were not up to standard at last pass, though the shade cover was improving. Sites cost US$5 for vehicle, tent, and up to four persons.

Residenciales Jujuy's budget accommodations are mostly near the old train station and bus terminal. Among the cheapest, friendly ***Residencial Río de Janeiro*** *(☎ 422-3700, José de la Iglesia 1356)*, west of the bus terminal, charges US$13 double with shared bath, US$14 with private bath; both have good hot showers. ***Residencial Chung King*** *(☎ 422-8142, Alvear 627)* charges US$12/14 for singles/doubles with shared bath, US$18/22 with private bath.

Residencial Los Andes *(☎ 422-4315, República de Siria 456)*, a few blocks east of the terminal, will do in a pinch for US$11/16 single/double with shared bath, US$13/19 with private bath. Across the street, ***Residencial San Carlos*** *(☎ 422-2286, República de Siria 459)* charges US$14/20 with shared bath, US$20/25 with private bath.

Places to Stay – Mid-Range

Mid-range accommodations start around US$27/42 for singles/doubles at recommended ***Hotel Avenida*** *(☎ 423-6136, Av 19 de Abril 469)*. ***Hotel Sumay*** *(☎ 423-5065, Otero 232)* charges US$36/48 including breakfast, while rooms at ***Hotel Augustus*** *(☎ 423-0203, Belgrano 715)* run from US$40/62 to US$50/68.

Places to Stay – Top End

Overlooking the Xibi Xibi, ***Hotel Fenicia*** *(☎ 423-1800, Av 19 de Abril 427)* costs US$52/80. High-rise ***Hotel Internacional*** *(☎ 423-1599, Belgrano 501)* charges about US$55/70. Rates at four-star ***Gran Hotel Panorama*** *(☎ 423-0186, Belgrano 1295)* are US$70/90 with breakfast. The only other four-star accommodations are ***Hotel Jujuy Palace*** *(☎ 423-0433, Belgrano 1060)*, which charges US$82/105.

Places to Eat

Upstairs at the ***Mercado Municipal***, at Alvear and Balcarce, several eateries serve inexpensive regional specialties that are generally spicier than elsewhere in Argentina – try *chicharrón con mote* (stir-fried pork with boiled maize). Another local favorite is the modest-looking but interesting ***La Sucreña***, at Leandro Alem and Av Dorrego, which serves a spicy sopa de maní.

Look for standard Argentine fare at parrillas like ***La Rueda*** *(☎ 422-7845, Lavalle 329)* and moderately priced ***Krysys*** *(☎ 423-1126, Balcarce 272)*. Misleadingly named ***Chung King*** *(☎ 422-8142, Alvear 627)* has an extensive Argentine menu and fine service.

La Ventana *(Belgrano 749)* serves regional specialties including pork, trout, goat, and homemade pasta. ***Ruta 9*** *(☎ 423-7043, Lavalle 287)* is a local classic. The ***Sociedad Española*** *(☎ 423-5065, Belgrano 1102)* is a traditional Spanish restaurant.

For vegetarian fare, try ***Madre Tierra*** *(☎ 422-9575)*, at the corner of Belgrano and Otero. ***El Pan Casero*** *(Belgrano 619)* is a natural-foods bakery.

On and near the Belgrano peatonal are numerous confiterías and excellent ice creameries, most notably ***Helados Pingüino***. Two bakeries prepare distinctive regional sweets ***El Humahuaqueño***, *(Güemes 920)* and ***La Quebrada*** *(Senador Pérez 476)*.

Entertainment

Theater Built in 1901, the Teatro Mitre *(☎ 422782, Alvear 1009)* sponsors plays and similar cultural events.

Cinema The ***Cine 1-2*** is a two screener on Alvear between Ramírez de Velasco and Senador Pérez. The ***Cine Teatro Alfa***, also a two-screener, is on Patricias Argentinas between Alvear and Belgrano.

Spectator Sports Jujuy's first-division soccer team, ***Gimnasia y Esgrima*** *(☎ 422-8011)*, has offices at Güemes 1031 but plays at the stadium at Av El Éxodo 78.

Shopping

La Hilandería (☎ 423-5121), Av Bolivia 1501, specializes in regional woolens, including blankets and ponchos.

Getting There & Away

Air Austral (☎ 422-7198), San Martín 735, flies twice daily to Buenos Aires' Aeroparque (US$97 to US$254) except Sunday (once only). LAPA (☎ 423-2244), Belgrano 616, flies daily except Sunday to Aeroparque (US$99 to US$209) and daily except Saturday to Salta (though this short hop doesn't make much sense).

Lloyd Aéreo Boliviano (LAB; ☎ 423-0699), Güemes 779, 2nd floor, flies Monday to Santa Cruz (Bolivia) via Tucumán, with onward connections to Cochabamba and La Paz; its Thursday Santa Cruz flight is nonstop.

Though it flies out of Salta, Dinar (☎ 423-7100), Senador Pérez 308, Local 3, provides overland transfers to and from Jujuy (US$10 each way). See the Salta entry for details.

Bus The Terminal de Ómnibus (☎ 422-3934), at Av Dorrego and Iguazú, has provincial and long-distance services, but Salta has more alternatives.

Sample fares include Purmamarca (US$4, one hour), Salta (two hours, US$8), Pocitos (five hours), Tucumán (US$15, five hours), La Quiaca (US$15, seven hours), Susques (US$16, 6½ hours), Córdoba (US$25), Catamarca (9½ hours), La Rioja (12 hours), San Juan (18 hours), Mendoza (US$45, 20 hours), Resistencia (US$42 to US$55), and Buenos Aires (US$64 to US$80, 22 hours).

International Chile-bound buses from Salta stop in Jujuy before crossing the Paso de Jama to Calama (US$50), Antofagasta (US$55), Iquique (US$70), and Arica (US$75). Make reservations as far in advance as possible at Tramaca (☎ 423-6438), which leaves Tuesday, Friday, and Sunday at 8:45 am.

Long Distance Panamericano (☎ 422-7143) goes south daily to Salta (three times), Tucumán, Córdoba, and Buenos Aires, and north to destinations in the Quebrada de Humahuaca as far as the Bolivian border at La Quiaca (twice). Atahualpa (☎ 422-8402) has many buses to Salta and also to the Bolivian border posts of La Quiaca and Pocitos. El Quiaqueño (☎ 425-0588) goes five times daily to La Quiaca.

Empresa Balut (☎ 423-1157) goes north to La Quiaca, to Orán and the other Bolivian border crossing at Pocitos, and south to Salta, Córdoba, and Buenos Aires. Alsimar (☎ 423-7942) goes daily to Tucumán, Córdoba, and Buenos Aires, as does La Internacional (☎ 423-6068).

La Estrella (☎ 423-4409) goes to Pocitos (three daily), Tucumán, Córdoba, and Buenos Aires at 4:30 pm and to Neuquén at 8 am daily. TAC goes to Patagonian destinations including Río Gallegos at 8 am, Esquel at 6 pm, and General Roca at 8 pm, and to Buenos Aires at 9:15 am.

Andesmar (☎ 423-3293) runs southbound buses to Salta, Tucumán, Catamarca, La Rioja, San Juan, and Mendoza (three daily), and also goes to Pocitos. Bosio (☎ 423-4043) goes twice daily to Mendoza and thrice to Pocitos. Autotransporte Mendoza goes three times daily to Mendoza.

La Veloz del Norte (☎ 423-2366) goes frequently to Salta, twice daily to Tucumán, to Resistencia at 4:30 pm, and to Córdoba at 8:30 pm. Empresa Itatí crosses the Chaco weekly to Corrientes and Puerto Iguazú.

Provincial Empresa Purmamarca (☎ 03886-423786) goes to Purmamarca and El Moreno (five hours) at 5:45 am daily, returning at 12:30 pm. It also goes to Susques at noon Wednesday, Saturday, and Sunday, returning the following day at noon, and frequently to Libertador General San Martín (for access to Parque Nacional Calilegua). Línea Vilte goes to Susques Monday, Wednesday, and Friday at 9:30 am.

Cota Norte (☎ 422-6911) goes to Tilcara and Maimará, and also to Humahuaca from Maimará, and to Purmamarca seven times daily.

Besides its long-distance services, Panamericano also goes to Purmamarca and to remote puna settlements like El Moreno, Susques, and Olaroz Chico. Balut also goes to Purmamarca.

Getting Around

To/From the Airport Tea Turismo, 19 de Abril 485, runs minibuses to Aeropuerto Internacional Dr Horacio Guzmán (☎ 491-1106), 32km southeast of town, for US$5. LAPA provides its own airport transfers, as does Dinar (to Salta).

Car Avis (☎ 423-0433) is at Hotel Jujuy Palace, Belgrano 1060.

AROUND JUJUY

Termas de Reyes

Don't leave Jujuy without visiting these thermal baths, northwest of town on the slopes of the scenic canyon of the Río Reyes. The surrounding mountains offer good hiking.

Rustic facilities are free, but for US$6 you can wallow in the enormous, comfortable tubs at ***Hotel Termas de Reyes*** *(☎ 492-2522)*. Although the hotel's public baths were not built for the view, it's still a worthwhile experience; its outdoor swimming pool also charges nonguests US$6 for day use.

The hotel restaurant is expensive, so take along some food. For those who prefer to overnight, room rates of US$42/58 single/double include breakfast and in-room facilities; for US$51/80 you get half-board, while full board costs US$65/119.

From Plaza Belgrano, six buses daily go to the baths, at 9:30 am and 12:30, 2:30, 4:30, 7:40, and 8:45 pm.

QUEBRADA DE HUMAHUACA

The long, narrow Quebrada de Humahuaca, north of Jujuy, is an artist's palette of color splashed on barren hillsides dwarfing the hamlets where Quechua peasants scratch a living from irrigated agriculture and scrawny livestock. Though less fertile than in past centuries, the valley still supports a way of life not so different from that described by Vásquez de Espinosa in the 17th century:

> Omaguaca is an Indian village; the valley is fertile and abounds in wheat, corn, potatoes, and other native and Spanish root crops and fruit; it is all covered with small Indian villages and Spanish ranches.... There are some large rivers which flow with great turbulence.

Because the Spaniards colonized this area from Peru in the late 16th century, it has many cultural features that recall the Andean countries, particularly the numerous historic adobe churches. Earthquakes leveled many of the originals, which were often rebuilt in the 17th and 18th centuries with thick walls, simple bell towers, and striking doors and paneling hewn from the wood of the unusual *cardón* cactus. Whether you come south from La Quiaca or head north from Jujuy, there's something interesting every few miles on this colonial post route between Potosí and Buenos Aires.

The valley's main settlement is the village of Humahuaca, 130km from Jujuy, but there are so many worthwhile sights that the convenience of an automobile would be a big plus if you have a group to share expenses. Otherwise, buses are frequent enough that you should be able to do the canyon on a 'whistle-stop' basis, flagging down a bus when you need one. Excellent accommodations are available in Tilcara, only 88km from Jujuy, if things go more slowly than expected.

It is best to visit the Quebrada in the morning, when there's little wind and before the afternoon heat. Northbound travelers recommend the right side of the bus for better views (southbound, the left side is better).

Purmamarca

Beneath the polychrome Cerro de los Siete Colores (Hill of Seven Colors), a few kilometers west of RN 9 via RP 52, this tiny village's outstanding asset is its 17th-century **Iglesia Santa Rosa de Lima**. The influx of traffic due to the paving of the highway across the Andes to Calama has the potential to disrupt its tranquillity.

There's a Mercado Artesanal on the east side of the plaza, where ***La Posta de Purmamarca*** also offers meals. A simple ***hospedaje***, behind the church, is the only accommodations. There are many buses to Jujuy, and others to Tilcara and Humahuaca.

La Posta de Hornillos

Part of a chain that ran from Lima to Buenos Aires during viceregal times, this beautifully restored way station, 11km north of the Purmamarca turnoff, was the scene of several important battles during the wars of independence. The informal but informative guided tours make this an obligatory stop on the way up the Quebrada; it's open daily except Tuesday, 9 am to 6 pm.

Maimará

From an overlook on RN 9, only a few kilometers south of Tilcara, the astounding hillside cemetery of this picturesque valley settlement beneath the hill known as La Paleta del Pintor (the Painter's Palette) is a can't-miss photo opportunity. The town also has a worthwhile anthropological and historical museum.

Uquía

The 17th-century **Iglesia de San Francisco de Paula** in this roadside village displays a restored collection of paintings from the Cuzco school, featuring the famous *Ángeles arcabuceros*, angels armed with Spanish colonial weapons. It is normally closed except during mass; intending visitors should ask at the house of Adriana Valdivieso, two blocks south of the plaza – she keeps the 17th-century key and will accompany visitors to the church.

TILCARA

At an elevation of 2461m, Tilcara's most conspicuous feature is a classic Andean *pucará*, a pre-Columbian fortification commanding unobstructed views of the Quebrada de Humahuaca in several directions. The town's several museums and other interesting characteristics, including its reputation as an artists' colony, make it a highly desirable stopover. Many jujeños have weekend houses here, where hiking in the surrounding hills is a popular diversion.

Travelers should note the large monolith marking the spot where RN 9 to Humahuaca crosses the Tropic of Capricorn.

Orientation

Tilcara (population 3300), on the east bank of the Río Grande, is connected by a bridge to RN 9, which leads south to Jujuy and north to Humahuaca and La Quiaca. Its central grid is irregular beyond the village nucleus, focused on Plaza Prado. As in many small Argentine villages, people pay scant attention to street names and numbers.

Information

Little formal information is available, but El Antigal, a hotel and restaurant half a block south of Plaza Prado, distributes a small, useful brochure about the town. There are

Telecabinas on Lavalle, on the north side of Plaza Prado. Tilcara's area code is ☎ 03882, the same as Jujuy's.

El Pucará

Rising above the sediments of the Río Grande valley, an isolated hill provided the site for this reconstructed pre-Columbian fortification, 1km south of the village center. Open 9 am to 6 pm daily, the Pucará and its associated Jardín Botánico de Altura (☎ 495-5073) charges US$2 admission.

There are even better views from the hill on the road leading to the fort; from the south end of the bridge across the Río Huasamayo, it's an easy 15-minute climb to the top.

Museo Arqueológico Doctor Eduardo Casanova

The Universidad de Buenos Aires runs this outstanding, well-displayed collection of regional artifacts. Located in a striking colonial house at Belgrano 445, on the south side of Plaza Prado, it's open daily 9 am to 6 pm; admission is US$2 (US$1.50 for retired people), but it's free Tuesday. Admission is also good for El Pucará (see above).

Museo Ernesto Soto Avendaño

Ernesto Soto Avendaño, a sculptor from Olavarría (Buenos Aires province) who spent most of his life in Tilcara, was the perpetrator of Humahuaca's appalling monument to the heroes of Argentine independence. Alongside the Museo Arqueológico, this collection of his better work is open Wednesday through Sunday, 9 am to 1 pm and 3 to 6 pm.

Museo José Antonio Terry

Also located in a colonial building on the east side of Plaza Prado, this museum features the work of a Buenos Aires-born painter whose themes were largely rural and indigenous – his oils depict native weavers, market and street scenes, and portraits. Hours are daily except Monday, 7 am to 7 pm. Admission is US$2, but Thursdays are free.

Museo Irureta de Bellas Artes

Tilcara's newest museum displays an appealing collection of paintings, drawings, engravings, and sculptures by a variety of contemporary Argentine artists. At the corner of Bolívar and Belgrano, half a block west of Plaza Prado, the museum (☎ 495-5124) is open 10 am to 1 pm and 3 to 6 pm daily. Admission is free.

Special Events

Tilcara celebrates several festivals throughout the year, the most notable of which is January's Enero Tilcareño, with sports, music, and cultural activities. February's Carnaval is equally important in other Quebrada villages, as is April's Semana Santa (Holy Week). August's indigenous Pachamama (Mother Earth) festival is also worthwhile.

Places to Stay & Eat

Autocamping El Jardín *(☎ 495-5128)*, at the west end of Belgrano near the river, is a congenial place with hot showers and attractive vegetable and flower gardens, all for US$3 per adult, US$2 per child. There's an adequate free site, with picnic tables, near the YPF petrol station along the highway, but it has neither potable water nor sanitary facilities.

For US$8 per person, relocated porteños Juan and Teresa Brambati offer excellent Hostelling International accommodation at secluded, hilltop ***Albergue Malka*** *(☎ 495-5197, fax 495-5200, malka@hostels.org.ar)*, four blocks from Plaza Prado at the east end of San Martín. Breakfast and dinner are extra; Juan also arranges trekking and vehicle tours.

One block west and two blocks south of the plaza, ***Hospedaje El Pucará Casa de Piedra*** *(☎ 495-5050)* has very clean rooms in a garden setting for US$9 per person with shared bath, US$12 with private bath.

Residencial El Antigal *(☎ 495-5020)*, half a block from the plaza on Rivadavia, seems to be living on its laurels and has drawn several reader complaints, mostly for disagreeable management. Rates are US$15/25 single/double with private bath; its restaurant is still worth trying for the *locro*, a spicy stew of maize, beans, beef, pork, and sausage. ***El Pucará***, at Rivadavia and Lavalle, is also popular.

Utilitarian, two-star ***Hotel de Turismo*** *(☎ 495-5002, Belgrano 590)* costs US$30/40 with private bath; its swimming pool is usually empty. The restaurant is mediocre but passable.

Alongside the archaeological museum, the ***Café del Museo*** seems appropriate to a more urbane setting, but it's an agreeable spot for coffee and croissants.

Entertainment

La Peñalta, on Lavalle on the north side of Plaza Prado, is a folkloric peña with live music.

Getting There & Away

All the bus companies have kiosks on Plaza Prado. There are 26 buses daily to Jujuy, six of which continue to Salta. Northbound services to Humahuaca (24 daily) and La Quiaca also stop in Tilcara, and there are several buses daily to Purmamarca.

HUMAHUACA

Picturesque Humahuaca, the largest settlement between Jujuy and the Bolivian border, is a village of narrow, cobbled streets and adobe houses, with a large Quechua Indian population among its 6200 inhabitants. Nearly 3000m above sea level, it's one of the most popular destinations for budget travelers exploring the Quebrada. Locals occasionally target tourists aggressively, offering unsolicited guide services, and public drunkenness (though not so aggressive) is becoming unfortunately more common.

Orientation

Straddling the Río Grande east of RN 9, Humahuaca is very compact, so everything is within easy walking distance. The town center is between the highway and the river, but there are important archaeological sites across the bridge.

Information

Tourist Offices The tourist office, in the cabildo at Tucumán and Jujuy, is rarely open.

Post & Communications Correo Argentino is on Buenos Aires, across from the plaza; the postal code is 4630. There's a Telecentro at Jujuy 399, behind the Municipalidad. Humahuaca's area code is ☎ 03887.

Medical Services Hospital Belgrano, Santa Fe 34, is open 8 am to 1 pm and 2 to 6 pm, but there's always someone on duty for emergencies.

Things to See

Built in 1641, Humahuaca's **Iglesia de la Candelaria** faces the plaza on Calle Buenos Aires. It contains an image of the town's patron saint as well as 18th-century oils by Marcos Sapaca, a painter of the Cuzco school.

Across from the church, municipal offices occupy the **Cabildo**, famous for its clock tower, where a life-size figure of San Francisco Solano emerges daily at noon to deliver a benediction. Both tourists and locals gather in the plaza to watch the spectacle, but be sure to arrive early – the clock is erratic and the figure appears only briefly.

From the plaza, a staircase climbs to the **Monumento a la Independencia**, a chauvinistic travesty that is not the best work of Tilcara sculptor Ernesto Soto Avendaño. The Indian statue is a textbook example of *indigenismo*, a twisted nationalist tendency in Latin American art and literature that romantically extols the virtues of native cultures overwhelmed by European expansion.

Local writer and Quechua activist Sixto Vázquez Zuleta, who prefers his Quechua name of Toqo, runs the private **Museo Folklórico Regional,** open 8 am to 8 pm daily for guided tours only, with a minimum group of three or four. Toqo speaks little English but passable German.

The museum is alongside the youth hostel at Buenos Aires 447. Price for admission and tour is US$2 per person.

Special Events

Besides the Carnaval Norteño, celebrated throughout the Quebrada in February, Humahuaca observes February 2 as the day of its patron saint, the Virgen de Candelaria.

Places to Stay

Camping The municipal site across the bridge remains closed. It's possible to park or pitch a tent there for free, but there are no facilities.

Hostels The ***Albergue Juvenil*** *(☎ 421064, Buenos Aires 435)* does not require an International Youth Hostel card. For US$7 per person, it offers hot showers and kitchen facilities, but reports are that standards have fallen.

The ***Posada del Sol*** *(☎ 490508)*, a short distance across the bridge, is run by the owners of its namesake café, half a block east of the plaza. It's a little ramshackle and improvised, but has personality, hot showers, homemade bread, and free tea and coffee, and costs only US$7 per person.

Hospedajes, Residenciales & Hotels

There are two simple, inexpensive hotels. ***Residencial Humahuaca*** *(☎ 421141, Córdoba 401)*, near Corrientes, half a block from the bus terminal, charges US$10/18 single/double with shared bath, US$18/30 with private bath. ***Residencial Colonial*** *(☎ 421007, Entre Ríos 110)* costs US$12/18 with shared bath, US$20/30 with private bath.

Two-star ***Hotel de Turismo*** *(☎ 421154, Buenos Aires 650)* is the town's top-end lodging at US$30/40 with private bath, despite its drabness.

Places to Eat

For regional dishes including tamales, empanadas, and chicken, try ***Cacharpaya*** on Jujuy between Santiago del Estero and Tucumán.

El Humahuaca *(Tucumán 22)* is only so-so but palatable. ***El Fortín***, on Buenos Aires just north of Salta, is worth a look, as is ***Cafetería Belgrano*** (good pizza) near the railway line. There's an acceptable confitería at the bus terminal.

Entertainment

Peña de Fortunato, at the corner of San Luis and Jujuy, has regional cuisine and live folk music.

Shopping

Visit the handicrafts market, near the train station, for woolen goods, souvenirs, and the atmosphere. The quality is excellent, but northbound travelers will probably find similar items at lower prices in Bolivia.

Getting There & Away

The Terminal de Ómnibus is at Belgrano and Entre Ríos. Panamericano, Balut, Cota Norte, and Atahualpa run numerous southbound buses to Salta and Jujuy, with northbound buses to La Quiaca (US$15, 2½ hours).

Transportes Mendoza (☎ 421016), at Belgrano and Salta, offers service to the Andean village of Iruya (US$7, three hours), daily except Tuesday and Thursday, at 10:15 am; these may not leave at all in summer when it rains. Buses return from Iruya the same days at 3 pm.

AROUND HUMAHUACA

Coctaca

Covering about 40 hectares, Coctaca is northwestern Argentina's most extensive pre-Columbian ruins. Although they have not yet been excavated, many of the ruins appear to have been broad agricultural terraces on an alluvial fan, but there are also obvious outlines of clusters of buildings. The nearby school is training guides to the site.

After rains, the road may be impassable. It's possible to hike 10km to the ruins, but leave before the heat of the day and take water. After crossing the bridge across the Río Grande in Humahuaca, follow the dirt road north and bear left until you see the village of Coctaca.

LA QUIACA

Near Abra Pampa, a forlornly windy town 90km north of Humahuaca, RN 9 becomes a dusty graveled road (gradually being paved) that climbs abruptly to the high steppe *(altiplano)* typical of western Bolivia. Except in the summer rainy season, nightly frosts make agriculture precarious, so people concentrate subsistence efforts on livestock that can survive on the sparse *ichu* grass – llamas, sheep, goats, and a few cows. Off the main highway, look for flocks of the

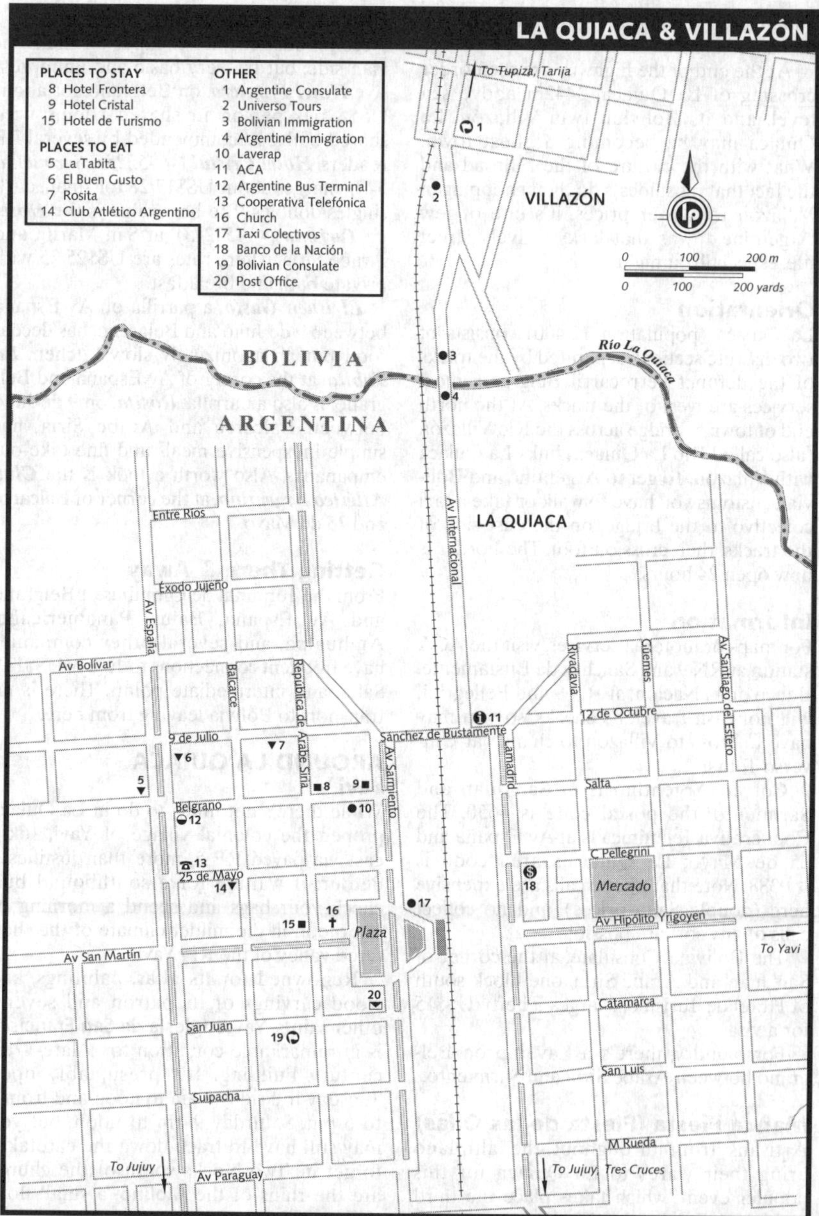
LA QUIACA & VILLAZÓN
PLACES TO STAY
8 Hotel Frontera
9 Hotel Cristal
15 Hotel de Turismo
PLACES TO EAT
5 La Tabita
6 El Buen Gusto
7 Rosita
14 Club Atlético Argentino
OTHER
1 Argentine Consulate
2 Universo Tours
3 Bolivian Immigration
4 Argentine Immigration
10 Laverap
11 ACA
12 Argentine Bus Terminal
13 Cooperativa Telefónica
16 Church
17 Taxi Colectivos
18 Banco de la Nación
19 Bolivian Consulate
20 Post Office
To Tupiza, Tarija
VILLAZÓN
BOLIVIA
ARGENTINA
Río La Quiaca
LA QUIACA
Av Internacional
Entre Ríos
Éxodo Jujeño
Av España
Av Bolívar
Balcarce
República de Árabe Siria
Av Sarmiento
Rivadavia
Güemes
Av Santiago del Estero
12 de Octubre
Sánchez de Bustamente
Lamadrid
9 de Julio
Salta
Belgrano
C Pellegrini
Mercado
25 de Mayo
Plaza
Av Hipólito Yrigoyen
To Yavi
Av San Martín
Catamarca
San Juan
San Luis
Suipacha
M Rueda
To Jujuy
Av Paraguay
To Jujuy, Tres Cruces
0 100 200 m
0 100 200 yards

endangered vicuña, a wild relative of the llama and alpaca.

At the end of the highway are the border crossing of La Quiaca, 3442m above sea level, and its Bolivian twin Villazón. La Quiaca may be becoming a ghost town. What with the closure of the railroad and the fact that most locals do their shopping in Villazón for lower prices, it's one of few Argentine towns that lacks a lively street life, especially at night.

Orientation

La Quiaca (population 12,400) consists of two discrete sections, separated by the tracks of the defunct Ferrocarril Belgrano; most services are west of the tracks. At the north end of town, a bridge across the Río Villazón (also called Río La Quiaca) links La Quiaca with Villazón. To get to Argentine and Bolivian customs you have to walk or take a taxi colectivo to the bridge, on the east side of the tracks, then cross on foot. The border is now open 24 hours.

Information

For maps or motorist services, visit the ACA station at RN 9 and Sánchez de Bustamente. Banco de la Nación, at RN 9 and Pellegrini, will not cash traveler's checks, so you may have to cross to Villazón to change at Universo Tours.

Correo Argentino is at San Juan and Sarmiento; the postal code is 4650. The Cooperativa Telefónica is at Av España and 25 de Mayo; La Quiaca's area code is ☎ 0388. Note that phone calls are expensive here (double Salta prices), and no collect calls of any sort are possible.

The Bolivian Consulate, at the corner of San Juan and Árabe Siria, one block south of Hotel de Turismo, charges a hefty US$15 for a visa.

For laundry, there's a Laverap on Belgrano between Árabe Siria and Sarmiento.

Manca Fiesta (Fiesta de las Ollas)

Artisans from throughout the altiplano bring their wares to La Quiaca for this popular event, which takes place the third and fourth Sundays of October.

Places to Stay & Eat

Accommodations are cheaper on the Bolivian side, but try very basic and unimpressive ***Hotel Frontera***, on Belgrano, for about US$8 per person in shared rooms with shared baths. Recommended by several LP readers, ***Hotel Cristal*** *(☎ 452255, Sarmiento 543)* charges about US$17/28 for small, dark singles/doubles. The best value is the ***Hotel de Turismo*** *(☎ 452243)*, at San Martín and Árabe Siria, where rates are US$25/35 with private bath and breakfast.

El Buen Gusto, a parrilla on Av España between 9 de Julio and Belgrano, has decent food but an agonizingly slow kitchen. ***La Tabita***, at the corner of Av España and Belgrano, is also a parrilla. ***Rosita***, on 9 de Julio between Balcarce and Árabe Siria, has simple inexpensive meals and fine take-out empanadas. Also worth a look is the ***Club Atlético Argentino***, at the corner of Balcarce and 25 de Mayo.

Getting There & Away

From the Terminal de Ómnibus at Belgrano and Av España, Balut, Panamericano, Atahualpa, and several other companies have frequent connections to Jujuy (US$14), Salta, and intermediate points. There is no transport to Bolivia leaving from here.

AROUND LA QUIACA

Yavi

While there's not much to do in La Quiaca proper, the colonial village of Yavi, 16km east via paved RP 5, more than justifies a detour; if waiting for a southbound bus, check your bags and spend a morning or afternoon in the milder climate of the sheltered valley of the Río Yavi.

Renowned for its altar, paintings, and wood carvings of its patron and several other saints, Yavi's **Iglesia de San Francisco** is in remarkable condition for a late-17th-century building. It's presumably open Tuesday to Friday 9 am to noon and from 3 to 6 pm, Saturday 9 am to noon, but you may still have to track down the caretaker to get in. Two blocks south of the church are the ruins of the **Molino**, a small flour mill.

Across the street from the church, in less than splendid condition, the **Casa del Marqués Campero** belonged to a Spanish noble whose marriage to the holder of the original encomienda in this reducción created a family that dominated the regional economy in the 18th century. Now a museum, it contains nothing of the Marqués' possessions, which are scattered around Jujuy, Hornillos, and Salta, but the eclectic contents (like an old Victrola) lend it a certain charm and there's an interesting antiquarian library. Ask directions to the caretaker's house to see the museum, which keeps erratic hours.

Near Yavi there are several short hikes in the **Cerros Colorados**, including one to rock paintings and petroglyphs at **Las Cuevas** and another to springs at **Agua de Castilla**. Alejandro Toro (☎ 03887-49112), who works in the park alongside the Casa del Marqués Campero, is a knowledgeable local guide. Free ***camping*** is possible in the park, which gets very crowded with people from La Quiaca on weekends.

Flota La Quinqueña provides regular public transport from La Quiaca to Yavi, but shared cabs are another alternative. Every half hour or so, there's a pickup truck that runs from La Quiaca's Mercado Municipal on Av Hipólito Yrigoyen.

MONUMENTO NATURAL LAGUNA DE LOS POZUELOS

Three species of flamingos plus coots, geese, ducks, and many other birds breed along the barren shores of this 16,000-hectare lake, at an altitude of nearly 4000m, where you may also see the endangered vicuña. There are archaeological sites as well.

Because the park is so isolated, a car is the best transportation option, but carry extra fuel; there is no gasoline available beyond Abra Pampa, midway between Humahuaca and La Quiaca. Heavy summer rains can make the unpaved routes off the main highway impassable.

From Abra Pampa, Panamericano and Vilte have mid-morning buses to Rinconada, west of the lake, where there are simple accommodations. Empresa Mendoza goes daily at 11:30 am (US$7). On request, the bus will drop you off at the Río Cincel ranger station, where it's a 7km walk over level puna to the laguna.

Camping is possible on very exposed sites, with basic infrastructure, at the ranger station. For the latest information, ask at the tourist office in Jujuy or at the Centro Cultural in Abra Pampa.

PARQUE NACIONAL CALILEGUA

On the eastern borders of Jujuy province, the high and arid altiplano gives way to the dense subtropical cloud forest of the Serranía de Calilegua, whose preservation is the goal of this accessible, 75,000-hectare park. At the park's highest elevations, about 3600m, verdant Cerro Hermoso reaches above the forest and offers boundless views of the Gran Chaco to the east. Bird life is abundant and colorful, but the tracks of rare mammals, such as puma and jaguar, are easier to see than the animals themselves.

As of late 1998, Calilegua and nearby Baritú were under threat of a gas pipeline construction, which was opposed by both the Argentine branch of Greenpeace and the local Aymara (Kolla) organization Tinkunaku.

Information

Park headquarters (☎ 03886-422046) is in the village of Calilegua just off RN 34, just north of Libertador General San Martín. Donated by the Ledesma sugar mill, the building includes a visitor center with exhibits on the region's national parks and monuments, including Calilegua, Baritú, El Rey, and Laguna Pozuelos. The staff can also provide the latest information on road conditions, since many areas are inaccessible during the summer rainy season. La Veloz del Norte buses between Salta and Orán stop at the excellent and reasonable restaurant belonging to the Club Social San Lorenzo, next door to park headquarters. There are many buses to Ledesma, only a couple kilometers south of Calilegua.

Another source of information is Restaurant del Valle, part of the new Hotel Posada del Sol, which also arranges backcountry tours and has an email address (rhbellon@cooperlib.com.ar).

Flora & Fauna

Receiving 2000mm of precipitation a year, but with a defined winter dry season, Calilegua comprises a variety of ecosystems correlated with altitude. The 'transitional *selva*,' from 350 and 500m above sea level, consists of tree species common in the Gran Chaco, such as lapacho and *palo amarillo*, which drop their leaves in winter. Between 550 and 1600m, the 'cloud forest' forms a dense canopy of trees more than 30m tall, punctuated by ferns, epiphytes, and lianas, covered by a thick fog in summer and autumn. Above 1200m, the 'montane forest' is composed of 'pines' (a general term for almost any conifer, such as cedar), *aliso*, and *queñoa*. Above 2600m this grades into moist puna grasslands, which become drier as one proceeds west toward the Quebrada de Humahuaca.

The 230 bird species include the condor, brown eagle, torrent duck, and the colorful toucan. Important mammals, rarely seen in the dense forest, include tapir, puma, jaguar, collared peccary, and otter.

Things to Do

Nature-oriented activities will be the focus of any visit to Calilegua. The best places to view birds and mammals are near the stream courses in the early morning or very late afternoon, just before dark. From the ranger station at Mesada de las Colmenas, follow the steep, rugged, and badly overgrown trail down to a beautiful creek usually marked with numerous animal tracks, including those of large cats. The descent takes perhaps an hour, the ascent twice that.

There are excellent views from 3600m Cerro Hermoso, although there are no detailed maps; ask rangers for directions. Ordinary vehicles cannot go far past the Mesada de las Colmenas, but the road itself offers outstanding views of Cerro Hermoso and the nearly impenetrable forests of its steep ravines.

From Valle Grande, beyond the park boundaries to the west, it's possible to hike to Humahuaca along the Sierra de Zenta or to Tilcara, but the treks take at least a week. For details, see the 3rd edition of Bradt Publications' *Backpacking in Chile and Argentina* (1994). It's also possible to do the hike in the other direction; see Juan Brambati at Tilcara's Albergue Malka for summer departures.

Places to Stay & Eat

Camping is the only alternative in the park itself. The developed free ***camping site*** at Aguas Negras, on a short lateral road near the ranger station at the entrance, has balky bathrooms and water shortages. Beware mosquitoes, which are a lesser problem at higher elevations. Although there are no other developed campsites, you can camp on a level area at the ranger station at Mesada de las Colmenas, which has great open views to the east.

There are several residenciales in nearby Libertador General San Martín, such as ***Residencial Gloria*** *(Urquiza 270)* for US$10 per person with shared bath, US$12 per person with private bath. Presently under construction, the new ***Hotel Posada del Sol*** also includes the ***Restaurant del Valle***.

Getting There & Away

Empresa Valle Grande goes from Libertador General San Martín at 7 am Tuesday and Saturday, returning at 11 am Thursday and Sunday. However, inquire at the park visitor center for the most current information.

Otherwise, it should be possible to hitch to the park and Valle Grande with the logging trucks that pass through the park on RP 83. Start from the bridge at the north end of the town of Libertador General San Martín, where there is a good dirt road through mostly shady terrain to Aguas Negras, 8km west.

Salta Province

In the Noroeste, Salta is the province with everything. Argentina's best-preserved colonial city, the provincial capital, is the center for excursions to the montane subtropical forests of Parque Nacional Finca El Rey, the polychrome desert canyons of El Toro and Cafayate, along with their vineyards, and the sterile but scenic salt lakes and volcanoes of the high puna. Hundreds of archaeological sites and colonial buildings testify to Salta's importance in both pre-Hispanic and colonial times, even though it declined with Argentine independence.

In colonial times, Salta's marshy but fertile Lerma valley pastured thousands of mules that were bred on the Pampas of Buenos Aires and sold at an annual fair – in the 17th and 18th centuries, up to 70,000 animals per year found their way to Bolivia and Peru, where they performed a wide variety of tasks in the mining industry. Independence and political fragmentation reduced this trade, a blow from which Salta has never completely recovered. In the early 20th century, it briefly reoriented itself toward Chile, supplying beef to the nitrate mines of the Atacama Desert across the Andes, but this trade declined as petroleum-based fertilizers supplanted mineral nitrates in the world economy. Today, Salta is primarily an agricultural province, dependent on sugar cane, tobacco, and bananas, plus an increasing tourist trade, with minor contributions from mining and petroleum.

SALTA

Founded in 1582 by Hernando de Lerma, Salta lies 1200m above sea level in a basin surrounded by verdant peaks. This valley's perpetual spring attracted the Spaniards, who could pasture animals in the surrounding countryside and produce crops that could not grow in the frigid Bolivian highlands, where the mining industry created enormous demand for hides, mules, and food. When extension of the Belgrano railroad made it feasible to market sugar to the immigrant cities of the Pampas, the city recovered slightly from its 19th-century decline.

Orientation

At the town of General Güemes, RN 9 veers sharply west, climbing gradually through endless cane fields before dropping steeply into the Lerma valley and the city of Salta. From the central Plaza 9 de Julio, Salta's conventional grid extends in all directions until it ascends the eastern overlooks of Cerro 20 de Febrero and Cerro San Bernardo, whose streets hug their contours.

Although Salta (population 374,000) has sprawled considerably over the past several years, most points of interest are within a few blocks of Plaza 9 de Julio. The commercial center is southwest of the plaza, where both Alberdi and Florida become pedestrian malls between Caseros and Av San Martín. North-south streets change their names on either side of the plaza, but the names of east-west streets are continuous.

Information

Tourist Office The provincial Secretaría de Turismo (☎ 431-0950), Buenos Aires 93, is open 8 am to 9 pm daily. It has some English-speaking staff, and brochures and maps, and is helpful in locating accommodations in private houses.

The Dirección Municipal de Turismo (☎ 437-3341), at the corner of Av San Martín and Buenos Aires, is open 8 am to 9 pm daily; in high season, at the bus terminal, it maintains a smaller office that closes from 1 to 4 pm.

The Administración de Parques Nacionales (☎ 431-0255), Santa Fe 23, has information on the province's several national parks.

ACA (☎ 431-0551) is at Rivadavia and Mitre.

Immigration Migraciones (☎ 422-0438) is at Maipú 35, 11 blocks west of Plaza 9 de Julio.

SANDRA BAO

On the road to Salta

Money Cambio Dinar, Mitre 101, changes cash and traveler's checks, the latter at a high commission. Banco Roberts, Mitre 143, cashes traveler's checks without commission; it and several other banks around Plaza 9 de Julio have ATMs.

Post & Communications Correo Argentino is at Deán Funes 170; the postal code is 4400. There are many Telecentros, including one on Buenos Aires just half a block south of Plaza 9 de Julio. Salta's area code is ☎ 0387.

Internet Resources Shownet, 20 de Febrero 28, has Internet access.

Travel Agencies Chicoana Turismo (☎ 431-4027), Zuviría 255, Local 1, is the AmEx representative. For city tours (US$20) and excursions in the Salta area, try Yaco Turismo (☎ 431-6704), Buenos Aires 39, which arranges trips to destinations like Cuesta del Obispo (US$33, seven hours), Valles Calchaquíes (US$90, two days), and Parque Nacional El Rey (US$100, two days).

Clark Expediciones (☎/fax 421-5390), Caseros 121, specializes in bird-watching trips to the province's national parks and more remote areas. It also doubles as a bookstore; English-speaking owner Ricardo Clark has authored several books on Argentine birds.

Bookstores There are three good downtown bookstores, Feria del Libro at Buenos Aires 83, Rayuela at Buenos Aires 94, and Plural Libros at Buenos Aires 220.

Laundry Lavandería Sol de Mayo (☎ 431-9718) is at 25 de Mayo 755.

Walking Tour

Several colonial buildings in Salta's historic downtown have become important museums, but even visitors arriving on Monday, when most are closed, can absorb the colonial atmosphere by walking around the area. To see most of the buildings, head north from the corner of Florida and Alvarado,

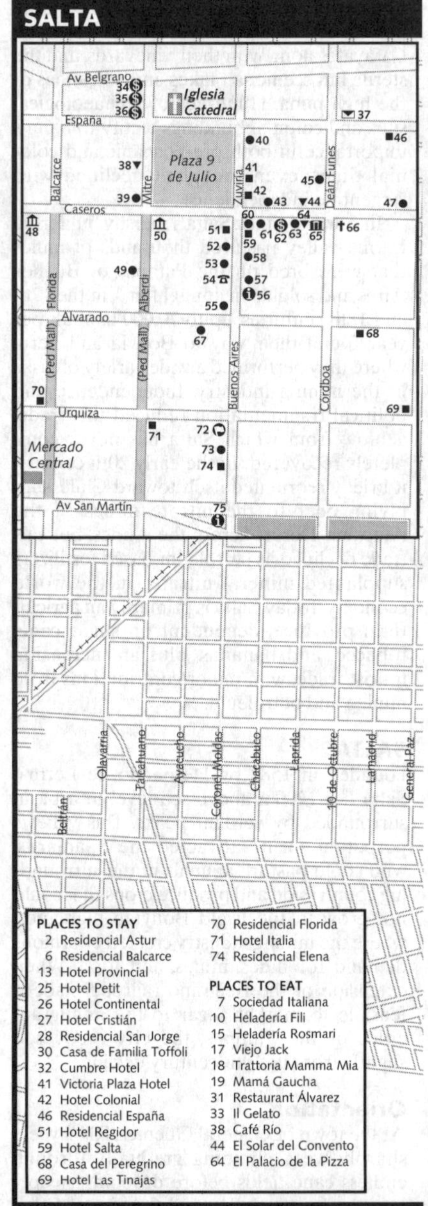

SALTA

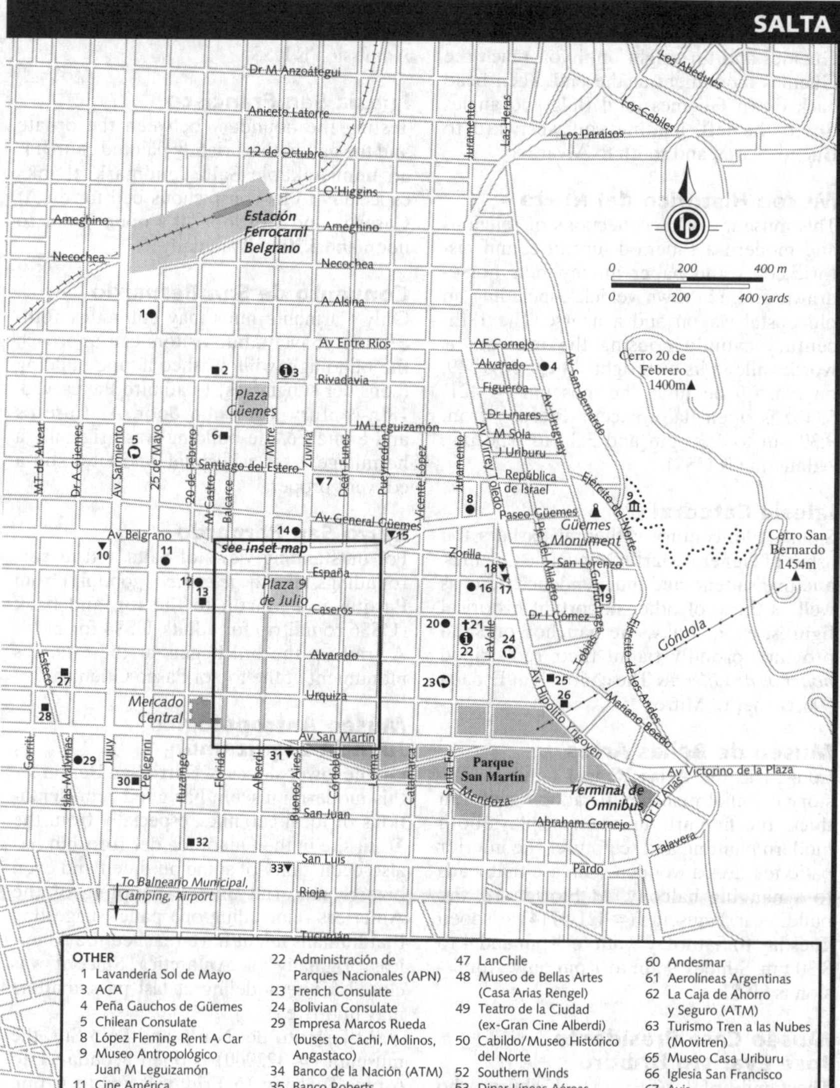

OTHER

1 Lavandería Sol de Mayo
3 ACA
4 Peña Gauchos de Güemes
5 Chilean Consulate
8 López Fleming Rent A Car
9 Museo Antropológico Juan M Leguizamón
11 Cine América
12 Shownet (Internet Access)
14 Chicoana Turismo (AmEx)
16 Dulces Regionales La Negrita
20 Clark Expediciones
21 Convento de San Bernardo
22 Administración de Parques Nacionales (APN)
23 French Consulate
24 Bolivian Consulate
29 Empresa Marcos Rueda (buses to Cachi, Molinos, Angastaco)
34 Banco de la Nación (ATM)
35 Banco Roberts
36 Cambio Dinar
37 Post Office
39 Casa de Gobierno
40 Cine Victoria
43 LAPA
45 Lloyd Aéreo Boliviano
47 LanChile
48 Museo de Bellas Artes (Casa Arias Rengel)
49 Teatro de la Ciudad (ex-Gran Cine Alberdi)
50 Cabildo/Museo Histórico del Norte
52 Southern Winds
53 Dinar Líneas Aéreas
54 Telecentro
55 Rayuela
56 Secretaría de Turismo
57 Feria del Libro
58 Yaco Turismo
59 Dollar Car Rental
60 Andesmar
61 Aerolíneas Argentinas
62 La Caja de Ahorro y Seguro (ATM)
63 Turismo Tren a las Nubes (Movitren)
65 Museo Casa Uriburu
66 Iglesia San Francisco
67 Avis
72 German Consulate
73 Plural Libros
75 Dirección Municipal de Turismo

turning east on Caseros past the plaza to Av Hipólito Yrigoyen. Head north to Paseo Güemes and turn right until you reach the Güemes monument at the end. Then head back down Güemes until Belgrano angles off to the left, leading you westward to Buenos Aires, and south to Alvarado.

Museo Histórico del Norte

This museum holds collections of religious and modern art, period furniture, and historic coins and paper money, plus horse-drawn and ox-drawn vehicles, including an old postal wagon and a hearse. The 18th-century cabildo housing the museum is worthwhile in its own right. At Caseros 549, on Plaza 9 de Julio, the museum (☎ 421-5340) is open daily except Tuesday from 9:30 am to 1:30 pm and 3:30 to 8:30 pm. Admission is US$1.

Iglesia Catedral

Salta's 19th-century cathedral harbors the ashes of General Martín Miguel de Güemes, a native salteño and independence hero, as well as those of other important historical figures; even today, the gauchos of Salta province proudly flaunt their red-striped *ponchos de Güemes*. The church is at España 596, corner of Mitre.

Museo de Bellas Artes

Lodged in the Arias Rengel family's two-story colonial mansion, its adobe walls 2m thick, the fine-arts museum displays both modern painting and sculpture. The interior patio features a wooden staircase that leads to a hanging balcony. At Florida 18, the building and museum (☎ 421-4714) are open Tuesday to Saturday 9 am to 1 pm and 4 to 8:30 pm, Sunday 9 am to 1 pm only. Admission is US$1.

Museo Casa Presidente José Evaristo Uriburu

The family of José Evaristo Uriburu, who was twice President of the Republic (both times briefly), lived in this 18th-century house at Caseros 417. Open Tuesday through Friday 9:30 am to 1:30 pm and 3:30 to 8:30 pm, Saturday 9:30 am to 1:30 pm only, the museum (☎ 421-5340) features a well-preserved collection of period furniture. Admission is US$1.

Iglesia San Francisco

Testing the boundary between the ornate and the gaudy, this brightly painted church is an unmistakable Salta landmark, thanks especially to its conspicuous bell tower. At Caseros and Córdoba, it's open 7 am to noon and 5:30 to 9 pm daily.

Convento de San Bernardo

Only Carmelite nuns may enter this 16th-century convent, but visitors can approach the blindingly whitewashed adobe building (consider sunglasses) to admire the carved, 18th-century algarrobo door. At Caseros and Santa Fe, the building was originally a hermitage, later a hospital, and later still a convent proper.

Cerro San Bernardo

For outstanding views of Salta and its surroundings, take the *teleférico* (gondola) from Parque San Martín to the top and back (US$6 roundtrip for adults, US$4 for kids). A trail up the hill begins at the Güemes monument at the top of Paseo Güemes.

Museo Antropológico Juan M Leguizamón

On the lower slopes of Cerro San Bernardo, this modern museum has good representations of local ceramics, especially from the Tastil site in the Quebrada del Toro, but has also been guilty of some outdated and even bizarre material on the peopling of the Americas – including one panel suggesting that humans might have reached the Americas originally via Antarctica. Since it was closed for remodeling at last pass, matters may improve.

At Ejército del Norte and Polo Sur, the museum (☎ 422960) is open Monday 1 to 6 pm, Tuesday to Friday 8 am to 6 pm, Sunday 10 to 1 pm. Admission is US$1.

Places to Stay – Budget

Camping One of Argentina's best campgrounds, ***Camping Municipal Carlos***

Xamena *(☎ 423-1341)* has 500 tent sites and one of the world's largest swimming pools (it takes a week to fill in the spring). Fees are US$2 per car, US$3 per tent, US$2 per adult, and US$1 per child. Its major drawback is that in summer, when salteños flock here to catch some rays, they play unpleasantly loud music for the swimmers and sunbathers. Mercifully, they switch off the sound system by early evening. You can purchase food and drinks at the nearby supermarket.

From downtown, take southbound bus No 13 ('Balneario'), which also connects with the train station.

Hostels The Hostelling International affiliate is ***Backpacker's Hostel*** *(☎/fax 423-5910, hostelsalta@impsat1.com.ar, Buenos Aires 930)*, 10 blocks south of Plaza 9 de Julio and 13 blocks from the bus terminal. Despite the hostel's cramped conditions, the enthusiastic Argentine-Israeli management has made it so popular that reservations are advisable. They offer Internet access to guests and arrange tours, and it's a good place to organize a group to rent a car to explore the high country. Rates are $8 per person with kitchen facilities for members; nonmembers pay US$9.

Bus No 12 from the terminal stops nearby, but the hostel also offers free transfers.

Another possibility is the ***Casa del Peregrino*** *(☎ 432-0423, Alvarado 351)*, which charges US$6 in six-bed rooms with shared bath, US$8 in four-bed rooms with private bath. Less central, but equally reasonable, the ***Residencia Universitaria Santa Bárbara*** *(☎ 425-2189, Av 17 de Junio)*, has comfortable facilities in the Ciudad del Milagro neighborhood, north of downtown. Bus No 20 goes there.

Casas de Familia, Residenciales & Hotels

The Secretaría de Turismo maintains a list of private houses that are an excellent alternative to bottom-end hotels. One of the most popular and central is run by María de Toffoli *(☎ 431-8948, Mendoza 915)*, one of three sisters. The other two let rooms in their own houses next door *(☎ 421-2233, Mendoza 917, and ☎ 421-7383, Mendoza 919)*. All have pleasant patios, kitchen facilities, and spotless bathrooms, for US$10 per person.

Despite the virtual disappearance of rail service, the area near the train station retains inexpensive accommodations like ***Residencial Astur*** *(☎ 421-2107, Rivadavia 752)* for US$18/25, and ***Residencial Balcarce*** *(☎ 421-8023, Balcarce 460)* for US$20/25.

Two blocks south and six blocks west of Plaza 9 de Julio, ***Residencial San Jorge*** *(☎ 421-0443, Esteco 244)* costs US$9 per person with shared bath, US$20/25 single/double with private bath. Take local bus No 3 or No 10 from the Terminal de Ómnibus.

Italian-run ***Hotel Italia*** *(☎ 421-4050, Alberdi 231)* is very central and charges US$19/27 for plain but spacious and sunny rooms. Attractive ***Residencial Elena*** *(☎ 421-1529, Buenos Aires 256)*, in a neocolonial building with an interior patio, offers rooms for US$20/28 but seems reluctant to accept single travelers.

Another possibility is ***Residencial España*** *(☎ 421-7898, España 319)* for US$20/30. For US$21/31 is the central but architecturally undistinguished ***Residencial Florida*** *(☎ 421-2133, Urquiza 718)*.

Places to Stay – Mid-Range

Prices for mid-range accommodation have risen recently except at a couple of places like ***Hotel Las Tinajas*** *(☎ 431-8197, Lerma 288)*, which charges US$25/35 for singles/doubles. ***Hotel Continental*** *(☎ 431-1083, Hipólito Yrigoyen 295)* costs US$30/50.

Rates at upgraded ***Hotel Petit*** *(☎ 421-3012, Hipólito Yrigoyen 225)* are US$40/55, while ***Hotel Colonial*** *(☎ 431-0760, Zuviría 6)* costs US$40/60. Downtown near Plaza 9 de Julio, try ***Hotel Regidor*** *(☎ 431-1305, Buenos Aires 8)* for US$43/65. Two new but well-regarded choices, both charging around US$40/65, are ***Cumbre Hotel*** *(☎ 431-7770, Ituzaingó 585)* and ***Hotel Cristián*** *(☎ 431-9600, Islas Malvinas 160)*.

Places to Stay – Top End

Another step up is the ***Victoria Plaza Hotel*** *(☎ 431-0334, Zuviría 10)*, which charges about US$65/82 for standard singles/doubles but US$75/92 for VIP quarters, and even more for suites.

At attractive, centrally located ***Hotel Salta*** *(☎ 421-1413, Buenos Aires 1)*, rates start at US$67/90 and rise as high as US$104/142, but several readers have found it a less than outstanding value. Try also ***Hotel Provincial*** *(☎ 421-8993, Caseros 786)*, ranging from US$85/110 up to US$145 double.

Places to Eat

One of the cheapest places to eat is Salta's large, lively ***Mercado Central***, Florida and San Martín, where you can supplement inexpensive pizza, empanadas, and humitas with fresh fruit and vegetables. Even if you're not a budget traveler, pay the market a visit.

Álvarez *(☎ 421-4523, Buenos Aires 302)* has large portions of palatable, cheap food. ***El Palacio de la Pizza*** Caseros 437, is a reasonable choice for pizza. The ***Sociedad Italiana***, Zuviría and Santiago del Estero, has quality four-course meals for about US$6. ***Café Río*** *(☎ 421-1296, Mitre 41)* comes reader-recommended.

Viejo Jack *(Av Virrey Toledo 145)* and ***Viejo Jack II*** *(☎ 439-2802, Av Reyes Católicos 1465)* are separate branches of a popular parrilla that has drawn enthusiastic readers' reviews. ***El Solar del Convento*** *(Caseros 444)* is an appealing downtown parrilla.

For superb, varied pasta at reasonable prices (US$4 to US$5 per entrée, check out ***Trattoria Mamma Mia*** *(☎ 422-5061, Pasaje Zorrilla 1)*; dessert prices are also good, and there's tobacco-free seating. Its very Argentine counterpart is ***Mamá Gaucha*** *(☎ 431-7307, Gurruchaga 225)*.

Salta has several fine ice creameries, including ***Heladería Rosmari*** *(Pueyrredón 202)*, ***Heladería Fili*** *(Av Güemes 1009)*, and ***Il Gelato*** *(Buenos Aires 606)*.

Entertainment

Cinema The ***Cine Victoria*** *(Zuviría 70)* charges only US$3 Monday through Thursday for current films. ***Cine América*** is at the corner of España and 25 de Mayo.

Theater The former Gran Cine Alberdi is now the ***Teatro de la Ciudad*** *(☎ 431-3330, Alberdi 56)*, which features live theater and music performances.

Live Music For impromptu entertainment, don't miss ***La Casona del Molino*** *(☎ 431-6079, Luis Burela 1)*, about 20 blocks west of Plaza 9 de Julio. This former mansion, a real Salta experience, also serves great empanadas and humitas in several spacious rooms, each with different performers – though the distinction between audience and performer is dubious in this participatory milieu. Meals cost from US$7 to US$17.

Another traditional place is the ***Peña Gauchos de Güemes*** *(☎ 421-0820, Av Uruguay 750)*, which is more expensive and less spontaneous.

Shopping

For souvenirs, the most noteworthy place is the provincially sponsored Mercado Artesanal (☎ 434-2808) at the west end of Av San Martín, reached by bus Nos 2, 3, or 7 from downtown. Articles for sale include native handicrafts like hammocks, string bags, ceramics, basketry, leather work, and the region's distinctive ponchos. It's open 9 am to 9 pm daily.

In the Cabildo, opposite Hotel Salta, Horacio Bertero is a protégé of silversmith Raúl Horacio Draghi, San Antonio de Areco's best-known artisan.

Dulces Regionales La Negrita (☎ 421-1833), España 79, sells local sweets.

Getting There & Away

Air Aerolíneas Argentinas (☎ 431-1331), Caseros 475, flies three times daily (except Sunday, with only two flights) to Buenos Aires' Aeroparque (US$139 to US$248). Dinar Líneas Aéreas (☎ 431-0606), Buenos Aires 46, Local 2, flies nonstop every weekday to Aeroparque (US$139 to US$219), and daily to Aeroparque via Tucumán. LAPA (☎ 421-0386), Caseros 492, flies twice each weekday and once on Saturday and on Sunday to Aeroparque (US$99 to US$209, and daily except Sunday to Jujuy.

Lloyd Aéreo Boliviano (☎ 431-0320), Deán Funes 29, flies Tuesday, Friday, and Sunday to Santa Cruz (Bolivia), with onward connections. LanChile (☎ 421-1500), Caseros 322, has seasonal flights across the Andes.

Andesmar (☎ 431-0875), at Caseros 489, flies daily except Sunday from Salta to Tucumán (US$24 to US$48), Córdoba (US$76 to US$100), and Mendoza (US$125 to US$159); Monday and Friday to Tucumán, Córdoba, and Rosario, and Sunday to Tucumán and Córdoba only.

Southern Winds (☎ 421-0808), Buenos Aires 28, flies twice each weekday, once Saturday and once Sunday to Córdoba (US$82 to US$109); daily to Rosario (US$119 to US$159) and Mendoza (US$127 to US$169); weekdays to Mar del Plata (US$149 to US$199); daily to Neuquén (US$142 to US$189); Tuesday, Wednesday, and Thursday to Tucumán; Wednesday and Saturday to Bariloche (US$157 to US$209); and Tuesday to Aeroparque (US$104 to US$139).

Bus Salta's Terminal de Ómnibus (☎ 431-5227), on Av Hipólito Yrigoyen southeast of downtown, has frequent services to all parts of the country. Most companies are located in the terminal, but a few have offices nearby or elsewhere in town.

Sample fares include Jujuy (US$6 to US$9, two hours), Cafayate (US$9 to US$10, three hours), San Antonio de los Cobres (US$14, five hours), Cachi (US$14, five hours), Tucumán (US$15 to US$18, four hours), Molino (US$20, 7½ hours), Santiago del Estero (US$20 to US$26, five hours), Angastaco (US$25, 9½ hours), Catamarca (US$26), La Quiaca (US$23, nine hours), Resistencia (US$32 to US$42, 13 hours), La Rioja (US$35), Córdoba (US$45, 12 hours), Santa Fe (US$50, 15 hours), San Juan (US$50, 17 hours), Mendoza (US$61, 19 hours), Rosario (US$57 to US$73, 17 hours), Buenos Aires (US$64 to US$86, 22 hours) and Mar del Plata (US$85, 19 hours).

International For US$55, Tramaca (☎ 431-2497) goes Tuesday and Friday to the Chilean destinations of San Pedro de Atacama (12 hours) and Calama, (14 hours). Buses depart at 7 am. There are connections to Antofagasta (US$60), Iquique (US$72), and Arica (US$75).

Empresa Godoy goes four times daily to Resistencia, continuing onward to Asunción, Paraguay.

Long Distance Many companies make the northbound run to Jujuy and up the Quebrada de Humahuaca to the Bolivian border at La Quiaca, among them Internacional (☎ 431-2430), Balut (☎ 432-0608), and La Veloz del Norte (☎ 431-7215). Atahualpa (☎ 431-3544) runs several buses daily on this route.

La Internacional and La Veloz del Norte both cross the Chaco to Resistencia daily, the former at 7:30 pm and the latter at 5 pm. La Veloz also goes three times daily to Santiago del Estero, Rosario, and Buenos Aires, and 10 times to Tucumán, with less frequent southbound service to La Rioja, Catamarca, Córdoba, San Juan, Mendoza, and Mar del Plata.

La Internacional also goes twice daily to Tucumán and twice daily to Santiago del Estero, Rosario, and Buenos Aires. Chevallier (☎ 431-2819) goes twice daily to Tucumán. Panamericano (☎ 431-1957) has frequent service to Tucumán, Santiago del Estero, and Córdoba, plus Mar del Plata.

Andesmar (☎ 431-0263) goes to Mendoza and other Cuyo destinations, and even farther south to Patagonia. TAC (☎ 431-0600) and Autotransportes Mendoza also go to Cuyo and Patagonia.

Provincial El Indio (☎ 431-9389) leaves five times daily for Cafayate except Sunday (four times), while El Cafayateño (☎ 431-3544) goes twice daily except Sunday (once). El Quebradeño (☎ 431-4068) goes daily to San Antonio de los Cobres.

Empresa Marcos Rueda (☎ 421-4447), Islas Malvinas 393, serves the altiplano village of Cachi twice daily except Monday and Wednesday, when it goes once only; it also goes daily except Monday to Molinos, and Thursday to Angastaco.

Train The Ferrocarril Belgrano (☎ 421-3161), Ameghino 690, no longer offers regular passenger services. One of Salta's popular attractions, though, is the scenic ride to and beyond the mining town of San Antonio de los Cobres on the famous Tren a las Nubes (Train to the Clouds) – contact Turismo Tren a las Nubes (☎ 431-4984, fax 431-6174), Caseros 431, or see the entry on San Antonio de los Cobres for details.

The local freight, leaving Friday at about 9:20 am (the ticket office opens at 8 am – reservations can't be made), is a cheaper alternative for getting to San Antonio de los Cobres. It also goes farther, on a 29-hour marathon ride to the Chilean border at Socompa (US$10 to San Antonio, US$30 to Socompa). From San Antonio de los Cobres you can catch a return El Quebradeño bus to Salta (departing at 9 am; $14), but see also the separate entry on Tren a las Nubes later in this chapter.

Getting Around

To/From the Airport Aeropuerto Internacional El Aybal (☎ 423-1648) is 9km southwest of town on RP 51; buses to and from the airport cost US$3.

To/From the Bus & Train Stations Local bus No 5 connects the train station and downtown with the bus terminal on Av Hipólito Yrigoyen, which is southeast of downtown. Bus No 13 connects the station with the municipal campground.

Car Renting a car is a good way to see Salta's countryside, but it's far from cheap – figure a minimum of US$27 per day plus US$0.27 per kilometer, plus US$17 for insurance. Three-day deals with 800km included are available for about US$280 plus insurance. Among the agencies are Avis (☎ 431-7575) at Alvarado 537, López Fleming (☎ 421-4143) at Av Güemes 92, and Dollar (☎ 431-8049) at Buenos Aires 1 in Hotel Salta.

NATIONAL PARKS OF SALTA PROVINCE

Salta has three important national parks, but only one, Los Cardones, is easily accessible. Finca El Rey is increasingly accessible, thanks to road improvements, while Baritú must be approached through Bolivia.

Parque Nacional Los Cardones

Occupying some 70,000 hectares on both sides of the winding highway from Salta to Cachi across the Cuesta del Obispo, Parque Nacional Los Cardones takes its name from the candelabra cactus known as the cardón *(Trichocereus pasacana)*, the park's most striking plant species. Only 100km from Salta, the park finally obtained official national park status in 1997, after several years in administrative limbo.

In the absence of forests in the Andean foothills and the puna, the cardón has long been an important source of timber for rafters, doors, window frames, and similar uses. As such, it is commonly found in native construction and in the region's colonial churches. According to Argentine writer Federico Kirbus, clusters of cardones can be indicators of archaeological sites – the Indians of the puna ate its sweet black seed, which, after passing through the intestinal tract, readily sprouted around their latrines.

Los Cardones still has no visitor services, but there is a ranger in Payogasta, 11km north of Cachi. Buses between Salta and Cachi will drop you off or pick you up, but verify times. If visiting Buenos Aires before going to Salta, drop by the Parques Nacionales office to check the latest information; otherwise, try the Secretaría de Turismo in Salta. Salta's Backpacker's Hostel (☎/fax 423-5910, hostelsalta@impsat1.com.ar), Buenos Aires 930, sometimes arranges trips to the park.

Parque Nacional Baritú

Hugging the Bolivian border in Salta province, Baritú is the most northerly of the three Argentine parks conserving subtropical montane forest. Like Calilegua (see the entry under Jujuy province) and Finca El Rey (see below), it protects diverse flora and harbors a large number of endangered or threatened mammals, including black howler and capuchin monkeys, the southern river otter, Geoffroy's cat, the jaguar, and the Brazilian tapir. The park's emblem is the *ardilla roja* (yungas forest squirrel), which inhabits the moist montane forest above 1300m.

It was here, in 1963, that Che Guevara's psychopathic disciple Jorge Ricardo Masetti tried to start the Argentine revolution by infiltrating from Bolivia. At present, the only road access to Baritú is through Bolivia, where southbound travelers from Tarija may want to inquire about entry via a lateral off the highway that goes to the border station at Bermejo/Aguas Blancas. For information in Argentina, contact the visitor center at Parque Nacional Calilegua (☎ 03886-422046) in the village of Calilegua, Jujuy province.

Parque Nacional Finca El Rey

Confined to a narrow strip, no wider than about 50km, Argentina's subtropical humid forests extend from the Bolivian frontier south of Tarija almost to the border between Tucumán and Catamarca provinces. Parque Nacional Finca El Rey, comprising 44,000 hectares almost directly east of Salta, is the southernmost Argentine park protecting this unusual habitat, the most biologically diverse in the country. It takes its name from the estancia that formerly occupied the area, whose expropriation led to the park's creation.

The park's emblem is the giant toucan, appropriate because of the abundant bird life, but the mosquito might be just as appropriate (check yourself for ticks, for that matter). Most of the same mammals found in Baritú and Calilegua are also present here. The staff maintain a vehicular nature trail along the Río Popayán and there's a foot trail (actually an abandoned road) to moss-covered **Pozo Verde**, a 2½-hour climb to an area teeming with bird life. There are several shorter trails.

There is free ***camping*** at park headquarters, in a grassy area with water and pit toilets, but no other infrastructure. At last pass, the park's comfortable hostería was closed, but contact the Parques Nacionales office in Salta for up-to-date information.

As the crow flies, Finca El Rey is only about 100km from Salta, but via paved RN 9, paved but rutted RP 5, and RP 20 it's more than 200km from the provincial capital. There is public transport as far as the junction of RN 9 and RP 5, but even if you can hitch to the second junction, there's little traffic for the last 46km to park headquarters. The latter road is much improved, but even 4WD vehicles are no sure bet in heavy summer rains.

QUEBRADA DE CAFAYATE

Salta's Lerma valley receives abundant rainfall from summer storms that drop their load on the slopes surrounding the city, but higher ranges of peaks to the south and west inhibit the penetration of subtropical storms. In several areas, the rivers that descend from the Andes have carved deep *quebradas* (canyons) through these arid zones, exposing the multicolored sedimentary strata that underlie the surface soils.

Many of these layers have eroded to strange, sometimes unearthly formations, which southbound travelers from Salta can appreciate from paved RN 68, but which are even more intriguing when explored up close. For its extraordinary scenery, the canyon deserves national or provincial park status.

Properly speaking, the Quebrada de Cafayate is the Quebrada del Río de las Conchas, after the river that eroded the canyon. Beyond the tiny village of Alemania, about 100km south of Salta, the scenery changes suddenly and dramatically from verdant hillsides to barren, reddish sandstones. To the east, the Sierra de Carahuasi is the backdrop for distinctive landforms bearing evocative names like Garganta del Diablo (Devil's Throat), El Anfiteatro (The Amphitheater), El Sapo (The Toad), El Fraile (The Friar; a nearby farm sells empanadas and cold drinks), El Obelisco (The Obelisk), and Los Castillos (The Castles). Just north of Cafayate, Los Médanos is an extensive dunefield.

Getting There & Away

Other than renting a car (possible in Salta but not in Cafayate) or the ideal alternative, riding a bicycle (rental bikes are available in Cafayate), the only ways to see the quebrada are to take the bus, hitch, or walk. Tours from Salta are brief and regimented. You can disembark from any El Indio bus and a succeeding bus will pick you up. Be aware of the schedules between Salta and Cafayate, as you probably don't want to get stuck in the canyon after dark (although if you have your tent along there are worse places to camp). The same holds if you hitch between the most interesting sites – you may want to catch one of the buses if it gets late.

Walking allows you to see the canyon at your own pace, but carry food and plenty of water in this hot, dry environment. A good place to start is the impressive box canyon of Garganta del Diablo. Remember that the most interesting portion is much too far to walk in a single day, so see as much as you can before continuing to Cafayate – you can always double back the next day.

CAFAYATE

Several major Argentine vintners have vineyards near Cafayate, whose warm, dry, and sunny climate is ideal for the cultivation of wine grapes – a local specialty is the fruity white *torrontés*. The most important town in extreme southwestern Salta province, Cafayate is a popular tourist destination, but rarely overrun with visitors except on weekends.

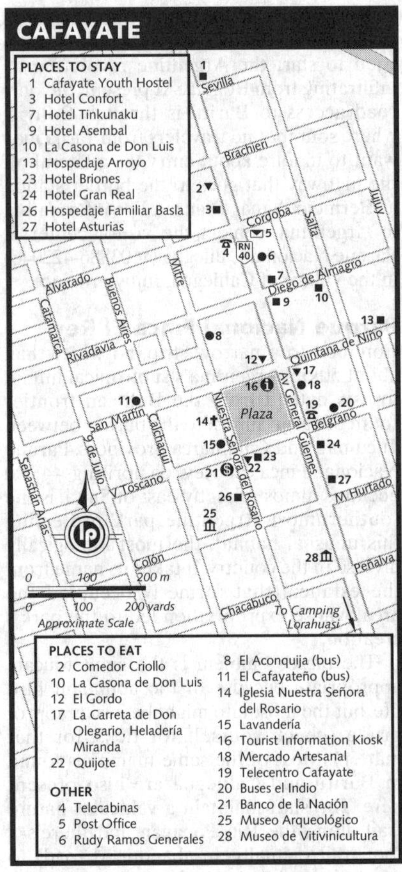

Orientation

Cafayate sits at 1660m at the foot of the Calchaquí valley, near the junction between RN 40, which goes northwest to Molinos and Cachi, and RN 68, which goes to Salta through the Quebrada de Cafayate. Through town, RN 40 is Av Güemes. As in many provincial towns, few people bother with street names.

Information

The tourist information kiosk at the northeast corner of Plaza San Martín is open weekdays 9 am to 8 pm, weekends 9 am to 1 pm and 3 to 9 pm. It's better to change money elsewhere, but try Banco de la Nación on the plaza, or the larger shops or hotels.

Correo Argentino is at Güemes and Córdoba; the postal code is 4427. Telecentro Cafayate is at the corner of Güemes and Belgrano, Telecabinas at the corner of Güemes and Alvarado. Cafayate's area code is ☎ 03868.

The lavandería at the corner of Toscano and Nuestra Señora del Rosario, washes clothes.

Museo Arqueológico

In this private museum, the late Rodolfo Bravo, a dedicated aficionado of and expert on the region, left an astounding personal collection of Calchaquí (Diaguita) ceramics, as well as colonial and more recent artifacts, such as elaborate horse gear and wine casks. While there's not much explication, the material itself is worth seeing. The museum is at the corner of Colón and Calchaquí; drop in at any reasonable hour, as his widow and son still give tours for US$1.

Wineries

On Güemes near Colón, the **Museo de Vitivinicultura** details the history of local wine production; it's open weekdays 10 am to 1 pm and 5 to 8 pm; admission is US$1.

Three nearby wineries offer tours and tasting. At the southern approach to town, Bodega Etchart (3000 hectares) is open for guided tours weekdays 7:30 am to noon and 3 to 6:30 pm, Saturday 8 am to noon only. At the north end of town, the smaller Bodega La Banda (800 hectares) offers cheerful tours, even for one person, 9 am to 1 pm and 3 to 6 pm daily.

Bodega La Rosa, belonging to Michel Torino and near the RP 68 junction to the Quebrada de Cafayate north of town, is open Monday through Thursday 8 am to 5 pm, Friday 8 am to 4 pm. The imposing **Casa de Alto**, an Italian-style villa at the junction, is no longer part of the Torino properties and is not open to the public.

Special Events

La Semana de Cafayate, at the end of February or beginning of March, is a three-day folklore festival. The annual Fiesta de la Virgen, in early October, is worthwhile if you're in the area.

Places to Stay

Camping Although it can be dusty when the wind blows, the municipal ***Camping Lorohuasi*** *(☎ 421051)*, on RN 40 at the south end of town, charges US$2 per car, per person, and per tent. Facilities are decent and include dependable hot showers and a swimming pool, though some of the toilets are a bit funky.

Lorohuasi also has claustrophobic four-bed cabañas for US$20 per night – OK for an intimate group, with two bunks on each side and limited storage space. There's a small grocery, but you can also buy food in town, which is just a 10-minute walk.

WAYNE BERNHARDSON

Vineyards, Cafayate

Hostels Despite the sign outside, the ***Cafayate Youth Hostel*** *(☎ 421440, Av Güemes Norte 441)* is not an official Hostelling International affiliate. Still, it's friendly and has good facilities for US$8 per person.

Residenciales & Hotels In an old adobe mansion at the corner of Salta and Diego de Almagro, with a particularly attractive patio, ***La Casona de Don Luis*** is one of Argentina's best hotel values, but it's hard to imagine that prices of US$10 per person, for spotless rooms with private bath, won't go up.

Hospedaje Familiar Basla *(☎ 421098, Nuestra Señora del Rosario 153)* charges US$10 per person in clean multibed rooms. ***Hospedaje Arroyo***, Quintana de Niño 160, is comparably priced.

Hotel Confort *(☎ 421091, Av Güemes Norte 232)* charges US$15 per person with private bath. Clean and spacious but a bit dark, ***Hotel Tinkunaku*** *(☎ 421148, Diego de Almagro 12)* charges US$20/38 single/double with breakfast, but ask about discounts.

For US$25/35, ***Hotel Briones*** *(☎ 421270, Toscano 80)*, on the plaza, is a lesser value than it once was, but still has a decent confitería. ***Hotel Asembal*** *(☎ 421065)*, at Güemes and Almagro, costs US$20 per person, while ***Hotel Gran Real*** *(☎ 421231, Güemes 128)* costs only US$15 per person except in summer, when rates rise to US$48 double. The dingy downstairs confitería does not enhance its appeal.

Hotel Asturias *(☎ 421040, Güemes 154)* costs US$20 per person except in summer, when rates climb to US$27. At US$30/43 with breakfast, ACA's ***Hostería de Cafayate*** *(☎ 421296)* on RN 40 north of town, is a bargain for members but costs US$35/50 for nonmembers.

Places to Eat

Besides La Casona de Don Luis, whose restaurant looks great but was unfortunately closed for a private party at last pass, ***La Carreta de Don Olegario*** *(☎ 421004, Av Güemes 2)* has an appealing menu with many regional dishes, but not everything is always available. Try also ***Quijote***, alongside Hotel Briones at the southwest corner of the plaza.

There are several cheaper places, such as ***El Gordo***, on the north side of the plaza, and ***Comedor Criollo***, on Güemes Norte between Alvarado and Brachieri, serving large portions of unexceptional Argentine food with occasional regional specialties.

Heladería Miranda, at Güemes and C. Quintana de Niño, has imaginative wine-flavored ice cream – torrontés and cabernet.

Shopping

Cafayate has many young artists and craftspeople; check the Mercado Artesanal, on Güemes across from the tourist office, for local handicrafts.

Getting There & Away

El Indio, on Belgrano between Güemes and Salta, has five buses daily to Salta (US$9, four hours), except Sunday when there are four. There are also five daily to San Carlos, up the Valle Calchaquí, and one to Angastaco (US$6). El Cafayateño, at the corner of San Martín and Buenos Aires, goes twice daily to Salta except Sunday (once).

Use the daily buses to Santa María to visit the important ruins at Quilmes (see later in this chapter), in Tucumán province. From Mitre 77, El Aconquija's twice-daily buses to Tucumán (US$17, 6½ hours) both pass through Tafí del Valle; one goes via Santa María.

Getting Around

For US$10, Rudy Ramos Generales, Av Güemes Norte 175, rents mountain bikes from 8:30 am to 3 pm, time enough to take an early Salta bus to El Anfiteatro and ride back to town through the Quebrada de Cafayate.

VALLES CALCHAQUÍES

In these valleys, north and south of Cafayate and one of the main routes across the Andes to Chile and Peru, Calchaquí Indians put up some of the stiffest resistance to Spanish rule. In the 17th century, plagued with labor shortages, the Spaniards twice tried to impose forced labor obligations on the Calchaquíes, but found themselves having to maintain armed forces to prevent the indigenes from sowing crops and attacking pack trains.

Military domination did not solve Spanish labor problems, since their only solution was to relocate the Indians as far away as Buenos Aires, whose suburb of Quilmes bears the name of one group of these displaced people. The last descendants of the 270 families transported to the viceregal capital had died or had dispersed by the time of Argentine independence.

When their resistance failed, the Calchaquíes lost the productive land that had sustained them for centuries and would have done so much longer. According to American geographer Isaiah Bowman, who visited the area in the 1920s, 'So fertile is the soil of the Calchaquí valley . . . that alfalfa lasts for twenty five years without resowing.' Those riches found their way into the hands of Spaniards who formed large rural estates, the haciendas of the Andes.

Definitely one of Argentina's most appealing off-the-beaten-track areas, the Valles Calchaquíes combine striking natural landscapes with unique cultural and historical resources. The vernacular architecture merits special attention – even modest adobe houses affect neoclassical columns and/or Moorish arches.

Quilmes

Although it is in the province of Tucumán, the pre-Columbian fortress of Quilmes is only 50km south of Cafayate and many travelers will approach it from this direction.

Probably the best-restored archaeological site in the country, this pucará deserves a visit despite its location 5km off the main highway. See the Tucumán section later in this chapter for details.

Angastaco

From Cafayate, paved RN40 continues north to San Carlos, beyond which it becomes a bumpy, dusty gravel surface passing among wildly tilted sedimentary beds even more interesting than the Quebrada de Cafayate. Angastaco (population 650), 74km north of Cafayate and 51km beyond San Carlos, resembles other oasis settlements placed at regular intervals in the Valles Calchaquíes, with vineyards, fields of peppers, and ruins of an ancient pucará. There is also an archaeological museum.

Hostería Angastaco *(☎ 03868-491123, 03868-1563-9016 cellular)* has rooms for US$20 per person with breakfast and a swimming pool; dinners costs about US$7, and the manager's daughter also organizes horseback rides for about US$7 per hour. In addition to the hostería, there's the cheaper but still very fine ***Pensión Cardón*** for just US$7 per person.

Friday at 11 am, Expreso Marcos Rueda has a bus to Molinos, Cachi, and Salta (US$25), returning to Angastaco Thursday afternoon. There's a daily bus to Cafayate.

Molinos

Dating from 17th-century encomiendas, Molinos (population 500) takes its name from the still-operative grain mill on the Río Calchaquí; its restored 18th-century **Iglesia de San Pedro de Nolasco**, in the Cuzco style, features twin bell towers and a traditional tiled roof. Like Angastaco, Molinos was a way station on the trans-Andean route to Chile and Peru, and well into the 20th century, pack trains passed here with skins, wool, blankets, and wood for sale in Salta and subsequent shipment to Buenos Aires. In a dispute with the federal government, La Rioja caudillo Felipe Varela occupied the town in 1867.

Also known as the **Casa de Isasmendi**, after encomendero Nicolás Severo de Isasmendi (1753-1857), the 18th-century ***Hostal Provincial de Molinos*** *(☎ 0387-431-1711 in Salta)* provides lodging for US$60/78 with breakfast. Isasmendi, Salta's last colonial governor, was born, lived, and died in this sprawling residence in a town that was a stronghold of royalist resistance. Restored in 1988, it features a small but worthwhile archaeology museum and a small artisans' shop. The patio, shaded by a spreading pepper tree, is also worth a stop.

Travelers lacking the wherewithal to stay at the Hostal can try the tidy ***Camping Municipal*** (US$3 per person), which has access to the showers and toilets at the adjacent ***Albergue Municipal***, an impeccable new facility with half a dozen rooms, each outfitted with two single beds, for US$10 per person.

About 1.5km west of Molinos is the **Criadero Coquera**, where INTA, Argentina's agricultural extension service, is raising vicuñas; alongside it is the **Casa de Entre Ríos**, part of the former Estancia Luracatao, where there's a very fine artisans' market with spectacular alpaca 'ponchos de Güemes' for sale.

Getting There & Away Daily except Thursday at 6:45 am, a Marcos Rueda bus goes to Salta (US$20, seven hours) via RN 40 through Cachi and RP33 through Parque Nacional Los Cardones.

Cachi

With its scenic surroundings, cobbled streets, 18th-century church, and archaeological museum, Cachi (population 1800) is probably the single most appealing stopover among the valley's more accessible settlements. On the west side of Plaza 9 de Julio, the **Centro de Artesanías** (☎ 03868-491053) is both a crafts market and the de facto tourist office, open 9 am to 2 pm and 3 to 8 pm weekdays, 10 am to 1 pm and 2 to 8 pm Saturday, and 10 am to 1 pm Sunday. It also rents mountain bikes for US$10 per day, US$5 per half day, and has its own website (www.salnet.com.ar/cachi/).

On the east side of the plaza, the simple but attractive **Iglesia San José** (1796) features a three-bell tower, graceful arches, and a tightly fitted ceiling of cardón wood. The confessional and other features are also made of cardón.

Directly south of the church, Cachi's **Museo Arqueológico Pío Pablo Díaz** offers a professionally arranged account of the surrounding area's cultural evolution. Except for the improbable suggestion that the first South American ceramics arrived by sea from Japan 5400 years ago, and the debatable assertion that settled agriculture improved the Diaguita diet, the museum is a welcome contrast to many provincial institutions that make little effort to interpret their materials in a regional context. It's open weekdays 8 am to 7 pm, Saturday 10 am to 2 pm and Sunday 10 am to 1 pm. Admission is US$1.

Places to Stay & Eat Cachi's ***Camping Municipal***, on a hilltop about 1km southwest of the plaza, has shaded sites surrounded by privet hedges for US$5; sites without hedges are slightly cheaper. On the same grounds is the ***Albergue Municipal***, where beds cost US$5 per person.

For US$10 per person, modest but central ***Hotel Nevado de Cachi*** *(☎ 03868-491004)* is the cheapest accommodations. For US$15 plus US$2 for breakfast, though, the best place is charming ***Hospedaje El Cortijo de María Luisa*** *(☎ 03868-491034)*, a recycled colonial-style building that's truly one of the best in the country. It's across from ACA's ***Hostería Cachi*** *(☎ 03868-491105)*, which has singles/doubles for US$28/43 for members, US$37/57 for nonmembers. The breakfast gets no raves, but there are several other restaurants.

Getting There & Away You can reach Cachi either from Cafayate or, more easily and frequently, by the Marcos Rueda bus from Salta. This route passes across the scenic Cuesta de Obispo past Parque Nacional Los Cardones (see above). There are two buses daily to Salta (US$15) except Tuesday and Wednesday (one only).

From Cachi, buses continue to La Poma, an old hacienda town that, for all practical purposes, is the end of the line. The road beyond, to San Antonio de los Cobres, is impassable except for vehicles with 4WD; it's much easier to approach San Antonio from Salta via the Quebrada del Toro.

San Antonio de los Cobres

In colonial times, transportation from northwestern Argentina depended on pack trains, most of which passed through the Quebrada de Humahuaca on the way to Potosí, but an alternative route crossed the rugged elevations of the Puna de Atacama to the Pacific and then continued to Lima. A member of Diego de Almagro's party, the first Spaniards to cross the puna, left an indelible account of the dismal 800km crossing, which took 20 days in the best of times:

> Many men and many horses froze to death, for neither their clothes nor their armor could protect them from the freezing wind. . . . Many of those who had died remained, frozen solid, still on foot and propped against the rocks, and the horses they had been leading also frozen, not decomposed, but as fresh as if they had just died; and later expeditions . . . short of food, came upon these horses and were glad to eat them.

For trans-Andean travelers, the area around the bleak mining town of San Antonio de los Cobres (altitude 3700m) must have seemed an oasis, though even as late as 1914 it had a population below 1000. Until well into this century, it continued to be an important way station for drovers moving their stock across the mountains to arid Chile, whose narrow alluvial valleys could not produce the food needed for the nitrate miners of the Atacama Desert. Later, railroads and rugged highways supplanted mules for shipping food and supplies to Argentine mining settlements and across the Andes.

San Antonio de los Cobres (population 3500) is a largely Indian town, but the posters and political graffiti scribbled on its adobe walls serve as reminders that it's still part of Argentina. For truly intrepid travelers, it still offers one of the most interesting border crossings in all of Argentina, paralleling the routes of the muleteers across the

Puna de Atacama to the Pacific coast of Chile via the famous Train to the Clouds.

Places to Stay & Eat Until recently, San Antonio had only the most basic accommodations and food – and still, for the most part, what you see is what you get. That's basic lodging at ***Hospedaje Belgrano*** (☎ *490-9025*) or ***Hospedaje Los Andes***, for about US$8 per night per person, with plenty of blankets (nights are always cold at this elevation) and shared bath. Hospedaje Los Andes has a restaurant, and limited food and drink are also available in the few shops.

Hostería de las Nubes (☎ *0387-490-9056/8*) has attempted to fill the accommodations gap with 12 rooms with private baths, double-glazed windows, and a total of 30 beds. It also has a restaurant, central heating, and a TV lounge; rates are US$40/50 single/double, including breakfast, but can rise by 20% in the July-August peak season. Make reservations at Tren a las Nubes Turismo (☎ 0387-431-4984, fax 431-1264, Caseros 443) in Salta.

Getting There & Away There are daily buses from Salta to San Antonio de los Cobres (US$14, five hours) with El Quebradeño. See below for details on the scenic Tren a las Nubes trip from Salta to San Antonio de los Cobres and beyond.

Do not waste time trying to hitch across the Andes because there are almost no vehicles; even the summer buses operated by Géminis and Atahualpa from Salta now go via Jujuy and the Paso de Jama.

EL TREN A LAS NUBES & THE CHILEAN CROSSING

From Salta, the Tren a las Nubes (Train to the Clouds) leaves the Lerma valley to ascend the multicolored Quebrada del Toro, continuing past the important ruins of Tastil as it parallels RN 51. To reach the heights of the puna on the Chilean border, 571km west (though the Tren a las Nubes travels less than half this distance), the track makes countless switchbacks and even spirals, passes through 21 tunnels more than 3000m in total length, and crosses 31 iron bridges

WAYNE BERNHARDSON

El Tren a Las Nubes

and 13 viaducts. The trip's highlight, a stunning viaduct 64m high and 224m long, weighing 1600 tons, and spanning an enormous desert canyon at La Polvorilla, is a magnificent engineering achievement unjustified on any reasonable economic grounds. At Abra Chorillos, an altitude of 4575m makes this the fourth-highest operating line in the world.

From April to October, Tren a las Nubes Turismo (☎ 0387-431-4984, fax 431-1264), Caseros 443 in Salta, operates the Tren a las Nubes service only as far as La Polvorilla; most trips take place weekends only, but they can be more frequent during the July holidays. The train leaves at 7:05 am and returns to Salta at 10:15 pm. The fare is US$95 for the 438km roundtrip, which reaches a maximum altitude of 4200m. Meals are additional, ranging from a US$11 fixed-price lunch in the dining car to sandwiches and hamburgers for US$3.50 to US$4.50. Some travelers have gotten slightly less comfortable 'discount carriage' tickets for US$50.

Freight trains from Salta, which you may be able to catch in Rosario de Lerma or San Antonio de los Cobres, are a cheaper alternative to the Tren a las Nubes; for more details, see the Getting There & Away entry for the city of Salta. Freights are the only possibility from October to April, passing the gigantic salt lakes of the puna to the Chilean border station at Socompa, where it is feasible to catch the Chilean freight to the Atacama Desert station of Baquedano on the Carretera Panamericana, about 100km from the port of Antofagasta. On the Chilean side, this is a rugged, uncomfortable trip, not for the squeamish.

At Socompa, 3900m above sea level, passengers must clear Argentine and Chilean immigration and customs before seeking permission to ride the infrequent westbound freights – it is not unusual to wait several days for a train. The Chilean station agent will radio for permission to carry passengers in the train's caboose; while permission is fairly routine, it is not guaranteed. Purchase some Chilean pesos before leaving Salta, since the agent may offer *very* unfavorable rates for US dollars.

From Socompa, the train descends with impressive views of 6051m Volcán Socompa to the east and 6739m Llullaillaco to the south, through vast monochrome deserts that few visitors to the continent ever see. At the abandoned mining station of Augusta Victoria, the crew may ask you to disembark while the train backtracks to another isolated mining outpost, but it will return. You may, however, wish to try hitching to Antofagasta – in this isolated area, mining trucks serve as informal public transport and almost certainly will stop. Otherwise, sleep in the abandoned station, which is far more comfortable than the caboose, until the train returns.

Tucumán Province

Tucumán is Argentina's smallest province, but its size belies its importance. From colonial times, when it was an important way station en route to Potosí, through the early independence period and into the present, Tucumán has played a critical role in the country's political and economic history.

In contemporary Argentina, Tucumán means sugar. Unlike areas to the north, Tucumán benefits from both its proximity to the high Sierra de Aconquija to the west and the absence of a front range to the east. This permits warm, easterly winds to drop their moisture on the sierra, bringing moderate winter temperatures – the area within 60km of its slopes is frost-free. These humid slopes and dense, subtropical forests give birth to permanent streams for irrigation. While sugar monoculture has enabled the province to develop secondary industry, it has also created tremendous inequities in wealth and land distribution, as well as ecological problems. Yields per hectare have fallen in comparison with Salta and Jujuy.

The extreme west of the province is a high, arid extension of the Valles Calchaquíes, but the scenic area around Tafí del Valle is a

Who's on the Train?

British capital and engineers built most of Argentina's railways, but the line from Salta to the Chilean border, used by the Tren a las Nubes, is one of few exceptions. New York-born Richard Maury, who also worked in Cuba, came to Argentina in 1906 at the age of 24. He modified an earlier design for the awesome La Polvorilla viaduct and, with a crew of 1300 laborers, built a two-section steel bridge over the Río Toro. Buried in the village of Campo Quijano, the North American engineer is also memorialized at a station known as Ingeniero Maury, 2358m above sea level. Still, a project first proposed in 1905 and not begun until 1921 was not completed until 1948.

Workers on the Huaytiquina line came from around the world. Legend says that one of the immigrant applicants was a taciturn Yugoslav exile, who started at Campo Quijano and worked his way up the Quebrada de Toro before returning to Buenos Aires and, later, to Europe. In World War II, Josip Broz led a guerrilla struggle against the Nazis and, after the war, became president of his country. Most know him as Marshal Tito.

Readers interested in more detail should consult Federico Kirbus' *El Fascinante Tren a las Nubes* (Buenos Aires: Editorial El Ateneo, 1993), on sale in both Buenos Aires and Salta.

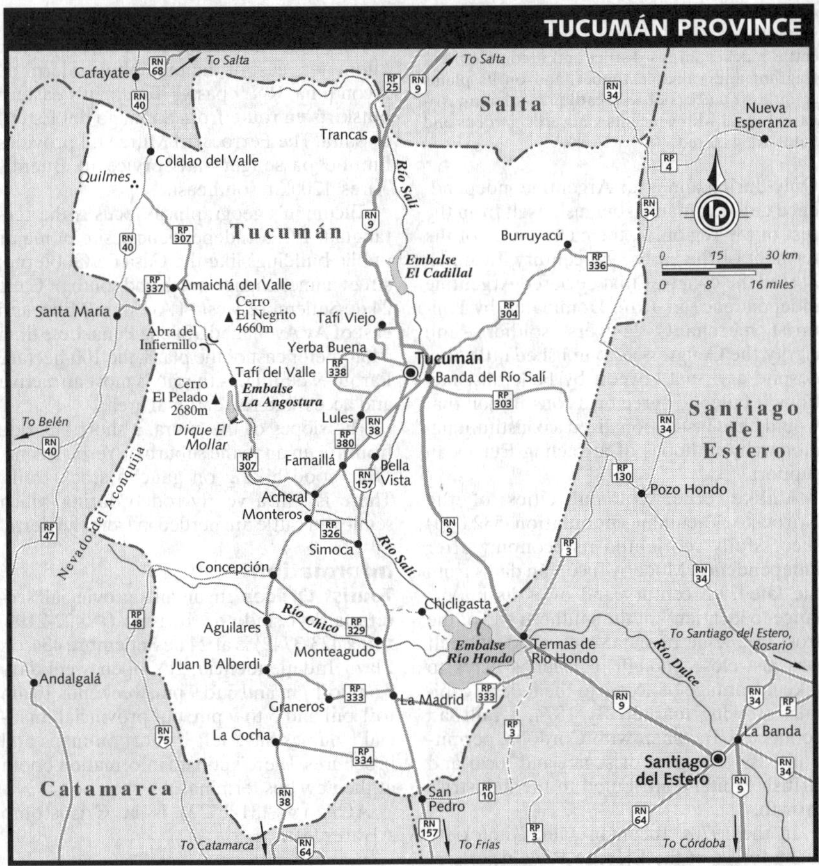

climatic anomaly, a cool, damp valley between subtropical mountains and arid puna, where potatoes are the most important crop. The precipitous mountain road (RN 38 to RP 307) from Tucumán to Tafí del Valle is a spectacular trip no visitor to the area should miss.

TUCUMÁN

Although Tucumán (formally known as San Miguel de Tucumán) is the commercial and administrative center for the sugar industry, visitors find its main appeal in its colonial and 19th-century historical sites and its access to the scenic Sierra de Aconquija. Founded in 1565 at the convergence of roads from Rosario, Córdoba, and Santa Fe, the city and its hinterland were oriented toward Salta and Bolivia for most of the colonial period. Vásquez de Espinosa's early-17th-century description paints Tucumán as the most prosperous of the early Spanish cities:

> It has as many as 250 Spanish residents; its climate is very hot and damp. It has in its neighborhood some Indian parishes in which are produced

> quantities of cotton cloth, canopies, bedspreads and other elaborate products. There are mule and cattle ranches in this district and it contains very fragrant and valuable timber, and on its plains countless numbers of wild cattle . . . It has an irrigation canal with which its vineyards, gardens and fields are watered.

Only during and after Argentine independence did Tucumán distinguish itself from the rest of the region. In the culmination of the ferment of the early 19th century, Tucumán hosted the congress that declared Argentine independence in 1816. Dominated by Unitarist merchants, lawyers, soldiers, and clergy, the Congress accomplished little else; despite a virtual boycott by Federalist factions, it failed to agree on a constitution that would have institutionalized a constitutional monarchy in hopes of attracting European support.

Unlike other colonial cities of the Noroeste, Tucumán (population 532,000) successfully reoriented its economy after independence. Modern Tucumán dates from the late 19th century and owes its importance to location – at the southern end of the frost-free zone of sugar-cane production, it was just close enough to Buenos Aires to take advantage of access to the federal capital's growing market. By 1874, a railroad connected Tucumán with Córdoba, permitting easy transport of sugar, and local and British capital contributed to the industry's growth.

In the 1970s, Tucumán gained notoriety when forces of the Ejército Revolucionario del Pueblo (ERP) in the forests of the Sierra de Aconquija waged a guerrilla campaign, ruthlessly suppressed by General Antonio Domingo Bussi – currently the province's elected governor. In early 1997, though, Bussi himself ran into problems when he was found to have hidden a Swiss bank account whose funds may have been illegal acquisitions during the Proceso. Though the provincial legislature was unable to impeach Bussi because his Fuerza Republicana party held enough seats to block such action, the governor was politically weakened and became vulnerable to prosecution in the courts.

Orientation

On the west bank of the Río Salí, only a few kilometers east of the precipitous Sierra de Aconquija, RN 9 passes Tucumán's eastern outskirts en route from Santiago del Estero to Salta. The Ferrocarril Mitre still provides limited passenger rail service to Buenos Aires, 1200km southeast.

Tucumán's geographical focus is the rectangular Plaza Independencia, site of major public buildings like the Casa de Gobierno; street names change north and south of Calle 24 de Setiembre, west of Av Alem/Mitre, and east of Av Avellaneda/Sáenz Peña. Less than a kilometer east of the plaza, the 100-hectare Parque 9 de Julio is the city's most attractive and accessible recreational area.

The slopes of the sierra, a short bus ride from Tucumán to the suburb of Yerba Buena, offer good hiking on gaucho stock trails. There is still a yearly rodeo during which semi-wild cattle are herded in from the sierra.

Information

Tourist Offices Tucumán's provincial Secretaría de Estado de Turismo (☎ 422-2199, ☎/fax 423-3742) is at 24 de Setiembre 484, on Plaza Independencia. It's open weekdays 7 am to 1 pm and 5 to 9 pm, weekends 10 am to 1 pm and 6 to 9 pm, but provincial financial troubles have left it short on maps and brochures. There's still no information booth at the new bus terminal.

ACA (☎ 431-1522) is at Crisóstomo Álvarez 901.

Foreign Consulates Tucumán has a substantial representation of foreign (mostly European) consulates. See the Facts for the Visitor chapter.

Money There are several cambios on San Martín between Maipú and Junín. Maguitur, San Martín 765, cashes traveler's checks for a 2% commission with a US$5 minimum exchange. Many downtown banks have ATMs.

Post & Communications Correo Argentino is at 25 de Mayo and Córdoba; the postal code is 4000. There's a Telecentro at

Maipú 480, and another on 25 de Mayo near San Martín; Tucumán's area code is ☎ 0381.

Internet Resources For Internet access, the Tucumán Cybercenter, San Juan 612, is open 9:30 am to 1 pm and 5 to 11 pm daily except Sunday, when it's open 5 to 11 pm only. Rates are US$8 to US$10 per hour.

Travel Agencies Patsa Turismo (☎ 421-6806), Chacabuco 38, is the AmEx representative. Duport Turismo (☎ 422-0000), Mendoza 720, Local 3, offers city tours (US$15) and excursions to Tafí del Valle (US$35); for another US$10, the Tafí trip can include the ruins at Quilmes.

Cultural Centers To learn what's happening in town, visit the Universidad Nacional de Tucumán's Centro Cultural Eugenio Flavio Virela (☎ 421-6024), 25 de Mayo 265, which has art exhibitions, an auditorium, and a small café that's a respite from the noisy downtown streets. There are also crafts for sale.

The Centro Cultural Doctor Alberto Rougués (☎ 422-7976), Laprida 31, has rotating exhibits of provincial painters. It's open 8:30 am to 12:30 pm and 5 to 9 pm weekdays, 10:30 am to 12:30 pm and 6:30 to 8:30 pm Saturday.

Laundry Lavandería Marva is at Santiago del Estero 694.

Medical Services Hospital Ángel C Padilla (☎ 422-1319) is at Alberdi 550.

Public Buildings & Museums

Tucumán is a historic city with a wealth of museums and other public buildings. The most imposing downtown landmark is the turn-of-the-century **Casa de Gobierno**, which replaced the colonial cabildo on Plaza Independencia. The **Basílica Santo Domingo** (1860), on 9 de Julio between Crisóstomo Álvarez and San Lorenzo, and the **Iglesia Catedral** (1845) at the corner of 24 de Setiembre and Congreso, are major ecclesiastical holdings; the latter contains the **Museo de Arte Sacro**, a collection of religious artwork.

The **Museo Iramain** (☎ 421-1874) has collections of Argentine paintings and sculpture; at Entre Ríos 27, it's open weekdays 8 am to noon and 2 to 7 pm, Saturday 8 am to noon only. Dating from 1905, the **Museo de Bellas Artes Timoteo Navarro** (☎ 422-7300), 9 de Julio 44, has changing exhibits, including some very imaginative sculpture; it's open weekdays 9:30 am to 12:30 pm and 5 to 8:30 pm, weekends 5:30 to 8:30 pm only.

Other noteworthy museums include the **Museo Histórico de la Provincia** (☎ 431-1039) at Congreso 56, President Nicolás Avellaneda's birthplace, open 9 am to 12:30 pm weekdays only and 5 to 8 pm daily; and the **Museo Arqueológico** (☎ 421-6024), 25 de Mayo 265, which displays collections on northwestern Argentine prehistory weekdays 8 am to noon and 5 to 9 pm.

Casa Padilla

Alongside the Casa de Gobierno, this partly restored mid-19th-century house first belonged to provincial governor José Frías (1792-1874), then to his mayor son-in-law Ángel Padilla and to the latter's son. At 25 de Mayo 36, its museum displays a collection of European art and period furniture weekdays 9:30 am to 12:30 pm and 5 to 8 pm, Saturday and holidays 9 am to 12:30 pm, and Sunday 5 to 8:30 pm.

Casa de la Independencia

Unitarist lawyers and clerics (Federalists boycotted the meeting) declared Argentina's independence from Spain on July 9, 1816, in this dazzlingly whitewashed late-colonial house. Portraits of the signatories line the walls of the room where the declaration was signed.

The interior patio is a pleasant refuge from Tucumán's commercial bustle. At Congreso 151, 1½ blocks south of Plaza Independencia, the casa (☎ 431-0826) is open Tuesday to Friday 9 am to noon and 5 to 7:30 pm, weekends and holidays 9 am to 1 pm and 3:30 to 7:30 pm. Admission is US$2; there's a light-and-sound show nightly except Tuesday at 8:30 pm.

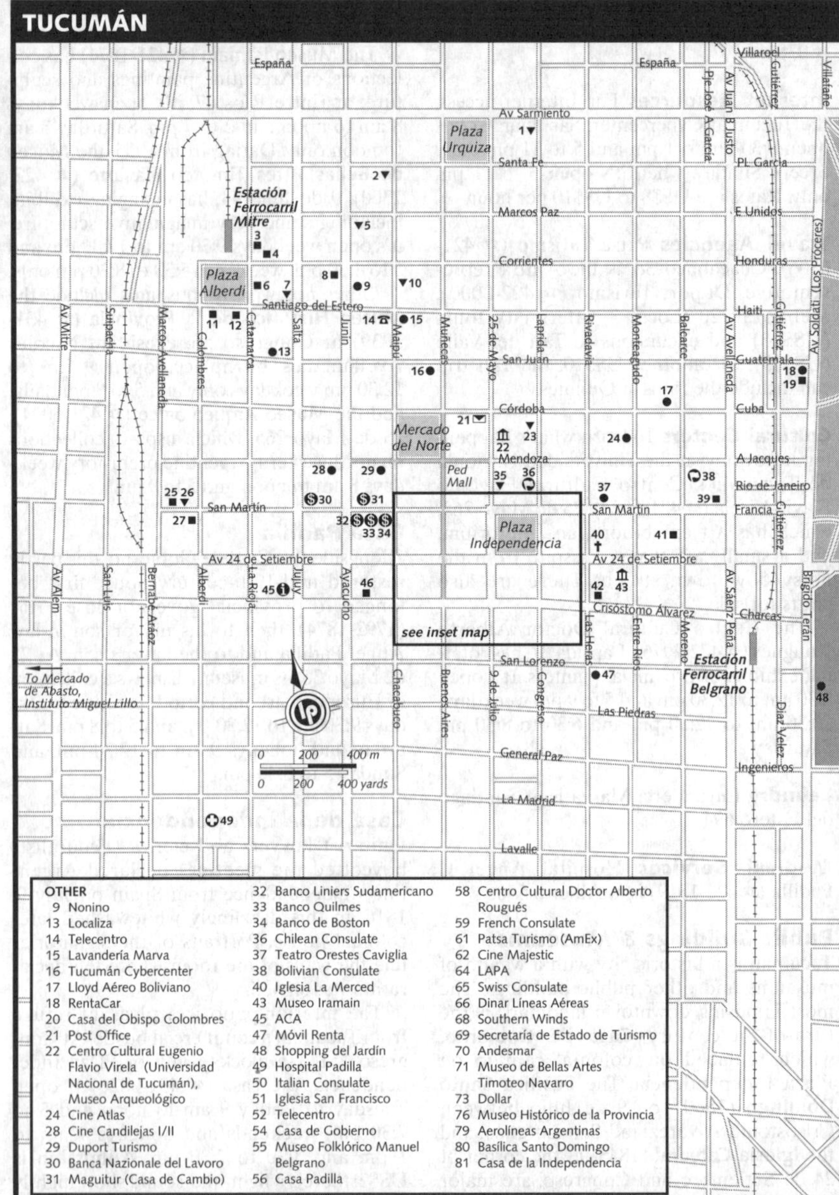
TUCUMÁN
OTHER
9 Nonino
13 Localiza
14 Telecentro
15 Lavandería Marva
16 Tucumán Cybercenter
17 Lloyd Aéreo Boliviano
18 RentaCar
20 Casa del Obispo Colombres
21 Post Office
22 Centro Cultural Eugenio Flavio Virela (Universidad Nacional de Tucumán), Museo Arqueológico
24 Cine Atlas
28 Cine Candilejas I/II
29 Duport Turismo
30 Banca Nazionale del Lavoro
31 Maguitur (Casa de Cambio)
32 Banco Liniers Sudamericano
33 Banco Quilmes
34 Banco de Boston
36 Chilean Consulate
37 Teatro Orestes Caviglia
38 Bolivian Consulate
40 Iglesia La Merced
43 Museo Iramain
45 ACA
47 Móvil Renta
48 Shopping del Jardín
49 Hospital Padilla
50 Italian Consulate
51 Iglesia San Francisco
52 Telecentro
54 Casa de Gobierno
55 Museo Folklórico Manuel Belgrano
56 Casa Padilla
58 Centro Cultural Doctor Alberto Rougués
59 French Consulate
61 Patsa Turismo (AmEx)
62 Cine Majestic
64 LAPA
65 Swiss Consulate
66 Dinar Líneas Aéreas
68 Southern Winds
69 Secretaría de Estado de Turismo
70 Andesmar
71 Museo de Bellas Artes Timoteo Navarro
73 Dollar
76 Museo Histórico de la Provincia
79 Aerolíneas Argentinas
80 Basílica Santo Domingo
81 Casa de la Independencia

Museo Folklórico Manuel Belgrano

Occupying a colonial house that once belonged to the family of Bishop José Eusebio Colombres, a major figure in the independence movement who also fostered local sugar cultivation, this pleasant and interesting museum features a good collection of River Plate horse gear, indigenous musical instruments and weavings, Toba wood carvings, Quilmes pottery, and samples of *randa* (an intricate lace resembling Paraguayan *ñandutí)* from the village of Monteros, 53km south of Tucumán. Some items are for sale in the museum shop (☎ 431-1039). At 24 de Setiembre 565, it's open weekdays 7 am to 1 pm and 3 to 9 pm, weekends 9 am to 1 pm and 4 to 9 pm. Admission is free.

Casa del Obispo Colombres

In the center of Parque 9 de Julio (formerly Bishop Colombres' El Bajo plantation), this 18th-century house contains the first ox-powered *trapiche* (sugar mill) of Tucumán's postindependence industry. Guided tours, in Spanish, explain the operation of the mill, some of whose equipment is still in working order. Hours are weekdays 8 am to 12:30 pm and 2 to 7 pm, weekends 7 am to 7 pm. Admission is US$1.

Instituto Miguel Lillo

Life-size replicas of dinosaurs and other fossils from San Juan's Parque Provincial Ischigualasto populate the garden of this natural history museum near the Mercado de Abasto (see below). At Miguel Lillo 205, the museum (☎ 433-0868, 423-9364) is open weekdays 9 am to noon and 5:30 to 9 pm.

Mercado de Abasto

Photographers should not miss this colorful wholesale/retail market, though the brightly painted horse carts that haul their goods from the countryside are fewer than they were even in the recent past. Unlike most markets, it's liveliest in mid- to late afternoon, when the city's restaurateurs go to purchase their produce. At San Lorenzo and Miguel Lillo, it's 10 blocks west and two blocks south of Plaza Independencia; the market cafés are very cheap places to eat.

Special Events

Celebrations of Día de la Independencia (Argentina's Independence Day) on July 9 are especially vigorous in Tucumán, the cradle of the country's independence. Tucumanos also celebrate the Batalla de Tucumán (Battle of Tucumán) September 24.

Activities

The staff at the Secretaría de Turismo has information on a variety of outdoor activities. Trekking and hiking are popular activities in the Sierra de Aconquija; one popular excursion is the four-day hike to Tafí del Valle. LP correspondents have enthusiastically recommended Héctor Heredia ('El Oso' or 'the Bear'; ☎ 422-6205, fax 430-2222) as a mountain guide for the Sierra, Tafí del Valle, and surrounding areas. Héctor can arrange extended treks in the provinces of Tucumán and Catamarca, and gives a good explanation of what to expect in advance. His address is Balcarce 1067, 4000 San Miguel de Tucumán, República Argentina.

Places to Stay

Tucumán's generally modern hotels lack character. The cheapest ones, near the old bus terminal, are pretty shabby, but the area around Plaza Alberdi and the Ferrocarril Mitre is experiencing something of a revival, with upgraded but still reasonably priced accommodations and restaurants.

Places to Stay – Budget

Camping Fees are traditionally very low at ***Las Lomitas***, which has reopened in Parque 9 de Julio, about 10 blocks from the new bus terminal via Av Benjamín Aráoz. The unfenced site is less secure than most Argentine campgrounds – although theft is unlikely, inform the attendant when you leave. If tent camping, choose your site carefully; lower-lying parts flood when it rains heavily.

Hostels Tucumán's AAAJ-affiliated ***Albergue Juvenil*** *(☎ 431-0265, Junín 580)* occupies part of the mid-range Hotel Miami. Rates are US$15 with breakfast included; the Hostelling International card is obligatory.

Hospedajes, Residenciales & Hotels Near the Mitre station, ***Hotel Norte*** *(Catamarca 639)* is cheap but seamy for US$10 per person, though the hot showers are good. One block south, try ***Hotel Tucumán*** *(☎ 422-1809, Catamarca 563)*, where singles/doubles cost US$12/15 with shared bath, US$15/25 with private bath. About five blocks south, ***Hotel Royal*** *(☎ 421-8697, San Martín 1196)* charges US$12/25.

Friendly ***Hotel Petit*** *(☎ 421-3902, Crisóstomo Álvarez 765)* has become the best budget choice in town at US$10 per person for small but tidy rooms with shared bath, US$15 for larger rooms with private bath.

Hotel Florida *(☎ 422-6674, 24 de Setiembre 610)*, just off Plaza Independencia, is friendly, quiet, and central, but very small; upstairs rooms have more and better light. Rooms with fans and shared bath cost US$15/25, slightly more with private bath.

Residencial Viena *(☎ 431-0313, Santiago del Estero 1054)*, opposite the Mitre station, charges US$20/25. ***Hotel Roni*** *(☎ 421-1434, San Martín 1177)* wins an award for one of the weirdest entrances to any Argentine hotel – a bridge leads from the hallway into the lobby – but rates are moderate at US$22/25.

Places to Stay – Mid-Range

Mid-range accommodations are more abundant, starting at US$25/30 for singles/doubles with private bath at downtown ***Hotel Independencia*** *(☎ 421-7038, Balcarce 56.)*. Modern, boxy ***Hotel Astoria*** *(☎ 421-3101, Congreso 92)*, just off Plaza Independencia, charges US$25/33; the street itself is very noisy.

Downtown ***Hotel Impala*** *(☎ 431-0371, Crisóstomo Álvarez 274)* is clean and modern for US$25/35 with private bath. Nearby ***Hotel Francia*** *(☎ 431-0781, Crisóstomo Álvarez 467)* costs US$26/36.

Hotel Colonial *(☎ 431-1523, San Martín 35)* comes very highly recommended for US$35/50 – though there's nothing remotely colonial about this very modern building. An equally good value is spiffy ***Hotel América*** *(☎ 430-0810, Santiago del Estero 1064)*, where basic rates are US$32/42 but more comfortable VIP rooms go for US$38/50.

For US$38/48, ***Hotel Miami****(☎ 431-0265, Junín 580)* is a better value at hostel rates (see above). Near the Mitre station, ***Hotel Dallas*** *(☎ 421-8500, Corrientes 985)* charges US$42/53.

Places to Stay – Top End

Opposite Plaza Independencia, the modern but attractive ***Hotel Mediterráneo*** *(☎ 431-0025, 24 de Setiembre 364)* charges US$50/65 for singles/doubles with cable TV and room service; English and French are spoken. ***Hotel Premier*** *(☎ 431-0381, Crisóstomo Álvarez 502)* charges US$60/70.

More expensive but perhaps a lesser value are the central high-rises like ***Hotel del Sol*** *(☎ 431-0393, Laprida 35)*, where rates are about US$70/90, and ***Hotel Metropol*** *(☎ 431-1180, 24 de Setiembre 524)*, for US$72/92.

Fronting on Parque 9 de Julio, five-star ***Gran Hotel de Tucumán*** *(☎ 424-5000, Av Los Próceres 370)* is the city's best and most expensive for US$100/120.

Places to Eat

One of the best places to explore for inexpensive food is the colorful Mercado de Abasto (see separate entry earlier in this chapter), but the more central ***Mercado del Norte***, at Mendoza and Maipú, is another possibility.

For breakfast, try ***Café de la Fuente*** *(☎ 422-2074, 25 de Mayo 183)*, where coffee or chocolate, two medialunas, a small glass of fresh-squeezed orange juice, and a glass of soda water costs only about US$2; it's also air-conditioned.

Half a block east of Plaza Independencia on 24 de Setiembre, try the chicken empanadas, humitas and other tasty regional specialties at modest-looking ***El Portal***, one of several small stands at the same address. Similar dishes are also available at ***Paquito*** *(☎ 422-9021, San Martín 1165)*.

La Corzuela *(☎ 421-6402, Laprida 866)*, serves parrillada but also regional specialties like locro, humitas, and empanadas. The ***Jockey Club*** *(San Martín 451)* serves traditional Argentine fare, especially parrillada.

Middle Eastern food is the rule at ***Doña Sara Figueroa*** *(☎ 422-6533, 24 de Setiembre 358)*, and at ***Restaurant Sirio Libanés***, on Maipú between Corrientes and Santiago del Estero.

For pizza, try moderately priced ***Ciao*** *(☎ 430-5576, 9 de Julio 63)* or the outstanding but more elaborate and expensive ***Pizzería Io*** *(☎ 422-1837, Salta 602)*.

Federico *(☎ 421-1857, Maipú 790)* has an extensive menu, including vegetarian meals, with reasonable prices; the fixed-price lunch or dinner costs about US$9. ***Kló & Kló*** *(☎ 422-3340, Junín 663)* offers fixed-price meals from US$8 to US$13, as well as pasta, seafood, and paella. ***Xing Wang*** *(Laprida 260)* is a Chinese tenedor libre.

Entertainment

Tucumán is large enough to have several cinemas showing recent international films. Among them are the two-screen ***Cine Candilejas*** *(☎ 430-1901, Mendoza 826)*, ***Cine Atlas*** *(☎ 422-0825, Monteagudo 250)* and the ***Cine Majestic*** *(☎ 421-7515, 24 de Setiembre 666)*.

The ***Teatro Orestes Caviglia*** is on San Martín between Las Heras and Entre Ríos. ***Nonino*** *(☎ 421-6098, Junín 545)* is a cultural center that presents live folkloric music, including tango, and theater.

Getting There & Away

Air Aerolíneas Argentinas (☎ 431-1030), 9 de Julio 112, flies daily to Salta (US$20) and Buenos Aires' Aeroparque (US$77 to US$228). LAPA (☎ 430-2630), Buenos Aires 95, flies twice daily to Aeroparque (US$79 to US$189) except Saturday and Sunday (once only).

Dinar Líneas Aéreas (☎ 422-9274), at 9 de Julio and 24 de Setiembre, flies twice each weekday and once Saturday and Sunday to Aeroparque (US$109 to US$199), and once a day to Salta except Sunday (twice).

Andesmar (☎ 430-4517), 9 de Julio 72, flies daily to Salta (US$24 to US$48) with an additional flight Monday and Friday, to

Córdoba twice each weekday and once Saturday and Sunday (US$53 to US$77), to Mendoza daily except Sunday (US$102 to US$149), weekdays to Rosario, and to La Rioja Tuesday, Wednesday, and Thursday.

Lloyd Aéreo Boliviano (LAB; ☎ 421-2090), Córdoba 131, flies Thursday to Jujuy and to Santa Cruz, Bolivia, with onward connections to Cochabamba and La Paz.

Southern Winds (☎ 422-5554), 9 de Julio 77, has two flights to Córdoba (US$67 to US$89) Monday, Tuesday, and Thursday, four on Friday, and one each on Saturday and Sunday; they also fly daily to Mendoza (US$119 to US$159); daily to Rosario (US$104 to US$139); weekdays to Mar del Plata (US$134 to US$179); daily except Sunday to Neuquén (US$127 to US$169); Wednesday and Saturday to Bariloche (US$142 to US$189); and Tuesday to Aeroparque (US$89 to US$119).

Bus At Brígido Terán 350, Tucumán's sparkling Estación de Ómnibus (☎ 422-2221) is a major public-works project with 60 platforms, a post office, telephone services, a supermarket, bars, and restaurants. In the complex, Shopping del Jardín's information booth (☎ 430-6400, 430-2060), open daily 6:30 am to 11:30 pm, provides information on the Estación and the shopping center only. The entire scheme was the brainchild of the province's ambitious former governor, Ramón (Palito) Ortega, a onetime crooner with presidential hopes, who was constitutionally ineligible for reelection.

Aconquija (☎ 422-7620) goes to Tafí del Valle at 10 am and 12:30 and 4 pm, to Amaichá del Valle four times daily, and to Cafayate at 6 am and 2 pm daily, with a transfer at Santa María.

El Tucumano (☎ 422-6442) goes south to Córdoba, north to Salta and Jujuy, and southeast to Termas de Río Hondo, Santiago del Estero, Rosario, and Buenos Aires. La Veloz del Norte (☎ 421-7860) has similar routes and also crosses the Chaco to Resistencia.

Panamericano (☎ 431-0544) heads north to Salta and Jujuy, and south to Córdoba. Bosio (☎ 422-8940) has similar routes and goes additionally to Mendoza and intermediate points. Atahualpa goes to Jujuy and Pocitos, on the Bolivian border; and to Córdoba, Rosario, and Buenos Aires. Chevallier (☎ 421-0805) serves Córdoba, Rosario, and Buenos Aires.

La Estrella (☎ 430-6090) goes daily to Mendoza via Catamarca, La Rioja, and San Juan; south to Córdoba; southeast to Santa Fe, Paraná, Rosario, Buenos Aires, and Mar del Plata; and north to Salta and Jujuy. It also crosses the Chaco to Posadas via Resistencia and Corrientes, and has limited Patagonian services to Neuquén.

TAC (☎ 430-6663) has interior routes to Catamarca, La Rioja, San Juan, Mendoza, Neuquén, San Martín de los Andes, and Bariloche; goes to Buenos Aires; and also has coastal Patagonian connections to Puerto Madryn, Trelew, Comodoro Rivadavia, and Río Gallegos. It also has international services to Santiago de Chile via Mendoza.

Andesmar (☎ 422-5702) passes through Tucumán on its routes between Mendoza and Jujuy, with connections to Bariloche, and also goes to Santiago de Chile with a change in Mendoza.

Cacorba (☎ 422-6111), El Ranchilleño (☎ 422-2220) and La Unión (☎ 423-3862) all go to Termas de Río Hondo and Santiago del Estero; Cacorba also goes to Córdoba and Buenos Aires, as does Balut (☎ 430-7153).

Gutiérrez (☎ 422-8801) goes to Buenos Aires, and to Belén Tuesday and Friday at 8 am, returning Tuesday and Thursday at noon.

Sample fares include Termas de Río Hondo (US$5, 1½ hours), Santiago del Estero (US$9, two hours), Tafí del Valle (US$9, three hours), Catamarca (US$9 to US$12, 4½ hours), Salta (US$21, 4½ hours), Jujuy (US$19, 5½ hours), La Rioja (US$17, six hours), Cafayate (US$20, seven hours), Córdoba (US$20, eight hours), Pocitos (US$30), Corrientes (US$34, 13 hours), San Juan (US$40, 13 hours), Mendoza (US$40 to US$48, 15 hours), Santa Fe/Paraná (US$44, 12 hours), Rosario (US$49, 11 hours), Posadas (US$55, 18½ hours),

Buenos Aires (US$30 to US$69, 15 hours), Neuquén (US$72 to US$80, 24 hours), Bariloche (US$106), Esquel (US$101, 38 hours), Puerto Madryn (US$111, 27 hours), Comodoro Rivadavia (US$132, 32 hours), Caleta Olivia (US$135, 34 hours), and Río Gallegos (US$151, 44 hours). International service to Santiago de Chile (24 hours) costs US$68.

Train From the Ferrocarril Mitre station (☎ 430-3895) at Catamarca and Corrientes, opposite Plaza Alberdi, El Tucumano goes to Buenos Aires via Santiago del Estero (La Banda) and Rosario Thursday and Sunday at 2:45 pm. Fares are US$25 primera, US$40 Pullman, and US$75 camarote.

Getting Around

To/From the Airport Aeropuerto Internacional Benjamín Matienzo (☎ 426-1122) is 8km east of downtown via Av Gobernador del Campo, the northern boundary of Parque 9 de Julio. Empresa Sáenz Alderete runs airport minibuses (US$2.50) that leave 75 minutes before flight time from opposite the entrance to Gran Hotel Corona on Calle 9 de Julio, half a block from Plaza Independencia.

Bus City buses do not accept cash, so you must buy cospeles (US$0.60) at downtown kiosks; they are less readily available elsewhere.

Car Try Móvil Renta (☎ 431-0550) at San Lorenzo 370, Dollar (☎ 430-4625) at Congreso 89, Localiza (☎ 431-1352) at San Juan 935, or RentaCar (☎ 421-1372) at Av Soldati 380.

AROUND TUCUMÁN

Ruins of San José de Lules

Until 1767, this mission 20km south of Tucumán was a Jesuit reducción among the region's Lule Indians. After the Jesuits' expulsion, the Dominicans assumed control of the complex, whose present ruins date from the 1880s and once served as a school. The small museum has replicas of colonial documents and a plethora of busts of various Argentine independence heroes. There are numerous ghost stories about the place, and legends of buried Jesuit treasure.

To get to Lules, a pleasant site for an afternoon outing, take the Trébol, Provincial, or El Centauro bus from downtown Tucumán.

TAFÍ DEL VALLE

From Tucumán, RN 38 heads southwest through sprawling cane fields, punctuated by the *ingenios* (industrial mills) of large sugar companies, before intersecting RP 307 at Acheral. From Acheral, RP 307 snakes up the narrow gorge of the Río de los Sosas where, in places, the rising river has so eroded the highway that even a single vehicle can barely pass. On all sides dense, verdant subtropical forest covers the hills – this is the refuge where, in the late 1970s, the controversial General Bussi's Argentine army wiped out the Ejército Revolucionario del Pueblo (ERP), ending their dreams of emulating Fidel Castro's success in Cuba's Sierra Maestra, another sugar-producing zone.

About 100km from Tucumán, the gorge opens onto a misty valley beneath the snowy peaks of the Nevados del Aconquija. When summer heat drives tucumanos out of the sweltering provincial capital, they seek refuge in the cool heights around the hill station of Tafí del Valle, whose permanent population of 6000 can swell to 15,000 or more. Beyond Tafí, the newly paved road zigzags over the 3050m pass known as Abra del Infiernillo (Little Hell Pass), an alternative route to Cafayate and Salta, passing the impressive Diaguita ruins at Quilmes.

Prior to the Spaniards' arrival, Calchaquí Indians inhabited the Tafí valley, raising potatoes and herding llamas in dispersed settlements. After the Spanish invasion and decline of the encomienda, the Jesuits acquired the valley, which enjoyed a new prosperity until their expulsion in 1767. With Argentine independence, the isolated valley declined economically for more than a century until a new highway made it possible to get crops to market and tourists to the valley.

A temperate island in a subtropical sea, Tafí del Valle produces seed potatoes and fruits (apples, pears, and peaches) for Tucumán. It also pastures cattle, sheep, and, at higher altitudes, llamas; overgrazing and other deplorable agricultural practices have turned some of the area into something resembling arid badlands, surprising considering the humid, midlatitude, high-altitude environment.

Typical products include sweets and dairy products – in early February, the town celebrates the **Fiesta Nacional del Queso** (National Cheese Festival). There is good fishing for trout and pejerrey in La Angostura, the reservoir formed by Dique El Mollar.

Orientation

At the north end of the reservoir formed by Dique El Mollar, Tafí del Valle sits 2000m above sea level. It is 70km from Quilmes and 113km from Cafayate via RP 307. Most public services are on or near the Centro Cívico, which features an unusual semicircular plaza.

Information

Tafí's helpful Casa del Turista (☎ 421020) is open weekdays 7:30 am to 7:30 pm, weekends 10 am to 4 pm. There is an excellent small café in the Centro Cívico, but the nearby peatonal is marred by a deafening video arcade.

Banco de la Provincia, in the Centro Cívico, changes US cash. Long-distance telephones are also here; Tafí's area code is ☎ 03867.

Capilla La Banda

This 18th-century Jesuit chapel, acquired by the Frías Silva family of Tucumán on the Jesuits' expulsion and then expanded in the 1830s, was restored to its original configura-

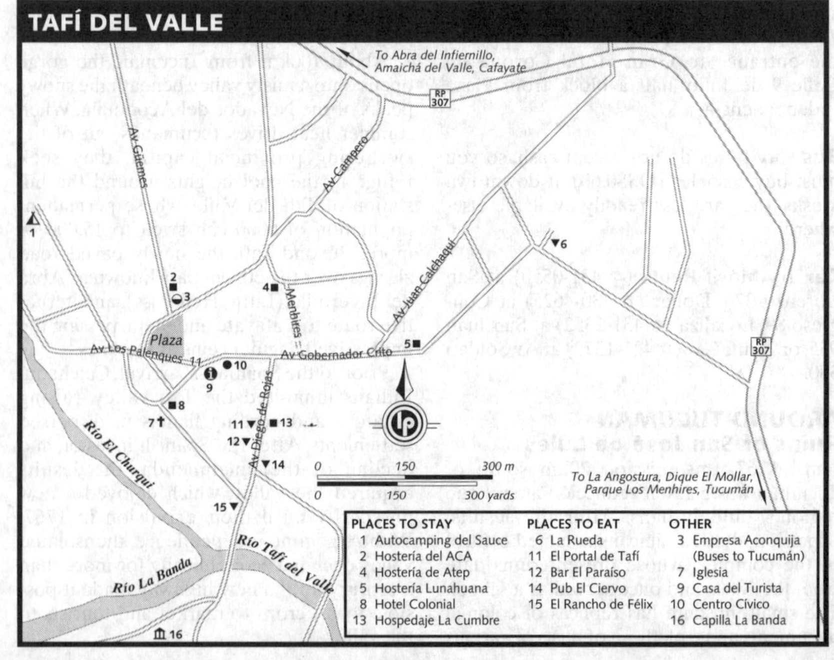

tion in the 1970s. Note the escape tunnel in the chapel. The small archaeological collection consists mostly of funerary urns, but also religious art of the Cuzco school, ecclesiastical vestments, and period furniture that once belonged to the Frías Silvas. Guided tours are available; admission is US$1.

The chapel is a short distance south of downtown, across the bridge over the Río Tafí del Valle and up the dirt road to the west.

Parque Los Menhires

More than 80 aboriginal granite monuments, resembling the standing stones of the Scottish Hebrides, cover the hillside at the southern end of La Angostura reservoir. Collected from various sites throughout the valley, these sculptures of human and animal forms had a ritual significance that archaeologists have not yet completely deciphered.

Hiking

Several nearby peaks and destinations make hiking in the mountains around Tafí del Valle an attractive prospect; try 3000m **Cerro El Matadero**, a four- to five-hour climb; 3800m **Cerro Pabellón** (six hours); and 4600m **Cerro El Negrito**, reached from the statue of Cristo Redentor on RN 307 to Acheral. The village of La Ciénaga is about seven hours away. The trails are badly marked, and no trail maps are available. Ask for more information at Casa del Turista.

Places to Stay

Tafí's ***Autocamping del Sauce*** *(☎ 421084)* is acceptable for US$2.50 per person, but toilets and showers are very run-down; although the grounds are well kept. Shade is limited (a lesser problem in overcast Tafí than elsewhere in the country). Bunks in small cabañas are available for US$5 per person, but these would be very claustrophobic at their maximum capacity of four persons.

Hospedaje La Cumbre *(☎ 421016, Av Diego de Rojas 311)* charges US$10 per person for rooms with shared bath, with meals additional; ***Hospedaje Celia Correa*** *(☎ 421170, Belgrano 443)* is comparable. Union-run ***Hostería de Atep*** *(☎ 421061)* costs just US$12 for accommodations only, US$25 with full board, while ***Hotel Colonial*** *(☎ 421443)* charges US$25 per person with half-board.

The well-kept ***Hostería del ACA*** *(☎ 421027)* theoretically accepts members only, for US$27/40 single/double, but in practice they're much less discriminating. Newer, more upscale accommodations cost US$49/59 at ***Hotel Tafí*** *(☎ 421007, Belgrano 137)* and for US$70/90 at ***Hostería Lunahuana*** *(☎ 421360, Av Gobernador Critto 540)*.

Places to Eat

Pub El Ciervo, on Diego de Rojas alongside the YPF station, has moderately priced minutas, including humitas. Nearby ***Bar El Paraíso*** is where locals congregate to dine cheaply and watch Seagal or Stallone videos. ***El Rancho de Félix***, which serves regional food, is probably the best choice, but ***La Rueda*** is also worth a look. ***El Portal de Tafí*** has repulsively kitschy decor, especially the animal skins stretched across the walls, but there's a good and varied menu of sandwiches, meat, and pasta.

Shopping

The crafts shop at the west end of the peatonal near the Centro Cívico has good pottery, jewelry, and blankets, but also a fair amount of dreck.

Getting There & Away

Tafí's bus station is on the north side of the plaza. Empresa Aconquija has buses to Tucumán at 4 and 6 am, and 1:30, 4:30, 6, and 10 pm. Buses From Tucumán also continue to Santa María and Cafayate.

Getting Around

Hourly in summer, every three hours in winter, local Aconquija buses do most of the circuit around Cerro El Pelado, in the middle of the valley. One goes on the north side, another on the south side, so it's possible to make a circuit of the valley by walking the link between them.

QUILMES

Dating from about 1000 AD, Quilmes was a complex urban settlement that occupied about 30 hectares and housed as many as 5000 people. The Quilmes Indians survived contact with the Incas, which occured from about 1480 AD onwards, but could not outlast the siege of the Spaniards who, in 1667, deported the last 2000 inhabitants to Buenos Aires.

Quilmes' thick walls underscore its defensive purpose, but clearly this was more than just a pucará. Dense construction sprawls both north and south from the central nucleus, where the outlines of buildings, in a variety of shapes, are obvious even to the casual observer. For revealing views of the form, density, and extent of the ruins, climb the trails up either flank of the nucleus, which offer vistas of the valley once only glimpsed by the city's defenders. Give yourself at least half a day, preferably more, to explore the nucleus and the surrounding area.

There is a small museum at the entrance, whose US$2 admission charge also entitles you to explore the ruins (which now feature hired tourist llamas). The museum shop features a good selection of artisanal goods at relatively small markups.

Places to Stay & Eat

It is possible to camp on site, but shade is limited. The new ***Hotel Ruinas de Quilmes*** *(☎ 03892-421075)* blends so well into its surrounding that it's surprisingly inconspicuous from outside, but its high ceilings and skylights manage to convey the expansiveness of the desert. Rates are US$60/80 single/double with breakfast.

The museum now has a ***confitería*** for basic meals.

Getting There & Away

Buses from Cafayate to Santa María or Tafí del Valle will drop passengers at the junction, but from there you'll have to walk or hitch (there is little traffic) 5km to the ruins. It will probably be easier to get a lift back to the highway, since you can approach any vehicle visiting the ruins.

Santiago del Estero Province

The hot, subtropical lowland province of Santiago del Estero is a transitional area between the Gran Chaco and the Andes; cotton is the dominant crop. Its eponymous capital is Argentina's oldest city, from which the region's other cities were founded. Termas de Río Hondo, the province's second city, is a popular winter resort known for its mild climate and thermal mineral waters.

SANTIAGO DEL ESTERO

Founded in 1553 by Francisco de Aguirre, the 'Madre de Ciudades' (Mother of Cities) was Spain's first urban settlement in what is now Argentina; for centuries it was an important stopover between the Pampas and the mines of Bolivia. The city and province rely on agriculture, cotton being the most important crop; irrigation supplements unreliable rainfall. Often crops are grown on seasonally inundated *bañados* as flood waters recede; these areas shift with the annual movements of the Río Dulce.

In December 1993, provincial employees, disgruntled at not having been paid for four months, set fires that destroyed the interiors of two historical buildings. Tourist office brochures describe the event as 'an energetic social protest,' but the conflict was serious enough to bring federal intervention to the province. The fires proved to be only the first incidents of ongoing unrest.

Orientation

Santiago del Estero (population 224,000) sits on the west bank of the Río Dulce, 1045km northwest of Buenos Aires, about 440km north of Córdoba by RN 9, and 170km southeast of Tucumán by the same highway.

Reflecting its early settlement, Santiago's urban plan is more irregular than most Argentine cities. The town center is Plaza Libertad, from which Av Libertad, trending southwest to northeast, bisects the city; at its northern end, woodsy Parque Aguirre offers relief from summer heat. North and south of the plaza, Av Independencia and

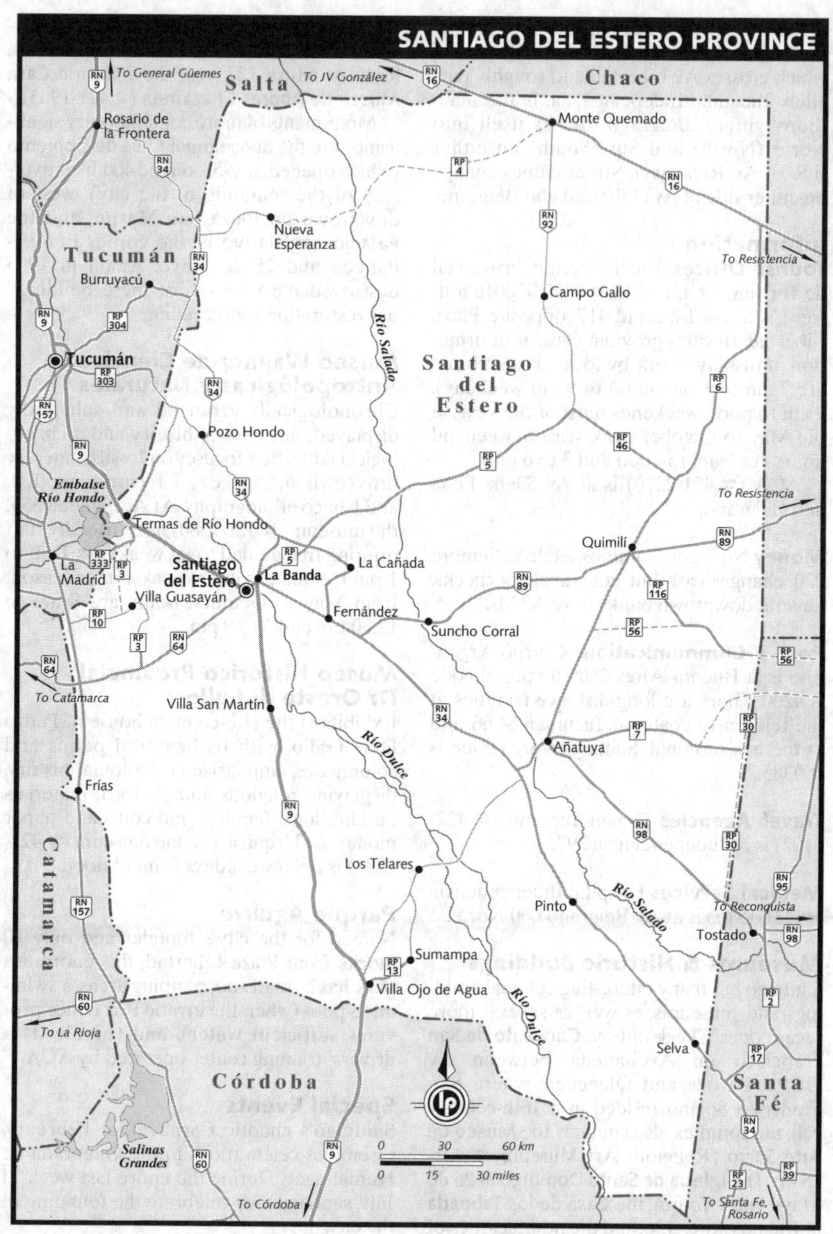
SANTIAGO DEL ESTERO PROVINCE
To General Güemes
To JV González
Salta
Chaco
Rosario de la Frontera
Monte Quemado
Nueva Esperanza
Tucumán
Burruyacú
Campo Gallo
To Resistencia
Tucumán
Río Salado
Santiago del Estero
Pozo Hondo
Embalse Río Hondo
Termas de Río Hondo
To Resistencia
Quimilí
La Madrid
Santiago del Estero
La Banda
La Cañada
Villa Guasayán
Fernández
Suncho Corral
To Catamarca
Villa San Martín
Añatuya
Río Dulce
Frías
Los Telares
Catamarca
Pinto
Río Salado
To Reconquista
Tostado
Sumampa
Villa Ojo de Agua
To La Rioja
Río Dulce
Selva
Córdoba
Santa Fé
Salinas Grandes
To Córdoba
To Santa Fe, Rosario
0 30 60 km
0 15 30 miles
RN 9
RN 16
RN 34
RP 4
RN 92
RP 304
RP 303
RN 157
RP 6
RN 46
RP 5
RN 89
RP 333
RP 3
RN 116
RP 10
RN 64
RP 56
RP 7
RP 30
RN 98
RN 95
RN 60
RP 13
RP 2
RP 17
RP 23
RP 39

the peatonal Av Tucumán become important commercial areas, but Av Belgrano, which crosses Av Libertad and roughly parallels Tucumán/Independencia, is the main thoroughfare. Belgrano divides itself into Norte (North) and Sur (South) on either side of Av Rivadavia. Street names change on either side of Avs Libertad and Belgrano.

Information

Tourist Offices The Dirección Provincial de Turismo (☎ 421-4243; ☎ 0800-450016 toll-free) is at Av Libertad 417, opposite Plaza Libertad. Besides providing visitor information, it displays work by local artists. Hours are 7 am to 1 pm and 3 to 9 pm weekdays, 9 am to noon weekends most of the year; in the May to October peak season, weekend hours are 9 am to noon and 3 to 6 pm.

ACA (☎ 421-2270) is at Av Sáenz Peña and Belgrano.

Money Noroeste Cambios, 24 de Setiembre 220, changes cash but not traveler's checks. Several downtown banks have ATMs.

Post & Communications Correo Argentino is at Buenos Aires 250; the postal code is 4200. There are long-distance facilities at the Telecentro Peatonal, Tucumán 64/66, and at the bus terminal. Santiago's area code is ☎ 0385.

Travel Agencies Pagani Turismo (☎ 422-0102) is at Independencia 397.

Medical Services Hospital Independencia (☎ 421-1515) is at Av Belgrano 660 Norte.

Museums & Historic Buildings

Santiago has many interesting colonial buildings and museums, as well as several more recent ones. Check out the **Convento de San Francisco** on Avellaneda between Av General Roca and Olaechea, where San Francisco Solano resided in a 16th-century cell; the complex also contains the **Museo de Arte Sacro** (Religious Art Museum; ☎ 421-1548). The **Iglesia de Santo Domingo** at 25 de Mayo and Urquiza, the **Casa de los Taboada** at Buenos Aires 136, and the new facilities of the **Museo Provincial de Bellas Artes** (☎ 421-1839) at Belgrano Sur 1537 also deserve a look. At Mitre 127, visit the folkloric **Casa Museo de Andrés Chazarreta** (☎ 421-1905).

Monuments of more contemporary significance are the neocolonial **Casa de Gobierno** (which opened in 1953, on the 400th anniversary of the founding of the city), west of downtown on Plaza San Martín; and the **Palacio Legislativo** at the corner of Avellaneda and 25 de Mayo. Arson in 1993 destroyed the interiors of these buildings, but restoration is proceeding.

Museo Wagner de Ciencias Antropológicas y Naturales

Chronologically arranged and splendidly displayed, this natural history and archaeological collection focuses on fossils, funerary urns (owls and snakes are recurring motifs), and Chaco ethnography. At Avellaneda 355, the museum (☎ 421-1380) has a friendly staff offering free guided tours weekdays 7 am to 1 pm in summer; in the peak winter season, from May to October, hours are 8 am to 12:30 pm and 3 to 9 pm.

Museo Histórico Provincial Dr Oreste di Lullo

Exhibits at the late-colonial house of Pedro Díaz Gallo, with its beautiful patios and colonnades, emphasize postcolonial history, displaying religious and civil art, materials on elite local families, and coins and paper money. At Urquiza 354, the museum (☎ 421-2893) is open weekdays 8 am to noon.

Parque Aguirre

Named for the city's founder and only 10 blocks from Plaza Libertad, this enormous park has a small zoo, camping areas, a swimming pool (when the erratic Río Dulce provides sufficient water), and (be alert!) a drivers' training center operated by ACA.

Special Events

Santiago's chaotic Carnaval, in February, resembles celebrations in the Quebrada de Humahuaca. During the entire last week of July, santiagueños celebrate the founding of the city.

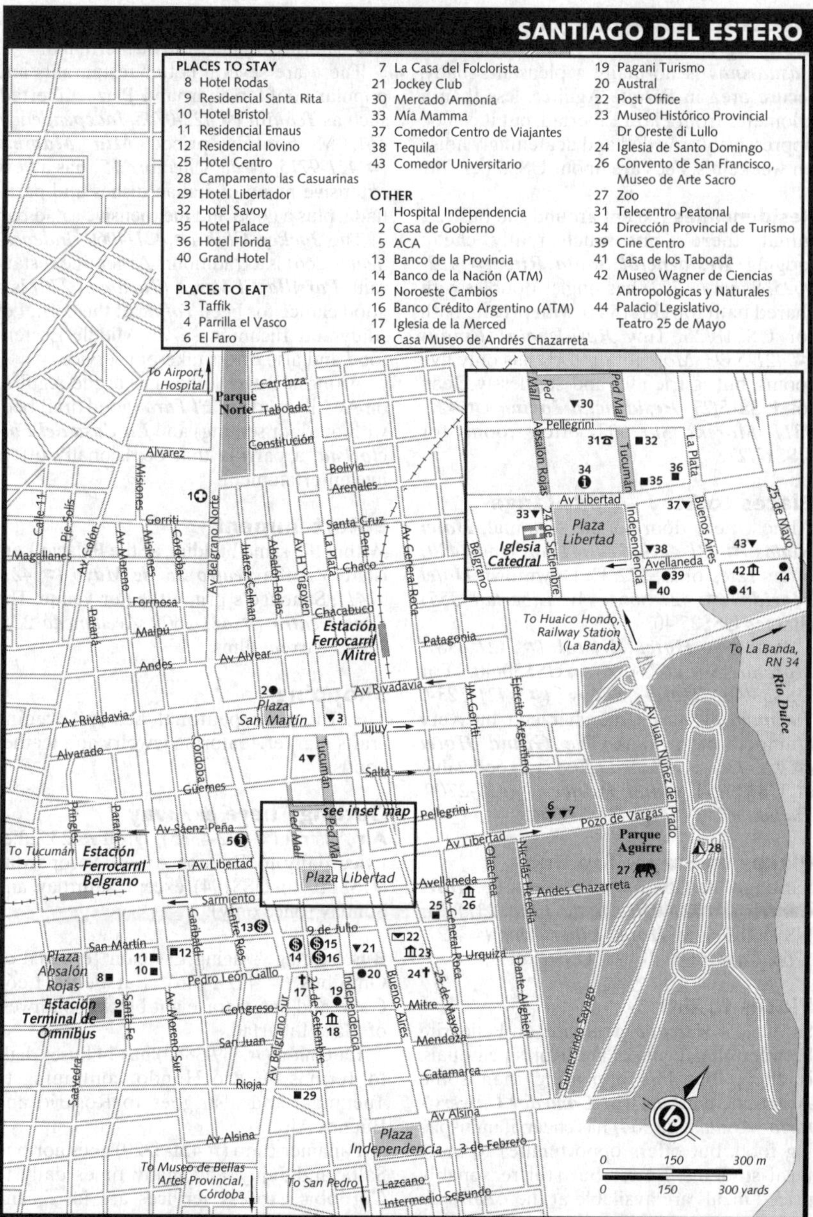
SANTIAGO DEL ESTERO
PLACES TO STAY
8 Hotel Rodas
9 Residencial Santa Rita
10 Hotel Bristol
11 Residencial Emaus
12 Residencial Iovino
25 Hotel Centro
28 Campamento las Casuarinas
29 Hotel Libertador
32 Hotel Savoy
35 Hotel Palace
36 Hotel Florida
40 Grand Hotel
PLACES TO EAT
3 Taffik
4 Parrilla el Vasco
6 El Faro
7 La Casa del Folclorista
21 Jockey Club
30 Mercado Armonía
33 Mía Mamma
37 Comedor Centro de Viajantes
38 Tequila
43 Comedor Universitario
OTHER
1 Hospital Independencia
2 Casa de Gobierno
5 ACA
13 Banco de la Provincia
14 Banco de la Nación (ATM)
15 Noroeste Cambios
16 Banco Crédito Argentino (ATM)
17 Iglesia de la Merced
18 Casa Museo de Andrés Chazarreta
19 Pagani Turismo
20 Austral
22 Post Office
23 Museo Histórico Provincial Dr Oreste di Lullo
24 Iglesia de Santo Domingo
26 Convento de San Francisco, Museo de Arte Sacro
27 Zoo
31 Telecentro Peatonal
34 Dirección Provincial de Turismo
39 Cine Centro
41 Casa de los Taboada
42 Museo Wagner de Ciencias Antropológicas y Naturales
44 Palacio Legislativo, Teatro 25 de Mayo
To Airport, Hospital
Parque Norte
Carranza
Taboada
Constitución
Alvarez
Bolivia
Arenales
Santa Cruz
Chaco
Chacabuco
Gorriti
Magallanes
Formosa
Maipú
Andes
Av Alvear
Patagonia
Av Rivadavia
Alvarado
Güemes
Jujuy
Salta
Pellegrini
Av Sáenz Peña
Av Libertad
Avellaneda
Sarmiento
9 de Julio
San Martín
Urquiza
Pedro León Gallo
Congreso
Mitre
San Juan
Mendoza
Catamarca
Rioja
Av Alsina
3 de Febrero
Lazcano
Intermedio Segundo
Calle 11
Pje Solís
Av Colón
Misiones
Av Moreno
Córdoba
Av Belgrano Norte
Juárez Celman
Absalón Rojas
La Plata
Av H Yrigoyen
Peru
Av General Roca
JM Gorriti
Ejército Argentino
Av Juan Núñez del Prado
Olaechea
Nicolás Heredia
Dante Alighieri
Gumersindo Sayago
Paraná
Pringles
Garibaldi
Entre Ríos
Av Moreno Sur
Santa Fe
Saavedra
Av Belgrano Sur
24 de Setiembre
Independencia
Buenos Aires
25 de Mayo
Tucumán
Ped Mall
Estación Ferrocarril Mitre
Plaza San Martín
see inset map
Plaza Libertad
To Tucumán
Estación Ferrocarril Belgrano
Plaza Absalón Rojas
Estación Terminal de Ómnibus
Plaza Independencia
To Museo de Bellas Artes Provincial, Córdoba
To San Pedro
To Huaico Hondo, Railway Station (La Banda)
To La Banda, RN 34
Río Dulce
Pozo de Vargas
Parque Aguirre
Andes Chazarreta
Iglesia Catedral
Belgrano
Av Libertad
Avellaneda
0 150 300 m
0 150 300 yards

Places to Stay – Budget

Camping The municipal ***Campamento Las Casuarinas*** is normally a pleasant, shady, secure area in Parque Aguirre, less than a kilometer from Plaza Libertad, but it can be oppressively crowded and deafeningly noisy on weekends. Fees are about US$5 per site.

Residenciales Except around the bus terminal, there's not much really cheap lodging. ***Residencial Santa Rita*** *(☎ 422-0625, Santa Fe 273)* has singles/doubles with shared bath for US$15/20, with private bath for US$18/25. Tiny ***Residencial Emaus*** *(☎ 421-5893, Moreno Sur 673)* has only five rooms, but is friendly and spotlessly clean for US$15/27. ***Residencial Iovino*** *(☎ 421-3311, Moreno Sur 602)* offers rooms for US$17/27.

Places to Stay – Mid-Range

Almost next door to the terminal, ***Hotel Rodas*** *(☎ 421-4229, Pedro León Gallo 430)* offers rates of US$22/33. Downtown ***Hotel Florida*** *(☎ 421-8664, Av Libertad 355)* charges US$25/40.

Rates at ***Hotel Bristol*** *(☎ 421-8387, Moreno Sur 677)* are US$30/40. For US$33/40, ***Hotel Savoy*** *(☎ 421-1234, Tucumán 39)* has some character but very cramped bathrooms. The ***Grand Hotel*** *(☎ 422-4283, Avellaneda 203)* is a good value at US$37/54. ***Hotel Palace*** *(☎ 421-2700, Tucumán 19)* charges US$42/54.

Places to Stay – Top End

Santiago has two upscale hotels, ***Hotel Centro*** *(☎ 421-9502, 9 de Julio 131)* for US$60/83, and ***Hotel Libertador*** *(☎ 421-5766, Catamarca 47)* for US$62/82.

Places to Eat

Santiago's ***Mercado Armonía***, on Pellegrini between the Tucumán and Rojas peatonals, is cheap but less appealing than some Argentine markets. The ***Comedor Universitario*** *(Avellaneda 364)* has cheap if uninspiring food, but offers opportunities to meet local students. Better but still reasonably priced meals are available at the ***Centro de Viajantes*** *(Buenos Aires 37)*. Other inexpensive eateries are near the bus terminal.

There are several better restaurants and popular confiterías around Plaza Libertad, such as ***Tequila*** *(☎ 422-0745, Independencia 46)*. Moderately priced ***Mía Mamma*** *(☎ 421-9715, 24 de Setiembre 15)* has a very extensive menu of Italian dishes and parrillada, plus a good and inexpensive salad bar.

The ***Jockey Club*** *(☎ 421-4060, Independencia 266)* is a traditional Argentine restaurant. ***Parrilla El Vasco*** *(Tucumán 270)* is a good choice for beef. ***Taffik***, at the corner of Jujuy and Tucumán, serves Middle Eastern food and also offers take-out service.

Alongside each other in Parque Aguirre on Av Libertad are ***El Faro*** (good draft beer with outdoor seating) and ***La Casa del Folclorista***, a parrilla that occasionally offers live entertainment.

Entertainment

Within the same building as the Palacio Legislativo is the ***Teatro 25 de Mayo*** *(☎ 421-4141)*, Santiago's prime theater venue. The ***Cine Centro*** *(☎ 421-2505, Avellaneda 225)* shows current films.

Shopping

The Tucumán peatonal has an evening crafts market, featuring jewelry and leather goods.

Getting There & Away

Air Austral (☎ 422-4335), Urquiza 235, flies twice daily to Buenos Aires' Aeroparque (US$119 to US$194) except Saturday and Sunday (once only).

Bus Santiago's aging Estación Terminal de Ómnibus (☎ 421-3746) is at Pedro León Gallo and Saavedra, eight blocks southwest of Plaza Libertad.

La Unión (☎ 439-3880) has 14 buses daily to Termas de Río Hondo, continuing to Tucumán, and also goes to Rosario and Buenos Aires.

Panamericano (☎ 421-5329) goes north to Salta and Jujuy, and many times daily to Córdoba; express services are faster and more comfortable, but only slightly costlier, than the local buses. La Veloz del Norte also goes north to Tucumán, Salta, and Jujuy, continuing to Pocitos on the Bolivian border, and south to Córdoba, Rosario, and Buenos Aires.

Central Argentino (☎ 427-4912) goes north to Tucumán and south to Buenos Aires, La Plata and intermediate points. El Santiagueño (☎ 421-5870) goes south to Córdoba, as does Cacorba (☎ 421-3454), which also goes daily to Buenos Aires. Chevallier (☎ 421-5880) goes north to Tucumán and south to Córdoba, Rosario, and Buenos Aires.

La Estrella (☎ 421-3004) serves Santa Fe, Paraná, Buenos Aires, and Mar del Plata, while Empresa Tata (☎ 421-8251) goes to Rosario and Buenos Aires.

El Rayo crosses the Chaco to Roque Sáenz Peña, Resistencia, and Corrientes, with connections to Puerto Iguazú, and also goes to Rosario and Buenos Aires. Cotal also crosses the Chaco, and goes west and southwest to Catamarca, San Juan, and Mendoza. Bosio has daily buses to Catamarca, San Juan, La Rioja, and Mendoza. TAC has additional services to the Cuyo region, while TAC and Gutiérrez both go to Buenos Aires. Libertador also serves La Rioja, San Juan, and Mendoza.

Patagonian carrier Ute Comahue goes to Neuquén, with connections to Bahía Blanca, Viedma, Bariloche, and Río Gallegos. Tus and Tup go to Santa Rosa de La Pampa and Patagonian destinations. Andesmar (☎ 421-5880) has extensive routes north to the Bolivian border, southwest to Cuyo, and south into Patagonia.

Sample fares include Termas de Río Hondo (US$4, one hour), Tucumán (US$7, two hours), Catamarca (US$14, four hours), Córdoba (US$19, five hours), La Rioja (US$20, six hours), Rosario (US$25), Resistencia (US$25, eight hours), Corrientes (US$27, nine hours), Salta (US$25, six hours), Jujuy (US$28, seven hours), Santa Fe (US$30, 10 hours), Paraná (US$32, 11 hours), San Juan (US$35, 12 hours), Mendoza (US$45, 14 hours), and Buenos Aires (US$45, 14 hours).

Train The Ferrocarril Mitre's station is in the suburb of La Banda. *El Tucumano*, which links Buenos Aires and Tucumán, stops here Monday, Wednesday, and Friday northbound, and Tuesday, Thursday, and Sunday southbound.

Getting Around

Central Santiago del Estero is compact and walking suffices for almost everything except connections to the train station and the airport.

To/From the Airport Bus No 19 goes to Aeropuerto Mal Paso (☎ 422-2386), 6km southwest of downtown on Av Madre de Ciudades.

Train From Moreno and Libertad in downtown Santiago, buses Nos 10, 14, 18, and 21 all go to the Ferrocarril Mitre station in La Banda.

TERMAS DE RÍO HONDO

With 12,000 beds in 190 hotels, plus rental apartments, houses, chalets, and three campgrounds in a town with just 25,000 permanent residents, Termas de Río Hondo lives and dies by tourism. Competition keeps prices reasonable, but outside the peak winter season, May to October, most accommodations and many businesses shut down.

Termas de Río Hondo's primary attraction is its thermal springs – even the most basic accommodations have hot mineral baths. Outside town, the 30,000-hectare Dique Frontal is a reservoir used for water sports like swimming, boating, fishing, and windsurfing.

The town proper has two unusual features – its triangular Plaza San Martín, and one of few monuments in the country with busts of both Juan and Evita Perón.

Orientation

Midway between Santiago del Estero and Tucumán, Termas de Río Hondo has an irregular city plan, but the main thoroughfare is Av Alberdi (RN 9). Perpendicular Av Perón leads south to the Dique Frontal.

Information

Tourist Office The helpful Dirección Municipal de Turismo (☎ 421721), Caseros 132 between Rivadavia and Sarmiento, is open 7 am to 9 pm daily except for lunchtime (1 to 3 pm in summer, 1 to 2 pm in winter). *El Frontal de Río Hondo*, the town's weekly newspaper, publishes a 24-page supplement (US$2) of information about thermal baths.

Money Only Banco de la Nación, on Caseros, does foreign exchange, but don't expect to change traveler's checks.

Post & Communications Correo Argentino is on Av Alberdi between 9 de Julio and Maipú; the postal code is 4220. There are several locutorios; Termas de Río Hondo's area code is ☎ 03858.

Laundry Laverap is at Av San Martín 465, between Fleming and Yrigoyen.

Medical Services The Hospital Rural (☎ 421578) is at Antonino Taboada and Buenos Aires, west of downtown.

Places to Stay

Camping Along the river, several campgrounds near downtown charge around US$3 per person: ***Camping Mirador** (☎ 421392)*, ***Camping del Río** (☎ 421985)*, and ***Camping La Olla** (☎ 421857)*. Several kilometers outside town, on the road to the Dique Frontal, ***Camping del ACA** (☎ 421648)* is friendly, shady, and spotless, but the noise from the *cucuyos* (insects in the trees) can be deafening in summer.

Hotels Most of Río Hondo's hotels close in summer, but a few remain open. Prices nearly double during the July-August high season; unless otherwise indicated, those below are low season, per person, and include breakfast.

Among the best bargains is ***Residencial El Parque*** *(☎ 422337)*, at Belgrano and Libertad, for US$10. ***Residencial Mon Petit*** *(☎ 421822, Alberdi 602)*, ***Hotel Las Vegas*** *(☎ 421010, Absalón Rojas 17)*, and ***Hotel Los Olivos*** *(☎ 421313, Mar del Plata 455)* are all in the US$11 range.

Hotel Termal Los Felipe *(☎ 421484, San Francisco Solano 230)* costs US$17 in summer, US$24 in winter. The ***Casino Center Hotel*** *(☎ 421346, Caseros 126)* charges US$25 with breakfast in summer, US$35 in winter. Rates at four-star ***Hotel Los Pinos*** *(☎ 421175, Maipú 201)* are US$50 in summer, US$80 in winter.

Places to Eat

Fish dishes, notably the *dorado a la portuguesa*, are the specialty at ***La Cabaña de los Changos***, at Av Alberdi and Libertad. For other regional specialties at moderate prices, try ***La Casa de Rubén*** *(Sarmiento 69)*, a parrilla, and ***Sabot*** *(☎ 421444, Caseros 64)*, serving parrillada and international dishes. ***Chorizo Loco***, at Alberdi and Sarmiento, specializes in grilled meats.

Try ***Heladería Trieste***, at Sarmiento and Caseros, to sample Río Hondo's best ice cream.

Getting There & Away

Air Austral (☎ 421631) is at Rivadavia 358. Flights from Buenos Aires to Santiago del Estero have a direct bus connection to Río Hondo.

Bus The Terminal de Ómnibus (☎ 421513) is on Las Heras between España and 12 de Octubre, half a dozen blocks west of the plaza and two blocks north of Av Alberdi.

Many of the buses between Tucumán (US$4, one hour) and Santiago del Estero (US$4, one hour) stop in Termas de Río Hondo, including those by La Unión (☎ 421722), which also goes to Buenos Aires (US$42, 15 hours) and La Plata. Chevallier (☎ 421085) has service to Tucumán, Buenos Aires, and La Plata, while Expreso Panamericano (☎ 421127) goes to Córdoba (US$23, six hours). La Estrella (☎ 421769) has buses to Buenos Aires and Mar del Plata, and San Cristóbal (also ☎ 421769) goes to Paraná, Entre Ríos, and Santa Fe. Libertador (☎ 421127) goes to Mendoza (19 hours, US$48) via Santiago del Estero, La Rioja, and San Juan.

Getting Around

Empresa 4 de Junio (☎ 421826) goes to the Dique Frontal for US$0.60. Catch it downtown along RN 9 or Av Perón.

La Rioja & Catamarca Provinces

Among modern Argentina's provinces, remote La Rioja and Catamarca are poor relations, but they are rich in scenery, folklore, and tradition. Both were home to several important pre-Columbian cultures, mostly maize cultivators, who developed unique pottery techniques and styles – the region has many important archaeological sites. Inca influence did not touch the Diaguitas until the late 15th century, just before the arrival of the Spaniards.

Given the area's current economic distress, it seems remarkable that, in the early 16th century, Vásquez de Espinosa described La Rioja as, literally, an oasis of prosperity:

> As one comes into the city, since the orange trees . . . are always covered and loaded down with blossoms, this entrance to the city for that distance of two leagues is a lovely cheering site, with the trees loaded with fruit the whole year round, and the great freshness and verdure; but what aids to make that spot seem the terrestrial Paradise or a bit of Heaven is the fragrance, sweetness, and perfume of the orange blossoms.

Irrigation brought water to the vineyards and fields, allowing cultivation of corn, wheat, sweet potatoes, and other root crops, but winemaking has proven to be La Rioja's most enduring industry. In the mid-19th century, Domingo Faustino Sarmiento compared the riojano landscape to that of the Middle East:

LA RIOJA & CATAMARCA PROVINCES

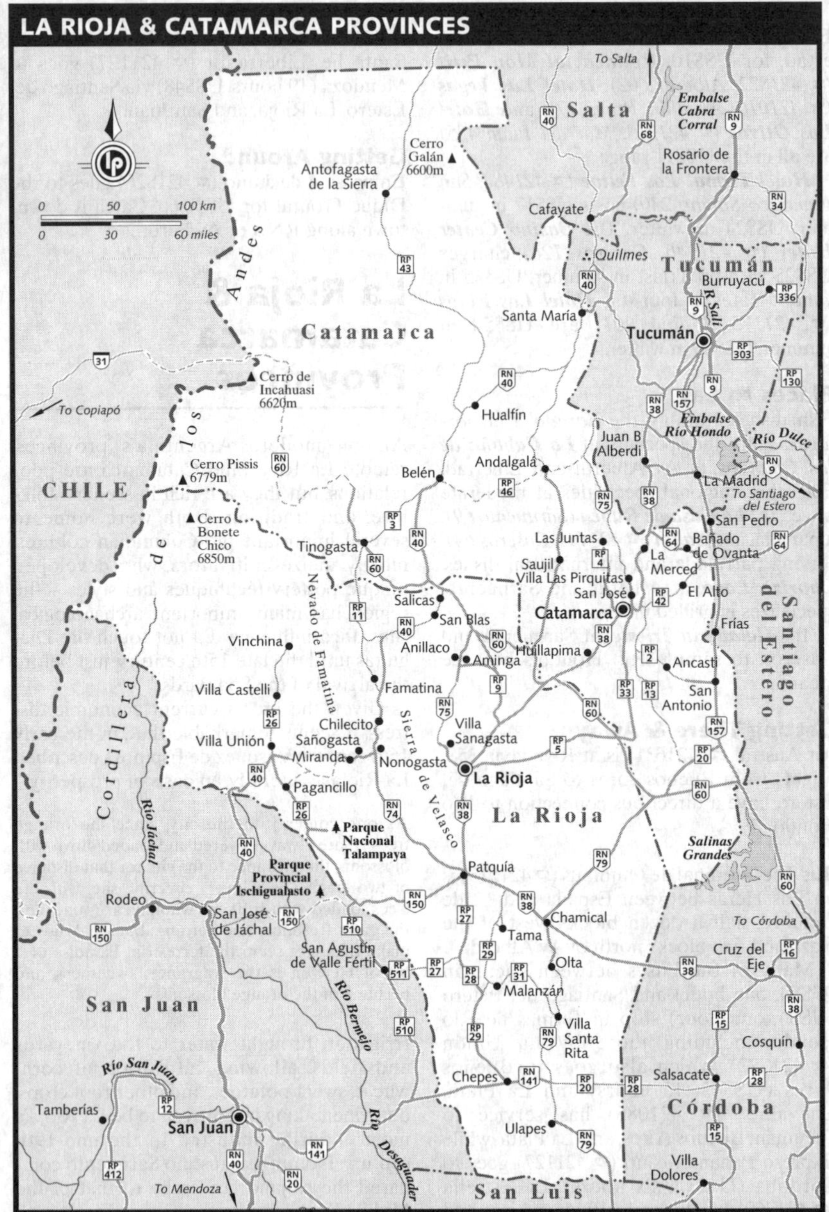

. . . in the reddish or ochreous tints of the soil, the dryness of some regions and their cisterns; also the orange-trees, vines and fig-trees bearing exquisite and enormous fruits, which are raised along the course of some turbid and confined Jordan. There is a strange combination of mountain and plain, fruitfulness and aridity, parched and bristling heights, and hills covered with dark green forests as lofty as the cedars of Lebanon.

Offering great beauty to visitors with a vehicle and time to explore, the region has also produced some of Argentina's most memorable historical figures, such as caudillos Facundo Quiroga, Chacho Peñaloza, and Felipe Varela – objects of Sarmiento's scorn in his famous diatribe against the rise of provincial strongmen. To balance the books, La Rioja also gave the country intellectuals like Joaquín V González, a writer, politician, and founder of La Plata university, and Arturo Marasso, writer and educator.

Presently, both provinces are economic backwaters with a low standard of living, especially in Catamarca, and people are leaving the countryside for the cities. The area is politically influential, though – President Carlos Menem and his mercurial family are riojanos, while the prominent Saadis have run Catamarca almost like a family fiefdom (at least until recent scandals outrageous even by Argentine standards). Both, to some degree, are modern counterparts of Facundo and his contemporaries, favoring personal loyalty and flagrant patronage over political principle.

Widespread corruption and nepotism often get out of hand – in 1990, when Governor Ramón Saadi of Catamarca appeared to have obstructed the rape/murder investigation of Guillermo Luque, the son of one of his political protégés, a Catholic nun led repeated local protests that finally forced Buenos Aires to intervene in the provincial courts. Not until 1998, though, did successful convictions send Luque and one of his accomplices to prison.

On the positive side, there is some evidence that the region may regain the oasis reputation it enjoyed in colonial times; at La Rinconada, north of the city of Catamarca, investors are planting extensive orchards of walnuts and pistachios under drip irrigation. To encourage commerce with Chile, paving of the highway from Catamarca over the 4726m Paso de San Francisco to Copiapó has commenced and should be finished by late 1999. While it may not make immediate economic sense, it could open up otherwise remote areas to adventurous travelers.

LA RIOJA

Juan Ramírez de Velasco founded Todos los Santos de la Nueva Rioja in 1591. Dominican, Jesuit, and Franciscan missionaries helped 'pacify' the Diaguita Indians and paved the way for Spanish colonization of what Vásquez de Espinosa called 'a bit of Paradise.'

The city's appearance reflects the conflict and accommodation between colonizer and colonized, the architecture combining European designs with native techniques and local materials. Many early buildings were destroyed in the 1894 earthquake, but the city has been entirely rebuilt. The recently restored commercial center, near Plaza 25 de Mayo, replicates colonial architecture, as do several churches and private homes.

Orientation

At the base of the picturesque Sierra de Velasco, La Rioja (population about 127,000) is 154km southwest of Catamarca and 460km northwest of Córdoba via RN 38, 515km northeast of San Juan via a combination of national and provincial routes, and 1167km north and west of Buenos Aires. It is relatively small, with all points of interest and most hotels within easy walking distance of each other.

Most public buildings, including the Palacio Legislativo, line the streets around Plaza 9 de Julio, but the city's commercial center surrounds Plaza 25 de Mayo and continues along east-west Pelagio Luna and north-south 25 de Mayo. North-south streets change their names at Rivadavia, but east-west streets are continuous.

Information

Tourist Offices The friendly, eager Dirección Municipal de Turismo (Dimutur;

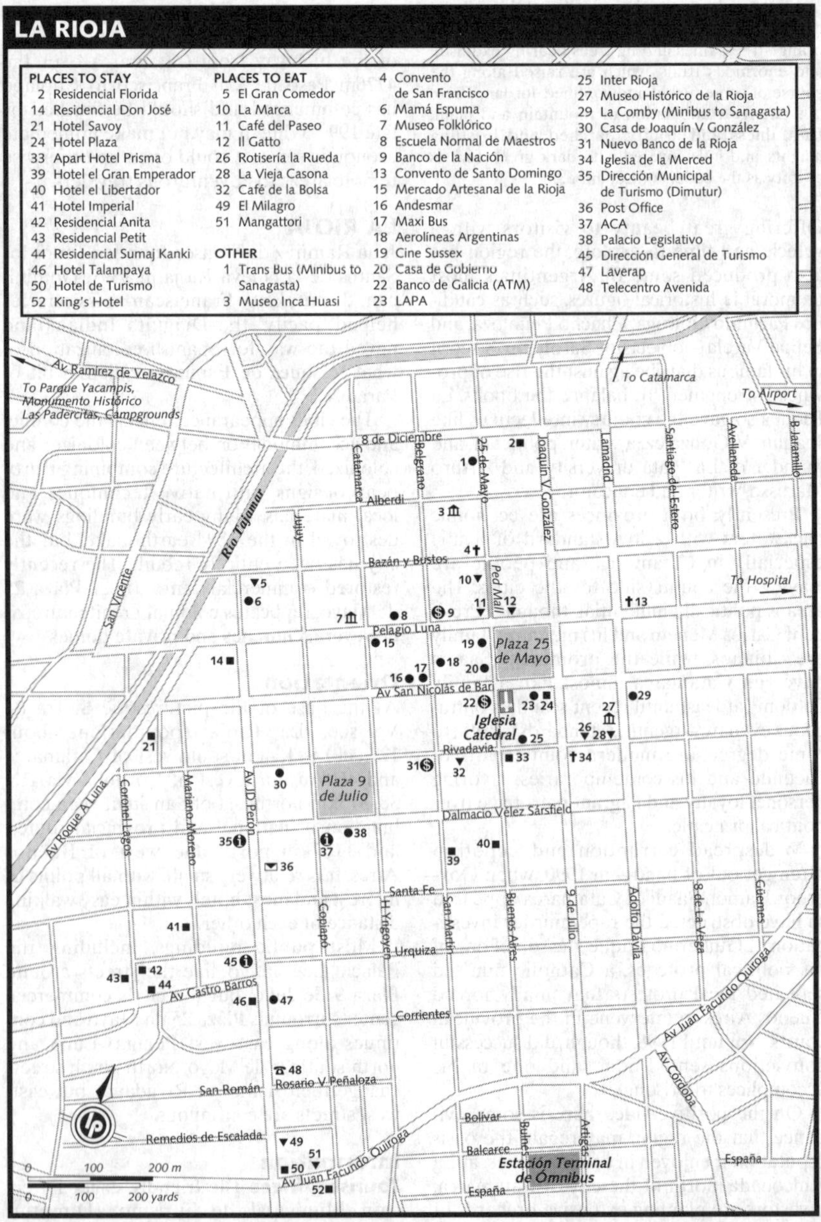

LA RIOJA
PLACES TO STAY
2 Residencial Florida
14 Residencial Don José
21 Hotel Savoy
24 Hotel Plaza
33 Apart Hotel Prisma
39 Hotel el Gran Emperador
40 Hotel el Libertador
41 Hotel Imperial
42 Residencial Anita
43 Residencial Petit
44 Residencial Sumaj Kanki
46 Hotel Talampaya
50 Hotel de Turismo
52 King's Hotel
PLACES TO EAT
5 El Gran Comedor
10 La Marca
11 Café del Paseo
12 Il Gatto
26 Rotisería la Rueda
28 La Vieja Casona
32 Café de la Bolsa
49 El Milagro
51 Mangattori
OTHER
1 Trans Bus (Minibus to Sanagasta)
3 Museo Inca Huasi
4 Convento de San Francisco
6 Mamá Espuma
7 Museo Folklórico
8 Escuela Normal de Maestros
9 Banco de la Nación
13 Convento de Santo Domingo
15 Mercado Artesanal de la Rioja
16 Andesmar
17 Maxi Bus
18 Aerolíneas Argentinas
19 Cine Sussex
20 Casa de Gobierno
22 Banco de Galicia (ATM)
23 LAPA
25 Inter Rioja
27 Museo Histórico de la Rioja
29 La Comby (Minibus to Sanagasta)
30 Casa de Joaquín V González
31 Nuevo Banco de la Rioja
34 Iglesia de la Merced
35 Dirección Municipal de Turismo (Dimutur)
36 Post Office
37 ACA
38 Palacio Legislativo
45 Dirección General de Turismo
47 Laverap
48 Telecentro Avenida
Av Ramírez de Velazco
To Parque Yacampis, Monumento Histórico Las Padercitas, Campgrounds
To Catamarca
To Airport
To Hospital
Río Tajamar
San Vicente
Jujuy
Catamarca
Belgrano
25 de Mayo
Joaquín V González
Lamadrid
Santiago del Estero
Avellaneda
B Jaramillo
8 de Diciembre
Alberdi
Bazán y Bustos
Ped Mall
Pelagio Luna
Plaza 25 de Mayo
Av San Nicolás de Bari
Iglesia Catedral
Rivadavia
Plaza 9 de Julio
Dalmacio Vélez Sarsfield
Av Roque A Luna
Coronel Lagos
Mariano Moreno
Av JD Perón
Copiapó
H Yrigoyen
San Martín
Buenos Aires
9 de Julio
Adolfo Dávila
8 de La Vega
Güemes
Santa Fe
Urquiza
Av Castro Barros
Corrientes
Av Juan Facundo Quiroga
Av Córdoba
San Román
Rosario V Peñaloza
Remedios de Escalada
Bolívar
Balcarce
Bulnes
Artigas
Estación Terminal de Ómnibus
España
0 100 200 m
0 100 200 yards

☎ 427103, fax 426648), Av Perón 715, distributes a good city map and brochures of other provincial destinations. Hotel information includes only officially registered hotels, excluding many cheaper possibilities, but there is a list of casas de familia. Hours are 8 am to 1 pm and 4 to 9 pm weekdays, 8 am to noon weekends.

The provincial Dirección General de Turismo (☎ 428839), at Av Perón and Urquiza, is also helpful. It's open 8 am to 1 pm and 4 to 9 pm weekdays, on weekends, there's usually a *guardia* (watchman) on hand.

ACA (☎ 425381) is at Vélez Sársfield and Copiapó.

Money La Rioja has no cambios, and bank hours are limited, but some travel agencies may change money. There are also several banks with ATMs.

Post & Communications Correo Argentino is at Av Perón 764; the postal code is 5300. Telecentro Avenida is at Av Perón 1066. La Rioja's area code is ☎ 03822.

Travel Agencies Yafar Turismo (☎ 423053) is at Pelagio B Luna 352.

Laundry Mamá Espuma is at Av Perón 324, Laverap at Av Perón 946.

Medical Services Hospital Presidente Plaza (☎ 427814) is at San Nicolás de Bari Este 97.

Landmark Buildings

La Rioja is a major devotional center, so most landmarks are ecclesiastical. Built in 1623 by Diaguita Indians under the direction of Dominican friars, the **Convento de Santo Domingo**, at Pelagio Luna and Lamadrid, is Argentina's oldest convent. The date appears in the carved algarrobo door frame, also the work of Diaguita artists.

At 25 de Mayo and Bazán y Bustos, the **Convento de San Francisco** houses the image of the Niño Alcalde, a Christ Child icon symbolically recognized as the city's mayor. The convent also contains the cell occupied in 1592 by San Francisco Solano, a priest known for educating native peoples and defending their rights.

The Byzantine **Iglesia Catedral** (1899), at San Nicolás de Bari and 25 de Mayo, contains the image of patron saint Nicolás de Bari, an object of devotion for both riojanos and the inhabitants of neighboring provinces. At the corner of Rivadavia and 9 de Julio, the **Iglesia de la Merced** replaced a Mercedarian church destroyed by the 1894 earthquake.

One of Argentina's greatest educators, founder of the Universidad de La Plata, lived in the **Casa de Joaquín V González**, at Rivadavia 952. The neoclassical **Escuela Normal de Maestros**, the teachers' school on Pelagio Luna between Catamarca and Belgrano, dates from 1884.

Museo Folklórico

While this museum credibly re-creates an authentic 19th-century house, with all the furnishings and objects necessary for everyday life, its thematic exhibits are even better. One hall displays ceramic reproductions representing mythological beings from local folklore, but it also contains particularly good Tinkunako materials (see Special Events later in this section), horse gear, an artisans' workshop and even diet statistics on criollo food (locro and humitas are much healthier than fatty empanadas).

At Pelagio Luna 811, the museum has a shady patio with comfortable benches that make it a good refuge from the heat. Hours are Tuesday to Sunday 9 am to noon, Tuesday to Friday 4 to 8 pm; admission is US$1.

Museo Inca Huasi

More than 12,000 pieces, including stone, wood, metal, and bone tools and artifacts, plus Diaguita ceramics and weavings, fill this paleontological and archaeological museum. Unfortunately, their poor arrangement and lack of interpretation diminish their interest except for specialists who really know what they're looking at. At Alberdi 650, Inca Huasi is open 9 am to noon daily except Monday; admission is US$1.

Museo Histórico de La Rioja

La Rioja was the land of the caudillos so deplored by Sarmiento, including the famous Facundo Quiroga, Felipe Varela, and Ángel (Chacho) Peñaloza; many Argentines say Carlos Menem modeled himself on Facundo (though Menem shaved his muttonchop sideburns some years ago). Offering some insight on the province's political development, this museum at Adolfo Dávila 79 contains Quiroga's stagecoach, military paraphernalia, and the die of the first coin used by his army. Hours are Tuesday to Saturday, 9 am to noon and 4 to 8 pm; admission is US$1.

Parque Yacampis

On the western edge of town at the foot of the Sierra de Velasco, this once neatly landscaped park has become increasingly rundown, but still has panoramic views, a small zoo where some local fauna such as rheas run free, and a popular swimming pool.

Special Events

El Tinkunako Taking place at midday December 31, this religious ritual reenacts the original ceremony of San Francisco Solano's 1593 mediation between the Diaguitas and the Spanish conquerors. For accepting peace, the Diaguitas imposed two conditions: resignation of the Spanish *alcalde* (mayor), and his replacement by the Christ Child. Some riojanos wear indigenous clothing and sing traditional songs in a procession carrying the image of their patron, San Nicolás de Bari, to meet the Niño Alcalde in front of the Casa de Gobierno. In deference to the mayor, the saint bows three times.

La Chaya This folkloric festival, the local variant of Carnaval, attracts people from throughout the country. Its name, derived from a Quechua word meaning 'to get someone wet,' should give you an idea of what to expect. The festival takes place around the figure of Pujllay, the indigenous deity responsible for the happiness of the poor, who is born at Carnaval, lives for three days, and dies on Sunday.

Festival del Viñador This festival, honoring local vintners, takes place at the beginning of the Villa Unión's March grape harvest. During the festival there is music, dancing, and tasting of regional wines, most notably the artisanal *vino patero*, made by traditional foot stomping of the grapes.

Places to Stay – Budget

Camping Parque Yacampis, at Av Ramírez de Velasco Km 3, has a free and shady but deteriorating ***campground*** whose swimming pool (not free) is its only redeeming feature, but at last pass it seemed that improvements were being made.

Several campgrounds occupy sites along RN 75 (formerly RP 1) west of town, including ***Country Las Vegas*** at Km 8 and ***Sociedad Siriolibanesa*** at Km 11. Rates are around US$5 per tent and US$4 per person; from Av Perón, city bus No 1 goes only as far as the Las Vegas before turning around.

Residenciales La Rioja lacks a large tourist infrastructure, especially in budget hotels, but the tourist office maintains a list of casas de familia offering accommodations for about US$12 per person.

Residencial Sumaj Kanki, at Av Castro Barros and Coronel Lagos, provides modest but clean accommodations for about US$10 per person with shared bath, but can get noisy. More central are ***Residencial Don José*** *(Av Perón 407)*, with small, dark, but clean rooms at US$10 per person with private bath, and ***Residencial Florida*** *(☎ 426563, 8 de Diciembre 524)* which has small but comfy rooms for US$15/26 with private bath.

Places to Stay – Mid-Range

The family-oriented ***Residencial Anita*** *(☎ 427008, Lagos 476)* is new and friendly for US$25 single or double. Across the street is ***Residencial Petit*** *(Lagos 427)*, which offers singles with shared bath for US$20 and singles/doubles with private bath for US$25/36. Once a grand place, the building conserves some of its past splendor, and the friendly, flexible management permits kitchen and laundry access.

In the same area, for about the same price and quality, are ***Hotel Talampaya*** *(☎ 424010, Av Perón 951)* and ***Hotel Imperial*** *(☎ 422478, Mariano Moreno 345)*. Along the river, ***Hotel Savoy*** *(☎ 426894, Av Roque A Luna 14)* charges US$25/35 with shared bath but has more comfortable rooms with private bath, air-con, and telephone for US$30/45; there's a bar and a confitería for breakfast.

In run-down Parque Yacampis, northwest of downtown, ACA's ***Motel Yacampis*** *(☎ 425216)* charges US$26/39 for members (good value) and US$39/55 for nonmembers (not-so-good value); it also has a restaurant and confitería. Other mid-range hotels are far from downtown. For US$48/56 with breakfast, ***Hotel de Turismo*** *(☎ 422005)*, Av Perón and Av Quiroga, is a bit more luxurious than others in this category, with a swimming pool and solarium.

Places to Stay – Top End

Affluent accommodations start around US$50/60 for singles/doubles at ***Hotel El Libertador*** *(☎ 426052, Buenos Aires 253)*, but there's a 10% cash discount for ACA members. ***Hotel El Gran Emperador*** *(☎ 438580, San Martín 250)* costs US$50/70. ***King's Hotel*** *(☎ 422122, Av Quiroga 1070)* charges US$70/95 and has a swimming pool.

Hotel Plaza *(☎ 425215, fax 422127)*, 9 de Julio and San Nicolás de Bari, offers rates of US$95/110, as well as room service, a swimming pool, and a bar. The new ***Apart Hotel Prisma*** *(☎ 421567)*, at the corner of Rivadavia and Buenos Aires, costs US$100 double.

Places to Eat

Regional cuisine, readily available at festivals and special events, can also be found at local restaurants. Some dishes to look for include: *locro* (stew), juicy and spicy empanadas differing from the drier ones of the Pampas, *chivito asado* (barbecued goat), *humita* (stuffed corn dough, resembling Mexican tamales), *quesillo* (a cheese specialty), and olives. Don't miss the local bread, baked in *hornos de barro* (adobe ovens). There is also a good selection of dried fruits, preserves, and jams from apples, figs, peaches, and pears. Don't hesitate to order house wines, which are invariably excellent.

Places serving regional specialties, as well as standard Argentine dishes like parrillada, include ***La Vieja Casona*** *(☎ 425996, Rivadavia 427)* and ***El Milagro*** *(☎ 430939, Av Perón 1200)*. ***El Gran Comedor*** *(☎ 422020, Bazán y Bustos 978)* also comes recommended.

Il Gatto *(☎ 421899, Pelagio Luna 555)* is part of a chain but still has very decent pizza and pasta at moderate prices. ***Mangattori*** *(☎ 422183, Av Quiroga 1131)* is one of the best Italian restaurants in town. ***La Marca*** is a diente libre parrilla on 25 de Mayo between Pelagio Luna and Bazán y Bustos.

Café del Paseo, at the corner of Pelagio Luna and 25 de Mayo, is an appealing Spanish-mission-style confitería. ***Café de la Bolsa*** *(☎ 421930, Rivadavia 684)* has fine fixed-price lunches including Middle Eastern dishes, while ***Rotisería La Rueda*** *(Rivadavia 461)* has good take-out food.

Entertainment

Performers of the stature of Leon Gieco perform at the ***Coliseo La Quebrada***, 5.5km west of downtown on Av San Francisco, where there are also theatrical performances.

Cine Sussex *(25 de Mayo 80)* shows current films.

Shopping

La Rioja has unique weavings that combine indigenous techniques and skill with Spanish designs and color combinations. The typical *mantas* (bedspreads) feature floral patterns over a solid background. Spanish influence is also visible in silverwork, including tableware, ornaments, religious objects, and horse gear. La Rioja's pottery is entirely indigenous – artists utilize local clay to make distinctive pots, plates, and flowerpots. Riojano wine has a national reputation; Saúl Menem, father of the president, founded one of the major bodegas.

The Mercado Artesanal de La Rioja, Pelagio Luna 792, exhibits and sells these items and other popular artworks at prices lower than most souvenir shops. It's open 8 am to noon and 4 to 8 pm Tuesday to Friday, 9 am to 1 pm weekends.

Getting There & Away

Air Aerolíneas Argentinas (☎ 426307), Belgrano 63, flies twice each weekday and once a day on weekends to Buenos Aires' Aeroparque (US$77 to US$190). LAPA (☎ 435197), San Nicolás de Bari Oeste 516, flies daily to Aeroparque (US$79 to US$149); Tuesday, Wednesday, Thursday, and Saturday flights stop in Catamarca (US$10 to US$17).

Andesmar (☎ 437995), San Nicolás de Bari Oeste 729, flies Tuesday, Wednesday, and Thursday to Córdoba (US$35 to US$59) and Rosario (US$85 to US$98).

Bus La Rioja's Estación Terminal de Ómnibus (☎ 425453) is at Artigas and España, though plans to build a new terminal are at the talking stage. A few companies, serving regional destinations, have separate downtown terminals.

El Cóndor (☎ 426436) travels daily to provincial destinations (Sanagasta and Chilecito), and has daily long-distance service to Córdoba, Catamarca, and San Luis. Cacorba (☎ 433967) also goes to Córdoba, as does Socasa (☎ 435841).

Socasa and Expreso Nacate both serve San Juan, while Autotransporte Mendoza (☎ 427395) goes three times weekly to Mendoza and to Pocitos, on the Bolivian border, with intermediate stops at Catamarca, Tucumán, Salta, and Jujuy. Bosio (☎ 421011) also goes to San Juan, Mendoza, and Pocitos; La Estrella (☎ 426306) has nearly identical routes. TAC goes to Tucumán, Mendoza, San Juan, and Neuquén.

Andesmar (☎ 422430) has extensive routes from Pocitos south to Mendoza, where it has connections to Patagonian destinations like Bariloche, Esquel, and Río Gallegos.

Empresa Ablo (☎ 426444) has buses to Córdoba, San Luis, Santa Fe, Buenos Aires, and Mar del Plata. Empresa General Urquiza (☎ 436272) serves Córdoba, Santa Fe, and Buenos Aires.

Inter Rioja (☎ 427878), Rivadavia 519, goes north to Anillaco and intermediate points via RN 1. La Riojana (☎ 435279), Buenos Aires 132, goes to Chilecito, as does Rioja Bus (☎ 430801), at San Nicolás de Bari 743. Maxi Bus (☎ 435979), San Nicolás de Bari 725, runs minibus service to Chilecito. Carhuva (☎ 436380), Dorrego 96, goes to Villa Unión, Vinchina, and Villa Castelli, in the province's western cordillera.

Sample fares include Catamarca (US$8, two hours), Chilecito (US$8, three hours), Tucumán (US$14, five hours), Córdoba (US$15 to US$17, five hours), Santiago del Estero (US$20, five hours), San Juan (US$22, six hours), Mendoza (US$26 to US$29, eight hours), San Luis (US$25, nine hours), Salta (US$24 to US$35, 11 hours), Jujuy (US$24 to US$36, 12 hours), Pocitos (US$43, 14 hours) and Buenos Aires (US$52 to US$62, 17 hours).

Getting Around

To/From the Airport From Plaza 9 de Julio, bus No 3 goes to Aeropuerto Vicente Almonacid (☎ 425483), 7km east of town on RP 5. An airport cab costs around US$6.

Car King's Rent A Car (☎ 422122) is in the King's Hotel, at Av Quiroga and Copiapó.

AROUND LA RIOJA

Monumento Histórico Las Padercitas

According to legend, San Francisco Solano converted many Diaguita Indians at the site of this Franciscan-built colonial adobe chapel, now sheltered by a stone temple, 7km west of town on RN 75. On the second Sunday of August, pilgrims convene to pay homage to the saint. Buses No 1 and 3 go to the site.

Dique Los Sauces

Beyond Las Padercitas, RN 75 climbs and winds past attractive summer homes, bright red sandstone cliffs, lush vegetation, and dark purple peaks whose cacti remind you that the area is semidesert. Balneario Los Sauces, 15km from La Rioja at the dam, is a pleasant place for a leisurely picnic or outing.

From Balneario Los Sauces you can hike or drive up the dirt road to 1680m Cerro de la Cruz, which affords panoramic views of the Yacampis valley and the village of Sanagasta.

The top also has a ramp for hang-gliding, a popular local activity. Sanagasta-bound buses can drop you off here.

VILLA SANAGASTA

At the end of paved RN 75 through the captivating valley of the Río Huaco, poplars line the narrow streets of summer homes and vineyards in the village of Sanagasta, 30km from La Rioja. The town has a small, well-restored **Iglesia de la Merced**, and the intriguing **Museo Rumy Mayo**.

Attractive ***Hostería Achay Sacat*** *(☎ 03822-492022)* is reasonably priced at US$20 per person with breakfast. For transportation from La Rioja, try La Comby (☎ 422360), Adolfo Dávila 20, or Trans Bus (☎ 426569), 25 de Mayo 368.

ANILLACO

Another 100km north of Sanagasta via RN 75, Anillaco has drawn unwelcome attention as, literally, a monument to corruption – President Carlos Menem's bucolic birthplace (population 900) features an international airport and an 18-hole professional golf course whose financing has been the subject of constant speculation in the Argentine press, and is likely to be investigated if the opposition Alianza wins the next election. Several TV journalists who exposed the scandal in a program entitled 'Menem's Disneyland' were fired by a station owner who declared 'I see nothing wrong with the country giving the president the gift of an airstrip.'

Something may be putrid here, but the scenery is worth a look and the highland climate is a refreshing change from sultry La Rioja. ACA's ***Hostería Anillaco*** *(☎ 03827-494064, Coronel Barros s/n)* charges US$20/32 single/double for members, US$30/48 for nonmembers. Nearby ***Hostería Los Amigos*** *(☎ 494107)* costs US$26/40. For transport from La Rioja, try Inter Rioja, Av Rivadavia 519.

CHILECITO

Founded in 1715 as Santa Rita de Casia, Chilecito was the takeoff point for a major 1817 expedition that crossed the Andes to Copiapó, Chile. It acquired its current name from the Chileans who worked the 19th-century gold mines of Famatina; later, the provincial government relocated here to escape intimidation by caudillo Facundo Quiroga. In 1892, the importance of the mines made Chilecito the site of the country's second branch of Banco de la Nación (locals responded vociferously to its proposed privatization in 1997).

In 1903, German contractors built one of the world's largest aerial engineering projects, the 35km cable car to La Mejicana mine, which reaches an altitude of 4603m. Although in the early 1900s there were 10 foundries in the area, agriculture has replaced mining as the main economic activity. The province's second-largest city (population 26,000), Chilecito is renowned for its wines, olives, and walnuts.

Orientation & Information

In a scenic valley at the foot of the massive Nevado de Famatina and Cerro Velazco, directly west of La Rioja, Chilecito is a roundabout 192km from the provincial capital via RN 38 and RN 74. Its compactness rewards walkers; most services are within a few blocks of Plaza Sarmiento.

Tourist Office Open weekdays 7 am to 1 pm and 3 to 9 pm, weekends 8 am to 9 pm, the Dirección Provincial de Turismo (☎ 422688), on Castro y Bazán between La Plata and Joaquín V González, has enthusiastic staff and good material. The municipal Dirección General de Turismo (Digetur) has a small office on Plazoleta Santa Rita, which is on Mitre between Castro Barros and Zelada y Dávila, and at the bus terminal.

Money Banco de la Nación and Nuevo Banco de La Rioja (ATM) are on opposite corners of Plaza Sarmiento. Banco de Salta has an ATM on Castro Barros between 25 de Mayo and 9 de Julio.

Post & Communications Correo Argentino is at Joaquín V González and Pelagio Luna; the postal code is 5360. Telecentro Audio 95 is on Joaquín V González near

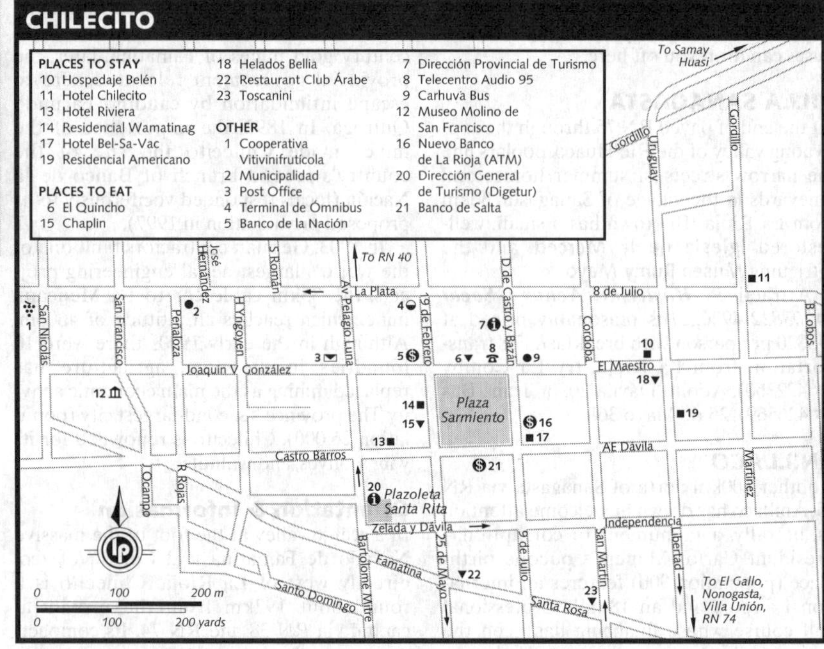

Castro y Bazán; Chilecito's area code is ☎ 03825.

Museo Molino de San Francisco

Chilecito founder Don Domingo de Castro y Bazán owned this colonial flour mill, whose museum houses an eclectic assemblage of archaeological tools, antique arms, early colonial documents, minerals, traditional wood and leather crafts, plus weavings and paintings. At J Ocampo 63, the building itself merits a visit, but the artifacts are a big plus. Hours are Tuesday to Sunday, 8 am to noon and 3 to 7 pm.

Samay Huasi

Joaquín V González, founder of the prestigious Universidad Nacional de La Plata, used this building, 3km from Chilecito past La Puntilla, as his country retreat. Now belonging to the university, the building houses a natural sciences, archaeology, and mineralogy museum, and a valuable collection of paintings by Argentine artists. It's open daily except Monday, 7 am to 8 pm; admission is US$1.

Cooperativa Vitivinifrutícola (Winery)

La Rioja is one of the best areas to taste the fruity white torrontés, though it's far from the only wine the province has to offer. One block north and five blocks west of Plaza Sarmiento, at La Plata 646, the province's largest winery (☎ 423150) is open to visitors weekdays for tours and tasting. Tours take place at 7:30 am, 9:30 am and 12:30 pm; there's an excellent selection of wine, as well as dried fruit, for sale.

Museo del Cablecarril

From the southern approach to Chilecito, about 2km southwest of Plaza Sarmiento, Estación No 1 del Cablecarril was the initial stop on the nine-station trip to La Mejicana. More than 260 towers sustained the 36km cable to its ultimate destination, 3510m higher than the town itself.

The cablecarril line was constructed in 1903; the *in situ* museum preserves the still-functional (though rarely used) wagons that carried men and supplies to the mine, in a little less than four hours, until 1935. A 39-step spiral staircase climbs to the platform, where ore carts and even passenger carts now wait silently in line. Alongside the platform is a wooden crane, built of Sitka spruce in 1913.

Well-versed municipal guides lead tours, in Spanish only, from the museum proper in the former mine offices, where there are mining artifacts, minerals, and communications equipment, including an early mobile phone. Admission is free, but a tip is appropriate. Hours are 7 am to 1 pm and 2 to 8 pm daily.

Places to Stay

The tourist office keeps a list of casas de familia, the cheapest accommodations in town, for about US$10 per person.

Otherwise, the cheapest in town is ***Hospedaje Belén*** *(☎ 422525, Maestro 198)* for US$10 with shared bath, US$12 with private bath. ***Residencial Americano*** *(☎ 422804, Libertad 68)* has singles/doubles for US$15/29 with shared bath. The very central ***Residencial Wamatinag*** *(☎ 423419, 25 de Mayo 87)* costs US$18/30.

For members and affiliates at least, the best value is ACA's utilitarian ***Hotel Chilecito*** *(☎ 422201, Timoteo Gordillo 101)*, which also has a good restaurant and pleasant common areas. Members' rates with private bath are US$20/32, but the non-member rates of US$30/48 are no bargain. Other choices include ***Hotel Riviera*** *(Castro Barros 158)* for US$24/35, and ***Hotel Bel-Sa-Vac*** *(☎ 422533)*, 9 de Julio and Dávila, for US$28/42.

Places to Eat

The hospitable owners of the ***Club Árabe***, 25 de Mayo and Santa Rosa, offer great food despite a limited menu; in summer, ask for grapes fresh off the vine. ***Chaplin*** *(25 de Mayo 54)* has good, inexpensive pasta.

Inexpensive ***El Gallo*** *(☎ 423427)*, at Libertad and Illia, on the south side of town, and ***Toscanini***, at San Martín and Santa Rosa, offer standard Argentine menus. ***El Quincho***, Joaquín V González 50, serves parrillada.

Helados Bellia, at the corner of El Maestro and Libertad, has fine ice cream.

Getting There & Away

The Estación Terminal de Omnibus is at La Plata and 19 de Febrero. Riojacor (☎ 422726) has daily buses to Villa Unión and La Rioja; Transporte Chilecito (☎ 422781), 19 de Febrero 194, goes to La Rioja many times daily. Ablo (☎ 422726) has three buses daily to Córdoba, Rosario, and Buenos Aires; General Urquiza (☎ 423279) runs the same route.

TAC (☎ 422943) goes Monday, Wednesday, and Friday at 8:30 pm to San Juan and intermediate points. Andesmar (☎ 424999) goes to Patquía, where it has extensive connections north and south. Empresa Vallecito goes to San Juan, Mendoza, and intermediate points.

Expreso Santa Rita (☎ 424566) serves nearby locations, including Miranda, Famatina, and Tinogasta. Carhuva Bus, at the corner of El Maestro and Castro y Bazán, has five buses weekdays to La Rioja, three Saturday and Sunday.

Samples fares include La Rioja (US$8, 2½ hours), Córdoba (US$17, seven hours), and Buenos Aires (US$45).

SECRETARÍA DE TURISMO ARGENTINA

Toucan

NONOGASTA

Only the roaring water of the acequias disrupts the peaceful, unpaved streets of this small town, birthplace of educator Joaquín V González. In a prosperous agricultural valley 16km south of Chilecito, Nonogasta features charming adobe architecture (including González's house and a 17th-century church), polite and friendly people, and good wines from Bodegas Nicarí.

CUESTA DE MIRANDA

With 800 turns, this mountainous stretch of RN 40 through the Sierra de Sañogasta, about 56km west of Chilecito, is one of the most spectacular in Argentina's northern Andes and one of the province's major scenic attractions. Although not paved, the surface is smooth and wide enough for vehicle safety; still, sounding the horn before the innumerable blind turns is a good idea. At the highest point, 2020m above sea level, there is a vista from which the Río Miranda looks like a frozen silver ribbon below.

PARQUE NACIONAL TALAMPAYA

Riojanos like to compare Talampaya, a 215,000-hectare reserve southwest of Chilecito, to Arizona's Grand Canyon of the Colorado. A better comparison would be southern Utah's arid canyon country, since only a trickle of permanent surface water winds through what, in the Quechua language, translates as the 'Dry River of the Tala' – a fitting description for this desert of scorching days, chilly nights, infrequent but torrential summer rains, and gusty spring winds.

Talampaya's recent upgrade from provincial to national park status has political implications – President Carlos Menem, himself a riojano, decreed it – but its natural landscape and cultural features, including pre-Columbian petroglyphs and mortars, are legitimate enough. As the park attracts more attention, visits are likely to increase and visitor services to improve, but for the moment both are limited.

Visitors may not use their own vehicles on park roads – only contracted guides with pickup trucks offer tours of sandy canyons where aboriginal petroglyphs and mortars adorn streambed sites and nesting condors scatter from cliffside nests as vehicles invade their otherwise undisturbed habitat. On the usual two-hour tour from park headquarters, the vehicle passes the dunes of **El Playón**, leading to the **Puerta de Talampaya** (Gate of Talampaya) entrance to the canyon. During a brief stop, passengers walk a sandy trail to the petroglyphs and mortars.

Back on the road, the truck enters the red sandstone canyon, whose eastern wall reveals a conspicuous fault. The next major stops are the **Chimenea del Eco**, an extraordinary echo chamber where your voice seems to come back louder than your original call, and a nature trail to the **Bosquecillo** (Little Forest), a representative sample of native vegetation. On the return the major point is **El Cañón de los Farallones** (Canyon of Cliffs) where, besides condors and turkey vultures, you may see eagles and other birds of prey 150m above the canyon floor. Longer four-hour excursions are possible to **Los Pizarrones** and other sites like **Los Cajones**, **Ciudad Perdida**, and **Los Chañares**.

Orientation & Information

Talampaya is 141km southwest of Chilecito via a combination of RN 40's scenic Cuesta de Miranda route, RP 18, and RP 26. Via RP 26, it is 55km south of Villa Unión and 58km north of Los Baldecitos, the turnoff to San Juan's Parque Provincial Ischigualasto.

From the junction with RP 26, a paved eastbound lateral leads 14km to the Puerta de Talampaya entrance, where there's a ***confitería*** (simple meals and cold drinks available) that may become the permanent visitor center; a ranger is usually on duty to collect the US$3 admission. There are some good dinosaur illustrations depicting the early Triassic, 250 million years ago.

Two-hour excursions cost US$35 for up to eight persons; proceeds go directly to guides. Four-hour trips cost US$110 for up to eight persons. If you can, sit in front with the guide one way, and in the back of the truck the other way.

Getting There & Away

Travelers without their own cars, on a limited budget, can take the Transportes Rápido bus from La Rioja to Pagancillo, 28km from Talampaya, where most of the park personnel reside; from there they will help you get to the park, where it is necessary to pay for the excursions.

In Pagancillo, Adolfo Páez (☎ 03825-470397, 03825-1567-1160 cellular) has good cabaña accommodation and offers free transportation to the park proper for visitors who take his tours. There are no accommodations at the park itself, though it's possible to camp informally at the confitería, which has toilets but no showers. There is speculation about construction of a hotel.

CATAMARCA

Spaniards founded Londres, the first city in present-day Catamarca province, as early as 1559, but hostile Indians delayed the permanent establishment of any city until 1683, when Don Fernando Mendoza de Mate de Luna founded San Fernando del Valle de Catamarca, or Catamarca for short. Like La Rioja, it's hot, but mountain breezes sometimes moderate the ambient temperature.

Economically, it has remained a provincial backwater, although major devotional holidays attract large numbers of visitors. Except for its magnificent cathedral (a landmark that looks better by night), Catamarca's cityscape is worn around more than just the edges.

Mirroring the province's economic distress and political corruption, the capital's drab peatonal Rivadavia, which becomes a neon-lit consumerist enclave by night, has few places to sit and relax, while its well-designed Plaza 25 de Mayo reveals seriously deferred maintenance. Slow progress on projects like the peatonal and modernization of the bus terminal reinforce the impression that La Rioja's future is less than promising. Though images and murals of the Virgen del Valle are everywhere, catamarqueños may be as fatalistic as they are faithful.

Orientation

Dense clouds often disrupt the view in the valley of the Río del Valle, which is flanked by the Sierra del Colorado in the west and the Sierra Graciana in the east. In the valley, Catamarca (population 138,000) sits 156km northeast of La Rioja, 238km from Tucumán via RN 38, and 218km from Santiago del Estero via RN 64.

Nearly everything is within walking distance in the city center, an area 12 blocks square circumscribed by four wide avenues: Av Belgrano to the north, Av Alem to the east, Güemes to the south, and Virgen del Valle to the west. The focus of downtown is the beautifully designed Plaza 25 de Mayo (the work of Carlos Thays, who also designed Parque San Martín in Mendoza and Tucumán's Parque 9 de Julio), a shady refuge from the summer heat. South of the plaza, Rivadavia is a permanent peatonal between San Martín and Mota Botello, while beyond Mota Botello to Av Güemes it's closed to auto traffic from 8 am to 1 pm and 3 to 11 pm. North of Av Belgrano along Tucumán is Parque Adán Quiroga, another green space in this relatively treeless city.

Streets in Catamarca often change names; the most recent is Av Urquiza, recently renamed Av Virgen del Valle, while Calle Vicente Saadi has reverted to its original name of República.

Information

Tourist Offices The Dirección Municipal de Turismo (☎ 437595), Sarmiento 535, is open weekdays 7 am to 8 pm, weekends 8 am to 8 pm. It has a decent downtown map, a good services brochure, and friendly, competent staff. For travelers intending to cross the Andes here, the Chilean national tourist agency Sernatur maintains an office in the same building.

Open weekdays 7 am to 8 pm, the provincial Subsecretaría de Turismo (☎ 437594) is in the Manzana del Turismo (Tourism Block) at the corner of Av Virgen del Valle and General Roca; the entrance is on General Roca.

ACA (☎ 424513) is at República 102.

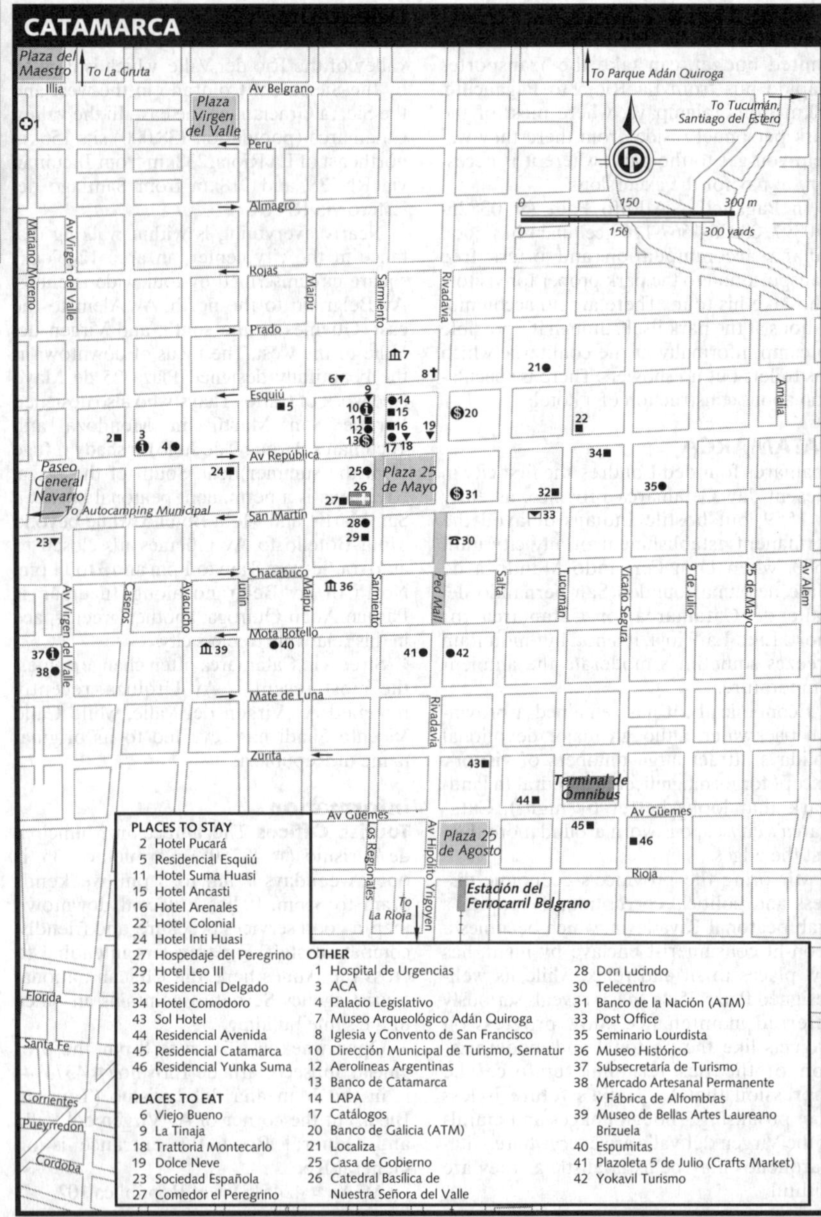

CATAMARCA
Plaza del Maestro
To La Gruta
To Parque Adán Quiroga
To Tucumán, Santiago del Estero
Plaza Virgen del Valle
Paseo General Navarro
To Autocamping Municipal
Plaza 25 de Mayo
Plaza 25 de Agosto
Terminal de Ómnibus
Estación del Ferrocarril Belgrano
To La Rioja
Ped Mall
0 150 300 m
0 150 300 yards
Illia
Av Belgrano
Peru
Almagro
Rojas
Prado
Esquiú
Av República
San Martín
Chacabuco
Mota Botello
Mate de Luna
Zurita
Av Güemes
Rioja
Florida
Santa Fe
Corrientes
Pueyrredon
Cordoba
Mariano Moreno
Av Virgen del Valle
Caseros
Ayacucho
Junín
Maipú
Sarmiento
Rivadavia
Salta
Tucumán
Vicario Segura
9 de Julio
25 de Mayo
Av Alem
Amalia
Los Regionales
Av Hipólito Yrigoyen
PLACES TO STAY
2 Hotel Pucará
5 Residencial Esquiú
11 Hotel Suma Huasi
15 Hotel Ancasti
16 Hotel Arenales
22 Hotel Colonial
24 Hotel Inti Huasi
27 Hospedaje del Peregrino
29 Hotel Leo III
32 Residencial Delgado
34 Hotel Comodoro
43 Sol Hotel
44 Residencial Avenida
45 Residencial Catamarca
46 Residencial Yunka Suma
PLACES TO EAT
6 Viejo Bueno
9 La Tinaja
18 Trattoria Montecarlo
19 Dolce Neve
23 Sociedad Española
27 Comedor el Peregrino
OTHER
1 Hospital de Urgencias
3 ACA
4 Palacio Legislativo
7 Museo Arqueológico Adán Quiroga
8 Iglesia y Convento de San Francisco
10 Dirección Municipal de Turismo, Sernatur
12 Aerolíneas Argentinas
13 Banco de Catamarca
14 LAPA
17 Catálogos
20 Banco de Galicia (ATM)
21 Localiza
25 Casa de Gobierno
26 Catedral Basílica de Nuestra Señora del Valle
28 Don Lucindo
30 Telecentro
31 Banco de la Nación (ATM)
33 Post Office
35 Seminario Lourdista
36 Museo Histórico
37 Subsecretaría de Turismo
38 Mercado Artesanal Permanente y Fábrica de Alfombras
39 Museo de Bellas Artes Laureano Brizuela
40 Espumitas
41 Plazoleta 5 de Julio (Crafts Market)
42 Yokavil Turismo

Money Catamarca has no cambios, but several downtown banks change cash and have ATMs.

Post & Communications Correo Argentino is at San Martín 753; the postal code is 4700. There's a Telecentro at Rivadavia 758; Catamarca's area code is ☎ 03833.

Travel Agencies Yokavil Turismo (☎ 430066), in the Galería Paseo del Centro at Rivadavia 916, arranges half-day tours to the Cuesta del Portezuelo (US$15) and the Gruta de la Virgen del Valle (US$15), and a full-day excursion to the eastern slopes of the Sierra de Ambato (US$35).

Bookstores Catálogos, República 518, has a quality selection of books on Argentine and regional history, as well as archaeology.

Laundry Espumitas (☎ 424504) is at Mota Botello 343.

Medical Services The Hospital de Urgencias (☎ 423964) is at Av Illia and Mariano Moreno.

Historic Buildings

Catamarca's provincial **Casa de Gobierno** (1859) is on the west side of Plaza 25 de Mayo, while the more recent, utilitarian **Palacio Legislativo** is on República between Caseros and Ayacucho.

The imposing neocolonial **Iglesia y Convento de San Francisco** (1892), at Esquiú and Rivadavia, holds the cell of Fray Mamerto Esquiú, a 19th-century priest celebrated for speeches in defense of the Constitution of 1853. A crystal box holding the priest's heart reposes in a locked room after being stolen and left on the roof some years ago.

Now occupied by a private school but dating from 1890, the former **Seminario Lourdista** (Lourdist Seminary) is a prominent landmark throughout the city, thanks to its conspicuous twin bell towers. It's on San Martín between Vicario Segura and 9 de Julio.

At the south end of Rivadavia, opposite Plaza 25 de Agosto, the **Estación del Ferrocarril Belgrano** is a striking landmark even though the trains no longer run.

Catedral Basílica de Nuestra Señora del Valle

Opposite Plaza 25 de Mayo, dating from 1859, the cathedral shelters the Virgen del Valle, Patron of Catamarca, one of northern Argentina's most venerated images since the 17th century. Her diamond-studded crown can be seen in early April and on December 8, when multitudes of pilgrims converge on Catamarca to pay her homage (she is also, in a curious juxtaposition of the sacred and profane, the *Patrona Nacional de Turismo)*.

The cathedral also contains an elaborately carved altar to Saint Joseph, an ornate baroque pulpit, and an exhibition of paintings of the virgin.

Museo Arqueológico Adán Quiroga

Mundane presentation and interpretive shortcomings keep this museum's three distinct collections from forming a coherent whole despite its impressive artifacts, and the most worthwhile items may be the contemporary paintings in the foyer. The first display hall contains assorted tools, ceramics, funerary pots, and mummies from 3000 BC to the 18th century, but the tedious descriptive chronologies of items in traditional glass cabinets detracts from their quality. The colonial-history room mixes disparate objects like rifles and musical instruments with fossils. The third room, also historical, presents ecclesiastical material and the personal effects of Fray Mamerto Esquiú.

At Sarmiento 450, the museum (☎ 437413) is open weekdays 7 am to 1 pm and 2:30 to 8:30 pm, weekends 8:30 am to 12:30 pm and 3:30 to 6:30 pm. Guides for large groups are available on request. Admission is US$1.

Museo Histórico

Occupying only a single room in a neoclassical building with Corinthian columns, the city's historical museum limits itself to nicely arranged portraits of provincial governors, supplemented by their personal artifacts. There is, however, almost no interpretation. At Chacabuco 425, the museum (☎ 437562) is open weekdays 8 am to noon and 3 to 7 pm, but you usually have to ask someone to open it up.

Museo de Bellas Artes Laureano Brizuela

Named for a prominent catamarqueño painter, the fine-arts museum exhibits his own works and those of Varela Lezama, Roberto Gray, Antonio Berni, Benito Quinquela Martín, Vicente Forte and others. The museum (☎ 437562) is at Mota Botello 239, between Ayacucho and Junín.

Special Events

Fiesta de Nuestra Señora del Valle For two weeks after Easter, in an impressive manifestation of popular religion, hordes of pilgrims come from the interior and from other Andean provinces to honor the Virgen del Valle. At the end of the *novena* (nine days of prayer), she is taken in procession around the plaza.

Fiesta Nacional del Poncho The last fortnight of July, a crafts and industrial fair accompanies this festival of folkloric music and dance celebrating the importance of the poncho in the province. The shows, which attract well-known musicians, and exhibitions take place in the Manzana del Turismo on Av Virgen del Valle. Don't miss the scattered *peñas*, informal gatherings with music, dance, and typical food – ask the tourist office for suggestions.

Día de la Virgen Pilgrims from throughout the country overrun Catamarca to pay homage to the Virgen del Valle on December 8, the city's patron saint's day.

Places to Stay – Budget

Camping Catamarca's ***Autocamping Municipal***, 4km west of town on RP 4, is a pleasant spot by the Río El Tala, in Sierra de Ambato foothills. It has two shortcomings: as the city's major recreation site, with two swimming pools, it gets loud and heavy weekend and holiday use (forget about sleeping), and it also has fierce mosquitoes.

Bathrooms and showers are clean, and there is electricity. The ***confitería*** has friendly staff and basic food, but it's cheaper to buy your own in town. Daily charges are US$5 per tent, plus US$2 per vehicle and US$1 per person.

From the Convento de San Francisco, on Esquiú, or from the bus terminal on Vicario Segura, take bus No 101.

Casas de Familia, Residenciales & Hotels The tourist office keeps a list of casas de familia offering inexpensive lodging. The cheapest option in town, however, is to share the pilgrims' dormitory accommodations at the ***Hospedaje del Peregrino*** *(☎ 431003, Sarmiento 653)* for US$5 per person (if you have your own sheets) or US$7 per person (with theirs). Otherwise, drab ***Residencial Yunka Suma*** *(☎ 423034, Vicario Segura 1255)* is suitable for one night only at US$10 per person with shared bath.

Not so good as it looks from outside, ***Hotel Comodoro*** *(☎ 423490, República 855)* rents small, dark rooms with shared bath for US$10 per person; better rooms with air-con and private bath cost US$20/30 single/double. Better than it looks from outside, for US$15/26 with private bath, cordial ***Residencial Delgado*** *(☎ 426109, San Martín 788)* is very central. Attractive ***Residencial Esquiú*** *(☎ 422284, Esquiú 365)* charges US$15/25.

Near the bus terminal, frayed but friendly ***Residencial Avenida*** *(☎ 422139, Av Güemes 754)* is not great value at US$15/23 with shared bath, US$18/26 with private bath. A block away, ***Residencial Catamarca*** *(☎ 422142, Av Güemes 841)* has rooms with bath at US$15/24.

Places to Stay – Mid-Range

For a pleasant place with friendly staff, try ***Hotel Colonial*** *(☎ 423502, República 802)* for US$27/37. The architecturally dreary but otherwise congenial ***Sol Hotel*** *(☎ 430803,*

WAYNE BERNHARDSON

Pottery market

Salta 1142) is a good value at US$21/28 with shared bath and kitchenette, US$28/38 with private bath; there are good views of town from the rooftop patio. The very central ***Hotel Suma Huasi*** *(☎ 425199, Sarmiento 541)*, with rates of US$35/42, offers discounts to ACA members.

Places to Stay – Top End

The modern ***Hotel Inti Huasi*** *(☎ 425005, República 297)* gives discounts to ACA members on its normal rates of US$40/50; prices are identical at central ***Hotel Ancasti*** *(☎ 425974, Sarmiento 520)*, though there are more commodious VIP rooms at US$50/65. ***Hotel Pucará*** *(☎ 430698/688, Caseros 501)* has pleasant rooms with television for US$40/54 for singles/doubles.

Top of the line are the downtown ***Hotel Leo III*** *(☎ 432080, Sarmiento 727)* for US$56/70, and ***Hotel Arenales*** *(☎ 430307, Sarmiento 544)* for US$64/79.

Places to Eat

The least-expensive eateries cater to pilgrims. In the gallery behind the cathedral, ***Comedor El Peregrino*** offers two courses (empanadas and pasta) for about US$4, or an option with meat for US$6. ***La Tinaja*** *(☎ 435853, Sarmiento 533)* also has low prices and sometimes live music. ***Viejo Bueno*** *(☎ 424224, Esquiú 480)* is a central parrilla. ***Trattoria Montecarlo*** *(☎ 423171, República 548)* specializes in pasta. The ***Sociedad Española*** *(☎ 431896, Av Virgen del Valle 725)* has traditional Spanish dishes, including seafood.

Dolce Neve, at the corner of República and Rivadavia, is a chain store but still serves good ice cream.

Shopping

For Catamarca's characteristic hand-tied rugs, visit the Mercado Artesanal Permanente y Fábrica de Alfombras at Virgen del Valle 945, next to the provincial tourist office. Besides rugs, the market sells ponchos, blankets, jewelry, red onyx sculptures, musical instruments, hand-spun sheep and llama wool, and basketry. It's open weekdays 8 am to 12:30 pm and 4 to 8:30 pm, Saturday 9 am to noon and 4:30 to 8 pm, and Sunday 9 am to noon. There's also a small, informal crafts market evenings on Plazoleta 5 de Julio, on Rivadavia.

Regional specialty shops are concentrated on Sarmiento, between Plaza 25 de Mayo and the Convento de San Francisco. Don Lucindo, on Sarmiento just south of San Martín, has a mixed selection – good stuff and kitsch – of pottery, basketry, wines, and fruits. Catamarca is the place to buy walnuts, including rich but tasty *nueces confitadas* (sugared walnuts), and olives, raisins, and wines.

Getting There & Away

Air Aerolíneas Argentinas (☎ 424460), Sarmiento 589, flies daily except Sunday to Buenos Aires' Aeroparque (US$77 to US$190). Austral, at the same office, flies daily except Saturday to Santiago del Estero (US$44) and Aeroparque. LAPA (☎ 434772), Sarmiento 506, flies Monday, Friday, and Sunday to La Rioja (US$10 to US$17) and Aeroparque (US$79 to US$159).

Bus The long-overdue facelift at Catamarca's privatized Terminal de Ómnibus (☎ 423415), Av Güemes 850, has been slower and less thorough than anticipated, but it's still an improvement on what used to be one of the country's grubbiest bus stations.

Chevallier (☎ 430921) has two buses each evening to Buenos Aires, via Córdoba and Rosario, with connections to Mar del Plata. Cacorba (☎ 423239) serves the same routes, and also goes to provincial towns like Aimogasta, Tinogasta, Andalgalá, Belén, and Fiambalá. Empresa Gutiérrez serves most of the same long-distance and provincial routes. Rubimar (☎ 428696) goes to provincial towns like Aimogasta, Belén, and Londres, and also to the Bolivian border at Pocitos.

La Estrella (☎ 430494) goes to Tucumán, San Juan, and Mendoza, also crossing the Chaco to Resistencia, Corrientes, and Posadas. Aconquija also goes to Tucumán, while Bosio (☎ 424334) services Tucumán, the Cuyo cities, and Santiago del Estero.

TAC (☎ 430253) covers destinations from Jujuy in the north to Mendoza (with connections to Chile) and into Patagonia, as well as crossing the Chaco to Resistencia and Corrientes. Andesmar (☎ 423777) has very extensive routes from the Bolivian border to Patagonia via Mendoza. Autotransportes Mendoza has similar Cuyo routes and also goes to Santiago del Estero.

General Urquiza (☎ 434980) goes to Córdoba and its Sierras, and to Mesopotamian destinations like Paraná. Ortiz (☎ 432641) goes to Rosario, Paraná, Corrientes, Buenos Aires, Santa Rosa de La Pampa, and Comodoro Rivadavia.

Sample fares include La Rioja (US$8, 2½ hours), Fiambalá (US$$11, four hours), Tucumán (US$11, 3½ hours), Santiago del Estero (US$12, five hours), Andalgalá (US$13, 4½ hours), Córdoba (US$16, 5½ hours), Salta (US$21, seven hours), Jujuy (US$24, eight hours), San Juan (US$21 to US$25, eight hours) Mendoza (US$27 to US$31, 10 hours), Resistencia/Corrientes (US$47. 14-15 hours) and Buenos Aires US$42 to US$54, 15 hours).

Getting Around

To/From the Airport For US$5, Aerolíneas' Servicios Diferenciales minibus goes to Aeropuerto Felipe Varela (☎ 430080, 435582), on RP 33, 22km east of town.

Car Localiza (☎ 435838) is at Esquiú 786.

AROUND CATAMARCA

Gruta de la Virgen del Valle

According to local legend, in 1619 or 1620 the image of the Virgen del Valle appeared in this grotto 7km north of downtown on RP 32. The present image is a replica of that in

Catamarca's Catedral, and a protective structure shelters the Gruta itself.

Empresa Cotca's bus No 104 goes to the Gruta every 40 minutes.

Cuesta de El Portezuelo

In 20km this hairpin road climbs more than 1000m to the top of the Sierras de Ancasti, affording increasingly distant views of the city of Catamarca. There are several turnouts for panoramic vistas and photography, but since passenger buses no longer take this route, a private car or an organized tour are the only alternatives; try Yokavil Turismo (see Travel Agencies in the Catamarca section).

Villa Las Pirquitas

The Sierra de Famatina, the province's highest mountain range, is visible from the road to this picturesque village near the dam of the same name, 29km north of Catamarca via RN 75. The foothills en route shelter small villages with hospitable people and interesting vernacular architecture. At the entrance to Villa Las Pirquitas, the house with the modest sign 'Hay Pan' sells Catamarca's best home-baked bread.

Camping is possible in the basic balneario, where the shallows are too muddy for swimming. The very attractive ***Hostería Municipal*** *(☎ 492030)* offers a great value at US$20/35 single/double with meals.

From Catamarca's bus terminal, Empresa Cotca's bus No 101 leaves hourly for the village.

ANDALGALÁ

At the north end of the Sierra de Sierra de Manchao, 200km from Catamarca via RN 75 and RP46, Andalgalá is a possible stopover on the scenic route from Catamarca to Belén via the Cuesta de Chilca; RP 46 continues west to the equally scenic Cuesta de Belén. There are accommodations at the plain ***Residencial Galileo*** *(Núñez del Prado 164)* and a good self-serve ***restaurant*** on the north side of the plaza. Gutiérrez buses from Catamarca to Belén take this very spectacular route.

BELÉN

Before the arrival of the Spaniards in the mid-16th century, the area around Belén was Calchaquí territory on the periphery of the Inca empire. After the Incas fell, it became the encomienda of Pedro Ramírez Velasco, founder of La Rioja, but its history is intricately intertwined with nearby Londres, a Spanish settlement shifted several times because of floods and Calchaquí resistance. More than a century passed before, in 1681, the priest José Bartolomé Olmos de Aguilera divided a land grant among veterans of the Calchaquí wars on the condition that they support evangelization in the area.

Orientation & Information

In the western highlands of Catamarca, Belén (population 8300) is 89km west of Andalgalá and 289km from the provincial capital, and 180km southwest of Santa María. The Oficina Municipal de Turismo is at the foot of Cerro de la Virgen, on the western edge of town. The postal code is 4750, the area code 03835.

Things to See & Do

The neoclassical brick church, the **Iglesia Nuestra Señora de Belén**, dates from 1907 and faces Plaza Olmos y Aguilera, well shaded by pines and colossal pepper trees. The provincial **Museo Cóndor Huasi**, with an impressive assortment of pre-Columbian materials, is due to move to new quarters.

December 20's **Día de la Fundación** celebrates the town's foundation, but festivities begin at least a week earlier with a dance at the foot of the **Cerro de la Virgen**, three blocks west of the plaza, where a steep 1900m trail leads to a 15m statue of the Virgin, side-by-side with a 4½m image of the Niño Jesús. Hauled to the site by muleback, the materials used to construct the statues included 400 cubic meters of gravel, 300 cubic meters of sand, 2 tons of iron, 2000 bags of cement, and 40,000 liters of water.

Shopping

Belén is one of the best places for woven goods, particularly ponchos, in Argentina.

Try both El Kollita, in the 200 block of Belgrano, and Regionales Los Antonitos (☎ 03835-461940), Lavalle 418.

Places to Stay & Eat

Free camping is possible on the shady, well-kept grounds of the ***Hotel Turismo*** *(☎ 461501)*, Belgrano and Cubas, but the toilets accessible to campers are not for the squeamish and there are no showers. The hotel proper is very reasonably priced at US$15/22 single/double. Other options include ***Hotel Gómez*** *(☎ 461388, Calchaquí 141)* for US$13/20, and ***Hotel Samay*** *(☎ 461320, Urquiza 399)* for US$35/45.

On summer nights, restaurants near Plaza Olmos y Aguilera set up tables on the plaza itself. ***Bar Sarmiento***, on Lavalle at the plaza's southwest corner, is cheap and popular throughout the day. Half a block south of the Plaza, on Lavalle, there's an anonymous ***bakery*** *(Lavalle 329)* producing exquisitely lemony *empanadas árabes*. There are several good ice creameries around the plaza.

El Único, at General Roca and Sarmiento, is a decent parrilla with an attractive quincho. ***Fénix***, at Sarmiento and Rivadavia opposite the bus terminal, serves palatable Middle Eastern food.

Getting There & Away

Belén's Terminal de Ómnibus, at the corner of Sarmiento and Rivadavia, one block south and one block west of the plaza, has both provincial and limited long-distance services.

Cacorba goes to Andalgalá, Pomán, and Chumbichá, to Catamarca (five hours) at 1:30 pm daily, and to Córdoba (14 hours) via Andalgalá Wednesday and Sunday at 6 pm. Transporte Parra goes to Salta (12½ hours) at 6 am Thursday, returning at 6 am Wednesday.

Empresa Ortiz, at Av Calchaquíes and Rivadavia, goes daily to Córdoba, Tinogasta, La Rioja, and Catamarca. Both Rubimar and Gutiérrez go to Catamarca (US$12, 4½ hours), the latter via the scenic Andalgalá route. San Cayetano goes Saturday to Andalgalá at 11 am, and Monday, Wednesday, and Friday at 2 pm to Santa María (five hours), returning Monday, Wednesday, and Friday at 7 am. Empresa Robledo connects Belén, Londres, El Salado, and Tinogasta (two hours), Tuesday and Sunday at 4 pm. El Antofagastino goes to Antofagasta de la Sierra at 10 am Friday.

AROUND BELÉN

Londres

Only 15km southwest of Belén, sleepy Londres (population 1800) is the province's oldest Spanish settlement, dating from 1558, though it moved several times before returning here in 1612; the inhabitants fled again during the Calchaquí uprising of 1632. The **Festival Provincial de la Nuez** (Provincial Walnut Festival) takes place here the first fortnight of February, but more interesting are the nearby Inca ruins at Shinkal.

From Belén, seven local buses daily go to Londres.

HUALFÍN

About 60km north of Belén via RN 40, the village of Hualfín features a colonial chapel beneath a small promontory whose 142-step staircase leads to a mirador with panoramic views of cultivated fields and the distant desert. The crumbling but atmospheric ***Hostería Hualfín*** charges US$10 per person in what was once an imposing late-colonial house, and also serves meals. Buses between Belén and Santa María stop here.

SANTA MARÍA

The northernmost settlement along RN 40 in Catamarca province, the crossroads town of Santa María de Yokavil lies in the midst of a richly endowed archaeological zone and is home to the **Museo Arqueológico Provincial Eric Boman**, named for the French archaeologist who did extensive pioneering research here in the early 20th century. With 11,000 inhabitants, this tidy oasis is 175km northeast of Belén, 35km south of the Ruinas de Quilmes, and 80km northwest of Tafí del Valle in Tucumán province.

There are several passable accommodations, starting at US$15/25 single/double at

Residencial Maturano *(Belgrano 146)*. The ***Hotel Provincial de Turismo*** *(☎ 03838-420240)*, charges US$30/35.

Some but not all buses en route between Tucumán, Tafí del Valle, and Cafayate stop here; for more information, see those entries. San Cayetano goes to Belén Monday, Wednesday, and Friday at 7 am.

Patagonia

For adventurous independent travelers, Argentina's most popular destination is Patagonia, that enormous region stretching south of the Río Colorado, just beyond the province of Buenos Aires, all the way to the Strait of Magellan. Beyond the strait, Argentina and Chile share the archipelago of Tierra del Fuego.

History

Despite its seemingly monotonous landscape, Patagonia has always held a place in the geography of European imagination. Charles Darwin saw many exotic lands in his five years on the *Beagle*, but Patagonia remained longest and most vividly in his memory:

In calling up images of the past, I find that the plains of Patagonia frequently cross before my eyes; yet these plains are pronounced by all wretched and useless. They can be described only by negative characters; without habitations, without water, without trees, without mountains, they support merely a few dwarf plants. Why then, and the case is not peculiar to myself, have these arid wastes taken so firm a hold on my memory? Why have not the still more level, the greener and more fertile Pampas, which are serviceable to mankind, produced an equal impression? I can scarcely analyze these feelings: but it must be partly owing to the free scope given to the imagination. The plains of Patagonia are boundless, for they are scarcely passable, and hence unknown; they bear the stamp of having lasted, as they are now, for ages, and there appears to be no limit to their duration during future time. If, as the ancients supposed, the flat earth was surrounded by an impassable breadth of water, or by deserts heated to an intolerable excess, who would not look at these last boundaries to man's knowledge with deep but ill defined sensations?

The origin of Patagonia's name is obscure, but one theory asserts that it derives from the region's native inhabitants, encountered by Magellan's crew as they wintered in 1520 at Bahía San Julián, in the present-day province of Santa Cruz. According to this explanation, the Tehuelche Indians, tall of stature and wearing moccasins that made their feet appear exceptionally large, may have led Magellan to apply the name after the Spanish word *pata*, meaning paw or foot. On encountering the Tehuelches, Antonio Pigafetta, an Italian nobleman on Magellan's crew, remarked with great hyperbole that one of them:

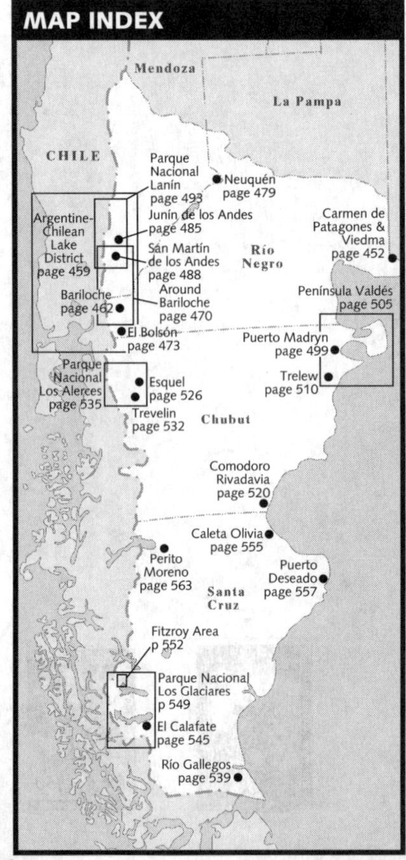

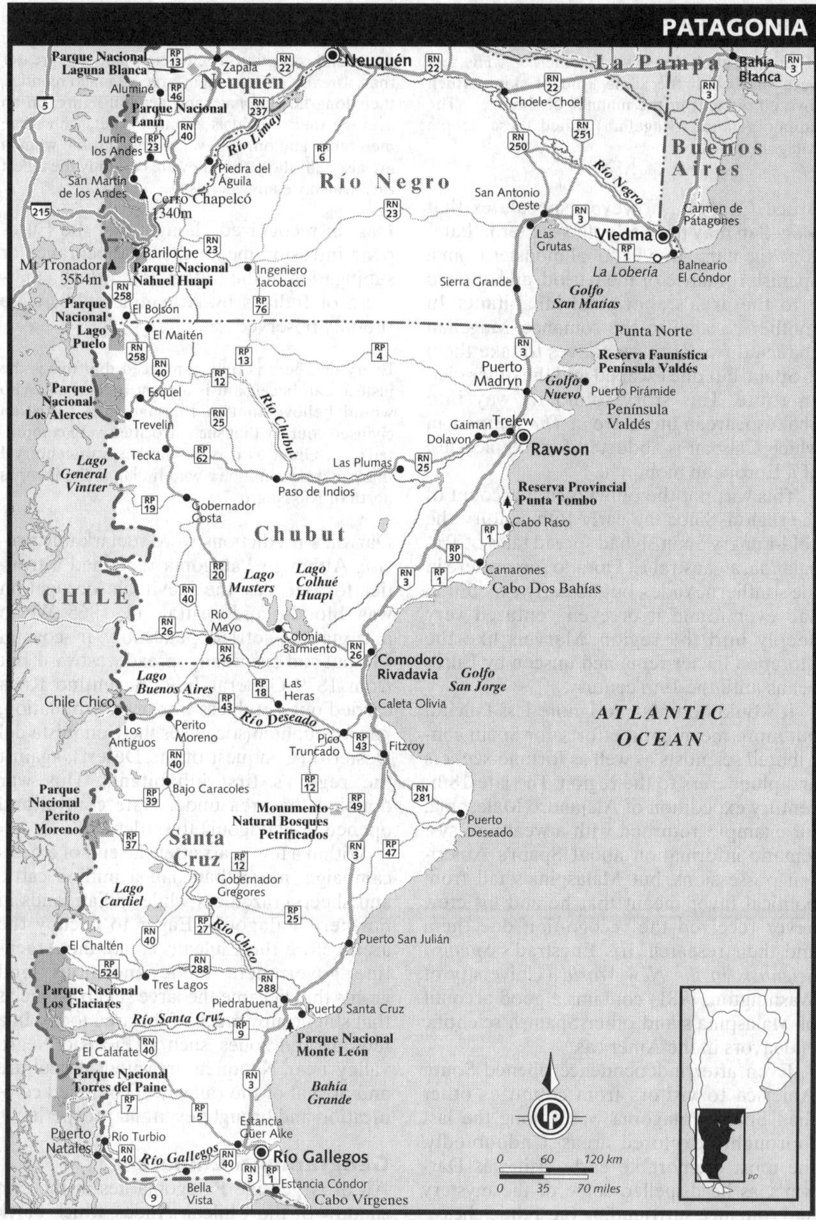
PATAGONIA
Parque Nacional Laguna Blanca
Zapala
Neuquén
Neuquén
La Pampa
Bahía Blanca
Aluminé
Parque Nacional Lanín
Junín de los Andes
Río Limay
Piedra del Águila
Choele-Choel
Buenos Aires
San Martín de los Andes
Cerro Chapelcó 1340m
Río Negro
Río Negro
San Antonio Oeste
Carmen de Patagones
Las Grutas
Viedma
Bariloche
Mt Tronador 3554m
Parque Nacional Nahuel Huapi
Ingeniero Jacobacci
La Lobería
Balneario El Cóndor
Sierra Grande
Golfo San Matías
Parque Nacional Lago Puelo
El Bolsón
El Maitén
Punta Norte
Reserva Faunística Península Valdés
Puerto Madryn
Golfo Nuevo
Puerto Pirámide
Península Valdés
Parque Nacional Los Alerces
Esquel
Trevelin
Río Chubut
Gaiman
Trelew
Dolavon
Rawson
Tecka
Las Plumas
Lago General Vintter
Paso de Indios
Reserva Provincial Punta Tombo
Gobernador Costa
Chubut
Cabo Raso
Lago Musters
Lago Colhué Huapi
Camarones
Cabo Dos Bahías
CHILE
Río Mayo
Colonia Sarmiento
Comodoro Rivadavia
Golfo San Jorge
Lago Buenos Aires
Las Heras
Chile Chico
Caleta Olivia
Río Deseado
Los Antiguos
Perito Moreno
Pico Truncado
Fitzroy
ATLANTIC OCEAN
Bajo Caracoles
Parque Nacional Perito Moreno
Monumento Natural Bosques Petrificados
Puerto Deseado
Santa Cruz
Gobernador Gregores
Lago Cardiel
Río Chico
El Chaltén
Puerto San Julián
Tres Lagos
Parque Nacional Los Glaciares
Piedrabuena
Puerto Santa Cruz
Río Santa Cruz
Parque Nacional Monte León
El Calafate
Parque Nacional Torres del Paine
Bahía Grande
Estancia Güer Aike
Puerto Natales
Río Turbio
Río Gallegos
Río Gallegos
Bella Vista
Estancia Cóndor
Cabo Vírgenes
0 60 120 km
0 35 70 miles

> was so tall we reached only to his waist, and he was well proportioned. . . . He was dressed in the skins of animals skillfully sewn together. . . . His feet were shod with the same kind of skins, which covered his feet in the manner of shoes. . . . The captain-general (Magellan) called these people Patagoni.

Bruce Chatwin, however, speculates that Magellan may have adopted the term 'Patagón,' the name of a fictional monster from a Spanish romance of the period, and applied it to the area's aboriginal inhabitants. In another parallel to the romance, Magellan abducted two of these natives to take them to Spain, but one escaped and the other died en route. This story found its way into Shakespearean literature in *The Tempest*, in which Caliban is abducted for the pleasure of a European monarch.

This was not the only fanciful account of the region. Since the early 16th century, the gold-hungry Spanish had spread tales of Trapalanda, an austral El Dorado somewhere in the southern Andes, but no early expedition had ever found it or even ventured very deeply into the region. Marvels like the Moreno Glacier remained unseen by Europeans until the 19th century.

It would be unfair to ignore less fanciful but more meaningful efforts, for Spain contributed scientists as well as fortune-seekers and plunderers to the region. The late-18th-century expedition of Alejandro Malaspina, for example, returned with a wealth of systematic information about Spain's American possessions, but Malaspina's fall from political favor meant that he and his crew never received the recognition due them and their research. Iris Engstrad's *Spanish Scientists in the New World* (University of Washington, 1981) contains a good account of Malaspina's and other Spanish scientific endeavors in the Americas.

Even after independence opened South America to visitors from countries other than Spain, Patagonia was among the last thoroughly explored areas. Undoubtedly, the most memorable early visit was Darwin's, as he dispelled some of the mystery and romance surrounding the Tehuelches:

> We had an interview at Cape Gregory with the famous so-called gigantic Patagonians, who gave us cordial reception. Their height appears greater than it really is, from their large guanaco mantles, their long flowing hair, and general figure; on an average their height is about six feet, with some men taller and only a few shorter; and the women are also tall; altogether they are certainly the tallest race which we anywhere saw.

Darwin recognized, though, that the European intrusion meant the disappearance or subjugation of the Indian. Recording a massacre of Indians by Argentine soldiers, he ruefully observed:

> Every one here is fully convinced that this is the justest war, because it is against barbarians. Who would believe that in this age in a Christian civilised country that such atrocities were committed? . . . Great as it is, in another half century I think there will not be a wild Indian in the Pampas north of Río Negro.

Darwin's predictions were remarkably precise. Although Patagonia remained a frontier for decades, the inevitable occupation was bloody and brutal. In 1865 Welsh nationalists settled peaceably in coastal Chubut and eventually spread westward, but from 1879 General Julio Argentino Roca carried out a ruthless war of extermination, known euphemistically as the Conquista del Desierto (Conquest of the Desert), against the region's first inhabitants. This war doubled the area under state control and opened up Patagonia to settlement.

Within a few years after the end of Roca's campaign, more than half a million cattle and sheep grazed erstwhile Indian lands in northern Patagonia. Eager to occupy the area before the Chileans could, the Argentine government made enormous land grants that became the large sheep estancias that still occupy much of the area today. In a few favored zones, such as the Río Negro valley near Neuquén, irrigated agriculture and arrival of the railway encouraged colonization and brought eventual prosperity.

Geography & Climate

All of Argentine Patagonia lies in the rain shadow of the Chilean Andes, which block most Pacific storms. Consequently, except in a few favored locations along the Andean divide, the region is semi-arid to arid; Chilean Patagonia, more vulnerable to these westerly storms, supports a denser forest cover.

Although they drop their moisture in Chile, powerful westerlies blow almost incessantly across the Patagonian plains. Because of oceanic influence where the South American continent tapers toward the south, the region's climate is generally temperate, but winter temperatures can drop well below freezing. The Campo de Hielo Sur (Southern Continental Ice Field), extending from Chile into parts of Argentina, is the site of the two countries' last remaining border dispute.

Economy

The economy's most conspicuous feature are the sprawling sheep estancias that occupy almost every part of the region south of the Río Negro all the way to Tierra del Fuego. Cattle are fewer and far less important. The irrigated Río Negro valley, east of the city of Neuquén, has an ideal climate for cultivation of temperate fruits such as apples, which are sold throughout Argentina and also processed into products like cider. Since extensive land uses like ranching employ relatively few people, the area south of the Río Negro is only thinly populated.

More important than sheep ranching is the contribution to Argentina's energy supply. Major oil fields near Comodoro Rivadavia in Chubut, Plaza Huincúl in Neuquén, and San Sebastián in Tierra del Fuego help make Argentina self-sufficient in petroleum, and the country even exports some to neighboring countries. The coal reserves at Río Turbio in Santa Cruz province are among the very few on the South American continent.

Tourism is a significant and growing part of the economy. The region contains most of the country's national parks, including three heavily visited units in the Andean lake district, where many Argentines spend their summer holidays: Nahuel Huapi and Los Arrayanes, near Bariloche; Lanín, near San Martín de los Andes; and Los Alerces, near Esquel. These areas are also popular winter sports centers. Some estancias are making a transition to the tourist economy, much like dude ranches in western North America.

Farther south, Los Glaciares, near El Calafate, is also a major attraction. Access to several lesser-known parks, like Perito Moreno and Bosques Petrificados, is difficult, but anyone who makes the effort to reach them will be well rewarded.

Río Negro & Neuquén Provinces

Taken together, Río Negro and Neuquén stretch from the Atlantic to the Andes. Most places of interest are near or along the Andes, but southbound visitors along the coast should at least stop over at Carmen de Patagones, a colonial relic.

Northern Patagonia's interior is mountainous, with alpine glaciers at the highest elevations. Near the Andean divide, diverse Valdivian forests cover the slopes, comprising extensive stands of southern beech, gigantic alerce, and the distinctive *pehuén*, known to English speakers as the monkey puzzle tree.

The native peoples of Río Negro and Neuquén were Puelches and Pehuenches (so called for their dependence on the pehuén, whose pine nuts formed the basis of their diet). Spaniards explored from the west in the late 16th century, but Mapuches who crossed the low Andean passes from Chile established their dominance in the region soon thereafter. As did North America's Plains Indians, Patagonia's native peoples soon learned to tame and ride the feral horses that had multiplied on the Pampas, and used their new mobility to make life hard on anyone who invaded their territory. Like the Plains Indians, they suffered when the state decided their presence was intolerable.

During colonial times, Spanish expeditions sought but never found the 'City of the Caesars,' the mythic Trapalanda, but they did reach Lago Nahuel Huapi, now the centerpiece of the country's best-known national park. The Jesuit and Franciscan missionaries penetrated the region as early as the 17th century, but few survived the Indians' organized resistance.

Only in the late 19th century did Argentina establish a permanent presence. The government placed such a high priority on settling the region that the Roca railway reached Neuquén before the turn of the

The Patagonian Estancia

Visually, Patagonia has little in common with urbane Buenos Aires and the verdant Pampas provinces that surround the capital. On eastern Patagonia's sparsely vegetated plain, visitors see a few straggling sheep and the occasional guanaco or rhea, but the few cities and towns are often hundreds of kilometers apart. Only a handful of sheltered and well-watered river valleys support any cultivation.

Historically, the sheep estancia was the most important economic institution. Like the cattle estancia of the Pampas, it represented the concentration of large amounts of land in the hands of relatively few people, who employed a dependent, resident labor force. As did the cattle estancia, the sheep estancia concentrated political power in the hands of a regional elite that, when threatened, showed no reluctance to use force to suppress discontent.

Estancia names can be quietly eloquent. Many are optimistic, contrasting with the bleak steppes that surround them: *La Esperanza* (Hope), *Bella Vista* (Beautiful View), *La Armonía* (Harmony), *La Confianza* (Trust). Frequently they bear women's names: *La Julia*, *La Margarita*, *La Sarita*. A few commemorate an important date: *Primero de Abril*, *Tres de Enero*. Others pay ironic homage to the aboriginal Tehuelches or Mapuches they dispossessed: *Pali Aike* (Place of Hunger), *Ototel Aike* (Place of Springs), *Choike Aike* (Place of the Rhea).

The estancia's nucleus usually consisted of a settlement cluster, including the owner's or manager's casco, family housing for foremen and other married employees, and a bunkhouse for single men. There were also garages, workshops, a *pulpería* or company store, corrals, and a woolshed for shearing the sheep and storing the clip. Outside the settlement, sheep grazed in *campos*, fenced paddocks often thousands of hectares in size. In the more remote parts of the estancia were isolated puestos, where resident shepherds tended the sheep. Only during the spring shearing season were the sheep gathered and brought into the settlement.

Most Patagonian cities, like Comodoro Rivadavia and Río Gallegos, grew as service centers for the estancias and the oil industry. Others, like Bariloche, became tourist destinations in their own right. Wages are often higher in Patagonia than elsewhere in the country, but few Argentines willingly relocate to what most perceive as an Argentine Siberia. When the Radical government of President Raúl Alfonsín proposed moving the seat of federal government from Buenos Aires to the northern Patagonian city of Viedma, shocked legislators and civil servants, accustomed to the capital's amenities, forced him to reconsider and abandon the project. Much of Patagonia is still gaucho country and, though pay and working conditions have improved in recent decades, the contemporary gaucho is a dependent laborer whose past is idealized by Argentines in urban folklore festivals.

Persistently low wool prices and environmental degradation have undercut the estancia's economic well-being in recent years. Some, in response, have sold out to corporate investors like Benetton, while others have passed into the hands of high-profile figures such as Ted Turner, his wife Jane Fonda, and Sylvester Stallone, for their personal pleasure. Others, like failing 19th-century cattle ranches in the western US, have begun to court the tourist trade in order to remain intact.

century, but it did not connect the area to the port of Bahía Blanca, in southern Buenos Aires province, until the 1930s. The Río Negro valley soon became, according to one account, 'a garden strip in a vast grazing region,' as the government granted 100-hectare plots on the condition that each settler build a house, fence the land, and plant poplar windbreaks that remain a conspicuous element of the agricultural landscape. The Plaza Huincul oilfields between Neuquén and Zapala have contributed significantly to Argentina's energy self-sufficiency; at the same time, paleontologists have made major dinosaur discoveries that have increased the area's tourist profile.

For travelers, the center of attraction is Bariloche in Río Negro province, convenient for exploring Parque Nacional Nahuel Huapi and other parks within a few hours north or south. The city itself has rapidly overdeveloped, losing much of its former charm, but the surrounding countryside is still tranquil and pleasant. Both winter and summer sports are popular.

CARMEN DE PATAGONES

Though in fact the southernmost city in Buenos Aires province, this small town along RN 3 is the gateway to Patagonia. Founded in 1779, it conserves much of its late colonial heritage; its name derives from its patron Virgen del Carmen and from the region's first inhabitants. The town itself is often referred to simply as Patagones, but the townspeople are called *maragatos*, reflecting the origins of early colonists from the Spanish county of Maragatería in León. In 1827, during the war with Brazil, they repelled invaders superior in numbers and weapons.

Orientation

On the north bank of the Río Negro, 950km south of Buenos Aires via RN 3, Carmen de Patagones (population 17,300) depends economically on the larger south-bank city of Viedma, capital of Río Negro province. Launches loaded with maragatos regularly cross the river for work, school, shopping, and entertainment; the centro cívico and most historical landmarks are within a few blocks of the passenger pier.

Two bridges also connect Carmen with Viedma. Both sides of the river have recreational balnearios, widely used for picnics and swimming in summer.

Information

Tourist Offices Much improved over recent years, the municipal Oficina de Información Turística (☎ 461777 interno 253), Bynon 186, is open weekdays 7 am to 9 pm, weekends 10 am to 1 pm and 4 to 9 pm.

Money Banco de la Nación, an architectural landmark, is at Paraguay 2, but for ATMs go to Viedma.

Post & Communications Correo Argentino is at Paraguay 38; Carmen's postal code is 8504. Locutorio 1 is at Olivera 9, Locutorio 2 at Rivadavia 379.

The area code is ☎ 02920.

Walking Tour

The tourist office distributes a brochure (Spanish only) describing the historic sites around Carmen de Patagones. Begin at **Plaza 7 de Marzo**; its original name, Plaza del Carmen, was changed after the 1827 victory over the Brazilians. Salesians built the **Iglesia Parroquial Nuestra Señora del Carmen** in 1883; its image of the Virgin, dating from 1780, is southern Argentina's oldest. Visitors can see two of the original seven Brazilian flags captured in 1827 on the altar. Just west of the church, the **Torre del Fuerte** is the last vestige of the fort, built in 1780, that once occupied the entire block. One block north, on 7 de Marzo, the elaborate **Teatro España** dates from 1875.

Below the Torre del Fuerte, twin cannon from forts that guarded the Patagonian frontier flank the 1960s **escalinata** (staircase) that leads to the riverside. At the base of the steps, **Rancho de Rial** (1820) is an adobe that belonged to Juan J Rial, the town's first elected mayor and later justice of the peace. At Mitre 27, the early-19th-century **Casa de la Cultura**, restored in 1981, was the site of a *tahona* (flour mill). Across the street, at the

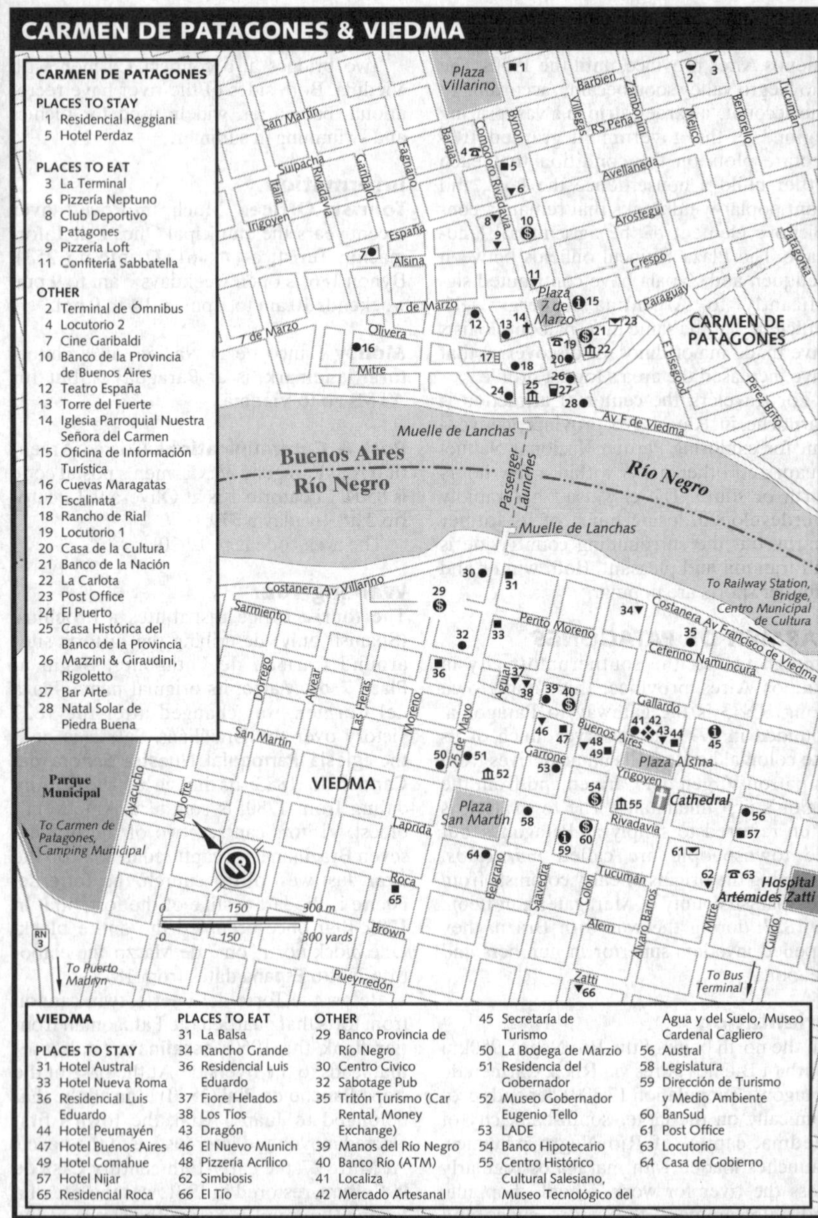
CARMEN DE PATAGONES & VIEDMA
CARMEN DE PATAGONES
PLACES TO STAY
1 Residencial Reggiani
5 Hotel Perdaz
PLACES TO EAT
3 La Terminal
6 Pizzería Neptuno
8 Club Deportivo Patagones
9 Pizzería Loft
11 Confitería Sabbatella
OTHER
2 Terminal de Ómnibus
4 Locutorio 2
7 Cine Garibaldi
10 Banco de la Provincia de Buenos Aires
12 Teatro España
13 Torre del Fuerte
14 Iglesia Parroquial Nuestra Señora del Carmen
15 Oficina de Información Turística
16 Cuevas Maragatas
17 Escalinata
18 Rancho de Rial
19 Locutorio 1
20 Casa de la Cultura
21 Banco de la Nación
22 La Carlota
23 Post Office
24 El Puerto
25 Casa Histórica del Banco de la Provincia
26 Mazzini & Giraudini, Rigoletto
27 Bar Arte
28 Natal Solar de Piedra Buena
Plaza Villarino
Plaza 7 de Marzo
CARMEN DE PATAGONES
San Martín
Suipacha
Italia
Ingoyen
Rivadavia
Garibaldi
Fagnano
España
Alsina
7 de Marzo
Olivera
Mitre
Baragas
Comodoro Rivadavia
Bynon
Villegas
Barbieri
Zambonini
RS Peña
Méjico
Bertorello
Tucumán
Avellaneda
Arostegui
Crespo
Paraguay
Patagonia
E Elsegood
Pérez Brito
Av F de Viedma
Muelle de Lanchas
Passenger Launches
Buenos Aires
Río Negro
Río Negro
Muelle de Lanchas
To Railway Station, Bridge, Centro Municipal de Cultura
Costanera Av Villarino
Sarmiento
Perito Moreno
Costanera Av Francisco de Viedma
Ceferino Namuncurá
Dorrego
Alvear
Las Heras
Moreno
San Martín
25 de Mayo
Aguiar
Gallardo
Buenos Aires
Garrone
Yrigoyen
Plaza Alsina
Cathedral
Rivadavia
Parque Municipal
VIEDMA
Ayacucho
M Jofre
Plaza San Martín
Laprida
Belgrano
Saavedra
Colón
Tucumán
Álvaro Barros
Mitre
Guido
Hospital Artémides Zatti
To Carmen de Patagones, Camping Municipal
Roca
Brown
Alem
Pueyrredón
Zatti
RN 3
To Puerto Madryn
To Bus Terminal
0 150 300 m
0 150 300 yards
VIEDMA
PLACES TO STAY
31 Hotel Austral
33 Hotel Nueva Roma
36 Residencial Luis Eduardo
44 Hotel Peumayén
47 Hotel Buenos Aires
49 Hotel Comahue
57 Hotel Nijar
65 Residencial Roca
PLACES TO EAT
31 La Balsa
34 Rancho Grande
36 Residencial Luis Eduardo
37 Fiore Helados
38 Los Tíos
43 Dragón
46 El Nuevo Munich
48 Pizzería Acrílico
62 Simbiosis
66 El Tío
OTHER
29 Banco Provincia de Río Negro
30 Centro Cívico
32 Sabotage Pub
35 Tritón Turismo (Car Rental, Money Exchange)
39 Manos del Río Negro
40 Banco Río (ATM)
41 Localiza
42 Mercado Artesanal
45 Secretaría de Turismo
50 La Bodega de Marzio
51 Residencia del Gobernador
52 Museo Gobernador Eugenio Tello
53 LADE
54 Banco Hipotecario
55 Centro Histórico Cultural Salesiano, Museo Tecnológico del Agua y del Suelo, Museo Cardenal Cagliero
56 Austral
58 Legislatura
59 Dirección de Turismo y Medio Ambiente
60 BanSud
61 Post Office
63 Locutorio
64 Casa de Gobierno

corner of Bynon and Mitre, **La Carlota** is a former private residence still decorated with typical 19th-century furnishings. It's open for guided tours at 10 and 11:30 am and 7:30 pm weekdays, Sunday 7:30 pm only; inquire at the Casa Historíca museum (see that section).

Once home to prosperous merchants who owned the shop across the street from the pier, **Mazzini & Giraudini's** facade was restored in 1985. The house was part of the **Zona del Puerto** (port) that connected the town with the rest of the viceroyalty. At **Solar Natal de Piedra Buena** is a bust of the naval officer and Patagonian hero Luis Piedrabuena; the site at the foot of Bynon once included the general store, bar, and naval supply stores of his father. One block west is the **Casa Histórica del Banco de la Provincia de Buenos Aires**, now a museum (see that section). Nearby is **El Puerto**, a former waterfront bar.

Things to See

The first locomotive to arrive at Carmen de Patagones, in 1921, **La Maragata** is across from the train station at Juan de la Piedra at the north end of Italia. On Olivera five blocks west of Plaza 7 de Marzo, the **Cuevas Maragatas** (Maragatas Caves), excavated in the riverbank, sheltered the first Spanish families who arrived in the 18th century. East of town, **Cerro de la Caballada**, where the battle with the Brazilians took place, offers a panoramic view.

The **Casa Histórica del Banco de la Provincia de Buenos Aires** originally housing naval stores, this riverside building became in succession a girls' school, a branch of Banco de la Provincia, and then of Banco de la Nación. Destroyed by a flood that ravaged Carmen de Patagones' riverside neighborhood and Viedma in 1899, it was rebuilt and occupied by several shops until its restoration by Banco de la Provincia in 1984.

A museum since 1988, the Casa displays an impressive collection of artifacts from Argentina's southern frontier. There's a disturbing subtext, however: an attempt to justify the cost of Patagonian settlement – the near extermination of the region's native population. The museum does acknowledge, grudgingly and patronizingly, the fact that Carmen once had a black slave population. Its greatest assets are the restored cueva maragata in the riverbank and a collection of photos from the 1899 flood, when residents of Viedma had to flee to Carmen's higher ground.

Open weekdays 9 am to noon, and daily 7 to 9 pm, the museum (☎ 462729) charges US$1 admission.

Places to Stay

Carmen de Patagones has only two hotels, so try Viedma for a wider choice. Probably the best value is ***Residencial Reggiani*** *(☎ 464137, Bynon 422)*, which has singles/doubles with shared bath for US$14/24 and with private bath for US$18/28. ***Hotel Perdaz*** *(☎ 461495, Comodoro Rivadavia 384)* charges US$28/39 and offers a reasonable breakfast.

Places to Eat

Restaurants include ***La Terminal*** at Barbieri and Bertorello and ***Club Deportivo Patagones*** at España and Rivadavia. ***Confitería Sabbatella*** *(Comodoro Rivadavia 218)* is a pleasant café for breakfast, while ***Pizzería Loft*** *(Alsina 70)* and ***Pizzería Neptuno***, at Rivadavia and España, are both worth a try.

Entertainment

Two attractive new bars have opened in recycled riverfront buildings on Av Viedma, near the Muelle de Lanchas: ***Bar Arte*** and ***Rigoletto***. The ***Cine Garibaldi*** *(España 206)* shows films.

Getting There & Away

Connections with the rest of the country by bus, train, or plane are more frequent in Viedma. Patagones' Terminal de Ómnibus (☎ 462666) is at Barbieri and Méjico. The *balsa* (passenger launch) crosses the river to Viedma (US$0.50) every few minutes.

VIEDMA

In 1779, with his men dying of fever and lack of water at Península Valdés, Francisco de Viedma put ashore to found the city that would later take his name, on the south bank of the Río Curru Leuvu (now the Río Negro). In 1879 it became the residence of the governor of Patagonia and the political and administrative locus of the country's enormous southern territory. After territorial division, Viedma became the provincial capital and remained an important administrative site. A mostly modern city, it's less picturesque than Carmen de Patagones, but also much livelier. It's also more flood-prone, though upstream hydroelectric dams now help control the spring runoff from the Andes.

In the 1980s, Viedma enjoyed 15 minutes of fame when the Alfonsín administration proposed moving the federal capital here from Buenos Aires. Although these plans never materialized, some migrants who anticipated the move have remained. Besides numerous secondary schools, Viedma (population 50,500) is home to a campus of the Universidad del Comahue, and a physical education center.

Orientation

On the south bank of the Río Negro, along RN 3 and only about 30km from the Atlantic, Viedma is 960km from Buenos Aires, 275km south of Bahía Blanca, and 180km east of San Antonio Oeste. It's a compact town, suitable for walking; the river itself is the focus of the city. Viedma's showpiece is the centro cívico at 25 de Mayo and the Costanera Av Villarino.

Key provincial public buildings cluster around Plaza San Martín, including the Casa de Gobierno, the dignified Residencia del Gobernador, and the hideous high-rise Legislatura. Street names change on either side of Colón, except for Buenos Aires, which is continuous between 24 de Mayo and Yrigoyen.

Information

Tourist Offices In summer the municipal Dirección de Turismo y Medio Ambiente (☎ 427171), Saavedra 456, is open 8 am to 2 pm and 6 to 9 pm. In summer, it maintains a tourist information office in the Centro Municipal de Cultura, on Av Viedma between 7 de Marzo and Urquiza; open 7 am to 9 pm daily. There's also an office at the bus terminal, open 5 to 9:20 pm daily.

The provincial Secretaría de Turismo (☎ 422150), Gallardo 121, has brochures and information for the whole province. Expoventa Patagónica (☎ 431395), a private information office at RN 3 Km 696 that also sells regional products, is open 8 am to 2 pm and 5 to 11 pm.

ACA (☎ 422441) is at RN 3 Km 692.

Money Tritón Turismo (see Travel Agencies, below) changes money, but several banks have ATMs.

Post & Communications Correo Argentino is at Rivadavia 151; the postal code is 8500. There's a locutorio at Mitre 531. Viedma's area code is ☎ 02920, the same as Carmen de Patagones.

Travel Agencies Tritón Turismo (☎ 430129), Namuncurá 78, also changes money and rents cars.

Medical Services Hospital Artémides Zatti (☎ 422333) is at Av Rivadavia 351.

Museums

Tehuelche tools, artifacts, and human remains, as well as exhibits on European settlement, are on display at the **Museo Gobernador Eugenio Tello**, which also functions as a research center in architecture, archaeology, physical and cultural anthropology, and geography. At San Martín 263, it's open weekdays from 10 am to noon and 3 to 9 pm.

At the corner of Colón and Rivadavia, the former **Vicariato de la Patagonia** (1890) is a massive brick structure containing the **Centro Histórico Cultural Salesiano**; it includes the **Museo Cardenal Cagliero**, Rivadavia 34, which tells the story of the Salesian order, which catechized Patagonian Indians. It's open weekdays 7:30 am to noon and 4 to 6 pm, weekends 5 to 9 pm. In the same building at Colón 498, the **Museo Tecnológico del Agua y del Suelo** (☎ 431569), an earth sciences collection, is open weekdays 9 to 11 am.

Organized Tours

Visitors should contact the municipal tourist office for walking tours on the **Circuito Histórico Cultural Viedma-Carmen de Patagones**, which covers the major historical landmarks and public buildings of both cities.

To get acquainted with the river, try the 1½-hour excursions on the catamaran *Curru Leuvu II*, which leaves from the Muelle de Lanchas (pier) Tuesday to Sunday at 5 pm. The excursion fare is US$5 per adult and US$3 for children up to 12 years old.

Special Events

The Regata del Río Negro, in the second half of January, includes a weeklong kayak race that begins in Neuquén and ends in Viedma, a distance of about 500km. In 1995, its 49 participants included several foreigners. For participants' information, contact the Dirección de Turismo y Medio Ambiente.

Places to Stay – Budget

Camping The friendly riverside ***Camping Municipal*** *(☎ 421341)* west of RN 3, easily reached by bus from downtown, charges US$4 per person and an additional US$4 per tent. The partially shaded grounds are tidy, though some plots are poorly marked. Beware mosquitoes in summer.

For noncampers, showers cost US$1; note that hot showers are available 7 pm to 7 am only – if you need an early shower, make it *very* early.

Hotels Except for camping, inexpensive accommodations are scarce and mostly inferior. Seedy ***Hotel Nuevo Roma*** *(☎ 424510, 25 de Mayo 174)* has singles/doubles with shared bath for US$12/15, with private bath for US$17/24; it also serves inexpensive meals. ***Hotel Buenos Aires*** *(☎ 424858, Buenos Aires 153)* is basic for US$20/25.

A step up, on a quiet block and with a good restaurant, is ***Residencial Luis Eduardo*** *(☎ 420669, Sarmiento 366)*, with rooms for US$20/30. Rates are identical at ***Residencial Roca*** *(☎ 431241, Roca 347)*.

Places to Stay – Mid-Range

Hotel Comahue *(☎ 423092, Colón 385)*, overlooking Plaza Alsina, costs US$30/50. Also on the Plaza, ***Hotel Peumayén*** *(☎ 425234, Buenos Aires 334)* charges US$33/55.

Places to Stay – Top End

Modern ***Hotel Nijar*** *(☎ 422833, Mitre 490)* charges US$39/56 (ACA discounts possible) for singles/doubles with TV, phone and aircon. Four-star ***Hotel Austral*** *(☎ 422615, Av Villarino 292)* features river views for US$59/63.

Places to Eat

Locals mob ***Pizzería Acrílico*** *(☎ 421530, Saavedra 326)* in the evening; it has flashy decor, good pizza, and mid-range prices except for the pasta, which is equally good but expensive by Argentine standards. Almost equally popular ***Los Tíos*** *(☎ 422790, Belgrano 265)* is nothing special. ***El Nuevo Munich*** *(Buenos Aires 161)* has good pizza, large tasty sandwiches, and good draft beer.

Local parrillas worth trying include ***El Tío*** at Av Zatti and Colón and ***Rancho Grande*** *(☎ 431944, Av Villarino 30)*. ***Simbiosis*** *(☎ 424796, Mitre 573)* has a more varied menu. ***La Balsa*** *(☎ 431974, Av Villarino 292)* is part of four-star Hotel Austral. ***Dragón*** *(Buenos Aires 366)* is a Chinese tenedor libre.

Fiore Helados, at Buenos Aires and Aguiar, is a good ice creamery.

Shopping

Viedma's Mercado Artesanal (☎ 423207), in the 300 block of Buenos Aires, stocks varied regional crafts including carvings, silverwork, ceramics, basketry, weavings, leather goods, and the like. Regional crafts are also available at Manos del Río Negro, Buenos Aires 108.

Expoventa Patagónica (☎ 431395), at RN 3 Km 696, is a private information office that also sells regional products. It is open 8 am to 2 pm and 5 to 11 pm. The best place for wine is La Bodega de Marzio (☎ 422087), San Martín 319, which offers *vinos de la zona fría* (cool-climate wines).

Entertainment

The ***Sabotage Pub*** *(Sarmiento 317)* has live rock & roll until the early hours.

Getting There & Away

Air Austral (☎ 422018), Mitre 402, flies weekdays to Buenos Aires' Aeroparque (US$109 to US$167).

LADE (☎ 424420), Saavedra 403, flies Monday to Esquel (US$73) and Comodoro Rivadavia (US$66); Monday to Puerto Madryn (US$28) and Trelew (US$32); Tuesday to Bahía Blanca (US$25), Mar del Plata (US$57), and Aeroparque (US$80); Thursday to Neuquén (US$40), San Martín de los Andes (US$69), and Bariloche (US$72); and Friday to Neuquén and Bariloche.

Bus Viedma's Terminal de Ómnibus (☎ 426850) is 13 blocks south of downtown, at Guido 1580 and Av General Perón.

La Puntual/El Cóndor (☎ 422748) has daily service north to Buenos Aires and to intermediate points. Fredes Turismo (☎ 430578), 7 de Marzo 726, also goes to the federal capital, while Transporte Mansilla (☎ 421385) goes to La Plata. TUS/TUP (☎ 425952) links Viedma with Bahía Blanca, Santa Fe, and Córdoba.

Transporte El Valle (☎ 422748) ascends the Río Negro valley to Neuquén and Bariloche, while Codao (☎ 422748) has Wednesday and Saturday service to Bariloche.

Transportes Don Otto (☎ 425952) reaches Patagonian destinations along RN 3 as far south as Río Gallegos; at the same office, Transportadora Patagónica serves coastal destinations in Buenos Aires province, from Necochea to Mar del Plata. Central Argentino stops in Viedma en route between Rosario and Comodoro Rivadavia.

Transportes Patagónicos (☎ 425952) goes often to the coastal resort of Las Grutas.

Sample fares include Las Grutas (US$10, 2½ hours), Bahía Blanca (US$13, four hours), Puerto Madryn (US$20, five hours), Trelew (US$22, 5½ hours), Neuquén (US$30, eight hours), Esquel (US$32, 10 hours), La Plata (US$34, 12 hours), Comodoro Rivadavia (US$37, 10 hours), Buenos Aires (US$35 to US$45, 13 hours), Bariloche (US$40 to US$52, 14 hours), and Río Gallegos (US$48, 20 hours).

Train From Estación Viedma, on the southeast outskirts of town, Sefepa (☎ 422130) still runs westbound trains to Bariloche (15 hours) at 6 pm Wednesday and Sunday. Fares are US$28 primera, US$46 Pullman; children 5 to 12 pay half.

Getting Around

To/From the Airport Aeropuerto Gobernador Castello (☎ 422001) is 15km southwest of town on RP 51. There's no airport bus service, but a cab or remise costs only about US$7.

Boat From the Muelle de Lanchas at the foot of 25 de Mayo, the launch *Ceferino Namuncurá* connects Viedma to Carmen de Patagones (US$0.50) on demand 6:30 am to 10 pm weekdays, 7 am to 9 pm Saturday, and 9 am to 9 pm Sunday.

Car Localiza (☎ 425314) is at the corner of Colón and Buenos Aires. Rent A Car (☎ 430129) is at Namuncurá 78, the same as Tritón Turismo.

COASTAL RÍO NEGRO

Río Negro's 400km of coastline attracts tourists with its many beaches, wildlife reserves, and summer resorts. The newly improved coastal highway RP 1 has opened up much of the area to recreation, but public transportation serves only a relatively small part of it.

Balneario El Cóndor

This small resort, 32km from Viedma, features a century-old lighthouse, Patagonia's oldest. It has limited accommodations and a few restaurants, but there is a free campsite, plus excellent fishing for the tasty corvina. After departure of the last tourists in late March, it shuts down for the winter.

Hospedaje Río de los Sauces *(☎ 497070)* charges US$20 per person, while ***Hotel Casino El Faro*** *(☎ 497046)* offers doubles with ocean views for US$60. Empresa Ceferino (☎ 424548) buses to the balneario depart from Scheroni 383 in Viedma and cost US$2, continuing to La Lobería (US$4).

Centro de Interpretación Faunística Punta Bermeja (La Lobería)

This permanent colony of about 2000 southern sea lions *(Otaria flavescens)* is some 60km south of Viedma via RP 1, on the north coast of Golfo San Matías. At one time, commercial slaughter threatened the colony's survival, but the reserve has encouraged conservation, education, and research. The striking scenery features high bluffs with distinct sedimentary strata and sandy beaches with occasional rock outcrops and tidal pools.

Peak numbers occur during the spring mating season, when fights between males are common as they come ashore to establish harems of up to 10 females each. From December onward, the females give birth. The observation balcony, directly above the mating beaches, is safe and unobtrusive.

Numerous coastal birds frequent the area, both seasonally and permanently. The most common migrants are snowy sheathbills, gulls, cormorants, oystercatchers, and sandpipers. Black eagles, peregrine falcons, turkey vultures, and chimangos prey on the parakeets and swallows that nest in the cliffs, while dunes provide habitat for guanacos, rheas, maras (Patagonian hares), wildcats, vizcachas, skunks, foxes, armadillos, small reptiles, and rodents.

The visitor center has a small interpretive exhibit on sea lions, a handful of stuffed pinnipeds and birds, and a confitería. It's possible to camp at barren, windy ***Camping La Lobería***, which has adequate sanitary facilities and a store, for US$2 per person as well as per tent.

West of La Lobería, RP 1 runs along dunes covered by low grasses and native shrubs, then continues as a very dusty dirt road via Bahía Creek (superb camping among immense dunes) to Punta Mejillón (site of another lobería with more difficult access). At Punta Mejillón the highway turns inland briefly before continuing west to intersect with paved RN 251, which returns to RN 3, near San Antonio Oeste.

Las Grutas

At the northwestern edge of the Golfo San Matías, 179km west of Viedma along RN 3, the crowded resort of Las Grutas owes its name (The Grottoes) to the caves that the sea has eroded in the cliffs. Because of an exceptional tidal range, the beaches can expand for hundreds of meters or shrink to just a few. Five formal *bajadas* (staircases) provide beach access.

In summer, the abundant but costly hotels, 25 campgrounds, and casino will discourage those in search of quiet and solitude – Las Grutas gets crowded! Outside peak season, though, the dunes, white sand beaches, and cliffs create a pleasant backdrop for walking, jogging, or simply relaxing; water sports like swimming, surfing, windsurfing, and diving are very popular.

The tourist office (☎ 02934-497470) at Galería Antares, Primera Bajada, has information on accommodations, as well as restaurant menus with prices. There are hourly buses to San Antonio Oeste, which is 15km away.

Sierra Grande

Eastern Río Negro's southernmost town is the northernmost spot on RN 3 to purchase gasoline at 'precios patagónicos' – less than half the price in Las Grutas/San Antonio Oeste. If at all possible, southbound motorists should avoid filling their tanks until they get here, and northbound motorists should not forget to fill up before continuing. It is 125km south of Las Grutas and 139km north of Puerto Madryn.

Sierra Grande is also making a unique attempt to attract tourists by exploiting the inactive Hierro Patagónico Rionegrino (Hiparsa for short) iron mine for conventional tours (US$15) or more adventurous alternatives that involve rappelling into the pit (US$25). For details, contact Hiparsa

(☎ 481212), which is just off RN 3 about 4km south of town.

The Subsecretaría de Turismo (☎ 02934-481910) is at Calle 2 No 300, parallel to the highway just off the main rotunda. Sierra Grande has several moderate hotels and restaurants, and all north-south coastal buses stop here.

BARILOCHE

Bariloche (formally San Carlos de Bariloche) is the urban center of the Argentine lake district and the base for exploring Parque Nacional Nahuel Huapi. In many ways, not all of them positive, it resembles European alpine resorts – the surrounding scenery is always pleasant and often spectacular, but crowds and traffic can be intolerable in ski season and in summer. Uncontrolled growth has cost the city much of its former character as quaint neighborhoods lose their views to multistory apartment buildings, and commercial development has impacted the lakefront like a wisdom tooth.

Prior to the European invasion, native peoples freely crossed the Andean divide between Chile and Argentina via the Paso de los Vuriloches, south of the landmark Monte Tronador, the area's highest peak. Until the late 19th century, the Mapuche nation successfully resisted Argentine occupation, but General Roca's Conquista del Desierto made the area safe for immigrant settlers, many of them Germans who have left a visible imprint on the cultural landscape. Officially founded in 1902, the city really began to attract visitors after the southern branch of the Ferrocarril Roca arrived in 1934 and architect Ezequiel Bustillo adapted Central European styles into a tasteful urban plan.

Between 1980 and 1991, the population grew from 60,000 to more than 80,000 (the next census figure should approach 100,000), but even those impressive numbers misleadingly understate the impact of the burgeoning hotels, time-shares, campgrounds, and the like. The last decade's deplorable orgy of construction has overwhelmed Bustillo's efforts and, consequently, Bariloche has lost much of its perceived exclusivity. The silver lining is that prices have remained reasonable, and some have even fallen in recent years. The influx of visitors from South America's largest country has led to the ironic nickname 'Brasiloche.'

Bariloche has acquired some notoriety in recent years because former SS officer Erich Priebke, who fled here after allegedly overseeing a massacre of 335 Italian civilians near Rome at the end of WWII, remained under house arrest while appealing extradition to Italy. The Menem administration, eager to mitigate Argentina's notoriety as a haven for war criminals, cooperated with the Italian request and even created a Bariloche-based Instituto Contra la Discriminación, Xenofobia y Racismo (Institute Against Discrimination, Xenophobia, and Racism) to investigate such matters.

Orientation

On the south shore of Lago Nahuel Huapi's eastern end, 770m above sea level, Bariloche is 460km southwest of Neuquén via RN 237. Entering the town from the east, RN 237 becomes the Costanera Av 12 de Octubre, continuing westward to the lakeside resort of Llao Llao. Southbound Calle Onelli becomes RN 258 to El Bolsón, on the border of Chubut province.

West of the Río Ñireco and east of Bustillo's centro cívico, the city has a fairly regular grid pattern, but north-south streets rise steeply from the lakeshore – some so steeply that they become staircases. The principal commercial area is along Av Bartolomé Mitre, but the new waterfront Puerto San Carlos, an overbuilt shopping center and marina, is taking some of the business a short distance north. Do not confuse similarly named Eduardo O'Connor (also known as Vicealmirante O'Connor) and John O'Connor, which cross each other near the lakefront, or Perito Moreno and Ruiz Moreno, which intersect near Diagonal Capraro, at the east end of the downtown area.

Information

Tourist Offices At the centro cívico, opposite the equestrian statue of General Roca,

ARGENTINE-CHILEAN LAKE DISTRICT

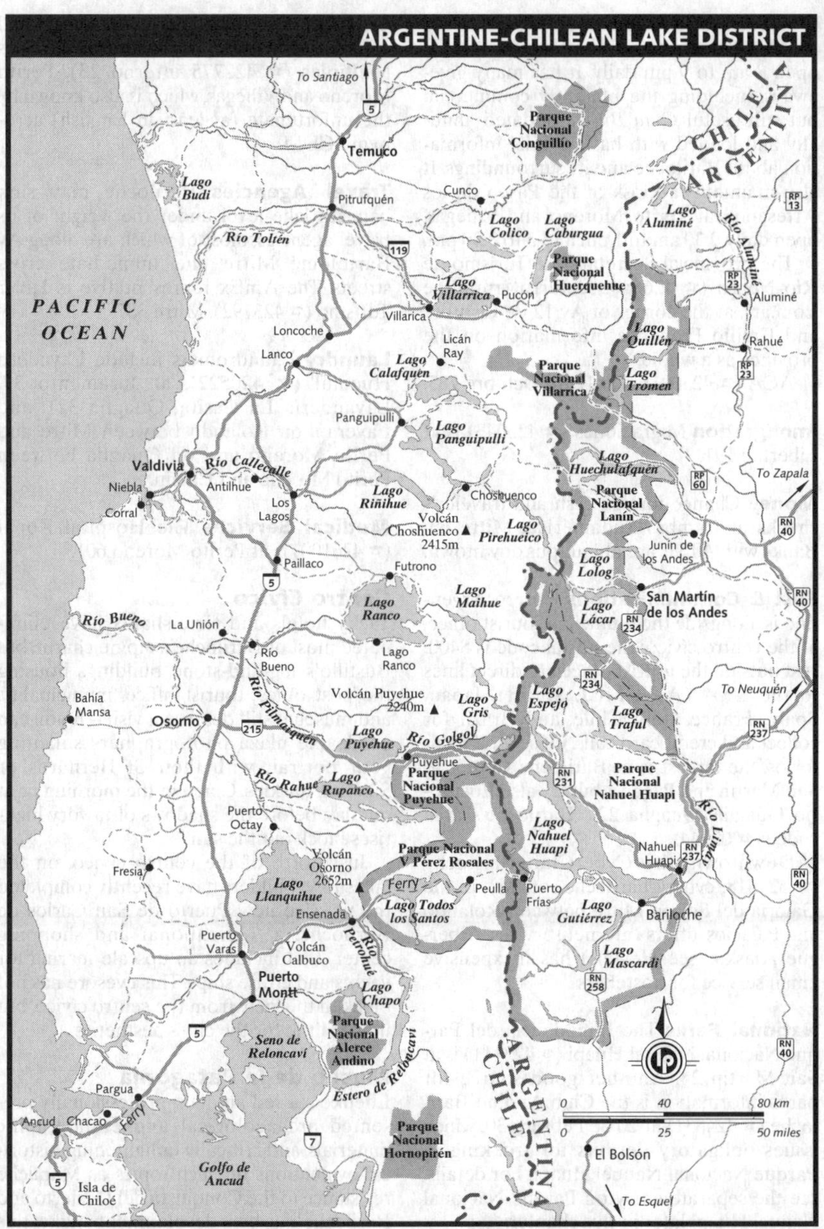

the Secretaría Municipal de Turismo (☎ 423122, secturismo@bariloche.com.ar) is open 8 am to 9 pm daily. It has many giveaways, including the blatantly commercial but still useful *Guía Busch*, updated annually and loaded with basic tourist information about Bariloche and its surroundings. It also maintains a kiosk at the Paseo de los Artesanos, at Perito Moreno and Villegas, open daily 9:30 am to 1 pm and 5 to 8:30 pm.

The provincial Secretaría de Turismo de Río Negro (☎ 426644, secturrn@rnonline.com.ar), at the corner of Av 12 de Octubre and Emilio Frey, has information on the province as a whole.

ACA (☎ 423001) is at 12 de Octubre 785.

Immigration Migraciones (☎ 423043) is at Libertad 191.

Money Change foreign cash and traveler's checks at Cambio Sudamérica, Mitre 63. Banks with ATMs are ubiquitous downtown.

Post & Communications Correo Argentino is alongside the municipal tourist office, at the centro cívico; the postal code is 8400. Just outside the tourist office are direct lines to the USA (ATT, MCI, Sprint), Japan, Spain, France, Italy, Chile, and Brazil for collect and credit card calls. Of several locutorios, the largest is at Bariloche Center at San Martín and Pagano, but try also Locutorio Quaglia, Quaglia 220. Bariloche's area code is ☎ 02944.

Downtown, the CyberClub Bariloche (☎ 421418, cyber@bariloche.com.ar), in the Galería del Sol on Mitre between Rolando and Palacios, offers Internet services. Albergue Alaska (see Hostels) has inexpensive email service for hostellers.

National Parks The Intendencia del Parque Nacional Nahuel Huapi (☎ 423111) is at San Martín 24. Another good source for parks information is the Club Andino Bariloche (☎ 424531) at 20 de Febrero 30, which issues obligatory permits for trekking in Parque Nacional Nahuel Huapi. For details, see the separate entry on Parque Nacional Nahuel Huapi later in this chapter.

Cultural Centers There are occasional exhibitions at the Salón Cultural de Usos Múltiples (☎ 422775 interno 23), Perito Moreno and Villegas, which is also known by the unfortunate (at least in English) acronym SCUM.

Travel Agencies Bariloche may sink beneath lake level under the weight of its travel agencies, most of which are along Av Bartolomé Mitre and immediate cross streets. The AmEx representative is Hiver Turismo (☎ 423792), Mitre 387.

Laundry Laundromats include Lavadero Huemul (☎ 420522), at Juramento 37, Lavandería La Casita, Quaglia 321, and Laverap, on Rolando between Mitre and Perito Moreno and on Quaglia between Perito Moreno and Elflein.

Medical Services The Hospital Zonal (☎ 426100) is at Perito Moreno 601.

Centro Cívico

Tacky hotels and time-shares have eliminated most of Bariloche's alpine charm, but Bustillo's log-and-stone buildings housing the post office, tourist office, municipality, and museum still deserve a visit – if you can evade the plaza photographers soliciting your portrait with their St Bernards or Siberian huskies. Come in the morning or at midday, before the shadows of tawdry highrises block out the sun.

Just north of the centro cívico, on the lakeshore, builders have recently completed the massive new Puerto de San Carlos de Bariloche, a 'recreational and shopping center' that includes an upscale marina for yachts and cruise ships. This eyesore has not blocked the view from the centro cívico, but it does little for the city's aesthetics.

Museo de la Patagonia

Lifelike stuffed animals, professionally presented archaeological and ethnographic materials, and critically enlightening historical evaluations on such topics as Mapuche resistance to the Conquista del Desierto and Bariloche's urban development make this diverse museum in the centro cívico one of the country's best. It has a specialized library, and there is a bookstore in the lobby.

Admission to the museum (☎ 422309) is US$2.50. Hours are Tuesday to Friday 10 am to 12:30 pm and 2 to 7 pm, Monday and Saturday 10 am to 1 pm only.

Activities

Bariloche and the Nahuel Huapi area are one of Argentina's major outdoor recreation areas, with several operators offering a variety of outdoor activities, particularly horseback riding, mountain biking, and white-water rafting. Among these operators, some of which are accessible by post office box *(casilla)*, phone, and fax only, are the following:

Adventure World (mountain biking, rafting, riding)
Casilla (PO Box) 234 (☎ 440154, fax 422637)

Aguas Blancas (rafting)
Morales 564 (☎ 432799)

Amuncar (rafting, trekking)
Av San Martín 82, 1st floor (☎ 431627, fax 423187, cecilia@bariloche.com.ar)

Bariloche Mountain Bike (mountain biking)
Gallardo 375 (☎ 462397)

Bariloche Rafting (rafting)
Mitre 86, Local 5 (☎/fax 424854)

Cabalgatas Carol Jones (riding)
Casilla (PO Box) 1436 (☎ 423646)

Cumbres Patagonia (fishing, rafting, riding)
Villegas 222 (☎ 423283, fax 431835, cumbres@bariloche.com.ar), and in Hotel Llao Llao (☎ 448350 interno 550)

Expediciones Náuticas (rafting)
Mitre 125, 1st floor, Oficina 126 (☎ 426677)

Karnak Expediciones (rafting, riding, trekking)
Mitre 265, Local 18 (☎/fax 425300)

La Bolsa del Deporte (mountain biking)
Elflein 385 (☎ 423529)

Rafting Adventure (rafting)
Mitre 161(☎ 432928)

Tom Wesley Viajes de Aventura (mountain biking, riding)
Av Bustillo Km 15.5 (☎/fax 448193)

Mountain Biking Bicycles are ideal for the Circuito Chico and other trips near Bariloche, where most roads are paved, even the gravel roads are good, and Argentine drivers are less ruthless, slowing and even stopping for the scenery. Mountain-bike rental, usually including gloves and helmet, costs about US$20 per day at a number of places.

For rentals, try Bariloche Mountain Bike (☎ 462397) at Gallardo 375, Bikeway (☎ 424202) at Eduardo O'Connor 867, Dirty Bikes (☎ 425616) at Eduardo O'Connor 681, or Martín Ferrer (☎ 1560-2515 cellular).

Fishing Fishing for both native and exotic species draws visitors from around the world to Argentina's accessible Andean-Patagonian parks, from Lago Puelo and Los Alerces in the south to Lanín in the north. The most popular introduced species are European brown trout, rainbow trout, brook trout, and landlocked Atlantic salmon, which reach impressive sizes. Native species, which should be thrown back, are generally smaller; these include *perca* (perch), *puyen*, Patagonian pejerrey, and the rare *peladilla*.

On larger lakes like Nahuel Huapi, trolling is the preferred method, while fly-fishing is the rule on most rivers. Night fishing is prohibited. The season runs mid-November to mid-April. For more information, contact the Club de Caza y Pesca (☎ 422785) at Costanera 12 de Octubre and Onelli. For rental equipment, try Baruzzi Deportes (☎ 424922), Urquiza 250, or Martín Pescador (☎ 422275), Rolando 257.

For non-Argentines, seasonal licenses, available from the Intendencia de Parques Nacionales at the centro cívico or the provincial department of Recursos Naturales at Morales and Elflein, cost US$100. Monthly licenses cost US$60 and weekly licenses US$30. There are surcharges for 'preferential' areas and trolling.

Horseback Riding Horseback excursions start at around US$20 for two hours or US$40 per half day. There are longer excursions around the lower Río Manso (US$75 full day) or several days into Chile (US$500).

Mountaineering & Trekking The Parques Nacionales office in Bariloche distributes a

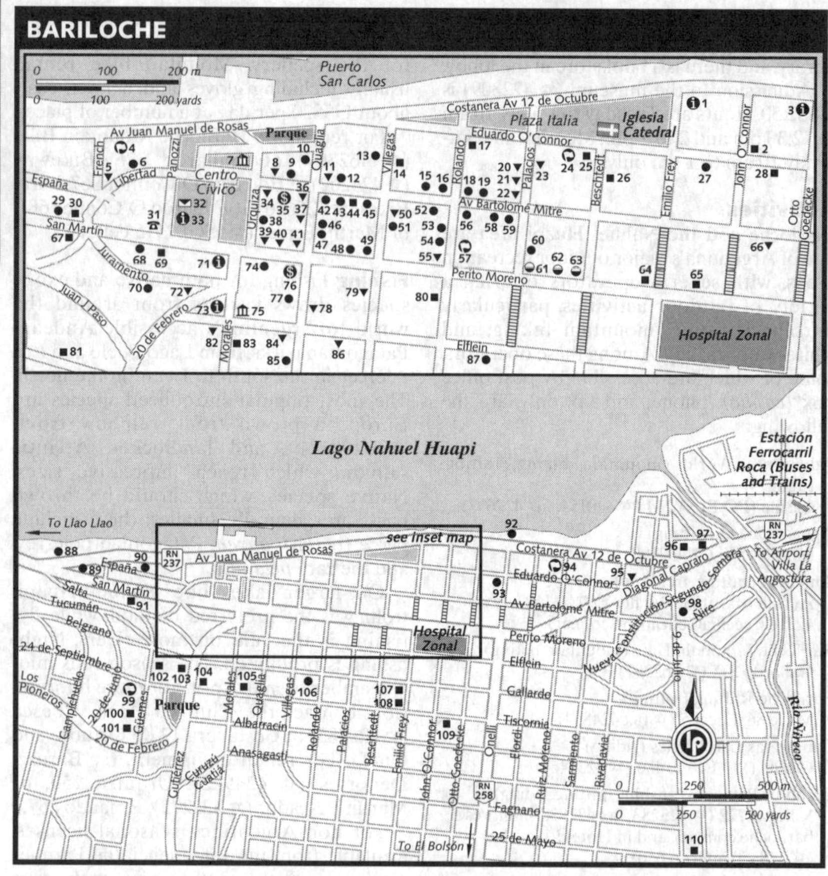

brochure with a simple map, adequate for initial planning, that rates hikes as easy, medium, or difficult and suggests possible loops. Many of these hikes are detailed in the 2nd edition of Clem Lindenmayer's *Trekking in the Patagonian Andes* (Lonely Planet, 1998).

The Club Andino Bariloche (☎ 422266), 20 de Febrero 30, provides information and issues obligatory permits for trekking in Parque Nacional Nahuel Huapi. For US$3, their *Mapa General de la Guía de Sendas y Picadas* is cartographically mediocre, but has good trail descriptions. Another good source of information and advice, especially for climbing the more difficult peaks, is the Asociación Argentina de Guías de Montaña (☎ 422567), Neumeyer 60. Both organizations also lead excursions in the area.

Skiing The runs around Bariloche were once South America's trendiest, but other areas in Argentina (especially Las Leñas, near Mendoza) and Chile (Portillo and Valle Nevado) have pretty much superseded the Nahuel Huapi area, which is more popular

BARILOCHE

PLACES TO STAY
- 2 Hostería El Ñire
- 14 Hostería Posada del Sol
- 17 Hotel Pucón
- 25 Hostería Sur
- 26 Hostería Piuké
- 28 Hospedaje Tito
- 30 Hotel Aconcagua
- 44 Hotel Internacional
- 64 Hostería Los Andes
- 65 Hotel Panorámico
- 67 Hotel Edelweiss
- 69 Albergue Mochilero's
- 80 Hotel Bella Vista
- 81 Hotel Campana
- 83 Hotel Carlos V
- 91 Hostería La Sureña
- 96 Casa de Familia Aguilar Cárdenas
- 97 Casa de Familia Lemos de Ferreyra
- 99 Casa de Familia Pirker
- 100 Casa de Familia Arko
- 101 Residencial Güemes
- 102 Residencial Wickter
- 103 Residencial Martín
- 104 Casa de Familia Lamouniere
- 105 Albergue Patagonia Andina
- 107 Hostería Ivalú
- 108 El Viejo Aljibe
- 109 Residencial Torres
- 110 Hospedaje Monte Grande

PLACES TO EAT
- 5 Helados Bari
- 8 La Andinita
- 11 El Viejo Munich
- 20 Ahumadero Familia Weiss
- 21 Bucaneros
- 22 Zona Sur
- 23 Pizzería Vogue
- 34 Cocodrilos
- 36 Melgari
- 37 Abuela Goye
- 39 Helados Jauja
- 40 Lennon
- 41 La Alpina
- 50 De la Granja
- 55 La Vizcacha
- 66 El Mundo de la Pizza
- 69 Rock Chicken
- 72 La Esquina de las Flores
- 78 Jauja
- 79 El Boliche de Alberto
- 82 El Vegetariano
- 84 La Andina
- 86 1810 (Parilla)
- 95 Bagdad Café

OTHER
- 1 Secretaría de Turismo de Río Negro
- 3 ACA
- 4 Chilean Consulate
- 6 Migraciones
- 7 Museo de la Patagonia
- 9 Bariloche Rafting
- 10 Localiza
- 12 Budget
- 13 LAPA
- 15 Southern Winds
- 16 Val Gardena
- 18 Del Turista
- 19 CyberClub Bariloche
- 24 Italian Consulate
- 27 Dirty Bikes
- 29 Al
- 31 Bariloche Center
- 32 Post Office
- 33 Secretaría Municipal de Turismo
- 35 Cambio Sudamérica
- 38 Baruzzi Deportes
- 42 Expediciones Náuticas
- 43 Rafting Adventure LADE
- 46 Aerolíneas Argentinas
- 47 TAN
- 48 Salón Cultural de Usos Múltiples (SCUM)
- 49 Paseo de los Artesanos
- 51 Cumbres Patagonia
- 52 Karnak Expediciones
- 53 Martín Pescador
- 54 Laverap
- 56 Fenoglio
- 57 Spanish Consulate
- 58 Hiver Turismo (AmEx)
- 59 Catedral Turismo
- 60 Kaikén Líneas Aéreas
- 61 Local Bus Station
- 62 Codao del Sur
- 63 Micro Ómnibus 3 de Mayo
- 68 Avis
- 69 Amuncar
- 70 Lavadero Huemul
- 71 Intendencia del Parque Nacional Nahuel Huapi
- 73 Club Andino Bariloche
- 74 Cine Arrayanes
- 75 Museo Arquitectónico
- 76 Banco de Galicia
- 77 Laverap
- 80 Quincho del Hotel Bella Vista
- 85 Lavandería La Casita
- 87 La Bolsa del Deporte
- 88 Grisú
- 89 Rockett
- 90 Cerebro
- 92 Club de Caza y Pesca
- 93 Bikeway
- 94 German Consulate
- 98 Pub Moritz
- 99 Austrian Consulate
- 105 Aguas Blancas
- 106 Bariloche Mountain Bike

with Argentines than foreigners. Gran Catedral, the largest and most popular area, amalgamates two formerly separate areas, Cerro Catedral and Lado Bueno, so skiers can buy one ticket valid for lifts in both areas. There is also the smaller Piedras Blancas area on Cerro Otto; for details, see the Parque Nacional Nahuel Huapi section later in this chapter.

If you need lessons, contact the ski schools at Cerro Catedral (☎ 423776), or the Club Andino Bariloche (☎ 424579) at 20 de Febrero 30. For rental equipment, try Baruzzi Deportes (☎ 424922) at Urquiza 250 or Martín Pescador (☎ 422275) at Rolando 257. Equipment is also available on site at Piedras Blancas and Gran Catedral.

In addition to downhill skiing, there are also cross-country opportunities.

Rafting & Kayaking Rafting and kayaking on the Río Limay (an easy Class II float, US$35) and the Río Manso (a generally Class III white-water descent with some

Class IV segments) have become increasingly popular in recent years. The latter are generally 20km day trips that usually cost around US$65, including transfers, a hearty lunch, and neoprene wet suits, helmets, and other equipment.

Other Water Sports Sailing, windsurfing, and canoeing have all become popular on Lago Nahuel Huapi and other nearby lakes and streams. For equipment rentals, see Fishing earlier in this chapter.

Organized Tours

Bariloche proper offers the opportunity to eat and drink well, and to see and be seen, but Parque Nacional Nahuel Huapi has greater possibilities. This section suggests some organized excursions, but consult the Parque Nacional Nahuel Huapi section for more detailed information.

City Tour Pochi's gaudy motorized *trencito* (little train) conducts regular city tours (US$5), starting at the centro cívico, but is hardly worthwhile unless you're too tired to walk. Trips to Isla Huemul, in Lago Nahuel Huapi, leave from Puerto San Carlos.

Half-day trips from Bariloche include Cerro Otto, Cerro Catedral (US$13 without chairlift access), the Circuito Chico west of town (US$13), and Cerro López (US$29).

Full-day trips include the delightful town of El Bolsón (US$29); Isla Victoria and Parque Nacional Los Arrayanes (US$30; for details on the latter, see Villa La Angostura, later in this chapter); San Martín de los Andes via Siete Lagos (US$34); and Cerro Tronador and Cascada Los Alerces via Lago Mascardi (US$35).

Catedral Turismo (☎ 425443, fax 426215), Av Bartolomé Mitre 399, covers all these destinations, but so do many other travel agencies. Catedral also arranges the scenic bus-boat combination over the Andes to Puerto Montt (US$110), which leaves weekdays at 9 am.

If you belong to ACA (☎ 423001) or any of their overseas affiliates, their office at Costanera 12 de Octubre 785 can arrange these excursions at discounts of at least 10%.

The Albergue Alaska *(☎/fax 461564, alaska@bariloche.com.ar; Lilinquen 328)*, 7½km west of town just off Av Bustillo, does a series of inexpensive camping tours ranging from the four-day Safari Siete Lagos (US$160 plus US$30 for the food kitty) and the identically priced four-day Safari Los Alerces to the 11-day Safari Patagónico (US$420 plus US$80 for food) and the 18-day Safari del Fin del Mundo (US$850 plus US$140 for food), which goes all the way to Tierra del Fuego. More information is available on their website (www.bariloche.com.ar/usuarios/alaska).

Special Events

In January and February, the Festival de Música de Verano puts on several different events, including the classical Festival de Música de Cámara (Chamber Music Festival), the Festival de Bronces (Brass Festival), and the Festival de Música Antigua (Ancient Music Festival).

In March, the Muestra Floral de Otoño allows the city's horticulturists to show off their green thumbs, while the Salón Cultural de Usos Múltiples (SCUM) has displays of three-dimensional arts in April. May 3 is the Fiesta Nacional de la Rosa Mosqueta, after the fruit of the wild shrub used in many regional delicacies.

During the ski season, Bariloche holds its Fiesta Nacional de la Nieve (National Snow Festival), while horticulturists show their early season colors at October's Fiesta del Tulipán (Tulip Festival) and the Muestra Floral de Primavera (Spring Flower Show).

A December event is the Navidad Coral (Christmas Chorus).

Places to Stay

Bariloche's abundant accommodations, ranging from camping and private houses to five-star hotels, make it possible to find good values even in high season, but it's sometimes necessary to be patient. Some visitors may wish to look outside of town, where the ambience is more pleasant.

The municipal tourist office maintains a computer database with current prices; the list below is only a cross-section of the many possibilities.

Places to Stay – Budget

Camping The nearest organized camping area is ***La Selva Negra*** *(☎ 441013)*, 3km west of town on the road to Llao Llao. Despite a few reports of unfriendly staff and imperfect maintenance, it has good facilities, and you can step outside your tent to pick apples in the fall. Fees are US$7 per site; ACA discounts are available. Other sites between Bariloche and Llao Llao include ***Camping Yeti*** *(☎ 442073)* at Km 5.6, where sites cost US$6, and ***Camping Petunia*** *(☎ 461969)* at Km 13.5, which also costs US$6.

Hostels The official Hostelling International facility is ***Albergue Alaska*** *(☎/fax 461564, alaska@bariloche.com.ar, Lilinquen 328)*, 7½km west of town just off Av Bustillo; buses Nos 10, 20, and 21 drop passengers nearby. Rates are US$10 per person (US$8 in off-season) with kitchen privileges and laundry facilities; prices are slightly higher for non-members. It has 44 beds, including three double rooms, rents mountain bikes, and arranges tours and ski transfers. Breakfast costs US$2 more.

There are two more central but unofficial hostels. Friendly ***Albergue Mochilero's*** *(☎ 431627, fax 423187, cecilia@bariloche.com.ar, San Martín 82)* charges US$5 for floor space, or US$8 with your own sleeping bag (US$10 with sheets) in smaller dorm rooms. There is also good luggage storage.

Albergue Patagonia Andina *(☎ 422783, Morales 564)* charges from US$8 to US$10 per person in an older house in an excellent location. Though some rooms are small, there are good common spaces.

Casas de Familia Bariloche's best values are casas de familia. Starting at US$10 to US$12 per person at the east end of town are the Lemos de Ferreyra family *(☎ 422556, Martín Fierro 1535)* and friendly Señora Heydée Aguilar Cárdenas *(☎ 425072, Martín Fierro 1541)* with firm beds, but cramped rooms. Both are near the bus/train station.

In the convenient, woodsy Barrio Belgrano, overlooking the centro cívico, are several slightly dearer but agreeable and comparable choices; the houses in this area help each other out, so if one is full they'll contact their neighbors. Try Marianne Pirker *(☎ 424873, 24 de Septiembre 230)*, who also has a one-bedroom apartment for US$20 (her husband is the Austrian Honorary Consul); Rosa Arko *(☎ 423109, Güemes 691)*; Carlotta Baumann *(☎ 429689, Av Los Pioneros 860)*; and Eloisa Lamouniere *(☎ 422514, 24 de Septiembre 71)*.

Hospedajes, Hosterías & Hotels The ***Hospedaje El Mirador*** *(☎ 422221, Perito Moreno 652)*, a converted private house, charges US$8 per person with shared bath and US$12 with private bath. At ***Hospedaje Monte Grande*** *(☎ 422159, 25 de Mayo 1544)* rates are US$15/24 single/double. ***Residencial Torres*** *(☎ 423355, Tiscornia 747)* charges US$15/25, but breakfast is extra.

Hostería Los Andes *(☎ 422222, Perito Moreno 594)* charges US$15/28 with shared bath, US$20 per person with private bath. For US$15 per person, the otherwise unimpressive ***Hospedaje Tito*** *(☎ 424039, Eduardo O'Connor 745)* is a friendly place that's often full. In Barrio Belgrano, ***Residencial Güemes*** *(☎ 424785, Güemes 715)* costs US$30 double.

Places to Stay – Mid-Range

Many mid-range accommodations are, for some inexplicable reason, overpriced compared to better low-end places. For US$40 double, for instance, attractive ***Residencial Wickter*** *(☎ 423248, Güemes 566)* is still a lesser value than other places in Barrio Belgrano. ***Hotel Pucón*** *(☎ 426164, Rolando 118)* is very central for US$22/40. For good views and moderate prices, there's ***Hotel Panorámico*** *(☎ 423468, Perito Moreno 646)*, for US$25/36.

Very centrally located ***Hotel Internacional*** *(☎ 425938, Mitre 171)* charges US$30/40. Convenient ***Hostería Posada del Sol*** *(☎ 423011, Villegas 148)* costs US$30/45 with breakfast, while ***Hotel Campana*** *(☎ 422162, Belgrano 165)* is comparably priced but friendlier, for US$30/49.

Hostería Sur *(☎ 422677, Beschtedt 101)* has very large beds in some very small rooms, with private bath, for US$30/50. This includes a generous breakfast, but even with a 10% discount for ACA members it's still a bit overpriced. Across the street, the unfortunately named ***Hostería Piuké*** *(☎ 423044, Beschtedt 136)* charges US$30/50.

Just a block from the cathedral, inviting ***Hostería El Ñire*** *(☎ 423041, Eduardo O'Connor 702)* charges US$35/45. Two attractive hillside hotels are lesser values than they once were: ***Hostería Ivalú*** *(☎ 423237, Frey 535)* for US$38/48 and ***El Viejo Aljibe*** *(☎ 423316, Frey 571)* for US$40/50, both including breakfast. Clean, quiet ***Hostería La Sureña*** *(☎ 422013, San Martín 432)* charges US$42/56.

Places to Stay – Top End

Upscale accommodations start around US$70/80 for singles/doubles at ***Hotel Aconcagua*** *(☎ 424718, San Martín 289)* and ***Hotel Carlos V*** *(☎ 425474, Morales 420)*. The ***Hotel Bella Vista*** *(☎ 422435, Rolando 351)* charges US$68/90. Five-star ***Hotel Edelweiss*** *(☎ 426165, San Martín 202)* charges US$110/115 plus IVA, while the budget-busters at ***Hotel Panamericano*** *(☎ 425846, San Martín 532)* extort US$170/180.

Places to Eat

For all its shortcomings, Bariloche has some of Argentina's best food. It's unlikely you'll have time or money enough to sample all the worthwhile restaurants, but a broad sample appears below. Note that most formal restaurants collect a *cubierto* (cover charge) for bread and cutlery.

Regional specialties deserve mention, including *jabalí* (wild boar), *ciervo* (venison), and *trucha* (trout); some places, like ***Ahumadero Familia Weiss*** *(☎ 424829, Palacios 167)* specialize in smoked game and fish. At the vegetarian end of the spectrum, ***La Esquina de las Flores***,. the landmark Buenos Aires restaurant and natural foods market, has a local branch at 20 de Febrero and Juramento. ***El Vegetariano***, at Neumeyer and Morales, serves full meals.

Decorated in a Beatles motif, ***Lennon*** *(☎ 423182, Perito Moreno 48)* is nominally a parrilla, but the menu is more imaginative than that would suggest; it's also inexpensive (no cubierto), with excellent service. The ***Bagdad Café***, Eduardo O'Connor 1348, is a pub with a midday lunch, usually something like ñoquis, for just US$3. ***Rock Chicken***, downstairs from Albergue Mochilero's at Av San Martín 82, serves moderately priced meals and drinks in a lively pub atmosphere.

La Vizcacha *(☎ 422109, Rolando 279)* is one of the country's best and cheapest parrillas, offering pleasant atmosphere and outstanding service. Its standard parrillada for two includes not only the usual beef but also chicken breast garnished with red peppers and parsley. Besides butter, you get deer pâté and Roquefort cheese spreads. With a liter of house wine, the total bill comes to about US$20.

Another parrilla is ***1810*** *(☎ 423922, Elflein 167)* but some readers have complained of high prices, indifferent service, and the staff's reluctance to allow diners to share portions. ***La Andina*** *(☎ 423017, Elflein 95)* has drawn praise for good food, large portions, and moderate prices – and no objections to portion-sharing. ***El Boliche de Alberto*** *(☎ 431433, Villegas 347)* is also a parrilla.

Recommended ***De la Granja*** *(☎ 435939, Villegas 220)* features farm-fresh ingredients at moderate prices. The more expensive ***Jauja*** *(☎ 422952, Quaglia 366)* has a good European-style menu but erratic service and relatively small portions.

There are many pizzerias. ***Cocodrilos*** *(☎ 426640, Mitre 5)* serves a very fine fugazzeta at a very reasonable price, as does ***La Andinita*** *(☎ 422257, Mitre 56)*. ***Bucaneros*** *(☎ 423674, Palacios 187)* is also a good inexpensive choice, but try also ***Pizzaiola*** *(☎ 426181, Pagano 275)* or ***El Mundo de la Pizza*** *(☎ 423461, Mitre 759)*. The food at ***Pizzería Vogue*** *(☎ 431343, Palacios 156)* has drawn some favorable comment, but the service can be atrocious.

La Alpina *(☎ 425693, Perito Moreno 98)* is a good, popular confitería, but there are innumerable others. ***Zona Sur*** *(☎ 434258, Mitre 396)* serves tasty coffee, hot chocolate, and fresh croissants at reasonable prices. Befitting its name, ***El Viejo Munich*** *(☎ 422336, Mitre 102)* has excellent draft beer, served with complimentary peanuts.

Outstanding ice cream is available at ***Helados Bari*** *(☎ 422305, España 7)*, a block from the centro cívico, ***Melgari*** at Mitre and Quaglia, and ***Abuela Goye*** *(☎ 422276, Quaglia 221)*. The best in town, though, is ***Helados Jauja*** *(Perito Moreno 14)*; the adventurous should try the exquisitely tasty *mate cocido* (boiled *mate)* flavor, which sounds strange even to Argentines.

Entertainment

Cinema ***Cine Arrayanes*** *(☎ 422860, Perito Moreno 39)* is Bariloche's only remaining cinema.

Dance Clubs Several dance clubs along Av Juan Manuel de Rosas appeal to a youngish crowd but tend to be expensive – usually charging around US$25 for cover, which at least includes one drink. Among them are ***Cerebro*** *(☎ 424965, Rosas 406)*, ***Rockett*** *(☎ 431940, Rosas 424)*, and ***Grisú*** *(☎ 422269, Rosas 574)*.

Pub Moritz *(Mitre 1530)* attracts a slightly older crowd, about 25 to 30 years old. The ***Quincho del Hotel Bella Vista*** *(☎ 422435, Rolando 351)* features salsa and other Latin American music. ***Cauquén***, at Km 13.8 on Av Bustillo, is a parrilla that also features music for dancing.

Shopping

Bariloche is renowned for its sweets and confections. Del Turista (☎ 422124) and Fenoglio (☎ 423119), across the street from each other at Mitre and Rolando, are virtual supermarkets of chocolate and also good places for a cheap stand-up cappuccino or hot chocolate, as well as dessert. Benroth, at Mitre and Quaglia, and Abuela Goye, at Quaglia 221, are also good outlets for chocoholics. Try also Val Gardena, Mitre 298, for chocolates.

Local craftspeople display their wares in wool, wood, leather, and other media at the Paseo de los Artesanos, Villegas, and Perito Moreno, between 10 am and 9 pm daily.

Getting There & Away

Air Aerolíneas Argentinas (☎ 422425), Quaglia 238, flies to Buenos Aires' Aeroparque (from US$97 to US$269) twice daily Monday through Wednesday and three times daily the rest of the week. LAPA (☎ 423714), Villegas 121, flies once each weekday and twice Saturday and Sunday to Aeroparque (US$99 to US$235).

TAN (☎ 427889), Quaglia 242, Local 11, flies Saturday to Comodoro Rivadavia (US$75 to US$88), and Tuesday and Friday to Puerto Montt, Chile (US$50 to US$62).

LADE (☎ 423562), Mitre 186, flies Monday to Neuquén (US$47) and Viedma (US$72); Wednesday to San Martín de los Andes (US$20), Zapala (US$26), and Neuquén, as well as to Mar del Plata (US$100 to US$130), and Aeroparque (US$110); Thursday to El Bolsón (US$20), El Maitén (US$20), and Esquel (US$20); Friday to Esquel, Puerto Madryn (US$53), Trelew (US$53 to US$74), and Comodoro Rivadavia (US$60 to US$80), and to San Martín de los Andes, Neuquén, Viedma, Bahía Blanca (US$81), and Aeroparque.

Kaikén Líneas Aéreas (☎ 433494), Palacios 266, flies daily except Sunday to Neuquén (US$56) and Mendoza (US$140 to US$170), and to Comodoro Rivadavia (US$80 to US$88), Río Gallegos (US$160 to US$310), Río Grande (US$196 to US$360), and Ushuaia (US$209 to US$380).

Southern Winds (☎ 423704), Mitre 260, flies Wednesday to Córdoba (US$127 to US$169), Rosario (US$149 to US$199), and Mendoza (US$134 to US$179), Saturday afternoon to Córdoba and Mendoza, Saturday evening to Córdoba only, Sunday morning to Córdoba and Rosario, and Sunday afternoon to Córdoba, Rosario, Mendoza, Tucumán (US$142 to US$189), and Salta (US$157 to US$209).

Bus Bariloche's bus terminal (☎ 426999) and train station are currently one and the same. Estación Ferrocarril Roca is across the Río Ñireco along RN 237. Most of the bus companies have downtown offices, some of them shared. Unless mentioned otherwise, offices below are at the terminal. Shop around for the best deals, since fares vary and there are frequent promotions.

International Several companies cover the route between Bariloche and Osorno (US$18) and Puerto Montt (US$19), with onward connections to northern Chilean destinations: Río de la Plata (☎ 424269, 421699), at Mitre 161; Bus Norte (☎ 23654), Tas-Choapa (☎ 26663, 432521), at Perito Moreno 138; Andesmar (☎ 422140, 430211), at Palacios 246; and Cruz del Sur (☎ 424163, 424044), at San Martín 453.

Domestic Chevallier (☎ 423090), Perito Moreno 107, has daily coche cama departures at 2:15 pm for Buenos Aires via Santa Rosa, La Pampa province, and has Tuesday, Friday and Sunday service to Rosario, connecting to Santa Fe and Paraná.

La Estrella (☎ 422140), at the same downtown office, leaves daily for Buenos Aires at 2 pm via Bahía Blanca. Tirsa (☎ 426076, 421699), Quaglia 197, goes Tuesday and Sunday to Rosario via Santa Rosa. With El Valle (☎ 431444), the daily 12:15 pm trip to Buenos Aires goes via Neuquén, Viedma, and Bahía Blanca, which has an additional service at 11:15 pm. La Unión del Sud (☎ 428589), Moreno 366, goes to Neuquén daily at noon.

Vía Bariloche (☎ 426181), Mitre 131, Local 1, has two or three services daily to Neuquén and Buenos Aires, with onward connections (after a nine-hour layover) to Posadas and Puerto Iguazú. TAC (☎ 426883, 432521), Perito Moreno 138, has daily service to Buenos Aires and La Plata, daily direct service to Córdoba (as well as connections in Neuquén), and goes daily to Mendoza via Neuquén, Zapala, and San Rafael.

Don Otto (☎ 424269, 421699), Mitre 161, goes daily to El Bolsón, Esquel, and Comodoro Rivadavia, with connections to Río Gallegos. Don Otto also has service to Trelew and Puerto Madryn, connecting in Esquel.

Andesmar (☎ 422140, 430211), Palacios 246, has connections in Neuquén for southbound Patagonian destinations like Puerto Madryn and Trelew. Andesmar's daily northbound services beyond Neuquén include stops in San Rafael and Mendoza, with connections to San Juan, La Rioja, Catamarca, Tucumán, Salta, and Jujuy.

TUS (☎ 424565, 422818), Elflein 320, serves Neuquén and Córdoba daily except Monday and Thursday. Mercedes (☎ 424269, 421699), Mitre 161, serves Neuquén and the Buenos Aires provincial beach resorts of Necochea and Mar del Plata.

Charter (☎ 426663, 421689), Perito Moreno 138, runs seven buses daily to El Bolsón; it also offers a faster minibus service. Vía Bariloche also runs six buses daily to El Bolsón, two of which (8 am and 6 pm) continue to Lago Puelo and Esquel.

Codao del Sur (☎ 423654), Perito Moreno 480, goes to El Maitén Tuesday at 8 am, and has a nightly service to Viedma.

Transportes Ko-Ko (☎ 423090), Perito Moreno 107, has buses to Junín de los Andes and San Martín de los Andes, mostly via the longer paved La Rinconada (RN 40) route rather than the more scenic but chokingly dusty Siete Lagos route, which usually has service in summer only. Ko-Ko has daily service on this route as far as Villa La Angostura all year, while Turismo Algarrobal (☎ 423081) goes to San Martín via Siete Lagos three times daily. Albus (☎ 430211) goes daily to San Martín via Villa Traful.

Sample fares include Villa La Angostura (US$6.50, two hours), El Bolsón (US$8 to US$11, two hours), El Maitén (US$14, 3½ hours), Junín de los Andes (US$16, four hours), San Martín de los Andes (US$17, 4½ hours), Esquel (US$18, 4½ hours), Neuquén (US$18 to US$22, seven hours), Viedma (US$40 to US$50, 16 hours), Bahía Blanca (US$45 to US$55, 14 hours), Trelew (US$40 to US$51, 13 hours), Puerto Madryn (US$48 to US$54, 14 hours), San Rafael (US$45, 17 hours), Santa Rosa (US$50, 11 hours), Mendoza (US$55 to US$62, 19 hours), Comodoro Rivadavia (US$47 to US$69, 14 hours), San Juan (US$63 to

US$72), Mar del Plata (US$65), La Rioja (US$74), Buenos Aires (US$75 to US$85, 23 hours), Córdoba (US$75 to US$79, 22 hours), Rosario (US$76, 23 hours), Catamarca (US$86), Tucumán (US$89), Río Gallegos (US$78 to US$104, 28 hours), Salta (US$105), Jujuy (US$106), Posadas (US$140), and Puerto Iguazú (US$155).

Train Sefepa (Servicio Ferrocarril Patagónico, ☎ 423172) leaves from the Estación Ferrocarril Roca, which is across the Río Ñireco along RN 237. Departures for Viedma (16 hours) are Tuesday and Friday at 5 pm; fares are US$28 primera, US$42 Pullman.

Boat Catedral Turismo (☎ 425443), Mitre 399, is the representative for the scenic bus-boat combination over the Andes to Puerto Montt (US$110), which leaves weekdays at 9 am; it's also possible to do the trip in segments: Bariloche to Puerto Pañuelo (US$5), Puerto Pañuelo to Puerto Blest (US$14), Puerto Blest to Puerto Frías (US$5), Puerto Frías to Peulla, Chile (US$54), Peulla to Petrohué (US$25), and Petrohué to Puerto Montt (US$7).

Getting Around

To/From the Airport Aeropuerto Teniente Candelaria (☎ 422767) is 15km east of town via RN 237 and RP 80. TAN runs its own airport minibus, while LADE, LAPA, and Aerolíneas use Transporte Alí, which leaves Aerolíneas' downtown offices, at Quaglia 238, 1½ hours before each flight. The price is US$3.

Bus From Perito Moreno between Palacios and Beschtedt, Codao del Sur (☎ 423654) and Ómnibus 3 de Mayo (☎ 433805) run hourly buses to Cerro Catedral for US$2.40 one-way. Codao uses Av de los Pioneros, while 3 de Mayo takes Av Bustillo. In summer 3 de Mayo goes four times daily to Lago Mascardi.

From 6 am to midnight, municipal bus No 20 leaves the local bus station at Perito Moreno and Palacios every 20 minutes for the attractive lakeside towns of Llao Llao (US$1.90) and Puerto Pañuelo. The Nos 10 and 11 buses also go to Colonia Suiza (US$2.20) 14 times daily. Three of these, at 8:05 am, noon, and 5:40 pm continue to Puerto Pañuelo, allowing you to do the Circuito Chico (see Parque Nacional Nahuel Huapi later in this chapter) on inexpensive public transport. Departure times from Puerto Pañuelo back to Bariloche via Colonia Suiza are 9:40 am and 1:40 and 6:40 pm. You can also walk any section and flag down buses en route.

Ómnibus 3 de Mayo's Nos 50 and 51 buses go to Lago Gutiérrez (US$1.10) every 30 minutes, while in summer the company's Línea Mascardi goes to Villa Mascardi (US$3.50) and Los Rápidos (US$5) three times daily. Their Línea El Manso goes twice Friday and once Sunday to Río Villegas and El Manso (US$7.50), on the southwestern border of Parque Nacional Nahuel Huapi.

Car Bariloche is loaded with all the standard car-rental agencies and a few local ones to boot: AI (☎ 426420, fax 427494), San Martín 235; Amuncar (☎ 431627), San Martín 82, 1st floor; Avis (☎ 431648, fax 431649), San Martín 130; Budget (☎ 422482), Mitre 106, 1st floor; and Localiza (☎/fax 423457), Quaglia 161.

PARQUE NACIONAL NAHUEL HUAPI

In bequeathing the lands that comprise Parque Nacional Nahuel Huapi to the Argentine state in 1904, Francisco Pascasio Moreno stipulated that they 'be conserved as a natural public park' and emphasized his desire that 'the current features of their perimeter not be altered, and that there be no additional constructions other than those that facilitate the comforts of the cultured visitor.' At present, though, as Argentina's oldest national park and one of its most heavily visited, Nahuel Huapi plays the same role as Yosemite in the United States, attracting so many people that the very values Moreno expressed are at risk. Some of Nahuel Huapi's problems stem from the fact that nearly half the park is a 'national reserve,' permitting and even encouraging certain commercial activities. Another

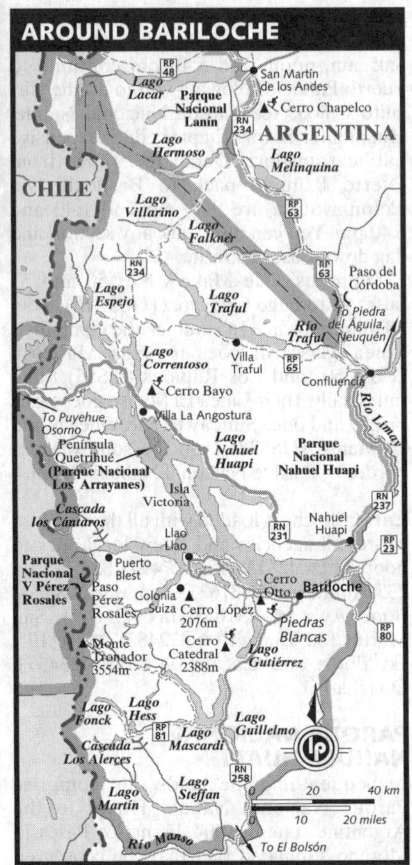

problem is nearby Bariloche's phenomenal growth from a modest village to an urban enclave that threatens its surrounding environment with noise, pollution, and sprawl.

Parque Nacional Nahuel Huapi occupies 750,000 hectares in mountainous southwestern Neuquén and western Río Negro provinces. Covering more than 500 sq km, the park's centerpiece is Lago Nahuel Huapi, a glacial remnant over 100km long that is the source of the Río Limay, a major tributary of the Río Negro. To the west a ridge of high peaks separates Argentina from Chile; the tallest is 3554m Tronador, an extinct volcano that still lives up to its name (which means 'Thunderer') when blocks of ice tumble from its glaciers. During the summer months, wildflowers blanket alpine meadows.

Besides its scenery, Nahuel Huapi was created to preserve local flora and fauna, including its Andean-Patagonian forests and rare animals. Tree species are much the same as those found in Parque Nacional Los Alerces (see that section later in this chapter), while the important animal species include the *huemul* or Andean deer *(Hippocamelus bisulcus)* and the miniature deer known as *pudú (Pudu pudu)*. Most visitors are not likely to see either of these, but several species of introduced deer are common, along with native birds. Both native and introduced fish species offer excellent sport.

The US-based National Outdoor Leadership School (NOLS; ☎ 307-332-6973), 288 W Main St, Lander, WY 82520, runs a 'Semester in Patagonia' program that lasts 75 days (university credit possible), taking place partly in Parque Nacional Nahuel Huapi. Most of the program takes place in Chile, however, where NOLS's base is the town of Coihaique.

Unless listed otherwise, all telephone numbers in this section have the area code ☎ 02944.

Books

For trekking maps and information about hiking in the region, see the 2nd edition of Clem Lindenmayer's LP guide *Trekking in the Patagonian Andes* or, if you read Spanish, the locally published *Las Montañas de Bariloche* (Guías Regionales Argentinas, 1993) by Toncek Arko and Raúl Izaguirre. Claudio Chehébar and Eduardo Ramilo's *Fauna del Parque Nacional Nahuel Huapi* (Administración de Parques Nacionales & Asociación Amigos del Museo de la Patagonia Francisco P Moreno) is a guide to the park's animal life.

Circuito Chico

One of the area's most popular excursions, with excellent views, this route begins on

Av Bustillo, on Bariloche's outskirts, and continues on to the tranquil resort of Llao Llao, named for the 'Indian bread' fungus. At **Cerro Campanario**, Av Bustillo Km 17, the Aerosilla Campanario (☎ 427274) lifts passengers to a panoramic view of Lago Nahuel Huapi for US$10.

Llao Llao's Puerto Pañuelo is the point of departure for the boat-bus excursion across the Andes to Chile. Have a look at the grounds of the state-built ***Hotel Llao Llao*** (☎ 448544), a national treasure that became a topic of political controversy when, in the summer of 1990-1991, two Italian businessmen who had given Argentine president Carlos Menem an expensive sports car a few months earlier sought government permission to take over the hotel. For a paltry US$230 per night, you, too, can enjoy what may be the country's single most prestigious lodging. In fact, that's the price for a 'senior' room, but bargain 'refugios' are available for US$155 double, suites from US$370 to US$580, and 'estudios' for US$350.

From Llao Llao you can double back to **Colonia Suiza**, named for its early Swiss colonists and the site of the annual Fiesta Nacional del Curanto (celebrating a typical dish made from red and white meat, or from vegetables; it bears no resemblance to its Chilean namesake, a seafood stew). A modest confitería has excellent pastries, and there are several campgrounds. The road passes the trailhead to 2076m **Cerro López**, a three-hour climb, before returning to Bariloche. At the top, it's possible to spend the night at the Club Andino Bariloche's ***Refugio López*** *(☎ 423750 in Bariloche for reservations)*, where meals are also available.

Although travel agencies operate this as a tour, it's easily done on public transportation. For details, see the Bariloche Getting Around section.

Isla Victoria

In Lago Nahuel Huapi, Isla Victoria is a large island on which the Argentine park service trains park rangers, attracting students from throughout Latin America. Boats to Isla Victoria and to Parque Nacional Los Arrayanes on Península Quetrihué leave from Puerto Pañuelo at Llao Llao, but you can visit Los Arrayanes more easily and cheaply from Villa La Angostura (see that section later in this chapter). From Bariloche's Puerto San Carlos, the trip costs US$30; from Puerto Pañuelo, it costs US$22.

Cerro Otto

Cerro Otto (altitude 1405m) is an 8km hike on a gravel road west from Bariloche (there's enough traffic that hitching is feasible; this is also a steep and tiring but rewarding bicycle route). The Teleférico Cerro Otto (☎ 441035), at Km 5 on Av de Los Pioneros, carries adult passengers to the summit for US$15, children for US$5; a free bus leaves from the corner of Mitre and Villegas or Perito Moreno and Independencia to the base of the mountain. Bring food and drink – prices at the summit confitería are truly extortionate.

Piedras Blancas (☎ 425720 interno 1708) is the nearest ski area to Bariloche, at Km 6 on the Cerro Otto road. There's a trail from Piedras Blancas to the Club Andino's ***Refugio Berghof*** *(☎ 1560-3201 cellular)*, at an elevation of 1240m; make reservations, since there are only 20 beds. Meals are also available here.

The Refugio Berghof also contains the **Museo de Montaña Otto Meiling**, named for a pioneering climber. Guided visits cost US$1.50.

The diminutive *pudú* is a rarely seen denizen of Parque Nacional Nahuel Huapi.

Cerro Catedral

This 2388m peak, 20km southwest of Bariloche, contains the area's most important ski center, the **Centro de Deportes Invernales Antonio M Lynch**. Several chairlifts and the Aerosilla Cerro Bellavista (US$16), which also operates during the summer from 10 am to 5 pm daily except Monday, carry passengers up to 2000m, where there is a restaurant/confitería offering excellent panoramas. Several trekking trails also begin here; one relatively easy four-hour walk goes to Club Andino's ***Refugio Emilio Frey*** *(☎ 424831)*, where 40 beds and simple meals are available. This refugio itself is exposed, but there are sheltered tent sites in what is also Argentina's prime rock-climbing area.

There is a good mix of easy, intermediate, and advanced skiing runs, with steep advanced runs at the top and some tree runs near the base. Lift lines can develop at this very popular resort, but the capacity is substantial enough that waits are not excessive. One complaint is that many Argentines crowd the lines, but the author's opinion is that they have a greater tolerance for this than do North Americans or Europeans.

Rates for lift passes vary from low to mid- to high season, starting at US$22 and going up to US$40 per day for adults, US$18 to US$32 for children; weekend passes get only small discounts, but one-week passes entail substantial savings at US$110 to US$200 for adults, US$90 to US$160 for children. Basic rental equipment is cheap, but quality gear is far more expensive.

Gran Catedral also has several ski schools at Villa Catedral, at the base of the lifts, including Robles Catedral (☎ 460050), Ski Club (☎ 460012), and Ski Total (☎ 460094).

Hostería del Cerro *(☎ 460026)*, at the base of the lifts, charges US$123/176 for singles/doubles in high season. Alternatively you can stay in Bariloche; public transport from there is excellent, consisting of hourly buses from downtown with Micro Ómnibus 3 de Mayo.

Monte Tronador

From Lago Mascardi, this full-day trip up a single-lane dirt road goes to Pampa Linda and visits the Ventisquero Negro (Black Glacier) and the base of Tronador. Traffic goes up in the morning (until 2 pm) and down in the afternoon (after 4 pm). For US$12 one-way, US$20 return, the Club Andino Bariloche organizes transport to Pampa Linda daily at 9 am, returning at 5 pm, with Transporte RM (☎ 423918); some have found the trip itself to be dusty and unpleasant.

The area around Tronador resembles, in some ways, Yosemite Valley – you have to set your sights above the hotels, confiterías, and parking lots to be able to focus on the dozens of waterfalls that plunge over the flanks of the extinct volcanoes. There is another irritation factor as well – at the end of the short trail from the parking lot at the end of the road, the park service places a whistle-blower to keep people from advancing into areas considered too hazardous for the average porteño.

From Pampa Linda, hikers can approach the Club Andino's snowline ***Refugio Meiling*** *(☎ 461861)* on foot and continue to Laguna Frías via the Paso de las Nubes; it's a five- to seven-hour walk to an elevation of 2000m.

It's also possible to complete the trip in the opposite direction via the bus-boat-bus combination from Llao Llao/Puerto Pañuelo to Puerto Blest, then hike up the Río Frías to Paso de las Nubes before descending to Pampa Linda via the Río Alerce.

Climbers intending to scale Tronador should anticipate a three- to four-day technical climb requiring experience on rock, snow, and ice. Hostería Pampa Linda (see below) arranges horseback riding in the area.

Places to Stay

Besides those campgrounds in the immediate Bariloche area, there are sites at Lago Gutiérrez, Lago Mascardi, Lago Guillelmo, Lago Los Moscos, Lago Roca, and Pampa Linda. Refugios charge US$6 per night, US$1.50 for day use, and US$3 extra for kitchen privileges.

Within the park are a number of hotels tending to the luxurious, but ***Hostería Pampa Linda*** *(☎ 423757, 422181)* is moderately priced at US$25/40 single/double with breakfast off-season, US$45/60 in peak season (January, February, March). Meals are also reasonable; full board costs an additional US$24 per person. At ***Hotel Tronador*** *(☎ 468127, fax 441062)* at the northwest end of Lago Mascardi on the Pampa Linda road, doubles cost US$88 per person including half-board.

EL BOLSÓN

According to its reputation, El Bolsón is a tolerant mecca for graying ponytailed hippies who live on woodsy communes, drive VW Kombis, eat macrobiotic food, and make a living peddling handmade jewelry and pottery on the streets. The limited substance to the stereotypical image of a sixties anachronism makes this town and its surroundings a welcome relief from Bariloche's vulgar commercialism – El Bolsón invites backpackers rather than the deluge of bourgeois porteños who overrun the Nahuel Huapi area throughout the year.

El Bolsón's 5000 townspeople and their government were the first in Argentina to declare their hometown a 'non-nuclear

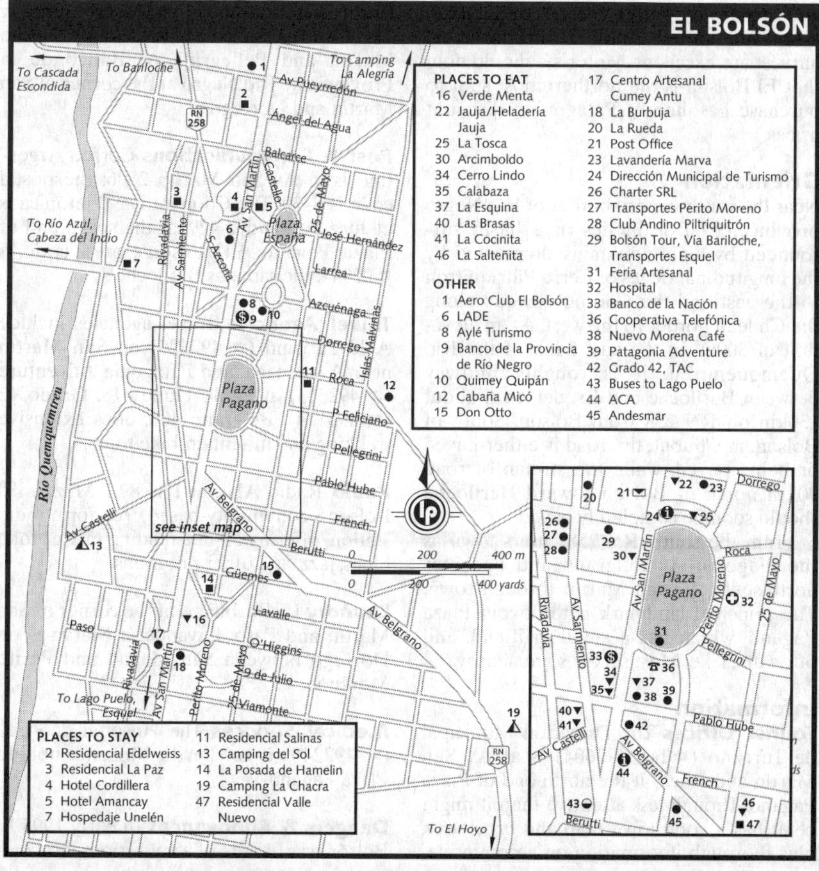

zone' and an 'ecological municipality.' This broadly supported policy was in part a response to the Menem administration's failed effort to locate a nuclear dump in nearby Chubut province. Communications are in fact better with northern Chubut than with Río Negro, though improvements in the traditionally dismal highway to Bariloche may yet reorient the community.

The local economy relies on tourism, agriculture, and forestry. Rows of poplars lend a Mediterranean appearance to the chacras, most of which are devoted to hops (nearly three-quarters of the country's production), soft fruits like raspberries and strawberries, and orchard crops like cherries and apples. Beer and sweets made from the local harvest are excellent. Motorists should note that El Bolsón is the northernmost spot to purchase gasoline at Patagonian discount prices.

Orientation

Near the southwestern border of Río Negro province, El Bolsón lies in a basin surrounded by high mountains, dominated by the longitudinal ridges of Cerro Piltriquitrón to the east and the Cordón Nevado along the Chilean border to the west. At an elevation of 300m on the east bank of the Río Quemquemtreu, it is roughly midway between Bariloche and Esquel, each about 130km on RN 258 from Bolsón. South of Bolsón, in Chubut, the road is either paved or being paved, while the stretch of road 90km north of Bolsón toward Bariloche should soon be completely paved.

From the south, RN 258 enters town as the diagonal Av Belgrano and becomes north-south Av San Martín through town. The principal landmark is the ovoid Plaza Pagano, which has a small artificial, and often dry, lake. Most services are nearby.

Information

Tourist Offices The Dirección Municipal de Turismo (☎/fax 492604) is at Av San Martín and Roca, at the north end of Plaza Pagano. Though less attentive than it might be, it has a good town map and brochures, plus thorough information on accommodations, food, tours, and services. Maps of the surrounding area, though, are very poor. In summer, it's open 8 am to 10 pm weekdays, 9 am to 10 pm Saturday, and 10 am to 10 pm Sunday. The rest of the year, hours are 9 am to 6 pm.

Visitors interested in the surrounding mountains – the main reason for coming to Bolsón – can contact the Club Andino Piltriquitrón on Sarmiento between Roca and Feliciano.

For motorists, ACA (☎ 492260) is at Avs Belgrano and San Martín.

Money It's better to change elsewhere, since El Bolsón has no ATMs or cambios. Try, however, Banco de la Nación at Av San Martín and Pellegrini, or Banco de la Provincia de Río Negro at the corner of San Martín and Dorrego.

Post & Communications Correo Argentino is at Av San Martín 2806; the postal code is 8430. The Cooperativa Telefónica is at Juez Fernández 429, at the south end of Plaza Pagano. El Bolsón's area code is ☎ 02944, the same as Bariloche's.

Travel Agencies Travel agencies include Aylé Turismo (☎ 492329) on San Martín near Azcuénaga, and Patagonia Adventure (☎ 492513) at Pablo Hube 418. Grado 42 (☎ 493124), Belgrano 406, does extensive trekking and mountain-bike tours.

Radio Radio Alas, at FM 89.1 Mhz, is El Bolsón's community-based, free-form radio station, offering an outstanding mix of folk, blues, jazz, and other programs.

Laundry La Burbuja is at the corner of San Martín and Paso. Lavandería Marva is on Dorrego between San Martín and Perito Moreno.

Medical Services The Hospital de Area (☎ 492240) is on Perito Moreno, behind Plaza Pagano.

Dangers & Annoyances In early 1995 El Bolsón was the site of a mysterious viral outbreak which soon claimed four lives. The culprit turned out to be rodent-borne hantavirus, which often kills its victims within 24 hours of infection. While the probability of contact is small, especially for tourists, visitors should avoid places such as sheds and ruined houses, which may be frequented by rats and mice. These rodents are just the carriers; victims inhale the airborne virus when droppings are disturbed.

Feria Artesanal

Tuesday, Thursday, and Saturday, local craftspeople sell their wares at the south end of Plaza Pagano from 10:30 am to 3 pm. It's one of your best chances to eat and drink local delicacies such as homemade empanadas and sausages, Belgian waffles with fresh raspberries, and locally brewed beer.

Festival Nacional del Lúpulo

Local beer gets headlines during the national hops festival, which takes place over four days in mid-February.

Places to Stay – Budget

Budget travelers are more than welcome in El Bolsón, where reasonable prices are the rule rather than the exception. The tourist office maintains a list of private houses that offer lodging.

Camping El Bolsón's most central campground is the dusty but shady municipal ***Camping del Sol***, at the west end of Av Castelli, which has hot showers, a small confitería, and swimming in the river. Rates are US$3 per person. For US$5, ***Camping La Chacra*** *(☎ 492111)*, off Av Belgrano on the eastern edge of town, has more grass, less dust, and less shade, though the trees are filling in quickly.

Hostels Local buses go hourly to Hostelling International affiliate ***Albergue El Pueblito*** *(☎ 493560, pueblito@hostels.org.ar)* in Barrio Luján, about 4km north of town. A good place to meet Argentine backpackers, this fine and friendly facility has beds for 40 people and places to camp as well. Rates are US$8 with hostel card, US$9 without.

Hospedajes, Residenciales & Hosterías ***Residencial Salinas*** *(☎ 492396, Roca 641)* has rooms for US$10 that include a private log fire, but the insulation is inadequate in winter. Rates are the same at ***Residencial Edelweiss*** *(☎ 492594, Ángel del Agua 360)* with shared bath, while ***Residencial La Paz*** *(☎ 492252, Sarmiento 3212)* charges US$12 per person with private bath.

For US$13/25 single/double, try ***Hospedaje Unelén*** *(☎ 492729, Azcuénaga 350)*. Slightly more expensive is ***Hostería Steiner*** *(☎ 492224, Av San Martín 600)*, at the south end of town, for US$15 per person.

Places to Stay – Mid-Range

Mid-range accommodations start around US$20/30 for singles/doubles at ***La Posada de Hamelin*** *(☎ 492030, Granollers 2179)*. ***Residencial Valle Nuevo*** *(☎ 492087, 25 de Mayo 2329)* charges US$26/36. Clean, comfy ***Hotel Amancay*** *(☎ 492222, Av San Martín 3217)* costs US$30/50 with private bath.

Places to Stay – Top End

At least until the autobahn from Bariloche brings the crowds, three-star ***Hotel Cordillera*** *(☎ 492235, Av San Martín 3210)* remains top of the line at US$51/64.

Places to Eat

El Bolsón's restaurants lack Bariloche's variety, but the food is a consistently good value and often outstanding, thanks largely to fresh, local ingredients and careful preparation. The best, most economical place to eat is at the ***Feria Artesanal***, held at the south end of Plaza Pagano from 10:30 am to 3 pm, Tuesday, Thursday, and Saturday. The goodies here range from fresh fruit to Belgian waffles (with raspberries and cream), very cheap empanadas and sandwiches, frittatas, milanesa de soja (vegetarian milanesa), regional desserts, and many other goodies. You'll be tempted to sample everything.

Calabaza *(☎ 492480, San Martín 2524)* has superb breakfasts for as little as US$2.50. ***La Esquina*** *(☎ 492136, San Martín 2537)* is a first-class confitería, while ***La Tosca***, behind the tourist office at Roca and

Moreno, has above-average offerings. ***Cerro Lindo*** *(☎ 492899, San Martín 2524)* has large, tasty pizzas, good music, and excellent, friendly service.

La Cocinita *(Sarmiento 2530)*, at Sarmiento and Castelli, is an inexpensive but indifferent parrilla, but ***Las Brasas*** *(☎ 492923)* at Sarmiento and Hube is a superb choice for beef, with excellent service. ***Arcimboldo*** *(☎ 492137)*, on San Martín between Roca and Feliciano, has very cheap pasta. For spicy northern empanadas, try ***La Salteñita*** *(25 de Mayo 2367)*. ***Verde Menta*** *(San Martín 2137)* is a health-food store.

For a splurge, ***Jauja*** *(☎ 492448, San Martín 2867)* remains one of Argentina's best values. Though it's not cheap, ingredients are first-rate, the preparation is excellent, the decor (including imaginative flower arrangements) appealing, the music good but not overbearing, and the service agreeable. Its very extensive menu includes pasta with tasty sauces, milanesa de soja, pizza, fish, vegetarian plates, homemade bread, and locally brewed beer. Save room to gorge yourself on the astoundingly good homemade, fruit-flavored ice cream next door at ***Heladería Jauja***, which is one of Argentina's very best.

Shopping

For fresh fruit and homemade jams and preserves, visit the berry plantations at Cabaña Micó (☎ 492691), Isla Malvinas 2753. Heladería Jauja (see Places to Eat, above) also sells outstanding chocolates.

Besides the twice-weekly Feria Artesanal (see that entry earlier in this section), there are several other outlets for local arts and crafts. Centro Artesanal Cumey Antú, Av San Martín 2020, sells Mapuche clothing and weavings; hours are 9 am to 1 pm. Taller Artesanal Sukal, 2km outside town on the road to Cerro Piltriquitrón, sells dried flower arrangements and painted wood products, such as jewelry boxes.

Entertainment

The ***Nuevo Morena Café*** *(☎ 492725)*, at San Martín and Pablo Hube, showcases live blues.

Getting There & Away

Air LADE (☎ 492206), on San Martín between José Hernández and Azcona, flies Wednesday to Bariloche (US$20), San Martín de los Andes (US$21), Zapala (US$35), and Neuquén (US$43); and Thursday to El Maitén (US$20), Esquel (US$20), and Comodoro Rivadavia (US$53). All flights leave from the Aero Club El Bolsón, at the north end of Av San Martín.

Bus El Bolsón has no central bus terminal, but most companies are on or near Av San Martín.

Andesmar (☎ 492178), at Belgrano and Perito Moreno, goes to Bariloche and points north, usually with a change in Neuquén, and to Esquel. Charter SRL (☎ 492333), at the corner of Sarmiento and Roca, also goes to Bariloche.

Bolsón Tour (☎ 492161), Roca 359, is the agent for Vía Bariloche, which goes to Esquel, Bariloche, and Buenos Aires. Transportes Esquel, at the same address, goes Tuesday and Friday at 8:30 am to Esquel. Grado 42 (☎ 493124), Belgrano 406, is the agent for TAC, which goes to Bariloche and combines in Neuquén for Mendoza, Córdoba, and other northern destinations.

Don Otto (☎ 493910), at the corner of Belgrano and Güemes, goes to Bariloche and Comodoro Rivadavia, with connections in Esquel for Trelew and Puerto Madryn.

Transportes Perito Moreno (☎ 492307), Sarmiento 2786, Local 1, goes to El Maitén, Bariloche, Los Alerces, and local destinations.

The most common destinations are Bariloche (US$10, two hours) and Esquel (US$16, three hours); to other destinations, southbound fares are slightly lower than those from Bariloche, northbound fares slightly higher.

Getting Around

Bus La Golondrina (☎ 492557) goes to Mallín Ahogado, leaving from the south end of Plaza Pagano, while buses to Río Azul depart Bolsón Tour (☎ 492161), at Roca 359.

Quimey Quipán (☎ 499172), Perito Moreno 2960, sends buses to Lago Puelo (30 minutes, US$2) and back at 7 and 9:30 am, and at 12:15, 3:30, 6, and 9 pm. The buses depart from the corner of San Martín and Sarmiento.

Taxi Some of Bolsón's taxi drivers have a reputation for avarice, but try Radio Taxi Glaciar (☎ 492892); their driver Diógenes has been recommended for local knowledge and reasonable prices.

Bicycle Rental bikes are available at La Rueda (☎ 492465), Sarmiento 2972.

AROUND EL BOLSÓN

Cabeza del Indio

On a ridge top 8km west of town, this metamorphic rock formation truly resembles a stereotypical profile of the 'noble savage.' Part of the trail traverses a narrow ledge that offers the best views of the formation itself, but by climbing from an earlier junction you can obtain better views of the Río Azul and, in the distance to the south, Parque Nacional Lago Puelo.

Cascada Mallín Ahogado

This waterfall on the Arroyo del Medio, a tributary of the Río Quemquemtreu, is 10km north of town, west of RN 258. Beyond the falls, a gravel road to the Club Andino Piltriquitrón's ***Refugio Perito Moreno*** *(☎ 493912)* offers lodging for US$5 to US$10 per night, with a capacity of 80 persons. Meals are an additional US$8.

From the refugio, it's 2½ hours to the 2206m summit of **Cerro Perito Moreno**. In winter months, there's skiing at the Centro de Deportes Invernales Perito Moreno, where the base elevation is 1000m. The T-bar lifts reach 1450m.

Cascada Escondida

Downstream from Cascada Mallín Ahogado, this waterfall is 8km from El Bolsón. There is a footpath beyond the bridge across the river at the west end of Av Pueyrredón.

Cerro Piltriquitrón

Dominating the landscape east of Bolsón, the 2260m summit of this granitic ridge yields panoramic views westward across the valley of the Río Azul to the Andean crest along the Chilean border. After driving or walking to the 1000m level (the 11km road costs about US$15 by taxi), another hour's steep, dusty walk leads to the Club Andino's ***Refugio Piltriquitrón*** *(☎ 492024)*, where beds cost US$6 per person – an outstanding value. Moderately priced meals are available, but bring your own sleeping bag.

Water is abundant along most of the summit route, but hikers should carry a canteen and bring lunch to enjoy at the top. From the refugio a steep footpath climbs along the rusted tow bar, then levels off and circles east around the peak before climbing again precipitously up loose scree to the summit, marked by a brightly painted cement block. On a clear day, the tiring two-hour climb (conspicuously marked by paint blazes) rewards the hiker with views south beyond Lago Puelo, northwest to landmark Cerro Tronador, and, beyond the border, the snow-topped cone of Volcán Osorno in Chile's Parque Nacional Vicente Pérez Rosales.

Cerro Lindo

Southwest of Bolsón, a trail from Camping Río Azul goes to ***Refugio Cerro Lindo*** *(☎ 492763)*, where you can get a bed for US$10; meals are extra. It's about four hours to the refugio, from which the trail continues to the 2150m summit.

El Hoyo

Just across the provincial border in Chubut, this town's microclimate makes it the local 'fresh fruit capital.' Nearby Lago Epuyén has good camping and hiking.

Parque Nacional Lago Puelo

In Chubut province, only 15km south of El Bolsón, this windy, azure natural lake is suitable for swimming, fishing, boating, hiking, and camping. There are regular buses from El Bolsón, but reduced service on Sunday, when you may have to hitch.

There are both free and fee campsites at the park entrance; Camping Lago Puelo (☎ 499186) charges US$5 per person, including tent and vehicle.

With all the hubris of military bureaucracy, the Argentine navy maintains a mobile prefecture in a trailer close to the dock, where the launches *Juana de Arco* (☎ 493415) and *Popeye 2000* take passengers across the lake to Argentina's Pacific Ocean outlet at the Chilean border (US$18 per person). From there it's possible to continue by foot or horseback to the Chilean town of Puelo on the Seno de Reloncaví, with connections to Puerto Montt. This is roughly a three-day walk; for details on guided trips, contact Grado 42 in El Bolsón.

For US$30, the launches also take passengers to El Turbio, at the south end of the lake, where there's a ***campground***.

NEUQUÉN

Established as the capital of its namesake province for its strategic location along the railroad at the junction of two major rivers, Neuquén is the gateway to the Andean lake district, and has good connections to Bariloche and Chile. A clean, modern city, it's also Patagonia's main financial center and the service locus for the agricultural towns of the Río Negro valley. Like many Patagonian towns, Neuquén is trying to make the most of its handful of historic buildings, most notably the railroad station and its remainders, and it's worth a day's stopover for the good restaurants and attractive parks.

Orientation

At the confluence of the Río Limay and the Río Neuquén, 265m above sea level, Neuquén (population 235,000) is the province's easternmost city. Paved highways go east to the Río Negro valley, west toward Zapala, and southwest toward Bariloche and the lake district.

Also known as Félix San Martín, east-west RN 22 is the main thoroughfare, a few blocks south of downtown (do not confuse Av San Martín, the obligatory homage to Argentina's national icon, with Félix San Martín). The principal north-south route is Av Argentina (Av Olascoaga south of the train station). Street names change on each side of Av Argentina and the old train station; most of the old railyard now constitutes the Parque Central. Several diagonals bisect the conventional grid.

Information

Tourist Offices The Dirección Provincial de Turismo (☎ 424089) is at Félix San Martín 182. It's open weekdays 7 am to 9 pm, weekends 8 am to 8 pm. Neuquén province generally provides free, up-to-date maps and brochures that contain truly useful material rather than glossy photos.

The municipal Dirección de Turismo maintains a kiosk on the median strip of Av Argentina between Rodríguez and Alberdi.

ACA (☎ 422325) is on the diagonal 25 de Mayo at Rivadavia.

Immigration Migraciones (☎ 422061) is at Santiago del Estero 466.

Money Neuquén has two cambios: Cambio Olano at the corner of JB Justo and Yrigoyen, and Cambio Pullman at Ministro Alcorta 144. Several banks along Av Argentina have ATMs.

Post & Communications Correo Argentino is at Rivadavia and Santa Fe; the postal code is 8300. There are many downtown locutorios, including one on Mitre across from the bus terminal.

Neuquén's area code is ☎ 0299.

Travel Agencies Neuquén's dozens of travel agencies are almost all near downtown. The AmEx representative is Zanellato (☎ 423741, fax 433337), Av Independencia 366.

Laundry Try Lavisec, on Roca between Brown and Yrigoyen.

Medical Services Neuquén is known throughout Argentina for quality medical services that, in some circumstances, are free. Do not hesitate to consult the Hospital Regional (☎ 431474), Buenos Aires 421.

Things to See

The **Sala de Arte Emilio Saraco** (☎ 481630), in the old cargo terminal at the railroad station, has current art exhibits and is well

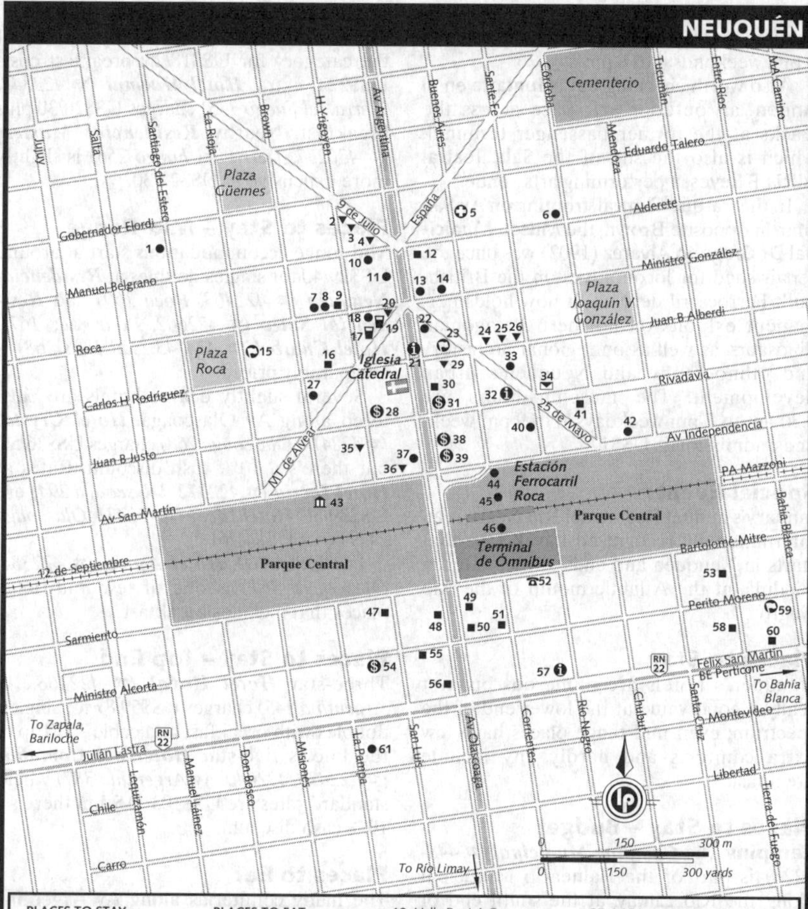

PLACES TO STAY
- 9 Residencial Neuquén
- 12 Hotel del Comahue
- 16 Residencial Suizo
- 30 Hotel Royal
- 41 Residencial Belgrano
- 47 Hotel Charbel
- 48 Hotel Ideal
- 49 Hotel Crystal
- 50 Hotel Iberia
- 51 Residencial Continental
- 53 Residencial Musters
- 55 Residencial Alcorta
- 58 Hotel Huemul
- 56 Hotel Apolo
- 60 Residencial Inglés

PLACES TO EAT
- 2 Chin Hwa
- 3 Fatto dalla Mamma
- 4 Franz y Peppone
- 20 Heladería Pire
- 24 La Rural
- 25 El Plato
- 26 La Fusta
- 29 La Tejuela
- 35 Pop Hot's Pizza
- 36 El Sótano

OTHER
- 1 Migraciones
- 5 Hospital Regional
- 6 AI
- 7 Artesanías Neuquinas
- 8 Lavisec
- 10 Valle Rent A Car
- 11 Municipalidad
- 13 Kaikén Líneas Aéreas, Southern Winds
- 14 Cine Quimey
- 15 Chilean Consulate
- 17 La Casona
- 18 Artesanías Mapuches
- 19 Tobago Bar
- 21 Dirección de Turismo (Kiosk)
- 22 Cine Teatro Español
- 23 Spanish Consulate
- 27 LADE
- 28 Cambio Olano
- 31 Banca Nazionale del Lavoro
- 32 ACA
- 33 TAN
- 34 Post Office
- 37 LAPA
- 38 Banco de La Pampa
- 39 Banco Provincia
- 40 Austral
- 42 Zanellato (AmEx)
- 43 Museo Municipal Dr Gregorio Álvarez
- 44 Paseo de los Artesanos
- 45 Juntarte en el Andén, Sala Teatral Alicia F Reyes
- 46 Sala de Arte Emilio Saraco
- 52 Locutorio
- 54 Cambio Pullman
- 57 Dirección Provincial de Turismo
- 59 Italian Consulate
- 61 Localiza

worth a look if you're waiting for a bus connection. It's free, and open weekdays 9 am to 8 pm, weekends 4 to 8 pm.

Also worth checking out is **Juntarte en el Andén**, an outdoor art space across the tracks at the former passenger terminal, which is also the site of the **Sala Teatral Alicia F Reyes**, a performing arts venue.

In the Parque Central, fronting on Av San Martín opposite Brown, the **Museo Municipal Dr Gregorio Álvarez** (1902) was once the repair shed for locomotives on the British-built Ferrocarril del Sud. It now holds permanent exhibits on northern Patagonian dinosaurs, as well as on regional prehistory and ethnography and Neuquén's urban development. The museum hours are 8:30 am to 7 pm weekdays, 6 to 9 pm weekends; admission is US$1.

Special Events

January's annual Regata del Río Negro is an internationally recognized kayak race that starts in Neuquén and ends a week later in Viedma, at the Atlantic mouth of the Río Negro.

Places to Stay

Neuquén's hotels are numerous but not really a good value at the lower end of the spectrum; even mid-range places have few extra comforts and hardly any include breakfast.

Places to Stay – Budget

Camping The ***Camping Municipal*** *(☎ 448-5228)* is part of the Balneario Municipal along the Río Limay, at the south end of town; take bus No 103 from downtown to Obreros Argentinos and Copahue. Rates are US$4 per tent, plus US$1 per person. It closes for camping after April 1.

Residenciales & Hotels Basic ***Residencial Continental*** *(☎ 423757, Perito Moreno 90)*, close to the bus terminal, has singles/doubles with private bath for US$15/20. ***Residencial Inglés*** *(☎ 422252, Félix San Martín 534)* costs US$15/25, about the same as the inviting ***Residencial Belgrano*** *(☎ 424311, Rivadavia 283)*.

The ***Residencial Alcorta*** *(☎ 422652, Ministro Alcorta 84)* is probably the pick of the category for US$18/25; breakfast costs US$2.50 extra. ***Hotel Huemul*** *(☎ 422344, Tierra del Fuego 335)* charges US$20/30 plus breakfast. Nearby ***Residencial Musters*** *(☎ 430237, Tierra del Fuego 255)* is slightly more expensive at US$22/30.

Places to Stay – Mid-Range

Mid-range accommodations start at around US$29/40 for singles/doubles at ***Residencial Neuquén*** *(☎ 422403, Roca 109)* and ***Residencial Suizo*** *(☎ 422602, Rodríguez 167)*. ***Hotel Charbel*** *(☎ 424143, San Luis 268)* is comparably priced.

Several slightly dearer hotels are clustered along Av Olascoaga. ***Hotel Crystal*** *(☎ 422414, Olascoaga 268)* charges US$36/56, but there's a 10% cash discount. Rates at ***Hotel Iberia*** *(☎ 422372, Olascoaga 294)* are US$39/56. ***Hotel Ideal*** *(☎ 422431, Olascoaga 243)* costs US$41/61.

For US$45/69, ***Hotel Apolo*** *(☎ 422334, Olascoaga 361)* is one of few mid-range places that includes breakfast.

Places to Stay – Top End

Three-star ***Hotel Royal*** *(☎ 422408, Av Argentina 145)* charges US$59/87 for singles/doubles with breakfast and cable TV. Top of the line is five-star ***Hotel del Comahue*** *(☎ 422439, 422440, Av Argentina 387)* where standard rates are US$103/115, but there's a 10% cash discount.

Places to Eat

The many confiterías along Av Argentina are all pleasant spots for breakfast and morning coffee. ***El Plato*** *(☎ 480359, Alberdi 158)* has a good reputation for its US$5 lunch specials. Nearby ***La Fusta***, Alberdi 176, has home-style Argentine cooking. ***Chin Hwa***, 9 de Julio 70, is a Chinese tenedor libre.

Franz y Peppone, at 9 de Julio and Belgrano, is a good but unusual combination of Italian and German cuisine. ***Fatto dalla Mamma*** *(☎ 425291, 9 de Julio 56)* has attractive decor in addition to outstanding pasta, but prices, especially for desserts, are on the high side. ***Pop Hot's Pizza*** *(☎ 488888, Yrigoyen 90)* has good music and ambience.

La Tejuela *(☎ 435435, Alberdi 59)* has a varied, reasonable meat and seafood menu. ***La Rural*** *(☎ 424297, Alberdi 126)* is a parrilla that deserves special mention for its surprisingly diverse menu at mid-range prices, cheap daily specials, pleasant environment, and attentive service. For parrillada, there's also ***El Sótano*** *(☎ 431112, Av San Martín 41)*.

Heladería Pire *(Diagonal Alvear 29)* has respectable ice cream.

Entertainment

The ***Cine Teatro Español*** *(☎ 422048, Av Argentina 271)* shows current films, as does the two-screener ***Cine Quimey*** *(Ministro González 30)*.

For barhoppers, there's occasionally live music at ***La Casona*** *(Alvear 59)* and the nearby ***Tobago Bar***, also on Alvear but closer to Yrigoyen.

Shopping

Neuquén offers a good selection of regional handicrafts – the biggest choice is at the Parque Central's Paseo de los Artesanos, on Av Independencia near Buenos Aires, north of the old train station. It's open Wednesday to Sunday, 10 am to 9 pm.

Good crafts shops include the provincially sponsored Artesanías Neuquinas (☎ 423806), Roca 155, and Artesanías Mapuches (☎ 432155), Roca 62.

Getting There & Away

Air Austral (☎ 422409), Santa Fe 52, flies to Buenos Aires' Aeroparque (US$57 to US$196) three times each weekday and twice Saturday and Sunday.

LAPA (☎ 438555), Av Argentina 30, flies weekdays to Bariloche (US$41 to US$76) and three times each weekday, twice Saturday and once Sunday to Aeroparque (US$59 to US$149).

Neuquén-based TAN (☎ 423076), 25 de Mayo 180, has extensive regional schedules and the only international flights. It flies at least daily to Comodoro Rivadavia (US$95 to US$115) and Bariloche (US$47 to US$85); five times weekly to San Martín de los Andes (US$40 to US$60) and Puerto Montt, Chile (US$80 to US$105); Tuesday, Wednesday, Friday (twice), and Saturday to Bahía Blanca (US$39 to US$63); Tuesday and Wednesday to Trelew (US$59 to US$70); and at least twice daily to Mendoza (US$85 to US$100), with daily connections to Córdoba (an additional US$69 to US$110). Three of the flights to Córdoba pass through San Juan (US$80 to US$90).

LADE (☎ 431153), Brown 163, flies Monday and Friday to Viedma (US$40); Wednesday and Friday to Mar del Plata (US$76) and Aeroparque (US$82 to US$107); Wednesday, Thursday, and Friday to Bariloche (US$36 to US$47); Thursday to Zapala (US$20), El Bolsón (US$43), El Maitén (US$43), Esquel (US$51), Comodoro Rivadavia (US$76 to US$120), and San Martín de los Andes (US$28); and Friday to Bahía Blanca (US$41).

Patagonian carrier Kaikén Líneas Aéreas (☎ 471333), Av Argentina 327, flies daily except Sunday to Bariloche (US$56), Comodoro Rivadavia (US$114 to US$160), Río Gallegos (US$175 to US$240), Río Grande (US$210 to US$295), Ushuaia (US$225 to US$315), and to Mendoza (US$96 to US$100). Southern Winds (☎ 487248), at the same address, flies daily to Córdoba (US$89 to US$119), Rosario (US$127 to US$169), Mendoza (US$104 to US$139), Tucumán (US$127 to US$169), and Salta (US$142 to US$189), and Wednesday to Bariloche.

Bus Neuquén's Terminal de Ómnibus (☎ 424903), on the south side of Parque Central at Bartolomé Mitre 147, is a major hub for provincial, national, and international bus services.

International Narbus (☎ 423661) and Igi Llaima (☎ 423661) alternate service to Temuco, Chile (US$45, 13 to 14 hours) via Zapala and the Pino Hachado pass, nightly except Wednesday at midnight. Igi Llaima/El Petróleo (☎ 423661) combine service to Temuco (US$45, 15 hours) over Paso Tromen via Junín de los Andes nightly at 11 pm.

Andesmar (☎ 422216) goes Tuesday, Thursday, and Saturday to Osorno and

Puerto Montt via Paso Cardenal Samoré (US$45, 14 hours).

Provincial & Long-Distance El Petróleo (☎ 484601) is the main provincial carrier, with frequent services to Zapala, Junín de los Andes and San Martín de los Andes. El Valle (☎ 425168) runs the same routes, as well as some to Bariloche, Bahía Blanca, Mar del Plata, and Buenos Aires. Mercedes (☎ 423661) and Vía Bariloche/La Puntual (☎ 427054) also serve Bariloche; Mercedes also goes to Mar del Plata. Vía Bariloche goes to Viedma and Bahía Blanca, while Tirsa (☎ 436327) goes to Rosario. Centenario (☎ 488778) has another three daily buses to Junín and San Martín de los Andes.

Empresa Pehuenche (☎ 421951) goes to Buenos Aires via Santa Rosa, La Pampa. La Estrella/Chevallier (☎ 423616) also serve the federal capital; both also go to Córdoba. Albus (☎ 473745) goes nightly to Buenos Aires, twice daily to San Martín de los Andes, and three times to Villa La Angostura. Transportes EC (☎ 420076) goes daily to Villa La Angostura and intermediate points.

TUS/TUP (☎ 420270) go daily to Córdoba and also to San Martín de los Andes and Bariloche. Alto Valle (☎ 434510) has service to Mendoza, as does TAC (☎ 431224), which goes four times daily to Buenos Aires, twice to Córdoba and to La Plata; Alto Valle also goes to Esquel and Paraná. Empresa del Sur y Media Agua (☎ 488778) goes to San Rafael, Mendoza, and San Juan.

Andesmar has the most extensive nationwide routes. Northbound, via Mendoza, it connects Neuquén with San Juan, La Rioja, Catamarca, Tucumán, Salta, and Jujuy. Southbound, it goes to Bariloche, El Bolsón and Esquel, and to the Patagonian coastal destinations of Puerto Madryn, Trelew, Comodoro Rivadavia, and Río Gallegos. Don Otto also goes to the deep south.

Sample fares include Zapala (US$9, three hours), Aluminé (US$20, six hours), Bariloche (US$15 to US$25, five hours), Junín de los Andes (US$22, seven hours), San Martín de los Andes (US$24, eight hours), Santa Rosa (US$25), Villa La Angostura (US$28, seven hours), Bahía Blanca (US$30, eight hours), Puerto Madryn (US$39, 10 hours), Trelew (US$42, 11 hours), El Bolsón (US$42, 10 hours), Mendoza (US$45, 12 hours), Esquel (US$51, 12 hours), Buenos Aires (US$45 to US$55, 16 hours), La Rioja (US$63), Comodoro Rivadavia (US$65, 15 hours), Catamarca (US$69), Córdoba (US$43 to US$72, 16½ hours), Rosario (US$75, 14 hours), Tucumán (US$80), Salta (US$95), Jujuy (US$96), and Río Gallegos (US$111, 28 hours).

Getting Around

To/From the Airport Turismo Lanín connects the main bus terminal with Aeropuerto Internacional Neuquén (☎ 431444), west of town on RN 22, which has extensive domestic services and international services to Chile only.

Car Neuquén is a good province to explore by automobile, but foreigners should be aware that RN 22, both east along the Río Negro valley and west toward Zapala, is a rough road with heavy truck traffic and some of Argentina's most dangerous drivers.

Local rental agencies include AI (☎ 422288) at Alderete 270; Avis (☎ 430216) at Lastra 1196; Localiza (☎ 420875) at La Pampa 462; and Valle Rent A Car (☎ 470186) at Belgrano 14.

ZAPALA

Windy, dusty, and economically depressed Zapala, once the end of the line for the northern branch of the Ferrocarril Roca, is an ordinary desert mining town, but there are several worthwhile destinations nearby. Locals dream that the rejuvenation and projected extension of the railroad to Las Lajas and to Lonquimay, across the Andes in Chile, will return prosperity to the area.

Orientation

Zapala (population 32,000) is a junction for several important highways, including RN 22 east to Neuquén and north to Las Lajas, RN 40 southwest to Junín de los Andes and San Martín de los Andes and north to Chos Malal, and RP 13 west to Primeros Pinos.

The main street is Av San Martín, which is an exit off the roundabout junction of RN 22 and RN 40.

Information

Tourist Offices The helpful Dirección Municipal de Turismo, a kiosk on the grassy median of Av San Martín at Almirante Brown, is open in summer 7 am to 8 pm weekdays, 8 am to noon and 4 to 7 pm weekends; the rest of the year it is open weekdays 8 am to 8 pm.

For information on Parque Nacional Laguna Blanca, visit the Parques Nacionales office at Ceballos 446.

Money There's no cambio but Banco de la Provincia del Neuquén, Cháneton 460, has an ATM.

Post & Communications Correo Argentino is at Av San Martín and Cháneton; the postal code is 8340. There's a Telecenter at Etcheluz 537; Zapala's area code is ☎ 02942.

Medical Services The Hospital Regional (☎ 421256) is at Luis Monti 155.

Museo Olsacher

In spacious new quarters near the bus terminal, this agreeably surprising mineralogical museum contains more than 3500 exhibits, including numerous fossils, from 80 different countries. At the corner of Etcheluz and Ejército Argentino, it's open weekdays 7 am to 2 pm and 6 to 9 pm; weekends 5 to 9 pm; admission is free.

Places to Stay & Eat

Zapala's limited but decent accommodations are fairly costly except for the free ***Camping Municipal***, on Calle Sapag south of the railroad tracks, which has hot showers but funky toilets.

Residencial Coliqueo *(☎ 421308, Etcheluz 165)* costs US$21/31. ***Residencial Huincúl*** *(☎ 421300, Av Roca 311)* charges US$23/37 single/double, as does strongly recommended ***Pehuén Hotel*** *(☎ 423135)*, at Etcheluz and Vidal, near the bus terminal.

The best in town, charging US$40/64, is three-star ***Hotel Hue Melén*** *(☎ 422391, Almirante Brown 929)*.

Residencial Huincul and ***Hotel Hue Melén*** both have restaurants. Try ***El Chancho Rengo*** *(☎ 422795)*, a confitería at Av San Martín and Etcheluz, for a light lunch, or ***La Zingarella*** *(☎ 422218)*, at the junction of RN 22 and Av San Martín, for a full meal.

Shopping

The Escuela de Cerámica (Ceramics School), Luis Monti 240, sells pottery made from local materials by students. Artesanías Neuquinas, at Av San Martín and Cháneton, sells regional crafts.

Getting There & Away

Air LADE (☎ 430134), Uriburu 397, flies Wednesday to Neuquén (US$20) and Thursday to Bariloche (US$26), El Bolsón (US$35), El Maitén (US$35), Esquel (US$44), and Comodoro Rivadavia (US$78).

Cabs to Aeropuerto Zapala (☎ 421879), southwest of town at the junction of RN 40 and RP 46, cost about US$5.

Bus The Terminal de Ómnibus (☎ 421370) is at Etcheluz and Uriburu. Westbound buses from Neuquén en route to Junín de los Andes, San Martín de los Andes and Temuco, Chile, pass through Zapala. Monday, Thursday, and Sunday at 3 am, Ruta Sur crosses the Andes to Temuco (US$35).

The only direct service to Buenos Aires (US$49) is El Petróleo's Sunday bus; all others require changing at Neuquén, including Chevallier. El Petróleo also has two buses daily to San Martín de los Andes and daily service to the resort of Copahue, on the Chilean border. El Valle (☎ 431286) also goes Buenos Aires, while Centenario goes to Buenos Aires and to ski areas at Copahue.

Ticsa serves San Juan and San Luis three times weekly, while TAC connects Mendoza (US$45) and Bariloche (US$20) via Zapala, also three times weekly in each direction.

Albus goes to Laguna Blanca (US$5) and Aluminé (US$10) Monday, Wednesday, and Friday at 9:20 pm, while Aluminé Viajes goes to Laguna Blanca (US$3.50) and Aluminé (US$11) at 7:30 pm.

The cisne de cuello negro (black-necked swan) stays year-round at Laguna Blanca.

AROUND ZAPALA

Parque Nacional Laguna Blanca

Only 30km southwest of Zapala, at 1275m above sea level and surrounded by striking volcanic deserts, Laguna Blanca is only 10m deep, an interior drainage lake that formed when lava flows dammed two small streams. Too alkaline for fish, it nonetheless hosts many bird species, including coots, ducks, grebes, upland geese, gulls, and even a few flamingos, but the 11,250-hectare park primarily protects habitat of the black-necked swan *Cygnus melancoryphus*, a permanent resident. Its breeding colonies, on a peninsula in the lake, have been fenced off to prevent disturbance by livestock.

Ten km south of Zapala, paved and well-marked RP 46 leads directly through the park toward the Andean town of Aluminé; for transport details, see Zapala. If these schedules do not serve you, a cab or remise is not unreasonable, and there's sufficient traffic to make hitching feasible.

There's a small improved campground with windbreaks, but bring all your own food – despite the unexpected rehabilitation of the once abandoned visitor center, there's still no place to eat.

Primeros Pinos

This ski resort near Las Lajas, 55km northwest of Zapala via RP 21, has a 700m vertical drop. For information, contact Parque Primeros Pinos (☎ 02942-421163) in Zapala.

Plaza Huincul

About an hour east of Zapala, not quite halfway to Neuquén on RP 22, Plaza Huincul is one of Argentina's major petroleum centers, but for visitors it's more significant for its **Museo Municipal Carlos Funes**, where there are partial remains of *Argentinosaurus huinculensis*, an herbivore 40m long and 18m high. While perhaps not worth a major detour in its own right, it certainly justifies a stop for travelers en route to or from Zapala and San Martín de los Andes.

The museum, open 8 am to 8 pm weekdays and 4 to 8 pm weekends, also features good historical materials on the local petroleum industry. There's a free municipal campground in nearby Cutral-Có. All buses between Neuquén and Zapala stop here.

ALUMINÉ

Aluminé, 103km north of Junín de los Andes via RP 23, offers access to the northern sector of Parque Nacional Lanín; the Río Aluminé, paralleling the highway for most of its length, is one of the country's most highly regarded trout streams.

For information, consult the Dirección de Turismo (☎ 02942-496154) or its Centro de Informes at RP 23 and San Juan Bosco. In early April, Aluminé (population 2500) celebrates the Fiesta del Pehuén in honor of the unique trees that cover the slopes of the Andes. Several nearby Mapuche reservations sell traditional weavings. For bus services, see Zapala.

JUNÍN DE LOS ANDES

Founded in 1883 as an army outpost during the Conquista del Desierto, this modest livestock center on the Río Chimehuín calls itself the 'trout capital' of Neuquén province. Less attractive but also less expensive than fashionable San Martín de los Andes, Junín (population 8800) can be a better base for exploring Parque Nacional Lanín, and also has a handful of interesting festivals and celebrations.

Orientation

Junín de los Andes is just south of the confluence of the Río Curruhue and the larger Río Chimehuín, which forms the city's eastern limit. Paved RN 234 (known as Blvd Juan Manuel de Rosas in town) is the main thoroughfare, leading 41km south to San

Martín de los Andes and 116km northwest to Zapala via RN 40. North of town, graveled RP 23 heads to the fishing resort of Aluminé, while several secondary roads branch westward to Parque Nacional Lanín.

The city center is between the highway and the river. Do not confuse Av San Martín, which runs on the west side of Plaza San Martín, with Félix San Martín, two blocks farther west.

Information

Tourist Offices The enthusiastically helpful Secretaría Municipal de Turismo (☎ 491160) is at Padre Milanesio 596, corner of Coronel Suárez, on Plaza San Martín. Hours are 8 am to 10 pm daily. Fishing permits are also available here.

In an adjacent office, fronting on Coronel Suárez, Parques Nacionales is open weekdays from 9 am to 8:30 pm and weekends 2:30 to 8:30 pm.

Money Banco de la Provincia de Neuquén is on Av San Martín, opposite the plaza, between Suárez and Lamadrid.

Post & Communications Correo Argentino is at Suárez and Don Bosco; the postal code is 8371. It's easiest to make local or long-distance calls from the locutorio on Padre Milanesio, opposite the plaza. Junín's area code is ☎ 02972.

Laundry Laverap Pehuén is at Ponte 340.

Medical Services The Hospital de Area (☎ 491162) is at Ponte and Padre Milanesio.

Things to See & Do

Junín's surroundings are more appealing than the town itself, but the Salesian-organized **Museo Mapuche** at Ginés Ponte 540 is worth a look. In addition to ethnographic and historical materials, it also

displays a selection of fossils and other natural history items. The **Museo Moisés Roca Jalil**, at the corner of Coronel Suárez and San Martín, is an offbeat private collection open Monday, Wednesday, and Friday 10 am to noon.

Nearby Parque Nacional Lanín (see later in this chapter) merits an extended visit for campers, hikers, climbers, and fishing enthusiasts. The Club Andino Junín de los Andes (☎ 491206), in the Paseo Artesanal at Padre Milanesio 568, can provide information on climbing Volcán Tromen and other excursions in the park, as can the Parques Nacionales office (see Information above).

Many North Americans and Europeans spend fishing holidays here; the Río Aluminé, north of Junín, is an especially choice area, but fishing is possible even within city limits. Catch-and-release is obligatory in many local streams. For detailed information and equipment, visit the Fly Shop (☎ 491548) at Illeras 378, across the highway. Neuquén fishing licenses cost US$100 for the season, US$60 monthly, or US$30 weekly; trolling licenses cost another US$60 for the season.

Special Events

Every year, Junín celebrates its own lively Carnaval del Pehuén with parades, costumes, live music, and the usual water balloons. No one will mistake it for Rio de Janeiro or Bahia, but if you're in the area it can be entertaining.

In January, the Feria y Exposición Ganadera displays the best of local livestock – cattle, horses, and sheep, along with poultry and rabbits. There are also exhibitions of horsemanship, and local crafts exhibits, but this is the estanciero's show – the peons and the people get their chance at mid-February's Festival del Puestero.

In early August, the Mapuche celebrate their crafts skills in the Semana de Artesanía Aborígen.

Places to Stay

Camping The municipal ***Camping La Isla*** *(☎ 491461)*, just three blocks east of the plaza on the banks of the Chimehuín, has the standard facilities for US$6 per person per day. Showers, available 8 to 10 am and 8 to 10 pm, cost US$1.

Residenciales, Hosterías & Hotels Junín's limited accommodations are modest in quality and generally no bargain. ***Residencial Marisa*** *(☎ 491175, Blvd Rosas 360)* charges US$20/30 single/double with private bath (breakfast extra), as do ***Posada Pehuén*** *(☎ 491569, Coronel Suárez 560)* and ***Hostería del Montañés*** *(☎ 491155, San Martín 555)*. ***Residencial El Cedro*** *(☎ 491182, Lamadrid 409)* costs US$22/40.

Overlooking the river at Coronel Suárez and 25 de Mayo, ***Hostería Chimehuín*** *(☎ 491132)* is an excellent value at US$23 per person with breakfast, US$40 with half-board, but there are also rooms with shared bath for US$15 per person. At ***Hotel Alejandro Primo*** *(☎ 491184)*, on busy Blvd Rosas at the northern outskirts of town, prices are US$30/50.

Places to Eat

Junín has fairly mediocre restaurants, though local specialties like trout, wild boar, or venison may be available. ***Ruca Hueney*** *(☎ 491113, Padre Milanesio 641)* has the most extensive menu, with entrées in the US$6 to US$12 range.

Roble Bar *(☎ 491124, Ponte 331)* is Junín's main pizzeria, offering baked empanadas and sandwiches as well. Just east of the plaza, ***Rotisería Tandil*** *(Coronel Suárez 431)* has excellent take-out empanadas.

Shopping

A wide selection of artisanal goods in various media, including wood, leather, wool, stone, and ceramics, is available at the Paseo Artesanal on Padre Milanesio, just north of the tourist office.

Getting There & Away

Air Aeropuerto Chapelco lies midway between Junín and San Martín de los Andes. For further information, see Getting There & Away for San Martín de los Andes later in this chapter.

Bus The Terminal de Ómnibus (☎ 491110) is at Olavarría and Félix San Martín. Centenario (☎ 491030) uses the Zapala route to Neuquén, as does El Petróleo (☎ 491713); both continue to Bahía Blanca and Buenos Aires (US$60, 22 hours). El Petróleo goes Tuesday to Aluminé (US$13, three hours) and to San Martín de los Andes, while Centenario goes three times daily to San Martín (US$3.50, one hour) except Sunday, when it goes twice.

Ko-Ko (☎ 491713) has service to Bariloche via both the paved Rinconada route and the dusty but also more scenic Siete Lagos alternative.

TAC (☎ 491861) heads north to Mendoza, as does Andesmar. TUS (☎ 491030) goes to Córdoba via Santa Rosa, La Pampa (US$80, 21 hours), Monday and Thursday, while Chevallier (☎ 491713) provides services to Buenos Aires (US$60, 22 hours).

Empresa San Martín (☎ 491030) links Junín with neighboring San Martín de los Andes and crosses the Andes to Temuco, Chile, via the Tromen pass. Other carriers serving Chile include Igi-Llaima and Buses JAC, at the same number.

SAN MARTÍN DE LOS ANDES

Thanks partly to a height limit on new construction, San Martín de los Andes retains some of the charm and architectural unity that once attracted people to Bariloche, but the burgeoning hotels and restaurants and the ominous, insidious time-shares are rapidly transforming it into a costly tourist trap. Founded as an army post in 1898, San Martín (population 20,600) grew so rapidly in recent years that an inadequate sewage system contaminated Lago Lácar's attractive beaches. A new treatment plant has made swimming safe again.

On nearly every corner in downtown San Martín, there's at least one attractive young woman trying to lure visitors into signing time-share contracts. Although they're less aggressive than their counterparts in, say, Cabo San Lucas, visitors might consider memorizing a phrase like 'Lo siento, pero el médico dice que me quedan sólo dos meses de vida' (I'm sorry, but the doctor says I have only two months to live).

Orientation

Nestled amid striking mountain scenery at the east end of Lago Lácar, 642m above sea level, San Martín straddles RN 234, which passes through town southbound to Villa La Angostura, on the north shore of Lago Nahuel Huapi. Northbound RN 234 heads to Zapala via Junín de los Andes.

Almost everything in San Martín de los Andes is within walking distance of the centro cívico, while the shady lakefront park and pier are a delightful place to spend the afternoon. Bounding the centro cívico plaza along with Av Roca, Mariano Moreno, and Capitán Drury, Av San Martín is the main commercial street, running from the lakefront north toward the highway to Junín.

Information

Tourist Offices In an airy, modern building at the centro cívico (Avs San Martín and Rosas), the well-organized Secretaría Municipal de Turismo (☎ 427347) provides surprisingly candid information. Open daily 8 am to 10 pm, it has details about hotels and restaurants, plus excellent brochures and maps, and also sells fishing licenses.

Money Weekdays try Banco de la Nación, Av San Martín 687, which has an ATM. The only official cambio is Andina Internacional at Capitán Drury 876.

Post & Communications Correo Argentino is at the centro cívico, Roca and Coronel Pérez; the postal code is 8370. The Cooperativa Telefónica is at Capitán Drury 761. San Martín's area code is ☎ 02972.

National Parks Open 7 am to 1 pm weekdays only, the Intendencia of Parque Nacional Lanín (☎ 427233) is at Emilio Frey 749, in the centro cívico. Limited maps and brochures are available here.

Travel Agencies Grupo 3 de Turismo (☎ 428453), San Martín 1141, Local 1, is the

SAN MARTÍN DE LOS ANDES

PLACES TO STAY
1 La Posta del Caminante
2 Hotel Crismalú
4 Residencial Laura
8 Club Cordillerano
9 Hotel Colonos del Sur
10 Hostería La Cheminee
11 Hotel Patagonia Plaza
19 Hostal del Esquiador
20 Residencial Italia
21 Residencial Villalago
22 Hostería del Chapelco
23 Residencial Los Pinos
24 Residencial Casa Alta
25 Hostería La Masía
26 Hostería Las Lengas
27 Hostería La Raclette
30 Hostería Las Lucarnas
49 Hostería Tisú
50 Hostería Anay
52 Hotel Rosa de los Viajes
56 Hostería Peumayén
57 Hotel Chapelco Ski
60 Hotel Caupolicán
68 Hostería Cumelén

PLACES TO EAT
6 Heladería Charlot
14 Rotisería Viviana
15 La Cabreada
18 Piscis
37 Abolengo
45 Heladería Andina
47 Café de la Plaza
48 Mendieta
51 Paprika
64 Trattoria Mi Viejo Pepe
65 Pura Vida
67 Las Catalinas

OTHER
3 Centro Cultural Amankay, Cine Amankay
5 Grego Tour (Airport Buses)
7 Grupo 3 de Turismo (AmEx)
12 La Colina
13 Hospital Rural Ramón Carrillo
16 Bumps
17 Ici Viajes
21 Fiocca
28 Casino
29 Post Office
31 Austral
32 Intendencia Parque Nacional Lanín
33 Museo Primeros Pobladores
34 Artesanías Neuquinas
35 Secretaría Municipal de Turismo
36 Cooperativa Telefónica
38 Fenoglio
39 TAN
40 Transportes Caleuche
41 Tiempo Patagónico, Mont Blanc, Cerro Torre
42 Al (By Mich)
43 Avis
44 Centro de Informes Cerro Chapelco
46 Banco de la Nación
53 Kosem Artesanías
54 Cambio Andina Internacional
55 Laverap
58 LADE
59 Pucará
61 Laverap
62 La Oveja Negra
63 HG Rodados
66 Claro Turismo

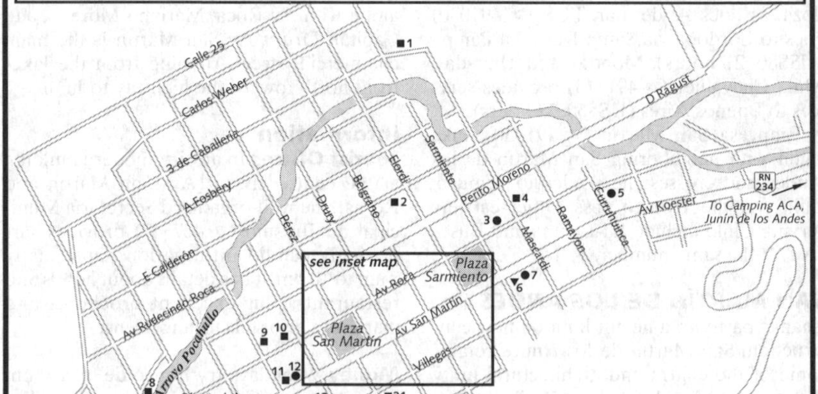

AmEx representative, but there are many other agencies along Av San Martín, Belgrano, and Elordi.

Cultural Centers The Centro Cultural Amankay (☎ 428399) is at Roca 1154; within it is the Cine Amankay (☎ 427274).

Laundry Laverap (☎ 428820) is at Capitán Drury 880 and Villegas 972.

Medical Services Hospital Rural Ramón Carrillo (☎ 427211) is at Coronel Rohde and Av San Martín.

Museo Primeros Pobladores

Regional archaeological and ethnographic items such as arrowheads, spear points, pottery, and musical instruments are the focus of this museum, next door to the tourist office. There are also mineral and fossil exhibits. It's open weekdays from 2 to 7 pm.

Activities

HG Rodados (☎ 427345), Av San Martín 1061 opposite Plaza Sarmiento, rents mountain bikes for about US$15 daily.

For rafting on the Río Hua Hum or Río Meliquina, contact Tiempo Patagónico (☎ 427113) at San Martín 950 (US$45 with transfers), Ici Viajes (☎ 427800) at Villegas 590, or El Claro Turismo (☎ 428876) at Villegas 977. A full day on the Class III Río Aluminé costs US$50 with Pucará (☎ 427862), Av San Martín 941.

Trekking and climbing are also important activities in Parque Nacional Lanín. Horacio Peloso, known by his nickname, 'El Oso,' is a highly regarded mountain guide who arranges trips and rents equipment for climbing Lanín. He can be found at Cerro Torre, San Martín 950, which is near Tiempo Patagónico.

Skiing at nearby Cerro Chapelco draws enthusiastic winter crowds (see Cerro Chapelco later in this chapter). In town, rental equipment is available at Bumps, Villegas 566; La Colina (☎ 427414), San Martín 532; Mont Blanc, San Martín 950; La Pista, San Martín 800; and Fiocca, Villegas 717.

Special Events

February 4 is Día de la Fundación, the anniversary of San Martín's founding, which is celebrated with speeches, parades, and other festivities; the city celebrated its centennial in 1998. The festival's parade itself is an entertainingly incongruous mix of military, firefighters, gauchos, polo players, and foxhunters.

Organized Tours

San Martín's several travel agencies offer tours to a number of outlying sights, among them Termas de Lahuén Co (US$30, full day); Siete Lagos and Villa La Angostura (US$30, full day); Lago Huechulafquen, Paimún, and Lanín (US$30, full day); and Cerro Chapelco (US$18, half-day).

Places to Stay

As a tourist center, San Martín is loaded with accommodations, but they're relatively costly in all categories except camping, especially in summer and during ski season. The quality, however, is generally high. Prices below reflect the high season, when single rates are often hard to find.

Places to Stay – Budget

Camping On the eastern outskirts of town *Camping ACA (☎ 427332, Av Koessler 2176)* is a spacious, attractive campground charging US$10 per site; even if it's very crowded, it's easy to find a quiet (though perhaps less aesthetically pleasing) site. Similar facilities, at comparable prices, are available at ***Playa Catritre*** *(☎ 426986)*, 4km south of San Martín in Parque Nacional Lanín, and ***El Molino*** *(☎ 426350)*, 5km north of town.

Hostels San Martín's ***La Posta del Caminante*** *(☎ 428672, 3 de Caballería 1164)* charges $10 per person but lacks kitchen facilities. The YPF's ***Club Cordillerano*** *(☎ 427431)*, on Juez del Valle just north of the arroyo, charges US$10 for shared rooms, US$15 per person for double rooms, with better facilities.

Residenciales Regular budget accommodations are few, starting around US$20 per person at ***Residencial Italia*** *(☎ 427590, Coronel Pérez 977)*, ***Residencial Laura*** *(☎ 427271, Mascardi 632)*, remodeled ***Residencial Villalago*** *(☎ 427454, Villegas 717)*, and nicely located ***Residencial Los Pinos*** *(☎ 427207, Almirante Brown 420)*, just outside the busy downtown.

Places to Stay – Mid-Range

Mid-range accommodations are more numerous and generally a reasonable value, though often without breakfast, from about US$30/50 single/double at ***Hostería Las Lucarnas*** *(☎ 427085, Coronel Pérez 632)*. The typical ***Hotel Colonos del Sur*** *(☎ 427224, Rivadavia 686)* charges US$33/50, which includes breakfast; they offer a 10% discount for cash.

Several places charge around US$35/50, including ***Hostería Tisú*** *(☎ 427231, Av San Martín 771)*, ***Hostería Cumelén*** *(☎ 427304, Elordi 931)*, and ***Rosa de los Viajes*** *(☎ 427484, Av San Martín 817)*.

Slightly dearer is ***Hostería Anay*** *(☎ 427514, Capitán Drury 841)* for US$37/55. Another step up are ***Hotel Crismalú*** *(☎ 427283, Rudecindo Roca 975)* for US$40/56; and ***Hostería Peumayén*** *(☎ 427232, Av San Martín 851)* for US$42/61.

Places to Stay – Top End

Top-end accommodations generally include breakfast and cable TV. ***Residencial Casa Alta*** *(☎ 427456, Obeid 659)*, a onetime budget choice, has long outgrown that category, charging US$50/65 single/double. ***Hostería La Raclette*** *(☎ 427664, Coronel Pérez 1170)* and ***Hotel Chapelco Ski*** *(☎ 427480, Belgrano 869)* both charge the same, while ***Hostería del Chapelco*** *(☎ 427610, Brown 297)* is slightly dearer at US$50/70. ***Hostería Las Lengas*** *(☎ 427659, Coronel Pérez 1175)* costs US$53/76.

Hotel Caupolicán *(☎ 427900, Av San Martín 969)* charges US$60/85, but offers a 10% cash discount. Rates at ***Hostería La Masía*** *(☎ 427688, Obeid 811)* are US$75/92.

San Martín's most luxurious accommodations are upscale places like five-star ***Hotel Sol de Los Andes***, on a hill overlooking the southern approach to town, at US$70/110. The ***Hostal del Esquiador*** *(☎ 427674, Coronel Rohde 975)* charges US$76/105. Tasteful ***Hostería La Cheminee***, downtown at Av Roca and Mariano Moreno, costs US$100 double, while the new luxury ***Hotel Patagonia Plaza*** *(☎/fax 422280)*, at San Martín and Rivadavia, goes for US$140/170.

Places to Eat

Though not inexpensive, the pleasant sidewalk ***Café de la Plaza*** *(☎ 428488)*, at Av San Martín and Coronel Pérez, is a decent breakfast choice. ***Rotisería Viviana*** *(☎ 428917, San Martín 489)* is an outstanding choice for take-out food, particularly the very cheap as well as superb baked empanadas.

For coffee, chocolate, and croissants, try ***Abolengo*** *(☎ 427732, Av San Martín 806)*.

San Martín has many parrillas, including traditional favorite ***Piscis*** *(☎ 427601, Villegas 598)*, which is mobbed in the evening. Long lines form outside ***Mendieta*** *(San Martín 713)*, a more upscale parrilla named for the dog of the famous cartoon gaucho, Inodoro ('Toilet') Pereyra. ***La Cabreada*** *(☎ 429376, Rivadavia 825)* is a popular parrilla.

Las Catalinas *(☎ 427203)*, at Villegas and Elordi, has a tenedor libre menu for US$6 to US$10. ***Pura Vida*** *(☎ 429302, Villegas 745)* has a small but good and mostly vegetarian menu, plus some chicken and fish items, and first-rate service.

Nearby, ***Trattoria Mi Viejo Pepe*** *(☎ 427415, Villegas 725)* is an expensive Italian restaurant; across the street, ***Paprika*** *(☎ 427056, Villegas 744)* serves pricey Central European food.

Heladería Andina, at Av San Martín and Mariano Moreno, serves good ice cream, as does ***Heladería Charlot*** *(San Martín 1017)*.

Shopping

Many local shops sell regional products and handicrafts. The Artesanías Neuquinas (☎ 428396), Rosas 790, offers local Indian weavings. La Oveja Negra (☎ 427248), Av San Martín 1045, and Kosem, Capitán Drury 846, also sell artisanal textiles. Chocolates are available at Fenoglio (☎ 427515), Av San Martín 836.

Getting There & Away

Air Austral (☎ 427003), Capitán Drury 876, flies daily except Wednesday to Buenos Aires' Aeroparque (US$159 to US$260); Monday, Tuesday, and Thursday flights go via Esquel (US$79).

LADE (☎ 427672), Av San Martín 915, flies Wednesday to Zapala (US$20) and Neuquén (US$28); Thursday to Bariloche (US$20); and Friday to Neuquén, Viedma (US$69), Bahía Blanca (US$78), Mar del Plata (US$95), and Aeroparque (US$102).

TAN (☎ 427872), Belgrano 760, flies Friday through Tuesday to Bariloche (US$30 to US$40) and Monday through Saturday to Neuquén (US$40 to US$60).

Bus The Terminal de Ómnibus (☎ 427044) is at Villegas and Juez del Valle. Regional carrier El Petróleo (☎ 427750) serves northern destinations (Aluminé, Junín de los Andes, Zapala), the Río Negro valley to the east, and has daily service to the Chilean border at Pirehueico (US$5.50). Aluminé buses leave Tuesday only, at 8 am.

Transportes Ko-Ko (☎ 427422) goes to Villa La Angostura and to Bariloche, sometimes by the scenic Siete Lagos route but usually by the longer but smoother Rinconada route. Albus (☎ 428799) also goes to Villa La Angostura, three times daily by the Siete Lagos route, twice to Bariloche, and once to Villa Traful. To Neuquén there is frequent service with Albus, El Petróleo, and Centenario (☎ 427294).

To Buenos Aires, there are daily services with Chevallier (☎ 427422), Vía Bariloche (☎ 427750), TAC (☎ 428874), Centenario, and Albus. TAC also goes to Mendoza nightly at 12:45 and 1 am, the latter with three hours layover in Cipoletti, and daily at 12:50 pm to Córdoba. TUS (☎ 491713) goes to Córdoba Monday and Thursday mornings.

Igi-Llaima (☎ 427750) goes Tuesday, Thursday, and Saturday at 6 am to Temuco, Chile (US$25), while Empresa San Martín (☎ 428508) goes Monday, Wednesday, and Friday at the same hour.

Sample fares include Junín de los Andes (US$3.50, one hour), Pirehueico (US$5.50, two hours), Villa Traful (US$13, 2½ hours), Villa La Angostura (US$13, three hours), Aluminé (US$13, four hours), Bariloche (US$19, 4½ hours), Neuquén (US$22, six hours), Temuco (US$25, eight hours), Buenos Aires (US$65 to US$75, 22 hours), Mendoza (US$67, 19½ hours), Córdoba (US$70, 21 hours).

Boat Plumas Verdes (☎ 428427, 427380) sails from the Muelle de Pasajeros (passenger pier) on the Av Costanera to Paso Hua Hum on the Chilean border daily at 10 am. The fare is US$30, plus a US$5 national park fee.

Getting Around

To/From the Airport Aeropuerto Chapelco (☎ 428398) is midway between San Martín and Junín, on RN 234. Transportes Caleuche (☎ 422115), Belgrano and San Martín, goes to Chapelco (US$6) Monday, Tuesday, Friday, and Saturday at 10 am, Sunday at 10:30 am. Grego Tour (☎ 428968), at Curruhuinca and Los Cipreses, also has airport buses.

To/From Parque Nacional Lanín Empresa Centenario goes twice daily to Lago Huechulafquen (US$9). Albus goes to Catritre (US$1.50) several times daily, while Transportes Ko-Ko runs four buses daily to Lago Lolog (US$2).

Car Agencies include AI (By Mich) (☎ 427997) at Av San Martín 960, Avis (☎ 427704) at Av San Martín 998, and El Claro (☎ 428876) at Villegas 977.

AROUND SAN MARTÍN DE LOS ANDES

Cerro Chapelco

Cerro Chapelco's Centro de Deportes Invernales (☎ 02972-427460) has a downtown Centro de Informes/Escuela de Ski at Av San Martín and Elordi. The site itself, 20km southeast of San Martín, is one of Argentina's principal winter sports centers, with runs for beginners and experts, at a maximum elevation of 1920m. Rental equipment is available on site as well as in town.

Depending on snow conditions, provincial skiing championships take place every

August. The first half of August also sees the Fiesta Nacional del Montañes, the annual ski festival.

Lift Tickets The season runs mid-June to mid-October; prices vary depending on when you go – peak, mid-, or low season. Season passes cost US$790 for adults, US$550 for children.

Half-day passes run from US$33 to US$18 for adults, US$26 to US$15 for children. Full-day passes range from US$37 to US$21 for adults and from US$30 to US$18 for children. A single lift ticket for adults/children is US$15/9. Three-day passes for adults are US$110 to US$61 and US$86 to US$52 for kids. Four-day passes are US$146 to US$81 for adults and US$114 to US$69 for kids. A weeklong pass for adults ranges from US$220 to US$126 and from US$178 to US$107 for children. For a 15-day pass expect to pay US$370 to US$210 for adults and US$296 to US$178 for children. Monthlong passes cost US$740 to US$420 for adults and US$533 to US$357 for children.

PARQUE NACIONAL LANÍN

Dominating the view in all directions along the Chilean border, the snowcapped cone of 3776m Volcán Lanín is the centerpiece of Parque Nacional Lanín, which extends 150km from Parque Nacional Nahuel Huapi in the south to Lago Ñorquinco in the north. Created in 1937 to protect 379,000 hectares of native Patagonian forest, tranquil Lanín has so far avoided the commercial blemishes of Nahuel Huapi and Bariloche.

Parque Lanín has many of the same species that characterize more southerly Patagonian forests, such as the southern beeches *lenga*, *ñire*, and *coihue*. More botanically unique to the area, though, are extensive stands of the broadleaf deciduous southern beech *raulí (Nothofagus nervosa)* and the curious pehuén or monkey puzzle tree *(Araucaria araucana)*, a pinelike conifer whose nuts have long been a dietary staple for the Pehuenches and Mapuches. Note that only Indians may gather piñon nuts from the pehuenes.

Besides the views of Volcán Lanín and these unusual forests, the park has recreational attractions in the numerous finger-shaped lakes carved by Pleistocene glaciers. Excellent campsites are abundant, though some of the less developed but more accessible places are unfortunately dirty and polluted.

Information

The Intendencia de Parques Nacionales in San Martín de los Andes produces brochures on camping, hiking, and climbing in various parts of the park that are widely distributed in the area's tourist offices. Scattered throughout the park proper are several ranger stations, but they usually lack printed materials.

Things to See & Do

From south to north, the towns of San Martín de los Andes, Junín de los Andes, and Aluminé are the best starting points for

WAYNE BERNHARDSON

The *pehuén* (araucaria or monkey puzzle tree)

exploring Lanín, its glacial lakes, and the backcountry. This section begins at San Martín and works northward.

Lago Lácar From San Martín, at the east end of the lake, there is a bus service on RP 48, which parallels the shoreline to the Chilean border at Paso Hua Hum. A boat excursion also goes from San Martín to Hua Hum, where there are numerous hiking trails, and free and organized ***campsites***.

Lago Lolog Fifteen km north of San Martín de los Andes, this largely undeveloped area has fishing, and good camping at ***Camping Puerto Arturo*** (US$2 per person) and ***Camping Lolog*** (US$3). Transportes Ko-Ko (☎ 427422) runs four buses daily (US$2) to Lago Lolog from San Martín.

Lago Huechulafquen The park's largest lake is also one of its most central and accessible areas, reached from San Martín and Junín de los Andes despite limited public transport. From a junction just north of Junín, RP 61 climbs west to Huechulafquen and the smaller Lago Paimún, along the way offering outstanding views of Volcán Lanín and access to trailheads of several excellent hikes. Source of the Río Chimehuín, Huechulafquen offers superb fishing at its outlet.

From the ranger station at Puerto Canoa, a good trail climbs to a viewpoint on Lanín's shoulder, where it's possible to hike across to Paso Tromen or continue climbing to either of two refugios. One belongs to the army's Regimiento de Infantería de Montaña (RIM) and the other to the Club Andino Junín de los Andes (CAJA), but either can be a staging point for attempting the summit (see Lago Tromen below for more detail, including permits and equipment). The initial segment follows an abandoned road, but after about 40 minutes it becomes a pleasant woodsy trail along the **Arroyo Rucu Leufu**, an attractive mountain stream; yellow paint blazes mark the route where it is not obvious. Be on the lookout for hares, lizards, and tarantulas. Halfway to the refugio is an extensive pehuén forest, the southernmost in the park, which makes

the walk worthwhile if you lack time for the entire route. The route to RIM's refugio, about 2450m above sea level, takes about seven hours one way, while the trail to CAJA's refugio takes a bit longer.

Another good backcountry hike circles **Lago Paimún**. This requires about two days from Puerto Canoa; you return to the north side of the lake by crossing a cable platform strung across the narrows between Huechulafquen and Paimún. A shorter alternative hike goes from the very attractive campground at Piedra Mala to **Cascada El Saltillo**, a nearby forest waterfall. If your car lacks 4WD, leave it at the logjam 'bridge' that crosses the creek and walk to Piedra Mala – the road, passable by any ordinary vehicle to this point, quickly worsens. Rental horses are available at Piedra Mala.

Along the highway are many campsites, some free and others inexpensive. Travelers camping in the free sites in the narrow area between the lakes and the highway must dig a latrine and remove their own trash. If you camp at the organized sites (which, though not luxurious, are at least maintained), you'll support Mapuche concessionaires who at least derive some income from lands that were theirs alone before the state usurped them a century ago.

Fees at ***Camping Raquithue*** are US$3 per person, while those at ***Camping Piedra Mala*** are US$4.50; ***Bahía Cañicul*** is dearer at US$6.50 with electricity, US$5.50 without. Limited supplies are available, but Junín de los Andes has a better selection at lower prices.

Noncampers with money can stay at ***Hostería Refugio Pescador*** *(☎ 02972-491132)* at Puerto Canoa or the three-star ***Hostería Paimún*** *(☎ 02972-491211)*, both catering to fishing parties and charging around US$90 per person with full board.

Lago Tromen This northern approach to Volcán Lanín, which straddles the Argentine-Chilean border, is also the shortest, and is usually the earliest in the season to open for hikers and climbers. En route from Junín, note the unique volcanic landforms, including the isolated El Mollar. Before climbing Lanín, ask permission at the Intendencia de Parques Nacionales in San Martín or, if necessary, of the Gendarmería (border guards) in Junín. It's obligatory to show equipment, including plastic tools, crampons, ice axe, and clothing – including sunglasses, sunscreen, gloves, hats, and padded jackets.

From the trailhead at the Argentine border station, it's five to seven hours to the ***CAJA refugio*** (capacity 14 persons) at 2600m on the Camino de Mulas route; above that point, snow equipment is necessary. There's a shorter but steeper route along the ridge known as the Espina del Pescado, where it's possible to stay at the ***RIM refugio*** (capacity 20 persons) at 2450m. Trekkers can cross the Sierra Mamuil Malal to Lago Huechulafquen via Arroyo Rucu Leufu (see the previous entry).

Hostería San Huberto *(☎ 02972-491238)*, on the north side of RP 60, offers accommodations with full board for US$400 double.

Lago Quillén Situated in the park's densest pehuén forests, this isolated lake is accessible by dirt road from Rahué, 17km south of Aluminé, and has many good ***campsites***. Other nearby lakes include Lago Rucachoroi, directly west of Aluminé, and Lago Ñorquinco on the park's northern border. There are Mapuche reservations at Rucachoroi and Quillén.

Getting There & Away

Although the park is close to San Martín and Junín, public transport is minimal; see the entries on those towns for details. With some patience, hitching is feasible in high season. Buses over the Hua Hum and Tromen passes from San Martín and Junín to Chile will carry passengers to intermediate destinations, but they are often full.

Pickup trucks from Junín carry six or seven backpackers to Puerto Canoas for about US$5 per person.

VILLA LA ANGOSTURA

On the north shore of Lago Nahuel Huapi, placid but fast-growing Villa La Angostura is a scenic lakeside resort whose permanent population has increased threefold, from about 2000 to 6000, in the past five years. Its most accessible natural asset is Parque Nacional Los Arrayanes, while nearby Cerro Bayo is a small but popular winter sports center.

Orientation

On the north shore of Lago Nahuel Huapi, about 100km south of San Martín de los Andes, Villa La Angostura (850m above sea level) is near the junction of RN 231 from Bariloche, which crosses the Andes to Puyehue and Osorno, Chile, and RN 234, which leads northward to San Martín de los Andes and Parque Nacional Lanín. Through town, RN 231 is known as Av Los Arrayanes and Av Los Lagos.

Villa La Angostura takes its name from the 91m-wide isthmus that connects it with Peninsula Quetrihué, which protrudes southward into the lake. In fact, the village consists of two distinct areas: El Cruce is the commercial center along the highway, while La Villa, 3km south, is more residential but still has hotels, shops, services, and lake access. Despite rapid growth, densely forested Villa La Angostura does not dominate its surroundings, so that, except along the highway, visitors are hardly aware of being in a town.

Information

Tourist Offices The helpful, well-organized Dirección Municipal de Turismo (☎ 494124), at Av Siete Lagos 93 in El Cruce, has a good selection of maps and brochures. It's open 8:30 am to 9 pm daily.

Money Banco de la Provincia is on Av Los Arrayanes between Las Mutisias and Los Notros.

Post & Communications Correo Argentino is in El Cruce; the postal code is 8407. There's a locutorio in the Galería Inacayal on Av Los Arrayanes, at El Cruce; the area code is ☎ 02944.

National Parks The local intendencia (☎ 494152) is on Nahuel Huapi, in La Villa.

Travel Agencies Angostura Turismo (☎ 494405), on Av Arrayanes, organizes local excursions and activities.

Things to See & Do

Both town and the surrounding area are best seen on foot. From the local terminal on Av Los Lagos, just north of Los Arrayanes, taxis and remises are now the only means of getting to the trailheads.

Parque Nacional Los Arrayanes This inconspicuous, overlooked park, encompassing the entire Quetrihué peninsula, protects remaining stands of the cinnamon-barked arrayán *(Myrceugenella apiculata)*, a member of the myrtle family. In Mapudungun, language of the Mapuche, the peninsula's name means 'Place of the Arrayanes.'

Park headquarters is at the southern end of the peninsula, near El Bosque, the largest concentration of arrayanes in the park. They are 12km away from La Villa, but it's an easy three-hour walk on an excellent interpretive nature trail (brochures are available in the tourist office at El Cruce). Since regulations require hikers to leave the park by 4 pm, you should start early in the morning. Another alternative is to rent mountain bikes at El Cruce for US$5 per hour, or at full-day rates (a better bargain). There are two small lakes along the trail; horses are not allowed.

From the park's northern entrance at La Villa, a very steep 20-minute hike leads to two panoramic overlooks of Lago Nahuel Huapi.

Cerro Belvedere This 4km walk to an overlook offers good views of Lago Correntoso, Nahuel Huapi, and the surrounding mountains, then continues another 3km to the 1992m summit. After visiting the overlook, retrace your steps to a nearby junction that leads to Cascada Inayacal, a 50m waterfall.

Centro de Ski Cerro Bayo From June to September, lifts carry skiers from the 1050m base up to 1700m at this relatively inexpensive winter resort (☎ 494189), 9km southeast of El Cruce via RP 66. All facilities, including rental equipment, are available on site. Rates during the season depend on when you come – during the peak time, midseason, or low season. Children ages six to 12 qualify for discounts, while children five or younger and adults 65 and older ski free.

A half-day pass for adults costs between US$16 and US$22 and for children, between US$10 and US$18. A full-day pass for adults is US$18 to US$26, for children US$12 to US$20. Weekend lift tickets are valid Friday, Saturday, and Sunday and cost US$49 to US$70 for adults, US$32 to US$54 for children. Weekly rates range from US$108 to

US$156 for adults and US$72 to US$120 for children. Season passes cost US$650 for adults, US$500 for children.

Siete Lagos From Villa La Angostura, RP 234 follows an eminently scenic but even more rough, narrow, and dusty route past numerous alpine lakes to San Martín de los Andes. Tours from Bariloche and San Martín regularly do this route, which might be more accurately called La Ruta de las Nubes de Polvo (Route of the Dust Clouds). There's also scheduled bus service; for details, see Getting There & Away below.

Special Events

In early February, the Fiesta de los Jardines (Garden Festival) is the main event. Late May's Fiestas Mayas celebrate local and national patriotic holidays.

Places to Stay

Camping ***Camping El Cruce*** *(☎ 494145)*, on Av Los Lagos 500m beyond the tourist office, charges US$5 per person. Their hot showers are dependable, but the toilets are sometimes dirty. Rates are US$6 at ***Camping Correntoso*** *(☎ 494829)*, on Lago Correntoso north of town. There are also free sites along Lago Nahuel Huapi.

Residenciales, Hosterías & Hotels

Except for camping, accommodations tend to the pricey, and in summer single rooms are almost impossible to find – expect to pay for two people. All rates include breakfast, which ranges from simple continental fare at budget places to elaborate buffets at more upscale lodgings.

Residencial Don Pedro *(☎ 494269)*, at the corner of Belvedere and Los Maquis in El Cruce, charges US$24/34 for singles/doubles. Also in El Cruce, at the north end of Topa Topa, rates are around US$30/40 at ***Residencial Río Bonito*** *(☎ 494110)*. On Nahuel Huapi in La Villa, rates are US$55/80 at lakeside ***Hotel Angostura*** *(☎ 494224)*, which also has an excellent restaurant. Also on the lakeside, a few kilometers south of El Cruce, three-star ***Hostería Las Balsas*** *(☎ 494308)* charges US$110 per person with breakfast.

Places to Eat

There are several restaurants and confiterías along Los Arrayanes and its cross streets in El Cruce. ***Parrilla Las Varas*** *(☎ 494405, Av Arrayanes 235)* is a favorite, but Lado Sur *(☎ 494322)* on Los Taiques is also well established. ***Rincón Suizo*** *(☎ 494248)*, on Av Los Arrayanes near Av Siete Lagos, serves fondue and has outdoor seating.

La Recova *(Av Arrayanes 51)* has decent food and excellent service; next-door ***Helados Melgari*** is worth a stop for ice cream.

Shopping

On weekends, artisans sell their own crafts at the Feria de Artesanos, on Belvedere between Av Los Arrayanes and Las Fucsias.

Getting There & Away

Villa La Angostura's new Terminal de Ómnibus is at the junction of Av Siete Lagos and Av Arrayanes in El Cruce.

Turismo Algarrobal (☎ 494360) has three buses daily in each direction between Villa La Angostura and Bariloche (US$6, two hours). Transportes Ko-Ko (☎ 494322) stops in El Cruce en route between Bariloche and San Martín de los Andes. Albus (☎ 494763) goes thrice daily to San Martín de los Andes (US$13, three hours) by the Siete Lagos route. Transporte EC goes twice daily to Neuquén (US$28, nine hours)

Río de La Plata (☎ 494999), Andesmar (☎ 494124), Tas-Choapa (☎ 494572), and Bus Norte pass through El Cruce en route from Bariloche to Osorno and Puerto Montt (Chile), but they are often full.

VILLA TRAFUL

On the south shore of Lago Traful, about 80km north of Bariloche on RP 65 in Parque Nacional Nahuel Huapi, Villa Traful offers excellent opportunities for camping, hiking, and fishing in a relatively undeveloped area.

Other than camping, the cheapest lodging is ***Hostería Villa Traful*** *(☎ 02944-479005)* at a modest US$18 per person with breakfast. The most extravagant is ***Rincón del Pescador*** *(☎/fax 02944-479028)*, appealing to fishermen for US$80 per night, but their trout dinners are worth a try.

Albus has daily services to San Martín de los Andes at 11:30 am daily, and to Bariloche.

Chubut Province

Argentina's third-largest province, after Buenos Aires and Santa Cruz, and a self-declared non-nuclear zone, Chubut takes its name from the Mapuche expression *Chupat*, meaning meandering river. Stretching from the Atlantic to the Andes and producing up to 22 million kg of wool yearly, the sheep estancias of its eastern steppe surround the prosperous, irrigated Río Chubut valley. Road and air communications with Buenos Aires are exceptional, while an excellent paved highway links the coast with Chubut's portion of the scenic Argentine lake district, which is also accessible from Bariloche, in Río Negro province to the north.

History

Magellan's celebrated 16th-century expedition entered the Golfo Nuevo, site of present-day Puerto Madryn, but Europeans mostly shunned Chubut until the mid-19th century. At that time Welsh nationalists, frustrated with English domination, sought a land where they could exercise sufficient political autonomy to retain their language, religion, and cultural identity. Deciding on desolate Patagonia, they appealed to the government of Argentina, which, after initial misgivings due partly to the British presence in the Falkland Islands, offered them a land grant in the lower part of the Río Chubut valley in 1863.

Disillusion and misfortune plagued the 153 first arrivals from the brig *Mimosa* in the winter of 1865. The Patagonian desert bore no resemblance to their verdant homeland, and several children died in a storm that turned a two-day coastal voyage into a 17-day ordeal. Only a handful of the immigrants were farmers in well-watered Wales, yet their livelihood was to be agriculture in arid Chubut. After near starvation in the early years, the colonists engineered suitable irrigation systems and increased their harvests, permitting the gradual absorption of more Welsh immigrants.

Eventually, the Welsh occupied the entire lower Chubut valley and founded the towns of Rawson (named for the Argentine minister who arranged their land grant), Trelew (after Lewis Jones, a founding member of the colony), Puerto Madryn (after colonist Love Parry, Baron of Madryn), and Gaiman (a Tehuelche word meaning Stony Point). Even so, by 1895 the territory's European population was fewer than 4000. Only after the turn of the century did immigration from central Argentina and Europe (Italy, Scotland, England, and elsewhere) completely transform the area.

All this immigration had been made possible by General Roca's ruthless Conquista del Desierto. To their credit, the Welsh did not participate in this slaughter of the Indians, but their settlements constituted a foothold for the Argentine state in an area previously outside its authority.

With the outbreak of WWI, Welsh immigration ceased and there began a gradual process of assimilation into Argentine society. The province's cultural landscape still reflects the Welsh presence, though, with its stone buildings and monuments in typical villages like Dolavon, near Gaiman, and Trevelin, near Esquel. Cultural traditions such as teahouses and the *Eisteddfod* (Folk Festival) in Gaiman endure. Younger people speak Spanish by preference (there are relatively few Welsh speakers under the age of 40), but a recent influx of tutors from Wales has led to a minor linguistic revival.

The most accessible book on the area is Anglo-Argentine writer Andrew Graham-Yooll's *The Forgotten Colony* (Hutchinson, London, 1981), a comprehensive account of British immigration into Argentina that contains a chapter on the Welsh settlements. More specialized and thorough is Glyn Williams' historical geography *The Desert and the Dream: A History of the Welsh Colonisation of Patagonia, 1865-1915* (University of Wales, 1975). More recently he has produced *The Welsh in Patagonia: The State and the Ethnic Community* (University of Wales, 1991).

PUERTO MADRYN

Founded by Welsh settlers in 1886, this sheltered desert port has taken off as a tourist destination because its proximity to the provincial wildlife sanctuary of Península Valdés attracts foreigners, and the good beaches appeal to domestic tourist traffic. The street names and little else proclaim Puerto Madryn's Welsh origins – it took its name from Love Parry, Baron of Madryn. Despite modernization, the city has not succumbed to the gaudiness of lake district destinations like Bariloche. Puerto Madryn prides itself on environmental consciousness – like the province of Chubut, it has declared itself a non-nuclear zone. The local campus of the Universidad de la Patagonia is known for its marine biology, computer science, and engineering departments.

Recent arrivals greatly outnumber self-identified 'NICs' *(nacido y criado*, or 'born and raised'). Between 1974, which saw the construction of the Muelle Storni (Storni Pier) and Argentina's first aluminum plant (Aluar), and 1988, the town's population multiplied nearly tenfold to 50,000; inadequate planning encouraged spontaneous housing and caused serious water and sewage problems. With closure of some fish-processing plants and the reduction of Aluar's activities, the population declined to about 45,000, but then rebounded to about 63,000 as the city staked its future on its natural appeal and the export of wool and maritime products. Madryn is now the country's second-largest fishing port.

One unanticipated effect of the increase in the local tourist trade is the influx of professionals from elsewhere in the country – even to the point that there's a surprising amount of work for psychologists and psychiatrists. The city has also developed cultural ambitions (or pretensions). Madrynenses enjoy theater and cinema, so much so that the revived Sociedad Italiana auditorium now hosts first-run films at a time when other towns of comparable size are closing such facilities.

Orientation

Puerto Madryn occupies a protected site on the Golfo Nuevo, just east of RN 3, 1371km south of Buenos Aires, 439km north of Comodoro Rivadavia, and only 65km north of Trelew. Unlike most Argentine cities, but like many other towns in Patagonia, its activities do not cluster around the central Plaza San Martín, which features only a handful of businesses despite a nightly crafts market. Madryn's broad sandy beaches and the costanera Av Roca/Brown are the principal areas of interest to visitors.

Information

Tourist Offices The Secretaría de Turismo y Medio Ambiente (☎ 453504, 452148, municipio_madryn@cpsarg.com) has a spacious visitor center at Av Roca 223, near the corner of 28 de Julio. It's open daily 7 am to 1 am from mid-December to mid-March, but the rest of the year hours are 8 am to 2 pm and 3 to 10 pm. The staff has a reputation for helpfulness and efficiency, and there's usually an English-speaker on duty.

During summer, the center offers a nightly series of videos and lectures – ask for the weekly program. Its personnel also lead a series of walking tours including the Circuito Galesa (Welsh Circuit), Circuito Ferrocarril (Railroad Circuit), Circuito Avenida Roca, and Circuito Punta Cuevas.

Money Local cambios, usually part of travel agencies, include La Moneda at 28 de Julio 21, Local 4; Cuyun-Co at Av Roca 161; and Turismo Puma (☎ 473063) at 28 de Julio 48.

Banco de la Nación, 9 de Julio 117, changes American Express traveler's checks, as does Banco Almafuerte, at Roque Sáenz Peña and 25 de Mayo, and there are also several ATMs.

Post & Communications Correo Argentino is at Belgrano and Gobernador Maíz; the postal code is 9120. Telefónica Patagónica, Marcos A Zar 289, permits overseas collect and credit card calls; there's another large locutorio at the corner of Av Roca and 9 de Julio.

Puerto Madryn's area code is ☎ 02965.

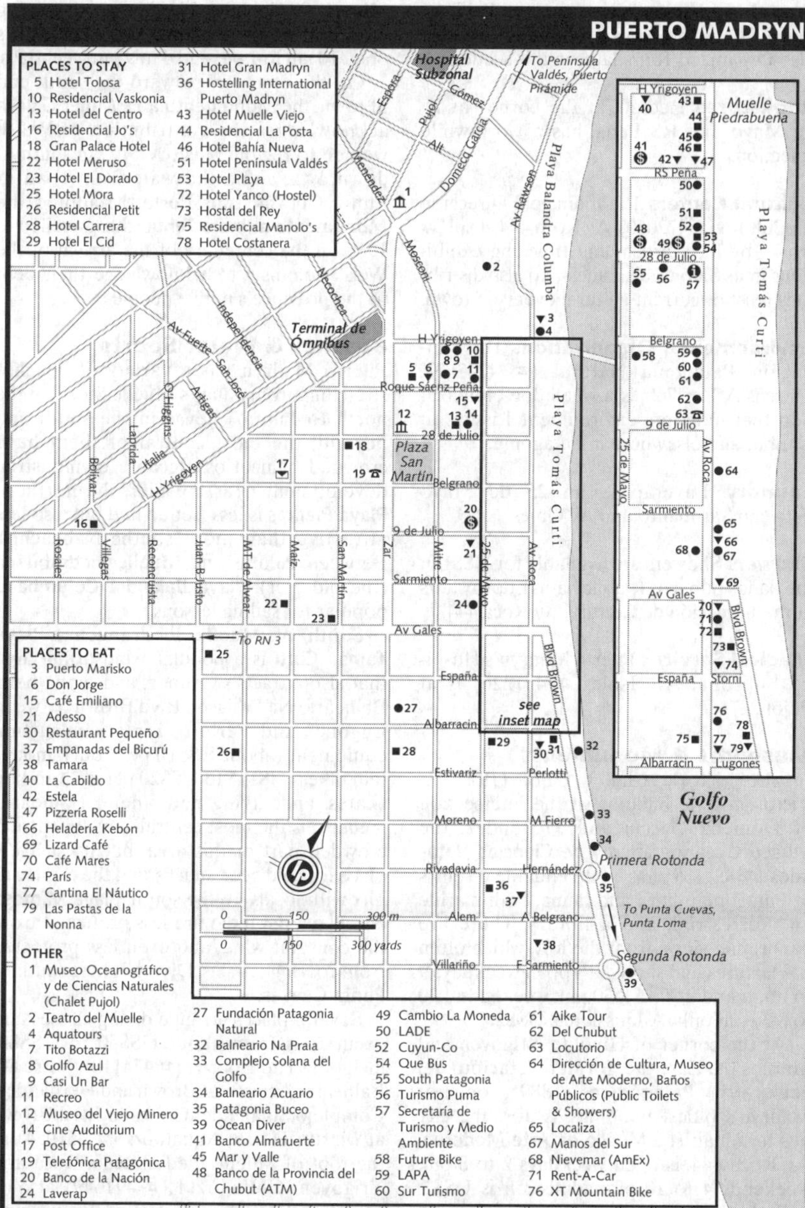
PUERTO MADRYN
PLACES TO STAY
5 Hotel Tolosa
10 Residencial Vaskonia
13 Hotel del Centro
16 Residencial Jo's
18 Gran Palace Hotel
22 Hotel Meruso
23 Hotel El Dorado
25 Hotel Mora
26 Residencial Petit
28 Hotel Carrera
29 Hotel El Cid
31 Hotel Gran Madryn
36 Hostelling International Puerto Madryn
43 Hotel Muelle Viejo
44 Residencial La Posta
46 Hotel Bahía Nueva
51 Hotel Península Valdés
53 Hotel Playa
72 Hotel Yanco (Hostel)
75 Hostal del Rey
73 Residencial Manolo's
78 Hotel Costanera
PLACES TO EAT
3 Puerto Marisko
6 Don Jorge
15 Café Emiliano
21 Adesso
30 Restaurant Pequeño
37 Empanadas del Bicurú
38 Tamara
40 La Cabildo
42 Estela
47 Pizzería Roselli
66 Heladería Kebón
69 Lizard Café
70 Café Mares
74 París
77 Cantina El Náutico
79 Las Pastas de la Nonna
OTHER
1 Museo Oceanográfico y de Ciencias Naturales (Chalet Pujol)
2 Teatro del Muelle
4 Aquatours
7 Tito Botazzi
8 Golfo Azul
9 Casi Un Bar
11 Recreo
12 Museo del Viejo Minero
14 Cine Auditorium
17 Post Office
19 Telefónica Patagónica
20 Banco de la Nación
24 Laverap
27 Fundación Patagonia Natural
32 Balneario Na Praia
33 Complejo Solana del Golfo
34 Balneario Acuario
35 Patagonia Buceo
39 Ocean Diver
41 Banco Almafuerte
45 Mar y Valle
48 Banco de la Provincia del Chubut (ATM)
49 Cambio La Moneda
50 LADE
52 Cuyun-Co
54 Que Bus
55 South Patagonia
56 Turismo Puma
57 Secretaría de Turismo y Medio Ambiente
58 Future Bike
59 LAPA
60 Sur Turismo
61 Aike Tour
62 Del Chubut
63 Locutorio
64 Dirección de Cultura, Museo de Arte Moderno, Baños Públicos (Public Toilets & Showers)
65 Localiza
67 Manos del Sur
68 Nievemar (AmEx)
71 Rent-A-Car
76 XT Mountain Bike
Hospital Subzonal
To Península Valdés, Puerto Pirámide
Terminal de Ómnibus
Plaza San Martín
Playa Balandra Columba
Playa Tomás Curti
Muelle Piedrabuena
Golfo Nuevo
Primera Rotonda
Segunda Rotonda
To Punta Cuevas, Punta Loma
To RN 3
see inset map
0 150 300 m
0 150 300 yards

Travel Agencies Nievemar (☎ 455544), Roca 549, is the AmEx representative. See also Organized Tours later in this section.

Bookstores Recreo, at the corner of 25 de Mayo and RS Peña, has a worthwhile selection.

Cultural Centers The municipal Dirección de Cultura (☎ 472060), Av Roca 444, displays works by local artists and traveling exhibitions in its Salón Luis James, and also distributes a list of current cultural events in town.

Environmental Organizations The Fundación Patagonia Natural (☎ 474363), Marcos A Zar 760, is a watchdog organization that monitors environmental issues in Chubut and elsewhere in Patagonia.

Laundry Laverap is on 25 de Mayo between Sarmiento and Av Gales.

Showers Showers are available for US$1 in the baños públicos (public baths), downstairs at the Dirección de Cultura, Av Roca 444.

Medical Services Puerto Madryn's Hospital Subzonal AR Isola (☎ 451226) is at Pujol 247.

Museums & Monuments

In the historic Chalet Pujol (1917), a Victorian-style building at the intersection of Domecq García and Menéndez, the **Museo Oceanográfico y de Ciencias Naturales** (☎ 451139) has commendable displays of Patagonian flora and fauna, both marine and terrestrial, and a library. There are panoramic views from the loft, which often has lectures and shows. It's open weekdays 9 to noon and 2:30 to 8:30 pm, weekends 4:30 to 8:30 pm only. Admission is US$2.

At the corner of Hipólito Yrigoyen and Marcos A Zar, the former **Estación del Ferrocarril Patagónico** (1889), one of Madryn's oldest buildings, is now the city bus terminal. The **Museo de Arte Moderno**, Av Roca 444, is open weekdays 2 to 8 pm, weekends 4 to 10 pm; admission is US$1, half that for kids. The **Museo del Viejo Minero**, 28 de Julio 293, is a small mining museum opposite Plaza San Martín; it's open 10 am to 1 pm and 4 to 9 pm weekdays.

On the costanera, toward the south end of town, the **Monumento a La Mujer Galesa** acknowledges the contribution of Welsh women to regional history. Six km south of downtown, along the waterfront road to Punta Cuevas, Luis Perlotti sculpted the **Monumento al Indio Tehuelche**, unveiled in 1965 on the centenary of the arrival of the Welsh colonists, to acknowledge their debt to the province's native peoples.

Beaches & Water Sports

Puerto Madryn has a variety of beaches stretching from Aluar's Muelle Storni in the north to Punta Cuevas in the south and beyond; the most central of them have crowded balnearios. Because of industrial development near the pier, the northern **Playa Piedras** is less frequented but also less attractive than more southerly beaches. Between Piedras and Muelle Piedrabuena (the old pier), **Playa Balandra Columba** is popular for sailing lessons.

South of Muelle Piedrabuena, **Playa Tomás Curti** is a popular windsurfing area that also attracts swimmers and sunbathers; Balneario Na Praia, on Blvd Brown between Lugones and Perlotti, rents windsurfing equipment (about US$10 per hour), mountain bikes (US$15 to US$20 per day), in-line skates, and diving equipment. Balneario Acuario is the most central, developed, and crowded part of this area, but it's a lively place for cold beer, snacks, and the chance to mix with locals. To the south, **Playa Mimosa** and **Playa del Indio** are less protected from the constant wind, and even less protected from roaring jet-skis. Diving is best south of **Punta Cuevas**.

Several places arrange diving classes and excursions from about US$50 to US$80, including Tito Botazzi (☎ 474110), Mitre 80; Balneario Acuario at Brown and Hernández; Complejo Solana del Golfo on Blvd Brown at Martín Fierro; Aquatours (☎ 451954) at the foot of Muelle Piedrabuena, Roca and Yrigoyen; Golfo Azul (☎ 471649) at Yrigoyen and Mitre and at Blvd Brown and

Sarmiento; Patagonia Buceo (☎ 452278), at Blvd Brown and Primera Rotonda; and Ocean Diver (☎ 471444) at Blvd Brown and Segunda Rotonda.

Mountain Biking

XT Mountain Bike (☎ 472232), Av Roca 742, conducts guided tours and also rents mountain bikes by the hour, half day, or full day. Future Bike (☎ 02682-465108), 25 de Mayo 302, charges US$25 per day.

Try also Pablo Neme Tours (☎ 471476), Humphreys 85.

Organized Tours

Tours of nearby attractions should be booked at least a day in advance. Aike Tour (☎ 450720), Av Roca 353, offers trips to Península Valdés or Punta Tombo for as little as US$20, but fares tend to be competitive at places like Mar y Valle (☎ 472872), Av Roca 37, and South Patagonia (☎ 455053), 25 de Mayo 226. Some stop for tea in Gaiman on the return from Punta Tombo.

Nearly all the guides speak English at Sur Turismo (☎ 473585), Av Roca 349, which organizes tours of the Madryn area and Península Valdés to match visitors' interests, including overland and submarine photographic safaris, educational tours, and whale watching. For small groups, Turismo Puma (☎ 471482), 28 de Julio 48, organizes nature walks, lasting about four hours, along the coast as well as in the countryside.

Special Events

See the tourist office for a list of current offerings and specific dates. The Fiesta Nacional del Cordero (National Lamb Festival) takes place the second week of February. The Semana de la Fauna (Fauna Week) coincides with the arrival of whales at Península Valdés.

Places to Stay

Besides the regular accommodations detailed below, the Secretaría de Turismo maintains a list of apartments for rent on a daily, weekly, or monthly basis. Prices usually range from US$10 to US$15 per day per person.

Note that budget to mid-range places do not generally include breakfast in their prices, while upscale places do.

Places to Stay – Budget

Camping Toward Punta Cuevas and the Monumento al Indio Tehuelche, the 800-site ***Camping ACA*** *(☎ 452952)* charges US$13 daily for up to four people with car, trailer, and tent, but US$16 for nonmembers. Of this area's several campgrounds, this is the only one with large trees offering shelter from the wind. It closes in winter.

Well designed but less sheltered, nearby ***Camping Municipal Sud*** *(☎ 455640)* has designated 'A' and 'B' areas for US$12 daily for four people, tent, car, and trailer, but their perfectly acceptable 'C' and 'D' areas cost only U$2.50 daily per person and US$2.50 per tent. It's open all year

The Club Náutico Atlántico Sud's ***El Golfito*** *(☎ 471602)* has 300 partially forested sites with direct beach access. Nonmember prices are US$10 for four people, tent, and car, plus US$3 per additional person. There's also an 85-bed hostel for US$5.50 per person.

From downtown, city bus No 2 goes to within 500m of the southern campgrounds.

Hostels On spacious grounds, ***Hostelling International Puerto Madryn*** *(☎/fax 474426, madrynhi@hostels.org.ar, hi-pm@satlink.com.ar, 25 de Mayo 1136)* has large rooms, some with private bath, for US$10 per person for HI members, US$12 for nonmembers. Office hours are 8 am to 1 pm and 4 to 9 pm only; it closes after Easter. It also rents mountain bikes.

Hotel Yanco *(☎ 471581, Av Roca 626)* has hostel accommodations for US$12 per person with breakfast, but offers no kitchen privileges, nor do they seem to encourage hostelers.

Residenciales & Hotels Basic ***Residencial Vaskonia*** *(☎ 472581, 25 de Mayo 43)* is perhaps the best budget value for US$15/24 single/double. Comparably priced, at US$15/25, are ***Hotel El Dorado*** *(☎ 471026, San Martín 545)* and ***Hotel del Centro***

(☎ 473742, 28 de Julio 149), which is friendly and pleasant despite its dark, narrow approach.

Residencial Petit *(☎ 451460, MT de Alvear 845)* has rooms with private bath at US$16 per person. Rooms at ***Residencial Jo's*** *(☎ 471433, Bolívar 75)* are a good value for US$20/30.

Places to Stay – Mid-Range

Hotel Meruso *(☎ 452222, Gobernador Maíz 545)* charges US$25/35. Slightly less central ***Hotel Mora*** *(☎ 471424, Juan B Justo 654)* is identically priced but mediocre.

Residencial La Posta *(☎ 472422, Av Roca 33)* charges US$30/40 for small but tidy rooms with bunk beds. For the same price, ***Gran Palace Hotel*** *(☎ 471009, 28 de Julio 390)* has good upstairs rooms, but the downstairs rooms are less appealing.

The attractive, central ***Residencial Manolo's*** *(☎ 472390, Av Roca 763)* costs US$30/45. Rates at ***Hotel Muelle Viejo*** *(☎ 471284, Yrigoyen 38)* are US$30/50. For US$38/55, ***Hotel Yanco*** *(☎ 471581, Av Roca 626)* has good views and a pleasant atmosphere, but the downstairs dance club makes sleep difficult some nights.

The ***Hotel Gran Madryn*** *(☎ 472205, Lugones 40)* is pleasant and well located for US$40/50. ***Hotel Carrera*** *(☎ 450759, Marcos A Zar 852)* is identically priced. ***Hotel El Cid*** *(☎ 471416, 25 de Mayo 850)* is a bit more expensive at US$45/55, while ***Hotel Costanera*** *(☎ 453000, Blvd Brown 759)* costs US$45/65.

Less central but with spacious rooms, ***La Posada de Madryn*** *(☎ 474087, Abraham Mathews 2951)*, south of downtown, charges US$48/65. Their restaurant offers a wide range of international dishes, and the hotel provides patrons with transportation to town and the airport. Still, beachfront ***Hostal del Rey*** *(☎ 471156, Blvd Brown 681)* may be the best mid-range value at US$50/60.

Places to Stay – Top End

Top-end hotels are primarily those with immediate beach access. The major exception is the newish but impersonal ***Hotel Tolosa*** *(☎ 471850, Roque Sáenz Peña 253)*, which charges US$67/78. ***Hotel Playa*** *(☎ 451446, Av Roca 181)* charges US$72/92, while the new three-star ***Hotel Bahía Nueva*** *(☎ 451677, Av Roca 67)* costs US$73/92. The priciest accommodations are at ***Hotel Península Valdés*** *(☎ 471292, Av Roca 155)*, which costs US$100/110.

Places to Eat

Puerto Madryn has a varied selection of quality food at reasonable prices. Although beef is more expensive here than in the Pampas, there are several good parrillas, among them the highly recommended ***Estela*** *(☎ 451573, Roque Sáenz Peña 27)*, ***París*** *(☎ 456558, Av Roca 672)*, and ***Don Jorge*** *(☎ 450356, Roque Sáenz Peña 214)*.

The deservedly popular ***Cantina El Náutico*** *(☎ 471404)*, at Av Roca and Lugones, serves particularly fine *vieiras* (scallops) *a la provenzal* and other seafood dishes, but drinks are expensive. ***Puerto Marisko*** *(☎ 450752, Av Rawson 4)*, just north of Muelle Piedrabuena, also serves seafood, as does ***Restaurant Pequeño*** *(☎ 472807, Av Roca 822)*, along with pasta and parrillada.

Adesso *(☎ 453070)*, at 25 de Mayo and 9 de Julio, is an outstanding pizza and pasta restaurant with pleasant, unpretentious decor, but note that the very low pasta prices are a bit misleading because the choice of sauce is additional. ***Las Pastas de la Nonna*** *(☎ 450108, Blvd Brown 775)*, on the beach, is comparable.

There are several other pizzerias, including ***Halloween II*** *(☎ 450909, Av Roca 1355)*, which has a variety of empanadas as well. ***Pizzería Roselli*** *(☎ 472451)*, at Av Roca and Roque Sáenz Peña, is also extremely popular, but perhaps the best pizzas are the large ones at ***La Cabildo*** *(☎ 471284, H Yrigoyen 36)*, which also serves great baked empanadas.

Downtown are several confiterías and trendy cafés, including the ***Lizard Café*** *(☎ 472182)*, at Avs Roca and Gales, and ***Café Emiliano*** *(Roque Sáenz Peña 112)*. For Welsh tea, Madryn's only choice is ***Tamara*** *(Av Roca 1250)*. ***Empanadas del Bicurú*** *(☎ 471046, Av Roca 1143)* serves 14 different styles of tasty take-out empanadas.

Ice cream at ***Café Mares*** *(Av Roca 600)*, rates with Buenos Aires' best – try the chocolate and lemon mousses, and the white and bittersweet chocolates. Some locals, though, swear by ***Heladería Kebón*** *(Av Roca 540)*.

Entertainment

In summer the ***Teatro del Muelle***, on Av Rawson (the northern extension of Av Roca) just beyond the Muelle Piedrabuena, has live theater and musical shows Friday, Saturday, and Sunday nights (and sometimes more frequently). For current offerings, contact the Dirección de Cultura *(☎ 472060, Av Roca 444)*.

The ***Cine Auditorium*** *(☎ 455653, 28 de Julio 129)* shows first-run movies and also theater productions.

Casi Un Bar *(Yrigoyen 144)* has live music.

Shopping

Del Chubut, Av Roca 369, produces *alfajores* (cookie sandwiches with sweet fillings like chocolate, dulce de leche, and fruit) and tasty *torta galesa* (Welsh black cake). Manos del Sur (☎ 472539), Roca 546, has an outstanding selection of souvenirs, natural foods, and artisanal products in ceramics, wood, wool, leather, and the like.

Getting There & Away

Air Though Puerto Madryn has had its own convenient Aeródromo El Tehuelche since 1989, nearly all commercial flights still arrive at Trelew, 65km south (see the Trelew's Getting There & Away). The local airport tax is US$2.

LADE (☎ 451256), Av Roca 119, flies Monday to Trelew (US$20), Esquel (US$51), Bariloche (US$53), Neuquén (US$55 to US$80), and Viedma (US$125); Tuesday to Viedma (US$32), Bahía Blanca (US$50), Mar del Plata (US$80), and Buenos Aires' Aeroparque (US$90); and Friday to Trelew and Comodoro Rivadavia (US$39).

LAPA (☎ 450893), Belgrano 12, has bus shuttle service to the airport at Trelew.

Bus In the historic railroad station, Puerto Madryn's Terminal de Ómnibus is on H Yrigoyen between MA Zar and San Martín. Línea 28 de Julio (☎ 472056) runs frequent buses to Trelew and back.

TAC (☎ 451537) goes north to Buenos Aires, Córdoba, Tucumán, and Jujuy; west to Mendoza; and south to Río Gallegos. Don Otto (☎ 451675) has one daily direct bus to Buenos Aires, three to Comodoro Rivadavia, and combinations to Río Gallegos and intermediate points It also goes to Neuquén and to Esquel (via Trelew) daily. La Puntual (☎ 471125) also has twice-daily service to Buenos Aires via Viedma and Bahía Blanca, and daily departures to Comodoro Rivadavia. Que Bus (☎ 455805), Av Roca 187, goes to La Plata and Buenos Aires.

El Pingüino goes to Buenos Aires daily at 2:45 pm, and to Río Gallegos at 3:45 pm. Andesmar (☎ 473764) has daily buses to Neuquén and Mendoza and to Caleta Olivia; three times weekly, this latter service continues to Río Gallegos. El Cóndor, at the same office, also goes to Bariloche, nightly at 8:10 pm. Central Argentino (☎ 473764) goes to Comodoro Rivadavia, Bahía Blanca, and three times weekly to Rosario. TUP (☎ 451962) travels three times weekly to Córdoba via Santa Rosa (La Pampa), and to Camarones, Comodoro Rivadavia, and Caleta Olivia.

Mar y Valle (☎ 472056) has buses Sunday through Friday to Esquel, and also goes to Trelew and to Puerto Pirámide daily at 8:55 am and 5 pm; the latter bus runs at peak times, in summer and during the whale-watching season.

Sample fares include Trelew (US$4, one hour), Puerto Pirámide (US$6.50, 1½ hours), Comodoro Rivadavia (US$18, six hours), Caleta Olivia (US$20, eight hours), Bahía Blanca (US$24, eight hours), Esquel (US$28, eight hours), Neuquén (US$32, 12 hours), Córdoba (US$55 to US$61, 18 hours), Bariloche (US$50, 14 hours), Río Gallegos (US$44 to US$52, 16 hours), Buenos Aires (US$35 to US$57, 20 hours), Rosario (US$76), and Mendoza (US$72, 23 hours).

Getting Around

To/From the Airport Aeródromo El Tehuelche (☎ 451909) is 5km west of town, at the junction with RN 3; cabs are not expensive.

Southbound Línea 28 de Julio buses from Puerto Madryn to Trelew, which run hourly Monday through Saturday between 6:15 am and 10:30 pm, will stop at Trelew's Aeropuerto Internacional Almirante Zar on request. Aerolíneas Argentinas also runs a bus from Almirante Zar to Puerto Madryn (US$10), leaving 30 minutes after the flight arrival. LAPA has its own airport shuttle, leaving two hours before flight time from its downtown offices and from the Monumento a la Mujer Galesa.

Car Renting a car is the best way to see Puerto Madryn and its surrounding area, especially Península Valdés. Rent-A-Car (☎ 452355), Av Roca 624, has vehicles for as little as US$100 daily, all-inclusive (except for gasoline). Localiza (☎ 456300) is at Av Roca 536, and Cuyun-Co (☎ 451845) at Av Roca 165.

AROUND PUERTO MADRYN

Reserva Faunística Punta Loma

This sea lion rookery, 17km southwest of Puerto Madryn via a good but winding gravel road, has a visitor center and an overlook about 15m from the animals. Some travel agencies organize tours; otherwise, hire a car or taxi.

Adult admission is US$3, but retired people and students pay only US$1.

RESERVA FAUNÍSTICA PENÍNSULA VALDÉS

Sea lions, elephant seals, guanacos, rheas, Magellanic penguins, and many other seabirds are present in large numbers on the

Isla de los Pájaros

While most visitors to Península Valdés focus on whales, elephant seals, sea lions, penguins, and other marquee species, the area has a wide variety of birdlife, most of which will be new to visitors from the Northern Hemisphere. Most of these birds are also common in the rest of Patagonia and in Chile; only a handful, most notably the rock cormorant, night heron, crested duck, and steamer duck, breed here. Note that Spanish common names can vary between Argentina and Chile – sometimes for nationalistic reasons.

Linnaean Name	*Spanish Common Name*	*English Common Name*
Spheniscus magellanicus	pingüino de Magallanes	Magellanic/jackass penguin
Phoenicopterus chilensis	flamenco austral	Chilean flamingo
Nycticorax nycticorax	garza bruja	black-crowned night heron
Haematopus ater	ostrero negro	black oystercatcher
H ostralegus	ostrero común	common oystercatcher
Phalacrocorax magallanicus	cormorán de cuello negro	rock cormorant
P olivaceus	biguá	olive cormorant
Charadrius falklandicus	chorlo doble collar	two-banded plover
Calidris fuscicollis	chorlito rebadilla blanca	white-rumped sandpiper
Egretta alba	garza blanca	great egret
Larus dominicanus	gaviota cocinera	Dominican/kelp gull
L maculipennus	gaviota capucho café	brown-hooded gull
Lophonetta specularioides	pato crestón	Patagonian crested duck
Tachyeres leucocephalus	pato vapor cabeza blanca	white-headed steamer duck
Sterna hirundinacea	gaviotín sudamericano	South American tern
S maxima	gaviotín real	royal tern
Calorsterna eurygnatha	gaviotín pico amarillo	yellow-beaked tern

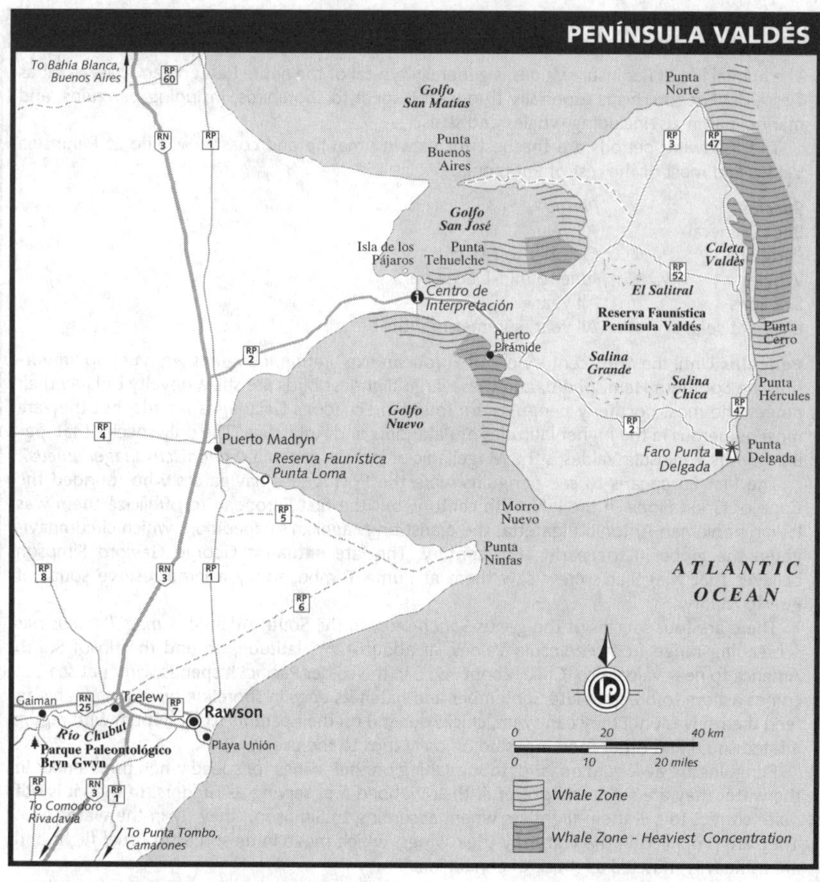

beaches and headlands of one of South America's finest wildlife reserves, but the biggest attraction – literally and figuratively – is the southern right whale *Eubalaena australis*, known in Spanish as the *ballena franca*. The right whale's presence has led the federal government to designate the breeding zones along the Golfo Nuevo, Golfo San José, and the Atlantic Ocean as the Monumento Natural Ballena Franca Austral.

Sheep estancias occupy most of the peninsula's interior, which includes one of the world's lowest continental depressions, the salt flats of Salina Grande and Salina Chica, 42m below sea level. At the turn of the century, Puerto Pirámide, the peninsula's only village, was the port of exit for salt from Salina Grande. Now dependent on tourism, it's an excellent base for exploring the peninsula. Visited by right whales between mid-June and mid-December, its sandy white beaches and the Golfo Nuevo's warm clear waters attract fishing and water-sports enthusiasts. For visitors without cars, there's a sea lion colony only 4km from town, with good

Fauna of Península Valdés & Patagonia

The animal life of Península Valdés is generally typical of the entire Patagonian coast as far as Tierra del Fuego. This is especially true with respect to shorebirds, including penguins, and marine mammals, including whales and seals.

The following periods are the best for viewing marine and coastal wildlife at Península Valdés and most of the rest of Patagonia.

Species	*Period*
Birds (general)	All year
Penguins	October to March
Whales	June to mid-December
Sea lions	All year
Elephant seals	All year; summer months best

Penguins Until the 16th-century era of European exploration, penguins were unknown outside the Southern Hemisphere, and these large flightless birds are still a novelty outside their range. The most northerly penguins are found in Ecuador's Galápagos Islands, but they are most numerous in the higher latitudes of Patagonia and Antarctica. The only species that regularly visits Península Valdés is the Magellanic or jackass penguin *(Spheniscus magellanicus)*.

The first Europeans to see penguins were the Portuguese navigators who rounded the Cape of Good Hope in the late 15th century, but the first European to publicize them was Italian nobleman Antonio Pigafetta, the diarist on Magellan's expedition, which circumnavigated the globe in the early 16th century. The late naturalist George Gaylord Simpson believes that Magellan's crew saw them at Punta Tombo, today a large reserve south of Puerto Madryn.

There are four species of the genus *Spheniscus*. In the South Atlantic, *S magellanicus* has a breeding range from Península Valdés, at about 42° S latitude, around the tip of South America to near Valparaíso, Chile, about 33° S in the colder Pacific. It spends winter at sea but comes ashore to breed in late September and hatch its eggs in shoreline burrows. Unable to feed themselves until they can swim, chicks depend on their parents to feed them with regurgitated squid and other food ingested on daily trips to the ocean.

Penguins are awkward on land, tobogganing on their wings for speed when threatened. In the water they are swift and graceful, their webbed feet serving as rudders. In fact, it is not quite correct to call them flightless when, according to Simpson, 'they fly in the water . . . . They are propelled in the water by their wings, which move in unison as in usual flight and are as heavily muscled as those of aerial fliers.'

Despite their enormous numbers, penguins have many predators. In the water, southern sea lions, leopard seals, and killer whales take adult birds. On land, eggs and chicks are vulnerable to gulls, skuas, and other large birds. Both aboriginal peoples, such as the Maori of New Zealand, and Europeans have consumed them for food; French naturalist Antoine Pernety, visiting the Falklands in the late 18th century, wrote that French colonists there ate penguins 'several times in ragouts, which we found to be as good as those made of hares.' Even today, Falkland Islanders collect penguin eggs in the spring, but no longer are penguins killed and boiled down for their oil, which was used to top off casks of whale and seal oil.

Magellanic penguins sometimes frequent the beach at Puerto Pirámide on Península Valdés. Otherwise you can see them along Caleta Valdés, although there are much larger numbers farther south at Punta Tombo and Cabo Dos Bahías. For information on other penguin species, see the Falkland Islands chapter. A readable account of the natural history of

Fauna of Península Valdés & Patagonia

penguins, as well as a history of human encounters with them, is Simpson's *Penguins: Past and Present, Here and There*.

Whales The world's largest living animals comprise two orders: The toothed whales (including dolphins, porpoises, and the killer whale *Orcinus orca)* feed mainly on fish and squid, while the baleen whales (including the southern right whale *Eubalaena australis)* trap plankton and krill (small crustaceans) as seawater filters through plates in their jaws. A layer of blubber beneath their skin insulates whales from the cold ocean waters.

Their bodies black with white underbellies, killer whales frequent the waters around Península Valdés in pods. Males can reach more than 9m in length and weigh as much as 5000kg, although most specimens of both males and females are considerably smaller. Their ominous dorsal fin can reach nearly 2m high. Near the top of the food chain, they prey on fish, penguins, dolphins, seals, and, on rare occasion, larger whales.

Exploited for meat and oil, the slow moving right whale was a favorite target of whalers because, unlike other species, it remained floating on the surface after being killed; after more than half a century of legal protection, South Atlantic right whale populations are slowly recovering.

Averaging nearly 12m in length and weighing more than 30 tons, right whales enter the shallow waters of the Golfo Nuevo and the Golfo San José in spring to breed and bear their young. Whale watching is possible from June to mid-December, but September and October are the best months. At Puerto Pirámide, launches take visitors out into the harbor for closer views.

Elephant Seals & Sea Lions The southern elephant seal *(Mirounga leonina)* and the southern sea lion *(Otaria flavescens)* belong to the order of pinnipeds, or eared seals, which are widely distributed throughout Patagonia and other southern midlatitude and sub-Antarctic areas and islands.

Elephant seals *(elefantes marinos* in Spanish) take their common name from the male's enormous proboscis, which does indeed resemble an elephant's trunk. These ponderous animals reach nearly 7m in length andcan weigh over 3500kg, but the females are so much smaller that it would be possible to mistake them for a different species. They spend most of the year at sea, and have been observed to dive to a depth of 1500m and stay submerged for over an hour in search of squid and other fish. (The average dive depth and duration are 1000m and 23 minutes).

Península Valdés has the only breeding colony of southern elephant seals on the South American continent. The bull elephant comes ashore in late winter or early spring, breeding shortly after the already pregnant females arrive and give birth. Dominant males known as 'beachmasters' control harems of up to 100 females but must constantly fight off challenges from bachelor males. Fights are frequent and spectacular, leaving many adult males disfigured.

In the course of these fights, bulls accidentally crush many seal pups. Those that survive gain weight rapidly for about three weeks before being abandoned by their mothers, and head to sea by the end of the year. There are substantial numbers of elephant seals at the Punta Norte reserve, but access to them is better on the gravel spit at Caleta Valdés.

Aggressive southern sea lions will sometimes drag away a helpless elephant seal pup, but they, too, feed largely on squid and the occasional penguin. The male is an imposing specimen, whose mane truly resembles that of an African lion. Like the African lion, it is surprisingly quick and aggressive on land. Do not approach them too closely for photographs.

views (and sunsets) across the Golfo Nuevo toward Puerto Madryn. In season, launches can approach right whales in the harbor.

About 18km north of Puerto Madryn, paved RP 2 branches off RN 3 across the Istmo Carlos Ameghino to the entrance of the Península Valdés reserve; provincial officials collect a visitor fee of US$5 per adult above 12 years of age (there are indications this fee may double). Open 8 am to 8 pm daily, the greatly improved **Centro de Interpretación** here focuses on natural history and includes a full right whale skeleton, but there's also informative material on colonization of the peninsula, from the Spanish Fuerte San José to later mineral exploration and the 34km narrow gauge railway that ran from Salina Grande to Puerto Pirámide. From the observation tower, there are views across the desert to Golfo San José to the north and Golfo Nuevo to the south.

In Golfo San José, 800m north of the isthmus, **Isla de los Pájaros** is a bird sanctuary off-limits to humans but visible through a powerful telescope; it also contains a replica of a chapel built at Fuerte San José, the area's first Spanish settlement.

To visit remaining wildlife sites beyond Puerto Pirámide, it's essential to have a car or take an organized tour; the much improved gravel roads still have occasional soft sand, but present no obstacle to prudent drivers. Just north of **Punta Delgada**, in the peninsula's southeast corner, a large colony of sea lions and elephant seals is visible from the cliffs, but the better sites are farther north.

WAYNE BERNHARDSON

Elephant seal.

On the eastern shore, **Caleta Valdés** is a sheltered bay with a long gravel spit onto which elephant seals haul themselves in the spring. They are easily photographed, but should not be approached too closely. Guanaco sometimes stroll along the beach. Between Caleta Valdés and Punta Norte is a substantial colony of burrowing Magellanic penguins. At **Punta Norte** itself is an enormous mixed colony of sea lions and elephant seals, with clearly marked trails and fences to discourage either side (human or animal) from too close an encounter. Punta Norte now has a small but surprisingly good museum, focusing on marine mammals (orcas are a local feature, present from mid-February through mid-April). There are also materials on sealing and, most importantly, on the aboriginal Tehuelche, acknowledging them as the province's first inhabitants.

Dangers & Annoyances

At most wildlife sites, it is foolish to attempt to descend the precipitous, unconsolidated cliffs to get close to the animals. Even should you make it down safely, male sea lions are quick, aggressive, and dangerous. Note that some areas are closed to all visitors, and you may have to be content to view them from a distance; ask park rangers for latest details.

Visitors contracting tours should know that frustrated travelers have found that some trips spend too much time at confiterías and too little time at wildlife sites; drivers apparently get kickbacks based on the amount of money spent at these stops. Before agreeing to any of these trips, speak to other travelers to learn about their experiences, discuss the tour with the operator to be sure that their expectations are the same as yours, and do not hesitate to relay complaints to the Secretaría de Turismo y Medio Ambiente in Puerto Madryn.

Activities

From June to mid-December, several operators in Puerto Madryn and Puerto Pirámide offer whale-watching excursions on the waters of the Golfo Nuevo for about US$20. These companies include Hydrosport (☎ 495006), Aquatours (☎ 495015), Sur

Turismo (☎ 473585), Tito Botazzi (☎ 495050), and Peke Sosa (☎ 471291).

Although most operators are scrupulous, provincial authorities have requested visitors to report to rangers (or to the Secretería de Turismo in Puerto Madryn) any instance of boats attempting to pursue, disperse, or round up whales; getting within 100m of any whale without cutting the motor; intercepting their course or navigating parallel with them; touching an animal with the boat; separating a mother from her young; and nearing an animal that is already under close observation by another boat.

Most of the same companies, as well as Patagonia Scuba (☎ 495030), in the *Hostería Pub Paradise*, (see Places to Stay & Eat) rent mountain bikes as well.

Places to Stay & Eat

Accommodations and other services in Puerto Pirámide are expanding and improving rapidly. Since Av Roca, the only street, parallels the beach, all hotels have good beach access; note that the beach almost disappears at high tide. Change money in Puerto Madryn or Trelew.

Sites at Puerto Pirámide's ***Camping Municipal***, though not well marked, are sheltered from the wind by dunes and trees. It has clean toilets, hot showers, and a store with groceries and cold beer, mineral water, and soft drinks. Prices are US$4 per person; because of the extreme water shortages, showers (US$1) are carefully timed. In summer, the place gets very crowded and somewhat noisy, but a persistent search should reward you with a quiet site.

There is basic but acceptable lodging at ***Hospedaje El Español*** *(☎ 495031)* for US$8 per person, with simple but clean rooms and toilets, plus hot showers. ***Hostería El Libanés*** *(☎ 495007)* has modest rooms in summer for US$23 per person with bath, slightly less the rest of the year, and a small confitería that serves a reasonable breakfast. The most expensive accommodations are the ***Hostería ACA*** *(☎ 495004)*, with singles/doubles for US$52/65 and a costly restaurant.

In attractive new facilities, the ***Hostería Pub Paradise*** *(☎ 495030, fax 495003, paradise@satlink.com)* offers B&B accommodations for US$53/73; the pub/restaurant serves sandwiches, a broad selection of pizzas, and fixed-price meals for US$12.

Camping is prohibited on Península Valdés outside of Puerto Pirámide. Thus the best base for exploration is the highly recommended ***Faro Punta Delgada*** *(☎ 02965-471910, office: Av Julio Roca 141, Puerto Madryn)*, at the northeastern edge of the peninsula, which has 30 double rooms with private bath on the site of the old lighthouse. Rates are US$60 per person with breakfast, US$80 with half-board, and US$100 with full board. The ***dining room*** is open to nonguests.

Getting There & Away

Daily at 8:55 am and 5 pm, the Mar y Valle bus goes from Puerto Madryn to Puerto Pirámide (US$6.50, 1½ hours), returning at 11 am and 7 pm. Bus tours from Puerto Madryn may allow passengers to get off at Puerto Pirámide and reboard another day for no additional charge, but verify that this is acceptable before doing so.

Getting Around

Hitchhiking in Península Valdés is nearly impossible, so to visit sites any distance from Puerto Pirámide, the alternatives are renting a car, hiring a remise, or taking an organized tour. For a group of three or four persons, sharing expenses can make a rental car or remise a relatively reasonable and more flexible alternative to bus tours.

Most travel agencies in Puerto Madryn organize day trips for about US$25 to US$30, but stiff competition means occasional bargains. Admission to the reserve is not included.

There are now several tour agencies in Puerto Pirámide itself, as well as rental bikes, very convenient for the immediate area. The major wildlife sites are too distant for most bike day trips, however, especially with the strong winds.

TRELEW

Actively courting tourists, Trelew is a convenient staging point for visits to the historic Welsh villages of Gaiman and Dolavon, as well as the massive Punta Tombo penguin reserve. Founded in 1886 as a railway junction to unite the Chubut valley with the beaches of the Golfo Nuevo, its Welsh name is a contraction of *tre* (meaning town) and *lew* (after Lewis Jones, who promoted railway expansion). The town's first Eisteddfod (a poetry and music event still held in October) took place in 1890, when the population did not exceed 80.

During the following 25 years, the railway reached Gaiman, the Welsh built their Salón San David, and Italian immigrants constructed the Teatro Verdi. By 1915 the population had reached 4400, but it stabilized at this level until 1956, when federal customs preferences promoted Patagonian industrial development. Trelew became very attractive to immigrants from all over the country and, by 1970, its population had risen to 24,000. Around that time, Trelew gained notoriety for the massacre of political prisoners who escaped from the local prison and took over the airport for some hours.

The 1980s witnessed another wave of immigration for which local authorities were unprepared – toward the end of the decade, the population had reached 90,000. After

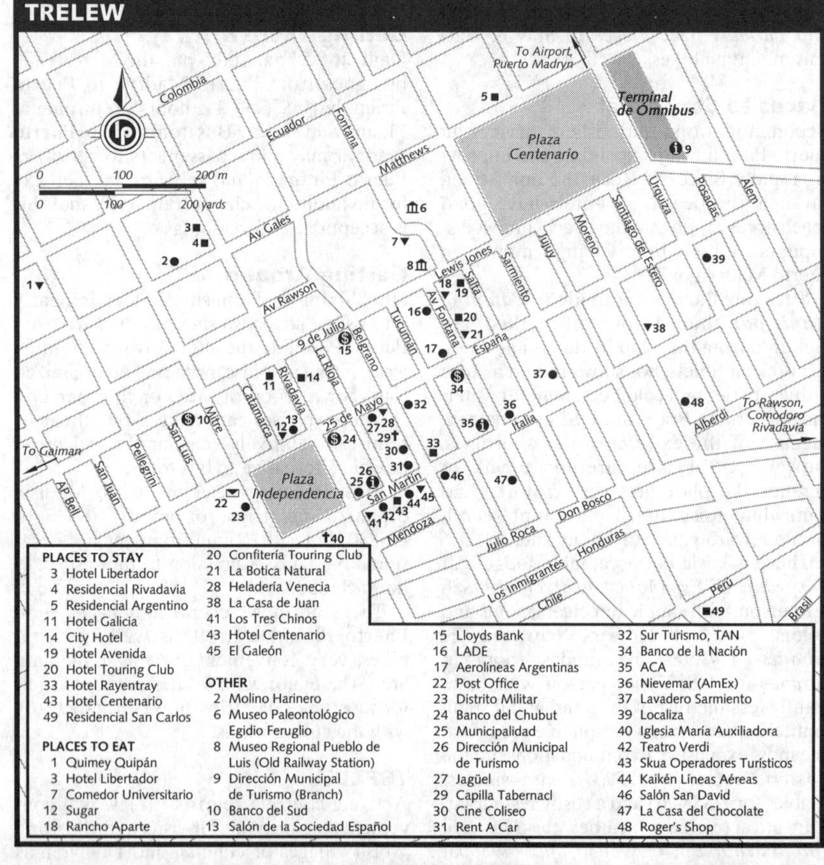

1989 the abandonment of industrial promotion policies forced many to leave the area, but the present population has rebounded to around 100,000. Like El Bolsón and Puerto Madryn, Trelew declared itself a 'non-nuclear municipality' in objecting to the federal government's plans to locate a nuclear waste dump in the province.

Orientation

In the Río Chubut valley, Trelew is 65km south of Puerto Madryn via RN 3. The center of Trelew's grid is Plaza Independencia, while most of the main sights are on Calles 25 de Mayo and San Martín, at the north and south ends of the plaza, and along Av Fontana, two blocks east. East-west streets change their names on either side of Av Fontana. One of the downtown's more appealing features is a series of semi-pedestrian passageways inaccessible to all but very small cars, traveling at very slow speeds.

Information

Tourist Offices The cheerful, competent Dirección Municipal de Turismo (☎ 420139), San Martín 171, is open 8 am to 8 pm weekdays; from September to March it is open weekends 10 am to 1 pm and 5 to 8 pm. The branch at the bus terminal (☎ 420121) is open 9:30 am to 12:30 pm and 6 to 9 pm weekdays, 6 to 8 pm Saturday. There's also an airport information booth (☎ 428021), open for incoming flights.

ACA (☎ 435197) is at Av Fontana and San Martín.

Money It's most efficient to change at travel agencies such as Sur Turismo (see below), which also changes traveler's checks. Banks are usually open 8 am to 1 pm, but there are several ATMs.

Post & Communications Correo Argentino is at Calle 25 de Mayo and Mitre; the postal code is 9100. There are many downtown locutorios; Trelew's area code is ☎ 02965.

Travel Agencies Local agencies such as Sur Turismo (☎ 434081) at Belgrano 330 and Skua Operadores Turísticos (☎ 420358) at San Martín 150 organize tours to Península Valdés and the penguin reserve at Punta Tombo. So does Nievemar (☎ 434114), Italia 20, which is the AmEx representative.

Laundry Lavadero Sarmiento is on Sarmiento between España and Italia.

Walking Tour

The Dirección Municipal de Turismo distributes an informative brochure, in Spanish and English, describing most but not all of the city's historic buildings. A good starting point is the **Museo Regional Pueblo de Luis** at the former railway station (1889), at the north end of Av Fontana. Half a block south, on Fontana, the **Touring Club** began in 1906 as Hotel Martino before expanding to become, at least briefly, Patagonia's best hotel (a description that may have been faint praise). While its glory days are past, it's still an interesting edifice and a popular gathering place.

Banco de la Nación started operations in 1899 after being relocated from Rawson following floods on the Río Chubut, but the present building at Fontana and 25 de Mayo dates from 1922; note the clock tower. One block south and one block west, at San Martín and Belgrano, the **Salón San David** (1913) is a Welsh community center that often hosts the Eisteddfod. Half a block north on Belgrano, the **Capilla Tabernacl** (1889), Trelew's oldest building, still has Welsh-language services on alternate Sundays. Italian immigrants inaugurated the **Teatro Verdi**, on San Martín between Belgrano and Rivadavia, as a skating rink in 1914.

At the southeast corner of Plaza Independencia, the **Municipalidad** (1931) houses city offices; the plaza's most interesting feature is its Victorian gingerbread **Kiosco**, dating from 1910. On the west side of the plaza, on Calle Mitre, the **Distrito Militar** (1903) housed Trelew's first school; on the north side, at 25 de Mayo 237, Spanish immigrants built the **Salón de la Sociedad Española** (1920), which hosted local theater productions. Three blocks north and half a block west, on Av Gales between Mitre and

Rivadavia, the **Molino Harinero** is a former flour mill dating from 1910.

Museo Regional Pueblo de Luis

In the former railway station at Av Fontana and 9 de Julio, historical photographs, clothing, and period furnishings are the strengths of this museum, whose fatal defect is the absence of any explanation for the Welsh departure from the United Kingdom or anything on their relationship to the Argentine state. The train itself stopped running in 1961, but the antique steam engine and other machinery outside are worth a stop.

The museum is open daily 7 am to 1 pm and 2 to 8 pm weekdays; admission is US$2 for adults, US$1 for children.

Museo Paleontológico Egidio Feruglio

Saber-toothed tigers, dinosaur eggs the size of bowling balls, and a fossil spider (so large that arachnophobes may exit screaming) are among the specimens in this well-organized museum, which takes its name from an Italian paleontologist who came to Argentina in 1925 as a petroleum geologist for YPF. The collections also include local dinosaurs, such as *Piatnitzkysaurus*, which are comparable to more celebrated Northern Hemisphere species like *Tyrannosaurus rex* and *Apatosaurus* (brontosaurus).

In spacious new quarters opposite the university, on Av Fontana north of 9 de Julio, the museum (☎ 420012, muspal@satlink.com) is open weekdays 8:30 am to 12:30 pm and 1:30 to 8 pm, Saturday 9 am to noon and 2 to 9 pm, and Sunday and holidays 2 to 9 pm. Admission is US$4 for adults, and US$2 for university students, retirees, and children under 12 years old.

The museum also offers excursions to Parque Paleontológico Bryn Gwyn, near Gaiman; for details, see that section later in this chapter.

Special Events

Trelew's major cultural event is the Eisteddfod de Chubut, celebrating Welsh traditions, in late October. October 20's Aniversario de la Ciudad commemorates the city's founding in 1886.

The most conspicuously commercial event is the Fiesta Provincial del Pingüino, coinciding with the flightless birds' arrival at Punta Tombo in late September. In late January, Trelew's Congreso de la Lana showcases local wool.

Organized Tours

Local travel agencies run excursions to most of the major sights in and around Trelew, including the city itself (US$20), Punta Tombo (US$30 plus the US$5 admission charge), and the lower Río Chubut valley (US$15; US$27 with Welsh tea in Gaiman). Day trips to Península Valdés (US$40 plus the US$10 admission charge) are more expensive here than those departing Puerto Madryn because it's an extra hour on the highway in each direction.

Places to Stay – Budget

Camping Open October to March, ***Camping Club Huracán*** *(☎ 434380)*, 4km south of town on RN 25 between the bridge and the traffic circle toward Comodoro Rivadavia, has hot showers and electricity, but is not very convenient because of limited public transport. Rates are US$3 per person.

Residenciales & Hotels Trelew's cheapest regular accommodations is ***Hotel Avenida*** *(☎ 434172, Lewis Jones 49)*, near Plaza Centenario. It is friendly, quiet, and clean for US$12/20 with shared bath and an inexpensive breakfast, but some of the beds sag. ***Residencial San Carlos*** *(☎ 421038, Sarmiento 758)* has small but tidy rooms at US$15/23 with bath, while the ***Residencial Argentino*** *(☎ 436134, Matthews 186)* is clean and comfy for US$15/25 single/double. Popular with travelers, the modest rooms at ***Residencial Rivadavia*** *(☎ 434472, Rivadavia 55)* are a good value for US$18/30 with private bath, but there are three singles with shared bath for US$13.

Places to Stay – Mid-Range

The best mid-range value – if only for its silent film-era atmosphere – is ***Hotel Tour-***

ing Club (☎ *433998, Av Fontana 240)*, which charges US$25/36 for singles/doubles. ***Hotel Galicia*** *(☎ 433803, 9 de Julio 214)* has pleasant rooms for US$25/40 with private bath, while ***City Hotel*** *(☎ 433951, Rivadavia 254)* costs US$30/40.

Places to Stay – Top End

Downtown ***Hotel Centenario*** *(☎ 420542, San Martín 150)* costs US$48/70 for singles/doubles and also has a restaurant, but the prices are not proportional to its standards. An alternative, for US$53/70, is ***Hotel Libertador*** *(☎ 420220, Rivadavia 31)*, which has a restaurant and a bar/confitería.

The most expensive and luxurious accommodation in town is four-star ***Hotel Rayentray*** *(☎ 434702)*, at San Martín and Belgrano, which has a decent restaurant, swimming pools, a gym, and a sauna. Rates are US$90/110.

Places to Eat

The ***Comedor Universitario***, on Fontana near 9 de Julio, offers wholesome meals at very low prices. For breakfast, the ***Confitería Touring Club***, part of its namesake hotel, has classic atmosphere even though the service can be lethargic. ***Sugar*** *(☎ 435978, 25 de Mayo 247)* is a good choice for sandwiches and minutas.

Trelew has several good tenedor libre values. For US$8, ***Rancho Aparte*** *(☎ 429263, Av Fontana 236)* specializes in Patagonian lamb. ***Los Tres Chinos*** *(☎ 437280, San Martín 188)* serves Chinese, while ***Quimey Quipán*** *(☎ 434350, Pellegrini 53 Norte)* has seafood.

La Casa de Juan *(☎ 421534, Moreno 360)* is nominally a pizzeria but has a far more varied menu. ***Delikatesse*** *(☎ 430716, AP Bell 434)*, west of downtown, serves mostly Italian cuisine and pizza, but also offers wild game and other unusual dishes. Recommended ***El Galeón*** *(☎ 420011, San Martín 118)* is a good seafood choice.

La Botica Natural is a natural-foods grocery on Av Fontana, alongside the Hotel Touring Club.

Heladería Venecia *(Belgrano 321)* is the spot for ice cream.

Entertainment

The ***Cine Coliseo*** *(☎ 425300, Belgrano 371)* shows first-run films.

Shopping

The area's most famous product is the Welsh fruitcake, sold at stores like Roger's Shop (☎ 430878), Moreno 488. More conventional sweets are available at La Casa del Chocolate, Av Fontana 455, Local 3.

For leather goods, horse gear, and woolens, try Jagüel (☎ 422949), 25 de Mayo 144.

Getting There & Away

Air At 25 de Mayo 33, Aerolíneas Argentinas (☎ 420210) flies twice a day to Buenos Aires' Aeroparque (US$77 to US$192) except Saturday and Sunday, when there's one flight only. LAPA (☎ 423440), Belgrano 206, flies twice daily to Aeroparque (US$79 to US$149).

TAN (☎ 434550), Belgrano 326, flies Tuesday and Wednesday to Comodoro Rivadavia (US$40 to US$50), and Monday, Wednesday, and Friday to Neuquén (US$59 to US$70).

LADE (☎ 435740), Av Fontana 227, flies Monday to Puerto Madryn (US$20), Esquel (US$47 to US$73), Bariloche (US$53 to US$74), Neuquén (US$53 to US$89), and Viedma (US$32 to US$125); Tuesday to Puerto Madryn, Viedma, Bahía Blanca (US$57 to US$73), Mar del Plata (US$88 to US$114), and Aeroparque (US$100 to US$147); Friday to Viedma, Neuquén, and Bariloche; and Friday to Comodoro Rivadavia (US$28 to US$43).

Kaikén Líneas Aéreas (☎ 421448), San Martín 146, flies daily to Bahía Blanca (US$60 to US$79), Comodoro Rivadavia (US$29 to US$43), Río Gallegos (US$89 to US$138), Río Grande (US$129 to US$157), and Ushuaia (US$132 to US$197), and daily except Sunday to Bariloche (US$76 to US$95), Neuquén (US$105 to US$140), and Mendoza (US$159 to US$189).

Bus Trelew's Terminal de Ómnibus (☎ 420121) is at Urquiza and Lewis Jones, six blocks northeast of downtown. Empresa 28 de Julio (☎ 432429) has frequent buses to

Puerto Madryn (US$4), and 20 daily to Gaiman (US$2.60) and Dolavon (US$1.40) between 7:20 am and 10:45 pm (weekend services are reduced). Empresas Rawson and 28 de Julio have buses to Rawson (US$1) every 15 minutes, starting at 5:30 am.

Empresa Mar y Valle (☎ 432429) has daily service to Puerto Pirámide, leaving Trelew at 7:45 am, with additional service in summer; for more detail, see Puerto Madryn Getting There & Away. Mar y Valle also goes daily to Esquel.

El Cóndor/La Puntual (☎ 433748) has daily buses to Buenos Aires. Que Bus (☎ 422760) offers nonstops to La Plata and to Buenos Aires. Empresa Don Otto (☎ 433748) has two buses daily to Buenos Aires, two to Bahía Blanca, two to Comodoro Rivadavia, one to Puerto Deseado, one to Rio Gallegos and one to Neuquén; it goes less frequently to Esquel (Tuesday, Friday, and Sunday). El Pingüino (☎ 422400) goes daily to Buenos Aires and Río Gallegos.

Andesmar (☎ 433535) goes daily to Neuquén, Mendoza, Comodoro Rivadavia, and Caleta Olivia, and three times weekly to Río Gallegos. Central Argentino, in the same office, goes to Viedma/Carmen de Patagones, Bahía Blanca and Rosario. Transportadora Patagónica (☎ 433748) goes to Bariloche and has two buses weekly to Mar del Plata.

TAC (☎ 431452) has extensive coastal routes, including Comodoro Rivadavia, Caleta Olivia, and Río Gallegos southbound, and Bahía Blanca, La Plata, and Buenos Aires northbound, plus interior routes to the Cuyo region and the Andean Northwest.

Empresa TUP (☎ 421343) travels to Santa Rosa and Córdoba three afternoons weekly, and to Comodoro Rivadavia three mornings a week.

Ñandú goes to Camarones weekdays at 8 am, returning at 5 pm.

Sample fares include Camarones (US$10, three hours), Puerto Pirámide (US$11, three hours), Comodoro Rivadavia (US$17 to US$22, five hours), Caleta Olivia (US$25, six hours), Viedma/Carmen de Patagones (US$28, seven hours), Esquel (US$35), Neuquén (US$38 to US$44, 10 hours), Bahía Blanca (US$45, 12 hours), Santa Rosa (US$46, 12 hours), Río Gallegos (US$51 to US$71, 17 hours), Buenos Aires (US$60 to US$80, 21 hours), Bariloche (US$56, 13 hours), La Plata (US$68 to US$78, 19 hours), Mar del Plata (US$72, 17 hours), Córdoba (US$78, 19 hours), Mendoza (US$78, 24 hours), and Rosario (US$100, 26 hours).

Getting Around

To/From the Airport Trelew's modern Aeropuerto Internacional Almirante Zar (☎ 428021) is on RN 3, 5km north of town; despite its designation, there are no scheduled international flights. Buses from Trelew to Puerto Madryn no longer enter the airport to drop off passengers, but cabs from downtown cost about US$8.

Car Included among local agencies are Rent A Car (☎ 420898) at San Martín 125, Avis (☎ 434834) at Paraguay 105, and Localiza (☎ 435344) at Urquiza 310.

GAIMAN

As Chubut's oldest municipality and one of few remaining demonstrably Welsh towns, Gaiman (population 4700) owes its name (Stony Point) to Tehuelche Indians who once wintered in the area. Contemporary visitors come to stuff themselves at its numerous Welsh teahouses.

The Welsh presence dates from 1874, but later immigrants, including criollos, Germans, and Anglos, also cultivated fruit, vegetables, and fodder in the lower Río Chubut valley. Industry followed later, including Argentina's only seaweed-processing plant, a nylon stockings factory, and a polyethylene packaging plant. Gaiman is 17km west of Trelew via RN 25.

In the sparkling new Casa de Cultura at Rivadavia and Belgrano, the Oficina de Informes Turísticos is open 7 am to 2 pm and 3 to 7 pm daily. It keeps a list of B&B accommodations and will make phone calls to arrange them.

The post office is at the corner of Juan Evans and Hipólito Yrigoyen, just north of the bridge over the river. There's a Fonofax office on Av Tello between 25 de Mayo and 9 de Julio; the area code is ☎ 02965, the same as Trelew.

Things to See & Do

Welsh culture is still evident in the cut stone buildings along Av Eugenio Tello, as well as in local customs. Numerous teahouses offer a variety of homemade cakes and sweets, and the **Eisteddfod**, with choral singing and poetry competitions, still takes place on a regular basis.

Architecturally distinctive churches and chapels of several denominations are scattered around town. The secondary school **Camwy** dates from 1899, while the **cemetery**, at the entrance to town, has many headstones with Welsh-language inscriptions. Nearby is the 300m **Túnel del Ferrocarril**, a brick tunnel through which the first trains to Dolavon passed in 1914; its top offers a good view of the valley and town.

The old railway station, at the corner of Sarmiento and 28 de Julio, houses the **Museo Histórico Regional de Gaiman** (☎ 491007), a fine small museum attended by Welsh- and English-speaking volunteers, with an intriguing collection of pioneer photographs and household items. Hours are 3 to 8 pm daily; admission is US$1.

One of the most amusingly offbeat sights anywhere in conformist Argentina is **Parque El Desafío** (☎ 491340), described by LP reader Paul Bruthiaux as

> Gaiman's answer to Disneyland. It's a wonderful, wild, wacky miniature theme park built by local political protester and conservationist Joaquín Alonso, exclusively from bits of string, bottles, cans, and other junk long before the rest of the world knew the meaning of recycling.

Admission is US$5 for adults (US$4 per person for groups larger than three), US$2 for children. Hours are dawn to dusk.

Places to Stay

Gaiman is mainly a day-trip destination from Trelew, but it has a small riverside campground and a growing number of B&Bs, some associated with teahouses.

The fire station's ***Camping Bomberos Voluntarios***, on Hipólito Yrigoyen between Libertad and Independencia, can be inaccessible when it rains, and the floodplain soil can be soggy. Still, it has good picnic tables, clean toilets, and excellent showers (lacking mirrors and hooks to hang your clothing) for US$2 per person.

Most B&Bs charge around US$15 per person and prefer to be phoned first – try Coca Horton's ***Man Aros*** *(☎ 491292)*, Ronald Foulkes *(☎ 491109)*, Delma Williams *(☎ 491086)*, Laura Alvarado *(☎ 491065)*, Ansel Roberts *(☎ 491250)*, or Moelona Drake *(☎ 491092)*.

Plas y Coed *(☎ 491133, Miguel Jones 123)* is a spinoff of Gaiman's most venerable teahouse; rates are US$50 double. The only formal hotel is ***Hotel Unelén***, at Av Eugenio Tello and 9 de Julio, which charges US$40 double with private bath and breakfast.

Places to Eat

One cannot leave Gaiman without visiting one of the local Welsh teahouses, with their abundant home-baked sweets. While tea costs around US$10 or more, portions are large and they're a good value. Note that almost all teahouses get uncomfortably crowded when tour buses arrive, so try to avoid places with buses outside – or do something else until they leave. The teahouses are really the only places to eat in town, besides a couple of rotiserías.

Most teahouses open by 3 pm, so don't eat more than a light lunch. The oldest is ***Plas y Coed*** *(☎ 491133, Miguel D Jones 123)*, run by English-speaking Marta Rees, the original owner's daughter-in-law and a charming and wonderful cook. She personally makes sure that every client is satisfied, even offering a doggy bag to those who can't finish the spread.

Other possibilities include ***Ty Gwyn*** *(☎ 491009, 9 de Julio 147)*, ***Ty Gaiman*** *(☎ 491131, Hipólito Yrigoyen 738)*, ***Te Newydd*** at the corner of Av Tello and 9 de Julio, and ***Ty Nain*** *(☎ 491126, Hipólito Yrigoyen 283)*, a beautiful house.

Set among its own irrigated fields in a tasteful new building with attractive gardens, ***Ty Caerdydd*** *(☎ 491287)* uses its own fresh produce, including raspberries and apples; prepares a particularly light egg custard; and sells cakes to take away. Recorded Welsh choral music adds to the atmosphere of Patagonia's largest teahouse, which does excellent business despite its relatively inconvenient location (at least for pedestrians) across the river; follow the signs along the bridge unless, as Princess Diana did on her visit, you have the privilege of helicopter service.

Shopping

Look for local crafts at the Paseo Artesanal Crefft Werin, at the corner of Av Tello and Miguel Jones, opposite Plaza Roca.

Getting There & Away

Stopping directly in front of Plaza Roca, Empresa 28 de Julio has 20 buses daily from Trelew via Gaiman to Dolavon, but weekend services are fewer. The return fare to Gaiman is US$2.80.

AROUND GAIMAN

Parque Paleontológico Bryn Gwyn

In the badlands along the Río Chubut, south of Gaiman via RP 5, Parque Paleontológico Bryn Gwyn is open to visitors for guided tours along a well-designed nature trail that is almost literally a walk through time, as the Río Chubut has exposed a wealth of fossils from as far back as the Tertiary, about 40 million years ago. While the oldest sediments here are too recent for dinosaurs, there are remains of terrestrial mammals in the volcanic Sarmiento formation, deposited prior to the building of the Andes, and later marine mammals and fish of the Puerto Madryn and Gaiman formations, when subtropical seas covered the low-lying area. Some of the fossils are in situ, while others have been excavated and mounted in display cases.

Affiliated with the Museo Feruglio (☎ 435464), on Av Fontana in Trelew, the park offers guided three-hour hikes for a fee. Admission is an additional US$4 for adults, US$2 for children, and US$3 for retired people. There is also a confitería in the park.

DOLAVON

Plentiful brick buildings line the streets of Dolavon, another 18km west of Gaiman by paved RN 25; the name means 'river meadow.' The major monument of this historic Welsh agricultural town is the **Molino Harinero** (1930), today a museum, with a still-functioning water wheel.

Dolavon has a dusty but free and otherwise acceptable ***Camping Municipal***, but the baths may be locked up. There is also one hotel, the ***Hotel Pierce*** *(☎ 02965-492013, 28 de Julio 45)*, and a single Welsh teahouse, ***Draig Goch***. Empresa 28 de Julio runs 10 buses daily to Dolavon, via Gaiman, from the Trelew bus terminal.

RAWSON

Named for Guillermo Rawson, the Argentine minister who granted the Welsh sanctuary, the city of Rawson (population 24,000) has always been politically important. The territorial capital since 1884, it became the provincial capital three years after Chubut attained provincial status in 1955. The modern centro cívico contains all government offices.

Since 1923 the long sandy beach has made the nearby suburb of Playa Unión a favorite holiday destination, but many visitors stay in Trelew, 20km west via paved RN 25, which is more important commercially as well as more interesting historically and culturally.

Fishing boats return every afternoon to Puerto Rawson, at the mouth of the Río Chubut, where you can taste the catch at the cantinas near the pier. Playa Unión has a couple of hotels, but can also be crowded with day-trippers from Trelew and area locals (mostly from the valleys) who keep summer houses at the beach.

Information

The Delegación Municipal de Turismo (☎ 496588) has a helpful office on the waterfront in Playa Unión. It's open from mid-December to mid-March, 8 am to 7 pm daily.

The provincial Secretaría de Turismo del Chubut (☎ 484144) is a friendly but bureaucratic office at 9 de Julio 280 in Rawson proper.

Banco del Chubut has an ATM at Rivadavia 615. Correo Argentino is on the central Plaza Rawson, at the corner of Mariano Moreno and Vacchina; the postal code is 9103. Rawson's area code is ☎ 02965, the same as Trelew's.

Things to See

The **Capilla Maria Auxiliadora**, a chapel with arresting architecture and fine murals, keeps very limited hours. So does the **Museo Regional Salesiano** (☎ 482623), in the Colegio Don Bosco at Don Bosco 248. It features a sample of weapons used in the Conquista del Desierto, as well as provincial fossils, minerals, and artifacts. The museum is open Tuesday and Friday 10 am to noon, and Monday, Wednesday, and Thursday 5 to 8 pm. Also worth a look is the **Museo de Rescate Histórico**, open 9 am to noon and 3 to 6 pm weekdays on Plaza Rawson.

Places to Stay & Eat

In Rawson proper, ***Hospedaje San Pedro*** *(☎ 481721, Belgrano 744)* has singles/doubles for US$15/25 with shared bath. ***Residencial Mara*** *(☎ 482082, Alejandro Maíz 377)* charges US$25/35 with private bath but no breakfast. Frequented by visiting politicians, the upgraded ***Hotel Provincial*** *(☎ 481300, Mitre 550)* has prices to match at US$70/80 with bath. Its restaurant and confitería are also very good.

At Playa Unión, beachfront ***Camping Siglo XXI*** *(☎ 481244)*, at the south end of Av Centenario, charges US$5 per person, with children ages eight and under free. ***Hotel Atlansur*** *(Costanera Av Rawson 339)* is a good value at US$15 per person. Modest ***Hostería Le Bon*** *(☎ 496638, Rifleros 68)* charges US$40 double with breakfast.

There are many restaurants and confiterías along Av Rawson in Playa Unión – for a variety of fish and shellfish dishes, try ***Cantina El Marinero*** *(☎ 496030)* or ***Cantina Marcelino*** *(☎ 496031)*, both near the pier at the south end of town.

Getting There & Away

Rawson has a new bus terminal on the Playa Unión road. Empresas Rawson and 28 de Julio run buses from Trelew every 15 minutes weekdays, every half-hour Saturday, and hourly Sunday and holidays. Buses run from 6 am to 1 am. Empresa Bahía connects downtown Rawson, Puerto Rawson, and Playa Unión.

There are more long-distance connections in Trelew, but La Puntual (☎ 483938) goes directly to Comodoro Rivadavia (five hours), Bahía Blanca (11 hours), and Buenos Aires (22 hours).

RESERVA PROVINCIAL PUNTA TOMBO

Half a million Magellanic penguins breed at Punta Tombo, continental South America's largest penguin nesting ground, and there are many seabirds and shorebirds, most notably king and rock cormorants, giant petrels, kelp gulls, flightless steamer ducks, and black oystercatchers.

Early-morning visitors will beat the numerous tour buses from Trelew. Most of the nesting area is fenced off; this does not prevent photographers from approaching the birds, since they pay no attention to the fences, but remember that penguins can inflict bites serious enough to require stitches. They remain on land from September to April. Provincial officials charge a US$5 entry fee per person. Camping is forbidden.

There are three ways to reach Punta Tombo, 110km south of Trelew via RP 1 and a short southeast lateral: by arranging a tour with a travel agency in Trelew (about US$30), hiring a taxi (about US$110), or renting a car, which permits you to remain as long as you wish.

Because of the speeds at which many Argentines drive, it is quite common on gravel roads for windshields to be broken by rocks kicked up by other vehicles (wire-mesh screens covering windshields are a common sight in Patagonia). Such damages are not always covered under the insurance policies offered by rental agencies; if they aren't, they will have to be paid out of your pocket. Be sure to check with the agency about coverage and deductibles. When you consider the cost of glass breakage or certain other uncovered damages that can occur on unpaved roads, hiring a remise for the day can be an appealing alternative. Rates are sometimes negotiable and will fluctuate with the season.

Graveled RP 1 is in very good condition; alternative routes are poorly marked and hard on vehicles. Motorists can proceed south to Camarones (see below) via scenic but desolate Cabo Raso.

Note that tours may be canceled if bad weather makes dirt roads impassable.

CAMARONES

Juan Perón's father operated a sheep estancia near Camarones, and the town figures, perhaps apocryphally, in Tomás Eloy Martínez's *The Perón Novel*. From RN 3, about 180km south of Trelew, newly paved RP 30 leads 72km to this small, dilapidated, but quaint fishing port (population 800), where any weekend is certain to be a quiet one. Motorists should know that the town's only petrol station rarely has fuel. There is an annual Fiesta Nacional del Salmón (National Salmon Festival) the second weekend of February.

At the eastern approach to town, the Oficina Turística Municipal (☎ 0297-4963104) is open 8 am to 9 pm daily in summer.

Places to Stay & Eat

Open all year, the privatized ***Camping Camarones*** near the Prefectura Naval on the waterfront charges US$4 per site, with electricity, hot showers, and some shade. ***Residencial Bahía del Ensueño*** *(☎ 0297-496-3077)*, Belgrano and 9 de Julio and ***Residencial Mar Azul***, 25 de Mayo and Urquiza, both cost US$12 per person. ***Hotel Kau-i-keukenk*** *(☎ 0297-496-3004)*, at Sarmiento and Roca, is slightly more expensive at US$15 per person with breakfast. Its restaurant, once exceptional, is still the best in town, but the US$10 tenedor libre parrillada is less appealing than the seafood specials it once served.

Getting There & Away

Ñandú buses to Camarones (US$10) leave Trelew at 8 am weekdays, returning at 5 pm.

AROUND CAMARONES

Cabo Dos Bahías

Attracting far fewer visitors than Punta Tombo, this scenic nature reserve, 30km southeast of Camarones, not only offers 30,000 nesting penguins in spring and summer, but also some of the largest concentrations of guanacos and rheas on the coast. Other marine and terrestrial wildlife includes a variety of seabirds, sea lions, fur seals, and foxes.

Camping is possible at beaches en route and at the reserve itself. If you have no car, try hiring a taxi in Camarones.

Cabo Raso

Just a few families eke out a bleak existence at this virtual ghost town, about 85km north of Camarones, on RP 1 to Punta Tombo. Camping is possible in the ruins near the shingle beach, where elephant seals sometimes haul themselves ashore.

COMODORO RIVADAVIA

While not a major destination in its own right, Comodoro Rivadavia is a frequent and worthwhile stopover for southbound travelers. Before its privatization the former state oil company, Yacimientos Petrolíferos Fiscales (YPF), spared no expense on the petroleum museum, in the suburb of General Mosconi; now operated by the Universidad de la Patagonia, it's one of the best of its kind in the world, and no visitor should miss it.

Fuel storage tanks and pipelines clutter the landscape nearly everywhere among the starkly scenic Atlantic beaches at the foot of steeply rising headlands like 212m Cerro Chenque. Chubut's southernmost city, Comodoro Rivadavia (population 150,000) is the powerhouse of the Argentine oil industry, providing about one-third of the country's production. Seismic survey lines crisscrossing the desert testify to subterranean blasting that may well have contributed to a massive landslide on Cerro

Chenque, an area of poorly consolidated marine sediments. The landslide destroyed sections of RN 3 in early 1995, isolating the northern suburbs and disrupting long-distance commerce.

The city's other questionable distinction is the prevalence of what may be the largest soft-drink murals anywhere in the country and perhaps in the world – one covers the entire west-facing wall of the 10-story Hotel Comodoro. At least they're not neon.

History

Founded in 1901, Comodoro (as it is commonly known) boomed a few years later after workers drilling for water serendipitously struck petroleum – the country's first major oil find. Foreign companies played a significant role in early development, but the state soon dominated the sector through YPF, 'the first vertically integrated state petroleum industry outside the Soviet Union,' according to historian David Rock. Though YPF lost money as a state enterprise, Argentina remains self-sufficient in petroleum and even exports small amounts to neighboring countries.

Orientation

Most of central Comodoro sits on a narrow wave-cut platform, behind which the hills rise steeply. RN 3 connects the city with Buenos Aires to the north and Río Gallegos to the south. Cerro Chenque, just north of downtown, is a stiff climb rewarded with panoramic views.

Unlike most Argentine cities, Comodoro has no central plaza around which major public buildings cluster. The principal commercial street is Av San Martín, which trends east-west below Cerro Chenque. San Martín, north-south Av Alsina (which becomes Av Chiclana), and the Atlantic shoreline form a triangle that circumscribes the downtown area.

Information

Tourist Offices Comodoro's helpful Dirección de Turismo (☎ 462376), Rivadavia 430, is open in summer 8 am to 9 pm weekdays, 2 to 7 pm weekends; winter hours are 8 am to 7 pm weekdays, 8 am to 3 pm weekends. It also has a space at the bus terminal, open Monday to Saturday 9 am to 7 pm, Sunday 5 to 9 pm only.

ACA (☎ 464036) has maps and information at its office at Dorrego and Alvear.

Money Most of Comodoro's numerous banks and ATMs are along Av San Martín. Travel agencies along Av San Martín may also change cash, but not traveler's checks.

Post & Communications Correo Argentino is at Av San Martín and Moreno; the postal code is 9000. Telefonía Patagonia is at Av San Martín and Belgrano; Comodoro's area code is ☎ 0297.

Travel Agencies Tur Ceferino (☎ 473805), 9 de Julio 880, 1st floor, is the AmEx representative, but there are many other agencies on or near Av San Martín.

Internet Resources The Sociedad Argentina de Escritores, on Rivadavia near 25 de Mayo, is a cybercafe, among other things.

Laundry Laverap is at Rivadavia 287.

Medical Services The Hospital Regional (☎ 462542) is at Hipólito Yrigoyen 950.

Museo Regional Patagónico

Conspicuously decaying natural history specimens nearly overshadow this museum's entertaining archaeological and historical items, including some good pottery and spear points, materials on early South African Boer immigrants, and a possible local encounter with members of Butch Cassidy's Wild Bunch. Still, compared with the state-of-the-art Museo de Petróleo, it's pretty insignificant. On the Av Rivadavia median, between Francia and Chacabuco, the museum (☎ 477-1017) is open 9 am to 7 pm weekdays, and is free of charge.

Organized Tours

Several agencies arrange city tours (around US$18) and trips to outlying sights like the

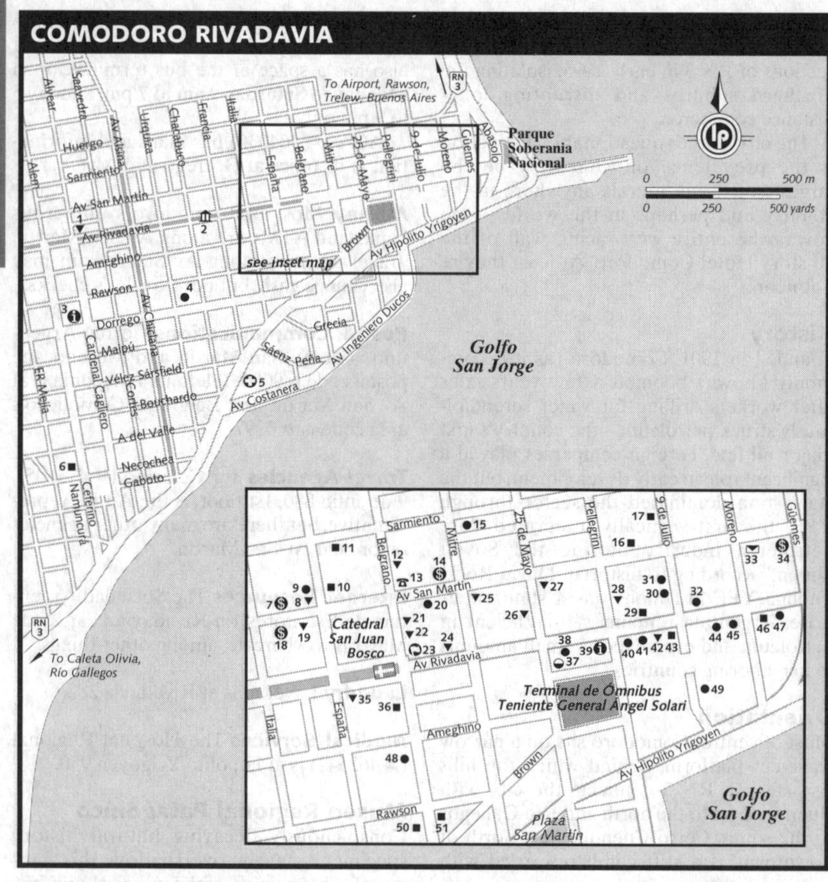

Bosque Petrificado Sarmiento (US$65, minimum three passengers; see Around Comodoro Rivadavia later in this chapter) and Cueva de las Manos (US$100, also minimum three passengers). Among the local operators are Total Travel (☎/fax 445464), Sarmiento 649, and Turismo Aonikenk (☎/fax 466768, aonikenk@satlink.com), Urquiza 573.

Mónica Jury and Pedro Mangini (☎ 451537, fax 460365) also arrange trips to Bosque Petrificado, Cueva de las Manos, and Patagonian estancias.

Places to Stay – Budget

Camping There's no campground in Comodoro Rivadavia proper, but the ***Camping Municipal** (☎ 452423)* at Rada Tilly, a windy beach resort 15km south on RN 3, charges US$2.50 per adult, US$1.50 per child, and US$3 per tent. Frequent local buses link Comodoro's Terminal del Ómnibus with Rada Tilly.

Hospedajes, Hosterías & Hotels Deservedly, the most popular budget hotel is ***Hotel Comercio** (☎ 472341, Rivadavia 341)*,

COMODORO RIVADAVIA

whose vintage bar and restaurant alone justify a visit. Rooms with shared bath cost US$15 per person. Well-located ***Hospedaje Cari-Hue*** *(☎ 472946, Belgrano 563)* charges US$15/25 for singles/doubles that have a private bath.

Charging US$18/30, ***Hotel Colón*** *(☎ 462283, Av San Martín 341)* has drawn some criticism for lack of cleanliness. Others in this category, for US$20/30 with private bath, include ***Hostería Rúa Marina*** *(☎ 468777, Belgrano 738)* and the quiet ***Hospedaje Belgrano*** *(☎ 478349, Belgrano 546)*.

Places to Stay – Mid-Range

Residencial Atlántico *(☎ 463145, Alem 30)* costs US$25/40 for singles/doubles with private bath, but has some budget singles for US$15 with shared bath. ***Hotel Español*** *(☎ 460116, 9 de Julio 850)* charges US$20 per person.

In a quiet location, ***Hotel Azul*** *(☎ 474628, Sarmiento 724)* charges US$35/56. Not to be confused with high-rise Hotel Comodoro (see below), the ***Residencial Comodoro*** *(☎ 462582, España 919)* costs US$36/55.

Places to Stay – Top End

Prices at ***Hotel Austral*** *(☎ 472200, Av Rivadavia 190)* have risen to US$50/83 but it offers a few bargain singles in the US$35 range. Remodeled ***Hotel Comodoro*** *(☎ 472300, 9 de Julio 770)* has top-of-the-line rooms at US$75/94.

Places to Eat

Dino *(☎ 463799, San Martín 592)*, on the 2nd floor, is a cheap confitería that's good for breakfast, while ***La Fonte D'Oro*** *(☎ 460804)*, San Martín at 25 de Mayo, is its more upscale counterpart. At the corner of Rivadavia and Alvear, ***Rotisería Andafama*** *(☎ 463882)* prepares a variety of exquisite empanadas for take-out; the more central ***La Chacha*** *(Pellegrini 827)* has less-diverse offerings.

Parrillas include ***La Rastra*** *(☎ 462140, Rivadavia 348)*, the very popular ***El Nazareno*** *(☎ 463725)* at San Martín and España, and ***Bom Bife*** *(☎ 467448)* at the corner of Rivadavia and España.

Gran Pizzería Romanella *(☎ 460823, 25 de Mayo 866)* serves standard fare, as does ***Pizzería Giulietta*** *(☎ 461201, Belgrano 851)*. Try also ***La Cantina*** *(Belgrano 845)*.

Peperoni *(☎ 469683, Rivadavia 619)* is a very good restaurant with friendly service, featuring minutas, pasta, and fish. ***La Barca*** *(Belgrano 935)* also serves seafood.

For ice cream, try ***La Fueguina***, Av San Martín 811.

Entertainment

The rehabbed ***Cine Español*** *(☎ 477700, Av San Martín 664)*, a classic, shows current films.

The ***Sociedad Argentina de Escritores***, located on Rivadavia near 25 de Mayo, is a multi-hybrid bookstore, cybercafe, and literary café.

El Galpón Pub *(Rivadavia 120)* has live rock music, while ***Café Colonial*** *(Belgrano 690)* has live jazz.

Getting There & Away

Comodoro Rivadavia has extensive air and road connections to coastal and interior destinations in Patagonia. RN 3 is entirely paved to Río Gallegos, while RN 26, RP 20, and RN 40 are paved to Esquel, the Andean foothill gateway to Parque Nacional Los Alerces.

Air Aerolíneas Argentinas (☎ 440050), 9 de Julio 870, flies daily except on Saturday to Trelew (US$29 to US$43), and nonstop to Buenos Aires' Aeroparque (US$77 to US$199) three times each weekday, twice Saturday, and once on Sunday. LAPA (☎ 472400), Rivadavia 396, flies to Aeroparque (US$79 to US$169) twice each weekday and once a day on weekends. Dinar Líneas Aéreas (☎ 441111), Rivadavia 242, flies daily except Saturday to Aeroparque (US$109 to US$170), with onward connections to Córdoba, Mendoza, Tucumán, and Salta.

Comodoro is the hub for LADE (☎ 476181), Rivadavia 360. Flights are frequently overbooked, but travelers stand a good chance of getting on at the airport itself. LADE flies Monday to Trelew (US$28), Puerto Madryn (US$39), Esquel (US$43), Bariloche (US$60 to US$80), Neuquén (US$76 to US$120), Viedma (US$66 to US$132), Puerto Deseado (US$25), San Julián (US$39), Gobernador Gregores (US$39), Santa Cruz (US$48), and Río Gallegos (US$66); Tuesday to Perito Moreno (US$28), Gobernador Gregores, El Calafate (US$62), Río Gallegos, Río Grande (US$89), and Ushuaia (US$100); Wednesday to Esquel (US$43), El Maitén (US$51), El Bolsón (US$53), Bariloche, San Martín de los Andes (US$70), Zapala (US$78), and Neuquén (US$76 to US$120); Thursday to Perito Moreno, Gobernador Gregores, El Calafate, Río Turbio (US$63), Río Mayo (US$21), and Río Gallegos; and Friday to Trelew, Viedma, Neuquén, and Bariloche.

TAN (☎ 477268), España 928, flies Tuesday, Friday, and Saturday to Puerto Montt, Chile (US$103 to US$107); the latter two flights stop in Bariloche (US$75 to US$88). It also flies Monday, Wednesday, and Friday to Trelew (US$40 to US$50) and Neuquén (US$95 to US$115), and nonstop to Neuquén Monday and twice Tuesday, Wednesday, Thursday, Saturday, and Sunday.

Kaikén Líneas Aéreas (☎ 472000), Rivadavia 240, flies daily except Sunday to Trelew (US$29 to US$43), Bariloche (US$76 to US$95), Neuquén (US$114 to US$160), and Mendoza (US$160 to US$260); and twice daily Monday through Saturday to Río Gallegos (US$69 to US$103), Río Grande (US$99 to US$126), and Ushuaia (US$119 to US$142); Sunday there is one flight to each.

Bus Comodoro's Terminal de Ómnibus Teniente General Ángel Solari (☎ 467305) is at Ameghino and 25 de Mayo.

La Puntual (☎ 469176) and El Cóndor (☎ 468894) both have daily buses to Buenos Aires and intermediate points via RN 3. Empresa Don Otto/Transportadora Patagónica (☎ 464118) has almost identical service to Buenos Aires, but also goes to Mar del Plata Tuesday and Friday, and daily to Río Gallegos, to Esquel, El Bolsón, and Bariloche, to Neuquén, and to Viedma and Bahía Blanca.

Central Argentino (☎ 468894) goes Tuesday to Viedma, Bahía Blanca and Rosario, and Friday to Viedma and Bahía Blanca only.

El Pingüino (☎ 479104) goes northbound to Buenos Aires and intermediate points at 9 am, and southbound at 9 pm to Río Gallegos and intermediate points, with connections to El Calafate, Río Turbio, and the Chilean towns of Punta Arenas and Puerto Natales.

TAC (☎ 443376) has extensive routes southbound to Río Gallegos and northbound to Bahía Blanca, La Plata, and Buenos Aires, but also serves Santa Rosa and the northwestern destinations of Córdoba, Santiago del Estero, Tucumán, Salta, and Jujuy. TUP (☎ 468493) goes daily southbound to Caleta Olivia and northbound to Santa Rosa, Córdoba, and intermediate points.

Andesmar (☎ 468894) goes south to Caleta Olivia and Río Gallegos, and north to Trelew, Puerto Madryn, Santa Rosa, San Luis, Mendoza, and San Juan, with connections to northwestern Argentina as well as to Chile.

Empresa Quebek (☎ 445674) goes southbound to Río Gallegos and intermediate points on uneven-numbered days, and northbound to Trelew, Santa Rosa, Córdoba, and intermediate points on even-numbered days.

Transportes Robledo (☎ 468187) has Tuesday and Friday service to Córdoba and to Catamarca, while Transportes Ortiz (☎ 465723) goes Monday and Thursday to Tinogasta, in Catamarca province.

Transportes La Unión (☎ 462822) goes hourly to Caleta Olivia, three times daily to Puerto Deseado, and twice daily to Perito Moreno and Los Antiguos. Transportes Sportsman (☎ 442988) goes daily at 6 am to Perito Moreno and Los Antiguos. Etap (☎ 474841) goes to Sarmiento and to Río Mayo daily, and to Esquel daily except for Saturday.

Transportes Giobbi (☎ 474841) departs at 1 am Monday and Thursday for Coihaique, Chile, via Río Mayo, but these buses are often very full.

Turibús (☎ 465723) goes to Coihaique Tuesday and Saturday at 8 am.

Sample fares include Caleta Olivia (US$4, one hour), San Julián (US$14), Trelew (US$15, six hours), Puerto Deseado (US$17, four hours), Puerto Madryn (US$20, seven hours), Los Antiguos (US$20, six hours), Esquel (US$29, eight hours), Río Gallegos (US$30, 11 hours), Viedma (US$35, 10 hours), Coihaique (US$40), Bahía Blanca (US$45), Bariloche (US$47, 14 hours), Buenos Aires (US$60, 24 hours), Mendoza (31 hours), Córdoba (US$80), and Catamarca/La Rioja (US$83).

Getting Around

To/From the Airport Aeropuerto General Mosconi (☎ 473355, ext 163) is north of the city, but the No 8 Patagonia Argentina (Directo Palazzo) bus goes there directly from the downtown bus terminal.

To/From Rada Tilly Expreso Rada Tilly (☎ 451363) links Comodoro to the nearby beach resort about every half-hour weekdays, less frequently weekends. The last bus leaves Comodoro's terminal at 11:30 pm weekdays, 12:30 am Saturday nights/Sunday mornings, and 11:20 pm Sunday evenings.

Car Rental cars are available at Localiza (☎ 460334), 9 de Julio 770, or at Avis (☎ 476382), 9 de Julio 687.

AROUND COMODORO RIVADAVIA

Museo del Petróleo

Built by the former state oil agency YPF but now managed by the Universidad Nacional de Patagonia, one of Argentina's best museums boasts vivid exhibits on the region's natural and cultural history, early and modern oil technology, and social and historical aspects of petroleum development. Historical photographs merit special mention, but there are also fascinating, detailed models of tankers, refineries, and the entire zone of exploitation. The grounds include the site of Comodoro's original gusher and an excellent display of restored antique drilling equipment and vehicles. The video salon offers an impressive slide show, which is marred slightly by its bombastic taped narration.

In the suburb of General Mosconi (named for YPF's first administrator), a few kilometers north of downtown, the museum (☎ 455-9558) is on Lavalle between Viedma and Carlos Calvo. From downtown Comodoro, take either the No 7 Laprida or 8 Palazzo bus.

Admission is US$2.50, US$3.50 with a guided tour. Hours are Tuesday to Friday 8 am to 1 pm, and Tuesday through Sunday 4 to 9 pm.

Museo Astra

About 15km north of Comodoro on RN 3, this open-air display of early oil-drilling equipment also holds a small but impressive semisubterranean exhibit on Patagonian paleontology and minerals. Admission is free, but the mineral exhibit has very limited hours: weekends 2 to 6 pm only.

Petrified Forests

South of Colonia Sarmiento, an agricultural town 148km west of Comodoro via paved RN 26 and RP 20, are two petrified forests more accessible than Monumento Natural Bosques Petrificados (see Santa Cruz province later in this chapter). From Sarmiento, easily reached by Etap bus (US$10 one-way), it's possible to arrange a car and driver (about US$40) to the Ormachea (30km) and Szlapelis (20km farther) reserves; there is an additional admission charge of US$5. See also the Organized Tours entry for Comodoro Rivadavia.

RÍO MAYO

Only gauchos and soldiers are likely to spend more than a night at this dusty western crossroads (population 2700), 274km from Comodoro Rivadavia via paved RN 26 and RP 20, but it has good travelers' services. Graveled RN 26 continues west to Coihaique, Chile, while rugged RN 40 heads south to Perito Moreno and Los Antiguos, and paved RP 22 and then RP 20 head north to Esquel, El Bolsón, and Bariloche.

The tourist office occupies new quarters in the Casa de la Cultura (☎ 420400) on Av Ejército Argentino s/n; it's open 9 am to noon and 3 to 6 pm daily.

Banco del Chubut has an ATM at the corner of Yrigoyen and Argentina. Río Mayo's postal code is 9030; the area code is ☎ 02903.

Things to See & Do

In the small **Museo Regional Federico Escalada**, relocated to an early-20th-century schoolhouse that also serves as the tourist office, the rather mundane objects – antique hair curlers, an espresso machine, plus the usual Tehuelche and Mapuche artifacts – lend it a homey attractiveness. It keeps the same hours as the tourist office.

Early January's Festival Nacional de la Esquila, held at the Predio Olegario Paillaguala (fairgrounds), features sheep-shearing competitions.

Places to Stay & Eat

Río Mayo has plenty of reasonably-priced accommodations, starting at US$10 per vehicle at the riverside ***Camping Municipal*** *(☎ 420121)* in the Predio Olegario Paillaguala. Otherwise, the cheapest is the marginal ***Hospedaje El Cóndor*** *(☎ 420310)*, Av Ejército Argentino and Yrigoyen, for US$8 per person with shared bath. ***Hotel San Martín*** *(☎ 420066, San Martín 400)* charges US$10 per person with shared bath, and also has a restaurant/bar with take-out food. Nicely remodeled ***Hotel Akatá*** *(☎ 420054, San Martín 640)* charges US$15 per person with private bath and also has a restaurant. ***Hotel Covadonga*** *(San Martín 573)* is comparably priced.

Getting There & Away

Air LADE (☎ 420060), San Martín 520, flies Friday to Comodoro Rivadavia (US$21).

Bus From the Terminal de Ómnibus (☎ 420164) at Fontana and Irigoyen, Angel Giobbi has daily buses to Comodoro Rivadavia (US$22, four hours) at 6 am, and goes to Coihaique, Chile (US$23), Monday and Thursday at 5:30 am; the latter services, which start in Comodoro Rivadavia, are often full.

Monday at 10 am and Thursday at 10 pm, Etap (☎ 420167) covers the 350km to Esquel (US$25, seven hours) via Río Senguer, San Martín, Gobernador Costa, and Tecka. There is no public transportation on RN 40 southward toward Perito Moreno and Los Antiguos, but patience may yield a lift.

GOBERNADOR COSTA

Midway between Río Mayo and Esquel, and also on the route between Esquel and Comodoro Rivadavia, this cattle town (population 1700) has good travelers' services, including its ***Camping Municipal*** for US$2 per person with hot water and electricity.

Both ***Residencial Jair*** and ***Hotel Vegas*** have singles for US$15 with bath; the latter has a modest restaurant. On February 28, the town celebrates its annual festival, the Día del Pueblo.

Twenty km west of town, RP 19 leads to Lago General Vintter, in a less-frequented part of the Argentine lake district, and several smaller lakes near the Chilean border. There is good trout and salmon fishing.

Getting There & Away

Several buses a week stop here between Trelew and Esquel, and between Comodoro Rivadavia and Bariloche. Etap serves Río Mayo (see above) via Alto Río Senguer.

ESQUEL

In the western Chubut foothills, sunny Esquel is the gateway to Parque Nacional Los Alerces and other Andean recreation areas, and the terminus for the picturesque narrow-gauge railway from Ingeniero Jacobacci in Río Negro province (this train no longer covers the entire route, however). Founded at the turn of the century, the town (population 23,000) is also the area's main commercial and livestock center. It takes its name from a Mapuche term meaning either 'place of the thistles' or 'bog.'

Orientation

On the north shore of the eponymous Arroyo Esquel, the town has a fairly standard grid pattern. RN 259 zigzags through town to a junction with RN 40, which heads north to El Bolsón and Bariloche, and southeast toward Comodoro Rivadavia. South of town, RN 259 leads to the Welsh settlement of Trevelin, with junctions to Parque Nacional Los Alerces and other Andean attractions.

Information

Tourist Offices Esquel's Dirección Municipal de Turismo (☎ 452369), at Sarmiento and Alvear, keeps a current price list of accommodations that includes hotels, casas de familia, and campgrounds both in town and in Parque Nacional Los Alerces. There are also details on travel agencies and tours, transportation, and recreation.

ACA (☎ 452383) is at 25 de Mayo and Ameghino.

Money Banco de la Nación, Alvear and Roca, changes AmEx traveler's checks only. Banco del Chubut has an ATM at Alvear 1131, Bansud on 25 de Mayo 737.

Post & Communications Correo Argentino is at Alvear 1192, across Fontana from the bus station; the postal code is 9200. Esquel has several convenient locutorios, including Su Central at 25 de Mayo 415 and Unitel at 25 de Mayo 526. Esquel's area code is ☎ 02945.

Travel Agencies Esquel Tours (☎ 452704), at Av Fontana 754, arranges the usual boat trips in Parque Nacional Los Alerces, but so do many others. Patagonia Verde (☎ 452251), 9 de Julio 926, deals in less conventional activities like hiking, climbing, and horseback riding.

Bookstores El Ágora (☎ 453799), 9 de Julio 999, has a wide selection of reading material in Spanish only.

Cultural Centers The Dirección Municipal de Cultura (☎ 451929), Belgrano 330, sponsors theater and music events.

Laundry Laverap is at Mitre 543.

Medical Services The Hospital Zonal (☎ 452131, 452226) is at 25 de Mayo 150.

Things to See & Do

Most of the area's attractions, notably Parque Nacional Los Alerces, are around rather than in Esquel. The **Museo Indigenista** (☎ 451929), part of the Dirección Municipal de Cultura, is at Belgrano 330. A modest collection, it's open 9 am to 1 pm weekdays and 4 to 9 pm daily. The **Museo de Arte Naif**, part of the Vestry teahouse at Rivadavia 1065, is open 9 am to 10 pm daily.

The **Estación Ferrocarril Roca**, at Brown and Roggero, is now also a museum, but

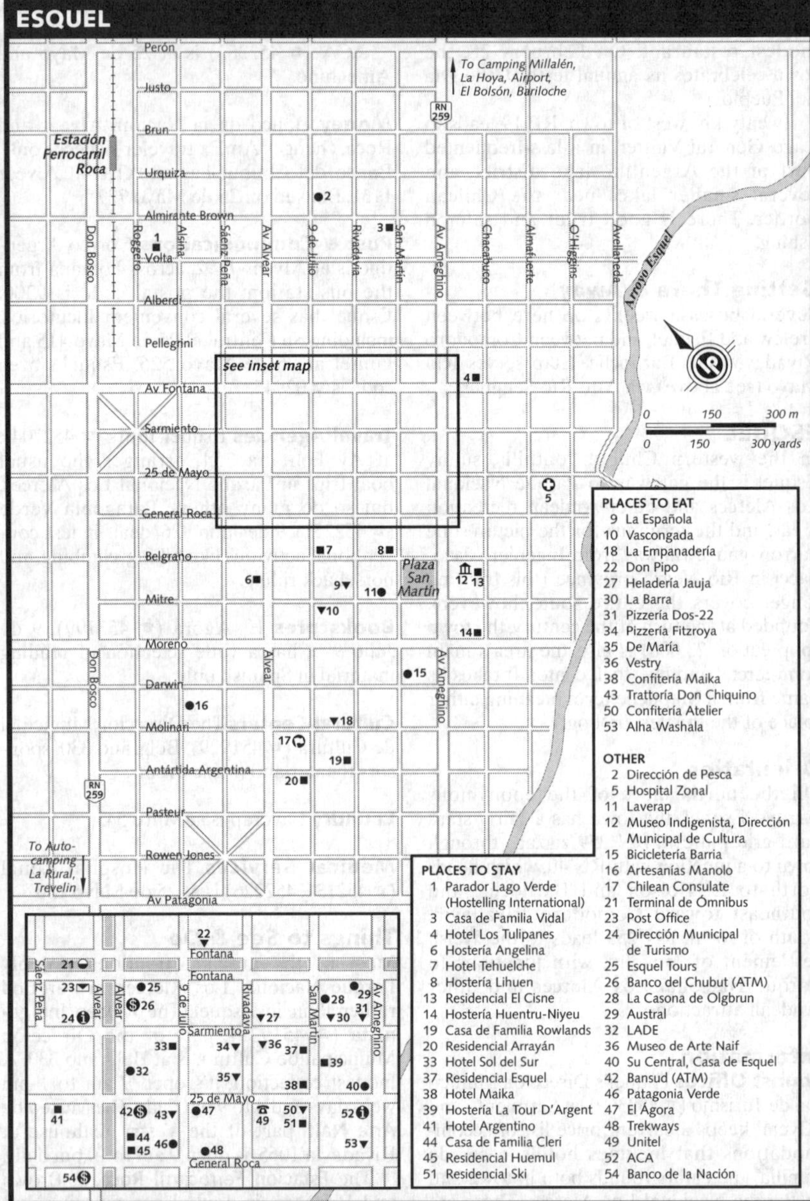
ESQUEL
To Camping Millalén, La Hoya, Airport, El Bolsón, Bariloche
Estación Ferrocarril Roca
Plaza San Martín
see inset map
Arroyo Esquel
To Auto-camping La Rural, Trevelin
PLACES TO EAT
9 La Española
10 Vascongada
18 La Empanadería
22 Don Pipo
27 Heladería Jauja
30 La Barra
31 Pizzería Dos-22
34 Pizzería Fitzroya
35 De María
36 Vestry
38 Confitería Maika
43 Trattoría Don Chiquino
50 Confitería Atelier
53 Alha Washala
OTHER
2 Dirección de Pesca
5 Hospital Zonal
11 Laverap
12 Museo Indigenista, Dirección Municipal de Cultura
15 Bicicletería Barria
16 Artesanías Manolo
17 Chilean Consulate
21 Terminal de Ómnibus
23 Post Office
24 Dirección Municipal de Turismo
25 Esquel Tours
26 Banco del Chubut (ATM)
28 La Casona de Olgbrun
29 Austral
32 LADE
36 Museo de Arte Naif
40 Su Central, Casa de Esquel
42 Bansud (ATM)
46 Patagonia Verde
47 El Ágora
48 Trekways
49 Unitel
52 ACA
54 Banco de la Nación
PLACES TO STAY
1 Parador Lago Verde (Hostelling International)
3 Casa de Familia Vidal
4 Hotel Los Tulipanes
6 Hostería Angelina
7 Hotel Tehuelche
8 Hostería Lihuen
13 Residencial El Cisne
14 Hostería Huentru-Niyeu
19 Casa de Familia Rowlands
20 Residencial Arrayán
33 Hotel Sol del Sur
37 Residencial Esquel
38 Hotel Maika
39 Hostería La Tour D'Argent
41 Hotel Argentino
44 Casa de Familia Cleri
45 Residencial Huemul
51 Residencial Ski

even travelers arriving by air or bus should try to witness the arrival or departure of **La Trochita**, the narrow-gauge steam train. Serious trainspotters will find the town of El Maitén, on the border of Río Negro province, even more interesting because of the extraordinary collection of antique rail equipment in its workshops.

Organized Tours

Travel agencies sell tickets for the Circuito Lacustre boat excursion in Parque Nacional Los Alerces; obtaining a ticket here assures a place on this often crowded trip. Full-day excursions including the lake cruise, described in detail in the separate entry on the park, cost US$57 when sailing from Puerto Chucao, US$68 from Puerto Limonao. This includes transportation to and from the park, but you can also buy the boat excursion separately if you have your own transportation.

There are also full-day trips to Futaleufú in Chile, Cholila/Lago Rivadavia (US$35), El Bolsón/Lago Puelo (US$48), and also Corcovado/Carrenleufú. Half-day trips include the La Hoya winter sports complex, the nearby Welsh settlement of Trevelin and the Futaleufú hydroelectric complex (US$22), and the narrow-gauge railway excursion to Nahuelpan (US$22).

Activities

Fishing The fishing season in local lakes and rivers runs from early November to mid-April. Seasonal licenses, valid throughout the Patagonian provinces of Chubut, Santa Cruz, Río Negro, and Neuquén, and in national parks, cost US$100. Weekly (US$30) and monthly (US$60) licenses are cheaper.

Licenses can be purchased at the Dirección de Pesca (☎ 451226), 9 de Julio 1643.

Mountain Biking Bicicletería Barria (☎ 454443), San Martín 515, has rental bikes for US$10 per day.

Rafting Trekways (☎ 451000), Roca 687, and Rafting Adventure (☎ 451891), north of the train station at Miguens 40, organize full-day Class II-IV rafting trips on the Río Corcovado for about US$70 including transfers and all equipment, as well as breakfast and lunch.

Special Events

February's Semana de Esquel celebrates the founding of the city in 1906. The Fiesta Nacional de Esquí (National Ski Festival) takes place in September.

Places to Stay – Budget

Camping ***Autocamping La Colina*** *(☎ 454962, Humphreys 554)*, two blocks west of Don Bosco, costs US$3.50 per person and also has hostel accommodations for US$8/15 single/double. ***Camping Millalén*** *(☎ 456164, Ameghino 2063)* charges US$4.50 per adult, US$3 per child age 10 or below.

Shady ***Autocamping La Rural*** *(☎ 0268-428-1429)*, just south of town on the Trevelin road, charges US$5 per person, plus a one-time charge of US$5 per car, tent, and family group.

Hostels Informally, ***Hotel Argentino*** *(☎ 452237, 25 de Mayo 862)* offers floor space for backpackers for US$3 per person.

The local affiliate of Hostelling International, Parador Lago Verde (☎ 452251, fax 453901, lagoverd@hostels.org.ar, Volta 1081) offers a small discount on its regular accommodations.

Casas de Familia The best values are the casas de familia (private homes). Check the tourist office for latest listings, but try Elvey Rowlands *(☎ 452578, Rivadavia 330)* for US$10 per person with shared bath, or identically priced Ema Cleri *(☎ 452083, Alvear 1021)*, which has rooms with private bath. Marta Vidal *(☎ 452847, San Martín 1590)* charges US$14/24 single/double with private bath, while Isabel Barutta (who speaks some English) runs highly regarded ***Parador Lago Verde*** *(☎ 452251, Volta 1081)* for US$15/24 with private bath.

Residenciales, Hosterías & Hotels The ***Hotel Argentino*** *(☎ 452237, 25 de Mayo 862)* is the cheapest of the formal lodgings

The Survival of La Trochita

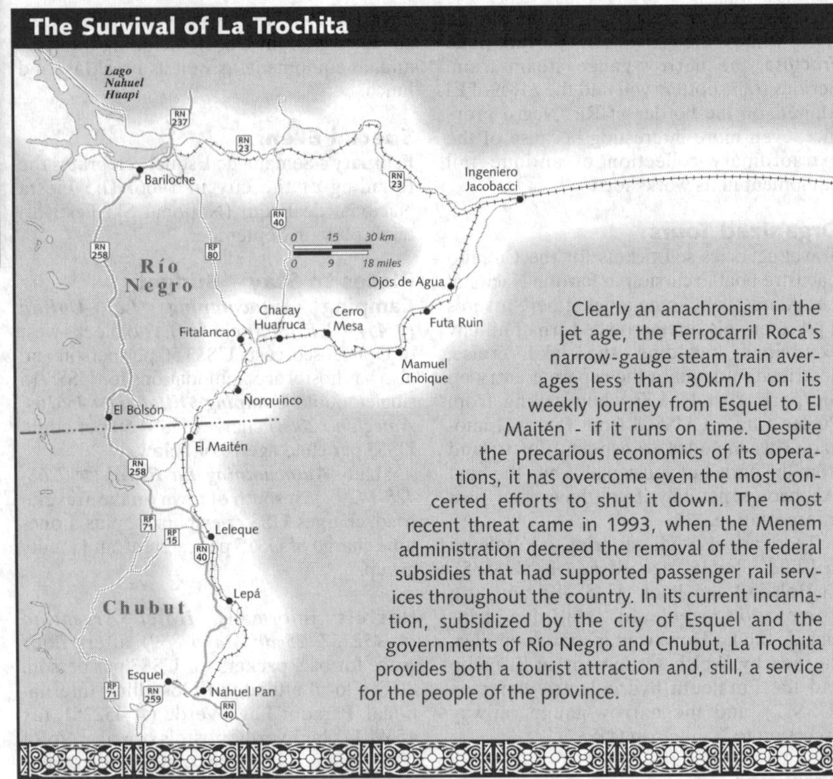

Clearly an anachronism in the jet age, the Ferrocarril Roca's narrow-gauge steam train averages less than 30km/h on its weekly journey from Esquel to El Maitén - if it runs on time. Despite the precarious economics of its operations, it has overcome even the most concerted efforts to shut it down. The most recent threat came in 1993, when the Menem administration decreed the removal of the federal subsidies that had supported passenger rail services throughout the country. In its current incarnation, subsidized by the city of Esquel and the governments of Río Negro and Chubut, La Trochita provides both a tourist attraction and, still, a service for the people of the province.

at US$12/18 with shared bath, US$18/28 for singles/doubles with private bath. ***Residencial El Cisne*** *(☎ 452256, Chacabuco 778)* costs US$12/20, while the ***Hostería Huentru-Niyeu*** *(☎ 452576, Chacabuco 606)* charges US$17/22.

The highly regarded ***Residencial Ski*** *(☎ 452254, San Martín 961)* charges US$20/25. Slightly dearer are ***Residencial Arrayán*** *(☎ 451051, Antártida Argentina 767)* for US$20/30, and ***Residencial Huemul*** *(☎ 452149, Alvear 1015)* for US$20/35.

Places to Stay – Mid-Range

Mid-range accommodations start around US$25/32 for singles/doubles at ***Hostería Lihuen*** *(☎ 452589, San Martín 822)*. Similar prices and quality are available for US$24/35 at ***Hotel Maika*** *(☎ 452457)*, 25 de Mayo and San Martín, and for US$25/35 at friendly but undistinguished ***Residencial Esquel*** *(☎ 452534, San Martín 1044)*. Recommended ***Hostería Los Tulipanes*** *(☎ 452748, Fontana 365)* is a good value at US$25/40. ***Hostería La Tour D'Argent*** *(☎ 454612, San Martín 1063)* charges US$28/42.

Hostería Angelina *(☎ 452763, Alvear 758)* has drawn praise for comfort, hospitality, and very substantial breakfasts, though some rooms are a bit small for US$30/40.

Places to Stay – Top End

At three-star ***Hotel Sol del Sur*** *(☎ 452189, 9 de Julio 1086)* rooms cost around US$40/48

The Survival of La Trochita

Like many other state projects, completion of the line seemed an interminable process. In 1906, the federal government authorized the southern branch of the Roca line between Puerto San Antonio, on the Atlantic coast, and Lago Nahuel Huapi, with the possibility of any spur lines considered convenient for economic development and colonization - in this case, to haul wool and other agricultural commodities to the main line. In 1922, Ferrocarriles del Estado began work on the narrow-gauge section that, due to poor route planning exacerbated by floods and other natural disasters, did not reach the halfway point of Ñorquinco until 1939. In 1941 it made it to the workshops at El Maitén, and in 1945 it reached the end of the line at Esquel.

Since then, the line has suffered some of the oddest mishaps in railroad history. Three times within a decade, in the late 1950s and early 1960s, it was derailed by high winds, and ice has caused other derailments. In 1979, when a collision with a cow derailed the train at Km 243 south of El Maitén, the engine driver was the appropriately named Señor Bovino.

In full operation until recently, La Trochita's 402km route between Esquel and Ingeniero Jacobacci was probably the world's longest remaining steam-train line, with half-a-dozen stations and another nine *apeaderos* (whistle stops); the Belgian Baldwin and German Henschel engines refilled their 4000-liter water tanks at strategically placed pumps *(parajes)* every 40 to 45km. Most of the passenger cars, heated by wood stoves, date from 1922, as do the freight cars.

From Esquel's train station (now a museum), the **Tren Turístico** goes to Nahuel Pan, the first station down the line, 20km east. This three-hour trip (US$15) departs twice daily except Thursday; for a small additional charge, you can return with travel agencies by minibus.

The best place to see and enjoy the variety of rolling stock and installations is the workshop at El Maitén, where there's a tourist excursion to Paraje Vuelta del Río and back Saturday at 2 pm, returning at 4:30 pm, also for US$15.

For details of the regular passenger service between Esquel and El Maitén, see Esquel's Getting There & Away.

for singles/doubles with breakfast. ***Hotel Tehuelche*** *(☎ 452420/1, 9 de Julio 825)* has a friendly young staff with some English-speakers; rates for comfortable rooms with large baths start around US$75/90, but fall to barely half that in the off-season. Ask for something facing away from the noisy street.

Places to Eat

Confitería Atelier *(☎ 453547)*, 25 de Mayo and San Martín, has excellent coffee and chocolate, and is open 24 hours. Try also lively ***Confitería Maika*** *(☎ 452457)*, part of Hotel Maika across the street.

El Bolsón's ***Heladería Jauja*** has a branch at the corner of Rivadavia and Sarmiento, serving extraordinary ice-cream flavors. For a variety of empanadas, there's ***La Empanadería*** *(Molinari 633)*.

Esquel has several worthwhile pizzerias, starting with ***Don Pipo*** *(☎ 453458, Fontana 649)*, ***Pizzería Fitzroya*** *(Rivadavia 1050)*, and ***Pizzería Dos-22*** *(☎ 454995)* at the corner of Ameghino and Sarmiento. The best Italian choice, though, is ***Trattoría Don Chiquino*** *(☎ 451508, 9 de Julio 964)*, which serves a variety of pasta specialties, in addition to pizza, amidst informal decor. The service is friendly and attentive, and the owner provides puzzle-lovers something to do while they wait.

Friendly and pleasant ***La Española*** *(☎ 451509, Rivadavia 940)* is a reasonable parrilla with a salad bar, as is ***La Barra***

(Sarmiento 638). ***De María*** *(☎ 452503, Rivadavia 1024)* has lamb, pork, and goat in addition to the usual Argentine beef.

Vascongada *(☎ 454609)*, 9 de Julio and Mitre, has good food in generous portions, with friendly and attentive service. ***Alha Washala*** *(Ameghino 924)* is also highly regarded.

Vestry *(Rivadavia 1065)* is Esquel's only Welsh teahouse, open 4:30 to 10 pm daily.

Shopping

The Asociación de Artesanos de Esquel has opened a new Feria Artesanal Permanente in Plaza San Martín, Thursday and Friday 7 to 10:30 pm, weekends 6 to 11:30 pm.

Artesanías Manolo, Alsina 483, specializes in woodcraft. La Casona de Olgbrun (☎ 453841), San Martín 1137, has attractive but expensive copperwork and other crafts, as well as chocolates, smoked salmon, and other delicacies. Casa de Esquel, 25 de Mayo 415, has books and crafts.

Getting There & Away

Air Austral (☎ 453413, 453614), Fontana 406, flies Monday, Tuesday, Thursday, Friday, and Saturday to Buenos Aires' Aeroparque (US$165 to US$282).

LADE (☎ 452124), Alvear 1085, flies Monday to Bariloche (US$20), Neuquén (US$51), and Viedma (US$73); Monday and Thursday to Comodoro Rivadavia (US$43 to US$116); Wednesday to El Maitén (US$20), El Bolsón (US$20), Bariloche, San Martín de los Andes (US$31), Zapala (US$44), and Neuquén; and Friday to Puerto Madryn (US$51), Trelew (US$47) and Comodoro Rivadavia.

Bus Esquel's congested Terminal de Ómnibus is at the corner of Avs Fontana and Alvear. Local authorities have long projected a new terminal for the northern part of town, in the block bounded by Av Justo, 9 de Julio, Av Brun, and Av Alvear, but there's still no firm commitment.

Empresa Don Otto (☎ 453012) goes daily to El Bolsón and Bariloche via Epuyén, to Comodoro Rivadavia nightly at 9 pm, with connections to Río Gallegos, and nightly at 9:30 pm to Trelew, with connections to Bahía Blanca and Buenos Aires. Empresa Mar y Valle (☎ 453712) has buses to Trelew Friday through Wednesday at 10 pm via Paso de Indios.

Andesmar (☎ 450143) goes daily to Bariloche and Mendoza, with connections to Salta, Jujuy, and other northwestern Argentine destinations, and to Osorno and Santiago, Chile. Vía Bariloche (☎ 453528) goes twice daily to Bariloche, at 7:30 am and 6 pm.

Etap (☎ 454756) goes to Comodoro Rivadavia Monday at 1 pm; Thursday, Friday, and Sunday at 9 pm; and to Río Mayo Monday at 1 pm and Thursday at 9 pm. It also has northbound service to El Bolsón. TAC (☎ 451110) goes to El Bolsón and Bariloche, with connections to Neuquén, Córdoba, Salta, and Jujuy.

Transportes Jacobsen (☎ 453528) connects Esquel with El Maitén at 6:30 am Monday and at 6:30 pm Monday, Wednesday, Thursday, and Friday, returning Monday, Tuesday, Friday, and Saturday at 8 am. Jacobsen also goes to Cholila Tuesday and Thursday at 12:30 pm, returning at 3 pm.

Codao (☎ 452924) serves the nearby provincial destinations of Trevelin (frequently); La Balsa (Monday at 8 am and Friday at 8 am and 5 pm); and Corcovado and Carrenleufú (Sunday, Monday, and Wednesday at 5 pm, Friday at 9 am).

Transportes Esquel (☎ 455059) goes to Parque Nacional Los Alerces and Lago Puelo daily at 8 am and 2 pm, plus a 7:30 pm that goes only as far as Lago Verde; the first service combines with lake excursions. Fares are US$3.50 to Futaleufú, US$4.50 to the Intendencia, US$5 to Bahía Rosales, US$7 to Lago Verde, US$8 to Lago Rivadavia, US$11 to Cholila, US$12.50 to Epuyén, US$15 to El Hoyo, and US$18 to Puelo (El Bolsón). Winter schedules may differ.

Typical fares include Trevelin (US$1.40, 30 minutes), El Bolsón (US$8, 2½ hours), Corcovado/Carrenleufú (US$10, 4½ hours), Bariloche (US$15, five hours), Neuquén (US$28, eight hours), Trelew (US$28, 8½ hours), Puerto Madryn (US$30, nine hours), Comodoro Rivadavia (US$33, nine hours), Osorno, Chile (US$33), Santiago, Chile

(US$53), Río Gallegos (US$64, 19 hours), Mendoza (US$70, 24 hours), Córdoba (US$76), Buenos Aires (US$91, 30 hours), Salta (US$98), and Jujuy (US$120).

Train The Ferrocarril General Roca (☎ 451403) is at the corner of Brown and Roggero. Its narrow-gauge steam train *El Trencito* or *La Trochita* has passenger service to El Maitén Thursday at 11 pm (US$15, 6½ hours), but it's now primarily a recreational tourist train; see The Survival of La Trochita for more details.

Getting Around

Esquel Tours runs minibuses according to flight schedules at Aeropuerto Esquel, 20km east of town on RN 40.

AROUND ESQUEL

La Hoya

Just 15km north of Esquel, 1350m above sea level, this winter sports area is cheaper and less crowded than Bariloche, but skilled and experienced skiers consider it pretty tame. The season lasts June to October, with the Fiesta Nacional del Esquí (National Ski Festival) the second week of September.

Full-day lift passes run from US$16 (low season) to US$20 (high season), with minimal children's discounts. Six-day passes cost US$80 to US$100 for adults, US$70 to US$90 for children, while season passes cost US$240 for adults, US$180 for children.

Equipment can be rented on site or in Esquel. For information, contact Trekways (☎ 451000), Roca 687 in Esquel.

Cholila

Bruce Chatwin's literary travel classic *In Patagonia* recounts Butch Cassidy and the Sundance Kid's ranching efforts near this small town at the northeast entrance to Parque Nacional Los Alerces. A few years ago, US author Anne Meadows located their house, just off RP 71 at Km 21 near the conspicuously marked turnoff to the Casa de Piedra teahouse, a short distance north of Cholila.

Transportes Esquel buses from Esquel to Parque Nacional Los Alerces and El Bolsón pass close enough for a fleeting glimpse of the house on the west side of the highway, but visitors with their own vehicle or time to spare can stop for a look at the overlapping log construction, typical of North America but unusual in this region. The occupant of the rapidly deteriorating house, which is reached by the first gate to the right, is Aladín Sepúlveda. Ask permission before looking around or taking photographs.

Follow the signs to the Calderón family's ***Casa de Piedra*** *(☎ 02945-498056)*, which offers tea, sweets, and preserves, as well as information; the Calderóns, of Spanish-Welsh-English-French Basque-Mapuche descent, also provide accommodations for US$25 per person, with breakfast, from December to the end of March, and during Semana Santa.

TREVELIN

Historic Trevelin, the only community in interior Chubut that retains any notable Welsh character, derives its name from the Welsh words for town *(tre)* and mill *(velin)*, after its first grain mill, now a museum. This pleasant town (population 4400) is suitable for either an overnight stay or a day trip from Esquel.

Orientation

Just 24km south of Esquel via paved RN 259, Trevelin's urban plan is very unusual for an Argentine city – at the north end of town, eight streets radiate like the spokes of a wheel from Plaza Coronel Fontana. The principal thoroughfare, Av San Martín, is the southward extension of RN 259, toward Corcovado and the Chilean border at Futaleufú.

Information

Tourist Offices From December to March, the exceptionally helpful Dirección de Turismo, Deportes y Actividades Recreativas (☎ 480120), directly on Plaza Coronel Fontana, is open daily 8 am to 10:30 pm. Winter hours are 8 am to noon and 2 to 8 pm. It has some English-speaking staff, and can help arrange guides, mountain bikes, and horses. Videos are available of activities like treks in Parque Nacional Los Alerces, organized by the Taller de Turismo Municipal. Showers are available here for US$0.50.

Money Banco del Chubut is at the corner of Av San Martín and Brown, but it's easier to change in Esquel.

Post & Communications Correo Argentino is on Av San Martín, just off Plaza Coronel Fontana; the postal code is 9203. There's a locutorio at the corner of San Martín and Holdich, one block south of 25 de Noviembre; Trevelin's area code is ☎ 02945.

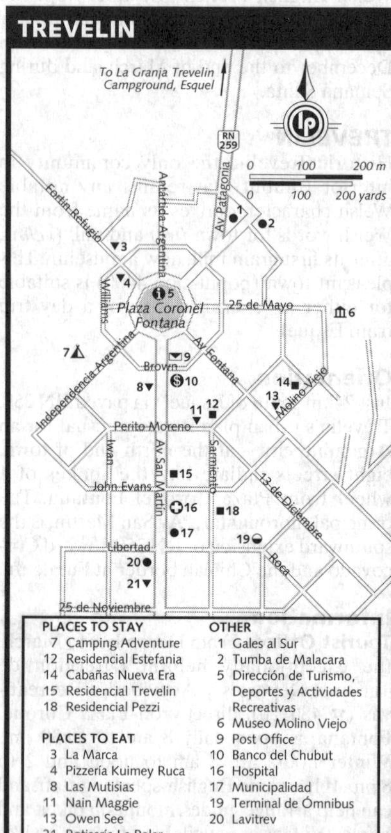

Travel Agencies Gales al Sur (☎ 480427), Av Patagonia 186, arranges a variety of tours in the area, including horseback riding, trekking, mountain biking, and rafting.

Laundry Lavitrev (☎ 480647) is at Av San Martín 448.

Medical Services Trevelin's hospital (☎ 480132) is at San Martín and John Evans.

Things to See & Do

Dating from 1918, the **Museo Molino Viejo** (☎ 480189) occupies the restored remains of the old grain mill (which was destroyed by fire). At the east end of 25 de Mayo, it's open 11 am to 9 pm daily from November to March; the rest of the year hours are 11 am to 6:30 pm. Admission is US$2 for adults, US$1 for children under age 12.

The Welsh chapel of **Capilla Bethel** (1910) is at the south end of town near ApIwan and Laprida. Two blocks northeast of Plaza Coronel Fontana, the monument **Tumba de Malacara** (☎ 480108) holds the carcass of a horse whose bravery enabled its Welsh rider, John Evans, to escape a retaliatory raid by Araucanians who had been attacked by the Argentine army during the Conquista del Desierto. Admission to the site costs US$2.

Every Sunday in summer and on alternate Sundays the rest of the year, there's an artisans' market in Plaza Coronel Fontana.

Special Events

March 19's Aniversario de Trevelin celebrates the city's founding. The Eisteddfod, a festival of Welsh choral singing, takes place the second week of October.

Places to Stay

Camping The most central campground is ***Camping Adventure*** *(☎ 480267)*, the former municipal site, only a block southwest of Plaza Coronel Fontana. It's less attractive than some Argentine campgrounds, but facilities include hot showers, electricity, running water at every site, and spotless toilets. Fees are US$4 per person.

Three km north, on RN 259 to Esquel, ***La Granja Trevelin*** *(☎ 480096)* charges US$5 per person for camping, but also has cabañas for US$30 double. There are also activities such as horseback riding and yoga.

Residenciales & Hotels Trevelin has limited, modest, but pleasant accommodations. Reservations are a good idea at ***Residencial Pezzi*** *(☎ 480146, Sarmiento 353)*, a pleasant, family-run hotel with a large garden, charging US$15 per person with private bath and breakfast. ***Residencial Estefania*** *(☎ 480148)*, at Perito Moreno and 13 de Diciembre, charges US$16/24 single/double and has a good ***restaurant***.

Residencial Trevelin *(☎ 480102, Av San Martín 327)* has rooms with shared bath for US$15 per person without breakfast, US$17 with; prices are slightly higher with private bath. For decent family accommodations, try ***Cabañas Nueva Era*** *(☎ 480295)*, on Molino Viejo just east of Av Fontana, for about US$45 double.

Places to Eat

Just as visitors to Trelew flock to Gaiman, so visitors to Esquel head to Trevelin for Welsh tea, which costs from US$10 to US$12.

The oldest teahouse is ***Nain Maggie*** *(☎ 480232, Perito Moreno 179)*, occupying a modern building but maintaining its traditional high standards. Along with a bottomless pot of tea, it offers sweets made from dulce de leche, chocolate, cream, rhubarb, cheese, traditional Welsh black cake, and scones hot from the oven. Service is attentive but unobtrusive. After a late afternoon here, you will probably skip dinner.

Other teahouses include ***Las Mutisias*** *(☎ 480165, Av San Martín 170)* or ***Owen See*** *(☎ 480295, Molino Viejo 361)*.

If you're hungry for more than tea, sweets, or cheese, try ***La Marca*** *(☎ 480643)*, the local parrilla, on Fortín Refugio one block north of Plaza Coronel Fontana, or the excellent ***Pizzería Kuimey Ruca*** *(☎ 480088, Av Fortín Refugio s/n)*.

Cheeseheads should seek out homemade queso de Chubut. ***Rotisería La Polar***, on San Martín between Libertad and 25 de Noviembre, has good take-out food.

Getting There & Away

The Terminal de Ómnibus is at the corner of Libertad and Roca. There are 11 Codao (☎ 452924) buses each weekday between Esquel and Trevelin, seven on weekends, for US$1.40. There are three weekly to Río Grande/Futaleufú (US$3), on the Chilean border, Monday, Wednesday, and Friday at 8:30 am, and five weekly to Carrenleufú, another Chilean border crossing, at 5:30 pm. To travel north, you must first go to Esquel.

AROUND TREVELIN

From 9:30 am to 5:30 pm daily, there are guided tours of the **Central Hidroeléctrico Futaleufú**, a dam project 18km west of Trevelin that submerged a chain of lakes in the southern part of Parque Nacional Los Alerces in order to provide electricity for the aluminum plant at Puerto Madryn, 550km to the east. ***Autocamping Aikén Leufú*** *(☎ 0268-428-1398)*, on the park boundary, charges US$5 per adult and also has cabañas for US$25 double.

On RN 259, 17km south of Trevelin, a 7km trail leads to a series of cascades in **Reserva Provincial Nant-y-Fall**, open 9:30 am to 5:30 pm daily. Trevelin's Dirección de Turismo arranges excursions but, unfortunately, a landowner dispute has made it impossible to start at the north end and get picked up at the southern end, on RP 17. At Arroyo Baguilt, on RN 259 near the Chilean border, is the provincial **Estación de Salmonicultura** (salmon hatchery), open for visits weekdays, 8 am to 1 pm.

Camping El Paso *(☎ 44403)*, 32km west of Trevelin on RN 259, costs US$6 per person (children free of charge), while ***Camping Puerto Ciprés***, 5km east of the border, charges US$5, with a one-time charge of US$5 per vehicle.

Near **Lago Rosario**, 24km southwest of Trevelin via a lateral off RP 17, is a Mapuche Indian reservation. Just to its north, the **Sierra Colorada** offers good hiking.

PARQUE NACIONAL LOS ALERCES

Resembling the giant sequoia of California's Sierra Nevada, the *alerce* or

Patagonian cypress *(Fitzroya cupressoides)* flourishes in the humid temperate forests of southern Argentina and Chile. Individual specimens of this strikingly beautiful and long-lived tree (one specimen may be more than 4000 years old) can measure over 4m in diameter and exceed 60m in height. Like the giant sequoia, it has suffered overexploitation because of its valuable timber. West of Esquel, this 263,000-hectare unit protects some of the largest remaining alerce forests.

Geography & Climate

Hugging the eastern slope of the Andes along the Chilean border, the peaks of Parque Nacional Los Alerces do not exceed 2300m, and their receding alpine glaciers are smaller and less impressive than the continental ice fields of Parque Nacional Los Glaciares to the south. They have left, however, a series of nearly pristine lakes and streams that offer attractive vistas, excellent fishing, and other outdoor recreation. Many local place names derive from Mapudungun, the Mapuche language, such as Lago Futalaufquen (Big Lake) and Futaleufú (Big River).

Because the Andes are relatively low here, westerly storms drop nearly 3m of rain annually to support the humid Valdivian forest. The eastern part of the park, though, is much drier. Winter temperatures average 2°C, but can be much colder. The summer mean high reaches 24°C, but evenings are usually cool.

Flora

While its wild backcountry supports some wildlife, Los Alerces exists primarily because of its botanical riches. Besides the alerce, other important coniferous evergreens and deciduous broadleaf trees characterize the dense, humid Valdivian forest, with its almost impenetrable undergrowth of *chusquea*, a solid rather than hollow bamboo. Conifers include another species of cypress *(Pilgerodendron uviferum)* and the aromatic Chilean incense cedar *(Austrocedrus chilensis)*.

The genus *Nothofagus* ('false beech,' but commonly known as 'southern beech'), to which most of the larger broadleaf tree species in the park belong, exists only in the Southern Hemisphere. Local species include ñire *(Nothofagus antarctica)*, coihue *(Nothofagus dombeyi)*, and lenga *(Nothofagus pumilio)*. Another interesting species is the arrayán, whose foliage and peeling, cinnamon-colored bark bear resemblance to the madrone *Arbutus menziesii* of the western US coastal states and British Columbia. More extensive stands can be found at Parque Nacional Los Arrayanes, near Villa La Angostura in Neuquén province.

Information

The Intendencia is at Villa Futalaufquen ('the Villa'), at the south end of Lago Futalaufquen; for an introduction to the park's natural history, visit the **Museo y Centro del Interpretación** here, which includes an aquarium and historical displays and documentation about the park's creation in 1937. It's open weekdays 8 am to 8 pm, weekends and holidays 8 am to 1 pm and 2:30 to 8 pm; rangers can supply park information.

Park admission is US$5.

Circuito Lacustre

Traditionally, Los Alerces' most popular excursion sails from Puerto Limonao up Lago Futalaufquen through the narrow channel of the Río Arrayanes to Lago Verde, but low water levels have eliminated part of this segment, making it necessary to hike the short distance between Puerto Mermoud, at the north end of Lago Futalaufquen, and Puerto Chucao on Lago Menéndez.

Launches from Puerto Chucao handle the second segment of the trip to the nature trail to **El Alerzal**, the most accessible stand of alerces. The voyage from Puerto Chucao to El Alerzal lasts about 1½ hours each way and costs US$35; purchase tickets in Esquel to assure a place on this popular trip. From Puerto Limonao, the excursion costs US$55. Scheduled departures are at 10 am from Limonao and noon from Chucao, returning to Chucao at 4 pm and to Limonao at 7 pm.

The launch remains docked over an hour, sufficient for a deliberate hike around the loop trail that also passes Lago Cisne and an attractive waterfall to end up at **El Abuelo** (The Grandfather), the finest alerce specimen along the route. Local guides are knowledgeable on forest ecology and conservation, but you may find the group uncomfortably large. If so, you may go ahead or lag behind the group, so long as you return to the dock in time for the return trip.

Unfortunately, because of the fire hazard authorities do not allow backcountry camping at El Alerzal or in other parts of the park's 'zona intangible,' which is open only to scientific researchers. There are several more interpretive trails near Lago Futalaufquen for day hikes, but the only trekking alternative is the trail from Puerto Limonao along the south shore of Futalaufquen to Lago Krüger (see below).

Things to See & Do

There are rock-art sites on the **Río Desaguadero** near the Los Maitenes campground near the Intendencia. Park rangers lead guided hikes to **Cerro Alto El Dedal** (US$7, six hours) from the trailhead near the Prefectura Naval at Puerto Bustillo, on the eastern shore of Lago Futalaufquen a few kilometers north of the Intendencia; another nearby alternative, from the same trailhead, is **Cinco Saltos** (2½ hours). Carry water and food.

Since so much of the park is designated as inaccessible zona intangible, the longest possible hike is the 25km trail along the south shore of Lago Futalaufquen to Refugio Krüger, a seven-hour trip that can be broken up by camping at Playa Blanca (rangers claim the trip takes 12 hours, but are known to exaggerate). Boat excursions from Puerto Limonao to Puerto Lago Krüger cost US$20 per person.

Places to Stay

Camping Los Alerces has several organized campgrounds accessible by road, all of which have hot showers, picnic tables, groceries, and restaurants on site or nearby. Another campground is accessible by foot or boat only. There are free campsites near some of these fee sites. Since park regulations do not control livestock, campers may be awakened by moos and cowbells rather than birdcalls.

At ***Camping Los Maitenes*** *(☎ 02945-451003)*, 200m from the Intendencia on the Puerto Limonao road, sites cost US$3 per person plus a one-time charge of US$4 per tent and/or vehicle. ***Camping Bahía Rosales*** *(☎ 02945-471004)*, at the north end of Futalaufquen 12km from the Intendencia, charges US$5 per day, while ***Camping Lago Verde*** *(☎ 02945-454421)* on the eastern shore of its namesake lake 30km from Villa Futalaufquen, charges US$2.50 per person with a one-time charge of US$2 for tent and/or vehicle, but also offers a 30% discount for backpackers not resident in Chubut. ***Camping Lago Rivadavia*** *(☎ 02945-454381)*, 42km north of the Villa at the south end of the lake, charges US$5 per person plus a one-time charge of US$3 per tent/vehicle.

Camping & Refugio Lago Krüger, on its namesake lake, is accessible only by the 25km foot trail that leaves from Hotel Futalaufquen, or by launch from Puerto Limonao. Camping costs US$5 per person, while its refugio, which has hot showers and other amenities, charges US$15 per person, US$8 if you have your own sleeping bag.

Cabañas & Hosterías Small- to medium-sized groups can rent cabins. ***Cabañas Los Tepúes***, 8km north of the Villa on the eastern shore of Lago Futalaufquen, rents cabins for US$80 per day for up to eight persons. Nearby ***Cabañas Tejas Negras*** *(☎ 02945-471046)*, 10km north of the Villa, has five-person cabins for US$160, six-person cabins for US$180.

Also on Lago Futalaufquen, ***Motel Pucón Pai*** *(☎ 02945-452828)*, by the campground of the same name, has singles/doubles with private bath for US$90/$104 including breakfast, US$104/118 with half-board. ***Hostería Quime Quipan*** *(☎ 02945-454134)* at the south end of the lake charges US$55 per person for half-board, with private bath, and also has cabins suitable for six or seven persons for US$120. ***Hostería Cume Hue*** *(☎ 02945-453639)*, 25km north of the Villa, offers full pension for US$60 with shared bath, US$70 with private bath. The very dignified, tasteful ***Hostería Futalaufquen*** *(☎ 02945-471008; 011-4394-3808 in Buenos Aires)*, 4km north of the Villa on the quieter western shore, is the park's most appealing accommodation, but it comes at a steep price – US$140 double with breakfast, plus 21% IVA.

Getting There & Away

For details of getting to and from the park, see the Esquel Getting There & Away section.

EL MAITÉN

In open range country on the upper reaches of the Río Chubut, about 70km southeast of El Bolsón, this small, dusty town deserves a visit primarily because of the workshops for La Trochita, the narrow-gauge train running between Esquel and Maitén. A graveyard for antique steam locomotives and other railroad hardware, it's an aficionado's dream and an exceptional subject for photography.

Every February, the Fiesta Provincial del Trencito commemorates the railroad that put El Maitén (population 3000) on the map and keeps it there; it now doubles as the Fiesta Nacional del Tren a Vapor (National Steam Train Festival). Drawing people from all over the province and the country, it features riding and horse-taming competitions, live music (earplugs should be mandatory during performances by the provincial police band of Rawson), and superb produce and pastries, including homemade jams and jellies.

Places to Stay

The ***Camping Municipal***, directly on the river, charges US$2 per person but gets crowded and noisy during the festival. ***Hostería La Vasconia***, on the plaza across from the train station, has rooms for US$15 per person, but vacancies are few during the festival.

Getting There & Away

Air LADE (☎ 02945-495159), Av San Martín s/n, flies Wednesday to El Bolsón (US$20), Bariloche (US$20), San Martín de los Andes (US$21), Zapala (US$35), and Neuquén (US$43). On Thursday it goes to Esquel (US$20) and Comodoro Rivadavia (US$43).

Bus Transportes Jacobsen (☎ 453528) connects El Maitén with Esquel Monday, Tuesday, Friday, and Saturday at 8 am. There's also minibus service to and from El Bolsón.

Train La Trochita (☎ 02945-495190) still goes to Esquel, Wednesday at 2 pm (US$15, six hours).

Santa Cruz Province

Santa Cruz province consists of three ecologically distinct zones: the Atlantic coast, the Patagonian *meseta* (steppe) extending several hundred kilometers inland, and the Andean lake district, famous for its rugged glacial terrain. The Río Santa Cruz, born in the Fitzroy Range and the glacial troughs of Lago Viedma and Lago Argentino, slices through the steppe to form a deep, broad, and scenic canyon, eventually reaching the sea at Puerto Santa Cruz. Several lesser rivers also originate in the glaciers and lakes of the Andes.

Santa Cruz's aboriginal inhabitants were nomadic Tehuelche Indians, hunters of guanaco, rhea, and lesser wildlife. The first Europeans to set foot in the province came from Magellan's 1520 expedition, which wintered at San Julián and eventually circumnavigated the globe. The arid, windy meseta failed to attract Europeans until the 18th century, when Spain established a series of outposts including a whaling station at Puerto Deseado, and missionaries began to penetrate the region.

Even after Argentine independence, settlement lagged until opportunities in wool attracted British pioneers. Many settlers came from the Falkland Islands, where large grazing units had already occupied all available pastoral land; their surnames are still common in both the Falklands and Santa Cruz.

Although vast Santa Cruz offered almost unlimited grazing over nearly 250,000 sq km, its human population grew slowly. In 1895, it barely surpassed 1,000, and in 1914 was still less than 10,000. The earliest towns were small ports such as San Julián, Santa Cruz, and Río Gallegos, which transferred the wool clip to oceangoing vessels.

Nowadays, the 7 million-plus sheep in Santa Cruz are still the most conspicuous sector of the economy, but the province has also diversified with coal, oil, and tourism. RN 3, the principal north-south highway in Argentina, connects the fast-growing provincial capital of Río Gallegos with Buenos Aires and intermediate destinations. RN 3 south of Río Gallegos, to the Chilean border and Tierra del Fuego, is still one of the worst roads in the country.

For both Argentines and foreigners, Santa Cruz is a popular summer destination because of Parque Nacional Los Glaciares, which features both the famous Moreno Glacier, one of few in the world that is actually advancing, and the spectacular granite pinnacles of the Fitzroy Range.

The coast and steppe, though much less popular, have their own charm; it is possible to see both maritime and terrestrial wildlife, and to visit the sheep estancias that made European settlement possible.

For information on visiting estancias in the province, try the website www.wam.com.ar/tourism/estancs/etsc/stacruz.htm (which includes most, but not all, the estancias open to travelers in the area).

RÍO GALLEGOS

Founded in 1885 on the south bank of its namesake river, near the southern tip of Argentina, this provincial capital and port of 70,000 is the country's largest city south of Comodoro Rivadavia. It continues its tradition of service to the wool industry, but has also become a center for energy development. While the narrow-gauge railway from the coal deposits at Río Turbio, 230km west near the Chilean border, now discharges its cargo to oceangoing vessels at nearby Punta Loyola rather than here, YPF still operates a refinery with the crude from its nearby oil fields. For most travelers, Río Gallegos will only be a stopover en route to El Calafate and the Moreno Glacier, Punta Arenas, or Tierra del Fuego, but a day spent here need not be a wasted one.

History

Bruce Chatwin's classic literary travelogue *In Patagonia* vividly retells the story of the Anarchist rebellion of 1921 and the Argentine army's subsequent massacre of laborers at Estancia La Anita. *La Patagonia Rebelde*, a fictionalized film version based on German-Argentine historian Osvaldo Bayer's polemical history of the period, depicts the powerful Menéndez family of southern Patagonia and the Anglo-Argentine woolgrowers of Río Gallegos in a very unfavorable light. Scenes from the film were shot in the Hotel París (see Places to Stay), once known as the Grand Hotel de Río Gallegos.

Orientation

Central Río Gallegos has a standard grid pattern, centered on two major avenues, Av Julio Roca and Av San Martín; street names change on both sides of these avenues. Most areas frequented by visitors are in and around the southwest quadrant formed by Roca and San Martín, although the attractive, newly developed riverfront park at the north end of San Martín also deserves a visit. The most central open space, Plaza San Martín, is one block south of the junction of the two main avenues. Don't confuse Bernardino Rivadavia with Comodoro Rivadavia.

Information

Tourist Offices The energetic Subsecretaría de Turismo de la Provincia (☎ 422702), Av Roca 1551, is open weekdays 9 am to 8 pm. It has maps and a helpful list of accommodations (omitting the very cheapest and most unsavory alternatives), transport, and excursions.

The Dirección Municipal de Turismo maintains a Centro de Informes (☎ 442159) at the bus terminal, open weekdays 8 am to 10 pm, weekends 10 am to 2 pm and 5 to 9 pm; there's another downtown at Av San Martín and Av Roca.

ACA (☎ 420477) is at Orkeke 10, near the river.

Immigration Migraciones (☎ 420205), Urquiza 144, is open from 8 am to 8 pm weekdays.

Money Cambio El Pingüino, Zapiola 469, changes cash dollars, traveler's checks (for a modest commission), and Chilean pesos. Sur Cambio is at Av San Martín 565.

Most banks are on or near Av Roca; there are several ATMs.

Post & Communications Correo Argentino occupies a historic building at Av Julio Roca 893; the postal code is 9400. There are numerous locutorios, including Telefax at Av Roca 1328. Río Gallegos' area code is ☎ 02966.

Travel Agencies Among Gallegos' many travel agencies are Escalatur (☎ 422466) at Roca 998 and Tur Aike (☎ 424503) at Zapiola 63.

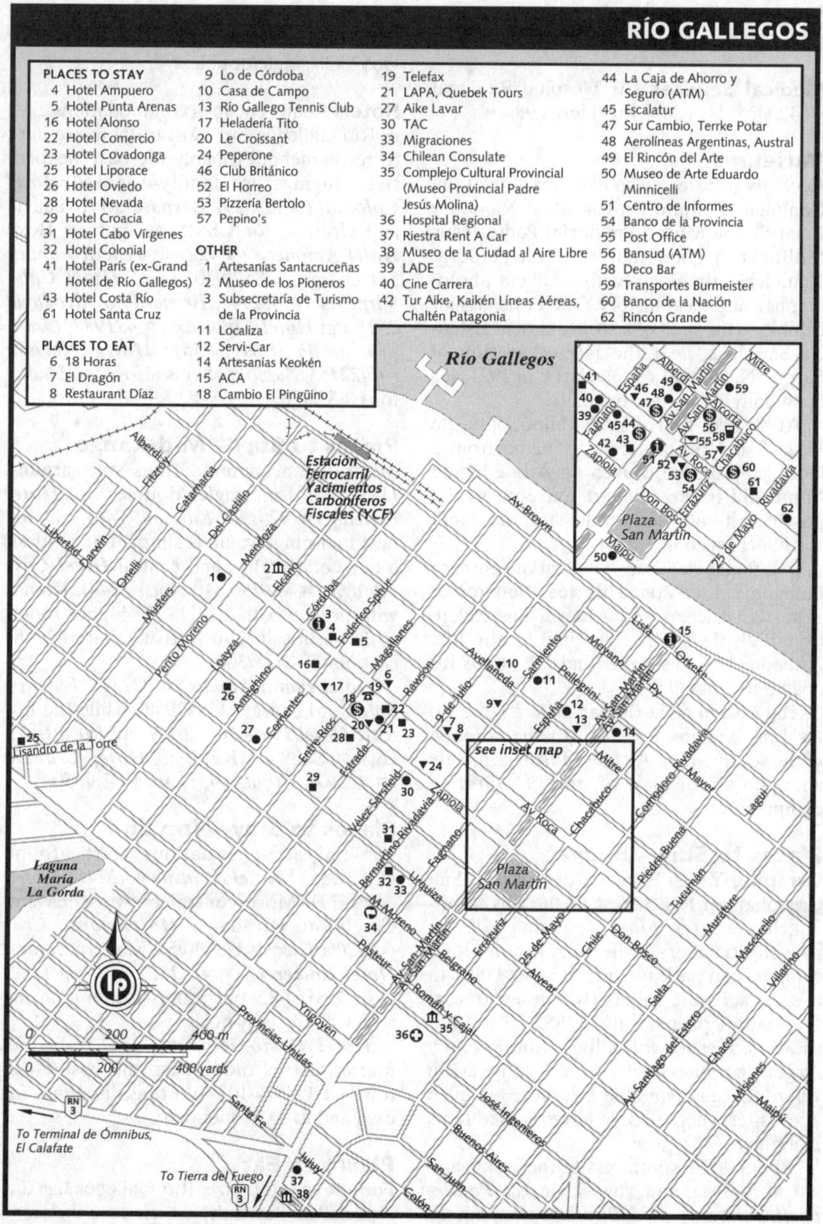

RÍO GALLEGOS

PLACES TO STAY
4 Hotel Ampuero
5 Hotel Punta Arenas
16 Hotel Alonso
22 Hotel Comercio
23 Hotel Covadonga
25 Hotel Liporace
26 Hotel Oviedo
28 Hotel Nevada
29 Hotel Croacia
31 Hotel Cabo Vírgenes
32 Hotel Colonial
41 Hotel París (ex-Grand Hotel de Río Gallegos)
43 Hotel Costa Río
61 Hotel Santa Cruz

PLACES TO EAT
6 18 Horas
7 El Dragón
8 Restaurant Díaz
9 Lo de Córdoba
10 Casa de Campo
13 Río Gallego Tennis Club
17 Heladería Tito
20 Le Croissant
24 Peperone
46 Club Británico
52 El Horreo
53 Pizzería Bertolo
57 Pepino's

OTHER
1 Artesanías Santacruceñas
2 Museo de los Pioneros
3 Subsecretaría de Turismo de la Provincia
11 Localiza
12 Servi-Car
14 Artesanías Keokén
15 ACA
18 Cambio El Pingüino
19 Telefax
21 LAPA, Quebek Tours
27 Aike Lavar
30 TAC
33 Migraciones
34 Chilean Consulate
35 Complejo Cultural Provincial (Museo Provincial Padre Jesús Molina)
36 Hospital Regional
37 Riestra Rent A Car
38 Museo de la Ciudad al Aire Libre
39 LADE
40 Cine Carrera
42 Tur Aike, Kaikén Líneas Aéreas, Chaltén Patagonia
44 La Caja de Ahorro y Seguro (ATM)
45 Escalatur
47 Sur Cambio, Terrke Potar
48 Aerolíneas Argentinas, Austral
49 El Rincón del Arte
50 Museo de Arte Eduardo Minnicelli
51 Centro de Informes
54 Banco de la Provincia
55 Post Office
56 Bansud (ATM)
58 Deco Bar
59 Transportes Burmeister
60 Banco de la Nación
62 Rincón Grande

Río Gallegos
Estación Ferrocarril Yacimientos Carboníferos Fiscales (YCF)
Laguna María La Gorda
Plaza San Martín
see inset map
To Terminal de Ómnibus, El Calafate
To Tierra del Fuego
0 200 400 m
0 200 400 yards

Laundry Aike Lavar (☎ 420759) is at Corrientes 277 near Urguiza.

Medical Services The Hospital Regional (☎ 420025) is at José Ingenieros 98.

Museums

Recently transferred to new quarters at the Complejo Cultural Provincial, at Ramón y Cajal 51, the **Museo Provincial Padre Jesús Molina** has good materials on geology, Tehuelche ethnology (with excellent photographs), and local history. One of its grislier exhibits is the skull of a striker shot at Estancia San José, near the Fitzroy section of Parque Nacional Los Glaciares, in 1921. It's open daily 10 am to 6 pm daily.

At Av San Martín and Maipú, opposite Plaza San Martín, taking its name from a local sculptor, the **Museo de Arte Eduardo Minnicelli** is the first art museum in the province; it once housed the staff of a landmark local school.

In a metal-clad house typical of southern Patagonia, the **Museo de los Pioneros** at Sebastián Elcano and Alberdi has exceptional displays on early immigrant life. Attended by Scots-Argentine volunteers, it's open 3 to 8 pm daily.

The **Museo de la Ciudad al Aire Libre**, on Av Los Inmigrantes close to the rotonda at the south end of Av San Martín, is mostly an open-air display of antique farming equipment.

Places to Stay – Budget

Camping YPF's Estación de Servicio San Cristóbal, on RN 3 west of the bus terminal, has a large ***playa*** (parking lot) for passing truckers, where self-contained campers can park for free; it costs US$1 to use the separate toilets (which are free at the station proper) and US$2.50 for hot showers. It's not formally a campground; Argentine backpackers generally crash where space is available, but there are even a few sites where people have pitched tents in a pinch.

About 400m southwest of the bus terminal, at Asturias and Yugoslavia, the ***Polideportivo Atsa*** *(☎ 442310)* offers camping for US$3 per person, US$3 per vehicle; showers cost US$2. There are also rooms for US$20/30 single/double.

Hotels Really cheap accommodations exist in Río Gallegos, but most of them are hard to recommend. Probably the best inexpensive lodgings are family-oriented ***Hotel Colonial*** *(☎ 422329)*, Bernardino Rivadavia and Urquiza, for US$15 per person. Boxy ***Hotel Ampuero*** *(☎ 422189, Federico Sphur 38)* charges US$20/30, as do ***Hotel Cabo Vírgenes*** *(☎ 422141, Bernardino Rivadavia 252)* and ***Hotel Liporace*** *(☎ 421937, Lisandro de la Torre 255)*. ***Hotel Nevada*** *(☎ 422155, Zapiola 486)* is also a good value for US$22/38.

Places to Stay – Mid-Range

Mid-range accommodations start around US$28/40 for singles/doubles at ***Hotel Oviedo*** *(☎ 420118, Libertad 746)*, but the best mid-range value is simple but spotless, quiet, comfortable, and central ***Hotel Covadonga*** *(☎ 420190, Av Roca 1244)*. Rooms with private bath are US$29/44, but rooms with washbasin and mirror (shared bath) cost only US$18/30.

Hotel Punta Arenas *(☎ 422743, Federico Sphur 55)* charges US$29/40, while the historic ***Hotel París*** *(☎ 420111, Av Roca 1040)* costs US$29/42. Rates at ***Hotel Croacia*** *(☎ 422997, Urquiza 431)* are US$30/50.

Places to Stay – Top End

Top-end accommodations start around US$39/56 at ***Hotel Alonso*** *(☎ 422414, Corrientes 33)*. More central at Av Roca and Comodoro Rivadavia, ***Hotel Santa Cruz*** *(☎ 420601)* costs US$40/54. Modern, central ***Hotel Comercio*** *(☎ 422172, Av Roca 1302)* costs US$54/82, but rooms fronting on the street can be very noisy.

Hotel Costa Río *(☎ 423412, Av San Martín 673)* is the newest and costliest in town at US$74/102, offering discounts for cash and to ACA members.

Places to Eat

For a town of its size, Río Gallegos has few especially noteworthy eateries, but the scene is improving. ***Le Croissant***, at Zapiola and Estrada, has a variety of attractive baked goods, prepared on the premises. ***Pepino's*** *(☎ 437100, Chacabuco 88)* features good fast food, sandwiches, and cheap draft beer. ***Restaurant Díaz*** *(☎ 420203, Av Roca 1143)* has reasonable minutas, as does ***18 Horas*** *(Av Roca 1315)*.

In the remodeled Sociedad Española, a historic building, is the attractive and highly regarded ***El Horreo*** *(☎ 420060, Av Roca 862)*. Directly alongside it, equally appealing ***Pizzería Bertolo*** *(Av Roca 858)* has very indifferent service. ***Peperone*** *(☎ 426991, Vélez Sarsfield 96)* features fine pizza, but the service can be careless.

The classic atmosphere at the ***Club Británico*** *(☎ 425223, Roca 935)* outshines the food, which, however, is more than passable. Comparable, at least in a historical sense, is the ***Río Gallego Tennis Club*** *(☎ 422507, Avellaneda 25)*. ***Lo de Córdoba*** *(☎ 424300, Sarmiento 124)* is a parrilla, while ***El Dragón*** *(☎ 429811, 9 de Julio 39)* is a Chinese tenedor libre.

Casa de Campo *(☎ 424622, Avellaneda 275)* serves an elaborate afternoon tea; reservations are advisable.

Heladería Tito, at Zapiola and Corrientes, has very good and imaginative ice-cream flavors, even by Argentine standards (try orange in white chocolate), but high prices as well.

Entertainment

The ***Cine Carrera*** *(☎ 420204, Av Roca 1012)*, upstairs, shows recent films.

The ***Deco Bar***, at Alcorta and Chacabuco, has good ambience for a drink.

Shopping

Local woolen goods, leather work, fruit preserves, sweets, and other items are available at Artesanías Keokén (☎ 420335), Av San Martín 336. Rincón Grande, Av Roca 619, specializes in horse gear and the like. For a varied selection, try Artesanías Santacruceñas at the corner of Av Roca and Perito Moreno.

For works by local artists, check out El Rincón del Arte, a gallery at Alberdi 12.

Getting There & Away

From Río Gallegos, there are several Patagonian options: west to Chile's Puerto Natales and Parque Nacional Torres del Paine via Calafate and Parque Nacional Los Glaciares, or via the Argentine coal-mining town of Río Turbio; or south to Punta Arenas and across the Strait of Magellan to Tierra del Fuego.

Air On its transpolar flight from Ezeiza to Auckland and Sydney, Aerolíneas Argentinas (☎ 422020), Av San Martín 545, makes a stopover at Río Gallegos Monday, Friday, and Sunday. Aerolíneas also flies daily to Buenos Aires' Aeroparque (US$107 to US$217) via Ushuaia (US$56), and twice daily except Sunday (once only) nonstop to Aeroparque.

LAPA (☎ 428382), Estrada 71, flies daily to Río Grande (US$27 to US$47); Tuesday, Thursday, and Saturday to Ushuaia (US$35 to US$61); daily to Bahía Blanca (US$97 to US$163), Trelew (US$62 to US$108), and Aeroparque in the capital (US$109 to US$217).

LADE (☎ 422316), Fagnano 53, flies Tuesday and Wednesday to Río Grande (US$26) and Ushuaia (US$36); Tuesday to Santa Cruz (US$20), Gobernador Gregores (US$32), San Julián (US$28), Puerto Deseado (US$49), and Comodoro Rivadavia (US$66); Wednesday to El Calafate (US$25); Thursday to El Calafate, Gobernador Gregores, Perito Moreno (US$58), and Comodoro Rivadavia; and Friday to Río Turbio (US$20), as well as El Calafate, Gobernador Gregores, Perito Moreno, and Comodoro Rivadavia.

Tur Aike (☎ 424503), Zapiola 63, is the agent for Kaikén Líneas Aéreas, which flies daily to Comodoro Rivadavia (US$89 to US$103), Trelew (US$89 to US$138), and Bahía Blanca (US$139 to US$175); daily except Sunday to El Calafate (US$44 to US$55), Bariloche (US$160 to US$310), Neuquén (US$175 to US$240), and Mendoza (US$215 to US$283); and two or three times daily to Ushuaia (US$50 to US$60), sometimes stopping in Río Grande (US$39 to US$48).

Bus Río Gallegos' Terminal de Ómnibus (☎ 442159) is at the corner of RN 3 and Av Eva Perón. Río Gallegos is a major hub for provincial, long-distance, and international bus travel. Some but not all companies have convenient downtown offices.

To/From Chile While travelers bound for northern Chile cannot board through buses from Punta Arenas here, Terrke Potar (☎ 422701), Av San Martín 565, sell tickets for these routes; it's necessary to take another bus south to the border at Monte Aymond and board the through bus there.

El Pingüino (☎ 442169) goes to Punta Arenas (US$20, 5½ hours) daily at 1 pm. Buses Ghisoni (☎ 442557) goes there Tuesday and Thursday at 9 am, Friday and Sunday at noon. Magallanes Tour goes Wednesday at noon.

El Pingüino also goes to Puerto Natales (US$18, six hours), Tuesday and Thursday at 11 am, while Bus Sur (☎ 442080) goes Tuesday and Thursday at 5 pm. Natales-bound travelers can also take buses to Río Turbio (see later in this chapter), where there are frequent buses across the border.

Provincial & Long-Distance El Pingüino (☎ 442169) goes daily to Río Turbio and twice daily to El Calafate. Their nightly service to Buenos Aires and intermediate points leaves at 9 pm. Ezquerra (☎ 442499) goes to Río Turbio at 9 am daily.

Nightly at 9:30 pm Transportes Patagónicos/Don Otto (☎ 442160) goes to Buenos Aires and intermediate points, with connections via Comodoro Rivadavia to Bariloche. Andesmar (☎ 442195) goes Tuesday, Thursday, and Saturday to Mendoza via northern Patagonian destinations including Neuquén and Zapala. TAC (☎ 442042), at Zapiola and Vélez Sarsfield, goes nightly at 8 pm to Córdoba and at 10 pm to Buenos Aires.

Quebek Tours (☎ 442194), Estrada 71, goes twice daily to Río Turbio, twice daily to El Calafate, and nightly at 8:30 pm to Córdoba. Interlagos (☎ 442080) goes to El Calafate and the Moreno Glacier. Buses to El Calafate leave from the airport 30 minutes after flight arrivals, but seats may be few.

Transporte Greco (☎ 442080) goes to Gobernador Gregores Tuesday and Friday at 1 pm (eight hours). Transportes Burmeister (☎ 420293), San Martín 470, goes directly to El Chaltén, bypassing El Calafate, Monday, Wednesday, and Friday, returning Tuesday, Thursday, and Saturday. Chaltén Patagonia (☎ 424503), Zapiola 63, does the same route.

Sample fares include San Julián (US$15, 4½ hours), Río Turbio (US$15, five hours), El Calafate (US$20, 4½ hours), Caleta Olivia (US$27, eight hours), Comodoro Rivadavia (US$31, nine hours), Trelew (US$45, 14 hours), Puerto Madryn (US$52, 15 hours), Viedma (US$70), Bariloche (US$88), Buenos Aires (US$70 to US$100, 40 hours), and Mendoza (US$117, 36 hours).

Getting Around

To/From the Airport There is no regular public transport to or from Aeropuerto Internacional Río Gallegos except for cabs, which cost about US$5 to US$8 to downtown. To save money, share a cab with other arrivals.

To/From the Bus Terminal Most long-distance companies have offices near downtown, but the Terminal de Ómnibus is on the southern outskirts, at Av Eva Perón and RN 3, reached by bus Nos 1 or 12 (the placard must say 'terminal') from Av Roca. Local buses in Río Gallegos are the country's most expensive at about US$1.20 per trip.

Car Localiza (☎ 424417), Sarmiento 237, rents cars for excursions to outlying places like Cabo Vírgenes. Other agencies include Riestra Rent A Car (☎ 421321) at Av San Martín 1504 and Servi-Car (☎ 427293) at España 311.

AROUND RÍO GALLEGOS

Estancia Güer Aike

At the junction of northbound RN 3 and westbound RP 5, about 30km west of Río Gallegos, this ***estancia*** has 12km of river frontage, offering trout-fishing holidays for $235 double per day with full board. For nonguests, lunch or dinner costs US$20

(US$10 for kids under 12), while afternoon tea costs US$8.

It's open November to April; for reservations, contact Truchaike *(☎ 02966-436127 in Río Gallegos; ☎/fax 011-4394-3486 in Buenos Aires)*, Esmeralda 719, 2° Piso B, 1007 Buenos Aires.

Reserva Cabo Vírgenes

Some 30,000 Magellanic penguins nest at this colony at the end of RP 1, about 120km southeast of Río Gallegos. There's no scheduled public transport, but it may be possible to catch a lift with sheep farmers or oil workers at the clearly marked junction off RN 3 about 15km south of town. Camping is possible near the attractive but exposed beach. There are no facilities or even running water, but the small, isolated naval detachment may help. Provincial authorities have established a small information center staffed by a ranger, and there's a new 1700m nature trail.

Estancias along RP 1 may provide a bed for the night, but try to arrange this in advance in Río Gallegos. Estancia Cóndor, a beautiful settlement midway to Cabo Vírgenes, has a store that may sell supplies to passersby; in season, you can also watch sheep shearing here. El Pingüino bus company in Río Gallegos may organize visits to the reserve.

The closest estancia to the pingüinera, ***Estancia Monte Dinero*** *(☎/fax 02966-426900 in Río Gallegos)* offers guided tours, meals, and lodging from October to April. By mail, contact Señor Ricardo Fenton, Casilla de Correo 86, 9400 Río Gallegos, Provincia de Santa Cruz, República Argentina. Rates for B&B are US$100 per night; with full board, the price is US$140.

RÍO TURBIO

During WWII energy shortages, local coal deposits (rare in South America) spurred the development of this grimy, desolate border town (population 8000), 270km west of Río Gallegos via RN 40. Many, if not most, YCF employees are Chileans who commute from Puerto Natales, 30km south. Paralleling RN 40, a narrow-gauge railway hauls the coal to the seaport at Punta Loyola, near Río Gallegos. Passenger services are difficult to arrange, but trainspotters will enjoy exploring the railyards, which date from 1951.

RN 40 north of Río Turbio, from Estancia Tapi Aike to the junction with paved RP 5 at El Cerrito, is much improved, permitting any vehicle to take this shortcut to El Calafate and avoid the much longer detour via La Esperanza. Buses between Puerto Natales and El Calafate also take this route now.

Río Turbio's Centro de Información Turística (☎ 421950), on the Plazoleta Agustín del Castillo in the center of town, is open 8 am to 8 pm weekdays. The postal code is 9407, the area code 02902.

With permission, it is possible to visit the mines; ask the tourist office about guided tours. In winter the Centro de Deportes de Invierno Valdelén is a small but lighted ski area outside town, at the Villa Dorotea border crossing. Hours are 10 am to 10 pm daily.

Places to Stay & Eat

Río Turbio's cheapest accommodation, usually occupied by miners, is the ***Albergue Municipal*** *(☎ 421160, Paraje Mina 1)*, where four-to-a-room dormitory beds cost US$10. About 5km east of town, at the junction with RN 40 at Julia Dufour, ***Hostería Capipe*** *(☎ 482930)* charges US$23/40 single/double with private bath and breakfast.

Hotel Nazo *(☎ 421800, Gobernador Moyano 100)* has comfortable rooms with private bath, breakfast, telephone, and cable TV for US$30/50 single/double. At the ski area, ***Hostería de la Frontera*** *(☎ 421979)* seems out of place in a grimy coal town, but it's an excellent value for US$35/58 in summer, US$39/70 in ski season.

El Guri *(☎ 421190)*, almost directly opposite the tourist office, prepares excellent pastas (particularly ñoquis) at reasonable prices, and has many other items.

Getting There & Away

Air The airport is close enough to town for taking a cab to be a reasonable alternative. LADE (☎ 421224), Av Mineros 375, flies

Thursday to Río Gallegos (US$20), and Friday to El Calafate (US$20), Gobernador Gregores (US$29), Perito Moreno (US$55), and Comodoro Rivadavia (US$63).

Bus Cootra (☎ 421448) runs a dozen buses every weekday to Puerto Natales (US$4, 1½ hours) from Mineros and Agustín del Castillo, but weekend and holiday service is reduced. Cootra also goes to El Calafate at 8 am daily (US$18).

TAC (☎ 421058), on Av Jorge Newbery near the YPF station, crosses the steppe to Río Gallegos (US$15, six hours) daily at 3 pm. Quebeck Tours (☎ 421422), at the corner of Hipólito Yrigoyen and Agustín del Castillo, about a block from the tourist kiosk, goes to Gallegos at 1 am and 10 am daily. El Pingüino (☎ 421203), Jorge Newbery 14, goes to Río Gallegos at 2 am daily.

ESTANCIA TAPI AIKE

At the junction of RN 40 and RP 7, about midway between Puerto Natales and El Calafate, YPF has installed a new gas station and, from November to April, ***Estancia Tapi Aike*** *(☎ 02966-420092 in Río Gallegos; 011-4801-0020 in Buenos Aires)* offers comfortable B&B accommodations for US$45 per person. English is spoken, and afternoon tea (US$10) and lunch or dinner (US$22) are available for nonguests as well as guests.

EL CALAFATE

Gradually overcoming its tourist-trap reputation, El Calafate remains an almost inescapable – but now more agreeable – stopover en route to some of Argentina's most impressive sights. Formally founded in 1927, this onetime stage stop takes its name from the wild barberry *(Berberis buxifolia)*, which grows abundantly in the area.

Once an oversized encampment of rapacious merchants bent on making a year's income in a few short months by maintaining high prices rather than increasing sales, El Calafate (population 4000) still swarms with porteño tourists who parade up and down the sidewalks of Av del Libertador San Martín, to the accompaniment of roaring motorcycles, before and after spending a few hours at the Moreno Glacier. In recent years, though, greater competition has slowed price rises and reduced gouging, and some merchants are even showing an unprecedented courtesy.

January and February are the most popular months, so, if possible, plan your visit just before or just after peak season. From May to September, visitors are fewer and prices may drop, but days are shorter and the main attractions less accessible (though not necessarily inaccessible).

Orientation

El Calafate is 320km northwest of Río Gallegos via paved RP 5 and RP 11, and 32km west of RP 5's junction with northbound RN 40, which heads toward the El Chaltén section of Parque Nacional Los Glaciares. Westbound RP 11 goes to the southern sectors of Parque Nacional Los Glaciares and the Moreno Glacier. RN 40 south to Río Turbio is greatly improved, permitting any vehicle to cut 100km off the trip to Torres del Paine (Chile) by avoiding the lengthy La Esperanza route.

El Calafate's main thoroughfare is Av del Libertador General San Martín, more conveniently known as 'Av Libertador' or 'San Martín.' Because the town is small, most everything is within easy walking distance of San Martín.

Information

Tourist Offices Calafate's Ente Municipal Calafate Turismo (Emcatur; ☎ 491090, 492884), at the bus terminal, is open 8 am to 10 pm November to March, 8 am to 8 pm the rest of the year. It keeps a list of hotels and prices; has maps, brochures, and a message board; and there's usually an English-speaker on hand.

ACA (☎ 449-1004) is at Primero de Mayo and Av Roca.

Money Though (or because) Calafate is a tourist destination, changing money has traditionally been problematic, but the federal government's rigid convertibility policy has curtailed foreign exchange profiteering by local merchants.

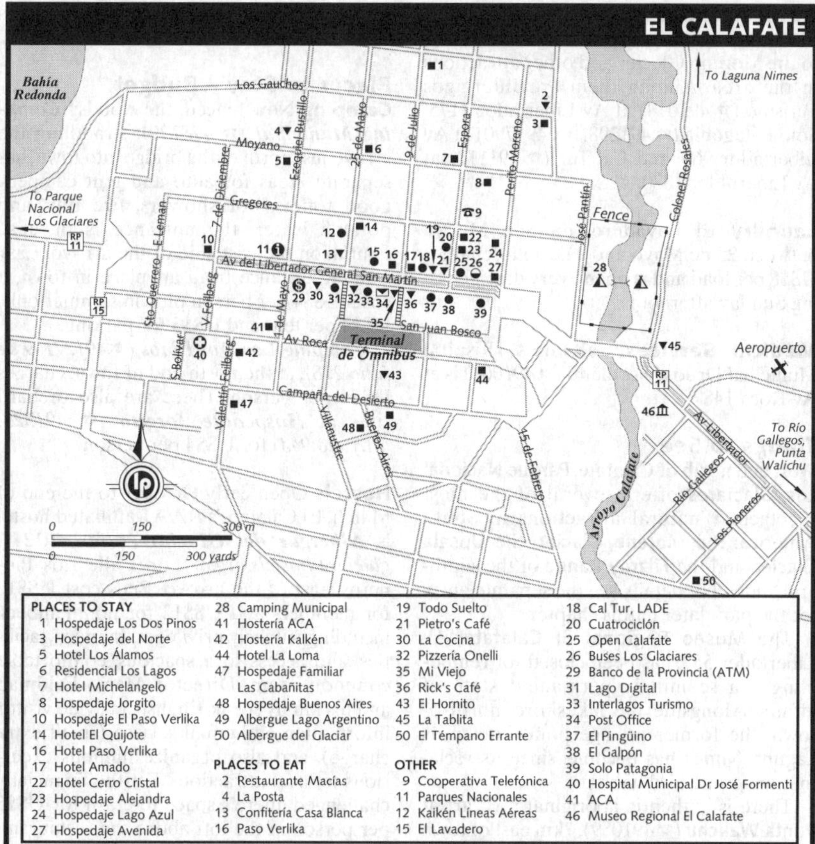

Banco de la Provincia de Santa Cruz, Av Libertador 1285, changes traveler's checks (with substantial commission), but it's open 10 am to 3 pm weekdays only; its ATM is often out of service. El Pingüino, Av Libertador 1025, also changes money, but also imposes a substantial commission on traveler's checks.

Post & Communications Correo Argentino is at Av Libertador 1133; the postal code is 9405. Calafate's Cooperativa Telefónica is at Espora 194; collect calls are not possible, and discounts are available only after 10 pm. The area code is ☎ 02902.

Internet Resources Calafate now has Internet access at Lago Digital (☎ 492328), on Av Libertador, opposite Casa Blanca

National Parks The Parques Nacionales office (☎ 491755, 491005), Av Libertador 1302, is open weekdays 7 am to 2 pm, and has brochures including a decent (though not adequate for trekking) map of Parque Nacional Los Glaciares.

Travel Agencies All of Calafate's numerous travel agencies can arrange excursions to the Moreno Glacier and other attractions in the area. Among them are Interlagos Turismo (☎ 491018) at Av Libertador 1175, Solo Patagonia (☎ 491298, fax 491790) at Av Libertador 963, and Cal Tur (☎ 491117) at Av Libertador 1080.

Laundry El Lavadero, on San Martín between 25 de Mayo and 9 de Julio, charges US$8 per load and is open every day, including Sunday afternoons.

Medical Services Calafate's Hospital Municipal Dr José Formenti (☎ 491001) is at Av Roca 1487.

Things to See

West and north of Calafate, **Parque Nacional Los Glaciares** offers several of the most spectacular natural attractions in South America: the **Moreno Glacier**, the **Upsala Glacier**, and the **Fitzroy Range** of the southern Andes. For details, see the separate entry for the park later in this chapter.

The **Museo Regional El Calafate**, Av Libertador 557, has been closed for remodeling – a seemingly permanent state of affairs. Alongside the lakeshore, north of town, the former sewage pond known as **Laguna Nimes** has become, since its reclamation, prime bird habitat.

There is authentic aboriginal rock art at **Punta Walichu** (☎ 491059), 7km east of town near the shores of Lago Argentino, but this grossly commercialized site is a reminder of old bad Calafate – its Disneyland reproductions of similar sites like northern Santa Cruz's Cueva de las Manos epitomize the Argentine slang term *trucho* (bogus). Whatever integrity it might have had before its privatization, its absurd US$7 admission fee and US$12 guided tour (plus US$4 for transfers) make it one of the country's most flagrant tourist rip-offs.

Places to Stay

Prices for accommodations can vary seasonally; the peak is usually January and February, but it can extend from early November to late March at some places. Many places close in winter.

Places to Stay – Budget

Camping Now fenced, the woodsy ***Camping Municipal*** *(☎ 498129)*, straddling the arroyo just north of the bridge into town, has separate areas for auto and tent campers, good toilets, hot showers, fire pits, and potable water; the entrance is on José Pantín, on the east side of the arroyo. Easy walking distance from anyplace in town, it costs US$4 per person plus, in summer only, US$4 per tent and US$3 for parking.

Camping Los Dos Pinos *(☎ 491271, 9 de Julio 218)*, at the north end of town, charges US$4 per person. There are also orchard sites at ***Hospedaje Jorgito*** *(☎ 491323, Moyano 943)* for US$4 per person.

Hostels Open early October to the end of March, El Calafate's RAAJ-affiliated hostel is ***Albergue del Glaciar*** *(☎/fax 491243, glaciar@hostels.org.ar)*, on Calle Los Pioneros, east of the arroyo. Beds cost US$10 for members and US$12 for nonmembers, including kitchen privileges, laundry facilities, and access to a spacious, comfortable common room. Director Mario Feldman and his family speak English, provide visitor information and email service (small extra charge), and also organize minibus excursions to local attractions. For the financially challenged, there's space to crash for US$5 per person in the loft above the restaurant, while those with bigger bucks will find comfortable private rooms.

There are also several unofficial hostels. ***Albergue Lago Argentino*** *(☎ 491423, Campaña del Desierto 1050)*, opposite the bus terminal, charges US$5 for those with their own sleeping bag, US$8 for those who need sheets. ***Los Dos Pinos*** *(☎ 491271, 9 de Julio 358)* has hostel accommodations for US$7 per person. ***Hospedaje El Paso Verlika*** *(☎ 491642)*, at the corner of Av Libertador and 7 de Diciembre, costs US$10 per person.

Hospedajes Prices vary considerably with the season, but the cheapest places are family inns like highly regarded ***Hospedaje Alejandra*** (☎ *491328, Espora 60)*, where rooms with shared bath cost US$10 per person.

Identically priced are ***Hospedaje Jorgito*** *(☎ 491323, Moyano 943)*, and ***Hospedaje Lago Azul*** *(☎ 491419, Perito Moreno 83)*.

Near the bus terminal, ***Hospedaje Buenos Aires*** *(☎ 491147, Ciudad de Buenos Aires 296)* has drawn mixed commentary; rates are US$15 per person. ***Hospedaje Avenida*** *(☎ 491159, Av Libertador 902)* also costs US$15, while ***Hospedaje Los Dos Pinos*** *(☎ 491271, 9 de Julio 358)* charges US$17.

Places to Stay – Mid-Range

Hospedaje del Norte *(☎ 491117, Los Gauchos 813)* charges US$20/30 for singles/doubles with shared bath, US$25/36 with private bath. Attractive ***Hotel Cerro Cristal*** *(☎ 491088, Gregores 989)* costs US$20/30 in the off-season, US$25/40 in peak season. Recommended ***Residencial Los Lagos*** *(☎ 491170, 25 de Mayo 220)* charges US$25/40 all year, as does ***Hotel Paso Verlika*** *(☎ 491009, Av Libertador 1108)*.

Hospedaje Familiar Las Cabañitas *(☎ 491118, Valentín Feilberg 218)* costs US$28/42 in peak season. Several readers have praised ***Cabañas del Sol*** *(☎ 491439, Av Libertador 1956)*, which charges US$30/34 in low season, US$35/44 in peak season.

Hotel La Loma *(☎ 491016, Av Roca 849)* costs US$35/50 to US$45/70 in the November to March high season, but is cheaper the rest of the year. ***Hotel Amado*** *(☎ 491134, Av Libertador 1072)* charges US$38/56. Members pay US$45/60 at the ***Hostería ACA*** *(☎ 491004, Primero de Mayo 50)*, while nonmembers are welcome for US$56/80.

Places to Stay – Top End

Several hotels charge upward of US$50 per night, including pleasant ***Hostería Kalkén*** *(☎ 491073, Valentín Feilberg 119)*, which serves an excellent breakfast. Rates are US$66/90 for singles/doubles in peak season, but only US$43/62 in October, April, and May.

Hotel Michelangelo *(☎ 491045, Moyano 1020)* charges US$87/105 with breakfast, but is about 20% cheaper in October and April. ***Hotel El Quijote*** *(☎ 491017, fax 491103, Gregores 1191)* charges US$95/120. In a class by itself is four-star ***Hotel Los Álamos*** *(☎ 491144, Moyano 1355)*, set among spectacular gardens, where rates are US$169/175 in peak season, plus US$5 for breakfast.

Places to Eat

There are several good values in Calafate's improving restaurant scene. ***Confitería Casa Blanca*** *(☎ 491402, Av Libertador 1202)* has good pizza and reasonable beer, but beware the US$3.50 submarino; ***Pizzería Onelli*** *(☎ 491184, Libertador 1197)*, across the street, also has its adherents. ***Paso Verlika*** *(☎ 491009, Av Libertador 1108)*, in the hotel of the same name, is popular and reasonably priced, especially the pizza. ***Pietro's Café*** *(Av Libertador 1640)* also serves pizza, as does ***El Hornito*** *(☎ 491443, Buenos Aires 155)*, half a block south of the bus terminal.

The kitchen at ***Hotel Michelangelo*** *(☎ 491045, Moyano 1020)* offers decent food but (unusually for Argentina) in microscopic portions, and it's not cheap. More reasonable are ***La Tablita*** *(☎ 491065, Coronel Rosales 24)*, near the bridge, and ***Restaurante Macías***, on Los Gauchos opposite Hospedaje del Norte.

La Cocina *(☎ 491758, Av Libertador 1245)* has an innovative Italian menu. ***Mi Viejo*** *(☎ 491691, Av Libertador 1111)* is a good and popular but pricey parrilla.

El Témpano Errante *(☎ 491243)*, the new restaurant at the youth hostel on Los Pioneros, is one of the best values in town, well worth a try even for visitors from upscale hotels. Much dearer, but perhaps not much better except for its upscale ambience, is ***La Posta*** *(☎ 491144)*, at Bustillo and Moyano (it's part of Hotel Los Álamos, across the street).

Rick's Café *(Av Libertador 1105)* is a new confitería that's worth a look. ***Todo Suelto*** *(Av Libertador 1044)* prepares a dozen types of empanadas, including trout.

Shopping

Open Calafate, Av Libertador 996, has books and souvenirs. In the past few years there has been a proliferation of shops on

Av Libertador offering good but expensive homemade chocolates.

Getting There & Away

Air As facilities improve at El Calafate's airport, it's likely some of the major airlines will fly directly here. For the moment, though, only two smaller airlines serve the town.

LADE (☎ 491262), Av Libertador 1080, flies Tuesday to Río Gallegos (US$25), Río Grande (US$49), and Ushuaia (US$56); Thursday to Río Turbio (US$20) and Río Gallegos; and Thursday and Friday to Gobernador Gregores (US$23), Perito Moreno (US$43), and Comodoro Rivadavia (US$62).

Kaikén Líneas Aéreas (☎ 491266), 25 de Mayo 23, flies daily except Sunday to Río Gallegos (US$55) and Ushuaia (US$93).

Bus El Calafate's hilltop Terminal de Ómnibus is on Av Roca, easily reached by a pedestrian staircase from the corner of Av Libertador and 9 de Julio.

El Pingüino (☎ 491273), Interlagos (☎ 491018), and Quebek Tours (☎ 491843) all cover the 320km of RP 5 and RP 11, which is now completely paved between Calafate and Río Gallegos (US$20, six hours). On request, they will drop you at the Río Gallegos airport, saving you a cab fare.

Turismo Zaahj (☎ 491631), along with Bus Sur, connects Calafate with Puerto Natales, Chile (US$23), daily except Monday and Thursday. Cootra (☎ 491444) goes daily except Saturday to Río Turbio (US$18) and Puerto Natales.

Daily at 7:30 am in summer, Buses Los Glaciares (☎ 491158) leaves Calafate for El Chaltén (US$25 one-way, US$50 with open return) and the Fitzroy Range. The return service leaves El Chaltén at 5 pm; winter schedules may differ. Cal Tur (☎ 491842) goes to Chaltén half an hour earlier, but returns at the same time, while Chaltén Travel (☎ 491833) leaves at 8 am and returns at 6 pm.

Almafuerte Travel's new Rotativo Patagónico service runs minibuses from Calafate to the town of Perito Moreno (US$50, 9½ hours) daily in January and February, less frequently the rest of the year. Service beyond Perito Moreno to Esquel (US$50 and nine hours more) involves an overnight at the passenger's expense in Perito Moreno. Service is reduced to one to three times weekly the rest of the year on this pilot route.

Getting Around

Cuatrociclón, on Espora near the corner of San Martín, rents mountain bikes for US$5 per hour, US$8 for two, US$15 for half a day, and US$20 for a full day.

AROUND EL CALAFATE

Estancia El Galpón

About 20km west of El Calafate, Estancia El Galpón is a working ranch that, like many others, has opened itself to the tourist trade. Afternoon excursions, including tea on arrival, observation of herding and sheep shearing, a birding walk, and a lamb asado for dinner, cost US$55 including transportation. They also offer horseback riding to nearby Cerro Frías (US$50) and even to the Moreno Glacier.

For more detail contact El Galpón (☎/fax 491793, elgalpon@cotecal.com.ar), at Av Libertador 1015 in El Calafate, or in Buenos Aires (☎ 011-4312-4473, fax 011-4313-0679) at Av Leandro Alem 822, 3rd floor.

PARQUE NACIONAL LOS GLACIARES

Nourished by awesome glaciers that descend from the Andean divide, Lago Argentino and Lago Viedma in turn feed southern Patagonia's largest river, the Río Santa Cruz. Along with the Iguazú Falls, this amalgam of ice, rock, and water is one of the greatest sights in Argentina and all of South America.

Its centerpiece is the breathtaking **Moreno Glacier** which, due to unusually favorable local conditions, is one of the planet's few advancing glaciers, though topography prevents it from making a net advance. A low gap in the Andes allows moisture-laden Pacific storms to drop their loads east of the divide, where they accumulate as snow. Over millennia, under

PARQUE NACIONAL LOS GLACIARES

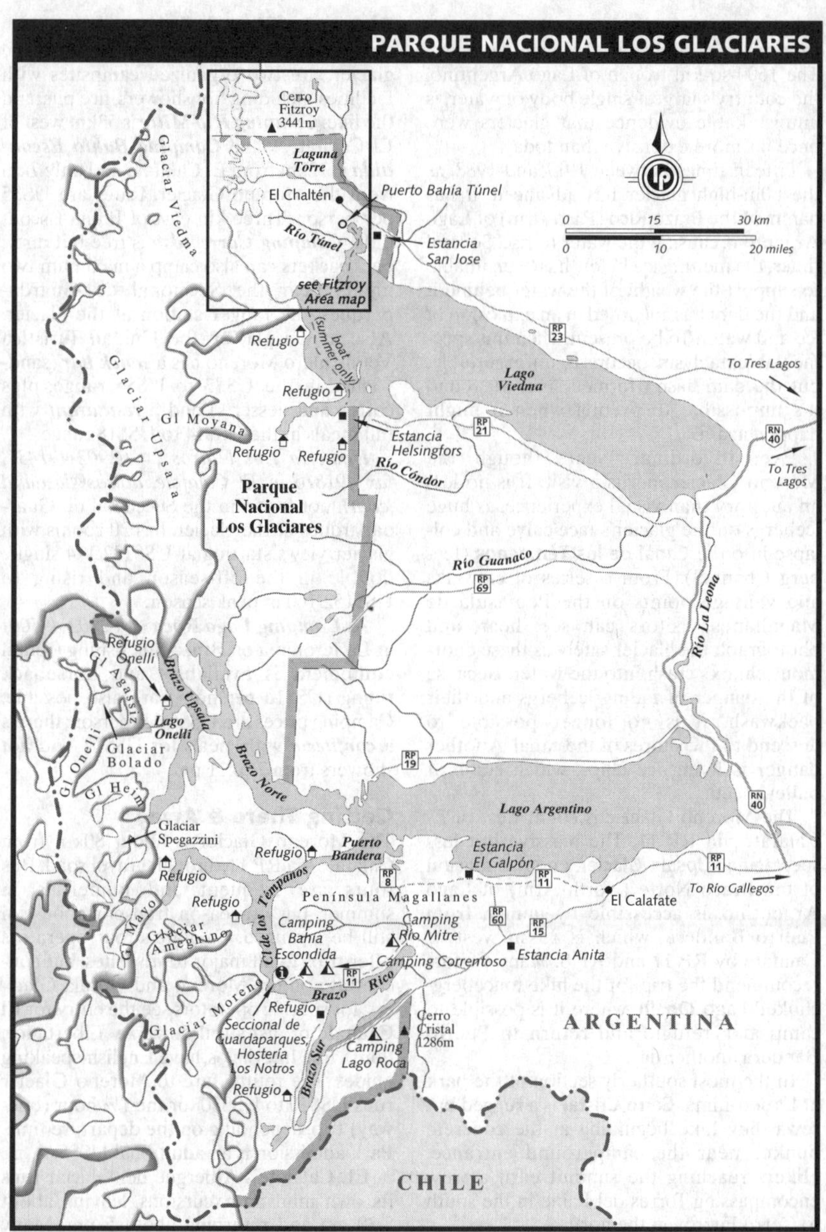

tremendous weight, this snow has recrystallized into ice and flowed slowly eastward. The 1600-sq-km trough of Lago Argentino, the country's largest single body of water, is unmistakable evidence that glaciers were once far more extensive than today.

Fifteen times between 1917 and 1988, as the 60m-high glacier has advanced, it has dammed the **Brazo Rico** (Rico Arm) of Lago Argentino, causing the water to rise. Several times, the melting ice below has been unable to support the weight of the water behind it and the dam has collapsed in an explosion of ice and water. To be present when this spectacular cataclysm occurs is unforgettable, but the dam hasn't formed since 1988 and it's impossible to predict when it might happen again.

Even in ordinary years, though, the Moreno Glacier merits a visit. It is no less an auditory than visual experience, as huge icebergs on the glacier's face calve and collapse into the **Canal de los Témpanos** (Iceberg Channel). From a series of catwalks and vantage points on the Península de Magallanes visitors can see, hear, and photograph the glacier safely as these enormous chunks crash into the water. Because of the danger of falling icebergs and their backwash, it is no longer possible to descend to the shores of the canal. Another danger is flying ice chips, which come at bullet speed.

The Moreno Glacier is 80km west of El Calafate via RP 11. The massive but less spectacular **Upsala Glacier**, on an extension of the Brazo Norte (North Arm) of Lago Argentino, is accessible by launch from Puerto Bandera, which is 45km west of Calafate by RP 11 and RP 8. Many visitors recommend the trip for the hike to iceberg-choked **Lago Onelli**, where it is possible to camp at a refugio and return to Puerto Bandera another day.

In the most southerly section of the park at La Jerónima, **Cerro Cristal** is a rugged but rewarding hike beginning at the concrete bunker near the campground entrance. Hikers reaching the summit earn a view encompassing Torres del Paine in the south to Cerro Fitzroy in the north.

Places to Stay & Eat

On Península Magallanes, en route to the glacier, are two organized campsites with facilities including hot showers, fire pits, and the like: ***Camping Río Mitre*** is 53km west of El Calafate, while ***Camping Bahía Escondida*** is 72km from El Calafate and only 7km from the Moreno Glacier. Rates are US$5 per person. Three km east of Bahía Escondida, ***Camping Correntoso*** is free but dirty; backpackers can also camp a maximum two nights near the Seccional de Guardaparques, the ranger station at the glacier. Also at the glacier, the Unidad Turística Ventisquero Moreno has a ***snack bar*** (sandwiches in the US$3 to US$5 range, plus coffee and desserts) and a ***restaurant*** with full meals in the US$14 to US$18 range.

Hostería Los Notros *(☎ 02902-491437, fax 491816 in El Calafate, notros@lastland.com)*, not far from the Seccional de Guardaparques at the glacier, has 20 rooms with glacier views starting at US$132/174 single/double in the off-season and rising to US$152/160 in peak season.

At ***Camping Lago Roca*** *(☎ 02902-49500)* at La Jerónima on Brazo Sur, fishing (rental equipment is available) and horseback riding (US$10 per hour) are also possible. Camping prices are US$6 per person; there's a ***confitería*** with meals for US$12, and hot showers from 7 to 11 pm.

Getting There & Away

The Moreno Glacier is about 80km from Calafate via RP 11, a rough gravel road. Bus tours are frequent and numerous in summer, but off-season transportation can still be arranged. Calafate's tour operators offer trips to all major tourist sites, but concentrate on the Moreno and Upsala Glaciers; for specific operators see the entry for El Calafate or just stroll down Av Libertador. Some, like Interlagos, have English-speaking guides. The return fare to Moreno Glacier runs US$20 to US$30 for the 1¼ hour (one-way) trip, depending on the departure time. Park admission is an additional US$5.

EL Calafate's Albergue del Glaciar runs its own minivan excursions, leaving about 8:30 am and returning about 5 pm. Many visitors feel that day trips allow insufficient time to appreciate the glacier, especially if inclement weather limits visibility. The changeable weather is almost sure to provide a window on the glacier at some time during your trip, but it's also worth exploring possibilities for camping nearby.

Several travel agencies offer brief hikes across the glacier itself. After crossing Brazo Rico in a rubber raft, you hike with guides through the southern beech forest and onto the glacier. This all-day 'minitrekking' excursion from El Calafate costs US$65. Full-day bus/motor launch excursions to the Upsala Glacier cost about $55. Meals are extra and usually expensive; bring your own food.

FITZROY RANGE (CERRO FITZROY)

Sedentary tourists can enjoy the Moreno Glacier, but the Fitzroy Range is the mecca for hikers, climbers, and campers. The staging point for most everything is the tiny settlement of **El Chaltén**, a monument to Argentina's prodigious capacity for bureaucracy. At one time in this town, where Chile and Argentina have settled all but one of their almost interminable border disputes, virtually every resident was a government employee.

Once a desolate collection of pseudochalets pummeled by the almost incessant wind, El Chaltén is becoming a village rather than just a bureaucratic outpost seemingly airlifted onto the exposed floodplain of the Río de las Vueltas. While it still has faults, its magnificent surroundings and improving services – hotels, hostels, campgrounds, restaurants, phones, even a pharmacy – make El Chaltén more agreeable every day. The name itself, signifying 'azure' in the Tehuelche language, was the name applied to Cerro Fitzroy.

Orientation & Information

While Chaltén is a bit spread out and there are no street addresses, everything is easy to find. Parques Nacionales (☎ 493004), at the entrance to town just before the bridge over the Río Fitzroy, provides information and issues climbing permits from 8 am to 8 pm daily. The several hostels in town are also good sources of information. The area code is ☎ 02962.

There's no place to change money, but there is phone service and, after many years, YPF has placed a gas station here.

Things to See & Do

One of many fine hikes in the area goes to **Laguna Torre**, and continues to the base camp for climbers of the famous spire of **Cerro Torre**. There's a signed trailhead between the chalets and the rustic Madsen campground along the road to the north. After a gentle initial climb, it's a fairly level walk through tranquil beech forests and along the Río Fitzroy until a final steeper climb up the lateral moraine left by the receding Glaciar del Torre. From Laguna Torre, there are stunning views of the principal southern peaks of the Fitzroy Range. Allow at least three hours one-way.

While clouds usually enshroud the summit of 3128m Cerro Torre, look for the 'mushroom' of snow and ice that caps the peak. This precarious formation is the final obstacle for serious climbers, who sometimes spend weeks or months waiting for weather good enough for an ascent. Protected ***campsites***are available in the beech forest above Laguna Torre.

Another exceptional but more strenuous hike climbs steeply from the pack station at the Madsen campground; after about an hour, there's a signed lateral to excellent backcountry ***campsites*** at **Laguna Capri**. The main trail continues gently to **Río Blanco**, a base camp for climbers of Cerro Fitzroy, and then climbs very steeply to **Laguna de los Tres**, a high alpine tarn named in honor of the three Frenchmen who first scaled Fitzroy. Condors glide overhead and nest in an area where, in clear weather, the views are truly extraordinary. Allow about four hours one-way, and leave time for contemplation and physical recovery after the last segment, on which high winds can be a real hazard.

If the weather doesn't permit climbing to the Laguna – or even if it does – consider a one-hour detour down the Río Blanco to

FITZROY AREA

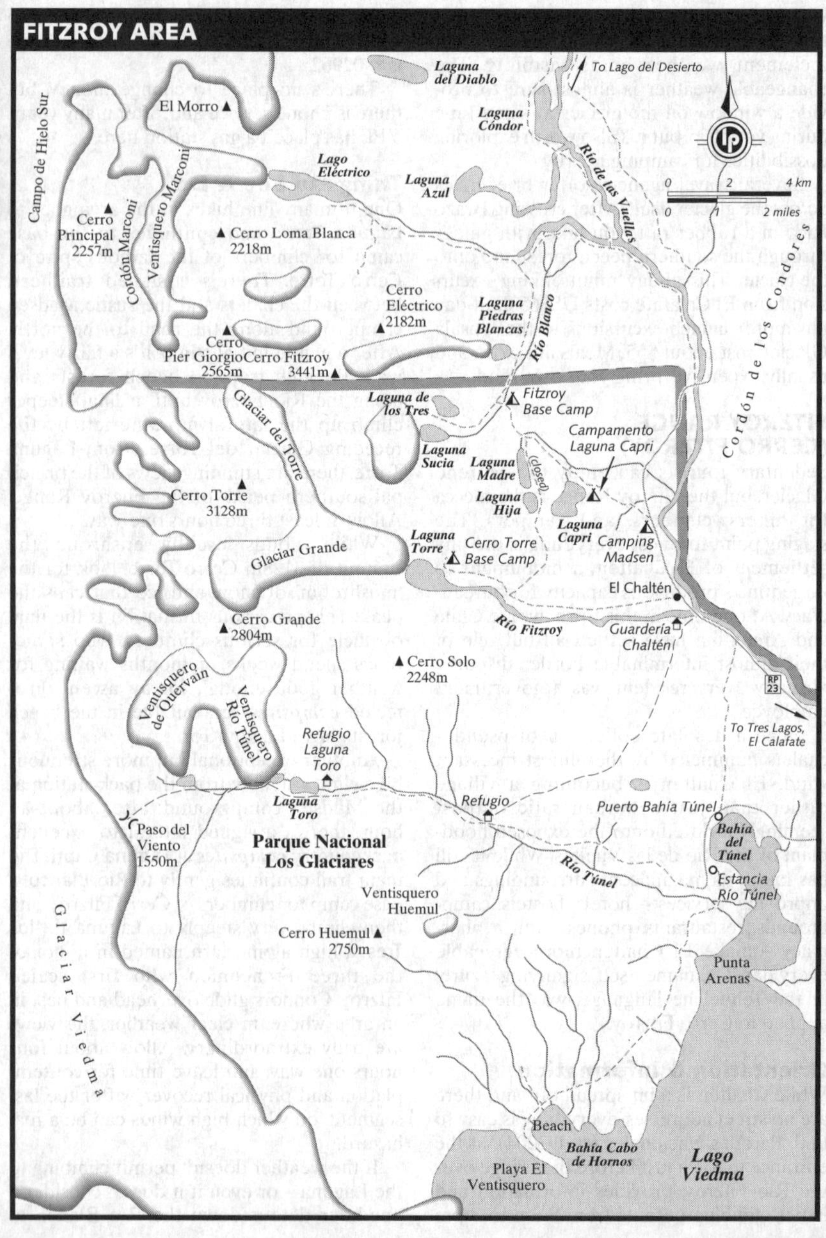

Glaciar Piedras Blancas, the last part of which is a scramble over massive granite boulders to a turquoise lake with dozens of floating icebergs and constant avalanches on the glacier's face.

More-ambitious hikers can make a circuit through the Fitzroy Range that is shorter than the one in Torres del Paine, but still worthwhile; another possibility is Laguna del Desierto, north of Chaltén. Recent reports suggest some restriction on hiking this loop; ask for details at the ranger station in Chaltén. The owner of ***Los Troncos***, a good private campground along the circuit, restricts access through his land, making it an obligatory overnight.

At **Lago del Desierto**, 30km north of El Chaltén, Argentina appears to be reinforcing its territorial claim against Chile with pretentious plaques, toilet paper, and cigarette butts. There is, however, a 500m trail to an overlook with fine views of the lake and surrounding mountains and glaciers, though the weather often intervenes against photography. Powered by twin outboards, the enclosed *Mariana II* (☎ 02902-491103 in El Calafate), cruises the length of the lake (80 minutes) thrice daily for US$30 return. Chaltén Travel minibus service to Lago del Desierto, leaving at 11 am and returning at 4:30 pm, costs US$15 return; hitching is feasible but not easy.

For more-adventurous hikers, it's possible to take three- to 15-day guided hikes over the **Hielo Patagónico Continental** (Continental Ice Field); for details, contact Parques Nacionales or the local representative of the Asociación Argentina de Guías de Montaña (☎ 493017). Rates range from US$75 to US$150 per day.

From the north shore of Lago Viedma, at Puerto Bahía Túnel, it's possible to visit the Finnish pioneer **Estancia Helsingfors**, on the south shore, on the *Embarcación Huemul*, which also passes the Viedma Glacier (see the PN Los Glaciares map). The eight-hour excursion costs US$55; it's possible to continue to El Calafate for another US$15. Buses to Puerto Bahía Túnel leave from Confitería La Senyera. It's also possible to get to Helsingfors and El Chaltén directly from El Calafate (US$65); make reservations at Nova Terra (☎ 02902-491726), 25 de Mayo 23.

Highly regarded ***Hostería Helsingfors*** *(☎/fax 011-4824-6623 in Buenos Aires, landsur@wam.com.ar)* has accommodations with full board for US$125/210 single/double from November to mid-December and in March, while prices in summer and at Semana Santa are US$140/260. Children under 12 pay half. There are also three-day, two-night packages, including transport from El Calafate, continuing on to El Chaltén, for US$345 double; two-day, one night packages cost US$225. For the latest details, see the Helsingfors home page (www.wam.com.ar/tourism/estancs/helsingfors/).

Places to Stay

Camping There's free camping at Parques Nacionales' ***Camping Madsen*** in Chaltén, with running water and abundant firewood, but no toilets – you must dig a latrine. There's another free, but less sheltered, site across the road from Parques Nacionales' information office. If you don't mind walking about 10 minutes, shower at Confitería La Senyera for about US$1.

Most paying campgrounds, like ***Posada Lago del Desierto*** and ***El Relincho***, charge about US$5 per person, sometimes charging extra for hot showers. ***Ruca Mahuida*** *(☎ 493018)* charges US$6 per person, has meals and hot showers, and arranges local excursions.

Hostels There are several hostels open all year. ***Albergue Los Ñires*** *(☎ 493009)* is a small (eight-bed) hostel that charges US$10 per person or US$5 per person for camping. The larger but homier Dutch-Argentine ***Albergue Patagonia*** *(☎ 493019, patagoni@hostels.org.ar)* charges US$12 plus US$2 for kitchen privileges; reasonable meals are also available. The spacious new 44-bed ***Rancho Grande Hostel*** *(☎ /fax 493005, bigranch@hostels.org.ar, rancho@cvtci.com.ar)* costs US$10 for HI members, slightly more for nonmembers.

Hotels & Cabañas The ***Posada Lago del Desierto*** *(☎ 493010)* has comfortable six-bed apartments, with kitchen facilities, private bath, and hot water, for US$100 per person; its hotel has doubles for US$60. Meals are expensive. ***Cabañas Cerro Torre*** *(☎ 493061)* has four-bed cabins with private bath for US$20 per person (US$25 with breakfast).

At the ***Fitzroy Inn*** *(☎ 493062)*, half-board accommodations cost US$53 per person, but you might want to opt for a US$70 package that includes return transportation from Calafate, one night's lodging, dinner, and breakfast; two-night packages cost US$95, while three nights cost US$120.

Places to Eat

Confitería La Senyera *(☎ 493063)* has enormous portions of tasty chocolate cake, plus other quality snacks and light meals. ***The Wall*** is a similarly popular pub-restaurant.

Confitería Carrilay Aike has good homemade bread, teas, and the like for breakfast. ***Josh Aike*** *(☎ 493008)* has drawn praise for its pizzas, desserts, and breakfasts, but the best place to eat is ***Ruca Mahuida*** *(☎ 493018)*, part of the eponymous campground, which has tasty and creative cuisine in a tobacco-free environment. ***La Casita*** *(☎ 493042)* comes recommended by locals, but the food can't match Ruca Mahuida and poor ventilation makes the smoke-laden atmosphere almost lethal even in the short term.

Groceries (including fresh bread) are available at ***Kiosko Charito*** and ***El Chaltén***.

Getting There & Away

El Chaltén is 220km from El Calafate via paved RP 11, rugged RN 40, and improved but still rugged RP 23. See the entry on El Calafate for details on daily buses to Chaltén; buses normally return from El Chaltén at 5 or 6 pm. There is also direct service from Río Gallegos with Transportes Burmeister, which stops at The Wall.

Northbound on RP 40, the nearest gas station is at Tres Lagos, 123km east of El Chaltén. Beyond the RP 23 junction, RN 40 is very bad and carries very little traffic, but in summer Daniel Bagnera (☎ 011-4302-9533 in Buenos Aires) operates the twice-weekly minibus service Itinerarios y Travesías to the small agricultural town of Perito Moreno, with a 2½-hour stop at Cueva de las Manos, for US$92 (18 hours elapsed time). While the price may seem steep, it's the only fixed transport on this route, which is rough on vehicles, and compared with backtracking to Río Gallegos it's pretty cheap.

Between Tres Lagos and Bajo Caracoles, the highway has been greatly improved, permitting speeds between 65 and 80kph en route to Perito Moreno and the junction to Los Antiguos.

CALETA OLIVIA

Less publicized than the Andean lake district, eastern Santa Cruz province, along the Atlantic coast and longitudinal RN 3, is not without interest. The oil port of Caleta Olivia, founded in 1901 to discharge cargo for the Buenos Aires-Cabo Vírgenes telegraph line, offers access to several petrified forests as well as the Andean oasis of Los Antiguos, a crossing point into Chile.

For southbound travelers on RN 3, Caleta Olivia (population 32,000) is the first stop in Santa Cruz province. Dominating the downtown traffic circle, in a style that might well be called 'Peronist realism,' is its most visible landmark, the **Monumento al Obrero Petrolero**, sculptor Pablo Daniel Sánchez's 10m monument of the muscular oil worker known colloquially as 'El Gorosito.' Other industries include seafood processing and wool. If heading south toward Tierra del Fuego or east toward the Andes, you might opt to spend a night here.

Orientation & Information

Entering Caleta Olivia from the north, RN 3 becomes part of Av Jorge Newbery and then Av San Martín (the main thoroughfare) before taking a dogleg at the monument, where it becomes Av Eva Perón. Many streets have recently been renamed.

The friendly, enthusiastic Coordinación de Turismo (☎ 485-1101 interno 234), on Av San Martín near the monument, is open 7 am to 9 pm in summer, 8 am to 5 pm the

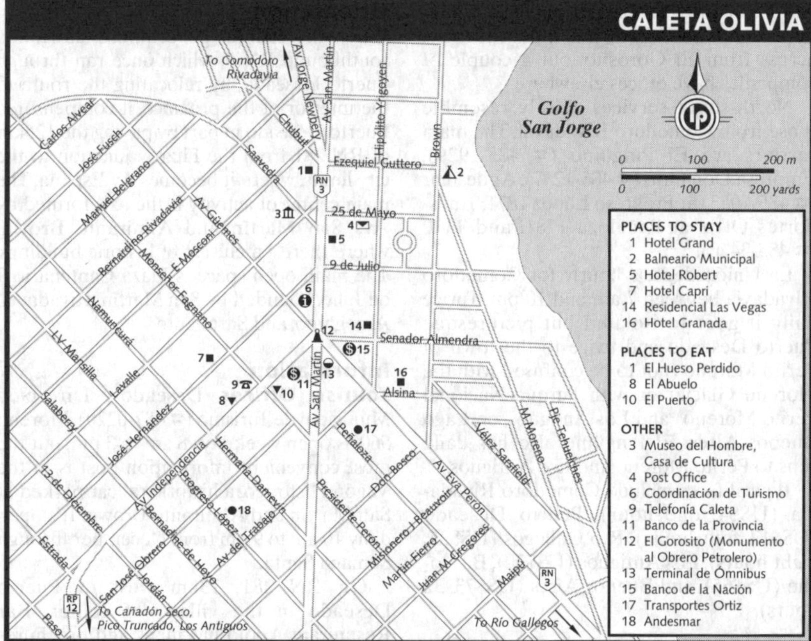

rest of the year. Correo Argentino is on 25 de Mayo at Hipólito Yrigoyen. The most convenient locutorio is Telefonía Caleta, Av Independencia 1147. Caleta Olivia's area code is ☎ 0297.

Things to See

In the Casa de Cultura, on Lavalle near San Martín, the **Museo del Hombre** (Museum of Man) is open 8 am to 4 pm daily.

Places to Stay

Camping at the ***Balneario Municipal*** *(☎ 485-1082 interno 249)*, at Brown and Guttero, costs US$6 per site. There is 24-hour hot water and other services.

Otherwise, the most reasonable accommodations are comfortable ***Residencial Las Vegas*** *(☎ 485-1177, Hipólito Yrigoyen 2094)*, one block from El Gorosito, where rates are US$15 per person with private bath, and ***Hotel Granada*** *(☎ 485-1512, Alsina 953)*, which costs US$20/36 single/double. ***Hotel Capri*** *(☎ 485-1132, José Hernández 1145)* charges US$25/35, while ***Hotel Grand*** *(☎ 485-1393)*, at Av San Martín and Chubut, is slightly more expensive at US$26/45. Rates at ***Hotel Robert*** *(☎ 485-1452, Av San Martín 2151)* range from US$41/62 to US$52/77.

Places to Eat

El Hueso Perdido, a parrilla, is downstairs at Hotel Grand. ***El Puerto*** *(☎ 485-1313, Av Independencia 1060)* has a good midday menu for US$6.50; nearby ***El Abuelo*** is probably the best (and priciest) in town.

Getting There & Away

Caleta Olivia is a hub for bus travel in northern Santa Cruz, as excellent paved roads lead north to Comodoro Rivadavia, south to Río Gallegos, and west to Perito Moreno and Los Antiguos. The Terminal de Ómnibus is at Avs San Martín and Independencia, across from El Gorosito, but a couple of companies have offices elsewhere.

North-south services closely resemble those from Comodoro Rivadavia. The main carriers are El Pingüino (☎ 485-1929), Empresa Don Otto (☎ 485-1237), Andesmar (☎ 485-1053) at Progreso López 1871, Transportes Ortiz at Peñaloza 1781, and TUP (☎ 485-3420).

La Unión departs hourly for Comodoro Rivadavia between 7 am and 10 pm. Thrice daily it goes to isolated but picturesque Puerto Deseado and twice to the town of Perito Moreno (not to be confused with the Moreno Glacier or with Parque Nacional Perito Moreno) and Los Antiguos, on Lago Buenos Aires. El Pingüino also has daily runs to Perito Moreno and Los Antiguos.

Typical fares include Comodoro Rivadavia (US$4, one hour), Puerto Deseado (US$17, four hours), Río Gallegos (US$25, eight hours), Los Antiguos (US$30), Bariloche (US$65), and Buenos Aires (US$73, 32 hours).

PUERTO DESEADO

Coastal Patagonia, with its barren steppes and bullet-riddled highway signs, has the look of Wyoming-by-the-Sea, and off-the-beaten-track Puerto Deseado is one of those agreeable surprises that makes travel rewarding. Once the port terminus of a railway projected to continue to Bariloche, in Río Negro province, this architecturally intriguing town of 8000 features a turn-of-the-century station that could have been plucked off the Great Plains, but it's within sight of the Ría Deseado, a submerged estuary that provides habitat for thousands of seabirds and other marine wildlife.

In colonial times, Spain established a whaling station at Puerto Deseado, but when the *Beagle* anchored here in 1833, Darwin found only 'ruins of an old Spanish settlement' where Indian attacks had 'compelled the colonists to desert their half-finished buildings.' In 1881 Argentina established a naval prefecture and, in 1884, the first permanent settlers arrived.

Orientation

When the federal government shortened southbound RN 3, which once ran through Puerto Deseado, by relocating the route to the interior of the province, it compensated Puerto Deseado in part by paving the 125km of RN 281 from the Fitzroy junction to the city limits, where it becomes Av España. The main center of activity is the axis formed by Avs San Martín and Almirante Brown, where there's a cluster of historic buildings. The main open space is Plaza Centenario 9 de Julio, bounded by San Martín, Rivadavia, Ameghino, and Sarmiento.

Information

Tourist Offices Deseado's Dirección Municipal de Turismo (☎ 487-0220), Moreno 560, is open weekdays 8 am to 3 pm, but the most convenient information post is in the Vagón Histórico, a historic railcar parked at San Martín and Almirante Brown. It's open daily 10 am to 9 pm from December through Semana Santa.

On RN 281, 13km west of Puerto Deseado in the village of Tellier, Bar Restaurant Apolo has maps and brochures of the town and the surrounding area. At the junction on RN 3 and RN 281 in Fitzroy, there's a helpful trailer office open 9 am to 8:30 pm daily from December through Semana Santa.

Money There are several banks clustered along San Martín.

Post & Communications Correo Argentino is at San Martín 1075; the postal code is 9050. Telefonía Deseado is at Almirante Brown 544; the telephone code is ☎ 0297.

Travel Agencies Hito 45 (☎ 487-0231) is at Don Bosco 970.

Medical Services The Hospital Distrital (☎ 487-0200) is at Brown and Colón.

Things to See

Puerto Deseado has three superbly restored historical monuments within a short distance of one another at Av San Martín and Almi-

rante Brown. The most notable is the **Vagón Histórico** (1898) of the Ferrocarril Patagónico, a mixed cargo and passenger route than once hauled wool and lead from Chilean mines from Pico Truncado and Las Heras, 280km northwest, and might have reached Bariloche had not the project been aborted. Colonel Héctor Benigno Varela used the car as his headquarters during the Anarchist rebellion of 1921; Varela, who personally executed gaucho rebel Facón Grande (Big Knife) at Jaramillo two days after reporting him killed in action, was himself assassinated by an anarchist in Buenos Aires. In the latter days of the Proceso in 1980, Deseado's townspeople demonstrated and blocked the roads out of town to keep the car here – an extraordinary event given its symbolism in militant labor history.

A supermarket now occupies the former site of the **Compañía Argentina del Sud** (1919), while the vintage **Banco de la Nación** across the street is built of imposing lava blocks quarried nearby. One block west, at San Martín 1176, the **Sociedad Española** dates from 1915.

To the east, on Oneto, the imposing **Estación del Ferrocarril Patagónico** was the coastal terminus for the line. The railroad closed in 1977, but the station is undergoing restoration as municipal offices.

Divers are working to recover more artifacts for the **Museo Regional Mario Brozoski**, best known for relics of the English corvette *Swift*, sunk off the coast of Deseado in 1776 and located in 1982 (ironically, only two months before the Falklands war). The museum (☎ 487-0220) is at Colón and Belgrano, but has been closed for remodeling.

Places to Stay

Puerto Deseado has plenty of moderately priced accommodations, ranging from camping to residenciales and hotels.

Camping Open all year, the ***Camping Municipal La Costanera*** *(☎ 487-2728)*, on the waterfront Av Marcelo Lotufo, charges only US$2 to US$3 per person and per tent, depending on the site, US$4 for self-contained campers. It has good toilets and showers, but the incessant winds can be a noisy nuisance and some tent sites are a bit stony. Inexpensive trailers/cabañas are available for US$7 per person.

There is also a new, sheltered, and woodsier ***Camping Cañadón Giménez***, at the western approach to town.

Hostels The ***Albergue Municipal*** *(☎ 487-0260, Colón 1147)* mostly attracts groups, but does offer rooms with private bath for US$12, US$8 without sheets. Rates for rooms with shared bath are US$8, US$5 without sheets.

Hotels & Residenciales The ***Hotel Oneto*** *(☎ 487-0455)*, at Doctor Fernández and Oneto, has singles/doubles with shared bath for US$13/22, while those with private bath go for US$24/40. Remodeled ***Hospedaje Los Olmos*** *(☎ 487-0077, Gregores 849)* is probably the best inexpensive alternative for US$23/36 with breakfast. Two hotels under the same management cost US$23/39: ***Residencial Sur 1*** *(☎ 487-0522, Ameghino 1640)* and ***Residencial Sur 2*** *(☎ 487-2350, Pueyrredón 367)*.

Rates at sparkling ***Hotel Chaffers*** *(☎ 487-2246, 487-2168)*, San Martín and Moreno, begin around US$45/62.

Under new ownership, the hilltop ***Hotel Los Acantilados*** *(☎/fax 487-2167)*, Pueyrredón and España, has the best views in town. Rates start at US$50/70; there's a 10% cash discount.

Places to Eat

Pizzería El Petrolero *(☎ 487-0114, San Martín 1294)* has basic fixed-price meals for US$8 – but they're no bargain and the service is not particularly good. ***Pizzería La Balsa*** *(☎ 487-1275, 12 de Octubre 641)* and ***Pronto Pizza*** *(☎ 487-2134, Don Bosco 1055)* are decent alternatives.

El Pingüino *(☎ 487-0373, Piedra Buena 958)* is a parrilla, but the best choice is seafood at places like ***Viejo Marino*** *(☎ 487-0509, Pueyrredón 224)*, ***Los Galenos*** at Ameghino and Rivadavia, and ***El Galeón*** in the Club Náutico, which offers homestyle cooking and good views of the port's historic Muelle de Ramón, at the foot of Almirante Zar.

Entertainment

The modernistic ***Jackaroe Boliche*** *(Moreno 633)*, a dance club, looks as out of place in sleepy Deseado as its Australian-derived name might suggest.

Getting There & Away

Air Taxis provide the only transportation to and from the airport, which is about 6km outside town. LADE (☎ 487-1204), Don Bosco 1580, flies Monday to San Julián (US$22), Gobernador Gregores (US$33), Santa Cruz (US$34), and Río Gallegos (US$49), and Tuesday to Comodoro Rivadavia (US$25).

Bus The new Terminal de Ómnibus is at Sargento Cabral 1302, at the northeast corner of town. Transporte La Unión, San Martín 1259, goes to Caleta Olivia (US$17, four hours) and Comodoro Rivadavia (US$19) at 7 am and 1 and 6 pm daily.

AROUND PUERTO DESEADO

Reserva Natural Ría Deseado

The intrusion of the South Atlantic into the former riverbed created several islands and other sites with nesting habitat for seabirds. These spots include Isla Chaffers (2000 pairs of Magellanic penguins), Banco Cormorán (good photo access to rock cormorants and the strikingly beautiful grey cormorant), and Isla de los Pájaros (nesting terns). The most interesting site, 30km offshore at Isla de los Pingüinos, has nesting rockhoppers and breeding elephant seals, but getting there costs a hefty US$575 for a maximum of five persons.

At the western approach to town, Gipsy Tours (☎/fax 487-2155, 487-2501; 15624-7554 cellular, gipsytms@patagonia.net.ar) runs reasonably priced regular Sunday excursions (US$22 to US$65) along the ría, but is also available for charter at other times. Their Buenos Aires office (☎/fax 021-4315-0779, 4312-4287, gipsy@starnet.com.ar) is at Leandro Alem 1067, 12th floor, Oficina 39.

Contact also Turismo Aventura Los Vikingos (15624-5141 cellular) for excursions of varying itineraries and prices, including trips to Monumento Natural Bosque Petrificado.

Balneario Las Piletas

When the tide is low enough on summer days to isolate enormous tidal pools from the cold South Atlantic a few kilometers northeast of town, Deseado residents take advantage of the warming water to swim. Penguins sometimes come ashore where rugged lava flows, unusual in this part of Patagonia, have created some picturesque shoreline caves.

Gruta de Lourdes

Pilgrims flock to and camp at the entrance to this sacred site in a volcanic canyon, about 10km west of Puerto Deseado via RN 281 and a short lateral, where there are plenty of devotional plaques and a pool at the base of a normally dry waterfall. Less-devout visitors have decorated the otherwise scenic spot with spray paint. It's still worth a brief detour for visitors with their own vehicle.

Cañadón Quitapeña

Five km north of town via Zar, this scenic sheltered canyon has good ***camping*** but no services; consequently, it's most suitable for those with their own vehicles, but it's worth a hike and a look.

MONUMENTO NATURAL BOSQUES PETRIFICADOS

In the Argentine national park system, natural monuments are the only units invulnerable to commercial exploitation, so the 15,000-hectare Petrified Forest Natural Monument contains no hotels, restaurants, confiterías, or other concessions, unlike Nahuel Huapi, Los Glaciares, and other overdeveloped parks. Bosques Petrificados has only its volcanic, polychrome desert landscape, fossilized forests, wildlife, and solitude to recommend it. Just off RN 3, 157km south of Caleta Olivia, an excellent gravel road (along which guanacos are a common sight) leads 50km west to the park.

During Jurassic times, 150 million years ago, this area enjoyed a humid, temperate climate, but intense volcanic activity leveled its flourishing forests and buried them in ash. Erosion later exposed the mineralized *Proaraucaria* trees (ancestors of the modern *araucaria*, unique to the Southern Hemisphere), up to 3m in diameter and 35m in length. A short interpretive trail leads from park headquarters to the largest concentration of petrified trees. Until its legal protection in 1954, the area was consistently plundered for some of its finest specimens; do not perpetuate this unsavory tradition by taking even the tiniest souvenir.

Other parts of the scenic desert park also merit exploration, but consult with park rangers before continuing far on the road toward the peak of Madre e Hijo (Mother and Son). You can pitch a tent for free near the dry creek, within sight of headquarters, which has a small display of local artifacts and fauna. Since there is no water at the site, bring your own if you have a vehicle. Otherwise, you *may* be able to obtain some from headquarters. Like the rest of Patagonia, it's extremely windy, but the southern night sky offers a spectacular display of stars.

There is no public transportation directly to the park, although you can rent a car in Comodoro Rivadavia or try hitching. From Puerto Deseado, Turismo Aventura Los Vikingos (see Reserva Natural Ría Deseado earlier in this section) runs tours to Bosques Petrificados.

Buses from Caleta Olivia will drop you at the junction, but you may wait several hours for a lift. Do not attempt hitching in winter, when the area is bitterly cold.

There is also ***camping***, as well as provisions, at La Paloma, midway between RN 3 and park headquarters.

PUERTO SAN JULIÁN

In the winter of 1520, Magellan's crew wintered in the sheltered harbor of San Julián, while in 1780 Antonio de Viedma established a colony that lasted only a few years. Only the wool boom of the late 19th century brought permanent settlement, thanks to pioneering Scots with surnames like Gleadell, MacCaskill, McRae, and Munro; from the turn of the century until the recent decline of wool prices in the past 20 years, the British-owned San Julián Sheep Farming Company was the area's most powerful economic force. Seafood processing is a secondary industry. If driving or hitching, you can break the long trip between Caleta Olivia and Río Gallegos here.

Orientation

San Julián (population 5500), 341km south of Caleta Olivia and a few kilometers east of RN 3, fills a small peninsula jutting into its protected namesake bay. Av San Martín, the main drag, is an eastward extension of the junction at RN 3.

Information

From mid-December to March, the Municipalidad maintains an information office in a trailer at the highway junction; it's open 8 am to 10 pm daily. The Dirección de Turismo (☎ 454396), downtown at Av San Martín 1125, is open 7 am to 1 pm weekdays.

Nearly all public services are near the east end of Av San Martín, close to the tip of the peninsula. Correo Argentino is at Av San Martín and Belgrano, while the only locutorio is at San Martín y Saavedra. Banco de la Nación occupies an attractive Victorian building at Mitre and Belgrano. San Julián's area code is ☎ 02962.

Things to See & Do

The **Museo Regional y de Arte Marino**, in a classic Magellanic house opposite the bus terminal on Vieytes between Rivadavia and Ameghino, features archaeological artifacts and historical materials (surprisingly weak on local sheep farming, though there's a handful of photos on the Tehuelche), as well as painting and sculpture. It's open weekdays 9 am to noon and 3 to 8 pm, weekends 10 am to noon and 5 to 10 pm.

Ten km west of town, on RP 25 toward Gobernador Gregores, are the ruins of **Floridablanca**, Viedma's short-lived colony of 1780; ask at the tourist trailer for keys to the locked site. The Swift **Frigorífico** (mutton freezer), which operated between 1912 and 1967, is north of town.

Hired launches are available for visiting harbor rookeries of penguins, cormorants, and other seabirds at Banco Cormorán and Banco Justicia. Some of these sites are accessible by foot at low tide, but otherwise contact Carlos Cedón's Pinocho Expediciones (☎ 452856), Brown 739; rates are US$15 per person for a maximum of eight persons.

Places to Stay & Eat

Possibly coastal Patagonia's best campground, San Julian's ***Autocamping Municipal** (☎ 452160)*, on the waterfront at the north end of Vélez Sarsfield, has hot showers, a laundry, a playground, and tall hedges for windbreaks, for US$3 per person, plus US$5 per tent or car. There are other beachfront sites at Cabo Curioso (20km north of town) and Playa La Mina, farther north, which has a sea lion rookery.

Hotel prices are fairly high. ***Hotel Álamo** (☎ 454031)*, at the RN 3 junction, charges US$30/43 single/double. ***Hotel Sada** (☎ 452013, Av San Martín 1112)* has rooms with bath for US$35/52, while the ***Hotel Municipal de Turismo** (☎ 452301, 25 de*

Mayo 917) costs US$38/59. ***Hotel Bahía*** *(☎ 454028, Av San Martín 1075)* is an attractive brick building with cable TV and breakfast for US$50/75.

Restaurant Sportsman *(Mitre 301)* has excellent parrillada and pasta (especially ñoquis) at reasonable prices. ***La Rural*** *(☎ 454149, Ameghino 811)* is a parrilla serving excellent beef but only occasionally local lamb. ***Stop Restaurant*** *(☎ 452673, Ameghino 1075)* is worth a look for fish, seafood, and minutas.

Entertainment

At San Martín and Ameghino, ***Casa Lara*** is an attractive new bar in a building dating from 1901.

Getting There & Away

Air The airport is at the highway junction. LADE (☎ 452137), Berutti 985, flies Monday to Gobernador Gregores (US$20), Santa Cruz (US$20), and Río Gallegos (US$28), and Tuesday to Puerto Deseado (US$22) and Comodoro Rivadavia (US$39).

Bus The Terminal de Ómnibus (☎ 452082) is on Vieytes between Rivadavia and Ameghino. Transportadora Patagónica's Río Gallegos-Buenos Aires services pick up passengers here, but any bus on RN 3 will take on passengers from the junction. Andesmar, TAC, and El Pingüino also operate from San Julián. Iceberg Turismo (☎ 452678, 02966-1562-4713 cellular) has door-to-door service to Piedrabuena (1½ hours) and Río Gallegos (4½ hours) at 5:30 am daily.

Transporte Cerro San Lorenzo (☎ 452403) has Tuesday, Wednesday, Saturday, and Sunday services to Laguna Posadas, near the Chilean border, via Gobernador Gregores and Bajo Caracoles. This passes the junction to otherwise inaccessible Parque Nacional Perito Moreno (see that section later in this chapter).

GOBERNADOR GREGORES

Gobernador Gregores is the nearest town to Parque Nacional Perito Moreno. Although it's still more than 200km east of the park, it's easier and cheaper to arrange a car and driver here rather than at the town of Perito Moreno, and it's a good place to stock up on supplies. The Administración de Parques Nacionales (☎/fax 02962-491477) maintains an office here; the postal address is Casilla de Correo 103, (9311) Gobernador Gregores.

The free ***Camping Municipal***, at Roca and Cañadón León, has hot showers. ***Hotel San Francisco*** *(☎ 02962-491039)*, at San Martín and Sánchez, has singles/doubles for US$20/30. The best place to eat, which also has accommodations for US$20/35 with shared bath, is ***Cañadón León*** *(☎ 491082, Roca 397)*.

LADE (☎ 491008), Colón 544, flies Monday to Santa Cruz (US$20) and Río Gallegos (US$32); Tuesday to El Calafate (US$23), Río Gallegos, Río Grande (US$58), Ushuaia (US$68), San Julián (US$20), Puerto Deseado (US$33), and Comodoro Rivadavia (US$39); Thursday to El Calafate, Río Turbio (US$29), and Río Gallegos; and Thursday and Friday to Perito Moreno (US$26) and Comodoro Rivadavia.

Transporte Cerro San Lorenzo buses leave Gregores for San Julián four times weekly. Transporte Greco goes to Gallegos Wednesday and Sunday at 2 pm, taking eight hours.

COMANDANTE LUIS PIEDRABUENA

On the north bank of the Río Santa Cruz, Piedrabuena is just east of RN 3, 127km south of San Julián, and 235km north of Río Gallegos. Despite a lack of major attractions, it's a common stopover. Hitchhikers, who often wait in line at the junction near the ACA service station, confitería, and motel, can at least get food and drink here. North of town is a large army camp.

At **Isla Pavón**, in the Río Santa Cruz about 3km south of the highway junction, a museum honors Piedrabuena, who first raised the Argentine flag here in 1859. Fishing, water-skiing, and other aquatic sports are popular.

Orientation & Information

From RN 3, Av Belgrano goes directly into town, where it intersects the riverfront Av

Gregorio Ibáñez, which becomes Av San Martín to the south. Tourist information (02966-15-62-3978 cellular) is available at the bus terminal, while Banco de la Provincia de Santa Cruz is on Av San Martín. The area code is ☎ 02962.

Places to Stay & Eat

Piedrabuena's ***Camping Municipal Isla Pavón*** *(☎ 497187, 02966-1562-3453 cellular)*, on the island itself, charges US$7 per site and has 24-hour electricity and hot water. Showers cost US$2 per person.

Hotel Internacional *(☎ 497197, Av Gregorio Ibáñez 99)*, across from the bus station, charges US$13/22 single/double with shared bath. ***Hostería El Álamo*** *(☎ 497249, Lavalle 8)* costs US$25/35 with private bath; some rooms have TV.

The ***ACA Motel*** *(☎ 497245)* is a good value at US$22/28 for members, but non-members pay US$30/38; because it's small and good, it usually fills early. Its restaurant is dependable and reasonable. ***Hotel Huayén*** *(☎ 497265, Belgrano 321)* is comparably priced at US$23/38.

Getting There & Away

Piedrabuena's Terminal de Ómnibus is at Ibáñez and Menéndez, but passing buses will also pick up passengers on RN 3. Long-distance companies with terminal offices include El Pingüino, Andesmar, and TAC (☎ 497018). El Greco goes to Gobernador Gregores Tuesday and Friday at 1 pm. Iceberg has door-to-door service to Río Gallegos at 7 am.

It may be possible to hitch to Calafate, 45km south of Piedrabuena, along RP 9, a decent gravel road that passes numerous estancias. The route has panoramic views of the canyon of the Río Santa Cruz, but hitching is generally difficult because of heavy competition.

AROUND COMANDANTE LUIS PIEDRABUENA

Parque Nacional Monte León

Only the second coastal national park to be established in Argentina (the first, and for decades only, was PN Tierra de Fuego), Monte León's sandy beaches and striking headlands are home to Magellanic penguins, sea lions, and unusual geographic features like La Olla (a huge cave-like structure eroded by the ocean). Perhaps its most interesting attraction is Isla Monte León, a high offshore stack once exploited by guano collectors – the cable tram that carried the guano over to the mainland wouldn't need much work to be operable again.

Now being recolonized by king cormorants, Dominican gulls, skuas, and other birds, Isla Monte León is accessible at low tide, when it's also possible to walk in La Olla, but the tidal range is great and the water returns fast, so take care not to get stranded – or worse. The surrounding hills are very scenic.

There is no public transport to Monte León, which is 58km south of Piedrabuena via paved RN 3 and graveled RP 63, rough in spots but passable for any vehicle in good weather. There is ***camping***, with limited services, but no other accommodations.

The park is also accessible, by foot, from Punta Quilla, 17km beyond the town of Puerto Santa Cruz, which is 26km west of Piedrabuena via paved RN 288. Puerto Santa Cruz itself has little to recommend it, but there's overland access, by foot, to a penguin colony at Punta Quilla, at least at low tide.

PERITO MORENO

Not to be confused with the Moreno Glacier in Parque Nacional Los Glaciares, nor with Parque Nacional Perito Moreno, this modest agricultural settlement is a brief stopover en route to the Andean oasis of Los Antiguos. Its main appeal is its relatively good access to the pre-Columbian rock art site of Cueva de las Manos, and to Parque Nacional Perito Moreno.

In early February, Perito Moreno (population 3000) celebrates its Festival Folklórico Cueva de las Manos, an annual musical event for the past 15 years.

Orientation

Perito Moreno's main thoroughfare, Av San Martín, leads north to RP 43, an excellent

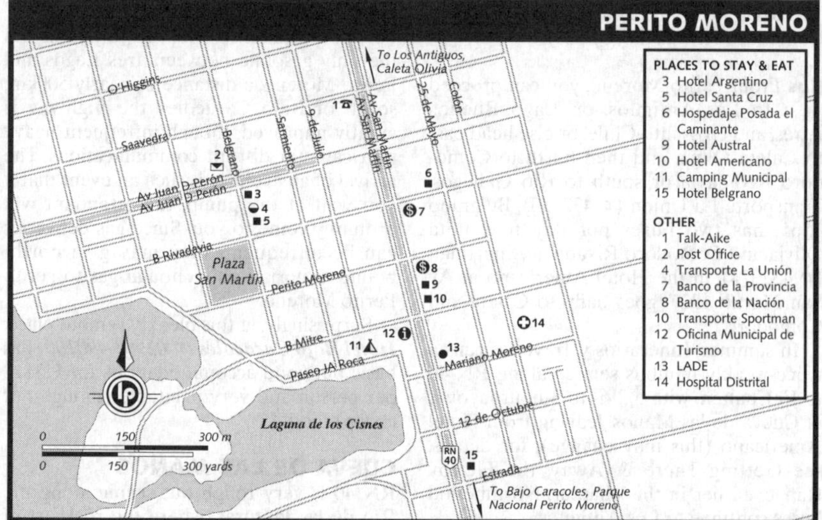

paved road that forks west to Los Antiguos and east toward Caleta Olivia. At the south end of town it becomes RN 40, a rough highway that leads to the bleak oasis of Bajo Caracoles and, beyond that, a junction to Parque Nacional Perito Moreno.

Information

The obliging Oficina Municipal de Turismo, San Martín 1222, is open daily 9 am to 8 pm except on weekends, when it closes from noon to 2 pm. Correo Argentino is on Av JD Perón, near Belgrano; the postal code is 9040. There are banks but no ATMs. Talk-Aike is a locutorio at San Martín and Saavedra.

Perito Moreno's area code is ☎ 02963.

The Hospital Distrital (☎ 432040) is at Colón 1237.

Places to Stay & Eat

The ***Camping Municipal*** *(☎ 432121)*, near the south end of town at Laguna de los Cisnes, is the cheapest place to stay and, moreover, has outstanding hot showers in heated bathrooms. Sites cost US$2 per person, plus US$1.50 per car or tent, or you can rent one of their rather claustrophobic six-bunk cabañas for US$10.

No-frills ***Hotel Argentino***, at JD Perón and Belgrano, charges US$10 per person; ***Hotel Santa Cruz***, around the corner on Belgrano, is similar. There are four other better and roughly comparable hotels: ***Hotel Americano*** *(☎ 432074, San Martín 1327)*, for US$20/30 per single/double; ***Hospedaje Posada el Caminante*** *(☎ 432204, Rivadavia 937)*, for US$22 per person; ***Hotel Belgrano*** *(☎ 432019, Av San Martín 1001)*, for US$25/36; and ***Hotel Austral*** *(☎ 432042, San Martín 1381)*, for US$25/35. All of the latter except for Posada el Caminante have ***restaurants***, with meals ranging from US$7 to US$17 for lunch or dinner.

Getting There & Away

Air Taxis are the only transportation between town and the airport, at the north end of town near the highway junction.

LADE (☎ 432055), San Martín 1207, flies Tuesday to Río Grande (US$84) and Ushuaia (US$94); Tuesday and Thursday to Gobernador Gregores (US$26), El Calafate (US$43), Río Gallegos (US$58), and Río

Turbio (US$55); and Thursday and Friday to Comodoro Rivadavia (US$28).

Bus From Perito Moreno, you can proceed west to Los Antiguos, on Lago Buenos Aires, and cross into Chile, or else head east to Caleta Olivia and then north to Comodoro Rivadavia or south to Río Gallegos. Transporte La Unión (☎ 432133), Belgrano 1565, has two buses per day to Caleta Olivia and Comodoro Rivadavia. Sportman (☎ 432074), in the Hotel Americano at Av San Martín 1327, goes daily to Caleta and Comodoro.

In summer, Itinerarios y Travesías runs a twice-weekly minibus service along RN 40 to El Chaltén, with a 2½- to 3-hour layover at Cueva de las Manos, leaving from Hotel Americano (this may change); for details, see Getting There & Away, the Fitzroy Range, earlier in this chapter. Northbound buses continue to Los Antiguos.

AROUND PERITO MORENO

There is limited public transport southward on RN 40 toward Cueva de las Manos and Parque Nacional Perito Moreno (see those sections later in this chapter), and very little traffic of any sort, but a group may hire a taxi and driver to go there. El Al Viajes (☎ 432839), San Martín 1494 in Perito Moreno, does tours to Cueva de las Manos.

About 28km south of Perito Moreno on RN 40, English is spoken at Dutch-run ***Estancia Telken*** *(☎ 02963-432079, fax 432373)*, which offers accommodations with breakfast and shared bath for US$34 per person, with private bath for US$40 per person; camping costs US$18 for two people with tent and vehicle, though cyclists pay only US$6 per person.

Meals, including afternoon tea, are also available, and the estancia offers hiking and inexpensive horseback riding, as well as excursions to Cueva de las Manos. Telken is open from September to April; the rest of the year check the Santa Cruz estancias website listed at the beginning of the Santa Cruz province section, or their Buenos Aires contact (☎ 011-4797-7216/1950).

BAJO CARACOLES

For motorists on RN 40, this tiny oasis has the only gasoline between Tres Lagos and Perito Moreno, a distance of nearly 500km; south of Bajo Caracoles the highway is greatly improved, though infrequent heavy rain can still disrupt communications. The arrival of any vehicle is such an event that if you wait at the pump, the attendant will promptly come to you. Since gas deliveries can be infrequent, they may give northbound motorists only enough gas to get to Perito Moreno.

Surprisingly, in this bleakly remote place, ***Hotel Bajo Caracoles*** *(☎ 02963-490100)* has basic but good accommodations for US$12 per person and very palatable (though not cheap) food.

CUEVA DE LAS MANOS

RN 40 is very rough but scenic along the Río de las Pinturas, where the rock art of Cueva de las Manos (Cave of Hands) graces the most notable of several archaeological sites. Dating from about 7370 BC, these polychrome rock paintings cover recesses in the near vertical walls with imprints of human hands as well as troops of guanacos and, from a later period, more-abstract designs.

There are two points of access, one from Bajo Caracoles, on the south side of the river, and another from Hostería Cueva de las Manos, on the north side, via a footbridge. Since the Municipalidad of Perito Moreno has suspended its Sunday bus trips, there is no regular public transport except for the weekly summer minibus service between El Chaltén and Perito Moreno. Perito Moreno's El Al Viajes (see Around Perito Moreno) does tours to the site, however.

The Municipalidad maintains a small information center and a ***confitería*** (cold beer, soft drinks, and simple meals) at the southern entrance, where it also offers a few rocky ***campsites*** (US$2 per tent). Admission to the site proper costs US$3.

Open November through March and for Semana Santa, ***Hosteria Cueva de las Manos*** *(☎ 011-4901-0436, fax 011-4903-7161* *in Buenos Aires)*, a short distance off RN 40 about 77km south of Perito Moreno, has four carpeted rooms with private bath, restaurant, and room service for US$55 double with breakfast; there is also hostel accommodation for US$19 per person without breakfast. ***Estancia Casa de Piedra*** *(☎ 02963-432-1990)*, on RN 3 80km south of Perito Moreno, allows camping for $2.50 per tent, plus US$2.50 for showers.

PARQUE NACIONAL PERITO FRANCISCO P MORENO

Beneath the Sierra Colorada, a painter's palette of sedimentary peaks, herds of guanacos graze peacefully alongside aquamarine lakes in this gem of the Argentine park system. Honoring the system's founder, this remote but increasingly popular park encompasses 115,000 hectares along the Chilean border, 310km by RN 40 and RP 37 from the town of Perito Moreno.

Besides guanacos, there are also pumas, foxes, wildcats, chinchillas, *huemul* (Andean deer), and many birds, including condors, rheas, flamingos, black-necked swans, upland geese *(cauquén)*, and crested caracaras *(caranchos)*. Predecessors of the Tehuelche Indians left evidence of their presence with rock paintings of guanaco and human hands in caves at Lago Burmeister. Beyond the park boundary, glacier-topped summits such as 3700m Cerro San Lorenzo hover above the landscape.

As precipitation increases toward the west, the Patagonian steppe grasslands of the park's eastern border become sub-Antarctic forests of southern beech, lenga, and coihue. Because the base altitude exceeds 900m, considerably higher than more-accessible southerly parks like Los Glaciares, weather can be severe. Summer visits are usually comfortable, but warm clothing and proper equipment are imperative at any season.

WAYNE BERNHARDSON

Cueva de las Manos features 9000-year-old rock paintings.

Perito Moreno's quiet and solitude are a blessing, but visitors should be especially careful with fire in the frequent high winds. Bring all food and supplies, though water is pure and plentiful, and dead wood may be collected for fuel.

Information

From its formal creation in 1936 until only a few years ago, Perito Moreno lacked visitor services, but it is now permanently staffed and has a progressive management plan. Rangers at the park's Centro de Informes, on the eastern boundary, have a good supply of informative maps and brochures, and offer a variety of guided hikes and visits; they can also be contacted through the Parques Nacionales office (☎/fax 02962-491477) in Gobernador Gregores.

Things to See & Do

Consult park rangers for guided walks to **Casa de Piedra**, on Lago Burmeister, where there are pictographs; to **Playa de los Amonites** on Lago Belgrano, where there are fossils; and to 1434m Cerro León. There are also several backpack trails; ask for latest details.

From Estancia La Oriental, it's a 2½ hour hike to the summit of 1434m **Cerro León**, a mostly gentle climb except just above and below the tree line, where it's very steep. Look for Patagonian woodpeckers among the lengas on the lower slopes. From the peak, where troops of guanacos can be among the climbers, there's a dazzling panorama of the surrounding mountain ranges and the meseta to the east. Immediately east of the summit, across a low saddle, the volcanic outcrop of **Cerro de los Cóndores** is a nesting site for the Andes' signature bird, while the marshes at its base harbor upland geese, ibis, snipe, and many other species. There have also been puma sightings in the area.

Places to Stay

Camping is an attractive possibility, but no longer the only one. Free ***sites*** are available at the park's Centro de Informes (barren and exposed) and at Lago Burmeister (far more scenic, and well sheltered among dense lenga forest). Neither has showers, but there are pit toilets.

From November to March, ***Estancia La Oriental***, at the foot of Cerro León on the north shore of Lago Belgrano, has sheltered camping for US$15 per site with hot showers. It also offers accommodations (US$70 double) and meals; the excellent dinners are pricey at US$20, but the abundant breakfasts (including scones, homemade bread and preserves, and ham and cheese) are a bargain at US$5. La Oriental also also arranges transportation and pack trips into the backcountry; for reservations, contact Manuel Lada *(☎ 02962-452196, Rivadavia 936)*, San Julián.

Getting There & Away

There is a possibility that public transport may begin from Hotel Las Horquetas, near the junction of RN 40 and RP 37, from mid-December to the end of February. For details, contact tourist offices in communities like Perito Moreno, Los Antiguos, El Calafate, and El Chaltén.

Hitching is possible from the highway junction on RN 40, at least in January, but even then the park is so large that getting to trailheads presents difficulties. From April to November, the road becomes impassable at times.

LOS ANTIGUOS

Picturesque rows of Lombardy poplars provide windbreaks for the irrigated chacras of Los Antiguos, a pleasant retreat on the southern shore of Lago Buenos Aires near the Chilean border, with good fishing and hiking in the surrounding countryside. Tourist facilities are good, but the area has not yet been overrun by outsiders; the abundant fresh fruit harvest, for lack of large nearby markets, is absurdly cheap.

Before the arrival of Europeans, Tehuelche Indians and their forerunners frequented this 'banana belt' in their old age – the town's name is a near-literal translation of a Tehuelche usage meaning Place of the

Elders. In August 1991, the eruption of Volcán Hudson on the Chilean side of the border covered both Los Antiguos and Chile Chico in volcanic ash and briefly forced their evacuation, causing the loss of as many as three harvests and the death of much livestock for lack of forage.

In 1997 Los Antiguos drew unwanted attention when a Chubut provincial tourist brochure inadvertently placed the town in Chile – an unpardonable gaffe in an area where geopolitics is virtually a religion – leading to protests from the Santa Cruz provincial legislature and the recall of tens of thousands of maps at a cost of roughly US$100,000.

Orientation & Information

Los Antiguos (population 2500) occupies the delta formed by the Río Jeinemeni, which constitutes the border with Chile, and the Río Los Antiguos. As in many smaller Argentine towns, there are few street signs and even fewer street numbers; most services are on or near east-west Av 11 de Julio, which runs the length of town. To the west, the avenue reaches and crosses the border to Chile Chico.

At the eastern portal to town, the Municipalidad maintains a tourist information office, open 8 am to 8 pm daily from October to March. The Subsecretaría de Turismo (☎ 491261, fax 491261), Av 11 de Julio 432, is open 7 am to 8 pm daily October to March, 9 am to 4 pm weekdays the rest of the year.

Correo Argentino is at Gobernador Gregores 19; the postal code is 9041. Locutorio Los Antiguos is at Perito Moreno and Patagonia Argentina; the area code is ☎ 02963. Banco de la Provincia is at Av 11 de Julio and Perito Moreno.

Things to See & Do

In summer, **Lago Buenos Aires** is warm enough for swimming from the beaches at the municipal campground at the east end of Av 11 de Julio. Juan Carlos Pellón, owner of Hotel Argentino, will guide fishermen to pejerrey and rainbow trout on the lake. **Monte Zeballos**, 50km south, offers good hiking in southern beech forests; the road to Monte Zeballos may be extended southward to Paso Roballos, permitting a scenic circuit around the volcanic Meseta del Lago Buenos Aires via Lago Posadas, Bajo Caracoles, and Perito Moreno.

Since 1989, Los Antiguos has held an annual Fiesta de la Cereza (Cherry Festival), lasting three days in the second week of January. Other local fruits, including raspberries, strawberries, apples, apricots, pears, peaches, plums, and prunes, are equally delectable. You can stop to purchase these, and homemade fruit preserves, directly from the farms. Señora Regina de Jomñuk's Chacra El Porvenir is easy walking distance from the main avenue, but there are many others, including Belgian-run Chacra El Paraíso on the lakeshore.

Other local festivals are Día del Lago Buenos Aires on October 29 and Día de los Antiguos, celebrating the town's anniversary, on February 5.

Places to Stay & Eat

Los Antiguos's ***Camping Municipal*** *(☎ 491265)*, on the lakeshore at the east end of Av 11 de Julio, is one of Argentina's best and cheapest. Forest plantings shelter the sites, each of which has tables and firepits, from the wind. Hot showers are available from 5:30 to 10 pm. Fees have recently risen but are still reasonable at US$3 per person, plus US$2.50 per tent and US$5 per vehicle. There are also a limited number of cabañas, which can hold up to six persons, for US$10.

Hotel Argentino *(☎ 491132, Av 11 de Julio 850)*, which charges US$19/35 single/double with private bath, also has excellent fixed-price dinners and lunches for US$8, with desserts of local produce and an outstanding breakfast for US$4. ***El Disco*** *(☎ 491254, Pallavicini 140)* is a parrilla.

Getting There & Away

LADE serves the nearest airport, at Perito Moreno 64km east; for details, see the Perito Moreno entry.

La Unión buses (☎ 491077) Alameda 451, go to Caleta Olivia (US$18, five hours) and

Comodoro Rivadavia (US$20, six hours) at 7 am and 3:30 pm daily. Sportman, Av 11 de Julio 666, goes to Caleta and Comodoro at 4:30 pm daily.

Transportes Padilla (☎ 491140), San Martín 44, and Acotrans cross the border to Chile Chico (US$3 return) several times daily.

Tierra del Fuego & Chilean Patagonia

Since the 16th-century voyages of Magellan to the 19th-century explorations of Fitzroy and Darwin on the *Beagle* and even to the present, this 'uttermost part of the earth' has held an ambivalent fascination for travelers of many nationalities. For more than three centuries, its climate and terrain discouraged European settlement, yet indigenous people considered it a 'land of plenty.' Its scenery, with glaciers descending nearly to the ocean in many places, is truly enthralling.

The Yahgan Indians, now few in number, built the fires that inspired Europeans to give this region its name, famous throughout the world. It consists of one large island, Isla Grande de Tierra del Fuego, and many smaller ones, few of them inhabited. The Strait of Magellan separates the archipelago from the South American mainland.

History

In 1520, when Magellan passed through the strait that now bears his name, neither he nor any other European explorer had any immediate interest in the land and its people. Seeking a passage to the spice islands of Asia, early navigators feared and detested the stiff westerlies, hazardous currents, and violent seas that impeded their progress. Consequently, the Ona, Haush, Yahgan, and Alacaluf peoples who populated the area faced no immediate competition for their lands and resources.

All these groups were mobile hunters and gatherers. The Onas, also known as Selknam, and the Haushes subsisted primarily on terrestrial resources, hunting the guanaco (relatives of the domesticated llama of the central Andes) and dressing in its skins, while the Yahgans and Alacalufes, known collectively as 'Canoe Indians', lived on fish, shellfish, and marine mammals. The Yahgans, also known as the Yamana, consumed the 'Indian bread' fungus *(Cytarria darwinii)* that parasitizes the ñire, a species of southern beech. Despite frequently inclement weather, they wore little or no clothing, but constant fires (even in their bark canoes) kept them warm.

As Spain's control of its American empire dwindled, the area slowly opened to settlement by other Europeans, ensuring the rapid demise of the indigenous Fuegians, whom Europeans struggled to understand. Darwin, visiting the area in 1834, wrote that the difference between the Fuegians ('among the most abject and miserable creatures I ever saw') and Europeans was greater than that between wild and domestic animals. On an earlier voyage, though, Captain Robert Fitzroy of the *Beagle* had abducted a few Yahgans whom he returned after several years of missionary education in England.

From the 1850s, Europeans attempted to catechize the Fuegians, the earliest such instance ending with the starvation death of British missionary Allen Gardiner. Gardiner's successors, working from a base at

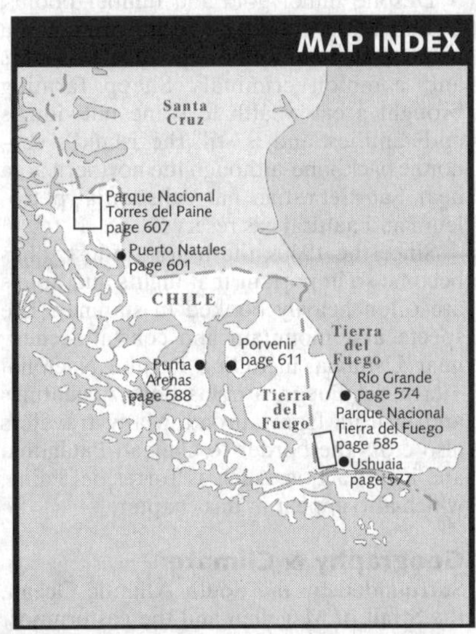

Keppel Island in the Falklands, were more successful despite the massacre of one party by Fuegians at Isla Navarino. Thomas Bridges, a young man at Keppel, learned to speak the Yahgan language and became one of the first settlers at Ushuaia, in what is now Argentine Tierra del Fuego. His son, Lucas Bridges, born at Ushuaia in 1874, left a fascinating memoir of his experiences among the Yahgans and Onas titled *The Uttermost Part of the Earth* (1950).

Since no other European power had had any interest in settling the region until Britain occupied the Falklands in the 1770s, Spain too paid little attention to Tierra del Fuego, but the successor governments of Argentina and Chile felt differently. The Chilean presence on the Strait of Magellan beginning in 1843 and increasing British evangelism spurred Argentina to formalize its authority at Ushuaia in 1884 and install a territorial governor the following year. In 1978 Argentina and Chile nearly went to war over claims to three small disputed islands in the Beagle Channel. International border issues in the area were only finally resolved in 1984, when an Argentine plebiscite ratified a diplomatic settlement.

Despite minor gold and lumber booms, Ushuaia was for many years primarily a penal settlement for both political prisoners and common criminals. Sheep farming brought great wealth to some individuals and families, and is still the island's economic backbone, although the northern area near San Sebastián has substantial petroleum and natural gas reserves.

Since the 1960s, the tourist industry has become so important that flights and hotels are often heavily booked in summer. The spectacular mountain and coastal scenery near Ushuaia, including Parque Nacional Tierra del Fuego, attracts both Argentines and visitors from abroad. Many travelers also cross the border to Chilean Patagonia and its attractions, such as Torres del Paine, which also appear in this chapter.

Geography & Climate

Surrounded by the South Atlantic Ocean, the Strait of Magellan and the easternmost

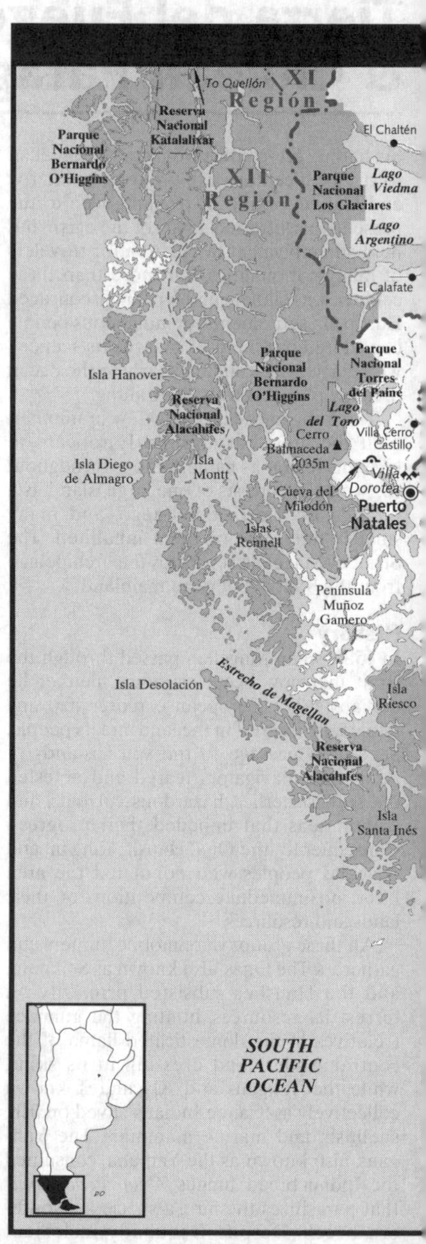

TIERRA DEL FUEGO & CHILEAN PATAGONIA
To Caleta Olivia
Tres Lagos
ARGENTINA
Cordillera de los Andes
Puerto Santa Cruz
Parque Nacional Monte León
Santa Cruz
Esperanza
Paso Cancha de Carreras
Bahía Grande
Río Turbio
Río Gallegos
Güer Aike
Paso Casas Viejas
Bella Vista
Parque Nacional Pali Aike
Estancia El Cóndor
SOUTH ATLANTIC OCEAN
Laguna Blanca
Villa Tehuelches
Estancia Kimiri Aike
Cabo Vírgenes
Punta Delgada
Río Verde
Estancia San Gregorio
Seno Skyring
Primera Angostura
Cerro Sombrero
Cabo Espíritu Santo
Pingüinera Otway
Monumento Natural Los Pingüinos
Seno Otway
Punta Arenas
Estrecho de Magellan
Porvenir
Reserva Forestal Magallanes
Reserva Forestal Laguna Parrillar
Onaisin
San Sebastián
Bahía Inútil
Península Brunswick
Camerón
Fuerte Bulnes
Río Grande
CHILE
Lago Blanco
Isla Dawson
Redman
Isla Clarence
Isla Capitán Aracena
Tierra del Fuego
Timaukel
Sierra de Beauvoir
Isla Grande de Tierra del Fuego
Lago Kami /Fagnano
Cordillera Darwin
PN Tierra del Fuego
Paso Garibaldi
Estrecho de Le Maire
Canal de Beagle
Lapataia
Ushuaia
Cockburn Channel
Estancia Harberton
Puerto Williams
Isla Hoste
Puerto Toro
Isla Picton
Isla de los Estados (Staten Island)
Isla Navarino
Isla Nueva
Isla Lennox
Parque Nacional Cabo de Hornos
Cabo de Hornos (Cape Horn)
0 50 100 km
0 30 60miles

The Guanaco

part of the Pacific Ocean, the archipelago of Tierra del Fuego has a land area of roughly 76,000 sq km, about the size of Ireland or South Carolina. The Chilean-Argentine border runs directly south from Cabo Espíritu Santo, at the eastern entrance of the Strait of Magellan, to the Beagle Channel (Canal de Beagle), where it trends eastward to the channel's mouth at Isla Nueva. Most of Isla Grande belongs to Chile, but the Argentine side is more densely populated, particularly around the substantial towns of Ushuaia and Río Grande. Porvenir (see the Chilean Patagonia section) is the only significant town on the Chilean side.

The plains of northern Isla Grande are a landscape of almost unrelenting wind, enormous flocks of Corriedales, and oil derricks, while the mountainous southern part offers scenic glaciers, lakes, rivers, and seacoast. The maritime climate is surprisingly mild, even in winter, but its changeability makes warm, dry clothing essential, especially on hikes and at higher elevations. The mountains of the Cordillera Darwin and the Sierra de Beauvoir, reaching up to 2500m in the west, intercept Antarctic storms, leaving the plains around Río Grande much drier than areas nearer the Beagle Channel.

The higher southern rainfall supports dense deciduous and evergreen southern *(Nothofagus)* forests, while the drier north consists of extensive native grasses and low-growing shrubs. Storms batter the bogs and truncated beeches of the remote southern and western zones of the archipelago. Guanaco, rhea, and condor can still be seen in the north, but marine mammals and shorebirds are the most common wildlife around tourist destinations along the Beagle Channel.

Books

Though its practical information is badly out of date, the 3rd edition of Rae Natalie Prosser Goodall's detailed bilingual guidebook *Tierra del Fuego* (1979) is still the most informed single source on the island's history and natural history. According to the author, separate new editions in English and Spanish are underway but with no immediate likelihood of publication; the old edition continues to be sold in local bookshops in Ushuaia.

Dangers & Annoyances

Collection of shellfish is not permitted because of toxic red tide conditions. Hunting is likewise illegal throughout the Argentine part of Tierra del Fuego.

Getting There & Around

Overland, the simplest route to Argentine Tierra del Fuego is via Porvenir, across the Strait of Magellan from Punta Arenas; for details, see the section on Chilean Patagonia. Transbordadora Austral Broom (☎ 061-218100, tabsa@entelchile.net), Anexo 21 in Punta Arenas, operates the roll-on, roll-off ferry *Bahía Azul*, which runs from Punta Delgada across the narrows at Primera Angostura to Chilean Tierra del Fuego, but there's no public transportation to it. The ferry operates daily 8:30 am to 11 pm; the 20-minute crossing costs US$2 for passengers and US$18 for automobiles and pickup trucks. Weather and tidal conditions sometimes cause delays.

The principal border crossing is San Sebastián, a truly desolate place about midway between Porvenir and Río Grande. Roads have improved considerably in recent years: They are unpaved on the

Chilean side, but RN 3 is smoothly paved from San Sebastián past Río Grande as far as Tolhuín on Lago Kami, and from Rancho Hambre to Ushuaia. This leaves a section of about 60km along the south shore of Lago Fagnano and over the Garibaldi pass, which is expected to be completed by press time.

Unlike the rest of Argentina, Tierra del Fuego has no designated provincial highways *(rutas provinciales)*, but has secondary roads known as *rutas complementarias*, modified by a lowercase letter. References to such roads in this chapter will be 'RC-a', for example.

Tierra del Fuego

RÍO GRANDE

Founded in 1894 on the estuary of its namesake river, this bleak, windswept wool and petroleum service center is making a genuine effort to beautify and improve itself, but still has far to go. A recent economic boom, sparked by duty-free status, has subsided and the local economy has stagnated. Most visitors pass through quickly en route to Ushuaia, but it has a good new museum and the surrounding countryside is not devoid of interest.

Orientation

Río Grande (population 59,813) faces the open South Atlantic on RN 3, which leads 190km southwest to Ushuaia and 79km north to the Chilean border at San Sebastián. The main street is Av San Martín, which runs northwest-southeast and crosses Av Islas Malvinas/Santa Fe, as RN 3 is known through town.

Most visitor services are along Av San Martín and along Av Manuel Belgrano between San Martín and the waterfront. Do not confuse the similarly named parallel streets 9 de Julio and 11 de Julio, which are two blocks (as well as two days) apart.

Information

Tourist Offices In the lobby of Hotel Los Yaganes, at Belgrano 319, the Instituto Fueguino de Turismo (Infuetur; ☎ 422887, infuerg@satlink.com) is open 10 am to 5 pm weekdays.

Money There are several banks with ATMs on and near Av San Martín.

Post & Communications Correo Argentino is on Rivadavia between Moyano and Alberdi; the postal code is 9420. Locutorio Cabo Domingo is at Av San Martín 458; the area code is ☎ 02964.

Laundry El Lavadero is located at Perito Moreno 221.

Medical Services Río Grande's Hospital Regional (☎ 422088) is at Av Belgrano 350.

Museo de Ciencias Naturales e Historia

Río Grande's new natural sciences and history museum challenges visitors' preconceptions about the region's aboriginal inhabitants ('could you maintain your family with these tools?'). It also has good displays on Fuegian natural history, cartography, communications (postal, aerial, and electronic), and even astronomy.

At Elcano 159, the museum is open 9 am to 5 pm daily.

Places to Stay

Patience and perseverance are necessary to find quality budget accommodations, which often fill up fast.

Places to Stay – Budget

Hospedaje Noal *(☎ 422857, Rafael Obligado 557)* charges US$13 per person with shared bath, US$15/35 single/double with private bath and breakfast. At ***Hostería Antares*** *(☎ 421853, Echeverría 49)* rates are US$15 per person.

One of Río Grande's better choices, ***Hotel Villa*** *(☎ 422312, San Martín 277)* charges US$17 single. ***Hotel Rawson*** *(☎ 425503, fax 430352, JM Estrada 750)* is probably the best budget choice at US$18/28 for small but spotless and well-heated rooms with cable TV.

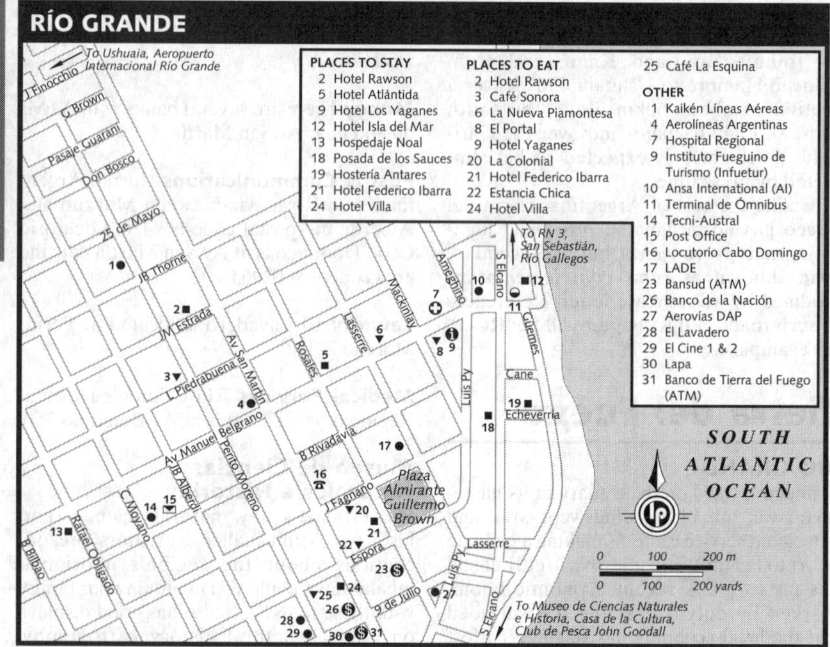

Places to Stay – Mid-Range & Top End

ACA's ***Hotel Los Yaganes*** *(☎ 430822, Belgrano 319)* costs US$38/46 for members, US$50/61 for nonmembers. ***Hotel Isla del Mar*** *(☎ 422883)*, at Güemes just north of the bus terminal, has ocean views for US$40/50.

Federico Ibarra Hotel *(☎ 430071, Rosales 357)* costs US$55/65, while rates at ***Hotel Atlántida*** *(☎ 422592, Av Belgrano 582)* are US$65/80. Enthusiastically recommended ***Posada de los Sauces*** *(☎ 432895, Elcano 839)* charges US$68/78.

Places to Eat

Hotel Villa, ***Hotel Federico Ibarra***, and ***Hotel Los Yaganes*** all have restaurants. For short orders and sandwiches, there are several ***confiterías*** in and around downtown, including one at ***Hotel Rawson*** and ***Café La Esquina***, at the corner of Perito Moreno and Espora. ***La Nueva Piamontesa*** *(☎ 421977, Av Belgrano 464)* is an outstanding rotisería with reasonable takeout meals.

Café Sonora *(Perito Moreno 705)* has fine pizza at reasonable prices. Popular ***La Colonial***, on J Fagnano between Av San Martín and Rosales, is primarily a pizzeria but also has other Italian dishes. ***El Portal*** *(Belgrano 383)* and ***Estancia Chica***, on Espora between Av San Martín and Rosales, are both parrillas.

Entertainment

El Cine 1 & 2 *(☎ 433260, Perito Moreno 211)* shows recent films.

Getting There & Away

Air Aeropuerto Internacional Río Grande is only a short cab ride from downtown.

Aerolíneas Argentinas (☎ 422748), San Martín 607, flies daily to Río Gallegos and to Aeroparque in Buenos Aires. Lapa

(☎ 432620), 9 de Julio 747, flies daily to Río Gallegos, Bahía Blanca, and Aeroparque.

LADE (☎ 421651), Lasserre 447, flies Tuesday and Wednesday to Ushuaia; Wednesday and Thursday to Río Gallegos and El Calafate; and Thursday to Gobernador Gregores, Perito Moreno, and Comodoro Rivadavia.

Kaikén Líneas Aéreas (☎ 430665), Perito Moreno 937, flies five times daily except Sunday (three times) to Ushuaia, four times daily to Río Gallegos, and also serves El Calafate, Comodoro Rivadavia, Trelew, Bariloche, Neuquén, Mendoza, and Bahía Blanca.

Aerovías DAP (☎ 430249), 9 de Julio 597, flies Monday, Wednesday, and Friday at 11 am to Punta Arenas, Chile (US$79).

Bus Río Grande's bus terminal (☎ 421339) is at the foot of Av Belgrano on the waterfront, but most companies have offices elsewhere in town as well.

Tecni-Austral (☎ 422620), Moyano 516, goes to Ushuaia daily (US$21) at 7:30 am and 6 pm, stopping en route at Tolhuin (US$10), and also goes to Punta Arenas Monday, Wednesday, and Friday at 11:30 am. It also sells tickets for Transporte Gesell (☎ 421339), which goes Wednesday and Saturday at 8 am to Porvenir (US$25, seven hours) in Chilean Tierra del Fuego, meeting the ferry to Punta Arenas.

Buses Pacheco (☎ 423382) goes to Punta Arenas (US$30) Tuesday, Thursday, and Saturday at 7:30 am. Prevensur (☎ 420465), at the terminal, goes to Tolhuin at 9 am and 3 pm.

Getting Around

Given limited public transportation, fishing and other excursions outside town are much simpler with a rental car, available from Ansa International (AI; ☎ 422657), at Ameghino 612.

AROUND RÍO GRANDE

The most interesting historic site is the **Museo Salesiano**, 10km north of town on RN 3, established by the missionary order that converted the Indians in this part of the island. Its several distinctive buildings contain a wealth of geological, natural history, and ethnographic artifacts, but unfortunately the order does little with them. It's open weekdays 10 am to 12:30 pm and daily 3 to 7 pm; admission is US$2 for adults, US$1 for children.

Historic **Estancia María Behety**, 17km west of town via RC-c, features the world's largest shearing shed. **Estancia José Menéndez**, 25km southwest of town via RN 3 and RC-b, is also one of the most historic ranches on the island.

The entire coastline of northeastern Tierra del Fuego, from south of Río Grande north to Bahía San Sebastián, is a migratory bird sanctuary known as **Reserva Provincial Costa Atlántica de Tierra del Fuego**; part of this area, near the San Sebastián border crossing, is the particularly dense marshland habitat **Refugio de Vida Silvestre Dicky**.

Lago Fagnano, also known as Lago Kami, fills the huge glacial trough on RN 3 between Río Grande and Ushuaia; about 100km from Ushuaia on the south shore, beautifully sited ***Hostería Kaikén*** *(☎ 02964-492208)* offers lodging for US$10/25 single/double on the ground floor, US$15/35 on the upper floor, but it's often full. Its restaurant has good but rather costly meals, with indifferent service (at best). Pasarela buses (US$25) go to Ushuaia at 2 pm daily, Antartur buses (US$20) at 4 pm, but the Tecni-Austral buses at 9:45 am and 8:15 pm costs only US$10.

Fishing

Fishing is a popular activity in many nearby rivers. For information on guided trips on the Fuego, Menéndez, Candelaria, Ewan, and MacLennan, contact the Club de Pesca John Goodall *(☎ 424324)*, Ricardo Rojas 606 in Río Grande.

One highly recommended place is ***Hostería San Pablo*** *(☎ 02964-424638)*, 120km southeast of Río Grande via RN 3 and RC-a, where there is good fly-fishing for trout and salmon on the Río Irigoyen. Rooms cost US$30/35 single/double with breakfast included, while lunch or dinner costs an additional US$13.

USHUAIA

Over the past two decades, fast-growing Ushuaia has mutated from a sleepy seaside village into a homely city of 42,000, sprawling and spreading from its original site, but the setting is still dramatic, with jagged glacial peaks rising from sea level to nearly 1500m. Its defects are tacky commercialism and shabby new construction, but the countryside offers activities like trekking, fishing, and skiing, as well as the opportunity to go as far south as roads go – RN 3 ends at Bahía Lapataia in Parque Nacional Tierra del Fuego, 3242km from Buenos Aires.

In 1870, the British-based South American Missionary Society made Ushuaia its first permanent outpost in the Fuegian region, but only artifacts, shell mounds, memories, and Thomas Bridges' famous dictionary remain of the Yahgan Indians who once flourished here. Nearby Estancia Harberton, now open to visitors, still belongs to descendents of the Bridges family.

Between 1884 and 1947, Argentina incarcerated many of its most notorious criminals and political prisoners here and on remote Isla de los Estados (Staten Island). Since 1950, the town has been an important naval base that Argentina has used to support its Antarctic claims, and in recent years it has become an important tourist destination.

Wages are higher than in mainland Argentina, thanks to industrial successes in electronics assembly, fishing, and food processing, but so are living expenses. The boom is subsiding, and the city is to lose the preferential tax treatment it now enjoys, with the imposition of IVA in 2003.

Orientation

Running along the north shore of the Beagle Channel, the beautified Av Maipú becomes Av Malvinas Argentinas west of the cemetery and, as RN 3, continues west to Parque Nacional Tierra del Fuego. The waterfront, its harbor protected by the nearby peninsula (site of the expanded airport), is a good place to observe shorebirds.

Ushuaia has no central plaza. Most hotels and visitor services are on or within a few blocks of Av San Martín, the principal commercial street, one block north of Av Maipú. North of Av San Martín, streets rise very steeply, offering good views of the Beagle Channel.

Information

Tourist Offices The municipal Dirección de Turismo (☎ 424550, 0800-333-1476 on the island), Av San Martín 660, also has an airport branch for arriving planes and another at the port for arriving ships. They maintain a complete list of accommodations with current prices and will assist in finding a room with private families; after closing time they post a list of available lodgings. They also have a message board, and the friendly, patient, and helpful staff usually includes an English speaker and less frequently a German, French, or Italian speaker. Hours are weekdays 8 am to 9 pm, weekends and holidays 9 am to 8 pm.

The Instituto Fueguino de Turismo (Infuetur; ☎ 423340) is on the ground floor of Hotel Albatros at Maipú and Lasserre. ACA (☎ 421121) is at Malvinas Argentinas and Onachaga.

Immigration Migraciones (☎ 422334) is at Beauvoir 1536.

Money Several banks on Maipú and San Martín have ATMs. The best bet for traveler's checks (2% commission) is Banco de la Provincia, San Martín 396. CrediSol, on San Martín between Rosas and 9 de Julio, takes 5%.

Post & Communications Correo Argentino is at Av San Martín and Godoy. The postal code is 9410. Locutorio del Fin del Mundo is at Av San Martín 957, Locutorio Cabo de Hornos at 25 de Mayo 112. Ushuaia's area code is ☎ 02901.

The Dirección de Turismo has a convenient line for collect and credit-card calls to Brazil, Chile, France, Italy, Japan, Spain, Uruguay, and the USA (ATT, MCI, Sprint). The Oficina Antarctica Infuetur (☎ 424431, antartida@tierradelfuego.ml.org), on the waterfront Muelle Comercial, has email

WAYNE BERNHARDSON

Magellanic penguins, Patagonia

SANDRA BAO

Elephant seals, Patagonia

FRANK S BALTHIS

Ushuaia

SANDRA BAO

Cuernos del Paine, Parque Nacional Torres del Paine, Chile

WAYNE BERNHARDSON

King cormorants, Sea Lion Island, Falkland Islands

WAYNE BERNHARDSON

Black-crowned night herons, Falkland Islands

WAYNE BERNHARDSON

Johnny rook, Pebble Island, Falkland Islands

WAYNE BERNHARDSON

Rockhopper & Macaroni penguins, Falkland Islands

SYLVIA STEVENS

Stanley, Falkland Islands

SYLVIA STEVENS

Sheep in yard, Stanley, Falkland Islands

SYLVIA STEVENS

Stanley, Falkland Islands

SYLVIA STEVENS

Ross Road, with Christ Church Cathedral, Stanley, Falkland Islands

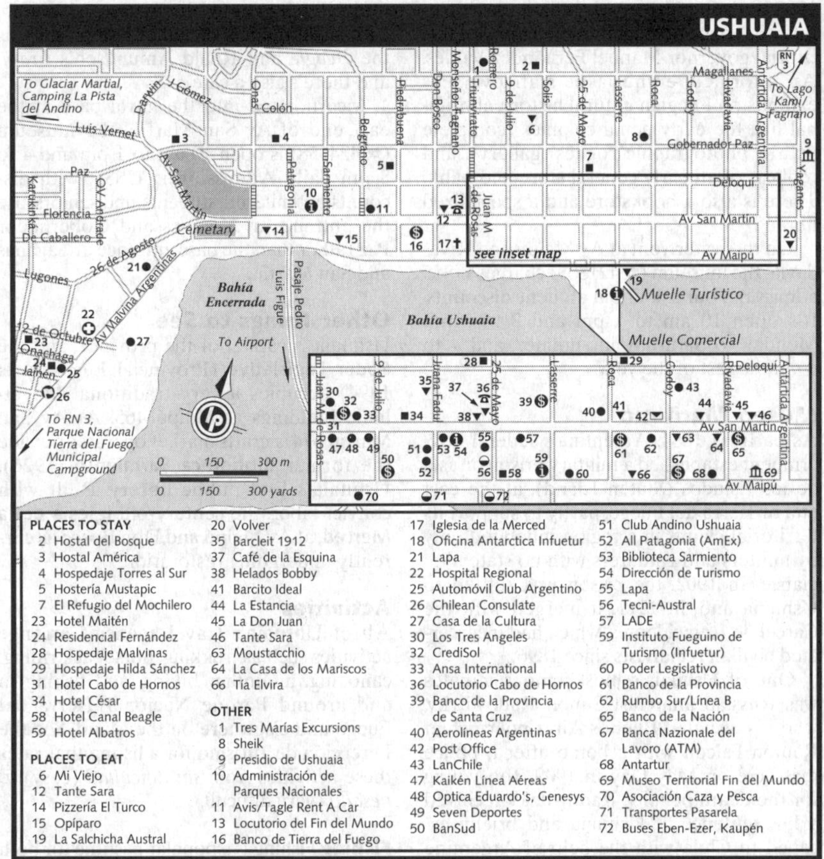

services for a small charge. Genesys, on San Martín near 9 de Julio, also offers email access.

National Parks The Administración de Parques Nacionales (☎ 421315), San Martín 1395, is open 9 am to noon weekdays.

Travel Agencies Ushuaia has nearly a score of travel agencies, among them: Rumbo Sur (☎ 422441), at Av San Martín 342 and at the Muelle Turístico; Antartur (☎ 423240), at Maipú 237; and All Patagonia (☎ 430725), Juana Fadul 26, which is the AmEx representative.

Laundry Los Tres Angeles (☎ 422687) is at Juan M de Rosas 139.

Medical Services Ushuaia's Hospital Regional (☎ 422950, 107 for emergencies) is at Maipú and 12 de Octubre.

Museo Territorial Fin del Mundo
The city has restored the original facade of this unusual block construction, dating from

1903 and atypical of Magellanic architecture, that once belonged to the family of territorial governor Manuel Fernández Valdés. An informed, enthusiastic staff oversees exhibits on Fuegian natural history, aboriginal life, the early penal colonies (complete with a photographic rogues' gallery), and replicas of an early general store and bank. There is also a bookstore and a specialized library.

On the waterfront at Av Maipú and Rivadavia, the museum (☎ 421863) charges US$5 admission, but ask about student discounts. It's open 10 am to 1 pm and 3 to 8 pm Monday to Saturday in summer, and 4 to 8 pm the rest of the year.

Museo Marítimo

As early as 1884, Argentina's federal government established a military prison on Isla de los Estados (Staten Island), at the east end of Tierra del Fuego, partly to support its territorial claims in a region inhabited only by hunters and gatherers with no state allegiance. In 1902, the prison was shifted to Ushuaia and, in 1911, it merged with the Carcel de Reincidentes, which had incarcerated civilian recidivists since 1896.

One of Ushuaia's most famous inmates was Russian anarchist Simón Radowitzky, who assassinated Buenos Aires police chief Ramón Falcón with a bomb after a police massacre on May Day in 1909. Too young for the death penalty, Radowitzky received a life sentence at Ushuaia and briefly escaped to Chile with the help of Argentine anarchists.

In 1930 Radical President Hipólito Yrigoyen ordered him released, but the military dictatorship that overthrew Yrigoyen shortly thereafter confined several Radical political figures to Ushuaia, including writer Ricardo Rojas, diplomat and former presidential candidate Honorio Pueyrredón, and Pueyrredón's vice-presidential candidate Mario Guido. Héctor Cámpora, who served as president before Juan Perón's last term, also did time here.

Closed as a penal institution since 1947, the present building held up to 800 inmates in 380 cells designed for one prisoner each. Officially, it is now the Museo Marítimo, with scale models of famous ships such as the *Beagle* and Roald Amundsen's *Fram*, and there's also a café.

Incorporated into the naval base at the east end of Av San Martín, the museum (☎ 424058) is open 10 am to 1 pm and 4 to 8 pm daily. Admission is US$5, with discounts for children, students, and seniors; use the entrance at Yaganes and Gobernador Paz rather than the base entrance at Yaganes and San Martín.

Other Things to See

Ushuaia is capital of the province, and the **Poder Legislativo** (Provincial Legislature; 1894) occupies a very traditional Magellanic buildings at Maipú 465. At Av San Martín 674, a crafts market operates outside the former **Biblioteca Sarmiento** (1926), Ushuaia's first public library. Built with convict labor, the century-old **Iglesia de la Merced**, at Av Maipú and Don Bosco, is currently undergoing restoration.

Activities

All of Uhsuaia's travel agencies arrange activities such as trekking, horseback riding, canoeing, mountain biking, and fishing in and around Parque Nacional Tierra del Fuego and elsewhere on the island. See the Dirección de Turismo for a listing that rates these activities from *sin dificultad* (easy) to *pesado* (very difficult).

Fishing Fishing is a popular pastime for both Argentines and foreigners; there are two kinds of permits, one for the national park and one for the island at large. For the former, which costs US$10 daily, US$30 weekly, US$60 monthly, and US$100 for the season, visit the Administración de Parques Nacionales (see Information). For the latter, visit the Asociación Caza y Pesca (☎ 423168), at Maipú 822, or try Optica Eduardo's (☎ 433252), at San Martín 830. These licenses cost US$10 daily, US$20 weekly, US$30 for 15 days, and US$40 monthly.

Spinning and fly casting are the most common means of hooking brown trout, rainbow trout, Atlantic salmon, and other species. The nearest site is Río Pipo, 5km west of town on RN 3. It is possible to visit the Estación de Piscicultura (trout hatchery) at Río Olivia, 2km east of town.

Mountain Biking From October to April, local operators arrange mountain-bike excursions ranging from a full day in Parque Nacional Tierra del Fuego to weeklong tours over Paso Garibaldi to Lago Kami, Lago Yehuin, and Río Grande. Distances range from 50 to 95km per day and, fortunately, the wind is usually at your back. For rentals, try Seven Deportes (☎ 437604), San Martín 802.

Skiing From June to mid-September, the nearby mountains provide opportunities for both downhill and cross-country skiing, although only the period around Argentine winter holidays in early July is really busy. The main downhill area is **Centro de Deportes Invernales Luis Martial** (☎ 421423, 423340), 7km northwest of town, which has one 1300m run on a 23° slope, with a double-seat chairlift (maximum capacity 244 skiers per hour). The Club Andino Ushuaia (☎ 422335), Fadul 50, has a smaller area only 3km from downtown on the same road.

East of Ushuaia, along RN 3 toward Paso Garibaldi, are cross-country ski areas at the Club Andino's Pista Francisco Jermán, 5km from town; at Valle de los Huskies (☎ 431902), 17km from town; at Tierra Mayor (☎ 437454), 21km from town; at Las Cotorras (☎ 499300), 26km from town; and at Haruwen (☎/fax 424058), 37km from town. Rental equipment is available at each site for around US$30 per day. Each center provides its own transportation from downtown Ushuaia.

Ushuaia's biggest ski event is the annual **Marcha Blanca**, a symbolic re-creation of San Martín's historic crossing of the Andes, taking place on August 17, the date of the great man's death. Attracting up to 450 skiers, it starts from Las Cotorras and climbs to Paso Garibaldi.

SANDRA BAO

Ushuaia

Organized Tours

Overland Trips Local operators (see Travel Agencies) offer tours to the principal attractions in and around Ushuaia, including Parque Nacional Tierra del Fuego. Trips to historic Estancia Harberton (US$55 to US$70), east of Ushuaia, can be arranged with sufficient notice, but no one should arrive unannounced; admission to the estancia costs an additional US$6 and includes a visit to the Bridges family cemetery. There are also half-day tours of the city (US$15 including the museum), tours to Lapataia/Parque Nacional Tierra del Fuego (US$15), and excursions over Paso Garibaldi to Lago Kami/Fagnano (US$30 full-day) and Río Grande.

Boat Trips Popular boat trips, with destinations such as the sea lion colony at Isla de los Lobos, leave from the Muelle Turístico (tourist jetty) on Maipú between Lasserre and Roca. The most commonly seen species is the southern sea lion *Otaria flavescens*, whose thick mane will make you wonder why Spanish speakers call it *lobo marino* (sea wolf). Fur seals, nearly extinct because of commercial overexploitation during the past century, survive in much smaller numbers; they usually arrive in early January. Isla de Pájaros, also in the Beagle Channel, has many species of birds, including extensive cormorant colonies.

See travel agencies for trips on the luxury catamarans *Ana B*, *Ezequiel B*, and *Luciano Beta*, which cost about US$30 for a 2½-hour excursion to Isla Lobos; with an extension to Bahía Lapataia or the pingüinera (penguin colony) near Estancia Harberton, they cost US$50. Trips to Estancia Harberton cost US$70.

Héctor Monsalve's Tres Marías Excursiones (☎/fax 421897), Romero 514 and at the Muelle Turístico, charges US$45 for a four-hour morning or afternoon excursion on the Beagle Channel, including the king cormorant colony on Isla Alicia, the fur seal and sea lion colony on Isla de Lobos, and a short but interesting hike on Isla Bridges, which has a rock cormorant colony, shell-mounds, and the occasional king penguin.

For weeklong sailboat excursions around Cape Horn or the Cordillera Darwin (for about US$1200 per person), contact travel agencies such as All Patagonia or Rumbo (see Information).

Places to Stay

In the summer high season, especially January and February, demand is very high and no one should arrive without reservations; at least, try to arrive early in the day before everything fills up. If nothing is available, the 24-hour confitería at the Hotel del Glaciar (at Km 3.5 on the road to Glaciar Martial) is a good place to stay up drinking coffee. The tourist office posts a list of available accommodations outside after closing time.

Places to Stay – Budget

Camping Ushuaia's ***Camping Municipal***, 8km west of town on RN 3 to Parque Nacional Tierra del Fuego, has minimal facilities but an attractive setting for US$1 per tent plus US$5 for use of their parrillas. The ***Camping del Rugby Club Ushuaia***, 5km west of town, charges US$5 per person up to a maximum of US$15 per tent. Far more central but still a steep uphill walk, ***La Pista del Andino*** *(☎ 02901 1556-8626, Alem 2873)*, at the Club Andino's ski area, charges US$5 per person and offers the first transfer free. It has a bar-restaurant with good atmosphere (you can also crash in the refugio upstairs), but could use more showers and toilets.

Other ***campsites***, both free and for a fee, are at Parque Nacional Tierra del Fuego plus others out RN 3 toward Río Grande and Valle de los Huskies. ***Camping Río Tristen***, at the Haruwen winter sports center, has a dozen sites, with bathrooms and showers, for US$5 per tent (two people).

Hostels The local affiliate of Hostelling International, highly regarded ***Torre al Sur Hostel*** *(☎ 430745, torresur@hostels.org.ar, Gobernador Paz 1437)* charges US$10 in low season, US$12 in summer.

Deservedly popular ***El Refugio del Mochilero*** *(☎ 436129, 25 de Mayo 241)* is not yet an official HI affiliate, but has excellent facilities and great ambience for US$13.

At the Martial Glacier, the Club Andino's ***Refugio de Alta Montaña*** offers hostel accommodations for US$7.

Casas de Familia The tourist office helps arrange rooms in private homes, which tend to be cheaper than hotels, but these are usually available only seasonally and change from year to year. Prices are typically in the US$20 per person range, occasionally slightly cheaper.

Hospedajes & Hosterías ***Hospedaje Torres al Sur*** (see Hostels) charges $15 single for nonhostelers. The Dirección de Turismo discourages visitors from ***Hospedaje Hilda Sánchez*** *(☎ 423622, Deloquí 391)*, but many travelers have found her place congenial, if crowded and a bit noisy at times. Rates are US$15 per person, and it's open all year.

Run by a Croat nationalist, ***Hostería Mustapic*** *(☎ 421718, Piedrabuena 230)* costs US$25/40 with shared bath, US$35/50 with private bath.

Places to Stay – Mid-Range

Mid-range accommodations start around US$33/45 at ***Hotel Maitén*** *(☎ 422745, 12 de Octubre 140)*. Nearby popular ***Residencial Fernández*** *(☎ 421192, Onachaga 72)* has rooms at US$35/50, as does ***Hostal América*** *(☎ 423358, Gobernador Paz 1665)*.

On the waterfront, ACA's ***Hotel Canal Beagle*** *(☎ 421117, Av Maipú 599)* is good value for members at US$40/60, but non-members pay US$54/80. Other possibilities in this range include ***Hospedaje Malvinas*** *(☎ 422626, Deloquí 609)* for US$50/60, and ***Hotel César*** *(☎ 421460, Av San Martín 753)* for US$50/65.

Places to Stay – Top End

Boxy ***Hotel Cabo de Hornos*** *(☎ 422187)*, Av San Martín at Rosas, costs US$60/70. On the hillside, ***Hostal del Bosque*** *(☎ 421723, Magallanes 709)* charges US$64/80. At ***Hotel Ushuaia*** *(☎ 430671, Lasserre 933)* rates are US$80/110, while quiet ***Hotel Tolkeyén*** *(☎ 434883)*, 5km west of town on RN 3, rents rooms for US$85/100.

Overpriced ***Hotel Albatros*** *(☎ 433446, Av Maipú 505)* charges US$162 single or double with breakfast, but the restaurant has great harbor views. For the same price ***Hotel del Glaciar*** *(☎ 430640, fax 430636)*, at Km 3.5 on the road to Glaciar Martial, is probably a better choice, but it's still hard to call it a good value. Five-star ***Las Hayas Resort Hotel*** *(☎ 430710)*, at Km 3 on the Glaciar Martial road, charges US$185/195, but sometimes lacks staff to provide all the services of a hotel in its category.

Places to Eat

On the waterfront near the Muelle Turístico, informal ***La Salchicha Austral*** *(☎ 424596)* is among the most reasonable places in town. ***Pizzería El Turco*** *(☎ 424711, San Martín 1440)* is also good and relatively inexpensive. ***Opíparo*** *(☎ 434022, Maipú 1255)* specializes in varied, moderately priced pizza and pasta. ***Barcleit 1912*** *(☎ 433422, Fadul 148)* is a pizzeria plus minutas that also has live music Friday and Saturday.

The US$10 *tenedor libre* (buffet) at lively ***Barcito Ideal*** *(☎ 430614, Av San Martín 393)* is no bargain, but some travelers making it their only meal of the day find it a good choice. ***Mi Viejo*** *(☎ 423565, Gobernador Campos 758)* also has a tenedor libre special, as does the traditional (but more expensive) favorite ***Moustacchio*** *(☎ 423308, Av San Martín 298)*.

At pricier restaurants, reservations are essential for groups of any size. ***La Don Juan*** *(☎ 422519, San Martín 193)* is Ushuaia's main parrilla, but ***La Estancia***, on San Martín between Godoy and Rivadavia, offers some competition.

La Casa de los Mariscos *(☎ 421928, San Martín 232)* specializes in fish and shellfish, most notably crab. ***Tía Elvira*** *(☎ 424725, Maipú 349)* also has a good reputation for seafood, along with ***Volver*** *(☎ 423977, Maipú 37)*.

Café de la Esquina *(☎ 421446, San Martín 601)* is Ushuaia's most popular confitería. ***Tante Sara*** *(San Martín 175)*, and at the corner of San Martín and Don Bosco, has outstanding ice cream and other desserts. ***Helados Bobby*** *(San Martín 621)* features deliciously unusual ice-cream flavors, like rhubarb and calafate.

Entertainment

Since the ***Cine Pakawaia*** burned to the ground in May of 1998, the only current cinema is at the ***Casa de la Cultura***, at Maipú and 12 de Octubre.

Sheik, at Gobernador Paz and Roca, is a good place for drinks and music.

Shopping

Ushuaia is ostensibly a duty-free zone, but overseas visitors will find few bargains compared to Punta Arenas. Locally made chocolates deserve a taste.

Getting There & Away

Air A new 3800m runway at Aeropuerto Internacional Malvinas Argentinas now permits planes larger than 737s to land safely, and Aerolíneas Argentinas' loss of a landing monopoly has allowed some long-distance competition. Note that airport taxes are the most expensive in the country: US$4 to Río Grande, US$13 elsewhere in Argentina, and US$20 international.

Aerolíneas Argentinas (☎ 421091), Roca 116, flies twice daily, with an additional flight on Monday, Thursday, and Sunday, to Buenos Aires' Aeroparque (US$147 to US$252); the Monday flight stops in Trelew (US$79 to US$157).

Lapa (☎ 422150), 25 de Mayo 64, flies daily except Saturday to Trelew (US$90 to US$156) and Aeroparque (US$149 to US$245); the flights on Tuesday, Thursday, and Sunday first stop at Río Gallegos (US$35 to US$61).

LADE (☎ 421123), in the Galería Albatros at Av San Martín 564, flies Wednesday and Thursday to Río Grande (US$20), Río Gallegos (US$35 to US$61), and El Calafate (US$56), continuing Thursday only to Gobernador Gregores (US$68), Perito Moreno (US$94), and Comodoro Rivadavia (US$100).

Kaikén Líneas Aéreas (☎ 432963), San Martín 880, flies daily to Río Grande (US$28 to US$36), Río Gallegos (US$39 to US$49), Comodoro Rivadavia (US$119 to US$142), Trelew (US$129 to US$157), and Bahía Blanca (US$180 to US$221); and daily except Sunday to Bariloche (US$209 to US$380), Neuquén (US$238 to US$355), and Mendoza (US$265 to US$350).

Bus Tecni-Austral (☎/fax 423396), in the Galería del Jardín at 25 de Mayo 50, goes to Río Grande (US$21, four hours) at 7:30 am and 6 pm daily. The Monday, Wednesday, and Friday morning services continue to Punta Arenas (US$51, 14 hours).

For transportation to Parque Nacional Tierra del Fuego, see the Getting There & Away entry for the park.

Boat The *MV Terra Australis* runs expensive sightseeing cruises, with accommodations and all meals included, to Punta Arenas; three-day trips cost US$681 to US$1272 in low season, September, October and April; US$858 to US$1611 in mid-season, November to mid-December and March; US$1078 to US$2036 in high season, mid-December through February. See travel agents for details.

The *Piratur* (☎ 423875), a 12-passenger boat, recently suspended service between Puerto Almanza, east of Ushuaia, and Puerto Williams, across the Beagle Channel in Chile. Check with the tourist office for an update.

Getting Around

To/From the Airport Aeropuerto Internacional Isla Malvinas is on the peninsula across from the waterfront. Cabs are moderately priced, and there's also bus service along Av Maipú.

Car Although rural public transport is better than at Río Grande, it is still limited. Rental rates for a Fiat Spazio start around US$30 per day plus US$0.30 per kilometer plus at least US$15 insurance daily. Rental companies include Avis/Tagle (☎ 422744), San Martín and Belgrano, AI (☎ 436388), at San Martín 847, and Localiza (☎ 430663), at Hotel Albatros. Rates go up to US$170 per day plus mileage and insurance for a 4WD pickup.

AROUND USHUAIA

Glaciar Martial

Just within the borders of Parque Nacional Tierra del Fuego lies Glaciar Martial, which hikers can reach via a magnificent walk that begins from the west end of Av San Martín, passes the Parques Nacionales office, and climbs the zigzag road (there are many hiker shortcuts) to the ski run 7km northwest of town. Transportes Pasarela (☎ 433712, 434706), leaving from the YPF station at Av Maipú and Fadul, runs five buses daily (US$5 return) to the Aerosilla del Glaciar, a chairlift that is open 10 am to 4:30 pm daily except Monday. Buses Eben-Ezer (☎ 431133) leaves Maipú and 25 de Mayo 10:30 am and 1, 2:30, and 4 pm, returning at 11 am and 1:30, 4 and 4:45 pm. Kaupén (☎ 434015) goes at 10:30 am and 12:30 and 3:30 pm.

From the base of the Aerosilla (which costs US$5 and saves an hour's walk), the glacier is about a two-hour walk, offering awesome views of Ushuaia and the Beagle Channel. The weather is changeable, so take warm, dry clothing and sturdy footwear.

Ferrocarril Austral Fueguino

Originally constructed to assist the logging industry during presidio days, Ushuaia's short-line, narrow-gauge railroad has reopened as a tourist train under a 30-year concession and now has permission to enter Parque Nacional Tierra del Fuego as far as Cañadón del Toro. It stops at Cascada La Macarena, whose tourist-trap reconstruction of a Selknam/Ona camp would fit better into Disneyland.

From Ushuaia's Plaza Cívica on the waterfront at the Muelle Turístico, Tranex (☎ 431600, fax 437696) sells tickets for the 3½-hour excursion, which would be a poor value at even a small fraction of the US$26 cost. A bus leaves for the starting point at the municipal campground, 8km west of town, 45 minutes before the 10 am and 3 and 5:30 pm departures.

Estancia Harberton

Fuegian pioneer Thomas Bridges, a missionary from the Falkland Islands, founded this historic estancia on the north shore of the Beagle Channel, 80km east of Ushuaia via RN 3 and RC-i, but his son Lucas made it famous with his memoir of life among the Yahgan Indians, *The Uttermost Part of the Earth*. Still owned by the Goodalls, direct descendents of the Bridges, the estancia now provides well-organized tours (English usually spoken) around the Bridges family cemetery, a small native botanical garden with replicas of Yahgan dwellings, and the estancia's wool shed, carpenter shop, boathouse, and gardens. The estancia itself has only about 1500 sheep on 20,000 hectares, since the severe winter of 1995.

Rae Natalie Prosser de Goodall, a North American biologist who married into the family, has also created a bone museum stressing the region's marine mammals. It's also possible to visit nearby penguin rookeries on the *Piratur*, the small vessel that also crosses to Puerto Williams, Chile.

SECRETARÍA DE TURISMO ARGENTINA

Estancia Haberton

Estancia Harberton (☎ 422742, fax 422743) is open to visitors (US$6 per person for tours) in the summer months. Its ***Casa de Té Mánacatush***, serving afternoon tea for US$9, can't match the Welsh teahouses of Chubut, but it's not bad and the setting is incomparable. The Goodalls permit ***camping*** at several sites on their property, but asking permission is obligatory. Several Ushuaia travel agencies offer boat tours (around US$70) of the Beagle Channel that make a short stop at Harberton, but overland visits are more leisurely.

PARQUE NACIONAL TIERRA DEL FUEGO

Its, bays, lakes, rivers, peaks, and glaciers attract many visitors and hikers to Argentina's first coastal national park, a 63,000-hectare unit extending from the Beagle Channel in the south along the Chilean border to beyond Lago Kami/Fagnano in the north. Just 18km west of Ushuaia via RN 3, the park lacks the integrated network of hiking trails of Chile's Torres del Paine. There are several short trails, but the one major trek is now off-limits because of misguided and inexplicable policies that have declared large but lightly impacted portions of the park a *reserva estricta*, closed to all access except for scientific research, while permitting the more accessible, so-called *zona de recreación* to have been trashed almost beyond belief.

Information

Parques Nacionales maintains a Centro de Información at the park entrance on RN 3, where visitors must also pay the US$5 admission charge.

Books

William Leitch's *South America's National Parks* (The Mountaineers, 1990) has a useful chapter on Parque Nacional Tierra del Fuego, emphasizing natural history. Several authors have contributed to Bradt Publications' *Backpacking in Chile & Argentina*, which describes treks in the area around Ushuaia but is skimpy on maps. The 2nd edition of Clem Lindemayer's *Trekking in the Patagonian Andes* (Lonely Planet, 1997) is much more detailed.

Two useful guides for bird watchers are Claudio Venegas Canelo's *Aves de Patagonia y Tierra del Fuego Chileno-Argentina* and Ricardo Clark's *Aves de Tierra del Fuego y Cabo de Hornos* (Buenos Aires: Literature of Latin America, 1986). Claudio Villegas' *Aves de Magallanes* is also a worthwhile purchase.

Flora & Fauna

Three species of the southern beech *(Nothofagus)*, known by their common names coihue, lenga, and ñire, dominate the dense native forests. The evergreen coihue and deciduous lenga thrive on heavy coastal rainfall at lower elevations, and the deciduous ñire tints the Fuegian hillsides red during the fall months. Other tree species are less significant and not so conspicuous.

Sphagnum peat bogs in low-lying areas support ferns, colorful wildflowers, and the insectivorous plant *Drosera uniflora*; these may be seen on the self-guided nature trail **Sendero Laguna Negra**. To avoid damage to the bog and danger to yourself, stay on the trail, part of which consists of a catwalk for easier passage across the swampy terrain.

The cauquén is also known as the upland goose.

Land mammals are scarce, although guanacos and foxes exist; marine mammals are most common on offshore islands. Visitors are most likely to see two unfortunate introductions, the European rabbit and the North American beaver, both of which have caused ecological havoc and proved impossible to eradicate. The former numbers up to 70 per hectare in some areas, while the latter's handiwork is visible in the ponds and by the dead beeches along the **Sendero de los Castores** (Trail of the Beavers) to Bahía Lapataia. Originally introduced at Lago Kami/Fagnano in the 1940s, beavers quickly spread throughout the island.

Birdlife is much more abundant, especially along the coastal zone, including Lapataia and Bahía Ensenada. The Andean condor and the maritime black-browed albatross overlap ranges here, although neither is common. Shorebirds such as cormorants, gulls, terns, oystercatchers, grebes, steamer ducks, and kelp geese are common. The large, striking upland goose *(cauquén)* is widely distributed farther inland.

Things to See & Do

Most park trails are very short, and the only remaining trek permitted is a mere 6km through lakeside lenga forest along the level northern shore of Lago Roca to the unimposing border marker at **Hito XXIV**. The extended trek from the Río Pipo campsite, across the Montes Martial and Sierra de Padre Mario Zavattaro to Lago Kami/Fagnano – a rugged 30km trip – should be simple for experienced, independent hikers, but Parques Nacionales' reclassification of the area has eliminated access.

Because of Argentina's perpetual fiscal crisis and the military's proprietary attitude toward border zones, there are no official, detailed, easily available maps, but the route is fairly straightforward. Probably the best detailed walking map is the one contained in LP's *Trekking in the Patagonian Andes*.

From Bahía Ensenada Isla Verde/Yishka Turismo runs boat circuits to and from Bahía Lapataia via Isla Redonda, a small island in the Beagle Channel, from 10 am to 6 pm daily.

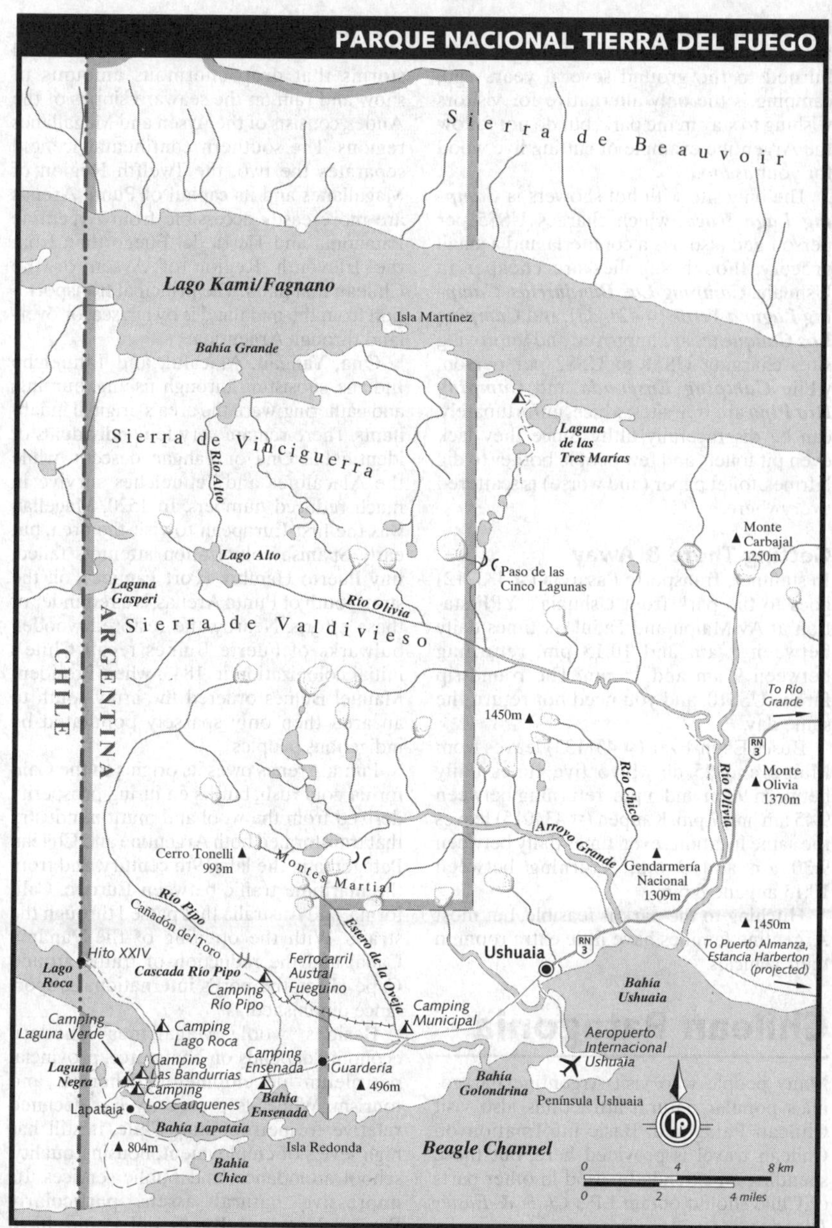
PARQUE NACIONAL TIERRA DEL FUEGO
Sierra de Beauvoir
Lago Kami/Fagnano
Isla Martínez
Bahía Grande
Laguna de las Tres Marías
Sierra de Vinciguerra
Río Alto
Lago Alto
Laguna Gasperi
Paso de las Cinco Lagunas
Monte Carbajal 1250m
Río Olivia
Sierra de Valdivieso
CHILE
ARGENTINA
To Río Grande
1450m
RN 3
Río Chico
Río Olivia
Monte Olivia 1370m
Arroyo Grande
Cerro Tonelli 993m
Montes Martial
Gendarmería Nacional 1309m
Río Pipo
Cañadón del Toro
Estero de la Oveja
1450m
Ushuaia
To Puerto Almanza, Estancia Harberton (projected)
Hito XXIV
Lago Roca
Cascada Río Pipo
Ferrocarril Austral Fueguino
Camping Río Pipo
Camping Municipal
Bahía Ushuaia
Camping Laguna Verde
Camping Lago Roca
Camping Ensenada
Guardería
Aeropuerto Internacional Ushuaia
Laguna Negra
Camping Las Bandurrias
Camping Los Cauquenes
496m
Bahía Ensenada
Bahía Golondrina
Península Ushuaia
Lapataia
Bahía Lapataia
804m
Isla Redonda
Beagle Channel
Bahía Chica
0 4 8 km
0 2 4 miles

Places to Stay

Since Hostería Alakush at Lago Roca burned to the ground several years ago, camping is the only alternative for visitors wishing to stay in the park, but do not follow the Argentine example of cutting live wood for your *asado*.

The only site with hot showers is ***Camping Lago Roca***, which charges US$5 per person and also has a confitería and a small grocery, though supplies are cheaper in Ushuaia. ***Camping Las Bandurrias***, ***Camping Laguna Verde*** *(☎ 421433)*, and ***Camping Los Cauquenes*** are improved and improving sites charging US$1 to US$2 per person, while ***Camping Ensenada*** and ***Camping Río Pipo*** are free sites, which, unfortunately, can be disgracefully filthy. Since they lack even pit toilets and few people bother to dig latrines, toilet paper (and worse) is scattered everywhere.

Getting There & Away

In summer, Transporte Pasarela (☎ 433712) goes to the park from Ushuaia's YPF station at Av Maipú and Fadul six times daily between 8 am and 10:15 pm, returning between 9 am and 11 pm. The roundtrip fare is US$10, and you need not return the same day.

Buses Eben-Ezer (☎ 431133) leaves from Maipú and 25 de Mayo five times daily between 9 am and 6 pm, returning between 9:45 am and 7 pm. Kaupén (☎ 434015) leaves the same location seven times daily between 9:30 am and 9 pm, returning between 10:15 am and 8 pm.

Hitching to the park is feasible, but most Argentine families have little extra room in their vehicles.

Chilean Patagonia

Many people who visit Argentine Patagonia's popular natural attractions also visit Chilean Patagonia. Basic information on Chilean travel is provided here, but those spending an extended period in other parts of Chile should obtain LP's *Chile & Easter Island*.

Chilean Patagonia, a rugged, mountainous area battered by westerly winds and storms that drop enormous amounts of snow and rain on the seaward slopes of the Andes, consists of the Aysén and Magallanes regions. The southern continental icefield separates the two; the Twelfth Region of Magallanes and its capital of Punta Arenas are more easily accessible from Argentine Patagonia and Tierra del Fuego than from the Eleventh Region of Aysén or the Chilean mainland. The principal transportation from the mainland is by air, sea, or overland through Argentina.

Ona, Yahgan, Alacaluf, and Tehuelche Indians, subsisting through fishing, hunting, and gathering, were the area's original inhabitants. There remain very few individuals of identifiable Ona or Yahgan descent, while the Alacalufes and Tehuelches survive in much reduced numbers. In 1520, Magellan was the first European to visit the area, but early Spanish colonization attempts failed; tiny Puerto Hambre (Port Famine), on the strait south of Punta Arenas, is a reminder of these efforts. Nearby, the restored wooden bulwarks of Fuerte Bulnes recall Chile's initial colonization in 1843, when President Manuel Bulnes ordered the army south to an area then only sparsely populated by indigenous peoples.

Punta Arenas owes its origins to the California gold rush, but its enduring prosperity derived from the wool and mutton industry that transformed both Argentine and Chilean Patagonia in the late 19th century, and from the maritime traffic between Europe, California, and Australia that passed through the straits. With the opening of the Panama Canal and the reduction of traffic around Cape Horn, the port's international importance diminished.

Besides wool, Magallanes' modern economy depends on commerce, provincial petroleum development, fisheries, and tourism. While its prosperity has declined relative to metropolitan Chile, it still has high levels of employment, housing quality, school attendance, and public services. Its impressive natural assets, particularly Parque Nacional Torres del Paine, have made it an increasingly popular destination for travelers.

Visas

Nationals of countries with which Chile has diplomatic relations, including the USA, Canada, Western Europe, Japan, Australia, and many others, need passports but not visas to enter the country. All visitors do need a tourist card, which is issued at the port of entry. Like the Argentine tourist card, it is valid for 90 days and renewable for another 90. Unlike the Argentine card, authorities take it very seriously, so guard it closely to avoid the hassle of replacing it. Chilean border officials are generally reasonable and friendly, however.

Note that the Chilean government now collects a US$45 processing fee from US citizens arriving by air, in response to the US government's imposition of a similar fee on Chilean citizens applying for US visas; this one-time payment is valid for the life of the passport. There is a similar fee for Australians (A$46) and Canadians (C$81).

Customs

Chilean customs permits the importation of personal belongings, 500 cigarettes, 100 cigars, and 2 liters of alcoholic beverages plus gifts and souvenirs. Normally customs officials are not difficult to deal with, although returning to Puerto Montt or Santiago from Punta Arenas (a free zone where electronic items are very cheap), you may encounter a thorough internal customs check. Unless you are carrying, say, half a dozen cameras of the same brand and model, you are not likely to be seriously inconvenienced.

Money

In 1998, the Chilean peso (Ch$) depreciated from approximately 400 to 470 pesos per US dollar, but the inflation rate pretty much offset the dollar's gains. Banknote denominations are Ch$500, Ch$1000, Ch$2000, Ch$5000, Ch$10,000, and Ch$20,000 pesos, although breaking notes CH$10,000 or larger can be a nuisance for small purchases. There are also coins of Ch$5, Ch$10, Ch$50, and Ch$100, but few items cost less than Ch$50.

For basic costs such as accommodations, food, and transport, foreign visitors will find Chile more expensive than the central Andean countries but cheaper than Argentina. Chilean Patagonia, however, generally has a higher cost of living than the rest of the country because of its remoteness and relative isolation.

Health

Conditions are much the same as in Argentina; see the section on health in the Facts for the Visitor chapter. Chile does not demand any unusual health precautions, and no vaccinations are required as a condition of entry.

Getting There & Away

Visitors to Chilean Patagonia must arrive by air, by sea from mainland Chile, or overland through Argentina. Chile's two major airlines, LanChile and Ladeco, are both comfortable and efficient, as is Avant, which has fewer flights and is slightly cheaper. Weekly ferry services link Puerto Montt, on mainland Chile, and Puerto Natales, in Magallanes.

Within Chilean Patagonia, Aerovías DAP serves both Chilean and Argentine Tierra del Fuego, Río Gallegos, and sometimes Antarctica. There are ferries between Punta Arenas and Porvenir, in Chilean Tierra del Fuego.

Comfortable buses connect Punta Arenas, Puerto Natales, and Parque Nacional Torres del Paine, the main visitor destinations in Chilean Patagonia.

PUNTA ARENAS

At the foot of the Andes on the western side of the Strait of Magellan, Patagonia's most interesting and liveliest city features many mansions and other impressive buildings dating from the wool boom of the late 19th and early 20th centuries. As the best and largest port for thousands of kilometers, Punta Arenas (population 113,000) attracts ships from the burgeoning South Atlantic fishery as well as Antarctic research and tourist vessels. Free port facilities have promoted local commerce and encouraged immigration from central Chile; luxury items

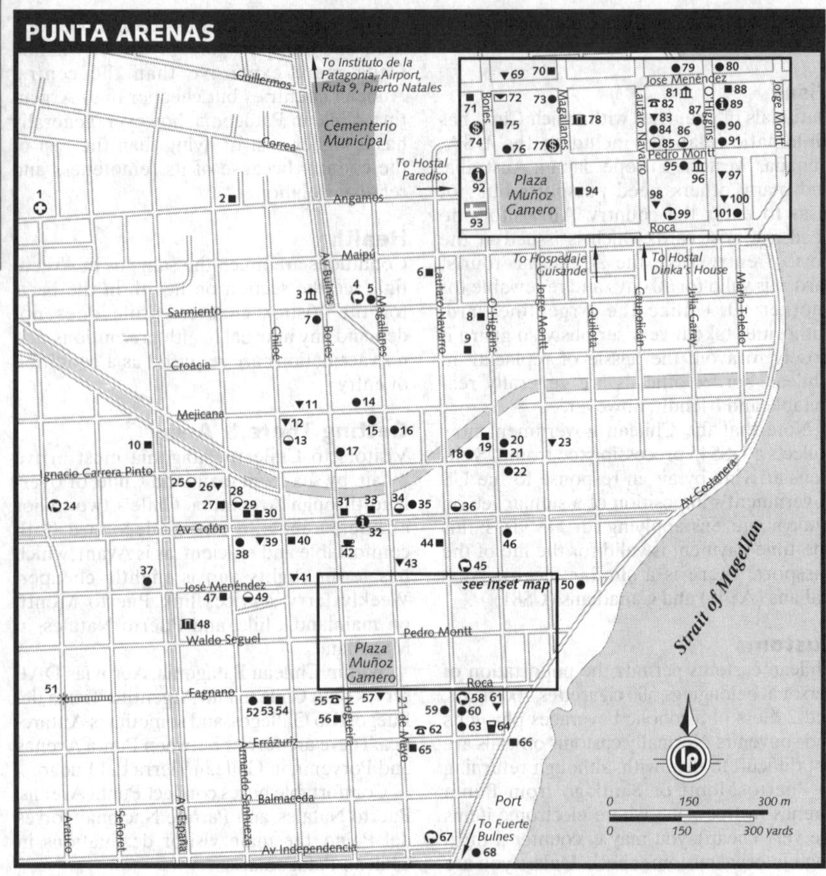

like automobiles are much less expensive here, but the basic cost of living is higher.

Punta Arenas has experienced a large influx of foreign visitors, compared to their relative paucity in Argentina, but the town is utterly dead on Sunday, which is a good day to explore some of the surrounding area or start a trip to Torres del Paine.

History

Founded in 1848, Punta Arenas was originally a military garrison and penal settlement that proved to be conveniently situated for ships headed to California during the gold rush. Compared to the initial Chilean settlement at Fuerte Bulnes, 60km south, the town had a better, more protected harbor, and superior access to wood and water. For many years, English maritime charts had called the site 'Sandy Point,' and this became its rough Spanish equivalent.

In Punta Arenas' early years, its economy depended on wild animal products, including sealskins, guanaco hides, and feathers; mineral products, including coal, gold, and guano; firewood, and timber. None of these

PUNTA ARENAS

PLACES TO STAY
2 Residencial Sonia (HI)
6 Hostal Carpa Manzano
8 ¡Ecole! Patagonia
9 Hostal de la Patagonia
10 Hostal Rubio
19 Hospedaje Manuel
21 Albergue Backpacker's Paradise
27 Residencial Coirón
29 Hostal de la Avenida
30 Hotel Cóndor de Plata
31 Hotel Tierra del Fuego
33 Hotel Finis Terrae
40 Hotel Montecarlo
44 Hostal Calafate
47 Hostal Oasis
53 Residencial Oasis
54 Hotel Mercurio
56 Hotel Plaza
65 Hotel Isla Rey Jorge
66 Hostal O'Higgins
70 Residencial Roca
71 Hotel Los Navegantes
75 Hotel José Nogueira
88 Hostal Calafate II
94 Hotel Cabo de Hornos

PLACES TO EAT
11 222
12 El Mercado
23 El Mesón del Calvo
26 Rotiserìa La Mam·
39 Golden Dragon
41 La Carioca
42 Café Calipso
43 El Infante
57 Centro Español
61 Sotito's Bar
69 Lomit's
83 Asturias
98 Quijote
99 La Taberna de Silver
100 El Beagle

OTHER
1 Hospital Regional
3 Museo Regional Salesiano Mayorino Borgatello
4 Netherlands Consulate
5 Internacional Rent A Car
7 Southern Patagonia Souvenirs & Books
13 Transportes Polo Sur
14 Solovidrios
15 Sala Estrella
16 Turismo Aonikenk
17 Austro Internet
18 Arka Patagonia
20 Canadian Institute
22 Chile Típico
24 Brazilian Consulate
25 Buses Punta Arenas
28 Buses Fernández, Buses Pingüino, Turibús, Queilén
32 Kiosko de Informaciones
34 Bus Sur
35 Operatur Patagónica
36 Buses Pacheco, Australmag Rent A Car
37 Turismo Cordillera Darwin
38 Turismo Comapa, Magallanes Tour
45 Spanish Consulate
46 Gabriela Mistral Mural
48 Milward's Stone Castle
49 Austral Bus
50 CONAF
51 Mirador La Cruz
52 Turismo Viento Sur
55 CTC
57 Teatro Cervantes
58 Belgian Consulate
59 Tercera Zona Naval
60 Turismo Pali Aike
62 Chilexpress
63 Ladeco
64 Olijoe Pub
67 Navimag, Norwegian Consulate
68 Pingüi Tour (Casa de Cambio)
72 Post Office
73 Lubag Rent A Car
74 Redbanc (ATM)
76 Club de la Unión
77 Citibank
78 Casa Braun-Menéndez
79 Turismo Pehoé
80 Aerovías DAP
81 Museo Militar de la Quinta División del Ejército
82 Entel
84 LanChile
85 Buses Ghisoni, Tecni-Austral
86 Buses Transfer
87 Budget Rent A Car
89 Automóvil Club de Chile
90 Lavasol
91 Hertz
92 Sernatur
93 Catedral
95 Disco Splash
96 Museo Naval y Marítimo
99 British Consulate, Avant
101 Emsa/Avis

was a truly major industry, and the economy did not take off until the last quarter of the 19th century, after the territorial governor authorized the purchase of 300 purebred sheep from the Falkland Islands. This successful experiment encouraged others to invest in sheep and, by the turn of the century, nearly 2 million animals grazed in the territory.

In 1875, Magallanes' population was barely 1000, but European immigration accelerated as the wool market boomed. Among the most notable immigrants were Portuguese businessman José Nogueira; Irish doctor Thomas Fenton, who founded one of the island's largest sheep stations; and José Menéndez, an Asturian entrepreneur who would become one of the wealthiest and most influential individuals not just in Patagonia, but in all of South America.

First engaged solely in commerce, Menéndez soon began to acquire pastoral property, founding the famous Sociedad Explotadora de Tierra del Fuego, which controlled nearly a million hectares in Magallanes alone and other properties across the border – one of

Argentina's greatest estancias, near Río Grande, bears the name of his wife María Behety. Together with another important family, the Brauns, the descendents of Menéndez figured among the wealthiest and most powerful regional elites in Latin America. Although few remain in Punta Arenas (having relocated to Santiago and Buenos Aires), their downtown mansions remain symbols of Punta Arenas' golden age.

Menéndez and his colleagues could not have built their commercial and pastoral empires without the labor of immigrants from many lands: English, Irish, Scots, Croats, French, Germans, Spaniards, Italians, and others. On all sides of José Menéndez' opulent mausoleum, modest tombstones in the municipal cemetery reveal the origins of those whose efforts made his and other wool fortunes possible. Since the expropriation of the great estancias, including those of the Sociedad Explotadora, in the 1960s, land tenure is more equitable, but energy has eclipsed wool in the regional economy.

Orientation

Punta Arenas sits on a narrow shelf between the Andes to the west and the Strait of Magellan to the east. Consequently, the city has spread north and south from its original center between the port and the Plaza de Armas, properly known as Plaza Muñoz Gamero. Street names change on either side of the plaza, but street addresses fronting on the plaza bear the name Muñoz Gamero. Most landmarks and accommodations are within a few blocks of here. Mirador La Cruz, at Fagnano and Señoret, four blocks west of the plaza, provides a good view of town and the strait.

Most city streets are one-way, though grassy medians divide Av Bulnes and a few other major thoroughfares. There are two main routes out of town: Av Costanera leads south to Fuerte Bulnes, and Av Bulnes heads north past the airport to become Ruta 9 to Puerto Natales, which branches off to Ruta 255 to Río Gallegos, Argentina. Travelers coming from Argentina will find Chilean traffic much less hazardous.

Information

Tourist Offices Sernatur (☎ 225385), the Chilean state tourist agency, is at Waldo Seguel 689, just off Plaza Muñoz Gamero. It's open weekdays 8:30 am to 5:45 pm, but has extended January and February hours: 8:30 am to 8 pm weekdays, 11 am to 7 pm Saturday, and 11 am to 3 pm Sunday. It has a friendly, helpful, and well-informed staff with English speakers, publishes an annually updated list of accommodations and transport, and provides a message board for foreign visitors.

The municipal Kiosko de Informaciones (☎ 223798), in the 700 block of Av Colón between Bories and Magallanes, is open weekdays 9 am to 7 pm all year, and Saturday 9 am to 7 pm in summer.

The Automóvil Club de Chile (Acchi; ☎ 243675), O'Higgins 931, is the equivalent of Argentina's ACA and honors other countries' auto club memberships.

Foreign Consulates The Argentine Consulate (☎ 261912), 21 de Mayo 1878, is open weekdays 10 am to 3 pm.

Several European and other South American countries have consulates in Punta Arenas, including:

Belgium
(☎ 241472)
Roca 817, Oficina 61

Brazil
(☎ 241093)
Arauco 769

Italy
(☎ 221596)
21 de Mayo 1569

Netherlands
(☎ 248100)
Sarmiento 780

Norway
(☎ 241437)
Av Independencia 830, 2nd floor

Spain
(☎ 243566)
José Menéndez 910

UK
(☎ 244727)
Roca 924

Money Money changing is easiest at cambios and travel agencies along Lautaro Navarro, which are open weekdays and Saturday mornings, but not on Sunday. Traveler's checks are easier to negotiate than in Argentina, but many hotels and restaurants also accept US dollars at a fair rate of exchange. Bus Sur, at Magallanes and Colón, cashes traveler's checks for Saturday afternoon arrivals.

Redbanc has an ATM at Bories 970, half a block north of the plaza, but there are several others in the area.

Post & Communications Correos de Chile, the central post office, is at Bories 911, one block north of Plaza Muñoz Gamero.

Long-distance telephone service is better and cheaper than in Argentina. CTC is at Nogueira 1116, on Plaza Muñoz Gamero, Chilexpress at Errázuriz 856, Entel at Lautaro Navarro 931. Chile's country code is ☎ 56, and Punta Arenas' area code is ☎ 61.

For Internet access, try Austro Internet, Bories 687, Oficina 3, the Canadian Institute (☎ 227943), O'Higgins 694, or Albergue Backpacker's Paradise hostel, at Ignacio Carrera Pinto 1022.

National Parks The Corporación Nacional Forestal (CONAF; ☎ 223841) is at José Menéndez 1147.

Travel Agencies In addition to the agencies listed under Organized Tours, try also Turismo Pehoé (☎ 241373), at José Menéndez 918, or Turismo Cordillera Darwin (☎/fax 224637), José Menéndez 386, which arranges trips to remote parts of Tierra del Fuego.

Photography A good, conscientious place for film developing, including slides, is Todocolor, Chiloé 1422 between Av Independencia and Boliviana.

Bookstores Southern Patagonia Souvenirs & Books, Bories 404, has a good selection printed material and maps, including some in English.

Laundry Lavasol (☎ 243607), O'Higgins 969, isn't as cheap as it used to be, but is still fast and efficient.

Medical Services The Hospital Regional (☎ 244040) is at Arauco and Angamos.

Walking Tour

Punta Arenas' compact downtown rewards walkers. The logical starting place is the lovingly maintained **Plaza Muñoz Gamero**, landscaped with a variety of exotic conifers and a Victorian kiosk (1910) that sometimes contains handicraft displays. In the plaza's center, donated by wool baron José Menéndez in 1920, is a monument to the 400th anniversary of Magellan's voyage; Magellan stands on a pedestal, flanked on a lower level by a Selknam Indian symbolizing Tierra del Fuego and a Tehuelche symbolizing Patagonia. Behind the Portuguese navigator are a globe and a copy of his log; beneath him is a mermaid with Chilean and regional coats of arms.

Around the plaza are the **Club de la Unión** (once the Sara Braun mansion, built by a French architect and currently a hotel/restaurant), the **Catedral** and other monuments to the city's turn-of-the-century splendor. At the northeast corner of the plaza, the present Citibank was the headquarters of the powerful Sociedad Menéndez Behety.

Half a block north, at Magallanes 949, is the spectacular **Casa Braun-Menéndez**, the famous family's mansion which is now a cultural center and regional history museum. Three blocks west of the plaza, the outlandish **stone castle** at Av España 959 belonged to Charly Milward, whose equally eccentric exploits inspired his distant relation Bruce Chatwin to write the extraordinary travelogue *In Patagonia*.

Four blocks south of the plaza, at the foot of Av Independencia, is the entrance to the **puerto** (port), which is open to the public. At the end of the pier, you may see ships and sailors from the Chilean navy, as well as from Spain, Poland, Japan, France, the USA, and many other countries, not to mention local fishing boats and countless seabirds. At the corner of Colón and O'Higgins, four blocks northeast of the plaza, is a very fine **mural** of Nobel Prize-winning poet Gabriela Mistral.

Six blocks north of the plaza, at Bories and Sarmiento, is the **Museo Salesiano** (Salesian Museum). Another four blocks north is the entrance to the **Cementerio Municipal** (Municipal Cemetery), an open-air historical museum in its own right.

Casa Braun-Menéndez

Also known as the Palacio Mauricio Braun, this opulent mansion testifies to the wealth and power of pioneer sheep farmers in the late 19th century. The last remaining daughter of the marriage between Mauricio Braun (brother of Sara Braun) and Josefina Menéndez Behety (daughter of José Menéndez and María Behety) died some years ago in Buenos Aires, but the family has donated the house to the state. Much of it, including original furnishings, remains as it did when still occupied by the family. At present, only the main floor is open to the public, but restoration may permit access to the upper floors.

The museum (☎ 244216) also has excellent historical photographs and artifacts of early European settlement. The admission fee is modest (US$2), but there's an extra charge for photographing the interior. Hours are Tuesday to Sunday 11 am to 2 pm in summer, 11 am to 1 pm the rest of the year. Access to the grounds is easiest from Magallanes, but the museum entrance is at the back of the house.

Museo Regional Salesiano Mayorino Borgatello

Especially influential in European settlement of the region, the Salesian order collected outstanding ethnographic artifacts, but their museum takes a self-serving view of the Christian intervention, portraying missionaries as peacemakers between Indians and settlers. The rotting natural history specimens are nothing to speak of, however; the best materials are on the mountaineer priest Alberto de Agostini and the various indigenous groups. A real surprise is the cross salvaged from the grave of Pringle Stokes, an officer who died on the *Beagle* in 1828; the rotting cross was replaced by another on site.

Hours at the museum (☎ 241096), Av Bulnes 374, are 9 am to noon and 3 to 6 pm daily except Monday. Admission is US$2.

Museo Naval y Marítimo

Despite its overbearing military music and romantic view of Chile's presence in the southern oceans, Punta Arenas' naval and maritime museum has varied exhibits on model ships, naval history (including the obligatory homage to patriotic icon Arturo Prat), the unprecedented visit of 27 US warships to Punta Arenas in 1908, material on southern Patagonia's Canoe Indians, and a very fine account of the Chilean mission that rescued British explorer Sir Ernest Shackleton's crew from Antarctica. The most imaginative display is a ship's replica, complete with bridge, maps, charts, and radio room, that really gives the sense of being on board a naval vessel.

At Pedro Montt 981, the museum (☎ 205558) is open Tuesday through Saturday 9:30 am to 12:30 pm and 3 to 6 pm. Admission is US$0.75.

Museo Militar de la Quinta División del Ejército

The army museum (☎ 244619), José Menéndez 961, is open daily except Monday 9 am to 5 pm. Admission is free.

Cementerio Municipal

In death as in life, Punta Arenas' first families flaunted their wealth – wool baron José

SANDRA BAO

Punta Arenas' Cementerio Municipal

Menéndez's extravagant tomb is, according to Bruce Chatwin, a scale replica of Rome's Vittorio Emanuele monument. But the headstones among the topiary cypresses in the walled municipal cemetery, at Av Bulnes 949, also tell the stories of Anglo, German, Scandinavian, and Yugoslav immigrants who supported the wealthy families with their labor. There is also a monument to the now nearly extinct Onas.

Open daily, the cemetery is about a 15-minute walk from Plaza Muñoz Gamero, but you can also take any taxi colectivo from the entrance of the Casa Braun-Menéndez on Magallanes.

Instituto de la Patagonia

Part of the Universidad de Magallanes, the Patagonian Institute's **Museo del Recuerdo** features an collection of antique farm and industrial machinery imported from Europe, a typical pioneer house and shearing shed (both reconstructed), and a wooden-wheeled trailer that served as shelter for shepherds. Visitors can wander among the outdoor exhibits at will, but ask the caretaker at the library for admission to the buildings.

The library also has a display of historical maps and a series of historical and scientific publications for sale to the public. A rather overgrown botanical garden, a small zoo, and experimental garden plots and greenhouses are also open to the public.

Admission to the museum (☎ 207196) is US$1. Hours are weekdays 8:30 am to 12:30 pm and 2:30 to 6 pm, Saturday 8:30 am to 12:30 pm only. Any taxi colectivo to the *zona franca* (duty-free zone) will drop you across the street.

Organized Tours

Several agencies run trips to the important tourist sites near Punta Arenas, as well as to more distant destinations such as Torres del Paine.

Turismo Pali Aike (☎/fax 223301), Lautaro Navarro 1129, goes to Cerro Mirador in the Reserva Forestal de Magallanes (US$5 return) west of town at 10:30 am and 2:30 pm Tuesday to Sunday, to the Seno Otway penguin colony (US$10 to US$12) daily at 4 pm, to Fuerte Bulnes (US$12) daily at 10 am, and to Río Verde (US$15). All tours include sandwiches and soft drinks. Other agencies running similar trips include Arka Patagonia (☎ 248167), at Ignacio Carrera Pinto 946; Turismo Aonikenk (☎ 228332), at Magallanes 619; Turismo Viento Sur (☎ 225167), at Fagnano 565; and Operatur Patagónica (☎ 240513), at Av Colón 822. Most of these companies can now do both the Otway and Fuerte Bulnes trips in the same day.

A better though more expensive alternative is Turismo Comapa's (☎ 241437, tcomapa@entelchile.net), Av Independencia 830, 2nd floor, trip to the Isla Magdalena penguin colony. They run Tuesday, Thursday, and Saturday from December to February and cost US$30. Total time on the island is less than two hours, and the crossing takes two hours each way.

Boat Cruises From September through April, Turismo Comapa (☎ 241437, fax 224526), Av Independencia 830, runs weeklong luxury cruises on the 100-passenger *Terra Australis* from Punta Arenas through the Cordillera de Darwin, the Beagle Channel, and Puerto Williams, Ushuaia (Argentina) and back. While these cruises are expensive, starting at US$1047 per person double occupancy in low season (September to October and April) and reaching $3132 for a high-season single (mid-December through February), all meals are included and they do offer a chance to visit parts of the region that are otherwise very difficult and even more expensive to reach independently. It is possible to do the leg between Punta Arenas and Ushuaia, or vice-versa, separately.

Special Events

At the end of March, the Carnaval de Invierno welcomes the winter with two days of parades and floats, also celebrating the city's anniversary.

Places to Stay – Budget

Prices for accommodations have risen recently, but there are still good values.

Sernatur maintains a very complete list of accommodations and prices. Note that at some hotels, guests paying in US dollars may be exempt from IVA.

Hostels Open November through March, the ***Albergue Backpacker's Paradise*** *(☎ 222554, Ignacio Carrera Pinto 1022)* charges US$6 for dark, crowded dormitory accommodations, but it has pleasant common rooms, a kitchen, Internet access, and cable TV.

The lively Pucón cooperative ¡Ecole! has recently opened the ***¡Ecole! Patagonia*** *(☎ 221764, O'Higgins 424)*, where singles cost US$14 with breakfast. It also plans to be a clearinghouse for environmental information in southern Chile and Argentina.

Six blocks south of Plaza Muñoz Gamero), ***Colegio Pierre Fauré*** *(☎ 226256, At Bellavista 697)* is a private school that operates as a hostel in January and February. Singles cost US$7 with breakfast, US$6 without, but campers can also pitch a tent in the side garden for US$4 per person. All bathrooms are shared, but there's plenty of hot water, and it's a good place to hook up with other travelers.

HI-affliated ***Hostal Sonia*** *(☎ 248543, Pasaje Darwin 175)*, north of downtown, charges US$10 with hostel card.

Hospedajes, Residenciales, Hostales & Hotels Sernatur has reclassified most of the city's hospedajes and residenciales as hostales, but this is pretty much a semantic issue. Popular ***Hostal Dinka's House*** *(☎ 226056, fax 244292, Caupolicán 169)*, on a quiet street, costs only US$7.50 with breakfast and shared bath, US$10 with private bath, but it's often full. Avoid their nearby annexes.

Homey ***Hospedaje Guisande*** *(☎ 243295, J M Carrera 1270)*, near the cemetery, has earned exuberant recommendations for US$9 with breakfast. ***Hospedaje Manuel*** *(☎ 220567, O'Higgins 648)* has similar accommodations for US$9/15 and also organizes tours. In the port zone south of downtown are ***Hospedaje Carlina*** *(☎ 247687, Paraguaya 150)* and ***Hospedaje Nena*** *(☎ 242411, Boliviana 366)* both charge about US$9 per person with breakfast.

At recommended ***Hostal O'Higgins*** *(☎ 227999, O'Higgins 1205)*, near the port, rates are US$12 per person. Perennial favorite ***Residencial Roca*** *(☎ 243903, Magallanes 888, 2nd floor)* has moved to new quarters and has singles/doubles for US$12/22 with breakfast and shared bath.

Other modest and modestly priced alternatives include ***Residencial Oasis*** *(☎ 223240, Fagnano 583)* for about US$13, and friendly ***Residencial Coirón*** *(☎ 226449, Sanhueza 730)*, across from the Fernández bus terminal, which has spacious, sunny singles for US$13 with breakfast. ***Hostal Rubio*** *(☎ 226458, Avenida España 640)* is good value at US$15/21 single/double with shared bath, US$25/40 with private bath, both with breakfast.

Recommended ***Hostal Calafate II*** *(☎ 241281, José Menéndez 1035)* charges US$16/30 with shared bath, while ***Hostal Oasis*** *(☎ 226849, José Menéndez 485)* is slightly dearer at US$17/30. ***Hostal Parediso*** *(☎/fax 224212, Angamos 1073)* is excellent value for US$18/20 with shared bath, US$25/30 with private bath. In addition to hostel accommodations, ***Hostal Sonia*** *(☎ 248543, Pasaje Darwin 175)* has regular rooms for US$22/40.

Rehabbed ***Hotel Montecarlo*** *(☎ 223438, Avenida Colón 605)* charges US$21/35 with shared bath, US$38/52 with private bath. Recommended ***Hostal Calafate*** *(☎ 248415, Lautaro Navarro 850)* charges US$25/38 with a substantial breakfast.

Places to Stay – Mid-Range

Mid-range accommodations are relatively scarce compared with budget and top-end places. ***Hostal de la Patagonia*** *(☎/fax 249970, Croacia 970)* costs US$30/44 with private bath, but has some doubles with shared bath for US$30. ***Hostal Carpa Manzano*** *(☎ 242296, fax 248864, Lautaro Navarro 336)* is also worth a try for US$36/44, as is ***Hostal de la Avenida*** *(☎/fax 247532, Colón 534)* for US$44/50.

Comfortably modern ***Hotel Cóndor de Plata*** *(☎ 247987, fax 241149, Avenida Colón*

556) costs US$48/60 – a better value than others charging considerably more. ***Hotel Mercurio*** *(☎ 223430, Fagnano 595)* is also modern, clean, and comfortable and charges US$49/63 with breakfast. Convenient ***Hotel Plaza*** *(☎ 241300, fax 248613, Nogueira 1116)* charges US$57/68.

Places to Stay – Top End

Once the best in town, the declining but still passable ***Hotel Los Navegantes*** *(☎ 244677, fax 247545, José Menéndez 647)* has rooms for US$96/120. The new ***Hotel Tierra del Fuego*** *(☎/fax 226200, Av Colón 716)* charges US$98/109 plus IVA. Another newish top-end choice is ***Hotel Isla Rey Jorge*** *(☎/fax 222681, 21 de Mayo 1243)*, for US$105/130.

On the east side of Plaza Muñoz Gamero, refurbished ***Hotel Cabo de Hornos*** *(☎ /fax 442134)*, charges US$130/154. It has a good but costly bar, and its solarium displays a number of stuffed birds, including macaroni and rockhopper penguins, which visitors to local penguin colonies are unlikely to see. ***Hotel Finis Terrae*** *(☎ 228200, fax 248124, Av Colón 766)* costs US$127/144.

Part of the Sara Braun mansion has become ***Hotel José Nogueira*** *(☎ 248840, fax 248832, Bories 959)*, half a block from Plaza Muñoz Gamero. Rooms cost US$151/180 plus IVA, but selective backpackers can still enjoy a drink or a meal in its conservatory/restaurant, beneath what may be the world's most southerly grape arbor.

Places to Eat

222 *(☎ 224704, Mejicana 654)* offers good pizza and sandwiches. ***Quijote*** *(Lautaro Navarro 1087)* also has reasonable lunches. ***La Carioca*** *(☎ 224809, José Menéndez 600)* has good sandwiches and lager beer, although its pizzas are, like most Chilean pizzas, smaller and more expensive than those in Argentina. ***Rotisería La Mamá*** *(☎ 225812, Sanhueza 720)*, across from the Fernández bus terminal, is a small family-run place with excellent, moderately priced lunches.

A good choice for breakfast, *onces* (afternoon tea), and people-watching is ***Café Calipso*** *(☎ 241782, Bories 817)*. Their 'selva negra' chocolate cake is a portion large enough for two, as are their sandwiches. ***Lomit's*** *(☎ 243399, José Menéndez 722)* also serves excellent sandwiches.

A local institution, ***El Mercado*** *(☎ 248420, Mejicana 617)*, an upstairs restaurant with an inconspicious ground-level entrance, prepares a spicy ostiones al pil pil and a delicate but filling *chupe de locos*; prices are generally moderate. It's also open 24 hours, but adds a 10% surcharge between 1 and 8 am.

The ***Centro Español*** *(☎ 242807)*, above the Teatro Cervantes on the south side of Plaza Muñoz Gamero, serves delicious *cóngrio* and ostiones among other specialties. ***Golden Dragón*** *(☎ 241119, Colón 529)*, a Chinese restaurant, is also very good.

Highly regarded ***Sotito's Bar*** *(☎ 245365, O'Higgins 1138)* serves outstanding if pricey dishes like *centolla*, but also has more reasonably priced items. The same holds for nearby ***El Beagle*** *(☎ 243057, O'Higgins 1077)*. Prices are moderate at ***La Taberna de Silver*** *(☎ 225533, O'Higgins 1037)*, though its fish is often deep fried. Another recommendation is ***El Mesón del Calvo*** *(☎ 225015, Jorge Montt 687)*, specializing in

Food from the Sea

If a constant diet of Argentine beef has become tiresome, visitors to Chilean Patagonia can feast on the superb and varied seafood that typifies Chilean cuisine – both finfish and shellfish. Popular regional dishes include *centolla* (king crab), *cholgas* (mussels), *congrio* (conger eel), *locos* (abalone, whose availability may be limited because of overexploitation), *ostiones* (scallops), and *erizos* (sea urchins, definitely an acquired taste). Travelers with a group should consider *curanto*, a tasty, filling stew with shellfish, chicken, mutton, potatoes, and vegetables. The traditional Chilean salad, consisting of tomatoes and onions, is simple but tasty.

lamb, but the food sometimes lags behind the atmosphere.

Asturias *(☎ 243763, Lautaro Navarro 967)* is worth a try at the upper end of the scale, as is ***El Infante*** *(☎ 241331, Magallanes 875)*.

Entertainment

Chilean nightlife is more exuberant than under the late military dictatorship, but no one will mistake Punta Arenas for Buenos Aires. ***Café Calipso*** (see Places to Eat) has a lively crowd late into the evening, and sometimes has live entertainment. Try ***Disco Splash*** *(☎ 223667, Pedro Montt 951)* and the ***Olijoe Pub***, at Errázuriz and O'Higgins.

Two central cinemas often show North American and European films: ***Teatro Cervantes*** *(☎ 223225)*, on the south side of Plaza Muñoz Gamero, and the ***Sala Estrella*** *(☎ 241262, Mejicana 777)*.

On the outskirts of downtown, on Avenida Bulnes, are the ***Club Hípico*** (municipal racetrack) and the ***Estadio Fiscal*** (stadium), where the local entry in the Chilean soccer league plays.

Shopping

Punta Arenas' *zona franca* (duty-free zone) is a good place to replace a lost or stolen camera and to buy film and other luxury items. Fujichrome slide film, 36 exposures, costs about US$5 per roll without developing, but it is increasingly difficult to find; print film is correspondingly cheap. Taxi colectivos run frequently from downtown to the Zona Franca, which is open daily except Sunday.

Chile Típico (☎ 225827), Ignacio Carrera Pinto 1015, offers artisanal items in copper, bronze, lapis lazuli, and other materials. Tres Arroyos (☎ 241522), Bories 448, sells a variety of chocolates.

To replace a shattered windshield on a private car – not an unusual occurence on Patagonia roads – head to Solovidrios (☎ 224835), Mejicana 762. Prices here are a fraction of what they are in Argentina.

Getting There & Away

Sernatur distributes a useful brochure with information on all forms of transportation including those which go to or through Argentina and their schedules to and from Punta Arenas, Puerto Natales, and Tierra del Fuego. Note that discount airfares are available from the major airlines between Punta Arenas and mainland Chile but usually involve some restrictions.

Air From Punta Arenas, there are flights to domestic destinations, including Chilean Antarctic bases, and to Argentine Patagonia and the Falkland Islands. Note that at press time flight to the Falklands were suspended, due to pressure from the Chilean government in regard to the Pinochet situation.

LanChile (☎ 241232), Lautaro Navarro 999, flies twice daily to Santiago via Puerto Montt, and Saturday to the Falkland Islands (US$200 one way). Ladeco (☎ 244544, 21100), Lautaro Navarro 1155, flies twice daily to Santiago via Puerto Montt except Wednesday and Saturday, when the afternoon flight stops in Concepción.

Avant (☎ 227221), Roca 924, flies twice daily to Santiago via Puerto Montt; most flights also stop in either Temuco or in Concepción.

Aerovías DAP (☎ 223340, fax 221693), O'Higgins 891, flies to Porvenir (US$22) and back at least twice daily except Sunday. Tuesday, Thursday, and Saturday, it flies to and from Puerto Williams on Isla Navarino (US$66 one way). In summer, it also flies daily except for Sunday to Río Grande (US$79). DAP also flies monthly to Chile's Teniente Marsh air base in Antarctica (US$1000); the schedule permits one or two nights in Antarctica before returning to Punta Arenas.

Bus Punta Arenas has no central bus terminal. Each bus company has its own office from which its buses depart, although most of these are within a block or two of Av Colón.

There are direct buses to Puerto Natales, to the Argentine cities of Río Gallegos, Río Grande, and Ushuaia, and to mainland Chilean destinations via Argentina. It makes sense to purchase tickets at least a couple hours in advance.

Buses Fernández (☎ 242313), Armando Sanhueza 745, has seven buses daily except Sunday to Puerto Natales (US$7, three hours) and a reputation for excellent service. Bus Sur (☎ 244464), at Magallanes and Colón, has three buses daily to Natales, and Transfer Austral (☎ 229613), Pedro Montt 966, goes at 5 and 6:30 pm daily.

Austral Bus (☎ 241708), José Menéndez 565, has buses at 8:30 am and 2 and 6 pm to Puerto Natales, and also goes Tuesdays to Puerto Montt (US$97). Buses Ghisoni (☎ 222078), Lautaro Navarro 971, goes Wednesday and Saturday to Puerto Montt (US$70). Buses Punta Arenas (☎ 249868), at Ignacio Carrera Pinto 457 and Magallanes 775, goes to Puerto Montt (US$71) Wednesday and Saturday at 8:30 am.

Turibús (☎ 227970), Armando Sanhueza 745, goes Monday, Thursday, and Saturday to Puerto Montt (US$75), Castro (US$85), Concepción (US$95), and also Santiago (US$100). These trips take up to two days, but the comfortable buses make regular meal stops.

There are numerous services to Río Gallegos, Argentina (US$13 to US$18, five hours; the fare in the opposite direction exceeds US$20). The most frequent is Buses Pingüino (☎ 221812, 242313), Armando Sanhueza 745, daily at 12:45 pm. Buses Ghisoni goes Monday, Wednesday, Thursday, and Saturday at 11 am, and Magallanes Tour (☎ 221936), Colón 521, departs on Tuesday at 9 am.

Buses Pacheco (☎ 242174), Av Colón 900, goes Monday, Wednesday, and Friday at 7:15 am to Río Grande (US$27) in with connections to Ushuaia. Tecni-Austral (☎ 223205), Lautaro Navarro 971, goes direct to Río Grande (US$30) and Ushuaia (US$51) Tuesday, Thursday, and Saturday at 7 am.

Boat Transbordador Austral Broom (☎ 218100, fax 212126), Av Bulnes 05075, ferries passengers (US$7) and automobiles (US$45) between Punta Arenas and Porvenir in 2½ hours; the *Melinka* sails Tuesday, Wednesday, and Friday at 9 am; Thursday and Saturday at 8 am; and Sunday at 9:30 am from the terminal at Tres Puentes, readily accessible by taxi colectivo from the Braun-Menéndez house. The return from Porvenir is normally at 2 pm; on Sundays and holidays, when the ferry returns at 5 pm, it's possible to do this as a day trip.

Broom is also the agent for the ferry *Patagonia*, which sails twice monthly to Puerto Williams on Isla Navarino. Seats on the 38-hour trip cost US$50 including meals; bunks cost US$80.

Navimag (☎ 224256, fax 225804), which offers ferry service from Puerto Natales to Puerto Montt via the spectacular Chilean fjords, has an office at Avenida Independencia 830. For schedules and fares, see the Puerto Natales entry.

Getting Around

To/From the Airport Aeropuerto Presidente Carlos Ibáñez del Campo is 20km north of town. Austral Bus runs airport minibuses from Hotel Cabo de Hornos, on Plaza Muñoz Gamero. DAP runs its own airport bus, while LanChile and Ladeco use local bus companies.

Transportes Polo Sur (☎ 243173), Chiloé 873, offers airport transfers for US$5, as does Buses Transfer (☎ 220766), Pedro Montt 966.

Bus & Colectivo Although most points of interest are within easy walking distance of downtown, public transportation is excellent to outlying sights, such as the Instituto de la Patagonia and the zona franca. Taxi colectivos, with numbered routes, are only slightly more expensive than buses (about US$0.40, a bit more late at night and on Sundays), much more comfortable, and much quicker.

Car Punta Arenas' numerous rental agencies include Hertz (☎ 248742), at O'Higgins 987; Emsa/Avis (☎ 222810, fax 226863), at Roca 1022; Budget (☎ 241696), at O'Higgins 964; the Automóvil Club de Chile (☎ 243675, fax 243097), at O'Higgins 931; Internacional (☎ 228323, fax 248865), at Sarmiento 790B; Australmag (☎ 242174, fax 226916), at Av Colón 900; and Lubag (☎ 242023, fax 214136), at Magallanes 970.

AROUND PUNTA ARENAS

Penguin Colonies

Also known as the jackass penguin for its characteristic braying sound, the Magellanic penguin *Spheniscus magellanicus* comes ashore in spring to breed and lay its eggs in sandy burrows or under shrubs a short distance inland. There are two substantial colonies near Punta Arenas: easier to reach is the mainland pingüinera at **Seno Otway** (Otway Sound), about an hour northwest of the city, while the larger (50,000 breeding pairs) and more interesting **Monumento Natural Los Pingüinos** is accessible only by boat to Isla Magdalena in the Strait of Magellan. Several cormorant and gull species are also common, along with rheas and southern sea lions.

Magellanic penguins are naturally curious and tame, though if approached too quickly they scamper into their burrows or toboggan awkwardly across the sand back into the water. If approached too closely, they will bite, and their bills can open a cut large enough to require stitches – never stick your hand or face into a burrow. The least disruptive way to observe or photograph them is to seat yourself near among the burrows and wait for their curiosity to get the better of them. At Otway, the grounds are fenced to prevent visitors from too close an encounter; a morning tour would be better for photography because the birds are mostly backlighted in the afternoon.

Penguins are usually present from October to April, but the peak season is December through February. Visitors who have seen the larger penguin colonies in Argentina or the Falkland Islands may find Punta Arenas-based tours less worthwhile than those who have not seen penguins elsewhere.

Since there is no scheduled public transport to either site, it's necessary to rent a car or take a tour to visit them. For details, see Organized Tours in Punta Arenas. Admission to the sites costs US$4 per person. There's a small snack bar at the Otway site.

Puerto Hambre & Fuerte Bulnes

Founded in 1584 by an overly confident Pedro Sarmiento de Gamboa, 'Ciudad del Rey don Felipe' was one of Spain's most inauspicious (and short-lived) American outposts. Not until the mid-19th century was there a permanent European presence at suitably named Puerto Hambre ('Port Famine'), where a plaque commemorates the 125th anniversary of the arrival of the Pacific Steam Navigation Company's ships *Chile* and *Peru* in 1965.

Named for the Chilean president who ordered occupation of the territory in 1843, the once remote outpost of Fuerte Bulnes is 55km south of Punta Arenas. Only a few years after its founding, it was abandoned because of its exposed site, lack of potable water, poor, rocky soil, and inferior pasture.

A good gravel road runs from Punta Arenas to the restored wooden fort, where a fence of sharpened stakes surrounds the blockhouse, barracks, and chapel, but there is no interpretive material whatsoever. Nor is there any scheduled public transport, but several travel agencies make half-day excursions to Fuerte Bulnes and Puerto Hambre, now a quiet fishing village where visitors can see the ruins of an early church; for details, see the Organized Tours entry for Punta Arenas. There are good picnic sites and pleasant trails along the coast.

Río Verde

About 50km north of Punta Arenas, a graveled lateral leads northwest toward Seno Skyring (Skyring Sound), passing this former estancia before rejoining Ruta 9 at Villa Tehuelches. Visitors with a car should consider this interesting detour to one of the best-maintained assemblages of Magellanic architecture in the region, including the impressive **Escuela Básica**, a boarding school for the surrounding area, and the shearing shed of Estancia La Mirna. The school's **Museo de Fauna** charges US$0.50 admission. Note the town's topiary cypresses.

Six km south of Río Verde proper, 90km from Punta Arenas, ***Hostería Río Verde*** *(☎ 311122)* is well-known for large portions of lamb, pork, or seafood at its Sunday lunches, for about US$10. Despite the rustic exterior, it also offers comfortable accommodations for US$30 with private bath.

Río Rubens

Roughly midway between Villa Tehuelches and Puerto Natales on Ruta 9, Río Rubens is a fine trout-fishing area and a ideal spot to break the journey from Punta Arenas, at least for travelers with their own transport. The cozy, comfy ***Hotel Río Rubens*** is the closest thing to an old country-style inn in the region, and at US$14 per person with breakfast and private bath, it's a bargain. The restaurant serves outstanding meals, including lamb and seafood.

Estancia San Gregorio

Some 125km northeast of Punta Arenas, straddling Ruta 255 to Río Gallegos (Argentina), this once enormous (90,000 hectares) estancia is now a cooperative. Since the abandonment of most of the main buildings (employee residences, warehouses, chapel, and *pulpería*, or general store), it has the aspect of an enormous ghost town. The casco still belongs to Alfonso Campos, a lawyer descendent of the influential Menéndez family, but the cooperative uses the large shearing shed. Also worth a look are the rusting shipwrecks on the beach.

The nearest accommodation is ***Hostería Tehuelche*** (*☎ 221270*), 29km northeast, where buses to and from Río Gallegos stop for lunch or dinner; this is also the junction for the road to the ferry that crosses the Strait of Magellan from Punta Delgada to Chilean Tierra del Fuego. Until 1968, the hostería was the casco for Estancia Kimiri Aike, pioneered by the Woods, a British immigrant family. It has clean, comfortable rooms for US$32/41 single/double, and a good restaurant and bar. Hotel staff will change US dollars at fair rates, but Argentine currency is better changed before leaving Río Gallegos.

Parque Nacional Pali Aike

Along the Argentine border, west of the Monte Aymond border crossing to Río Gallegos, this 5030-hectare park is an area of volcanic steppe where, in the 1930s, Junius Bird's excavations at **Pali Aike Cave** yielded the first Paleo-Indian artifacts associated

The Frozen South

One of the unanticipated, ironic dividends of the end of the Cold War has been the increasing accessibility of Antarctica at relatively reasonable prices. About 60% of Antarctic tourists leave from Ushuaia, where it's possible to arrange visits to the frozen continent with research vessels that once benefitted from subsidies but must now pay their own way. To do so, they have begun to take paying passengers on 10- to 21-day Antarctic cruises on well-equipped, remodeled vessels.

The season runs from November to March. Most cruises are expensive, but if space is available it's sometimes possible to get on for as little as US$2000 to US$2500 or even less. The Oficina Antarctica Infuetur (☎ 424431, fax 430694, antartida@tierradelfuego.ml.org), on Ushuaia's waterfront Muelle Comercial, serves as a clearing house for Antarctic tours; it's open 8 am to 5 pm weekdays, weekends only if there are boats. Try also local tourist agencies such as All Patagonia, Antartur, and Rumbo Sur.

Overseas operators arranging Antarctic tours include Mountain Travel Sobek (☎ 510-527-8100 or 800-227-2384), 6420 Fairmount Ave, El Cerrito, CA, USA 94530; Marin Expeditions (☎ 416-964-9069, fax 416-964-2366, 800-263-9147), 13 Hazelton Ave, Toronto, Ontario, Canada M5R 2E1; Nature Expeditions International (☎ 800-869-0639), PO Box 11496, 474 Willamette, Eugene, OR, USA 97440; and Natural Habitat Adventures (☎ 800-543-8917), 2945 Center Green Court S, Suite H, Boulder, CO, USA 80301-9539.

For more details on Antarctic travel, see Lonely Planet's *Antarctica*.

with extinct New World fauna like the milodon and the native horse *Onohippidium*. Bird, a self-taught archaeologist affiliated with the American Museum of Natural History, spent 2½ years here and also excavated **Fell's Cave**, just outside the park boundaries, where recent research has suggested that environmental change rather than hunting pressure was responsible for these extinctions.

The park has several hiking trails, including a 1700m path through the rugged lava beds of the **Escorial del Diablo** to the impressive **Crater Morada del Diablo**; wear sturdy shoes or your feet could be shredded. There is ample wildlife along the road, including guanaco, fox, bandurria, and rhea, but the real treat is the volcanic landscape. There's also a 9km trail from Cueva Pali Aike to **Laguna Ana**, where there's another shorter trail to a site on the main road, 5km from the park entrance.

Cueva Pali Aike itself measures 5m high and 7m wide at the entrance, while it is 17m deep. Bird's excavations in 1936-7 unearthed three cremated human skeletons plus milodon and native horse bones some 9000 years old.

Parque Nacional Pali Aike is 196km northeast of Punta Arenas via Ch 9, Ch 255, and a graveled secondary road from Cooop-erativa Villa O'Higgins, 11km north of Estancia Kimiri Aike. There's also an access road from the Chilean border post at Monte Aymond. There is no public transport, but Punta Arenas travel agencies can arrange tours.

There's a ranger at the main park entrance, but no regular accommodation nor food and water; ***camping*** is permitted but fires are not.

PUERTO NATALES

Black-necked swans paddle serenely around the gulls and cormorants that perch on the rotting jetties of scenic Puerto Natales, on the eastern shore of Seno Última Esperanza (Last Hope Sound). Traditionally dependent on wool, mutton, and fishing, this port of 18,000 people is the southern terminus for the scenic ferry from Puerto Montt and an essential stopover for hikers and other visitors en route to Parque Nacional Torres del Paine. It also offers the best access to Glaciar Serrano in Parque Nacional Bernardo O'Higgins and the famous Cueva del Milodón, and many travelers continue to Argentina's Parque Nacional Los Glaciares via the coal-mining town of Río Turbio.

The visitor season starts in October and runs until April, though the peak is January and February. During the rest of the year, access to attractions such as Torres del Paine and the Balmaceda Glacier may be much reduced.

History

The first Europeans to visit Última Esperanza were the 16th-century Spaniards Juan Ladrillero and Pedro Sarmiento de Gamboa, in search of a route to the Pacific, but their expeditions left no permanent legacy. In part because of Indian resistance, no Europeans located here until the late 19th century, when German explorer Hermann Eberhard established a sheep estancia near Puerto Prat, the area's initial settlement, later superseded by Puerto Natales.

The dominant economic enterprise was the slaughterhouse and meat packing plant at Bories, operated by the Sociedad Explotadora de Tierra del Fuego, which processed livestock from throughout southwestern Argentina as well. This factory still operates, though its importance has declined.

Orientation

About 250km northwest of Punta Arenas via Ruta 9, which should be completely paved by the time this book appears, Puerto Natales is compact enough that walking suffices for nearly all purposes.

Although its street grid is more irregular than many Chilean cities, most destinations are easily visible from the waterfront, where the Costanera Pedro Montt runs roughly east-west. The city's other main commercial streets are north-south Av Manuel and east-west Av Baquedano. Bories and the Cueva del Milodón are north of town on the graveled highway to Torres del Paine.

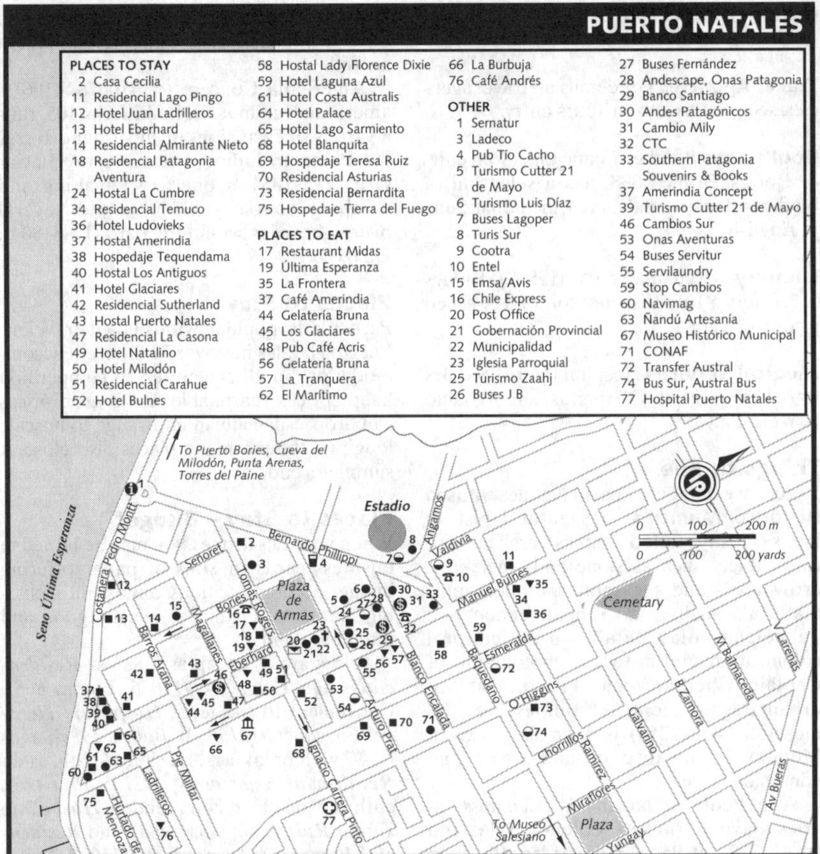

Information

Tourist Offices Sernatur (☎ 412125), which has maps and hotels, restaurant, and transport information, occupies a chalet on the Costanera Pedro Montt near the Philippi diagonal. Hours are 8:30 am to 1 pm and 2:30 to 6:30 pm weekdays all year, 9 am to 1 pm weekends in summer (December to March) only.

Money Several cambios change US dollars and checks: try Stop Cambios, Baquedano 380; Cambio Mily, Blanco Encalada 266; and Cambios Sur, Eberhard 285. Banco Santiago, Bulnes 598, has an ATM.

Post & Communications Correos de Chile is directly on the Plaza de Armas at Eberhard 429.

CTC, Blanco Encalada 169, operates long-distance telephone services 8 am to 10 pm daily, as does Chile Express, at Tomás Rogers 143. Entel is on Baquedano between Valdivia and Bulnes.

The area code is ☎ 61 (the same as Punta Arenas).

National Parks CONAF (☎ 411438) is at O'Higgins 584.

Travel Agencies For details on travel agencies, see the Organized Tours entry.

Bookstores Southern Patagonia Souvenirs & Books, Bulnes 688, has a selection of books and maps on the area, including some in English.

Laundry Servilaundry (☎ 412869), Bulnes 513, offers a 10% discount for loads washed prior to 10 am.

Medical Services Hospital Puerto Natales (☎ 411533) is at O'Higgins and Ignacio Carrera Pinto.

Things to See

Recently expanded, Puerto Natales' **Museo Histórico Municipal** has natural history items (mostly stuffed animals), archaeological artifacts, such as stone and whalebone arrowheads and spearpoints, ethnographic materials such as a Yahgan canoe and Tehuelche bolas, details on agricultural colonization, and historical photographs of Captain Eberhard and Puerto Natales' urban development. At Bulnes 285, the museum (☎ 411263) is open daily except Monday, 10 am to noon and 3 to 6 pm; admission is free.

As in Punta Arenas, the Salesian missionaries have a **Museo Colegio Salesiano** (☎ 411258), at Padre Rosas 1456. It's open 9 am to 1 pm and 3 to 6 pm daily except Monday; admission is free.

Organized Tours

Puerto Natales' many travel agencies offer visits to the main local attractions, including Bories, the Cueva del Milodón, and Torres del Paine. Among them are Andes Patagónicos (☎/fax 411594), Blanco Encalada 226, a good place to confirm airline reservations; Turismo Luis Díaz (☎ 411654, fax 411050), at Blanco Encalada 189, which also goes to Argentina's Parque Nacional Los Glaciares; and Onas Aventuras (☎ 412707), Bulnes 453, which also does sea kayaking and trekking trips. All these and other companies rent camping equipment as well.

Amerindia Concept (☎ 410678, 410679, amerindia@chilnet.cl), Ladrilleros 105, runs a variety of excursions in and around Torres del Paine, including a traverse of Glaciar Grey (US$85), a one-day kayaking and climbing course (US$100), and several overnights trips within the park (US$180 to US$280).

Places to Stay

Particularly popular with budget travelers, Puerto Natales has over 70 different accommodations in all categories, so competition keeps prices reasonable. Off-season prices can drop, especially in mid-range to upscale lodgings, though many places also close at summer's end.

Places to Stay – Budget

When your bus arrives, you may be buried in business cards or slips of paper offering budget accommodations, almost all including breakfast. Quality is usually good and often excellent.

Prices are as cheap as US$5 at ***Residencial Lago Pingo*** *(☎ 411026, Bulnes 808)*. Convenient to the ferry, ***Hospedaje Tierra del Fuego*** *(☎ 412138, Av Bulnes 23)* charges US$7 with breakfast and shared bath, as do ***Residencial Asturias*** *(☎ 412105, Prat 426)*, enthusiastically recommended ***Hospedaje Teresa Ruiz*** *(Esmeralda 483)*, and ***Residencial Patagonia Aventura*** *(☎ 411028, Tomás Rogers 179)*.

Charging US$9 per person, Swiss-Chilean ***Casa Cecilia*** *(☎ 411797, Tomás Rogers 64)* has become famous for delicious breakfasts with fresh bread and sweets, though some rooms are small. It also runs a cheaper nearby annex in summer. Comparably priced ***Hospedaje Tequendama*** *(☎ 412951, Ladrilleros 141)* is very obliging and serves a good breakfast, but rooms are basic and some very dark for US$9.

In the same range are recommended ***Residencial Almirante Nieto*** *(☎ 411218, Bories 206)*, attractive ***Residencial La Casona*** *(☎ 412562, Bulnes 280)*, ***Residencial Cara-***

hue *(☎ 411339, Bulnes 370)*, and ***Residencial Bernardita*** *(☎ 411162, O'Higgins 765)*. Just slightly more expensive, around US$10, are ***Residencial Temuco*** *(☎/fax 411120, Ramírez 310)* and friendly, Scots-Chilean ***Residencial Sutherland*** *(☎ 410359, Barros Arana 155)*.

Hostal Amerindia *(☎ 410678, Ladrilleros 105)* is becoming a traveler's hangout, partly due to the downstairs pub/café (which closes early enough, however, for a good night's sleep) and the climbing wall outside. Rates are US$12 in multibed rooms or US$30 double, but if it's not crowded they'll give you a single at the lower price.

More businesslike than friendly, well-kept ***Hostal Los Antiguos*** *(☎ 411885, Ladrilleros 195)* charges US$13 single. Comparably priced ***Residencial La Bahía*** *(☎ 411297, Serrano 434)*, three blocks south of Yungay, also has a superb restaurant.

Hostal Puerto Natales *(☎ 411098, Eberhard 250)* charges US$16/27 with private bath. ***Hostal La Cumbre*** *(☎ 412422, Eberhard 533)* costs US$17/29. ***Hotel Bulnes*** *(☎ 411307, Bulnes 407)* charges US$12 per person with shared bath, US$20/29 with private bath.

Places to Stay – Mid-Range

At recommended ***Hotel Natalino*** *(☎ 411968, Eberhard 371)* rooms with shared bath cost US$18/25, while those with private bath are US$22/32. ***Hotel Blanquita*** *(☎ 411674, Ignacio Carrera Pinto 409)* charges US$24/29 with private bath.

Hotel Laguna Azul *(☎ /fax 411207, Baquedano 380)* costs US$38/47, but there are several other good values: ***Hotel Lago Sarmiento*** *(☎ 411542, Bulnes 90)* for US$40/60, ***Hotel Milodón*** *(☎ 411727, Bulnes 356)* for US$42/60, and ***Hotel Ludovieks*** *(☎ 412580, Ramírez 324)* for US$45/68. At the upper end of range, set back off the street, the attractive ***Hostal Lady Florence Dixie*** *(☎ 411158, Bulnes 659)* charges US$57/75.

Places to Stay – Top End

Clearly showing its age, the well-worn ***Hotel Palace*** *(☎ /fax 411134, Ladrilleros 209)* costs US$67/76, while rates at the stylishly new ***Hotel Glaciares*** *(☎/fax 412189, Eberhard 104)* are US$77/89. Somewhere between the two in quality, but more expensive than both, ***Hotel Juan Ladrilleros*** *(☎ 411652, fax 412109, Pedro Montt 161)* goes for US$85/95.

For US$106/117, the waterfront ***Hotel Eberhard*** *(☎ 411208, fax 411209, Costanera Pedro Montt 25)* is overpriced despite an excellent dining room with panoramic harbor views. Also on the waterfront, at the corner of the Costanera Pedro Montt and Manuel Bulnes, rooms at the attractive ***Hotel Costa Australis*** *(☎ 412000, 411881)* start at US$146/165 with a town view, rising to US$185/204 with harbor view. Note that these prices do not include the 18% IVA, which foreign visitors are not charged if they pay with a credit card or in US dollars.

Places to Eat

For a small provincial town, Puerto Natales provides excellent dining, specializing in good and reasonably priced seafood. Open for lunch only, recommended ***La Frontera*** *(Bulnes 819)* has superb home-cooked meals for only US$4, but the service can be a bit haphazard.

Popular ***El Marítimo*** *(Costanera Pedro Montt 214)*, a moderately priced seafood choice, is still doing excellent business, but has become self-consciously touristy, particularly its overbearing troubadours.

Its walls covered with bric-a-brac worthy of some regional museums, popular ***La Tranquera*** *(☎ 411039, Bulnes 579)* has good food, friendly service, and reasonable prices. Another good and lively place is ***Restaurant Midas*** *(☎ 411045, Tomás Rogers 169)*, on the Plaza de Armas. Only a handful of foreigners patronize the excellent ***Última Esperanza*** *(☎ 411391, Eberhard 354)*, which has huge portions (salmon is a specialty), fine service, and is less costly than it looks.

Another good seafood choice is ***Café Andrés*** *(☎ 412380, Ladrilleros 381)*, whose hard-working cook-owner keeps long hours. Other possibilities include ***La Burbuja*** *(☎ 411159, Bulnes 291)* and ***Los Glaciares*** *(☎ 412007, Eberhard 261)*.

The dining room at unpretentious ***La Bahía** (☎ 411297, Serrano 434)* can accommodate large groups for a superb curanto, with sufficient notice. It's less central than most other restaurants in town, but still reasonable walking distance.

***Pub Café Acris** (☎ 412710, Eberhard 351)* serves excellent pizza, but the tobacco-laden atmosphere is a serious negative. Rhubarb-flavored ice cream is a local specialty at ***Gelatería Bruna** (☎ 411656, Bulnes 585, Eberhard 217)*.

Entertainment

In addition to good food, ***Pub Café Acris** (☎ 412710, Eberhard 351)* offers live music on weekends. Another pub worth visiting is ***Tío Cacho** (☎ 411021)*, Philippi 553. Downstairs, the nightly slide shows at ***Café Amerindia** (Ladrilleros 105)* are complemented by food and drinks and offer a good introduction to the Natales area.

Shopping

Ñandú Artesanía, at Manuel Bulnes 44, has a small but good selection of crafts, and also sells local maps and books.

Getting There & Away

Air Puerto Natales' small airfield, a few kilometers north of town on the road to Torres del Paine, has no regularly scheduled flights, though rumors persist of future commercial service.

The local Ladeco office (☎ 411236) is at Tomás Rogers 78. Andes Patagónicos has a computerized airline information service for reservations and information on other airlines, such as LanChile and DAP. Buses from Puerto Natales will drop passengers at Punta Arenas' Aeropuerto Presidente Carlos Ibáñez del Campo.

LADE, the Argentine air force passenger service, has flights to and from Río Turbio, just across the border.

Bus Puerto Natales has no central bus terminal, though several companies stop at the junction of Valdivia and Baquedano.

To Punta Arenas (US$7, three hours), Buses Fernández (☎ 411111), Eberhard 555, and Bus Sur (☎ 411325), Baquedano 534, provide eight buses Monday to Saturday, four on Sunday. Austral Bus (☎ 411859), also at Baquedano 534, goes to Punta Arenas daily at 8 am and 2 and 6 pm. Transfer Austral (☎ 412616), Baquedano 414, goes at Monday to Saturday 7:30 am and 1 pm daily except for Sunday, when the morning bus leaves at 8 am.

In summer, Bus Sur goes daily to Parque Nacional Torres del Paine (US$9 single, US$16 return), weekdays to Río Turbio (US$4), and Tuesday and Thursday at 6:30 am to Río Gallegos (US$19). El Pingüino, at the Fernández terminal, goes Wednesday and Sunday at 11 am to Río Gallegos (US$18). Other companies going to Paine include Servitur (☎ 411858), Prat 353, and Buses J B (☎ 412824), Prat 258.

Turismo Zaahj (☎ 412260), Prat 236, runs buses to El Calafate (5½ hours, US$23) in summer only, Tuesday, Thursday, and Saturday at 10 am, and does a long one-day tour to the Moreno glacier (US$70). These services are increasing since the improvement of RN 40 on the Argentine side, but the Moreno Glacier is a very long and tiring day trip. Bus Sur goes daily except Wednesday and Sunday to El Calafate at 9 am.

Buses Lagoper (☎ 411831), at Angamos 640, and Cootra (☎ 412785), at Baquedano 244, have frequent buses to Río Turbio (US$4), where it's possible to make connections to both Río Gallegos and Calafate. Bus Sur has two buses daily to Río Turbio, while Turis Sur, on Angamos near Valdivia, also goes there.

Car Emsa/Avis (☎/fax 412770), in Hotel Martín Gusinde at Bories 278, charges around US$80 per day.

Boat Navimag (☎ 411421, fax 411642), Costanera Pedro Montt 380, operates the car and passenger ferry *MV Puerto Edén* to Puerto Montt every seven to 10 days all year, though dates and times vary according to weather and tides. The four-day, three-night voyage is heavily booked in summer, so try to reserve as far ahead as possible. Thursday is the usual departure day from

Puerto Natales, Monday from Puerto Montt.

Accommodation in all categories is comfortable (though some have found the cheapest class cramped) and includes breakfast, lunch, and dinner, but incidentals like drinks and snacks are extra. There are many activities on board, but no laundry facilities. High season is November through February, while mid-season is September-October and March-April. Per person fares, which vary according to view and private or shared bath, are as follows:

	High Season	Mid-Season
Cabina Armador	US$551	US$515
AA	US$398	US$354
A	US$345	US$302
B	US$318	US$275
Económica	US$200	US$170

AROUND PUERTO NATALES

Puerto Bories

Built in 1913 with British capital, the Sociedad Explotadora's Puerto Bories **Frigorífico** (meat freezer), once processed enormous quantities of beef and mutton, and also shipped tallow, hides, and wool from estancias in Chile and Argentina for export to Europe. Its operations, 4km north of Puerto Natales, are now much reduced, but there remain several unique metal-clad buildings and houses, classic representatives of hybrid Victorian-Magellanic architecture.

Monumento Natural Cueva del Milodón

In the 1890s, Hermann Eberhard discovered the well-preserved remains of an enormous ground sloth in a cave at this national monument, 24km northwest of Puerto Natales. Twice the height of a human, the milodon was an herbivorous mammal that pulled down small trees and branches for their succulent leaves; like the mammoth and many other American megafauna, it became extinct near the end of the Pleistocene.

Bruce Chatwin's classic literary travelogue *In Patagonia* recounts the many fanciful stories that surround the milodon, including legends that Indians kept it penned as a domestic animal and that some specimens remained alive into the last century. Paleo-Indians existed simultaneously with the milodon, occupying the cave as a shelter, and possibly contributed to the animal's extinction through hunting. The best summary information on the milodon occurs in US archaeologist Junius Bird's *Travel and Archaeology in South Chile* (University of Iowa Press, 1988), edited by John Hyslop of the American Museum of Natural History.

A new **Museo de Sitio** at the cave is open 8 am to 8 pm daily. A tacky full-size replica of the animal stands in the cave, which is 30m high, 80m wide, and 200m deep. The cave itself formed at the base of a Cretaceous conglomeratic submarine channel fill of the Lago Sofia formation, overlying more easily eroded mudstones and sandstones of the Cerro Toro Formation, later uplifted from depths between 1000 and 2000m.

Although the closest hotel accommodation is at Puerto Natales, ***camping*** and picnicking are possible near the site. CONAF charges US$4 admission, less for Chilean nationals and children. Buses to Torres del Paine will drop you at the entrance, which is several kilometer walk from the cave proper. Alternatively, take a taxi or hitch from Puerto Natales.

Parque Nacional Bernardo O'Higgins

This otherwise inaccessible park is the final destination of a dramatic four-hour boat ride from Puerto Natales through Seno Ultima Esperanza, passing Glaciar Balmaceda (Balmaceda Glacier), to the jetty at Puerto Toro, where a footpath leads to the base of Glaciar Serrano (on a clear day, the Torres del Paine are visible in the distance to the north). En route, passengers glimpse the frigorífico at Bories, several small estancias whose only access to Puerto Natales is over water, numerous glaciers and waterfalls, a large cormorant rookery, a smaller sea lion rookery, and occasional Andean condors. The return trip takes the same route.

Daily in summer, weather permitting, Turismo Cutter 21 de Mayo, at Eberhard 554

(☎ 411978) and Ladrilleros 171 (☎ 411176) in Puerto Natales, runs its namesake cutter or the motor yacht *Alberto de Agostini* to the park, and will go at other times if demand is sufficient. At US$45 per person, the trip is approaching its maximum value, and any additional increases would make the trip marginal for most travelers, but it's possible continue upriver to Torres del Paine, a unique way to approach the park. Decent meals are available on board for about US$6, as are hot and cold drinks. For more information, contact Onas Patagonia (☎/fax 412707, onas@chileaustral.com), Eberhard 599, in Puerto Natales.

PARQUE NACIONAL TORRES DEL PAINE

Soaring almost vertically more than 2000m above the Patagonian steppe, the Torres del Paine (Towers of Paine) are spectacular granite pillars that dominate the landscape of what may be South America's finest national park, a miniature Alaska of shimmering turquoise lakes, roaring creeks, rivers and waterfalls, sprawling glaciers, dense forests and abundant wildlife. The issue is not whether to come here, but how much time to spend.

Before its creation in 1959, the park was part of a large sheep estancia, and it's still recovering from nearly a century of overexploitation of its pastures, forests, and wildlife. Part of the United Nations' Biosphere Reserve system since 1978, it shelters large and growing herds of guanacos, flocks of the flightless ostrich-like rhea (known locally as the ñandú), Andean condors, flamingos, and many other species.

The park's outstanding conservation success has undoubtedly been the guanaco *(Lama guanicoe)*, which grazes the open steppes where its main natural enemy, the puma, cannot approach undetected. After more than a decade of effective protection from hunters and poachers, the guanaco barely flinches when humans or vehicles approach. The elusive huemul, or Andean deer, is difficult to spot.

For hikers and backpackers, this 240,000-hectare reserve is an unequaled destination, with a well-developed trail network as well as opportunities for cross-country travel. The weather is changeable, with the strong westerlies that typify Patagonia, but very long summer days make outdoor activities possible late into the evening. Good foul-weather gear is essential, and a warm sleeping bag and good tent are imperative for those undertaking the extremely popular Paine circuit.

Guided daytrips from Puerto Natales are possible, but permit only a glimpse of what the park has to offer. It's better to explore the several options for staying at the park, including camping at both backcountry and improved sites, or staying at the guest houses and hotels near park headquarters and at Lago Pehoé. Roads into the park are much improved, largely for the benefit of the new luxury hotels.

Orientation & Information

Parque Nacional Torres del Paine is 112km north of Puerto Natales via a decent but sometimes bumpy gravel road that passes Villa Cerro Castillo, where there is a seasonal border crossing into Argentina at Cancha Carrera, and continues 38km north, where there's a junction with a 27km lateral along the south shore of Lago Sarmiento de Gamboa to the little-visited Lago Verde sector of the park.

Three km north of this junction the highway forks west along the north shore of Lago Sarmiento to the Portería Sarmiento, the park's main entrance; it's another 37km to the Administración (Park Headquarters). About 12km east of Portería Sarmiento, another lateral forks north, and, 3km farther, forks again; the northern branch goes to Guardería Laguna Azul, and the western branch goes to Guardería Laguna Amarga, the starting point for the Paine Circuit, and continues to the Administración.

At the Administración, the CONAF visitor center features a good exhibit on the park's carnivores, including the puma, two species of foxes, and Geoffroy's cat, all of which depend largely on the introduced European hare (though half the puma's diet consists of chulengos, or juvenile guanacos).

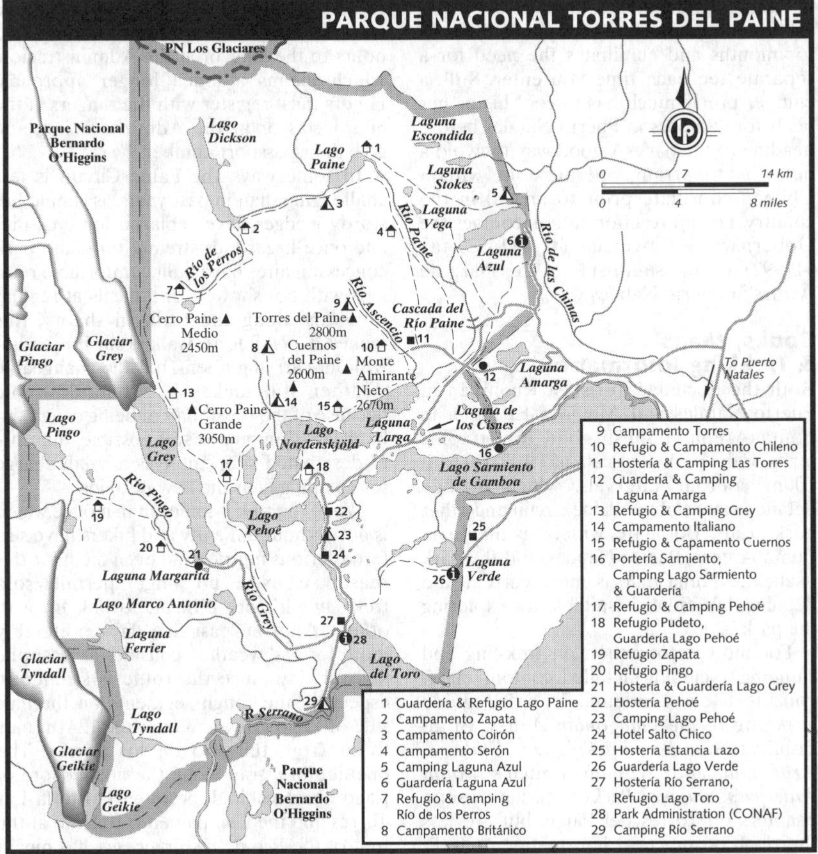

Entry There is an entry charge of US$14 per person, US$7 in low season (less for Chilean nationals). The entrance fee is collected at the Portería Sarmiento, where maps and informational brochures are available, or at Guardería Laguna Amarga (where most buses now stop inbound), Guardería Lago Verde, or Guardería Laguna Azul.

Visitors should be aware that, because of pressure on park resources, CONAF is likely to institute restrictions during periods of heavy usage, especially in January and February, when reservations may be necessary in some parts of the park.

Climbing Climbers headed for the Torres should know that CONAF charges a climbing fee of US$100 (a considerable reduction of the former US$825 fee for a maximum of seven climbers). Before being granted permission, climbers must present current résumés, emergency contact numbers, and authorization from their consulate.

Climbers must also get permission from the Dirección de Fronteras y Límites (Difrol) in Santiago, which takes 48 hours, but if you ask for enough time it keeps you in the park for months and eliminates the need for a separate fee each time you enter. Still, a climber pretty much has to cool his or her heels for 48 hours in Puerto Natales before heading to the park. A good way to avoid a delay is to arrange permissions with a Chilean consulate prior to arrival in the country. For more information, contact the Gobernación Provincial (☎ 411423, fax 411992), on the south side of the Plaza de Armas in Puerto Natales.

Books, Maps & Trekking Information

Both the Sociedad Turística Kaonikén in Puerto Natales and Almacén El Puma in Punta Arenas publish good topographic maps of the park at a scale of 1:100,000 with 100m contour intervals, which include detailed routes of the Paine circuit and other park trails. Both are widely available in Punta Arenas, Puerto Natales, and the park itself; the Puma map is more current and detailed, but either is suitable for exploring the park.

For more information on trekking and camping, including detailed contour maps, consult Clem Lindenmayer's LP guide *Trekking in the Patagonian Andes*. Bradt Publications' *Backpacking in Chile & Argentina* and William Leitch's *South America's National Parks* both have useful chapters on Torres del Paine, but are less thorough on practical information. A well-intentioned but awkwardly translated brochure titled *Guide, Pathway of Excursions National Park Torres del Paine* is also available.

On wildlife, LP readers have recommended *The Fauna of Torres del Paine* (1993), by Gladys Garay N and Oscar Guineo N, available in the Museo Salesiano in Punta Arenas.

Paine Circuit

Fast approaching gridlock, this inordinately popular trek usually begins at Guardería Laguna Amarga, where most intending hikers disembark from the bus and do the route counterclockwise. It's also possible to start at Portería Sarmiento, adding two hours to the hike, or at the Administración, which means a much longer approach. Hikers must register with the rangers at the guarderías or at the Administración, and give their passport number.

In some ways, the Paine Circuit is less challenging than in past years, as simple but sturdy bridges have replaced log crossings and once-hazardous stream fords, and park concessionaires have built comfortable refugios with hot showers and meals at regular intervals along the trail. In theory, this makes it possible to walk from hut to hut without carrying a tent, but the changeable weather still makes it a tent desirable because of the possibility of being caught in-between. Camping is still possible, but only at designated sites; there is a small charge for camping near the new refugios.

While the trek is tamer than it once was, it is not without difficulty and hikers have suffered serious injuries and even died; for this reason, CONAF no longer permits solo treks, but it's not difficult to link up with others. Allot at least five days, preferably more for bad weather; consider at least one layover day, since the route is strenuous, especially the rough segments on the east side of Lago Grey and over the 1241m pass to or from the Río de los Perros. The opening of a trail along the north shore of Lago Nordenskjöld, between Hostería Las Torres and the Campamento Italiano at the foot of the Río de los Franceses, has meant it's no longer necessary to start from park headquarters, and it's possible to exit as well as enter at Laguna Amarga.

Be sure to bring food, since prices at the small grocery at Posada Río Serrano near park headquarters are at least 50% higher than in Punta Arenas or Puerto Natales, and the selection is minimal. In late summer, the abandoned garden at Refugio Dickson still produces abundant gooseberries.

Andescape (☎ 412877, fax 412592, andescape@chileaustral.com), Eberhard 599 in Puerto Natales, has opened refugios at Lago Pehóe, Lago Grey, and Lago Dickson, as well as a campground at Río de los

Perros. For trekkers from Guardería Laguna Amarga, this would mean roughly an 11-hour hike to the first refugio at Dickson, though there is a rustic shelter at Campamento Coirón, about three hours earlier.

Andescape's refugios have 32 bunks for US$18 per night, including kitchen privileges and hot showers, but not sheets or sleeping bags. Breakfast is available for US$4.50, lunch for US$7.50, and dinner for US$10, or full board for US$20.50. A bunk plus full board costs US$34.50.

Campers pay US$4 per person at Andescape sites, with showers an additional US$2. Rental equipment is also available at reasonable prices.

Other Paine Trails

Visitors lacking time to hike the circuit or preferring a bit more solitude both have alternatives within the park. The next best choice for seeing the high country is the shorter but almost equally popular trail up the **Río Ascencio** to a treeless tarn beneath the eastern face of the Torres del Paine proper. From Guardería Laguna Amarga, there's a narrow but passable road to the trailhead beyond Hostería Las Torres, where a footbridge avoids a sometimes hazardous river ford, before the trail continues up the canyon to Refugio & Campamento Chileno and Refugio & Campamento Cuernos, the only legal campsites (US$5 per sites). Both refugios cost about US$15 and are spacious and comfortable, with excellent meals. The estancia runs a minibus between Guardería Laguna Amarga and the trailhead (US$4), which saves two hours' walking.

From Campamento Torres, a steep and sometimes ill-marked trail climbs through patchy beech forests to the barren tarn above, which provides dramatic views of the nearly vertical Torres. This is a feasible day hike from Laguna Amarga, and a fairly easy one from Hostería Las Torres, but it's also an exceptional area for camping despite its popularity (try to arrive early to get the best sites).

Comparable to Río Ascencio trail is the trail up the **Valle Francés**, between 3050m Paine Grande to the west and the lower but still spectacular Cuernos del Paine (Horns of Paine) to the east. It's a seven-hour, one-way hike from the Administración, but also accessible by a new but still rugged trail from Hostería Las Torres along the north shore of Lago Nordenskjöld. Trekkers can pitch tents at the Campamento Italiano at the foot of the valley, at the Campamento Británico at its head, or at the estancia's Camping y Refugio Los Cuernos, about an hour's walk east of the Campamento Italiano, which is comparable to Andescape's facilities.

Floods in the early 1980s destroyed several bridges, requiring CONAF to relocate the part of the Paine Circuit that formerly crossed the Río Paine at the outlet of **Lago Paine**, whose northern shore is now accessible only from Laguna Azul. This four-hour, one-way hike, offering considerably greater solitude than the Paine Circuit, leads to the rustic Refugio Lago Paine, a former outside house on the former estancia.

From the outlet of Lago Grey, 18km northwest of the Administración by a passable road, a good trail leads to **Lago Pingo**, on the eastern edge of the Campo de Hielo Sur (Southern Continental Ice Field). Much less frequented than other park trails, this route has two very rustic refugios en route.

For a shorter day hike, try the walk from Guardería Lago Pehoé, on the main park highway, to **Salto Grande**, a powerful waterfall between Lago Nordenskjöld and Lago Pehoé that destroyed an iron bridge that once was a key part of the Paine circuit. From Salto Grande, an easy hour's walk

SANDRA BAO

Grazing guanacos

leads to **Mirador Nordenskjöld**, an overlook with superb views of the lake and cordillera.

Horseback Riding

At Río Serrano, contact Baqueano Zamora (☎ 412911). Rates are about US$15 for two hours or US$55 per full day, the latter with lunch included.

Places to Stay & Eat

See also the Paine Circuit for Places to Stay along the route.

Camping The most central organized campsites are ***Camping Lago Pehoé*** *(☎ 4410684)*, which charges US$21 for up to six people, and ***Camping Río Serrano***, which costs US$15. Fees include firewood and hot showers, the latter available in the morning (evenings only by request).

At Guardería Laguna Amarga, CONAF has a free ***camping area*** with a very rustic refugio and pit toilets. Only river water is available at this site, which is usually frequented by recent arrivals or people waiting for the bus to or from Puerto Natales.

On the grounds of Estancia Cerro Paine, ***Camping Las Torres*** charges US$5 per person and is popular with hikers taking the short trek up the Río Ascencio before doing the Paine Circuit. Though covered with cow patties, the sites themselves are pleasant and scenic, but the inadequate water supply has put pressure on the modern but overburdened toilet and shower facilities.

At the more remote ***Camping Laguna Azul***, rates are US$21 per night.

Hotels & Hosterías Despite a construction boom within park boundaries, accommodations are crowded in summer and reservations are a good idea. Low cost and even free accommodations exist, however – a short walk from the Administración, ***Refugio Lago Toro*** has bunks for US$6 plus US$2 for hot showers. A sleeping bag is essential. Other refugios are free but *very* rustic; the refugio at Pudeto on Lago Pehoé may start to charge a fee in the near future.

Hostería Río Serrano *(☎ 410684, fax 412349)*, a remodeled estancia house near the Administración, has rooms with shared bath for US$40/70, while those with private bath go for US$50 per person. It has a reasonably priced restaurant and bar, with occasional informal, live entertainment, but several readers consider it poor value and report that management has attitude problems. ***Hostería Mirador del Paine*** (formerly Hostería Estancia Lazo), with eight cabins and a spacious farmhouse at the park's Laguna Verde sector, costs US$88/99 and has drawn some very favorable commentary. Its Punta Arenas representative is Operatur *(☎/fax 240513, Av Colón 822, Oficina E)*.

Well worth considering is ***Hostería Lago Grey*** *(☎ 248167, fax 241504)*, at the outlet of its namesake lake, which costs US$130/150. ***Hostería Pehoé*** *(☎ 244506)*, on a small island in the lake of the same name and linked to the mainland by a footbridge, charges US$120/135 plus IVA for panoramic views of the Cuernos del Paine and Paine Grande, but the rooms are small and simple. It has a restaurant and bar, both open to the public, but service can be shoddy. ***Hostería Las Torres*** *(☎ 226054, fax 222641)*, 7km west of Guardería Laguna Amarga, charges US$105/119 to US$123/134 and also has a restaurant/bar.

The most extravagant lodging is ***Hotel Salto Chico*** *(☎ 02-206-6060, fax 228-4655 in Santiago, 61-411247 in Puerto Natales, explora@entelchile.net)*, near the Salto Chico waterfall at the outlet of Lago Pehoé, which specializes in packages ranging from four days and three nights for US$1347/2080 single/double in the least expensive room, to eight days and seven nights for US$5388/6738 in the most expensive suite, including transfers from Punta Arenas. In the off-season, accommodation may be available on a daily basis. While the building's exterior is unappealing, its relatively unobtrusive site limits the blight on the landscape; its real strength is the extraordinary view of the entire Paine massif across the lake.

Getting There & Away

For details of transportation to the park, see the Puerto Natales entry. Bus services drop you at the Administración at Río Serrano, although you can disembark at Portería Lago Sarmiento or Guardería Laguna Amarga, to begin the Paine circuit, or elsewhere upon request. Hitching from Puerto Natales is possible, but competition is heavy.

There are sometimes summer bus services between Torres del Paine and El Calafate, Argentina, the closest settlement to Parque Nacional Los Glaciares. Inquire at the Administración.

Getting Around

Hikers to Lago Grey or Valle Francés can save time and effort by taking the launch (US$14) from Refugio Pudeto, at the east end of Lago Pehoé, to Refugio Pehoé, at the west end of the lake. At press time the launch was run by Tzonka, known for its erratic service, but CONAF was in search of a more reliable concessionaire.

Service on the 38-passenger *Tetramarán Grey I*, which makes a three-hour excursion between Hostería Grey and Glaciar Grey (US$45), was suspended, though expected to resume.

PORVENIR

Founded barely a century ago to service the new sheep estancias across the Straits of Magellan from Punta Arenas, Porvenir is the largest settlement on Chilean Tierra del Fuego. Many of its 5083 inhabitants claim Yugoslav descent, dating from the brief 1880s gold rush and commemorated by several monuments and a pleasant waterfront park.

Porvenir becomes visible only as the ferry from Punta Arenas approaches its sheltered, nearly hidden harbor. The waterfront road, or costanera, leads from the ferry terminal to a cluster of rusting, metal-clad Victorians that ironically belie the town's optimistic name ('the future'). The beautifully manicured Plaza de Armas has a worthwhile

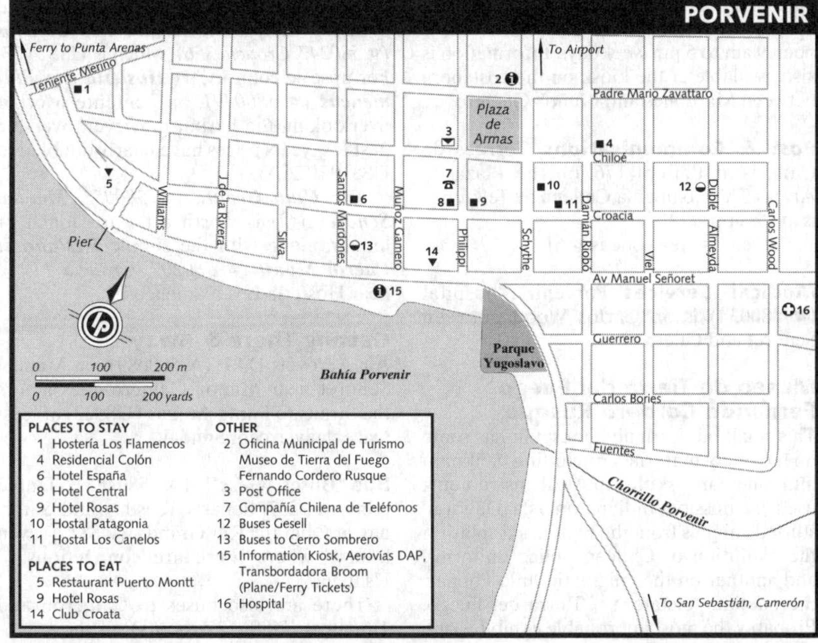

museum, but for most travelers Porvenir is a brief stopover en route to or from Ushuaia, on the Argentine side of Tierra del Fuego.

Motorists will find the gravel road east, along Bahía Inútil to the Argentine border at San Sebastián, in excellent condition, though a bit narrow in spots. Northbound motorists from San Sebastián should take the equally good route from Onaisín to Cerro Sombrero and the crossing of the Strait of Magellan at Punta Delgada-Puerto Espora, rather than the heavily traveled and rutted truck route directly north from San Sebastián.

Major changes may be in store for Porvenir. The multinational Trillium Corporation's controversial forestry initiative in southern Tierra del Fuego, presently on hold for its alleged environmental shortcomings, may result in construction of US$35 million worth of new port facilities.

Information

Tourist Offices The much improved Oficina Municipal de Turismo (☎ 580636), upstairs at Padre Mario Zavattaro 402, is open 9 am to 5 pm weekdays. Information is also available at the kiosk on the costanera between Mardones and Muñoz Gamero.

Post & Communications Correos de Chile is at Phillipi 176, on the Plaza de Armas. The Compañía Chilena de Teléfonos is at Philippi 277.

Porvenir's area code is ☎ 61.

Medical Services Porvenir's hospital (☎ 580034) is on Carlos Wood between Señoret and Guerrero.

Museo de Tierra del Fuego Fernando Cordero Rusque

This small but intriguing museum has some unexpected materials, including Selknam mummies and skulls, musical instruments used by mission Indians on Isla Dawson, stuffed animals from the region, a display on the evolution of Chilean police uniforms, and another on the enigmatic Julio Popper, the onetime 'dictator' of Tierra del Fuego. Probably the most improbable exhibit is one on early Chilean cinematography. On the Plaza de Armas, in the same building as the tourist office, museum hours are weekdays 9 am to 5 pm; in January and February, it's also open 11 am to 5 pm weekends.

Places to Stay & Eat

For its size, Porvenir has good accommodation and food, but prices have recently risen. The cheapest rooms are at ***Residencial Colón*** *(☎ 580108, Damián Riobó 198)*, where singles with shared bath and breakfast cost US$7. ***Hotel España*** *(☎ 580160, Croacia 698)* has singles for US$12 per person with shared bath, singles/doubles for US$14/26 with private bath. ***Hotel Central*** *(☎ 580077)*, at Phillippi and Croacia, is a good value for US$19/33 per person with shared bath, US$24/35 with private bath.

Across the street, ***Hotel Rosas*** *(☎ 580088, Philippi 296)* charges US$24/37 with private bath and has a good seafood restaurant. Two newer choices are ***Hostal Patagonia*** *(☎ 580372, Schythe 230)*, which charges US$24/30 but has some doubles with shared bath for US$18, and ***Hostal Los Canelos*** *(☎ 580247, Croacia 356)*, which is US$24/33. For upscale comfort, try ***Hostería Los Flamencos*** *(☎ 580049)*, on Teniente Merino overlooking the harbor, however, over the past few years prices have nearly doubled to US$105/126.

The ***Club Croata*** *(☎ 580053, Manuel Señoret 542)* is worth a try for lunch or dinner, along with the simple ***Restaurant Puerto Montt*** *(☎ 580207, Croacia 1199)*, near Hostería Los Flamencos.

Getting There & Away

Air Aerovías DAP (☎ 580089), on Manuel Señoret near Muñoz Gamero, flies across the Straits to Punta Arenas (US$22) at least twice daily except Sunday.

Bus Buses Gesell (☎ 580488), Dublé Almeyda 257, departs Tuesday and Saturday at 2 pm for Río Grande, (US$17, seven hours), where there are connections to Ushuaia.

There are also buses to Camerón and Timaukel (US$6, 2½ hours), in the southwestern part of the island, Wednesday at 3 pm; these leave from the DAP offices on Señoret. Monday, Wednesday, and Thursday at 5 pm, there's a bus to Cerro Sombrero (US$6, 1½ hours), departing from Santos Mardones 330.

Boat Transbordadora Broom (☎ 580089) operates the car-passenger ferry *Melinka* to Punta Arenas (2½ hours, US$7 per person, US$45 per vehicle) Tuesday through Saturday at 2 pm, Sundays and holidays at 5 pm.

Getting Around

The bus to the ferry terminal, departing from the waterfront kiosk about an hour before the ferry's departure, provides a farewell tour of Porvenir for US$1. Taxis cost at least four times as much.

CERRO SOMBRERO

This orderly but half-abandoned town at the north end of Tierra del Fuego, 43km south of the ferry crossing at Primera Angostura, is a company town belonging to Chile's Empresa Nacional de Petróleo (ENAP, National Petroleum Company). It has oddball '60s architecture, a bank, a modern cinema, cheap lodging, a restaurant open until 3 am, and, of all things, an astronomical observatory. The only scheduled public transport comes from Porvenir; return buses to Porvenir leave Monday, Wednesday, and Thursday at 8 am.

On the highway outside of town ***Restaurant El Conti*** serves a chicken soup that's the perfect choice for a cold, windy day (buses between Río Grande and Punta Arenas stop here).

LAGO BLANCO

In the southern part of Chilean Tierra del Fuego, accessible only by private car, Lago Blanco has excellent fishing. The nearest formal lodging is in the village of Timaukel, just south of the large estancia at Camerón (which, despite the Spanish accent, takes its name from a Scottish pioneer sheepfarming family that first settled in the Falkland Islands). The native forests in this area are presently under pressure from a controversial forestry project, which would allow the US-based Trillium Corporation to log substantial areas in return for replanting and preserving others.

PUERTO WILLIAMS

Captain Robert Fitzroy encountered the Yahgan Indians who accompanied the *Beagle* back to England for several years near this Chilean naval settlement on Isla Navarino, directly across the Beagle Channel from Argentine Tierra del Fuego. Missionaries in the mid-19th century and fortune-seekers during the local gold rush of the 1890s established a permanent European presence.

A few people of Yahgan descent still reside near Puerto Williams (population 1800), which is named for the founder of Fuerte Bulnes.

A dispute over the three small islands of Lennox, Nueva, and Picton, east of Navarino, nearly brought Argentina and Chile to war in 1978, but papal intervention defused the situation and the islands remain in Chilean possession.

Information

There is a cluster of public services, including a telephone, post office, supermarket, and tourist office, on President Ibáñez.

Money exchange is possible at Turismo Isla Navarino (☎ 621140) in the Centro Comercial.

Things to See & Do

The **Museo Martín Gusinde**, honoring the German priest and ethnographer who worked among the Yahgans from 1918 to 1923, has exhibits on natural history and ethnography. It's open weekdays 9 am to 1 pm, and daily 3 to 6 pm.

East of town, at **Ukika**, live the few remaining Yahgan people. There is good hiking in the surrounding countryside, but the changeable weather demands warm, water-resistant clothing.

Places to Stay & Eat

Central ***Hostería Camblor*** (*☎ 621033*) is basic but clean and comfortable for US$13 single with breakfast, US$31 with full board, both with private bath. ***Residencial Onashaga*** *(☎ 621081)* and ***Pensión Temuco*** *(☎ 621113)* charge slightly more, with shared bath.

Camping is possible near the upscale and highly recommended ***Hostería Wala*** *(☎ 621114)*, which has single/double rooms at US$40/50. During the winter prices may be negotiable. Both hotels serve meals.

Getting There & Away

Aerovías DAP flies to and from Punta Arenas Monday, Wednesday, and Friday (US$67 one way). Seats are limited and advance reservations essential. DAP flights to Antarctica make a brief stopover here.

Regular connections between Ushuaia/Almanza and Puerto Williams are suspended for the foreseeable future, though some developments are under discussion.

FALKLAND ISLANDS

SYLVIA STEVENS

Falkland Islands (Islas Malvinas)

Surrounded by the South Atlantic Ocean and centuries of controversy, the Falkland Islands lie some 300 miles (500km) east of the Patagonian mainland. Consisting of two main islands, East and West Falkland, and several hundred smaller ones, they support a permanent population of about 2000, most of whom live in the capital of Stanley. The remainder live on widely dispersed sheep stations.

FACTS ABOUT THE FALKLANDS

History

Although there is some evidence that Patagonian Indians may have reached the Falklands in rudimentary canoes, the Islands were uninhabited when Europeans began to frequent the area in the late 17th century. Their Spanish name, Islas Malvinas, derives from early French navigators from the Channel port of St Malo.

No European power established a settlement until 1764, when the French built a garrison at Port Louis on East Falkland, disregarding Spanish claims under the papal Treaty of Tordesillas, which divided the New World between Spain and Portugal. Britain soon planted, unbeknownst to either France or Spain, a West Falkland outpost at Port Egmont, on Saunders Island. Spain, meanwhile, discovered and then supplanted the French colony after an amicable settlement between the two European states. Spanish forces then detected and expelled the British in 1767. Under threat of war, Spain restored Port Egmont to the British, who a few years later abandoned the area without, however, formally renouncing territorial claims.

For the rest of the 18th century, Spain maintained the Islands as one of the world's most secure penal colonies. After it abandoned them in the early 1800s, only maverick whalers and sealers visited until the early 1820s, when the United Provinces of the River Plate sent a military governor to assert its claim as successor to Spain. Later, the naturalized Buenos Aires entrepreneur Louis Vernet initiated a project to monitor uncontrolled sealers and exploit local fur seal populations in an ostensibly sustainable manner, as well as tame the numerous feral cattle and horses that had multiplied on the islands since the Spaniards' departure.

Vernet's seizure of three American sealers triggered reprisals from hot-headed US naval officer Silas Duncan, who vandalized the Port Louis settlement beyond restoration in 1831. After Vernet's departure, Buenos Aires maintained a token force until early 1833, when it was expelled by British forces. Vernet pursued his claims for property damages in British courts for nearly 30 years, with little success. Argentina has since asserted its territorial claim to the Islands by diplomacy and, in 1982, by force.

Under the British, the Falklands languished until the mid-19th century, when sheep began to replace cattle, and wool became an important export commodity. Founded by Samuel Lafone, an Englishman from Montevideo, the Falkland Islands Company became the Islands' largest landholder, but other immigrant entrepreneurs occupied all available pastoral lands in extensive holdings by the 1870s.

The steady arrival of English and Scottish immigrants augmented the early population, which was a mix of stranded mariners and holdover gauchos from the Vernet era.

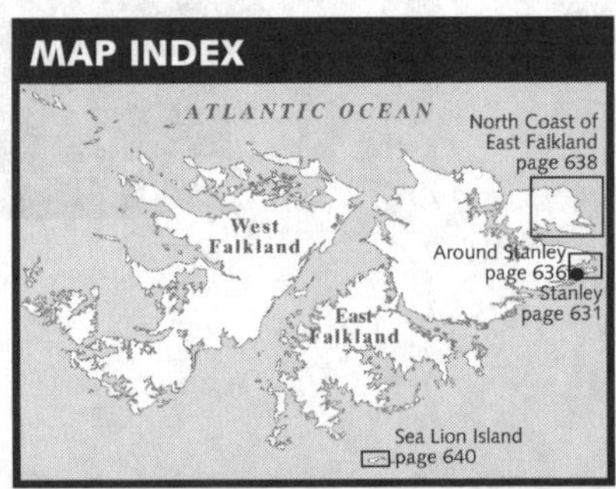

The Warrah, the Yahgans & the Discovery of the Falklands

Who discovered the Falklands? Opinions depend, it seems, on who's speaking and what that person's native language is. Spanish speakers argue forcefully, almost without exception, that a ship from Magellan's 1520 expedition wintered at the Islands, while English speakers strongly assert that privateer John Davis discovered them in 1592. Unfortunately, no Yahgan speakers remain to tell us whether the 'Canoe Indians' of Tierra del Fuego might have been the first to set foot on the Islands.

The evidence, admittedly, is slim and the idea seems at first unconventional and unlikely. The Yahgans navigated the waters of the Beagle Channel and the Strait of Magellan in simple beech bark canoes held together with whalebone and shredded saplings. By all accounts, these leaky vessels required constant bailing, but the Yahgans did use sealskin sails in favorable winds. In these canoes they certainly arrived at Staten Island at the eastern tip of Tierra del Fuego and, some speculate, more than 500 miles northeast in the Falklands. Early settlers found canoes washed up on the shores of West Falkland, but the most concrete evidence for at least a temporary Indian presence was the Islands' only native land mammal, the *warrah* or Falklands fox, *Dusicyon australis.*

When Europeans first landed, the Falklands were unpeopled, but the warrah (its name probably derived from the Australian Aboriginal word *warrigal*, used to describe the dingo) aroused the interest of visitors like Darwin, who wrote:

> There is no other instance in any part of the world of so small a mass of broken land, distant from a continent, possessing so large an aboriginal quadruped peculiar to itself . . . Within a very few years after these islands shall have become regularly settled, in all probability this fox will be classed with the dodo, as an animal which has perished from the face of the earth.

Darwin and others remarked on the animal's extraordinary tameness, a characteristic that would support British biologist Juliet Clutton-Brock's conclusion that the warrah was a feral dog or a cross of feral dog and South American fox. Analyzing the animal's physical characteristics from specimens in the British Museum, she concluded that, like the Australian dingo, the warrah had been domesticated and likely brought across several hundred miles of open ocean in Yahgan canoes.

Was this possible? No one can be absolutely positive. Indigenous peoples did navigate thousands of miles of the open Pacific, although their watercraft were more sophisticated than the Yahgans'. But the Yahgans were a hardy people, and chances are that a canoe or two might have ridden the prevailing winds and currents from the Strait of Lemaire to the Falklands. If, as was usual, they carried a dog or two, perhaps a pregnant bitch, it is reasonable to believe those animals might have bred on the Islands. Whether these presumed discoverers of the Falklands were able to return to Tierra del Fuego is even more speculative, but just considering the idea makes us rethink, once again, the myth of European 'discovery.' As Darwin predicted, the warrah itself did not survive European settlement – perceived as a threat to sheep, the last individual was shot on West Falkland in the 1870s.

Roughly half resided in the new capital and port of Stanley, founded in 1844, while the remainder became resident laborers on large sheep stations resembling those in Australia. Until the 1996 census, the population had never exceeded its 1931 maximum of 2392.

Most of the original landowners lived and worked in the Falklands, but in time they or their descendants returned to Britain and ran their businesses as absentees. For nearly a century the Falkland Islands Company, owner of nearly half the land and livestock, dominated the local economy.

Until the late 1970s, when local government began to encourage the sale and subdivision of large landholdings to slow high rates of emigration, little changed in the Islands' only industry. Since then, nearly every unit has been sold to local family farmers. Beginning in 1982, change became even more rapid with the Falklands War and the subsequent expansion of long-distance, deep-sea fishing in the surrounding South Atlantic. By mid-1998, the Anglo-Dutch Shell Corporation had found preliminary indications, but not commercial quantities,

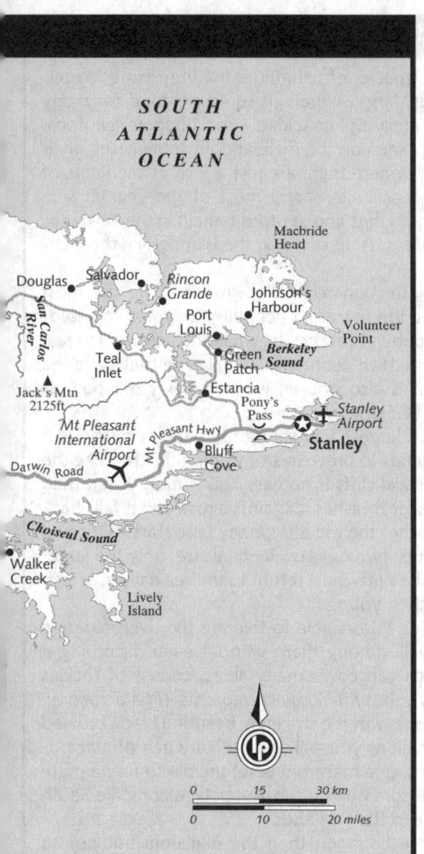

of offshore petroleum in the islands' northern maritime zone.

The Falklands War Although Argentina has persistently affirmed its claims to the Falklands since 1833, successive British governments never publicly acknowledged their seriousness until the late 1960s when, apparently, the Foreign & Commonwealth Office had begun to see the islands as a politically burdensome anachronism to be discarded with all judicious speed. By then, the FCO and the military government of General Juan Carlos Onganía reached a communications agreement giving Argentina a significant voice in matters affecting Falklands transportation, fuel supplies, shipping, and even immigration, beginning in 1971.

Islanders and their supporters in Britain saw the Argentine presence as an ominous development. Only a few years earlier, right-wing guerrillas had hijacked an Aerolíneas Argentinas jet, which crash-landed on the Stanley racecourse (the Islands had no airport at the time); afterward, the guerrillas briefly occupied parts of town. Concerned about Argentina's chronic instability, Falklanders suspected the FCO of secretly arranging transfer of the Islands to Argentina, and they were probably correct.

This process dragged on for over a decade, during which Argentina's brutal Dirty War gave Falklanders good reason to fear increasing Argentine presence. What was too fast for the Islanders was too slow for the Argentines, especially for General Leopoldo Galtieri's desperate military government, which invaded the lightly defended Islands on April 2, 1982.

Galtieri's disintegrating regime had come under increasing pressure from Argentines fed up with the corruption, economic chaos, and totalitarian ruthlessness of the Proceso, but his seizure of the Malvinas briefly united a divided country and made him an ephemeral hero. Galtieri and his advisers did not anticipate that British Prime Minister Margaret Thatcher, herself in precarious political circumstances, would respond so decisively. In a struggle whose loser would not survive politically, the Argentine sought diplomatic approval of his *fait accompli*, while the Briton organized an enormous naval task force to recover lost territory.

The military outcome was one-sided, despite substantial British naval losses, as experienced British troops landed at San Carlos Bay and routed ill-trained and poorly supplied Argentine conscripts. The most serious fighting took place at Goose Green, on East Falkland, but the Argentine surrender at Stanley averted the destruction of the capital. Near Stanley, and at a few other sites around the Islands, unexploded mines

Penguins & Their Feathered Friends

On the Patagonian mainland, the only breeding species of penguin is the burrowing Magellanic. In the cooler waters around the Falklands, large schools of squid are food for many more species of these fascinating birds of the family Spheniscidae – rockhoppers, gentoos, kings, and macaronis – plus other seabirds rarely seen on the mainland. In some cases, their numbers are almost incomprehensible, while elsewhere there are just a few, at the limits of their sub-Antarctic range. Rockhoppers and Magellanics spend most of the year at sea, coming ashore to breed in the southern spring, but kings and gentoos remain in the Falklands throughout the year. Occasionally a lone wanderer sets up camp on the Islands, like the chinstrap in a gentoo colony on Saunders Island.

Rockhopper penguins *(Eudyptes crestatus)*, affectionately called 'rockies,' are the most common Falklands species. Although resembling the macaroni penguin *(Eudyptes chrysolophus)*, rockies are easily distinguished by their floppy yellow crests, while the macaroni's crest is orange and more erect, resembling the foppish 18th-century male hairstyle that gave the bird its common English name. The rockhopper is also smaller, weighing only 5.5 pounds (2.5kg), while the macaroni reaches 10 pounds (4.5kg).

Falklands rockhopper colonies are the world's largest – in spring, perhaps as many as 5 million birds climb rugged, wave-battered headlands to breed in stony amphitheaters like the one on Sea Lion Island. Scaling these nearly vertical cliffs is no easy task – more often than not, as soon as the rocky leaves the water a breaker thrashes it against a rock and it falls back into the sea. Persistence triumphs, as the bird reaches the top after many false starts. Once on the headlands, male and female mate and produce two eggs of unequal size, only the larger of which usually hatches and reaches maturity. The birds must return to the sea daily in search of squid, which they digest and regurgitate for their young.

While rockhoppers can be pugnacious, careful visitors able to tolerate the overpowering odor of ammonia from penguin excreta can walk among them without even disturbing a nesting mother. Rarely do these colonies, which can cover many acres, consist of rockies alone. In their eastern breeding sites, rockies mix with king cormorants *(Phalacrocorax albiventer)*, while in the west they share their space with the strikingly beautiful black-browed albatross *(Diomedea melanophris)*. On rare occasions you will see a solitary pair of macaronis among the breeding rockhoppers, or even a single macaroni who, unable to find a mate of its own species, has nested with a rocky. More common on sub-Antarctic islands like South Georgia, the macaroni is at the limits of its range in the Falklands.

The gentoo *(Pygoscelis papua)* is much more common than the macaroni but not so common as the rocky. Its distinguishing features are its size (although smaller than the king, it weighs up to 13.5 pounds or 6kg), its bright orange bill, and the white band that connects the eyes across the crown. For nesting, it favors open, level sites some distance from the ocean; gentoo routes to and from the sea are like ant trails, often long and indirect. Traditionally, Falkland Islanders have collected gentoo eggs in the spring but, unlike the rockhopper, the gentoo may lay a second egg if the first is removed.

remain, but minefields are clearly marked and pose no danger to anyone exercising caution.

Postwar Politics & Development Since the end of the war, most Islanders have wanted little or nothing to do with Argentina, preferring to emphasize their political, economic, and cultural links with Britain and to renew long-standing commercial ties with the southern Chilean city of Punta Arenas.

In early 1995, however, Islanders Graham Bound and Janet Robertson toured Argen-

Penguins & Their Feathered Friends

Gentoos are popular with Falklands farmers, since they uproot the common *diddle-dee* shrub *(Empetrum rubrum)*, which has no pasture value, while fine pasture grasses quickly colonize abandoned gentoo nesting sites. The application of the popular name gentoo to the species is obscure, since the word describes a non-Muslim inhabitant of India – one speculation is that the band across the gentoo's head bears resemblance to a turban.

The undisputed monarch of Falklands penguins is, appropriately, the king *(Aptenodytes patagonicus)*. This enormous, regal bird is unmistakable, standing more than 3 feet (nearly a meter) in height and weighing more than 35 lb (16kg), with a bright orangeish ear patch connecting to a golden patch on the breast. It resembles the much larger emperor penguin *(Aptenodytes forsteri)* of Antarctica. Once nearly extinct in the Falklands, the king has reappeared at several sites throughout the Islands, most notably Volunteer Point, which has a breeding colony with perhaps as many as 700 birds. There is also a growing colony at Saunders Island.

King penguins breed on flat, open areas among gentoos, but they do not nest, instead incubating their single egg on their feet and protecting it among loose folds of skin. The most extraordinary thing about the bird is its erratic breeding cycle, which is not synchronized with the seasons or the year – no scientist has successfully explained why 14 to 16 months pass between eggs. Because of the kings' beauty and rarity, Falklands farms that have breeding populations take great pride in their presence.

Many other birds are worth seeing, but one deserves special mention: the black-browed albatross, which nests on precipitous, west-facing headlands on New Island, West Point, Saunders Island, and a few other places. Tiny but inaccessible Beauchene Island, an isolated southern outlier of East Falkland, has an astonishing 2 million birds. In total, the Falklands have more than three-quarters of the world's population of the species.

With an 8-foot (nearly 2.5m) wingspan and flat webbed feet, this enormous bird is ungainly on land, getting airborne only by leaping off cliffs into the prevailing westerlies. It spends most of the winter at sea, and some individuals migrate across the entire South Atlantic in a circular pattern. Like the penguins among which it nests, the black-browed albatross has little fear of humans. By sitting near the colony, you will arouse enough interest that this curious bird will come to you instead of your having to go to it.

Unfortunately, all is not idyllic in this wildlife paradise. Since 1986, revenue from fishing licenses has brought the Islands unprecedented prosperity, but Asian and European fleets may have overexploited the stocks of squid and finfish upon which penguins, black-browed albatrosses, and many other birds feed. Oil exploration in offshore waters poses an additional hazard, though local government has proceeded very deliberately in encouraging petroleum development.

Falklands Conservation, a pro-wildlife organization, with branches in both Stanley and the UK, is currently conducting seabird monitoring and research projects to determine the threat that commercial fishing and oil development pose to local wildlife. For more information, see the listing under Useful Organizations in this chapter.

tina as private citizens, under the auspices of the nongovernmental Consejo Argentino de Relaciones Internacionales (Argentine International Relations Council), to establish dialog and to explain the recent developments on the Falkland Islands to the Argentine public. While many Islanders opposed the visit, the Argentine audiences generally treated the visitors cordially and respectfully.

Official Argentina, at the same time, continues to send mixed messages to the

Islanders. President Carlos Menem has repeatedly renounced the use of force to support his country's claim to the Malvinas, yet he has also bragged that the Islands will once again be Argentine by the turn of the century. Foreign minister Guido di Tella, meanwhile, has pursued an ineffective policy of buttering up the Islanders by sending Christmas cards, gifts like children's videos, and even Queen's birthday greetings, while simultaneously proposing indemnities of US$100,000 or more per Islander should they vote to accept Argentine sovereignty in a referendum. Though nearly all Falklanders angrily dismiss di Tella's efforts to purchase their allegiance as insulting and patronizing, many have no objection to a strictly economic relationship with their larger neighbor.

In mid-1998, a private Argentine pilot made an unofficial and unscheduled flight to the Islands from the mainland in his own plane and was immediately deported (the pilot, a naturalized US citizen, could have entered freely on his US passport). Later in the year, Argentine television journalist Mariano Grondona became the first individual to enter the Islands with an Argentine passport, other than on a memorial trip, since 1982.

Geography & Climate

The Falkland Islands' total land area encompasses 4700 sq miles (12,173 sq km), about the same as that of Northern Ireland or the US state of Connecticut. There are two main islands, East and West Falkland, separated by the Falkland Sound; only a handful of the many smaller islands are large enough for human habitation. Despite a reputation for dismal weather, the Islands' oceanic climate is temperate, although with frequent high winds. Maximum temperatures rarely reach 75°F (24°C), while even on the coldest winter days the temperature usually rises above freezing at some time during the day. The average annual rainfall at Stanley, one of the Islands' most humid areas, is only about 24 inches (610mm).

Except for the low-lying southern half of East Falkland, known as Lafonia, the terrain is generally hilly to mountainous, although the highest peak of Mt Usborne, is a mere 2312 feet (705m). Among the most interesting geological features are the 'stone runs' of quartzite boulders that descend from many of the ridges and peaks on East and West Falkland. The numerous bays, inlets, estuaries, and beaches present an often spectacular coastline, with abundant, accessible, and remarkably tame wildlife.

Because the settlements are so far apart, often separated by water, and the Islands' road network is so limited, light aircraft remains the easiest way to visit areas beyond the immediate Stanley area. In some areas, riding is still a common means of travel, but the Land Rover and the motorcycle have mostly supplanted the horse. New East Falkland roads from Stanley to Darwin/Goose Green and to San Carlos, and from Estancia to Port San Carlos and the West Falkland road from Port Howard to Fox Bay, with a spur from Chartres to Hill Cove and Roy Cove, have improved overland communications. Walking is feasible for adventurous travelers, but trekkers must be prepared for changeable and sometimes inclement weather.

Flora & Fauna

Grasslands and prostrate shrubs dominate the flora; there are no native trees. At the time of European discovery, extensive stands of the native tussock grass *Parodiochloa flabellata* dominated the coastline and provided nutritious livestock fodder, but it proved highly vulnerable to overgrazing and fire. Today, very little tussock remains on East or West Falkland, although well-managed farms on offshore islands have preserved significant areas of it. Most of the native pasture is rank white grass *(Cortaderia pilosa)*, which supports only about one sheep per 4 or 5 acres.

Most visitors will find the Falklands' fauna more varied and interesting, and remarkably tame and accessible – only the Galápagos or the Everglades are comparable. The Islands' beaches, headlands, and offshore waters support the largest and finest concentrations of South Atlantic wildlife north of South Georgia and Antarctica. The Magellanic penguin, the only species that visits the South American continent, is common, but four other species breed regularly in the Falklands: the rockhopper, the closely related macaroni, the gentoo, and the king. Four other species have been recorded, but do not breed here.

Many other birds, equally interesting and uncommon, breed in the Falklands; for visitors from the Northern Hemisphere, almost all of them will be new. Undoubtedly the most beautiful is the black-browed albatross, but there are also caracaras, cormorants, gulls, hawks, oystercatchers, peregrine falcons, snowy sheathbills, sheldgeese, steamer ducks, and swans – among others. Most are present in large and impressive breeding colonies and are easy to photograph.

Also present, in locally large numbers, are marine mammals. Elephant seals, southern sea lions, and southern fur seals breed on the beaches, while six species of dolphins have been observed offshore. Killer whales are common, but the larger species of South Atlantic whales are rarely seen.

While the Falklands have no formally designated national parks, there are many outstanding wildlife sites. Over the past decade, local government has encouraged nature-oriented tourism, constructing small lodges near some of the best areas, but there are also less-structured opportunities away from these places. Hiking and trekking possibilities are excellent.

Government & Politics

In international politics, the Falklands remain a colonial anachronism, administered by a governor appointed by the Foreign & Commonwealth Office (FCO) in London, but in local affairs the eight-member, elected Legislative Council (Legco) exercises considerable power. Five of the eight members come from Stanley, while the remainder represent the camp, or countryside. Selected Legco members advise the governor as part of the Executive Council (Exco), which also includes the Chief Executive and the Financial Secretary. The present governor is Richard Ralph.

Economy

From the mid-19th century, the Falklands' economy has depended almost exclusively on the export of wool. Since 1986, however, fishing has eclipsed agriculture as a revenue producer under a licensing scheme established by the local government with the approval of the FCO. Asian and European fleets seeking both squid and finfish have brought as much as £25 million per year into the Islands, most of which has gone to fund improvements in public services such as roads, telephones, and medical care. Tourist traffic is numerically small, but facilities in Stanley and at some wildlife sites are more than adequate and often excellent. Local government began permitting offshore seismic surveys for oil in 1993 and issued the first licenses for exploration in 1996, though the potential environmental impact has left some Islanders ambivalent abut these developments.

Most of Stanley's population works for the local government (FIG) or for the Falkland Islands Company (FIC), which has been the major landowner and economic power in the Islands for more than a century. FIC has sold all its pastoral property to the government for subdivision and sale to local people, but continues to provide shipping and other commercial services for ranchers and other residents of the Islands. In the countryside, known colloquially as 'camp,' nearly everyone is involved in wool-growing on relatively small, widely dispersed family-owned units.

Population & People

According to the 1996 census, the population of the Falklands is 2564, of whom about two-thirds live in Stanley and the remainder in camp (including nonmilitary personnel at Mt Pleasant Airport). About 60% of the permanent residents are native-born, some tracing their ancestry back six or more generations, while the great majority of the remainder are immigrants or temporary residents from the United Kingdom. Islanders' surnames indicate that their origins can be traced to a variety of European backgrounds, but English is both the official language and the language of preference, though a few people speak and understand Spanish. There is a handful of immigrants from South America, nearly all of them Chilean.

Because of the Islands' isolation and small population, Falklanders are traditionally versatile and adaptable. Almost every male, for example, is an expert mechanic, while lack of spare parts has encouraged many to become improvisational machinists. This adaptability has also been a virtue for individuals who rely on seasonal labor such as sheep shearing and peat cutting, both of which are well paid. Many camp women also perform a variety of tasks, including shearing. There is, however, an increasing number of professionals among both sexes.

The Islands' history of colonial rule and the paternalistic social system (see the Stanley section) of the large sheep stations and other workplaces left an unfortunate legacy of public timidity in the face of authority, even when private opinions are very strong. At the same time, Falkland Islanders are extraordinarily hospitable, often welcoming visitors into their homes for 'smoko,' the traditional midmorning tea or coffee break, or for a drink. This is especially true in camp, where visitors of any kind can be infrequent. When visiting people in camp, it is customary to bring a small gift – rum is a special favorite. Stanley's several pubs are popular meeting places.

No visitor should miss the annual summer sports meetings, which consist of horse racing, bull riding, and similar competitions. These take place in Stanley between Christmas and New Year's, and on West Falkland at the end of the shearing season, usually in late February. The West Falkland sports rotate yearly among the settlements.

Approximately 2000 British military personnel, commonly referred to as 'squaddies,' reside at the Mt Pleasant airport complex, about 35 miles (56km) southwest of Stanley, and at a few other scattered sites around the Islands. Civilian-military relations are generally cordial but now rather distant.

FACTS FOR THE VISITOR

Although the Falklands are small and Islanders are few, in many ways the Islands are a small country, with their own immigration regulations, customs requirements, currency, and other unique features. Bureaucracy is generally not odious or cumbersome, but some government officials play things 'by the book.'

Planning

When to Go Since the Islands' primary attraction is wildlife, the best season is October to March, when migratory birds (including penguins) and marine mammals return to the beaches and headlands. December and January are the best months, since very long days permit outdoor activities even if inclement weather spoils part of the day.

Maps Excellent topographic maps, prepared by the Directorate of Overseas Surveys, are available from the Secretariat in Stanley for about £2 each. There is a two-sheet, 1:250,000 map of the entire Islands that is suitable for most purposes, but for more detail, obtain the 1:50,000 sheets. For maritime charts, contact the Customs & Immigration Department (☎ 27340) on Ross Rd in Stanley.

More readily available overseas is the 1st edition of ITMB's *Falkland Islands/Islas Malvinas* travel map, at a scale of 1:300,000, including the most current roads and detailed information on wildlife sites. It's widely available from bookstores or from International Travel Maps, 345 W Broadway, Vancouver BC, Canada V5Y 1P8.

What to Bring Since the weather is cool and changeable, visitors should bring good waterproof clothing, such as warm sweaters and an anorak, suitable for spring in the northern British Isles. A pair of rubber boots can be useful in wet weather. While summer never gets truly hot, and the wind can lower the ambient temperature considerably, the climate does not justify Antarctic preparations. For trekkers, a *very* sturdy tent with rain fly and a warm sleeping bag are essential.

Tourist Offices

The local tourist office is the Falklands Islands Tourist Board (☎ 22215, fax 22619) in

Stanley, but the Islands also have representation in the UK, Europe, and the Americas. The Tourist Board also has an informative website (www.tourism.org.fk).

Chile
Avant Airlines
(☎ 61-228312)
Roca 924, Punta Arenas. This is also the British consul's office.

Germany
HS Travel & Consulting
(☎/fax 61-05-1304)
PO Box 1447, 64529 Moerfelden. This is no longer officially affiliated with the Tourism Board, but still provides up-to-date information.

United Kingdom
Falkland House
(☎ 0171-222-2542,
020-7222-2542 starting April 2000)
14 Broadway, Westminster, London SW1H 0BH

USA
Tread Lightly Travel
(☎ 860-868-1710, fax 868-1718, patread@aol.com)
1 Titus Road, Washington Depot, CT 06794

Visas & Documents

All nationalities, including British citizens, must carry valid passports. For non-Britons, visa requirements are generally the same as those for foreigners visiting the UK, though Argentines must obtain an advance visa (not easily accomplished, though some have traveled on second passports). For details, consult Falkland House (☎ 0171-222-2542, 02-7222-2542 after April 1999, rep@figo.u-net.com), 14 Broadway, Westminster, London SW1H 0BH, or the Falkland Islands Tourist Board (☎ 22215, fax 22619, manager@tourism.org.fk). In Punta Arenas, Chile, contact LanChile (☎ 247079), at Lautaro Navarro 999, or British consul John Rees (☎ 228312), at Roca 924.

Local officials normally allow a four-month visitor's permit on arrival in the Islands, but may ask to see a return or onward ticket.

Customs

Customs regulations are few except for limits on importation of alcohol and tobacco, which are heavily taxed but readily available locally.

Money

The legal currency is the Falkland Islands pound (£), on a par with sterling. There are bank notes for £5, £10, £20, and £50, and coins for 1p, 2p, 5p, 10p, 20p, 50p, and £1.

Sterling notes and coins circulate alongside local currency, but Falklands currency is not legal tender in the UK, nor on Ascension Island, where flights to and from the UK make a brief refueling stop. Ascension/St Helena bank notes and coins are not legal tender in either the Falklands or the UK.

Credit cards are increasingly widely used in the Islands, but traveler's checks are also accepted with a minimum of bureaucracy. Britons with guarantee cards from Barclays, Lloyds, Midland, and National Westminster Banks can cash personal checks up to £50 at Stanley's Standard Chartered Bank.

Recent tourist development has encouraged short-stay, top-end accommodations and services at prices up to £50 or more per day (with full board), but there are cheaper alternatives, such as B&Bs in Stanley from about £15. In camp, there are low-cost, self-catering cabins for about £10, and opportunities for trekking and camping at little or no cost. Camp families in some isolated areas still welcome visitors without charge.

Food prices are roughly equivalent to the UK, but fresh meat (chiefly mutton) is extremely cheap. Restaurant meals are generally expensive, but inexpensive short orders and snacks are available in Stanley.

Post & Communications

Postal services are reliable. There are two airmail services weekly to and from the UK, but parcels larger than about 1lb (0.45kg) arrive or depart by sea four to five times yearly. The Government Air Service delivers the post to outer settlements and islands. If you're expecting mail in the Islands, instruct correspondents to address their letters to the 'Post Office, Stanley, Falkland Islands, via London, England.'

Cable and Wireless PLC operates both local and long-distance telephone services; all local numbers have five digits.

The Falklands' international country code is ☎ 500, which is valid for numbers in Stanley and in the camp.

Local calls cost 5p per minute, calls to the UK 15p for six seconds, and calls to the rest of the world 18p per six seconds. Operator-assisted calls cost the same but have a three-minute minimum. Collect calls are possible only locally and to the UK.

Books

Many books have been written since the 1982 war, but the most readily available general account is the 3rd edition of Ian Strange's *The Falkland Islands* (David & Charles, 1983), which deals with the geography, history, and natural history of the Islands. More recent are Paul Morrison's *The Falkland Islands* (Aston Publications, 1990), and Tony Chater's *The Falklands* (Penna Press, 1993), the latter with large format photographs.

Based on unpublished materials from Cambridge University archives and other sources, Patrick Armstrong's recent *Darwin's Desolate Islands: A Naturalist in the Falklands, 1833 and 1834* (Picton, 1992) is of great historical interest. Michael Mainwaring's *From the Falklands to Patagonia* (Allison & Busby, 1983) is a worthy historical work on pioneer sheep farming in the South Atlantic, based on private correspondence.

For a good contemporary account of the Falklands, see Robert Fox's *Antarctica and the South Atlantic: Discovery, Development and Dispute* (BBC Books, 1985). Of the numerous books on the war, one of the best is Max Hastings and Simon Jenkins' *Battle for the Falklands* (London, Pan, 1983).

Visitors interested in wildlife should acquire Robin Woods' *Falkland Islands Birds* (Anthony Nelson, 1982), which is a suitable field guide with excellent photographs, or his more detailed *Guide to Birds of the Falkland Islands* (Nelson, 1988), though the latter's format is less suited to field use. Strange's *Field Guide to the Wildlife of the Falkland Islands and South Georgia* (HarperCollins, 1992) is also worth a look. Bluntisham Books, a small British specialty house, has published TH Davies and JH McAdam's *Wild Flowers of the Falkland Islands* (1989) and Julian Fisher's *Walks and Climbs in the Falkland Islands* (1992).

Newspapers

The only print media are the weekly newspapers *Penguin News* and *Teaberry Express*, both available from Stanley shops.

Radio & TV

Radio is the most important communications medium. The Falkland Islands Broadcasting Service (FIBS) produces local programming and also carries news from the BBC and programs from the British Forces Broadcasting Service (BFBS). Do not miss the nightly public announcements, to which locals listen religiously – the Falklands may be the only place in the world where the purchase of air time is within anybody's reach. Frequencies are 550 kHz on the AM band and 96.5 MHz on the FM band.

Television is available through BFBS, which broadcasts same-day programs from the UK, and there is also cable TV (CNN, BBC World, ESPN, HBO, TNT, and Discovery) in the principal Stanley hotels.

Photography

Color and B&W print film are readily available at reasonable prices, although they're cheaper in the UK and the USA. Color slide film is less dependably available, so you may want to bring all you need. Color print processing is available in the Islands.

Time

The Falklands are four hours behind GMT. In summer, Stanley goes on daylight saving time, but camp remains on standard time.

Electricity

Electric current operates on 220/240 V, 50 cycles. Plugs are identical to those in the UK.

Weights & Measures

The metric system has become official, but in everyday matters people more commonly use English measurements. Since elevations on the Directorate of Overseas Survey maps are given in feet and most tourist literature uses English units, this chapter uses the English system, with the metric equivalent given in parentheses.

Health

No special health precautions need be taken in the Falklands, but carry adequate insurance. There are excellent medical and dental facilities at the King Edward VII Memorial Hospital, a joint civilian-military facility in Stanley.

Despite relatively cool temperatures, unsuspecting visitors may suffer severe sunburn after experiencing the deceptive combination of wind and sun. In the event of inclement weather, the wind can contribute to hypothermia.

Because flights from Brize Norton to Mt Pleasant may be diverted to West Africa or Brazil due to bad weather, the British Ministry of Defence (MOD) recommends that passengers on its flights make sure their yellow-fever vaccinations are up-to-date.

Useful Organizations

Based in both the UK and Stanley, Falklands Conservation is a nonprofit organization promoting wildlife conservation research, as well as the preservation of wrecks and historic sites in the Islands. Membership, which costs £15 per year, is available from Falklands Conservation (☎ 181-346-5011, 020-8346-5011 after April 1999), 1 Princes Rd, Finchley, London N3 2DA, England. Its local representative (☎ 22247, fax 22288) is on Ross Rd, opposite Malvina House Hotel.

The Falkland Islands Association (☎ 171-222-0028, 020-7222-0028 after April 2000), 2 Greycoat Place, Westminster, London SW1P 1SD, is a political lobbying group that publishes a quarterly newsletter on the Falklands with much useful information.

Dangers & Annoyances

Near Stanley and in a few camp locations on both East and West Falkland, there remain unexploded plastic land mines, but mine fields are clearly marked and, in the 17 years since the Falklands War, no civilian has been injured. *Never* even consider entering one of these fields – the mines will bear the weight of a penguin or even a sheep, but not of a human. Report any suspicious object to the Explosive Ordnance Disposal (EOD; ☎ 22229), opposite the Stanley police station, which distributes free minefield maps (which, incidentally, are handy for walks in the Stanley area).

Trekking in the camp is safe for anyone with confidence in his or her abilities, but it's better not to trek alone. The camp is so thinly populated that the consequences of an accident, however unlikely, could be very serious. Walkers in camp should be aware that so-called soft camp, covered by white grass, is boggy despite its firm appearance. This is not quicksand, but step carefully.

Business Hours

Falkland Islands government offices are open weekdays 8 am to noon and 1:15 to 4:30 pm. Most large businesses in Stanley, such as the FIC's West Store (a supermarket with some general interest items), stay open until 7 or 8 pm, but smaller shops are often open only a few hours a day. On weekends, business hours are much reduced. The few stores in camp, such as those at Fox Bay East and Port Howard, have a very limited regular schedule but will often open on request.

Public Holidays & Special Events

On both East and West Falkland, the annual sports meetings have been a tradition since the advent of sheep farming in the 19th century. In a land where most people lived a very isolated existence, they provided a regular opportunity to get together and share news, meet new people, and participate in friendly competitions such as horse racing, bull riding, and sheep-dog trials.

The rotating camp sports meeting on West Falkland carries on this tradition best, hosting 'two-nighters' during which Islanders party till they drop, go to sleep for a few hours, and get up and start all over again. Independent visitors should not feel shy about showing up at one of these events, although it is best to arrange for accommodations in advance – this will usually mean floor space for your sleeping bag.

National holidays include the following:

January 1
New Year's Day

Late February (dates vary)
Camp Sports

March/April (date varies)
Good Friday

April 21
Queen's Birthday

June 14
Liberation Day

August 14
Falklands Day

December 8
Battle of the Falklands (1914)

December 25
Christmas Day

December 26/27
Boxing Day/Stanley Sports

Activities

Wildlife is the major attraction for most visitors. Penguins, other shorebirds, and marine mammals are tame and easily approached even at developed tourist sites, such as Sea Lion Island and Pebble Island, but there are other equally interesting, undeveloped sites. Keep a respectful distance from these animals, especially the dangerous southern sea lion (see the Península Valdés boxed text in the Patagonia chapter).

Fishing for sea trout, mullet, and smelt is also popular; the most convenient site is the Murrell River, which is walking distance from Stanley. There are many other suitable places in camp, some easily accessible from the Mt Pleasant Hwy. Early March to late April is best for fishing for sea trout, which requires a license (£10) from the Stanley Post Office; it is obligatory to return the accompanying logbook to the Fisheries Department (☎ 27260) at the Falkland Islands Port and Storage System (FIPASS), anchored in Stanley Harbor east of town. The season runs from September 1 to April 30.

Trekking and camping are possible, but many landowners and the tourist board now discourage camping because of fire danger and disturbance to stock and wildlife. Hikers can visit the 1982 battlefields on both East and West Falkland.

Windsurfing is possible in sheltered waters such as Stanley Harbour (wet suits essential), but probably only the truly adept can avoid sailing to South Africa on the prevailing winds. Experienced divers may find it interesting to explore some of the Falklands' numerous wrecks; for information, contact Dave Eynon's South Atlantic Marine Services (☎ 21145, fax 22674, sams@horizon.co.fk), PO Box 140, Stanley, or in person at the boathouse on Ross Rd.

A current Falklands fad is golf, with courses in Stanley and several camp settlements hosting popular tournaments. No one will mistake Stanley Golf Course or any other for St Andrews, but the Falklands' gales and rolling terrain make for a challenging experience.

Work

Stanley's labor shortage has eased over the last few years, and work is more difficult to obtain. In the past, it was possible to obtain seasonal work on the large sheep stations belonging to the Falkland Islands Company and other companies, but agrarian reform has nearly eliminated this option. The major employers are FIC and FIG. There is a chronic housing shortage, and rental housing is difficult to come by, except for short-term stays.

Killer Whale

Accommodations

Accommodations are limited and improvised in some areas, but are still reasonably good everywhere. Stanley has several B&Bs and two hotels. Several farms have converted surplus buildings into lodges, some very comfortable, to accommodate tourists, but there are also self-catering cottages. A few have caravans or surplus Portakabin shelters (modular shell units that are similar to cargo containers but with doors and windows) obtained from the British military. They can be outfitted with beds or more elaborate furnishings, and sometimes with plumbing and electricity.

In areas not frequented by tourists, Islanders often welcome houseguests; in addition, many farms have 'outside houses' or shanties that visitors may use with permission. Some outside houses, traditionally used by shepherds on distant parts of a farm, are very comfortable if a bit old, while others are very run-down. Camping is possible only with permission.

Food & Drinks

Wool has long been the staple of the Falklands economy and mutton the staple of the Falklander's diet. While it is not true that Islanders eat mutton 365 days a year, it is nearly true – on Christmas Day they eat lamb, or so the story goes. Beef is generally available only in winter. Vegetarians will have a hard time of it, but meat is at least cheap.

Locally grown vegetables and fruits rarely appear on the market, since people grow their own produce in kitchen gardens, but a hydroponic market garden has begun to produce aubergines (eggplant), tomatoes, lettuce, and other salad greens throughout the year.

Stanley snack bars offer fast food such as fish and chips, mutton burgers (better than they sound), sausage rolls, and pasties. There are surprisingly good hotel restaurants, but nothing of international stature. Stanley has several well-patronized pubs, where beer and hard liquor (whiskey and rum) are the favorites, though wine has gained popularity in recent years. All drinks are imported.

GETTING THERE & AWAY

Air

Since 1986, with the completion of Mt Pleasant International Airport (MPA) 35 miles (56km) southwest of Stanley, regular flights have connected the Falklands to the Brize Norton air-force base, near Burford, Oxfordshire, England, via the tiny South Atlantic island of Ascension. Southbound, these flights leave Brize Norton every Monday and three Thursdays per month, arriving Tuesday and Friday; northbound, they leave Mt Pleasant Wednesday and three Saturdays per month, arriving Thursday and Sunday. The flight takes 18 hours, including an hour's stopover for refueling on Ascension.

The economy roundtrip fare is £2302, but there is a reduced APEX roundtrip fare of £1414 with 30-day advance purchase, as well as a £1192 fare for groups of six or more. Travelers continuing to Chile can purchase one-way tickets at half the above fares. For reservations in the UK, contact Gail Spooner at Falkland House (☎ 0171-222-2542, 020-7222-2542 after April 1999), 14 Broadway, Westminster, London SW1H 0BH. In Stanley, contact the FIC (☎ 27633, fax 27603), on Crozier Place, or International Tours & Travel Ltd (☎ 22041, fax 22042, int.travel@horizon.co.fk), in the Beauchene Complex on John St. The baggage limit is normally 44 lbs (20kg); enforcement is lax, but overweight charges run about £10 per pound.

Travelers visiting southern South America can reach the Falklands with LanChile (☎ 247079), Lautaro Navarro 999 in Punta Arenas, every Saturday. From Santiago, fares are US$410 one way, US$680 return (US$370 one way, US$630 with seven-day advance purchase); from Punta Arenas, fares are US$320 one way, US$490 return (US$280 one way, US$420 return with seven-day advance purchase).

Mount Pleasant has duty-free facilities, as does Wideawake Airfield on Ascension Island.

Stanley Services Limited (☎ 22622, fax 22623, sslcab@horizon.co.fk), on Airport Rd in Stanley, arranges excursions and itineraries for independent travelers; contact Carole Bedford, Manager, Travel Division.

Sea

Byron Marine Ltd (☎ 22245), fax 22246), at Waverly House in Stanley, occasionally sails the *MV Tamar* to Punta Arenas, Chile.

Berths are limited; the fare (£180 single, £300 return) is not much cheaper than flying, but it's probably more exciting unless you're prone to seasickness.

GETTING AROUND

Outside the Stanley/Mt Pleasant area, transportation is not cheap, since roads are few and the only regular public transportation is the Falkland Islands Government Air Service (FIGAS), an on-demand service that flies a 10-passenger Norman-Britten Islander aircraft to grass airstrips throughout the Islands. The approximate charges of £1 per minute would make the fare to Carcass Island, off West Falkland, about £145 roundtrip. The baggage limitation of 30 lbs (14kg) per passenger is strictly enforced for safety reasons.

Rental vehicles are available in Stanley, while lodges at Pebble Island, Sea Lion Island, Port Howard, and San Carlos have comfortable County Land Rovers available with drivers/guides for guests. Visitors may use their own state or national driver's licenses in the Falklands for up to 12 months.

Byron Marine Ltd (☎ 22245, fax 22246), carries a small number of passengers on its freighter *MV Tamar* as the latter makes its rounds to pick up and deliver wool and other goods to settlements around the Islands. Berths are limited; day trips cost £20, while overnights cost £25.

Stanley

In reality Stanley, the Falklands' capital, is barely a village which, by historical accident, acquired a political status totally out of proportion to its size. Because many of its houses were built from available materials, often locally quarried stone and timber from shipwrecks, it has a certain ramshackle charm, as the houses' metal cladding and brightly painted corrugated-metal roofs contrast dramatically with the surrounding moorland. Nearly all the houses have large kitchen gardens, where residents grow much of their own food and enough ornamentals to give the townscape a spot of color. The sweetish fragrance of peat fuel still permeates the town on calm evenings, though many households now use oil, gas, and electricity.

Stanley dates from 1844, when the Colonial Office ordered the removal of the seat of government from Port Louis, on Berkeley Sound, to the more sheltered harbor of Port Jackson, since renamed Stanley Harbour. Originally a tiny outpost of colonial officials, vagabond sailors, and British military pensioners, the town grew slowly as a supply and repair port for ships rounding Cape Horn en route to the California gold rush. Some damaged vessels were forced to limp back into port, their cargoes legitimately being condemned and sold, but ships began to avoid the port when others were scuttled under such questionable circumstances that the town acquired an unsavory reputation that undoubtedly discouraged growth. Only as sheep replaced cattle in the late 19th century did Stanley begin to grow more rapidly, as it became the transshipment point for wool between camp and the UK.

As the wool trade grew, so did the influence of the Falkland Islands Company (FIC), already the Islands' largest landowner. FIC soon became the town's largest employer, especially after acquiring the property of JM Dean, its only commercial rival, in the late 19th century. Over the next century, FIC's political and economic dominance was uncontested, as it ruled the town no less absolutely than the owners of the large sheep stations ruled the camp. At the same time, the company's relatively high wages and good housing provided a paternalistic security, although these 'tied houses' were available only so long as the employee remained with the company.

During the 1982 war, the capital escaped almost unscathed despite its occupation by thousands of Argentine troops. The two major exceptions were both ironic: a British mortar hit a house on the outskirts of town, killing three local women, while Argentine conscripts rioted against their officers after the surrender and burned the historic Globe Store, a business whose Anglo-Argentine owner had died only a few years earlier.

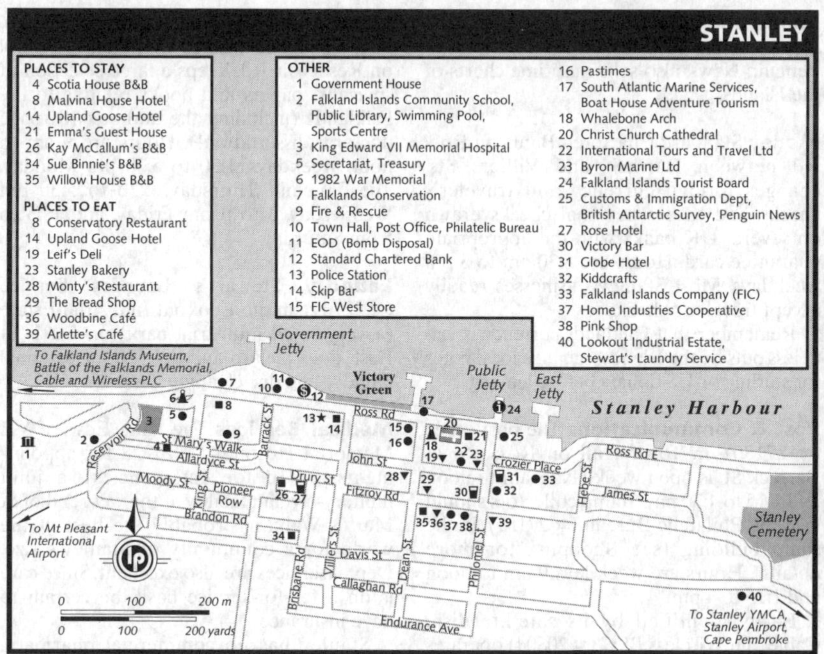

Stanley remains the service center for the wool industry, but since the declaration of a fisheries protection zone around the Islands, it has become an important port for the deep-water fishing industry, and many Asian and European fishing companies have offices here. The potential oil boom promises further changes.

Orientation

On a steep hillside on the south shore of Stanley Harbour, Port William's sheltered inner harbor on East Falkland, Stanley is surrounded by water and low hills. To avoid the prevailing southwesterlies, the town has sprawled east and west along the harbor rather than onto the exposed ridge of Stanley Common to the south. Ross Rd, running the length of the harbor, is the main street, but most government offices, businesses, and houses are within a few blocks of each other in the compact town center. Most Stanley roads are paved, but outside town they are invariably graveled. The only good roads outside Stanley are those to Mt Pleasant airport, to Darwin/Goose Green, with a spur to San Carlos, from Pony's Pass to Estancia and Port San Carlos, and from Estancia to Port Louis.

Information

Tourist Offices The Falkland Islands Tourist Board (☎ 22215, 22281, fax 22619, manager@tourism.org.fk) at the Public Jetty distributes an excellent guide to Stanley, as well as other useful brochures, including a list of accommodations throughout the Islands. Hours are 8 am to noon and 1:15 to 4:30 pm weekdays.

The Mount Pleasant Travel Office (☎ 76691) is at 12 Facility Main Reception, at Mt Pleasant International Airport.

FALKLAND ISLANDS

Immigration The Customs & Immigration Department (☎ 27340), on Ross Rd next to Penguin News, also sells maritime charts of the Islands.

Money Standard Chartered Bank, on Ross Rd between Barrack and Villiers Sts, changes foreign currency and traveler's checks, and cashes personal checks drawn on several UK banks with the appropriate guarantee card. Hours are 8:30 am to 3 pm weekdays. Most Stanley businesses readily accept traveler's checks.

Remember that Falklands currency is valueless outside the Islands – change local notes for sterling or US dollars before leaving.

Post & Communications The post office (☎ 27180), in Town Hall on Ross Rd at Barrack St, is open weekdays 8 am to noon and 1:15 to 4:30 pm. Stamp collectors should visit the Philatelic Bureau (☎ 27159), in the same building (see Shopping for more details). Hours are weekdays 9 am to noon and 1:15 to 4 pm.

Easily identified by its satellite dish, Cable and Wireless PLC (☎ 20804) operates the Falklands' phone, telegram, telex, and fax services from offices on Ross Rd near Government House. To make an overseas call from the booths in the office, purchase a magnetic card over the counter – this is cheaper than an operator-assisted call. Counter hours are 8:30 am to 5 pm weekdays, but public booths are open 24 hours.

Travel Agencies For special itineraries or assistance for groups or individuals within the Islands, contact Carole Bedford at Stanley Services (☎ 22622, fax 22623, sslcab@horizon.co.fk), on Airport Rd. For overseas travel, try International Tours & Travel Ltd (☎ 22041, fax 22042), in the Beauchene Complex on John St.

Photography Falkland Printz (☎ 32185), at Mt Pleasant Airport, stocks and develops both color print and slide film. In Stanley, leave your film at Pastimes, on Dean St near Ross Rd behind the FIC's West Store, for 36-hour service.

Libraries Stanley Public Library (☎ 27290), in the Falkland Islands Community School on Reservoir Rd, keeps a large selection of specialist papers and books relating to the Falklands (including the author's 781-page doctoral dissertation!). Hours are 9 am to noon weekdays, 1:30 to 5:30 pm Monday, Tuesday, and Thursday, 2:30 to 5:30 pm Wednesday, 3 to 6 pm Friday, and 1:45 to 5 pm Saturday.

Laundry Stewart's Laundry Service (☎ 22704), in the Lookout Industrial Estate (a very small industrial park) on Davis St East, does pickup and delivery of personal laundry and dry-cleaning.

Medical Services The King Edward VII Memorial Hospital (☎ 27328 for appointments, 27410 for emergencies), a joint military-civilian facility at the west end of St Mary's Walk, is probably the best in the world for a community of Stanley's size. Dental services are also excellent. Since care is on a fee-for-service basis, be certain to have insurance.

Stanley has no commercial pharmacy, but the hospital dispensary (☎ 27315) fills prescriptions weekdays 10 am to noon, Monday and Thursday 2:30 to 4:30 pm, Wednesday 1:30 to 5:30 pm, and Tuesday and Friday 3 to 5 pm.

Emergency The police (☎ 27222) are on Ross Rd, and Fire & Rescue (☎ 27333) is on St Mary's Walk.

Government House

Probably Stanley's most photographed landmark, rambling Government House has been home to London-appointed governors since the mid-19th century.

It is traditional for all visitors to the Falkland Islands to sign the register of visitors, but this custom has declined with the increased passenger traffic of the postwar period. Once a very minor post within the FCO, the governorship is currently much more significant.

Government House is on Ross Road West, set back about 50 yards from the street.

Christ Church Cathedral

Completed in 1892 and undoubtedly the town's most distinguished landmark, the cathedral, on Ross Rd near Dean St, is a massive brick-and-stone construction with a brightly painted, corrugated-metal roof and attractive stained-glass windows. Several interior plaques honor the memory of local men who served in the British Forces in WWI and WWII. On the small square next to the cathedral, the restored **Whalebone Arch** commemorates the 1933 centenary of British rule in the Falklands.

Battle of the Falklands Memorial

On Ross Rd West, just past Government House, this obelisk memorial commemorates a 1914 naval engagement between British and German forces in WWI. Nine British ships, in Stanley for refueling, quickly responded to sink four of five German cruisers that had earlier surprised them in southern Chile.

1982 War Memorial

Just west of the Secretariat on Ross Rd is a wall honoring the victims of the 1982 Falklands conflict. Designed by a Falkland Islander living overseas, it was paid for by public subscription and built with volunteer labor. Somber ceremonies take place here every June 14.

Stanley Cemetery

At the east end of Ross Rd, Stanley Cemetery is the final resting place for both the Islands' tiny elite and working class. Note the tombstones of three young Whitingtons, children of an unsuccessful 19th-century pioneer, whose eventual departure must have been a sad one. Other surnames, such as Felton and Biggs, are as common in the Islands as Smith and Jones are in the UK.

Falkland Islands Museum

Ironically, the facility that houses the Falklands museum was built for the Argentine Air Force officer who was the local representative of LADE, which until 1982 operated air services between Comodoro Rivadavia and Stanley. For several years after the war, it was the residence of the Commander of British Forces Falkland Islands (BFFI), but after the garrison moved to Mt Pleasant it became the new home of the local museum (☎ 27428), on Holdfast Rd south of Ross Rd W, just beyond the 1914 battle memorial.

Today the museum contains a professionally presented collection of artifacts from everyday life in the Falklands, in addition to natural history specimens. Curator John Smith is especially conversant with the Islands' maritime history; his booklet *Condemned at Stanley* relates the stories of the numerous shipwrecks that dot the harbor. Hours are Tuesday to Friday 10:30 am to noon and 2 to 4 pm, Sunday 10 am to noon. Admission costs £1.50 for adults, but is free for children.

Activities

Stanley's new public **swimming pool** (☎ 27291), on Reservoir Rd near the Mt Pleasant Hwy, has become a very popular recreational resource. Hours vary – check at the pool or with the tourist office.

Fishing for sea trout, mullet, and smelt is also a popular pastime; the nearest site is the Murrell River, which is walking distance from Stanley. There are many other suitable places in the camp, some easily accessible from the Mt Pleasant Hwy. Fishing for sea trout requires a license, available from the post office for £10. The season runs September 1 to April 30.

Mel Lloyd's Falcon Tours (☎ 32220) offers **horseback riding**, as does Gardner Fiddes' Tumbledown Trekking (☎ 21494).

Special Events

The capital's most noteworthy public event is the annual Stanley Sports between Christmas and New Year's, which features horse racing (betting is legal), bull riding, and other competitions.

Every March, the Falkland Islands Horticultural Society presents a competitive Horticultural Show, displaying the produce of kitchen gardens in Stanley and camp, plus a wide variety of baked goods. At the end of the day, the produce is sold in a spirited auction.

In August, the annual Crafts Fair in the gymnasium displays the work of local weavers, leather workers, photographers, and other artists (there are many talented illustrators and painters). Particularly interesting is the horsegear, whose origins lie in 19th-century gaucho traditions.

Places to Stay

Accommodations in Stanley are good but limited – reservations are advisable. Several B&Bs also offer the option of full board. Prices are for orientation only and subject to change.

The ***Stanley YMCA*** *(☎ 21074)*, with separate facilities on 'Squid Row,' at 12 Scoresby Close, and 21 Shackleton Drive, has single rooms with private bath and communal living and kitchen areas for £15 per night. However, it's often full with long-term tenants, so it's necessary to contact manager Terry Peck well in advance.

Otherwise, the most economical, and perhaps the best, is ***Kay McCallum's B&B*** *(☎ 21071, fax 21148, 14 Drury St)*, charging £16 per person; excellent lunches and dinners are available for a small additional charge, but Kay's heavy smoking has bothered some guests. Nick and Sheila Hadden's ***Willow House B&B*** *(☎/fax 21014, 27 Fitzroy Rd)* costs £16, while Bob and Celia Stewart's ***Scotia House B&B*** *(☎ 21191, 12 St Mary's Walk)* costs £19. ***Sue Binnie's B&B*** *(☎ 21051, 3 Brandon Rd)* charges £25. Popular ***Emma's Guest House*** *(☎ 21056, 36 Ross Rd)*, near Philomel St, costs £43 for B&B.

The venerable ***Upland Goose Hotel*** *(☎ 21455, 20-22 Ross Rd)*, a mid-19th-century building, charges from £38 per person for an economy room to £63 per person for a twin/double with breakfast and private bath.

The ***Malvina House Hotel*** *(☎ 21355, fax 21357, malvina@horizon.co.fk; 3 Ross Rd)*, has Stanley's most congenial ambience, with beautiful grounds and a conservatory restaurant. Rates are £57 single with breakfast.

Places to Eat

Most of Stanley's eateries are modest and inexpensive snack bars with limited hours. Two bakeries serve bread, snacks, and light meals: ***The Bread Shop*** *(☎ 21273)*, on Dean St (open daily 7:30 am to 1:30 pm), and ***Stanley Bakery*** *(☎ 22692)*, Waverley House, Philomel St (open weekdays 8:30 am to 3:30 pm, Saturday 9 am to 12:30 pm).

The ***Woodbine Café*** *(☎ 21002, 29 Fitzroy Rd)* serves fish and chips, pizza, sausage rolls, and similar items. It's open Tuesday to Friday 10 am to 2 pm, Wednesday and Friday 7 to 9 pm, and Saturday 10 am to 3 pm. ***Arlette's Café*** *(☎ 22633)*, Atlantic House, Fitzroy Rd, is open daily except Wednesday, from 9 am to 9 pm. ***Leif's Deli*** *(☎ 22721, 23 John St)* has specialty foods and snacks; it's open weekdays 9 am to 5 pm, Saturday 9:30 am to noon and 1 to 4 pm. The varied menu at ***Monty's Restaurant***, on John St, includes vegetarian dishes.

Most Stanley hotels also have restaurants, but meals should be booked in advance (see Places to Stay). ***Emma's Guest House*** has more elaborate lunches for £6.50 and dinner for £11. The outstanding ***Conservatory Restaurant***, at Malvina House Hotel, and the ***Upland Goose Hotel*** both serve three-course meals and bar snacks; Malvina has an excellent Chilean cook.

Entertainment

Stanley is no nightlife mecca but has several pubs, open Monday to Saturday 10 am to 2 pm, Monday to Thursday 5:30 to 11 pm, Friday and Saturday 5:30 to 11:30 pm, and Sunday noon to 2 pm and 7 to 10 pm. When cruise ships are in port, pubs are open all day.

The most popular is the ***Globe Hotel*** *(☎ 22703)*, at Crozier Place and Philomel St, which serves bar meals. Try also the ***Rose Hotel*** *(☎ 21067)*, on Brisbane Rd, the ***Victory Bar*** *(☎ 21199)*, on Philomel St at Fitzroy Rd, and the ***Stanley Arms*** *(☎ 22258)*, on John Biscoe Rd at the far western end of town. The Upland Goose Hotel's ***Ship Bar*** *(☎ 21455)* is open to the public, as is Monty's bar, ***Deano's*** *(☎ 21292)*.

In winter Stanley pubs sponsor a popular darts league, and darts tournaments take place in the Town Hall auditorium. For more information on such events, contact the Darts Club *(☎ 21199)*.

Many dances, with live music, and discos also take place throughout the year usually at the town hall. Listen to the nightly FIBS announcements for dates and times. There are no cinemas, but most hotels and guesthouses have video lounges.

Shopping

There are a few Falklands souvenirs, but most come from the UK. The exception is locally spun and knitted woolens, some of which are outstanding. Try the Home Industries Cooperative on Fitzroy Rd, open weekdays 9:30 am to noon and 1:30 to 4:30 pm. Kiddcrafts (☎ 21301), 2A Philomel St, makes stuffed penguins and other soft toys appealing to kids.

The Pink Shop (☎/fax 21399), 33 Fitzroy Rd, sells gifts and souvenirs in general, Falklands and general-interest books (including a selection of Lonely Planet guides), excellent wildlife prints by owner-artist Tony Chater, and work by other Falklands artists.

Postage stamps, available from the post office and from the Philatelic Bureau, are popular with collectors. The bureau also sells stamps from South Georgia and the British Antarctic Territory, and accepts Visa credit cards. The Treasury (☎ 27141), in the Secretariat on Thatcher Drive behind the 1982 War Memorial, sells commemorative Falklands coins.

Getting There & Away

Air For information on international flights, see the general Getting There & Away earlier in this chapter.

The Falkland Islands Government Air Service (FIGAS; ☎ 27219), at Stanley Airport, east of the city, sets up itineraries according to demand; as soon as you know when and where you wish to go, contact them, and listen to the FIBS announcements at 6:30 pm the night before your departure to learn your departure time. Flight plans depend on demand; if only one or two people are headed to a destination, FIGAS may delay a flight until other passengers join the group. On rare occasions, usually around holidays, flights are heavily booked and you may not get on. Because some grass airstrips can only accept a limited payload, luggage is restricted to 30 lbs (13.5kg) per person.

Passages may also be arranged through Stanley Services Ltd (☎ 22622, fax 22623, sslcab@horizon.co.fk), International Tours & Travel Ltd (☎ 22041, fax 22042, int.travel@horizon.co.fk), and the FIC (☎ 27633, fax 27603), on Crozier Place.

Sample roundtrip fares from Stanley include Salvador (£50), Darwin (£76), San Carlos (£78), Port Howard (£94), Sea Lion Island (£95), Pebble Island (£106), Fox Bay East or West (£121), and Carcass Island (£145).

Getting Around

To/From the Airport The Falklands have two main airports. Mt Pleasant International Airport is 35 miles (56km) southwest of Stanley via a good graveled road, while Stanley Airport (☎ 27303), for local flights, is about 3 miles (5km) east of town. Falkland Islands Tours & Travel (☎/fax 21775) takes passengers to Mt Pleasant for £13 single; call for reservations the day before. They will also take groups to Stanley Airport or meet them there.

Taxi For cabs, contact Ben's Taxi Service (☎ 21191) or Lowe's Taxis (☎ 21381), but be aware that they're expensive.

Car The improving road network has made this a more attractive alternative for getting around, but drivers without local experience often get stuck in the boggy soft camp on off-road tracks. This problem is so common even for experienced drivers that locals often carry a 2-meter ('ham') radio to call for help if they 'get bogged.'

Land Rovers are available from Ian Bury (☎ 21058), at 63 Davis St; Ben Claxton (☎ 21437), on Ross Rd E; and the Upland Goose Hotel (☎ 21455), on Ross Rd.

AROUND STANLEY

Stanley Harbour Maritime History Trail

See the tourist office on the Public Jetty for Graham Bound's informational brochure on the various wrecks and condemned ships in Stanley Harbour. There are now informational panels near the remains of vessels such as the *Jhelum* (a sinking East Indiaman deserted by her crew in 1871), the *Charles Cooper* (an American packet from 1866 still used for storage by FIC), and the *Lady Elizabeth* (a striking three-masted freighter that limped into Stanley after hitting a reef in 1913).

Gypsy Cove

About 200 pairs of Magellanic penguins breed at Gypsy Cove, about a 1½ hour walk northeast of Stanley, but there are also upland geese, kelp geese, and many other shorebirds. From the east end of Ross Rd, beyond the cemetery, cross the bridge over the inlet known as the Canache, continuing past the wreck of the *Lady Elizabeth* and Stanley Airport. Local tour operators will take you all the way to the cove, but taxi drivers may drop you some distance from the colony.

Gentoo penguins crowd the large sand beach at Yorke Bay north of the airport, where, unfortunately, the Argentines anticipated a British frontal assault and buried countless plastic mines. Do not climb over clearly marked fences into the minefields; apart from the obvious danger to your health, this is an illegal act with stiff penalties.

Battlefields

AD (Tony) Smith (☎ 21027, discovery51@hotmail.com) offers tours of 1982 battlefield sites near Stanley, including Wireless Ridge, Mt Tumbledown, and Sapper Hill.

Cape Pembroke Lighthouse

Built in 1855 and rebuilt in 1906, this recently restored lighthouse is a full-day's walk east from Stanley Airport. In the late 19th century, the entire Cape Pembroke peninsula constituted one of few small farms on the Islands, leased by the government to Stanley resident James Smith, a vocal advocate of agrarian reform, which finally came about a century later.

Kidney Island

This small nature reserve north of Port William is covered with tussock grass, forming the habitat for a wide variety of wildlife, including rockhopper penguins, sea

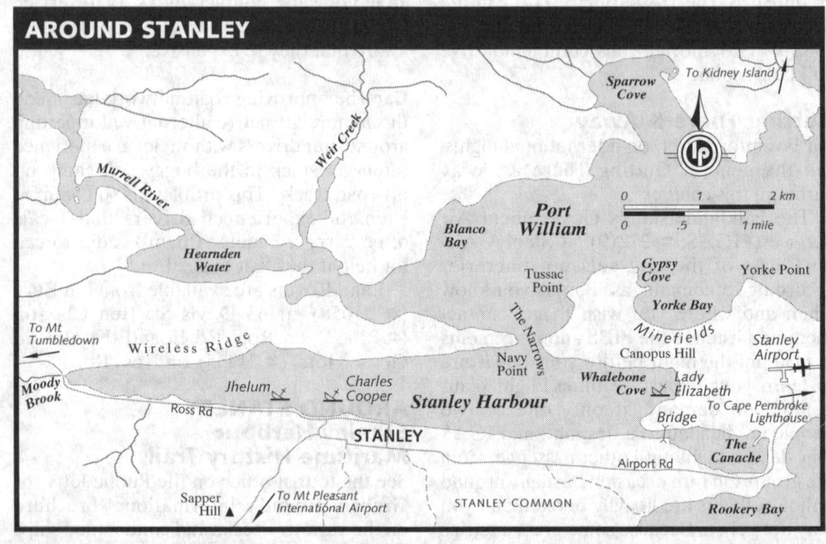

lions, and other species. Arrange carefully planned visits through the Agricultural Officer (☎ 27355). Dave and Carol Eynon's South Atlantic Marine Services/Boat House Adventure Tourism (☎ 21145, fax 22674, sams@horizon.co.fk), on Ross Rd, offers boat transportation, or contact Andrew Miller (☎ 22669, 22651, dicksoul@recol.es), Polar Warehouse, Stanley.

The Camp

Every part of the Falklands outside Stanley is 'camp,' including those parts of East Falkland accessible by road from Stanley, all of West Falkland, and the numerous smaller islands, only a few of which are inhabited. Nearly everyone in camp is engaged in sheep ranching, though a few work in tourism and minor cottage industries.

Since the advent of the large sheep stations in the late 19th century, rural settlement in the Falklands has consisted of tiny hamlets, really company towns, near sheltered harbors where coastal shipping could collect the wool clip. In fact, these settlements were the models for the sheep estancias of Patagonia, many of which were founded by Falklands emigrants. On nearly all of them, shepherds lived in 'outside houses' that still dot the countryside. Since the agrarian reform of the late 1970s and 1980s, this pattern of residence has not changed greatly despite the creation of many new farms.

Many but not all of the Islands' best wildlife sites are on offshore islands such as Sea Lion Island and Pebble Island, where there are comfortable but fairly costly tourist lodges. These are described in detail below, but there are also alternatives for budget travelers. Some of the most interesting islands have few or no visitor facilities and very difficult access, but it is worthwhile asking at the Tourist Board about them when you arrive in the Falklands.

EAST FALKLAND

East Falkland has the Islands' most extensive road network, consisting of a good highway to Mt Pleasant International Airport and Goose Green, with a spur to San Carlos. From Pony's Pass on the Mt Pleasant Hwy, there is also a good road north to the Estancia (a farm west of Stanley) and Port Louis, and an excellent road west from Estancia toward Douglas and Port San Carlos. Most other tracks are usable for 4WDs only.

Several Stanley operators runs day trips to East Falkland settlements, including Tony Smith's Discovery Tours (☎ 21027, fax 22304), Sharon Halford's Ten Acre Tours (☎ 21155, fax 21950), South Atlantic Marine Services (☎ 21145, fax 22674, sams@horizon.co.fk), and Montana Short's Photographic Tours (☎/fax 21076).

Salvador

Originally founded by Andrés Pitaluga, a Gibraltarian who arrived in the Islands via South America in the 1830s, Salvador is East Falkland's oldest owner-occupied sheep farm. On the station's north coast are colonies of five different species of penguins and many other shorebirds and waterfowl, while Centre Island in Port Salvador (also known as Salvador Water) has breeding populations of elephant seals and sea lions. Trekking along the north coast is possible with permission.

Owner Rob Pitaluga of ***Salvador Lodge*** *(☎ 31199)* offers self-catering accommodations (they provide the bedding, you provide and cook your own food) for £10 per person per night, £5 for children under 12.

Trekking the Northeast Coast

If you can do only one trek in the Islands, the hike from Seal Bay to **Volunteer Point** on the north coast of East Falkland is the one, offering a mixture of broad, sandy beaches and rugged headlands, with penguins always in view. Most but not all of the Stanley operators mentioned at the beginning of the East Falkland section do day trips to Volunteer Point for about £50 per person with a four-person minimum; rates include the owners' £10 per person visitor fee.

Port Louis to Seal Bay Port Louis is the starting point, reached by car – ask around town for a vehicle – or on foot from Stanley

FALKLAND ISLANDS

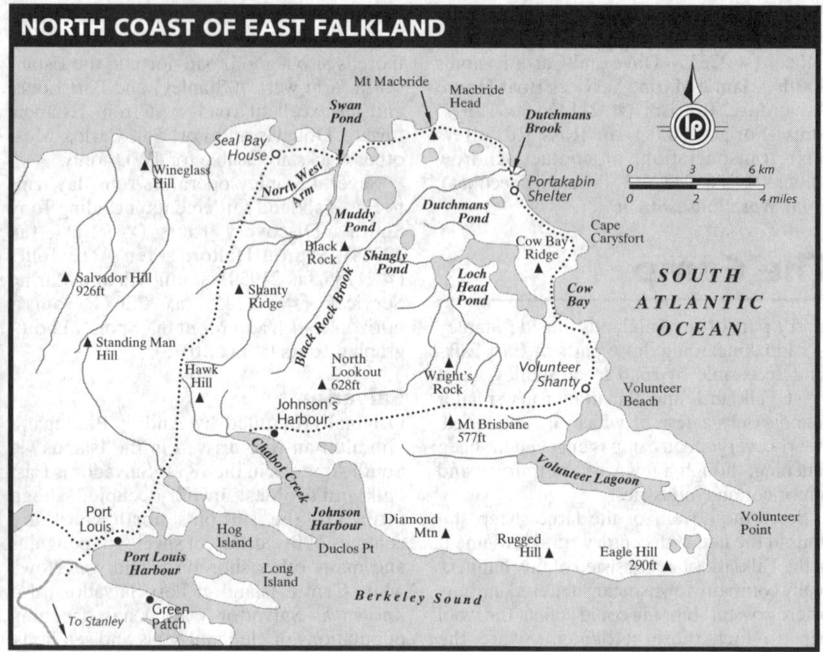

in one very long day. You will need permission from station manager Peter Gilding at Port Louis (☎ 31004) and owner George Smith of Johnson's Harbour (☎ 31399).

Port Louis is the Falklands' oldest settlement, dating from the French foundation of the colony by Louis de Bougainville in 1764. One of the oldest buildings in the colony is the ivy-covered 19th-century farmhouse, still occupied by farm employees, but there are also ruins of the French governor's house and fortress and Louis Vernet's settlement scattered nearby. Visit the grave of Matthew Brisbane, Vernet's lieutenant, who was murdered by gauchos after British naval officer JJ Onslow left him in charge of the settlement in early 1833.

From Port Louis, Seal Bay is a six- to eight-hour walk, depending on weather – with luck, the wind will be at your back. A Land Rover track follows a fence line almost all the way; be sure to close gates whenever you pass through them. Since much of the hiking is through soft white grass camp, choose your route to avoid sinking in.

Ask Peter Gilding's permission to stay or camp at Seal Bay House, which has a peat-burning Rayburn stove, before beginning the hike along the coast proper. Here, in the solitude of the north coast, you can get an idea of what it was to be a shepherd in the 19th century.

Seal Bay to Dutchmans Brook After leaving Seal Bay House, carry as much fresh water as possible, since penguins have fouled most of the watercourses along the way. Follow the arc of the coast eastward, past several colonies of rockhopper penguins and king cormorants, to the sea lion colony at Macbride Head. En route, there are also thousands of burrows of Magellanic penguins and occasional macaronis and gentoos.

Although the 1:250,000 map of East Falkland indicates a large inlet at Swan Pond, there is a broad, sandy beach there that only requires wading one shallow creek. The best ***campsite*** is Dutchmans Brook, where there is a Portakabin shelter but no dependable source of fresh water.

Dutchmans Brook to Volunteer Shanty

About 1½ hours south of Dutchmans Brook, in a patch of white grass along a fence line near a colony of gentoo penguins, a tiny spring is the only likely source of fresh water until Volunteer Shanty, another four hours south. On the way, you will see many more penguins, elephant seals, nesting turkey vultures, upland and kelp geese, and many other birds. Despite its name, Volunteer Shanty is a well-kept outside house, and George Smith now permits nonfarm personnel to use it; for details, contact him or Sharon Halford. It may also be possible to camp nearby, collect fresh water from the tap, and use its very tidy outhouse.

Volunteer Shanty to Johnson's Harbour

Volunteer Beach has the largest concentration of the photogenic king penguin in the Falklands, where the species is at the northern limit of its range. This colony has grown steadily over the past two decades and now contains about 150 breeding pairs. At Volunteer Point, several hours' walk from the shanty, an offshore breeding colony of southern fur seals is visible through binoculars. Return along Volunteer Lagoon to see more birds and elephant seals.

From Volunteer Beach, the settlement at Johnson's Harbour is an easy four- to five-hour walk along Mt Brisbane. If you are trekking back to Stanley, the small store at Johnson's Harbour may provide some supplies. FIGAS now stops at Johnson's Harbour only for emergencies.

San Carlos

British forces in the 1982 conflict first came ashore at San Carlos settlement, at the south end of San Carlos Water on the Falkland Sound side of East Falkland; there is a small military cemetery nearby. Until 1983, when it was subdivided and sold to half a dozen local families, San Carlos was a traditional large sheep station – the isolated 'big house,' with its lengthy approach, will give you some idea how farm owners and managers distanced themselves from laborers.

There is fishing on the San Carlos River, north of the settlement, while the comfortable ***Blue Beach Lodge*** *(☎ 32205, fax 32202)*, operated by William and Lynda Anderson, charges £55 per person with full board, with discounts for children; William Anderson also runs boat tours to wildlife sites such as Fanning Head and the San Carlos River.

Across San Carlos Water, on Ajax Bay, are the fascinating ruins of the **Ajax Bay Refrigeration Plant**, a Colonial Development Corporation (CDC) boondoggle of the 1950s that failed when farmers did not provide it with sufficient high-quality mutton from flocks raised primarily for wool. After its abandonment, prefab houses that were imported for laborers were dismantled and moved to Stanley, where they can be seen on Ross Rd W. Gentoo penguins occasionally wander through the ruins, which served as a military field hospital during the 1982 conflict. Take a flashlight if you plan to explore the ruins, which are about a four-hour walk around the south end of San Carlos Water.

Darwin & Goose Green

Darwin, at the narrow isthmus separating the southern peninsula of Lafonia from the northern half of East Falkland, was the site of Samuel Lafone's saladero, where the Montevideo merchant's local agents slaughtered feral cattle and processed their hides; later it became the center of the Falkland Islands Company's camp operations and, with nearby Goose Green, the largest Falklands settlement outside Stanley.

Built across Bodie Creek in 1926 to improve communications between Goose Green and Darwin, the world's southernmost suspension bridge is an unexpected sight. The heaviest ground fighting of the Falklands war took place at Goose Green, where there are several military landmarks, including an Argentine military cemetery

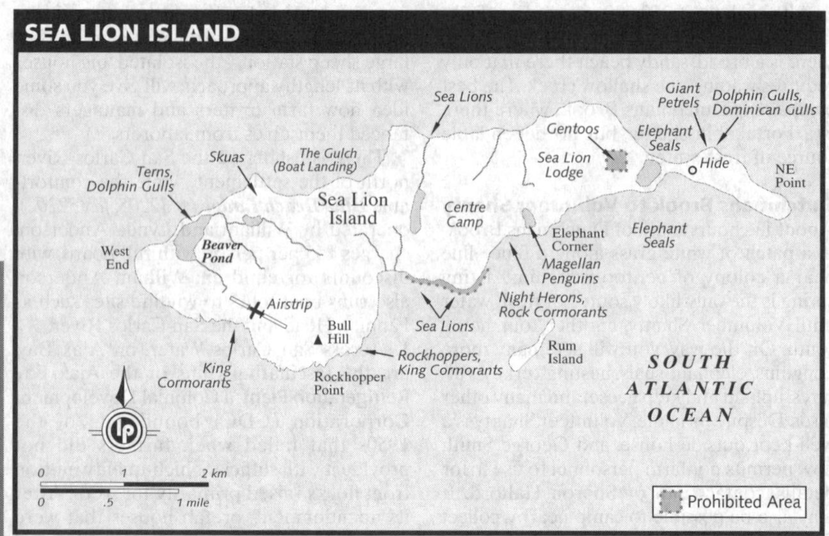

and a memorial to British Colonel H Jones. Darwin also has a golf course.

Sea Lion Island

The most southerly inhabited island in the Falklands is barely a mile across at its widest point, but still has more wildlife in a smaller area than almost anywhere in the Islands, including all five species of Falklands penguins, enormous colonies of cormorants, giant petrels, and the remarkably tame and charming predator known locally as the 'Johnny rook,' more properly the striated caracara *(Phalcoboenus australis)*. Hundreds of elephant seals haul up to breed on the island's sandy beaches every spring, while sea lions line the narrow gravel beaches below the southern bluffs and lurk among the towering tussock grass.

For most of its history, Sea Lion's isolation and difficult access undoubtedly contributed to the continuing abundance of wildlife, but much credit also goes to Terry and Doreen Clifton, who farmed Sea Lion Island since the mid-1970s before selling it in the early 1990s – the Cliftons developed their 2300-acre farm with the idea that wildlife habitat, and livestock were compatible uses. Sea Lion retains a substantial cover of native tussock, which once covered the coastal fringe of both East and West Falkland and many offshore islands before careless fires and overgrazing nearly eliminated it.

Through improved fencing and other conscientious management decisions, the Cliftons made the island both a successful sheep station and a popular tourist site, mostly for day trips from Stanley and the military base at Mt Pleasant. Since 1986 the modern ***Sea Lion Lodge*** *(☎ 32004, fax 32003)*, operated by Dave and Pat Grey, has offered twin-bedded rooms with full board for £55 per person, including access to a County Land Rover for visiting wildlife sites, although almost anyone can walk the length of the island in a few hours. To see the island in its entirety, allow at least two full days.

WEST FALKLAND

Nearly as large as East Falkland, West Falkland has an improving road system that runs from Port Howard on Falkland Sound to Fox Bay, with a spur from Chartres to Hill Cove and Roy Cove, and an extension is planned from Fox Bay to Port Stephens. In the meantime, a system of rough tracks is also suitable for Land Rovers and motorcycles.

Although offshore Saunders Island was the site of the first British garrison in 1765, West Falkland was settled permanently only in the late 1860s, when pioneer sheep farmer JL Waldron founded Port Howard. In short order, British entrepreneurs established stations at Hill Cove, Fox Bay, Port Stephens, Roy Cove, Chartres, and many smaller offshore islands. One of the most interesting experiments was the founding of a Keppel Island mission for Indians from Tierra del Fuego.

West Falkland has outstanding wildlife sites (as do adjacent islands) and good trekking in its interior, which is generally more mountainous than East Falkland. Only a few of these sites have formal tourist infrastructure, but independent travelers should look into visiting all parts of the island. Trekkers must obtain permission to walk across local farmers' properties.

Port Howard

West Falkland's oldest farm is the largest sheep station to survive the major agrarian reform of the 1980s. For more than a century it belonged to JL Waldron Ltd, but in 1987 it was sold to local managers Robin and Rodney Lee, who have kept the farm and settlement intact rather than subdividing it. About 40 people live on the 200,000-acre station, which has 42,000 sheep, 800 cattle, and its own dairy, grocery, abattoir, social club, and other amenities. Unusually for the Falklands, employees have been given the opportunity to purchase their houses, and at least one has chosen to retire here rather than move to Stanley. Port Howard will be the West Falkland terminus of the projected ferry across Falkland Sound.

Port Howard is a very scenic settlement at the foot of 2158-foot Mt Maria, at the north end of the Hornby range (the summit, about 3 miles (5km) west, makes a good afternoon hike). Although there is wildlife, most of it is distant from the settlement, whose immediate surroundings offer opportunities for hiking, horseback riding, and fishing. It is also possible to view summer shearing and other camp activities, and there is a small **museum** of artifacts from the 1982 war, when Argentine forces occupied the settlement.

The ***Port Howard Lodge*** *(☎/fax 42187)* is the former manager's house, a classic of its era with a beautiful conservatory that feels like the tropics when the sun comes out – see also the antique West Falkland telephone exchange, which no longer functions. Accommodations cost £55 per person with full board. Guest may also use the nine-hole golf course.

From Port Howard it's possible to hike up the valley of the Warrah River, a good trout stream, and past the Turkey Rocks to the Blackburn River and Hill Cove settlement, another pioneer 19th-century farm. Where the track is unclear, look for the remains of the old telephone lines. Ask permission to cross property boundaries, and remember to close gates. There are other, longer hikes south toward Chartres, Fox Bay, and Port Stephens.

Pebble Island

Elongated Pebble, off the north coast of West Falkland, has varied topography; a good sampling of wildlife, including Magellanic, gentoo, and rockhopper penguins; and extensive wetlands. ***Pebble Island Hotel*** (☎/fax 41093) charges £48 per person for room with full board, but if you're on a tight budget contact Raymond Evans (☎ 41098, fax 41099) about ***self-catering cottages*** at the settlement and ***Marble Mountain Shanty***, at the west end of the island.

Keppel Island

In 1853, the South American Missionary Society established an outpost on Keppel Island to catechize Yahgan Indians from Tierra del Fuego and teach them to become potato farmers instead of hunter-gatherers. The mission was controversial because the government suspected that Indians had been brought against their will, but it lasted until 1898, despite the Indians' susceptibility to disease – contrast the unmarked but discernible Yahgan graves with the marked ones of the mission personnel. One Falklands governor attributed numerous Yahgan deaths from tuberculosis to their

> delicacy of constitution ... developed owing to the warm clothing which they are for the sake of decency required to adopt after having been for 15 or 20 years roaming about in their canoes in a very cold climate without clothing of any kind.

It's likely that hard physical labor, change of diet, European contagion, and harsh living conditions in their small, damp stone houses played a greater role in the Yahgans' demise than any inherent delicacy of constitution. The mission was undoubtedly prosperous, though, bringing in an annual income of nearly £1000 from its herds of cattle, flocks of sheep, and gardens by 1877.

Although Keppel is now exclusively a sheep farm, there remain several interesting ruins. The former chapel is now a wool shed, while the stone walls of the Yahgan dwellings remain in fairly good condition. The mission bailiff's house stands intact, though in poor repair. Keppel is also a good place to see penguins. Visitors interested in exploring the island should contact owner LR Fell (☎ 41001), but FIGAS cannot fly there unless there is already someone on the island.

Saunders Island

Only a few miles west of Keppel, Port Egmont on Saunders Island was the site of the first British garrison on the Falklands, built in 1765. In 1767, after France ceded its colony to Spain, Spanish forces dislodged the British from Saunders and nearly precipitated a general war between the two countries. After the British left voluntarily in 1774, the Spaniards razed the settlement, including its impressive blockhouse, leaving the still remaining jetties, extensive foundations, and some of the buildings' walls, plus the garden terraces built by the British marines.

One British sailor left a memoir indicating how well developed the settlement was:

> The glory of our colony was the gardens, which we cultivated with the greatest care, as being fully convinced how much the comforts of our situation depended on our being supplied with vegetables ... We were plentifully supplied with potatoes, cabbages, broccoli, carrots, borecole, spinach, parsley, lettuce, English celery, mustard, cresses, and some few, but very fine cauliflowers.

Saunders Island continued to be controversial into the late 1980s because the property passed by inheritance into the hands of Argentine descendants of Scottish pioneer sheep farmer John Hamilton, who also had extensive properties near Río Gallegos in Santa Cruz province. For years, Islanders agitated for the farm's expropriation, but the owners finally consented to sell the island to its local managers in 1987.

In addition to historical resources, Saunders Island has an excellent sample of Falklands wildlife and offers good trekking, especially out the north side of Brett Harbour to The Neck. About four hours' walk from the settlement, this sandspit beach connects Saunders Island to Elephant Point peninsula, once a separate island. The Neck has a Portakabin shelter close to a large colony of black-browed albatrosses and rockhopper penguins, plus a few king penguins. Farther on, toward Elephant Point proper, are thousands of Magellanic penguins, breeding kelp gulls, skuas, and a colony of elephant seals in a very scenic area. From The Neck, Elephant Point is about a four-hour walk one way.

David and Suzan Pole-Evans on Saunders (☎ 41298, fax 41296) rent a comfortable ***self-catering cottage*** in the settlement for £10 per person per night, as well as a Portakabin at The Neck, which sleeps six (bedding supplied) and has a gas stove and a chemical toilet outside. Fresh milk and eggs are usually available in the settlement, but otherwise visitors should bring their own food. Depending on the farm workload, transportation to The Neck is available for £10 per person; the Pole-Evanses also rent mountain bikes for £4 per day.

Carcass Island

Despite its apparently unappealing name (which it owes to a ship rather than a dead animal), Carcass is a small, scenic island west of Saunders with a good variety of wildlife;

it's a popular weekend and holiday vacation spot for Stanleyites.

A couple of ***self-catering cottages*** in the settlement rent for £15/25 single/double, plus £5 per additional person; for details, contact Rob McGill on Carcass (☎ 41106).

Port Stephens

Open to the blustery South Atlantic and battered by storms out of the Antarctic, Port Stephens' rugged headlands are unquestionably the most scenic part of the Falklands. Thousands upon thousands of rockhopper penguins, cormorants, and other seabirds breed on the exposed coast, only a short distance from the settlement's sheltered harbor, until recently the center of one of the FIC's largest stations. Like many other settlements, Port Stephens has no formal tourist facilities, but is well worth a visit.

Less than an hour's walk from the settlement, Wood Cove and Stephens Peak are excellent places to see both gentoo and rockhopper penguins and other local birds. The peak of Calm Head, about two hours' walk, has superb views of the jagged shoreline and the powerful South Atlantic.

One interesting longer trek goes from the settlement to the abandoned sealing station at Port Albemarle and huge gentoo penguin colonies near the Arch Islands. Hoste Inlet, where there is a habitable outside house, is about five hours' walk in good weather, while the sealing station, another post-WWII Colonial Development Corporation blunder, is four hours farther. Like the Ajax Bay freezer, the sealing station is a monument to bureaucratic ineptitude, but photographers and aficionados of industrial archaeology will find its derelict power station, boilers, rail track, water tanks, jetty, and Nissen huts surrealistically intriguing. There is a habitable shanty with a functional Rayburn stove nearby, but unfortunately squaddies from the radar station on Mt Alice have vandalized the larger outside house.

The massive penguin colonies are an hour's walk beyond the sealing station. The Arch Islands, inaccessible except by boat, take their name from the opening that the ocean has eroded in the largest of the group – and it is large enough to allow a good-sized vessel to pass through it.

Visitors interested in exploring Port Stephens and trekking in the vicinity should contact Peter or Anne Robertson (☎ 42307) at the settlement, or Leon and Pam Berntsen (☎ 42309) at Albemarle Station.

South Georgia

One of the great stories of Antarctic adventure is British explorer Ernest Shackleton's rowing across several hundred miles of open ocean to the sub-Antarctic island of South Georgia from the Antarctic Peninsula, where his crew, low on provisions, wintered in 1916. Visitors to the Falklands are *relatively* close – about 800 miles (1300km) – to South Georgia, a onetime whaling base with several historic sites, including Shackleton's grave and the Norwegian station at Grytviken, which was also the site of British-Argentine confrontations during the 1982 Falklands War.

Only private cruises and yacht tours normally visit South Georgia, which is home to millions of seabirds and marine mammals, and some of the most spectacular mountain scenery in the circumpolar regions. It is under the administration of the Commissioner for South Georgia and the South Sandwich Islands (☎ 27433, fax 27434) at Government House in Stanley; for details on visiting, see Sally Poncet and Craig Shelton's *Information for Visitors to South Georgia*, published by the Government Printing Office in the Falklands' capital.

Weddell Island

Scottish pioneer John Hamilton, also a major landholder in Argentine Patagonia, acquired this western offshore island and others nearby to experiment on various agricultural improvement projects, including the replanting of tussock grass, forest plantations, the importation of Highland cattle and Shetland ponies, and the well-meaning but perhaps misguided introduction of exotic wildlife like guanacos (still present on Staats Island), Patagonian foxes (common on Weddell proper, and the cause of high lamb losses), and otters (apparently extinct). The third-largest island in the archipelago, Weddell still hosts abundant local wildlife, including gentoo and Magellanic penguins, great skuas, night herons, giant petrels, and striated caracaras. Farm owners John and Steph Ferguson do 4½ hour Land Rover tours to Loop Head, the best wildlife site, for £35 to £45 for a maximum of six persons.

Unfortunately, Hamilton's original farmhouse, which had spectacular interior woodwork, burned to the ground several years ago, but the Fergusons (☎ 42398, fax 42399) welcome guests at ***Seaview Cottage***, ***Hamilton Cottage***, or newly remodeled ***Mountain View House*** for £15 per person per night self-catering or £30 per person per night with full board.

New Island

Having been a refuge for whalers from Britain and North America from the late 18th century well into the 19th, despite the objections of Spanish and British authorities, the Falklands' most westerly inhabited island has great historic interest in addition to abundant wildlife. There remain ruins of a shore-based, turn-of-the-century Norwegian whaling factory that failed because there simply were not enough whales.

On the precipitous western coast are large colonies of rockhopper penguins and black-browed albatrosses, plus a substantial rookery of southern fur seals. Facilities are few and access is difficult, but potential visitors should contact Tony or Annie Chater (☎ 21399), or Ian or María Strange (☎ 21185) in Stanley. The Stranges maintain the southern half as the New Island South Nature Reserve.

URUGUAY

WAYNE BERNHARDSON

Facts about Uruguay

Roughly the size of Buenos Aires province, Uruguay is a classic political buffer between the South American megastates of Argentina and Brazil. Increasing numbers of independent travelers are visiting the country – from Buenos Aires, it's only a short hop across the Río de la Plata to the fascinating colonial contraband center of Colonia and only a little farther to Montevideo, one of South America's most interesting capitals.

East of Montevideo, sandy Atlantic beaches attract many Uruguayans and Argentines for summer holidays, but the less-frequented towns up the Río Uruguay, opposite Argentine Mesopotamia, are also clean and attractive. Uruguay's hilly interior is agreeable but rarely visited gaucho country.

Known officially as the República Oriental del Uruguay (Eastern Republic of Uruguay, often abbreviated as ROU), the area was long called the Banda Oriental or 'Eastern Shore' of the River Plate. For most of this century, foreigners considered Uruguay the 'Switzerland of South America,' but political and economic crises in the 1970s and 1980s undermined this favorable image.

HISTORY

Uruguay's aboriginal inhabitants were the Charrúa, a hunting and gathering people who also fished extensively. Hostile to outsiders, they discouraged settlement for more than a century by killing Spanish explorer Juan de Solís and most of his party in 1516. In any event, there was little to attract the Spanish who, according to William Henry Hudson, 'loved gold and adventure above everything, and finding neither in the Banda, they little esteemed it.'

In the 17th century, the Charrúa acquired the horse and prospered on wild cattle, eventually trading with the Spanish. Never numerous, they no longer exist as a definable tribal entity, though there remain some mestizo people in the interior along the Brazilian border. As on the Argentine Pampas, the gauchos subsisted on wild cattle, but in time, the establishment of estancias pushed them back into the interior.

European Colonization

The first Europeans on the Banda Oriental were Jesuit missionaries who settled near present-day Soriano, on the Río Uruguay. In 1680 the Portuguese established a beachhead at Nova Colônia do Sacramento, opposite Buenos Aires on the estuary of the Rió de la Plata. As a fortress and contraband center, Colonia posed a direct challenge to Spanish authority, forcing the Spanish to build their own citadel at the sheltered port of Montevideo.

This rivalry between Spain and Portugal led eventually to Uruguayan independence. José Gervasio Artigas, Uruguay's greatest national hero, allied with the United Provinces of the River Plate against Spain, but was unable to prevent Uruguay's takeover by Brazil. Exiled to Paraguay, he inspired

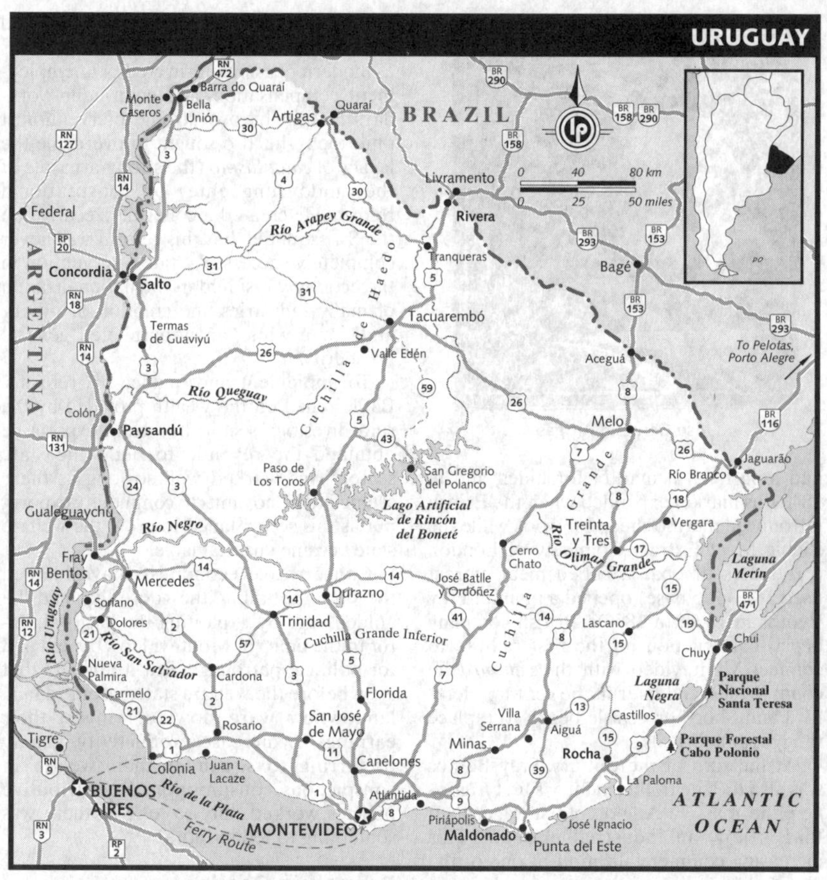

the famous '33 Orientales,' Uruguayan patriots under General Juan Lavalleja, who, with Argentine support, launched a campaign to liberate the Banda from Brazilian control. In 1828, after three years' struggle, a British-mediated treaty established Uruguay as a small independent buffer between the emerging continental powers.

Independence & Development

For most of the 19th century, Uruguay's independence was fragile, threatened politically and militarily by Argentina and Brazil, and economically by Britain. Federalist forces, supported by the Argentine dictator Rosas, besieged Montevideo from 1838 to 1851. From this period, Uruguay's two major political parties, the Blancos and the Colorados, can trace their origins as armed gaucho sympathizers of the Federalist and Unitarist causes. As Hudson wrote in *The Purple Land* (1922), 'Endless struggles for mastery ensued, in which the Argentines and Brazilians, forgetting their solemn compact, were for ever taking sides.'

British interest in the Banda, first aroused by that country's occupation of Montevideo in 1807, grew after independence. The UK

José Gervasio Artigas

had long been a market for hides, and in 1840 this market expanded when the British introduced merino sheep for wool, while the Liebig Meat Extract Company of London (producers of Oxo, a cubed meat extract used as a soup base) opened a plant at Fray Bentos in 1864. In 1868 a British company began construction on the first railway to connect Montevideo with the *campo* (the countryside), and later in the century Hereford and Shorthorn cattle began to replace rangy criollo breeds.

At the turn of the century, Fray Bentos was also the site of the country's first *frigorífico*, the massive Anglo cold storage plant that is now an industrial museum. This increasing commercialization of one of the country's few abundant resources brought about the demise of the independent gaucho who, as in Argentina, became attached to estancias, whose boundaries soon became fixed by barbed wire. As elsewhere in Latin America, large landholdings *(latifundios)* became a way of life in Uruguay, and these made a major, if reluctant, contribution to the general welfare in the form of taxes.

Batlle & Modernization

One of the most visionary politicians in Latin American history was Uruguay's José Batlle y Ordóñez, who devised the region's first comprehensive social welfare state. During two terms as president (1903-7 and 1911-5), he accomplished such innovations as modern pensions, farm credits, unemployment compensation, and eight-hour workdays. Despite his own strong, interventionist philosophy, he also sought to overcome the legacy of *caudillismo* (the strong-arm rule of the landowning elite) by constitutional reform. He created a collegial executive on the Swiss model, but this reform was never completely successful. State intervention in the economy resulted in the nationalization of many industries, the creation of others, and, for a while, an unparalleled general prosperity.

To implement and finance his reforms, Batlle relied on the wealth provided by the rural livestock sector; by taxing exports he obtained the revenue to build the state sector. This worked well so long as there seemed to be no limits to commodity exports, but as this sector failed to grow, the welfare state became unsustainable.

Conservative economists have blamed the state for 'killing the goose that laid the golden egg,' by exploiting the pastoral sector to the limit for Montevideo's benefit and for political patronage. But it appears that even before the welfare state became a fact, landowners were slow to reinvest their earnings to increase productivity, mainly preferring to squander their wealth in conspicuous consumption. Redistributive policies worked only so long as there was something to redistribute.

Economic Decline & Political Breakdown

From the mid-20th century, economic stagnation affected the entire country, but particularly the city of Montevideo, which had become accustomed to middle-class prosperity. State-supported enterprise became riddled with patronage and corruption, and the economy was unable to support a pensioner class numbering over 25% of the total workforce. By the mid-1960s this imbalance had reached crisis proportions, with serious political unrest, but the 1966 election of Colorado presidential candidate Oscar Gestido, a highly regarded retired general, appeared to give some cause for optimism and recovery. Gestido died shortly after taking office, however, to be replaced by Vice-President Jorge Pacheco Areco, a virtual unknown who proved to have disturbing authoritarian tendencies.

Under Pacheco, the country slid into dictatorship as he outlawed leftist parties, closed newspapers, and invoked state-of-siege measures because of guerrilla activity. The major guerrilla force was the Movimiento de Liberación Nacional (National Liberation Movement), more commonly known as the Tupamaros, a clandestine socialist faction who had organized as early as 1963 but did not reveal their existence publicly until 1967. Although an urban, middle-class movement in a country populated almost exclusively by descendants of Europeans, the Tupamaros took their name from a Peruvian Indian who led an 18th-century rebellion against the Spanish crown.

At first, the Tuparmaros enjoyed public support, but this eroded quickly as Uruguayans began to blame them for the Pacheco government's excesses, which included the dismissal of a police official who openly disapproved of torture. After the Tupamaros kidnapped and executed suspected CIA agent Dan Mitrione (an incident dramatized in Costa-Gavras' 1973 film *State of Siege)*, and then engineered the escape of more than 100 of their comrades from prison, Pacheco placed the military rather than the police in charge of the counterinsurgency.

Presidential elections occurred as scheduled in November 1971, but Pacheco's hand-picked successor, Juan M Bordaberry, invited the military to participate in government, ruling with a National Security Council and eventually dissolving the legislature.

Military Dictatorship & Aftermath

While the Uruguayan military takeover exhibited neither the shocking suddenness of the Chilean coup nor the sustained brutality of Argentina's Dirty War, it was perhaps even more insidious in the context of Uruguayan history. Virtually eliminating free expression, the armed forces occupied almost every position of importance in the entire country and ballooned the military budget to bolster 'national security.'

Torture or threat of torture became routine; eventually more than 60,000 citizens were detained. The military established a political classification system that determined eligibility for public employment, subjected all political offenses to military courts, actively censored public libraries, and even required prior police approval for large family gatherings.

Attempting to institutionalize their political role, the armed forces drafted a constitution, but the electorate rejected it in a plebiscite in 1980 despite warnings that rejection would delay any return to civilian rule. Four more years passed before voters could elect Colorado presidential candidate Julio María Sanguinetti under the Constitution of 1967. Sanguinetti, though not a tool of the military, won only because they prohibited the candidacy of Blanco leader Wilson Ferreira Aldunate, a vocal and popular opponent of the dictatorship.

Sanguinetti's presidency, while unspectacular, seemed to indicate a return to Uruguay's democratic traditions. He did, however, support a controversial amnesty bill for military human rights violations that was submitted to a referendum of all Uruguayans in April 1989. Despite serious misgivings on the part of many, a majority of voters approved the amnesty. Later that year, Blanco presidential candidate Luis Lacalle succeeded Sanguinetti in a peaceful transition of power. Sanguinetti returned to office as the head of a coalition government in the elections of November 1994.

GEOGRAPHY & CLIMATE

One of South America's smallest countries, Uruguay is still large by European standards. Its area of 187,000 sq km is greater than England and Wales combined, or about the size of the US state of North Dakota. Lacking energy resources (except for a few hydroelectric sites), minerals, and commercial forests, its principal natural asset is agricultural land, which is abundant but less fertile than the Argentine Pampas. For the most part, the country's rolling topography is an extension of southern Brazil, with two main ranges of interior hills, the Cuchilla de Haedo, west of Tacuarembó, and the Cuchilla Grande, south of Melo, neither of which exceeds 500 meters in height. West of Montevideo, the level terrain resembles the Pampas, while the coastal area east of the capital has impressive beaches, dunes, and headlands. There are some large lagoons near the Atlantic border with Brazil, including the huge Laguna Merín.

The climate is mild, even in winter, and frosts are rare. Along the coast, daytime temperatures average 28°C in January and 15°C in June, while nighttime temperatures average 17°C in January and 7°C in June. Annual rainfall, evenly distributed throughout the year, averages about 1m over the whole country.

FLORA & FAUNA

Consisting mostly of grasslands and gallery forests, Uruguay's native vegetation does not differ greatly from that of the Argentine Pampas or southern Brazil. Some areas of palm savanna remain in the southeast along the Brazilian border, but only a very small percentage of the land is forested.

Wild animals of any size are uncommon, although rhea can still be found in areas close to the Río Uruguay. Uruguay's nature reserves are few and offer little out of the ordinary, although the seal colonies near Punta del Este and at Cabo Polonio make worthwhile visits.

GOVERNMENT & POLITICS

Uruguay's 1967 constitution establishes three separate branches of government. The president heads the executive branch, while the legislative Asamblea General (General Assembly) consists of a 99-seat Cámara de Diputados (Chamber of Deputies) and a 30-member Senado (Senate). Elections for these seats take place every five years. The Corte Suprema (Supreme Court) is the highest judicial power. Administratively, Uruguay consists of 19 departments organized much like the national government.

The electoral system is complex. While the legislature is chosen by proportional representation, each party may offer several presidential candidates. The winner is the candidate with the most votes of the party with the most votes. This means that the winner almost certainly will not win a majority (even within his own party) and may not even be the candidate with the most votes overall. In eight elections between 1946 and 1984, no winning candidate obtained more than 31% of the vote.

The two major political parties are the Colorados, the inheritors of the legacy of *Batllismo*, and the generally more conservative Blancos. Julio María Sanguinetti of the Colorado party, the first post-military president, ruled between 1984 and 1989, while his successor, Luis Lacalle, who ruled until the 1994 elections, belonged to the Blancos. A third force, growing in power, is the Frente Amplio, or Encuentro Progresista, a center-left coalition that controls the mayorship of Montevideo. Ironically, its most prominent figure is a retired general, Liber Seregni. In the presidential election of November 1994, Frente Amplio candidate Tabar Vásquez actually won more votes than any other candidate, but the fact that his party had fewer total votes than the Colorados denied him the presidency.

This closely contested election returned Sanguinetti to the presidency at the head of a Colorado-Blanco coalition that has divided important cabinet posts between the two parties and constitutes, at least in theory, a substantial legislative majority. Whether the coalition of these traditional opponents will hold together for long remains an open question, but Frente Amplio now constitutes the official opposition. Despite continuing links to leftists (when ex-Tupamaro José Mujica, now an elected deputy, parked his motorcycle at Montevideo's Palacio Legislativo, he responded to staff inquiries as to how long he planned to remain with, 'Five years, unless the military returns'), it has made surprising inroads into wealthier barrios like Carrasco. As Frente Amplio mayor of Montevideo, Mariano Arana is one of the country's most powerful individuals outside the national government.

The major issues facing the government are reform of the overburdened social security system and the country's response to its membership in Mercosur as a junior partner, for all practical purposes, to economic giants Brazil and Argentina. The next elections will take place in late 1999.

ECONOMY

Uruguay is underpopulated and resource-poor. Historically, the dominant and most productive part of the Uruguayan economy has been the pastoral sector. Cattle and sheep estancias occupy over three-quarters of the land, grazing over 9 million cattle and 23 million sheep, but as the pastoral economy has stagnated from estancieros' unwillingness to invest in improvements, the country has been unable to sustain the progressive social programs established by José Batlle. The low international price for wool, the country's primary export, has been a major factor in recent years. Only along the southwest littoral does the country support intensive agriculture, although wet-rice cultivation has increased around Laguna Merín near the Brazilian border. Cropland occupies a relatively small area, but makes a disproportionately high contribution to the economy.

Manufacturing is restricted mostly to the area around Montevideo. In part because of Batlle's legacy of encouraging self-sufficiency despite a tiny internal market, many state-supported industries produce inferior products at very high cost, surviving only because of protective tariffs. Among the economic activities traditionally controlled by the government are railroads, banking, insurance, telephone service, electricity, water supply, oil refining, fisheries, and Montevideo's meat supply. This extensive control makes the country's economy the most state-dominated in Latin America. Social security pensions consume 60% of public expenditure.

Tourism plays an increasingly important economic role, as the beaches east of Montevideo attract wealthy Argentines. In many ways, Uruguay is an economic satellite of both Brazil and Argentina as well as a political buffer between these two major powers. The Mercosur common market, which went into effect in 1995, joined these two countries' economies with those of Paraguay and Uruguay; conceivably, by encouraging investment, this opening could reduce the emigration that has deprived Uruguay of many of its most youthful and capable people, who have sought employment in neighboring countries. In some ways, Uruguay remains the most maddeningly bureaucratic of South American states, with a bloated and unmotivated state sector.

Hyperinflation has twice required the introduction of new currencies in the past two decades. Inflation has fallen but is still high by European standards – for the 1997 calendar year, it was roughly 15%, but gradual devaluation of the peso is keeping prices relatively stable in US dollar terms. Foreign debt is still a major concern, as Uruguay has one of Latin America's largest per capita burdens. Historically, liberal banking laws have made Uruguay a destination for capital from neighboring countries, but usually only as a stop en route to Switzerland or the USA.

Uruguay's minimum wage is approximately US$95 per month, and the unemployment rate about 12%. In 1997, the per capita annual income was about US$6000.

POPULATION & PEOPLE

With a population of just over 3.2 million, Uruguay is South America's smallest Spanish-speaking country. It is highly urbanized, with 90% of Uruguayans residing in cities. Nearly half live in Montevideo, leading one political scientist to call Uruguay a 'city-state,' even though, historically, the rural sector has produced most of its wealth. The second-largest city, Salto, has barely 100,000 inhabitants.

By world standards, the welfare of Uruguayans ranks high. Infant mortality rates are low, and the life expectancy of 75 years matches Chile's as South America's highest, only slightly below that of the US and many Western European countries. Yet limited economic opportunity has forced half a million Uruguayans to live outside the country, mostly in Brazil and Argentina. The natural increase is less than 1%, with a doubling time of 88 years.

Most Uruguayans are predominantly of Spanish and Italian origin. European immigration has overwhelmed the small but still visible Afro-Uruguayan population of perhaps 60,000, descendents of slaves brought to the country in the 19th century who once constituted nearly 20% of Montevideo's population.

EDUCATION

For more than a century, primary education has been free, secular, and compulsory, with per capita government expenditures among the highest in Latin America. Uruguay's literacy rate is among the foremost in the region, and enrollment in free secondary schools is also very high.

Montevideo's Universidad de la República is the only public university. Since a disproportionate number of students pursue degrees in law or medicine, the country lacks trained personnel in more technically oriented professions.

ARTS

For such a small country, Uruguay has an impressive literary and artistic tradition. Uruguay's best-known contemporary writers are Juan Carlos Onetti, whose novels *No Man's Land* (Tierra de Nadie), *The Shipyard* (El Astillero), *Body Snatcher* (Juntacadáveres; New York, Pantheon, 1991), and *A Brief Life* (Una Vida Breve) are available in English. Poet, essayist, and novelist Mario Benedetti is another luminary. Journalist Eduardo Galeano, whose *Open Veins of Latin America* is mentioned in the section on Argentine history (see the Facts for the Visitor chapter), is also Uruguayan.

Uruguay's most famous writer is probably José Enrique Rodó, whose turn-of-the-century essay *Ariel*, contrasting North American and Latin American civilizations, is a classic of the country's literature (it's available in a paperback English translation). While none of 19th-century writer Javier de Viana's work has been translated into English, he and his 'gauchesco' novels are the subject of John F Garganigo's biography *Javier de Viana*.

Theater is a popular medium, and playwrights are very prominent. One is Mauricio Rosencof, a Tupamaros founder whose plays have been produced since his release from prison, where he was tortured by the military government in the 1970s.

Uruguayan artists such as Pedro Figari, who paints rural scenes, have earned recognition well beyond the country's borders. Punta Ballena, near Punta del Este, is well known as an artists' colony.

RELIGION

Uruguayans are almost exclusively Roman Catholic, but church and state are officially separate. There is a small Jewish minority, numbering around 25,000 and living almost exclusively in Montevideo. Evangelical Protestantism has made some inroads, and Sun Myung Moon's Unification Church owns the afternoon daily, *Últimas Noticias.*

LANGUAGE

Spanish is the official language and is universally understood. Uruguayans fluctuate between use of the *voseo* and *tuteo* (see the El Voseo boxed text in the Language chapter) in everyday speech, but either is readily understood. In the north, along the Brazilian border, many people are bilingual in Spanish and Portuguese, or speak *fronterizo*, an unusual hybrid of the two. See the Language chapter for more information on Latin American Spanish.

Facts for the Visitor

Although Uruguay is a very distinct country, traveling there is similar to traveling in Argentina. Only those facts differing significantly from those for travelers in Argentina are mentioned below.

HIGHLIGHTS

For most visitors, Montevideo and the Atlantic beach resorts will be Uruguay's main attractions. The narrow streets and port zone of Montevideo's Ciudad Vieja (Old City), currently being redeveloped, have immense colonial charm, while its hilly topography adds a dimension that even Buenos Aires' more picturesque neighborhoods lack. Besides its sophisticated resorts and broad sandy beaches, the Atlantic coast also has scenic headlands.

Up the estuary of the Río de la Plata, the colonial contraband port of Colonia is one of the continent's least-known treasures – every visitor to Buenos Aires should plan at least a day trip and preferably a weekend here. Farther up, on the Río Uruguay, there is first-rate river fishing. Uruguay's undulating interior literally offers relief from the comparative monotony of the Argentine Pampas.

PLANNING

When to Go

Since Uruguay's major tourist attraction is its beaches, most visitors come in summer and dress accordingly, but the year-round temperate climate requires no special preparations. In ritzy resorts like Punta del Este, people often dress their best when going out for the evening, but even Punta is casual most of the time.

Visitors to Montevideo can enjoy its urban attractions in any season. Along the Río Uruguay in summer, temperatures can be smotheringly hot, but the interior hill country is slightly cooler, especially at night.

Maps

Uruguayan road maps are only a partial guide to the highways, but see the Automóvil Club Uruguayo, and Shell and Ancap service stations for the best ones. For more detailed maps, try the Instituto Geográfico Militar (☎ 481-6868), at 12 de Octubre and Abreu in Montevideo.

TOURIST OFFICES

As in Argentina, almost every department and municipality has a tourist office, usually on the main plaza or at the bus terminal. Although Uruguayan maps are not quite so good as those in most Argentine tourist offices, many of the brochures have excellent historical information.

A few departments and municipalities maintain offices in Montevideo. The Intendencia Municipal de Maldonado, which includes the key resort of Punta del Este, runs a Centro de Información (☎ 903-0272) in the Pluna building, Colonia 1021. The Intendencia Municipal de Rocha (☎ 902-0133) maintains an information office on the 5th floor of the Galería Kambarrere, 18 de Julio 907 at Convención.

The larger Uruguayan consulates, such as those in New York and Los Angeles, usually have a tourist representative in their delegation, but they are not especially helpful.

Australia – There is no specific tourist information office in Australia. Direct tourist inquiries to the Uruguayan Consulate-General
(☎ 02-232-8029)
GPO Box 717, Sydney, NSW, 2001

Canada
(☎ 613-234-2937)
130 Albert St, Suite 1905, Ottawa, Ontario

UK – Tourist information can be obtained from the Uruguayan Embassy
(☎ 0171-584-8192, 020-7584-8192 after April 2000)
140 Brompton Rd, 2nd floor, London SW31HY

USA
(☎ 212-755-1200 ext 346)
541 Lexington Ave, New York, NY
(☎ 310-394-5777)
429 Santa Monica Blvd, Suite 400, Santa Monica, CA 90401
(☎ 202-331-1313)
1918 F St NW, Washington, DC 20006

URUGUAY

VISAS & DOCUMENTS

Uruguay requires visas of all foreigners, except nationals of neighboring countries, who need only national identification cards, and those of Western Europe, Israel, Japan, and the USA, who need passports.

All visitors need a tourist card, which is valid for 90 days and renewable for another 90. To extend your visa or tourist card, visit the Dirección Nacional de Migración (☎ 02-916-0471), at Misiones 1513 in Montevideo. The summer hours are between 7:15 am and 1 pm.

Uruguay has imposed visa requirements on Canadians in response to Canada's visa requirements for Uruguayans. The visa requires a return ticket, photograph, and payment of C$47 to an Uruguayan consulate, which can make a day trip to Colonia from Buenos Aires a costly and time-consuming process.

Passports are necessary for many everyday transactions, such as cashing traveler's checks and checking into hotels.

Theoretically, Uruguay requires the Inter-American Driving Permit rather than the International Driving Permit, but this appeared to make no difference in the one instance in which police asked me for identification.

URUGUAY

EMBASSIES & CONSULATES

Uruguayan Embassies & Consulates

Uruguay has diplomatic representation in neighboring countries and overseas, although its network is less extensive than Argentina's.

Argentina
(☎ 01-4803-6030)
Las Heras 1907, Recoleta, Buenos Aires
(☎ 03446-426168)
Rivadavia 510, Gualeguaychú
(☎ 0345-421-0380)
Pellegrini 709, 1ºC, Concordia
Consular offices in Córdoba, Mar del Plata, Mendoza, Rosario, and Salta.

Australia
(☎ 06-282-4800)
MLC Tower, 1st floor, Suite 107 (GPO Box 318), Woden, ACT, 2606

Brazil
(☎ 224-2415)
SES Av Das Naçoes, Lote 14, Brasilia DF
(☎ 553-6033)
Praja de Botafogo 242, 6 Andar, CEP 22250, Rio de Janeiro

Canada
(☎ 613-234-2937)
130 Albert St, Suite 1905, Ottawa, Ontario

Chile
(☎ 02-223-8398)
Pedro de Valdivia 711, Santiago

Paraguay
(☎ 021-203-864)
25 de Mayo 1894, Esquina Gral, Aquinto, Asunción

UK
(☎ 0171-584-8192, 020-7584-8192 after April 2000)
140 Brompton Rd, 2nd floor, London SW31HY

USA
(☎ 202-331-4219)
1918 F St NW, Washington, DC 20006
(☎ 310-394-5777)
429 Santa Monica Blvd, Suite 400, Santa Monica, CA 90401
(☎ 415-986-5222)
546 Market St, Suite 221, San Francisco, CA 94104

Embassies & Consulates in Uruguay

South American countries, the USA, and most Western European countries have diplomatic representation in Montevideo, though most are in outer barrios rather than downtown. Both Argentina and Brazil also have consulates in border towns.

Argentina
(☎ 0589-902-8623)
WF Aldunate 1281, Montevideo
(☎ 22266)
Franklin D Roosevelt 442, Carmelo
(☎ 0522-22093)
General Flores 350, Colonia
(☎ 535-2638)
Sarandí 3193, Fray Bentos
(☎ 0722-222536)
Leandro Gómez 1034, Paysandú
(☎ 042-46193)
Edificio Santos Dumont, Las Focas (30), Punta del Este
(☎ 07332931)
Artigas 1162, Salto

Belgium
(☎ 0589-916-2719)
Rincón 625, Montevideo

Bolivia
(☎ 0589-903-3109)
4th floor, WF Aldunate 1320, Montevideo

Brazil
(☎ 0589-901-2024)
6th floor, Convención 1343, Montevideo
Fernández 147, Chuy

Canada
(☎ 0589-901-5755)
Plaza Cagancha 1335, Montevideo

Chile
(☎ 0589-902-6316)
1st floor, Andes 1365, Montevideo

Denmark
(☎ 0589-908-3793)
Colonia 981, Oficina 405, Montevideo

France
(☎ 0589-902-0077)
Av Uruguay 853, Montevideo

Germany
(☎ 0589-902-5222)
La Cumparsita 1435, Montevideo

Israel
(☎ 0589-400-4164)
Bulevar Artigas 1585, Montevideo

Italy
(☎ 0589-708-1245)
JB Lamas 2857, Montevideo

Japan
(☎ 0589-408-7645)
Bulevar Artigas 953, Montevideo

Netherlands
(☎ 0589-771-2956)
Leyenda Patria 2880, Montevideo

Paraguay
(☎ 0589-408-5810)
Bulevar Artigas 1191, Montevideo

Peru
(☎ 0589-902-1113)
Soriano 1124, Montevideo

Spain
(☎ 0589-708-0048)
Libertad 2738, Montevideo

Sweden
(☎ 0589-916-2320)
5th floor, Sarandí 693, Montevideo

Switzerland
(☎ 0589-710 4315)
11th floor, Federico Abadie 2936, Montevideo

United Kingdom
(☎ 0589-622-3630)
Marco Bruto 1073, Montevideo

USA
(☎ 0589-203-6061)
Lauro Muller 1776, Montevideo

CUSTOMS

Uruguayan customs regulations permit the entry of used personal effects and other items in 'reasonable quantities.'

MONEY

The Uruguayan chapters refer to US dollars for prices because the dollar is more stable than the *peso uruguayo*. While US dollars are not the currency of convenience that they are in Argentina, they are commonly accepted as payment. Even some budget hotels give travelers their prices in US dollars, and better restaurants always accept dollars (or Argentine pesos at present, though usually at a slightly lower rate than the dollar). Away from major coastal tourist centers, dollars are less frequently accepted on an everyday basis.

Currency

The unit of currency is the peso uruguayo (Ur$), which replaced the *peso nuevo* (N$) in 1993 (the peso nuevo had replaced an older peso in 1975 after several years' hyper-inflation). Peso uruguayo notes come in denominations of 5, 10, 20, 50, 100, 200, 500, and 1000, while there are coins of 50 *centésimos*, and one and two pesos. Older banknotes of N$5000 and N$10,000 are still in circulation but gradually disappearing (to get current values, deduct three zeros).

Exchanging Money

Money is readily exchanged at casas de cambio in Montevideo, Colonia, and the Atlantic beach resorts, but banks are the rule in the interior. Casas de cambio accept traveler's checks at slightly lower rates than cash dollars, and sometimes charge commissions, although these are not so high as those levied in Argentina; there are some indications that cashing traveler's checks is getting more difficult. There is no black market for dollars or other foreign currency, which can be purchased without difficulty. Most better hotels, restaurants, and shops accept credit cards, but Uruguayan ATMs will not accept North American or European credit cards.

Exchange Rates

Because the peso is declining against the dollar, exchange rates are likely to work in your favor. At press time exchange rates were the following:

country	unit		peso
Argentina	Arg$1	=	Ur$11.10
Australia	A$1	=	Ur$6.99
Bolivia	Bol$1	=	Ur$1.95
Brazil	BraR$1	=	Ur$6.46
Canada	C$1	=	Ur$7.34
Chile	Ch$100	=	Ur$2.30
Euro	€1	=	Ur11.91
France	1FF	=	Ur$1.81
Germany	DM1	=	Ur$6.09
Italy	L1000	=	Ur$6.15
Japan	¥100	=	Ur$9.31
Netherlands	fl	=	Ur$5.40
New Zealand	NZ$1	=	Ur$5.92
Paraguay	₲1000	=	Ur$3.82
Spain	100pta	=	Ur$7.16
Switzerland	SF1	=	Ur$7.46
United Kingdom	UK£1	=	Ur$17.89
United States	US$1	=	Ur$11.09

Costs

Inflation, at a rate of 15% in 1997, is still running higher than in Argentina, but steady devaluations keep prices from rising substantially in dollar terms. Travel costs are slightly lower than in Argentina, especially with respect to accommodations and transportation; still, prices are approaching Argentine levels. Prices in this book are given in US dollars.

POST & COMMUNICATIONS

Rates are reasonable, but Uruguay's postal and telephone services are no better than in Argentina.

Post

As in Argentina, letters and parcels are likely to be opened, and the contents appropriated if they appear to be anything of value. If something is truly important, send it by registered mail or private courier.

For poste restante, address mail to the main post office in Montevideo. It will hold mail for up to a month, or up to two months with authorization.

Telephone

Uruguay's country code is ☎ 569.

Antel is the state telephone monopoly, with central long-distance offices resembling those in Argentina, but there are private locutorios as well. As in Argentina, public telephones take *fichas* (tokens, each good for about three minutes) rather than coins. More convenient magnetic cards are also available in values of 50, 100, 200, 300, and 500 *pesos*.

Discount rates (40% off) for international calls are in effect between 9 pm and 9 am weekdays, and all day Saturday, Sunday, and holidays.

Making credit-card or collect calls to the US and other overseas destinations is cheaper than paying locally.

The list below gives the numbers of foreign direct operators.

Argentina	☎ 000454
Belgium	☎ 0004320
Brazil	☎ 000455
Canada	☎ 000419
Chile	☎ 0004561
France	☎ 000433
Germany	☎ 000449
Italy	☎ 000439
Netherlands	☎ 000431
Paraguay	☎ 0004595
Spain	☎ 000434
Switzerland	☎ 000441
UK	☎ 000444
USA	☎ 000410 AT&T
	☎ 000412 MCI
	☎ 000417 Sprint

BOOKS

For more on Uruguayan literature see the Arts in Facts about Uruguay chapter.

History

Compared to neighboring countries, surprisingly little material is available on Uruguay in English. For a discussion of the rise of Uruguay's unusual social-welfare policies, see George Pendle's *Uruguay, South America's First Welfare State*, and Milton Vanger's *The Model Country: José Batlle y Ordóñez of Uruguay, 1907-1915*.

The country's agrarian history is covered in RH Brannon's *The Agricultural Development of Uruguay*. Even those with great patience and a command of Spanish will find José Pedro Barrán and Benjamín Nahum's seven-volume *Historia Rural del Uruguay Moderno* imposing, but the authors summarize their conclusions in 'Uruguayan Rural History,' an article in the *Hispanic American Historical Review* (November, 1984). William Henry Hudson's novel *The Purple Land* (1916) is a classic portrait of 19th-century Uruguayan life.

For a sympathetic explanation of the rise of the 1960s guerrilla movements, see María Esther Gilio's *The Tupamaro Guerrillas*.

Contemporary Government & Politics

A good starting point for looking at the politics of modern Uruguay is Henry Finch's collection *Contemporary Uruguay: Problems and Prospects* (Institute for Latin American Studies, 1980). See also Luis González's *Political Parties and Redemocratization in Uruguay*, and Martin Weinstein's *Uruguay, Democracy at the Crossroads*. For an account of Uruguay's Dirty War, see Lawrence Weschler's *A Miracle, A Universe: Settling Accounts with Torturers*.

FILMS

Costa-Gavras' famous and engrossing film *State of Siege*, filmed in 1973 in Allende's Chile, deals with the Tupamaro guerrillas' kidnapping and execution of suspected American CIA officer Dan Mitrione.

NEWSPAPERS

Newspapers are very important in Uruguay, which ranks second on the continent (behind Argentina) in total circulation per 1000 inhabitants. Montevideo has a variety of newspapers, including the morning dailies *El Día* (founded by José Batlle), *La República*, *La Mañana*, and *El País*.

Gaceta Comercial is the voice of the business community, as is *El Observador Económico*. Afternoon papers are *El Diario* and *Últimas Noticias*, the latter operated by followers of Reverend Sun Myung Moon. For the most part, newspapers are identified with specific political parties, but the weekly *Búsqueda* takes a more independent stance with respect to political and economic matters.

The *Buenos Aires Herald* and other porteño newspapers are readily available in Montevideo, Punta del Este, and Colonia.

RADIO & TV

Radio and television are popular, with 20 television stations (four in Montevideo) and 100 radio stations (about 40 in the capital) for Uruguay's 3 million people. While freedom of speech and the press are generally respected, in 1994 the government revoked the license of a radio station operated by the Tupamaros.

HEALTH

Note that Uruguayan hospitals generally demand cash and refuse to accept insurance coverage; travelers needing hospitalization or other medical services may have to pay first and then ask their insurance companies for reimbursement.

SENIOR TRAVELERS

Elderhostel runs several educational programs to Uruguay, all of which begin with a short orientation stay in Montevideo. Course topics include flora and fauna, and tours of Montevideo and Punta del Este. Participants must be at least 55 years of age. For more information or a catalog, contact Elderhostel (☎ 617-426-8056), 75 Federal St, Boston, MA 02110-1941.

USEFUL ORGANIZATIONS

Uruguay's youth hostel network, while limited, is a good alternative to standard accommodations, and a youth hostel card may prove worthwhile; for US$24, membership is reasonable. Accommodations cost around US$6.50 to $11 per night. For more information, contact the Asociación de Alberguistas del Uruguay (☎ 400-4245), the local affiliate of Hostelling International, at Pablo de María 1583, Montevideo. It's open weekdays from 11:30 am to 7 pm.

BUSINESS HOURS & PUBLIC HOLIDAYS

Most shops are open weekdays and Saturday 8:30 am to 12:30 or 1 pm, then close until midafternoon and reopen until 7 or 8 pm. Food shops also open on Sunday mornings.

Government office hours vary with the season – in summer, from mid-November to mid-March, offices are open 7:30 am to 1:30 pm, while the rest of the year their hours are noon to 7 pm. Banks are open weekday afternoons in Montevideo, but outside the capital they are usually open mornings only. Exceptions are noted in the text.

On public holidays, most stores and all public offices are closed. Public transportation does run, but schedules are usually limited. The year's public holidays are as follows:

January 1
: Año Nuevo (New Year's Day)

January 6
: Epifanía (Epiphany)

March/April (dates vary)
: Viernes Santo/Pascua (Good Friday/Easter)

April 19
: Desembarco de los 33 (Return of the 33) honors the exiles who returned to Uruguay in 1825 to liberate the country from Brazil with Argentine support.

May 1
: Día del Trabajador (Labor Day)

May 18
: Batalla de Las Piedras (Battle of Las Piedras) commemorates a major battle of the fight for independence.

June 19
: Natalicio de Artigas (Artigas' Birthday)

July 18
: Jura de la Constitución (Constitution Day)

August 25
: Día de la Independencia (Independence Day)

October 12
: Día de la Raza (Columbus Day)

November 2
: Día de los Muertos (All Souls' Day)

December 25
: Navidad (Christmas Day)

Uruguay's Carnaval, which takes place the Monday and Tuesday before Ash Wednesday in April, is livelier than its Argentine counterparts but not so lively as in Brazil. Visit Montevideo's Barrio Sur, where the city's black population celebrates with traditional *candombe* (Afro-Uruguayan dance) ceremonies.

Holy Week (Easter) is also La Semana Criolla, during which traditional gaucho activities like *asados* (barbecues) and folk music take place. Most businesses close for the duration.

FOOD

Per capita, Uruguayans consume even more beef than Argentines, and the *parrillada* (beef platter) is a standard here. Likewise, the kinds of eating places are very similar – *confiterías* (cafés), pizzerias, and restaurants closely resemble their Argentine counterparts. There are good international restaurants in Montevideo, Punta del Este, and some other beach resorts, but elsewhere the food is fairly uniform. Uruguayan seafood is almost always a good choice.

The standard of Uruguayan short orders is *chivito*, which is not goat but rather a tasty and filling steak sandwich with a variety of additions – cheese, lettuce, tomato, bacon, or other odds and ends. Even more filling is the *chivito al plato*, in which the steak is served topped with a fried egg, with potato salad, green salad, and french fries on the side. Other typical Uruguayan short orders include *olímpicos*, which are club sandwiches, and *húngaros*, which are spicy sausages on a hot-dog roll (probably too spicy for young children, who will prefer the blander *panchos*).

DRINKS

Uruguayans consume even more mate (Paraguayan tea) than Argentines and Paraguayans, many lugging a thermos wherever they go. Uruguayan wines are very decent, especially in the form of *clericó*, a mixture of white wine and fruit juice. Another popular alcoholic drink is the *medio y medio*, a mixture of sparkling wine and white wine. Beers are equally good.

ENTERTAINMENT

Cinema is extremely popular in Montevideo and throughout the country, although the domestic film industry is very limited. Live theater is also very well patronized, especially in Montevideo.

Tango is nearly as popular as in Argentina, while Afro-Uruguayan *candombe* music and dance adds a unique dimension not present in Uruguay's dominating neighbor.

SPECTATOR SPORTS

Uruguay has won soccer's World Cup twice in this century, once shocking a heavily favored Brazilian side in Brazil. But the national team suffered in recent years until it once again upset Brazil in the 1995 Copa de las Américas. Soccer remains the most popular spectator and participant sport; the most notable teams are Montevideo-based Nacional and Peñarol.

SHOPPING

Most shoppers will be interested in leather clothing and accessories, woolen clothing and fabrics, agates and gems, ceramics, wood crafts, and decorated gourds.

One of the most popular places for shoppers is the artisans' cooperative Manos del Uruguay, with several locations in Montevideo. For more details, see the listings under Montevideo.

Getting There & Away

For getting there and away, Uruguay is almost a satellite of Argentina. Most international flights to and from the country go to Buenos Aires' Ezeiza Airport before continuing to Montevideo, while all river transport and the great majority of land transport also passes through Argentina. There are several direct land crossings from Brazil.

AIR

Departure Tax

International passengers leaving from Aeropuerto Carrasco pay a departure tax of US$6 if headed to Argentina, and US$12 to other destinations.

The USA

Only Lloyd Aéreo Boliviano has direct flights to and from Miami – four times weekly – though they pass through La Paz, Santa Cruz de la Sierra, and Buenos Aires. Other airlines require a change of plane at Ezeiza; otherwise, the best connections are probably through São Paulo, Brazil.

Continental Europe

Pluna, an Uruguayan carrier, has twice-weekly flights from Madrid, stopping in Rio de Janeiro before continuing to Montevideo and Ezeiza. Iberia flies four times weekly to Montevideo via Barcelona, Madrid, and Ezeiza.

Neighboring Countries

There are frequent flights between Montevideo's Aeropuerto Internacional Carrasco and Buenos Aires' Aeroparque Jorge Newbery, as well as between Aeroparque and Punta del Este. Although it's possible to fly between Carrasco and Ezeiza, it's more expensive and less convenient unless your ticket is valid for an ongoing flight.

Pluna flies from Montevideo to Brazilian destinations, including Porto Alegre (daily), Florianópolis (twice weekly), Rio de Janeiro (daily), and São Paulo (two or three times daily). Varig flies daily to Porto Alegre and Rio de Janeiro, and daily to São Paulo continuing on to Rio de Janeiro.

Other South American Countries

Pluna also flies to Asunción, Paraguay, Monday and Saturday, and to Santiago, Chile (four times weekly). TAM flies Tuesday, Friday, and Sunday to Asunción.

Lloyd Aéreo Boliviano flies four times weekly to Santa Cruz de la Sierra and La Paz via Ezeiza. LanChile flies daily except Wednesday to Santiago, Chile, and has an additional Sunday flight.

Cubana stops Mondays in Montevideo en route to Buenos Aires, whence it returns to Havana.

LAND

Uruguay shares borders with the Argentine province of Entre Ríos and the southern Brazilian state of Rio Grande do Sul. Major highways and bus services are generally good, but there are no rail services.

Argentina Border Crossings

There are direct buses from Montevideo to Buenos Aires via Gualeguaychú, but these are slower and less convenient than the land/river combinations across the Río de la Plata. For more details on the bridge crossings of the Río Uruguay, see the Getting There & Away chapter for Argentina.

Brazil Border Crossings

Chuy to Chui & Pelotas The most frequently used border crossing from Uruguay into Brazil is connected to Montevideo by an excellent paved highway. Chuy and Chui are twin cities whose parallel main streets are separated only by a median strip, but Uruguayan immigration is about 1km before the actual border and Brazilian immigration 2km beyond it. If continuing any distance into Brazil, complete border formalities on both sides.

Río Branco to Jaguarão Less frequently used than the crossing at Chuy, this is an alternative route to Pelotas and Porto Alegre via the town of Treinta y Tres, in the department of the same name, or Melo, in the department of Cerro Largo. There are buses from Jaguarão to Pelotas.

Rivera to Livramento The crossing at Rivera and Livramento is frequented by travelers heading from Colón, Argentina, to Brazil, via Paysandú and the interior city of Tacuarembó. There are regular buses from Livramento to Porto Alegre.

Artigas to Quaraí This route crosses the Puente de la Concordia over the Río Quareim, but the principal highway goes southeast to Livramento.

Bella Unión to Barra do Quaraí In the extreme northwest corner of Uruguay, this crossing leads to the Brazilian city of Uruguaiana, from which you can cross into the Argentine province of Corrientes and head north to Paraguay or to Iguazú Falls. Overland travel to Iguazú Falls through southern Brazil is slow and difficult.

RIVER & SEA

The most common means of crossing from Montevideo to Argentina is by ferry or hydrofoil, sometimes involving bus combinations to Colonia. Ferry passengers embarking at Montevideo pay a US$5 port terminal and departure tax, while those at Colonia pay US$3.

Montevideo to Buenos Aires The so-called Buqueaviones are very comfortable, high-speed ferries that connect the two capitals in about 2½ hours for US$52 turista, US$67 primera. The main passenger salon is tobacco-free.

Colonia to Buenos Aires From Montevideo you can make direct bus connections to Colonia (three hours), where Ferrytur and Buquebus make several daily ferry crossings to Buenos Aires (US$23, 2½ hours). Ferrytur hydrofoils take only an hour from Colonia to Buenos Aires (US$32).

Carmelo & Nueva Palmira to Tigre There are launches across the estuary of the Río de la Plata to the Buenos Aires suburb of Tigre. Launches from Carmelo cost US$11 and take about 2½ hours, while those from Nueva Palmira cost US$15 and take slightly longer.

ORGANIZED TOURS

Organized tours to Uruguay are fairly rare, but for travelers at least 55 years of age, Elderhostel (☎ 617-426-8056), 76 Federal St, Boston, MA 02110, operates two-week tours of the country, starting at around US$3200. They also offer multicountry trips, which take in parts of Argentina, Brazil, and Paraguay, for about the same price.

Getting Around

AIR

Since the military airline Tamu suspended services, there are no flights within Uruguay except for the domestic leg of international flights from Punta del Este via Montevideo to Brazil.

BUS

Buses are not quite so comfortable as those in Argentina, but the rides are shorter and they are perfectly acceptable; many companies publish accurate timetables. Most Uruguayan cities do not have central bus terminals, but the companies are always within easy walking distance of each other, usually around the main plaza. Montevideo, however, has a new, spacious, and busy terminal.

Buses are frequent to destinations all around the country, so reservations should only be necessary on or near holidays. Fares are very reasonable – for example, the trip from Montevideo to Fray Bentos, a distance of about 300km, costs only about US$11.

TRAIN

Passenger services on Uruguayan trains ceased completely in 1988.

CAR

Uruguayans are less ruthless on the road than Argentines, although it has been said that dividing lines are mere decoration. There are, in any event, plenty of Argentine drivers on the road, so watch out for Argentine license plates. Outside Montevideo and coastal areas, traffic is minimal and poses few problems, but some interior roads are very rough. Visitors lulled to sleep by the endlessly flat Pampas must pay close attention on Uruguay's winding roads and hilly terrain.

Uruguay ostensibly requires the Inter-American Driving Permit, rather than the International Driving Permit, in addition to a state or national driver's license, but the police usually pay little attention as long as you have something that looks official. Arbitrary police stops and searches are less common than in Argentina, but the police are not above soliciting a bribe for minor traffic violations.

Driving can be even more expensive in Uruguay than in Argentina, since Uruguay imports all its oil and cars – there is no domestic automobile industry. Consequently, you will see so many lovingly maintained, truly antique *cachilas* on the streets of Montevideo that you may think you've stumbled onto the set of a gangster movie. If you plan to purchase a car, Argentina is a better bet. Leaded regular petrol costs about US$0.85 per liter, while unleaded premium (the only grade available) costs about US$1. Car rentals are just as costly as in Argentina.

The Automóvil Club del Uruguay (☎ 02-901-1251), at the corner of Colonia and Yi in Montevideo, is the equivalent of Argentina's ACA, although it's less widespread. It does have good maps and information.

LOCAL TRANSPORT

Taxi

Taxis have meters, and drivers correlate the meter reading with a photocopied fare chart. Between midnight and 6 am fares are higher. There is a small additional charge for luggage, and passengers generally round off the fare to the next even number.

Montevideo

Uruguay's capital dominates the country's political, economic, and cultural life even more than Buenos Aires does Argentina's. Nearly half the country's 3.2 million citizens live here, but there's a logic to this: Montevideo's fine natural port links the country to overseas commerce, and the almost exclusively rural economy hardly requires a competing metropolis for trade and administration.

In many ways, economic stagnation has left modern Montevideo a worn-out city where key public buildings are undistinguished, utilitarian constructions that would not be out of place in Eastern Europe – according to one graffito, it's *'un necrópolis de sueños rotos'* (a necropolis of broken dreams). Still, the municipal administration is sprucing up public spaces like Plaza Cagancha and promoting restoration of the Ciudad Vieja, the colonial core that is the city's most appealing feature.

If Montevideo is to experience a significant renaissance, even more important may be the emergence and growth of Mercosur, the nascent common market of Brazil, Argentina, Paraguay, and Uruguay. As Mercosur's administrative headquarters, Montevideo figures to benefit more directly than any other single location in the four-country customs union – even if it just takes the city's traditional bureaucratic functions to another level.

HISTORY

Spain's 1726 founding of Montevideo was a response to concern over Portugal's growing influence in the River Plate area; since 1680, the fortress and contraband port of Colonia had been a thorn in Spain's side. Montevideo was in turn a fortress against the Portuguese, as well as the British, French, and Danish privateers who came in search of hides in the Banda Oriental. Even more isolated than Buenos Aires, it was modest and unimpressive despite its official status as port of call for ships en route to the Pacific. In 1797, a British visitor to present-day Plaza Zabala observed:

> The fort seems to be the only object on which any attention has been bestowed; it is large, handsomely built, and consists of four bastions, on which are apparently very good brass cannon . . . .
>
> The church is the next principal building; it is large and clean, but has nothing remarkable about it: the houses, many of which lie scattered about in a very irregular manner, with very pleasing gardens and little plantations attached to them, are all low and meanly built, very few being higher than the ground floor; but their tiled tops, with the green trees waving over them, have, taken altogether, rather a pretty effect.

Many of Montevideo's early residents were Canary Islanders. The city's port, superior to Buenos Aires' in every respect except its access to the Humid Pampa, soon made it a focal point for overseas shipping. An early-19th-century construction boom resulted in a new Iglesia Matriz, Cabildo, and other neoclassical late-colonial monuments, but after independence authorities demolished many of these buildings and planned a new center east of Ciudad Vieja (Old City) and its port. No wonder, since it could be an insalubrious place – one British visitor in 1807 described the hazards of walking in the city at night:

> through long narrow streets so infested with voracious rats as to make it perilous sometimes to face them . . . Around the offals of carrion, vegetables, and stale fruit accumulated there, the rats absolutely mustered in legions. If I attempted to pass near those formidable banditti, or to interrupt their meals or orgies, they gnashed their teeth upon me like so many evening wolves. So far they were from running in affright to their numerous burrows, that they turned round, set up a raven cry, and rushed at my legs in a way to make my blood run chill.

Montevideños had other worries, though. During the mid-19th century, the city

URUGUAY

endured an almost constant state of siege by the Argentine dictator Rosas, who was determined to create a small client state to Buenos Aires. After Rosas' fall in 1851, normal commerce resumed and, between 1860 and 1911, the British-built railroad network assisted Montevideo's growth. Like Buenos Aires, the city absorbed numerous European immigrants in the early 20th century, mostly from Spain and Italy; by 1908, 30% of Montevideo's population was foreign-born.

Around this time, the country became ever more closely linked to the export trade; construction of the city's first locally financed *frigorífico* (cold storage plant) was followed by two similar foreign-backed enterprises. Growth has continued to stimulate agricultural expansion near Montevideo in response to the demands of the rapidly increasing urban population. Much of this population, consisting mostly of refugees from rural poverty, lives in *conventillos*, large, older houses converted into multifamily slum dwellings. Many of these are in the Ciudad Vieja, but even this population is being displaced as urban redevelopment usurps the picturesque and valuable central area.

WAYNE BERNHARDSON

Coventillo, Ciudad Vieja, Montevideo

ORIENTATION

Montevideo lies on the east bank of the Río de la Plata, almost directly east of Buenos Aires on the west bank. For most visitors, the most intriguing area will be the Ciudad Vieja, the colonial grid on a small peninsula near the port and harbor that was once surrounded by protective walls. The city's functional center is Plaza Independencia to the east, with many historic public buildings of the republican era. Av 18 de Julio, a major thoroughfare and traditionally the capital's main commercial and entertainment zone, begins here and, to the east, runs through Plaza Cagancha and divides the tree-shaded barrio known as El Córdon (in earlier times El Cardal, the birthplace of Artigas). Some streets change their name on either side of Av 18 de Julio. Most inexpensive accommodations are on side streets around Plaza Cagancha, though some are in the Ciudad Vieja.

From Plaza del Entrevero, on Av 18 de Julio, the diagonal Av Libertador General Lavalleja leads to the imposing Palacio Legislativo site of the Asamblea General. From the 11th-floor terrace of the Palacio Municipal, at Av 18 de Julio and Ejido, there are spectacular views of the city. At the northeastern end of Av 18 de Julio is Parque José Batlle y Ordóñez, a large public park containing the Estadio Centenario, a 75,000-seat stadium built to commemorate the country's centenary in 1930. Running perpendicular to its terminus is Bulevar Artigas, another major artery, while the nearby Av Italia is the main highway east to Punta del Este and the rest of the Uruguayan Riviera.

Many points of interest are beyond downtown, a result of Montevideo's sprawl both east and west along the river. Across the harbor to the west, the 132m Cerro de Montevideo ('a conical mountain of a stupendous height' according to an easily impressed 18th-century English visitor) was a landmark for early navigators and still offers outstanding views of the city. To the east, the Rambla, or riverfront road, leads past attractive residential suburbs with numerous public parks, including Parque Rodó at the south end of Bulevar Artigas.

Farther on, but well within the city limits, are numerous sandy beaches frequented by the capital's residents in summer and on weekends throughout the year.

INFORMATION

Tourist Offices

The Ministerio de Turismo (☎ 409-7399) has a cubbyhole information office on the ground floor at Av Libertador General Lavalleja 1409; it's open 9 am to 6:30 pm weekdays. Look, however, for a new office that is due to open in the former Pluna headquarters, at Colonia and Lavalleja.

The Oficina de Informes (☎ 601-1757) at Terminal Tres Cruces, the bus station at Bulevar Artigas and Av Italia, is open 9 am to 9 pm daily and is well prepared to deal with visitor inquiries. The very useful weekly *Guía del Ocio*, which lists cultural events, cinemas, theaters, and restaurants, comes with the Friday edition of the daily *El País*.

If your Spanish is good, dial ☎ 124 for general information on virtually anything in Montevideo. For entertainment information, call Espectáculos (☎ 0900-2323; the call costs US$0.60 per minute).

Immigration

The Dirección Nacional de Migracion (☎ 916-0471) is at Misiones 1513.

Money

There are many exchange houses around Plaza Cagancha and on Av 18 de Julio. Exprinter, Sarandí 700 on Plaza Independencia, is very dependable. American Express (☎ 902-0829), locally represented by Turisport at San José 930, no longer cashes its own traveler's checks, but Cambio Gales at 18 de Julio 1048 will do so.

Post & Communications

The Correo Central (main post office) is at Buenos Aires 451 in the Ciudad Vieja, with a branch on Ejido between San José and Soriano. Antel has Telecentros at Rincón 501 in the Ciudad Vieja, at San José 1102, and at the Tres Cruces bus terminal. Montevideo's area code is ☎ 02.

Travel Agencies

Among many others, Viajes COT (☎ 902-1605), Plaza Cagancha 1124, arranges trips in and out of Montevideo and to neighboring countries. Argentina's nonprofit student travel agency Asatej, an affiliate of STA Travel, has a Montevideo branch (☎ 908-0509, fax 908-4895) at Río Negro 1354, 2nd floor.

Photography

Kilómetro Cero, 18 de Julio 1180 on Plaza Cagancha, and Kodak Uruguaya, Yí 1532, offer dependable developing. Technifilm, at 18 de Julio 1202, is the place to go for camera repairs.

Bookstores

Montevideo has several fine bookstores. Linardi y Risso (☎ 915-7129), at Juan Carlos Gómez 1435 in the Ciudad Vieja, is the equivalent of Buenos Aires' Platero, offering outstanding selections in history and literature, including many out-of-print items. The city's largest book dealer is Librerías Barreiro (☎ 915-0150), at Juan Carlos Gómez 136 in the Ciudad Vieja, with branches at Av 18 de Julio 941 and in the suburbs of Pocitos and Carrasco.

Two worthwhile hybrid bookstore-cafés in Pocitos are Libertad Libros (☎ 711-3460), Libertad 2433, and Casa Gandhi (☎ 707-5870), JB Blanco 975.

Cultural Centers

Run by the United States Information Service, the Biblioteca Artigas-Washington (☎ 901-5232), Paraguay 1217, is a very substantial library with books and newspapers in English. The center also sponsors special programs and lectures.

The Anglo-Uruguayan Cultural Institute (☎ 900-3708), San José 1426, also operates an English-language library. Montevideo has branches of the Instituto Goethe, at Canelones 1524, and the Alianza Francesa (☎ 903-0805), at Soriano 1180. At the corner of 18 de Julio and Julio Herrera y Obes is the Centro Cultural Uruguayo-Brasileiro.

In the 1820s, escaped Brazilian slaves formed Montevideo's Afro-Uruguayan community in the capital's Barrio Sur; their descendants have built their own downtown cultural center, the Centro de Estudios e Informes Afros (☎/fax 915-0247) upstairs in the Mercado Central, Ciudadela 1229.

Medical Services

The most convenient medical facility is Hospital Maciel (☎ 915-6810), at 25 de Mayo and Maciel in the Ciudad Vieja. Línea SIDA (☎ 402-1010) is Montevideo's AIDS hot line.

Dangers & Annoyances

While Montevideo is pretty sedate by most standards, visitors will note symptoms of increasing street crime – private security guards now lurk at many cafés and restaurants, and all cabs now have a plastic shield between passenger and driver. Take the usual precautions, especially around the Ciudad Vieja's Mercado del Puerto.

WALKING TOUR

To orient yourself in downtown Montevideo, take a walk from **Plaza Independencia** through the Ciudad Vieja to the port. On the plaza, an honor guard keeps 24-hour vigil over the **Mausoleo de Artigas**, topped by a 17m, 30-ton statue of the country's independence hero. The 18th-century **Palacio Estévez**, on the south side, was the Government House until 1985. On the east side, the baroque, 26-story **Palacio Salvo** was the continent's tallest building when it opened in 1927 and is still the tallest in the city; from here, in 1939, British agents spied on the German destroyer *Graf Spee*, then at anchor in Montevideo harbor but later scuttled by its captain. Just off the plaza is the **Teatro Solís** (see separate entry).

At the west end of the plaza is **La Puerta de la Ciudadela**, a modified remnant of the colonial citadel which dominated the area before its demolition in 1833. Calle Sarandí, part of which is now a peatonal, leads to **Plaza Constitución**, also known as Plaza Matriz, where a central sculpture, by the Italian Juan Ferrari, commemorates the establishment of Montevideo's first waterworks. On the east side of Plaza Constitución, a historical museum occupies the

URUGUAY

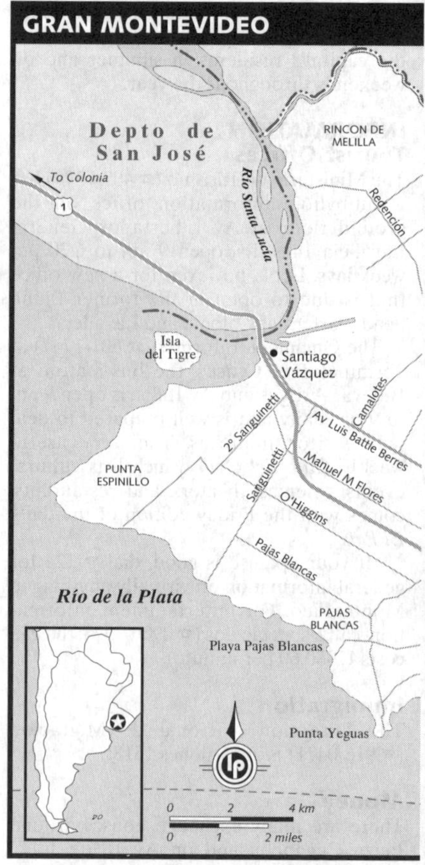

Cabildo (finished in 1812), a neoclassical stone structure designed by Spanish architect Tomás Toribio. Begun in 1784 and completed in 1799, the **Iglesia Matriz**, at the corner of Sarandí and Ituzaingó, is Montevideo's oldest public building, the work of Portuguese architect José de Sáa y Faría.

Detour one block north of Plaza Constitución to see Edmundo Prati's remarkable bas-reliefs on the **Banco La Caja Obrera** (1941), 25 de Mayo at Ituzaingó. Returning to Calle Rincón, continue west to the Casa Rivera at Rincón and Misiones, the Museo Romántico at 25 de Mayo 428, and the Casa

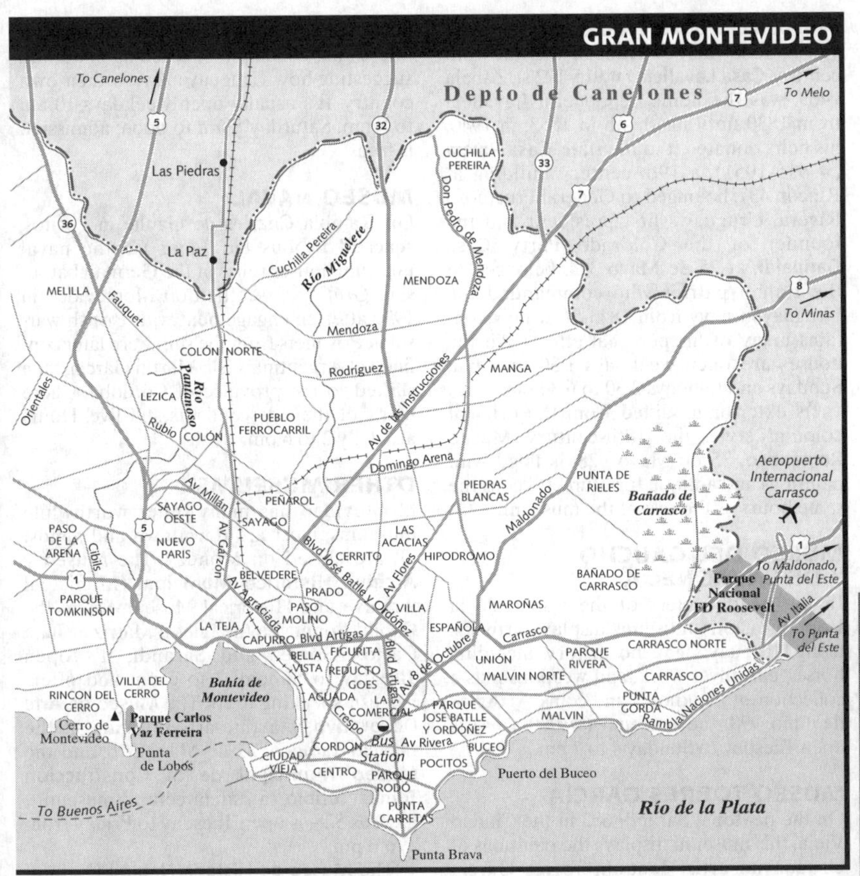

Lavalleja at Zabala and 25 de Mayo, all part of the **Museo Histórico Nacional** (see Museums & Landmarks). The **Palacio Taranco** (1910), at 25 de Mayo and Primero de Mayo, was built in an 18th-century European style by French architects commissioned by a wealthy merchant and now houses the **Museo de Arte Decorativo**, open weekdays 2 to 6 pm. From there, visit **Plaza Zabala**, site of the colonial governor's house until its demolition in 1878; there is a statue to Bruno Mauricio de Zabala, Montevideo's founder, by Spanish sculptor Lorenzo Coullant Valera. From the plaza, continue west along Washington and north to Colón and 25 de Mayo, where the **Casa Garibaldi** once sheltered the Italian hero, and then to Piedras and the Mercado del Puerto.

Travelers interested in more detail on the Ciudad Vieja's architecture should look for Julio C Gaeta's *Guía Ciudad Vieja Montevideo* (Montevideo, Guías Elarqa de Arquitectura, 1994), which has unfortunately gone out of print.

MUSEO HISTÓRICO NACIONAL

The national history museum actually consists of four different Ciudad Vieja houses, most of them former residences of Uruguayan national heroes. Built in the late 18th century, **Casa Lavalleja** (☎ 915-1028), Zabala 1469, was the home of General Lavalleja from 1830 until his death in 1853; in 1940, his heirs donated it to the state. **Casa Rivera** (☎ 915-1051), a 19th-century building at Rincón 437, belonged to General Fructuoso Rivera, Uruguay's first president and the founder of the Colorado Party. **Casa Garibaldi**, at 25 de Mayo 314, belonged to the Italian patriot who commanded the Uruguayan navy from 1843-51; it now contains many of his personal effects. All the houses are open weekdays 1:30 to 6 pm, Sundays and holidays 2:30 to 6:30 pm.

Its exterior modified from the original colonial style, the 18th-century **Museo Romántico**, 25 de Mayo 428, is filled with paintings and antique furniture. It keeps the same hours as the rest of the museum.

MUSEO DEL GAUCHO Y DE LA MONEDA

In the headquarters of the Banco de la República, this museum displays artifacts from Uruguay's gaucho history, including horse gear, silver work, and weapons plus a collection of banknotes and coins. At Av 18 de Julio 998, the museum (☎ 900-8764) is open Tuesday to Sunday 4 to 7 pm.

MUSEO TORRES GARCÍA

On the peatonal Sarandí 683 in the Ciudad Vieja, this museum displays the paintings of Uruguayan artist Joaquín Torres García (1874-1949), who spent much of his career in France producing abstract and even cubist work (like that of Picasso), as well as idiosyncratic portraits – almost caricatures – of historical figures such as Columbus, Mozart, Beethoven, Bach, and Rabelais. Open weekdays 3 to 7 pm and Saturday 11 am to 1 pm, the museum (☎ 916-2663) also has a small gift shop and bookstore. Admission is free.

MUSEO PEDAGÓGICO JOSÉ PEDRO VARELA

Named for the man who devised Uruguay's public education system, this museum at the northeast corner of Plaza Cagancha has an interesting collection of teaching materials, suggesting how Uruguayans view their own country. It's usually open weekdays 10 am to 8 pm, Saturday 8 am to noon; admission is free.

MUSEO NAVAL

On Rambla Charles de Gaulle in Pocitos, reached by bus No 14 or 62, the naval museum houses relics of the German battleship *Graf Spee*, scuttled off Montevideo in 1939 after an engagement with British warships. Prisoners from the ship were later confined at Argentina's Isla Martín García, then shifted to the province of Córdoba, where many of their descendants still live. Hours are daily 2 to 6 pm.

OTHER MUSEUMS

Montevideo has many other worthwhile museums; most are downtown and almost all are closed on Monday. The **Museo y Archivo Histórico Municipal** (Municipal Archive and Historical Museum) is in the Cabildo, opposite the Iglesia Matriz at Juan Carlos Gómez and Sarandí; it's open Tuesday to Sunday 2 to 6 pm and offers English-speaking tours. The **Museo de Arte Decorativo** is a fine-arts museum in the Palacio Taranco, 25 de Mayo 376; and the **Museo Municipal de la Construcción Tomás Toribio** (an architectural museum), Piedras 528, is open Tuesday to Friday from 2 to 6 pm.

The **Museo de Historia Natural** (Natural History Museum) is in the Teatro Solís building, Buenos Aires 652. The Automóvil Club del Uruguay's **Museo del Automóvil**, 6th floor, Colonia 1251, has a superb collection of vintage cars, including a mint 1910 Hupmobile. It's open 5 to 9 pm Tuesday to Friday, and weekends 3 to 9 pm. Admission is free.

Across the harbor, the **Museo del Cerro**, in Parque Carlos Vaz Ferreira, has an excellent weapons collection and offers good views of the city; take bus No 125 from downtown. Hours are Thursday and Friday 1:30 to 5:45 pm, Sunday 9:30 am to noon and 2 to 5:45 pm. The **Jardín Zoológico** (zoo) and

Planetario Municipal (planetarium) are at Rivera 3245, reached by No 60 tram from Av 18 de Julio.

The **Museo Zoológico Larrañaga**, Rambla República de Chile 4215 in the barrio of Buceo, has exhibits of stuffed animals, birds, and other fauna from Uruguay and neighboring countries. The building, with its gilded tower and tiles, deserves a visit in its own right; it's open 3 to 7 pm daily except Monday. The **Museo Juan M Blanes**, Av Millán 4016 in the suburb of Prado, shows the work of Uruguay's most famous painter, including many historical scenes not just of Uruguay but of the entire River Plate region. Hours are 2 to 7 pm daily except Monday. The Estadio Centenario's **Museo del Fútbol** is open Thursday, weekends, and holidays from noon to 5 pm.

PALACIO LEGISLATIVO

Dating from 1908, the neoclassical legislature was the work of Victor Meano, who won an international competition, and several other Italian architects who modified his plan over the next several years.

At the north end of Av Libertador General Lavalleja, brilliantly lighted at night, the three-story building is one of the city's most impressive landmarks. Available in English as well as Spanish, guided tours (☎ 200-1334) take place hourly between 8:30 am and 6:30 pm on weekdays only.

TEATRO SOLÍS

Named for the first Spaniard to set foot in what is now Uruguayan territory, Montevideo's leading theater opened in 1856 (construction actually began in 1842 but was delayed by Rosas' siege of Montevideo). Artists who have performed here include Caruso, Toscanini, Pavlova, Nijinski, Sarah Bernhardt, Rostropovich, and Twyla Tharp.

At the southwest corner of Plaza Independencia, at Buenos Aires 678, the Solís (☎ 915-1968) has superb acoustics and offers concerts, ballet, opera, and plays throughout the year. It is also home to the Comedia Nacional, the municipal theater company. You can usually get tickets a few days before events, but the earlier the better.

MERCADO DEL PUERTO

At its opening in 1868, Montevideo's port was the continent's finest, but its market now survives on personality and atmosphere. About 40 years ago, local entrepreneurs began to add more sophisticated restaurants to the grills that even then fed the people who brought their produce to the market, and the market gradually became a local phenomenon.

No visitor should miss the old port market building at the foot of Calle Pérez Castellano, whose impressive wrought-iron superstructure still shelters a gaggle of reasonably priced *parrillas* (choose your cut off the grill) and some more upmarket restaurants with outstanding seafood. Especially on Saturday afternoons, it's a lively, colorful place where the city's artists, craftspeople, and street musicians hang out. *Café Roldos*, at the same site since 1886, serves the popular *medio y medio*, a mixture of white and sparkling wines.

The Mercado restaurants are open into the late afternoon only; this is not a place for dinner. Note that there have been armed robberies near the Mercado, even during daylight hours, so be sure to take the usual precautions.

ORGANIZED TOURS

Free Way Viajes (☎ 900-8931), Colonia 994, runs a recommended city tour (US$13) and another by night for US$24 (US$35 dinner included). It organizes additional tours throughout the country and has guides available in several languages.

SPECIAL EVENTS

Much livelier than its Buenos Aires counterpart, Montevideo's late summer Carnaval is well worth the trip for those who can't make it to Rio de Janeiro.

Semana Criolla festivities during Semana Santa (Holy Week) take place at the Parque Prado, north of downtown. Because Uruguay is a secular country, official Holy Week celebrations are more nationalistic than religious. The festivites include displays of gaucho skills, *asados* (barbecues), and other such events.

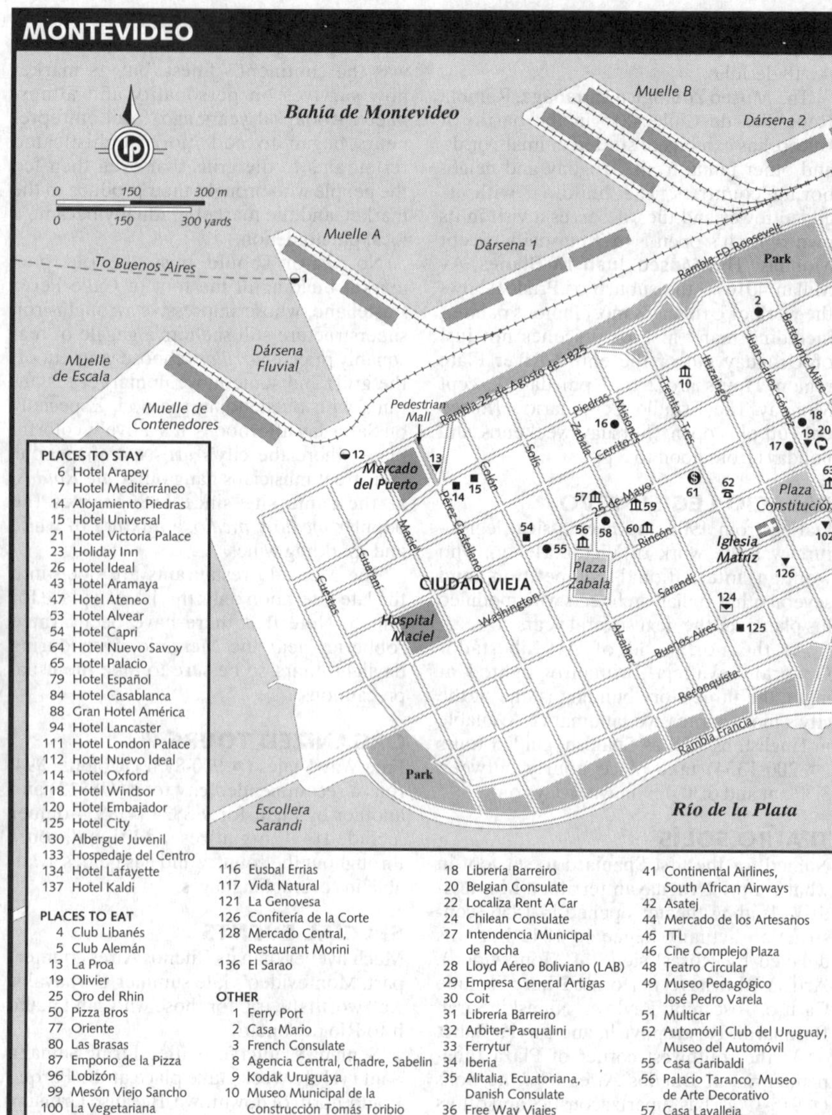
MONTEVIDEO
Bahía de Montevideo
Muelle B
Dársena 2
0 150 300 m
0 150 300 yards
Muelle A
Dársena 1
To Buenos Aires
Rambla FD Roosevelt
Park
Muelle de Escala
Dársena Fluvial
Muelle de Contenedores
Pedestrian Mall
Rambla 25 de Agosto de 1825
Piedras
Misiones
Zabala
Cerrito
Solís
Colón
Treinta y Tres
Ituzaingó
Juan Carlos Gómez
Bartolomé Mitre
Mercado del Puerto
Pérez Castellano
Maciel
Guaraní
Cuestas
25 de Mayo
Rincón
Plaza Constitución
Iglesia Matriz
Plaza Zabala
CIUDAD VIEJA
Washington
Sarandí
Alzaibar
Buenos Aires
Hospital Maciel
Reconquista
Rambla Francia
Park
Escollera Sarandí
Río de la Plata
PLACES TO STAY
6 Hotel Arapey
7 Hotel Mediterráneo
14 Alojamiento Piedras
15 Hotel Universal
21 Hotel Victoria Palace
23 Holiday Inn
26 Hotel Ideal
43 Hotel Aramaya
47 Hotel Ateneo
53 Hotel Alvear
54 Hotel Capri
64 Hotel Nuevo Savoy
65 Hotel Palacio
79 Hotel Español
84 Hotel Casablanca
88 Gran Hotel América
94 Hotel Lancaster
111 Hotel London Palace
112 Hotel Nuevo Ideal
114 Hotel Oxford
118 Hotel Windsor
120 Hotel Embajador
125 Hotel City
130 Albergue Juvenil
133 Hospedaje del Centro
134 Hotel Lafayette
137 Hotel Kaldi
PLACES TO EAT
4 Club Libanés
5 Club Alemán
13 La Proa
19 Olivier
25 Oro del Rhin
50 Pizza Bros
77 Oriente
80 Las Brasas
87 Emporio de la Pizza
96 Lobizón
99 Mesón Viejo Sancho
100 La Vegetariana
101 Mesón del Club Español
102 Confitería La Pasiva
109 La Vegetariana
110 El Fogón
115 Ruffino
116 Eusbal Errias
117 Vida Natural
121 La Genovesa
126 Confitería de la Corte
128 Mercado Central, Restaurant Morini
136 El Sarao
OTHER
1 Ferry Port
2 Casa Mario
3 French Consulate
8 Agencia Central, Chadre, Sabelin
9 Kodak Uruguaya
10 Museo Municipal de la Construcción Tomás Toribio
11 Budget Rent A Car
12 Buquebus
16 Dirección Nacional de Migracion
17 Linardi y Risso
18 Librería Barreiro
20 Belgian Consulate
22 Localiza Rent A Car
24 Chilean Consulate
27 Intendencia Municipal de Rocha
28 Lloyd Aéreo Boliviano (LAB)
29 Empresa General Artigas
30 Coit
31 Librería Barreiro
32 Arbiter-Pasqualini
33 Ferrytur
34 Iberia
35 Alitalia, Ecuatoriana, Danish Consulate
36 Free Way Viajes
37 Pluna/Varig
38 Ministerio de Turismo (Projected New Office)
39 Ministerio de Turismo
40 Buquebus
41 Continental Airlines, South African Airways
42 Asatej
44 Mercado de los Artesanos
45 TTL
46 Cine Complejo Plaza
48 Teatro Circular
49 Museo Pedagógico José Pedro Varela
51 Multicar
52 Automóvil Club del Uruguay, Museo del Automóvil
55 Casa Garibaldi
56 Palacio Taranco, Museo de Arte Decorativo
57 Casa Lavalleja
58 Teatro El Picadero
59 Museo Romántico
60 Casa Rivera
61 Banco La Caja Obrera
62 Telecentro Antel

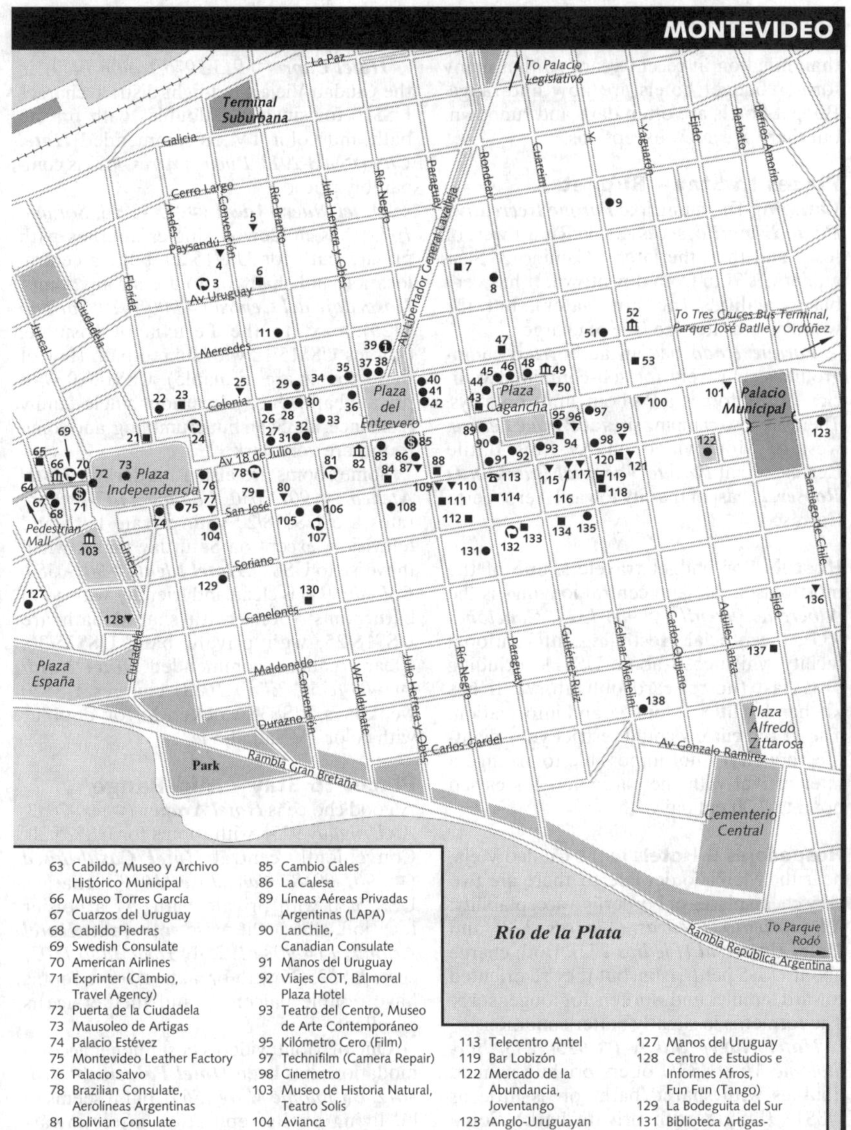
MONTEVIDEO
La Paz
To Palacio Legislativo
Terminal Suburbana
Galicia
Cerro Largo
Paysandú
Av Uruguay
Mercedes
Colonia
Av 18 de Julio
San José
Soriano
Canelones
Maldonado
Durazno
Rambla Gran Bretaña
Carlos Gardel
Av Gonzalo Ramírez
Rambla República Argentina
Andes
Convención
Río Branco
Julio Herrera y Obes
Río Negro
Paraguay
Av Libertador General Lavalleja
Rondeau
Cuareim
Yí
Yaguarón
Ejido
Barbato
Barrios Amorín
Florida
Ciudadela
Juncal
Liniers
W.F. Aldunate
Gutiérrez Ruiz
Zelmar Michelini
Carlos Quijano
Aquiles Lanza
Santiago de Chile
To Tres Cruces Bus Terminal, Parque José Batlle y Ordóñez
Plaza del Entrevero
Plaza Cagancha
Plaza Independencia
Palacio Municipal
Pedestrian Mall
Plaza España
Park
Plaza Alfredo Zittarosa
Cementerio Central
Río de la Plata
To Parque Rodó
63 Cabildo, Museo y Archivo Histórico Municipal
66 Museo Torres García
67 Cuarzos del Uruguay
68 Cabildo Piedras
69 Swedish Consulate
70 American Airlines
71 Exprinter (Cambio, Travel Agency)
72 Puerta de la Ciudadela
73 Mausoleo de Artigas
74 Palacio Estévez
75 Montevideo Leather Factory
76 Palacio Salvo
78 Brazilian Consulate, Aerolíneas Argentinas
81 Bolivian Consulate
82 Museo del Gaucho y de la Moneda, Centro Cultural Uruguayo-Brasileiro
83 Sala Zitarrosa
85 Cambio Gales
86 La Calesa
89 Líneas Aéreas Privadas Argentinas (LAPA)
90 LanChile, Canadian Consulate
91 Manos del Uruguay
92 Viajes COT, Balmoral Plaza Hotel
93 Teatro del Centro, Museo de Arte Contemporáneo
95 Kilómetro Cero (Film)
97 Technifilm (Camera Repair)
98 Cinemetro
103 Museo de Historia Natural, Teatro Solís
104 Avianca
105 Turisport (Amex)
106 Leather Corner
107 Argentine Consulate
108 Carlos Andersen (Jeweler)
113 Telecentro Antel
119 Bar Lobizón
122 Mercado de la Abundancia, Joventango
123 Anglo-Uruguayan Cultural Institute, Teatro del Anglo
124 Correo Central (Main Post Office)
127 Manos del Uruguay
128 Centro de Estudios e Informes Afros, Fun Fun (Tango)
129 La Bodeguita del Sur
131 Biblioteca Artigas-Washington
132 Peruvian Consulate
135 Alianza Francesa
138 Mil Años

PLACES TO STAY

Prices for accommodations have risen faster than inflation in recent years, so that many former budget hotels are now mid-range. Budget hotels are often dark and rundown, but there are a few exceptions.

Places to Stay – Budget

Camping The municipal ***Parque Recreativo Punta Espinillo***, accessed via Ruta 1 west of town and then the lateral Camino 2° Sanguinetti, is 7km from downtown. It has very basic facilities (no hot water), but it's woodsy, and sites are free of charge.

Parque Rodó has an authorized campground exclusively for self-contained vehicles, but enforces a 24-hour limit on stays. There are also camping sites at ***Parque Lecocq***, west of Montevideo on Av Luis Batlle Berres, and at ***Parque Nacional Franklin D Roosevelt***, east of the city toward Aeropuerto Carrasco.

Hostels For budget travelers, one of the most reasonable and central lodgings is the ***Albergue Juvenil*** *(☎ 908-1324, Canelones 935)*, the official Hostelling International facility, which costs about US$11, including breakfast (hostel card obligatory). It has kitchen facilities, a lounge, and information. The 11 pm curfew could restrict your nightlife, though it's not impossible to arrange a later arrival with the caretaker. It's closed noon to 7:30 pm daily.

Hospedajes & Hotels In the Ciudad Vieja, near the Mercado del Puerto, there are two very cheap places of borderline acceptability: ***Alojamiento Piedras*** *(Piedras 270)* and ***Hotel Universal*** *(Piedras 272)*. Both charge about US$5 per person, but they're oriented toward families and workers for longer stays. The former is in slightly better condition.

Hotel Nuevo Savoy *(☎ 915-7233, Bartholomé Mitre 1371)* offers brightly painted doubles with shared bath for as little as US$13 (US$18 with private bath). Some rooms are windowless and the presence of children means occasional noise, but it's friendly and well-run. The ***Hotel Windsor*** *(☎ 901-5080, Zelmar Michelini 1260)* charges US$11/14 for singles/doubles with shared bath, US$14/19 with private bath.

Hotel Capri *(☎ 915-5970, Colón 1460)*, in the Ciudad Vieja's red-light district, charges US$16 for singles or doubles with private bath and color TV. Recommended ***Hotel City*** *(☎ 908-2913, Buenos Aires 462)* is comparably priced.

Hotel Nuevo Ideal *(☎ 908-2913, Soriano 1073)* has mildewed singles/doubles with private bath for US$15/20, but its central location and shady patio are strong points. ***Hospedaje del Centro*** *(☎ 900-1419, Soriano 1126)*, next to the Peruvian Consulate, charges US$15/18 with shared bath (few of these rooms are available), US$18/20 with private bath. Once a luxurious single-family residence, it's clean but crumbling, and some rooms are very dark.

Some rooms are also a bit dark at ***Hotel Ateneo*** *(☎ 901-2630, Colonia 1147)*, where rates are US$18/20 with private bath and television, except on Saturday nights when they rise to US$29. ***Hotel Ideal*** *(☎ 901-6389, Colonia 914)* is clean and friendly, with good bathrooms; rooms with shared bath are US$18/25, with private bath US$25/30. Clean, reader-recommended ***Hotel Kaldi*** *(☎ 903-0365, Ejido 1083)* charges US$20 weekdays, US$30 weekends, for doubles with color TV and phone.

Places to Stay – Mid-Range

A good choice is ***Hotel Arapey*** *(☎ 900-7032, Av Uruguay 925)*, with rooms for US$25/30. Conveniently central ***Hotel Casablanca*** *(☎ 901-0918, San José 1039)* charges US$25/30 with private bath. At a noisier location, the otherwise pleasant ***Hotel Aramaya*** *(☎ 908-6192, Av 18 de Julio 1103)* costs US$25/35 with breakfast; some rooms have double balconies, and the service is excellent.

One of Montevideo's best budget accommodations has been ***Hotel Palacio*** *(☎ 916-3612, Bartolomé Mitre 1364)*, but it seems to be living on its reputation after unwarranted price increases. Singles with brass beds (some of them sagging), antique furniture, and balconies cost US$31 single or double with shared bath – though the water pressure can be erratic. Ask, however, for accommodations on the 6th floor, where the balconies are nearly as large as the rooms themselves and provide exceptional views of the Ciudad Vieja. Still a good place, it's not the value it once was.

Probably the best mid-range value is ***Hotel Mediterráneo*** *(☎ 900-5090, Paraguay 1486)*, which charges US$30/40 for well-kept rooms with breakfast and excellent service. Enjoying literary cachet as the site of Julio Cortázar's short story 'La Puerta Condenada,' ***Hotel Español*** *(☎ 900-3816, Convención 1317)* charges US$35/45 for interior rooms, US$40/55 for those facing the street.

The central ***Hotel Lancaster*** *(☎ 902-0029, Plaza Cagancha 1334)* has good service and rooms starting at US$45/65 with breakfast. Accommodating ***Gran Hotel América*** *(☎ 902-0392, Río Negro 1330)* charges from US$55/68, while ***Hotel Alvear*** *(☎ 902-0244, Yí 1372)* costs about the same. Reader-recommended ***Hotel Tres Cruces*** *(☎ 402-3474, Migueletes 2356)*, an eight-story, three-star high-rise near the bus terminal, costs US$55/75 with breakfast and satellite TV.

Places to Stay – Top End

Montevideo's top-end hotels lack the luxury of those in Buenos Aires, but there are some decent values; all include breakfast in their rates. Rates at the ***Hotel London Palace*** *(☎ 902-0024, Río Negro 1278)* run US$64/85 with a buffet breakfast. The ***Hotel Embajador*** *(☎ 902-0009, San José 1212)* starts at US$60/80 and rises to US$80/100. The refurbished ***Hotel Oxford*** *(☎ 902-0046, Paraguay 1286)* charges US$72/87, which includes an outstanding breakfast.

The relatively new ***Hotel Lafayette*** *(☎ 902-2351, Soriano 1170)* is Montevideo's only real luxury hotel, charging US$111/129 to US$129/137, though the Moonie-operated ***Hotel Victoria Palace*** *(☎ 902-0111, Plaza Independencia 759)* makes an effort to be one. Rates at the latter are US$143/165. The recently established ***Holiday Inn*** *(☎ 900-5794, Colonia 823)*, in fact, the upgraded former Hotel Internacional, costs US$140 single or double.

PLACES TO EAT

Montevideo falls short of Buenos Aires' sophistication and variety, but its numerous restaurants are unpretentious and offer excellent values. Reasonably priced, worthwhile downtown restaurants include ***Morini*** *(☎ 915-9733, Ciudadela 1229)* and ***Mesón Viejo Sancho*** *(☎ 900-4063, San José 1229)*. ***La Genovesa*** *(☎ 900-8729, San José 1242)* has good seafood and abundant portions, but note that IVA may not be included in the listed prices, nor the *cubierto*, or service.

Lobizón, on Zelmar Michelini between Av 18 de Julio and San José, has inexpensive lunch specials and a great informal atmosphere. There's even better bar atmosphere at its namesake ***Bar Lobizón*** *(☎ 901-1334, Zelmar Michelini 1264)*, a block south, but on the opposite side of the street; it's open only at night, with both food and entertainment.

Uruguayans eat even more meat than Argentines, so parrillada is always a popular choice. Central parrillas include ***El Fogón*** *(☎ 900-0900, San José 1080)*, ***Las Brasas*** *(☎ 900-2285, San José 909)*, and the many stalls at the Mercado del Puerto. If you've OD'd on meat, there are several vegetarian alternatives, including ***La Vegetariana*** *(☎ 900-7661, Yí 1334; 901-0558, San José 1056)* and ***Vida Natural*** *(San José 1184)*.

Seafood is another possibility. ***La Posada del Puerto*** *(☎ 915-4279)* has two stalls in the Mercado del Puerto, while ***La Tasca del Puerto*** is outside on the peatonal Pérez Castellano. ***La Proa*** *(☎ 916-2578)*, a sidewalk café on the peatonal Pérez Castellano, has entrées from about US$8; with drinks, dinner for two should cost about US$20. It serves as many as 800 people per day, but the service is still friendly and attentive. Another popular place in the Mercado is ***El Palenque*** *(☎ 915-4704)*. The reader-recommended ***Martín Pescador*** *(☎ 707-2941, Obligado 1392)*, near Rivera a few blocks south of Tres Cruces, has also drawn praise for its seafood.

As in Argentina, Italian immigration has left its mark on the country's cuisine. For pizza, try ***Emporio de la Pizza*** *(☎ 901-4681, Río Negro 1311)*. Less traditional is ***Pizza Bros*** *(Plaza Cagancha 1364)*, a lively place with good pizza and bright but not overpowering decor. For more elaborate dishes in addition to tasty pizzas, visit ***Ruffino*** *(☎ 908-3384, San José 1166)*, which offers a 10% discount for cash.

Olivier *(☎ 915-0617, JC Gómez 1420)*, just off Plaza Constitución, is a very highly regarded but expensive French restaurant. Spanish food is available at ***Mesón del Club Español*** *(☎ 901-5145, Av 18 de Julio 1332)* and ***El Sarao*** *(☎ 901-7688, Santiago de Chile 1137)*, which has flamenco shows Fridays. For Basque food, visit ***Eusbal Errias*** *(☎ 902-3519, San José 1168)*.

For German cuisine, try the ***Club Alemán*** *(☎ 902-3982, Paysandú 935, 4th floor)*. There's Middle Eastern food at the ***Club Libanés*** *(☎ 900-1801, Paysandú 898)*. ***Oriente*** *(Andes 1311)* has a good all-you-can-eat Chinese menu, though some á la carte dishes are expensive.

Confitería La Pasiva, on Plaza Constitución at JC Gómez and Sarandí in the Ciudad Vieja, has excellent, reasonably priced minutas and superb flan casero in a very traditional atmosphere (except for the digital readout menu on one wall); the 'pasiva entrecote' has been highly recommended as sufficient for two.

Other decent confiterías include ***Oro del Rhin*** *(☎ 902-2833, Convención 1403)*, the oldest in the city, and ***Confitería de la Corte*** *(Ituzaingó 1325)*, just off Plaza Constitución, with fine, moderately priced lunch specials.

URUGUAY

ENTERTAINMENT

Most of the entertainment venues listed below are in the Ciudad Vieja and the central barrio of El Cordón, but the focus of Montevideo's nightlife is shifting eastward toward Pocitos and Carrasco, where there are plenty of clubs and restaurants, and good beach access.

Tango

The legendary Argentine Carlos Gardel spent time in Montevideo, where the tango is no less popular than in Buenos Aires. The very informal ***Fun Fun*** *(☎ 915-8005, Ciudadela 1229)*, in the Mercado Central, offers a good mix of young and old. ***Mil Años*** *(☎ 901-1373, Zelmar Michelini 1054)* has tango and *candombe* (Afro-Uruguayan) dancing; the show and dinner run about US$20 per person. There's also ***La Casa de Becho*** *(☎ 924-4757, Nueva York 1415)*, north of Terminal Tres Cruces in the former home of Gerardo Matos Rodríguez, composer of the tango 'La Cumparsita.' Visitors interested in lessons can try ***Joventango*** *(☎ 901-5561)*, in the Mercado de la Abundancia at the corner of San José and Yaguarón.

Folk & Rock

For live folkloric music, Cuban salsa, and the like, the best place to go is ***La Bodeguita del Sur*** *(☎ 902-8649, Soriano 840)*. For rock music and occasional live theater, try the ***Sala Zitarrosa*** *(☎ 901-7303)*, at the corner of Av 18 de Julio and Jullo Herrera y Obes, opposite Plaza del Entrevero.

Cinema

Montevideo's commercial cinemas offer films from around the world and Latin America, lagging only a little behind Buenos Aires. Most cinemas are along or near Av 18 de Julio and Plaza Cagancha. The film club ***Cinemateca Uruguaya*** *(☎ 408-2460, Lorenzo Carnelli 1311)* has a modest membership fee that allows unlimited viewing at the five cinemas it runs.

Theater

Like Buenos Aires, Montevideo has a lively theater community. Besides the ***Teatro Solís***, there is the ***Casa del Teatro*** *(☎ 402-0773, Mercedes 1788)*, ***Teatro Circular*** *(☎ 908-1953, Rondeau 1388)*, ***Teatro del Anglo*** *(☎ 902-3773, San José 1426)*, and ***Teatro de la Candela*** *(☎ 710-9298, 21 de Setiembre 2797)*, in Pocitos; ***Teatro El Picadero*** *(☎ 915-2337, 25 de Mayo 390)*, in the Ciudad Vieja; ***Teatro del Centro*** *(☎ 902-8915, Plaza Cagancha 1164)*; and ***Teatro El Galpón*** *(☎ 408-3366, Av 18 de Julio 1618)*. Prices are very reasonable, starting at about US$5.

SPECTATOR SPORTS

Soccer, an Uruguayan passion, inspires large and regular crowds. The main stadium, the Estadio Centenario in Parque José Batlle y Ordóñez off Av Italia, opened in 1930 for

Horse-drawn carriage with a full load

the first World Cup. Later declared a historic monument, it also contains the Museo del Fútbol.

SHOPPING

Central Montevideo's main shopping area is Av 18 de Julio, although the Ciudad Vieja is becoming more attractive as it is redeveloped. Outlying barrios increasingly offer shopping malls like the unlikely Punta Carretas Shopping, a erstwhile prison remodeled into an upscale mall that attracts both locals and foreigners. It's near Rambla Mahatma Gandhi at José Ellauri and Solano García; bus No 121 from downtown is the most convenient public transportation.

At the other end of the spectrum, El Cordón's Feria De Tristán Narvaja, a 60-year tradition begun by Italian immigrants, is a Sunday morning outdoor market that sprawls from Av 18 de Julio along Calle Tristán Narvaja to Galicia, spilling over onto side streets. Besides groceries, you can find many interesting trinkets, antiques, and souvenirs in its dozens of makeshift stalls.

For attractive artisanal items, at reasonable prices in an informal atmosphere, visit Mercado de los Artesanos on Plaza Cagancha, which is also a hangout for younger Uruguayans. Another outlet is the recycled Mercado de la Abundancia, at the corner of San José and Yaguarón, with upstairs and downstairs groceries and crafts. Manos del Uruguay, at San José 1111 (☎ 900-4910) and Reconquista 602 (☎ 915-9522), is famous for its quality goods.

As in Argentina, leather is a popular item. Shops worth checking out include Casa Mario (☎ 916-2356), at Piedras 641 in the Ciudad Vieja; the Leather Corner (☎ 900-7922), a branch of Casa Mario, at San José 950; and the Montevideo Leather Factory (☎ 901-6226), at Plaza Independencia 832, 2nd floor.

For footwear, visit Arbiter-Pasqualini, at 18 de Julio 943, or Impel (☎ 709-8176), at Luis B Cavia 2898 in Pocitos, both of which make shoes to order.

Uruguayan woolens are excellent. Besides Manos del Uruguay, other good places to try are La Calesa, on Río Negro between 18 de Julio and San José, or Uruwool (☎ 401-2868), Tacuarembó 1531.

Uruguay's very limited mining industry produces some worthwhile gemstones, particularly amethysts and agates. Good jewelers include Cabildo Piedras, at Sarandí 610; Cuarzos del Uruguay (☎ 915-9210), at Sarandí 604, and Carlos Andersen (☎ 908-2742), at Julio Herrera y Obes 1284.

GETTING THERE & AWAY

Air

Many more airlines fly via Ezeiza in Buenos Aires than directly to Montevideo's Aeropuerto Internacional Carrasco, although many still have offices in Montevideo. Commuter airlines also provide international services between the two countries. Airlines flying out of Carrasco without stopping in Ezeiza include Pluna (to Buenos Aires' Aeroparque, several Brazilian destinations, Paraguay, Chile, and Spain), LAPA (to Aeroparque), TAM (to Paraguay), LanChile (to Santiago), and Varig (to Brazil). Pluna and LAPA offer the cheapest fares to Buenos Aires.

Aerolíneas Argentinas
(☎ 901-9466)
Convención 1343, 4th floor

Alitalia
(☎ 908-5828)
Colonia 981, 2nd floor

American
(☎ 916-3979)
Sarandí 699 bis

Avianca
(☎ 908-4851)
Andes 1293, 8th floor

Continental
(☎ 908-5828)
Río Negro 1380, Oficina 104
Ecuatoriana
(☎ 902-5717)
Colonia 981
Iberia
(☎ 908-1032)
Colonia 873
LanChile
(☎ 908-1032)
Plaza Cagancha 1335, Oficina 801
LAPA
(☎ 900-8765)
Plaza Cagancha 1339
Lloyd Aéreo Boliviano (LAB)
(☎ 902-2656)
Colonia 920, 2nd floor
Pluna/Varig
(☎ 902-1414)
Colonia 1001
South African Airways
(☎ 900-8000)
Río Negro 1380, Oficina 104
Transportes Aéreos Mercosur (TAM)
(☎ 916-6044)
Bacacay 1321

Bus

Still reasonably close to downtown, Montevideo's modern Terminal Tres Cruces (☎ 401-8998), at Bulevar Artigas and Av Italia, is a big improvement on the individual bus terminals that once cluttered Plaza Cagancha and nearby side streets. It has tourist information, decent restaurants, clean toilets, a luggage check, public telephones, a casa de cambio, and many other services.

Some companies have kept downtown ticket offices; addresses are included below when appropriate. They usually add a small *tasa de embarque* (terminal charge) of around US$0.50 in addition to the ticket price.

International Bus de la Carrera (☎ 402-1313) has three direct buses daily to Buenos Aires. Bus de la Hidrovía (☎ 402-5129) goes Tuesday and Sunday to Corrientes (14 hours).

Several companies go elsewhere in Argentina, including Empresa General Artigas (EGA; ☎ 402-5164 or 902-5335) at Río Branco 1409, which travels to Rosario and Mendoza at 10 am Saturday, and to Santiago de Chile at 12:30 Monday; Tas Choapa (☎ 409-8598) also goes to Santiago.

El Rápido Internacional (☎ 401-4764) also goes to Rosario and Mendoza, with connections to Chile, at noon Thursday. Expreso Encon (☎ 408-6670) goes to Rosario, Paraná, Santa Fe, and Córdoba, while Cora (☎ 409-8799) goes to Córdoba four times weekly.

Brújula (☎ 401-9350) goes to Asunción, Paraguay, on Tuesday, Friday, and Sunday, while Coit (☎ 401-5628, 901-6619), at Río Branco 1389, goes Monday, Wednesday, and Saturday via Uruguaiana (Brazil) and Posadas (Argentina). Both have a reputation for excellent service.

Cauvi (☎ 401-9196) goes to Buenos Aires and the Brazilian cities of Porto Alegre, Curitiba, and São Paulo. TTL (☎ 401-1410, 901-7142), at Plaza Cagancha 1385, goes nightly to Pelotas and Porto Alegre and to Florianópolis, Camboriú, Curitibá, and São Paulo. EGA also goes to Brazilian destinations, including Pelotas and Porto Alegre nightly at 8 pm; and Florianópolis, Camboriú, Curitiba, and São Paulo on Sunday, Wednesday, and Friday at 4 pm. Planalto (☎ 1717) also serves Brazilian destinations.

Sample fares include Buenos Aires (US$25, eight hours), Porto Alegre (US$40, 11 hours), Rosario (US$42, 15 hours), Corrientes (US$45, 14 hours), Florianópolis (US$56, 17½ hours), Camboriú (US$58, 18½ hours), Curitibá (US$67, 23 hours), Asunción (US$70, 18 hours), Mendoza (US$75, 21 hours), São Paulo (US$80, 29 hours), and Santiago de Chile (US$95, 28 hours).

Domestic COT (☎ 409-4949) sends more than 20 buses daily to Punta del Este, via Piriápolis, Pan de Azúcar, San Carlos, and Maldonado; Copsa (☎ 408-1521) also goes to Maldonado. COT also has 10 buses daily to Colonia and also goes to Rocha and La Paloma.

Agencia Central (☎ 1717, 900-5661), downtown at Rondeau 1475, goes to Mercedes, Paysandú, Salto, and Tacuarembó. Turil (☎ 1990) goes three times daily to Tacuarembó and Rivera, and eight times daily to Colonia.

Chadre (☎ 1717, 900-5661), at Rondeau 1475, Sabelín (☎ 1717, 900-5661), at Rondeau 1475, Copay (☎ 400-9926), and Intertur (☎ 409-7098) all serve Littoral destinations such as Colonia, Carmelo, Mercedes, Fray Bentos, Paysandú, and Salto.

Rutas del Sol (☎ 402-5451) goes to Rocha and La Paloma 10 times daily, and five times to Barra de Valizas. Cita (☎ 402-5425) goes to Chuy, as do COT and Rutas del Sol. Rutas del Plata (☎ 402-5129) goes to Minas, Treinta y Tres, and Río Branco four times daily.

Núñez (☎ 408-6670) serves interior destinations such as Minas, Treinta y Tres, Melo, Río Branco, Salto, and Rivera, while El Norteño (☎ 908-9212) goes to Salto and Bella Unión. Sharing offices with Núñez, Cynsa (☎ 408-6670) has five buses daily to Chuy, six to La Paloma, and also goes to Paysandú. Other companies going to Minas include Cita, Corporación (☎ 402-1920), Cota (☎ 402-1307), Cromín (☎ 402-5451), Emdal (☎ 409-7098), and Expreso Minuano (☎ 402-5075).

CUT/Corporación (☎ 402-1920) goes five times daily to Mercedes and Fray Bentos and twice to Artigas. Turismar (☎ 409-0999) goes to Treinta y Tres and Melo three times daily, as does Cota. Buses Nossar (☎ 1880) has five daily buses to Durazno, one of which continues to Paso de los Toros and Tacuarembó.

Sample fares include Minas (US$5, two hours), Pan de Azúcar (US$5.50, 1½ hours), Maldonado/Punta del Este (US$6, 2½ hours), Colonia (US$7, 2½ hours), Rocha (US$8, three hours), La Paloma (US$ 10, 3½ hours), Mercedes (US$10), Treinta y Tres (US$10, four hours), Fray Bentos (US$11, five hours), Chuy (US$13, five hours), Paysandú (US$15, five hours), Tacuarembó (US$15, 5½ hours), Rivera (US$18), and Salto (US$20, six hours).

River

Buquebus (☎ 902-0170) is downtown at Río Negro 1400 but also has port offices (☎ 916-8801) at the entrance to Dársena 1 on the Rambla 25 de Agosto, at the foot of Pérez Castellano in the Ciudad Vieja. It runs 'Buqueaviones' (high-speed ferries) across the river to Buenos Aires (2½ hours) four times daily. Fares are US$52 in turista, US$67 in primera; children ages two to nine pay US$17.

Ferrytur, at Río Branco 1368 (☎ 900-6617) and at Tres Cruces (☎ 409-8198), does bus-boat combinations to Buenos Aires (US$40, four hours) on their *Sea Cat* hydrofoil, with four departures weekdays and three on weekends.

Cacciola (☎ 401-9350), at Terminal Tres Cruces, runs a bus-launch service to Buenos Aires, via the riverside town of Carmelo and the Argentine Delta suburb of Tigre (US$29 one-way, US$55 return, eight hours; ask about off-season promotions). Services from Montevideo leave at 12:40 am Monday through Saturday, 4 pm Sunday, and daily at 8:30 am.

GETTING AROUND

To/From the Airport

For US$4, Ibat (☎ 601-0207) runs a special airport bus from Pluna's downtown offices opposite Plaza del Entrevero. From the Terminal Suburbana at the corner of Rambla 25 de Agosto and Río Branco, the No 209 Cutesa and Copsa buses go to the airport every 15 minutes (US$1.20).

Bus

Montevideo's improving fleet of buses less frequently leaves you gasping for breath, due to noxious diesel fumes, and still goes everywhere for about US$0.65. The *Guia de Montevideo Eureka*, available at bookshops or kiosks, lists routes and schedules, as do the yellow pages of the Montevideo phone book. As in Argentina, the driver or conductor will ask your destination. Retain your ticket, which may be inspected at any time. This is not Buenos Aires, however – most routes cease service by 10:30 or 11 pm. For information, contact Cutesa (☎ 200-9021, 200-7527).

Car

Uruguayan car-rental costs have risen dramatically and now approach Argentine prices; before signing a contract, verify whether insurance and IVA are included. Rental agencies include Budget (☎ 902-5353), at Mercedes 935; Dollar (☎/fax 402-6427), at J Barrios Amorin 1186; Localiza (☎ 902-3920), at Colonia 813; and Multicar (☎ 900-5079), at Colonia 1227.

Taxi

Montevideo's black-and-yellow taxis are all metered; it costs about US$1 to drop the flag and US$0.60 per 600m. Between 10 pm and 6 am, and on weekends and holidays, fares are 20% higher. There is a small additional charge for luggage, and riders generally round off the total fare to the next higher peso.

Uruguayan Littoral

West of Montevideo, the Littoral is that portion of Uruguay that fronts the Río de la Plata and the Río Uruguay, opposite Argentine Mesopotamia. Originally Indian and gaucho country, it has become the country's most important agricultural area, whose wheat fields and gardens feed the capital's growing population.

The region has one can't-miss attraction, the 17th-century Portuguese contraband port and fortress of Colonia opposite Buenos Aires, and several lesser sights that make worthwhile day trips from either Colonia or Montevideo. Overland travelers from Argentine Mesopotamia will find the towns along the Río Uruguay – Salto, Paysandú, Fray Bentos, and Mercedes – pleasant enough to justify a stopover en route to Colonia and Montevideo.

COLONIA

Only an hour or two from Buenos Aires, Colonia (full name Colonia del Sacramento) is one of the Southern Cone's unappreciated gems, attracting many thousands of Argentines but only a handful of the many foreign tourists who visit the Argentine capital.

Founded in 1680 by the Portuguese Manoel Lobo, it occupied a strategic position almost exactly opposite Buenos Aires across the Río de la Plata, but its major importance was as a source of contraband, undercutting Spain's jealously defended mercantile trade monopoly. British goods made their way from Colonia into Buenos Aires and the interior through surreptitious exchange with the Portuguese in the Paraná delta; for this reason, Spanish forces intermittently besieged Portugal's riverside outpost for decades. The Jesuit father Martin Dobrizhoffer vividly described mid-18th-century Colonia:

> The houses are few and low, forming a village, rather than city, yet it is far from despicable; opulent merchants, wares of every kind, gold, silver, and diamonds are concealed beneath its miserable roofs. Surrounded with a single and very slender wall . . . the land under Portuguese authority is of such small circumference that the most inactive person might walk round it in half an hour. Portuguese ships, laden with English and Dutch wares, and Negro slaves . . . crowd to this port, and the Spanish sentinels, either bribed or deceived, convey the goods to Paraguay, Peru, or Chili. It is incredible how many millions are lost to the Spaniards in this forbidden traffic.

Although the two powers agreed over the cession of Colonia to Spain around 1750, the agreement failed when Jesuit missionaries on the upper Paraná refused to comply with the proposed exchange of territory in their area. Spain finally captured the city in 1762, but failed to hold it until 1777, when authorities created the Viceroyalty of the River Plate. From this time, the city's commercial importance declined as foreign goods proceeded directly to Buenos Aires.

The capital of its department, Colonia is a pleasant town of about 30,000, with the streets of its historic colonial core shaded by sycamores from the summer heat. In the course of the day, the town discloses its many aspects as sunlight strikes whitewashed colonial buildings and the river; the latter, living up to its name, is silvery in the morning but turns brownish by midday. The townspeople are extremely polite – motorists even stop for pedestrians.

Colonia served as the fictional San José de los Altares in Argentine director María Luisa Bemberg's offbeat 1993 film *I Don't Want to Talk About It*, starring Marcelo Mastroianni as an enigmatic Italian immigrant who falls in love and marries a dwarf, the daughter of the widow of the town's mayor, who eventually deserts him to join the circus.

Big changes may be in store for Colonia if, as proposed, a massive bridge crosses the Río de la Plata from Punta Colorada, midway between Buenos Aires and the city of La Plata. The bridge project, which has

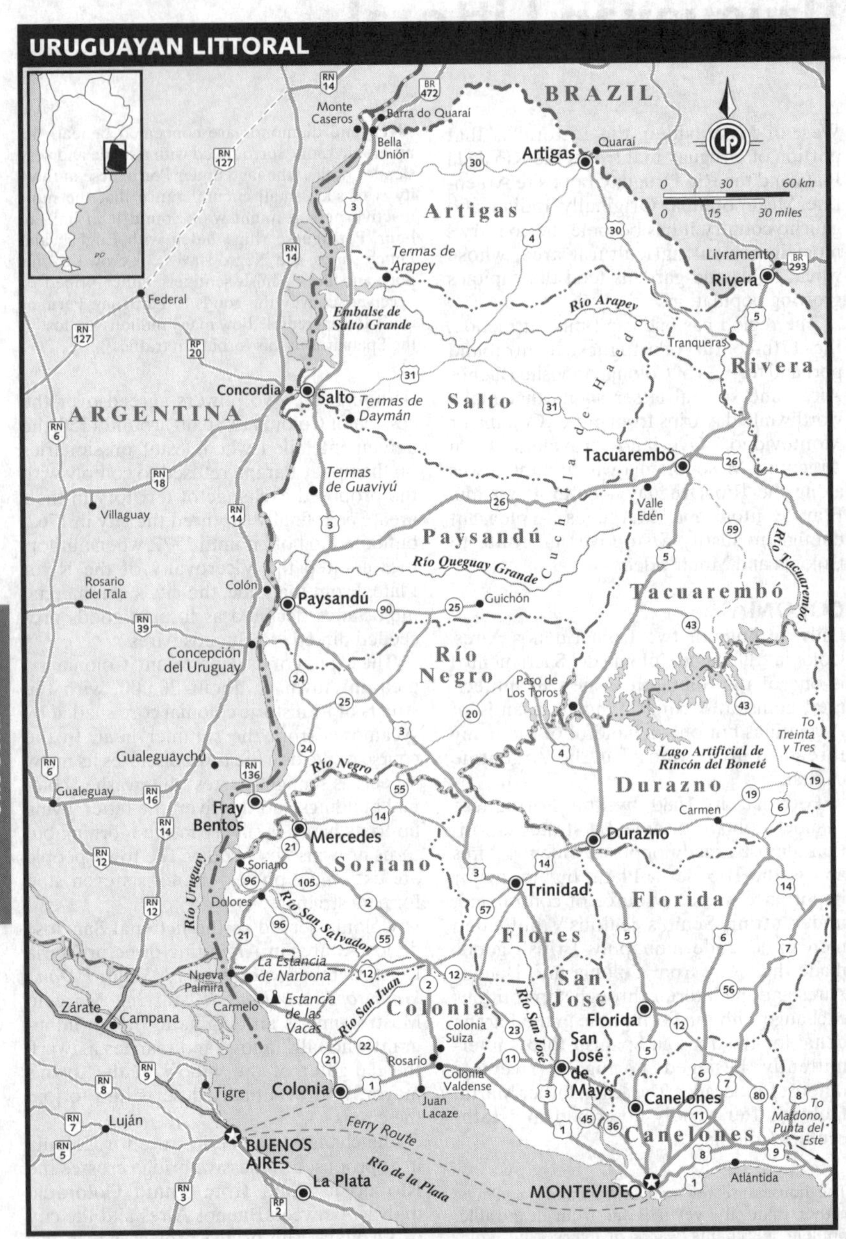
URUGUAYAN LITTORAL
BRAZIL
ARGENTINA
Artigas
Salto
Paysandú
Río Negro
Soriano
Colonia
Flores
San José
Florida
Durazno
Tacuarembó
Rivera
Canelones
Monte Caseros
Barra do Quaraí
Bella Unión
Quaraí
Artigas
Livramento
Rivera
Tranqueras
Termas de Arapey
Embalse de Salto Grande
Federal
Concordia
Salto
Termas de Daymán
Termas de Guaviyú
Tacuarembó
Valle Edén
Villaguay
Colón
Paysandú
Guichón
Rosario del Tala
Concepción del Uruguay
Paso de Los Toros
Lago Artificial de Rincón del Boneté
To Treinta y Tres
Gualeguaychú
Gualeguay
Fray Bentos
Mercedes
Carmen
Durazno
Trinidad
Soriano
Dolores
La Estancia de Narbona
Nueva Palmira
Carmelo
Estancia de las Vacas
Zárate
Campana
Colonia Suiza
Florida
San José de Mayo
Rosario
Colonia Valdense
Tigre
Colonia
Juan Lacaze
Canelones
Luján
BUENOS AIRES
La Plata
MONTEVIDEO
Atlántida
To Maldono, Punta del Este
Ferry Route
Río de la Plata
Río Uruguay
Río San Salvador
Río San Juan
Río San José
Río Negro
Río Queguay Grande
Río Arapey
Río Tacuarembó
Cuchilla de Haedo
0 30 60 km
0 15 30 miles

URUGUAY

drawn criticism on economic, environmental, and social grounds, is still in the early planning stages.

Orientation

Colonia del Sacramento sits on the east bank of the Río de la Plata, 180km west of Montevideo via Ruta 1, but only 50km from Buenos Aires by ferry or hydrofoil. Like Montevideo, it features an irregular colonial nucleus of narrow cobbled streets (now known as the Barrio Histórico) on a small peninsula jutting into the river. The town's commercial center, around Plaza 25 de Agosto, and the river port are a few blocks east, while the Rambla Costanera leads north along the river to the Real de San Carlos, another area of interest to visitors. The diagonal Av Roosevelt is the main highway to Montevideo.

Information

Tourist Offices The municipal Dirección de Turismo (☎ 26141) is at General Flores 499. Both helpful and increasingly well informed, the staff has numerous brochures difficult to obtain elsewhere. Hours are weekdays 7 am to 8 pm, weekends 10 am to 7 pm. The national Ministerio de Turismo (☎ 24897) maintains a ferry port branch, open 9 am to 3 pm daily.

Money Arriving at the port from Buenos Aires, you can change money at Banco República, which charges US$1 commission for traveler's checks. Downtown, try Cambio Colonia, at General Flores and Alberto Méndez, or Cambio Viaggio, at General Flores 350. Banco Acac, at the corner of General Flores and Washington Barbot, has an ATM.

Post & Communications The post office is at Lavalleja 226. Antel, at Rivadavia 420, has direct fiber-optic lines to the USA (AT&T and MCI) and the UK. Colonia's area code is ☎ 052.

Travel Agencies Receptivos Colonia (☎ 23388), General Flores 507, arranges air tickets, tours, and car rentals.

Walking Tour

Also known as La Colonia Portuguesa (the Portuguese Colony), Colonia's Barrio Histórico begins at the **Puerta de Campo**, the restored entrance to the old city on Calle Manoel Lobo, which dates from the governorship of Vasconcellos in 1745. A thick fortified wall runs south along the Paseo de San Miguel to the river. A short distance west is **Plaza Mayor 25 de Mayo**, off of which is the narrow, cobbled **Calle de los Suspiros** (Street of Whispers), lined with tile-and-stucco colonial houses. Just beyond this street, the **Museo Portugués** has good exhibits on the Portuguese period, including Lusitanian and colonial dress. Colonia's museums are generally open 11:30 am to 6 pm, but closed on Tuesday and Wednesday.

At the southwest corner of the Plaza Mayor are the **Casa de Lavalleja**, once the residence of General Lavalleja, and the ruins of the 17th-century **Convento de San Francisco** and the 19th-century **faro** (lighthouse). Open 10:30 am to noon weekends, the lighthouse provides an excellent view of the old town. At the west end of the Plaza Mayor, on Calle del Comercio, is the **Museo Municipal**; next door is the so-called **Casa del Virrey**, the Viceroy's House, although no viceroy ever lived in Colonia (maybe one slept here). At the northwest corner of the plaza, on Calle de las Misiones de los Tapes, the **Archivo Regional** contains a small museum and bookshop.

At the west end of Misiones de los Tapes is the **Museo de los Azulejos** (Museum of Tiles), a 17th-century house with a sampling of colonial tile work (the museum was closed at last pass). From there, the riverfront Paseo de San Gabriel leads to Calle del Colegio, where a right to Calle del Comercio leads to the **Capilla Jesuítica**, the ruined Jesuit chapel. Going east along Av General Flores and then turning south on Calle Vasconcellos, you reach the landmark **Iglesia Matriz** on the Plaza de Armas, also known as Plaza Manoel Lobo.

Across General Flores, at España and San José, the **Museo Español** has exhibitions of replica colonial pottery, clothing, and maps. At the north end of the street is the

Puerto Viejo, the old port. One block east, at Calle del Virrey Cevallos and Rivadavia, the **Teatro Bastión del Carmen** is a theater building that incorporates part of the city's ancient fortifications.

Iglesia Matriz

Begun in 1680, Uruguay's oldest church has undergone many changes over three centuries. It came to occupy its present perimeter between 1722 and 1749, under Portuguese Governor Pedro Vasconcellos. Nearly destroyed by fire in 1799, it was rebuilt by Spanish architect Tomás Toribio, who also designed the Cabildo of Montevideo.

The church suffered further misfortune when, during the Brazilian occupation of 1823, lightning struck a powder magazine in the sacristy, producing an explosion that destroyed part of the lateral walls, two-thirds of the vault, the altar, and the posterior wall, and left cracks in many other parts of the building. Between 1836 and 1842, under the direction of Padre Domingo Rama and sponsored by General Fructuoso Rivera, the church was again rebuilt; changes since then have been primarily cosmetic. It's on Calle Vasconcellos, between General Flores and the Plaza de Armas.

Real de San Carlos

At the turn of the century, naturalized Argentine entrepreneur Nicolás Mihanovich spent US$1.5 million to build an immense tourist complex 5km west of Colonia at Real de San Carlos, a spot where Spanish troops once camped before attacking the Portuguese outpost. Among the attractions erected by Mihanovich, a Dalmatian immigrant, were a 10,000-seat bullring (made superfluous after Uruguay outlawed bullfights in 1912), a 3000-seat jai alai frontón, a hotel-casino with its own power plant (the casino failed in 1917 when the Argentine government began to tax every boat crossing the river), and a racecourse.

Only the racecourse functions today, but the ruins make an interesting excursion. There is also the **Museo Municipal Real de San Carlos**, which focuses on paleontology, and unfortunately keeps no fixed hours.

Places to Stay

As Colonia has become a more popular destination for Argentine and international travelers, innkeepers have upgraded accommodations and prices have risen, but there are still reasonable alternatives. The municipal tourist office, on General Flores, may help find B&B lodgings when all else is full. Some hotels charge higher rates Friday through Sunday than Monday through Thursday.

Places to Stay – Budget

Camping The ***Camping Municipal de Colonia*** *(☎ 24444)* sits in a eucalyptus grove at Real de San Carlos, 5km from the Barrio Histórico. Close to the Balneario Municipal, its excellent facilities are open all year and are easily accessible by public transport. Fees are about US$4 per person.

Hospedajes & Hotels Except for camping, really cheap accommodations have nearly

SARAH J HAWKINS

Bullring ruins, Real de San Carlos

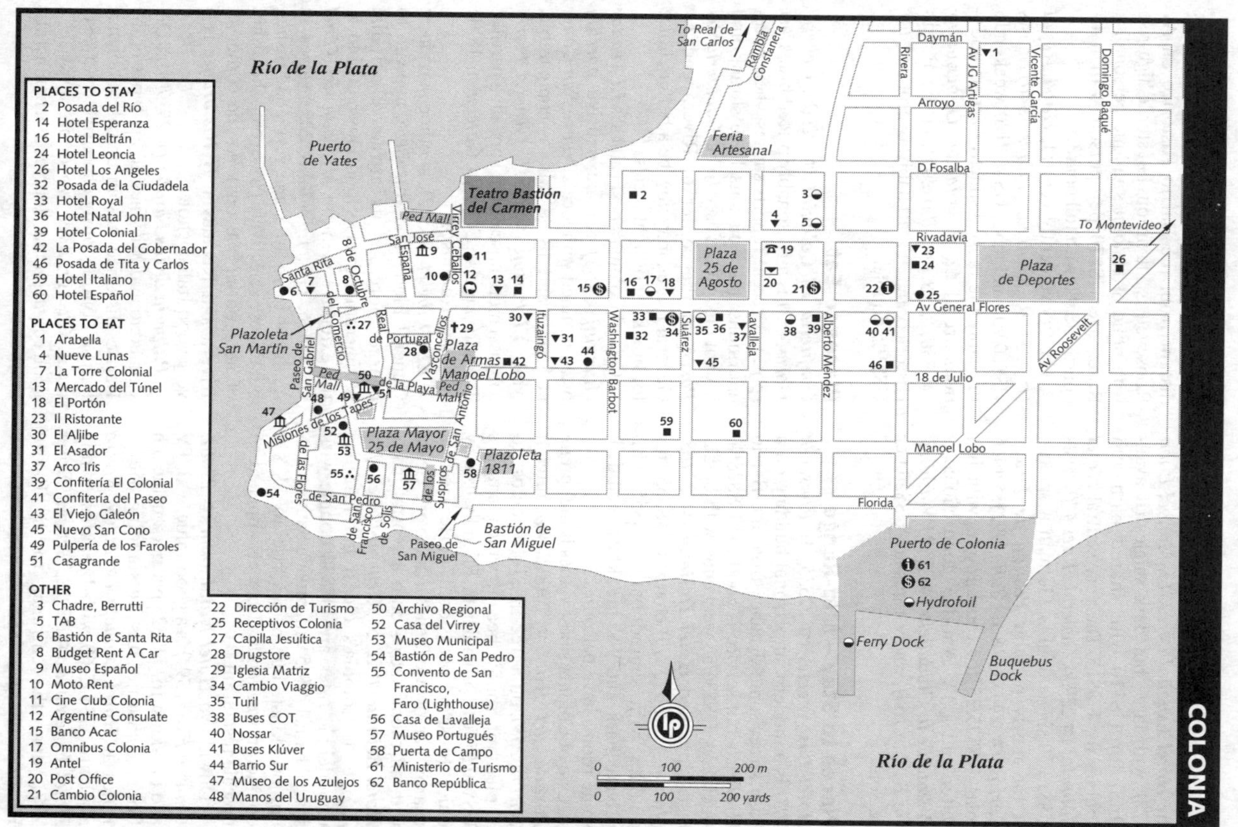

COLONIA
PLACES TO STAY
2 Posada del Río
14 Hotel Esperanza
16 Hotel Beltrán
24 Hotel Leoncia
26 Hotel Los Angeles
32 Posada de la Ciudadela
33 Hotel Royal
36 Hotel Natal John
39 Hotel Colonial
42 La Posada del Gobernador
46 Posada de Tita y Carlos
59 Hotel Italiano
60 Hotel Español
PLACES TO EAT
1 Arabella
4 Nueve Lunas
7 La Torre Colonial
13 Mercado del Túnel
18 El Portón
23 Il Ristorante
30 El Aljibe
31 El Asador
37 Arco Iris
39 Confitería El Colonial
41 Confitería del Paseo
43 El Viejo Galeón
45 Nuevo San Cono
49 Pulpería de los Faroles
51 Casagrande
OTHER
3 Chadre, Berrutti
5 TAB
6 Bastión de Santa Rita
8 Budget Rent A Car
9 Museo Español
10 Moto Rent
11 Cine Club Colonia
12 Argentine Consulate
15 Banco Acac
17 Omnibus Colonia
19 Antel
20 Post Office
21 Cambio Colonia
22 Dirección de Turismo
25 Receptivos Colonia
27 Capilla Jesuítica
28 Drugstore
29 Iglesia Matriz
34 Cambio Viaggio
35 Turil
38 Buses COT
40 Nossar
41 Buses Klüver
44 Barrio Sur
47 Museo de los Azulejos
48 Manos del Uruguay
50 Archivo Regional
52 Casa del Virrey
53 Museo Municipal
54 Bastión de San Pedro
55 Convento de San Francisco, Faro (Lighthouse)
56 Casa de Lavalleja
57 Museo Portugués
58 Puerta de Campo
61 Ministerio de Turismo
62 Banco República
Río de la Plata
Puerto de Yates
Teatro Bastión del Carmen
Feria Artesanal
To Real de San Carlos
Rambla Costanera
Plaza 25 de Agosto
Plaza de Deportes
To Montevideo
Plaza de Armas Manoel Lobo
Plaza Mayor 25 de Mayo
Plazoleta 1811
Plazoleta San Martín
Bastión de San Miguel
Paseo de San Miguel
Puerto de Colonia
Hydrofoil
Ferry Dock
Buquebus Dock
Dayman
Rivera
Av JG Artigas
Vicente García
Domingo Baqué
Arroyo
D Fosalba
Rivadavia
Av General Flores
18 de Julio
Manoel Lobo
Florida
Av Roosevelt
Ituzaingó
Washington Barbot
Suárez
Lavalleja
Alberto Méndez
Virrey Ceballos
Vasconcellos
Real
San José
España
8 de Octubre
Santa Rita
del Comercio
de Portugal
de la Playa
Ped Mall
San Antonio
Paseo de San Gabriel
Misiones de los Tapes
de las Flores
de San Pedro
de San Francisco
de Solís
de los Suspiros
0 100 200 m
0 100 200 yards

URUGUAY

disappeared. The cheapest in town, undergoing renovation at the time of writing, is the ***Hotel Español*** *(☎ 22314, Manoel Lobo 377)*, with large but dark singles (if available) for US$10 with shared bath and doubles for US$15. The very central ***Hotel Colonial*** *(☎ 22906, General Flores 440)* costs US$13/20 single/double. German is spoken at the newly popular ***Posada de Tita y Carlos*** *(☎ 24438, 18 de Julio 491)*, which costs US$25/35 for clean rooms with hot water and a TV. Another good choice is ***Posada de la Ciudadela*** *(☎ 22683, Washington Barbot 164)*, where rates are US$20 per person.

Places to Stay – Mid-Range

Hotel Los Angeles *(☎ 22335, Av Roosevelt 203)* is a modern, impersonal building on a busy street some distance from the Barrio Histórico, but service is good for US$28/40 weekdays, US$36/58 weekends, with breakfast. Upgraded ***Hotel Italiano*** *(☎ 22103, Manoel Lobo 341)* charges US$35 for doubles with shared bath, US$55 with private bath and TV, breakfast included; some rooms have balconies.

One of Colonia's best values is the serene ***Posada del Río*** *(☎ 23002, Washington Barbot 258)*, on a tree-lined street close to a pleasant sandy beach, which charges US$40/55 with private bath. Friendly, usually quiet (despite occasional noise from a nearby bar on weekends), and very clean, with all rooms facing onto a central patio, ***Hotel Beltrán*** *(☎ 22955, General Flores 311)* is one of Colonia's oldest hotels. Since remodeling, rates are US$36 double with shared bath, US$45 with private bath, including breakfast, but prices rise to US$70 double on weekends. It has also opened an upscale restaurant.

Downtown ***Hotel Natal John*** *(☎ 22081, General Flores 394)* is a good value, with TV and breakfast for US$25 per person; the 6th floor restaurant has outstanding views. Rates at ***Hotel Leoncia*** *(☎ 22369, Rivera 214)* are US$45/60 with breakfast, while ***Hotel Esperanza*** *(☎ 22922, General Flores 237)*, near the entrance to the Barrio Histórico, charges US$55/75 with breakfast.

Places to Stay – Top End

Gran Hotel Casino El Mirador *(☎ 22004)*, distant from the Barrio Histórico on Av Roosevelt, is a luxurious but sterile high-rise with none of Colonia's unique personality. Rates are US$70 per person with half-board, US$80 with full board.

The conveniently central, ***Hotel Royal*** *(☎ 23139, General Flores 340)* costs US$60/90 weekdays, US$80/120 weekends. Probably the most distinctive accommodations are at ***La Posada del Gobernador*** *(☎ 23018, 18 de Julio 205)*, in the Barrio Histórico, but it's arguably overpriced for US$105 double.

Places to Eat

Confitería El Colonial *(☎ 22906, General Flores 432)* is a reasonably priced breakfast spot, but recent reports suggest their once-enormous hot croissants have shrunk and it's not the value it used to be. ***Confitería del Paseo***, at the corner of Rivera and Av General Flores, may now be a better choice for breakfast or light meals.

One of Colonia's best values is ***El Asador*** *(Ituzaingó 168)*, an inexpensive *parrilla* often jammed with locals. ***Nuevo San Cono***, at Suárez and 18 de Julio, is comparable, while ***El Portón*** *(☎ 25318, General Flores 333)* is a more upscale but appealing parrilla. Try also popular ***El Viejo Galeón***, at 18 de Julio and Ituzaingó.

El Aljibe *(☎ 25342)*, another parrilla at General Flores and Ituzaingó, appears to charge more for its attractive colonial setting rather than its food. Down the block, the extensive menu at ***Mercado del Túnel*** *(☎ 24666, General Flores 229)* varies in quality – there are some very good dishes, but choose selectively (try eyeing the dishes of neighboring patrons). At the corner of Rivera and Rivadavia, ***Il Ristorante*** is a very good Italian choice.

Pulpería de los Faroles *(☎ 25399)*, at Del Comercio and Misiones de los Tapes in the Barrio Histórico, has an upscale ambience but isn't outrageously expensive for a tasty meal. ***Casagrande***, two doors away, is a good *confitería* that doubles as a handicrafts market.

At the tip of the Barrio Histórico, ***La Torre Colonial*** *(☎ 24639)* is a good pizzeria in a remodeled tower. Readers' recommendations include the pizza at ***Nueve Lunas*** *(Rivadavia 413)*, just off Plaza 25 de Agosto, and ***Arabella*** *(Avenida Artigas 384)*.

For ice cream, try ***Arco Iris***, on Lavalleja near General Flores.

Entertainment

Colonia's liveliest nightspot, also a good place to eat, is ***Drugstore*** *(Vasconcellos 179)*. ***Barrio Sur*** *(18 de Julio 267)* has snacks and live music.

For occasional films, check out the ***Cine Club Colonia*** *(Virrey Cevallos 236)*.

Shopping

Colonia's Feria Artesanal (Crafts Fair) has moved from its former site on the Plaza Mayor, in the Ciudad Vieja, to a new permanent spot at the corner of Suárez and Fosalba; it's open 9:30 am to 7:30 pm daily. Manos del Uruguay has an outlet at the corner of San Gabriel and Misiones de los Tapes, in the Ciudad Vieja.

Getting There & Away

Bus Colonia has no central bus terminal. COT (☎ 23121), General Flores 440, has at least nine buses daily to Montevideo (US$7, 2½ hours), and 10 buses daily to Colonia Suiza, Rosario, and Juan Lacaze.

Turil (☎ 25246), at General Flores and Suárez, one block east of Hotel Beltrán, goes eight times daily to Montevideo. Klüver (☎ 22934), at Av General Flores and Rivera, goes twice each weekday and once Saturday and Sunday to Mercedes, via Carmelo and Nueva Palmira.

Chadre, on Méndez between Fosalba and Rivadavia, goes twice daily to Montevideo and to Nueva Palmira, Carmelo, Salto, Paysandú, and Bella Unión. Berrutti, at the same offices, goes 10 times each weekday to Nueva Palmira, less frequently on weekends.

TAB, at the corner of Méndez and Rivadavia, serves interior destinations including Nueva Helvecia. Omnibus Colonia (☎ 22033), Av General Flores 323, goes to Nueva Helvecia and Colonia Suiza many times daily.

Nossar, on Av General Flores between Méndez and Rivera, goes to Durazno.

River Colonia has ferry and *aliscafo* (hydrofoil) services to Buenos Aires from the port at the foot of Av Roosevelt. Passengers leaving from Colonia's ferry terminal pay a US$3 departure tax.

Buquebus (☎ 22975) has two daily ferry sailings to Buenos Aires (2½ hours) on the *Eladia Isabel*, at 4 am and 7 pm. Regular one-way fares are US$23 adult, US$17 for children ages three to nine; slightly more expensive first-class service is also available. Buquebus also runs high-speed 'Buqueaviones' to Buenos Aires (45 minutes) seven times daily. One-way fares are US$32 adult, US$24 children ages three to nine; again, slightly more expensive first-class service is also available.

Ferrytur (☎ 22919) makes two ferry crossings to Buenos Aires (2½ hours) every weekday, and one every Saturday and Sunday, with the *Ciudad de Buenos Aires*. These depart at noon and 8 pm weekdays, 6:59 pm Saturdays and 7 pm Sundays. Regular fares are the same as Buquebus,' while day trips are available from US$31, including lunch and a city tour; there are also senior citizen discounts.

Ferrytur's hydrofoil *Sea Cat* goes to Buenos Aires (45 minutes) four times weekdays, three times daily on weekends for the same prices as Buquebus's Buqueaviones. Fares may be higher on selected peak days and in summer. There are also US$50 day trips, including lunch and a city tour.

Getting Around

The local bus companies Cotuc and ABC go to the Camping Municipal and the Real de San Carlos (US$0.40) from Av General Flores. Otherwise, Colonia'a compactness encourages walking.

Motor scooters are an inexpensive, popular means of getting around town – check Moto Rent, on Virrey Cevallos near Av General Flores, or Budget Rent A Car (☎ 25319), at Av General Flores 91. Prices are as low as US$15 for a Peugeot scooter, US$35 for a car.

COLONIA SUIZA

In the department of Colonia, Colonia Suiza (also known as Nueva Helvecia) is 120km west of Montevideo and 60km east of the city of Colonia del Sacramento along a short lateral off Ruta 1. Settled by Swiss immigrants in 1862, it was the country's first interior agricultural colony, providing wheat for the mills of Montevideo. A quiet, pleasant destination with a demonstrably European ambience, its dairy products are known throughout the country – 60% of Uruguay's cheese comes from here.

Information

Colonia Suiza has a formal tourist office at the entrance to town, but there's also a particularly helpful one at Artesanos Ciudad Jardín cooperative at Colonial Valdense, Km 120 of Ruta 1, about 6km from Colonia Suiza.

To change cash, try Banco La Caja Obrera, on 18 de Julio. Antel is at Artigas and Dreyer, across from the landmark OSE water tower. Colonia Suiza's area code is ☎ 055. The hospital (☎ 44057) is at 18 de Julio and C Cunier.

Things to See

The center of the town is the Plaza de los Fundadores, with an impressive sculpture, *El Surco*, commemorating the original Swiss pioneers. Interesting buildings include the ruins of the **Molino Quemado** (the first flour mill) and the historic **Hotel del Prado**, which also functions as a youth hostel.

Places to Stay & Eat

Dating from 1884, the 80-room ***Hotel del Prado*** *(☎ 44169)*, in the Barrio Hoteles on the outskirts of town, is a magnificent if declining building with huge balconies. Rooms cost US$25 per person, but it is also the youth hostel, offering beds with shared bath for US$8 with a hostel card.

Dating from 1872, the ***Granja Hotel Suizo*** *(☎ 44002)*, on Av Federico Fischer, is the country's oldest tourist hotel and has a renowned restaurant; doubles cost US$60. Without a doubt, though, the top of the line is luxurious ***Hotel Nirvana*** *(☎ 44052, 900-3823 in Montevideo)*, on Av Batlle y Ordóñez, where high-season (December 15 to April 1) accommodations cost US$56 per person with breakfast. It offers a swimming pool, tennis courts, horseback riding, facilities for children, and 25 hectares of beautifully landscaped grounds.

Colonia Suiza has several excellent restaurants. Besides Hotel Suizo, try ***La Gondola*** *(☎ 44474)*, Luis Dreyer and 25 de Agosto, ***L'Arbalete*** at Hotel Nirvana, and ***Don Juan*** *(☎ 45099, 18 de Julio 1214)*.

Getting There & Away

COT (☎ 44093), Berna 1268, has services to Montevideo, Colonia, Fray Bentos (three daily), and Paysandú (one daily). Ómnibus Colonia (☎ 44541), 25 de Agosto and Berna, goes to Colonia, while Turil (☎ 44998), 18 de Julio 1232, goes to Montevideo.

COLONIA VALDENSE

Colonia Valdense was founded by mid-19th century evangelical Christians, who earlier fled religious persecution in France and economic hardship Piedmont, Italy. The small town straddling Ruta 1 at the junction to Colonia Suiza is known as Uruguay's 'Garden City.' It also has fine craftspeople, whose works are on display at the headquarters of the Artesanos Ciudad Jardín, at Km 120 of Ruta 1, which doubles as a regional tourist office. The **Museo Valdense Sudamericano** documents the group's history.

Buses between Colonia and Montevideo pass through the town, but the nearest accommodations are at Colonia Suiza.

CARMELO

Where the Río Uruguay broadens and becomes the Río de la Plata, Carmelo sits opposite the Paraná delta, 75km northwest of Colonia del Sacramento and 235km from Montevideo. Launches connect it to the Buenos Aires suburb of Tigre. Part of the department of Colonia, it's a center for yachting, boating, and exploring the delta.

Carmelo dates from 1816, when residents of the village of Las Víboras petitioned

Artigas (for whom the town's original central plaza is named) for permission to move to the more hospitable Arroyo de las Vacas. The local economy depends on tourism, livestock, and agriculture – local wines have an excellent reputation.

Orientation

Carmelo straddles the Arroyo de las Vacas, a sheltered harbor on the Río de la Plata. North of the Arroyo, shady Plaza Independencia is now the commercial center. Most of the town's businesses are along 19 de Abril, which leads to the bridge across the arroyo, where a large park offers open space, camping, swimming, and a huge, tacky casino.

Information

Tourist Offices The municipal Oficina de Turismo (☎ 22001) has moved to Shopping Suhr, a gallery at 19 de Abril and Solís, near the bridge over the arroyo.

Money Carmelo has two exchange houses: Lerga, at 19 de Abril 300, and Viaggio, at 19 de Abril and 12 de Febrero, which is open 10 am to 6 pm weekdays but does not cash traveler's checks.

Post & Communications The post office is at Uruguay 368. Carmelo's area code is ☎ 54.

Medical Services The hospital (☎ 22107) is at Uruguay and Artigas.

Things to See

The **Santuario del Carmen**, at Lavalleja and El Carmen, dates from 1830. Next door is **Archivo y Museo Parroquial**, with documents and objects of local historical importance. Dating from 1860, the **Casa de Ignacio Barrios**, at Barrios and 19 de Abril, once belonged to one of San Martín's lieutenants, also a signer of Uruguay's declaration of independence.

Special Events

Early February's Fiesta Nacional de la Uva (National Grape Festival) has been an established event for more than 20 years.

Places to Stay

Camping ***Camping Náutico Carmelo*** *(☎ 22058)*, on the south side of Arroyo de las Vacas, charges US$3 per person. ***Camping Don Mauro*** *(☎ 22390)* is at Ignacio Barros and Arroyo de las Vacas, six blocks from downtown; it's open December to March, and has cold showers only. The fee is also US$3 per person.

Hotels The cheapest in town is basic ***Hotel Oriental*** *(19 de Abril 284)*, where adults pay US$7 plus an additional US$3 for children, in multibed rooms. ***Hotel Paraná*** *(☎ 22480, 19 de Abril 585)* has singles for US$8 with private bath. At tidy ***Hotel La Unión*** *(☎ 22028, Uruguay 368)*, alongside the post office, singles with shared/private bath cost US$9/12, doubles with private bath US$20.

Friendly ***Hotel San Fernando*** *(☎ 22503, 19 de Abril 161)* has clean rooms with private bath for US$14/20. At the ***Palace Hotel*** *(☎ 22622, Sarandí 308)* double rooms cost US$25.

The modern and clean but ugly ***Hotel Bertoletti*** *(☎ 22030, Uruguay 171)* has rooms for US$15/25 with shared bath, US$20/25 with private bath. At ***Hotel Rambla*** *(☎ 22390, Uruguay 55)*, conveniently close to the launch docks, rates are US$21/39 with breakfast. Top of the line is the ***Hotel Casino Carmelo*** *(☎ 22314)*, on Av Rodó across the Arroyo de las Vacas, which costs US$75 double with breakfast, US$123 with half-board, and US$135 with full board.

Places to Eat

El Vesubio *(☎ 22258, 19 de Abril 451)* serves an enormous, tasty *chivito al plato* plus a variety of other dishes. Other restaurants include ***Perrini*** *(☎ 22519, 19 de Abril 440)* and the ***Yacht Club*** *(☎ 22340)*, ***Morales*** *(☎ 22649)*, and ***El Refugio*** *(☎ 22325)*, all across the bridge in the park.

Getting There & Away

Bus All the bus companies are on or near Plaza Independencia. Chadre (☎ 22987), at Uruguay and 18 de Julio, goes to Montevideo (US$9, four hours) and north to Fray

Bentos, Paysandú, and Salto; Sabelín, at the same address, goes to Nueva Palmira six times daily. Turil goes to Colonia (US$2, one hour), as do Klüver (☎ 23411) and Intertur, both at 18 de Julio and Uruguay. Klúver also goes to Nueva Palmira and Mercedes, while Intertur goes as far as Nueva Palmira.

River Movilán/Deltanave, Constituyentes 263, has two crossings daily to the Buenos Aires suburb of Tigre, at 4 am and 10:30 am. Cacciola, Constituyentes 219, goes at 4 am and noon except Sundays, when departures are at noon and 7:30 pm. The fare is US$11 one-way for adults, US$9.35 one-way for children.

AROUND CARMELO

La Estancia de Narbona

Despite the deteriorating condition of its buildings, this 18th-century estancia on the Arroyo Víboras, about 20km west of Carmelo on the road to Nueva Palmira, is deservedly a national historical monument. Its estancia. and chapel, with a three-story bell tower, sit on the summit of a small hill about 2km from the main road. At the junction and near a hydraulic mill erected to process local wheat, the **Puente Castells**, the first bridge of its kind in the country, has stood for more than 130 years.

Estancia de las Vacas

Just east of Carmelo, Estancia de las Vacas was an 18th-century Jesuit enterprise, probably the most advanced of its kind in the Banda Oriental, with its chapel, patios, lodging, blacksmiths' and carpenters' workshops, looms, bakery, dairy, brick and tile factories, Uruguay's first vineyards, and 30,000 cattle. More than 200 people, including Indian peons and black slaves, lived here.

After expulsion of the Jesuits in 1767, Juan de San Martín (father of the Argentine hero) was the estancia's administrator until 1774. After his departure, it passed into the hands of another monastic order that proved much less capable, and the estanica fell into disrepair. It is now a national historical monument, also known as the Calera de las Huérfanas.

URUGUAY

FRAY BENTOS

Capital of Río Negro department, about 300km northwest of Montevideo, Fray Bentos is the southernmost overland crossing point from Argentina, reached by the Libertador General San Martín bridge over the Río Uruguay. It lies on the east bank of the river, opposite the Argentine city of Gualeguaychú.

In 1864, Fray Bentos was the site of the country's first meat extract plant; in 1902 British interests located Uruguay's first *frigorífico* here. The enormous Anglo plant in this former company town has closed, but the Uruguayan government is preserving it as a museum.

Orientation

Fray Bentos has a very regular grid pattern centered on the surprisingly open Plaza Constitución, where scattered palms surround a Victorian bandshell, a replica of London's Crystal Palace donated by the Liebig Meat Company in 1902. The main commercial street is 18 de Julio, leading east to Ruta 2 toward Mercedes and Montevideo; northbound 25 de Mayo passes the shadier Plaza Hargain, toward the bridge to Argentina.

Information

Tourist Offices The municipal Oficina de Turismo (☎ 2233) occupies an office in the Museo Solari, on the west side of Plaza Constitución. It has a friendly, helpful, and knowledgeable staff and is open weekdays 8 am to 1 pm and 2 to 8 pm, with summer hours of 7:30 am to 1:30 pm and 4 to 9 pm.

Post & Communications The post office is at Treinta y Tres 3271. Antel is at Zorrilla 1127. Fray Bentos' area code is ☎ 562.

Medical Services The Hospital Salúd Pública (☎ 2742) is at Echeverría and Lavalleja.

Things to See

Fray Bentos' most architecturally distinguished landmark, the 400-seat **Teatro Young** bears the name of the Anglo-Uruguayan

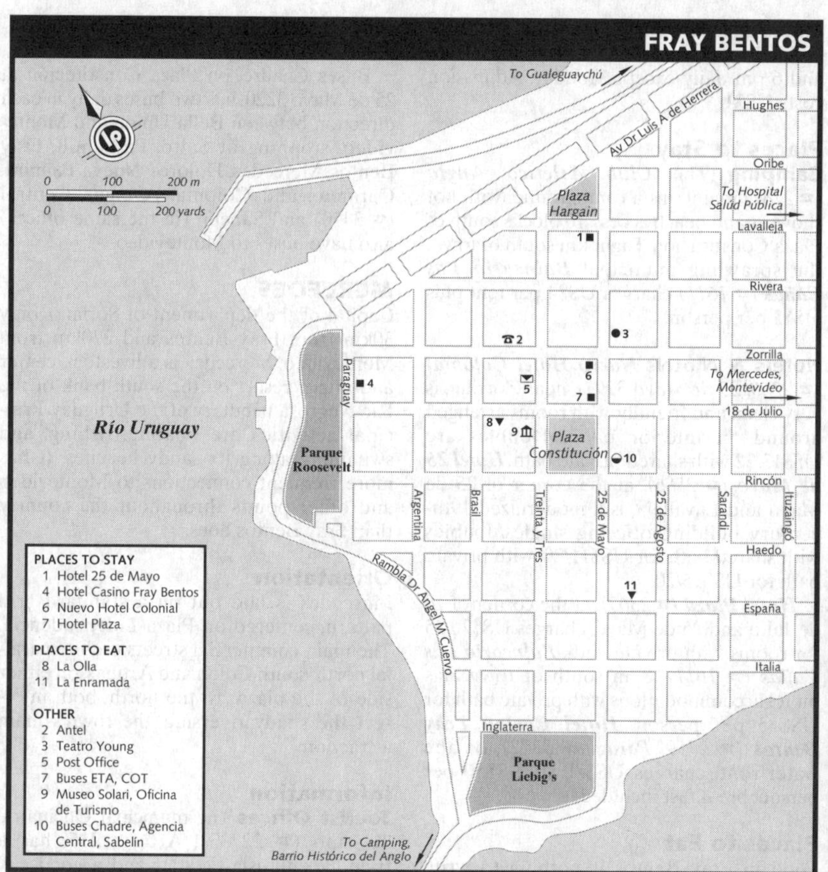

estanciero who sponsored its construction between 1909 and 1912. Now municipal property, it hosts cultural events throughout the year and can be visited upon request; ask at the theater itself or at the tourist office. It's a block north of Plaza Constitución at 25 de Mayo and Zorrilla.

The municipal **Museo Solari**, Treinta y Tres on the west side of Plaza Constitución, has changing exhibits. In Parque Roosevelt, on the banks of the river at the west end of town, the open-air **Teatro Municipal de Verano** seats 4000 and has excellent acoustics.

In 1865, the Liebig Extract of Meat Company located its pioneer South American plant, which soon became the most important industrial complex in Uruguay, southwest of downtown Fray Bentos. Most installations of the now defunct Frigorífico Anglo del Uruguay make up the dominant landmark in the **Barrio Histórico del Anglo**. Note especially the manager's residence and the former British Consulate.

The landscape and street life of this bustling neighborhood offer great photographic opportunities, as the former plant buildings are undergoing restoration as the

Museo de la Revolución Industrial (☎ 2918). Guided tours take place at 9:30 and 11 am and 6 pm daily except Monday. Admission costs US$1.

Places to Stay

Camping The ***Club Atlético Anglo*** *(☎ 2787)* maintains a campground, with hot showers and beach access, 10 blocks south of Plaza Constitución. Eight km south of town, the sprawling municipal ***Balneario Las Cañas*** *(☎ 1611)* charges US$4 per tent plus US$2 per person.

Hotels & Motels ***Nuevo Hotel Colonial*** *(☎ 2260, 25 de Mayo 3293)*, near Zorrilla, is very clean and friendly, with rooms arranged around an interior patio. Doubles are US$13/22 with shared/private bath. ***Hotel 25 de Mayo*** *(☎ 2586)*, at the corner of 25 de Mayo and Lavalleja, is a modernized 19th-century building offering singles/doubles with shared bath for US$11/20, with private bath for US$15/20.

Hotel Plaza *(☎ 2363)*, at the corner of 18 de Julio and 25 de Mayo, charges US$20/35 for rooms with private bath. ***Balneario Las Cañas*** *(☎ 1611)*, 8km south of town, has motel accommodations with private bath for US$35 per person. ***Hotel Casino Fray Bentos*** *(☎ 2359, Paraguay 3272)*, on the waterfront, charges US$40 to US$50 per person, breakfast included.

URUGUAY

Places to Eat

Food in Fray Bentos is nothing to write home about. ***La Enramada*** *(☎ 4036)*, on España between 25 de Mayo and 25 de Agosto, is cheap and friendly but basic. Try instead ***La Olla*** *(☎ 3365, 18 de Julio 1130)*. The best in town may be the ***Club de Remeros***, where the yacht crowd hangs out, near Parque Roosevelt.

Getting There & Away

There's a new terminal at 18 de Julio and Varela, but most bus companies still use offices on Plaza Constitución, 10 blocks west. ETA, with offices at the Hotel Plaza, has three buses daily to Gualeguaychú (US$4). CUT (☎ 2286), at the same location, has five daily to Mercedes (US$1.50) and Montevideo (US$11, five hours).

Buses Chadre, on Plaza Constitución at 25 de Mayo 3220, has two buses daily in each direction between Bella Unión and Montevideo, stopping at Salto, Paysandú, Fray Bentos, Mercedes, Dolores, Nueva Palmira, Carmelo, and Colonia. Agencia Central (☎ 3470) and Sabelín (in the same offices) also have buses to Montevideo.

MERCEDES

Capital of the department of Soriano, only 30km from Fray Bentos and 270km from Montevideo, Mercedes is a livestock center and minor resort on the south bank of the Río Negro, a tributary of the Uruguay. Principal activities are boating, fishing, and swimming along its sandy beaches. It has more frequent connections to Montevideo and other points throughout the country than Fray Bentos does.

Orientation

Mercedes is laid out on a standard grid pattern, centered on Plaza Independencia. The main commercial streets are the parallel north-south Colón and Artigas, on either side of the plaza. To the north, both intersect the shady riverside, the town's main attraction.

Information

Tourist Offices The municipal Oficina de Turismo (☎ 22733), Artigas 215, has a friendly, enthusiastic staff and a good city map. It's open Monday through Thursday 12:30 to 6:30 pm, and Friday through Sunday 9:30 am to 8:30 pm.

Money Cambio Fagalde, Giménez 709, or Cambio España, Colón 262, will change cash but not traveler's checks.

Post & Communications The post office is at Rodó 650, at the corner of 18 de Julio. The Centro Telefónico is at Artigas 290. Mercedes' area code is ☎ 53.

Medical Services Hospital Mercedes (☎ 22177) is at Sánchez 204.

Things to See & Do

The **Catedral de Nuestra Señora de las Mercedes**, south of Plaza Independencia, dates from 1788. The **Biblioteca Museo Eusebio Giménez**, on Giménez between Sarandí and 25 de Mayo, displays paintings by the local artist. Some distance west of town is the **Museo Paleontológico Alejandro Berro**, displaying a valuable fossil collection. It's open daily except Mondays from 7:30 am to 6:30 pm and is accessible by public transport. On Sunday mornings, there's a flea market and crafts fair east of downtown in Plaza Lavalleja.

Places to Stay

Camping Only eight blocks from Plaza Independencia, Mercedes' spacious ***Camping del Hum*** occupies half the Isla del Puerto in the Río Negro, connected to the mainland by a bridge. One of the best campgrounds in the region, it offers excellent swimming, fishing, and sanitary facilities, but the floods of 1997-8 have disrupted things here. Fees are just US$1 per person plus US$1 per tent.

Hostels There's a youth hostel at the ***Club Remeros Mercedes*** *(☎ 22534, De la Rivera 949)*, at Gomensoro.

Hotels Improved ***Hotel Mercedes*** *(☎ 23204, Giménez 659)* has singles with shared/private bath for US$9/12. Quiet, friendly ***Hotel Marín*** *(☎ 22987, Rodó 668)* has singles for US$10; its annex *(☎ 2115, Roosevelt 627)*, between 18 de Julio and 25 de Mayo, has more character but is slightly more expensive at US$12 plus US$2 for air-conditioning.

Despite its drab exterior, ***Hotel Brisas del Hum*** *(☎ 22740, Artigas 201)* is the closest to a luxury hotel in town. Rates are US$40/55 single/double with breakfast.

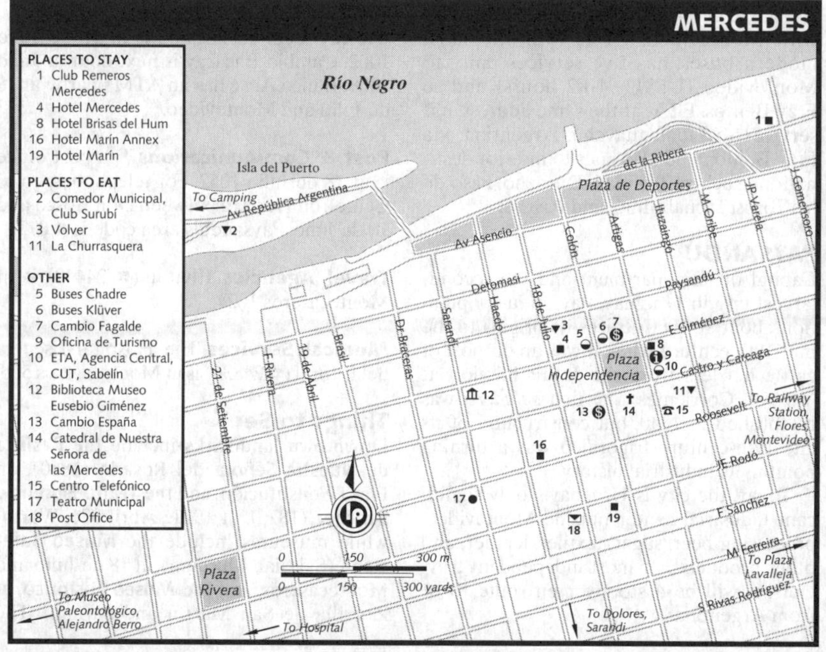

URUGUAY

Places to Eat

La Churrasquera *(☎ 24036, Castro y Careaga 790)* is a moderately priced parrilla with large portions, offering discounts to ACA members. ***Volver*** *(☎ 22366, 18 de Julio 185)* is also a parrilla.

On the Isla del Puerto, near the campground, the ***Comedor Municipal*** and ***Club Surubí*** both have good inexpensive food, including river fish selections. The outdoor seating is spartan but the surroundings are relaxing.

Getting There & Away

Klüver (☎ 22046), on Plaza Independencia at Giménez 701, has two buses daily to Colonia except Saturday and Sunday, when it has one only. It also has Monday, Wednesday, and Friday service to Durazno. For Buses Chadre, across the street at Colón and Giménez, Mercedes is a stopover en route from Bella Unión to Montevideo (see Fray Bentos for details).

Agencia Central, CUT, and Sabelín, all at Artigas 233 (☎ 23766), connect Mercedes with Montevideo. CUT, with the most modern buses, has five services daily to Montevideo (US$11, 4-1/2 hours) and to Fray Bentos. ETA, at the same address, has services to Gualeguaychú, Argentina, via Fray Bentos, and also goes to interior destinations, such as Trinidad, Durazno, Paso de los Toros, Tacuarembó, and Rivera.

URUGUAY

PAYSANDÚ

Capital of its department and the second-largest city in Uruguay, Paysandú (population about 100,000) traces its origins to the mid-18th century, when it was an outpost of cattle herders from the Jesuit mission at Yapeyú, Corrientes. The first *saladero* was established in 1840, but construction of its late-19th-century frigorífico was a turning point in its industrial history.

Today, the city is Uruguay's only significant industrial center outside Montevideo, processing beer, sugar, textiles, leather, and other products. For most independent travelers, it will be a stopover en route to or from Argentina.

Orientation

On the east bank of the Río Uruguay, Paysandú is 370km from Montevideo via Ruta 3 and 110km north of Fray Bentos via Ruta 24. The Puente Internacional General Artigas, 15km north of town, connects it with the Argentine city of Colón.

The city is laid out in a slightly irregular grid; the center of activity is Plaza Constitución, while 18 de Julio, the main commercial street, runs east-west along the south side of the plaza. Except for a small area around the port, directly west of downtown, the entire riverfront remains open parkland due to regular flooding, but it provides a welcome refuge from the oppressive summer heat.

Information

Tourist Offices The Dirección Municipal de Turismo (☎ 26221) is opposite Plaza Constitución at 18 de Julio 1226. Open 7 am to 7 pm weekdays, 8 am to 6 pm weekends, it has one of the best city maps in Uruguay and a selection of useful brochures.

Money Cambio Fagalde is at 18 de Julio 1002, Cambio Bacacay is next door at Julio 1008. Banco Acac has an ATM nearby at 18 de Julio and Montevideo.

Post & Communications The post office is at 18 de Julio 1052. For telephones, go to Centel, on Herrera between Don Bosco and 18 de Julio. Paysandú's area code is ☎ 072.

Travel Agencies Elvitur (☎ 24449) is at Montecaseros 1024.

Medical Services The Hospital Escuela del Litoral (☎ 24836) is at Montecaseros 520.

Things to See

Downtown landmarks include the **Basílica de Nuestra Señora del Rosario** (1860), on Plaza Constitución, and the **Teatro Florencio Sánchez** (1876), at 19 de Abril 926. Worthwhile museums include the **Museo Salesiano** (Salesian Museum), at 18 de Julio and Montecaseros, and the **Museo Histórico**, at Zorrilla de San Martín and Sarandí. The

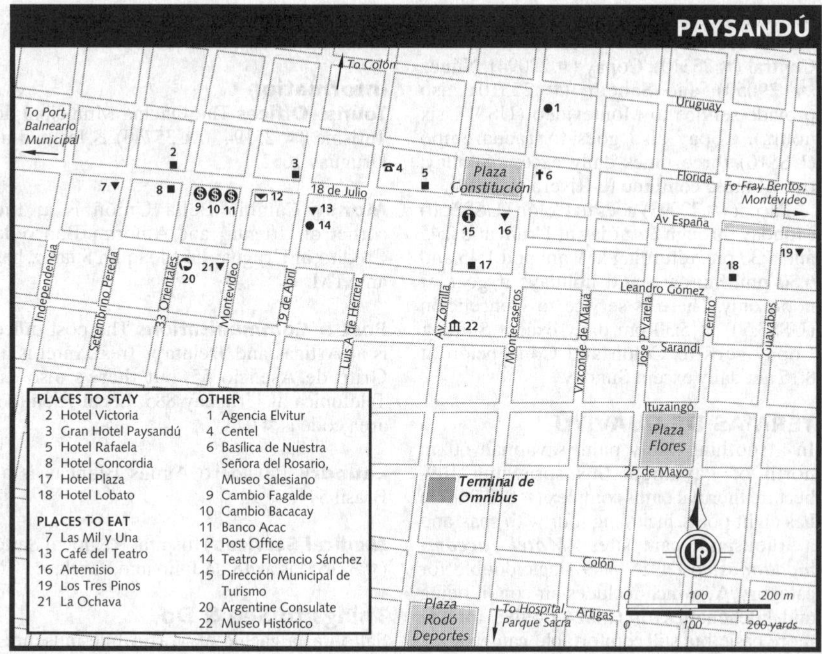

latter is open 11 am to 5 pm weekdays, 7 am to noon weekends.

Places to Stay

The cheapest lodging in town, and one of the friendliest, is ***Hotel Victoria*** *(☎ 24320, 18 de Julio 979)*. Rooms with shared bath cost US$7 per person, with private bath US$10. Across the street, the comparable ***Hotel Concordia*** *(☎ 22417, 18 de Julio 984)* charges US$8 with shared bath, US$9 with private bath.

Attractively remodeled ***Hotel Plaza*** *(☎ 22022, Leandro Gómez 1211)* charges as little as US$13/16 single/double with shared bath, US$16/29 with private bath, but better rooms cost US$24/32 to US$27/35. At the modern, comfortable ***Hotel Lobato*** *(☎ 22241, Leandro Gómez 1415)* singles/doubles with private bath cost US$18/30. ***Hotel Rafaela*** *(☎ 24216, 18 de Julio 1181)* is similar in price and standards.

Acknowledged as the best in town is ***Gran Hotel Paysandú*** *(☎ 23400, 18 de Julio 1103)*, for US$51/72 with breakfast.

Places to Eat

Good eating spots include highly regarded ***Artemisio*** *(18 de Julio 1248)*, near the tourist office, and ***Los Tres Pinos*** *(☎ 22302, Av España 1474)*, which serves outstanding pasta (particularly the *ñoquis)*, though prices tend toward the upper end.

La Ochava *(☎ 23342, Gómez 1050)* is a parrilla, while ***Las Mil y Una***, at 18 de Julio and Pereda, is a pizzeria. For snacks and coffee, try ***Café del Teatro***, at 18 de Julio and 19 de Abril.

Getting There & Away

Paysandú's bus station (☎ 23325) is at 25 de Mayo and Zorrilla de San Martín, directly south of Plaza Constitución. Buses Chadre (☎ 25310) passes through Paysandú en route between Bella Unión and Montevideo; for details, see the Fray Bentos entry. Agencia Central (☎ 25310), Copay (☎ 22094), Núnez (☎ 29050), and Sabelín (☎ 25310) also provide service to Montevideo (US$17, six hours). Copay also goes to Tacuarembó (US$10) three times daily except Sunday; two of these continue to Rivera (US$14).

Paccot (☎ 22093) goes to Colón (US$2.50) Monday through Saturday at 11 am and 2:45 and 7:30 pm, returning at 9 am and 1:45 and 6:30 pm; Sundays and holidays it goes at noon only. There is service to Concepción (US$3.50) at 5:30 pm daily except Sunday. Copay goes to Colón and Concepción at 8:15 am daily except Sunday.

TERMAS DE GUAVIYÚ

In a soothing yatay palm savannah 60km north of Paysandú, this sprawling 109-hectare thermal baths complex (☎ 072-26677) has eight pools, including four with spas, and a thousand campsites. ***Motel accommodations*** cost US$45/49 single/double for category 'A,' which includes air-conditioning and kitchenettes, or US$24 double for the more basic, but still comfortable, category 'B.' ***Camping*** costs US$2.50 per person, and saunas are available for US$5.

Buses between Montevideo and Salto will drop passengers at the Termas, which are directly on Ruta 3 at Km 441.5.

SALTO

Directly across the Río Uruguay from Concordia, Entre Ríos, Salto is the most northerly crossing point into Argentina and site of the enormous Salto Grande hydroelectric project, 520km from Montevideo via Ruta 3. The reservoir behind the dam is a very conventional recreational resource attracting some visitors, while the surrounding area is known for citrus, mostly oranges. Horacio Quiroga, who spent most of his life in Argentine Misiones, and novelist Enrique Amorim are major literary figures associated with Salto.

Orientation

Salto has a very regular grid centered on Plaza Artigas. Most points of interest are along Uruguay, the principal street, which runs west toward the port.

Information

Tourist Offices The Oficina Municipal de Turismo (☎ 25194, fax 35740) is located at Uruguay 1052.

Money Cambio Bella Unión is at the corner of Uruguay and Amorim. Banco de Crédito, at Uruguay and Joaquín Suárez, has an ATM.

Post & Communications The post office is at Artigas and Treinta y Tres. Antel is at Grito de Asencio 55, but there's also La Telefónica at Uruguay 885, Local 3. Salto's area code is ☎ 073.

Laundry Lavadero Aguas Blancas is at Brasil 544.

Medical Services Hospital Regional Salto (☎ 32155) is at 18 de Julio and Varela.

Things to See & Do

Salto has a gaggle of worthwhile museums. Northeast of downtown at Enrique Amorim and Blandengues, the **Museo Histórico Municipal** contains the ashes of cremated writer Horacio Quiroga (see the San Ignacio entry in the Mespotamia chapter for more on Quiroga). It's open 1 to 6 pm Tuesday through Saturday.

Open 1 to 7 pm weekdays, the **Museo del Teatro Larrañaga** (☎ 32158), Joaquín Suárez 51, is part of Salto's prime performing arts venue. The **Museo de Bellas Artes y Artes Decorativas** (☎ 29898), Uruguay 1067, is open 2 to 7 pm Tuesday through Saturday.

At Brasil and Zorrilla, the erstwhile Mercado Central (Central Market) has become the **Museo del Hombre y la Tecnología** (☎ 29898), featuring excellent displays on local cultural development and history; the basement **Museo Arqueológico** isn't bad, but doesn't measure up to the former. Both are open 3 to 8 pm Tuesday through Saturday.

The **Museo Escultórico Edmundo Pratti** (☎ 25220), a three-dimensional arts museum

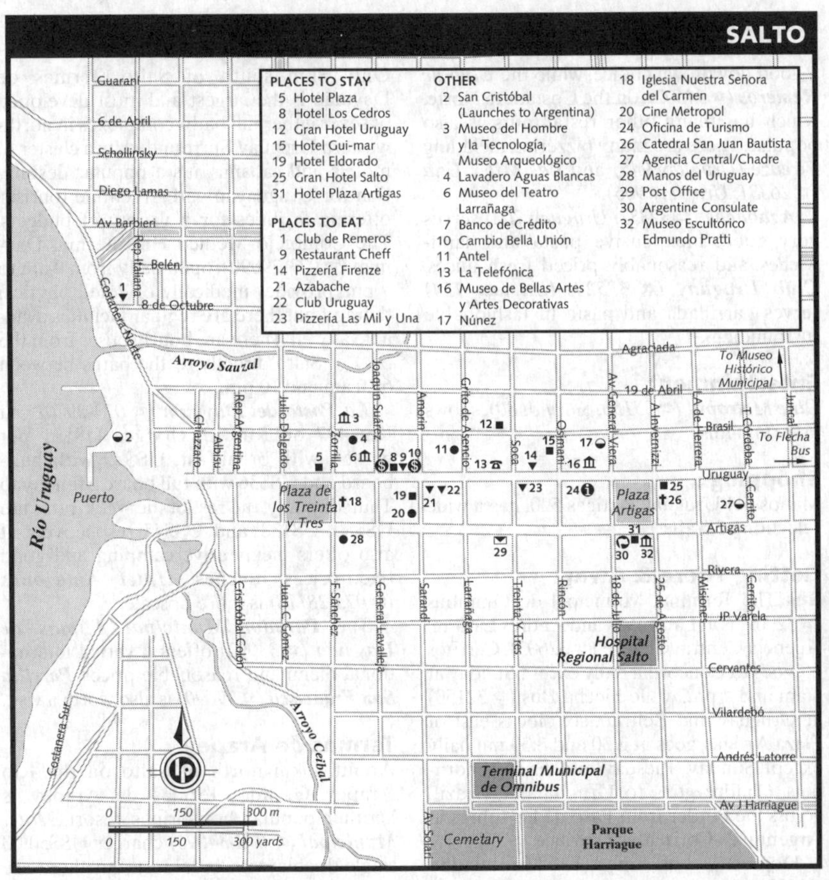

at Artigas and 25 de Agosto, honors one of Uruguay's finest sculptors. It's open 8 am to noon and 2 to 7 pm daily.

Guided visits of the **hydroelectric project** at Salto Grande (☎ 26131) take place 7 am to 2 pm daily except Sunday.

Places to Stay

Rundown but friendly ***Hotel Plaza Artigas*** *(☎ 34824, Artigas 1146)* costs US$9/12 per person with shared/private bath. The best budget choice, though, is rehabbed ***Hotel Plaza*** *(☎ 33744, Uruguay 465)*, for US$12. ***Hotel Gui-mar*** *(☎ 32223, Osimani 69)* is another option with rates of US$12, US$15 with breakfast.

Mid-range accommodations, including breakfast, start around US$33/50 at ***Hotel Los Cedros*** *(☎ 33984)*, at Uruguay and Joaquín Suárez. For US$35/60, rooms at ***Gran Hotel Uruguay*** *(☎ 33051, Brasil 891)* have cable TV, air-con, and phone. ***Hotel Eldorado*** *(☎ 35450, eldorado@saltoweb.com, Sarandí 20)* has comparable facilities for US$39/55.

Rooms at ***Gran Hotel Salto*** *(☎ 34333, 25 de Agosto 5)* cost US$38/50, or US$45/60 including a substantial buffet breakfast.

Places to Eat

Restaurant Cheff *(☎ 35328, Uruguay 639)* is a good downtown choice, while the ***Club de Remeros*** *(☎ 34607)*, on the Costanera Norte, which has many other restaurants, is also popular. There are many pizzerias, including ***Firenze*** *(Uruguay 945)* and ***Las Mil y Una*** *(☎ 26331, Uruguay 906)*.

Azabache *(☎ 32337, Uruguay 702)* serves very good, inexpensive pasta and sandwiches, and reasonably priced fresh juices. ***Club Uruguay*** *(☎ 33524, Uruguay 754)* serves parrillada and pasta in fashionable surroundings.

Entertainment

Cine Metropol *(☎ 33150, Sarandí 80)*, shows first-run films.

Shopping

Manos del Uruguay, Artigas 520, has a wide selection of crafts.

Getting There & Away

Bus The Terminal Municipal de Omnibus (☎ 32909) is at Larrañaga and Andrés Latorre. Agencia Central/Chadre (☎ 32603), Cerritos 66, goes to Concordia daily except Sunday at 8 am and 2 pm, while Flecha Bus (☎ 32150) at Uruguay and Beltrán, six blocks east of Plaza Artigas, goes at 2:30 and 8:30 pm daily except Sunday. Tuesday and Friday mornings, Chadre goes to Uruguaiana, Brazil, across the border from Paso de los Libres in Argentina's Corrientes province.

Domestic bus lines to Montevideo (US$20, six hours) include Chadre/Agencia Central, Núnez (☎ 35581), at Viera 42; and El Norteño (☎ 32150), Beltrán 19, which also goes to Bella Unión (US$5.50). Alonso (☎ 34821) goes to Paysandú (US$5, 1½ hours), while Agencia Central goes to interior destinations like Tacuarembó and Rivera.

River From the port at the foot of Brasil, San Cristóbal launches cross the river to Concordia (US$3) five times daily Monday through Saturday, but only twice on Sunday and holidays.

URUGUAY

AROUND SALTO

Termas de Daymán

Only 8km south of Salto, Termas de Daymán is the largest and most developed of several thermal baths complexes in northwestern Uruguay. Surrounded by a cluster of motels and cabañas, it's a popular destination for Uruguayan and Argentine tourists, offering facilities for a variety of budgets. The Complejo Médico Hidrotermal Daymán (☎ 073-29090), open daily from 9 am to 9 pm, provides medically oriented physical therapy, but there are regular facilities available as well. There are hourly buses from the port of Salto directly to the baths between 6:10 am and 10 pm.

La Posta del Daymán *(☎ 073-29701)*, at Km 487 on Ruta 3, charges US$21 per person with breakfast, US$29 with half-board and US$36 with full board Monday to Thursday only; the rest of the week, rates are US$30, US$38, and US$45 respectively. It also offers inexpensive camping and good fixed-prices lunches. ***Hotel Amazonas*** *(☎ 073-28118)* is more upscale.

The ***Parador Municipal Termas de Daymán*** *(☎ 33992)* offers a varied international menu and reasonable prices. ***Parrilla San Francisco*** *(☎ 29690)* is also worth a visit.

Termas de Arapey

About 45km north of Salto on the Río Arapey Grande, Termas de Arapey is another popular hot-springs resort. ***Hotel Municipal*** *(☎ 073-34096)* charges US$50/60 single/double with breakfast, but there are also cheaper motel and bungalow accommodations, as well as inexpensive camping.

TACUAREMBÓ

Capital of its department, Tacuarembó has sycamore-lined streets and attractive plazas that make it one of the most agreeable towns in Uruguay's interior. Since its founding in 1832, authorities have kept sculptors busy on busts and monuments that pay tribute to the usual military heroes as well as to writers, clergy, and educators. The economy relies on livestock, both cattle and sheep, but local producers also grow rice, sunflowers, peanuts, linseed, tobacco, asparagus, and strawberries. The late-March gaucho festival merits a detour if you're in the area.

Orientation

In the rolling hill country along the Cuchilla de Haedo, on the banks of the Río Tacuarembó Chico, Tacuarembó is 230km east of Paysandú and 390km north of Montevideo. It's a major highway junction for the Uruguayan interior, as Ruta 26 leads west to Argentina and east to Brazil and the Uruguayan coast, while Ruta 5 from Montevideo continues north to Rivera and Brazil.

The town center is Plaza 19 de Abril, but the streets 25 de Mayo and 18 de Julio both lead south past the almost equally important Plaza Colón and Plaza Rivera.

Information

Tourist Offices The municipal Oficina de Turismo (☎ 7144), Joaquín Suárez 215, is open 7 am to 7 pm daily. The friendly, helpful staff offer a simple map and limited brochures.

Post & Communications The post office is at Ituzaingó 262. Antel is at Sarandí 240; the area code is ☎ 0632.

Medical Services The Hospital Regional (☎ 2955) is at Treinta y Tres and Catalogne.

Museums

Tacuarembó's **Museo del Indio y del Gaucho Washington Escobar**, at Flores and Artigas, pays romantic tribute to Uruguay's nearly forgotten Indians and gauchos and their role in the country's rural history. The **Museo de Geociencias** is an earth-sciences facility at Suárez and 18 de Julio.

Special Events

In late March, the three-day Fiesta de la Patria Gaucha attracts visitors from around the country to exhibitions of traditional gaucho skills, music, and other activities. It takes place in Parque 25 de Agosto, at the north end of town.

Places to Stay

Camping The densely forested ***Balneario Municipal Iporá*** *(☎ 5344)*, alongside a reservoir 7km north of town, has both free and US$2 sites. The free sites have clean toilets but lack showers, and you may decide that shower access justifies the costlier alternative. Buses to the campground leave from near Plaza 19 de Abril.

Pensiones & Hotels Friendly ***Pensión Paysandú*** *(☎ 2453, 18 de Julio 154)*, opposite Plaza 19 de Abril, offers good, clean, but basic accommodations for US$9 per person in a shared room, US$12/15 single/double for a private room with shared bath.

Hotel Central *(☎ 2341, Flores 300)* charges US$19 per person with private bath and breakfast. ***Hotel Tacuarembó*** *(☎ 2104, 18 de Julio 133)*, is more comfortable but also more impersonal, with rooms for US$29/38 with private bath.

Places to Eat

Hotel Tacuarembó has a good restaurant serving parrillada, the regional standard, and other dishes. Two other parrillas include ***La Rueda***, at Beltrán and Flores, and ***La Cabaña*** *(25 de Mayo 217)*. A reasonable confitería is ***La Sombrilla***, at 25 de Mayo and Suárez. ***Rotisería del Centro***, on 18 de Julio near Plaza Colón, sells an enormous, tasty chivito that's a meal in itself.

Getting There & Away

The Terminal Municipal is on the northeastern outskirts of town, at the junction of Ruta 5 and Av Victorino Perera. To Montevideo (US$14, 5-1/2 hours), try Buses Chadre/Agencia Central (☎ 4122) or Turil (☎ 3305). Chadre/Agencia Central also serves interior destinations and connects Tacuarembó with the Littoral cities of Salto and Paysandú. Copay also sends buses to Salto and Paysandú (US$10) three times daily.

VALLE EDÉN

Valle Edén, 30km west of Tacuarembó on Ruta 26 to Paysandú, is a scenic area featuring a unique hanging bridge over the Arroyo

Jabonería and the unusual Cerro Cementerio, a granite outcrop on whose sides locals have entombed their dead.

RIVERA

Across the border from Livramento, Brazil, Rivera is 114km north of Tacuarembó via Ruta 5. The Oficina de Turismo (☎ 6860) is at the bus terminal, on Presidente Viera between Agraciada and Sarandí; it's open 6:30 am to 12:30 pm and 2:30 to 11:30 pm daily.

The post office is at Sarandí 501. Antel is at Artigas 1046. There are several exchange houses, and Brazil has a consulate (☎ 3278) at Ceballos 1159. The area code is ☎ 0622.

Places to Stay & Eat

The free ***Camping Municipal*** *(☎ 3803)*, on Agraciada near Presidente Viera, has hot showers.

There's also a youth hostel, ***Albergue Frontera de la Paz*** *(☎ 6660, Uruguay 735)*. ***Hotel Sarandí*** *(☎ 3521, Sarandí 770)* charges US$15 single.

Churrasquería El Rancho *(☎ 3974, Brasil 1071)* is a parrilla, as is ***El Telégrafo*** *(☎ 2111, Uruguay 531)*.

Getting There & Away

Local bus services are an extension of those to Tacuarembó.

Uruguayan Riviera

East of Montevideo, innumerable beach resorts dot the scenic Uruguayan coast, where sandy river beaches, vast dunes, and dramatic ocean headlands extend all the way to the Brazilian border. The area attracts hordes of summer tourists, but relatively few after wealthy Brazilians and Argentines end their holidays in early March. Its showplace is exclusive Punta del Este, where Argentina maintains a summer consulate and the Buenos Aires daily, *La Nación*, even opens a temporary bureau. Nearby Maldonado offers more reasonably priced accommodations and facilities, but other resorts slightly farther out are just as attractive and more affordable. After summer ends, prices fall, the weather is still ideal, and the pace is much more leisurely.

The modern department of Rocha, between Maldonado and the Brazilian border, was subject to a constant tug-of-war between Portugal and Spain in colonial times, and between Brazil and Argentina up to the mid-19th century. This conflict left several valuable historical monuments, such as the fortresses of Santa Teresa and San Miguel, while discouraging rural settlement and sparing some of Uruguay's wildest countryside. No one will compare it to trackless Amazonia, but it does have nearly undeveloped areas like Cabo Polonio, with extensive dunes and a large colony of southern sea lions, and Parque Nacional Santa Teresa (more a cultural than a natural park, however). The interior has a varied landscape of palm savannas and marshes rich in bird life.

Not often visited by foreigners, the interior departments of Treinta y Tres and Cerro Largo offer several alternatives for crossing into Brazil. The route north from the city of Treinta y Tres to Melo is one Uruguay's most beautiful highways.

This chapter starts with resorts immediately east of Montevideo, following the Ruta Interbalnearia (coastal highway) east and then north toward the Brazilian border, describing interior destinations where appropriate. Technically, beaches west of Punta del Este are river beaches, but most visitors will note little difference between these and the ocean beaches to the east, except for the river's gentle surf.

ATLÁNTIDA

In the department of Canelones, only 50km from Montevideo, Atlántida is the first major resort along the Interbalnearia. The municipal Oficina de Turismo (☎ 2736) is at the intersection of Calles 14 and 1. Atlántida's area code is ☎ 0372. COT (☎ 2039), Calle 22 and Av Artigas, has regular buses to Montevideo and on down the coast.

Camping El Ensueño *(☎ 2371)* is nine blocks from Playa Brava, Atlántida's most popular beach. Fees are about US$6 for two persons and include 24-hour hot water and sanitary facilities.

Accommodations start around US$21 per person, breakfast included, at ***Hotel Rex*** *(☎ 2009)*, on the waterfront Rambla at the corner of Calle 1. Just west of town is highly regarded ***Hostería del Fortín de Santa Rosa*** *(☎ 0376-7376)*, a popular hideaway for well-heeled folks from Montevideo, where single/double rates are US$80/100 with breakfast, US$95/130 with half-board.

PIRIÁPOLIS

The westernmost beach resort in Maldonado department, about 100 kilometers from Montevideo, Piriápolis is less pretentious and more affordable than Punta del Este. Founded in 1893, it was developed as a tourist resort in the 1930s by Argentine entrepreneur Francisco Piria, who built the imposing landmark Hotel Argentino and an eccentric residence known as 'Piria's Castle' (the latter now part of a city park). At one time Piria's ferries brought tourists directly from Argentina – a crossing that has recently resumed.

In the surrounding countryside are many interesting features, including Cerro Pan de

URUGUAY

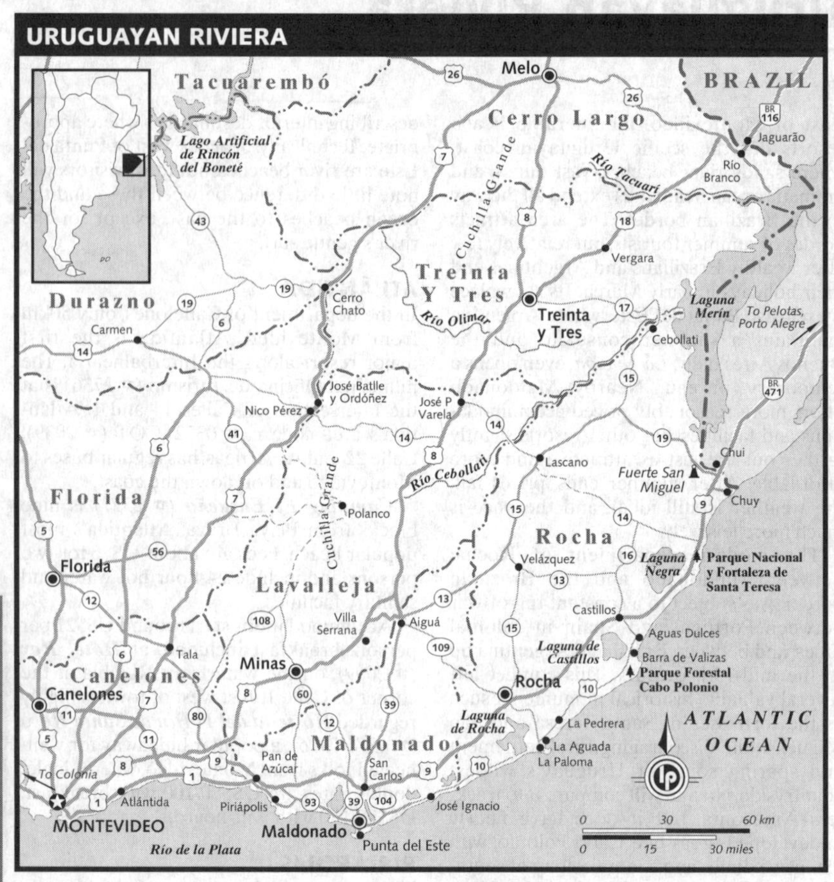

Azúcar, one of Uruguay's highest points, and the hill resort of Minas.

Orientation

With a permanent population of only about 6000, Piriápolis is very compact. Almost everything is within reasonable walking distance in an area bounded by the waterfront Rambla de los Argentinos to the south, Bulevar Artigas in the west, Calle Misiones in the north, and Av Piria on the east. Most local residents give directions by noting a site's proximity to Hotel Argentino.

Information

Tourist Offices The private Asociación de Fomento y Turismo (☎ 22560), at Rambla de los Argentinos 1348, near Hotel Argentino, has maps, brochures, and a listing of current hotel prices. In January and February, it's open 9 am to 11 pm daily; in March and April, hours are 9 am to 9 pm. The rest of the year, it's open daily from 10 am to 1 pm and 3 to 8 pm.

Money There's an ATM at the corner of Piria and Buenos Aires. You can change cash, but not traveler's checks, at Hotel Argentino.

Post & Communications The post office is on Rambla de los Argentinos, between Armenia and Manuel Freire. Antel is on Tucumán, behind the enormous skyscraper near the corner of Manuel Freire. Piriápolis' area code is ☎ 043.

Laundry Lavadero Piria (☎ 21324), at Piria and Chacabuco, is open 7 am to midnight daily.

Things to See & Do

The landmark **Hotel Argentino** is an attraction in itself. For a good view of Piriápolis, climb the **Cerro del Inglés** (also known as Cerro San Antonio) at the east end of town. For real lazybones, there is a chairlift to the top, open only on weekends except in summer.

Swimming and **sunbathing** are the most popular activities, but there is good **fishing** off the rocks at the west end of the Playa de Piriápolis, where Rambla de los Argentinos becomes Rambla de los Ingleses.

Places to Stay

In Piriápolis and most of the Uruguayan Riviera, there are abundant accommodations, but prices and availability are highly seasonal. Many places open only between December and April, and nearly all raise prices dramatically between December 15 and March 1 – after which prices drop, the weather is delightful, and the crowds are gone. From April 1 to December 1, prices are extremely reasonable.

Places to Stay – Budget

Camping Open mid-December to late April, ***Camping Piriápolis FC*** *(☎ 23275)* is at Misiones and Niza, 350m behind Hotel Argentino. It has every necessary facility, including electricity and hot showers, for US$5 per person, while there are a few rooms with shared bath available for US$9 per person.

Hostels Piriápolis has two spacious hostels close behind Hotel Argentino: ***Albergue Piriápolis 1*** *(☎ 20394, Simón del Pino 1106)*, and the ***Asociación de Alberguistas de Piriápolis*** *(☎ 22157, Simón del Pino 1136)*. Both charge around US$8 per person with an HI card and are open all year, but reservations are essential in January and February.

Pensiones & Hotels ***Hostal La Casona*** *(☎ 22441)*, at Freire and Defensa, costs US$25 double with private bath in mid-season, US$35 in summer. Otherwise, the cheapest in town is ***Residencial Uruguay*** *(☎ 22424, Uruguay 1026)*, which charges US$12 off-season but rises to US$26 in summer. At ***Hotel El Paso*** *(☎ 22632)* at Piria and Chacabuco, off-season singles cost US$15 and climb to US$22 in summer. Highly recommended, family-run ***Petite Pensión*** *(☎ 22471, Sanabria 1084)* is an intimate (seven-room), clean, and friendly hotel near Ayacucho, two blocks from the beach. Rates are US$18 off-season, US$22 per person in summer.

Places to Stay – Mid-Range

There are abundant mid-range accommodations, such as ***Hotel San Sebastián*** *(☎ 22546, Sanabria 942)*, charging US$15 to US$20 per person off-season, US$25 to US$30 in summer. At ***Hotel Alcázar*** *(☎ 22507)*, Piria and Tucumán, rates are US$16 to US$26 per person off-season, US$38 in summer.

Similar choices include ***Hotel Danae*** *(☎ 22594, Rambla de los Argentinos 1270)*, for US$18 off-season and US$27 in summer; and ***Hotel Sierra Mar*** *(☎ 22613, Sanabria 1051)*, for US$18 to US$20 off-season, US$22 to US$25 in summer. ***Hotel Centro*** *(☎ 22516, Sanabria 931)* ranges from US$25 off-season to US$45 in summer.

Quieter but less central than most mid-range hotels, highly recommended ***Hotel Colonial*** *(☎ 23366, Piria 790)*, near the verdant Cerro del Inglés, costs US$30 to US$35 off-season with half-board, and US$45 to US$55 in summer.

Places to Stay – Top End

Even if you don't stay at ***Hotel Argentino*** *(☎ 22791)*, you should visit this elegant, 350-room European-style spa on the Rambla de los Argentinos, with thermal baths, a casino, a classic dining room, and other luxuries. Rates are US$137/196 with half-board, US$158/238 with full board.

Places to Eat

La Langosta *(☎ 23382, Rambla de los Argentinos 1212)* has fine seafood and *parrillada* at moderate prices. Other appealing restaurants along the rambla include ***La Goleta*** *(☎ 22501)*, at the corner of Trápani, and ***Delta*** *(☎ 22364)*, at the corner of Atanasio Sierra.

Entertainment

Nuevo Cine Miramar *(☎ 20600, Rambla de los Argentinos 1126)*, shows current films. Tickets cost around US$5.

Shopping

For artisanal items, visit the Paseo de la Pasiva, an attractive colonnaded gallery along the Rambla de los Argentinos.

Getting There & Away

Bus The town's Terminal de Ómnibus is at Misiones and Niza, about three blocks from the beach. In high season, COT (☎ 24141) and Copsa (☎ 22571) run up to 27 buses daily from Montevideo to Punta del Este and back via Piriápolis. Guscapar (☎ 49253) has 20 buses daily to Pan de Azúcar, where there are connections to Minas. The fare to Montevideo is about US$3.

Boat Buquebus (☎ 23340), at the passenger pier on Rambla de los Ingleses, sails the ferry *Juan L* to Buenos Aires at 2 am Saturday and 6:30 pm Sunday. Fares are US$73 for adults, US$63 for retired people, US$53 for minors, and US$23 for infants.

PAN DE AZÚCAR

West of the highway between Piriápolis and the town of Pan de Azúcar, 10km to the north, an obvious hiking trail reaches the 493m summit of **Cerro Pan de Azúcar**, the country's third-highest point. At the nearby Parque Municipal is a small but well-kept **Reserva de Fauna Autóctona** of native species such as the capybara, grey fox, and ñandú. On the opposite side of the highway is the **Castillo de Piria**, Francisco Piria's opulent, outlandish residence. Both are open 10 am to 8 pm Tuesday to Sunday, noon to 6 pm weekends; admission is free.

MINAS

In the Cuchilla Grande of the department of Lavalleja, 120km northeast of Montevideo and 60km north of Piriápolis, Minas is an agreeable hill town offering a change of pace from Argentina's unrelentingly flat Pampas. It draws its name from the nearby quarries of building materials, but its most popular attraction is **Parque Salus**, 10km west of town, source of Uruguay's best-known mineral water and also site of a brewery. Every April 19, up to 70,000 pilgrims visit the **Cerro y Virgen del Verdún**, 6km west of town.

The municipal Oficina de Turismo (☎ 4118) is at Lavalleja 572, but visit also the **Casa de la Cultura**, at Lavalleja and Rodó. The post office is at Rodó 571; Antel at Beltrán and Rodó.

Minas' area code is ☎ 0442.

Places to Stay

Camping is possible at woodsy ***Parque Arequita*** *(☎ 0440-2503)*, 9km north of town on the road to Polanco (public transport is available from Minas). Sector 'A' is ridiculously cheap at US$2 per person per day, while Sector 'B' has the luxury of a swimming pool for US$5 per person per day. A limited number of two-bed cabañas, with shared bath, are available for US$11 per night; others with private bath cost US$17.

Hotel Verdún *(☎ 2110, 25 de Mayo 444)*, charges US$25 per person; for cheaper lodging, try ***Residencial 25*** *(☎ 4272, 25 de Mayo 525)*, charging US$22/30 single/double. At Parque Salus, accommodations are available at ***El Parador Salus*** *(☎ 5730)* for US$55/70 with breakfast, US$70/100 with half-board, and US$80/120 with full board.

Getting There & Away

The Terminal de Ómnibus is on Treinta y Tres, between Sarandí and Williman. Olivera Hermanos (☎ 4111) goes twice

URUGUAY

daily to Maldonado (US$3), a trip that Coom does eight times daily. Cota (☎ 2256) links Montevideo with Minas, Treinta y Tres (US$7, three hours), and Melo (US$10, four hours). Emdal (☎ 2405), Núñez, and CUT/ Corporación (☎ 2070) also go frequently to Montevideo (US$5, two hours).

AROUND MINAS

In **Villa Serrana**, 23km northeast of Minas, there are hostel accommodations at *Chalet Las Chafas* (no phone), with kitchen facilities, a swimming pool, and a lake. Buses from Minas pass no closer than 3km from the hostel, so you'll need to walk or hitch; make reservations, which are essential, through the Asociación de Alberguistas in Montevideo. Weekends and holidays can be uncomfortably crowded.

MALDONADO

Capital of its namesake department, Maldonado is a popular beach resort that has retained a semblance of colonial atmosphere despite virtually merging with fashionable Punta del Este. It remains a more economical alternative to Punta del Este, which is easily accessible by public transport.

Maldonado dates from 1755, when Governor JJ de Viana of Montevideo sent the first settlers to establish an outpost to provision ships at the mouth of the Río de la Plata. British forces occupied the town during the siege of Buenos Aires in 1806, and in 1832 Darwin used it as a base during 10 weeks spent collecting natural history specimens.

Because Maldonado and Punta del Este have grown together, only convenience separates them in this book, and readers will find themselves referring back and forth between the two entries.

Orientation

Maldonado is 130km east of Montevideo and only 30km from Piriápolis; most points of interest (except the beaches) are within a few blocks of its central Plaza San Fernando. The original city plan is a standard rectangular grid, but toward Punta del Este it becomes highly irregular.

To the west, along the Río de la Plata, Rambla Claudio Williman is the main thoroughfare, while to the east Rambla Lorenzo Batlle Pacheco follows the Atlantic coast. Locations along each of these routes are usually identified by numbered *paradas* (bus stops). There are many attractive beaches along both, but the ocean beaches have rougher surf. For beach details, see the Punta del Este entry.

Information

Tourist Offices Open weekdays 12:30 to 6:30 pm, the Dirección de Turismo (☎ 20847) is in the Intendencia Municipal, on Sarandí between Juan A Ledesma and Enrique Burnett. At the bus terminal, there's an Oficina de Informes (☎ 25701) that keeps longer hours.

Immigration The Dirección Nacional de Migraciones (☎ 37624), on Ventura Alegre between Sarandí and Román Guerra, is open 12:30 to 7 pm weekdays.

Money Maldonado has several exchanges houses, including Cambio Maldonado, at Dodero and Florida; Cambio Bacacay, on Florida near 18 de Julio; Cambio Dominus, at 25 de Mayo and 18 de Julio; and Cambio Porto, at Florida 764, in the same building as Hotel Le Petit. Banco Sudamerís has an ATM at the Ancap gas station, at Gorriti and Av Roosevelt.

Post & Communications The post office is at Ituzaingó and San Carlos. Antel is at the corner of Joaquín de Viana and Florida. Maldonado's area code is ☎ 042.

Travel Agencies Outdoors-oriented tours – birding, horseback riding, and hiking – are the forte of Natural (☎ 25409), located at Sarandí 643.

Laundry Espumas del Virrey (☎ 20582) is at Sarandí 679.

Medical Services Hospital Maldonado (☎ 25889) is on Ventura Alegre, about eight blocks west of Plaza San Fernando.

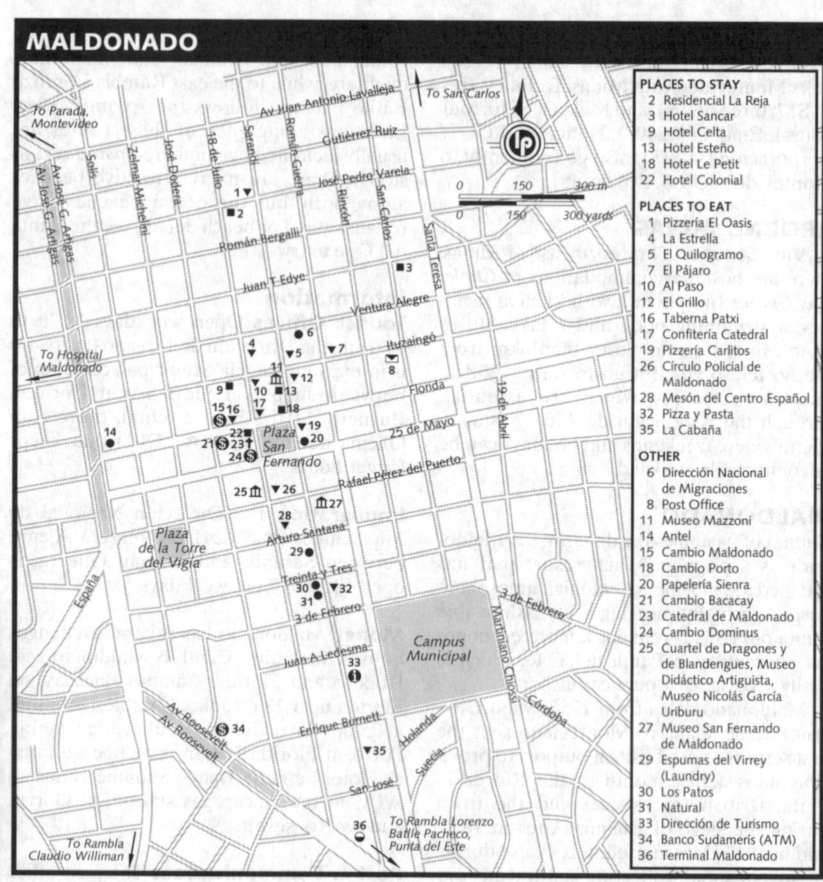

Things to See & Do

On Plaza San Fernando is the **Catedral de Maldonado**, completed in 1895 after nearly a century of construction. At Gorriti and Pérez del Puerto, the **Plaza de la Torre del Vigía** features a colonial watchtower built with peepholes for viewing the approach of hostile forces or other suspicious movements.

Another colonial relic, the **Cuartel de Dragones y de Blandengues** is a block of military fortifications with stone walls and iron gates, built between 1771 and 1797. It's located along 18 de Julio and Pérez del Puerto. Its **Museo Didáctico Artiguista** (☎ 25378), in honor of Uruguay's hero of independence, is open daily. It also contains the fine-arts **Museo Nicolás García Uriburu**.

The recently renovated **Museo San Fernando de Maldonado** (☎ 25929) is a fine arts museum at the corner of Sarandí and Pérez del Puerto, open Monday to Saturday 12:30 to 8 pm, Sunday 4:30 to 8 pm.

Maldonado's most unusual sight is the eclectic, eccentric Mazzoni house, dating from 1782. With all the family's furniture and belongings, and a particularly weird natural history room, the **Museo Mazzoni** defies description – see, for instance, the sculpted rockhopper penguin on the patio fountain. At Ituzaingó 789, the museum (☎ 21107) is open Tuesday to Friday 4 to 10 pm. Admission is free.

Activities

Sport fishing for corvina, conger eel, bonito, shark, and other species is a popular pastime along the coast, at sea, and on Isla Gorriti and Isla de Lobos. The tourist office publishes a brochure with a map of recommended fishing spots. Other water sports include surfing, windsurfing, and diving; another brochure recommends sites for each of these activities.

Places to Stay

Accommodations in the Maldonado/Punta del Este area are abundant but generally costly. Prices decline considerably after the summer high season, but can vary even within it – the first three weeks of January tend to be very expensive, but prices begin dropping after mid-February. Much depends on economic conditions in Argentina – if Argentina's economy and currency are weak, prices will drop in Uruguay. Unless otherwise indicated, prices below are high-season, per person (singles are difficult to find in season, though) and can be volatile. For Punta del Este proper, see the separate entry.

Camping ***Camping San Rafael*** *(☎ 86715)*, on the outskirts of Maldonado beyond Aeropuerto El Jagüel, has well-kept facilities on woodsy grounds, complete with store, restaurant, automatic laundry, 24-hour hot water, and other amenities. It's organized almost to the point of regimentation, but at least you can expect quiet after midnight. Sites cost US$17 for two in January and February, US$12 the rest of the year. It accepts Uruguayan pesos, US dollars, and almost all credit cards. Bus No 5 from downtown Maldonado drops you off at the entrance.

Residenciales & Hotels At ***Residencial La Reja*** *(☎ 23717, 18 de Julio 1092)*, singles/doubles with private bath cost US$25/35, but off-season it's only US$15 per person.

Irish-owned ***Hotel Celta*** *(☎ 30139, Ituzaingó 839)*, is a popular choice for foreign travelers. Standard rates are US$40 to US$55, but cheaper budget rooms are available, especially outside peak season. Rates are US$50 double at ***Hotel Sancar*** *(☎ 23563, Juan Edye 597)*.

Hotel Colonial *(☎ 23346, on 18 de Julio)*, near the cathedral, charges US$60 double with breakfast, but half that off-season (though without breakfast). ***Hotel Le Petit*** *(☎ 23044)*, at Florida and Sarandí opposite Plaza San Fernando, charges US$60 double in peak season, but just US$20 per person off-season. ***Hotel Esteño*** *(☎ 25222, Sarandí 881)* charges the same in low season, but US$68 double in peak season.

Places to Eat

Maldonado restaurants are often better values than their pricier and more prestigious counterparts in Punta del Este. The modest ***El Pájaro*** *(☎ 38934)*, Ituzaingó and Román Guerra, serves pizza, chivitos, and seafood. ***El Quilogramo*** *(☎ 38804)*, on Sarandí between Ventura Alegre and Ituzaingó, is a buffet that charges by weight; though it's not that cheap, the quality is good.

Other economical choices include the ***Círculo Policial de Maldonado*** *(☎ 22670, Pérez del Puerto 780)*, ***La Estrella***, on 18 de Julio between Ventura Alegre and Ituzaingó (standard Uruguayan menu specializing in chicken, particularly good for takeout); and ***El Grillo***, at Ituzaingó and Sarandí (chivitos). ***Confitería Catedral*** *(☎ 20101)*, at Florida and 18 de Julio, is fine for snacks.

Maldonado has a wealth of pizzerias. ***Pizzería Carlitos*** *(☎ 21727, Sarandí 834)*, on Plaza San Fernando, is inexpensive but ordinary. Try also ***Pizzería El Oasis*** *(☎ 34794)* at Sarandí and Varela or, for more elaborate Italian meals with better atmosphere, ***Pizza y Pasta*** *(at Sarandí 642)*, on the grounds of the Circolo Italiano.

Al Paso *(☎ 22881, 18 de Julio 888)*, a favorite parrilla, is relatively pricey but still a good value. More upmarket is ***Mesón del Centro Español*** *(☎ 24107, 18 de Julio 708)*, with excellent but costly Spanish seafood. ***Taberna Patxi*** *(☎ 38393, Florida 828)*, serves

Basque food, including fish and shellfish. Try also, at the upper end, ***La Cabaña*** *(☎ 20567)*, on Sarandí near Enrique Burnett.

Shopping

Los Patos, Sarandí 643, has a selection of artisanal goods.

Getting There & Away

Air There are flights to Maldonado/Punta del Este from Argentina all year, but mostly in summer, when there are also services to Brazil and sometimes Paraguay and Chile. For details, see the Punta del Este entry.

Aeropuerto Carlos Curbelo (☎ 78386), at Laguna del Sauce west of Maldonado, cannot handle aircraft larger than 737s at present, but there are plans to expand it to international standards. (Aeropuerto Carlos Curbelo is also known as Aeropuerto Laguna del Sauce.)

Bus Terminal Maldonado (☎ 25701) is at Av Roosevelt and Sarandí, eight blocks south of Plaza San Fernando. Long-distance and international services closely resemble those from Punta del Este, but some companies are at Maldonado or Punta del Este only. Among the companies with offices here are COT (☎ 25026), Copsa (☎ 34733), Expreso del Este (☎ 20040), Tur-Este (☎ 37323), Transporte Núnez (☎ 30170), Coom, and Olivera Hermanos (☎ 28330).

Both COT and Copsa go frequently to Montevideo, while COT goes northeast to the Brazilian border. Tur-Este (☎ 37323) goes to Rocha and Treinta y Tres. Transporte Núnez has two buses daily to Montevideo. Olivera Hermanos goes twice daily to Minas (US$3), while Coom makes eight trips there.

Getting Around

Codesa (☎ 23481), on Av Velásquez, runs local buses to Punta del Este, La Barra, Manantiales, and San Carlos. Olivera (☎ 24039) connects Maldonado and Punta del Este (US$0.50) with Punta Ballena, Portezuelo, and Aeropuerto Carlos Curbelo, in Laguna del Sauce, westbound, and with José Ignacio eastbound. Maldonado Turismo (☎ 37181) goes to La Barra and Manantiales.

URUGUAY

AROUND MALDONADO

Casa Pueblo

At Punta Ballena, a scenic headland 10km west of Maldonado, Uruguayan artist Carlos Páez Vilaró built this unconventional, sprawling, multilevel Mediterranean hillside villa and art gallery using no right angles. For an admission charge of US$3, visitors can tour the gallery, view a slide presentation on the building's creation, and dine or drink at the bar-cafeteria. Parts of Casa Pueblo (☎ 78041) are open to member-patrons only, but you can sneak a view from the outside. Regular hours are 10 am to 6 pm daily.

There is now accommodation at the ***Club Hotel Casapueblo*** *(☎ 042-79386, fax 78485)* starting at US$70/85 single/double Monday to Thursday, US$90/120 Friday to Sunday from October through mid-December. Summer prices are about double, but even higher between Christmas and New Year's.

There is also camping, starting around US$12 for two persons, at ***Camping Internacional Punta Ballena*** *(☎ 78902)*. Tent cabins are also available here for around US$25.

José Ignacio

Still pretty quiet, this once utterly tranquil fishing village, 30km east of Maldonado, has become the latest 'in' spot among upscale beach towns on the Uruguayan Riviera. There are two to three buses daily from Maldonado, and the number of restaurants and accommodations is growing.

PUNTA DEL ESTE

Where an early Jesuit visitor once commented that 'you see nothing here but a few cabins, the abodes of misery,' one of South America's most glamorous summer resorts typically swarms with upper-class Argentines who disdain Mar del Plata since the latter lost its exclusivity. Strictly speaking, Punta del Este is part of Maldonado, but economically and socially, its elegant seaside homes, yacht harbor, and expensive hotels and restaurants make it a world apart.

Punta's main street, Av Juan Gorlero, is a clutter of neon and plastic signs so dense it's hard to make sense of them – Uruguay's

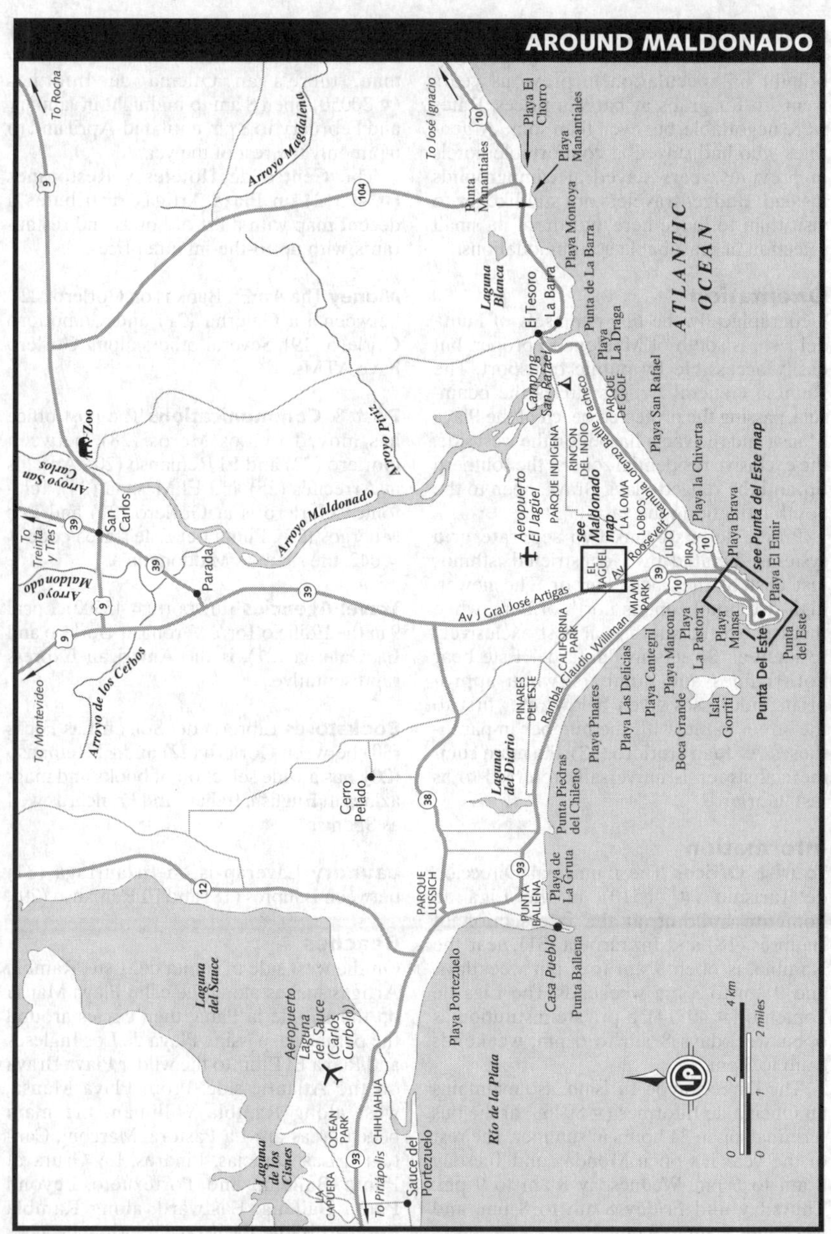
AROUND MALDONADO
To Rocha
Arroyo Magdalena
To José Ignacio
Playa El Chorro
Playa Manantiales
Punta Manantiales
Playa Montoya
ATLANTIC OCEAN
Laguna Blanca
El Tesoro
La Barra
Punta de La Barra
Playa de La Barra
Playa La Draga
Camping San Rafael
PARQUE DE GOLF
Playa San Rafael
RINCON DEL INDIO
Rambla Lorenzo Batlle Pacheco
PARQUE INDIGENA
Arroyo Pitiz
Zoo
Arroyo San Carlos
San Carlos
Arroyo Maldonado
To Treinta y Tres
Parada
Aeropuerto El Jagüel
see Maldonado map
LA LOMA
LOBOS
EL JAGÜEL
Av Roosevelt
LIDO
PIRA
Playa la Chiverta
Playa Brava
Playa El Emir
see Punta del Este map
Av J Gral José Artigas
MIAMI PARK
CALIFORNIA PARK
Rambla Claudio Williman
Playa Mansa
Punta Del Este
Punta del Este
Playa La Pastora
Playa Marconi
Playa Cantegril
Playa Las Delicias
Boca Grande
Isla Gorriti
Arroyo de los Ceibos
To Montevideo
PINARES DEL ESTE
Playa Pinares
Laguna del Diario
Punta Piedras del Chileno
Cerro Pelado
PARQUE LUSSICH
PUNTA BALLENA
Playa de La Gruta
Casa Pueblo
Punta Ballena
Laguna del Sauce
Aeropuerto Laguna del Sauce (Carlos Curbelo)
Playa Portezuelo
Río de la Plata
Laguna de los Cisnes
OCEAN PARK
CHIHUAHUA
LA CAPUERA
To Piriápolis
Sauce del Portezuelo
0 2 4 km
0 1 2 miles

URUGUAY

counterpart to the Las Vegas Strip. After a bad summer in 1995, much of the property bought on speculation in previous years went up for grabs at bargain prices. Rates were negotiable, but even then some Argentines who had stayed at comfortable hotels in previous years stayed at campgrounds instead. Budget travelers are still likelier to visit than to lodge here, but there's a small selection of reasonable accommodations.

Orientation

Geographically, the tiny peninsula of Punta del Este is south of Maldonado proper, but easily accessible by public transport. The Rambla General Artigas circles the peninsula, passing the protected beach of the Playa Mansa and the yacht harbor on the west side, the exclusive residential zone at the southern tip, and the rugged Playa Brava, open to the South Atlantic, in the east.

Punta del Este has two separate grid systems, dictated by a constricted isthmus just east of the yacht harbor. The newer, high-rise hotel zone is north of here, while the area to the south is almost exclusively residential. Streets in Punta del Este bear both names and numbers; when appropriate, addresses given below refer first to the street name, with the number in parentheses. Av Juan Gorlero (22), the main commercial street, is universally referred to as just 'Gorlero.'

URUGUAY

Information

Tourist Offices The municipal Dirección de Turismo (☎ 46510), in the Liga de Fomento building at the intersection of Baupres (18) and Inzaurraga (31), near the Rambla, is open 9 am to 9 pm weekdays, and 9 am to 3 pm weekends. The Liga de Fomento (☎ 40514), a private institution, is open weekdays 8 am to 6 pm, weekends 8 am to 3 pm.

The Dirección de Turismo also maintains an Oficina de Informes (☎ 89468) at the bus terminal, open 24 hours in summer. The rest of the year it's open Monday and Tuesday 8 am to 6 pm, Wednesday 8 am to 9 pm, Thursday and Friday 8 am to 8 pm, and weekends 9 am to 9 pm.

On the western approach to town, at Parada 24 (Las Delicias) on Rambla Williman, there's an Oficina de Informes (☎ 30050) open 8 am to midnight in January and February, to 8 pm until mid-April and to 6 pm only the rest of the year.

The Centro de Hoteles y Restoranes (☎ 40512) on Plaza Artigas, distributes a decent map with a list of hotels and restaurants, with up-to-the-minute prices.

Money The AmEx Bank is on Gorlero (22), between La Galerna (21) and Comodoro Gorlero (19). Several others along Gorlero have ATMs.

Post & Communications The post office has moved to Los Meros (28), between Gorlero (22) and El Remanso (20). Antel is at Arrecifes (25) and El Mesana (24); Telefónica Gorlero is at Gorlero (22) and Los Muergos (27). Punta del Este's area code is ☎ 042, the same as Maldonado's.

Travel Agencies Turisport (☎ 45500), Local 9 in the Edificio Torre Verona at Gorlero and La Galerna (21), is the American Express representative.

Bookstores Librería del Sol, on Las Focas (30) between Gorlero (22) and El Remanso (20), has a wide selection of books and magazines in English, Italian, and French, as well as Spanish.

Laundry Laverap is on Inzaurraga (31) between Baupres (18) and El Remanso (20).

Beaches

On the west side of Punta del Este, Rambla Artigas snakes along the calm Playa Mansa on the Río de la Plata, then circles around the peninsula, passing Playa de Los Ingleses and Playa El Emir to the wilder Playa Brava on the Atlantic side. From Playa Mansa, west along Rambla Williman, the main beach areas are La Pastora, Marconi, Cantegril, Las Delicias, Pinares, La Gruta at Punta Ballena, and Portezuelo, beyond Punta Ballena. Eastward, along Rambla Lorenzo Batlle Pacheco, the prime beaches

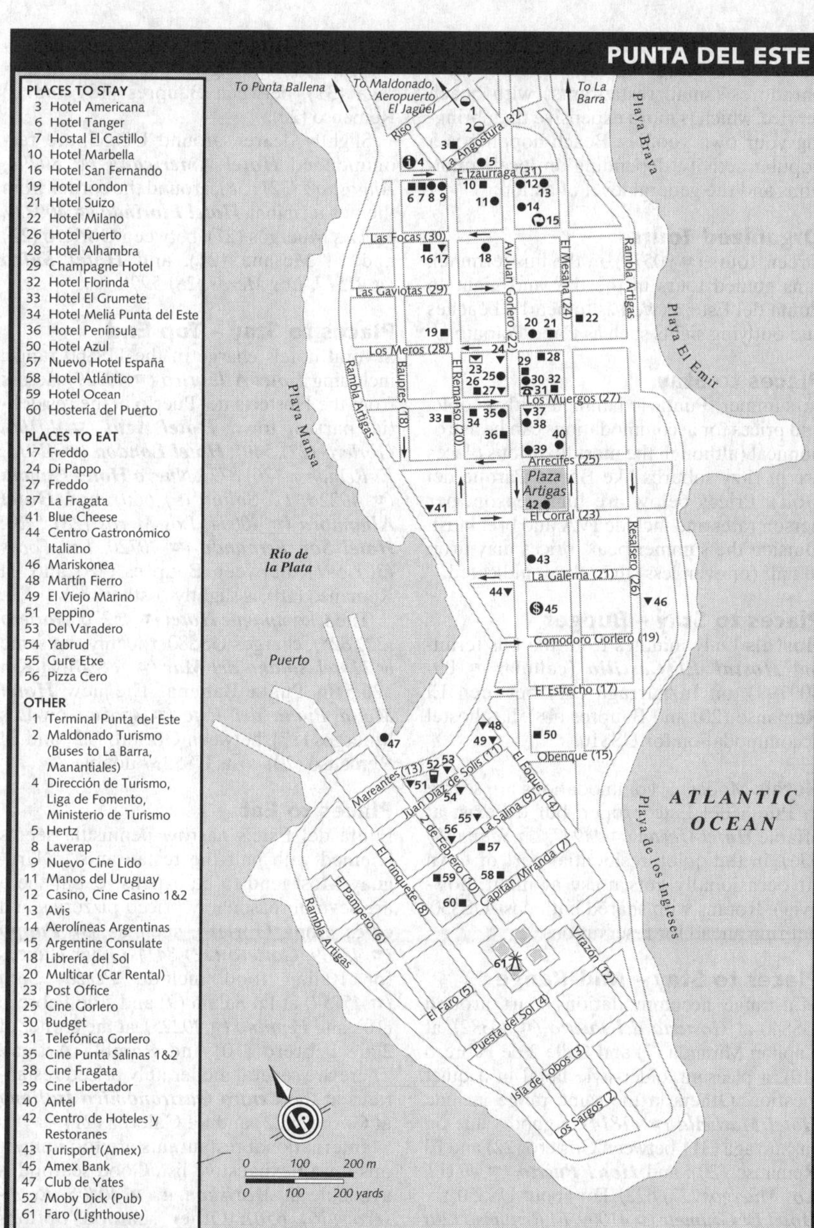
PUNTA DEL ESTE
PLACES TO STAY
3 Hotel Americana
6 Hotel Tanger
7 Hostal El Castillo
10 Hotel Marbella
16 Hotel San Fernando
19 Hotel London
21 Hotel Suizo
22 Hotel Milano
26 Hotel Puerto
28 Hotel Alhambra
29 Champagne Hotel
32 Hotel Florinda
33 Hotel El Grumete
34 Hotel Meliá Punta del Este
36 Hotel Península
50 Hotel Azul
57 Nuevo Hotel España
58 Hotel Atlántico
59 Hotel Ocean
60 Hostería del Puerto
PLACES TO EAT
17 Freddo
24 Di Pappo
27 Freddo
37 La Fragata
41 Blue Cheese
44 Centro Gastronómico Italiano
46 Mariskonea
48 Martín Fierro
49 El Viejo Marino
51 Peppino
53 Del Varadero
54 Yabrud
55 Gure Etxe
56 Pizza Cero
OTHER
1 Terminal Punta del Este
2 Maldonado Turismo (Buses to La Barra, Manantiales)
4 Dirección de Turismo, Liga de Fomento, Ministerio de Turismo
5 Hertz
8 Laverap
9 Nuevo Cine Lido
11 Manos del Uruguay
12 Casino, Cine Casino 1&2
13 Avis
14 Aerolíneas Argentinas
15 Argentine Consulate
18 Librería del Sol
20 Multicar (Car Rental)
23 Post Office
25 Cine Gorlero
30 Budget
31 Telefónica Gorlero
35 Cine Punta Salinas 1&2
38 Cine Fragata
39 Cine Libertador
40 Antel
42 Centro de Hoteles y Restoranes
43 Turisport (Amex)
45 Amex Bank
47 Club de Yates
52 Moby Dick (Pub)
61 Faro (Lighthouse)
To Punta Ballena
To Maldonado, Aeropuerto El Jagüel
To La Barra
Playa Brava
Playa El Emir
Playa Mansa
Playa de los Ingleses
ATLANTIC OCEAN
Río de la Plata
Puerto
Plaza Artigas
Riso
La Angostura (32)
E Izaurraga (31)
Las Focas (30)
Las Gaviotas (29)
Los Meros (28)
Los Muergos (27)
Arrecifes (25)
El Corral (23)
La Galerna (21)
Comodoro Gorlero (19)
El Estrecho (17)
Obenque (15)
Av Juan Gorlero (22)
El Mesana (24)
Rambla Artigas
Baupres (18)
El Remanso (20)
Resalsero (26)
Mareantes (13)
Juan Díaz de Solís (11)
El Foque (14)
La Salina (9)
2 de Febrero (10)
Capitán Miranda (7)
El Trinquete (8)
El Pampero (6)
Virazón (12)
El Faro (5)
Puesta del Sol (4)
Isla de Lobos (3)
Los Sargos (2)
0 100 200 m
0 100 200 yards

URUGUAY

are La Chiverta, San Rafael, La Draga, and Punta de la Barra. All these beaches have paradores (small restaurants) with beach service, which is more expensive than bringing your own goodies. Beach-hopping is a popular activity, depending on local conditions and the general level of action.

Organized Tours

Green Tours (☎ 90570), in the bus terminal, runs guided tours in the day and night to Punta del Este, as well as to nearby beaches and outlying sights such as Cabo Polonio.

Places to Stay

In summer, Punta is jammed with people, and prices for accommodations can be astronomical (although the most luxurious places are in ritzy suburbs like Barrio Parque del Golf). Prices below are high-season, per person rates and include IVA and breakfast. Outside the summer peak, prices may drop to half (or even less) than those indicated.

Places to Stay – Budget

Hostels Only minutes from the bus terminal ***Hostal El Castillo*** (cellular ☎ 09-409799), on Inzaurraga (31) between El Remanso (20) and Baupres (18), has hostel accommodation for US$10.

Hotels Modest accommodations are scarce in Punta del Este proper, but do exist at affable ***Hotel Ocean*** *(☎ 44947, La Salina (9) 636)*, in the quiet, residential part of town (it occasionally gets noisy at night, however). Rooms with shared bath cost US$30, but ring ahead for reservations.

Places to Stay – Mid-Range

Mid-range accommodations start around US$40 at ***Hostería del Puerto*** *(☎ 40332)*, at Capitán Miranda (7) and Calle 2 de Febrero (10), a pleasant, older-style hotel in a quiet location. Others in the same range include ***Hotel Marbella*** *(☎ 41814)*, a good value on Inzaurraga (31), between Gorlero (22) and El Remanso (20); and ***Hotel Puerto*** *(☎ 40332, Los Muergos (27) 622)*. For about US$50, try ***Hotel El Grumete*** *(☎ 41009, El Remanso (20) 797)*, ***Hotel Península*** *(☎ 41533, Gorlero (22) 761)*, ***Hotel Milano*** *(☎ 40039, El Mesana (24) 880)*, and ***Hotel Tanger*** *(☎ 40601)*, at Inzaurraga (31), between Baupres (18) and El Remanso (20).

Slightly dearer, around US$55, are recommended ***Hotel Americana*** *(☎ 80794, Angostura (32) 638)*, around the corner from the bus terminal, ***Hotel Florinda*** *(☎ 40022)*, on Los Muergos (27), between Gorlero (22) and El Mesana (24); and ***Hotel Suizo*** *(☎ 41517, Los Meros (28) 590)*.

Places to Stay – Top End

Several hotels charge in the US$60 range, including ***Hotel Atlántico*** *(☎ 40229)*, across from the Hostería del Puerto in the residential part of town; ***Hotel Azul*** *(☎ 40106, Gorlero (22) 540)*; ***Hotel London*** *(☎ 41911, El Remanso (20) 877)*, ***Nuevo Hotel España*** *(☎ 40228, La Salina (9) 660)*; and ***Hotel Alhambra*** *(☎ 40094, Los Meros (28) 573)*. ***Hotel San Fernando*** *(☎ 40720, Las Focas (30) 691)*, between Baupres (18) and El Remanso (20), is slightly costlier.

The ***Champagne Hotel*** *(☎ 45276, Gorlero (22) 828)*, charges US$80, roughly the same as ***Hotel Solana del Mar*** *(☎ 78888)*, at Km 126.5 in Punta Ballena. The new ***Hotel Meliá Punta del Este*** *(☎ 45656)*, on Los Muergos (27), between Gorlero (22) and El Remanso (20) costs US$237 double.

Places to Eat

Punta del Este's narrow peninsula seems jammed with half the restaurants in Uruguay. Most tend to be expensive, but there are several reasonably priced pizzerias and cafés along Gorlero, such as ***Di Pappo*** *(☎ 42869, Gorlero (22) 841)*. Other choices for Italian food include ***Pizza Cero*** *(☎ 45954)* at La Salina (9) and 2 de Febrero (10), and ***Peppino*** *(☎ 40225)*, at the corner of 2 de Febrero (10) and Rambla Artigas. There are several moderately priced restaurants at the ***Centro Gastronómico Italiano*** at Gorlero (22) and La Galerna (21).

International restaurants are too numerous for an exhaustive list. Good seafood is available at ***Mariskonea*** *(☎ 40408, Resalsero (26) 650)*. Other seafood options include ***La Fragata*** *(☎ 4000, Gorlero (22)*

800), at Los Muergos (27); ***Del Varadero*** *(☎ 40235)*, Rambla Artigas between 2 de Febrero (10) and Virazón (12); and ***El Viejo Marino*** *(☎ 43565)*, at Solís (11) and El Foque (14).

Between Punta and Maldonado, the very expensive ***La Bourgogne*** *(☎ 82007)*, at Pedragosa Sierra and Av del Mar, imports its chefs from France. Another highly regarded but expensive French restaurant is ***Blue Cheese*** *(☎ 40354)*, Rambla Artigas and El Corral (23). Montevideo's ***Bungalow Suizo*** *(☎ 82358)* has a local branch on Rambla Batlle Pacheco at Parada 8, near Av Roosevelt.

Martín Fierro *(☎ 45960)* at Rambla Artigas and El Foque (14), is a parrilla. For variety, try the Arab-Armenian ***Yabrud*** *(☎ 46463)*, at Solís (11) and Virazón (12), owned by Argentine President Carlos Menem's sidekick Armando Gostanian (see the 'Menem Trucho' boxed text in Facts for the Visitor chapter), or the Basque ***Gure Etxe*** *(☎ 46858)*, at Virazón (12) and La Salina (9).

The Argentine ice creamery ***Freddo*** has a branch at Las Focas (30) and El Remanso (20), and another at Gorlero (22) and Los Muergos (27).

Entertainment

Many cinemas line Av Gorlero, with pubs concentrated near the port. Cinemas include ***Cine Fragata*** *(☎ 40002, Gorlero (22) 798)*, ***Cine Gorlero*** *(☎ 44437)*, on Gorlero (22) between Los Meros (28) and Los Muergos (27); ***Cine Libertador*** *(☎ 44437)*, on Gorlero (22) near Arrecifes (25); ***Cine Punta Salinas 1&2*** *(☎ 46406/7)*, at Gorlero (22) and Los Muergos (27); and the five-screen ***Nuevo Cine Lido*** *(☎ 40911)*, at Inzaurraga (31) and El Remanso (20).

Punta's ***Casino***, at Gorlero (22) and Inzaurraga (31), also contains the ***Cine Casino 1&2*** *(☎ 41908)*.

Near the yacht harbor, ***Moby Dick***, on Rambla Artigas between Virazón (12) and 2 de Febrero (10), is an entertaining pub. Most dance clubs are along Rambla Batlle Pacheco, east of Playa Brava, including ***La Plage*** *(☎ 84869)*, at Parada 12.

Shopping

For souvenirs and handicrafts, visit the Feria de los Artesanos (once known as the 'Feria de los Hippies') on Plaza Artigas. In high season (December to March) hours are 6 am to 1 pm daily, while the rest of the year it's open 11 am to 5 pm weekends only – later if business is good. Much of the material is tacky, but there are some worthwhile items.

Manos del Uruguay has a leather outlet on Gorlero (22), between Inzaurraga (31) and Las Focas (30).

Getting There & Away

Air Pluna (☎ 90101), at Parada 8½ on Rambla Batlle Pacheco near Roosevelt, has 29 weekly flights to Buenos Aires' Aeroparque. In summer it has flights to Sáo Paulo and other Brazilian destinations, sometimes via Montevideo.

Aerolíneas Argentinas (☎ 43801), in the Edificio Santos Dumont on Gorlero between Inzaurraga (31) and Las Focas (30), flies to Aeroparque 19 times weekly. Lapa (☎ 90840), in the Torre Punta del Este at Av Roosevelt Parada 14½, flies to Aeroparque Friday and Sunday.

Bus Terminal Punta del Este (☎ 89467) is at Riso and Bulevar Artigas. Most bus services to Punta del Este are an extension of those to Maldonado; see the Getting There & Away for Maldonado as well.

International carriers here include TTL (☎ 86755) to Porto Alegre, Florianópolis, and São Paulo; and EGA (☎ 92380) to the same Brazilian destinations as well as to Rosario and Mendoza, Argentina, and Santiago de Chile.

Encon (☎ 90012) goes to Rosario, Santa Fe, Paraná, and Córdoba; and Cora, to the same Argentine destinations. There are more possible connections in Montevideo.

Domestically, COT (☎ 86810) covers the entire Uruguayan coast from Montevideo to the Brazilian border at Chuy. Copsa (☎ 89205) goes to Montevideo and to José Ignacio. Coom (☎ 86812) goes to Minas eight times daily, while Olivera goes there twice.

Getting Around

To/From the Airport Maldonado and Punta del Este share two airports. Aerolíneas Argentinas and Pluna use Aeropuerto Laguna de Sauce (aka Aeropuerto Carlos Curbelo), west of Portezuelo, reached by Buses Olivera (☎ 24039) from Maldonado.

Bus Maldonado Turismo (☎ 37181), Gorlero (22) and Las Focas (30), connects Punta del Este with La Barra and Manantiales. Its buses leave from La Angostura behind the bus terminal.

Car Budget (☎ 46363) has offices at Los Muergos (27) and Gorlero (22); Avis (☎ 42020) on Inzaurraga (31), between Gorlero (22) and El Mesana (24); and Hertz (☎ 89778) on Inzaurraga (31), between Gorlero (22) and El Remanso (20). Local agencies include Multicar (☎ 43143), at Gorlero (22) 860, and Uruguay Car (☎ 41036), in the Galería Sagasti alongside the Casino on Gorlero.

AROUND PUNTA DEL ESTE

Isla Gorriti

Boats leave every half hour or so from the yacht harbor for this nearby island, which has excellent sandy beaches and ruins of the **Baterías de Santa Ana**, an 18th-century fortification. It also has two restaurants, Parador Puerto Jardín and Playa Honda.

Isla de Lobos

About 6 miles offshore, the nature reserve of Isla de Lobos hosts a population of some 200,000 southern sea lions. During the invasion of 1806, British forces stranded numerous prisoners here without food or water, and many perished while attempting to swim to Maldonado. To arrange trips to the reserve, contact the Unión de Lanchas (☎ 42594) in Punta del Este.

ROCHA

Founded in 1793 by Rafael Pérez del Puerto, picturesque Rocha is capital of its namesake department and merits at least an afternoon visit for those staying on the beach at La Paloma. In the narrow alleyways off Plaza Independencia are a number of interesting houses from late colonial and early independence times.

Virtually everything of interest, as well as hotels and transport, is on or near Plaza Independencia. The municipal Oficina de Turismo (☎ 5008) is in the Intendencia at General Artigas 176. The post office is at 18 de Julio 131. Antel is at General Artigas and Rodó. The area code is ☎ 472. Money can be exchanged at Banco de la República or Banco Comercial.

Places to Stay & Eat

Accommodations are very reasonable, perhaps enough so to justify staying here rather than in La Paloma. Try the tidy ***Hotel Municipal Rocha*** *(☎ 2404, 19 de Abril 87)*, a block off the plaza, which was undergoing renovation at the time of writing. ***Hotel Trocadero*** *(☎ 2267)*, at 25 de Agosto and 18 de Julio, charges US$33/48 plus 14% IVA, including a buffet breakfast and cable TV.

Getting There & Away

Rocha is a hub for bus travel between Montevideo and the Brazilian border. Rutas del Sol (☎ 3541), at Ramírez and 25 de Agosto, runs 10 buses daily to Montevideo (US$8); five daily to Chuy (US$5), via La Paloma, La Pedrera, and Castillos; and six daily to Barra de Valizas (US$3.50). Cynsa has 10 daily to La Paloma and nine from La Paloma back to Rocha, where you can catch the service to Chuy. COT also serves Rocha.

LA PALOMA

Some 28km south of Rocha and 250km from Montevideo, placid La Paloma (population 5000) is less developed, less expensive, and much less crowded than Punta del Este, but still has almost every important comfort and amenity except for Punta's hyperactive nightlife. As elsewhere on the coast, there are attractive sandy beaches in town and beyond – those to the east are less protected from ocean swells.

Orientation

La Paloma occupies a small peninsula at the south end of Ruta 15. Its center, flanking

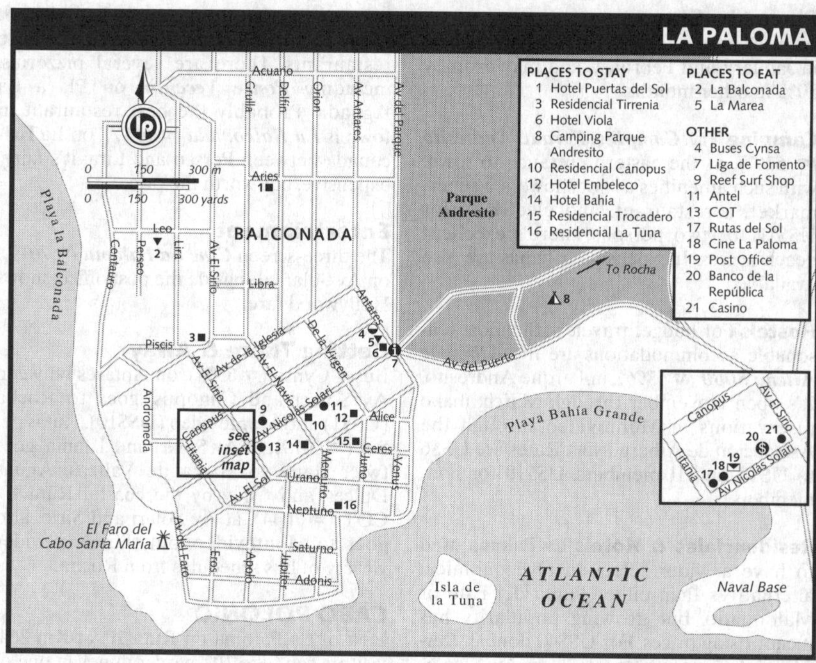

Av Nicolás Solari, is small and compact. Although the streets are named, the buildings, including hotels and restaurants, lack numbers and are more easily located by their relationship to prominent intersections and other landmarks. At the eastern entrance to town, on the highway to Rocha, the woodsy and spacious Parque Andresito is an appealing camping area with excellent facilities.

Information

Tourist Offices The Liga de Fomento (☎ 6008) is on the traffic circle at the east end of Av Nicolás Solari. In summer, it's open 10 am to 10 pm. The rest of the year hours are 10 am to 9 pm, except from April to October, when it's open weekends only.

Money Banco de la República is on Av Nicolás Solari near El Sirio, next door to the Casino.

Post & Communications The post office is on Av Nicolás Solari, just east of the former Onda bus terminal. Antel is on Av Nicolás Solari between Av El Navío and De La Virgen.

The area code is ☎ 0479.

Things to See & Do

In 1874, construction of **El Faro del Cabo Santa María**, the local lighthouse, marked the beginning of La Paloma's growth as a summer beach resort. It's open to the public 4:30 to 7:30 pm in summer and weekends only the rest of the year.

Laguna de Rocha, 10km west of La Paloma, is an ecological reserve with populations of black-necked swans, storks, and waterfowl.

Uruguay isn't widely known for its surfing, but the Reef Surf Shop, on Av Solari between Sirio and Navío, can offer suggestions for the best local spots.

URUGUAY

Places to Stay

As elsewhere on the coast, rates are highest in January and February, and may drop by 50% in other months.

Camping Try ***Camping Parque Andresito*** *(☎ 6107)*, at the eastern entrance to town, with such amenities as hot showers, a supermarket, a restaurant, and electricity for US$12 for two persons; there's excellent beach access. Inexpensive cabanas are also available.

Hostels For budget travelers, the most reasonable accommodations are the ***Albergue Altena 5000*** *(☎ 6396)*, in Parque Andresito. It's open November through March; make reservations in Montevideo through the Asociación de Alberguistas. Rates are US$6 to US$8 for HI members, US$10 for nonmembers.

Residenciales & Hotels La Paloma used to have a wider selection of economical alternatives than either Punta del Este or Maldonado, but growing popularity has meant rising prices. For US$40 double, ***Residencial Canopus*** *(☎ 6068)*, on Av Nicolás Solari near El Navío, is now one of the best values. ***Hotel Viola*** *(☎ 6020)* on Av Nicolás Solari near Antares, charges US$50.

Hotel Puertas del Sol *(☎ 6066)*, on Delfín near Aries, charges US$40 to US$60 in summer but only US$15 per person off-season. Most others are in the US$60 range, including ***Residencial Trocadero*** *(☎ 6007)*, on Juno near Ceres, ***Residencial Tirrenia*** *(☎ 6230)*, on Av El Sirio near Piscis, and ***Residencial La Tuna*** *(☎ 6083)*, on Neptuno between Juno and Av El Navío. ***Hotel Bahía*** *(☎ 6029)*, at Av El Navío and Av El Sol, charges US$65 double.

More upscale accommodations are available at ***Hotel Embeleco*** *(☎ 6108)*, at Av El Sol and De La Virgen, which costs US$80 per double with breakfast, and US$110 with half-board.

Places to Eat

La Marea, on Av Antares between Av Solari and Canopus, has reasonably priced seafood, but slow service from overworked waiters. ***Hotel Bahía*** and ***Hotel Embeleco*** also have restaurants. There are several pizzerias, including ***Ponte Vecchio***, on Playa La Aguada. Probably the best restaurant in town is ***La Balconada*** *(☎ 6197)*, on La Balconada between Perseo and Lira; it's fairly expensive, but worth the price.

Entertainment

The three-screen ***Cine La Paloma*** *(☎ 7079)*, on Av Solari alongside the post office, shows Hollywood fare.

Getting There & Away

Buses Cynsa (☎ 6304), on Antares between Av Solari and Canopus, goes to Rocha (US$1) and Montevideo (US$10). Rutas del Sol (☎ 6019), at Av Solari and Titania, goes twice daily to Barra de Valizas, Aguas Dulces, and Chuy by the coastal Rùta 10. COT (☎ 7044), at Av Solari and Sirio, also goes to Montevideo, but there's a wider variety of bus schedules from Rocha.

CABO POLONIO

East of La Paloma on Ruta 10, at Km 264, visitors can hike 10km over dunes in one of Uruguay's wildest areas to visit a sea lion colony. Near the entrance to the dunes, many people advertise rides to the reserve, which otherwise is a hefty but feasible full day's walk. Dune walking is very tiring – be sure to take water.

It's also possible to arrange 4WD tours from La Paloma with Tour Unidos La Pedrera; for details contact the tourist office.

AGUAS DULCES

This quaint fishing village, 11km directly southeast of the town of Castillos, is the place for a *really* quiet seaside holiday. Its only accommodations are the modest *Hotel Gainfor* and an equally modest municipal campground. Sample the seafood at any of several restaurants, and do not leave without tasting the messy but flavorful fruit of the *butía* palm, for sale in almost every tiny shop.

At nearby Barra de Valizas, the youth hostel *Albergue Artigas* (no phone), for which you must make reservations with the

Asociación de Alberguistas in Montevideo, has kitchen facilities and hot showers. Rutas del Sol buses from Montevideo stop nearby.

PARQUE NACIONAL SANTA TERESA

More a historical than a natural attraction, this coastal park, 35km south of Chuy, incorporates the hilltop **Fortaleza de Santa Teresa**, which was begun by the Portuguese in 1762 but finished by the Spaniards after its capture by Governor Cevallos of Montevideo in 1793. Across Ruta 9, the enormous Laguna Negra and the marshes of the Bañado de Santa Teresa support abundant bird life.

By international standards, Santa Teresa is a very humble unit, but it attracts many Uruguayan and Brazilian visitors for its relatively uncrowded beaches. It offers decentralized camping in forest plantations so irregular that they would seem natural – if you didn't know that eucalyptus is native to Australia and pine to the Northern Hemisphere only. Other features include a small zoo, an indoor plant nursery, and a shade nursery. The park gets very crowded during Carnaval, but most of the time it absorbs visitors without difficulty.

The camping fee is US$10 per site, for up to six people, and includes basic facilities such as hot showers. At park headquarters, there are abundant services, including phone and post offices, a supermarket, a bakery, a butchery, and a restaurant.

CHUY

Chuy is a grubby but energetic Uruguayan-Brazilian border town at the terminus of Ruta 9, 340km from Montevideo. Pedestrians and vehicles cross freely between the Uruguayan and Brazilian sides, which are separated only by a median strip along the main avenue (on the Uruguayan side, it's Av Brasil; on the Brazilian side, it's Av Uruguay).

Seven km west of Chuy, the restored **Fuerte San Miguel**, a pink-granite fortress built in 1734 during hostilities between Spain and Portugal, merits a visit. Its entrance, guarded by a moat, overlooks the border from an isolated high point. It's closed Monday, but you can still glimpse the interior and visit the nearby gaucho museum.

Information

If proceeding beyond Chuy into Brazil, complete Uruguayan emigration formalities at the border post on Ruta 9, 1km south of town. Entering Uruguay, you will find an extremely helpful and well-informed tourist office (☎ 2554), where, with a little polite cajoling, you can get a computer printout of up-to-date hotel and restaurant information for the whole department.

If you need a visa, Brazil has a consulate at Fernández 147. Change your Uruguayan money before entering Brazil, as Uruguayan currency is worthless any distance into Brazil. There are several exchange houses along Av Brasil, though changing traveler's checks is problematical.

Chuy's area code is ☎ 0474.

On the Brazilian side, there's a Uruguayan consulate (☎ 651151) at Rua Venezuela 311. Visas cost a whopping US$45 for those who need them.

Places to Stay & Eat

Singles cost only US$15 at ***Hotel Internacional*** *(☎ 2055, Río San Luis 121)*, but accommodations are usually cheaper at ***Rivero Hotel*** or ***Hotel e Restaurante São Francisco*** (see below), on the Brazilian side. ***Nuevo Hotel Plaza*** *(☎ 2309, Av Artigas 553)* has singles/doubles from US$36/55 and a restaurant. For dining, try also ***Parrillada Jesús*** *(☎ 2766, Av Brasil 603)* or the nearby ***Bar Restaurante Opal*** for pasta.

On the Brazilian side, the best cheapie is ***Rivero Hotel*** *(☎ 651271, Colombia 163)*, where bright *apartamentos* cost US$7 per person. ***Hotel y Restaurante São Francisco*** *(☎ 651096, Colombia 191)* charges the same prices.

Ten km south of Chuy, a coastal lateral leads to well-equipped ***Camping Chuy*** *(☎ 2425)*, which charges US$12 per site, and ***Camping de la Barra*** *(☎ 1611)*, which costs US$4 per person, with all facilities. Local buses from Chuy go directly to both.

Getting There & Away

Several bus companies connect Chuy with Montevideo (US$14, five hours) including Rutas del Sol (☎ 2048), at Av Internacional; COT (☎ 2009), at Av Brasil 595; and Cynsa, also on Av Brasil. There is also bus service to Treinta y Tres.

Brazilian buses have a central *rodoviária* (terminal) three blocks north of the border. There are regular buses to Pelotas, and two daily buses to Rio Grande (US$11, four hours), at 7 am and 3:30 pm. To Porto Alegre (US$22, 7½ hours), there are two buses daily, at noon and 11 pm.

TREINTA Y TRES

Little-visited Treinta y Tres (population 30,000) is a gaucho town in the scenic hill country of the Cuchilla Grande, on the Río Olimar. Founded in 1853 on the interior route to Brazil, via Río Branco or Melo (the route north to Melo is one of the most beautiful in Uruguay), it is also the department capital. The town is 150km northwest from Chuy via Ruta 14, and 290km northeast of Montevideo via Ruta 8.

The Oficina de Turismo (☎ 0452-2911), at Lavalleja and Echeveste, is open 6 am to 1 pm weekdays. For money changing, try Cambio España, at Lavalleja 1283.

On the plaza at Lavalleja 564, simple but clean and friendly ***Hotel Olimar** (☎ 0452-2115)* has singles for US$19 private bath, US$16 with shared bath. Slightly dearer is ***Hotel Treinta y Tres** (☎ 0452-2325, Lavalleja 688)*. ***Restaurant London***, also on the plaza at Lavalleja and Zufriátegui, has good, filling, and inexpensive meals.

Núñez, Expreso Minuano (☎ 0452-5364), at Araujo 242; Cota (☎ 0452-3617), at Manuel Freire 3617; and Rutas del Plata have eight buses daily to Melo and to Montevideo via Minas. Tur-Este (☎ 0452-3516) at Zufriátegui 209 goes daily to Maldonado (four hours).

MELO

Founded in 1795, the capital of Cerro Largo department is 110km north of Treinta y Tres via Ruta 8. Featuring a few late-colonial buildings and a stone post construction now housing the **Museo del Gaucho**, Melo is a transport hub for Uruguay's interior, with bus connections to Río Branco, Aceguá, and Rivera, all of which have border crossings to Brazil.

The post office is at Herrera 671, Antel at 18 de Julio and Herrera; the area code is ☎ 0462. There's a Brazilian consulate (☎ 2136) at Del Pilar 786.

Parque Rivera has a public ***campground***, while the ***Crown Hotel** (☎ 2261, Ituzaingó 609)*, has rooms starting at US$30/50 single/double with breakfast. For meals, try the ***Parillada El Pepe** (☎ 2022, Saravia 606)*, or ***Pizzería Aroztegui** (☎ 2570, Saravia 588)*.

Cota (☎ 2253), at Colón 627, Núnez, and Turismar have buses to Montevideo and also provide local services.

PARAGUAY

KEN LAFFAL

Facts about Paraguay

Paraguay is South America's 'empty quarter,' poorly known even to its neighbors. For much of its history, sustained by geographical isolation, it has distanced itself from the Latin American mainstream, but economic developments since the 1970s and political developments since the late 1980s appear to have brought about irrevocable changes, despite some recent glitches.

Once South America's most notorious and durable police state, the country now welcomes foreign visitors and offers many worthwhile sights, including the riverside capital of Asunción and its scenic surroundings, the Jesuit missions of the upper Río Paraná, the massive Argentine-Paraguayan and Brazilian-Paraguayan hydroelectric projects at Itaipú and Yacyretá, and several national parks, although access to most of them is difficult. The Gran Chaco, west of the Río Paraguay, is a paradise for bird watchers and other nature-oriented travelers.

HISTORY

Paraguay's pre-Columbian cultural patterns were more complex than either Argentina's or Uruguay's. At European contact, Guaraní-speaking people inhabited most of what is now eastern Paraguay, while west of the Río Paraguay a multitude of Indian groups, known collectively as 'Guaycurú' to the Guaraní, inhabited overlapping territories in the Chaco. Among these groups were the Tobas, Matacos, Mbayás, Abipones, and many others, some of whom are now extinct.

The Guaraní were semisedentary cultivators, while groups of hunter-gatherers such as the Aché (Guayakí) lived in enclaves of dense tropical and subtropical forests near the borders of present-day Brazil. The Chaco Indians were mostly hunter-gatherers who also fished along the Río Pilcomayo and other permanent watercourses.

Although predominantly a peaceful people, the Guaraní did not always refrain from venturing into Guaycurú territory and battling with them. They even raided the foothills of the Andes, where they obtained gold and silver objects that later aroused the Spaniards' interest. The Guaycurú, for their part, did not hesitate to fight back, and later Spanish-Guaraní expeditions into the Chaco were frequently violent. Well into this century, Indian hostility deterred settlement of many parts of the region.

European Exploration & Settlement

Europeans first entered the upper Paraná in 1524 when Alejo García, a survivor of Juan de Solís' ill-fated expedition to the Banda Oriental, walked across southern Brazil and Paraguayto the foothills of Bolivia with Guaraní guides. García found silver in the Andes, but he died on the return journey. His discoveries resulted in the renaming of the Río de Solís as the Río de la Plata (River of Silver).

Sebastián Cabot sailed up the Río Paraguay in 1527, however, Pedro de Mendoza's

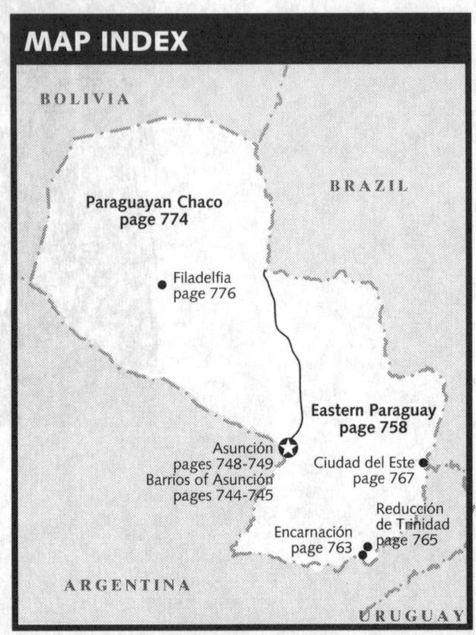

PARAGUAY

expedition made the major advance: After failing to establish a permanent settlement at Buenos Aires, his men founded a fortress called Nuestra Señora de la Asunción on the east bank of the Río Paraguay. At Asunción, the Guaraní were far more tolerant of the Spanish presence and made a military alliance with them against the hostile Chaco peoples.

The Guaraní were more sedentary than the nomadic Chaco tribes, though not as settled as the civilizations of the Andes, so relations between Indians and Spaniards took an unusual course. The Guaraní absorbed 350 Spaniards (and a few other Europeans) into their social system by providing them with women and, therefore, with food, since women bore the major responsibility for Guaraní agriculture. The Spaniards, in effect, became the heads of the household, and the *encomienda*, when it was introduced, merely ratified this informal arrangement. The Spaniards adopted Guaraní food, customs, and even language, but cultural assimilation was a two-way process. Gradually there emerged a hybrid, Spanish-Guaraní society in which the Spaniards were politically dominant. The mestizo children of the Spaniards adopted Spanish cultural values, and at the same time used the Guaraní language and followed other local customs.

The Jesuit Missions

In the colonial period, Paraguay comprised a much larger area than it does now and included large parts of present-day Brazil and Argentina. In this area, on both sides of the upper Paraná, Jesuit missionaries conducted a remarkable experiment, creating a series of highly organized settlements in which the Guaraní learned many aspects of European high culture as well as new crafts, crops, and methods of cultivation. For more than a century and a half, until the expulsion of the Jesuits in 1767 because of the local jealousies and Madrid's concern that their power had become too great, Jesuit organization deterred Portuguese intervention and protected the interests of the Spanish crown. (For more information on the missions themselves, see the Argentine Mesopotamia chapter.)

Jesuit influence was less effective among the non-Guaraní peoples of the Chaco, whose resistance to the Spaniards discouraged any proselytizing. Martin Dobrizhoffer, an Austrian Jesuit who spent nearly 20 years in the region, wrote about these people:

> The savage Guaycurus, Lenguas, Mocobios, Tobas, Abipones, and Mbayas, wretchedly wasted the province with massacres and pillage, without leaving the miserable inhabitants a place to breathe in, or the means of resistance. To elude their designs, little fortlets are every where erected on the banks of the Paraguay, fitted up with a single cannon, which, being discharged whenever the savages come in sight, admonishes the neighbours to fight or fly.

For these Indians, admitted Dobrizhoffer, the Chaco was a refuge 'which the Spanish soldiers look upon as a theatre of misery, and the savages as their Palestine and Elysium.' There, he wrote, they had 'mountains for observatories, trackless woods for fortifications, rivers and marshes for ditches, and plantations of fruit trees for storehouses.' Having acquired the horse, groups like the Abipones and Tobas were mobile and flexible in their opposition, while the riverine Payaguá could prey upon riverboats:

> These atrocious pirates, infesting the rivers Paraguay and Parana, had for many years been in the habit of intercepting Spanish vessels freighted with wares for the port of Buenos-Ayres . . . and of massacring the crews . . . .
>
> They have two sorts of canoes; the lesser for fishing and daily voyages, the larger for the uses of war. If their designs be against the Spaniards, many of them join together in one fleet, and are the more dangerous from their drawing so little water, which enables them to lurk within the shelter of the lesser rivers, or islands, till a favourable opportunity presents itself of pillaging loaded vessels, or of disembarking and attacking the colonies . . . . For many years they continued to pillage the Spanish colonies, and all the ships that came in their way, from the city of Asumpcion, forty leagues southwards.

Several Jesuit missionaries, some of them, like Dobrizhoffer, excellent amateur ethnographers and naturalists, managed to live among the Chaco tribes from the mid-17th century, but the area remained an Indian refuge even into the mid-20th century. After secular Spaniards realized that the Chaco route promised neither gold nor silver, they abandoned the area entirely, and the most important political and economic developments occurred east of the Río Paraguay.

Independence & the Reign of El Supremo

When Paraguayans deposed their Spanish governor and declared independence in 1811, the Spanish crown declined to contest the action, since the colony was so isolated and economically insignificant. Within a few years, José Gaspar Rodríguez de Francia emerged as the strongest member of the governing junta. From 1814 to 1840, the autocratic Francia ruled the country as El Supremo.

In the late 16th century, Spanish official López de Velasco wrote that Paraguay had 'all which is necessary for sustenance, but no wealth in money, for . . . all their wealth is in the agriculture of the country.' Even in

18th-century Asunción, wrote Dobrizhoffer, money was so scarce that the 'want or ignorance of metals may be reckoned among the divine blessings and advantages of Paraguay.' Francia, recognizing Paraguay's inability to compete with its neighbors, made a virtue of necessity by virtually sealing off the country's borders to commerce and promoting self-sufficiency – subsistence on a countrywide scale.

To accomplish his goals, Francia expropriated the properties of landholders, merchants, and even the Church (converting monasteries into army barracks), establishing the state as the dominant economic as well as political power. The small agricultural surplus – mostly *yerba mate* and tobacco – was state controlled. Like his successors almost to the present day, Francia ruled by fear, confining his opponents in what JP Robertson, who claimed to be the first Englishman to visit Paraguay during the Francia dictatorship, described as 'state dungeons':

> They are small, damp vaulted dungeons, of such contracted dimensions that to maintain an upright posture in them is impossible, except under the centre of the arch.
>
> Here it is, that loaded with irons, with a sentinel continually in view, bereft of every comfort, left without the means of ablution, and under a positive prohibition to shave, pare their nails, or cut their hair – here, in silence, solitude, and despair, the victims of the Dictator's vengeance . . . pass a life to which death would be preferable . . . . The wretched, and in most cases innocent victim is left to pine away his hours in darkness and solitude.

In a precocious example of newspeak that anticipated Orwell by more than a century, Francia called his most notorious dungeon the 'Chamber of Truth.'

Francia himself was not immune to the climate of terror. After escaping an assassination attempt in 1820, El Supremo so feared assassination that his food and drink were consistently checked for poison, no one could approach him closer than six paces, the streets were cleared for his carriage, and he slept in a different place every night. In 1840 he died a natural death and was replaced by Carlos Antonio López. In 1870, political opponents who knew how to hold a grudge disinterred Francia's remains and threw them into the Río Paraguay.

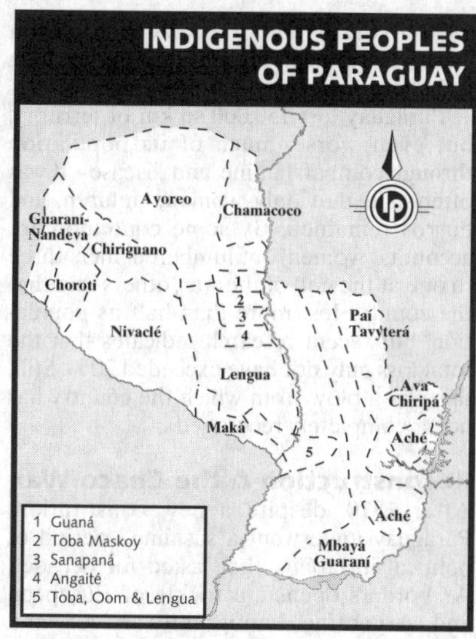

The López 'Dynasty' & the War of the Triple Alliance

With the income from state enterprises, Carlos Antonio López ended Paraguay's extreme isolation, building railways, a telegraph, an iron foundry, a shipyard, and – most importantly – an army. No less autocratic than Francia, he amassed a standing army of 28,000 men and another 40,000 reserves by the early 1860s (Argentina, at the time, had only 6000 men in uniform). His megalomaniacal son Francisco Solano López succeeded him and led the country into the catastrophic War of the Triple Alliance against Argentina, Uruguay, and Brazil.

Supporting a federalist Blanco faction in Uruguay, Solano López marched his forces across the Argentine territory of Misiones and even captured Corrientes, but Triple Alliance forces destroyed his navy and, after four years, captured Asunción. Solano López retreated into the bush but died in

1870 at the hands of Brazilian forces at Cerro Corá, near present-day Pedro Juan Caballero.

Paraguay lost 150,000 sq km of territory, but even worse, much of its population through combat, famine, and disease – it was often said that only women, children, and burros remained. By some contemporary accounts, women outnumbered men three to one at the end of the war; others said that the country lost more than half its population, but recent research indicates that the total loss may not have exceeded 20%. Still, this was a blow from which the country has never completely recovered.

Reconstruction & the Chaco War

After 1870, despite a new constitution, Paraguay underwent a sustained period of political instability that lasted for decades. As borders opened, a trickle of European and Argentine immigrants arrived and slowly resuscitated the agricultural economy. The Colorado Party, formed in 1887, helped reestablish the country as a sovereign state, encouraged agricultural development, and brought about reforms in public education. The other major party, the Liberals, took power after the turn of the century.

About this time, tension began to arise between Paraguay and Bolivia over the ill-defined borders of the Chaco, which neither country effectively occupied. As early as 1907, both began to build fortifications in anticipation of war, but full-scale hostilities did not erupt until 1932. After a 1935 ceasefire that left no clear victor, a peace treaty awarded Paraguay three-quarters of the territory in dispute. The country paid dearly, however, both financially and in the loss of another sizable portion of its population.

The reasons underlying the war remain unclear. The Paraguayans, by encouraging Mennonite immigrants to settle in the Chaco, certainly provoked the Bolivian government. However, Bolivia's war effort was rumored to have been underwritten by oil companies – one Paraguayan tourist brochure even makes the extraordinary claim that maverick United States Senator Huey Long, for whom a settlement on the Trans-Chaco highway is named, was assassinated for openly criticizing Standard's involvement on behalf of Bolivia. In any event, no oil was ever discovered, and the region is still a thinly populated backwater.

Modern Developments

After the end of the Chaco War, Paraguay endured more than a decade of disorder until the end of a brief civil war, which returned the Colorados to power in 1949. A military coup in 1954 removed the constitutional president and brought to power General Alfredo Stroessner, who despite completely bogus elections ('guided democracy'), ruled the country for 35 years in a manner that, in the former Soviet Union, might have been denounced as a 'cult of personality.'

Since Stroessner's overthrow by General Andrés Rodríguez in 1989, the government has made a concerted effort to eradicate the thousands of monuments to General Stroessner and his relatives, even renaming the city of Puerto Presidente Stroessner as Ciudad del Este, but reminders of his brutal regime linger. Some Paraguayans even express a certain nostalgia for the now elderly Stroessner (now suffering poor health in Brazilian exile), who has publicly sought permission to return to Asunción. Most, though, appreciate the demise of the Stroessner police state even if they are skeptical that it will bring any benefits beyond the freedom to say publicly what they have always thought. (For more information on the Stroessner regime and its successors, see Government later in this chapter.)

GEOGRAPHY & CLIMATE

Landlocked and isolated in the South American heartland, surrounded by gigantic Brazil, Argentina, and Bolivia, Paraguay appears much smaller than it really is. Its area of 407,000 sq km makes the country slightly larger than Germany and almost exactly the size of California. More than half of it is forested, but most of the timber has little commercial value.

The Río Paraguay, which connects the capital of Asunción with the Río Paraná, the rest of the River Plate drainage, and the Atlantic Ocean, divides the country into two unequal halves. In the smaller eastern sector, comprising about 40% of the country's territory and containing the great majority of the population, a well-watered, elevated plateau of rolling grasslands and patches of subtropical forest separates the valley of the Río Paraguay from the upper Paraná.

These rivers and the Río Pilcomayo form much of Paraguay's borders with Brazil and Argentina. The Paraná constitutes an outstanding hydroelectric resource, whose development may turn Paraguay into an energy colony of its larger neighbors. Mineral resources, including petroleum, are almost nonexistent.

Eastern Paraguay's climate is humid, with rainfall distributed fairly evenly throughout the year. In the east, near the Brazilian border, it averages an abundant 2000mm per annum, declining to about 1500mm near Asunción. Since elevations do not exceed 600m, temperatures are almost uniformly hot in summer – the average high in December, January, and February is 35°C. Winter temperatures are milder, with an average high of 22°C in July, the coldest month, although frosts are not unknown.

Paraguay is vulnerable to cold fronts known as *pamperos*, which work their way north from temperate Argentina in the spring and fall, causing temperatures to drop dramatically – as much as 20°C in only a few hours.

Paraguay's western sector is an extensive plain, known as the Gran Chaco, rising gradually toward the Bolivian border. Only about 4% of all Paraguayans live in the Chaco, whose principal economic activity is cattle ranching on very large *estancias*. Temperatures are even higher than in eastern Paraguay, often exceeding 40°C, and rainfall is erratic; precipitation does not exceed 1000mm. This, combined with high evaporation rates, makes rain-fed agriculture undependable. German Mennonite settlers have nevertheless successfully raised cotton, sorghum, and other commercial crops, as well as dairy cattle, in the region.

FLORA & FAUNA

Paraguay's vegetation correlates strongly with rainfall and diminishes from east to west. Its humid subtropical forest is densest in the moist valleys of eastern Paraguay, near the Brazilian frontier, and sparser on the thinner upland soils. The most important tree species are lapacho *(Tabebula* spp), quebracho colorado *(Schinopsis balansae)*, trébol *(Amburana cearensis)*, peroba *(Aspidosperma polyneuron)*, and guatambú *(Balfourodendron riedelanium)*. Between this forest and the Río Paraguay, the dominant vegetation is savanna with occasional gallery forests along watercourses, while west of the Río Paraguay, caranday palm savanna gradually gives way to scrub and thorn forest, including the valuable quebracho, a source of natural tannin. Throughout the country, there is a particular abundance of aroid plants (such as philodendrons) and orchids.

Paraguayan wildlife is equally diverse, but the dense human population of rural eastern Paraguay has put great pressure on the local fauna. Paraguayan mammals in danger of extinction include the giant anteater, giant armadillo, maned wolf, river otter, Brazilian tapir, jaguar, pampas deer, and marsh deer. One modest but notable wildlife success has been the rediscovery in the mid-1970s of the Chacoan peccary, which was thought to be extinct for at least half a century, and its nurture by a joint effort of Paraguayan and international conservationists.

Bird life is abundant, especially in the Chaco, and Paraguay has 365 bird species, including 21 species of parrots and parakeets, jabirú and wood storks, plumed ibis, and waterfowl, among many others. In the riverine lowlands, there are numerous reptiles, including two species of caiman, anacondas, and boa constrictors. Short-term visitors are unlikely to see the truly rare species, but they have a good chance of seeing many reptiles they have never seen before.

NATIONAL PARKS & RESERVES

Paraguay has several national parks and lesser reserves protecting an impressive diversity of habitats throughout the country, but only a few are easily accessible to travelers. The three largest are in the Chaco, while the smaller and more biologically diverse units are in eastern Paraguay. For information on Paraguayan parks and reserves, try contacting the Dirección de Parques Nacionales y Vida Silvestre (☎ 445-214), in the Edificio Ayfra, at Ayolas and Presidente in Asunción, though they're not well prepared to deal with the public. The Fundación Moisés Bertoni (☎ 608-790, mbertoni@pla.net.py), Prócer Carlos Argüello 208 in Asunción, is a private organization that works with landowners and the government in the interest of environmental conservation, and is also a good source of information on biological conservation in Paraguay.

Unfortunately, because of corruption, economic pressure, and a traditionally weak political commitment, some of Paraguay's parks have experienced serious disruption. Despite these difficulties, organizations like the Fundación Bertoni have accomplished a great deal by publicizing environmental issues both locally and abroad.

Reserva de Recursos Ypacaraí

Surrounding Lago Ypacaraí, only 30km east of Asunción, this 16,000-hectare reserve consists primarily of wetlands, but urban development is rapidly encroaching, and parts are seriously polluted.

Reserva de Recursos Ybytyruzú

Near the town of Villarrica, in the department of Guairá, this 24,000-hectare unit possesses diverse forest flora and some wetlands.

The giant armadillo is in danger of extinction.

Monumento Natural Moisés Bertoni

Only 25km south of Ciudad del Este, this small (200-hectare) unit of Alto Paraná rain forest memorializes the well-known Swiss-Paraguayan naturalist.

Monumento Natural Macizo Acahay

In the department of Paraguarí, southeast of the town of Carapeguá, 2500-hectare Acahay consists of hilly subtropical rain forest that, so far, is more a park on paper than in actual preserved green space.

Parque Nacional Ypoá

Also in the department of Paraguarí, 150km south of Asunción, this 100,000-hectare unit is a prime wetland site for migratory birds.

Refugio de Vida Silvestre Yabebyry

On the north bank of the Paraná, directly west of the town of Ayolas, this 30,000-hectare reserve includes wetland areas and forested islands in the river.

Reserva Natural del Bosque Mbaracuyú

Managed in conjunction with the Nature Conservancy and the Fundación Moisés Bertoni, this 64,000-hectare unit in Canindeyú department holds the largest remaining extents of Alto Paraná rain forest. Contact the Fundación Bertoni about guided trips.

Parque Nacional Serranía San Rafael

In hilly terrain in the southwestern departments of Itaipúa and Caazapá, San Rafael includes forests and wetlands, as well as historical sites and indigenous communities on 78,000 hectares.

Parque Nacional Tinfunqué

On the Río Pilcomayo, 300km from Asunción, this 280,000-hectare unit of savanna and marshlands is the country's second-largest park. Consisting entirely of private estancias, it is effectively a paper park, with neither a management plan nor direct protective activities, but landowners do not object to visitors. Wildlife includes capybara, swamp deer, caiman, and a great variety of bird life.

Parque Nacional Teniente Enciso

In semiarid upper Chaco, 665km from Asunción on the Ruta Trans-Chaco, 40,000-hectare Teniente Enciso features low, dense thorn forest and wildlife (similar to that of the larger and less accessible Defensores del Chaco) and also preserves Chaco War battle sites. Managed jointly by the Ministerio de Defensa and Ministerio de Agricultura y Ganadería, it has resident rangers and some visitor facilities.

Parque Nacional Defensores del Chaco

In semiarid northwest Chaco, 830km from Asunción, this 780,000-hectare park is by far the country's largest, although direct protective activities are minimal over most of the area. Its dominant vegetation is thorn forest of *quebracho*, *algarrobo*, and *palo santo*; and large mammals include jaguar, puma, tapir, peccary, and monkeys. Access is difficult but not impossible.

Parque Nacional Caaguazú

Tripled in size by recent acquisitions, 16,000-hectare Caaguazú is an area of mixed secondary Brazilian rain forest with considerable historical and anthropological interest, situated 250km southeast of Asunción in the department of Caazapá. The most common wildlife species are the coatimundi, deer, and reptiles, and there are several cave sites with aboriginal inscriptions. Because of pressure from agricultural colonists, its size has been reduced from an original 200,000 hectares, and direct protective activities are few.

Parque Nacional Cerro Corá

In the department of Amambay, 500km from Asunción, 22,000-hectare Cerro Corá is probably the most scenic of Paraguay's parks, with transitional humid subtropical forest among isolated peaks up to 450m high. It also features numerous cave sites and was the scene of the famous battle at which Francisco Solano López died during the War of the Triple Alliance. The park has a visitor center, camping area, and several *cabañas* (cabins) where visitors can lodge.

Parque Nacional Ybycuí

In the department of Paraguarí, only 150km from Asunción, 5000-hectare Ybycuí, with its humid subtropical forest, is the most accessible and probably best managed of Paraguay's parks, despite the presence of agricultural colonists and problems with timber poachers. There are several self-guided nature trails, a longer backpack trail, a visitors center, and a campground plus the ruins of Paraguay's first iron foundry. A small restaurant serves meals on weekends.

Parque Nacional Serranía San Luis

In the department of Concepción, 670km north of Asunción, 10,000-hectare San Luis is an area of rugged subtropical forest near the Brazilian border. It has limited visitor infrastructure.

Bosque Protector Ñacunday

In the department of Alto Paraná, just south of Monumento Natural Moisés Bertoni, this 1000-hectare reserve protects a small segment of Brazilian rain forest, surrounding the scenic Salto Ñacunday, an impressive waterfall.

GOVERNMENT & POLITICS

On paper, Paraguay is a republic with a 1992 constitution that establishes a strong president, popularly elected for a five-year term, who in turn appoints a seven-member cabinet to assist in governing. Congress consists of a lower Cámara de Diputados (Chamber of Deputies) and an upper Senado (Senate), elected concurrently with the president. The Corte Suprema (Supreme Court) is the highest judicial authority. Administratively, the country comprises 17 departments, the counterparts of states or provinces in other countries.

For most of the post-WWII era, however, Paraguay has been one of the Western Hemisphere's most odious and long-lasting dictatorships, whose extremely corrupt electoral politics has been controlled by a government that has allowed only token opposition. Lack of any limitation to presidential or congressional terms helped solidify the Stroessner dictatorship for 35 years until his overthrow in early 1989.

Historically, the electoral system has been simple and unrepresentative. The party with the most votes automatically gained two-thirds of the seats in Congress, effectively marginalizing the opposition. Controlling the machinery of government, the Colorado Party has been the dominant formal organization in Paraguayan political life since winning the civil war of 1947. For most of this period, the Colorados relied on Stroessner and the Paraguayan military for their privileged status. Political torture and assassination were common in those years.

Shortly after deposing Stroessner in 1989, General Andrés Rodríguez won the presidency, unopposed, in an election in which the entire spectrum of opposition parties obtained a larger percentage of congressional seats than ever before. In December 1991, in what was probably the fairest election ever held in Paraguay (undoubtedly faint praise) to that point, General Rodríguez's Colorado Party won a legislative majority. Even before the 1991 election, however, political activity and dialogue had flourished on a scale unprecedented in recent Paraguayan history.

Both the Liberals and the Febreristas, a moderate labor-oriented party, operated within the stringent bounds of acceptable public dialogue under the Stroessner regime, but others, including Liberal and Colorado factions, boycotted bogus elections. With the Liberals and Febreristas, the Christian Democrats and Mopoco (a dissident Colorado faction) now constitute the Alianza Democrática (Democratic Alliance) of political opposition.

Paraguay's 45 senators are now chosen by proportional representation in nationwide elections, while the 80 deputies are chosen geographically, by department; thanks to political decentralization, the various departments now choose their own civilian governors. The Colorados also did well in Congress, winning 24 of 45 Senate seats and 44 of 80 seats in the lower house in recent elections. Fourteen of 17 departmental governorships are under Colorado control.

Whether these promising developments will result in an enduring democracy is still uncertain because of Paraguay's authoritarian tradition and continuity among the entrenched Colorado elite. One of the great ironies of Stroessner's overthrow was Rodríguez's triumphant appearance on Paraguayan television with his daughter and grandchildren, who are also Stroessner's grandchildren since Rodríguez's daughter is married to Stroessner's son, Gustavo – so far, Paraguayans have managed to keep it in the family. A faction of the Colorado Party has lobbied for an amnesty to permit Stroessner's return from Brazilian exile.

Juan Carlos Wasmosy, Paraguay's first elected civilian president in eons, was nominated by the then ruling Colorados as a figurehead, but soon came into conflict with the still-powerful military, most notably coup-monger General Lino Oviedo. Nicknamed the 'bonsai horseman' for his diminutive stature and cavalry background, Oviedo once dressed as Julius Caesar at a costume party, but one senator remarked that the general more closely resembled Caligula.

After threatening a coup in 1996, the populist Oviedo drew a 10-year prison sentence from the military, making him ineligible for the 1998 presidential election, but his vice-presidential candidate, Raúl Cubas, took over the top spot on the ticket as the general's stalking horse. After handily defeating Alianza Democrática candidate Domingo Laíno, whose campaign focused on Colorado corruption, Cubas almost immediately pardoned Oviedo, enraging even some ardent Colorados, including his vice president, Luis María Argaña, who called for his impeachment.

In March 1999, Argaña was assassinated in Asuncíon, and Cubas resigned amid accusations that he masterminded the killing. With the support of the army and hailed by cheering crowds Senate chief Luis Angel González Macchi became the country's new president. Though Paraguayan politics remain unstable, the upheavals so far pose little threat to tourists.

Cubas, meantime, joined Stroessner in Brazilian exile, while Oviedo fled to Argentina, whose President Carlos Menem, despite vigorous criticism, granted him political asylum (Oviedo's wife is Argentine). Should the opposition Alianza take power in Argentina's 1999 presidential elections, chances are that Oviedo will flee elsewhere since Paraguay has asked for the general's extradition.

ECONOMY

Historically, Paraguay's economy has depended on agriculture and livestock. Its principal exports have been beef, maize, sugar cane, soybeans, lumber, and cotton, but a large proportion of the rural populace cultivates subsistence crops on small landholdings, selling any surplus at local markets and laboring on large estancias and plantations to supplement the household income. High transport costs, due primarily to Paraguay's landlocked isolation, have driven up the cost of its exports in comparison with other Latin American countries.

While Paraguay lacks mineral energy resources, it has begun to develop its abundant hydroelectric potential over the past 15 years through participation with Brazil and Argentina in enormous dam projects. Brazil takes most of the electricity from Itaipú, on the upper Paraná above Ciudad del Este, while corruption-plagued Yacyretá, on the border with the Argentine province of Corrientes, may never be finished (see Argentine Mesopotamia chapter). So far Paraguay has benefited by playing South America's two major economic and military powers off each other, but it risks becoming an energy colony, especially if the price of competing sources of energy drops and Paraguay cannot repay its share of capital costs, which Brazil and Argentina have already paid, and maintenance.

Paraguayan industry, which consists for the most part of the processing of agricultural products, benefits little from this enormous hydroelectric capacity. The slowdown in construction with Itaipú's completion and Yacyretá's continuing problems have nearly eliminated the economic growth of the 1970s. The economic growth rate for 1997 fell to 2%, though inflation also dropped, to about 6%. The official minimum wage is about US$240 monthly, but the Ministerio de Justicia y Trabajo (Ministry of Justice and Labor) is unable to enforce regulations, and probably 70% of Paraguayan workers fall below this level.

Paraguay's major 'source of income' is contraband including electronics and agricultural produce, most of which passes through Ciudad del Este to or from Brazil. Stolen cars, firearms, and illegal drugs, including cocaine, are other unfortunate goods that pass into or through Paraguay.

The gradual reduction of tariffs in Mercosur (see Economy in the Facts about Argentina chapter), of which Paraguay is a charter member, may reduce the prevalence of smuggling by making imported goods cheaper in the neighboring member countries of Argentina, Brazil, and Uruguay. Some Paraguayans envision the country becoming a financial center, but the *Wall Street Journal* has noted that financial irregularities are widespread, quoting the president of the Asunción stock exchange to the effect that 'Paraguayan corporate accounting statements typically contain certain anomalies. Assets are misrepresented, sales are misrepresented, and profits are misrepresented.'

Unlike most of the continent, where privatization has reduced opportunities for corruption, much of Paraguay's economy remains under state control and political influence.

POPULATION & PEOPLE

Paraguay's population of 5.2 million is about one-sixth that of the state of California, which has roughly the same area. With 500,000 residents, Asunción is by far the largest city, but only 52% of Paraguayans live in urban areas, compared with 90% in

Argentina and Uruguay. Many Paraguayans are peasant cultivators who produce a small surplus for sale.

By global and even South American welfare standards, Paraguayans rank comparatively low. Infant mortality rates are relatively high – though significantly lower than in Bolivia, Brazil, Ecuador, Guyana, Suriname, and Peru – and the life expectancy of 69 years is lower than any other South American country except Brazil, Bolivia, and Guyana. Population growth is 2.7% per annum, with a doubling time of only 26 years.

For both political and economic reasons, many Paraguayans live outside the country, mostly in Brazil and Argentina – between 1950 and 1970, more than 350,000 Paraguayans sought work in Argentina. Many political exiles have returned since the overthrow of the Stroessner dictatorship.

More than 75% of Paraguayans are mestizos, of mixed Spanish-Guaraní heritage. Almost all of these are bilingual, speaking Guaraní by preference, although Spanish is the official language of government and commerce. Even upper-class Paraguayans speak Guaraní, however.

Approximately 20% of Paraguayans are descendants of European immigrants, including about 100,000 Germans. Since the 1930s, agricultural settlement by German Mennonites, who have prospered in the difficult environment of the central Chaco, has caused ethnic friction and continuing problems with some Indian groups. Japanese immigrants have settled in parts of eastern Paraguay, along with Brazilian agricultural colonists, many of German origin, who have moved across the border in recent years. Asunción has seen a substantial influx of Koreans, mostly involved in commerce. Since the end of apartheid, a number of South Africans have moved to the department of Caaguazú.

In the Chaco and in scattered areas of eastern Paraguay, there are small but significant populations of indigenous people, some of whom, until very recently, still relied on hunting and gathering for their livelihood. According to many credible accounts, the Stroessner dictatorship conducted an active campaign of genocide against the Aché (Guayakí) Indians of eastern Paraguay in the 1970s.

Most of Paraguay's Indians live in the Chaco, where isolated groups such as the Ayoreo roamed almost untouched by European civilization until very recently. The largest groups are the Nivaclé and Lengua, both of whom number around 10,000. Many of them have become dependent labor for the region's agricultural colonists. In total, Indians comprise about 3% of the population.

EDUCATION

Education is compulsory only to the age of 12. In the country as a whole, literacy is only 90%, lowest of the River Plate republics but higher than all the Andean countries. Higher education is largely the responsibility of the Universidad Nacional and the Universidad Católica in Asunción, but both have branches throughout the country.

ARTS

In general, very little Paraguayan literature is available to English-speaking readers, but novelist and poet Augusto Roa Bastos put Paraguay on the international literary map by winning the Spanish government's Cervantes Prize in 1990. Despite having spent much of his adult life in exile from the Stroessner dictatorship, Roa Bastos focuses on Paraguayan themes and history in the larger context of politics and repressive government. He returned to Paraguay in 1996.

Some of Roa Bastos' best work is available in English. *Son of Man*, originally published in 1961, is a novel tying together several episodes in Paraguayan history, including the Francia dictatorship and the Chaco War. *I the Supreme* is a historical novel about the paranoid dictator Francia.

Works by other important Paraguayan writers, such as novelist Gabriel Casaccia and poet Elvio Romero, are not readily available in English. Josefina Pla's historical and critical works on Guaraní-Baroque art and the British in Paraguay have been translated, but her poetry has not. For books on history and other aspects of Paraguay, see Books in the Paraguay Facts for the Visitor chapter.

As in Buenos Aires and Montevideo, theater is a popular medium, with occasional offerings in Guaraní as well as Spanish. In 1933, during the Chaco War, theatergoers in Asunción swarmed to see the Guaraní dramatist Julie Correa's *Guerra Ayaa*. The visual arts are very important and popular; Asunción has numerous galleries, most notably the Museo del Barro, which emphasizes modern, sometimes very unconventional, works. Both classical and folk music are performed at venues in Asunción.

Paraguay's most famous traditional craft is the production of multicolored *ñandutí* (spider-web lace) in the Asunción suburb of Itauguá. Paraguayan harps and guitars, as well as filigree gold and silver jewelry and leather goods, are made in the village of Luque, while other high-caliber artisanal goods come from the Indian communities of the Chaco. While production for sale rather than for use may have debased the quality of certain items, such as spears and knives, wood carvings are truly appealing (the eastern Paraguayan village of Tobatí is well known for this).

SOCIETY & CONDUCT

English-speaking visitors will find Paraguay, in some ways, more 'exotic' than either Argentina or Uruguay due to the country's unique racial and cultural mix; however, Paraguayans in general are eager to meet and speak with foreign visitors. Take advantage of any invitation to drink *mate*, often in the form of ice-cold *tereré*, which can be a good introduction to Paraguay and its people.

In the Mennonite colonies of the Chaco, an ability to speak German helps dissolve barriers in this culturally insular community. It's more difficult, though, to make contact with the region's indigenous people, and it's undiplomatic to probe too quickly into the relations between the two, which are a controversial subject. From contact with the Mennonites, some Chaco Indians speak German rather than Spanish as a second language.

LANGUAGE

Paraguay is officially bilingual in Spanish and Guaraní, a legacy of colonial times when vastly outnumbered Spaniards had no alternative but to interact with the indigenous population. Though undoubtedly influenced

Common Guaraní Words & Phrases

The following is a small sample of Guaraní words and phrases that travelers may find useful, if only to break the ice. Those given are not so consistently phonetic as Spanish but are still fairly easy to pronounce. A few have obviously been adapted from Spanish.

I	*che*	many	*hetá*	water	*y*	road	*tapé*
you	*nde*	big	*guazú*	meat	*soó*	rain	*amá*
we	*ñande*	small	*mishí*	hot	*hakú*	cloud	*araí*
this	*péva*	one	*peteí*	cold	*roí*	mountain	*sero*
that	*amóa*	two	*mokoi*	woman	*kuñá*	new	*piahú*
no	*nahániri*	eat	*okarú*	man	*kuimbaé*	good	*porá*
all	*entéro*	drink	*hoiú*	person	*hente*	name	*héra*

How are you?	*Mba'eichapa?*	Where are you from?	*Moõguápa nde?*
Fine, and you?	*Iporãiterei, ha nde?*	I'm from Australia.	*Che Australia gua.*
I'm fine, too.	*Iporaãiterei avei.*	Where do you live?	*Moõpa reiko?*
		I live in California.	*Che aiko California*

PARAGUAY

by Spanish, Guaraní has also modified the European language in its vocabulary and pattern of speech. During the Chaco War of the 1930s, Guaraní enjoyed resurgent popularity when, for security purposes, field commanders prohibited Spanish on the battlefield. Listeners tuned to Paraguayan radio will hear otherwise familiar soft-drink jingles in Guaraní rather than Spanish.

Several other Indian languages are spoken in the Chaco and isolated parts of eastern Paraguay, including Lengua, Nivaclé, and Aché.

RELIGION

Roman Catholicism is Paraguay's official religion, but folk variants are important, and the Church is weaker and less influential than in most other Latin American countries. One 19th-century visitor, undoubtedly a Protestant, wrote that:

> Paraguayans were steeped in religious ignorance and floundering in idolatry . . . . The priests were ignorant and immoral, great cockfighters and gamblers, possessing vast influence over the women, a power which they turn to the basest of purposes.

Traditionally, Paraguay's isolation and the state's indifference to religion have resulted in a wide variety of irregular religious practices – according to one anthropologist, rural Paraguayans view priests more as healers or magicians than spiritual advisers. Women express greater religious devotion than men.

Protestant sects have made fewer inroads in Catholic Paraguay than in some other Latin American countries, although fundamentalist Mennonites have proselytized among Chaco Indians since the 1930s. Other evangelical groups, including the highly controversial New Tribes Mission, used to operate with the collusion and, some say, active support of the Stroessner dictatorship. This regime was no friend to the country's indigenous people, who, of course, have their own religious beliefs, many of which they have retained or only slightly modified, despite nominal allegiance to Catholicism or evangelical Protestantism.

Facts for the Visitor

Travelers will find Paraguay similar to Argentina and Uruguay in some respects but very different in others. Only facts that differ significantly from the other River Plate republics are mentioned in this chapter.

HIGHLIGHTS

For independent travelers with open minds, little-visited Paraguay has much to offer. As one of Latin America's oldest cities, Asunción's historical significance is considerable, even though it has relatively few colonial remains. Southeastern Paraguay, between Asunción and Encarnación, has important colonial remains, including those of Jesuit missions like Jesús and Trinidad, which in some ways surpasses that of Argentina's San Ignacio Miní. Fishing along the Río Paraná and the Río Paraguay is, obviously, similar to that in Argentina.

On the Brazilian frontier, the massive binational hydroelectric complex at Itaipú deserves a visit, if only to mourn Sete Quedas, a series of falls that dwarfed even Iguazú before their disappearance under a massive reservoir. Iguazú itself is easily visited from Ciudad del Este, but Paraguay has natural assets of its own in several widely dispersed national parks. The most accessible of these is Ybycuí, which preserves a representative sample of subtropical rain forest. Other reserves can be found both in eastern Paraguay and the nearly vacant Chaco region, one of South America's great wildernesses. Paraguay's bird life is exceptionally rich both in eastern Paraguay and the Chaco, although mammals and reptiles have suffered by comparison.

PLANNING

When to Go

Because of Paraguay's intense summer heat, visitors from midlatitudes may prefer the winter months from, say, May to August or September, when the country seems positively springlike. Days will normally be warm, but nights can be very cool, and frosts are not unusual.

Maps

The best maps come from the Instituto Geográfico Militar, on Av Artigas in Asunción, but the *Guía Shell* (see Travel Guides later in this chapter) contains the most useful road map of the country (despite the distracting Shell logos indicating their service station locations). The guide also includes a good general country map at a scale of 1:2,000,000, and a very fine map of Asunción, with a street index, at a scale of 1:25,000.

The Dirección de Turismo in Asunción distributes a very good city map, which includes an even more detailed *microcentro* (downtown) section, free of charge. In Filadelfia, it's possible to purchase an excellent, detailed map of the Mennonite colonies, but other maps of the country's interior towns and cities are hard to come by.

What to Bring

During the summer heat, Paraguayans dress very informally. Light cotton clothing suffices for almost all conditions except in winter, but a sweater or light jacket is advisable for changeable spring weather. If you're spending any time outdoors in the brutal subtropical sun, do not neglect a wide-brimmed hat or baseball cap, a lightweight long-sleeved shirt, and sunblock. Mosquito repellent is imperative in the Chaco and many other places.

TOURIST OFFICES

Paraguayan tourist offices are fewer than in Argentina or Uruguay and less well organized. They can be found in Asunción, Encarnación, Ciudad del Este, and a handful of other places.

The larger Paraguayan consulates, such as in New York and Los Angeles (see Embassies & Consulates), usually have a tourist representative in their delegation.

VISAS & DOCUMENTS

Paraguay requires visas of all foreigners except those from neighboring countries and Chileans (who need only national identification cards), and nationals of most Western European countries and the USA. According to the Paraguayan Consulate in Los Angeles, California, Canadians, Australians, and New Zealanders need advance visas but there is no longer any fee. Canadians should apply through the Paraguayan Consulate in New York.

Paraguay has dispensed with the tourist card it formerly required, and there are no longer any border charges except for airport departure taxes. However, be sure to get your passport stamped upon entering the country, or you may be subject to fines on leaving.

Passports are necessary for many everyday transactions, such as cashing traveler's checks, checking into hotels, and passing the various military and police checkpoints in the Chaco. Paraguay requires that foreign drivers possess the International Driving Permit, although document checks are usually perfunctory.

EMBASSIES & CONSULATES

Paraguayan Embassies & Consulates

Paraguay has diplomatic representation in neighboring countries and overseas, but its network is less extensive than Argentina's.

Argentina
(☎ 011-4812-0075)
Viamonte 1851, Buenos Aires
(☎ 03783-426576)
Gobernador Ruiz 2746, Corrientes
(☎ 03752-423850)
San Lorenzo, between Santa Fe and Sarmiento, Posadas

Australia
Paraguay does not have diplomatic representation in Australia.

Bolivia
(☎ 322018)
Av Arce, Edificio Venus, La Paz

Brazil
(☎ 045-523-2898)
Bartolomeu de Gusmão 738, Foz do Iguaçu
(☎ 242-9671)
No 1208, Rua do Carmo 20, Centro, Rio de Janeiro
(☎ 255-7818)
10th floor, Av São Luis 112, São Paulo

Chile
(☎ 639-4640)
Huérfanos 886, Santiago

UK
(☎ 0171-937-1253, 020-7937-1253 after April 2000)
Braemar Lodge, Cornwall Gardens, London SW7 4AQ

Uruguay
(☎ 400-3801)
Bulevar Artigas 1256, Montevideo

USA
(☎ 202-483-6960, fax 202-234-4508)
2400 Massachusetts Ave NW, Washington, DC 20008
(☎ 305-374-9090, fax 374-5522)
2800 Biscayne Blvd, Suite 9078A, Miami, FL
(☎ 212-682-9441)
675 3rd Ave, Suite 1604, New York, NY 10017
(☎ 310-203-8920, fax 203-8927)
1801 Ave of the Stars, Suite 421, Los Angeles, CA 90007

Embassies & Consulates in Paraguay

South American countries, the USA, and most Western European countries have diplomatic representation in Asunción, but Australians and New Zealanders must rely upon their consulates in Buenos Aires or the British Consulate.

Argentina
(☎ 442151)
Banco Nación, 1st floor, Palma 319, Asunción
(☎ 203446)
Mallorquín 788, Encarnación

Belgium
(☎ 610603)
5th floor, Juan O'Leary 409, Asunción

Bolivia
(☎ 210676)
Eligio Ayala 2002, Asunción

Brazil
(☎ 448084)
3rd floor, General Díaz 521, Asunción
(☎ 203950)
Memmel 452, Encarnación
(☎ 512308)
Pampliega 337, Cuidad del Este

Canada
(☎ 226196)
Profesor Ramírez and Juan de Salazar, Asunción

Chile
(☎ 600671)
Guido Spano 1687, Asunción

France
(☎ 212439)
Av España 893, Asunción

Germany
(☎ 214009)
Av Venezuela 241, Asunción
(☎ 204041)
Memmel 631, Encarnación

Israel
(☎ 495097)
8th floor, Edificio San Rafael, Yegros 437, Asunción

Italy
(☎ 207429)
Luis Morales 680, Asunción

Japan
(☎ 604616)
Av Mariscal López 2364, Asunción
(☎ 202288)
Carlos Antonio López 1290, Encarnación

Netherlands
(☎ 492137)
Chile 668, Asunción

Peru
(☎ 200949)
Av Mariscal López 648, Asunción

Spain
(☎ 490686)
6th floor, Yegros 437, Asunción

Switzerland
(☎ 490848)
4th floor, Juan O'Leary 409, Asunción

UK
(☎ 496067)
4th floor, Presidente Franco 706, Asunción

Uruguay
(☎ 203864)
25 de Mayo 1894, Asunción

USA
(☎ 213715)
Av Mariscal López 1776, Asunción

CUSTOMS

Paraguayan customs officially admit into the country 'reasonable quantities' of personal effects, alcohol, and tobacco; since contraband is the national sport, though, officials at overland crossings wink at anything that's not flagrantly illegal.

Nevertheless, foreign motorists may run into corrupt customs officials who claim that their vehicles may not enter the country without posting a bond of half the vehicle's local value – which is much higher than it is overseas. Anyone encountering such a problem should politely but firmly remind them that Mercosur regulations, which establish a common external tariff between Brazil, Argentina, Uruguay, and Paraguay, do not require this. Keep photocopies of vehicle documentation from neighboring countries for proof and reference when crossing borders.

MONEY

The unit of currency is the *guaraní* (plural *guaraníes)*, indicated by a capital letter G with a forward slash (/). Banknote values are 500, 1000, 5000, 10,000, 50,000, and 100,000 guaraníes; there are coins for 50, 100, and 500 guaraníes.

Annual inflation has fallen to about 6%, and prices in general are slightly lower than in Uruguay. Money is readily exchanged at casas de cambio in Asunción, Ciudad del Este, Encarnación, and Pedro Juan Caballero, but banks are the rule in the interior. Street changers give slightly lower rates than cambios, but they can be helpful on weekends or in the evening, when cambios are closed.

Most better hotels, restaurants, and shops in Asunción accept credit cards, but their use is less common outside the capital. Paraguayan ATMs generally do not recognize foreign credit cards.

Exchange Rates

Exchange houses accept traveler's checks at slightly lower rates than cash dollars, and sometimes charge commissions, although these are not as high as those levied in Argentina. German marks are more welcome in Asunción than in other South American capitals, although prices are given in US dollars, still the most popular foreign currency. There is no black market. Some travelers have reported that exchange houses will not cash traveler's checks without the bill of sale.

At press time exchange rates were as follows:

country	unit		guaranies
Argentina	Arg$1	=	₲2920
Australia	A$1	=	₲1855
Bolivia	Bol$1	=	₲513
Brazil	BraR$1	=	₲1702
Canada	C$1	=	₲1926
Chile	Ch$1	=	₲6.05
Euro	€1	=	₲3145
France	1FF	=	₲502
Germany	DM1	=	₲1680
Italy	L1	=	₲1.7
Japan	¥1	=	₲20.8
Netherlands	f1	=	₲1490
New Zealand	NZ$1	=	₲1563
Spain	1pta	=	₲19.8
Switzerland	SFr1	=	₲2033
UK	UK£1	=	₲4803
Uruguay	Ur$1	=	₲267
USA	US$1	=	₲2825

POST & COMMUNICATIONS

Postal rates are cheaper in Paraguay than in Argentina or Uruguay, but as elsewhere in Latin America, truly essential mail should be registered. Paraguayan post offices charge about US$0.25 per item for poste restante services.

Antelco, the state telephone monopoly, has central long-distance offices resembling those of Uruguay's Antel; it may soon undergo privatization. Central offices in Asunción have fiber-optic lines with direct connections to operators in the USA (ATT, MCI, Sprint), Britain, Australia, Germany, Argentina, Uruguay, Brazil, and Japan. Credit card or collect calls to the US and other overseas destinations are cheaper than paying locally. For local calls, public phone boxes (which take fichas rather than coins) are few and far between.

For an international operator, dial ☎ 0010; for Discado Directo Internacional (DDI), dial ☎ 002. The country code is ☎ 595.

BOOKS

History

Despite a slightly misleading title, J Richard Gorham's edited collection *Paraguay: Ecological Essays* (Academy of the Arts and Sciences of the Americas, 1973) contains excellent material on pre-Columbian and colonial Paraguayan history and geography.

For a standard historical account of rural Paraguay, see Elman and Helen Service's *Tobatí: Paraguayan Town*. Harris Gaylord Warren's *Rebirth of the Paraguayan Republic* tells the story of Paraguay's incomplete recovery, under the direction of the Colorado Party, from the disastrous War of the Triple Alliance.

For a general account of human rights abuses under Stroessner, see *Rule by Fear: Paraguay After Thirty Years Under Stroessner* (Americas Watch, 1985). Richard Arens' edited collection *Genocide in Paraguay* is an account of the Paraguayan government's role in the attempted extermination of the Aché Indians. Carlos Miranda's *The Stroessner Era* is a thoughtful, nonpolemical analysis of Stroessner's rise and consolidation of power, plus a short political obituary.

Natural History

Birders may want to acquire Floyd E Hayes' *Status, Distribution and Biogeography of the Birds of Paraguay* (American Birding Association, Monographs in Field Ornithology No 1, 1995).

Travel Guides

While its tourist information is limited and conventional, the local *Guía Shell* contains the most useful road map of the country. It also includes a good general country map and a very fine map of Asunción. A worthwhile acquisition for anyone spending more than a few days in the country, the guide and maps cost about US$8, but the Touring y Automóvil Club Paraguayo sells it for a slight discount to its members and to members of its international affiliates.

NEWSPAPERS & RADIO

The Stroessner dictatorship severely punished press criticism, closed opposition papers, jailed and tortured editors and reporters, and monitored foreign press agencies. Nevertheless, Asunción's daily *ABC Color* made its reputation as nearly the sole opposition to Stroessner, despite being subject to severe restrictions. An independent radio station, Radio Ñandutí, also criticized the Stroessner regime. The editorially bold newspaper *Última Hora* is very independent, breaking stories such as the deaths of army conscripts – usually termed 'suicides' – under suspicious circumstances; it also has an excellent cultural section.

El Pueblo, a small circulation organ of the Febrerista party, is independent of the government but has had little impact. *Hoy* and *Patria* (the official Colorado Party newspaper) are controlled by Stroessner relatives.

Asunción's German-speaking community publishes a twice-monthly newspaper, *Neues für Alle*, which is widely distributed throughout the country, and the weekly *Rundschau*. The *Buenos Aires Herald* and other Argentine newspapers are available in Asunción, at a kiosk on the corner of Chile and Palma, but they are hard to find elsewhere.

FILM & PHOTOGRAPHY

Asunción is one of the best places in South America to buy film, with Fujichrome 100 slide film readily available for about US$5 per roll without developing, but beware outdated rolls. This is suitable for Paraguay's tropical light conditions and verdant greens, although in the dense subtropical rain forests of eastern Paraguay it would be useful to have high-speed film, which is much more expensive and best brought from overseas.

TIME

Paraguay is three hours behind GMT except in winter (April 1 to September 30), when daylight-saving time adds an hour.

HEALTH

According to US Peace Corps volunteers, who have close contact with both rural and urban health conditions, Paraguay presents few health problems for travelers. Peace Corps officials recommend that volunteers follow the '20-meter rule' with respect to drinking water in rural areas – if the water source is within 20 meters of a latrine, do not drink it. The author has drunk tap water from Ciudad del Este all the way to Filadelfia with no ill effects, but if you have any doubts, stick to mineral water, which is readily available.

Malaria is not a major health hazard in Paraguay, but the monstrous Itaipú hydroelectric project on the Brazilian border appears to have created a new habitat for mosquitoes. The US Centers for Disease Control in Atlanta recommend chloroquine for malaria prophylaxis.

Other causes for concern, but not hysteria, are Chagas' disease, tuberculosis, typhoid, hepatitis, and hookworm *(susto)* – avoid going barefoot. Cutaneous leishmaniasis *(ura)*, a malady transmitted by sandflies that bite and resulting in open sores, is very unpleasant and can be dangerous if untreated. Yellow fever is uncommon, and there is a low risk of mosquito-transmitted dengue fever.

WOMEN TRAVELERS

Paraguay is generally safe for women travelers, but modesty is important, and women should, in general, avoid eye contact with unfamiliar males, especially in the countryside. Single women should also avoid even 'friendly' conversation with men on buses. There have been reports of kidnap and rape attempts on single women.

USEFUL ORGANIZATIONS

For visitors interested in natural history and conservation, the Fundación Moisés Bertoni (☎ 600855), Prócer Carlos Argüello 208, Asunción, is an indispensable organization that welcomes foreign visitors. Named for a 19th-century Swiss-Paraguayan naturalist, it sponsors projects that encourage biological diversity and restoration of degraded ecosystems, cooperates with the state in strengthening national parks and other reserves, promotes environmental education and research, and tries to involve Paraguayan citizens and private enterprise in conservation. Many if not most of the staff speak English.

The government organization in charge of Paraguay's national parks, working in concert with the Fundación Bertoni and the US Peace Corps, is the Ministerio de Agricultura's Dirección de Parques Nacionales y Vida Silvestre (☎ 445214). It's in the Edificio Ayfra, at Ayolas and Presidente in Asunción.

For motorists, the Touring y Automóvil Club Paraguayo is less widespread than its Argentine equivalent, but it's still a useful resource, providing information, road services, and excellent maps and guidebooks for its members and those of overseas affiliates. The Asunción office (☎ 210550, 210553) is on Calle Brasil, between Cerro Corá and 25 de Mayo.

DANGERS & ANNOYANCES

In the Chaco, especially, watch for poisonous snakes. As elsewhere in the world, you're not likely to find them unless you go looking, but the consequences of snakebite are so serious that you won't care to chance it. Differing from its northern counterparts, the Brazilian rattlesnake *(Crotalus durissus)* transmits a highly potent neurotoxin causing paralysis so severe that neck muscles cannot hold up the head, and the neck appears broken. However, you are more likely to be troubled by mosquitoes, so bring repellent, lightweight long-sleeved shirts, and a hat to protect yourself from both them and the sun.

Since the end of the Stroessner dictatorship, the police operate with less impunity than formerly, but it's unwise to aggravate either them or the military. Surprisingly, highway police appear less arbitrary than in Argentina; however, at Chaco highway checkpoints you will encounter teenage conscripts with automatic rifles as big as they are – although the rumor is that officers don't dare issue them ammunition for fear of being turned upon. Be polite, show your papers, and you are unlikely to be seriously inconvenienced. There is tension between the pacifist Mennonites and the Paraguayan military and police in the Chaco.

BUSINESS HOURS & PUBLIC HOLIDAYS

Most shops are open weekdays and Saturdays from 7 am to noon, then close until midafternoon and stay open until 7 or 8 pm. Banking hours are usually 7:30 to 11 am weekdays, but exchange houses keep longer hours.

Because of the summer heat, Paraguayans go to work very early – in summer, from mid-November to mid-March, government offices open as early as 6:30 am and usually close before noon. The following is a list of national holidays on which government offices and businesses are closed.

1 January
: Año Nuevo (New Year's Day)

3 February
: Día de San Blas (Patron Saint of Paraguay)

February (date varies)
: Carnaval – Paraguay's celebration of this popular Latin American festival is liveliest in Asunción, Encarnación, Ciudad del Este, Caacupé, and Villarrica

1 March
: Cerro Corá (Death of Mariscal Francisco Solano López) – commemorates the War of the Triple Alliance in the 1860s

March/April (dates vary)
: Viernes Santo/Pascua (Good Friday/Easter)

1 May
: Día de los Trabajadores (Labor Day)

15 May
: Independencia Patria (Independence Day)

12 June
: Paz del Chaco (End of Chaco War)

15 August
: Fundación de Asunción (Founding of Asunción)

29 September
: Victoria de Boquerón (Battle of Boquerón) – commemorating the Chaco War of the 1930s

8 December
: Día de la Virgen (Immaculate Conception) – the religious center of Caacupé is the most important site for this widespread Roman Catholic holiday

25 December
: Navidad (Christmas Day)

FOOD

The Paraguayan diet resembles that of Argentina and Uruguay in many aspects, but differs greatly in others. Meat consumption is much lower than in either of the other River Plate republics, although *parrillada*

D DONNE BRYANT

Palacio Salvo, Plaza Independencia, Montevideo, Uruguay

WAYNE BERNHARDSON

Teatro Young, Fray Bentos, Uruguay

WAYNE BERNHARDSON

Palacio Legislativo, Montevideo, Uruguay

WAYNE BERNHARDSON

Cachila, Colonia, Uruguay

WAYNE BERNHARDSON

Colonia, Uruguay

KEN LAFFAL

Casa Pueblo, Punta Ballena, Uruguay

Palacio de Gobierno, Asunción, Paraguay

KEN LAFFAL

Dancing, Asunción, Paraguay

SARAH J HAWKINS

WAYNE BERNHARDSON

Ruins of Jesuit mission, Trinidad, Paraguay

WAYNE BERNHARDSON

Horsecart builder, Piribebuy, Paraguay

(grilled meat) is still a restaurant standard. Tropical and subtropical foodstuffs, originating in the country's Guaraní heritage, play a greater role in the Paraguayan diet.

Grain, particularly maize, and tubers such as *mandioca* (manioc or cassava) are part of almost every meal. *Locro* is a maize stew resembling its Argentine namesake, while *mazamorra* is a corn mush. *Sopa paraguaya*, the national dish and a dietary staple, is not soup but rather a cornbread with cheese and onion. *Chipa guazú*, a recommended choice, is a variant of sopa paraguaya – it's a sort of cheese soufflé. *Mbaipy so-ó* is a hot maize pudding with chunks of meat, while *bori-bori* is a chicken soup with cornmeal balls. *Sooyo sopy* is a thick soup of ground meat, accompanied by rice or noodles. *Mbaipy heé* is a dessert of corn, milk, and molasses.

Manioc dishes are the province of the rural poor, since the crop yields abundantly on poor to mediocre soils. *Chipa de almidón* resembles chipa guazú, but manioc flour dominates instead of cornmeal. *Mbeyú*, also known as *torta de almidón*, is a plain grilled manioc pancake that in some ways resembles the Mexican tortilla. During Holy Week, the addition of eggs, cheese, and spices transforms ordinary food into a holiday treat.

Paraguay may be the best place in South America, other than the Guianas, to sample a variety of Asian food – Chinese, Korean, and Japanese – after a wave of immigration over the past decade. It certainly has the widest selection of any Spanish-speaking country on the continent.

DRINKS

Like Argentines and Uruguayans, Paraguayans consume enormous amounts of *mate*, but more commonly in the form of *tereré*, served refreshingly ice cold in the withering summer heat. A common story says that tereré became popular among soldiers during the Chaco War, when it was used to filter the region's muddy water, but as early as the 18th century, a Jesuit father noted that mate 'assuages both hunger and thirst, especially if . . . drunk with cold water without sugar.'

Throughout eastern Paraguay, roadside stands offer *mosto* – sugar-cane juice. *Caña*, cane alcohol, is a popular alcoholic beverage.

ENTERTAINMENT

Cinema and live theater are popular in Asunción, and the capital's cultural life is much livelier since the overthrow of Stroessner.

SPECTATOR SPORTS

Paraguayans in general are very sports-minded; the most popular soccer team, Olimpia, has beaten the best Argentine sides. Tennis and basketball have also become popular spectator sports, but golf and squash are exclusively the province of the elite.

SHOPPING

Paraguay's most well-known handicraft is ñandutí lace, ranging in size from doilies to bedspreads. The women of Itauguá, a village east of Asunción, are the best-known weavers. In the town of Luque, artisans produce stunningly beautiful handmade musical instruments, particularly guitars and harps, for surprisingly reasonable prices.

Paraguayan leather goods are excellent, and bargains are more readily available than in either Argentina or Uruguay. Chaco Indians produce carvings of animals from the aromatic wood of the palo santo, replicas of spears and other weapons, and traditional string bags *(yiscas)*.

Asunción and Ciudad del Este are good places to look for electronics, particularly to replace a lost or stolen camera. The selection is not so great as the *zona franca* (free zone) of Iquique, Chile, but prices are very reasonable.

Getting There & Away

Paraguay is a hub of sorts for Southern Cone air traffic, but overland travelers to destinations other than Iguazú Falls and Posadas will find it a bit out of the way. There is a time-consuming but intriguing and increasingly popular land crossing from Bolivia.

AIR

For North Americans and Europeans, there are more frequent air connections to Asunción's Aeropuerto via Buenos Aires or São Paulo than directly to Asunción.

Departure Tax

Paraguay collects a departure tax of US$17 for international flights from Asunción's Aeropuerto Silvio Pettirossi.

The USA

American Airlines flies twice daily to and from Miami (once via São Paulo), and daily to and from New York and Dallas. Lloyd Aéreo Boliviano (LAB) has Tuesday and Friday flights to Miami via Santa Cruz, Bolivia, but there's a long layover.

The UK & Continental Europe

Lufthansa has the most flights, which are from Frankfurt via Rio de Janeiro, São Paulo, or Ezeiza. Iberia flies daily from Madrid via Buenos Aires, but sometimes requires a change to Aerolíneas Argentinas at Ezeiza.

Neighboring Countries

Transportes Aéreos Mercosur (TAM), the successor to the former Lapsa (Líneas Aéreas Paraguayas), is rebuilding its network with a regional rather than overseas focus. It flies twice daily to Buenos Aires; daily to Brazilian destinations including Rio de Janeiro, São Paulo, and Brasilia; several days every week to the Brazilian cities of Curitiba, Porto Alegre, and Belo Horizonte; and less frequently to Santa Cruz, Bolivia.

Aerolíneas Argentinas flies three times weekly to Buenos Aires' Ezeiza. Lloyd Aéreo Boliviano flies Tuesday and Friday to Santa Cruz, with onward connections. Varig flies daily to São Paulo and Rio de Janeiro, Saturday to São Paulo only, and Thursday and Sunday to Florianópolis and Curitiba.

Other South American Countries

TAM flies several times weekly to Montevideo and Punta del Este (Uruguay), Santiago (Chile), and Lima (Perú). LanChile flies four times weekly to Santiago and three times to Iquique. The Chilean carrier Avant has recently acquired the routes of Santiago-based National Airlines, which had similar services to LanChile.

LAND

Paraguay's relatively few overland crossings underscore the country's geographical isolation. There are only three legal border crossings from Argentina, two from Brazil, and one from Bolivia.

Argentina Border Crossings

There are two direct border crossings between Paraguay and Argentina plus one that requires a brief detour through Brazil. If the corruption-plagued Yacyretá hydroelectric project on the Río Paraná is ever completed, another crossing will open from Ayolas to Ituzaingó via a bridge over the top of the dam.

Asunción to Clorinda There is frequent bus service via the Puente Internacional Ignacio de Loyola between Asunción and Clorinda, in the Argentine province of Formosa, which is renowned for ferocious customs checks.

Encarnación to Posadas Frequent bus service across the Paraná has facilitated this crossing on the Puente Internacional Beato Roque González to Posadas, in the Argentine province of Misiones. It remains possible to take a launch between the river docks, even as the Yacyretá Dam floods low-lying parts of both cities.

Ciudad del Este to Puerto Iguazú

Frequent buses connect Ciudad del Este (ex-Puerto Presidente Stroessner) to Puerto Iguazú in the Argentine province of Misiones, via the Brazilian city of Foz do Iguaçu.

Brazil Border Crossings

Ciudad del Este to Foz do Iguaçu This is the most frequently used overland border crossing between the two countries. Vehicles and pedestrian traffic move freely across the Puente de la Amistad (Friendship Bridge) that connects the two cities across the Paraná. If you plan to spend more than a day in either country, be sure to complete immigration procedures.

Pedro Juan Caballero to Ponta Porã Pedro Juan Caballero is a small town on the Paraguayan-Brazilian border, while Ponta Porã is its Brazilian counterpart. Each town has a consulate of the neighboring country. There are a regular air and bus services from Asunción to Pedro Juan Caballero, to which Ruta 5 is being paved. From the Brazilian city of Campo Grande, there are several buses and two trains daily.

Bolivia Border Crossings

This has long been one of South America's most difficult overland border crossings, lacking regular public transport between Estancia La Patria, on the Ruta Trans-Chaco, 85km from the border, and the Bolivian town of Boyuibe, 135km farther west. There is now, however, relatively reliable bus service to the Bolivian city of Santa Cruz de la Sierra. Beyond Filadelfia, the unpaved road is still subject to long delays in the event of heavy, if infrequent, rains.

In the absence of a bus, there are countless military checkpoints where you can wait for days in the hope of catching a truck across the border. One alternative is the Nasa bus from Asunción to Estancia La Patria, although Mariscal Estigarribia, where there is lodging, food, and a petrol station, would be a more comfortable place to wait.

RIVER

There are no regularly scheduled international boat services, but it's still possible to catch naval supply vessels upriver toward Brazil. See the Asunción chapter for further information.

ORGANIZED TOURS

Intertours (☎ 211747), Perú 436, Asunción, is Paraguay's largest and most experienced tour operator, offering brief or extended excursions to Asunción and its surroundings, the Jesuit mission area around Encarnación, and the Iguazú Falls of Brazil and Argentina.

Getting Around

Public transport in Paraguay is generally cheap and efficient, if not always quite so comfortable as in Argentina or Uruguay.

AIR

Domestic air services are limited. Transportes Aéreos Mercosur (TAM) has only international flights, but its affiliate Arpa and the new private carrier Ladesa serve Ciudad del Este and perhaps Encarnación. Transporte Aéreo Militar (TAM), the air force's passenger service, flies to isolated parts of the Chaco. A one-way ticket from Asunción to Ciudad del Este costs around US$75. For further details, see the appropriate geographical entries.

BUS

The quality of bus services varies considerably, depending on whether you take *servicio removido*, which makes flag stops, or *servicio directo*, which stops only at fixed locations in each city or town. Other common terms are *regular* (buses that stop at every shady spot along the highway), *común* (a basic bus that stops in only a limited number of places), and *ejecutivo* (a faster, deluxe bus with toilets, tea and coffee service, and other facilities). Larger Paraguayan cities have central bus terminals, but in those cities that do not, bus companies are within easy walking distance of one another, usually around the plaza.

Buses run very frequently to destinations all around the country, and only on or near holidays should reservations be necessary. Fares are very reasonable – for example, Asunción to Filadelfia, a distance of about 450km, costs only about US$11.

TRAIN

Paraguay's antique, wood-burning trains are more entertaining than practical. Visitors to Asunción should not miss the short ride to Areguá, on the shores of Lago Ypacaraí, but it's basically a day excursion.

CAR

Unfortunately, Paraguayans appear to be taking driving lessons from their Argentine neighbors, with all the hazards that implies – like high-speed tailgating and passing on blind curves. Driving in Paraguay also presents some problems that are less common to Argentina and Uruguay, most notably the presence of high-wheeled wooden oxcarts and livestock on the road. For the most part, carts stick to tracks that parallel the highway, but on occasion they must cross. Everywhere in the country, but especially in the Chaco, watch for cattle on the road. Such hazards make driving at night inadvisable.

Paraguay formally requires the International Driving Permit, as well as a state or national driver's license, but cars with foreign number plates are rarely stopped except at military checkpoints in the Chaco. Car theft is common, and many so-called *mau* vehicles are 'imported' illegally from Argentina and Brazil, with authorities turning a blind eye. If your vehicle is conspicuous, be especially certain it is secure.

Operating a car in Paraguay is more economical than in either Argentina or Uruguay because the price of super petrol, at US$0.50 per liter, is about half that in Argentina. The country also offers an abundance of cheap spares; if you need to purchase tires, Asunción is the place to do so. If you need repairs, competent Paraguayan mechanics are much cheaper than those in Argentina.

The Touring y Automóvil Club Paraguayo (☎ 215011), on Brasil between Cerro Corá and 25 de Mayo, Asunción, is the equivalent of Argentina's ACA. Though less widespread than ACA, they are nonetheless friendly and helpful.

BOAT

Upriver services from Asunción are unpredictable, but see the Asunción chapter for suggestions.

LOCAL TRANSPORT

To/From the Airport

Except in Asunción, air travel is infrequent in Paraguay, but Asunción city buses go to Aeropuerto Silvio Pettirossi. For details, see the Asunción chapter.

Bus

Asunción has an extensive public transport system, but late-night buses are less frequent than in Buenos Aires. As in Argentina, the driver or conductor will ask your destination. Retain your ticket, since an inspector may check it. The standard fare is about US$0.40.

Buses to Asunción suburbs like San Lorenzo, Villa Hayes, and Areguá leave from downtown as well as from the bus terminal. See the Asunción section for details.

Taxi

Cabs operate on the basis of direct meter readings. Fares are slightly cheaper than Argentina and Uruguay, but after midnight drivers are likely to levy a surcharge. There is often a small luggage surcharge as well.

Asunción

From its central location on the Río Paraguay, Asunción has always been landlocked Paraguay's link to the outside world and the pivot of its political, economic, and cultural life. Even though only about 20% of the country's population lives in the capital and its suburbs, most of the remainder lives within about 150km of here. Unlike Buenos Aires and other Latin American metropolises, Asunción has sprouted relatively few skyscrapers, so the sun still reaches the sidewalks of narrow downtown streets – a mixed blessing in summer's overpowering heat, relieved only by shady plazas. Although Asunción has some industry on its outskirts, mostly the processing of agricultural materials, its economy is really administrative and commercial.

HISTORY

Founded in 1537 by Juan de Salazar, an officer from Pedro de Mendoza's failed colony at Buenos Aires, Asunción enjoyed abundant food supplies and a hospitable Guaraní population. By 1541, its European residents numbered about 600 and, until the refounding of Buenos Aires in 1580, it was the River Plate region's most important settlement. Spaniards initially expected Asunción to be the gateway to Perú, but the hot, dry Chaco, with its hostile Indians, proved to be an insuperable barrier to travel and was superseded by the route down the eastern side of the Andes to Salta, Tucumán, Córdoba, and Buenos Aires.

By European standards, colonial Asunción was a stagnant backwater. Austrian Jesuit missionary Martin Dobrizhoffer, who visited in the mid-18th century, was unimpressed with the city and its society:

> Neither splendid edifices nor city fortifications are here to be found. Many of the houses are of stone or brick, and roofed with tiles, but none of them are above one story high. The monasteries are nearly of the same description, possessing nothing by which you could recognise the church. The streets are crooked, and impeded with ditches and stones thrown out of their places, to the imminent peril of both men and horses. It has but one market-place, and that covered with grass. The governor and bishop have resided here since the time of Charles V, though neither has any proper seat . . . Even matrons of the higher rank, boys, girls, and all the lower orders speak Guarany, though the generality have some acquaintance with Spanish. To say the truth, they mingle both, and speak neither correctly . . . . The Spanish miserably corrupted the Indian, and the Indian the Spanish language.

After independence in 1811, little changed during José Gaspar Rodríguez de Francia's isolationist dictatorship. Englishman JP Robertson, during a visit near the end of Francia's rule, also saw the capital through European eyes, but thought more highly of its residents:

> In extent, architecture, convenience, or population, it does not rank with a fifth-rate town in England . . . . Its government-house, with the title of palace, is a mean, low, whitewashed, though extensive structure. Its largest buildings – though anything but sumptuous – are the convents . . . while the great bulk of the dwellings were simple huts, constituting narrow lanes, or standing apart, surrounded by a few orange-trees. There could not be said to be more than one street in the town, and that was unpaved . . . .
>
> The inhabitants of Assumption and its suburbs amounted . . . to ten thousand . . . . The great bulk of the population was of a breed between Spaniards and Indians, so attenuated . . . as to give the natives the air and appearance of descendants from Europeans. The men were generally well made and athletic; the women almost invariably pretty.

Only with Francia's death in 1840 did Asunción's isolation end, as Carlos Antonio López opened the country to foreign influence and nearly obliterated all colonial remains in the process. López and his son, Francisco Solano López, built Asunción's major public buildings, including the Palacio de Gobierno (once intended as Francisco Solano López's residence, now housing the Congress), the Panteón de los Héroes, the train station, and an opera house modeled on La Scala (now the internal revenue building). But Francisco Solano López effectively ended this brief era of material progress by foolishly plunging Paraguay into the War of the Triple Alliance.

Ten years after the war, in 1880, a British journalist commented that these López family legacies were nothing more than 'extravagant luxuries' that stuck out like sore thumbs among their surroundings:

> These ruins of past greatness, glaring at the wretched buildings all around, looking down on the poverty-stricken people that wander under their rumbling pillars, tottering arcades, and dangling rafters, are unique. They are not grand, rather the reverse, but they must have appeared colossal to a people living in primitive dwellings.

Public improvements were indeed slow to come in the capital. Well into the 20th century, much of central Asunción went unpaved, although from 1873 a horse-drawn tramway, later upgraded to a steam locomotive, operated into Villa Morra and the northeast of the city. As European immigrants trickled in, the city gradually improved its appearance and developed exclusive residential suburbs to the east.

The Chaco War of the 1930s further retarded progress, but the city has since sprawled to encompass ever more distant areas, such as the university center of San Lorenzo. In recent decades, there's been a minor boom in high-rise downtown office and hotel construction, but the city still retains much of its 19th-century structure, with low buildings lining narrow streets. At the same time, the influx of people from the impoverished countryside has resulted in enormous shantytowns along the riverfront, the railway, or anywhere else there happens to be a vacant lot.

ORIENTATION

Asunción sits on a bluff above the east bank of the Río Paraguay. Like most colonial cities, it features a conventional grid pattern, refashioned by the irregularities of a riverside location, a slightly hilly topography, and some modern developments. Like Buenos Aires and Montevideo, the city consists of numerous barrios, but most key sights, as well as inexpensive hotels and restaurants, lie within an area bounded by the riverfront, Av Colón in the west, Haedo and Luis A Herrera in the south, and Estados Unidos to the east. There are few colonial remains.

The city center is Plaza de los Héroes, bounded by Independencia Nacional to the east, Palma to the north, Chile to the west, and Oliva to the south. Street names change on either side of Independencia Nacional. The city's commercial and financial institutions are concentrated along Palma and its eastward extension, Mariscal Estigarribia; from Plaza de los Héroes to Plaza Uruguaya, Palma and Mariscal Estigarribia are being redeveloped as a pedestrian walk.

Plaza Uruguaya is bounded by Eligio Ayala to the north, México to the west, 25 de Mayo to the south, and Antequera to the east (do not confuse Eligio Ayala with Eusebio Ayala, a major arterial leading east out of town). Although Plaza Uruguaya is a shady refuge from the midday heat, prostitutes frequent the area at night and single women will probably prefer to avoid it.

To the north, along the riverfront, irregular Plaza Constitución is bounded by Independencia Nacional to the east, El Paraguayo Independiente to the south, and 14 de Mayo to the west. It contains the Palacio Legislativo, but below the bluff, subject to flooding, lie the so-called *viviendas temporarias*, Paraguay's shantytown equivalent to Argentina's *villas miserias*. El Paraguayo Independiente, a diagonal, leads west to the Palacio de Gobierno, the presidential palace.

Asunción's most prestigious residential areas are east of downtown, out Avs España and Mariscal López toward Aeropuerto Silvio Pettirossi (ex-Aeropuerto Presidente Stroessner). Most of the capital's embassies and its best restaurants are here, in barrios such as Recoleta and Villa Morra. Northeast of downtown, at the end of Av Artigas, the Jardín Botánico was once the López family estate and is now the city's largest open space, a popular site for weekend outings.

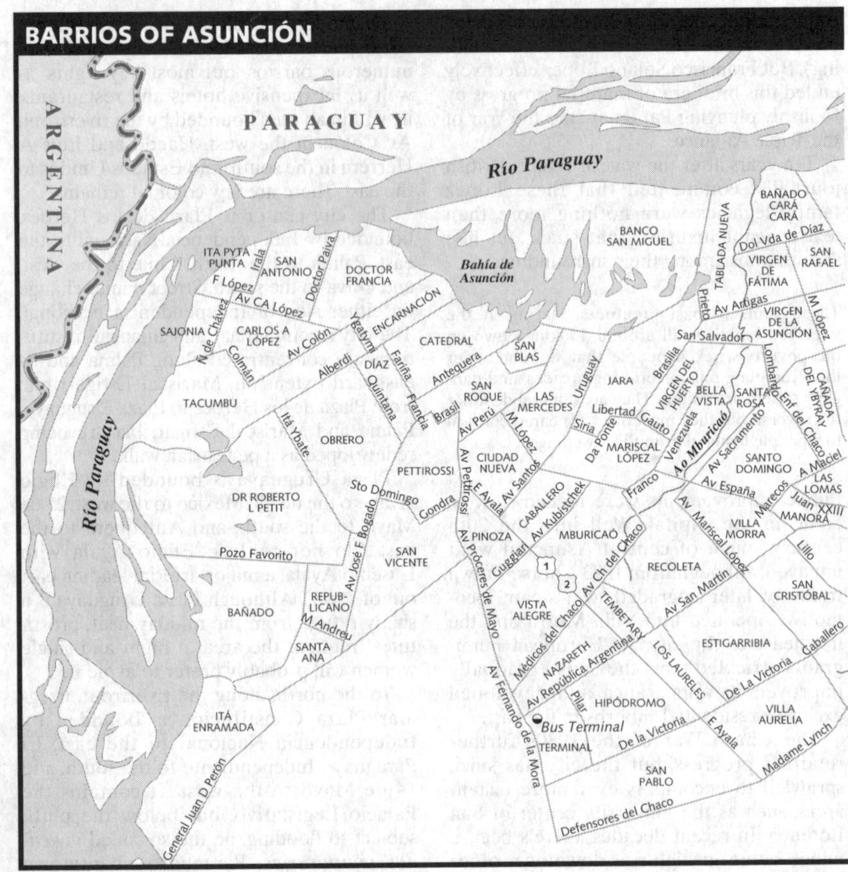

INFORMATION

Tourist Offices

The Dirección General de Turismo (☎ 441530, 441620, ditur@infonet.com.py), Palma 468 between Alberdi and 14 de Mayo, is friendly but not especially knowledgeable or helpful. It has a good city center map/brochure and several loose-leaf notebooks full of tourist information you can consult. It's open weekdays 7 am to 7 pm and Saturday 8 to 11:30 am; there's a satellite office at the bus terminal.

The Touring y Automóvil Club Paraguayo (☎ 215011) is located on Brasil, between Cerro Corá and 25 de Mayo. It sells the *Guía Shell* and its accompanying maps at a discount to members of its organization and those of affiliated overseas clubs. The staff is happy to provide other member services as well.

For more detailed maps, visit the Dirección del Servicio Geográfico Militar (☎ 206344), Av Artigas 920 at Perú.

Immigration

The Dirección de Migraciones (☎ 493646) is at the corner of Juan O'Leary and General Díaz, on the 1st floor.

Money

Cambios Guaraní is at Palma 449, but there are several other exchange houses on Palma and nearby side streets: Internacional Cambios (which does not insist on a bill of sale for cashing traveler's checks) is at Palma 364, and Banco Alemán is at Estrella and 14 de Mayo. There are also money changers with name tags near ticket offices on the 2nd floor of the bus terminal.

Post & Communications

The main post office, at Alberdi and El Paraguayo Independiente, is open weekdays 7:30 am to noon and 2:30 to 7:30 pm, Saturday 8 am to 1 pm. It also has an attractive patio garden, a museum (worthwhile if you're already in the building or nearby), and good rooftop views of downtown Asunción.

Antelco, at 14 de Mayo and Oliva, has direct fiber-optic lines to connect with operators in the USA (ATT, MCI, Sprint), Britain, Australia, Germany, Argentina, Uruguay, Brazil, and Japan for collect or credit-card calls. There is another office, much less state-of-the-art, at the bus terminal. Asunción's area code is ☎ 021.

Centro Cultural Paraguayo-Americano (☎ 224772), at Av España 352, charges US$1 to send or receive email. For more comprehensive Internet services, try the Patio de Luz (☎ 449741, pegaso@uninet.com.py), México 650, a café open 4 pm to midnight weekdays, 4 pm to 1 am Saturdays.

For private international mail service, try DHL Express, Av España 676.

Cultural Centers

Asunción's several international cultural centers offer artistic and photographic exhibitions, as well as films, at little or no cost. These include the Casa de la Cultura Paraguaya (ex-Colegio Militar), at the corner of 14 de Mayo and El Paraguayo Independiente; the Centro Juan de Salazar (☎ 449221), at Herrera 834; the Alianza Francesa (☎ 210382), at Estigarribia 1039; the Instituto Cultural Paraguayo Alemán (☎ 226242), at Juan de Salazar 310 off Av España; and the Centro Cultural Paraguayo-Japonés (☎ 661914), at Julio Correa and Portillo in Barrio San Miguel, near Av Santísima Trinidad. The Centro Cultural Paraguayo-Americano (☎ 224772), Av España 352, has American books, magazines, videos, a small café, and email access.

Travel Agencies

Asunción has a multitude of downtown travel agencies, including Inter-Express (☎ 490111), the AmEx representative, at Yegros 690. Americana Tours (☎ 490672), Alberdi 517, has English-speaking staff.

Paula Braun at Paula's Tours (☎ 446021), Cerro Corá 795, is an English-speaking

Mennonite travel agent who's a good source of information on the Chaco and will help arrange bus tickets through to Bolivia. Menno Travel (☎ 441210), República de Colombia 1042, is also Mennonite-operated.

Bookstores

Librería Comuneros, Cerro Corá 289, offers a good selection of historical and contemporary books on Paraguay. Another good shop is Librería Internacional, on Estigarribia 270 next to the Chaco Hotel. There are open-air bookstalls on Plaza Uruguay.

Laundry

Laverap is downtown at Hernandarias 636, at Teniente Fariña and Caballero, and at San José 313.

Medical Services

Asunción's Hospital de Clínicas (☎ 80982) is at the corner of Av Dr J Montero and Lagerenza, about 1km west of downtown.

WALKING TOUR

Asunción's compact downtown has a handful of remaining colonial buildings and a number of respectable museums, most of which keep erratic opening hours – it's better to phone before visiting, unless you're already in the area.

Begun in 1860 but not completed until 1892, the **Palacio de Gobierno** (presidential palace), on El Paraguayo Independiente between Ayolas and O'Leary, was intended as a residence for Francisco Solano López, who died in the War of the Triple Alliance. It is safe to approach it for photographs, at least since the ousting of Stroessner, who apparently followed the precedent of his 19th-century counterpart Francia – according to JR Robertson, El Supremo once ordered that 'every person observed gazing at the front of his palace should be shot in the act.' A flag ceremony takes place daily at sunset.

One of few colonial buildings to survive the Francia years, the restored **Casa Viola** (1750), across the street at Ayolas and El Paraguayo Independiente, is part of the **Centro Cultural de la Rivera** (☎ 442448), open weekdays 8 am to 1:30 pm and 4 to 8 pm. It presents art exhibitions, distributes a free event calendar, and houses a café and the **Museo Memoria de la Ciudad**, which chronicles Asunción's urban development. Two blocks east, at 14 de Mayo, the **Casa de Cultura Paraguaya** is a remnant of late Jesuit times that most recently served as the Colegio Militar. Overlooking the river, on Plaza Constitución at the foot of Alberdi, the **Palacio Legislativo**, begun in 1844 and completed in 1857, is home to both houses of the legislature.

At the east end of Plaza Constitución is the neoclassical **Catedral Metropolitana** (1845), whose **Museo del Tesoro de la Catedral** is open daily 8 to 11 am except Sundays. South of Plaza Constitución, on Alberdi between El Paraguayo Independiente and Benjamín Constant, the turn-of-the-century **Edificio de Correos** is the central post office and also the site of the **Museo Postal Telegráfico**. At Alberdi and Presidente Franco, the **Teatro Municipal** (1893) rests on foundations of an earlier theater that faced the river. One block west, at Presidente Franco and 14 de Mayo, Paraguayans declared independence in 1811 at the **Casa de la Independencia** (1772), which also has a museum (☎ 493918), open 7 am to 7 pm weekdays, 8 am to noon Saturday.

On the Plaza de los Héroes, at Chile and Palma, the **Panteón de los Héroes** is a public mausoleum for the country's greatest military figures, several of whom led the country into disastrous wars. Four blocks east, the small and disappointing **Museo de Bellas Artes** (☎ 447716), at Iturbe and Mariscal Estigarribia, is open Tuesday through Friday 7 am to 7 pm, Saturday 7 am to noon. Next door, the **Archivo Nacional** has fabulous woodwork and an interesting spiral staircase. At the foot of Iturbe are the remains of the **Cárcel Pública**, one of the dungeons in which Francia kept political enemies such as Pedro Juan Caballero, who committed suicide here. Two blocks east, on the north side of Plaza Uruguaya, the British-built **Estación Ferrocarril Central** dates from 1856 and displays antique steam locomotives, some of which still function on the short line to Areguá. The building served as a hospital during the Chaco War with Bolivia.

Political activists with a macabre sense of history may want to visit the site of the assassination of former Nicaraguan dictator Anastasio Somoza, on Av España between América and Venezuela. Interestingly and fittingly, this segment of Av España is officially 'Generalísimo Franco,' probably the only street in Latin America named for the late Spanish dictator. The name itself may fall victim to the de-Stroessnerization process, since most people prefer and continue to use 'Avenida España.'

PANTEÓN DE LOS HÉROES

On the Plaza de los Héroes, at Chile and Palma, a somber honor guard protects the remains of Carlos Antonio López, his son Francisco Solano López, Bernardino Caballero, José Félix Estigarribia, and other key figures (it's difficult to call most of them heroes) of Paraguay's catastrophic wars. Work commenced on the Panteón, originally intended as a religious shrine, during the rule of Francisco Solano López in 1863, but it was not finished until after the end of the Chaco War in 1936.

MUSEO ETNOGRÁFICO ANDRÉS BARBERO

Founded by and named for the former president of the Sociedad Científica del Paraguay, this anthropological and archaeological museum displays Paraguayan Indian tools, ceramics, weavings, and a superb collection of photographs, with good maps to indicate where everything comes from. For US$2, there's an excellent illustrated guide to accompany your tour. One of Asunción's best, the museo (☎ 441696), Av España 217, is open weekdays 7:30 to 11:30 am and 3 to 5:30 pm.

MERCADO PETTIROSSI & MERCADO CUATRO

The Mercado Pettirossi is a lively Saturday morning market lining both sides of several blocks east along Av Pettirossi from its beginning at Brasil. It deserves a visit, but don't make the mistake of trying to drive through it or, even worse, attempting to park. Farther east, at Pettirossi and Eusebio Ayala, is the similar Mercado Cuatro.

JARDÍN BOTÁNICO

Once the López family estate, Asunción's botanical gardens are no longer really what the name implies, but they are the city's largest open space and a popular area for weekend outings. The park contains a zoo (home to exotic rather than Paraguayan species), is the site of the municipal campground, and is also home to the displaced Maká Indians of the Chaco, for whose plight no one seems to take responsibility. Attendants collect a modest admission charge at the garden entrance, at Av Artigas and Av Primer Presidente, near the house where Uruguayan independence hero José Artigas spent his later years in exile.

Within the park, the **Museo de Historia Natural** (☎ 291255) is a vintage building housing an impressive collection of specimens, but the exhibits are poorly labeled and displayed, with no attempt to place them in any ecological context. The collection is worth seeing for the spectacular display of insects – one butterfly has a wingspan of 274mm – but some visitors may find the variety of bugs outdoors nearly as impressive. The museo is open weekdays 8 am to 4 pm, weekends 8 am to 1 pm.

From downtown, the most direct bus to the Jardín is the No 44B ('Artigas') from Oliva and 15 de Agosto, which goes directly to the gates. Or take No 23 or No 35.

MUSEO DEL BARRO

Asunción's foremost modern-art museum, in the newly developed area of Isla de Francia, displays some very unconventional work, but there are also other interesting exhibits from the 18th century to the present, including political caricatures of prominent Paraguayans. The Museo del Barro (☎ 607996) is open Wednesday to Sunday 3:30 to 8 pm.

To get there, take any No 30 bus beyond the end of Av San Martín out Av Aviadores del Chaco and look for the prominent sign – otherwise it's difficult to locate. It occupies a new facility at Callejón Cañada and Calle 1,

ASUNCIÓN

PLACES TO STAY	
7	Residencial Ambassador
26	Hotel América
32	Hotel Embajador
36	Plaza Hotel
47	Ñandutí Hotel
57	Chaco Hotel
64	Hotel de la Paz
69	Gran Hotel Renacimiento
75	Hotel Cecilia
80	Hotel Asunción Palace
81	Hotel Zaphir
82	Hotel Sahara
84	Hotel Continental
91	Hotel Hispania
93	Gran Hotel Paraná
94	Hotel Miami
99	Hotel Nova Itapúa
100	Hotel Internacional
109	Hotel Guaraní
124	Hotel Azara
126	Hotel España
127	Hotel La Española
129	Residencial Itapúa
131	Hotel Amalfi
135	Hotel Excelsior
138	Hotel Manduvirá Plaza
142	Hotel Tayí

PLACES TO EAT	
5	Formosa
12	Confitería El Molino
15	Don Vito
16	Il Capo
17	La Pérgola Jardín
27	Anahi
34	4-D
39	La Flor de Canela
40	Deutsche Bäckerei
41	Heladería Venecia
49	Confitería El Molino
52	Lido Bar
54	Munich
72	Talleyrand
73	Rincón Chileno
76	La Preferida
77	Café San Francisco
78	Buon Appetito
79	Chiquilín
87	Bolsi Bar
88	Bar San Marcos
96	Vieja Bavaria
112	Rincón Latino
114	Taberna El Antojo
122	Nick's
130	Jazmín
134	Alexander Grill
136	Patio de Comidas (Excelsior Mall)

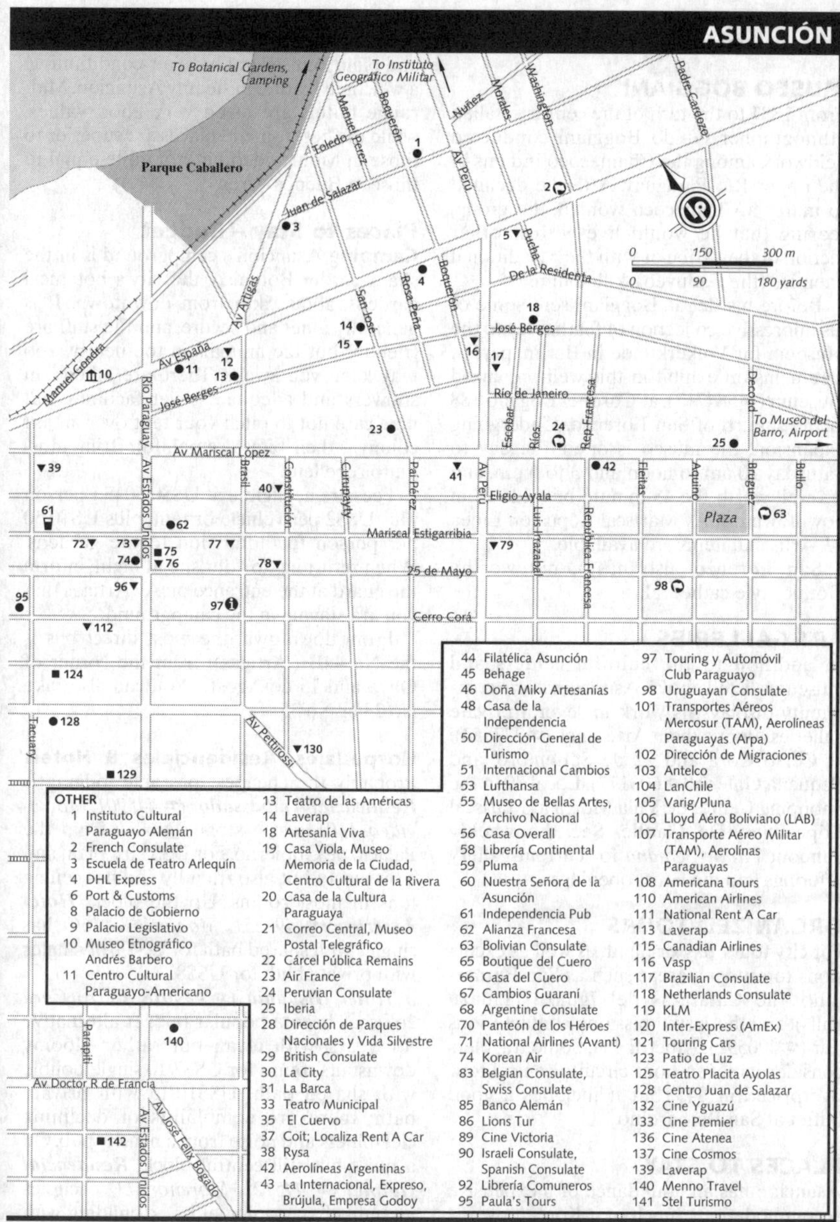
ASUNCIÓN
To Botanical Gardens, Camping
To Instituto Geográfico Militar
Parque Caballero
Toledo
Manuel Pérez
Boquerón
Nuñez
Morales
Washington
Padre Cardozo
Av Perú
Juan de Salazar
Pucha
De la Residenta
0 150 300 m
0 90 180 yards
Av Artigas
San José
Rosa Peña
José Berges
Av España
Manuel Gondra
Río Paraguay
Río de Janeiro
Escobar
Ríos
Rep Francesa
Decoud
To Museo del Barro, Airport
Av Mariscal López
Brasil
Constitución
Curupayty
Pai Pérez
Av Estados Unidos
Eligio Ayala
Luis Irrazabal
República Francesa
Brugez
Bello
Aquino
Flietas
Plaza
Mariscal Estigarribia
25 de Mayo
Cerro Corá
Tacuary
Av Pettirossi
Paraptí
Av Doctor R de Francia
Av José Félix Bogado
OTHER
1 Instituto Cultural Paraguayo Alemán
2 French Consulate
3 Escuela de Teatro Arlequín
4 DHL Express
6 Port & Customs
8 Palacio de Gobierno
9 Palacio Legislativo
10 Museo Etnográfico Andrés Barbero
11 Centro Cultural Paraguayo-Americano
13 Teatro de las Américas
14 Laverap
18 Artesanía Viva
19 Casa Viola, Museo Memoria de la Ciudad, Centro Cultural de la Rivera
20 Casa de la Cultura Paraguaya
21 Correo Central, Museo Postal Telegráfico
22 Cárcel Pública Remains
23 Air France
24 Peruvian Consulate
25 Iberia
28 Dirección de Parques Nacionales y Vida Silvestre
29 British Consulate
30 La City
31 La Barca
33 Teatro Municipal
35 El Cuervo
37 Coit; Localiza Rent A Car
38 Rysa
42 Aerolíneas Argentinas
43 La Internacional, Expreso, Brújula, Empresa Godoy
44 Filatélica Asunción
45 Behage
46 Doña Miky Artesanías
48 Casa de la Independencia
50 Dirección General de Turismo
51 Internacional Cambios
53 Lufthansa
55 Museo de Bellas Artes, Archivo Nacional
56 Casa Overall
58 Librería Continental
59 Pluma
60 Nuestra Señora de la Asunción
61 Independencia Pub
62 Alianza Francesa
63 Bolivian Consulate
65 Boutique del Cuero
66 Casa del Cuero
67 Cambios Guaraní
68 Argentine Consulate
70 Panteón de los Héroes
71 National Airlines (Avant)
74 Korean Air
83 Belgian Consulate, Swiss Consulate
85 Banco Alemán
86 Lions Tur
89 Cine Victoria
90 Israeli Consulate, Spanish Consulate
92 Librería Comuneros
95 Paula's Tours
97 Touring y Automóvil Club Paraguayo
98 Uruguayan Consulate
101 Transportes Aéreos Mercosur (TAM), Aerolíneas Paraguayas (Arpa)
102 Dirección de Migraciones
103 Antelco
104 LanChile
105 Varig/Pluna
106 Lloyd Aéro Boliviano (LAB)
107 Transporte Aéreo Militar (TAM), Aerolínas Paraguayas
108 Americana Tours
110 American Airlines
111 National Rent A Car
113 Laverap
115 Canadian Airlines
116 Vasp
117 Brazilian Consulate
118 Netherlands Consulate
119 KLM
120 Inter-Express (AmEx)
121 Touring Cars
123 Patio de Luz
125 Teatro Placita Ayolas
128 Centro Juan de Salazar
132 Cine Yguazú
133 Cine Premier
136 Cine Atenea
137 Cine Cosmos
139 Laverap
140 Menno Travel
141 Stel Turismo

just off Av Aviadores del Chaco; ask the driver to drop you at Av Molas López.

MUSEO BOGGIANI

From 1887 to the turn of the century, Italian ethnographer Guido Boggiani conducted fieldwork among the Chamacoco Indians of the upper Río Paraguay. After he declined to marry a Chamacoco woman, the group, fearing that he would live with another faction of their tribe or with their traditional enemies (the Caduveo), killed him.

Before his death, Boggiani sent some of his impressive collection of feather art to the Museum für Volkerkunde in Berlin; part of it remains on exhibit in this well-organized museum (☎ 584717), at Coronel Bogado 888 in the suburb of San Lorenzo. Undergoing expansion, the museo is open Tuesday to Saturday 10 am to noon and 3 to 6 pm, and it's well worth the 45-minute bus ride from downtown out Av Mariscal López on Línea 27. Artisanal items are available.

San Lorenzo also has a noteworthy Gothic-style cathedral.

ART GALLERIES

In addition to the cultural centers and museums listed above, Asunción's arts community displays its work in several private galleries, among them Artesanos (☎ 227853), at Cerro Corá and 22 de Setiembre; and Pequeña Galería (☎ 603177), Local 39 in the Shopping Center de Villa Morra at Mariscal López and De Gaulle. See the weekly handout *Fin de Semana* for current gallery offerings and the latest openings.

ORGANIZED TOURS

For city tours, day or night, as well as excursions to outlying areas such as San Bernardino, the Cataratas del Iguazú (Iguazú Falls), and the Jesuit missions, contact Lions Tur (☎ 490591), Alberdi 454. Some travelers consider its seven-hour circuito central tour overpriced at $45, but it includes a good buffet at San Bernardino.

PLACES TO STAY

Asunción has an abundance of inexpensive accommodations, much of it Korean-owned after heavy immigration over the past decade-plus. Most of these hotels are clean and plain, but several have air-conditioning, a welcome feature in steamy Asunción. Midrange hotels are often very good values, while the best top-end places are superior to those in Montevideo but not quite equal to those in Buenos Aires.

Places to Stay – Budget

Camping Asunción's campground is in the shady Jardín Botánico, the city's botanical gardens, about 5km from downtown. It is generally quiet and secure, and the staff are friendly, but the animals in the nearby zoo may keep you awake. There are lukewarm showers and adequate toilet facilities, but take care not to pitch your tent over an ant colony – their bites are painful. Bring mosquito repellent.

Fees are negligible at US$0.50 per person plus US$2 per vehicle or tent, plus US$0.50 per person for admission to the gardens. When returning to your site at night, inform the guard at the entrance on Av Artigas that you are staying in the campground.

From downtown, the most direct bus is the No 44B ('Artigas') from the corner of Oliva and 15 de Agosto. You can also take No 23 or No 35.

Hospedajes, Residenciales & Hotels Probably the cheapest passable lodging is ***Residencial Ambassador*** *(☎ 445901, Montevideo 110)*, just a stone's throw from the Palacio de Gobierno. For US$5 it's plain and a bit musty, but also friendly and has ceiling fans in most rooms. Up the block, ***Hotel América*** *(☎ 493251, Montevideo 160)* has singles with shared bath for US$5, or singles with private bath for US$8.

Hotel Hispania *(☎ 444018, Cerro Corá 265)* has been a popular budget alternative for years, with clean but rather gloomy downstairs rooms for US$7/10 single/double with shared bath, US$10/13 with private bath; there are complaints of declining cleanliness and noise from a nearby pub. On a quiet but still central block, ***Residencial Itaipúa*** *(☎ 445121, Moreno 943)* occupies an unlikely neocolonial brick building with spacious, comfortable common spaces. Rates are US$7/12 with shared bath and breakfast. Just outside the busy downtown area, ***Hotel Tayí*** *(☎ 490147, Simón Bolívar 930)* costs US$10 per person.

Hotel Azara *(☎ 449754, Azara 850)*, in a garden setting, has rooms with private bath, fridge, and air-con for US$10/12. Clean and spacious, with high ceilings, ***Hotel Embajador*** *(☎ 493393, Presidente Franco 514)* has doubles with private bath starting around US$11 per person.

Hotel Nova Itapúa *(☎ 493327, General Díaz 932)* is the latest US Peace Corps hangout. Rates are US$10/18 with shared bath, US$12/20 with private bath. The congenial ***Ñandutí Hotel*** *(☎ 446780, Presidente Franco 551)* offers excellent value for US$12 per person with shared bath, US$16 with private bath. At the recommended ***Hotel Miami*** *(☎ 444950, México 449)* rates are US$14/18 with private bath, breakfast, and air-con; ask for a room away from the busy front door.

If catching an early bus, you may prefer a place across from the terminal – try friendly and quiet ***Hotel Familiar Yasy*** *(☎ 551623, Fernando de la Mora 2390)*, which charges US$7 per person with private bath; next door is an anonymous restaurant with outstanding chicken empanadas.

Places to Stay – Mid-Range

Opposite Plaza Uruguaya and next to the train station, the ***Plaza Hotel*** *(☎ 444772, Eligio Ayala 609)* is clean, quiet, secure, and also friendly, charging US$14/21 with shared bath, US$21/28 with private bath. Near the bus terminal, ***Hotel 2000*** *(☎ 551628, Fernando de la Mora 2332)* charges US$16/26.

Hotel España *(☎ 443192, Haedo 667)* is slightly more expensive at US$22/26, while ***Hotel La Española*** *(☎ 447312, Luis A Herrera 142)* charges US$23/25. At downtown ***Hotel Sahara*** *(☎ 494935, Oliva 920)* rates are US$22/36 with bath and breakfast; the street is noisy but interior rooms are quiet.

The very agreeable ***Hotel Amalfi*** *(☎ 494154, Caballero 877)* costs US$32/42. The ***Hotel Asunción Palace*** *(☎ 600966, Av Colón 415)* has undertaken improvements and is now charging US$34/44 with air-con and private bath; rooms facing the street have pleasant balconies. One of downtown's older hotels, ***Gran Hotel Renacimiento*** *(☎ 445165, Chile 388)*, opposite Plaza de los Héroes, has more personality than most others. Rates are US$35/44 with breakfast, television, telephone, and other amenities.

Roughly comparable are ***Hotel Zaphir*** *(☎ 490025, Estrella 955)*, charging about US$34/43, and ***Hotel de la Paz*** *(☎ 490786, Av Colón 350)*, for US$35/48.

At the upper end of the range, the high-rise ***Hotel Manduvirá Plaza*** *(☎ 447533, Manduvirá 345)* charges US$40/48, ***Hotel Continental*** *(☎ 493760, 15 de Agosto 420)* costs US$43/52, and ***Gran Hotel Paraná*** *(☎ 444545)*, at 25 de Mayo and Caballero, has rooms for US$55/69.

Places to Stay – Top End

In recent years, prices have risen considerably at top-end places. ***Hotel Internacional*** *(☎ 496587, Ayolas 520)* costs US$74/83, while the modern ***Chaco Hotel*** *(☎ 492066, Caballero 285)* has rooms for US$80/102 with breakfast plus use of a rooftop swimming pool.

Another step up, the ***Hotel Cecilia*** *(☎ 210365, Estados Unidos 341)* charges US$99/112. High-rise ***Hotel Guaraní*** *(☎ 491131)*, opposite Plaza de los Héroes at Oliva and Independencia Nacional, has standard rooms for US$110/134. Rates at the extravagant ***Hotel Excelsior*** *(☎ 495632, Chile 980)* start at US$150/165.

Asunción's very best is the ***Yacht y Golf Club Paraguayo*** *(☎ 906117)*, whose very name implies its price: US$143/169. It's at Av del Yacht 11 in the ritzy western suburb of Lambaré.

PLACES TO EAT

From modest snack bars to formal international restaurants, Asunción has a surprising variety of quality food. The best dining areas are downtown and the eastern barrios, around Avs Mariscal López and España.

One of Asunción's best breakfast and lunch choices is the ***Lido Bar***, opposite the Panteón de los Héroes at the corner of Chile and Palma, which offers a variety of tasty, reasonably priced Paraguayan specialties. Packed with locals, it is good for snacks at any hour. The similar ***Bolsi Bar*** *(☎ 491841, Estrella 399)* is a tobacco-free, diner-style place with attentive service. ***Bar San Marcos***, at Alberdi and Oliva, is a local classic.

Anahi, at the corner of Presidente Franco and Ayolas, is an outstanding *confitería*, with good food and ice cream at moderate prices; it's open Sunday, when most downtown restaurants close. A few doors west, toward Montevideo, is an outstanding German bakery. ***Nick's*** *(Azara 348)* is a good and inexpensive lunch or dinner choice.

Another worthwhile stop is ***Confitería El Molino***, with branches at Palma 488 and at Av España 382 *(☎ 210671)*. For Asunción's best coffee, visit the hole-in-the-wall ***Café San Francisco***, at the corner of Brasil and Estigarribia.

Rincón Chileno *(Estados Unidos 314)* has good, moderately priced Chilean food and is popular with US Peace Corps volunteers (a good source of information on the country), but the owner can get hostile if you question his mathematics. One block south, ***Vieja Bavaria*** *(Estados Unidos 422)* has good beer and short orders. It's a hangout for German visitors, but everyone is welcome. ***Munich*** *(☎ 447604, Eligio Ayala 163)* also comes recommended. The ***Deutsche Bäckerei*** *(Eligio Ayala 1189)* serves German pastries.

As elsewhere in the River Plate republics, *parrillas* are the standard. The ***Alexander Grill***, at Alberdi and Teniente Fariña, is a buffet parrilla. There are several along Av Brasilia, north of Av España, in the barrio of Mariscal López: ***La Paraguaya*** *(Av Brasilia 624)*, ***Maracaná*** at the corner of Av Brasilia and Salazar, and ***Anrejó*** *(Av Brasilia 572)*, which is also a pizzeria. ***La Paraguayita***, at Av Brasilia and República Siria, belongs to the owners of La Paraguaya, across the street.

For Italian food, try the excellent, congenial ***Buon Appetito*** *(25 de Mayo 1199)*, which is a pleasant garden setting. Also try ***Il Capo*** *(☎ 213022, Perú 291)*, ***La Stampa*** *(☎ 606085)*, at Austria and Viena in Villa Morra, or the ***Spaghettoteca*** *(Av San Martín 893)*, at Austria in Villa Morra. ***Pizzometro*** *(Bruselas 1789)*, in Barrio Luis Herrera, has good all-you-can-eat pizza. Another attractive dinner choice is ***La Pérgola Jardín*** *(☎ 210219, Perú 240)*. ***Chiquilín***, at Av Perú and Estigarribia, serves pizza and pasta.

Highly regarded ***Talleyrand*** *(☎ 441163, Estigarribia 932)*, a French-international restaurant, is expensive but worthwhile for a special occasion. ***La Maison des Alpes***, at Bruselas and Viena in Villa Morra, and ***La Preferida*** *(☎ 441637, 25 de Mayo 1005)*, a German restaurant, also merit a visit.

With its walls covered with proverbs, and shells, bottles, and bells hanging from the ceiling, ***Taberna El Antojo*** *(☎ 441743, Ayolas 631)* has great ambience and good fixed-price meals for US$7, as well as live music and dance. Service is only so-so, however.

In new quarters near Mariscal López, ***La Flor de Canela*** *(☎ 498928, Tacuary 167)* serves excellent Peruvian food – try the *surubí al ajo*, a well-prepared river fish. ***Rincón Latino*** *(Cerro Corá 948)* serves equally good but more reasonably priced Peruvian fare, including tasty pisco sours.

Asunción probably has better Asian food and greater variety than either Buenos Aires or Montevideo because of the influx of Koreans – in the area around Mercado Cuatro, at Pettirossi and Rodríguez de Francia, try ***Copetín Koreano***, on Eusebio Ayala, one block from Rodríguez de Francia and Perú. For Chinese food, check out ***Jazmín*** *(Constitución 763)*, at Av Pettirossi, ***Formosa*** *(☎ 211075, Av España 780)*, near Perú, or ***Kung Fu*** *(Luis Herrera 1031)*.

Asunción's popular ice creamery ***4-D*** has a downtown branch at Eligio Ayala and Independencia Nacional, but the original at Av San Martín and Olegario Andrade (take bus Nos 12, 16, and 28) carries a wider selection of flavors. ***Heladería Venecia*** *(☎ 23861, Mariscal López 458)*, at Perú, also has good ice cream.

The Patio de Comidas at the Excelsior Mall, on Chile close to Manduvirá, offers fast-food versions of various ethnic cuisines: ***Sugar*** (outstanding ice cream), ***Don Vito*** (empanadas), ***Sabor Brasil***, ***Chopp y Compañía***, ***Taberna Española***, ***Shangri-La***, and ***Ali Baba***. ***Don Vito*** has another branch at José Berges 595.

ENTERTAINMENT

The weekly *Fin de Semana*, a calendar of entertainment and cultural events, is widely distributed throughout the city.

Cinemas

Most downtown cinemas rarely offer anything more challenging than cheap porno or the latest Arnold Schwarzenegger flick, but a few are worth checking out. First-run films cost about US$4 to US$5 at ***Cine Premier*** *(☎ 491106)*, at Montevideo and Piribebuy; ***Cine Yguazú*** *(☎ 494427)*, at Colón and Piribebuy; ***Cine Cosmos*** *(☎ 490306)*, at Independencia Nacional and Manduvirá; ***Cine Victoria*** *(☎ 448603)*, at Oliva and Chile; and ***Cine Atenea*** *(☎ 443015)*, in the Mall Excelsior at Chile and Manduvirá.

The capital's many cultural centers (see the Information section) offer the best of foreign cinema; check *Fin de Semana* for current listings. In summer, the ***Patio del Aguacate del Teatro Municipal***, at Alberdi and Presidente Franco, offers good films outdoors (rain or not) for US$3.

Bars

For live rock and roll, try ***El Cuervo*** *(Paraguarí 120)*. The ***Independencia Pub*** *(Estigarribia 127)* also features live music.

Clubs

Several readers have praised the shows, including traditional harp music, at ***Jardín de la Cerveza*** *(☎ 600752)*, at República Argentina and Castillo in the barrio of Recoleta (opposite the elite cemetery of the same name). Most were unimpressed with the food, however. The ***Patio de Luz*** *(☎ 449741, pegaso@uninet.com.py, México 650)* is a café offering live music as well as Internet services.

Downtown, try ***Piano Bar*** *(Ayolas 520)*, at the Hotel Internacional; ***La City***, at the corner of Presidente Franco and 15 de Agosto; and ***La Barca***, on Presidente Franco between 15 de Agosto and 14 de Mayo. Most others are in residential neighborhoods east of downtown, such as the ***Muzak Mall*** *(☎ 662792)* at Ocampos and Bertoni in Villa Morra.

Theater

Asunción has numerous venues for live theater and music; the season generally runs March to October. Possibilities include the Casa de la Cultura Paraguaya (see Cultural Centers under Information); the ***Teatro Arlequín*** *(☎ 605107)*, at De Gaulle and Quesada in Villa Morra; ***Escuela de Teatro Arlequín***, at Salazar and Av Artigas; the ***Teatro de las Américas*** *(☎ 224772, José Berges 297)*; and the ***Teatro Placita Ayolas***, at the corner of Ayolas and Humaitá.

SHOPPING

Most shops are open weekdays 8 am to noon and 3 to 7 pm, mornings only on Saturday. Some keep slightly longer hours.

Artesanía Viva, José Berges 993, features Chaco Indian crafts, including ponchos, hammocks, and bags, plus books and information on Chaco Indian groups. For woodcrafts, try Behage (☎ 493279), Ayolas 222, or carver Zenón Páez (☎ 490717), Lillo 1360 in Villa Morra. There's also Doña Miky Artesanías, on Juan O'Leary between Presidente Franco and Palma.

Casa Overall (☎ 448694), Estigarribia 397, has a good selection of *ñandutí* and leather goods. For leather goods, also try Boutique del Cuero (☎ 495239), at Montevideo 329, or Casa del Cuero (☎ 492701), at Montevideo and Estrella.

For books in and on Guaraní, try Guaraní Raity (☎ 227234), Eligio Ayala 3562 in Recoleta (this is a discontinuous street from downtown). Stamp collectors should visit Filatélica Asunción (☎ 446218), Presidente Franco 845.

The open-air market on Plaza de los Héroes is a good place for crafts, but remember that items made with feathers are probably subject to endangered species regulations overseas.

GETTING THERE & AWAY

Air

Aeropuerto Internacional Silvio Pettirossi (☎ 646083) is in the suburb of Luque, east of Asunción, but is easily reached by buses out Av Aviadores del Chaco.

Airlines with representatives in Asunción, though some have their connections through neighboring countries, include the following:

Alitalia
(☎ 660435)
General Genes 490

National Airlines (Avant)
(☎ 492000)
Independencia Nacional 365

Aerolíneas Argentinas
(☎ 491011, 491012)
Av Mariscal López 706

Air France
(☎ 448442)
San José 136

American Airlines
(☎ 443331)
Independencia Nacional 557

Canadian Airlines
(☎ 448917)
Juan O'Leary 690

Iberia
(☎ 214246)
Av Mariscal López 995

KLM
(☎ 449393)
Chile 680

Korean Air
(☎ 495059)
Estados Unidos 348

LanChile
(☎ 490782)
15 de Agosto 588

Lloyd Aéreo Boliviano (LAB)
(☎ 441586)
14 de Mayo 563

Lufthansa
(☎ 447962)
Nuestra Señora de la Asunción 208

Transportes Aéreos Mercosur (TAM)
(☎ 495265)
Oliva 761

Varig/Pluna
(☎ 497351)
General Díaz and 14 de Mayo

VASP
(☎ 490555)
Juan O'Leary 689

Aerolíneas Paraguayas (Arpa), in the same offices as TAM, links Asunción with Ciudad del Este five to seven times daily and with Encarnación daily except Sunday. Líneas Aéreas del Este (Ladesa; ☎ 600948), Mariscal López 4531 in Barrio San Cristóbal, also flies to Ciudad del Este.

The air force's Transporte Aéreo Militar (TAM; ☎ 445843; yes, there are two airlines calling themselves TAM), at Oliva 471, serves off-the-beaten-track destinations in the Chaco and along the northern Río Paraguay, including Concepción, Valle Mí, La Victoria, Fuerte Olimpo, San Carlos, and Bahía Negra.

Bus

Asunción's Terminal de Omnibus (☎ 551728, 551740) is at Av Fernando de la Mora and República Argentina in the Barrio Terminal. From downtown take bus Nos 8, 10, 25, 31, or 38 from Oliva. Asunción-bound passengers should note that the toilets at the terminal charge for the privilege, so use the ones on board before you arrive.

Asunción has excellent and frequent international as well as national connections; fares vary depending on the quality of the service. Some companies continue to operate ticket offices near the port or on Plaza Uruguaya, enabling you to avoid an unnecessary trip to the terminal.

Traveling into Argentina or Brazil, it may be slightly cheaper to take a local bus across the border (for example, Asunción to Clorinda or Encarnación to Posadas) and then to purchase a long-distance bus ticket. The inconvenience of changing buses usually offsets the minor financial advantage.

Argentina Border Crossings Nuestra Señora de la Asunción (☎ 551667) and Expreso Brújula (☎ 551662, 491720), at Presidente Franco 995, run buses to Falcón, on the Argentine border, from downtown Asunción (US$2). These leave from the corner of Presidente Franco and Av Colón, hourly from 5 to 11 am and 12:30 to 5:30 pm. Nuestra Señora, Brújula, and Empresa Godoy (☎ 491720) also run eight to 10 buses daily from the terminal directly to Clorinda.

Nuestra Señora also has frequent service to Posadas (US$11, five hours); Buenos Aires (US$56, 20 hours; US$73 in *coche cama* sleeper); and daily service (except Monday) to Rosario, Argentina (US$40 to US$56, 12 hours). Chevalier Paraguaya (☎ 551660) serves Buenos Aires via Formosa and Santa Fe. Expreso Brújula also serves Resistencia and Buenos Aires frequently. La Internacional (☎ 551662, 491720), at Presidente Franco 995, goes to Buenos Aires via Formosa. In the same offices, Empresa Godoy serves Resistencia via Formosa and Buenos Aires via both Formosa and Encarnación.

La Encarnaceña (☎ 551745) also has daily service to Buenos Aires, as does Expreso Río Paraná (☎ 551733). Singer has twice-weekly buses to Córdoba (US$46, 18 hours), as does Cacorba, in the same offices as Brújula.

Brazil Border Crossings Pluma (☎ 551758, 445024), at Mariscal Estigarribia and Antequera, and Nuestra Señora frequently connect Asunción with Foz do Iguaçu (US$10, five hours). Pluma continues to São Paulo (18 hours), Río de Janeiro (US$50, 22 hours), Curitiba (14 hours), and Paranaguá (16 hours). Rápido Yguazú (Rysa; ☎ 551601, 442244) also goes to Foz and São Paulo nine times weekly and to Rio de Janeiro twice weekly, while Expreso Brújula serves São Paulo five times weekly. Catarinense (☎ 551738) provides a service to Florianópolis (US$35) via Blumenau.

Bolivia Border Crossings Stel Turismo (☎ 450043, 390340), Caballero 1340, and Yacyretá (☎ 551725) now operate three to four services weekly to the Bolivian destinations of Boyuibe (24 hours) and Santa Cruz (US$56, 30 hours), and sometimes on to La Paz. Meals are included, but carry extra water on this hot, dusty trip. If wishing to explore the Paraguayan Chaco before continuing to Bolivia, it's still a good idea to purchase your ticket in Asunción, even if you wish to board in Filadelfia or Mariscal Estigarribia.

Uruguay Border Crossings Expreso Brújula goes to Montevideo Tuesday and Friday at 1:30 pm. Coit (☎ 551738, 496197), at Eligio Ayala 693, goes to Montevideo Monday, Wednesday, and Saturday morning (US$70, 18 hours).

Chile Border Crossings Expreso Pullman Sur (☎ 551553) goes to Santiago (30 hours) Tuesday and Friday. Expreso Brújula goes there Sundays at 1 pm.

Domestic Routes There are countless buses to Ciudad del Este (US$10 to US$14, 4½ hours): try Rysa, downtown at Eligio Ayala and Antequera; Rápido Caaguazú (☎ 551665); and Nuestra Señora de la Asunción (☎ 551667, 492274), at Mariscal Estigarribia 727. To Encarnación (US$10, five hours), try Rysa, Nuestra Señora, Flecha de Oro (☎ 551641), or La Encarnaceña (☎ 551745).

For Pedro Juan Caballero, try San Jorge (☎ 554782), Cometa del Amambay (☎ 551657), La Santaniana (☎ 551607), or La Ovetense (☎ 551737). Connections between Asunción and Concepción are offered by Nueva Asunción (Nasa; ☎ 551731), La Ovetense, San Jorge, La Santaniana, and Ciudad de Concepción (☎ 551912).

La Chaqueña serves nearby Chaco destinations such as Presidente Hayes and Benjamín Aceval. Long-distance Chaco carriers are Nasa (☎ 551731), Stel Turismo (☎ 390340), at Caballero 1340, and Ecmetur (☎ 555725), with services to Pozo Colorado and Concepción (weather permitting on the dirt road from Pozo), Filadelfia (US$12, eight hours), Neuland, Mariscal Estigarribia (US$14), and Estancia La Patria, the last stop on the Ruta Trans-Chaco. Nasa is the only company to travel this route in partial daylight.

Destinations near Asunción, such as San Bernardino and Caacupé, have such frequent services that it would be awkward to list them all here; instead, refer to the destination itself for such information.

Train

Built in 1856, the Estación Ferrocarril Central (☎ 447316) is on Plaza Uruguay, at the corner of Eligio Ayala and México. Its historic steam train to Lago Ypacaraí tours the backyards of Asunción's shantytowns en route to the Jardín Botánico, Luque, Isla Valle, and Areguá. The fare to Areguá, a US Peace Corps training center, is about US$0.70 return, but services over the past few years have been so erratic that it's misleading to publish anything about schedules – go to the station in person.

Boat

An alternative way of crossing to Argentina is the launch from Puerto Itá Enramada, west of downtown, to Puerto Pilcomayo, Formosa. These leave every half hour weekdays 7 am to 5 pm, and irregularly Saturday 7 to 10 am. It's possible to return by bus from Clorinda.

As many as a dozen naval supply boats per week carry passengers up the Río Paraguay as far as Concepción; inquire at the port at the river end of Calle Montevideo, direct east of the Aduana (Customs) at the port of Asunción. These go to Isla Margarita on the Brazilian border, then cross to Porto Murtinho, Brazil, with buses to Corumbá.

GETTING AROUND

To/From the Airport

From downtown, bus No 30A takes 50 to 60 minutes to Aeropuerto Silvio Pettirossi and costs US$0.25. Taxis cost about US$15.

To/From the Bus Terminal

Bus No 8 runs from Cerro Corá to the bus terminal, as does No 25 from Colón and Oliva, No 38 from Haedo, and No 42 from Rodríguez de Francia.

Buses

Asunción city buses go almost everywhere for around US$0.25, but Paraguayans are less night people than Argentines or Uruguayans, and buses are few after about 10 or 11 pm. Plan your late-night trip well or else take a cab. On the other hand, buses start running very early in the morning, since Paraguayans start work around 6:30 or 7 am. Around noon, buses are jammed with people going home for an extended lunch, so avoid travel into outlying barrios or suburbs at this hour.

Car

Asunción has several car rental agencies: Hertz (☎ 605708), at Eusebio Ayala, Km 4.5, or at Aeropuerto Silvio Pettirossi (☎ 645600); National (☎ 491379, national@infonet.com.py), at Yegros 501; Localiza (☎ 446233), at Eligio Ayala 695; and Touring Cars (☎ 447945), at Iturbe 682. Rates start around US$40 per day with 100km included.

Taxi

Cabs are metered and reasonable, but may tack on a surcharge late at night. A cab from downtown to the bus terminal costs about US$5, to the airport about US$15.

Eastern Paraguay

East of the Río Paraguay and beyond Asunción is the nucleus of historical Paraguay, the homeland of the Guaraní people among whom the Spaniards began to settle in the 16th century. More than 90% of the country's population now lives here, mostly within 100km of Asunción, but the border towns of Encarnación, across the Río Paraná from the Argentine city of Posadas, and Ciudad del Este (formerly Puerto Presidente Stroessner), across the Paraná from the Brazilian city of Foz do Iguaçu, have grown dramatically because of the enormous binational hydroelectric projects at Itaipú and Yacyretá.

Many of Paraguay's finest cultural, historical, and natural attractions are within a short distance of Asunción, on a convenient and popular circuit from the capital. These include the weaving center of Itauguá, the lakeside resorts of San Bernardino and Areguá, the celebrated shrine of Caacupé, colonial villages like Piribebuy and Yaguarón, and, a bit farther, Parque Nacional Ybycuí. On and near the highway between Asunción and Encarnación, numerous Jesuit ruins are in equal or better repair than those in Argentine Misiones. The fast-growing contraband center of Ciudad del Este is Paraguay's gateway to the Cataratas del Iguazú, and the gigantic Itaipú hydroelectric project is itself a tourist attraction of sorts.

Circuito Central

With great hyperbole, tourist brochures label this itinerary, roughly a 200km roundtrip from Asunción, the Circuito de Oro (Golden Circuit), but its lack of truly glittering attractions should not deter you from making day trips, weekend excursions, or even longer outings from the capital.

In most of these towns and villages, people pay little attention to street names, if indeed there are any.

AREGUÁ

On the south shore of Paraguay's largest lake, Lago Ypacaraí, the resort town of Areguá is slightly higher and cooler than Asunción, just 28km away. But it is also a US Peace Corps training center, and volunteers warn that pollution from a nearby fertilizer plant has made the lake unsuitable for swimming. On the main avenue from the train station to the lake, *Hospedaje Ozli* has rooms with fans for US$6 per person, pleasant gardens, and good food at reasonable prices.

Train service is erratic (but worthwhile if it's running; inquire at the station in Asunción). There are also frequent buses on Línea 11 from Av Perú in Asunción.

ITAUGUÁ

Founded in 1728 and only 30km from Asunción, Itauguá is the home of Paraguay's famous *ñandutí* lace, a cottage industry practiced by skilled women from childhood to old age. On both sides of Ruta 2, the main highway to Ciudad del Este, weavers display their multicolored merchandise, ranging in size from doilies to bedspreads. It's possible to visit the artisans' houses, where you can see the women working on their latest project.

There are two cooperatives, the Mutual Tejedoras, at Km 28, and the Taller Artesanal, at Km 29, both open daily from 9 am to 5 pm except Sunday. Lessons and demonstrations are free. Across from the Taller, Casa Myriam is a good choice for anyone in search of a US$1500 wedding dress, hand sewn for nine months by four women. Smaller pieces cost only a few dollars; larger ones range from US$50 upward, but you can bargain with shopkeepers. Casa Servín also has quality ñandutí.

Two blocks south of the highway, opposite the plaza, the **Museo Parroquial San Rafael** displays religious and secular relics from colonial times to the present, including Jesuit- and Franciscan-influenced indigenous artwork as well as very early samples

EASTERN PARAGUAY
1 Reserva Natural del Bosque Mbaracayú
2 Reserva de Recursos Ypacaraí
3 Parque Nacional Ypoá
4 Monumento Natural Macizo Acabay
5 Reserva de Recursos Ybytyruzú
6 Monumento Natural Moisés Bertoni
7 Bosque Protector Ñacunday
8 Refugio de Vida Silvestre Yabebyry
Alto Paraguay
Río Apa
Puerto Valle Mí
Puerto Pinasco
Parque Nacional Serranía San Luis
Amambay
Parque Nacional Cerro Corá
Ponta Porã
Pedro Juan Caballero
Concepción
Río Paraguay
Cordillera de Amambay
BRAZIL
0 40 80 km
0 20 40 miles
Concepción
Horqueta
Presidente Hayes
San Pedro
San Pedro
Cordillera de Mbaracayú
Salto del Guairá
Canindeyu
Embalse Itaipú
Alto Paraná
Río Pilcomayo
Espinillo
Villa Hayes
Cordillera
Lago Ypacaraí
Tobatí
Areguá
San Bernardino
ASUNCIÓN
Caacupé
Itauguá
Piribebuy
Itá
Yaguarón
San José
Caaguazú
Lago del Río Yguazú
Itaipú Dam
Coronel Oviedo
Caaguazú
Río Monday
Foz do Iguaçu
Ciudad del Este
Puerto Iguazú
Central
Paraguarí
Chololó
Carapeguá
Villarrica
Guairá
ARGENTINA
Paraguarí
Parque Nacional Caaguazú
Formosa
Parque Nacional Ybycuí
Caazapá
Villa Florida
Caazapá
Eldorado
Río Bermejo
Parque Nacional Serranía San Rafael
San Juan Bautista
Itapúa
Santa María
Pilar
San Ignacio Guazú
Jesús
Trinidad
Neembucú
Misiones
Capitán Miranda
Río Paraná
Encarnación
San Ignacio Miní
Ayolas
Posadas
ARGENTINA

PARAGUAY

of ñandutí. Although it's dark and the musty conditions are less than ideal for preservation, the quality of the artifacts definitely justifies a visit. It's open daily 8 to 11:30 am and 3 to 6 pm. In July the town celebrates the annual **Festival del Ñandutí**.

Meals are available in the local market for less than US$1, mostly for spaghetti with meat and manioc or rice. From the Asunción bus terminal, Itauguá, Caacupé, Tobatí, and Atyrá buses leave for Itauguá (US$0.50, one hour) about every 15 minutes all day and night.

SAN BERNARDINO

In 1881, German colonists settled San Bernardino, on the eastern shore of Lago Ypacaraí, 48km from Asunción on a northern spur off Ruta 2. It soon became a recreational refuge from the capital, and it's still a weekend resort for Asunción's elite, with a wide selection of restaurants, cafés, and hotels along its shady streets and the lakeshore. There are some reasonable budget alternatives, and the lake is cleaner here than at Areguá. Artisans in the nearby village of Altos create exceptional wood carvings, particularly animal masks.

The distinguished ***Hotel del Lago*** *(☎ 2201)*, at Caballero and Teniente Weiler, has rooms for US$12 per person. More upscale lodging is available at the relatively new ***San Bernardino Pueblo Hotel*** *(☎ 2195)*, at Paseo del Pueblo and Mbocayá, for US$36/48, or ***Hotel Acuario*** *(☎ 2375)*, at Km 45 on Ruta 2. ***Restaurant Las Palmeras*** and the German ***bakery*** on Colonos Alemanes are good places to eat in town. At Km 44 on Ruta 2, ***Cuckaroochoo***, run by an American, serves burgers and apple, pecan, and lemon pies.

From the Asunción terminal, Transporte Villa del Lago (Línea 210) runs buses to San Bernardino every 20 to 30 minutes most of the day. Transporte Cordillera de los Andes (Línea 103) has slightly less frequent service.

CAACUPÉ

Every December 8 since the mid-18th century, hordes of pilgrims have descended upon Caacupé, Paraguay's most important religious center, for the **Día de la Virgen** (Immaculate Conception), but the faithful continue to arrive throughout the year. After ending their tour of duty in the Chaco, military conscripts from eastern Paraguay often walk the length of the Ruta Trans-Chaco and the last 54km across Asunción and its suburbs to the imposing **Basílica de Nuestra Señora de Los Milagros**. The basilica dominates the townscape, presiding over a huge cobblestone plaza that easily accommodates the up to 300,000 pilgrims who sometimes gather here.

Basilica de Nuestra Señora de Los Milagros

Hospedaje Uruguayo *(☎ 0511-2977)*, at Eligio Ayala and Asunción, midway between Ruta 2 and the basilica, has comfortable rooms in a subtropical garden setting for US$12/16 single/double with private bath and fan, slightly more with air-conditioning. ***Hotel La Giralda*** *(☎ 0511-2227)*, at Alberdi and 14 de Mayo, has rooms for US$12/14.

Opposite the plaza is a block of cheap restaurants and tacky souvenir stands; try also ***Restaurant Edelweiss*** for meals. At Km 69 on Ruta 2, American-owned ***Casa de Maní*** has good food.

Transporte La Caacupeña (Línea 119) and Transporte Villa Serrana (Línea 110) run buses from Asunción almost every 10 minutes between 5 am and 10 pm.

AROUND CAACUPÉ

Tobatí

About 20km north of Caacupé, this village's skilled artisans produce outstanding wood carvings – a comparatively recent development, since the craft is not even mentioned in Elman and Helen Service's classic 1954 ethnography, *Tobatí: Paraguayan Town*.

For carvings, contact Zenón Páez (☎ 0516-202), who also has a studio in Asunción (see shopping in Asunción).

PIRIBEBUY

During the War of the Triple Alliance, the village of Piribebuy briefly served as the national capital and also saw serious combat. Founded in 1640, it features a mid-18th century church in excellent repair, which retains some of the original woodwork and sculpture. The **Museo Histórico Comandante Pedro Juan Caballero**, opposite the church on the plaza, has valuable but deteriorating artifacts on local history and the Chaco War; it's open daily 7:30 am to noon and 1 to 6 pm except Sunday.

Only 74km from Asunción, on a southern branch off Ruta 2, Piribebuy is a good place for a glimpse of rural Paraguay. At its northern entrance is the government's experimental sugar-cane plantation, with a nearby mill, while across the highway peasants grow maize, beans, and manioc. At the south end of town, a skilled carpenter produces up to five traditional wooden-wheeled oxcarts of hard lapacho wood per year.

Hotel Rincón Viejo *(☎ 0515-251, Teniente Horacio Giní 502)*, a block east of the plaza, has singles/doubles with private bath for US$12/14 including breakfast. ***Hotel Los Carlos*** *(☎ 0515-223, Mariscal Estigarribia 668)* charges US$12/21.

Transporte Piribebuy (Línea 197) has buses from Asunción every half hour between 5 am and 9 pm.

AROUND PIRIBEBUY

Chololó

South of Piribebuy, the narrow, scenic paved road leads to Chololó, less a village than a series of riverside campgrounds in a verdant, relatively undeveloped area. There's a branch road to the modest **Saltos de Piraretá**, a waterfall with nearby camping areas.

Paraguarí

The landscape around Paraguarí, where the road connects with Ruta 1 back to Asunción, consists of attractive hill country, but the town itself is notable only for having expunged 'Presidente Stroessner' as a street name – though the children's playground still bears a plaque honoring Stroessner's wife, Eligia. ***Hotel Chololó*** *(☎ 0531-242)* offers reasonable rooms for US$16/20 single/double. Transporte Ciudad Paraguarí (Línea 193) has buses to Asunción every 15 minutes between 5 am and 8 pm.

About 21km south of Paraguarí on Ruta 1, the village of **Carapeguá** is noted for its cotton hammocks, known by the Guaraní term *poyvi*. The **Festival del Poyvi** takes place in November.

YAGUARÓN

Yaguarón's pride is its landmark 18th-century Franciscan church, a wooden structure 70m long and 30m wide, with a baroque altar (the free-standing bell tower is a 20th-century reconstruction, however). It's open daily 7:30 am to noon and 2 to 5 pm except Sunday, when it's open for mass only.

Yaguarón is also home to the **Museo del Doctor Francia**, 2 ½ blocks from the church in a well-preserved colonial house where Francia was appointed colonial administrator. Its collection of colonial and early independence portraiture includes likenesses of El Supremo at different ages. It's open daily 7 to 11 am and 2 to 5 pm except Sunday.

Across Ruta 1 from the church is an inexpensive, unnamed restaurant that has mediocre food but excellent homemade ice cream. It also provides basic accommodation for US$5 per person. From Asunción, 48km north, Transporte Ciudad Paraguarí (Línea 193) has buses every 15 minutes between 5 am and 8:15 pm.

ITÁ

Founded in 1539 by Domingo Martínez de Irala, Itá is known for its *gallinita* pottery of local black clay. There are frequent buses to and from Asunción, 37km away, with Transporte 3 de Febrero (Línea 159).

Southeastern Paraguay

PARQUE NACIONAL YBYCUÍ

In the department of Paraguarí, 5000-hectare Parque Nacional Ybycuí preserves one of eastern Paraguay's last remaining stands of Brazilian subtropical rain forest. Its rugged topography consists of steep hills, reaching up to 400m, dissected by creeks that form a series of attractive waterfalls and pools. In structure and species composition, the forests resemble those of Argentina's Parque Nacional Iguazú. Created in 1973, Ybycuí is the most accessible unit in the Paraguayan system.

Wildlife, though abundant, is rarely seen because the mostly secondary forest is so dense; animals are so difficult to spot that they usually hide rather than run. The exception is a remarkable assemblage of stunningly colorful butterflies. Annual rainfall is about 1500mm, while temperatures average around 22°C to 24°C.

Things to See & Do

Ybycuí is tranquil and undeveloped, although the influx of weekenders from Asunción can disrupt its peacefulness. When this happens, you can take refuge on any of several hiking trails, which are more extensive and accessible than those at Iguazú. There is a visitor center, with rangers on duty, and a brochure for a self-guided nature hike.

Sendero Mirador West of the campground, on the opposite side of the road from the ranger's house, this short but steep trail to an overlook doesn't quite repay the climb, since the forest is so dense it's hard to see out. There is wildlife, but you are likelier to hear it than see it.

Salto Guaraní Below this waterfall near the campground, a bridge leads to a pleasant creekside trail that continues to the old iron foundry at La Rosada. You will see a wealth of butterflies, including the large metallic blue morpho. Watch for poisonous snakes, but bear in mind that the rattler and coral snake are not normally aggressive, and the very aggressive yarará is nocturnal.

La Rosada The first of its kind in South America, this iron foundry was built during the government of Carlos Antonio López, but Brazilian forces destroyed it during the War of the Triple Alliance. The old waterwheel is of special interest. Located at the park entrance, 2km west of the campground, it has an adjacent museum that keeps irregular hours.

Much of Ybycuí's forest is secondary, having recovered from overexploitation during the years when the foundry operated on wood charcoal, two tons of which were required to produce a single ton of iron. Engineers dammed Arroyo Mina to provide water and power for the bellows, while oxcarts hauled ore from several different sites more than 25km away.

Places to Stay

The park has no hotels, so your only alternative is to ***camp*** at Arroyo Mina, which has adequate sanitary facilities, cold showers, and a confitería serving meals on weekends. Level sites are scarce. Fortunately, mosquitoes are also few, but swarming moths and flealike insects are a nighttime nuisance, even though they do not bite.

At the cotton-mill village of Ybycuí, ***Hotel Pytu'u Renda*** (no phone) charges US$10 double.

Getting There & Away

Parque Nacional Ybycuí is 151km southeast of Asunción. Ruta 1, the paved highway to Encarnación, leads 84km south to Carapeguá, where there is a turnoff to the park, which is a further 67km via the villages of Acahay and Ybycuí. From Asunción, Transporte Emilio Cabrera has eight buses daily to Acahay, where it is necessary to make local connections to the village of Ybycuí – a bus leaves daily at noon for the park entrance, returning to the village every morning at 7 am and 2 pm. Covered trucks also continue through the park to the village of Sargento Barrientos.

If driving, do not mistake Parque Nacional Bernardino Caballero, a historical monument with a semiabandoned museum, for Parque Nacional Ybycuí, which is several kilometers farther down the road.

VILLA FLORIDA

On the banks of the Río Tebicuary, 161km southeast of Asunción, Villa Florida is a popular but relatively expensive ***balneario*** (bathing resort) and fishing and camping spot. Several hotels charge in the US$30/40 single/double range, including the ***Hotel Nacional de Turismo*** *(☎ 083-207)*.

ENCARNACIÓN

Nothing remains of Encarnación's early Jesuit *reducción* (settlement) of Itaipúa, and this lively city of 50,000, Paraguay's southern gateway, is still a town in limbo. As the rising waters behind Yacyretá inundate its oldest barrios, with their decaying public buildings and housing, most established businesses have moved onto high ground. This migration has left the old town center as a tawdry but vibrant bazaar of cheap imported trinkets – digital watches, personal cassette players, and the like – which Argentines swarm to buy at bargain prices.

Orientation

Encarnación sits on the north bank of the Río Paraná, directly opposite the much larger city of Posadas, Argentina. The Puente Internacional Beato Roque González, built by Argentina at Paraguay's insistence as part of the Yacyretá agreement, links the two cities.

Encarnación now comprises two very different parts: an older, colonial-style quarter along the flood-prone riverfront and a newer section on the bluff overlooking the river. From the riverside, Av Mariscal JF Estigarribia leads from the old commercial center to the new one around Plaza Artigas, site of the original Jesuit mission. Most government offices and businesses have relocated to higher ground, but a few hang on.

PARAGUAY

Information

Tourist Offices The Dirección General de Turismo, Monseñor Wiessen 345, is open weekdays only. The Touring y Automóvil Club Paraguayo (☎ 202203) is on Av Caballero between Mallorquín and Av Estigarribia.

Money Cambios Guaraní is at Av Estigarribia 1405, and Banco Continental across the street at Av Estigarribia 1418. Outside regular hours and on weekends, the bus terminal is loaded with money changers. Travelers with ATM or credit cards will have to cross the river to Posadas.

Post & Communications The post office is at Capellán Molas 337, in the old city. Antelco is at PJ Caballero and Carlos Antonio López, next to Hotel Viena. Encarnación's area code is ☎ 071.

Travel Agencies El Dorado Turismo (☎ 202558) is at Av Estigarribia 964. Also try Aruba Tour (☎ 205158) at Tomás Romero Pereira 347.

Photography Serpylcolor, on the corner of Av Estigarribia and Curupayty, has cheap print film, but slide film is harder to come by. Still, travelers in Posadas may want to cross the border to load up before continuing to Iguazú or Buenos Aires.

Laundry Lavamatic is on Carlos Antonio López between Monseñor Wiessen and Curupayty. Laverap is at 25 de Mayo 485.

Medical Services The Hospital Regional (☎ 202272) is at Independencia and General Bruguez.

Things to See

At Carlos Antonio López and General Gamarra, the **Feria Municipal** (municipal market) is a warren of stalls staffed by petty merchants intent on milking every last peso out of visiting Argentines before the flood. This description may sound pejorative, but in truth the place has a vitality that transcends the dubious quality of the baubles

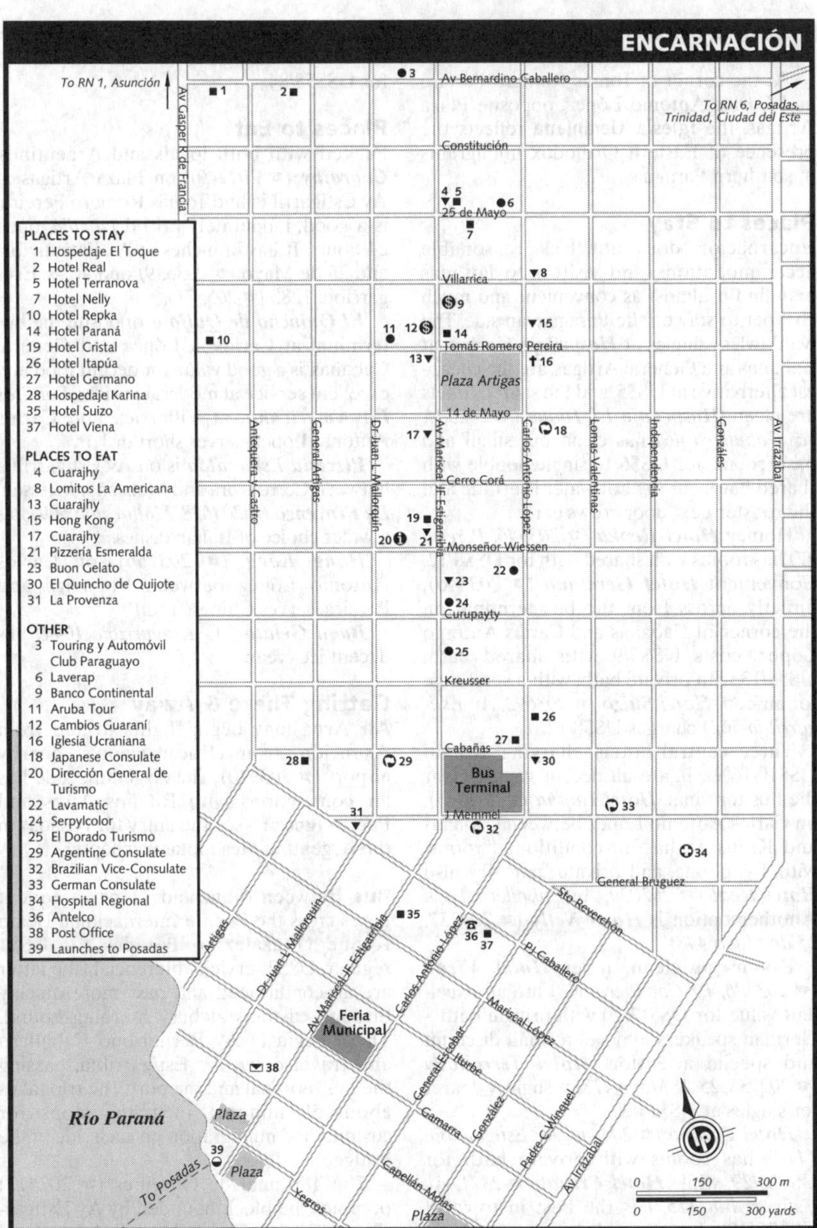
ENCARNACIÓN
To RN 1, Asunción
To RN 6, Posadas, Trinidad, Ciudad del Este
Av Bernardino Caballero
Constitución
25 de Mayo
Villarrica
Tomás Romero Pereira
Plaza Artigas
14 de Mayo
Cerro Corá
Monseñor Wiessen
Curupayty
Kreusser
Cabañas
Bus Terminal
J Memmel
General Bruguez
Av Gasper R de Francia
Antequera y Castro
General Artigas
Dr Juan L Mallorquín
Av Mariscal JF Estigarribia
Carlos Antonio López
Tomás Valentinas
Independencia
Gonzáles
Av Irrazábal
Sto Reverchon
PJ Caballero
Mariscal López
Iturbe
General Escobar
Gamarra
González
Padre C Winquel
Capellán Molas
Yegros
Artigas
Feria Municipal
Río Paraná
Plaza
To Posadas
PLACES TO STAY
1 Hospedaje El Toque
2 Hotel Real
5 Hotel Terranova
7 Hotel Nelly
10 Hotel Repka
14 Hotel Paraná
19 Hotel Cristal
26 Hotel Itapúa
27 Hotel Germano
28 Hospedaje Karina
35 Hotel Suizo
37 Hotel Viena
PLACES TO EAT
4 Cuarajhy
8 Lomitos La Americana
13 Cuarajhy
15 Hong Kong
17 Cuarajhy
21 Pizzería Esmeralda
23 Buon Gelato
30 El Quincho de Quijote
31 La Provenza
OTHER
3 Touring y Automóvil Club Paraguayo
6 Laverap
9 Banco Continental
11 Aruba Tour
12 Cambios Guaraní
16 Iglesia Ucraniana
18 Japanese Consulate
20 Dirección General de Turismo
22 Lavamatic
24 Serpylcolor
25 El Dorado Turismo
29 Argentine Consulate
32 Brazilian Vice-Consulate
33 German Consulate
34 Hospital Regional
36 Antelco
38 Post Office
39 Launches to Posadas
0 150 300 m
0 150 300 yards

PARAGUAY

and gadgets that change hands here. It's also a good, inexpensive place to eat.

At the corner of Tomás Romero Pereira and Carlos Antonio López, opposite Plaza Artigas, the **Iglesia Ucraniana** reflects the presence of Eastern Orthodox immigrants in southern Paraguay.

Places to Stay

Encarnación does not lack reasonable accommodations, and visitors to Posadas may find it almost as convenient and much cheaper to stay on the Paraguayan side. The windowless singles at ***Hospedaje Karina***, at Cabañas and General Artigas, are the cheapest alternative at US$5, and the shared toilets are clean. ***Hospedaje El Toque*** *(☎ 202604, Av Caballero 46)* has clean but small and basic rooms for US$6/10 single/double with shared bath, but the hot water is erratic and the rooster next door crows early.

Homey ***Hotel Repka*** *(☎ 203546, Pereira 47)* has rooms with shared bath for US$8/12. Convenient ***Hotel Germano*** *(☎ 203346)*, directly across from the bus terminal on the corner of Cabañas and Carlos Antonio López, costs US$6/9 with shared bath, US$8/13 with private bath, with a surcharge for air-con. ***Hotel Suizo*** *(☎ 203692, Av Estigarribia 562)* charges US$8/12.

Three central hotels, charging around US$10/16 each, are all decent values. Near the bus terminal, ***Hotel Itapúa*** *(☎ 205045)*, on Carlos Antonio López between Cabañas and Kreusser, has air-conditioned rooms with TV, phone, and private bath. Try also ***Hotel Real*** *(☎ 202020, Av Caballero 170)*. Another option is ***Hotel Nelly*** *(☎ 204737, 25 de Mayo 448)*.

Rooms at clean, quiet ***Hotel Viena*** *(☎ 203486, PJ Caballero 568)* are an excellent value for US$12/20 with private bath – German speakers may get a small discount and special attention. ***Hotel Terranova*** *(☎ 202038, 25 de Mayo 413)* is slightly dearer for singles at US$14/20.

Hotel Paraná *(☎ 204440, Av Estigarribia 1414)* has rooms with private bath for US$20/29, while ***Hotel Cristal*** *(☎ 2371, Av Estigarribia 1157)* is the best in town at US$35/48. Just outside town, in Villa Quitería at Ruta 1, Km 361, the ***Novotel*** *(☎ 207248)* has first-class accommodations for US$55/84.

Places to Eat

Packed with both locals and Argentines, ***Cuarajhy*** *(☎ 204249)*, on Plaza Artigas at Av Estigarribia and Tomás Romero Pereira, is a good, moderately priced *parrilla*, open 24 hours. It has branches at Av Estigarribia and 25 de Mayo *(☎ 203639)* and at Av Estigarribia 1285 *(☎ 205571)*.

El Quincho de Quijote, opposite the bus terminal at Carlos A López and General Cabañas, is a good value for decent food and excellent service at moderate prices. ***Lomitos La Americana***, at Villarrica and Carlos Antonio López, serves short orders.

Pizzería Esmeralda is on Av Estigarribia between Cerro Corá and Monseñor Wiessen. ***La Provenza*** *(☎ 204618, Mallorquín 609)* has a wider choice of Italian dishes.

Hong Kong *(☎ 203166)*, on Carlos Antonio López between Villarrica and Pereira, serves Chinese food.

Buon Gelato *(Av Estigarribia 1044)* has decent ice cream.

Getting There & Away

Air Arpa may begin flights to and from Asunción from Encarnación's nearby airport (☎ 203940). The Argentine side has air connections with Buenos Aires and Puerto Iguazú – see the entry for Posadas in the Argentine Mesopotamia chapter.

Bus Between 6 am and 11 pm, frequent buses cross the Puente Internacional Beato Roque González to Posadas for US$1 regular, US$2 servicio diferencial (the latter are air-conditioned and pass more quickly through customs at busy morning hours). These begin at Av Bernardino Caballero and travel down Av Estigarribia, passing the bus terminal and the port. The trip takes about 50 minutes, including stops for customs and immigration on each side of the bridge.

The Terminal de Ómnibus (☎ 202412) occupies the block bounded by Av Estigarribia, Cabañas, Carlos Antonio López, and

Memmel. The Oficina de Control at the Terminal posts a complete list of long-distance buses.

Several companies offer daily service to Buenos Aires (US$42, 18 hours), including La Encarnaceña (☎ 203448), Río Paraná (☎ 202606), and Rysa (☎ 203311). There are many more departures from Posadas, where prices are slightly lower.

Domestically, there are numerous buses to Asunción (US$10, five hours), with Flecha de Oro, La Encarnaceña, Nuestra Señora (☎ 203527), and Rysa. Ten companies, including La Encarnaceña, Rysa, Transparanaense (☎ 204121), and Yacyretá (☎ 204563), run some 30 buses daily to Ciudad del Este (US$8, four to five hours). There are also connections to Ayolas, San Cosme y Damián, Villarrica, and many lesser destinations.

Boat Launches still cross the Paraná to Posadas every half-hour between 7 am and 5 pm; the 30-minute trip costs US$1. The former dock is now submerged, so passengers board from the temporary floating dock at the foot of Av Estigarribia.

Getting Around

Encarnación has a good local bus system, but for all practical purposes, your feet should get you around town. Most buses to the old town use Carlos Antonio López and return by General Artigas. There are both horse-drawn and petrol-powered cabs.

AROUND ENCARNACIÓN

Trinidad & Jesús

Paraguay's best-preserved Jesuit reducción, Trinidad occupies an imposing hilltop site 28km northeast of Encarnación via Ruta 6. Though its church is smaller and its grounds are less extensive than those at San Ignacio Miní, in Argentine Mesopotamia, Trinidad is in many ways its equal. From its bell tower,

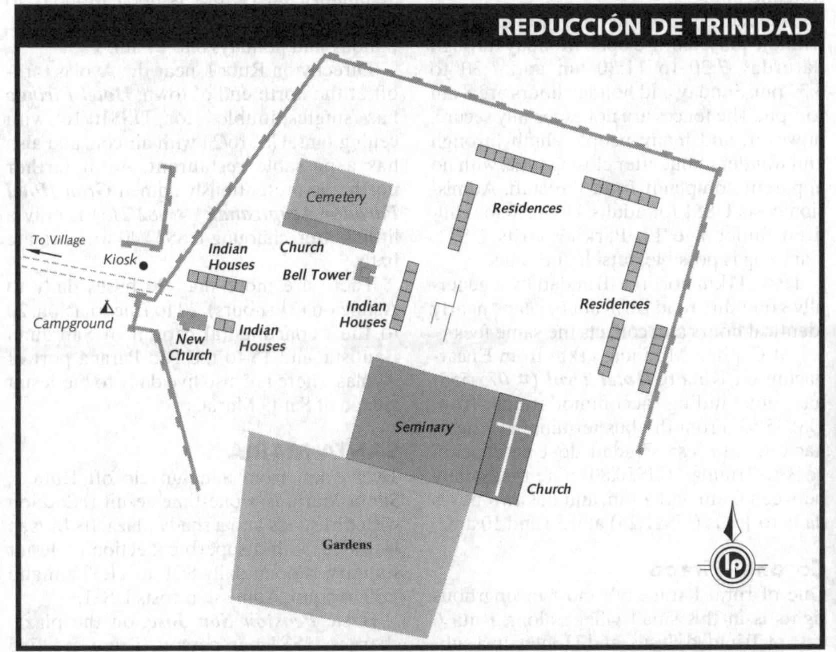

the Jesuit mission at Jesús de Tavarangue, 10km north as the crow flies, is easily visible – Jesús is, strictly speaking, not ruins but rather an incomplete construction project, interrupted by the Jesuits' expulsion in 1767.

Founded only in 1706, Trinidad was one of the later Jesuit establishments, but by 1728 it boasted a Guaraní population of more than 4000. Designed by Italian Jesuit architect Juan Bautista Prímoli, who spent 12 years on the project, it was not finished until 1760, less than a decade before the Jesuit expulsion in 1767. Its church, whose truly elaborate pulpit, frescos, statues, and other adornments remain in excellent repair, was the centerpiece of the reducción.

As elsewhere, the Jesuits introduced European crafts and industry, so that Trinidad became famous for the manufacture of bells, organs, harps, and statuary. It also operated three cattle *estancias*, two large *yerba mate* plantations, and a sugar plantation and mill.

The fenced grounds at Trinidad, along with the museum, are open Monday through Saturday 7:30 to 11:30 am and 1:30 to 5:30 pm; Sunday and holiday hours are 8 am to 5 pm. The fences are not especially secure, however, and many people climb through and wander about after closing time, with no apparent complaint from the staff. Admission costs US$1 for adults, US$0.50 for children under age 12. Parking costs US$1. Camping is possible outside the ruins.

Jesús, 11km north of Trinidad by a generally good dirt road off Ruta 6, keeps nearly identical hours and collects the same fees.

At Capitán Miranda, 21km from Encarnación on Ruta 6, ***Hotel Tirol*** *(☎ 075-555)* has outstanding accommodations from US$45/63. From the bus terminal at Encarnación, Empresa Ciudad de Encarnación goes to Trinidad (US$0.80) nine times daily between 6 am and 7 pm, and has two buses daily to Jesús (US$1.25) at 6:30 and 10 am.

Coronel Pirapó

One of rural Paraguay's most incongruous sights is in this small village along Ruta 6 east of Trinidad, Jesús, and Hohenau: a substantial stadium, seating well over a thousand people, with an electronic scoreboard. Here you will hear not Spanish, not Guaraní, but Japanese, thanks to immigrants who designed the park not for soccer but for baseball. Paraguayan participants are not unusual, however. The town also has Japanese gardens and fruit plantations.

Hotel Pirapó *(☎ 0768-507)*, directly on the highway, has modest accommodations for US$6/10 single/double. All buses between Encarnación and Ciudad del Este pass through town.

SAN IGNACIO GUAZÚ

About 140km northwest of Encarnación on Ruta 1, San Ignacio was also an 18th-century Jesuit reducción. It preserves only a modest sample of ruins, but has two commendable museums. The **Museo Jesuítico**, open daily 8 to 11:30 am and 2 to 5 pm, holds a valuable collection of Guaraní Indian carvings; admission costs US$1. The **Museo Histórico Semblanza de Héroes** is open Monday to Saturday 7:45 to 11:45 am and 2 to 5 pm, Sunday and holidays 8 to 11 am.

Directly on Ruta 1, near the Ayolas turnoff at the north end of town, ***Hotel Piringo*** has singles/doubles for US$10/16 with ceiling fans, US$16/24 with air-con, and also has a passable restaurant. A bit farther north, the pretentiously named ***Gran Hotel Parador Arapizandú*** *(☎ 082-213)* is only a little better, charging US$22/40 with private bath.

There are more than 30 buses daily to Asunción (3½ hours), 20 to Encarnación, 20 to the departmental capital of San Juan Bautista, and 15 to the Río Paraná port of Ayolas. There are also five daily to the Jesuit village of Santa María.

SANTA MARÍA

Twelve km from San Ignacio off Ruta 1, Santa María is a one-time Jesuit reducción with dirt roads and a shady plaza. Its **Museo Jesuítico**, with a superb collection of Jesuit statuary, is open daily 8:30 to 11:30 am and 1:30 to 5 pm. Admission costs US$1.

Basic ***Pensión San José***, on the plaza, charges US$4 per person. There are five buses daily from San Ignacio Guazú, the most convenient of which leave at 11:30 am and 4:30 pm.

Northeastern Paraguay

Easternmost Paraguay, along the Brazilian frontier, is Paraguay's economic boom zone. The world's largest hydroelectric project, at Itaipú, has spurred this development, and while it's a marvelous object lesson in Third World debt and environmental catastrophe, it has also propelled the town of Ciudad del Este into unprecedented, if ephemeral, prosperity (based also on contraband). Brazilian agricultural colonists are moving across the border and deforesting the countryside for coffee and cotton while squeezing out Paraguayan peasants and the region's few remaining Aché Indians.

CIUDAD DEL ESTE

Formerly Puerto Presidente Stroessner, Ciudad del Este is a key border crossing, a transportation hub, and one of the gateways to the world-famous Cataratas del Iguazú. It is perhaps more significant, in the words of the *Wall Street Journal*, as the site of '15,000 shops jammed into 20 blocks,' a 'chaos of mass consumption' that turns over up to US$55 billion per year in contraband – five times the size of the official Paraguayan economy.

While it's hard to ignore its ragged and undisciplined squalor, Ciudad del Este has an infectious boomtown vitality. Hidden behind handtrucks piled high with cardboard boxes holding imported VCRs and stereos, young boys wheel their merchandise up and down the sloping streets, while

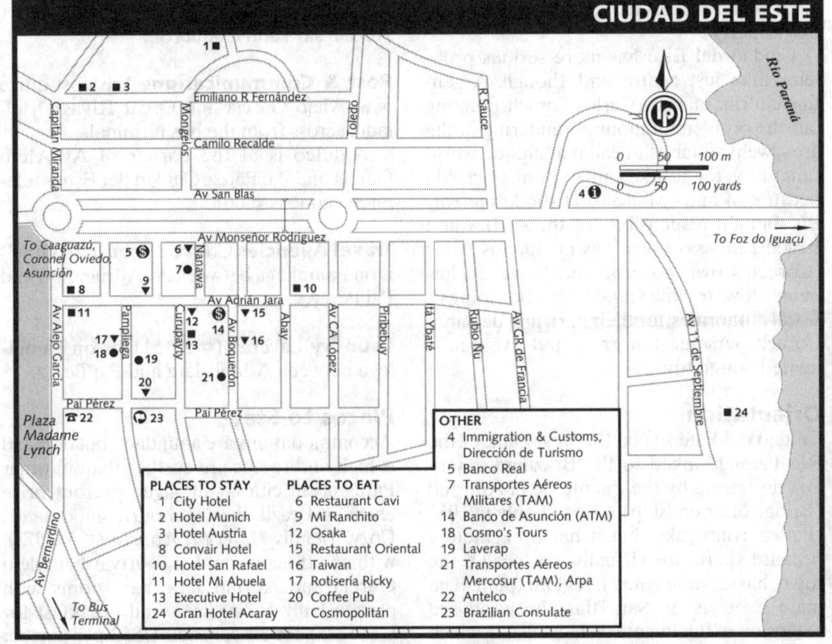

PARAGUAY

frenzied Brazilians stagger like overloaded porters burdened with enormous satchels holding everything acquired on shopping sprees financed with overvalued reals. There is extensive counterfeiting of items like brand-name cell phone batteries and CD-ROMs, and even President Raúl Cubas admits that 'one of Merocosur's major concerns is that Paraguay is involved in *intermediación*' – a euphemism for smuggling. You can buy or sell just about anything in Ciudad del Este, so long as it's not made in Paraguay.

Asian immigrants play a major role in legitimate commerce, but some locals worry that Mercosur tariff reductions may undercut the lawless contraband sector. One 'businessman,' quoted in the *Journal*, expressed it this way: 'As I understand it, we will no longer be able to live by smuggling products but will have to begin producing things.' Still, according to *The New York Times*, former Alto Paraná governor Carlos Barreto has been under investigation for a clandestine airstrip and two unmarked planes found on his property.

Ciudad del Este has more serious problems than just contraband, though. Argentine interior minister Carlos Corach, pointing out the problem of money laundering in the area, went so far as to call it a 'unique world sanctuary for crime and impunity,' partly because of murky links to Hizbollah terrorists thought responsible for the AMIA and Israeli Embassy bombings in Buenos Aires (Corach's own government, however, has been slow to investigate the bombings). Local authorities, for their part, first declared Corach persona non grata, but eventually invited him to town.

Orientation

Ciudad del Este sits on the west bank of the Río Paraná, linked to the Brazilian city of Foz do Iguaçu by the Puente de la Amistad (Bridge of Friendship). Created only in 1957 (Paraguayans joke that it has no cemetery because there are virtually no locals), the town has a somewhat irregular plan. The main street is Av San Blas, the westward extension of the Puente de la Amistad, which becomes Ruta 7 to Caaguazú, Coronel Oviedo, and Asunción (via Ruta 2). While a bit complex, irregular, and very disorderly, the center is compact and easily manageable on foot.

Information

Tourist Offices The Dirección de Turismo (☎ 512417, 516051) at the immigration border post is friendly but not particularly well informed or well supplied with printed matter.

The Touring y Automóvil Club Paraguayo (☎ 512340) is on Av San Blas, at the Shell station about 1km west of Plaza Madame Lynch, on Ruta 7 to Asunción. It sells the *Guía Shell*, which includes the best available road maps of Paraguay, for US$8.

Money Money changers are everywhere, especially at the border, but they give poorer rates than banks or cambios. Banco Real has an ATM at Av Monseñor Rodríguez and Tte Coronel Pampliega, while Banco de Asunción has one at Av Adrián Jara and Boquerón.

Post & Communications The post office is at Alejo García and Oscar Rivas Ortellado, across from the bus terminal.

Antelco is at the corner of Av Alejo García and Paí Pérez. Ciudad del Este's telephone code is ☎ 061.

Travel Agencies Cosmo's Tours (☎ 511068) is on Pampliega between Av Adrián Jara and Pai Pérez.

Laundry Laverap (☎ 561511) is on Pampliega between Adrián Jara and Paí Pérez.

Places to Stay

Accommodations are abundant, but demand is high and rooms are costlier than in other Paraguayan cities; still, given present price levels in Brazil, they're a fairly good value. Cozy, friendly ***Hotel Mi Abuela*** *(☎ 512373)*, with an attractive garden courtyard at Alejo García and Adrián Jara, has rooms with private bath, ceiling fans, and breakfast for US$12/20; for air-con, add US$3 per person.

Since it's been up for sale, changes may be in the offing.

Also good value is German-run ***Hotel Munich*** *(☎ 500347)*, at Emiliano Fernández and Capitán Miranda, where rooms with private bath, good breakfast, and air-con cost US$13/18. Down the block, enthusiastically recommended ***Hotel Austria*** *(☎ 504213, Emiliano Fernández 165)* is slightly dearer at US$16/18. ***City Hotel*** *(☎ 500415, Regimiento Sauce 301)*, at Capitán Miranda, charges US$20/30.

Hotel San Rafael *(☎ 500804)*, at the corner of Av Adrián Jara and Abay, charges US$25/35 for rooms with breakfast and air-con, while the modernistic ***Executive Hotel*** *(☎ 500942)*, at Av Adrián Jara and Curupayty, is slightly dearer at US$28/34. Upgraded ***Convair Hotel*** *(☎ 500342)*, across the street from Hotel Mi Abuela, has rooms with air-conditioning, television, telephone, and other amenities for US$34/42. ***Gran Hotel Acaray*** *(☎ 500252)*, on Av 11 de Septiembre near the river, is also Ciudad del Este's casino; rooms cost US$44/55. It's quieter because it's away from the rowdy downtown.

Places to Eat

The pleasant surprise in Ciudad del Este is the outstanding Asian food – Japanese, Chinese, and Korean – at reasonable prices. ***Restaurant Oriental***, on Adrián Jara near Av Boquerón, has Japanese/Chinese food, with an especially fine *agropicante* (hot-and-sour) soup. Alongside it, ***Osaka*** has an equally appealing menu but keeps shorter hours. ***Taiwan*** *(☎ 510635)*, on Boquerón between Adrián Jara and Pai Pérez, serves Chinese.

Rotisería Ricky, on Pampliega between Adrián Jara and Paí Pérez, has a variety of short orders and take-out foods. ***Mi Ranchito***, a sidewalk parrilla at Curupayty and Av Adrián Jara, offers good, complete meals for around US$4. ***Restaurant Cavi***, at Monseñor Rodríguez and Nanawa, is a popular Paraguayan choice. For snacks and sandwiches, there's ***Coffee Pub Cosmopolitan***, on Pai Pérez opposite the Brazilian consulate.

Getting There & Away

Air Ciudad del Este's new Aeropuerto Internacional Guaraní is 30km west of town on Ruta 7, but flights are still limited. Arpa (☎ 512646), Boquerón 310, flies several times daily to Asunción (US$60 to US$90) with onward international connections; in the same office, TAM (Transportes Aéreos Mercosur) flies Monday, Wednesday, Friday, and Sunday to Porto Alegre and Curitiba (Brazil); and Tuesday, Thursday, and Saturday to Iquique (Chile). The military airline TAM (☎ 518352), in the Edificio SABA on Nanawa, just off Monseñor Rodríguez, occasionally flies to Asunción.

There are also major airports at Foz do Iguaçu in Brazil and Puerto Iguazú in Argentina. From Foz, Varig and other Brazilian airlines have flights to São Paulo, Curitiba, Rio de Janeiro, and Asunción; from Puerto Iguazú, Aerolíneas, Austral, and LAPA have regular services to Aeroparque in Buenos Aires.

Bus Catch buses for Foz do Iguaçu, which leave every 10 minutes weekdays and Saturday, and every half hour Sunday and holidays, at the entrance to the bridge over the Paraná after going through Paraguayan immigration. On the other side, unless just crossing for the day, disembark to go through Brazilian immigration; if you hold onto your ticket, any following bus will take you to Foz. Direct buses to Puerto Iguazú, in Argentina, are almost as frequent.

There are half a dozen international services daily to São Paulo (18 hours), Rio de Janeiro (25 hours), Florianópolis (15 hours), and Curitiba (13 hours) on Pluma (☎ 510343), Rysa (☎ 500458), Catarinense, and La Paraguaya. There is, of course, a wider selection of Brazilian bus services in Foz. Pluma also goes to Buenos Aires, along with Rápido Caaguazú (☎ 510397), Rysa, and La Internacional.

From Ciudad del Este to Asunción, there are 34 buses daily with Rysa, Rápido Caaguazú (☎ 518124), Beato Roque González (☎ 510283), Ciudad del Este (☎ 510397), Nuestra Señora de la Asunción (☎ 510095), Pycasu (☎ 514910), La Paraguaya, and

Crucero del Sur. There are nearly as many to Encarnación, with Carepegueña (☎ 510178), La Pilarense (☎ 513637), Santa Rita del Monday (☎ 510089), Yacyretá (☎ 510897), Nuestra Señora, Crucero del Sur, La Sampedrana, Transporte Paraná, Rysa, Ciudad del Este, and others.

Salto Cristal has two per day, via Villarrica, to Ybycuí, convenient for Parque Nacional Ybycuí, while Piribebuy and La Guaireña (☎ 510181) also go to Villarrica several times daily. Empresa Piribebuy goes to Carapeguá via Piribebuy and Paraguarí, while Ciudad del Este goes five times daily to Caaguazú. Several carriers go to Pedro Juan Caballero, including Cometa del Amambay, García Hermanos, and Rysa.

Sample fares include Encarnación (US$8, 4½ hours), Villarrica (US$6, 3½ hours) and Asunción (US$10 to US$14, five hours).

Getting Around

Ciudad del Este's public transport system has managed to keep pace with the city's rapid development, but for most travelers the central area is compact enough that it's unnecessary to use it. The exception is the long-distance bus terminal on Av Bernardino Caballero, 2km south of downtown; take the 'Mburucuyá' bus from Av Alejo García or a cab for about US$3.

AROUND CIUDAD DEL ESTE

Itaipú Dam

With an installed capacity of 12.6 million kilowatts, the binational Itaipú Dam is the world's largest hydroelectric project. It's also an extraordinary illustration of the ways in which massive development projects have plunged countries like Brazil many billions of dollars into debt without hope of repayment. Paraguay, though, has benefited economically from Itaipú because of the construction boom, its own low domestic demand (in 1997, Itaipú's record 89,237,001 Mwh production was 18 times Paraguay's total domestic consumption), and Brazil's need to purchase the Paraguayan surplus.

Paraguay, though, risks becoming an energy colony of its mammoth neighbor. At the same time, should the price of competing energy sources drop, reduced Brazilian demand could saddle Paraguay with the repayment of an unexpected share of the project's enormous capital and maintenance costs.

Project propaganda omits any reference to the costs of the US$25 billion project, and environmental concerns figured not at all into the Itaipú equation. The dam created a 220m-deep reservoir covering 1350 sq km, which drowned the falls at Sete Quedas, a larger and even more impressive natural feature than Iguazú. Research indicates that the reservoir's stagnant waters have provided new habitat for anopheline mosquitoes, posing an increased malaria risk in an area where the disease had nearly been eradicated.

On both sides of the border, well-rehearsed guides lead tours that stop long enough for visitors to take photographs. On the Paraguayan side, these leave from the Centro de Recepción de Visitas, north of Ciudad del Este near the town of Hernandarias. Hours are Monday to Saturday at 8, 9, and 10 am, and 2:30 and 3:30 pm; passports are required. There is a documentary film, also available in English-language video format, a half hour before the tour departs.

From Ciudad del Este, take any Hernandarias Transtur or Tacurú Pucú bus from the roundabout at the intersection of Av San Blas and Av Alejo García. These leave every 10 to 15 minutes throughout the day – ask to be dropped at the entrance to the conspicious project.

Salto Monday

They're not Sete Quedas, but these falls on the Río Monday, near Puerto Presidente Franco, are the best Paraguay now has to offer. They're only 10km from Ciudad del Este, but there is no scheduled public transport, so taxi is the best alternative. Otherwise it should be possible to catch one of the frequent buses from Ciudad del Este to Puerto Presidente Franco and to walk to the falls from there.

Colonia Iguazú

Forty km west of Ciudad del Este on Ruta 7 to Asunción, Colonia Iguazú is a Japanese agricultural colony specializing in cotton that was established in 1960 with the assistance of the Japanese government. Buses from Ciudad del Este stop at the Esso Servicentro, where the restaurant serves excellent Japanese food along with Paraguayan dishes.

CORONEL OVIEDO

Just off Ruta 2 midway between Asunción and Ciudad del Este, Coronel Oviedo is a major crossroads in eastern Paraguay – long-distance buses pass through town at least every 15 minutes all day. Ruta 3 goes north toward Pedro Juan Caballero (with branches to Salto del Guairá and Concepción), while Ruta 8 heads south to Villarrica, center of an area of German colonization on the Asunción-Encarnación railway.

At the crossroads, ***Hotel Alemán*** *(☎ 0521-202374)* is a reasonable place to stay for US$10/12 per single/double, while nearby ***Parador La Tranquera*** has good food. In the town proper, 3km north of the crossroads, highly recommended ***Hotel Colonial*** *(☎ 0521-202393)* has singles for US$14/18. ***Hotel del Rey*** *(☎ 0521-202117, Av Mariscal JF Estigarribia 213)* charges US$14/24.

Between Coronel Oviedo and San José, a branch road off Ruta 2 leads to the frequently renamed town of **Nueva Australia**, a short-lived socialist experiment populated by the descendants of late-19th-century Australian immigrants. Named Hugo Stroessner, for Alfredo's immigrant father, on some maps, the dissension-ridden agricultural colony attracted its earliest participants with exaggerated propaganda on the area's economic potential until it finally broke apart in 1896. Colonia Cosme, an offshoot south of Villarrica, struggled on a few years more.

VILLARRICA

Settled by German agricultural immigrants, Villarrica is a quiet provincial town known as one of Paraguay's cultural capitals, due partly to the impressive Franciscan church that dates from colonial times. It is about 40km south of Coronel Oviedo via paved Ruta 8, which becomes Av Thompson past the plaza and then Av Carlos Antonio López at Bulevar Ayolas.

The nearby village of Yataity is renowned for artisans who produce *ao po'i* or *lienzo* (loose-weave cotton) garments. The **Fiesta del Ao po'i** takes place in November.

For budget lodgings, try ***Hotel Guairá*** *(☎ 0541-2369)*, at Talavera and Av. Mariscal Estigarribia, which charges US$8/12 single/double. ***Hotel Ybyturutzú*** *(☎ 0541-2390)*, at Carlos Antonio López and Dr Bottrell, has clean, spacious rooms with breakfast, private bath, and air-con for US$18/24, but some downstairs rooms are slightly musty. Good meals are available, and it has pleasant gardens and common spaces. For breakfast, try ***Tirol*** down the block.

Villarrica's only night spot is ***Petroleo's Pub***, also on Carlos Antonio López.

PEDRO JUAN CABALLERO

Capital of the department of Amambay, 532km northeast of Asunción by Ruta 3 and Ruta 5 from Coronel Oviedo, Pedro Juan Caballero is the Paraguayan counterpart of the Brazilian town of Ponta Porã. There is no clearly marked border, and locals cross from one side to the other at will. You can do the same, but before continuing any distance into either country, visit immigration at Naciones Unidas 144, open daily from 8 am to noon except Sunday. There are reports of contraband drug traffic, so beware unsavory characters.

Exchange houses are numerous, including Guaraní Cambios on Rodríguez de Francia. The Brazilian Consulate (open weekdays 8 am to noon and 2 to 6 pm) is in the ***Hotel La Siesta*** *(☎ (036-3021)*, at Alberdi and Dr Francia, which has singles/doubles for US$36/48. More economical accommodations are available at several hotels along Mariscal López: the recommended ***Hotel Guavirá*** *(☎ 2743, Mariscal López 1325)* charges US$6 single with shared bath, US$10 with private bath; ***Hotel Peralta*** *(☎ 2346, Mariscal López 1257)* has rooms for US$10/16; and ***Hotel La Negra*** *(☎ 2262, Mariscal López 1342)* for US$14 per person. ***Hotel Eiruzú*** *(☎ 2259, Av Mariscal JF Estigarribia 48)* charges US$31/46, and ***Hotel Casino Amambay*** *(☎ 2718, Rodríguez de Francia 1)* is the town's best for US$66/93.

Getting There & Away

Ten buses daily connect Pedro Juan Caballero with Asunción via Coronel Oviedo, with San Jorge, Cometa del Amambay, La Santaniana and La Ovetense; the trip traditionally takes eight to 12 hours, depending on weather and road conditions, but the highway is now almost entirely paved.

There are also 10 buses daily to Concepción, where it's conceivable to travel downriver to Asunción, and one per day to Ciudad del Este. Nasa goes daily to Campo Grande, Brazil, but there are more bus services plus two trains per day, across the border in Ponta Porã.

PARQUE NACIONAL CERRO CORÁ

Visitors passing through northeastern Paraguay should not bypass 22,000-hectare Parque Nacional Cerro Corá, only 40km southwest of Pedro Juan Caballero, which protects an area of dry tropical forest and savanna grasslands in a landscape of steep, isolated hills rising above the central plateau. Besides a representative sample of Paraguayan flora and fauna, the park also has cultural and historical landmarks, including pre-Columbian caves and petroglyphs, and was the site of the battle in which a Brazilian soldier killed Francisco Solano López at the end of the War of the Triple Alliance.

The park has nature trails, a camping area, and a few basic cabañas where travelers can lodge. There are rangers, but no formal visitor center.

CONCEPCIÓN

On the east bank of the Río Paraguay, 310km upstream from Asunción, the small provincial town of Concepción conducts considerable river trade with Brazil and has an interesting market. The least expensive lodgings are ***Hospedaje Boquerón*** *(☎ 031-2263)*, at Boquerón and Iturbe, for US$4 per person. ***Hotel Victoria*** *(☎ 031-2826)*, at Presidente Franco and Juan Pedro Caballero, costs around US$12/20 for singles/doubles with private bath, while the recommended ***Hotel Francés*** *(☎ 031-2750)*, at Presidente Franco and Carlos Antonio López, charges US$22/30 with a good breakfast.

Getting There & Away

Air TAM, the Paraguayan air force passenger service, flies to Asunción, Valle Mí, La Victoria, Fuerte Olimpo, San Carlos, and Bahía Negra.

Boat For details of boat traffic from Asunción to Corumbá, Brazil, see the Getting There & Away entry under Asunción.

Bus Bus services to Asunción, subject to suspension due to road conditions, can go either via Pozo Colorado in the Chaco or via Coronel Oviedo, the latter a nine- to 11-hour trip. The main carriers are Nasa, La Ovetense, San Jorge, La Santaniana, and Ciudad de Concepción. There are daily Nasa buses to Pedro Juan Caballero (US$8.50, 5½ hours, continuing to Campo Grande, Brazil), and others to Ciudad del Este.

Paraguayan Chaco

With more than 60% of the country's territory and only 4% of its population, the Gran Chaco is the Paraguayan frontier, where great distances separate tiny settlements. Paved Ruta 9, popularly known as the Ruta Trans-Chaco, leads 450km to the town of Filadelfia, center of an area colonized by European Mennonite immigrants since the late 1920s. Beyond Filadelfia, the pavement ends but the highway continues to the Bolivian border at Eugenio Garay, another 300km northwest.

Geographically, the Paraguayan Chaco is the northernmost segment of an almost featureless plain rising slowly from southeast to northwest, its surface consisting of sediments eroded from the Andes. It comprises three rather distinct zones that emerge gradually as one travels east to west. Immediately west of the Río Paraguay, the Low Chaco landscape becomes a soothing, verdant savanna of caranday palms with scattered islands of thorny scrub, commonly known as *monte*. In this poorly drained area, ponds and marshes shelter large numbers of colorful birds, including the ungainly South American storks. Peasant farmers build picturesque houses of palm logs, but the primary industry is cattle ranching, as Paraguayan *gauchos* herd scrawny cattle on *estancias* even larger than many in Argentina or Uruguay.

As the Ruta Trans-Chaco continues northwest, rainfall declines and the drought-tolerant monte expands, with substantial groves of quebracho, palo santo, and the unique *palo borracho*, which conserves water in its bulbous trunk. Despite erratic environmental conditions, Mennonite colonists have built successful agricultural communities in the Middle Chaco, but no one has yet established anything but army bases and cattle estancias in the High Chaco beyond Mariscal Estigarribia, where the thorn forest is denser and rainfall even more undependable.

Historically, the Chaco has been the last refuge of indigenous peoples such as the Ayoreo and Nivaclé, who managed an independent subsistence until very recently by hunting, gathering, and fishing. Later industries included cattle ranching and extraction of the tannin-rich quebracho. It was the Mennonite colonists, first arriving in 1927, who proved that parts of the Chaco were suitable for more intensive agriculture and permanent settlement. The first Mennonite settlers arrived in the heart of the Chaco not by the Ruta Trans-Chaco (which wasn't completed until 1964 or paved until the 1980s), but rather by railway from Puerto Casado, on the upper Río Paraguay.

A glance at the map reveals an inordinate number of Chaco place names that begin with the word *Fortín*; these were the numerous fortifications and trenches, many of which remain nearly unaltered, from the Chaco War (1932-5) with Bolivia. Most of these sites are abandoned, but small settlements have grown up near a few. The Paraguayan military still retains a visible presence throughout the region.

The Chaco War gave Paraguay the incentive to build a network of dirt roads, most of which have deteriorated since hostilities ended. This generality does not apply in the Mennonite communities, which have done an outstanding job of maintaining those roads within their autonomous jurisdiction. Most others are impassable except to 4WD vehicles.

Travel in the Chaco can be rough, and accommodations are scarce outside the few main towns; it is possible to camp almost anywhere, but beware of snakes. In a pinch, the estancias or the *campesinos* (peasants) along the Trans-Chaco will put you up in a bed with a mosquito net if they have one. Otherwise, you're on your own.

VILLA HAYES

Only a short distance from Asunción across the Puente Remanso, Villa Hayes takes its name from one of the most obscure and undistinguished US presidents, who, oddly,

is a hero in the hearts and minds of Paraguayans. Many consider him an honorary Paraguayan.

Rutherford Birchard Hayes (pronounced 'eye-zhess' in Paraguay's River Plate accent) occupied the White House from 1877-81, leaving office without even seeking a second term. Even in his hometown of Delaware, Ohio, the only monument to his memory is a modest plaque on the site of his birthplace – now a gasoline station. In Paraguay, by contrast, he is commemorated by the Club Presidente Hayes, which sponsors the local soccer team, an Escuela Rutherford B Hayes, and a separate monument outside the school. In 1928 and 1978, the town held major festivities to honor Hayes.

Why this homage to a man almost forgotten in his own country, who never even set foot in Paraguay, 7400km to the south? At the end of the War of the Triple Alliance, Argentina claimed the entire Chaco, but after delicate negotiations, both countries agreed to submit claims over a smaller area, between the Río Verde and the Río Pilcomayo, to arbitration. In 1878, Argentine and Paraguayan diplomats traveled to

Washington to present their cases to Hayes, who decided in Paraguay's favor; in gratitude, the Congreso in Asunción immortalized the American president by renaming the territory's largest town, Villa Occidental, in his honor.

To attend the Hayes sesquicentennial in 2028, take bus No 46 from Estados Unidos or Av España in downtown Asunción. It leaves every half hour between 5:30 am and noon, and every 45 minutes from noon to 9 pm.

POZO COLORADO

Pozo Colorado, 274km northwest of Asunción, has little of interest, but it's the only major crossroads in the entire Chaco. From here, Ruta 5 is a dry-weather route east to Concepción, where it's possible to catch a bus back to Asunción or onward to the Brazilian border at Pedro Juan Caballero. There's a military checkpoint just before Pozo Colorado.

Parador Pozo Colorado, on the north side of the highway, has decent food and very cold beer; it may be able to offer a bed for the night, but if not, try the Shell station across the highway. From Concepción, Nasa runs two buses daily to Asunción via Pozo Colorado, at 7:30 am and 11 pm. These should arrive 2½ to 3 hours later in Pozo. Several other buses continue from Pozo on to the Mennonite settlements at Filadelfia, Loma Plata, and Neu-Halbstadt.

FILADELFIA

Filadelfia, the administrative and service center for the Mennonite farmers of Fernheim colony, is the most visited of the three colonies, with the most reasonable accommodations and outgoing people. In some ways, it resembles the cattle towns of the Australian outback or the American West, but dairy products and cotton are the primary products rather than beef. Just as Aboriginal people work Australia's cattle stations, so Nivaclé, Lengua, Ayoreo, and other indigenous people work the Mennonite farms. The very controversial New Tribes Mission, an evangelical group not related to the Mennonites, maintains an office in town.

Filadelfia is still a religious community and shuts down almost completely on Sunday. On weekday mornings, you will see Mennonite farmers drive to town in their pickup trucks in search of Indians for day labor, returning with them in the afternoon. At noon, when the heat can be overpowering, the town is exceptionally quiet, as Mennonites have adopted the custom of the tropical siesta.

Orientation

Filadelfia is about 450km northwest of Asunción via the Trans-Chaco. The town itself lies about 20km north of the highway, on a spur whose pavement ends about 1km south of town.

Filadelfia's dusty, unpaved streets form a very orderly grid. The *Hauptstrasse* (main street) is north-south Hindenburg, named after the German general and president whose government helped the Fernheim refugees escape the Soviet Union. The other main thoroughfare is Trébol, which leads east to Loma Plata, the center of Menno colony, and west to the Trans-Chaco and Fortín Toledo. Nearly every important public service is on or near Hindenburg.

Information

Tourist Offices Filadelfia has no formal tourist office, but Hotel Florida shows a video on the Mennonite colonies.

Money To change cash, try the Cooperativa Mennonita supermarket, near the corner of Unruh and Hindenburg.

Post & Communications The post office and Antelco are both at Hindenburg and Unruh. Filadelfia's area code is ☎ 091.

Medical Services Filadelfia's modern hospital (☎ 2851) is at Hindenburg and Trébol.

Museo Unger

This well-arranged museum, opposite Hotel Florida on Hindenburg, tells the story of Fernheim colony from its foundation in 1930 to the present, and it also contains ethnographic materials on the Chaco Indians. It keeps no regular schedule, but Hartmut Wohlgemuth, manager of the hotel, provides guided tours in Spanish or German when his schedule permits. There is an admission charge of about US$1.

Places to Stay

Camping Camping is possible free of charge in shady ***Parque Trébol***, 5km east of Filadelfia, but there is no water and only a single pit toilet. While camping there one evening, we saw a highly venomous (but timid) coral snake.

Hotels Filadelfia's most established accommodation is ***Hotel Florida*** *(☎ 2476)*, at the corner of Hindenburg and Unruh. Motel-style double rooms with private bath and air-con cost US$28 per person with breakfast. But its budget annex is an excellent bargain at US$6 per person, with comfortable beds, shared bath with cold showers (not a bad idea here), and fans; rooms with private bath cost US$10 (breakfast costs an extra US$3).

The newish ***Hotel Safari*** *(☎ 2218)*, on Industrie between Hindenburg and Miller, charges US$22/29 single/double and also has a pool.

FILADELFIA

Bender
To Fortín Toledo, Airport
To Parque Trébol, Loma Plata
Trébol
Mariscal Estigarribia
Hindenburg
Miller
Unruh
Industrie
Chaco Boreal
Boquerón
To Hotel Edelweiss, Ruta Trans-Chaco
0 50 100 m
0 50 100 yards

PLACES TO STAY
5 Hotel Florida
12 Hotel Safari

PLACES TO EAT
6 La Estrella
9 Girasol

OTHER
1 New Tribes Mission Office
2 Monument
3 Hospital
4 Museo Unger
7 Cooperativa Mennonita
8 Post Office
10 Antelco
11 Librería El Mensajero
13 Stel Turismo
14 Ecmetur
15 Dipar (Car Rental)
16 Nasa Bus Terminal

Places to Eat

Hotel Florida has a very decent restaurant, while several shops along Hindenburg offer snacks and homemade ice cream. Try also the *parrillada* at ***La Estrella***, around the corner from the Hotel Florida on Unruh, which has a shady outdoor dining area. ***Girasol***, across the street, also serves a good *asado*. The modern Cooperativa Mennonita supermarket has excellent dairy products and other groceries.

Shopping

Librería El Mensajero, behind Antelco and across from the Mennonite cooperative, is an evangelical bookstore that also offers a good selection of Chaco Indian crafts. There's a better crafts selection at Neu-Halbstadt.

Getting There & Away

Nasa, on Chaco Boreal near the corner of Miller, goes daily at 2:30 and 9:30 pm to Asunción (seven hours) and at 2 am to Mariscal Estigarribia (two hours) and Estancia La Patria (five hours), the last public transport stop on the Trans-Chaco before the Bolivian border. It also has a 1 pm Saturday minibus service (US$4) to Mariscal Estigarribia for those who care to see the landscape.

Stel Turismo, on the east side of Hindenburg between Industrie and Chaco Boreal, connects Filadelfia with Asunción at noon daily except Saturday. Ecmetur, at the corner of Hindenburg and Chaco Boreal, has buses to the capital daily at 7 or 8 pm.

Local bus line Expreso CV connects Filadelfia with Loma Plata (25km) daily at 8 am, returning at 9 am. Nasa minibuses go Monday, Wednesday, and Friday at 11:30 am to Neu-Halbstadt, returning at 1 pm.

Nasa buses from Asunción also stop at Loma Plata and most continue onward to

Neu-Halbstadt if there's no rain, while Stel Turismo buses stop in Loma Plata and Neu-Halbstadt, rain or not.

Hitching or asking for a lift is worth a try if you plan to go anywhere else, like Fortín Toledo, Neu-Halbstadt, or Loma Plata, at odd hours.

Getting Around

Dipar (☎ 2450), on Chaco Boreal between Hindenburg and Miller, rents air-conditioned cars for US$50 per day with 100km included, but they may be used only within the Mennonite colonies.

AROUND FILADELFIA

Cruce de los Pioneros

A traditional stopping place on the Trans-Chaco, ***Hotel Cruce de los Pioneros*** *(☎ 094820, 605740 in Asunción)* has good accommodations and a restaurant, and the owner will organize trips into the Chaco interior. Singles/doubles cost US$24/32.

Fortín Toledo

About 40km west of Filadelfia, Fortín Toledo saw extended trench warfare during the Chaco conflict. It is now home to the **Proyecto Taguá**, a small reserve nurturing a population of the Chaco or Wagner's peccary *(Catagonus wagneri)*, thought extinct for nearly half a century until its rediscovery in a remote area in 1975. The current project managers, Jakob and María Unger, are English-speaking Mennonites who welcome visits if their schedule permits.

The peccaries are confined within a large fenced and forested area with a large pond, which attracts many Chaco birds. Directors of the project, sponsored in part by the San Diego Zoo (some of the mammals are now on display there), hope to be able to expand the reserve, but there are legal problems with acquisition of adjacent property, which is part of an inheritance dispute. Nearby you can visit the fortifications of Fortín Toledo, some of which are still in excellent repair, and a Paraguayan military cemetery. Try to imagine yourself in the dusty or muddy trenches, awaiting the charge of the Bolivians.

To get to Fortín Toledo from Filadelfia, hitch or take a bus (such as the Nasa bus to Estancia La Patria) out Calle Trébol to the intersection with the Ruta Trans-Chaco. From there, cross the highway and continue about 3km to an enormous tire on which are painted the words 'pasar prohibido.' Continue on the main road another 7km, passing several buildings occupied by squatters on an old estancia, before taking a sharp right that leads to a sign reading 'Proyecto Taguá' (if walking, avoid the midday heat). You may be able to hitch this segment as well.

At Rosaleda, near Fortín Toledo, the ***Hotel Suiza*** *(☎ 0951-355)* has accommodations from US$10 per person and a good restaurant.

LOMA PLATA

Loma Plata, 25km east of Filadelfia, is the administrative and service center of Menno colony, the oldest and most traditional of the Mennonite settlements. It has an excellent museum with an outdoor exhibit of early farming equipment and a typical pioneer house plus an outstanding photographic exhibit on the colony's history. Ask for the key at the Secretariat, the large building next door to the museum.

Accommodations are available at ***Hotel Loma Plata*** for about US$10 with shared bath. There's also the new ***Hotel Algarrobo*** *(☎ 0918-353)*, 1km outside town, for US$12 per person with private bath, air-con, and breakfast. It has two restaurants: ***Churrascaría Amambay*** and ***La Carreta***.

It's also possible to make a day trip from Filadelfia, where there are daily bus connections. Buses from Filadelfia to Asunción stop half an hour later in Loma Plata. Likewise, buses from Asunción to Filadelfia stop first in Loma Plata.

NEU-HALBSTADT

Founded in 1947 by Ukrainian-German Mennonites, 33km south of Filadelfia, Neu-Halbstadt is the service center of Neuland colony. ***Hotel Boquerón*** *(☎ 0951-311)* has singles/doubles for US$15/22 and a good restaurant, and there's also a ***campground***

The Mennonite Colonies

Mennonites are Anabaptists, believing in adult rather than infant baptism. This might sound harmless enough today, but in 16th-century Holland and Switzerland it got them into serious trouble with both Catholics and other Protestants. As pacifists, the Mennonites also believed in separation of church and state and rejected compulsory military service, making their situation even worse and leading them to flee to Germany, Russia, and Canada. By the early 20th century, political upheaval once again caused them to seek new homes, this time in Latin America. Their primary destinations were Mexico and Paraguay.

For Mennonites, Paraguay's attractions were large extents of nearly uninhabited land, where they could follow their traditional agricultural way of life, and the government's willingness to grant them political autonomy under a Privilegium: They were responsible for their own schools (with German-language instruction) and community law enforcement, and enjoyed separate economic organization, freedom from taxation, religious liberty, and exemption from military service. The first group to arrive in Paraguay, in 1927, were the *Sommerfelder* (Summerfield) Mennonites from the Canadian prairies, who left after Canadian authorities failed to live up to their promise of exemption from military service. These Sommerfelder formed Menno colony, the first of three distinct but territorially overlapping Mennonite groups. Centered around the town of Loma Plata, it is still the most conservative and traditional of the colonies.

Only a few years after the founding of Menno colony, refugees from the Soviet Union established Fernheim (Distant Home), with its 'capital' at Filadelfia. Neuland (New Land) was founded in 1947 by Ukrainian-German Mennonites, many of whom had served unwillingly in the German army in WWII and had managed to stay in the west after being released from prisoner-of-war camps. Its largest settlement is Neu-Halbstadt.

Mennonite immigrants obtained major concessions under the Privilegium, but they soon found that the Paraguayans had exploited their desire to live in peaceful isolation by granting them land in the midst of a zone of conflict. Since the early part of the century, Paraguay and Bolivia had been building fortifications in anticipation of armed conflict over an area that had been a cause of antagonism since colonial days. In 1932, this erupted into open warfare, with Mennonite settlements the scene of ground fighting and even Bolivian air attacks.

Because of their isolation, the Mennonites saw Paraguayans only infrequently, but regularly came into contact, and sometimes conflict, with Chaco Indians. During the war, nomadic Indians, who felt allegiance to neither country, were targets for both the Bolivians and

north of town. Nearby Fortín Boquerón preserves a sample of Chaco War trenches.

South of Neuland are the largest Indian reserves, where many Lengua and Nivaclé have settled with the assistance of the Asociación del Servicio de Cooperación Indígena Menonita (ASCIM) to become farmers. Neu-Halbstadt is a good place to obtain Indian handicrafts, including bags and hammocks, and woven goods, including belts and blankets colored with natural dyes. For excellent information on local Indians and access to a great selection of crafts, contact Verena Regehr (☎ 286) in Neu-Halbstadt, who distributes Indian crafts on a nonprofit basis and also owns Artesanía Viva in Asunción. Heinrich Braun (☎ 319) is also a good source of information on Neu-Halbstadt.

Several buses from Asunción to Filadelfia continue to Neu-Halbstadt, while others come directly from Asunción. Stel Turismo leaves for the capital daily at 6:30 pm except Saturday, when it leaves at noon.

PARAGUAY

The Mennonite Colonies

Paraguayans. Some found refuge with the Mennonites, but others so strongly resented the Mennonite intrusion that they resisted violently. As late as the 1940s, Ayoreo hunter-gatherers attacked and killed members of a Mennonite family in the northwestern Chaco, although it is not clear who was at fault.

Such extreme cases were unusual, but more than a few Indians thought the Mennonites invaders and did not hesitate to let their cattle graze on Mennonite crops. From motives that were both religious and expedient, Mennonites encouraged the Indians to become settled cultivators, following their own example. But the Mennonites also distanced themselves from the Indians – those who adopted the Mennonite religion were encouraged to form their own church and to integrate more closely into Paraguayan rather than Mennonite society. Over time, many Lengua and Nivaclé (Chulupí) Indians became seasonal laborers on Mennonite farms. This opportunistic exploitation and a some Mennonites patronizing attitude alienated many Indians whose cultural system was more egalitarian and reciprocal. There is no doubting the sincerity of the Mennonites' Christian convictions and their pacifism, but as one member of the community said, 'Not all of us live up to our ideals.'

As more Paraguayans settle in the Chaco, the Mennonite communities have come under pressure from authorities, and there is concern that the government may abrogate the Privilegium. Few Mennonites are reinvesting their earnings in Paraguay, and some are openly looking for alternatives elsewhere. On the other hand, the election of a Mennonite governor of the department of Boquerón, whose capital is Filadelfia, perhaps indicates a desire to participate more directly in a wider Paraguayan context.

Some Mennonites are disgruntled, however, with developments in Filadelfia, whose material prosperity has contributed to a generation more interested in motorbikes and videos than traditional Mennonite values. Beer and tobacco, once absolutely *verboten* in Mennonite settlements, are now sold openly, although only non-Mennonites would normally consume them in public.

There are perhaps 15,000 Mennonites and a slightly larger number of Indians in the region. Among themselves, Mennonites prefer to speak *Plattdeutsch* (Low German) dialect, but they readily speak and understand *Hochdeutsch* (High German), the language of instruction in the schools. Most adults now speak Spanish and a number speak passable English. Local Indians are as likely to speak German as Spanish, although most prefer their native language.

PARQUE NACIONAL DEFENSORES DEL CHACO

Created in 1980, the High Chaco park of Defensores del Chaco is Paraguay's largest (780,000 hectares) and most remote unit. Once the exclusive province of nomadic Ayoreo foragers, it is mostly a forested alluvial plain about 100m in elevation, but the isolated 500m peak of Cerro León is the park's greatest landmark.

Quebracho, algarrobo, palo santo, and cactus are the dominant species in the dense thorn forest, which harbors populations of important animal species despite illicit hunting, which has proved difficult to control over such a large, thinly populated area. This is the likeliest place in Paraguay to view large cats such as jaguar, puma, ocelot, and Geoffroy's cat, plus other unique species, although, as everywhere, such species are only rarely seen.

Defensores del Chaco is 830km from Asunción over roads that are impassable to most ordinary vehicles, especially after rain.

Park headquarters are reached by a road north from Filadelfia to Fortín Teniente Martínez and then to Fortín Madrejón, another 213km north. Further facilities are at Aguas Dulces, 84km beyond Madrejón.

As there is no regular public transportation to Defensores del Chaco, access is difficult, but not impossible. Inquire at the Dirección de Parques Nacionales (☎ 021-445214) in Asunción, which may be able to put you in contact with rangers who must occasionally travel to Asunción. They will sometimes, if space is available, take passengers on the return trip. Getting away may present some difficulty, but have patience – you are unlikely to be stranded forever.

MARISCAL ESTIGARRIBIA

In the words of LP reader Jerry Azevedo, the last sizeable settlement on the Trans-Chaco before the Bolivian border has '300 soldiers, half that many civilians, and an equal number of roosters.' Mariscal Estigarribia is 540km from Asunción; motorists should bear in mind that there is no dependable source of gasoline beyond here, so be sure to fill up and carry extra gas, food, and water.

Lodging is available at ***Hotel Alemán*** for US$16 double, and food can be had at ***Restaurant Achucarro*** (which also has simple accommodations).

There is also a police checkpoint and a gas station, which is a good place to try to catch a lift onward to Bolivia. It's conceivable to board buses to Santa Cruz (Bolivia) here, but it's advisable to purchase your ticket in Asunción.

Every Friday at 8 am, a Nasa bus goes to Estancia La Patria (three hours), the last Trans-Chaco outpost accessible by public transport. Buses to Asunción (US$12.50, 10 hours) leave daily, twice on Sunday.

ESTANCIA LA PATRIA

Only 85km from the Bolivian border, Estancia La Patria is being developed as a rural service center for the estancias of the High Chaco, with running water, a power station, school, hospital, phone system, motel, and petrol station. Every Friday at 2 pm, eastbound buses go to Mariscal Estigarribia (three hours), Filadelfia (five hours), and Asunción (14 hours). Gasoline may be available here.

Language

Spanish in Argentina, and the rest of the River Plate region, has characteristics that readily distinguish it from the rest of Latin America. Probably the most prominent are the usage of the pronoun *vos* in place of *tú* for 'you,' and the trait of pronouncing the letters 'll' and 'y' as 'zh' (as in 'azure') rather than 'y' (like English 'you') as in the rest of the Americas. Note that in American Spanish, the plural of the familiar 'tú' or 'vos' is *ustedes* rather than *vosotros*, as in Spain. Argentines understand continental Spanish but may find it quaint or pretentious.

There are many vocabulary differences between European and American Spanish, and among Spanish-speaking countries in the Americas. The speech of Buenos Aires, in particular, abounds with words and phrases from the colorful slang known as *lunfardo*. Although you shouldn't use lunfardo words unless you are supremely confident that you know their *every* implication (especially in formal situations), you should be aware of some of the more common everyday usages. Argentines normally refer to the Spanish language as *castellano* rather than *español*.

Every visitor should make an effort to speak Spanish, whose basic elements are easily acquired. If possible, take a brief night course at your local university or community college before departure. Even if you can't speak very well, Argentines are gracious hosts and will encourage your use of Spanish, so there is no need to feel self-conscious about vocabulary or pronunciation. There are many common cognates, so if you're stuck, try Hispanicizing an English word – it is unlikely you'll make a truly embarrassing error. Do not, however, admit to being 'embarrassed' *(embarazada)* unless you are in fact pregnant; see the list of 'false cognates' below for other usages to be avoided.

Phrasebooks & Dictionaries

Lonely Planet's *Latin American Spanish phrasebook* by Anna Cody is a worthwhile addition to your backpack. Another exceptionally useful resource is the *University of Chicago Spanish-English, English-Spanish*

Cognates & Condoms

False cognates are words that appear very similar but have different meanings in different languages; in some instances, these differences can lead to serious misunderstandings. The following is a list of some of these words in English with their Spanish cousins and their meaning in Spanish. Note that this list deals primarily with the River Plate region, and usages may differ in other areas.

English	Spanish	Meaning in Spanish
actual	*actual*	current (at present)
carpet	*carpeta*	looseleaf notebook
embarrassed	*embarazada*	pregnant
introduce	*introducir*	introduce (as an innovation)
notorious	*notorio*	well-known, evident
present (verb)	*presentar*	introduce (a person)
precise	*preciso*	necessary
preservative	*preservativo*	condom
violation	*violación*	rape

¡POR FAVORO, NO PRESERVATIVO, PLEASE!

Dictionary; its small size, light weight and thorough entries make it perfect for travel.

Pronunciation

Spanish pronunciation is, in general, consistently phonetic. Speak slowly to avoid getting tongue-tied until you become confident of your ability.

Vowels Vowels are very consistent and have easy English equivalents.

a is like 'a' in 'father'
e is like 'ai' in 'sail'
i is like 'ee' in 'feet'
o is like 'o' in 'for'
u is like 'u' in 'food'; after consonants other than 'q' it is more like English 'w,' as it also is when the vowel sound is modified by an umlaut, as in 'Güemes'
y is a consonant except when it stands alone or appears at the end of a word, in which case its pronunciation is identical to Spanish 'i'

Consonants Spanish consonants resemble their English equivalents, with some major exceptions. Pronunciation of the letters *f*, *k*, *l*, *m*, *n*, *p*, *q*, *s* and *t* is virtually identical to English. Although *y* is identical in most Latin American countries when used as a consonant, most Argentines say 'zh' for it and for *ll*, which is a separate letter. *Ch* and *ñ* are also separate letters, with separate dictionary entries.

b resembles its English equivalent but is indistinguishable from 'v.' For clarity, refer to the former as 'b larga,' the latter as 'b corta' (the word for the letter itself is pronounced like English 'bay').
c is like the 's' in 'see' before e and i, otherwise like English 'k.'
d closely resembles 'th' in 'feather.'
g is like a guttural English 'h' before Spanish 'e' and 'i,' otherwise like 'g' in 'go.'
h is invariably silent. If your name begins with this letter, listen carefully when immigration officials summon you to pick up your passport.
j most closely resembles English 'h' but is slightly more guttural.
ñ is like 'ni' in 'onion.'
r is a short 'tap r' except at the beginning of a word and after 'l,' 'n,' or 's,' when it is often rolled.
rr is very strongly rolled.
v resembles English, but see 'b,' above.
x is like 'x' in 'taxi' except for very few words for which it follows Spanish or Mexican usage as 'j.'
z is like 's' in 'sun.'

Diphthongs Diphthongs are vowel combinations forming a single syllable. In Spanish, the formation of a diphthong depends on combinations of 'weak' vowels ('i' and 'u') or strong ones ('a,' 'e,' and 'o'). Two weak vowels or a strong and a weak vowel make a diphthong, but two strong ones are pronounced as separate syllables.

A good example of two weak vowels forming a diphthong is the word *diurno* (during the day). The final syllable of *obligatorio* (obligatory) is a combination of weak and strong vowels.

Stress Stress, often indicated by visible accents, is very important, since it can

Lunfardo

Below are a few of the more common, and innocuous, lunfardo usages that you may hear on the streets. Visitors interested in more detail can look for Tino Rodríguez's *Primer Diccionario de Sinónimos del Lunfardo* (Buenos Aries, Editorial Atlántida 1987) and/or contact the Academia Porteña del Lunfardo (☎ 011-4383-2393), Estados Unidos 1379, Buenos Aires.

guita	money
laburo	work
macanudo	terrific
morfar	to eat
palo	ten pesos
pibe	guy, dude
piola	cool
pucho	cigarette

change the meaning of words. In general, words ending in vowels or the letters 'n' or 's' have stress on the next-to-last syllable, while those with other endings have stress on the last syllable. Thus *vaca* (cow) and *caballos* (horses) both have stress on their penultimate syllables.

Written accents will almost always appear in words that do not follow the above rules, such as *sótano* (basement), *América*, and *porción* (portion). When counting syllables be sure to remember that diphthongs constitute only one. When words appear in capitals, the written accent is generally omitted but still pronounced.

Greetings & Civilities

In their public behavior, Argentines are very conscious of civilities, sometimes to the point of ceremoniousness. Never, for example, approach a stranger for information without extending a greeting like *buenos días* or *buenas tardes*.

yes	*sí*
no	*no*
thank you	*gracias*
you're welcome	*de nada*
hello	*hola*
good morning	*buenos días*
good afternoon	*buenas tardes*
good evening	*buenas noches*
good night	*buenas noches*
goodbye	*adiós*, *chau* (informal)

I understand.	*Entiendo.*
I don't understand.	*No entiendo.*

I don't speak much Spanish.
Hablo poco castellano.

Useful Words & Phrases

and	*y*
to/at	*a*
for	*por, para*
of/from	*de, desde*
in	*en*
with	*con*
without	*sin*
before	*antes*
after	*después*
soon	*pronto*
already	*ya*
now	*ahora*
right away	*en seguida*
here	*aquí*
there	*allí*
Where?	*¿Dónde?*
Where is/are ...?	*¿Dónde está/están ...?*
When?	*¿Cuándo?*
How?	*¿Cómo?*

I would like ...	*Me gustaría/Quisiera ...*
coffee	*café*
tea	*té*
beer	*cerveza*
wine	*vino*

How much?	*¿Cuánto?*
How many?	*¿Cuántos?*
Is/Are there ...?	*¿Hay ...?*

Do you speak English?
¿Habla Usted inglés?
Speak (Drive) slowly, please
Despacio, por favor

Getting Around

airplane	*avión*
train	*tren*
bus	*colectivo,micro, ómnibus*
ship	*barco, buque*
ferry	*barca de pasaje*
hydrofoil	*aliscafo*
car	*auto*
taxi	*taxi*
truck	*camión*
pickup	*camioneta*
bicycle	*bicicleta*
motorcycle	*motocicleta*
hitchhike	*hacer dedo*

I would like a ticket to ...
Quiero un boleto/pasaje a ...
What's the fare to ...?
¿Cuánto cuesta el pasaje a ...?
When does the next bus leave for ...?
¿Cuándo sale el próximo ómnibus para ...?
Is there a student/university discount?
¿Hay descuento estudiantil/universitario?

Do you accept credit cards?
¿Trabajan con tarjetas de crédito?

first/last/next
primero/último/próximo

first/second class	*primera/segunda clase*
single/return (roundtrip)	*ida/ida y vuelta*
sleeper	*camarote*
luggage storage	*guardería, equipaje*

Accommodations

Below you will find English phrases with useful Spanish equivalents for Argentina, most of which will be understood in other Spanish-speaking countries.

hotel	*hotel, pensión, residencial*
single room	*habitación para una persona*
double room	*habitación doble, matrimonio*

How much does it cost?
¿Cuánto cuesta?

per night	*por noche*
full board	*pensión completa*
shared bath	*baño compartido*
private bath	*baño privado*
too expensive	*demasiado caro*
discount	*descuento*
cheaper	*mas económico*
May I see it?	*¿Puedo verla?*
I don't like it.	*No me gusta.*
the bill	*la cuenta*

Around Town

tourist information	*oficina de turismo*
airport	*aeropuerto*
train station	*estación de ferrocarril*
bus terminal	*terminal de ómnibus*
bathing resort	*balneario*
post office	*correo*
letter	*carta*
parcel	*paquete*
postcard	*postal*
airmail	*correo aéreo*
registered mail	*certificado*
express mail	*puerta a puerta*
stamps	*estampillas*
person to person	*persona a persona*
collect call	*cobro revertido*

Toilets

The most common word for toilet is *baño*, but *servicios sanitarios* (services) is a frequent alternative. Men's toilets usually bear a descriptive term like *hombres*, *caballeros*, or *varones*. Women's restrooms have a *señoras* or *damas* sign.

Countries

The list below contains only countries whose spelling differs significantly in English and Spanish.

Denmark	*Dinamarca*
England	*Inglaterra*
France	*Francia*
Germany	*Alemania*
Great Britain	*Gran Bretaña*
Ireland	*Irlanda*
Italy	*Italia*
Japan	*Japón*
Netherlands	*Holanda*
New Zealand	*Nueva Zelandia*
Peru	*Perú*
Scotland	*Escocia*
Spain	*España*
Sweden	*Suecia*
Switzerland	*Suiza*
United States	*Estados Unidos*
Wales	*Gales*

Numbers

Should hyperinflationary times return, you may have to learn to count in very large numbers.

0	*cero*
1	*uno*
2	*dos*
3	*tres*
4	*cuatro*
5	*cinco*
6	*seis*
7	*siete*
8	*ocho*
9	*nueve*

10 *diez*
11 *once*
12 *doce*
13 *trece*
14 *catorce*
15 *quince*
16 *dieciséis*
17 *diecisiete*
18 *dieciocho*
19 *diecinueve*
20 *veinte*
21 *veintiuno*
22 *veintidós*
30 *treinta*
31 *treinta y uno*
32 *treinta y dos*
40 *cuarenta*
50 *cincuenta*
60 *sesenta*
70 *setenta*
80 *ochenta*
90 *noventa*
100 *cien*
101 *ciento uno*
110 *ciento diez*
120 *ciento veinte*
200 *doscientos*
300 *trescientos*
400 *cuatrocientos*
500 *quinientos*
600 *seiscientos*
700 *setecientos*
800 *ochocientos*
900 *novecientos*

El Voseo

Spanish in the Río de la Plata region differs from that of Spain and most of the rest of the Americas, most notably in the familiar form of the second person singular pronoun. Instead of the tuteo used everywhere else, Argentines, Uruguayans, and Paraguayans commonly use the voseo, a relict 16th-century form requiring slightly different endings. Regular and most irregular verbs differ from tú forms; regular verbs change their stress and add an accent, while irregular verbs do not change internal consonants, but add a terminal accent. This is true for -ar, -er, and -ir verbs, examples of which are given below, with the tú forms included for contrast. Imperative forms also differ, but negative imperatives are identical in both the tuteo and the voseo.

In the list below, the first verb of each ending is regular, while the second is irregular; the pronoun is included for clarity, though most Spanish-speakers normally omit it.

Verb	**Tuteo/Imperative**	**Voseo/Imperative**
hablar (to speak)	*tú hablas/habla*	*vos hablás/hablá*
soñar (to dream)	*tú sueñas/sueña*	*vos soñás/soñá*
comer (to eat)	*tú comes/come*	*vos comés/comé*
poner (to put)	*tú pones/pon*	*vos ponés/poné*
admitir (to admit)	*tú admites/admite*	*vos admitís/admití*
venir (to come)	*tú vienes/ven*	*vos venís/vení*

Note that some of the most common verbs, like *ir* (to go), *estar* (to be) and *ser* (to be) are identically irregular in both the tuteo and the voseo, and that Argentines continue to use the possessive article *tu* (*Vos tenés tu lápiz?*) and the reflexive or conjunctive object pronoun *te* (*Vos te das cuenta?*).

An Argentine inviting a foreigner to address him or her informally will say *Me podés tutear* (you can call me 'tú') rather than *Me podés vosear* (you can call me 'vos'), even though the expectation is that both will use 'vos' forms in subsequent conversation.

1000	*mil*
1100	*mil cien*
2000	*dos mil*
5000	*cinco mil*
10,000	*diez mil*
50,000	*cincuenta mil*
100,000	*cien mil*
1,000,000	*un millón*

Time

Telling time is fairly straightforward. Eight o'clock is *las ocho*, while 8:30 is *las ocho y treinta* (literally, eight and thirty) or *las ocho y media* (eight and a half). However, 7:45 is *las ocho menos quince* (literally, eight minus fifteen) or *las ocho menos cuarto* (eight minus one quarter). Times are modified by morning *de la manaña* or afternoon *(de la tarde)* instead of am or pm. Transportation schedules commonly use the 24-hour clock.

Days of the Week

Monday	*lunes*
Tuesday	*martes*
Wednesday	*miércoles*
Thursday	*jueves*
Friday	*viernes*
Saturday	*sábado*
Sunday	*domingo*

Glossary

Unless otherwise indicated, the terms below apply to all three River Plate countries of Argentina, Uruguay, and Paraguay. Terms specific to the Falkland Islands are also noted. The list includes common geographical and biological terms plus slang terms from everyday speech. The latter includes *lunfardo*, the street slang of Buenos Aires (see the Lunfardo boxed text in the Language appendix).

AAA – Argentine Anti-Communist Alliance, a right-wing death squad probably organized by Perón's mysterious advisor José López Rega.
AAAJ – Asociación Argentina de Albergues de la Juventud. One of two Argentine youth hostel organizations. The other, RAAJ, has a smaller and generally better list of hostels than AAAJ, and is a more energetic outfit.
ACA – Automóvil Club Argentino, which provides maps, road service, insurance, and other services, and operates hotels, motels, and campgrounds throughout the country. A valuable resource even for travelers without motor vehicles.
acequia – irrigation canal, primarily in the Cuyo region.
Acuerdo Nacional – in Paraguay, a broad coalition of opponents of the Stroessner dictatorship.
aerosilla – chairlift.
alameda – street lined with poplar trees.
albergue transitorio – not to be mistaken for an *albergue juvenil* (youth hostel), this is very short-term accommodations normally utilized by young couples in search of privacy. Some places cater exclusively to this trade, while some budget hotels rely on it in part for financial viability. An alternative euphemism, used in Uruguay, is *hotel de alta rotatividad*.
alerce – large coniferous tree, resembling a California redwood, from which Argentina's Parque Nacional Los Alerces takes its name.
alfajores – biscuit sandwiches with chocolate, dulce de leche, or fruit.
alíscafo – hydrofoil from Buenos Aires across the Río de la Plata to Colonia, Uruguay.
altiplano – high Andean plain, often above 4000m, in the northwestern Argentine provinces of Jujuy, Salta, La Rioja, and Catamarca.
apunamiento – altitude sickness.
argentinidad – emotional but nebulous concept of Argentine national identity, often associated with extreme nationalism.
arrayán – tree of the myrtle family, from which Argentina's Parque Nacional Los Arrayanes takes its name.
arroyo – creek, stream.
asado – barbecue, usually a family outing in summer.
autopista – freeway or motorway.

bache – pothole (in a road or highway).
balneario – bathing resort or beach.
balsa – a launch or raft.
bañado – marsh or seasonally flooded zone on the rivers of northern Argentina. Bañados are good habitat for migratory birds, but are also often used for temporary cultivation.
banda negativa – low-cost air tickets in Argentina, where limited seats on particular flights are available for up to 40% below the usual price.
baqueano – back-country tracker.
barrio – neighborhood or borough.
bencina – white gas, used for campstoves. Also known as *nafta blanca*.
BFFI – British Forces Falkland Islands.
bicho – any small creature, from insect to mammal.
biota – the fauna and flora of a region.
boga – tasty fish from the rivers of Argentine Mesopotamia.
boleadoras – heavily weighted thongs, used by Pampas and Patagonian Indians for hunting guanaco and rhea. Also called *bolas*.
bonos – bonds used as legal currency in the provinces of Jujuy, Salta, and Tucumán, but

worthless outside the province of issue. Bonos usually have a date of expiration, beyond which they have no value.

cabildo – colonial town council; also, the building housing the council.
cachila – in Uruguay, an antique automobile, often beautifully maintained.
cacique – Indian chief.
cajero automático – automated teller machine (ATM).
caldén – *Prosopis caldenia*, a characteristic tree of the Dry Pampa.
calle – street.
Camp, the – in the Falkland Islands, the area beyond Stanley, ie, the countryside. Anglo-Argentines use the same term to refer to the countryside, but it can also mean a given field or paddock, in both Falklands or Anglo-Argentine usage.
campo – the countryside. Alternately, a field or paddock.
caracoles – a winding road, usually in a mountainous area.
característica – telephone area code.
carapintada – in the Argentine military, extreme right-wing, ultranationalist movement of disaffected junior officers, responsible for several attempted coups during the Alfonsín and Menem administrations.
carpincho – capybara, a large aquatic rodent that inhabits the Paraná and other subtropical rivers.
cartelera – an office selling discount tickets.
casa de familia – modest family accommodations, usually in tourist centers.
casa de gobierno – literally 'government house,' a building now often converted to a museum, offices, etc.
casco – 'big house' of a cattle or sheep estancia.
cataratas – waterfalls.
caudillo – in 19th-century Argentine politics, a provincial strongman whose power rested more on personal loyalty than political ideals or party organization.
cerro – mount, mountain.
chachacoma – Andean shrub whose leaves produce an herbal tea that relieves symptoms of altitude sickness.
chacra – small, independent farm.
chivito – Uruguayan steak sandwich.
chopp – draft or lager beer.
chopperia – an establishment serving *chopp* and food.
chusquea – solid bamboo of the Valdivian rain forest in Patagonia.
ciervo – deer.
coima – a bribe. One who solicits a bribe is a *coimero*.
comedor – basic cafeteria or dining room in a hotel.
CONAF – Corporación Nacional Forestal, Chilean state agency in charge of forestry and conservation, including management of national parks like Torres del Paine.
confitería – café that serves coffee, tea, desserts, and simple food orders. Many confiterías are important social centers in Argentina.
congregación – in colonial Latin America, the concentration of dispersed native populations in central settlements, usually for purposes of political control or religious instruction (see also *reducción*).
congrio – conger eel, a popular and delicious Chilean seafood.
Conquista del Desierto – 'Conquest of the Desert,' a euphemism for General Julio Argentino Roca's late-19th-century war of extermination against the Mapuche of northern Patagonia.
conventillo – tenements that housed immigrants in older neighborhoods of Buenos Aires and Montevideo. On a reduced scale, these still exist in the Buenos Aires barrio of San Telmo and the Ciudad Vieja of Montevideo.
cordobazo – 1969 uprising against the Argentine military government in the city of Córdoba, which eventually paved way for the return of Juan Perón from exile.
cospel – token used in Argentine public telephones in lieu of coins. Cospeles are also common in Uruguay and Paraguay.
costanera – sea-, river-, or lakeside road.
criollo – in colonial period, an American-born Spaniard, but the term now commonly describes any Argentine of European descent. The term also describes the feral cattle of the Pampas.
cuatrerismo – cattle rustling.

curanto – Chilean seafood stew. Also an unrelated Argentine Andes dish made of red or white meat, or vegetables.

démedos – literally 'give me two,' a pejorative nickname for Argentines who travel to Miami, where everything is so cheap that they buy things they don't need.
DDI – Discado Directo Internacional (International Direct Dialing), which provides direct access to home-country operators for long-distance collect and credit-card calls. This is cheaper than the Argentine companies Telecom and Telefónica, but is not yet available in all areas.
dique – a dam. The reservoir created by a dique is often used for recreational purposes. In some cases, dique refers to a drydock.
Dirty War – see *Guerra Sucia*.
dulce de leche – caramelized milk, an Argentine invention and obsession, often spread on bread or crackers and stuffed in pastries.
dorado – large river fish in the Paraná drainage, known among fishing enthusiasts as the 'Tiger of the Paraná' for its fighting spirit. The fish is tasty but rather bony.

encomienda – colonial labor system, under which Indian communities were required to provide workers for Spaniards *(encomenderos)*, in exchange for which the Spaniards were to provide religious and language instruction. In practice, the system benefited Spaniards far more than native peoples.
EOD – Explosive Ordnance Disposal, British army unit in charge of dealing with unexploded land mines and other weapons from the Falklands War of 1982.
ERP – Ejército Revolucionario del Pueblo, revolutionary leftist group that mimicked Cuban-style revolution in the sugar-growing areas of Tucumán province in 1970s. Wiped out by the Argentine army during the Dirty War.
escrache – tactic of human-rights advocates, plastering the city with posters publicizing the faces and addresses of Dirty War criminals and demonstrating outside their residences.
esquí alpino – downhill skiing.
esquí de fondo – Nordic or cross-country skiing.
estancia – extensive grazing establishment, either for cattle or sheep, with a dominating owner or manager and dependent resident labor force.
estanciero – owner of an estancia.

facturas – pastries.
ficha – token used in the Buenos Aires subway system (Subte) in lieu of coins.
FIBS – Falkland Islands Broadcasting Service.
FIC – Falkland Islands Company.
FIDC – Falkland Islands Development Corporation.
FIG – Falkland Islands Government.
FIGAS – Falkland Islands Government Air Service.
forro – slang term for condom or, when used to describe a person, a 'scumbag'; to be avoided in polite conversation.
frigorífico – meat-freezing factory.
fronterizo – hybrid Spanish-Portuguese dialect spoken along the border between Uruguay and Brazil.

gardeliano – fan of the late tango singer Carlos Gardel.
gas-oil – diesel fuel.
gasolero – motor vehicle that uses diesel fuel, which is much cheaper than ordinary gasoline in Argentina.
guapoy – strangler fig of subtropical forests.
guardaganado – cattle guard (on a road or highway).
guardería – In Chile, a park ranger station.
Guerra Sucia – the Dirty War in the 1970s, of the Argentine military against left-wing revolutionaries and anyone suspected of sympathizing with them.
guita – in lunfardo, money.
gurí – Guaraní word meaning 'child' that has been adopted into regional speech in Argentine Mesopotamia and Paraguay.

hacienda – in the Andean Northwest, a large but often underproductive rural landholding, with a dependent resident labor force, under a dominant owner. In Argentina, a less common form of *latifundio* than in other Latin American countries.

ichu – bunch grass of the Andean steppe (altiplano).
ida – one-way.
ida y vuelta – roundtrip.
iglesia – church.
indigenismo – movement in Latin American art and literature that extols aboriginal traditions, usually in a romantic or patronizing manner.
ingenio – industrial sugar mill.
interno – extension off a central telephone number or switchboard.
IVA – *impuesto de valor agregado*, value added tax (VAT), often added to restaurant or hotel bills in Argentina and Uruguay. If there is any question, ask whether IVA is included in the bill.

jabalí – wild European boar, a popular game dish in Argentine Patagonia.
jineteada – any horseback riding competition, as in a rodeo.

lapacho – important timber tree in subtropical northern Argentina.
latifundio – large landholding, such as a cattle or sheep estancia.
legua – vernacular 'league' of about 5km, commonly used to measure distance in rural Argentina.
literatura gauchesca – literature *about* idealized gauchos and their values, usually written by urban and rural elites, as opposed to literature *by* gauchos, whose traditions were oral rather than written.
lunfardo – street slang of Buenos Aires, with origins in turn-of-the-century immigrant neighborhoods.

manta – a shawl or bedspread.
mara – Patagonian hare.
maragato – native or resident of the city of Carmen de Patagones, in southern Buenos Aires province.
mazamorra – thickish maize soup, typical of the Northwest Andean region.
mate – see *yerba mate.*
mazorca – political police of 19th-century Argentine dictator Juan Manuel de Rosas.
mediero – sharecropper, a tenant who farms another's land in exchange for a percentage of the crop.
meseta – interior steppe of eastern Patagonia.
mestizo – a person of mixed Indian and Spanish descent.
minifundio – small landholding, such as a peasant farm.
minuta – in restaurant or confitería, a short order such as spaghetti or milanesa.
mirador – viewpoint, usually on a hill but often in a building.
Montoneros – left-wing faction of the Peronist party that became an underground urban guerrilla movement in 1970s.
monte – scrub forest. The term is often applied to any densely vegetated area.
municipalidad – city hall.
museo – museum.

nafta – gasoline or petrol.
novela – television soap opera.

ñandú – rhea; large, flightless bird, resembling the ostrich. There are two Argentine species.
ñandutí – delicate 'spiderweb' lace woven by the women of Itauguá, a small town near Asunción, Paraguay.
ñoqui – a public employee whose primary interest is collecting a monthly paycheck. So-called because potato pasta, or ñoquis (from the Italian *gnocchi)*, are traditionally served in financially strapped Argentine households on the 29th of each month, the implication being that the employee shows up at work around that time.

oligarquía terrateniente – derogatory term for the Argentine landed elite.
onces – 'elevenses,' Chilean afternoon tea.

pampero – South Atlantic cold front that brings dramatic temperature changes to Uruguay, Paraguay, and the interior of northern Argentina.
parada – bus stop.

parrillada, parrilla – respectively, a mixed grill of steak and other beef cuts, and a restaurant specializing in such dishes.
paseaperros – professional dog-walker in Buenos Aires.
pasarela – catwalk across a stream or bog.
paseo – an outing, such as a walk in the park or downtown.
peatonal – pedestrian mall, usually in the downtown area of major Argentine cities.
pehuén – araucaria, or 'monkey puzzle' tree of southern Patagonia.
peña – club that hosts informal folk-music gatherings.
peones golondrinas – 'swallows,' term frequently applied to seasonal laborers from Bolivia in the Tucumán sugar harvest, but also used in similar contexts elsewhere in Argentina.
picada – in rural areas, a trail, especially through dense woods or mountains; in the context of food, hors d'oeuvres.
pingüinera – penguin colony.
piropo – sexist remark, ranging from complimentary and relatively innocuous to rude and offensive.
Portakabin – modular shelter unit similar to a cargo container but with doors and windows. Many left on the Falkland Islands by the British military are now used to accommodate travelers or hikers.
porteño – inhabitant of Buenos Aires, a 'resident of the port.'
precordillera – foothills of the Andes.
primera – 1st class on a train.
Privilegium – agreement between the Paraguayan government and Mennonite agricultural colonists, granting the latter land and political autonomy, including the right to German-language schools, freedom of religion, exemption from military service, cooperative economic organization, and independent law enforcement.
Proceso – in full, 'El Proceso de Reorganización Nacional,' a military euphemism for its brutal attempt to remake Argentina's political and economic culture between 1976 and 1983.
propina – a tip, for example, in a restaurant or cinema.
pucará – in the Andean Northwest, a pre-Columbian fortification, generally on high ground commanding an unobstructed view in several directions.
puchero – soup combining vegetables and meats, served with rice.
puesto – 'outside house' on a cattle or sheep estancia.
pucho – in lunfardo, a cigarette or cigarette butt.
pulpería – rural shop or 'company store' on cattle or sheep estancia.
puna – Andean highlands, usually above 3000m.
puntano – a native or resident of Argentina's San Luis province.

quebracho – literally, 'axe-breaker'; tree *(Quebrachua lorentzii)* of the Chaco, a natural source of tannin for the leather industries of the River Plate.
quilombo – in lunfardo, a mess. Originally a Brazilian term describing a settlement of runaway slaves, it came to mean a house of prostitution in Argentina.
quinoa – a native Andean grain, the dietary equivalent of rice in pre-Columbian times.

RAAJ – Red Argentina de Alojamiento para Jóvenes. The more robust of the two Argentine youth hostel organizations.
rambla – avenue or shopping mall.
rancho – a rural house, generally of adobe, with a thatched roof.
recargo – additional charge, usually 10%, that many Argentine businesses add to credit-card transactions because of delays in payment.
reducción – like congregación, the concentration of native populations in towns modeled on the Spanish grid pattern, for purposes of political control or religious instruction. The term also refers to the settlement itself.
refugio – a usually rustic shelter in a national park or remote area.
remise – (also *remís)*a taxi with a radio connection to a dispatcher.
río – river.

RN – Ruta Nacional, in Argentina, a national highway.
RP – Ruta Provincial, in Argentina, a provincial highway.
ruta – highway.

sábalo – popular river fish in the Paraná drainage.
saladero – establishment for salting meat and hides.
salar – salt lake or salt pan, usually in the high Andes or Argentine Patagonia.
SIDA – AIDS.
siesta – lengthy afternoon break for lunch and, occasionally, a nap.
s/n – 'sin número,' indicating a street address without a number.
smoko – in the Falkland Islands, midmorning tea or coffee break, usually including cakes and other homemade sweets.
sobremesa – after-dinner conversation.
soroche – altitude sickness.
Southern Cone – in political geography, the area comprising Argentina, Chile, Uruguay, and parts of Brazil and Paraguay. So-called after the area's shape on the map.
squaddies – British enlisted men on four-month tours-of-duty in the Falkland Islands.
Subte – the Buenos Aires underground.
surubí – popular river fish in Argentine Mesopotamia and in the River Plate drainage. It is frequently served in restaurants.

taguá – Wagner's peccary, a species of wild pig thought extinct but recently rediscovered in the Paraguayan Chaco.
tapir – large hoofed mammal of subtropical forests in northern Argentina and Paraguay, a distant relative of the horse.
teleférico – gondola cable-car.
tenedor libre – 'all-you-can-eat' restaurant. Also known as *diente libre*.
tereré – cold mate, as consumed by Paraguayans.
todo terreno – mountain bike.
tola – high-altitude shrubs in the altiplano of northwestern Argentina.
trapiche – antique sugar mill.
trasnochador – one who stays up very late or all night, as do many Argentines.
trucho – bogus, a term widely used by Argentines to describe things that are not what they appear to be.
turco – 'Turk,' an often derogatory term for any Argentine of Middle Eastern descent.
turismo aventura – term used to describe nontraditional forms of tourism, such as trekking and river rafting.
turista – 2nd class on a train, usually not very comfortable.
tuteo – use of the pronoun *tú* in Spanish and its corresponding verb forms.
two-nighter – in the Falkland Islands, a traditional party for visitors from distant sheep stations, who would invariably stay the weekend.

vado – dip (in a road or highway).
vicuña – wild relative of domestic llama and alpaca, found in Argentina's Andean Northwest only at high altitudes.
villas miserias – shantytowns on the outskirts of Buenos Aires and other Argentine cities.
vinchuca – biting insect, living in thatched dwellings with dirt floors, that is a vector for Chagas' disease.
viviendas temporarias – riverfront shantytowns of Asunción, Paraguay.
vizcacha – wild relative of the domestic chinchilla. There are two common species in Argentina, the mountain vizcacha *(Lagidium vizcacha)* of the Andean highlands and the plains vizcacha *(Lagostomus maximus)* of the subtropical lowlands. Some regard the latter as a pest.
voseo – the use of the pronoun *vos* and its corresponding verb forms in the River Plate republics of Argentina, Uruguay, and Paraguay.

warrah – the now extinct but possibly once domesticated Falklands fox or wolf, *Dusicyon australis*, presumptive evidence of Yahgan Indian presence on the Falklands.

yacaré – South American alligator, found in humid, subtropical parts of Argentina, Uruguay, and Paraguay.
YCF – Yacimientos Fiscales Carboníferos, Argentina's state coal company.

yerba mate – 'Paraguayan tea' *(Ilex paraguariensis)*, which Argentines consume in very large amounts. Many Paraguayans, Uruguayans, and Brazilians also use it regularly. Taking *mate* is an important everyday social ritual.
yisca – bag made of vegetable fiber, traditional among the Toba Indians of the Chaco.
YPF – Yacimientos Fiscales Petrolíferos, Argentina's former state oil company.
yungas – in northwestern Argentina, transitional subtropical lowland forest.
yuyos – 'herbs,' mixed with *yerba mate* in northern Argentina.

zafra – sugar harvest.
zona franca – duty-free zone.
zonda – in the central Andean provinces, a powerful, dry north wind like the European *Föhn* or North American *Chinook*.

Climate Charts

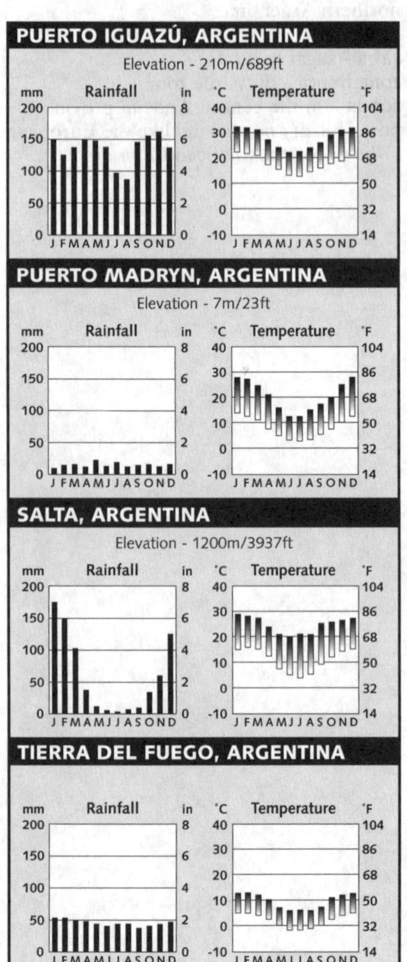

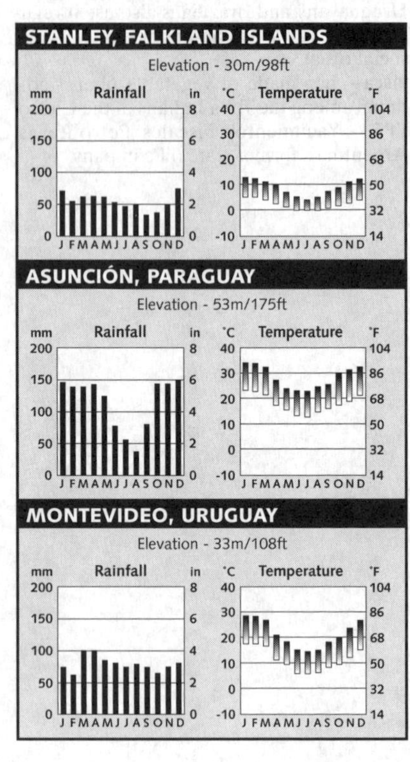

Internet Resources

Argentina (Buenos Aires in particular) has spawned a growing mass of Internet resources. In this fast-moving field, however, change is the rule, and addresses and content can change quickly. Remember that there is a great deal of inaccurate or misleading information on the Internet, and that many websites are updated far less frequently than guidebooks (including this one!).

Government & Information

Cancillería Argentina
www.mrecic.gov.ar/pag1/pagina.htm
Argentina's foreign ministry homepage, with up-to-date information on visa requirements and diplomatic missions, including both embassies and consulates

Centers for Disease Control & Prevention
www.cdc.gov/travel/index.html
Official US government website with information on worldwide travel-related health issues

Dirección de Museos
www.buenosaires.gov.ar/cultura/museos/index.html
Current information on municipal museums in the city of Buenos Aires

Gobierno de la Ciudad de Buenos Aires
www.buenosaires.gov.ar/
General information on the city of Buenos Aires, including government, tourism, and business

Grippo – El Directorio de Argentina
www.grippo.com/
Private Argentine Internet directory with a huge number of links organized by categories, including arts and humanities, news and media, and science; in Spanish and English

Instituto Nacional de Estadísticas y Censos
www.indec.mecon.ar/default.htm
Homepage for the Argentine federal government's major statistical agency, though the online census material is insufficiently organized to be very useful

Museo Nacional de Bellas Artes
www.startel.com.ar/bellasartes/mnba.htm
Homepage for Argentina's major fine-arts facility

Páginas Amarillas
www.paginasamarillas.com.ar
Searchable business phone directory, but may not list all the numbers you need

Language Schools

Instituto de Lengua Española para Extranjeros
www.studyabroad.com/ilee

Tradfax
www.tradfax.com

Media

Ámbito Financiero
www.ambitofinanciero.com
Buenos Aires' leading financial daily

Buenos Aires Herald
www.buenosairesherald.com
Abbreviated but still informative weekly version of the capital's venerable English-language daily

Clarín
www.clarin.com.ar
Very complete version of the world's largest-circulation Spanish-language daily, but the graphics overkill often means very slow downloading

La Nación
www.lanacion.com.ar
One of Buenos Aires' oldest and most prestigious dailies

Página 12
www.pagina12.com
Left-of-center daily known for the capital's best investigative journalism

UkiNet
www.ukinet.com/
Human rights-oriented website by a committed and talented independent journalist

Travel & Tourism

Aconcagua
www.aconcagua.com.ar
Information for climbers of highest peak in the Americas; in Spanish, English, German, French, and Portuguese

Aerolíneas Argentinas
www.aerolineas.com.ar/
Homepage for Argentina's traditional carrier

Business Travel to Argentina
www.invertir.com
Information geared toward business travelers to Buenos Aires and some provincial cities

Council Travel
www.ciee.org
Homepage for widespread network of discount

travel agencies; also includes information on study programs

Ente Municipal de Turismo (Mar del Plata)
www.argenet.com.ar/~emtur
Official site of Buenos Aires province's major beach resort

Instituto Fueguino de Turismo
http://tierradelfuego.ml.org/indexseng.htm
Official site for Tierra del Fuego, including up-to-date prices and material on Antarctica

Lonely Planet
www.lonelyplanet.com
Succinct summaries on traveling to most places on earth, postcards from other travelers, travel news, updates, and links, along with the Thorn Tree bulletin board, where you can ask questions of other travelers or post advice

Red Argentina de Alojamiento para Jóvenes (RAAJ)
www.hostels.com.ar/
Official website for local affiliate of Hostelling International

Secretaría de Turismo de Río Negro
www.rnonline.com.ar
Official site of Río Negro province, including Bariloche

STA Travel
www.sta-travel.com.html
Similar to Council Travel, a widespread network of discount travel agencies

Worldski Argentina
www.worldski.com.ar/
Homepage for several Argentine ski resorts, including Las Leñas

Uruguay

Dieciocho – Gran Directorio de Recursos Uruguayos en Internet
www.civila.com/uruguay/
Guide to Uruguayan Internet resources

Mercopress News Agency
www.falkland-malvinas.com/index.html
Montevideo-based Internet news agency covering politics and business in the Mercosur countries of Argentina, Brazil, Uruguay, and Paraguay, as well as Chile and the Falkland Islands; in English and Spanish

Montevideo Comm
www.montevideo.com.uy/mvd/
Uruguayan Internet provider offering a good choice of links

Usenet Discussion Groups

Soc.culture.argentina
Wide-ranging, sometimes trivial, but often polemical and irritating discussion group

Rec.travel.latin-america
Regional travel discussion group

Acknowledgements

THANKS

Many readers wrote with helpful information and suggestions, including Jadwiga Adamzuk, Dai and Daniel Alford, Lucy W de Alió, Rune E Alkstrand, Miriam Allen, Spencer Allman, Tim Allman and Rebecca Lush, Miguel Angel Alonso, C Gabriel Alperovich, Federico Amorim, Katrine Helsing Andersen, Charles and Julian Anderson, Cherie Anderson and Dairne Fitzpatrick, Debbie Anderson, Matt Anderson, Claus B Andersson, Tom Andre, Belinda Andrews, Dominique Argenson, Dudley Arnold, Bob Aronoff, Chris Ashton, Valeria Axelrad, Ed and Gloria Azarian, Jerry Azevedo, Christine Badre, Bernard Badzioch and Sylwia Zablocka, Daniel Bagnera, Joze Balas, Carolyn Barnato, Craig Barrack and Carolyn Johnson, Nick Barraud, Susan Barreau, Tim Barrett, Dom Barry, Lee Barry, Jonathan Bear, John Beaven, John Becken, Michael Beckmann, Anja Behrendt and Alexander Sturm, Suzanne Belson, Carlos Benedit, Anne-Trine Benjaminsen, Kate Berg, Marloes Bergmans and Stefan Rooyackers, Steve Bergren, Góran Berntsson, John Beswetherick and Kath Jones, Ragnhild and Antoon Beyne-Pille, Loretta Biasutti, Frances and Paul Black, Ray Black, Colleen Blake, Marisa Blumhagen and David Sutter, Cristián Boiero Sutter, Alastair Bool, Charlotte and Paul Boorje, Anthony Boult, Patrick Bowes, Christoph Braun, Gert-jan Bremer, Marianne Brito, Linda Broschofsky, Berne Broudy, Suzanne Brown, Vanessa Brown, Maud Bruemmer, Alexandra Bucka, Ian Bunton, Rollo Burgess, Matthew Burke, Stephen D Busack, Jasper F Buxton, Marcelo Caballero, Frank Campbell, Colin S Carr, Ana Valeria Carranza, John Carrington-Birch, Carmel Castellan and Alexandra Taylor, Pablo Castelli, Mike Cavendish, Roberto Chatfield, Walt Clayton, Andrew and Karen Cockburn, Jane C Coffey, David Connor, Dale and Kevin Coghlan, Pat Coleman and Sara Tizard, Patrick Collins, Richard Collyer-Hamlin, Anne Cook, Peter Coutts, Aaron Corcoran, Gianluca Corsini, Bryce Coulter, Julie Coulthard, Keith Crandall, Lenora Crane, Paula Crotty, Paul Crovella and Julia Pike, Guillermo Cumini, Sebastián Cwilich, Phillip A Dale, Paul R Danneberg, Bill Davis, Alan and Leanne Dawson, Dee and Bob Day, Jorge DeJean, Mark Dekkers, Jennifer Delagneau, Hernán Demb, Myriam Deshaies, Jason Diautz, Enrique Díaz, Miguel Dijkman, Juan Carlos Dima, Carole Dixon, Andres Dörr, Marion Drexler, Michael and Phyllis Dyer, Bernd Ebner, David Edelstein, Mats Ekelund, Dana Ellerbrock, Marie Engelstad, Donald C Erbe, Martin Erdmann, Dave Eynon, Igor Fabjan, Gustavo Faigenbaum, Michael Falk, Douglas Fears, Jochen Feinhals, Natasha Fellowes, María José Fernández Mendy, Marcelo Ferrante, John Ferreira, Pablo Fisch, Jean-Marc Fiton, Steve Flint, Carolyn Foreman, John L Franklin, Jonathan Freeman, Daniel Freitas, Marjolein Friele, Roberta Friend, Christián Adolfo Frungieri, Gabriela Furlotti, Lesley Furness, Carlos Gajardo and Lenka Hodrová, Andrés Garcia, Gabriel Garriga, Ricard Gavaldà, Anne Geddes, Bert Geigengack, Fabrice Gendre, Klaus Gierhake, Diego Giles, Juan Bernardo Gimelli Santos, Thomas and Alcke Girtz, Christian Ezequiel Golman, Lorenzo Gordon, Robert Grant, Claudia von Graevenitz, Moira Greaven, Gaye Greenwald, DN Griffiths, David P Grill, Danile Grujic, Michael K Gschwind and Valentina Salapura, Wade Guthrie, Jacqueline Gygax, Alicia Haber, Deta Hadorn-Planta, Patrick Hagans, Victor Håkansson, Christopher Hall, Ross Hamilton, Rhonda Hankins, Brad Hanson, Christiane Hanstein, James Hardy, Joan Harelik, Lynda Harpley, Bill Hart, Holger Hartmeier, Boris Hasselblatt, Michelle Hecht and Bob Redlinger, Cyndi Heller, Michele Heymann, Julius Heinis, Elisabeth Herrería, Fernando Hevia, Magda Belén Hinojosa, Jochen Hoettcke, Brett Hogan, Michael Hogue, Andrew Holmes, William Hood, Dawn and Kevin Hopkins, Russell Hopp, Joseph Horan, Martin Howard, James and Kathleen Howley, Melvyn Huckaby, Bernhard Humpert, Jason Humphreys, Lyndsay Humphries, David L Huntzinger, Ernestien Idenburg, Peter Irvine, Nuria Ivorra and Michiel Kraak, Felicia Jalomo, Marie Jenneteg, Dr Jiri Jerabek, Ken Jewkes, Keith Johnson, Ripton Johnson, Sharon Johnson and Kiki Kolesedis,

Raphaël Joliat, Carole Jones, Erika Jones, Todd Jones, Horst Jung, Kristine Jürs, Dale Kabat, Phyllis Kangas, Harry Kangassolo, Marie-Therese Karlen, James C Kautz, Elilsa Kelly, Jane Kelly, Steve Kennedy, Wolfgang Kessler, Bernd Klett, Josef Klimek, Rob Knapen, Steven Koenig, Daniel Alberto Korman, Dale and Adrienne de Kretser, Thomas Krusekamp, Peter Kunkel, Steven Kusters, Steven Kuypers, Oda Karen Kvaal and Gavin Tanguay, Fred "Chico" Lager, Nadia Landolt, Julianne de Lange, Chris Larkin, Judith R Lave, Robin Lee, Eric and Brenda Legget, Barbara Leighton, Conny Leiß, Raphael Leite, Brian and Lorna Lewis, Federico Lifsichtz, John Lilley, Jill Liu, Sarah Llewelyn, Karl H Loring, Jessica Lowe and Nathan Kesteven, Agnes and Antoine Lorgnier, Karl Loring, Francesco Lulli, Mari Tomine Lunden, DF Luond, Hermann Luyken, Tamsin Lyle, Gordon Machin, Iain Mackay, Andy Mackenzie, Alejandra Mallol, Richard Manasseh, Will Markle, Kirsten and Mike Martin, Pablo M Martínez, William Massie, Mario Mathieu, Luis Mazarrasa, Jim McAdam, M McDonald, Denise and Malcolm McDonough, Jane McKenzie, Arend Meischke and Marco Vijverberg, Ed Menning, John and Tessa Messenger, Martie Meyer and Albert van der Rooy, J Michael Miller, Mark Miller, Patrick Miller, Carlos Mocorrea, Jones Monaghan, Jamie Monk, Eduardo Montuani, Werner Moosbrugger, María Florentín Morel, Fernando Miguel Moreno Olmedo, Chris and Janet Morris, Lori Murphy, Linda Murray, James Musick, Julio Muslera, Gavin Nathan, Bruce and María Nesbitt, Vera Neuman, Jan Nielsen, Leo and Marita Niemenen, Anna Noakes, Miguel Nogales, Betty Odell, Beat Oppliger, Shannon Orton, José Orviz, Jennifer Oswalt, Eric Otterson, Dieter Ottlewski, Olav Østrem, David Owen, Miguel Oyarzo Oyarzún, Anthony Palmer, Patrick Paludan, Victorio Panzica, Julie and Spiros Pappas, David Parsons, Gennaro Pastore, Jim Patterson, Douglas Peacocke, Marc Peake, Grace Peng, Neil Pepper, Mónica Pérez, Marco Perezzani, Catarina Perrone, Giorgio Perversi, Alison Peters, Laura Pezzano, Kathie Piccagli, Carsten Pieper, Roberto Pizzo and Rubén Bellón, Andreas Poethen, Michael Pößl, Julianne Power, Marcus Pussel, Alberto Quesada, Malcolm Reid, Tonje Reitan, Juliet Rhodes, Elise Richards, Mary A Richards, Amy Risley, Doug Robinson, Vanessa Rodd, Maureen Roe, Roy and Becey Rogers, Jorge A Romero Lozano, Egon Conti Rossini, Hans R Roth, Verle Roovers, Matt Rowland and Nicole Böttcher, Annette Rudolph, MH Rudolph, Robert Runyard, Michael Ruppert, Gabriel Saiz, Roberto F Salinas, Alicia Sánchez Yubero, Karen Santangelo, Volker Sauer, Dirk Scharlevsky, Josee and Manfred Schick, Henrik Schinzel, Doreen Schreiber and René Sorbe, Toralf Schrinner, Rolf Schröder, Lisa Schroeder, Dirk Schulze, Martin Sczendziva, Sigrid Seel, Franz and Gabi Seibold, Jerome Sgard, Daniel Sherr, Karen Shouse, Tira Shubart, Sarah Simmons, Vlad Sinayuk, Udo Skladny, Clark Smeltzer, Neil Smit, TJ Snow, Charlotte Snowden, Erland Sommerskog, Robert E Sonntag, Sebastian Sorge, Claudio de Sousa, Cecilia Spiegel, Paul Stang, Urs Steiger, Paul Steng, Patrick Sterckx, Ralph E Stone, Ian and Maria Strange, Heather Staveley, Hubert Strasser, Mark and Kathie Sund, Charlotte Sutton, Walter Svagelj, Wilbert Sybesma, Alison Teeman and G Michael Yovino-Young, Idshe ten Dyk and Mireille Bos, Christine Terashita and Adriana Rossini, Rich Thom, Andreas Tölke, Debbie Triff, Eleonora Troksberg, Arnood Troust and Fenna den Hartog, Heidi Tschanz, Vivien Turner, Lorena Uriarte, Ricardo Uribe and Adolfo González, Lian van Berkel, Koosje van der Horst, Sandra van Heyste and Gert van Lancker, Enrique Vargas, CA Veerman, Alvaro Vega, Natalie Vial, Christophe Vidal and Jens Birk, Laverne Waddington, Pam Wadsworth, Kaspar Waelti, Michael Walensky, Jeannette Ward, Juan Warouiers, Boyd Warren, Nicole Washburn, JP Watney, Jonathan Weber, Judit Wessel, Reto Westermann and María-José Blass, Jennifer Williams, Rob and Lee Williams, Russell Willis, Anne Wilshin, Joy Wintersteen, Campbell Wood, Jane Woodill, Andrew Woolley, Monty Worth, Ana Zimel de Algazaburo.

Phrasebooks

Lonely Planet phrasebooks are packed with essential words and phrases to help travellers communicate with the locals. With color tabs for quick reference, an extensive vocabulary and use of script, these handy pocket-sized language guides cover day-to-day travel situations.

- handy pocket-sized books
- easy to understand Pronunciation chapter
- clear & comprehensive Grammar chapter
- romanization alongside script to allow ease of pronunciation
- script throughout so users can point to phrases for every situation
- full of cultural information and tips for the traveller

'...vital for a real DIY spirit and attitude in language learning'
– Backpacker

'the phrasebooks have good cultural backgrounders and offer solid advice for challenging situations in remote locations'
– San Francisco Examiner

Arabic (Egyptian) • Arabic (Moroccan) • Australian *(Australian English, Aboriginal and Torres Strait languages)* • Baltic States *(Estonian, Latvian, Lithuanian)* • Bengali • Brazilian • Burmese • Cantonese • Central Asia • Central Europe *(Czech, French, German, Hungarian, Italian, Slovak)* • Eastern Europe *(Bulgarian, Czech, Hungarian, Polish, Romanian, Slovak)* • Ethiopian (Amharic) • Fijian • French • German • Greek • Hill Tribes • Hindi/Urdu • Indonesian • Italian • Japanese • Korean • Lao • Latin American Spanish • Malay • Mandarin • Mediterranean Europe *(Albanian, Croatian, Greek, Italian, Macedonian, Maltese, Serbian, Slovene)* • Mongolian • Nepali • Papua New Guinea • Pilipino (Tagalog) • Quechua • Russian • Scandinavian Europe *(Danish, Finnish, Icelandic, Norwegian, Swedish)* • South-East Asia *(Burmese, Indonesian, Khmer, Lao, Malay, Tagalog Pilipino, Thai, Vietnamese)* • Spanish (Castilian) *(also includes Catalan, Galician and Basque)* • Sri Lanka • Swahili • Thai • Tibetan • Turkish • Ukrainian • USA *(US English, Vernacular, Native American languages, Hawaiian)* • Vietnamese • Western Europe *(Basque, Catalan, Dutch, French, German, Greek, Irish)*

Guides by Region

Lonely Planet is known worldwide for publishing practical, reliable and no-nonsense travel information in our guides and on our Web site. The Lonely Planet list covers just about every accessible part of the world. Currently there are 16 series: Travel guides, Shoestring guides, Condensed guides, Phrasebooks, Read This First, Healthy Travel, Walking guides, Cycling guides, Watching Wildlife guides, Pisces Diving & Snorkeling guides, City Maps, Road Atlases, Out to Eat, World Food, Journeys travel literature and Pictorials.

AFRICA Africa on a shoestring • Cairo • Cairo City Map • Cape Town • Cape Town City Map • East Africa • Egypt • Egyptian Arabic phrasebook • Ethiopia, Eritrea & Djibouti • Ethiopian (Amharic) phrasebook • The Gambia & Senegal • Healthy Travel Africa • Kenya • Malawi • Morocco • Moroccan Arabic phrasebook • Mozambique • Read This First: Africa • South Africa, Lesotho & Swaziland • Southern Africa • Southern Africa Road Atlas • Swahili phrasebook • Tanzania, Zanzibar & Pemba • Trekking in East Africa • Tunisia • Watching Wildlife East Africa • Watching Wildlife Southern Africa • West Africa • World Food Morocco • Zimbabwe, Botswana & Namibia
Travel Literature: Mali Blues: Traveling to an African Beat • The Rainbird: A Central African Journey • Songs to an African Sunset: A Zimbabwean Story

AUSTRALIA & THE PACIFIC Auckland • Australia • Australian phrasebook • Australia Road Atlas • Bushwalking in Australia •Cycling New Zealand • Fiji • Fijian phrasebook • Healthy Travel Australia, NZ and the Pacific • Islands of Australia's Great Barrier Reef • Melbourne • Melbourne City Map • Micronesia • New Caledonia • New South Wales & the ACT • New Zealand • Northern Territory • Outback Australia • Out to Eat – Melbourne • Out to Eat – Sydney • Papua New Guinea • Pidgin phrasebook • Queensland • Rarotonga & the Cook Islands • Samoa • Solomon Islands • South Australia • South Pacific • South Pacific phrasebook • Sydney • Sydney City Map • Sydney Condensed • Tahiti & French Polynesia • Tasmania • Tonga • Tramping in New Zealand • Vanuatu • Victoria • Walking in Australia • Watching Wildlife Australia • Western Australia
Travel Literature: Islands in the Clouds: Travels in the Highlands of New Guinea • Kiwi Tracks: A New Zealand Journey • Sean & David's Long Drive

CENTRAL AMERICA & THE CARIBBEAN Bahamas, Turks & Caicos • Baja California • Bermuda • Central America on a shoestring • Costa Rica • Costa Rica Spanish phrasebook • Cuba • Dominican Republic & Haiti • Eastern Caribbean • Guatemala • Guatemala, Belize & Yucatán: La Ruta Maya • Healthy Travel Central & South America • Jamaica • Mexico • Mexico City • Panama • Puerto Rico • Read This First: Central & South America • World Food Mexico • Yucatán
Travel Literature: Green Dreams: Travels in Central America

EUROPE Amsterdam • Amsterdam City Map • Amsterdam Condensed • Andalucía • Austria • Baltic States phrasebook • Barcelona • Barcelona City Map • Berlin • Berlin City Map • Britain • British phrasebook • Brussels, Bruges & Antwerp • Brussels City Map • Budapest • Budapest City Map • Canary Islands • Central Europe • Central Europe phrasebook • Corfu & the Ionians • Corsica • Crete • Crete Condensed • Croatia • Cycling Britain • Cycling France • Cyprus • Czech & Slovak Republics • Denmark • Dublin • Dublin City Map • Eastern Europe • Eastern Europe phrasebook • Edinburgh • Estonia, Latvia & Lithuania • Europe on a shoestring • Finland • Florence • France • Frankfurt Condensed • French phrasebook • Georgia, Armenia & Azerbaijan • Germany • German phrasebook • Greece • Greek Islands • Greek phrasebook • Hungary • Iceland, Greenland & the Faroe Islands • Ireland • Istanbul • Italian phrasebook • Italy • Krakow • Lisbon • The Loire • London • London City Map • London Condensed • Madrid • Malta • Mediterranean Europe • Mediterranean Europe phrasebook • Moscow • Mozambique • Munich • the Netherlands • Norway • Out to Eat – London • Paris • Paris City Map • Paris Condensed • Poland • Portugal • Portuguese phrasebook • Prague • Prague City Map • Provence & the Côte d'Azur • Read This First: Europe • Romania & Moldova • Rome • Rome City Map • Russia, Ukraine & Belarus • Russian phrasebook • Scandinavian & Baltic Europe • Scandinavian Europe phrasebook • Scotland • Sicily • Slovenia • South-West France • Spain • Spanish phrasebook • St Petersburg • St Petersburg City Map • Sweden • Switzerland • Trekking in Spain • Tuscany • Ukrainian phrasebook • Venice • Vienna • Walking in Britain • Walking in France • Walking in Ireland • Walking in Italy • Walking in Spain • Walking in Switzerland • Western Europe • Western Europe phrasebook • World Food France • World Food Ireland • World Food Italy • World Food Spain
Travel Literature: Love and War in the Apennines • The Olive Grove: Travels in Greece • On the Shores of the Mediterranean • Round Ireland in Low Gear • A Small Place in Italy • After Yugoslavia

Lonely Planet Journeys

JOURNEYS is a unique collection of travel writing – published by the company that understands travel better than anyone else. It is a series for anyone who has ever experienced – or dreamed of – the magical moment when they encountered a strange culture or saw a place for the first time. They are tales to read while you're planning a trip, while you're on the road or while you're in an armchair in front of a fire.

These outstanding titles explore our planet through the eyes of a diverse group of international writers. JOURNEYS books catch the spirit of a place, illuminate a culture, recount a crazy adventure or introduce a fascinating way of life. They always entertain, and always enrich the experience of travel.

FULL CIRCLE
A South American Journey
Luis Sepúlveda (translated by Chris Andrews)

'A journey without a fixed itinerary' with Chilean writer Luis Sepúlveda. Extravagant characters and extraordinary situations are memorably evoked: gauchos organising a tournament of lies, a scheming heiress on the lookout for a husband, a pilot with a corpse on board his plane . . . *Full Circle* brings us the distinctive voice of one of South America's most compelling writers.

WINNER 1996 Astrolabe – Etonnants Voyageurs award for the best work of travel literature published in France.

GREEN DREAMS
Travels in Central America
Stephen Benz

On the Amazon, in Costa Rica, Honduras and on the Mayan trail from Guatemala to Mexico, Stephen Benz describes his encounters with water, mud, insects and other wildlife – and not least with the ecotourists themselves. With witty insights into modern travel, *Green Dreams* discusses the paradox of cultural and 'green' tourism.

DRIVE THRU AMERICA
Sean Condon

If you've ever wanted to drive across the USA but couldn't find the time (or afford the gas), *Drive Thru America* is perfect for you. In his search for American myths and realities – along with comfort, cable TV and good, reasonably priced coffee – Sean Condon paints a hilarious road-portrait of the USA.

'entertaining and laugh-out-loud funny'– *Alex Wilber, Travel editor, Amazon.com*

SEAN & DAVID'S LONG DRIVE
Sean Condon

Sean and David are young townies who have rarely strayed beyond city limits. One day, for no good reason, they set out to discover their homeland, and what follows is a wildly entertaining adventure that covers half of Australia.

'a hilariously detailed log of two burned out friends' – *Rolling Stone*

Lonely Planet Travel Atlases

Lonely Planet has long been famous for the number and quality of its guidebook maps. Now we've gone one step further and produced a handy companion series: Lonely Planet travel atlases – maps of a country produced in book form.

Unlike other maps, which look good but lead travellers astray, our travel atlases have been researched on the road by Lonely Planet's experienced team of writers. All details are carefully checked to ensure the atlas corresponds with the equivalent Lonely Planet guidebook.

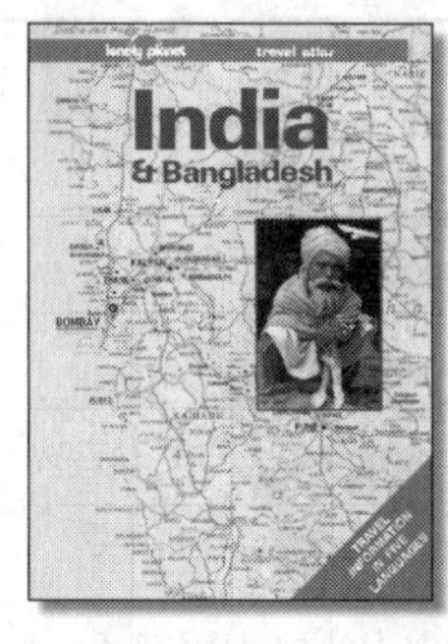

- full-colour throughout
- maps researched and checked by Lonely Planet authors
- place names correspond with Lonely Planet guidebooks
- no confusing spelling differences
- legend and travelling information in English, French, German, Japanese and Spanish
- size: 230 x 160 mm

Available now: Chile & Easter Island • Egypt • India & Bangladesh • Israel & the Palestinian Territories • Jordan, Syria & Lebanon • Kenya • Laos • Portugal • South Africa, Lesotho & Swaziland • Thailand • Turkey • Vietnam • Zimbabwe, Botswana & Namibia

---

Lonely Planet TV Series & Videos

Lonely Planet travel guides have been brought to life on television screens around the world. Like our guides, the programs are based on the joy of independent travel, and look honestly at some of the most exciting, picturesque and frustrating places in the world. Each show is presented by one of three travellers from Australia, England or the USA and combines an innovative mixture of video, Super-8 film, atmospheric soundscapes and original music.

Videos of each episode – containing additional footage not shown on television – are available from good book and video shops, but the availability of individual videos varies with regional screening schedules.

Video destinations include: Alaska • American Rockies • Australia – The South-East • Baja California & the Copper Canyon • Brazil • Central Asia • Chile & Easter Island • Corsica, Sicily & Sardinia – The Mediterranean Islands • East Africa (Tanzania & Zanzibar) • Ecuador & the Galapagos Islands • Greenland & Iceland • Indonesia • Israel & the Sinai Desert • Jamaica • Japan • La Ruta Maya • Morocco • New York • North India • Pacific Islands (Fiji, Solomon Islands & Vanuatu) • South India • South West China • Turkey • Vietnam • West Africa • Zimbabwe, Botswana • Namibia

The Lonely Planet TV series is produced by: Pilot Productions
The Old Studio
18 Middle Row
London W10 5AT, UK

Index

Abbreviations

A – Argentina
B – Brazil
C – Chile
F – Falkland Islands
P – Paraguay
U – Uruguay

Text

A

Abipones 720
ACA 55, 126–7
accommodations 94–6
Aché 767
Aconcagua (A) 330, 347–9, 350
acute mountain sickness (ACM) 80
Aguas Dulces (U) 714–5
air travel
  to/from Argentina 104–14
  within Argentina 120–2, **121**
  baggage 108–9
  courier flights 110
  glossary 106–7
  to/from Paraguay 738
  within Paraguay 740
  tickets 104–8, 112–3
  travelers with special needs 108
  to/from Uruguay 661
  within Uruguay 663
Alacalufes 569, 586
Alfonsín, Raúl 27, 38, 130, 450, 454
Almagro, Diego de 373, 404
Alta Gracia (A) 326–7
altitude sickness 80
Alto Verde (A) 236
Aluminé (A) 484
Andahazi, Federico 48
Andalgalá (A) 443
Andean Northwest (A) 30, 373–5, **374**. *See also* Catamarca; Jujuy; La Rioja; Salta; Santiago del Estero; Tucumán
Angastaco (A) 403
Anillaco (A) 433
Antarctica 599, 643
Aramburu, Pedro 152
Araucanians 186, 247
araucaria. *See* pehuén
architecture 48
Areguá (P) 757
Argentina **18, 19, 30**. *See also* *specific locations*
  arts 45–52
  border crossings 114–7, 294, 311, 405–6
  business hours 91
  customs 63
  dangers & annoyances 90–1
  ecology & environment 32, 283
  economy 41–3
  education 45
  electricity 76
  embassies & consulates 58–61
  entertainment 100–2
  food & drinks 96–101, 159
  geography & climate 29–32, **30**
  government & politics 37–41, 72–3
  highlights 54
  history 16–7, 20–9, 71–3
  holidays & special events 91
  language 53, 781–6
  literature & books 47–8, 70–3
  maps 55
  money 63–7
  newspapers & magazines 74–5
  parks & reserves 34–7, **18**
  population & people 43–5
  post & communications 67–70
  provinces **19**
  radio & TV 75–6
  religion 52–3
  society & conduct 52
  sports 92–3, 102
  suggested itineraries 55
  time 76
  tourist offices 56–7
  tourist traps 56
  transportation to/from 106–19
  transportation within 120–8, **121**
  useful organizations 89–90
  weights & measures 76
  what to bring 55–6
  when to go 55
  work 93–4
art
  murals 239, 268
  painting 48–50
  sculpture 48–50, 300, 301
Artigas, José Gervasio 646, 648
Asunción (P) 743–56
  accommodations 750–1
  attractions 747–50
  barrios **744–5**
  entertainment 751–3
  history 743–4
  information 744–6
  maps **744–5, 748–9**
  organized tours 750
  orientation 743
  restaurants 751–3

shopping 753
transportation to/from 754–6
transportation within 756
walking tour 746–7
Atlántida (U) 699
ATMs 64
Automóvil Club Argentino (ACA) 55, 126–7
Automóvil Club del Uruguay 662
Avendaño, Ernesto Soto 384
Ayoreo 773
Aysén (C) 586

B

Bahía Blanca (A) 220–4, **221**
Bajo Caracoles (A) 564
Balneario El Cóndor (A) 456–7
Balneario Las Piletas (A) 559
Barbieri, Gato 46
bargaining 66
Bariloche (A) 56, 458–69, **462**, **470**
Baritú (A) 398–9
Basílica de Nuestra Señora de Los Milagros (P) 759
Basílica Nuestra Señora de Luján (A) 195–6
Batlle y Ordóñez, José 648, 651
Beagle Channel 32, 570, 572, 617
bedbugs 87
Belén (A) 443–4
Belgrano, Manuel 238, 376
Bemberg, María Luisa 50, 203, 679
Benedetti, Mario 652
Benoit, Pedro 188, 192
Bertoni, Moisés 724, 735
bicycling 92, 127–8, 294, 338, 461
Bioy Casares, Adolfo 47, 48
Bird, Junius 599–600, 605
birds 345, 389, 390, 457, 504, 598. *See also* penguins

Bold indicates maps.

bites 86–7
boat cruises 579–80, 593, 599
Boggiani, Guido 750
Bolívar, Simón 21
Bolivian border crossings 116, 739, 755
Bonpland, Amado 268, 272–3
books. *See also* literature
on Argentina 70–3
on Falkland Islands 626
on Paraguay 734
on Uruguay 657
border crossings
Argentina-Bolivia 116
Argentina-Brazil 116, 294
Argentina-Chile 114–6, 405–6
Argentina-Paraguay 116, 311, 738–9, 754–5
Argentina-Uruguay 116, 660
Paraguay-Bolivia 739, 755
Paraguay-Brazil 739, 755, 771
Uruguay-Brazil 660–1, 715–6
Borges, Jorge Luis 47, 208
Bosque Protector Ñacunday (P) 725
Bosques Petrificados (A) 559–60
Brazil
border crossings 116, 294, 660–1, 715–6, 739, 755, 771
Foz do Iguaçú 295–8, **295**
Itaipú Dam 296
Parque Nacional do Iguaçú 294–5
Villazón 388, **387**
Bridges, Lucas 71, 153, 569, 583
Bridges, Thomas 569, 576, 583
Brizuela, Laureano 440
Buenos Aires (city) (A) 130–78
accommodations 155–8
attractions in 138–51
attractions near 179–83
barrios 138, **134**
entertainment 163–8
history 22, 23, 130–1
information 133–8
language courses 151
maps 133, **132**, **134**, **140–1**, **144–5**, **148–9**
organized tours 151, 154
orientation 131, 133
restaurants 158–63
shopping 169–70
special events 154–5
sports 168–9
transportation to/from 170–5
transportation within 175–9, **176–7**
Buenos Aires (province) (A) 188–229, **189**
Atlantic coast beaches 203–20
northern 188–203
southern 220–9
buses
within Argentina 122–3, 128
within Paraguay 740, 741, 756
within Uruguay 662, 667
Bussi, Antonio Domingo 29, 408, 415
Bustillo, Ezequiel 458, 460

C

Caacupé (P) 759
Caaguazú (P) 725
Cabeza de Vaca, Álvar Núñez 290–1, 292
Cabeza del Indio (A) 477
Cabezas, José Luis 75, 215
Cabo Dos Bahías (A) 518
Cabo Polonio (U) 714
Cabo Raso (A) 518
Cabo Vírgenes (A) 543
Cacheuta (A) 344–5
Cachi (A) 403–4
Cafayate (A) 400–2, **400**
Calchaquíes 402, 415, 443
Caleta Olivia (A) 554–6, **555**
Calilegua (A) 389–90
Calvario de la Carrodilla (A) 344

Camarones (A) 518
Camp (F) 637–44
camping 94
Cámpora, Héctor 25, 578
Cañadón Quitapeña (A) 559
Candelaria (A) 327
Candonga (A) 325
Canoe Indians 569, 592, 617
Cañon del Atuel (A) 353
Cape Pembroke Lighthouse (F) 636
Capilla La Banda (A) 416–7
Carcass Island (F) 642–3
Carmelo (U) 686–8
Carmen de Patagones (A) 451–3, **452**
cars
 in Argentina 63, 124–7
 in Paraguay 740, 741, 756
 in Uruguay 662, 678
Casa Braun-Menéndez (C) 592
Casa de Horacio Quiroga (A) 285–6
Casa de la Independencia (A) 409
Casa de San Martín (A) 274
Casa de Sarmiento (A) 358
Casa Padilla (A) 409
Casa Pueblo (U) 706
Cascada Escondida (A) 477
Cascada Mallín Ahogado (A) 477
Cassidy, Butch 531
Catamarca (A)
 city 437–42, **438**
 province 425–7, 437–45, **426**
Cataratas del Iguazú (A) 249, 278, 290–4, **290, 293**
Catedral Metropolitana (A) 139, 142
caudillos 20, 21
Cavallo, Domingo 39, 42, 45
Caverna de Las Brujas (A) 354
Cayastá (A) 236
cemeteries 152–3
Centro de Interpretación Faunística Punta Bermeja (A) 457
Cerro Aconcagua (A) 330, 347–9, 350
Cerro Belvedere (A) 495
Cerro Catedral (A) 472
Cerro Chapelco (A) 491–2
Cerro Corá (P) 725, 772
Cerro Fitzroy (A) 551–4, **552**
Cerro Lindo (A) 477
Cerro Otto (A) 471
Cerro Piltriquitrón (A) 477
Cerro San Bernardo (A) 394
Cerro Sombrero (C) 612
Cerro Tres Picos (A) 226
Chacarita (A) 152–3
Chaco (province) (A) 299–308. *See also* Gran Chaco
Chaco War 722, 725, 743, 773
Chagas' disease 85–6
Chamacoco 750
Charrúa 646
Chatwin, Bruce 70, 531, 538, 591, 593, 605
children, traveling with 62, 88–9
Chile
 border crossings 114–6, 405–6
 customs 587
 food 595
 money 587
 Patagonia 449, 586–611
 Tierra del Fuego 611–4
 visas 587
Chilecito (A) 433–5, **434**
cholera 82–3
Cholila (A) 531
Chololó (P) 760
Christ Church Cathedral (F) 633
Chubut (province) (A) 497–537
Chuy (U) 715–6
Ciudad del Este (P) 767–70, **767**
Civit, Emilio 332, 337
climbing & mountaineering
 in Argentina 92–3, 320, 338, 347–9, 461–2
 in Chile 607–8
Clorinda (A) 311
Coctaca (A) 386
Colón (A) 260–1
Colonia (U) 679–85, **683**
Colonia Iguazú (P) 770–1
Colonia Suiza (U) 686
Colonia Valdense (U) 686
colonial period 17, 20, 278
Comandante Luis Piedrabuena (A) 561–2
Comechingones 16, 313, 315, 326
Comodoro Rivadavia (A) 518–23, **520**
Complejo Museográfico Enrique Udaondo (A) 196
Concepción (A) 259–60
Concepción (P) 772
Concordia (A) 263–5, **263**
Conquista del Desierto 17, 448, 458, 460, 497
Convento y Museo de San Francisco (A) 233
Córdoba (A)
 city 313, 315–23, **318**
 province 313–29, **314, 316**
Coronel Oviedo (P) 771
Coronel Pirapó (P) 766
Corrientes (A)
 city 266–70, **267**
 province 265–74
Cortázar, Julio 47–8
Cosquín (A) 324
credit cards 64–5
Cristo Redentor (A) 350
Cruce de los Pioneros (P) 777
Cuesta de El Portezuelo (A) 443
Cuesta de los Terneros (A) 352–3
Cuesta de Miranda (A) 436
Cueva de las Manos (A) 564–5
Cueva del Milodón (C) 605
customs
 Argentine 63
 Chilean 587
 Falkland Islands' 625
 Paraguayan 733
 Uruguayan 655
Cuyo (A) 330, **331**. *See also* Mendoza; San Juan; San Luis
cycling. *See* bicycling

D

dams 283, 296, 727, 757, 770
Darwin, Charles
in Argentina 131, 159, 186, 332, 346, 446, 448, 556, 569
in Falkland Islands 617
in Uruguay 703
Voyage of the Beagle 71
Darwin (F) 639–40
Defensores del Chaco (P) 725, 779–80
Delta del Paraná (A) 179–80, **180**
Diaguitas 16, 373, 425, 427, 429, 430, 432
diarrhea 83
Difunta Correa Shrine (A) 363, 364
Dique Los Sauces (A) 432–3
Dique Ullum (A) 361–2
Dirty War (Guerra Sucia) 14, 26, 28, 40, 73
disabled travelers 88
'Disappeared, The' 26–7
Dolavon (A) 516
drinks
in Argentina 99–101
in Falkland Islands 629
in Paraguay 736–7
in Uruguay 658
driving
in Argentina 63, 124–7
in Paraguay 740, 756
in Uruguay 662, 678
Duhalde, Eduardo 39, 215
dysentery 83

E

East Falkland (F) 637–40, **638**
Eberhard, Hermann 600, 604, 605
El Bolsón (A) 473–7, **473**
El Calafate (A) 56, 544–8, **545**
El Fogón de los Arrieros (A) 301
El Hoyo (A) 477
El Leoncito (A) 363

Bold indicates maps.

El Maitén (A) 536–7
El Palamar (A) 261–2
El Supremo. *See* Francia, José Gaspar Rodríguez de
electricity 76, 626
elephant seals 506, 507, 508, 640, 642
email 69–70
embassies & consulates
in Argentina 58–61
in Paraguay 732–3
in Uruguay 654–5
Encarnación (P) 762–5, **763**
encomiendas 16
entertainment
in Argentina 100–2
in Paraguay 737
in Uruguay 659
Entre Ríos (province) (A) 251–65
Ejército Revolucionario Popular (ERP) 26, 408, 415
Esquel (A) 525–31, **526**
Esquiú, Mamerto 319, 439
estancias 17, 22, 96, 450
Acelain (A) 229
de las Vacas (U) 688
de Narbona (U) 688
El Galpón (A) 548
Güer Aike (A) 542–3
Harberton (A) 583
La Cinacina (A) 201–2
La Patria (P) 780
near San Antonio de Areco (A) 203
San Gregorio (C) 598
Tapi Aike (A) 544
Telken (A) 564
Esteros del Iberá (A) 271–2
Estomba, Ramón 220

F

Falkland Islands 616–44, **618–9**. *See also* Camp; Stanley
accommodations 628–9
activities 628
books 626
business hours 627
customs 625
dangers & annoyances 627
economy 623
electricity 626
flora & fauna 622–3
food & drinks 629
geography & climate 622
government & politics 623
health 627
history 616–22
holidays & special events 627
maps 624
money 625
newspapers 626
population & people 623–4
post & communications 625–6
radio & TV 626
time 626
tourist offices 624–5
transportation 629–30
useful organizations 627
visas & documents 625
weights & measures 626–7
what to bring 624
when to go 624
work 628
Falklands War 14, 27, 619
Falla, Manuel de 326, 327
Fangio, Juan Manuel 212
fax services 69
Ferrocarril Austral Fueguino 582–3
Figari, Pedro 652
Filadelfia (P) 775–7, **776**
films
Argentine 50, 73–4
Uruguayan 657
Finca El Rey (A) 399
fireworks 90
fishing
in Argentina 254, 270, 461, 484, 486, 575, 578
in Falkland Islands 633
in Paraguay 731
in Uruguay 705
Fitzroy, Robert 569
Fitzroy Range (A) 551–4, **552**
flora & fauna. *See also* wildlife viewing

of Argentina 32–4, 292, 294, 506–7, 534, 584
of Falkland Islands 622–3
of Paraguay 723
of Uruguay 650
food
in Argentina 79, 96–9, 159
in Chile 595
in Falkland Islands 629
in Paraguay 736–7
in Uruguay 658
Formosa (A)
city 308–11, **309**
province 299, 308–12
Fortín Toledo (P) 777
Foz do Iguaçú (B) 295–8, **295**
Francia, José Gaspar Rodríguez de 720–1, 742, 746, 760
Fray Bentos (U) 688–90, **689**
Fuerte Bulnes (C) 586, 598
Fundación Moisés Bertoni735
fungal infections 80–1

G

Gaiman (A) 514–6
Galeano, Eduardo 71, 652
Galtieri, Leopoldo 27, 619
Garay, Juan de 130, 195, 203
García, Charly 46
García, Joaquín Torres 668
Gardel, Carlos 45, 73, 152–3, 166–7, 674
gauchos 20, 22, 159, 186, 199, 200–1, 358, 363, 450
gay & lesbian travelers 88, 168
General Alvear (A) 353
giardiasis 84
Gil, Gaucho Antonio 271
Glaciar Martial (A) 582
Gobernador Costa (A) 524–5
Gobernador Gregores (A) 561
golf 93
González, Joaquín V 188, 427, 429, 434, 436
Goose Green (F) 639–40
Government House (F) 632
Gran Chaco 30
Argentine 30–1, 299–312, **300**
Paraguayan 773–80, **774**
Gruta de la Virgen del Valle (A) 442–3
Gruta de Lourdes (A) 207, 559
Gualeguaychú (A) 257–9, **257**
Guaraní
in Argentina 16, 249, 251, 274, 276–7, 284, 291
language 729–30
in Paraguay 718–20, 757
Guaycurú 299, 718
Guerra Sucia. *See* Dirty War
Guevara, Ernesto 'Che' 49, 71, 236, 239, 278, 326, 327, 399
Güiraldes, Ricardo 199–200
Gypsy Cove (F) 636

H

hantavirus 86
Haushes 569
Hayes, Rutherford B 774–5
health 76–87
basic 79–80
cuts, bites & stings 86–7
diseases 82–6
environmental hazards 80–2
food & water 79
guides 77
immunizations 77–8
insurance 78
medical kit 78–9
women's 87
heat exhaustion 81
heatstroke 81
hepatitis 84
Hernández, José 147, 200, 201
hiking
in Argentina 92, 294, 417, 461–2
in Chile 608–10
in Falkland Islands 637–9
hitchhiking 128
homestays 95–6
horseback riding 461, 608
hospedajes 95
hostels 63, 89, 94–5, 658
hotels 95
Hualfín (A) 444
Huarpe 330, 336, 356
Humahuaca (A) 385–6
hydatidosis 85
hypothermia 81–2

I

Iglesia Matriz (U) 682
Iguazú Falls. *See* Cataratas del Iguazú
immunizations 77–8
Incas 347, 373, 375–6, 418
Internet resources 70, 795
Isasmendi, Nicolás Severo de 403
Ischigualasto (A) 367
Isla de Lobos (U) 712
Isla Gorriti (U) 712
Isla Martín García (A) 180–3, **181**
Isla Victoria (A) 471
Islas Malvinas. *See* Falkland Islands
Itá (P) 760
Itaipú Dam (P, B) 296, 757, 770
Itauguá (P) 757, 759

J

Jáchal (A) 363–5
Jardín Botánico (P) 747
Jesuits
in Argentina 249, 251, 276–8, 284–5, 325
in Paraguay 720, 765–6
in Uruguay 688
Jesús (P) 765–6
Jesús María (A) 325–6
jet lag 82
José Ignacio (U) 706
Jujuy (A)
city 376–82, **379**
province 375–90, **376–7**
Junín de los Andes (A) 484–7, **485**

K

kayaking 93, 463–4
Keppel Island (F) 641–2
Kidney Island (F) 636

L

La Calera (A) 323
La Falda (A) 324–5

La Hoya (A) 531
La Lobería (A) 457
La Paloma (U) 712–4, **713**
La Pampa (province) (A) 242–8, **243**
La Paz (A) 256–7
La Plata (A) 188, 190–4, **191**
La Posta de Hornillos (A) 383
La Quiaca (A) 386–8, **387**
La República de los Niños (A) 194
La Rioja (A)
  city 427–32, **428**
  province 425–37, **426**
La Trochita 527, 528–9
Lago Blanco (C) 613
Lago Huechulafquen (A) 493
Lago Lácar (A) 493
Lago Nahuel Huapi (A) 449, 470, 471
Lago Puelo (A) 477–8
Lago Quillén (A) 494
Lago Tromen (A) 494
Laguna Blanca (A) 484
Laguna de los Pozuelos (A) 388–9
Lake District (A, C) 31, 458, **459**
language 781–6
  in Argentina 53
  in Paraguay 729–30, 779
  in Uruguay 652
language courses 93, 151
Larreta, Enrique 150–1, 229
Las Grutas (A) 457
Las Heras, Gregorio de 346
Las Leñas (A) 355–6
laundry 76
Lengua 778, 779
lice 87
Lihué Calel (A) 246–8
Liniers, Santiago 326
literature. *See also* books
  Argentine 47–8
  Paraguayan 728–9
  Uruguayan 652
Littoral (U) 679–98, **680**

Bold indicates maps.

Loma Plata (P) 777
Londres (A) 444
López, Carlos Antonio 721, 742, 747
López, Estanislao 229, 233
López Rega, José 25–6
Loreto (A) 284
Los Alerces (A) 533–6, **535**
Los Antiguos (A) 566–8
Los Arrayanes (A) 495
Los Cardones (A) 398
Los Molles (A) 354–5
Los Penitentes (A) 346, 349
Luján (A) 195–7
Lules 373, 415
Luro, Pedro 246

M

Madres de la Plaza de Mayo 27, 29, 40, 138, 139
Magallanes (C) 586, 589
Magellan, Ferdinand 446, 448, 506, 537, 560, 569, 591
Maimará (A) 383
Malargüe (A) 353–4
malaria 86, 735
Malaspina, Alejandro 448
Maldonado (U) 703–6, **704**, **707**
Mapuches 45, 449, 450, 458, 460
Mar Chiquita (A) 212
Mar del Plata (A) 56, 203–12, **204**
Maradona, Diego 102, 146
Marasso, Arturo 427
Mariscal Estigarribia (P) 780
Martín, Benito Quinquela 48, 146, 147
Matacos 45, 299
mate 52, 100–1, 659, 737
Maury, Richard 406
medical kit 78–9
medical problems. *See* health
Melo (U) 716
Mendoza, Pedro de 17, 130, 249, 718
Mendoza (A)
  city 332–46, **334**
  province 330–56

Menem, Carlos 28–9, 38, 42–4, 49, 220, 251, 283, 427, 430, 433, 458, 471
Menéndez, José 589–90, 591, 592–3
Mennonites 722, 723, 730, 773, 778–9
Mercedes (A) 270–1
Mercedes (U) 690–2, **691**
Mercosur 43, 651, 768
Merlo (A) 371–2
Mesopotamia (A) 30–1, 249–51, **250**. *See also* Corrientes; Entre Ríos; Misiones
military 90
Mina Clavero (A) 327–9
Minas (U) 702–3
Misiones (province) (A) 275–98, **275**
missions 250, 274, 276–8, 284–5, 415, 720, **277**
Mitre, Bartolomé 143
Mocoví 229, 299
Molinos (A) 403
money
  in Argentina 63–7
  in Chile 587
  in Falkland Islands 625
  in Paraguay 733–4
  in Uruguay 655–6
monkey puzzle tree. *See* pehuén
Monte León (A) 562
Monte Tronador (A) 472–3
Montecarlo (A) 286
Montevideo (U) 663–78, **666–7**, **670–1**
  accommodations 672–3
  attractions 667–9
  entertainment 674
  history 663–4
  information 665–6
  organized tours 669
  orientation 664–5
  restaurants 673–4
  shopping 674
  special events 669
  sports 674–5
  transportation to/from 675–7

transportation within 677–8
walking tour 666–7
Montoneros 26
Monumento Histórico Las Padercitas (A) 432
Monumento Nacional a la Bandera (A) 238–9
Monumento Natural Bosques Petrificados (A) 559–60
Monumento Natural Cueva del Milodón (C) 605
Monumento Natural Laguna de los Pozuelos (A) 388–9
Monumento Natural Macizo Acahay (P) 724
Monumento Natural Moisés Bertoni (P) 724
Moreno, Francisco P 34, 192, 469
Moreno Glacier (A) 548, 550–1
motion sickness 82
mountain biking. *See*bicycling
mountaineering. *See* climbing & mountaineering
murals 239, 268
museums
Complejo Museográfico Enrique Udaondo (A) 196
Convento y Museo de San Francisco (A) 233
El Fogón de los Arrieros (A) 301
Museo Arqueológico La Laja (A) 362–3
Museo Boggiani (P) 750
Museo de la Patagonia (A) 460–1
Museo de La Plata (A) 192–3
Museo de Motivos Argentinos José Hernández (A) 147
Museo del Automovilismo Juan Manuel Fangio (A) 212
Museo del Barro (P) 747, 750
Museo del Gaucho y de la Moneda (U) 668–9
Museo del Petróleo (A) 523
Museo del Puerto (A) 222
Museo Etnográfico Andrés Barbero (P) 747
Museo Fundacional (A) 336
Museo Histórico General San Martín (A) 337
Museo Histórico Nacional (A) 145–6
Museo Histórico Nacional (U) 667–8
Museo Histórico Provincial Marqués de Sobremonte (A) 319–20
Museo Marítimo (A) 578
Museo Mitre (A) 143
Museo Nacional de Bellas Artes (A) 147
Museo Naval (U) 668
Museo Paleontológico Egidio Feruglio (A) 512
Museo Pedagógico José Pedro Varela (U) 668
Museo Roscen (A) 329
Museo Torres García (U) 668
Parque Criollo y Museo Gauchesco Ricardo Güiraldes (A) 199–201
music 45–7

N

Nahuel Huapi (A) 469–73
ñandutí 729, 737
native people. *See also specific groups*
of Argentina 16–7, 44–5, 448, **17**
of Paraguay 718–20, **721**
of Uruguay 646
Necochea (A) 217–20, **218**
Neu-Halbstadt (P) 777–8
Neuquén (A)
city 478–82, **479**
province 449–51, 478–97
New Island (F) 644
newspapers
in Argentina 74–5
in Falkland Islands 626
in Paraguay 734–5
in Uruguay 657
Nivaclé 773, 778, 779
Nonogasta (A) 436
Noroeste Andino. *See* Andean Northwest

O

Ocampo, Victoria 47, 208
Omaguaca 373
Onas 569, 586, 593
Onetti, Juan Carlos 652
Onganía, Juan Carlos 315, 619
Oviedo, Lino 726–7

P

Pacheco Areco, Jorge 649
painting 48–50
Palacio del Congreso (A) 142–3
Palacio Legislativo (U) 669
Palacio San José (A) 260
Pali Aike (C) 599–600
Pampas (A) 31, 185–8, **187**. *See also* Buenos Aires (province); La Pampa (province); Santa Fe
Pan de Azúcar (U) 702
Panteón de los Héroes (P) 747
Paraguarí (P) 760
Paraguay 718–80, **719**, **758**. *See also specific locations*
arts 728–9
border crossings 116, 311, 738–9, 754–5, 771
business hours & holidays 736
customs 733
dangers & annoyances 736
economy 727
education 728
embassies & consulates 732–3
entertainment 737
flora & fauna 723
food & drinks 736–7
geography & climate 722–3
government & politics 725–7
health 735

highlights 731
history 718–22, 734
language 729–30, 779
literature & books 728, 734
maps 731
money 733–4
newspapers & radio 734–5
parks & reserves 723–5
population & people 727–8
post & communications 734
religion 730
shopping 737
society & conduct 729
sports 737
time 735
tourist offices 731
transportation to/from 738–9
transportation within 740–1
useful organizations 735–6
visas & documents 732
what to bring 731
when to go 731
Paraná (A) 251–6, **252**
parks, national 34–7, 723–5, **19**. *See also* natural monuments; reserves
Baritú (A) 398–9
Bernardo O'Higgins (C) 605–6
Caaguazú (P) 725
Calilegua (A) 389–90
Cerro Corá (P) 725, 772
Chaco (A) 305–6
Defensores del Chaco (P) 725, 779–80
do Iguaçú (B) 294–5
El Palamar (A) 261–2
Finca El Rey (A) 399
Iguazú (A) 290–4
Lago Puelo (A) 477–8
Laguna Blanca (A) 484
Lanín (A) 492–4, **493**
Lihué Calel (A) 246–8
Los Alerces (A) 533–6, **535**
Los Arrayanes (A) 495
Los Cardones (A) 398
Los Glaciares (A) 548–51, **549**
Monte León (A) 562
Nahuel Huapi (A) 469–73
Pali Aike (C) 599–600
Perito Moreno (A) 565–6
Río Pilcomayo (A) 311–2
Santa Teresa (U) 715
Serrania San Luis (P) 725
Serrania San Rafael (P) 724
Sierra de las Quijadas (A) 371
Talampaya (A) 436–7
Teniente Enciso (P) 725
Tierra del Fuego (A) 583–6, **585**
Tinfunqué (P) 724–5
Torres del Paine (C) 606–11, **607**
Ybycuí (P) 725, 761–2
Ypoá (P) 724
parks, provincial 34–7, **19**. *See also* reserves
Aconcagua (A) 347–50, **348**
Ernesto Tornquist (A) 226–7
Ischigualasto (A) 367
Volcán Tupungato (A) 346
Parque Criollo y Museo Gauchesco Ricardo Güiraldes (A) 199–201
Parque General San Martín (A) 337
Parque Los Menhires (A) 417
Parque Paleontológico Bryn Gwyn (A) 516
Parque Zoológico y Complejo Ecológico (A) 308
Paseo del Bosque (A) 192
Paso de la Patria (A) 270
Paso de los Libres (A) 272–4, **273**
Patagonia. *See also* Chubut; Neuquén; Rio Negro; Santa Cruz
Argentine 31, 446–9, 450, **447**
Chilean 449, 586–611
fauna of 506–7
Paysandú (U) 692–4, **693**
Pebble Island (F) 641
Pedro Juan Caballero (P) 771–2
pehuén 346, 449, 492
Pehuenches 353, 449
Peñaloza, Ángel 'Chacho' 427, 430
penguins 506–7, 508, 510, 517, 543, 559, 583, 598, 620–1
Península Valdés (A) 504–9, **505**
pensiones 95
Pérez Esquivel, Adolfo 27
Perito Moreno (A)
national park 565–6
town 562–4, **563**
Perón, Evita 24, 25, 72, 152, 194
Péron, Isabelita 26, 40
Perón, Juan 23–6, 72, 152, 182, 283, 356, 518
petrified forests 524, 559–60
photography 76, 626, 735
Piazzolla, Astor 45–6
Pigafetta, Antonio 446, 506
Pinamar (A) 215–7
Piriápolis (U) 699–702
Piribebuy (P) 760
Plaza Huincul (A) 484
police 90
polo 93
Port Howard (F) 641
Port Stephens (F) 643
Porvenir (C) 611–3, **611**
Posadas (A) 279–84, **280**
postal services
in Argentina 67–8
in Falkland Islands 625
in Paraguay 734
in Uruguay 656
Potrerillos (A) 345
Pozo Colorado (P) 775
pregnancy 87
Primeros Pinos (A) 484
Proceso 26
pucarás 384, 402–3, 418
Puelches 449
Puente del Inca (A) 349–50

Bold indicates maps.

Puerto Bories (C) 605
Puerto Deseado (A) 556–8, **557**
Puerto Hambre (C) 598
Puerto Iguazú (A) 286–90, **287**
Puerto Madryn (A) 498–504, **499**
Puerto Natales (C) 600–5, **601**
Puerto San Julián (A) 560–1
Puerto Williams (C) 613
Puig, Manuel 47
Punta Arenas (C) 586, 587–97, **588**
Punta de Este (U) 706, 708–12, **709**
Punta Tombo (A) 517–8
Purmamarca (A) 383

Q

Quebrada de Cafayate (A) 399–400
Quebrada de Humahuaca (A) 382–3
Quechua 45, 373
Querandí 17, 130, 185, 195
Quilmes (A) 402, 418
Quilmes Indians 418
Quiroga, Facundo 326, 358, 427, 430, 433
Quiroga, Horacio 285–6, 694

R

rabies 86
radio
  in Argentina 75
  in Falkland Islands 626
  in Paraguay 734–5
  in Uruguay 657
Radowitzky, Simón 578
rafting 93, 294, 338, 345, 463–4
Rawson, Franklin 358
Rawson (A) 516–7
Real de San Carlos (U) 682
Recoleta Cemetery (A) 152–3
Reducción de Trinidad 765–6, **765**
refugios 94
religion
  in Argentina 52–3, 363, 364
  in Paraguay 730
  in Uruguay 652
reserves **19**
  Bosque Protector Ñacunday (P) 725
  Cabo Dos Bahías (A) 518
  Cabo Vírgenes (A) 543
  de Recursos Ybytyruzú (P) 724
  de Recursos Ypacarai (P) 724
  de Vida Silvestre Yabebyry (P) 724
  del Bosque Mbaracuyú (P) 724
  El Leoncito (A) 363
  Parque Luro (A) 246
  Península Valdés (A) 504–9, **505**
  Punta Loma (A) 504
  Punta Tombo (A) 517–8
  Ría Deseado (A) 559
residenciales 95
Resistencia (A) 301–5, **303**
Ría Deseado (A) 559
Río Gallegos (A) 538–42, **539**
Río Grande (A) 573–5, **574**
Río Mayo (A) 524
Río Negro (province) (A) 449–78
Río Pilcomayo (A) 311–2
Río Rubens (C) 599
Río Santiago (A) 194–5
Río Turbio (A) 543–4
Río Verde (C) 598
Rivadavia, Bernardino 20, 315
river excursions 254, 258
Rivera (U) 698
Riveria (U) 699–716, **700**
Roa Bastos, Augusto 728
Roca, Julio Argentino 448, 458
Rocha, Dardo 188, 190, 192
Rocha (U) 712
Rodríguez, Andrés 722, 726
Roque Sáenz Peña (A) 306–8, **307**
Rosario (A) 185, 229, 236–42, **237**
Rosas, Juan Manuel de 20, 22, 131, 150, 199–201, 251, 358, 664
Rosencof, Mauricio 652
rugby 93

S

Saadi, Ramón 427
Sábato, Ernesto 27, 47
Salina Chica (A) 505
Salina Grande (A) 505
Salomé, Madre María 153
Salta (A)
  city 391–8, **392–3**
  province 390–406, **376–7**
Salto (U) 694–6, **695**
Salto Monday (P) 770
Salvador (F) 637
San Agustín de Valle Fértil (A) 365–7, **366**
San Antonio de Areco (A) 197–203, **198**
San Antonio de los Cobres (A) 404–5
San Bernardino (P) 759
San Carlos (F) 639
San Clemente del Tuyú (A) 217
San Ignacio Guazú (P) 766
San Ignacio Miní (A) 277, 284–5, **285**
San José de Jáchal (A) 363–5
San José de Lules (A) 415
San José del Rincón (A) 236
San Juan (A)
  city 356–63, **357**, **362**
  province 356–67
San Luis (A)
  city 368–71, **369**
  province 368–72
San Martín, José de 20, 21, 142, 150, 265, 271, 332, 337, 359
San Martín de los Andes (A) 487–91, **488**
San Rafael (A) 350–2, **351**
San Salvador de Jujuy (A) 376–82, **379**
Sanguinetti, Julio María 649, 650
Santa Ana (A) 284
Santa Catalina (A) 326
Santa Cruz (province) (A) 537–68

Santa Fe (A)
city 229–36, **232**
province 229–42, **230**
Santa María (A) 444–5
Santa María (P) 766–7
Santa Rosa (A) 242–6, **245**
Santa Teresa (U) 715
Santiago del Estero (A)
city 418–23, **421**
province 418–25, **419**
Santo Tomé (A) 274
Sarmiento, Domingo Faustino 20, 22, 150, 200–1, 358, 363, 425, 427, 430
Sarmiento de Gamboa, Pedro 598, 600
Saunders Island (F) 642
sculpture 48–50, 300, 301
Sea Lion Island (F) 640, **640**
sea lions 457, 506, 507, 508, 640, 712
senior travelers 63, 88, 657
sexually transmitted diseases 85
Shackleton, Ernest 592, 643
shellfish poisoning 86
shopping
in Argentina 103
in Paraguay 737
in Uruguay 659
Sierra de la Ventana (A) 224–6, **225**
Sierra de las Quijadas (A) 371
Sierra Grande (A) 457–8
Sierras de Córdoba (A) 313, 320, **316**
skiing 92, 338, 345–6, 355, 462–3, 472, 491–2, 495–6, 579
smoking 91
soccer
in Argentina 92, 102, 168–9, 194, 241, 321, 381
in Paraguay 737
in Uruguay 659, 674
Socompa (C) 406
softball 256

Bold indicates maps.

Solano, San Francisco 430, 432
Solano López, Francisco 721–2, 725, 742–3, 747
Solís, Juan de 646, 718
Soriano, Osvaldo 41, 47, 48
Sosa, Mercedes 46
South Georgia 643
sports. *See also specific sports*
in Argentina 92–3, 102
in Paraguay 737
in Uruguay 659
Stanley (F) 630–7, **631**, **636**
stings 86–7
Strait of Magellan 569, 617
Stroessner, Alfredo 13, 14, 722, 726, 746
student & youth cards 63
sunburn 81

T

Tacuarembó (U) 696–7
Tafí del Valle (A) 415–7, **416**
Talampaya (A) 436–7
Tandil (A) 227–9
tango 45–6, 165, 166–7, 674
taxes & refunds 67
taxis
within Argentina 129, 179
within Paraguay 741, 756
within Uruguay 662, 678
Teatro Colón (A) 143
Teatro Solís (U) 669
Tehuelches 446, 448, 450, 537, 566, 586
telephones
in Argentina 68–70
in Falkland Islands 625–6
in Paraguay 734
in Uruguay 656
Teniente Enciso (P) 725
Termas de Arapey (U) 696
Termas de Daymán (U) 696
Termas de Guaviyú (U) 694
Termas de Reyes (A) 382
Termas de Río Hondo (A) 423–5, **424**
Termas de Sáenz Peña (A) 308
Termas Villavicencio (A) 345
terrorism 90–1
Terry, José Antonio 384
tetanus 86
Thatcher, Margaret 27, 619
theater
in Argentina 51–2
in Paraguay 729
in Uruguay 652
thermal baths
in Argentina 308, 344–5, 365, 382, 423
in Uruguay 694, 696
ticks 87
Tierra del Fuego 32, 569–73
Argentine 573–86
Chilean 611–4
Tigre (A) 179–80, **180**
Tilcara (A) 383–5
tipping 66
Tito, Marshal 406
Tobas 45, 229, 299, 302, 720
Tobatí (P) 759–60
toilets 76
Tonocote 373
Torres del Paine (C) 606–11, **607**
Touring y Automóvil Club Paraguayo 736, 740
tourist offices
of Argentina 56–7
of Falkland Islands 624–5
of Paraguay 731
of Uruguay 653
tourist traps 56
tours, organized
to Argentina 117–9
within Argentina 129
to Paraguay 739
to Uruguay 661
trains
within Argentina 123–4, 128
historic 405–6, 527, 528–9, 582–3
within Paraguay 740, 741
within Uruguay 662
transportation
to/from Argentina 106–19
within Argentina 120–8, **121**
to/from Falkland Islands 629–30
within Falkland Islands 630

to/from Paraguay 738–9
within Paraguay 740–1
to/from Uruguay 660–1
within Uruguay 662
Trapalanda 448, 449
travel insurance 63
traveler's checks 64
Treinta y Tres (U) 716
Trelew (A) 509–14, **510**
Tren a las Nubes 405–6
Trevelin (A) 531–3, **532**
Trinidad (P) 765–6, **765**
Tronador (A) 472–3
Tucumán (A)
city 407–15, **410–1**
province 406–18, **407**
Túnel Subfluvial Uranga Silvestre Begnis (A) 254
Tuparmaros 649, 657
Tupungato (A) 346, 349
TV
in Argentina 75–6
in Falkland Islands 626
in Uruguay 657

U

Upsala Glacier (A) 550
Upsallata (A) 346–7
Uquía (A) 383
Urquiza, Justo José de 150, 251, 259, 260
Uruguay 646–716, **647**, **680**, **700**. *See also specific locations*
arts 652
border crossings 117, 660–1, 715–6
business hours & holidays 658
customs 655
economy 651
education 652
embassies & consulates 654–5
entertainment 659
flora & fauna 650
food & drinks 658–9
geography & climate 649–50
government & politics 650–1, 657
health 657
highlights 653
history 646–9, 657
language 652
literature & books 652, 657
maps 653
money 655–6
newspapers 657
population & people 651–2
post & communications 656
radio & TV 657
religion 652
shopping 659
sports 659
tourist offices 653
transportation to 660–1
transportation within 662
useful organizations 658
visas & documents 654
when to go 653
Ushuaia (A) 570, 576–82,**577**

V

Valle Edén (U) 697–8
Vallecito (A) 363, 364
Vallecitos (A) 345
Valles Calchaquíes (A) 402–5
Varela, Felipe 403, 427, 430
Varela, José Pedro 668
Vásquez de Espinosa, Antonio 330, 332, 356, 373, 376, 382, 407, 425
Vernet, Louis 616
Viedma (A) 453–6, **452**
Villa Carlos Paz (A) 56, 323–4
Villa de las Rosas (A) 329
Villa Florida (P) 762
Villa General Belgrano (A) 327
Villa Gesell (A) 212–5
Villa Hayes (P) 773–5
Villa La Angostura (A) 494–6
Villa Las Pirquitas (A) 442
Villa Sanagasta (A) 433
Villa Serrana (U) 703
Villa Traful (A) 496–7
Villa Ventana (A) 226
Villarrica (P) 771
Villavicencio (A) 345
Villazón (B) 388, **387**
Virgen de Luján 195
Virgen del Valle 439, 440, 442–3
visas & documents
in Argentina 62–3
in Chile 587
in Falkland Islands 625
in Paraguay 732
in Uruguay 654
Volcán Tupungato (A) 346, 349
von Humboldt, Alexander 272

W

War of the Triple Alliance 278, 721–2, 725, 774
warrah 617
water 79
water sports 254, 464, 500–1
waterfalls 290–4, 477, 770
Weddell Island (F) 643–4
weights & measures 76, 626–7
Welsh immigrants 497–8
West Falkland (F) 640–4
whales 505, 506–7
wildlife viewing 262, 271–2, 504, 506–7, 628. *See also* flora & fauna; *specific animals*
wineries 344, 353, 359, 401, 434
women travelers 87–8, 735
work 93–4

Y

Yabrán, Alberto 75, 215
Yacanto (A) 329
Yacyretá Dam (A) 283, 727
Yaguarón (P) 760
Yahgans 16, 569, 576, 583, 586, 613, 617, 641–2
Yapeyú (A) 274
Yavi (A) 388–9
Ybycuí (P) 725, 761–2
yellow fever 86
Yrigoyen, Hipólito 40, 131, 182, 578
Yrurtia, Rogelio 49, 151

Z

Zapala (A) 482–3

Boxed Text

Air Travel Glossary 106–7
Breaking Your Diet 98
Common Guaraní Words & Phrases 729
Difunta Correa 364
Embassies & Consulates 58–61
Endangered Species 33
Fauna of Península Valdés & Patagonia 506–7
Food from the Sea 595
Freedom of the Press? 75
The Frozen South 599
Gardel & the Tango 166–7
Gaucho Antonio Gil 271
Isla de los Pájaros 504
The Jesuit Missions 276–7
The Legend of Che Guevara 49
Let Them Eat Beef 159
Life & Death in Recoleta & Chacarita 152–3
Mate & Its Ritual 100–1
Meatless Meals in Cattle Country 97
Megawatts for Megabucks 283
The Menem Trucho 65
The Mennonite Colonies 778–9
The Number You Dialed Has Been Changed... 68
The Patagonian Estancia 450
The Paths of the Liberators 21
Penguins & Their Feathered Friends 620–1
The Rise & Romance of the Gaucho 200–1
South Georgia 643
The Survival of La Trochita 528–9
Teniente General Juan Domingo Perón 24
Ticket Options 112–13
Tourist Traps 56
The Warrah, the Yahgans & the Discovery of the Falklands 617
Who's on the Train? 406

Bold indicates maps.

MAP LEGEND

BOUNDARIES

International
Province
County

HYDROGRAPHY

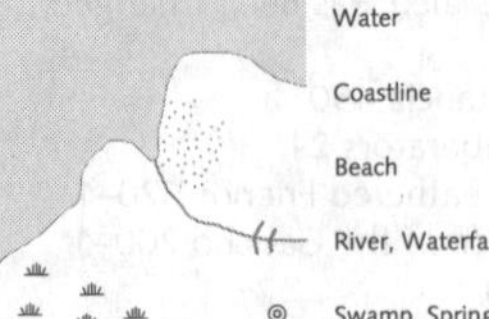

ROUTES & TRANSPORT

Freeway
Toll Freeway
Primary Road
Secondary Road
Tertiary Road
Unpaved Road
Pedestrian Mall
Trail
Walking Tour
Ferry Route
Railway, Train Station
Mass Transit Line & Station

ROUTE SHIELDS

RN 3 Argentina Ruta Nacional
RP 21 Argentina Ruta Provincial
1 Highway
10 State Highway
5 Chile Ruta Nacional
BR 116 Brazil Highway

AREA FEATURES

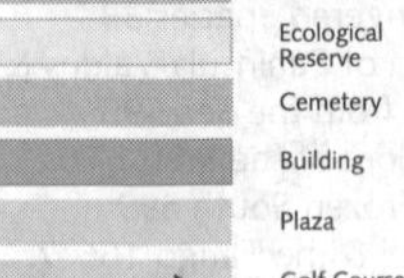

NATIONAL CAPITAL
State, Provincial Capital
LARGE CITY
Medium City
Small City
Town, Village
Point of Interest

Place to Stay
Campground
RV Park
Refugio

Place to Eat
Bar (Place to Drink)
Café

MAP SYMBOLS

Airfield
Airport
Archaeological Site, Ruins
Bank
Baseball Diamond
Beach
Border Crossing
Bus Depot, Bus Stop
Cathedral
Cave
Church
Dive Site
Embassy
Foot Bridge
Fish Hatchery
Gas Station
Hospital, Clinic
Information
Lighthouse
Live Music
Lookout

Mission
Monument
Mosque
Mountain
Museum
Observatory
One-Way Street
Park
Parking
Pass
Picnic Area
Police Station
Pool
Post Office
Shopping Mall
Skiing (Nordic)
Skiing (Alpine)
Stately Home
Trailhead
Winery
Zoo

Note: Not all symbols displayed above appear in this book.

LONELY PLANET OFFICES

Australia
PO Box 617, Hawthorn, Victoria 3122
☎ 03 9819 1877 fax 03 9819 6459
email: talk2us@lonelyplanet.com.au

USA
150 Linden St, Oakland, CA 94607
☎ 510 893 8555 TOLL FREE: 800 275 8555
fax 510 893 8572
email: info@lonelyplanet.com

UK
10a Spring Place, London NW5 3BH
☎ 020 7428 4800 fax 020 7428 4828
email: go@lonelyplanet.co.uk

France
1 rue du Dahomey, 75011 Paris
☎ 01 55 25 33 00 fax 01 55 25 33 01
email: bip@lonelyplanet.fr
www.lonelyplanet.fr

World Wide Web: www.lonelyplanet.com *or* AOL keyword: lp
Lonely Planet Images: lpi@lonelyplanet.com.au